Modern Management Control Systems

THE ROBERT S. KAPLAN SERIES IN MANAGEMENT ACCOUNTING

Robert S. Kaplan, Consulting Editor

MANAGEMENT ACCOUNTING, 2/E
Atkinson / Banker / Kaplan / Young

THE DESIGN OF COST MANAGEMENT SYSTEMS
Cooper / Kaplan

MODERN MANAGEMENT CONTROL SYSTEMS
Merchant

ADVANCED MANAGEMENT ACCOUNTING, 3/E
Kaplan / Atkinson

To Gail, Abbidee, and Madelyn

Modern Management Control Systems

Text and Cases

Kenneth A. Merchant

University of Southern California, Los Angeles

PRENTICE HALL, Upper Saddle River, New Jersey 07458

Library of Congress Cataloging-in-Publication Data

Merchant, Kenneth A.
Modern management control systems : text and cases / Kenneth A. Merchant.
p. cm.
Includes bibliographical references and index.
ISBN 0-13-554155-7
1. Industrial management. 2. Industrial management—Case studies. 3. Cost control. 4. Cost control—Case studies. I. Title.
HD31.M3973 1997
658.15—dc21 97-15527
CIP

Editor-in-Chief: P. J. Boardman
Editorial Assistant: Jane Avery
Editorial Director: James Boyd
Marketing Manager: Deborah Hoffman Emry
Production Editor: Lynda Paolucci
Production Coordinator: Cindy Spreder
Managing Editor: Katherine Evancie
Senior Manufacturing Supervisor: Paul Smolenski
Manufacturing Manager: Vincent Scelta
Interior Design: Ann France
Cover Design: Lorraine Castellano
Cover Art: Marjory Dressler
Composition: Progressive Publishing Alternatives

A Simon & Schuster Company
Upper Saddle River, New Jersey 07458

Prentice-Hall International (UK) Limited, *London*
Prentice-Hall of Australia Pty. Limited, *Sydney*
Prentice-Hall Canada, Inc., *Toronto*
Prentice-Hall Hispanoamericana, S. A., *Mexico*
Prentice-Hall of India Private Limited, *New Delhi*
Prentice-Hall of Japan, Inc., *Tokyo*
Simon & Schuster Asia Pte. Ltd., *Singapore*
Editora Prentice-Hall do Brasil, Ltda., *Rio de Janeiro*

Printed in the United States of America

10 9 8 7 6 5 4

Contents

Preface

This book provides materials for a comprehensive course on management control systems (MCS). MCS are defined broadly to include everything managers do to help ensure that their organization's strategies and plans are carried out, or, if conditions warrant, that they are modified.

All students interested in business or management can benefit from this book because control is a core function of management. However, courses based on the materials in this book should be particularly useful for those who aspire to be general managers, management consultants, financial specialists (for example, controller, financial analyst, auditor), or human resource specialists (for example, personnel director or compensation consultant).

This book includes sixty cases as classroom materials. The case method, which stimulates learning through the analysis of actual (or sometimes hypothetical) events, is generally recognized to be the best method for teaching a MCS course. Because MCS, the contexts in which they operate, and the outcomes they produce are complex and multidimensional, simple problems and exercises cannot capture the essence of the issues managers face in designing and using MCS. Students must develop the thinking processes that will guide them successfully through decision tasks with multiple embedded issues and large amounts of relatively unstructured information. They must learn to develop problem finding skills, as well as problem resolution skills. Case analyses provide the best method available for simulating these tasks in a classroom.

The discussions in this book assume a basic level of knowledge of management accounting (for example, variance analysis) and core MCS elements (for example, budgeting). The book was designed primarily for graduate students and practicing professionals, but the book in manuscript form has also been used successfully with undergraduate students who have had a prior management accounting course. It should be recognized, however, that some of the cases in this book are too challenging for most undergraduate students. Cases for use in an undergraduate course have to be chosen carefully.

This book is different from other MCS texts in several important ways. First, the basic organizing framework is different. The first major module of the book discusses controls based on the object of control—actions, results, or personnel/culture. The object-of-control framework has considerable advantages over other possible organizing frameworks. It has clean, clearly distinguishable categories. It is all-inclusive; readers can relate all controls and other control classifications and theories (for example, proactive vs. reactive controls; prevention vs. detection controls; agency theory) to it. And it is intuitive: Students can easily see that managers must make choices among these categories of controls. Researchers and instructors in both MBA and executive education courses have been using this object-of-control framework for nearly 20 years, but the framework had not, until now, been made operational in a complete textbook.

Second, the treatment of MCS is broad. Like all MCS textbooks, this book focuses intensively on the use and effects of "financial results controls"—that is, those which involve measurement and evaluation of performance in financial terms—which dominate in importance at managerial levels in all but the smallest organizations. But this book also provides a broad treatment of controls (organized around the object-of-control framework) to put the financially-oriented controls in proper perspective. For example, the book describes many situations where financial results controls are not effective and discusses the alternatives that managers can use in those situations (for example, non-financial performance indicators, centralization of authority, internal audits, and/or creation of a team-oriented culture).

A third important difference is that the significant concepts, theories, and issues are not discussed just in abstract terms. They are illustrated with a large number of real-world examples, far more than are included in any other MCS textbook. The examples make the textual discussion more concrete and bring the complex MCS subject to life.

Fourth, the mix of cases included in this book differs from those in other MCS textbooks in three important ways:

1. A vast majority of the cases are real (not "armchair" cases). Further, a high proportion of the cases are undisguised (that is, they use the companies' real names and describe the facts of the actual situations). Reality and lack of disguise enhance student interest and "secondary learning" (that is, about companies, industries, and specific people).
2. Most of the cases include rich descriptions of the context within which the MCS are operating. The descriptions give students opportunities to try to identify and address control problems and issues within the multidimensional situations within which practicing managers have to deal with them. The rich descriptions make some of the cases relatively long. Case length, by itself, is an undesirable characteristic, but quite a few relatively lengthy cases were included in the book because of the pedagogical advantages they provide. Few of the cases included here are intended as management accounting technique-oriented problems. Some of the cases in this book can be used to review and reinforce knowledge about some basic management accounting techniques, but if student knowledge about a specific technique (for example, variance analysis, or even accrual accounting) is deficient, instructors will have to provide extra lectures and review exercises to bring the students "up-to-speed."
3. Most of the cases are of relatively recent vintage. They are not 1950s cases which have had their dates "updated." They have also been chosen to ensure coverage of the latest MCS topics and issues, such as how to minimize management myopia, how to motivate all employees to maximize shareholder value, and whether or not to use the EVA™ or "balanced scorecard" measurement approaches. However, despite their relative recency, all of the cases included in this book have been classroom tested.

The cases included in this book permit the exploration of the control issues in a broad range of settings. Included in the course package are cases on both large and small firms, manufacturing and service firms, U.S.-domestic and foreign firms, and profit-seeking and not-for-profit organizations. The cases present issues faced by personnel in both line and staff roles at corporate, divisional, and functional levels of the organization. Instructors can use the cases to teach a MCS course which is broad in scope or has a more narrowly defined focus (for example, MCS in service organizations).

The cases provide considerable scheduling flexibility. Most of them cut across multiple topic areas because MCS are inherently multi-dimensional. The focus of a given case might be on, for example, the setting of performance targets. Such a case must also describe the organization structure, the characteristics of the people in key positions, the planning processes, performance measures, and incentive systems. As a consequence, the ordering of the cases in the book is not intended to be rigid. Many alternatives are possible.

In developing the materials that led to the writing of this book, I have benefited from the insightful comments, helpful suggestions, and cases of many people. I owe special thanks to the two professors who served as my management control systems "mentors" at the Harvard Business School: William Bruns and Richard Vancil. I also benefited from contributions from many of my other former colleagues at Harvard, including George Baker, Norman Berg, Thomas Bonoma, Robin Cooper, William Fruhan, Julie Hertenstein, Regina Herzlinger, Robert Kaplan, Krishna Palepu, and Robert Simons. I wish also to thank Francisco Arenas and Pedro Suãrez (both at the Instituto Panamericano de Alta Direcction de Empresa, Mexico City), Peter Brownell (University of Melbourne, Australia), Chee Chow (San Diego State University), Lourdes Ferreira (University of Baltimore), Tom L. C. M. Groot (Free University, Amsterdam), Frank Hartmann (University of Limburg, Maastricht, the Netherlands), Kevin Murphy and Mark Young (both at the University of Southern California), Anne Wu (National Chengchi University, Taiwan), and the reviewers of the rough manuscripts of this book: Kung Chen (University of Nebraska), Terry Dancer (Arkansas State University), Alf Eastergard (Bloomsburg University), Jane Finley (Belmont University), Donald Madden (University of Kentucky), Sakthi Mahenthiran (Butler University), Gary Mann (University of Texas at El Paso), William Rotch (Darden Graduate School at the University of Virginia), Michael Shields (University of Memphis), and Bor-Yi Tsay (University of Alabama at Birmingham).

Valuable research and clerical assistance were provided by Salma Majeed, Elizabeth Orozco, and Rachel Osborn, all at USC.

I owe a special thanks to the Harvard Business School for their permission to use the many Harvard cases which are included in this text. Requests to reproduce cases copyrighted by Harvard should be directed to the Permissions Manager, Harvard Business School Publishing Division, Boston, MA 02163.

Finally, I wish to acknowledge that there is certainly no one way to convey the rich subjects related to MCS. I have presented one useful scheme in the best way I know how, and I welcome comments regarding context, organization, or specific errors. Please direct them to me at the Leventhal School of Accounting, University of Southern California, Los Angeles, CA 90089-1421. Phone (213) 740-4841; Fax: (213) 747-2815.

K.A.M.
Dean of Leventhal School of Accounting,
University of Southern California

Modern Management Control Systems

Section I: The Control Function of Management

CHAPTER 1

Management and Control

INTRODUCTION

Control is a critical function of management. Control problems can lead to large losses and possibly even to organizational failure. Here are some recent examples:

- In 1993, General Electric Company (GE) ended its streak of fifty-one consecutive quarters of earnings gains (excluding accounting changes). The company had to take a $210 million after-tax write-off in the first quarter of 1994 because of problems at Kidder Peabody, its securities unit. In the most serious of the incidents, a single Kidder Peabody government bond trader, Joseph Jett, reported over $350 million in fictitious trading profits over a two-year period, masking losses of up to $100 million so that he could earn greater recognition and larger bonuses (which, in 1993 alone, totalled $9 million).[1] The poor controls cost Kidder Peabody and GE many millions of dollars in losses, serious public relations problems, and the services of a number of talented people, including some in top management, who were fired or pressured to resign. A subheadline in *The Wall Street Journal* asked how Kidder Peabody could get "so far out of control."[2]
- In early 1996 at Baby Superstore, Inc., a retailer of baby and young children's products with sixty-three stores in eighteen states and annual sales of just under $300 million, managers discovered that an accounting error had caused cash reserves to be overstated in the last fiscal year. Although this single mistake was not terribly costly by itself, Baby Superstore's stock price fell 19 percent on the day the mistake was publicly disclosed. Why? Some analysts concluded that the mistake probably revealed a lack of internal controls, and that deficiency placed significant portions of the company's assets at risk.[3]
- In the late 1980s and early 1990s, Apple Computer suffered major performance problems. An article on Apple's "sad decline" placed much of the blame on Apple's culture which is "unharnessed and uncontrolled." The article's author noted that Apple did not have a well-organized strategic plan and that many of the company's employees, particularly the technical "wizards," were difficult to direct. These control problems caused many analysts to question whether Apple could survive as an independent company.[4]

Because of its importance, control is mentioned often in management literature. Numerous books and articles describe companies as having, for example, excellent, inadequate, lax, excessive, weak, or nonexistent controls, or as having tightened or loosened their controls. Management critics have complained that more controls are not leading to better control, that the controls in common use are stifling, and, particularly in U.S. companies, that the controls being used cause managers to be excessively short-term oriented.

Understanding and comparing the views in the books and articles written on control is difficult, however, because the language of control is imprecise. The term *control,* as it applies to a management function, does not even have a universally accepted definition. An old, narrow view of a management control system (MCS) is that of a simple *cybernetic* system; that is, a system involving a single feedback loop. In describing this process, authors in management literature often use a thermostat analogy. Thermostats include a single feedback loop; they measure the temperature, compare those measurements with the desired standard, and, if necessary, take a corrective action (turn on, or off, a furnace or air conditioner). In an MCS feedback loop, managers measure performance, compare that measurement with a pre-set performance standard, and, if necessary, take corrective actions.

This book, however, like many other recent control writings, takes a broader view of MCS.[5] It recognizes, for example, that many controls in common use, such as direct supervision, employee hiring standards, and codes of conduct, do not focus on measured performance. They focus instead on encouraging, enabling, or, sometimes, forcing employees to act in the organization's best interest. This book recognizes that some controls are *proactive,* rather than *reactive.* Proactive means the controls are designed to *prevent* control problems before the organization suffers any adverse effects on performance. Examples of proactive controls include planning processes, required expenditure approvals, computer passwords, and segregation of employees' duties. Controls, then, include all the devices managers use to ensure that the behaviors and decisions of people in the organization are consistent with the organization's objectives and strategies.[6]

Designed properly, control devices individually and collectively influence employees' behaviors in desirable ways and, consequently, increase the probability that the organization will achieve or exceed its goals. That is, the primary *function* of controls is to influence behaviors in desirable ways. The *benefit* of the controls is the increased probability that the organization's objectives will be achieved.

MANAGEMENT AND CONTROL

Control is the back end of the management process. This can be seen by looking at the various ways in which the broad topic of management is disaggregated.

Management

Management literature includes many definitions of management, all of which relate to the processes of organizing resources and directing activities for the purpose of achieving organizational objectives. Here is a representative definition: *Management* is "the process of integrating resources and tasks toward the achievement of stated organizational goals."[7]

Inevitably, those who study and teach management have broken the subject into smaller, more manageable elements. The most prominent classification schemes are shown in Table 1-1. The first column identifies the basic management functions: product (or service) development, operations (making things or performing services), marketing/sales (finding buyers and making sure the products and services fulfill a customer's needs), and finance (raising money). Virtually every school of management offers courses focused on only one, or only part of one, of these individual functions.

The second column of Table 1-1 identifies the major types of resources with which managers must work: people, money, machines, and information. Manage-

TABLE 1-1 Different Ways of Breaking Down the Broad Area of Management into Smaller Elements

Functions	*Resources*	*Processes*
product (or service) development	people	objective setting
operations	money	strategy formulation
marketing/sales	machines	control
finance	information	

ment schools also offer courses organized using these classifications. These courses are often called human resource management, finance, production, and information systems, respectively.

The term *control* appears in the third column of Table 1-1, which separates the management functions along a process continuum involving objective setting, strategy formulation, and control. Many management courses, including business policy, strategic management, and management control systems, focus on elements of the management process. To focus on control, we must distinguish the concept from the objective-setting and strategy-formulation processes.

Objective Setting

Knowledge of *objectives* is a necessary prerequisite for the design of any control or MCS and, indeed, for any purposeful activities. The objectives do not have to be quantified in terms such as 20 percent annual return on equity, nor do they have to be financial. A not-for-profit organization's primary objective might be providing shelter for homeless people, for example. In any organization, however, employees must have some understanding of what the organization is trying to accomplish. Otherwise no one could claim that any of the employees' actions are purposive, and no one could ever support a claim that the organization was successful.

In most organizations the employees know the objectives, but rarely do all employees agree on how to balance their organization's responsibilities to all of their stakeholders (including owners, debtors, employees, suppliers, and customers). Early in their histories, organizations develop compromise mechanisms to resolve conflicts among stakeholders and reach some level of agreement about the objectives they will pursue.

Strategy Formulation

Strategies define how organizations should use their resources to meet their objectives. We can view strategies as constraints that managers place on themselves and their subordinates so they will focus their activities on what their organizations do best; particularly in areas where they have advantages over their competitors. Well-conceived strategies, which result from analyzing the organizations' strengths and weaknesses in its marketplaces, guide managers in directing and controlling their organizations.

Larger, more complex organizations often specify two levels of strategy: a corporate diversification strategy and business strategies within each operating unit. Strategies at both levels constrain managers to focus on what their organizations do best (or must do best).

Corporate diversification strategies specify the market or geographical areas in which the organization will operate. They include statements like this: Of all the ways in which it is possible to create value (or fulfill other organizational missions, such as provide education or house the needy), we are going to focus on these few specialties (businesses or markets) and leave the rest to others. Diversification strategies provide direct inputs into corporate decisions about investments, acquisitions, divestments, organization structures, and financing.

Business strategies describe how operating units should focus their resources to convert distinctive competencies into competitive advantages in specific businesses (individual markets). Business strategies take this form: Of all the ways in which it is possible to create value (or provide service) in this business, we are going to focus in this particular way, such as by producing at the lowest cost or by differentiating our products in useful ways.

Both levels of strategies can be specified formally or left largely unspecified. Many organizations develop formal strategies through systematic, relatively open, often elaborate planning processes. Other organizations, however, do not have formal, written strategies. Instead, they try to respond effectively to opportunities.[8] Major elements of these latter organizations' strategies *emerge* from a series of interactions between management, employees, and the environment; from decisions made spontaneously; and from local experimentation designed to learn what activities lead to the greatest success. Nonetheless, if some decision-making consistency exists, a strategy can be said to have been formed, regardless of whether managers planned or even intended that particular consistency.[9]

It is sometimes difficult to judge an organization's strategy. Spontaneous decisions at times conflict directly with the organizations' formal strategic statements, not because of control problems but because the formal strategic statements have become obsolete and employees have decided to take actions that are better than the formal strategy suggests. In the early 1980s Intel's stated plan was to be a major player in memory chips (as well as microprocessors), but in 1985 it exited the dynamic random access memory (DRAM) business. In retrospect, Andrew Grove, Intel's CEO, observed that the company was "fooled by its own strategic rhetoric." Its marketing, pricing, and investment decisions as early as 1983 made it clear that some key employees had made a decision to retreat from memory chips.[10] This shows that the actual strategy a firm enacts may be different from its formal strategic statements.

Not even the most elaborate strategic visions and statements are complete to the point where they detail every desired action and contemplate every possible contingency. However, for purposes of designing an MCS, it is useful to have strategies that are as specific and detailed as possible, if those strategies are well thought out and can be kept current. The formal strategic statements make it easier for upper management both to identify the feasible control alternatives and to implement them effectively. The controls can be targeted to the organization's critical strategic factors, such as developing new products, keeping costs down, or enhancing market share, rather than aiming more generally at improving corporate profitability. Formal strategic statements are not mandatory for control purposes, however. Many organizations with largely emergent strategies have effective control systems, although their control alternatives are often more limited.

Strategic Control Versus Management Control

In the broadest sense, control systems can be viewed as having two basic functions: strategic control and management control. *Strategic control*[11] involves managers addressing the question: Is our strategy valid? Or, more appropriately in changing environments, they ask: Is our strategy still valid, and if not, how should it be changed? All firms must be concerned with strategic control issues, but the concern that a strategy may have become obsolete is obviously greater in firms operating in more dynamic environments.

Management control involves addressing the general question: Are our employees likely to behave appropriately? This question can be decomposed into several parts. First, do our employees understand what we expect of them? Second, will they work consistently hard and try to do what is expected of them? That is, will they implement the organization's strategy as was intended and not steal the organization's assets or otherwise allow them to be dissipated (such as through carelessness)? Third, are they capable of doing a good job? Finally, if the answer to any of these questions is no, what can be done to solve the management control problems? All managers who must rely on employees to accomplish organizational objectives must deal with management control issues.

The tools for addressing strategic and management control issues are quite different. Managers addressing strategic control issues have a focus primarily external to the organization; they examine the industry and their organization's place in it. They think about how the organization, with its particular combination of strengths, weaknesses, and limitations, can compete with the other firms in its industry. On the other hand, managers addressing management control issues primarily have an internal focus; they think about how they can influence employees' behaviors in desired ways.

This book focuses on management control. From a management control perspective, strategies should be viewed as useful, but not absolutely necessary, guides to the proper design of an MCS. As is shown later, when strategies are formulated more clearly, more control alternatives become feasible, and it becomes easier to implement each form of management control effectively. Managers can, however, design and operate some types of controls without having any clear strategies in mind.

EFFECTS OF MANAGEMENT CONTROLS ON BEHAVIOR

As was mentioned earlier, management control involves managers taking steps to help ensure that the organization's employees do what is best for the organization. This is an important function because it is people in the organization who make things happen. Controls are necessary to guard against the possibilities that people will do something the organization does not want them to do or fail to do something they should. It makes little sense to talk about cost control, for example, without reference to people because costs do not control themselves, people control them.

This behavioral orientation is an area of agreement in the recent management control literature. One control book observed that

> the crucial aspect of any control system is its effect on behavior. . . . The system needs to be designed in a way that assists, guides, and motivates management to make decisions and act in ways that are consistent with the overall objectives of the organization.[12]

The behavioral orientation of controls has also long been recognized by managers and controllers. When Bill McElroy, finance director and board member of Toyota Motor Corporation of Australia, was asked what he would study if given the opportunity for some formal learning, he replied,

> I would like to know more about psychology—in terms of why people are the way they are and why they behave the way they behave. If I had studied this in my university days, I think I would have gained significant benefits all the way through my career.[13]

If all personnel could always be relied on to do what is best for the organization, there would be no need for an MCS. Unfortunately, individuals are sometimes unable or unwilling to act in the organization's best interest, so managers must take steps to guard against the occurrence, and particularly the persistence, of undesirable behaviors and to encourage desirable behaviors.

CAUSES OF MANAGEMENT CONTROL PROBLEMS

Given this behavioral focus of controls, the next logical question to ask is: What is it about the people on whom the organization must rely that creates the needs for managers to implement controls? The causes of the needs for control can be classified into three main categories: lack of direction, motivational problems, and personal limitations.

Lack of Direction

Some people perform poorly simply because they do not know what the organization wants from them. When this *lack of direction* occurs, the likelihood of the desired behaviors occurring is obviously small. Thus, one control system function involves informing employees as to how they can maximize their contributions to the fulfillment of overall organizational objectives.

Motivational Problems

Even where all involved individuals clearly understand what they are expected to do, some choose not to perform as the organization would have them perform because of *motivational problems.* Motivational problems are common because individuals' objectives and organizations' objectives do not naturally coincide; individuals are self-interested.[14]

Most, if not all, employees sometimes act in their own personal interest at the expense of their organization's interest. Frederick Taylor, one of the major figures in the "scientific management movement" that took place early in the twentieth century wrote, "Hardly a competent worker can be found who does not devote a considerable amount of time to studying just how slowly he can work and still convince his employer that he is going at a good pace."[15] Taylor's point still has some validity today. In 1982, wasting time on the job was estimated to have cost U.S. employers $125 billion.[16] A study of employees in three industry sectors (retail, hospital, and electronics) found that more than two-thirds engaged in counterproductive activities, such as long lunches, use of sick leaves when not sick, and use of drugs on the job.[17]

Employees, particularly managers, are also prone to make decisions that serve their interests, but not those of their organization. They tend to overspend on things that make their lives more pleasant (for example, office accoutrements).

They often play "games" to make their performance reports look good even when they know the actions they are taking have no economic value to the company and, in many cases, are actually harmful. They also tend to be excessively risk averse and reluctant to make even good investments because of fear that if the investments do not pay off, they may lose their job. (Those and other related problems are discussed in detail in Chapter 6 and in the chapters in Section IV of this book.)

Employee fraud and theft are the most extreme examples of motivational problems. Although accurate data about employee crime do not exist because many crimes are not reported, estimates suggest that fraud and theft are very serious problems. In a recent speech at an American Institute of Certified Public Accountants' conference, John J. Hall, a fraud expert, "almost guaranteed" that every firm was losing to fraud *at least* 1 percent of the amounts that move through their books and records.[18] A survey of 330 companies showed that 76 percent of the company respondents admitted having experienced fraud during the prior year, with the median loss estimated at $200,000.[19] A study conducted by the Association of Certified Fraud Examiners found that businesses (with fewer than 100 employees) which were victimized by fraud lost an average of $120,000; an amount that threatens the life of these small organizations.[20]

Estimates of losses from even specific types of fraud are sizable. Estimates of total losses from *white-collar* crime in the United States range from $50 billion[21] to $200 billion a year.[22] The FBI estimated that annual losses from *computer-related crime* was perhaps as large as $5 billion.[23] Banks were estimated to be losing $10 billion per year due to check fraud, and $712 million per year due to credit card fraud.[24]

These huge fraud and theft costs can be traced back to human weaknesses (and, probably, to the lack of effective controls). Brian McNally, the manager of the fashionable "44" restaurant in the Royalton Hotel in New York, said, "Every single person in your restaurant is trying to steal from you."[25] Randolph D. Brock III, president of Brock International Security Corporation, estimated, more conservatively

> Between 10 and 20 percent of a company's employees will steal anything that isn't nailed down. Another 20 percent will never steal. They would say it is morally wrong. The vast majority of people are situationally honest. They won't steal if there are proper controls.[26]

These estimates are supported by research findings. One author concluded that 50 percent of all employees steal to some degree; 25 percent take important items; 8 percent steal in volume.[27] Another author concluded that one in three employees steal, and he showed evidence suggesting that employee theft is rising by 5 percent a year.[28] A polygraph-test study found that 76 percent of a sample of workers admitted involvement in employee theft.[29] A survey study found that 80 percent of the 9,000 employee respondents admitted to having stolen company property. Controls are obviously needed to protect the organization against these behaviors.

Personal Limitations

The final behavioral problem that controls must address occurs when people who know what is expected of them and are highly motivated to perform well are simply unable to do a good job because of certain personal limitations. Many of these limitations are person-specific. They may be caused by a lack of requisite intelligence, training, experience, stamina, or knowledge for the tasks at hand. The U.S. Social Security Administration suffered some major operating problems that caused it to send many erroneous and tardy checks to recipients. The problems were blamed on a "chronic lack of trained computer technicians."[30]

Marriott International's "Pathways to Independence" program faced personal limitation problems head-on.[31] The company has put nearly 600 former welfare recipients through training, counseling, and coaching sessions and has offered jobs to those who complete the program. Many of the trainees become good employees; but others (those with severe personal limitations), are unable to do so. "[Some of] the trainees often show up late, work slowly, fight with co-workers and go AWOL, for reasons as simple as a torn stocking."[32] Said one of the trainers with the program, "It's enough to drive you nuts."[33] One of the managers of the program said,

> You just can't believe how differently a lot of these people think. There's a mentality that they are not responsible for what happens to them; It's always somebody else's fault.[34]

The best-selling book *The Peter Principle* publicized and labeled the too-common situation where employees are promoted above their level of competence.[35] Where employees are "over their heads," problems are nearly inevitable.

Another common personal limitation is lack of knowledge or information. Many control problems occur because key personnel did not have the information necessary to do a good job. Osborne Computer was criticized for having poor controls because, among other things, its managers "didn't know how much inventory they had [and] they didn't know how much they were spending."[36] Management at American Bakeries described the company as being in a "state of disarray" because of the absence of critical information about delivery routes, depots, bakeries, and divisions.[37] Some major firms in the romance novel publication industry were described as being "out of control" because the key managers in the firms did not have the information necessary to make good publication decisions, and costly mistakes were being made.[38]

Some jobs just are not designed properly. These jobs may cause even the most physically fit people to get tired or stressed and, in turn, lead to on-the-job accidents and decision errors.

Some jobs require people to perform duties or to make judgments that even the most talented among us are unable to perform. A significant and growing body of psychological research has demonstrated that all individuals—even very intelligent, well-trained, experienced individuals—have some severe limitations on their abilities to perceive new problems, to remember important facts, and to process new information properly.[39] In looking at the future it has been shown that people tend to overestimate the likelihood of most-likely events and events that have occurred relatively recently (both of which are easier to remember) as compared with relatively rare events and those that have not occurred recently. Sometimes training can be used to reduce the severity of these limitations; but in most situations multiple biases and limitations remain. These limitations are a problem because they reduce the probability that employees will make the correct decisions or even that they will observe the problems about which decisions should be made. Researchers are just beginning to explore the control implications of these limitations.

These three management control problems, lack of direction, motivational problems, and personal limitations, can obviously occur simultaneously. A person in a job may not understand what is expected, may not be motivated to perform well, and may not be capable of performing well even if he or she both understand what is being asked for and is highly motivated to achieve it.

CHARACTERISTICS OF GOOD MANAGEMENT CONTROL

To have a high probability of success, organizations must maintain good management control. *Good control* means an informed person can be reasonably confident that no major, unpleasant surprises will occur. The label *out of control* is used to describe a situation where there is a high probability of forthcoming poor performance, either overall or in a specific performance area, despite a reasonable operating strategy.

Good control still allows for some probability of failure because *perfect control* does not exist, except perhaps in very unusual circumstances. Perfect control would require complete assurance that all individuals on whom the organization must rely always act in the best way possible. Perfect control is obviously not a realistic expectation because it is virtually impossible to install controls so well designed that they guarantee good behaviors. Furthermore, as controls are costly, it is rarely, if ever, cost effective to try to implement enough controls even to approach perfect control.

The good-control concept can be applied to an entire organization or entity within that organization or to a specific organizational function. Good inventory control usually requires that employees know accurately the quantities and locations of the inventory on hand, that a low risk of loss or damage exists, and that the right quantities are stocked (proper balancing of benefits and costs). Similarly, good cost control means that the operating costs being incurred are appropriate.

A state of good control can be achieved if the following characteristics are considered. First, control is *future oriented;* the goal is to have no unpleasant surprises in the future. The past is not relevant except as a guide to the future.

Second, controls are *objectives driven.* Objectives[40] are things which the organization seeks to attain. Good control is not established over an activity or entity with multiple objectives unless performance on all significant dimensions has been considered. Thus, control of a production department cannot be considered good unless all of its major performance dimensions, such as efficiency, quality, and asset management, are well controlled.

Finally, better control, meaning tighter assurances of attainment of objectives, is *not always economically desirable.* Like any other economic good, control devices are costly and should be implemented only if the expected benefits exceed the costs.

The cost of not having a perfect control system can be called a "control loss." It is the difference between the performance that is theoretically possible given the strategy selected and the performance that can be reasonably expected with the control system in place. More or better controls should be implemented only if the amount by which they would reduce the control loss is greater than their cost. Optimal control can also be said to have been achieved if the control losses are expected to be smaller than the cost of implementing more controls. Because of control costs, perfect control is rarely the optimal outcome; what is optimal is control that is good enough and at a reasonable cost.

Assessing whether good control has been achieved is difficult and subjective. An informed expert may make a judgment that the control system in place is adequate because no major, unpleasant surprises are likely. This judgment is subject to error, not only because the expert possesses innate human limitations and biases, but also because adequacy must be measured against a future that can be very difficult to predict. As difficult as this assessment of control is, however, it should be done because organizational success depends on a good control system.

Organizations that have not achieved good control, either because they have not implemented a control system or because they have not implemented one well, are likely to face severe repercussions. They can suffer loss or impairment of assets, deficient revenues, excessive costs, inaccurate records, and reports that can lead to poor decisions, legal sanctions, or business interruptions. At the extreme, if they do not control performance on one or more critical performance dimensions, these organizations can fail.

CONTROL PROBLEM AVOIDANCE

Implementing some combination of the behavior-influencing devices commonly known as controls is not always the best way to achieve good control; sometimes the problems can be avoided. *Avoidance* means eliminating the possibility that the control problems will cause the organization harm. Organizations can never avoid all their control problems, but they can often avoid some of them by limiting exposure to certain types of problems or to a smaller number of problem sources (that is, particular persons or groups) or by reducing the maximum potential loss if the problems occur. Four prominent avoidance strategies are activity elimination, automation, centralization, and risk sharing.

Activity Elimination

Managers can sometimes avoid the control problems associated with a particular entity or activity by turning over the potential profits, and the associated risks, to a third party through such mechanisms as subcontracts, licensing agreements, or divestment. This form of avoidance can be called *activity elimination.*

Managers who are not able to control certain activities, perhaps because they do not have the required resources, because they do not have a good understanding of the required processes, or because they face legal or structural limitations, are those most likely to eliminate activities.[41] General Motors (GM) turned its Clark, New Jersey, rollerbearing operations over to the plant's employees. The plant had not performed within limits acceptable to GM managers. The GM managers hoped the employees would soon understand an important message that they had been unable to get them to understand—that productivity improvements were necessary for the plant to survive.[42]

When managers do not wish to completely avoid an area they cannot control well, they are wise at least to limit their investments, and hence their risks, in that area. Chase Manhattan Bank was left with a potential $135 million after-tax write-off because of its involvement in the government-securities lending business with Drysdale Government Securities. In retrospect, bank executives admitted they had not understood this business and its risks very well and that they had not been wise to become so heavily involved in it.[43] Limiting risk is partial avoidance of problems that might arise.

The economics-oriented field of study which focuses on whether specific activities (or transactions) can be controlled more effectively and efficiently through markets or through organizational hierarchies has come to be known by the term *transaction cost economics.*[44] A detailed examination of the theories and evidence in this field of study is outside the scope of this book. Nonetheless, it should be noted that activity eliminations represent MCS failures because activities which are eliminated have to be controlled instead through either legal contracts or markets. In general, however, MCSs have been found to be effective in a broad range of settings. The worldwide growth and success of large, integrated organizations has depended on good MCSs.

Automation

Automation is a second avoidance possibility. Managers can sometimes use computers, robots, expert systems, and other means of automation to reduce their organization's exposure to some control problems. These automated devices can be set to behave appropriately (that is, as the organization desires), and when they are operating properly, they usually perform more consistently than humans. Computers eliminate the human problems of inaccuracy, inconsistency, and lack of motivation. Once programmed, computers are absolutely consistent in their treatments of transactions, and they never have any dishonest or disloyal motivations.

As technology has advanced, companies have substituted machines and expert systems for people who have been performing quite complex actions and making sophisticated judgments and decisions. An artificial intelligence system called Discern is able to perform many of the tasks doctors and nurses had to perform. The system monitors patients' conditions and trends and alerts the medical staff of possible problems, assists in making diagnoses, orders the needed drugs, and checks for potential drug interactions and allergic reactions.[45] Discern allows organizations to avoid one of the behavioral problems—the personal limitations of the medical staff. In the vast majority of situations, Discern is more likely than the members of the medical staff to recall all the details of every condition, medication, and possible complication and to initiate the proper response. The system makes it more likely that no major, unpleasant surprises will occur.

Mrs. Fields' Cookies provides one of the best examples of a corporate control system dominated by automation.[46] The company runs 600 company-owned stores located in shopping malls in thirty-seven states and six other countries. Total sales are in excess of $100 million. The 5,000 store-level employees are mostly young and inexperienced. The company has a small headquarters staff (120 people).

The Mrs. Fields' Cookies corporate control system is built around a computer application that directs and assists the store managers. The computer makes hourly sales projections and tells the managers what to bake—how many batches of cookies, of what type, and when. It gives the managers volume-increasing suggestions. If customer counts are down, it might suggest giving away cookie samples to shoppers in the mall. If customer counts are normal but sales are down, it might present ideas for suggestive selling. The computer schedules the crew. It helps interview applicants by having applicants type answers to questions into the computer, where an expert system analyzes the responses. It assists with personnel administration by generating the personnel folder and reminding the manager of paperwork requirements. It helps with maintenance by making suggestions regarding repairs, and if the suggestions do not work, by preparing a work order and selecting a vendor. The computer system is designed to make it possible for even inexperienced store managers to run their stores just as Debbie Fields, the successful founder of the company, would.

In most managerial situations, however, automation can provide only a partial control solution, at best. One limitation is feasibility. Humans have many talents, particularly those involving complex, intuitive judgments, that no machines or decision models have been able to duplicate. A second limitation is cost. Automation often requires major investments that may be justifiable only if improvements in productivity, as well as in control, are forthcoming, or if the automation investments can be marketed to others, as Mrs. Fields' Cookies has done. Finally, automation may just replace some control problems with others. Computer automation often increases control risks. The elimination of source documents can obscure the audit trail; the concentration of information in one location increases security risks; and placing greater reliance on computer programs exposes the company to the risks of programmer errors or fraud.

Centralization

Centralization of decision making is a third avoidance possibility, and it can even be one of the central elements of a company's control system. Extreme forms of centralization, in which all the key decisions are made at top management levels, are common in small businesses which are run by a strong leader, who is also often a founder. Amerada Hess Corporation is one example. The company's controls were considered tight because its then-chairman, Leon Hess, was said to run the business "like a family store, with an iron grip on authority."[47] Extreme forms of centralization also exist in some large businesses whose top managers have reputations for being "detail oriented." Data General Corporation's ex-president, Edson de Castro, maintained centralized control. A former manager in the company observed that "all the real decisions in that company go to one desk—de Castro's."[48] Hess and de Castro reserved the important, and sometimes the not-so-important, decisions for themselves because they apparently did not trust their subordinates to take the proper actions. In so doing, they avoided some control problems.

Some managers centralize decision making in some areas of their companies at specific points in their histories to improve control. Managers at Tandem Computers, became aware of "overly aggressive sales practices" and an "apparent lack of accounting controls," which led to a downward restatement of its annual results. One of Tandem's responses was to add a layer of management to centralize the control of manufacturing, product management, and international marketing.[49]

Similarly, many companies which have become concerned about the multimillion dollar losses on complex derivative plays suffered by Procter & Gamble, Gibson Greetings, Piper Jaffray, Metallgeseellschaft, and Orange County California, to name a few, have responded by centralizing risk management activities. In the banking industry alone, Morgan Stanley, J.P. Morgan, Citicorp, and Swiss Bank Corporation are among the companies that have appointed corporate risk managers to perform this important activity.[50]

Centralization exists to some extent in all functional areas and at all levels of management, as managers tend to reserve for themselves many of the most critical decisions that fall within their authority. In fact, one study found that (1) identification of the key risk areas and (2) centralization of decision making in these areas are characteristics of the MCSs used by "excellent" Canadian companies.[51]

Common candidates for centralization are decisions regarding diversification strategy (such as major acquisitions and divestments), major capital expenditures, negotiation of pivotal sales contracts, organization changes, and hiring and firing of high-level executives. However, in most organizations of even minimal size, it is not possible to centralize all critical activities, and other control solutions are necessary.[52]

Risk Sharing

A final, partial avoidance possibility is risk sharing. Sharing risks with outside entities can bound the losses (or forgone opportunities) that could be incurred by inappropriate employee behaviors. Risk sharing can involve buying insurance to protect against certain types of large, potential losses they might not be able to afford. Many companies purchase fidelity bonds on employees in sensitive positions (such as bank tellers) to reduce the firm's exposure. These insurance contracts pass at least a portion of the risk of large losses, errors, and defalcations to the insurance companies. Another way to share risks with an outside party is to enter into a joint venture agreement. This shares the risk with the joint venture partner.

These avoidance alternatives are often an effective partial solution to, or bounding of, many of the control problems managers face. It is rarely possible to avoid all risk because firms are rewarded for bearing risk, but most firms use some forms of elimination, automation, centralization, and risk sharing in order to limit their areas of exposure to the control problems.

CONTROL ALTERNATIVES

For the control problems that cannot be avoided, and those for which decisions have been made not to avoid, managers must (or probably should) implement one or more types of mechanisms which are generally called *controls*. The collection of control mechanisms that are used is generally referred to as a *control system* or an MCS.

Controls vary considerably among companies and among the areas of any single company. Table 1-2 shows some of the individual controls used in a manufacturing firm. Table 1-3 shows some of the controls used in a computer facility.

TABLE 1-2 Examples of Controls Used in a Manufacturing Firm

1. The cash payment and cash receipt functions are segregated.
2. A check protector is used, and signature plates are kept under lock and key.
3. The accounting department matches invoices to receiving reports or special authorizations prior to payment.
4. Checks are mailed by someone other than the person making out the check.
5. The accounting department matches invoices to copies of purchase orders.
6. The blank stock of checks is kept under lock and key.
7. Impress accounting is used for payroll.
8. Bank reconciliations are to be accomplished by someone other than the one who writes checks and handles cash.
9. Surprise counts of cash funds are conducted periodically.
10. Orders can be placed with approved vendors only.
11. All purchases must be made by the purchasing department.

TABLE 1-3 Examples of Controls Used in a Computer Facility

1. Written standards exist for documentation of systems, operations, and administration.
2. Access to the computer system and all online data terminals is restricted at all times to authorized personnel only.
3. Data is secured through tape file protection rings, file labels, cryptographic protection, duplication procedures, and requirement of storage of duplicates at a remote site.
4. Hardware controls include duplicate circuitry, dual reading, echo checks, preventative maintenance, and uninterruptible power systems.
5. Major risks are insured against.
6. Backup systems and procedures are developed.

The control systems of some firms consist primarily of trying to hire people who can be relied upon to serve the firm well. Other firms provide modest performance-based incentives, and still others offer incentives that can more than double base salaries. Some firms assign the incentives based on the accomplishment of targets defined in terms of financial accounting numbers, others use nonfinancial measures of performance, and still others evaluate performance only subjectively. Some firms have elaborate sets of policies and procedures that they expect all, or maybe some, employees to follow, whereas others have no such procedures or they allow the procedures that were once in place to get out of date. Some firms make extensive use of a large, highly professional internal audit staff, while others do not have an internal audit function. These are just examples. The distinctions that can be made among the MCS in use are many.

Managers' control choices are not random. They are based on a number of factors. Some controls are not effective, or are not cost-effective, in certain situations. Some types of controls are better at addressing particular types of problems, and different organizations and different areas within each organization often face quite different mixes of control problems. Some types of controls have undesirable side effects which can be particularly dangerous in some settings. Some controls merely suit particular managers' styles better than others. A major purpose of this book is to describe the factors affecting one or more control choice decisions and the effects on the organization when better or worse choices are made.

BOOK OUTLINE

This book discusses controls and MCSs from four different angles, each the focus of one major section of the book. The second section distinguishes controls based on the *object of control,* which can focus on the actions taken *(action control),* the results produced *(results control),* or the types of people employed and their shared norms and values *(personnel/cultural control).*[53] Chapters 2 through 7 discuss each of these forms of control, the positive and negative outcomes they can produce, and the factors that lead managers to choose one object of control over another.

The third section of the book, Chapters 8 through 11, focuses more intensively on the major elements of *financial results control systems,* an important type of results control in which results are defined in financial terms. Included in this section of the book are discussions of alternate financial performance measurements and financial responsibility structures, planning and budgeting systems, and financial performance-dependent rewards and punishments.

The fourth section of the book, Chapters 12 through 15, discusses some major problems managers face when they use financial results control systems and some of the major approaches they use in solving these problems. These problems include the tendency of accounting measures to cause managers to be excessively short-term oriented (myopic), the tendency for return-on-investment measures of performance to cause bad investment and performance evaluation decisions, the likelihood of negative behavioral reactions from managers who are held accountable for factors over which they have less than complete control, and the likelihood of misleading performance signals and dysfunctional internal competition if transfer prices are not set appropriately.

The fifth section of the book, Chapters 16 and 17, discusses some key organizational control roles, including those of controllers, auditors, and audit committees of the board of directors. It also discusses some common control-related ethical issues and how to analyze them.

The final section of the book, Chapters 18 through 20, discusses some of the contextual factors that have significant effects on either the choices of control systems or the effectiveness of the systems in specific settings. Chapter 18 discusses the effects of three of the most important factors that cause control systems to be different: uncertainty/lack of programmability, corporate diversification strategy, and business strategy. Chapter 19 focuses on control problems unique to international and multinational contexts. Chapter 20 focuses on some control problems unique to not-for-profit organizations.

Notes

1. M. Siconolfi, "Report Faults Kidder for Laxness in Jett Case," *Wall Street Journal* (August 5, 1994), p. C1.
2. W. M. Carley, M. Siconolfi, and A. K. Haj, "How Will Welch Deal with Kidder Scandal?: Problems Keep Coming," *Wall Street Journal* (May 3, 1994), p. A1.
3. "Super Slipup," *Forbes* (March 25, 1996), p. 16.
4. K. Rebello, P. Burrows, and I. Sager, "The Fall of an American Icon," *Business Week* (February 5, 1996), p. 39.
5. Even auditors have broadened their definition of control beyond narrow internal financial control to include many behavioral considerations. For the approach in the United States, see the so-called COSO report: Committee of Sponsoring Organizations, *Integrated Control—Integrated Framework* (New York: Committee of Sponsoring Organizations, 1992). Similar broader internal control approaches were also recently developed by the United Kingdom's Cadbury Commission and the Canadian Criteria of Control Committee (CoCo).
6. For example, D. J. Galloway, "Control Models in Perspective," *Internal Auditor,* 51, no. 6 (December 1994), pp. 46–52; E. G. Flamholtz, T. K. Das, and A. Tsui, "Toward an Integrative Framework of Organizational Control," *Accounting, Organizations and Society,* 10 (1985), pp. 35–50; and K. A. Merchant, *Control in Business Organizations* (Marshfield, Mass.: Pitman, 1985).
7. A. D. Szilagyi, *Management and Performance* (Glenview, Ill.: Scott, Foresman and Company, 1981), p. 6.
8. See H. Mintzberg, "Crafting Strategy," *Harvard Business Review,* 65 (July–August 1987), pp. 66–75.
9. H. Mintzberg, "The Strategy Concept I: Five Ps for Strategy," *California Management Review,* 30, no. 1 (1987), pp. 11–24.

10. R. Henkoff, "How to Plan for 1995," *Fortune* (December 31, 1990), p. 76.
11. The strategic control task has been discussed by, among others, M. Goold, "Strategic Control in the Decentralized Firm," *Sloan Management Review,* 32, no. 2 (Winter 1991), pp. 69–81; J. F. Preble, "Towards a Comprehensive System of Strategic Control," *Journal of Management Studies,* 29, no. 4 (July 1992), pp. 391–409; G. Schreyögg and H. Steinmann, "Strategic Control: A New Perspective," *Academy of Management Review,* 12, no. 1 (1987), pp. 91–103; and J. H. Horovitz, "Strategic Control: A New Task for Top Management," *Long Range Planning,* 12 (June 1979), pp. 2–7.
12. E. E. Lawler III and J. G. Rhode, *Information and Control in Organizations* (Pacific Palisades, Calif.: Goodyear, 1976), p. 6.
13. W. Birkett, "The Changing Role of the CFO: An Interview with Bill McElroy," *A View of Tomorrow: The Senior Financial Officer in the Year 2005* (New York: International Federations of Accountants, 1995).
14. Many management accounting and management control textbooks refer to *lack of goal congruence* as a general problem category which subsumes both lack of direction and lack of motivation.
15. F. Taylor, *The Principles of Scientific Management* (New York: Harper, 1929).
16. "Time Stealing," *Forbes* (December 20, 1982), p. 9.
17. R. D. Hollinger and J. P. Clark, *Theft by Employees* (Lexington, Mass.: Lexington Books, 1983).
18. K. Rankin, "Fraud Expert: Accountants Must Hone Detection Skills," *Accounting Today* (July 24–August 6, 1995), p. 12.
19. KPMG Peat Marwick, *Fraud Survey Results 1993* (KPMG Peat Marwick, 1993).
20. J. R. Emshwiller, "Small Business is the Biggest Victim of Theft by Employees, Survey Shows," *Wall Street Journal* (October 2, 1995), p. B2.
21. W. McGowan, "The Great White-Collar Crime Coverup," *Business and Society Review* 45 (Spring 1983), pp. 25–31.
22. W. S. Albrecht and M. B. Romney, "Deterring White-Collar Crime in Banks," *Banker's Magazine,* 163, no. 6 (November–December 1980), pp. 60–64.
23. W. G. Flanagan and McMenamin, "The Playground Bullies are Learning How to Type," *Forbes* (December 21, 1992), p. 186.
24. K. Holland, "Bank Fraud, The Old-Fashioned Way," *Business Week* (September 4, 1995), p. 96. Data from American Bankers Association.
25. K. B. Lewis, "Thou Better Not Steal," *Forbes* (November 7, 1994), p. 170.
26. D. Gillmor, "Crime Is Headed Up—And So Is Business," *Boston Globe* (February 15, 1983), p. 47.
27. M. Lipman, *Stealing: How America's Employees are Stealing Their Companies Blind* (New York: Harper's Magazine Press, 1973).
28. K. C. Bettencourt, *Theft and Drugs in the Workplace* (Saratoga, Calif.: R&E Publishers, 1993).
29. R. R. Schmidt, "Executive Dishonesty: Misuse of Authority for Personal Gain," in S. Leininger, ed., *Internal Theft: Investigation and Control* (Los Angeles: Security World, 1975), pp. 69–81.
30. J. J. Fialka, "Ailing Computers Give Social Security System Another Big Problem," *Wall Street Journal* (October 5, 1981), p. 1.
31. This example taken from D. Milbank, "Hiring Welfare People, Hotel Chain Finds, Is Tough but Rewarding," *Wall Street Journal* (October 31, 1996), p. A1.
32. Milbank, p. A1.
33. Ibid.
34. Ibid, p. A6.
35. L. J. Peter and R. Hull, *The Peter Principle: Why Things Go Wrong* (New York: William Morrow & Co., 1969).

36. E. Larson and K. Wells, "Shaken Osborne Computer Seeking Suitor in the Face of Possible Failure," *Wall Street Journal* (September 12, 1983), p. 35.

37. "American Bakeries: A New Chef Cleans Up the Kitchen," *Business Week* (June 27, 1983), p. 52.

38. "Why Book Publishers Are No Longer in Love with Romance Novels," *Business Week* (December 5, 1983), p. 157.

39. See summaries by R. E. Nisbett and L. Ross, *Human Inference: Strategies and Shortcomings of Social Judgment* (Englewood Cliffs, N.J.: Prentice-Hall, 1980); R. Libby, *Accounting and Human Information Processing: Theory and Applications* (Englewood Cliffs, N.J.: Prentice-Hall, 1981); and R. H. Ashton, *Human Information Processing in Accounting,* Studies in Accounting Research no. 17 (Sarasota, Fla.: American Accounting Association, 1982).

40. Confusion has long reigned as to how to use the terms "objectives" and "goals." In this book, the term objectives refers to broad things the organization wants to achieve (such as "be a leader in information services industry"). The term goals refers to specific things the organization wants to achieve in a specified time period (such as earn a 20 percent return on net assets in the coming year). Objectives are relatively stable. Goals may change every planning period.

41. Issues related to whether activities are better managed internally through organizational hierarchies or externally through market contracting are outside the scope of this book. By definition, MCSs include only internal control devices. The fact that all organizations of any size struggle with MCS issues is testament to the failure of arms-length, market-based transactions with entities external to the firm to solve the control problems satisfactorily. The economic issues related to hierarchical vs, market controls are discussed in a body of literature called "transaction cost economics." Oliver Williamson is generally recognized as the most prominent theoretical contributor in this area. For an overview of this literature, see O. Williamson, "Transaction Cost Economics," in R. Schmalensee and R. Willig, eds., *Handbook of Industrial Economics* (New York: North Holland, 1989), chapter 3.

42. A. Sloan, "Go Forth and Compete," *Forbes* (November 23, 1981), pp. 41–42.

43. J. Salamon, "How New York Bank Got Itself Entangled in Drysdale's Dealings," *Wall Street Journal* (June 11, 1982), p. 1.

44. See O. Williamson, *The Economic Institutions of Capitalism* (New York: Free Press, 1985).

45. S. Oliver, "Take Two Aspirin; the Computer Will Call in the Morning," *Forbes* (March 14, 1994), pp. 110–111.

46. This example is taken from T. Richman, "Mrs. Fields' Secret Ingredient," *Inc.* (October 1987), pp. 67–72.

47. S. Mufson, "Amerada Hess Chief Keeps Controls Tight, Emphasizes Marketing," *Wall Street Journal* (January 11, 1983), p. 1.

48. "Data General's Management Trouble," *Business Week* (February 9, 1981), p. 58.

49. "An Acid Test for Tandem's Growth," *Business Week* (February 28, 1983), p. 64.

50. "Managing Risk," *Business Week* (October 31, 1994), p. 92.

51. T. Cawsey, G. Deszca, and H. D. Teall, *Management Control Systems in Excellent Canadian Companies* Management Accounting Issues Paper no. 5 (Hamilton, ON: The Society of Management Accountants of Canada, 1994).

52. Williamson (1985) discusses "transaction cost economics" which deals theoretically with the trade-offs between the efficiencies created by controlling activities through organizational hierarchies or through market contracting. See O. Williamson, *The Economic Institutions of Capitalism* (New York: Free Press, 1985).

53. This framework was discussed by W. Ouchi, "A Conceptual Framework for the Design of Organizational Control Mechanisms," *Management Science,* 25, no. 9 (September 1979), pp. 833–848. It was elaborated on by K. Merchant, *Control in Business Organizations* (Cambridge, Mass.: Ballinger, 1985). The first section of this book presents a refined and expanded discussion of the material in the 1985 book.

Leo's Four-plex Theater

Leo's Four-Plex Theater was a single-location, four-screen theater located in a small town in west Texas. Leo Antonelli bought the theater a year ago and hired Bill Reilly, his nephew, to manage it. Leo was concerned, however, because the theater was not as profitable as he had thought it would be. He suspected the theater had some control problems. He asked Park Cockerill, an accounting professor at a college in the adjacent town, to study the situation and provide suggestions.

Park found the following:

1. Customers purchased their tickets at one of two ticket booths located at the front of the theater. The theater used general admission (not assigned) seating. The tickets were color coded to indicate which movie the customer wanted to see. The tickets were also dated and stamped "good on day of sale only." The tickets at each price (adult, child, matinee, evening) were prenumbered serially, so that the number of tickets sold each day at each price for each movie could be determined by subtracting the number of the first ticket sold from the ending number.
2. The amounts of cash collected were counted daily and compared with the total value of tickets sold. The cash counts revealed, almost invariably, less cash than the amounts that should have been collected. The discrepancies were usually small, less than $10 per cashier. However, on one day two weeks before Park's study, one cashier was short by almost $100.
3. Just inside the theater's front doors was a lobby with a refreshment stand. Park observed the refreshment stand's operations for a while. He noted that most of the stand's attendants were young, probably of high school or college age. They seemed to know many of the customers, a majority of whom were of similar ages, which was not surprising given the theater's small town location. But the familiarity concerned Park because he also observed several occasions where the stand's attendants either failed to collect cash from the customers or failed to ring up the sale on the cash register.
4. Customers entered the screening rooms by passing through a turnstile manned by an attendant who separated the ticket and placed part of it in a locked "stub box." Test counts of customers entering and leaving the theater did not reconcile either with the number of ticket sales or the stub counts.

   Park found evidence of two specific problems. First, he found a few tickets of the wrong color or with the wrong dates in the ticket stub boxes. And second, he found a sometimes significant number of free theater passes with Billy Reilly's signature on them. These problems did not account for all of the customer test count discrepancies, however. Park suspected that the ticket collectors might also be admitting friends who had not purchased tickets, although his observations provided no direct evidence of this.

When his study was complete, Park sat down and wondered whether he could give Leo suggestions which would address all the actual and potential problems, yet not be too costly.

Professor Kenneth A. Merchant wrote this case as the basis for class discussion rather than to illustrate either effective or ineffective handling of an administrative situation.

Wong's Pharmacy

Thomas Wong was the owner/manager of Wong's Pharmacy, a small, single-location drug store. The store was founded by Thomas' father, and it had operated in the same location for 30 years. All of the employees who worked in the store were family members. All were hard workers, and Thomas had the utmost trust in all of them.

Although the store thrived in its early years, performance in the last few years had not been good. Sales and profits were declining, and the problem was getting worse. The performance problems seemed to have begun approximately at the time when a large drugstore chain opened a branch two blocks away.

Professor Kenneth A. Merchant wrote this case as the basis for class discussion rather than to illustrate either effective or ineffective handling of an administrative situation.

---

33 Dunster Street (A)

In September 1983, Molly Hoagland, owner and manager of 33 Dunster Street, a restaurant/bar in Cambridge, Massachusetts, was considering investing $46,000 in a new state-of-the-art, computerized information and control system. She explained:

> I'm a firm believer of the 3 Cs of the restaurant business: control, consistency, and cleanliness. Control is necessary to protect what we have and what we earn; consistency is important because people like to know that what they liked last time is what they'll receive the next time; and the importance of cleanliness is obvious. Maintaining consistency and cleanliness are relatively easy, but maintaining good control is a constant struggle.
>
> We have several control problems that we have had difficulty solving. First, we have too much food wastage. I can tell that because our food purchases are too high for our level of sales, and I can see it in what we have to throw out. Second, we have too much paperwork. Our staff spends too little time serving customers because they are so busy filling out and completing the checks. Third, I am convinced that we could improve our purchasing if we had accurate information about customer traffic and the demand for specific menu items. A new computerized control system should help us address these problems, but these systems cost a lot of money, and the judgments involved in deciding whether or not they are worth it are difficult.

THE OPERATION

33 Dunster Street was a popular restaurant/bar located in Harvard Square, in the midst of the Harvard University campus. The restaurant offered a broad menu and reasonable prices.

The restaurant was purchased in 1975 by Ralph and Molly Hoagland, a Boston business couple. A restaurant known as the Spaghetti Em-

This case was prepared by Research Assistant Chris S. Paddison, under the supervision of Associate Professor Kenneth A. Merchant, as the basis for class discussion rather than to illustrate either effective or ineffective handling of an administrative situation.

porium had operated on the 33 Dunster Street site for several years, but despite the excellent location, that restaurant had failed. The Hoaglands, who owned a successful regional pharmacy chain, purchased the restaurant as the first in a diversification strategy.

The Hoaglands improved the restaurant's atmosphere and broadened the menu. With a new decor of bookshelf-lined walls, hanging plants, and a Tiffany lamp over every table, 33 Dunster Street became a popular restaurant appealing particularly to students and young professionals.

The restaurant's floor plan reflected the emphasis on table service over bar sales. Seating was provided for 328 people at 72 tables. A large stand-up bar area could accommodate 38 people. A floor plan is shown in Exhibit 1. The restaurant operation was designed to handle any size of group and to ensure that under normal conditions customers could be seated, have dinner, and leave in 45 minutes, if need be. The average turnover, including drinks, was approximately one hour in normal periods, and 1½ hours in busy periods.

33 Dunster Street was open for lunch and dinner. The average per-person check, including food and beverage, was approximately $6 at lunch and $12 at dinner. The same food items were offered for both meals, but the lunch menu offered lower prices on average because smaller portions were provided and daily luncheon specials were offered. Still, lunch was considered an important revenue source as it accounted for about 30 percent of the restaurant's total dollar volume.

Since its opening, 33 Dunster Street had been a very successful operation. The restaurant served 7,000 customers per week, with weekends the busiest days. The estimated annual revenues for 1983 were expected to be around $2,000,000 up 20 percent from the prior year, and operating ratios and profitability were approximately at the midpoint of the industry ranges shown in Exhibit 2.

PEOPLE/ORGANIZATION

The 33 Dunster Street staff included approximately 85 full-time and part-time employees. The tasks were divided among the employees to ensure good customer service. When customers descended into the restaurant's underground location, they were greeted by a host or hostess and showed to their table. Within minutes of the seating, a server would arrive at the table and offer to get drinks. Servers did not deliver food and drink to the tables, however; that was done by runners so that the servers could focus on order taking and customer service. After customers had paid and left, the tables were cleared and prepared by busboys. The manager on duty helped ensure excellent customer service by supervising the staff and attending to any problems that surfaced.

A majority of the servers were college graduates who worked in the restaurant while they sought more permanent work. They were paid a low salary plus tips. The kitchen staff, which included cooks, dishwashers and pot washers, were mostly people with relatively little formal education. Although the Hoaglands treated their employees well and offered job security, turnover was high, as it was in most Boston-area restaurants. In fact, average annual turnover in the restaurant industry in the U.S. was approximately 350%.

The administrative staff included Mrs. Hoagland, three managers, all of whom had been promoted from server or bartender positions, and a part-time bookkeeper. Bob Lenson, the head manager, was responsible for personnel scheduling. He based his schedule on historical traffic patterns adjusted for any special events that might be taking place in the area (e.g. Harvard reunion, neighborhood festival). Staffing of the restaurant could be done on a flexible basis because employees in 33 Dunster Street were not represented by a union. Mr. Lenson and Mrs. Hoagland were jointly responsible for planning the menu, although with the exception of the daily specials, few changes were made from month to month.

WORK FLOW AND RECORD KEEPING

The procedures in use at 33 Dunster Street were designed to ensure good control of food orders and the accompanying cash flow. Of particular concern were mistakes by the staff and thefts by staff or customers.

At the beginning of each shift, servers were given a stack of preprinted, prenumbered, two-part order tickets. As customers ordered, the servers wrote the food orders on the front of the tickets and drinks on the back. They then went to one of two electronic cash registers (ECRs) located on either side of the restaurant, placed the ticket in the ECR and entered the ticket number, their server number, the table number, and the order. The ECRs printed the dollar amounts on the order ticket and prepared an order chit that the food runners were to use to pick up the food and drink from the kitchen and bar. The ECRs had 40 preset keys for popular food items, but some of the items were input in their dollar amount only.

The preset ECR keys were used to track the sales of certain items by server. Mrs. Hoagland noted that "There is a big difference between the servers who actively sell and those who just take orders." To encourage the servers to be sellers, she sometimes provided special awards, such as coupon books and free dinners, for good performances. Among the items that were sometimes tracked for special award purposes were drinks, desserts, and the "daily special," particularly when the restaurant made a quantity purchase of a particular food item such as a crate of lobsters.

After the ECR entry, the server delivered one copy of the order ticket to the kitchen and the other to the bar. The kitchen staff and bartenders prepared the food and drink and placed it in staging areas for the runners to pick up. Access to the kitchen was restricted, so the kitchen staff passed the food to the runners across a chest-high counter. The runners delivered the orders to the table noted on the order ticket.

The cooks and bartenders were supposed to perform two control functions at the time the food and drink was picked up. First, they were to check the dollar amounts printed on the ticket. Second, they were to check that the runners picked up the correct order by matching the order ticket with the chit brought by the runner and then "spindling the chit" by putting a hole in it so that it could not be used again. These control functions were not being done reliably, especially during busy periods.

When a meal was completed, the server totalled the bill in the ECR, gave the printed ticket to the customer, and collected the money. They kept all the money and tickets until the end of the shift, although periodically the manager on duty would "bleed" the servers, meaning that he or she would give them a receipt in exchange for some of the cash so that they would not be carrying amounts of cash that could be as large as $1,000 each.

At the end of their shift, the servers would count their money, have the amount verified by a witness, and then seal it in a cash envelope. The manager would tally the order tickets and pay the servers their tips. During busy periods, this process could take up to an hour, and the servers were paid their hourly rate while they waited.

After the servers were paid, the manager completed an employee time sheet and a daily reconciliation form which displayed the food and alcohol sales, gross profit, and the numbers of checks, tables and guests. He or she would also initial the cash envelopes and drop them in a locked deposit box. In the morning the bookkeeper would count the receipts and reconcile them with the ECR totals. If the receipts did not reconcile, the servers were held responsible for the difference. Differences were usually relatively minor, not totalling more than $10 per day.

THE BAR AREA

The bar area presented some somewhat unique control problems because bartenders had access to both money and inventory. 33 Dunster Street had an attractive 40-foot wooden bar, with polished bottles and glasses displayed on shelves behind and above the bar. Two ECRs were located behind the bar. A larger inventory of alcohol was stored in a room located behind the bar area. Normally the bar was run by one or two bartenders, each assigned his or her own ECR. But sometimes in very busy times, three bartenders had to be used and an ECR had to be shared.

For drink orders taken by the waitresses, the bartenders would prepare the drinks and deliver them to one of two serving areas. At these serving areas, a runner would pick them up, add garnishment if necessary, and deliver them to the table. The bartender would not record these sales in the ECR as the server had already done so. But when a patron at the bar requested a drink, the bartender would ring up the sale and collect the money.

CONCERNS WITH SYSTEM

Mrs. Hoagland identified three primary concerns with the present system:

> The greatest problem we face is human error. For example, servers sometimes fail to charge for an item, or they charge the wrong amount. Cooks sometimes attach an order to the wrong chit or the servers deliver food to the wrong table, and the customer will start

eating before the error is discovered. And busboys, in their haste, sometimes throw silverware into the garbage. To address this latter problem, I installed giant magnets over the garbage cans to retrieve the silverware that had been discarded.

The second greatest problem is trying to control dishonest employees. We know of lots of ways to "beat" the system. For example, servers have several means of stealing. They can key their food order onto another server's bill and pocket the cash, or they can sell a meal that has been returned to the kitchen because of an error or a customer complaint. Bartenders can sell drinks to bar customers without recording the sale; they can vary the quantity of alcohol in the drinks they serve; or they can register the drink on the other bartender's register. And if we allowed access to the kitchen, the cooks could give food to the servers for sale without an order ticket.

Another concern is customers trying to cheat the restaurant. A lot of our customers are students who appear to be willing to take advantage of any mistakes our employees make, from incorrect adding of a bill to delivering additional food or drinks. People also try to abuse the salad bar. People are supposed to order either a small or large salad from the server and then go and serve themselves. Well, some customers try to order a small salad and then use a large salad plate, or they share their salad with other diners. I don't know of any restaurant that doesn't hate their salad bar.

My strategy is to "divide and conquer." I want to make it very difficult for any one person to steal from us, and I want to make collusion as difficult as possible. To control the special problems in the bar area, we hire professional spotters to pose as patrons and watch the bartenders. We are quick to fire any employee we catch doing something illegal.

People get the wrong impression about the food business. They think that it is all marketing and maintenance of food quality. Well that's not enough. If you want to make money in this business, you have to control it almost as tightly as a bank. With our margins, unless we control everything tightly, we'll be out of business. We do a weekly inventory of our food and bar stocks, and I spend a lot of time trying to figure out how my employees and my customers might be beating us.

THE INVESTMENT DECISION

In early 1983 Mrs. Hoagland became interested in rethinking her control system after reading in a trade magazine about recent improvements in restaurant cash register systems. The new systems provided a more complete set of routine financial and operating reports. Most also offered summary statistics that were available at any time for any operating period and an array of detailed reports, such as sales of each item on the menu and sales by server.

Mrs. Hoagland thought this information could be useful for managing 33 Dunster Street. The summary statistics would allow restaurant managers to evaluate operations from the back room during the shift. The menu item sales numbers could be useful for planning purposes because 33 Dunster Street managers had been estimating the popularity of its menu items based on food purchases, not sales. And the server-sales numbers could be useful for motivational purposes. If server sales were tracked, extra compensation could be provided and the best servers could be rewarded and used to their best advantage by assigning them to the best tables. Among the statistics thought to be useful were number of customers served, order size per customer, and the liquor to food ratio.[1]

Mrs. Hoagland investigated several different systems on the market and decided to focus her attention on a system manufactured by the Remanco Company, a Canadian firm. Her choice was influenced by several factors. Remanco had an excellent reputation and nine years of experience providing control systems to restaurants in the high end of the food-service business. They manufactured all of their equipment and had a good quality record. They claimed to have the most software available and promised that additional programs could be added easily if needed. They offered excellent training for both management and staff. And finally, two local businesses had purchased computer-aided systems and claimed

---

[1]Liquor sales were more profitable than food sales.

they had provided profit improvements: Legal Seafood, the leading Boston seafood chain used the Remanco system in all three of its operations; and Au Bon Pain, a rapidly growing coffee and pastry chain, claimed a similar system had saved it approximately two percent of sales.

In an initial discussion, a Remanco representative claimed that the system was readily adaptable to 33 Dunster's current operation and that it would yield some major improvements in control and efficiency. In his view, the new system should consist of four (instead of two) serving stations, each with a small terminal with display screen and printer, a CPU, memory drive and printer to be installed in the restaurant office, and two extra print-only stations located in the kitchen and bar areas.

Under the sales representative's conception of the system, servers would take orders and then go to a serving station into which they would insert a magnetic key permitting access only to their individual files. The servers would enter the table number, number of guests and the quantity and three-digit codes of each item being ordered. The name and price of each item on the menu would be recalled from memory automatically. The computer would transmit the drink orders to a printer located behind the bar and the food orders to a printer located in the kitchen. (Exhibit 3 shows two sample orders as they would appear on the bartender's printer.) The server had the option of printing the order at the server station for purposes of verification. When the meal was complete, the server would close the file, and the computer would tabulate the bill and print out a check for the table (see Exhibit 4).

The Remanco system promised many advantages over the ECR system, as follows:

1. The system offered a complete set of reports available on both routine and special-request bases. For example, Exhibit 5 shows a sample of a hypothetical server report that could be produced. Exhibit 6 shows a hypothetical sample statistics report.
2. The Remanco system promised to be easier to use because the server had less information to input into the system, and if so, the servers would have more time available with which to provide better service or to manage more tables. Mrs. Hoagland estimated that servers talked to customers a total of five times each, and each interaction was an opportunity to sell more food and beverages. So she thought that if a new system provided servers with additional time, enough to talk to a table six times during an average meal, then food and beverage sales could increase by as much as 2–5%.
3. The new system would also speed up the preparation of food and drinks, as the orders were printed out immediately in the kitchen and bar. This could save as much as 10 minutes per order during busy periods.
4. Some server errors would be eliminated, particularly those involving the charging of the wrong price or not charging for an item at all.
5. The new system allowed the "telescoping down" of tables. This meant that as business slackened, some servers could be sent home and their tables reassigned to other servers. This reassignment of tables could not be done with the ECR system.
6. The new system promised time-saving features for management. Currently it took the night manager approximately one to two hours to prepare the daily reports. The manager had to complete the time cards on all the employees, summarize the tallies from all of the envelopes received throughout the day, and prepare a report of the daily business, all manually. The new system would reconcile the daily business automatically and print out the reports desired by the next morning.
7. Storage of customer order tickets would be simplified. Restaurants were required by the tax authorities to store all customer checks until they were audited or, in the absence of an audit, indefinitely. On a busy evening, 2,500 checks, or more, were produced at 33 Dunster Street, and storing these checks was a burden. With the new systems, however, the checks could be stored on disk.

To protect against power failures, the system would be equipped with a five-minute battery back-up. If a power failure lasted more than five minutes, the restaurant would have to revert to a manual operation.

Mrs. Hoagland was impressed with the Remanco system, but she still had some concerns. One was simply that she was accustomed to hearing sales representatives exaggerate the claims for a product, and she wondered how the system would really perform in place. Second, she wondered if the benefits would be worth the investment of $46,000 plus additional expenses, such as for service and supplies, estimated to be approximately $5,000 per year. Finally, she wondered how easy it would be to train the staff to operate the system, and how the staff would react.

EXHIBIT 1 Restaurant Floor Plan

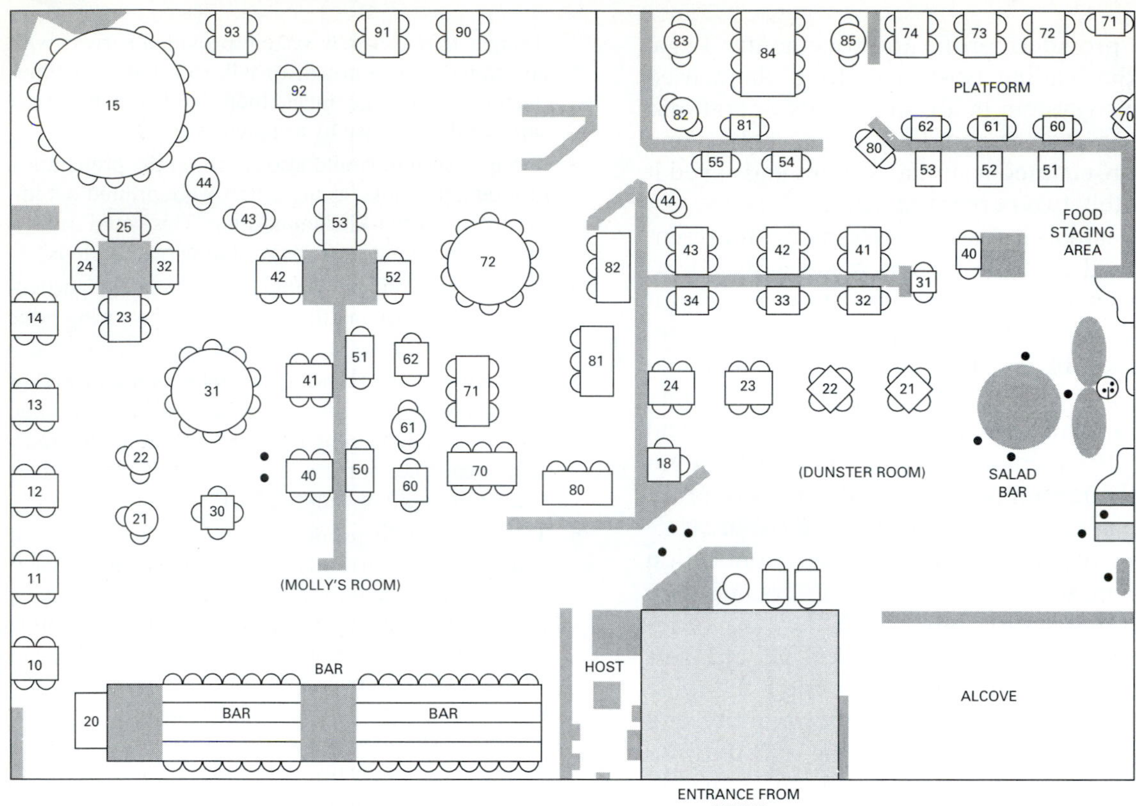

EXHIBIT 2 Restaurant Industry Income Statement Ratios

Sales:	
Food	70.0–80.0
Beverages	20.0–30.0
Total sales	100.0
Cost of sales:	
Food costs (raw food from suppliers, percent of food sales)	38.0–48.0
Beverage cost (percent of beverage sales)	25.0–30.0
Total cost of sales	35.0–45.0
Gross profit	55.0–65.0
Operating expenses:	
Controllable expenses:	
Payroll	30.0–35.0
Employee benefits	3.0–5.0
Employee meals	1.0–2.0
Laundry, linens, uniforms	1.5–2.0
Replacements	0.5–1.0
Supplies (guests)	1.0–1.5
Menus and printing	0.25–0.5
Miscellaneous contract expenses (cleaning, garbage, extermination, equipment, rental)	1.0–2.0
Music and entertainment (where applicable)	0.5–1.0
Advertising and promotion	0.75–2.0
Utilities	1.0–2.0
Management salary	2.0–6.0
Administration expenses (including legal and accounting)	0.75–2.0
Repairs and maintenance	1.0–2.0
Occupation expense:	
Rent	4.5–9.0
Taxes (real estate and personal property)	0.5–1.0
Insurance	0.75–1.0
Interest	0.3–1.0
Depreciation	2.0–4.0
Franchise royalties (where applicable)	3.0–6.0
Total operating expenses	55.0–65.0
Net profit before income tax	0.5–9.0

Source: Bank of America, *Small Business Reporter,* 8, no. 2, 1968.

EXHIBIT 3 Sample Bar Orders

```
37:44 ID    11 TBL   172/ 1AREA=C          19.50
CHECK #      2                           4 GUESTS

       1    10 HEINEKEN LIGHT
```

```
37:54 ID    11 TBL   170/ 1AREA=C          15.40
CHECK #      3                           8 GUESTS

      1     1 MILLER LIGHT
      2     1 ROLLING ROCK
      3     1 STOLICHNAYA      FZ
      4     1 REMY USOP
```

EXHIBIT 4 Sample Table Check

```
                GUEST CHECK
SERVER  11     TABLE  170/    1   TIME   08:05

         1  1 MILLER LIGHT              1.55
         4  ROLLING ROCK                7.20
         1  STOLICHNAYA                 2.85
         1  REMY USOP                   3.80

                    TOTAL              15.40
                      TAX               0.77
           PAID BY DCUP                −2.00

           GRAND TOTAL                 14.17

           DCUP NUMBER 0

              33 DUNSTER STREET
        HARVARD SQUARE—CAMBRIDGE
        THANK YOU—PLEASE PAY SERVER
DON'T MISS OUR SUNDAY BRUNCH BUFFET 10–3
HAVE AN AFTER DINNER DRINK AT OUR BAR!
```

EXHIBIT 5 Hypothetical Daily Server Sales Report

Server Name	*ID#*	*Income*	*Over/Short*	*Entrees Q/D*	*APPS/DESS Q/D*	*Liquor Q/D*	*Beer Q/D*	*Wine Q/D*	*Other Items*	*Guests $S/Average*
Rybar, Danny	11	$795.89	( )	41	105	21	57	13	11	106
			-----	295.75	215.05	57.00	110.50	43.00	34.80	756.10
HIGH SALES			$/Guest	2.79	2.03	0.54	1.04	0.41	0.33	7.14
			% Mix	39.00	99.00	20.00	54.00	12.00	10.00	******
Athanasiou, Leslie	14	603.74	( )	35	59	29	46	17	1	71
			-----	223.35	135.10	83.65	83.10	47.90	0.00	573.10
			$/Guest	3.15	1.90	1.18	1.17	0.67	0.00	8.07
			%/Mix	49.00	83.00	41.00	65.0	24.00	1.00	******
Wells, Dorothy	16	140.85	( )	23	31	0	0	0	1	21
			-----	100.95	32.65	0.00	0.00	0.00	0.50	134.10
			$/Guest	4.81	1.55	0.00	0.00	0.00	0.02	6.38
			%/Mix	110.00	148.00	0.00	0.00	0.00	5.00	******
Cyr, Danielle	22	202.56	( )	32	33	0	5	0	10	35
			-----	138.25	37.10	0.00	9.85	0.00	3.00	188.20
			$/Guest	3.95	1.06	0.00	0.28	0.00	0.09	5.38
			%/Mix	91.00	94.00	0.00	14.00	0.00	29.00	******
Doolin, Bill	28	238.12	( )	4	6	7	68	10	0	3
			-----	21.80	16.85	22.20	123.85	20.00	0.00	204.70
			$/Guest	7.27	5.62	7.40	41.28	6.67	0.00	68.24
			%/Mix	133.00	200.00	233.00	2,267.00	333.00	0.00	******
Weiss, Karen	32	682.65	( )	37	93	18	67	16	6	82
			-----	221.55	205.65	51.05	127.35	39.35	5.10	650.05
			$/Guest	2.70	2.51	0.62	1.55	0.48	0.06	7.92
			%/Mix	45.00	113.00	22.00	82.00	20.00	7.00	******

EXHIBIT 6 Hypothetical Sample Statistics Report

	House Sales			
Category Name	*Quantity Sold*	*Dollar Value*	*Dollar/ Guest*	*Percent Mix*
Entrees	327	$1,776.20	3.29	61.00%
APPS/DESS	531	957.70	1.77	98.00
Liquor	128	364.25	0.67	24.00
Beer	346	648.75	1.20	64.00
Wine	73	199.50	0.37	14.00
Other items	46	64.55	0.12	9.00
House average check			7.42	

Section II: Control Alternatives and Their Effects

CHAPTER 2
Action Controls

One common and important category of controls, *action controls,* involves ensuring that employees perform (or do not perform) certain actions known to be beneficial (or harmful) to the organization. Action controls are the *most direct* form of control because control involves taking steps to make certain that employees act in the organization's best interest. With action controls, the actions themselves are the focus of the controls.

Although they are commonly used in business organizations, action controls are not effective in every situation. They are usable and effective only when managers know what actions are desirable (or undesirable) and have the ability to make sure that the desirable actions occur (or that the undesirable actions do not occur).

TYPES OF ACTION CONTROLS

Action controls take four basic forms: behavioral constraints, preaction reviews, action accountability, and redundancy.

Behavioral Constraints

Behavioral constraints are a negative form of action control. They make it impossible, or at least more difficult, for people to do things that should not be done. The constraints can be applied physically or administratively.

Most companies use multiple forms of *physical constraints,* including locks on desks, computer passwords, and limits on access to areas where valuable inventories and sensitive information are kept. Some behavioral constraint devices are technically sophisticated, such as magnetic identification-card readers, voice-pattern detectors, fingerprint readers, and eyeball-pattern readers.

Administrative constraints can also be used to place limits on an individual's abilities to perform all or a portion of specific acts. One common form of administrative control involves the restriction of decision-making authority. Managers at a low level may be allowed to approve expenditures of up to $100; those at a higher level up to $500; and so on. Above those limits, the purchasing department is instructed not to place the order. The senior managers who restrict the decision-making rights in this way are trying to minimize the risk that untrained or uninformed employees will make major mistakes.

Another common form of administrative control is generally referred to as *separation of duties.* This involves dividing up the tasks necessary for the accomplishment of certain sensitive duties, thus making it impossible, or at least difficult, for one person to complete certain tasks that should not be completed.

Separation of duties comes in many forms. One common example involves making sure the person who makes the payment entries in the accounts receivable ledger is different from the person who receives the checks. If one employee who was diverting company checks to a personal account had only the payment-entry duties; that is, opening the mail and listing, endorsing, and totaling incoming checks, customers would eventually complain about being dunned for amounts they had already paid. A person with both check-receiving and payment-entry duties could divert the checks and cover the action by making fictitious entries of returns of goods or, perhaps, price adjustments.

Separation of duties is described by auditors as one of the basic requirements of what they call good *internal control.* The effectiveness of separation of duties is limited, however, because it does not prevent negative actions produced by collusion between two or more key individuals, such as those with the check-receiving and payment-entry duties.

Sometimes physical and administrative constraints can be combined into what has been labeled as *poka-yokes,* which are designed to make an operation or system *foolproof.*[1] A poka-yoke is a step built into a process to prevent deviation from the correct order of steps.[2] It must be performed before the next step can be completed. A simple mechanical poka-yoke example is the inclusion of a switch in the door of a microwave oven so that the oven cannot be operated with the door open. Similar mistake-preventing poka-yokes can also be built into some production and administrative processes. For example, it might be possible to have a signature-verifying computer generate the paperwork necessary for making a cash distribution only after all the approvals for that distribution have been secured.

Preaction Reviews

Preaction reviews are a second form of action controls. These reviews involve scrutiny of the action plans of the individuals being controlled. Reviewers can approve or disapprove the proposed actions, ask for modifications, or ask for a more carefully considered plan before a final approval is granted.

Preaction reviews come in many forms, some formal and some informal. A common form of formal preaction review is the requirement of approvals for expenditures of certain types. Most managers are able to spend only a certain amount of money without review by a higher authority, and the review limit often varies by type of expenditure (such as capital or expense). Another set of formal preaction reviews takes place during organizational planning and budgeting processes, as there are usually multiple levels of reviews of planned actions. The state enterprise control office in Brazil was struggling to bring the giant state companies, including the oil company Petrobras, "under control" and it used both of these formal preaction reviews.[3] The office decided to conduct detailed reviews of all company budgets and to require company personnel to secure written permission before borrowing money.

Informal reviews of actions are also an important part of most organizations' control systems. These reviews may involve nothing more than a hallway chat between a superior and a subordinate, perhaps checking on the progress of a specific project.

Action Accountability

A third form of action control, *action accountability,* involves holding employees accountable for the actions they take. The implementation of action accountability controls requires (1) defining what actions are acceptable or unacceptable, (2) communicating those definitions to employees, (3) observing or otherwise tracking what happens, and (4) rewarding good actions or punishing actions that deviate from the acceptable.

The actions for which people are to be held accountable can be communicated either administratively or socially. Administrative modes of communication include the use of work rules, policies and procedures, contract provisions, and company codes of conduct. It is common in chains of fast-food franchises, such as McDonald's, Wendy's, and Burger King, to prescribe and communicate in writing and clarify through training classes how virtually everything should be done, including how to handle cash, how to hire new employees, where to buy supplies, and what temperature to keep the oil while cooking french fries. Similarly, nurses use "preoperative checklists" to help ensure that they prepare patients thoroughly for surgery. These checklists may remind them to check on the patient's allergies, recent drug-taking history, and time of last meal. Department store managers also have sets of procedures they are expected to follow. At Sears, Roebuck and Company, store managers are rebuked if empty merchandise cartons are not broken down before they are sent to the trash room (because employees could use the cartons to steal merchandise).[4]

Line-item input budgets, which place an upper constraint on the amount to be spent in a given time period, are also common and powerful ways to hold people accountable. They set limits on the areas in which managers may behave. If the managers exceed those limits, they are punished. Managers whose capital expenditures exceed their targets will likely be punished through verbal admonishment, loss of trust from superiors, or loss of bonus.

The desired actions do not have to be communicated in written form, of course. They can be communicated orally, in meetings, or in private, face-to-face discussions. Andrew Grove, Intel's CEO, recognizes that to keep "his generals and his troops marching in the same direction requires constant cajoling and quarreling up and down the ranks."[5]

Sometimes the actions desired are not communicated explicitly at all. In many operational (or performance) audits, post audits of capital investment decisions, and peer reviews of auditors, lawyers, doctors, and managers, people are held accountable for their actions which involved professional judgment. The desirability of these actions is not, and could not be, clearly delineated in advance. The effects (both desirable and undesirable) of these actions might never have been known had it not been for the audit or review.[6] Nonetheless, these people are held accountable for their actions.

Although action accountability controls are most effective if the desired actions are well communicated, communication is not enough by itself to make these controls effective. The affected individuals must understand what is required and feel reasonably sure that what they do will matter; that their individual actions will be noticed and rewarded or punished in some significant way.

Actions can be tracked in several ways. Employee actions can be observed directly and nearly continuously as is done by direct supervisors on production lines. They can be tracked periodically, such as retail stores do when they use "mystery shoppers" to critique the service provided by store clerks. They can also be tracked by examining evidence of actions taken, such as activity reports or expense documentation. Auditors, particularly internal auditors, spend much of their time examining evidence about compliance with preestablished action standards.

Action accountability is usually implemented with negative reinforcements. That is, the actions defined are more often linked with punishments than with rewards. Steelmaker Nucor links several contract elements to actions as part of the production workforce's incentive compensation agreement. Specifically, anyone late for a shift loses a day's bonus, and anyone who misses a shift loses the bonus for the week.[7]

Redundancy

A fourth form of action control is *redundancy*. Redundancy involves assigning more people (or machines) to a task than is theoretically necessary, or at least having backup people available to increase the probability that a task will be accomplished. Redundancy is common in computer facilities and security and other critical operations, but it is rarely used in other areas. It is expensive, and assigning more than one person to the same task usually results in conflict and frustration.

ACTION CONTROLS AND THE CONTROL PROBLEMS

Action controls work because they, like the other types of controls, address one or more of the three control problems. Table 2-1 shows the types of problems addressed by each of the action controls.

Behavioral constraints are primarily effective in eliminating motivational problems. Individuals who might want to do undesirable things can be prevented from doing so.

Preaction reviews can address all three of the control problems. Because they often involve communications from superiors to the individuals being controlled, they can help alleviate a lack of direction. They can provide motivation, as the threat of the impending review usually prompts extra care in the preparation of an expenditure proposal or a plan. They can also mitigate the potentially costly effects of the personal limitations, because a good reviewer can add expertise if it is needed. The reviews can prevent mistakes or other harmful actions from happening.

TABLE 2-1 Control Problems Addressed by Each of the Action Control Types

	Control Problem		
Type of Action Control	*Lack of Direction*	*Motivational Problems*	*Personal Limitations*
Behavioral constraints		x	
Preaction reviews	x	x	x
Action accountability	x	x	x
Redundancy		x	x

Action accountability controls can also address all of the control problems. The prescriptions of desired actions can help provide direction and alleviate the types of personal limitations due to inadequate skills or experience. The rewards or punishments help provide motivation.

Redundancy is the most limited of these controls in its application. It can be effective in helping to accomplish a particular task if there is some doubt as to whether the person assigned to the task is both motivated to perform it satisfactorily and capable of doing so.

PREVENTION VERSUS DETECTION

Action controls can also be usefully classified according to whether they serve to *prevent* or to *detect* undesirable behaviors. This distinction is important because controls that prevent the undesired errors and irregularities from occurring are, when they are effective, the most powerful form of control because *none* of the costs of the undesirable behaviors will be incurred. Detection-type action controls differ from prevention-type controls in that they are applied *after* the occurrence of the behavior. Still, they can be effective if the detection is made in a timely manner and if it results in a cessation of the behavior and a correction of the effects of the harmful actions. Also, the promise of prompt detection of harmful actions is, itself, preventative; it discourages individuals from purposefully engaging in such behaviors.

Most action controls are aimed at preventing undesirable behaviors. The exception is action accountability controls. Although action accountability controls are designed to motivate employees to behave appropriately, the company personnel are not sure the appropriate actions were taken until evidence of the actions taken is gathered. However, if the evidence gathering is concurrent with the activity, as it is with direct supervision, then action accountability control can approach the desired state of prevention of undesired actions. Table 2-2 shows examples of common forms of action controls classified according to whether their purpose is to prevent or detect problems.

TABLE 2-2 Examples of Action Controls Classified by Purpose

	Control Purpose	
Type of Action Control	*Prevention*	*Detection*
Behavioral constraints	Locks on valuable assets Separation of duties	N/A
Preaction reviews	Expenditure approvals Budget reviews	N/A
Action accountability	Prespecified policies, linked to expectations of rewards/ punishments	Compliance-oriented internal audits Cash reconciliations Peer reviews
Redundancy	Assigning multiple people to an important task	N/A

CONDITIONS DETERMINING THE EFFECTIVENESS OF ACTION CONTROLS

Action controls cannot be used effectively in every situation. They are effective only when both of the following conditions exist, at least to some extent:

1. Managers know what actions are desirable (or undesirable); and
2. Managers are able to ensure that the desirable actions occur (or that the undesirable actions do not occur).[8]

Knowledge of Desired Actions

Lack of knowledge as to what actions are desirable is the constraint that most limits the use of action controls. This knowledge is often difficult to obtain. Although it may be easy to define relatively completely the actions required of employees on a production line, the definitions of preferred actions in highly complex and uncertain task environments, such as those of research engineers or top-level managers, cannot be as complete or as precise.

Lack of knowledge or desirable actions definitely limits the application of action controls. A small manufacturing firm that was considering a change in the controls over its sales function faced this knowledge-limitation problem. A consulting firm hired to evaluate the effectiveness of the sales controls recommended implementing an elaborate set of reports to track how the salespeople were allocating their time among types of customers and between direct sales and general market development for action control purposes. The company's managers resisted collecting this information, however, primarily because they did not know how to use it. They did not have a good idea as to how salespeople *should* spend their time. Without that knowledge, the managers did not consider the information about the actions the salespeople actually took to be useful.[9]

Knowledge of the desired actions can be discovered or learned in either of two basic ways. One is by analyzing the actions or results patterns in a specific situation or similar situations over time to learn what actions produce the best results. Store location decisions for most large chains are now highly structured. Over time, the store managers observe which of their stores thrive and which fail. In so doing they learn which locations best fit their store's concept. They can then specify an ideal store-location-decision protocol, delegate the decision to lower-level employees, and control the employees' behaviors by monitoring their adherence to the desired decision protocol. Another way managers can learn which actions are desirable is to be informed by others. Indeed, that is a major role played by consultants. They share their detailed knowledge of best practices.

It is important that the actions for which the individuals are to be held accountable be, in fact, the actions that will lead to the highest probability of accomplishment of one or more of the organization's objectives, or at least the proper implementation of the strategy that is being followed. Dictating a procedure for bank loan officers to follow is correct only if it either leads the officers to perform superior analyses of prospective clients' ability to pay back the loans or it facilitates superiors' and loan committee reviews of those analyses. Many companies have actually found themselves holding employees accountable for taking the *wrong* actions. This problem is discussed in detail in Chapter 6.

Ability to Ensure That Desired Actions Are Taken

Knowing what actions are desirable is not enough to ensure good control; managers must have some ability to ensure that the desired actions are taken. This ability varies widely among the different action controls.

The effectiveness of the behavioral constraints and preaction reviews varies directly with the reliability of the physical devices or administrative procedures the organization has in place to ensure that the desired (undesired) actions are taken (not taken). In many cases, these devices and procedures are not effective. Most firms have implemented administrative constraints to prevent unauthorized personnel from completing foreign currency transactions. However, at Spectra-Physics, a manufacturer of gas lasers, an unauthorized employee was able to bind the company to a number of large foreign-exchange contracts and to conceal the practice from the company. The losses were approximately $10 million.[10] Dai-Ichi Kangyo Bank, Japan's largest commercial bank, suffered a $36 million loss because of unauthorized foreign-exchange speculation over a four-year period in its Singapore branch.[11]

Action tracking often provides a significant challenge that must be faced in making action accountability controls effective. Even where employees' actions cannot be observed directly, usually some actions can be tracked. This tracking is not always effective, however. The criteria that should be used to judge whether the action tracking is effective are precision, objectivity, timeliness, and understandability. If any of these measurement qualities cannot be achieved, action accountability control will not be effective in evoking the desired behaviors.

Precision refers to the amount of error in the indicators used to tell what actions have taken place. If action tracking involves direct supervision, can the supervisors accurately distinguish good from bad actions? If action tracking involves examination of transaction records, do those records reliably tell whether the proper actions were taken? Consider this action-tracking example: A firm was considering requiring salespeople to spend a certain percentage of their time in market development activities, as opposed to direct sales activities. This control effort was doomed to failure until precise definitions could be developed as to which actions fell into each of these two areas.

Another precision failure of an action control occurred with the U.S. Foreign Corrupt Practices Act. This act was intended to make significant bribes to foreign officials illegal, but to allow "facilitating payments to lower-level officials." The distinction between "bribes" and "facilitating payments" was not made clear, however. The vagueness of this law has caused much concern among corporate officials who cannot be sure that their real-time interpretations of the act would match those made by independent observers (such as, a jury) at a later date.[12] Precision problems also limit the effectiveness of many companies' codes of conduct.

Objectivity, or freedom from bias, is a concern because reports of actions prepared by those whose actions are being controlled cannot necessarily be relied upon. Project-oriented personnel are frequently asked to prepare self-reports of how they spend their time. In most cases, these reports are precise, as the allocations may be in units of time as small as one tenth of an hour, but the reports are not objective. If the personnel involved want to obscure the true time patterns, perhaps to cover a bad performance or to allow some personal time, it is relatively easy for them to report that most of their time was spent on productive activities. Most companies use direct supervisors and internal auditors to provide objectivity checks on such reports. Without objectivity, management cannot be sure whether the action reports reflect the actual actions taken, and the reports lose their value for control purposes.

Timeliness in tracking actions is important. If the tracking is not timely, interventions are not possible before harm is done. Further, much of the motivational effect of the feedback and rewards is lost.

Finally, it is important that the actions for which individuals are to be held accountable be *understandable.* Most action prescriptions are understandable. Employees can easily understand prescriptions to "Show up for work on time" or "Don't steal," but understandability does become a problem where the action is defined in aggregate terms and the individual involved does not understand everything implied by the aggregate prescription. Auditors who are held accountable for "testing an accounts receivable balance" may not understand that their tests will be judged based on the satisfactory accomplishment of a series of generally accepted steps, including inspections of documentation, confirmations, computations, reconciliations of general-ledger balances, and clerical checks. If the employees do not understand the detailed procedures, the overall behavioral effect will be unsatisfactory even though the aggregate action is defined correctly and the tracking of whether or not the steps have been performed adequately can be done precisely, objectively, and on a timely basis.

Implementing action controls where one of these action-tracking qualities cannot be achieved will lead to some undesirable effects. These, too, are discussed in Chapter 6.

CONCLUSION

This chapter has provided an overview of the most direct type of controls: action controls. Action controls take any of several different forms: behavioral constraints, preaction reviews, action accountability, and redundancy. It is useful to discuss the action controls together because they are all focused on the same object of control (actions), and they have the same basic feasibility constraints.

Action controls are the most direct type of controls because action controls serve the control objective—ensuring the proper actions of the people on whom the organization must rely—by focusing directly on the actions themselves.

The next chapter focuses on results controls, an indirect, but important form of control. Results controls focus on the results produced by the actions taken.

Notes

1. D. Stewart and R. Chase, *Mistake-Proofing: Designing Errors Out* (Portland, Oreg.: Productivity Press, 1995).
2. Poka-yoke is the Japanese term for foolproof. It was introduced to the management literature by the Japanese quality guru Sigeo Shingo.
3. N. Ulman, "Brazilian Oil Company Has Much of the Clout of Government Itself," *Wall Street Journal* (November 17, 1983), p. 1.
4. V. Govindarajan and J. G. San Miguel, "Sears, Roebuck and Co. (C): The Internal Audit Function," case no. 9-179-125 (Boston: HBS Case Services, 1979).
5. R. Henkoff, "How to Plan for 1995," *Fortune* (December 31, 1990), p. 74.
6. For example, a report of the Special Committee On Operational and Management Auditing of the American Institute of Certified Public Accountants [American Institute of Certified Public Accountants, *Operational Audit Engagements* (New York: American Institute of Certified Public Accountants, 1982)] listed one of the benefits of an operational audit as "identification of previously undefined organizational policies and procedures." Manage-

ment may, however, be held accountable for not having had these policies and procedures in place if it is judged that they are part of what might be called "generally accepted management practice," as was the case, for example, with an operational audit of Portland General Electric Company by auditors from Arthur D. Little, Inc. See R. D. Banker and J. G. San Miguel, "Portland General Electric Company," case no. 9-170-171 (Boston: HBS Case Services, 1978).

7. F. K. Iverson, "Effective Leadership: The Key is Simplicity," in Y. K. Hsetty and V. M. Buehler, eds., *The Quest for Competitiveness* (New York: Quorum, 1991).
8. This is referred to in the economic literature as "observability."
9. K. A. Merchant and T. V. Bonoma, "Macon Prestressed Concrete Company (A)-(D)," case nos. 9-182-175, 9-182-176, 9-182-177, 9-182-178 (Boston: HBS Case Services, 1982).
10. "Spectra-Physics See Fiscal '83 Loss, Cites a $10 Million Charge," *Wall Street Journal* (August 9, 1983), p. 18.
11. "Singapore Slings—and Arrows," *Economist* (October 2, 1982), p. 90.
12. See, for example, R. N. Holt and R. E. Fincher, "The Foreign Corrupt Practices Act," *Financial Analysts Journal* 37 (March–April 1981), pp. 73–76; and L. Landro, "Analysis of ITT's Report Shows Problems in Halting Questionable Foreign Payments," *Wall Street Journal* (June 3, 1982), p. 27.

Macon Prestressed Concrete Company, Inc. (A, B, C Condensed)

Alone in his office, Paul Jones, president of Macon Prestressed Concrete Company, Inc. (MPCC), reflected on his June 10, 1981 meeting with consultants from Marketing Planning Associates (MPA). MPA, a New York City based consulting firm, had just completed an extensive project suggesting major revisions in MPCC's sales control and marketing information systems. At this point, Jones had very mixed feelings about the MPA control system recommendations. Certainly there were some valuable suggestions, but many of their ideas struck him as "fancy notions" better suited to a sprawling $100 million corporation than to his $20 million concrete company, a regional competitor in the southeastern United States. Jones couldn't help but wonder whether he had really received $70,000 of value from his one and a half-year association with MPA.

BACKGROUND INFORMATION

Prestressed Concrete Production

Concrete was a class of masonry made from varying proportions of cement, sand, gravel or coarse aggregate, and water. Generally, the smaller the ratio of water to cement, the stronger the concrete. For construction purposes, concrete often was poured "in place" at the construction site into wood or steel forms with the desired shape. All poured concrete—no matter how strong the cement mixture—had load limits above which it could not function. Concrete was especially vulnerable to tensile loads, which tended to cause cracking, as opposed to compressive loads.

Prestressed concrete was developed early in the 20th century, becoming the latest in a series of innovations to increase the load limits of concrete. The principle of prestressing was to induce compression forces in load-bearing concrete at the points where tensile forces were likely to be the greatest. While its primary advantage was its ability to carry greater loads at lower cost and weight, prestressed concrete offered the additional benefits of faster construction, lower maintenance, and expansion flexibility.

To make prestressed concrete, steel strands were stretched under high tension. Wet concrete was then placed into forms or molds which encased the strands. As the concrete set, it bonded to the tensioned steel. When the concrete reached a specified strength, the tension on the strands was released, putting the concrete under compressive stress and creating a built-in resistance to loads.

Prestressed concrete products were manufactured and finished at the plant. Prefabricated construction members were transported by truck to the construction job site. A sampling of typical prestressed concrete products is shown in Exhibit 1. MPCC produced a relatively small number of products, all of which were produced to customer order (not inventoried) because of the varied sizes and finishes available.

The manufacture of prestressed concrete was not especially capital-intensive. The requirements for production were a large piece of land, a concrete mixer, molds or forms into which the concrete could be poured, hydraulic equipment for stretching the cable, and transport equipment for moving the finished members. Skilled labor requirements were low for the basic structural

This case originally was prepared by Assistant Professor Kenneth Merchant and Associate Professor Thomas Bonoma as the basis for class discussion rather than to illustrate either effective or ineffective handling of an administrative situation. The current revision was prepared by Research Associate Shirley Spence, under the supervision of Associate Professor Thomas Bonoma.

pieces, but increased if special finishes (e.g., exposed aggregate) or special shapes (e.g., curved) were needed.

The Market

The prestressed concrete industry was launched in 1950 in the wake of publicity about the successful completion of a major bridge structure in Philadelphia. Growth was rapid. By 1979, industry sales had reached $1.5 billion, with approximately 250 plants producing prestressed members, primarily in the U.S., Canada, and Mexico. The high cost of transporting a bulky and heavy product limited all competing firms to a relatively small geographical area around their plants.

Prestressed concrete was considered a commodity product by buyers. Bidding was the most common pricing mechanism, and the lowest competitive bid generally won. The closest competitor to the eventual job site had a significant transportation cost advantage on bidding that job.

Sometimes, however, deals were negotiated between a manufacturer and a building contractor or customer (e.g., a large company). This was most common in the case of special "architectural" products which were constructed with special decorative finishes such as white concrete, or relief textures such as brick patterns. Producer margins were generally higher for negotiated work than for bid work; the profit margin on a job could range from 0 to 20 percent.

The buying process for prestressed concrete was complicated and the decision-making chain a long one, involving as major parties an owner, architect, general contractor, and subcontractors. The basic structural materials choice placed prestressed concrete in competition with such alternative materials as exposed structural steel or poured-in-place concrete. Choices often were made on the basis of total cost, aesthetics, and maintenance requirements. Assuming prestressed concrete was selected, further decisions regarding specific concrete shapes, sizes, and finishes would be made as the preliminary construction design became better formulated.

For example, the owner of a parking lot might decide to build a parking garage on an adjacent lot. An architectural design firm would be retained to specify a preliminary plan. The architect, in consultation with the owner, would make a primary materials choice among steel girder construction, concrete poured in place at the construction site, and prestressed concrete members. Similar choices between prestressed and other materials (e.g., brick) would be made for walls and other components.

Next, a general contractor would be hired to manage the entire construction process from ground-breaking to final detail after the building was released to the owner for use. The general contractor would review and possibly recommend changes in the project design or basic materials choice, and would hire and manage a number of subcontractors. Subcontractors specialized in a particular phase of construction. There were, for example, excavation and foundation subs, mechanical subs (heating, ventilating, air conditioning) and special subs for every subphase of the project. MPCC's goal was to be the subcontractor of choice to manufacture and, if possible, erect the prestressed concrete building's exterior structure.

Various selling strategies were used by prestressed concrete manufacturers. Most firms maintained a commodity orientation by keeping their costs low and trying to submit low bids for desired jobs. This was especially effective for winning government contracts, which were always assigned on a bid basis. A less frequently used approach was to enter the buying process early (e.g., by showing the owner or architect the advantages of prestressed concrete) and act as a consultant to the customer. This was a higher cost strategy since it required relatively more salesmen and engineers, but was particularly well-suited to negotiated work or in situations where there was a high degree of product differentiation (e.g., unique surface finishes).

MPCC

MPCC began operations in 1956 with a single plant in Macon, Georgia. In 1957, the first full year of operation, the company had 30 workers and sales of approximately $300,000. By the end of 1980, MPCC had plants in four locations: Macon, Jonesboro, and Atlanta in Georgia, and Columbia in South Carolina, and maintained in-house capabilities for transporting and erecting all products manufactured. Sales had grown to about $20 million. The company now had over 400 people on the payroll and was organized functionally. (See Exhibit 2 for 1980 organization, and backgrounds of key managers.)

The company had experienced slow but

steady growth through mid-1975, but suffered a 46 percent drop in sales in 1976 when the 1974–76 recession hit the construction market in the southeastern United States. Consistent with industry trends, MPCC experienced losing years from 1976 to 1978. Although the company became solidly profitable again in the last half of 1979, sales for that year returned only to 1975 levels.

In 1980, MPCC sales were double 1979 figures and profits were healthy (see Exhibit 3). This rebound was due to: (1) the late 1980 acquisition of the Atlanta plant, which was one of the largest in the world and increased MPCC's capacity by about 65 percent; and (2) improved market conditions. In 1981, however, sales were forecast to be flat versus 1980, and profits down slightly.

Sales and Marketing

MPCC operated with a customer focus rather than a low-cost production orientation. It encouraged its customers to let MPCC personnel coordinate and supervise the job through the erection stage, even if the work was performed by outside suppliers.

MPCC's primary market area was in the states of Georgia and South Carolina, with secondary marketing efforts in Alabama, North Carolina, Tennessee, and northern Florida. Because of minimal competition, MPCC was dominant in southern Georgia, but significant competition was present in all other market areas.

Eight salespeople, called district sales managers (DSMs), reported to the marketing and sales manager, Mr. Phil Beard. Each DSM was assigned a separate geographical area, except in Atlanta where each DSM was assigned a specific list of potential customers (including architects, contractors, and customer companies). Each DSM was assigned an annual sales quota based on the sales manager's judgment of the area's sales potential.

Salespeople paid their own expenses, and were compensated on a commission basis. Up to 120 percent of quota, commissions were set at approximately 3 percent of sales, depending on the sales representative's individual compensation package. Above the quota level, the sales representative was allowed to earn more money, but the commission percentage on incremental sales was lowered to approximately 1.5 percent to protect the company against an excessive payout in any given year.

A commission-sharing procedure had been implemented because two DSMs might be working to sell the same job; one with the job architect and the other with the contractor. In those situations, one-third of the job commission went to the DSM working with the architect and two-thirds to the DSM working with the contractor. This percentage was set both to encourage "promotion" of prestressed concrete to individuals in the earlier stages of the buying process (e.g., architects) and to reflect the fact that making the sale was all-important.

The pricing of jobs was not a marketing function. The estimates and bids were supervised by the operations vice president, Mr. William (Billy) Boswell, with input from engineering, the plant managers, and sales representatives. The first step in the pricing process was to estimate the direct costs of the job, which included: direct materials, direct labor, special items needed on the job (e.g., custom-made forms, special transporting equipment), transportation, erection (if included), and a contingency factor[1] (if desired).

The second step was to scale the total direct cost figure up by a factor designed to cover plant and corporate overhead and provide a profit margin. Company analyses had shown that, at a 1980 volume level, multiplying by 1.6 would provide a total contribution sufficient to cover all plant overhead and supply no contribution to corporate overhead. A factor of 1.65 would provide a corporate break-even, and 1.7 would provide the desired Return on Invested Capital (ROIC—with replacement of equipment in like kind).

The actual multiplication factors used varied widely, depending on the backlogs in each plant and the expected competitive bids. The factor would be reduced if a plant needed the work or wanted work of a particular type. It would also be reduced if the DSM or sales manager indicated that competition for the job was likely to be stiff. In 1980, actual pricing multipliers ranged from 1.3 to 3.0, with an average of 1.78.

THE SALES AND MARKETING AUDIT

In May 1980, Paul Jones attended a marketing seminar taught by Tom Barron, a vice president of Marketing Planning Associates. Mr. Jones felt that

[1]The contingency factor was designed to protect the company against the risk of cost overruns on any job.

MPCC might have some weaknesses in marketing and, at the end of the seminar, he asked Tom Barron about the possibility of having MPA perform an overall review of marketing at MPCC. Paul Jones explained:

> Our company was doing very well. Our backlog was in good shape, and we were setting new production records every month, but I wasn't sure we were really creating optimal opportunities. I was worried that we were doing well in spite of ourselves and that if things got tight, it might all fall in on us. I wanted someone to take a look at it and say: "You're all right. You don't have anything to worry about." Or, "You do have some problems; you need to make some changes."

After several discussions between Paul Jones, Tom Barron, and Mike Rubenstein, a senior consultant at MPA, it was decided that MPCC's greatest need was for an examination of the sales portion of MPCC's marketing effort. In August 1980, MPA presented Paul Jones with a proposal for what was called a "sales and marketing audit" (see Exhibit 4). Mike Rubenstein had these comments on the audit approach:

> Now obviously, this is just a piece of the overall marketing activity of the company. It would have been nice to be able to do the complete job. By that I mean I would have liked to have had more time to examine the market environment, the company marketing strategy, advertising and promotion policies, and so on. But MPCC is a fairly small company, and they just couldn't afford a full-blown study.

The proposal was presented to Paul Jones in August 1980, and promptly accepted. MPA began work immediately. Tom Barron served as project supervisor and quality control officer, while Mike Rubenstein managed the project on a day-to-day basis. Since an early completion of the study was desired, two MPA staff consultants were assigned to help Rubenstein with data collection.

Method

The audit had three phases: data gathering, analysis, and report preparation. Most of the data gathering involved field interviews. Mike Rubenstein explained:

> Interviews were the best way to collect most of the needed information. This is not like a CPA audit where most of the relevant information is right in the financial records and back-up files. Most of what I was interested in was not written down. But even if it were, I would still have interviewed the key personnel because people are often a large part of any problems that might exist.

A considerable amount of planning preceded the data collection effort. The budget was considered tight, so the process had to be designed to gather data efficiently, yet provide enough overlap to allow any perceptual differences to appear. A list of interviewees was prepared including: (1) all key MPCC managers and salesmen, (2) a sample (14 total) of customers and potential customers of all types (i.e., architects, contractors, government, large corporations) and in all sales districts, (3) the president of a major competitor, and (4) several senior personnel in a major but noncompeting prestressed concrete firm. Interview guides or lists of questions were prepared for each interview type (see Exhibit 5). Actual interviews were conducted by the consulting team, either singly or in groups of two.

The Report

MPA presented its final audit report in November 1980. The report indicated that MPA found a relatively strong company that was limited in its ability to react to market changes because of weaknesses in its planning and control systems.

Three main recommendations were made. First, MPA recommended that an experienced person be given responsibility for heavy construction sales, which primarily involved bidding on contracts for highway or railroad bridge construction. Heavy construction business accounted for a significant portion of MPCC's revenue and contributions (20 to 25 percent), but company attention to the development of this segment was small compared to that devoted to the building markets. MPCC had been handling the heavy construction business by dividing the responsibility among three plant managers, with coordination provided by the VP for operations. (These were considered "house accounts.") MPA also observed that it was risky for MPCC to have such a high proportion of sales concentrated in accounts that it did not service.

Second, MPA recommended that the sales management function be strengthened. Mike Rubenstein explained:

> Although direct comparisons are difficult to make, the efficiency and effectiveness of the sales organization seem low. MPCC's district sales managers seem to pursue short-term goals. They scramble for jobs without much organization or advanced planning. The vice president of sales is really not doing any managing. He spends half his time preparing bids and does not really get involved in directing the sales force, something that is very important because the key selling skills vary widely among individuals.
>
> The implication of not having a sales force control system is that the salesmen may be ineffective, or at least inefficient, in their use of time. The lack of information and direction makes it difficult for the DSMs to set priorities among activities or accounts, and without effective controls, management has no way to determine if the sales force is doing its job.
>
> I think MPCC has a strong need to do the following:
>
> - Develop the basis for a control system by developing standards for certain key measures; such as market penetration, numbers and costs of different types of sales calls, and number of orders per 100 sales calls.
> - Develop a reporting system to track key measures, such as those listed above, on a regular basis.
> - Develop an annual sales budget.
> - Develop a programmatic approach for sales and promotional activities.
> - Move the sales manager function to Atlanta, where five of the salesmen are located, to provide better supervision and direction.

The third major recommendation was to improve the marketing information system. MPA observed that very little marketing information was gathered, and that what was gathered was not shared among the DSMs. Thus, MPA suggested that a system be designed to organize efforts to gather, analyze, and communicate information that could be supplied by salesmen and other sources. MPA expected that such a system would require hiring a staff person to gather and process the information, and that much of the communication could be done best by increasing the role of sales meetings.

Company Reaction

Paul Jones gave his impression of the report:

> The MPA audit report confirmed some things that I had a gut feeling about. They put some things into words that had been in the back of my mind, and they stated it in a way that made it more urgent.

MPCC responded almost immediately to the first recommendation and part of the second via a reorganization announced in December 1980. Phil Beard, the former vice president of sales, was assigned responsibility for the heavy construction accounts. Mickey Briel, a former plant manager who also had sales experience, was promoted to sales manager for all building markets. Mickey kept his primary office in Atlanta, where most of the salesmen were located, and began to exert a more active sales management role.

MPA suggestions regarding the design of improved control and information systems, however, met with resistance from MPCC management. This task was felt to be too complex for MPCC to tackle at that time, given the planned sales reorganization and the fact that the company was still adjusting to the acquisition of the Atlanta plant.

The New Proposal

MPA had anticipated this implementation problem, and on November 25 offered a proposal for a follow-up study to design a new information and control system (see Exhibit 6). The aims of the project were to increase sales force productivity, and to enable MPCC to improve market control and penetration. The project was divided into two sequential parts: (1) Phase 1 would culminate in an MPA report on the design of the proposed system; (2) Phase 2 would involve a one-month trial implementation period and subsequent system refinements, as necessary. Estimated cost was $32,000, plus expenses.

A considerable amount of time and effort went into the development of the proposal. Mike Rubenstein explained:

> In order to be specific in the proposal, I practically had to design the complete system, be-

cause the assignment was novel to MPA and we didn't have an established, structured process that we knew would get us to where we wanted to go. Altogether, I spent about 15 solid working days in the library of a local business school doing a fairly complete literature search to find out how other companies controlled their sales forces.

MPCC wasn't even aware that this was happening and, in fact, Tom Barron didn't even know how much time I had invested in preparing to write the proposal. While Tom was strongly encouraging Paul to go ahead with the job, it wasn't to protect our investment. He strongly felt MPCC needed the system.

Paul Jones' reaction to the proposal was somewhat ambivalent:

> MPA wants to go right ahead with the follow-up study, but I'm not sure we're ready for it. We've already got a lot to do in assimilating the new Atlanta plant and the new organization. And we couldn't implement the suggestions until we hire a new marketing person, as the audit report suggested, anyway. Also, I'm disappointed in the cost figure. It's more expensive than I wanted.
>
> On the other hand, the fact is that we have a fairly large fixed investment here which we need to keep busy. We've had good results recently, but I'm afraid we may start another downswing. That's why I have to be concerned about the effectiveness of our sales function. We've got to capitalize on current opportunities, or the next downturn will put severe strains on the company.

Over the next month, there were a number of telephone conversations between Paul Jones and Tom Barron to clarify MPCC's needs and refine the proposed MPA project approach. In January 1981, despite his still moderately strong reservations about the project, Paul Jones formally authorized MPA to proceed with the design of a new marketing control system for MPCC.

THE MARKETING CONTROL SYSTEM

Since so much of the system design work had been done during the preparation of the project proposal, there was relatively little left to do once MPA technically "started" the job. Mike Rubenstein spent no more than a couple of days organizing his thoughts and writing the initial report draft. Since he had just finished the MPCC audit, the company's situation was still clear in his mind. He knew Paul Jones was worried about the cost, so he spent only one day total at MPCC in Atlanta before the presentation of the final report, although he did make a number of phone calls to clarify some details and to get preliminary company reactions to his ideas.

Rationale for the System

In explaining the thinking behind the system he designed for MPCC, Mike Rubenstein said:

> I was struck by how MPCC, like a typical commodity product manufacturer, thinks they make their profit at the plant level, by keeping the plant busy. They're always thinking: "We've got to find enough customers to pay our bills." They may survive that way, with ups and downs as the economy fluctuates, but to thrive, I think they've got to segment the market and go after a more profitable mix of jobs. They need to learn what their most profitable products are, or could be, and channel their sales efforts in the right directions. The first step is to get some information about whether the market already has some higher margin segments. This may be by product (e.g., architectural), by customer type (e.g., negotiated versus bid), or by geographical region. My system is designed to help get that information.
>
> I also think that the salesman's role should be much broader than just direct selling at the time the job is imminent. I think the salesman should be trying to identify potential buyers and then educating them so that they become regular buyers of prestressed concrete from MPCC. I call this general promotion work, as opposed to direct sales. Right now, MPCC is probably doing 10 percent or less general promotion, and I'd say that's too low.
>
> Coming up with an ideal sales/promotion mix, though, requires a lot more information about both the market opportunity and the extent to which it's been developed.

That's why I've recommended that MPCC start formally collecting market intelligence information and using it in their planning. They also need to develop more customer-related information, both on a general level (i.e., how customers made decisions about their materials) and more specifically (e.g., a checklist on each potential customer to rate how well the DSM knows the people and how comfortable they are with MPCC's product offerings).

Of course, even assuming MPCC is able to develop reasonable sales/promotion mix goals for each territory, there's still the question of how to make sure the DSMs implement the plan as intended. To a large extent, I think implementation successes result simply from having good people and telling them what you would like them to do, of course. I would deliver the message about what I expect through the compensation system to emphasize, for example, current growth or market development for the future.

It's dangerous, though, to just rely on people controlling themselves. A more formal control system is good protection. For the sales function, tracking results alone is not adequate. Results are measured in terms of bookings and purchase orders received, which are easy to measure but arrive irregularly in chunks that can be very large, up to $2 million each. So feedback based on results is not very timely. That's why I recommended that MPCC track both results and sales activities.

The Report

The new control system design was presented to MPCC in April 1981. The system focused on two types of measurable resources: time allocation of the sales and marketing personnel, and expense involved in supporting their activities.

An overview of the control system process is provided in Exhibit 7. The first column shows four major *data streams* MPA felt MPCC needed to get and keep good control over the marketing and sales function. The second column outlines specific *analytic tasks* needed to process the data streams. The third column shows the major *decision processes* that would be improved by making use of the analysis of superior information, including goal-setting and resource allocation. The last column shows the *programs* that could be developed to help each responsibility area accomplish its plans.

The critical first step in the implementation of the control system was the development of better information for each of the four major data streams. Rubenstein offered sample report formats for gathering that information. To formalize market intelligence information, he proposed collecting data on the key attributes of each proposed construction project in the market area (Exhibit 8). For better financial visibility, he suggested that summaries be provided on a marketing function basis (Exhibit 9) and by individual job (Exhibit 10). For sales force information, eight suggested reports provided raw sales call information, summaries by type of activity over various time frames, and some indications of results such as bookings, margins, market share (Exhibit 11). For backlog, a proposed weekly report broke down data by plant, type of product, and length of run.

To ensure that MPCC effectively used all this information, Rubenstein presented some techniques for analyzing the collected data at periodic intervals. These seven "analytic tasks" included: market size and share analysis, market and segment forecasting, job cost analysis, sales force calling analysis, marketing productivity analysis, jobs lost analysis, and backlog trend analysis. For each analytic task, the report provided a "general description" that clarified the purpose of the task, identified relevant data sources, and offered examples. Exhibit 12 shows a sample "general description."

Company Reaction

On June 10, Paul Jones and Mickey Briel met with Tom Barron and Mike Rubenstein to discuss MPCC reactions to the report. The meeting was held in the Kon-Tiki Lounge in a motel near Newark, New Jersey. After exchanging amenities and feeding the exotic parrot chained to a post near the table, the men turned their attention to the control system report.

While Paul Jones' overall reaction to the control system report was positive, he made it clear in a somewhat heated discussion with Tom

Barron that he did not believe in and would not implement the job costing system which MPA felt was essential for segmentation purposes. Excerpts from their exchange follow:

PAUL JONES: I think we're basically in agreement with what you've presented in the report, although I'm not sure we're in a position to implement all the suggestions at the present time. I've just hired a marketing manager, Deborah Perdue. Debby, who is 24 years old, is just finishing an MBA in marketing from Georgia State University. She'll join us in July, and I think she'll be a big help.

There is one suggestion in the report which we have decided not to implement. That is the detailed analysis of job costs. To collect that data would take a major change in our accounting procedures, and we just don't have enough accountants to do all that. Actually, some years ago, we used to produce information just like this, but it caused us major problems. We tended to lose sight of the real direct costs of a job because they were interspersed among the accounting allocations.

Our present system computes the gross margin on each job. We think we can use these data usefully by evaluating each job on both the gross margin and the PV ratio (gross margin divided by revenue).

TOM BARRON: Paul, I think these job cost data are a key part of the system. I feel very strongly that the marketing people need to know the profitability of different jobs so that they can allocate the salesmen's efforts and other resources in the direction they want to take the company. You know that the jobs have different cost structures, especially between architectural and structural products. Architectural products have a much higher value added and higher margin, but they also involve more sales time, more engineering, and remakes. The size of those costs may be small when compared to revenue, but you're in a low margin business, and they're very large when compared to profits. We're talking about effective segmentation here, and without that, you're not going to be a well-managed company.

Here's what's going to happen. Macon manages to backlog, and in bad times without segmentation, you'll take too much marginally profitable business to keep the backlog up. In good times, all that marginally profitable backlog will keep you from getting the really profitable jobs because you won't have production capacity. Good segmentation and good management is the art of saying "no" to marginally profitable business. Unless you know the costs, you'll keep falling into the trap of saying "yes."

PAUL JONES: Sure, there are some real differences in products and customers. We know we have problems with architectural work, and we reflect that in our pricing. I just don't think it's worth a lot of work to track it on a job basis. Architectural is a very small part of our business (about 10 percent). Besides, we don't price on a product basis. We price a whole *job,* which may involve a large number of structural products, and maybe a few architectural pieces.

Tom, I see what you want, but I still think we can get that by computing the gross margin on each job. If we find out we can't, we can then consider revising and expanding our accounting procedures to go down to a theoretical job profit on each job.

In any case, the information wouldn't do us any good now. We're facing another construction slowdown, and that puts us in the position of having to sell whatever's available. We can't afford to wait for the high margin jobs.

TOM BARRON: That's just the problem. You. . . .

PAUL JONES: Let me change the subject. Since I've got you here, let me get your reaction to another change we're thinking about. As you know, we presently set our sales commissions at roughly 2 percent of revenue. All your talk about job profitability suggested to Mickey and me that perhaps a revenue-based commission schedule provides the wrong motivation. We're thinking about basing the commissions on job margins. To hold the total compensation package about constant, the percentage would have to be increased, to about 6 to 7 percent of the job margins. Do you have any reaction to that?

EXHIBIT 1 Typical Prestressed Concrete Products

SINGLE TEE:

Typical Uses:
Roof and floor systems, wall panels, bridges and conveyors.

Standard Sizes of Tees:
Depth: 12″–48″
Widths: 6′, 8′ and 10′ are standard. Other widths can be provided to custom specifications.

DOUBLE TEE:

Typical Uses:
Roof and floor systems, wall panels, pier decks, tank covers, conveyors, bridges and catwalks.

Standard Sizes:
14″ deep × 4′ wide
14″ deep × 8′ wide
24″ deep × 8′ wide
36″ deep × 10′ wide

WALL PANELS:

All of the standard double tee, single tee, and flat slab products are available as wall panels, curtain walls and load-bearing walls. Mixing products provides an unlimited number of patterns. Connections can be designed for easy demounting in case of movement or future expansions or modifications.

FLAT SLABS:

Typical Uses:
Short-span roof and floor systems where flat ceiling or minimum structural depth is particularly desired, wall panel, and tank and tunnel covers.

Standard Sizes:
Depths: 4″ and 7″
Widths: 8′ and 10′

RAIL CROSSTIES:

Typical Uses:
High quality support for high-speed and heavy-duty rail.

Standard Sizes:
8′6″ long, 11″ wide
7″ high in midsection
9½″ at the rail seats.

BRIDGE SECTIONS:

Typical Uses:
Long, medium, and short-span highway and railway bridges, and other heavily loaded deck situations.
Standard Sizes:
Standard AASHTO Type II, III and IV beams, and flat deck slabs in widths of 48″ and various depths.

EXHIBIT 2 1980 Organization

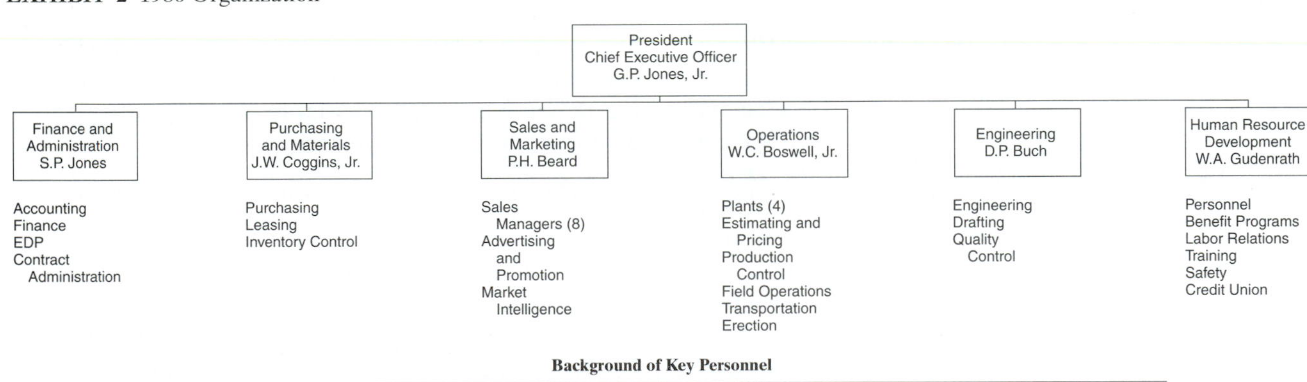

Background of Key Personnel

G. Paul Jones, Jr.—President, 51 years old, Bachelor's degree in mechanical engineering, Georgia Institute of Technology, 1952. In 1956, after serving in Korea with the U.S. Army Corps of Engineers, he assisted in forming Macon Prestressed Concrete Company. Has served as president of the Prestressed Concrete Institute and is currently a member of the executive committee and board of directors. Is also serving as vice chairman of the National Construction Industry Council.

William C. Boswell, Jr.—Vice President (Operations), 45 years old, Bachelor of Civil Engineering degree, Georgia Institute of Technology, 1958. Started with company in 1958, elected vice president in 1973. Served with Corps of Engineers through 1965. Completed the AMA management course sponsored by the American Management Association.

Philip H. Beard—Vice President (Sales), 44 years old, Bachelor of Science degree in industrial management, Auburn University. Employed by company in 1961, and elected in 1973 to present position. Served on the marketing committee of Precast Systems, Inc. Currently serves as vice chairman of the board of directors of Precast Systems, Inc., and president of the Georgia Prestressed Concrete Association. Completed the AMA management course sponsored by the American Management Association.

Samuel P. Jones—Secretary—Treasurer, 37 years old, Bachelor's degree in civil engineering, Davidson College/Georgia Institute of Technology, 1968. Employed in 1970 as an engineer after serving with the U.S. Army, First Cavalry Division. Was elected to the board of directors of Cornell-Young Co. and Macon Prestressed Concrete Co., 1971. Elected to present position in 1973. A member of the following affiliations: National Society of Professional Engineers, Macon Chapter of the Georgia Society of Professional Engineers, American Concrete Institute.

Dharmendra P. Buch—Chief Engineer, 45 years old, Bachelor of Civil Engineering degree, Gujarat University (India), 1956; Master of Science degree, University of California, 1959. Spent nine years employed by consulting engineers in Florida, Virginia, and India. Joined company in June 1979. Is a registered professional engineer in several states and a member of the American Concrete Institute and Prestressed Concrete Institute.

EXHIBIT 3 Summary Income Statements for 1970 through 1981

(Numbers in Millions)	*1981**	*1980*	*1979*
Sales	$20.0	$19.9	$8.9
Cost of sales	16.4	16.1	7.2
Gross profit	$ 3.6	$ 3.8	$1.7
Selling, general, and administrative expenses	$ 2.7	$ 2.5	$1.3
Profit before taxes	.9	1.3	.4
Income taxes	.4	.5	—
Profit after taxes	$ .5	$ .8	$ .4

*Estimated from three months' data.

EXHIBIT 4 Proposal for Sales and Marketing Audit

August 14, 1980

Mr. G. Paul Jones, Jr.
Macon Prestressed Concrete Co.
4496 Mead Road
Macon, GA 31206

Dear Paul:

As we agreed at our last meeting, we have prepared a proposal as to how we might approach some of the issues you raised in a consulting project designed to provide you with specific recommendations.

The rising tide of sunbelt prosperity may be increasing the company's sales and profitability while masking unknown managerial weaknesses. If that is the case, these weaknesses make the company more vulnerable than management suspects to competitive or recessionary forces.

Management has asked the question, "Are we doing it right?" Management's sense of the situation is that more information and outside expertise is needed to assist management in answering that question.

APPROACH

We at MPA suggest that the proper approach to this problem is to do a partial audit of the company's marketing effort, focusing on the sales effort. Paul, you may prefer to call this study a Sales Opportunity Analysis in discussions with your staff, rather than an audit.

In general terms, the steps are:

1. Analyzing the MPCC operation and its sales management needs.
2. Sharing our perceptions of the problems with you.
3. Preparing recommendations that are specific and actionable so that you can implement them directly without further work on our part.

Specifically, MPA will look at the key environmental trends affecting MPCC and the sales levers that management can pull to influence its sales performance. These include:

1. Learning the strategic goals that management has set for the company.
2. Looking at the overall market to verify the emergence of those desirable segments MPCC would prefer to serve.
3. Looking at one market area with specific problems to determine what opportunities exist for MPCC.

(Continued)

EXHIBIT 4 Proposal for Sales and Marketing Audit *Continued*

4. Examining customer purchase decision patterns, to see if they are changing.
5. Determining the nature of the MPCC sales task and how it must change to meet management's goals in a changing environment.
6. Addressing the problem of how internal order-taking through house accounts affects external selling and performance.
7. Analyzing the company's systems that support the accomplishment of the sales task:
   a. Sales force goal setting, control, and performance measurement;
   b. Sales force motivation and compensation;
   c. Recruiting, selecting, and training the sales force, and how the company manages underperforming salesmen;
   d. Time management and direction;
   e. Assessing, from these observations, the nature of the sales management task and the types of resources that would be required to assure successful managerial performance.

We will analyze this information and draw conclusions and make recommendations from our analysis. Our recommendations to you will have two parts: an informal oral report in the form of a discussion, preceding a final written report.

WORKPLAN

We have outlined a proposed workplan for the project. This we will make more specific with your help once we have your go-ahead. This plan is as follows:

Week of:

August 18—Project go-ahead approval and initial planning by telephone
August 25—Tom Barron visits Macon, meets with top managers informally
September 1—Project planning and scheduling
September 8–15—MPA project team meets with MPCC managers in Macon for initial introductory overview of the company and its operations
—Interviews planned for remainder of the month
—Internal interviews (10–15) completed
—Literature review completed—field interviews in some market areas (10–15)
September 22—Interim analysis and final interview scheduling
September 29—Final field interviews (8–12)
—Follow up internal interviews by telephone
—Telephone interviews with customers (10–15)
October 6–13—Analysis and oral report preparation
October 20—Oral final report
October 27—Project completion and preparation of final report
November 3—Delivery of written report

STAFFING, TIMING, AND COSTS

As we have already discussed, Tom Barron will provide the overall conceptual leadership for this project. Tom will dedicate four days of his time to this project, with the emphasis on participating in the initial planning, in the analysis phase, and in making recommendations. I will manage the project on a day-to-day basis and will coordinate closely with Tom and you. I may ask one or more MPA consultants to help me in the industry and market analysis and in interviewing.

You expressed interest in a speedy beginning and early completion of the project. I have made sure necessary staff resources are available. Accordingly, we are ready to begin the project as soon as we receive approval from you, providing you let us know by August 20, at the latest.

(Continued)

EXHIBIT 4 Proposal for Sales and Marketing Audit *Continued*

We have estimated the total professional fees involved in this project to be $26,000. In addition, it is our practice to bill for out-of-pocket expenses (travel, clerical, telephone, etc.) separately. Such expenses generally run about 20 to 25 percent of fees on this type of project.

You are free to cancel the project at any time and pay only those fees and expenses actually accrued to that date. To begin the project, please sign one copy of this proposal as indicated below, and return it to me.

We are excited about this project, Paul, and the opportunities for MPCC. We look forward very much to working with you.

Sincerely,

Michael Rubenstein
Senior Consultant

______________________________ Date ______________

Accepted for Macon Prestressed Concrete Co.
G. Paul Jones, President

EXHIBIT 5 Sales and Marketing Audit—Interview Guide

1. Level of Service
  a. In the customers' terms, what is Macon giving them?
  b. Is rapport important (would they rather see one DSM, or doesn't it matter?)
  c. How much contact do they want/need with DSM?

2. Information Exchanged
  a. Type of information exchanged.
  b. Does it meet customers' needs?

3. Preparation, Organization, Expertise of Sales Force
  a. In client's view, are DSMs prepared? What is level of expertise that they perceive in DSMs? Is the DSM doing a good job for Macon and for customer?

4. Amount of Engineering Contact
  a. Would customer prefer to see an engineer, or is DSM enough most of the time?

5. Opportunity for Coordination
  a. Does customer want to work with Macon, or just buy from Macon?
    i. If work with, when?
    ii. Is this involvement by Macon changing? Should it?

6. Bid vs. Negotiated Work
  a. What does customer prefer?
  b. Where is the market going?
  c. Key criteria.

7. Customers' Strategy and Macon
  a. What role can Macon play in helping its customers implement their strategies? (e.g., if more engineered work is the goal, will customers use Macon more?)

8. Macon's Competitors
  a. How are they different?
  b. How are they better or less effective?

9. Other
  a. New products.
  b. Butler concept.*
  c. Trends in industry.

*The Butler concept referred to a strategy used by another building company, in which prefabricated concrete building components were used to construct complete customer buildings. Butler acted as a general contractor on such work.

EXHIBIT 6 Proposal for Marketing Control System Study

November 25, 1980

Mr. G. Paul Jones, Jr.
Macon Prestressed Concrete Co., Inc.
4496 Mead Road
Macon, GA 31206

Dear Paul:

It has been a real pleasure to work with you and Macon's employees these past few months on the sales audit. The sales force has been most cooperative with us. Please thank them on our behalf for helping to make the job go smoothly.

One of our key findings in that study was that Macon did not have a marketing control system. At our presentation to you on October 29, you expressed an interest in hearing more from MPA on how we would develop such a system for Macon. This letter shares with you our understanding of your needs and how MPA would approach this project. It also includes some of the changes we discussed in our recent telephone conversations.

BACKGROUND

Macon has two immediate needs: first, to improve your marketing productivity, which means making sure your sales force is efficient; and second, obtaining the tools to accomplish market penetration on a regional basis for better profitability and greater control of your markets. Your current concerns, therefore, lie with managing your existing resources more effectively.

You also are planning to acquire other firms in your industry, located in other regions. As Macon acquires other firms, you will have to manage Macon's dispersed operations. Your needs then will be to coordinate and compare activities across regions, and to develop standards for guiding and evaluating your managers' performance. One of your concerns is to have the control system designed and in place before you start working actively on the next acquisition.

Management control has two chief purposes. The first is to motivate individuals to take the right actions as uniquely defined for their responsibility area. Their goals need to be consistent with your goals. This aspect of control is primarily behavioral. The second purpose is to allow you to compare performance—of regions, programs, approaches, salesmen, managers, products—after the fact. This comparison becomes the basis of resource allocation decisions on budget, staffing, investment, bonuses, promotion expenses, and the like. This aspect of control is normally informative and analytical. Firms of Macon's size typically have control systems that reflect a managerial style midway between the highly directive managerial style that characterizes the small, entrepreneurial company, and the very hands-off, purely results-oriented style found among the best-managed, decentralized conglomerates. Taking the step of installing a control system is entirely appropriate for a threshold firm such as Macon.

APPROACH

A control system will be most valuable to Macon if it accomplishes three goals:

1. Assures that performance is consistent with agreed-upon objectives.
2. Supplies reasons for performance deviations that occur and provides a basis for taking corrective action.
3. Provides performance measures to help assess both the competence of managers and the effectiveness of business strategies.

We propose to design a control system for Macon that will successfully address these three performance goals.

We believe that four critical constraints must be imposed on the design of the completed control system:

1. Simple. The system should run with an absolute minimum of employee time and effort. We anticipate that the process will be paper-based. It should occupy only part of the time of one lower-level employee.

(Continued)

EXHIBIT 6 Proposal for Marketing Control System Study *Continued*

2. Familiar. The system should deal with common data of which employees and managers have a sound working knowledge.
3. Understandable. The content, flow, and resulting output of the system must be easily comprehensible to all users.
4. Implementable. The final system must be practicable and readily usable by your people without further MPA input.

We propose to divide this project into two phases (see chart 1). The first phase covers design and is primarily analytic work. MPA will be responsible for the work in this phase. Phase 1 will culminate in a report on the proposed design of the control system.

Phase 2 is the specification and implementation phase. Since the control system involves a "buy-in" and commitment by Macon people, we will shift primary responsibility for this phase to your employees. We will, of course, work closely with them and oversee the process as they complete it. We foresee your people being responsible for 80 percent of the work in Phase 2 and MPA for 20 percent.

STAFFING AND FEES

We estimate that professional fees involved in developing a control system for Macon will be $32,000 plus expenses, which we expect will run approximately 15% on this project. As you know, once the project has begun, you are free to cancel the project at any time and pay only the fees and expenses actually accrued.

Paul, we are very enthusiastic about this project and eager to continue working with you and Macon. If this proposal in its present form meets your needs, please sign one copy of this letter and return it to me for project commencement. If you have any questions, please give me a call.

Sincerely,

Michael Rubenstein
Senior Consultant

APPROVED:

____________________________ ____________________

G. Paul Jones, Jr. (For Macon Prestressed Concrete Co., Inc.) — Date

Chart 1: Workplan

PHASE 1*

Week of	*Activity*
December 8	Planning and preparation for data gathering.
December 15	Group interview with Macon top management on plans and measures; Group interview with sales force; Obtain and review market information and budget systems.
December 22 & January 5	Analysis, system flow design, and initial development of key variables; Interviews with managers of well-controlled companies in similar circumstances for purposes of comparison.
January 12–19	Complete analysis, prepare report.
January 26	Report delivered in working document form.

PHASE 2

Period	*Activity*
February 2–20	Work with Macon employees to provide detail of reporting flows and content, form development, and support system.
March	Begin trial period.
April	Review of experience after first month; tune and refine system as necessary.

*Due to the holiday season, Phase 1 timing should be regarded as somewhat flexible.

EXHIBIT 7 Overview of the Design of the Control System Process

MAJOR DATA STREAMS	ANALYTIC TASKS	MAJOR DECISION PROCESSES	ACTION AREAS
1. Market Intelligence	1. Market Size and Share	1. Marketing Planning and Budgeting —Segmentation —Strategy —Compensation —Territory —Marketing Efficiency —New Products and Processes —Administrative	1. Market Growth Programs
	2. Market & Segment Forecasting		2. Market Penetration Programs
2. Financial Results	3. Job Cost Analysis		3. Marketing Productivity Programs
	4. Sales Force Calling Analysis		4. Key Account Management
3. Sales Force Activities Data	5. Marketing Productivity Analysis		5. Management Programs —Territory Assign ments —Compensation —DSM Training
	6. Jobs Lost Analysis		
4. Backlog	7. Backlog Trend Analysis	Bid Development (not part of system)	

EXHIBIT 8 Market Intelligence Suggested Data Format

	Job one	*Job Two*
Description	Sherwin Grinder Corp. Manufacturing plant—200,000 sq. ft. factory 10,000 sq. ft. attached office	
Location	Sherwin, GA—I-85 Exit	
Building type or purpose	Heavy manufacturing	
Total dollar amount	$38,000,000	
Material type	Structural steel with P/S skin	
Potential for P/S	$1,000,000	
Final proportion P/S	$880,000	
Explanation of difference	Office went to metal building	
Segment type	Insulated flat wall panel	
Structural vs. architectural	Architectural	
Construction method	Conventional	
Bid/negotiated	Bid	
If bid, Macon's price	$880,000	
Macon high (low) by	($31,000)	
Owner	Sherwin Grinder	
Contractor	Instabilt	
Architect	A, B, & C Design	
P/S competitors	Tindall	
Producer(s)	Macon, Butler	
Time schedule	December 1980–May 1981	
Macon's backlog at bidding time	16 weeks	
Other data elements	Lost office space to metal building competitor; owner wanted special color.	

EXHIBIT 9 Marketing Budget Summary

1. Macon should separate marketing expense from corporate expense on the operating statement.

2. Marketing should be consolidated for review and control by the sales manager.

3. Current marketing accounts in the chart of accounts are:
   a. 761—Sales Expense
   b. 763—Sales Salaries
   c. 764—Sales Commission (Accrual)
   d. 768—Sales and Promotion

Macon should use the detail it has available and break down the marketing expense further for use in analyzing the marketing expenditures.

4. One possible breakdown of the summary of marketing expenses is as follows:

	Budget		*Actual*
Sales Salaries			
1. Supervision	$ 5		—
2. DSMs	20		—
3. Support	2		—
4. Total salaries		27	—
5. Sales Commissions		11	—
6. Travel		5	—
7. Telephone		1	—
8. Training		2	—
9. Promotion materials expense		2	—
10. Other expenses		1	—
11. Total marketing expense		$49	

EXHIBIT 10 Detailed Job Cost Data

		Garfield Stadium	*Job Two*
1. Revenue		$100	
Direct expenses			
Marketing			
2. Selling	3		
3. Servicing	2		
4. Travel allocation	2		
5. Other	1		
6. Total marketing direct		(8)	
7. Engineering & estimation		(3)	
8. Transportation & erection		(25)	
Plant costs			
9. Labor	15		
10. Materials	20		
11. Other	5		
12. Total plant direct		(40)	
13. Repair Costs		0	
14. Job contribution		24	
Allocated costs			
15. Marketing		(3)	
16. Plant		(10)	
17. Corporate overhead		(6)	
18. Job profit		$5	

EXHIBIT 11 Sales Force Reports

1. Weekly Call Report Summary

District Manager ____________________
Week Ending ____________________

Number of customers contacted ____________________
Number of in-person calls ____________________
Number of telephone contacts ____________________

Hours spent:

		Percent of Total
1. Prospecting—new customers	____________ hrs.	____________%
2. Promoting prestressed and Macon	____________	____________
3. Selling jobs	____________	____________
4. Servicing bids	____________	____________
5. Servicing jobs	____________	____________
6. Total customer contact	____________	____________
7. Travel	____________	____________
8. Other support	____________	____________
9. Total hours spent	____________	100%

Bookings:

Exception items for Sales Manager's attention:

2. Weekly Call Report Detail
(for DSM's file and reference)

Date	Customer	Job	Ph.	Pur-pose	Time	Notes
4-10	Higgins Constr.	ABC WHSE.	✓	4	.25	discussed specs. change for bid

3. DSM Monthly Summary

DSM ____________________
Month ____________________

Customer	*Job*	*# Calls*	*# Hours*
Hanson Mfg.	123	4	6
	234	1	1
	general	1	4
Iota Corp.	456	20	20
Jackson	567	3	8
Logare Architects	promo	1	4
Total 29	17	148	130
		Travel	51
		Training	—
		Internal/Customer	12
		Other	17
		Support Total	80

Bookings:

Acme Printing	$1,000,000
Justin Twine Corp	280,000

(Continued)

4. Sales Manager's Weekly Summary of Call Activity

Number of customers contacted	________
Total number of customer contacts	________
Total hours spent	________
Proportion of time spent:	________
1. Prospecting—new customers	________%
2. Promoting prestressed and Macon	________
3. Selling jobs	________
4. Servicing bids	________
5. Servicing jobs	________
6. Total customer contact	80
7. Travel	15
8. Other support	5
TOTAL	100%

Bookings ________

5. Sales Managers' Quarterly Financial Summary

____ Quarter, 198_

	Total Hours		*Std. Hourly Cost*		*Functional Costs*
Total prospecting hours	____	×	____	=	____
Promotional hours	____		____		____
Selling hours	____		____		____
Service hours	____		____		____
Customer hours	____		____		____
Support hours	____		____		____

Percent distribution of costs Customer ________% Support ________%
Bookings for the quarter: ________
Planned contribution of quarter's bookings: ________

6. Quarterly Marketing Productivity Report

	This Quarter	*Last Quarter*	*Year Ago*
1. Bookings	$____	____	____
2. Number of jobs	____	____	____
3. Marketing expense	____	____	____
4. Marketing expense per $1,000 of bookings	____%	____%	____%
5. Average margin of bookings	____%	____%	____%
6. Corporate earnings	____	____	____
7. Marketing expense as a percentage of corporate earnings	____%	____%	____%
8. Number of calls	____	____	____
9. Costs per call	____	____	____
10. Number of DSM hours	____	____	____
11. Cost per hour	____	____	____
12. Calls per job	____	____	____
13. Calls per $1,000 of bookings	____	____	____

(Continued)

EXHIBIT 11 Sales Force Reports *Continued*

7. Quarterly Market Share Report

Markets & Segments	*Total Purchases*	*Macon's Bookings*	*Macon's Share*	*Macon's Share Last Year*	*Chief Competitors*
					A B C
______	______	______	______	______	__% __% __%
______					
______					

DSM Territory	*Total Purchases*	*Macon's Bookings*	*Macon's Share*	*Macon's Share Last Year*	*Chief Competitors*
______					
______					
______					

8. Quarterly Profitability Report

Segment	*Macon Bookings*	*Planned Contribution*	*Percent Contribution*
______	$______	$________	_______%
______			
______			
DSM Territory			
______	$______	$________	_______%
______			
______			
Product Line			
______	$______	$________	_______%
______			
______			

EXHIBIT 12 Sample "General Description of the Analytic Task"

Market and Segment Forecasting

Purpose:
To develop the ability to anticipate changes in the market and, to the extent possible, make sure that Macon is positioned to take advantage of these changes.

Example:
Review changes in customer needs determined from information gathered by the sales force. Estimate what the purchases of key customers and segments will be 3, 6, 12, and 24 months into the future. Estimate changes in the product mix. Update estimates periodically. Distinguish high-opportunity from low-opportunity segments. Identify possible responses the firm can make to serve and control the market more effectively. Determine what obstacles the firm will encounter. Improve the marketing staff's skill at customer-based forecasting of sales.

Frequency:
Quarterly.

Sources:
Market intelligence.

Rohm and Haas (A)

"Every November, we have our usual dissatisfying meeting. Each year, the committee approves the budget, although with greater reluctance each time. This year, however, things came to a screeching halt."

Bill Groetzinger, the director of Information Systems and Management (ISMS) of Rohm and Haas was describing the annual budget approval meeting. The November 1984 budget approval meeting had resulted in the postponement of the two major capital expenditures which the ISMS group had requested for 1985; a second mainframe computer and a new data center. In July 1985, Groetzinger was starting the cycle for the 1986 ISMS strategic plan and budget, which would include resubmitted requests for the new mainframe and data center.

ROHM AND HAAS

Rohm and Haas, a chemical company based in Philadelphia, was founded in 1909. In the early 1900s Dr. Otto Rohm, an analytical chemist in Stuttgart, Germany, had developed a standardized bate for tanning leather that was vastly superior to traditional tanning materials. Rohm persuaded his friend, Otto Haas, to help him sell the new chemical, a difficult task since tanners were reluctant to make any changes in the traditional leather tanning process. The two entrepreneurs formed a partnership in 1907. After two years of

This case was prepared by Lily Chu, Research Assistant, under the supervision of Assistant Professor Julie H. Hertenstein as the basis for class discussion rather than to illustrate either effective or ineffective handling of an administrative situation.

intense selling, they succeeded in establishing the product in the European tanning markets.

Haas then established a new branch of the partnership in Philadelphia, the center of the U.S. leather tanning industry. Although the entry of the United States into World War I in 1917 forced separate incorporation of the Philadelphia-based Rohm and Haas, to make it independent of the German firm, close ties were reestablished between the two companies following the war. After the leather tanning bate was established in American markets, Rohm and Haas expanded into other chemicals, including dye solvents, varnishes and insecticides. In 1932, Rohm began to find commercial applications for a new clear acrylic material which he named Plexiglas. Otto Haas quickly obtained the U.S. rights. It was the demand for Plexiglas, officially approved for U.S. military aircraft, that caused Rohm and Haas' sales to increase 500% from 1938 to 1945.

Otto Haas defined Rohm and Haas' strategy as combining technological excellence with a strong sales effort based on solving customer problems. Rohm and Haas' technological expertise was in chemicals, and it was there that the company concentrated its efforts.

During the 1960s and early 1970s, Rohm and Haas, like many other companies, followed a strategy of business diversification. The company entered unrelated businesses, including polyester and nylon fibers and various health products, through acquisitions and internal projects. Faced with operating losses in a number of new businesses, Rohm and Haas returned to its core strengths; by the mid-1970s the company began to divest losing businesses and concentrate once more on its chemical-related areas.

By 1984, Rohm and Haas had sales of over $2 billion (Exhibits 1 and 2). Its products included: paint additives, plastics, water purifiers, oil additives, and pesticides (Exhibits 3 and 4). In the 1982–84 period, Rohm and Haas' major capital expenditures included new plants and large investments in its herbicide, fungicide, and plastics businesses, and it made acquisitions to bolster its water treatment businesses.

In addition, acquisitions were made in two promising new business areas: electronic chemicals and seeds. In the first, Rohm and Haas produced chemicals used in the assembly and packaging of electronic components which managers viewed as a potentially high-growth area. In the second, Rohm and Haas had developed a special hybridization technology for wheat seed, and was looking for ways to exploit this technology; thus, several seed companies were acquired. Both of these businesses were expected to continue to grow.

In the second half of 1984, the chemical industry was facing a slowdown in demand for its products. This forced reconsideration of capital availability and allocation at Rohm and Haas. Corporate goals, such as expansion into promising new business areas and the renewed focus on projects designed to improve product quality, were considered very important. At the same time, top management decided to reduce the total pool for 1985 capital expenditures; the pool was set at $165 million.

ORGANIZATION STRUCTURE

The organization chart shown in Exhibit 5 disguises a matrix organization; Rohm and Haas was organized both by business group and by geographical region. Managers in the product groups reported to both their business group and their region. The same was true of the corporate functions; for example, corporate Accounting reported both to the corporate controller and to the financial manager of the North American Region.

ISMS was a corporate staff group. About 150 of the 300 ISMS employees were in data processing or management information services (MIS) at the home office. An additional 150 employees served in MIS functions in the field-plants and subsidiaries or other noncorporate groups. They reported dually to ISMS and to their assigned business group. For example, computer applications developers in the European Region reported dually to the region and to ISMS.

ISMS was divided primarily into two groups: MIS and non-MIS (Exhibit 6). The MIS group was responsible for mainframe computer services in the Corporate Data Center and for the purchase or development of information systems in Computer Systems. The MIS group evaluated and recommended appropriate commercial computer software; if appropriate software was not available, the group developed the software internally. Similarly, they evaluated hardware needs; they also determined whether use of the company mainframe computer or personal computers was more appropriate for applications. Examples of mainframe computer applications they were responsible for included inventory management, budgeting systems, payroll, and health and safety records.

The non-MIS groups handled services such as office automation, voice and data communications, and operations research for the corporation, as well as the ISMS administrative and planning functions.

ISMS USERS

Almost everyone in the company was in some way a "user" of ISMS services. ISMS services could be requested for entire divisions, or for individual plants or product groups.

Research, the largest single user of ISMS resources, felt that computer applications were essential to the success of the Research Division, and thus to the company. As Joe Gilbert, manager of Computer Applications Research, described it, "The computer will be the primary tool in research in the future. It will impact every phase of research." Gilbert listed several important applications which ranged from using the computer as an electronic notebook to using the computer to do advanced modeling and simulation. The computer could even be used to predict the properties of molecules, thereby reducing the research effort and the trouble of actually creating many new substances that would turn out to have no practical value. Further, once a usable new molecule had been identified, the computer could help determine under which conditions the production process should be run.

Less dramatic computer applications such as electronic communications could also be important to research. According to Gilbert:

> Text messaging allows us to communicate not only between different buildings and departments, but between different countries as well. We have a research lab in France and right now there's only a two-hour window when our scientists in France and our scientists in Philadelphia are both working. Having text messaging is a tremendous time-saver. Without this electronic mail, it's hard to catch them at their phones and it's hard to transmit a lot of information at once. Now, we can communicate a lot more information at any time.

Gilbert estimated that there were over 600 computer terminals in the Research Division and of the 1500 Research employees, over 1000 of them used the computer on a regular basis in mid-1985. Research was so committed to the computer as a tool that they planned to add 200 terminals each year until everyone who needed one had one. Gilbert estimated that the cost, including the terminal, computer time, and other support costs, was about $7800/year for each person with a terminal. Research was also investigating the possibility of having terminals installed in scientists' homes as well.

Dave Stitely, financial manager of the North American Region, had a somewhat different view of computers. He felt it was necessary for computer projects to be justified but he believed the era when computer projects could easily be justified on hard financial grounds was past. Historically, systems projects had allowed for the reduction in clerical or other personnel which resulted in direct cost savings. By 1984, systems projects could rarely be justified on a ROI basis, and Stitely had to apply "softer" measurements:

> Take the voice messaging system. That's a perfect example of a project that you'll never be able to quantifiably justify. We put that in about two years ago, and we're out of capacity on the system now. We approved an increase in capacity last week by bringing together the six prime users, (that's the six managers whose people are using it the most) and asking "Do you people agree this is worth $100,000 to you?" You end up with a subjective opinion, but if you can get six senior managers in a room to agree that an expenditure is going to pay for itself qualitatively, then it's probably justified.

ISMS PLANNING

ISMS charged users of its systems development and computer services on a full cost basis, with the goal that it would show zero profit at the end of each fiscal year. For the Corporate Data Center, unit charges were calculated at the beginning of each year, based on estimated levels of various types of usage and Data Center costs (Exhibit 7). In the event that the Data Center overcharged users and actually showed a "profit," the excess was credited back to users (Exhibit 8).

In order to determine the proper unit charges and to forecast needed computer acquisitions, accurate estimates of user demand were necessary. Each June, several ISMS managers, led by Tom Rife (ISMS planning manager) and Al Sciscio (ISMS facilities planning manager) interviewed managers and MIS in each user group to prepare a personnel three-year plan. The data from these interviews, in conjunction with projections based on historical trends, were used to estimate future needs. According to Al Sciscio:

> In the past, we used to rely exclusively on user input for our mainframe computer capacity projections, but we found that it wasn't very accurate. Users almost always underestimated their needs. We have found that computer usage has been increasing at a rate of about 50% each year. Of course, no user thinks that his usage is going to increase that much. Users particularly have a hard time making usage estimates for new projects. So we use our historical projections for the basic estimates, and adjust them according to user input. For example, if we know a user has a big project coming up, we'll adjust the historical projection to take that into account. Another thing we take into account is the number of terminals that will be used. We've found that mainframe computer usage is pretty closely correlated to the number of terminals. So even if a user can't estimate how much computer time his department will use, if we are told that ten new terminals will be installed in his department, we can make a reasonable estimate of the increase in usage.

Another consideration in the planning process was the corporate guidelines. In 1976 the company had placed an MIS personnel cap of 300 and had set a target "MIS ratio" (worldwide MIS costs as a percent of worldwide sales) of .8%. While the personnel cap had proved not to be an encumbrance, the target MIS ratio, in Groetzinger's view, was somewhat unrealistic. Although the MIS ratio had dropped to .9% in 1984 from a previous high of 1.1%, the unending growth in demand for computer services made a further decline unlikely.

Upon completion of the user interviews, the ISMS planners used all available data to construct a three-year plan. The three-year plan included the ISMS operating budget, a listing of user projects which identified the estimated costs and manpower requirements, and a schedule of necessary hardware and software acquisitions.

Next the planners developed the one-year plan in greater detail for the year beginning the following January. This one-year plan was basically a subset of the three-year plan. The one-year plan included the budget for the following year, projects scheduled for the following year, and the acquisitions, expenditures, and staffing requirements necessary to meet user needs.

Projects included in the ISMS plan had already been authorized by the user groups. For example, when purchasing, which reported to both corporate and the North American Region, wanted a Purchasing/Accounts Payable system, it had to get approval from both groups. The request to spend the money on the development of this new system was included in the budget requests for both corporate and the North American Region. These budget requests were reviewed and approved formally by a committee of top managers. Only after the project had been formally approved in the budgeting process of both groups was it included in the ISMS budget.

Based on its estimate of user needs, ISMS projected the staffing, equipment and facilities required to meet these needs. For 1985, two major expenditures were determined to be necessary: a second mainframe computer and the construction of a new data center.

According to projections of usage, the current mainframe would be at capacity by the fourth quarter of 1985. The second mainframe would cost an estimated $6 million, plus an additional $4 million for peripherals, software and expenses such as maintenance and sales tax. Upgrading or expanding the existing mainframe would have been considered a preferable solution to adding a second computer because some redundancy is encountered in areas such as peripherals and staffing when a second computer is added. Unfortunately, the capacity problem could not be solved by upgrading to the next larger size: the Rohm and Haas mainframe was already the largest IBM mainframe available. Groetzinger refused to "manage demand by decreasing quality," that is, by allowing response time to grow. Since user needs were projected to outgrow the current mainframe within the year, and since usage was expected to continue growing at the compound annual growth rate of 50% as it had since 1979, a second computer was required.

Similarly, projected computer capacity indicated that additional floor space was necessary. In 1984, the total home office space required for ISMS needs was in excess of 17,000 square feet. An additional 1500 square feet was estimated to be required each year until at least 1990. Of this additional space, the second mainframe and related peripherals would require less than 700 square feet. The ISMS group evaluated several possible ways to obtain the necessary floor space. Alternatives ranged from taking space from other Rohm and Haas departments to constructing a new building capable of housing the data center. If a new building was constructed, the most likely site was at Spring House, Pennsylvania, located only fifteen miles north of the company's Philadelphia home office. The Rohm and Haas Research Center was located at Spring House; additional land was available at that site for the data center. Obtaining additional space at the home office would mean inconveniencing other departments and would require the expenditure of about $4 million in conversion costs for what was at best a temporary solution. ISMS planning believed that constructing a separate data center facility, with an estimated cost of $6 million, was the best solution.

THE BUDGET APPROVAL MEETING

In November 1984, Bill Groetzinger brought the ISMS one-year plan to be reviewed by the top managers at Rohm and Haas. The budget approval meeting was attended by:

NAME	TITLE
Don Felley	President & Chief Operating Officer
Larry Wilson	Group Vice President, Administration & Finance
Jack Mulroney	Group Vice President, Director Corporate Business Department
Norm Harberger	Vice President & General Manager of Administration
Fred Shaffer	Vice President & Chief Financial Officer
Bill Groetzinger	Director of Information Systems and Management Services

Felley, Wilson, Mulroney, and Shaffer reviewed the budgets for all the business groups in the company and were responsible for approving both the budgets and major capital expenditures for the entire company.

At the meeting, Groetzinger presented the ISMS personnel requests, operating budget and capital requests for the 1985 fiscal year (summarized in Exhibit 9) as well as a listing of user projects to be undertaken or continued. The detailed request listed user projects ranging from user-friendly inquiry systems in regular English to companywide inventory management systems; the proposed capital expenditures ranged from a few thousand dollars for a new software package to two $6 million projects: the mainframe and the data center.

Almost all the capital and personnel requests were approved. However, the two major requests, the addition of a second mainframe computer and the construction of a new data center, were denied. Groetzinger was asked to develop alternatives that would allow the postponement of the two projects.

REACTIONS

A particularly bewildering aspect of the rejections was that the ISMS budget was based on user requests that had been approved by senior user management. The ISMS group believed it was not asking for anything beyond what was needed to meet those prior approved user requests; through the full-cost billing system, the costs had been accepted as worthwhile by the users. There were several reactions to the projects being rejected. According to Al Sciscio:

> I think the reason it's harder for us to get our budget requests through than it is for users to get their ISMS requests through is the difference in accounting. The users are making "below the line" payments; they're just sending money to another department in the company. We're making "above the line" payments. When we make a capital request, the top managers realize that it's real money the company has to pay out, and that's when they start to balk.

Jack Mulroney shared his views:

> It's a fallacy to think that full-cost billing works as a de facto approval system. A lot of

> managers don't really understand what they're being billed for when they get their computer bill. If I'm a manager with a department budget of $10 million, maybe $1 million is overhead. That includes the computer as well as the normal sales and administrative charges. If the computer charge is $100,000, it kind of gets lost in the shuffle. What am I gonna do about it? Tell Bill I don't want my seven people to have voice messaging? Then my people wonder why everyone else gets voice messaging and they don't. And Bill may say that having incremental people on the voice messaging system doesn't cost much, so dropping those seven people from voice messaging only saves my department $250. At that point, the managers just don't bother. But multiply that $100,000 a hundred times over, and *that's* the number I have to see.

Larry Wilson agreed that it was difficult for managers to control computer usage:

> We can't even give them guidelines. With other things we can say, "Don't make it unless it has x profit margin." What do we tell them about computers, "Don't use the computer unless you're making at least $100 per minute with it?"

To Jack Mulroney, it was just one more in a series of budget cuts they had to make for 1985. Thinking ahead, he said:

> For next year (1986), we're planning to make about $180 million in capital expenditures. Now, in mid-1985, we've already received requests for over $325 million. While $6 million for a particular project might be small potatoes, we've got to cut somewhere.
>
> It's like the electric companies in the sixties who felt everyone should switch to electric heat when there was nothing wrong with gas heat. We're being told from all directions that the information explosion, the never-ending growth in computer usage, is good. My personal opinion is that people are beginning to doubt the business value of that extra computer unit.
>
> The other thing to keep in mind is the environment we're in. The economy is essentially flat. In the chemical industry, from 1979 to 1985 there has been little or no net growth in sales; that's unit growth not dollar growth. Yet, year after year, ISMS comes up with thirty, forty percent growth over the previous year. What we have to decide is what part of that growth we want to support and what part of that growth we are willing to forego.
>
> We, the top few managers of the company, got tired of going to the annual budgeting meeting, listening to the MIS proposals for the coming year which were always up another 30%, sitting there asking the same questions, and not understanding the answers. During the year, we had seen the R&D budget, the manufacturing budget. We'd see that the plant would cost $50 million dollars, or recruiting was off. So when it came to the end of the year, we had some kind of personal experience with the R&D budget, the selling and administrative budget, or whatever. Then we'd go into the ISMS meeting and we'd see computer curves, peripherals, laser printers, smart terminals, dumb terminals, hardware, software, . . . big deal. All you can do is not like the result.

Dave Stitely of the North American Region agreed with the decision to postpone the two major capital expenditures, even at the cost of postponing a few user projects. He believed that other departments, like the North American Region, could easily cut back on proposed projects. Stitely and his boss, Samuel Talucci, North American regional director began their MIS allocation process by establishing priorities the North American Region's MIS projects. Keeping the target MIS ratio of .8% firmly in mind, they would begin to cut projects. Stitely said that they succeeded in cutting out 25–50% of the proposed MIS projects. He admitted that the priorities and the resulting cutting process were "relatively arbitrary," but argued that they were necessary.

> Even though each department is within its MIS budget, once you add up all those individual projects, we've overflowed. We're now at a crucial break point. We're faced with spending $15 million for MIS. At this point, it behooves every one of those managers to go back and look at his projects and see if they're essential. The only way to deal with

this is to cap the top and force managers to establish priorities at the bottom.

Joe Gilbert of Research had a different perspective.

> We need computers to compete in research with other companies. And, all those extra applications, like messaging or word processing are important. For example, if a scientist has some ideas that he wants to write up and knows that if he waits he can do it on the computer instead of writing and rewriting it on paper, he'll wait to do it. The differences in efficiency are amazing. Computers, or the lack of them can also impact recruiting. The best people coming from school expect to have a computer ready for their use. If we can't provide it, they'll go to some company that can.

Larry Wilson's wry response was, "I do think it's important to remain competitive with other companies. But somehow I don't think that the company that's on the leading edge of the text messaging technology is going to have an appreciable advantage over its competitors."

EXHIBIT 1 Income Statements

Rohm and Haas Company and Consolidated Subsidiaries
Statements of Consolidated Earnings
Years ended December 31, 1984, 1983 and 1982

(Thousands of dollars)	*1984*	*1983*	*1982*
Current Earnings			
Net sales	$2,042,011	$1,875,937	$1,828,027
Cost of goods sold	1,364,838	1,275,842	1,345,113
Gross profit	677,173	600,095	482,914
Selling and administrative expense	285,941	254,999	256,318
Research and development expense	109,492	100,428	95,516
Interest expense	43,523	37,160	28,135
Facility disposals and termination benefits, net	—	—	11,850
Equity in net earnings of affiliates	4,482	6,059	552
Other income, net	42,887	32,293	9,551
Earnings before income taxes	285,586	245,860	128,898
Income taxes	113,367	108,257	43,293
Net earnings	$ 172,219	$ 137,603	$ 85,605
Net earnings per share, *in dollars*	$ 6.73	$ 5.33	$ 3.32
Retained Earnings			
Retained earnings at beginning of year	$ 620,029	$ 517,676	$ 468,229
Adjustment resulting from change in foreign currency translation	—	3,527	—
Beginning, as restated	620,029	521,203	468,229
Net earnings for the year	172,219	137,603	85,605
	792,248	658,806	553,834
Cash dividends paid ($1.80, $1.50 and $1.40 per share in 1984, 1983 and 1982 respectively)	46,184	38,777	36,158
Retained earnings at end of year	$ 746,064	$ 620,029	$ 517,676

See accompanying summary of significant accounting policies (page 45) and notes to consolidated financial statements (pages 49–57).

Financial Ratios			
As a percent of sales			
Gross profit	33.2%	32.0%	26.4%
Selling, administrative and research expense	19.4	18.9	19.0
Net earnings	8.4	7.3	4.7
Debt-to-equity ratio at year-end	31.9%	30.6%	37.1%

EXHIBIT 2 Balance Sheets

Rohm and Haas Company and Consolidated Subsidiaries
Consolidated Balance Sheets

December 31, 1984 and 1983

(Thousands of dollars)	*1984*	*1983*
Assets		
Current assets		
Cash and marketable securities	$ 155,708	$ 260,208
Accounts receivable, net	271,065	252,592
Inventories	356,245	292,338
Prepaid expenses and other assets	45,119	47,538
Total current assets	828,137	852,676
Investments in and advances to unconsolidated subsidiaries and affiliates		
Investments	79,937	73,376
Advances	1,922	668
Total investments and advances	81,859	74,044
Land, buildings and equipment, net	555,945	518,360
Other assets	167,088	66,164
	$1,633,029	$1,511,244
Liabilities and Stockholders' Equity		
Current liabilities		
Notes payable	$ 135,446	$ 48,730
Accounts payable and accrued liabilities	254,878	219,507
Federal, foreign and other income taxes	10,718	31,579
Total current liabilities	401,042	299,816
Long-term debt	172,193	227,586
Deferred income taxes and other liabilities	94,648	79,449
Stockholders' equity		
Common stock; par value—$2.50; authorized—100,000,000 shares; issued—26,217,460 shares	65,544	65,544
Additional paid-in capital	232,182	234,446
Retained earnings	746,064	620,029
	1,043,790	920,019
Less cost of reacquired common shares held in treasury (1984—1,448,119 shares; 1983—411,630 shares)	78,644	15,626
Total stockholders' equity	965,146	904,393
	$1,633,029	$1,511,244

EXHIBIT 3 Business Segments

(Millions of dollars)	*1984*	*1983*	*1982*
Sales to customers			
Polymers, Resins and Monomers	$ 765	$ 745	$ 707
Plastics	419	390	353
Industrial Chemicals	419	341	331
Agricultural Chemicals	359	337	336
Miscellaneous	80	63	101
Total	$2,042	$1,876	$1,828
Operating profit (loss)			
Polymers, Resins and Monomers	$ 156	$ 149	$ 78
Plastics	76	63	15
Industrial Chemicals	50	40	21
Agricultural Chemicals	51	34	35
Miscellaneous	(11)	(12)	9
Total	$ 322	$ 274	$ 158
Identifiable assets at year-end			
Polymers, Resins and Monomers	$ 409	$ 372	$ 360
Plastics	262	235	234
Industrial Chemicals	337	192	163
Agricultural Chemicals	285	257	262
Miscellaneous	65	82	92
Total	$1,358	$1,138	$1,111
Depreciation and depletion expense			
Polymers, Resins and Monomers	$ 32	$ 34	$ 33
Plastics	19	18	17
Industrial Chemicals	13	11	12
Agricultural Chemicals	17	17	10
Miscellaneous	8	10	9
Corporate	4	3	2
Total	$ 93	$ 93	$ 83
Capital additions			
Polymers, Resins and Monomers	$ 44	$ 24	$ 41
Plastics	36	13	18
Industrial Chemicals	24	14	16
Agricultural Chemicals	24	14	17
Miscellaneous	1	4	21
Corporate	5	3	13
Total	$ 134	$ 72	$ 126

EXHIBIT 4 Geographical Segments

(Millions of dollars)	*1984*	*1983*	*1982*
Total sales			
United States	$1,515	$1,366	$1,303
Canada	97	100	84
Europe	388	360	367
Latin America	121	112	116
Pacific	100	119	125
Adjustments and eliminations	(179)	(181)	(167)
Total	$2,042	$1,876	$1,828
Operating profit (loss)			
United States	$ 204	$ 173	$ 104
Canada	10	10	6
Europc	66	50	18
Latin America	47	44	26
Pacific	(3)	(1)	—
Adjustments and eliminations	(2)	(2)	(4)
Total	$ 322	$ 274	$ 158
Identifiable assets at year-end			
United States	$ 998	$ 830	$ 806
Canada	27	26	24
Europe	285	234	235
Latin America	78	66	68
Pacific	35	46	46
Adjustments and eliminations	(65)	(64)	(68)
Total	$1,358	$1,138	$1,111

EXHIBIT 5 Organization Chart

ROHM AND HAAS COMPANY

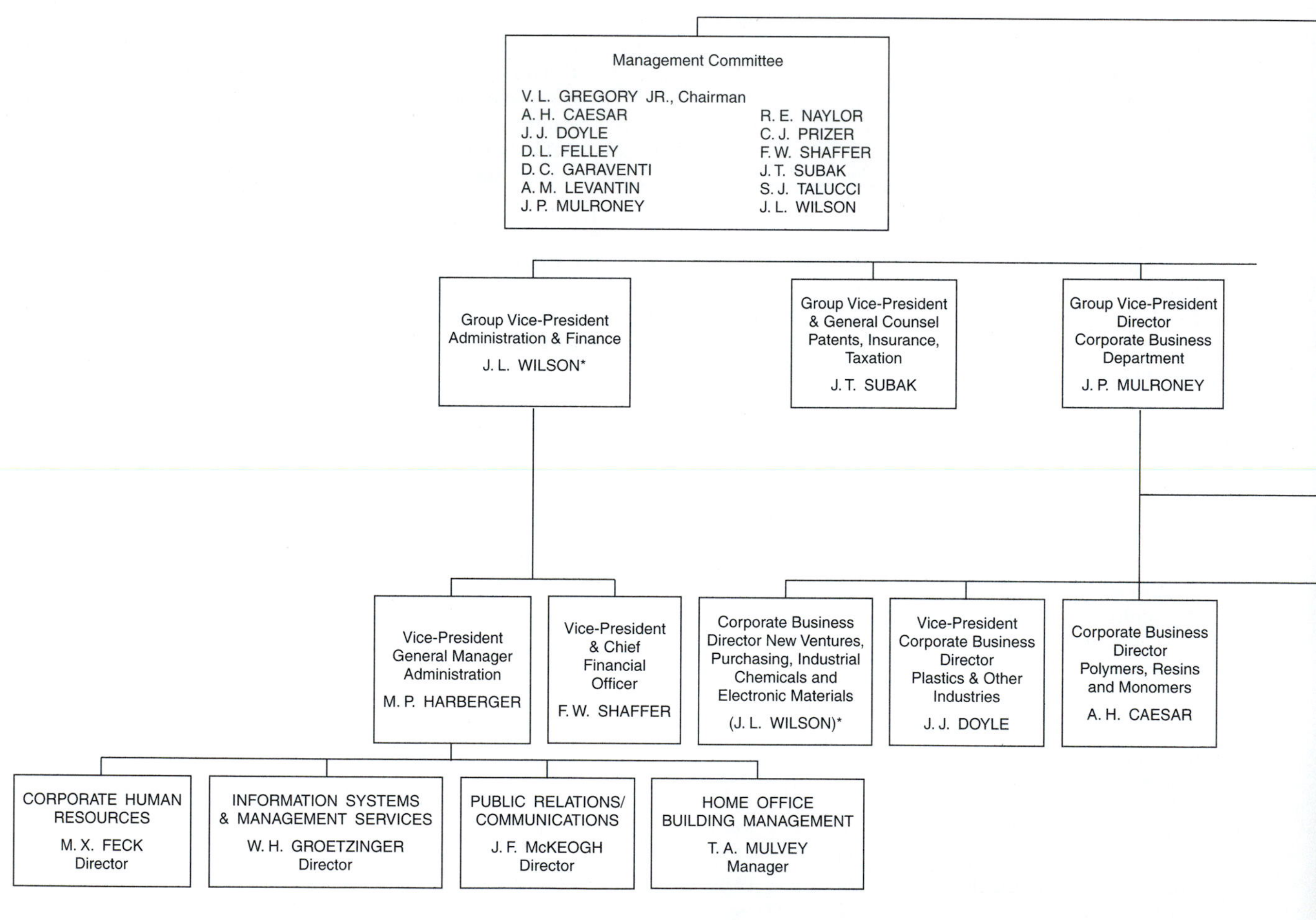

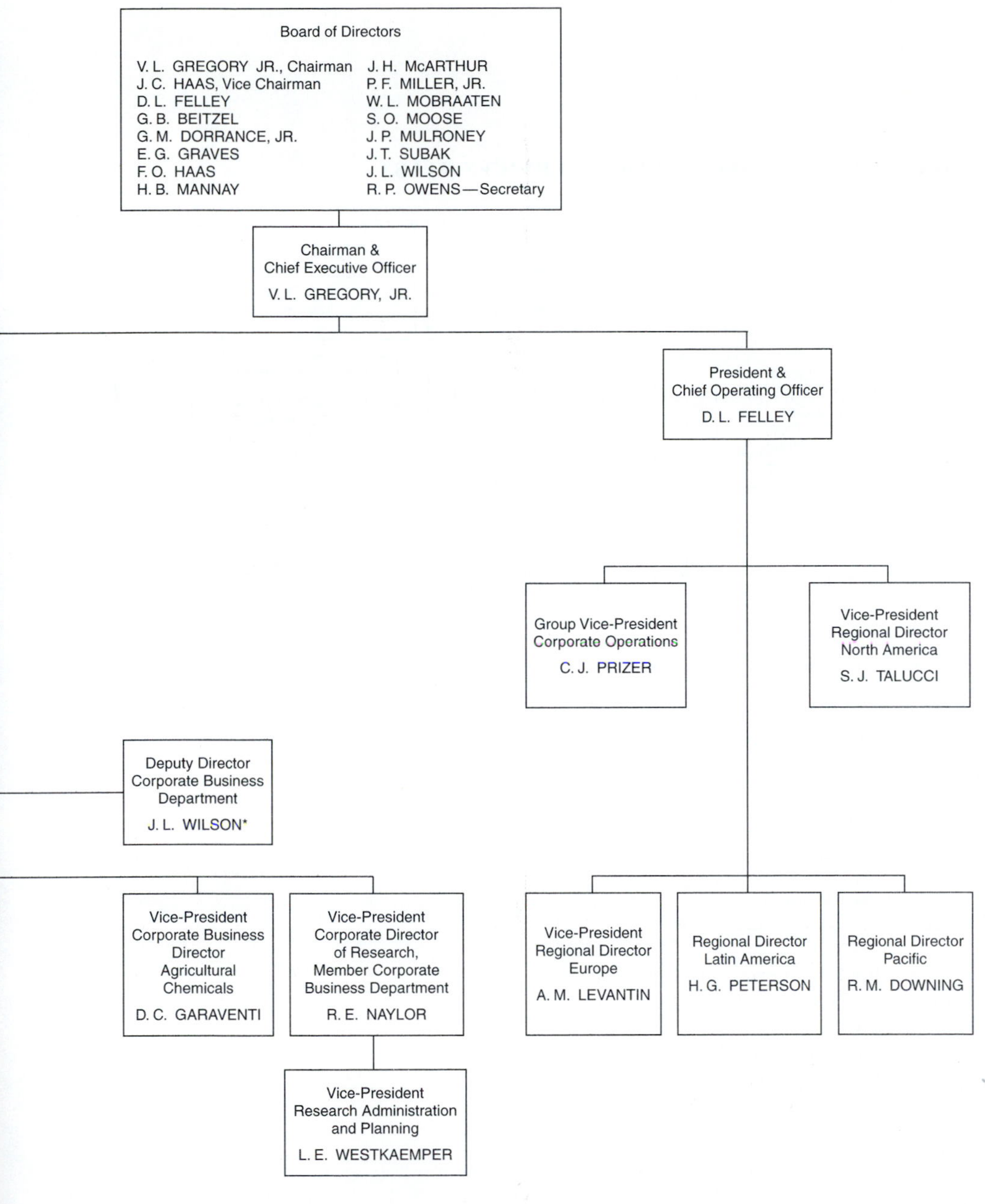
Board of Directors
V. L. GREGORY JR., Chairman
J. C. HAAS, Vice Chairman
D. L. FELLEY
G. B. BEITZEL
G. M. DORRANCE, JR.
E. G. GRAVES
F. O. HAAS
H. B. MANNAY
J. H. McARTHUR
P. F. MILLER, JR.
W. L. MOBRAATEN
S. O. MOOSE
J. P. MULRONEY
J. T. SUBAK
J. L. WILSON
R. P. OWENS—Secretary
Chairman & Chief Executive Officer
V. L. GREGORY, JR.
President & Chief Operating Officer
D. L. FELLEY
Group Vice-President Corporate Operations
C. J. PRIZER
Vice-President Regional Director North America
S. J. TALUCCI
Deputy Director Corporate Business Department
J. L. WILSON*
Vice-President Corporate Business Director Agricultural Chemicals
D. C. GARAVENTI
Vice-President Corporate Director of Research, Member Corporate Business Department
R. E. NAYLOR
Vice-President Research Administration and Planning
L. E. WESTKAEMPER
Vice-President Regional Director Europe
A. M. LEVANTIN
Regional Director Latin America
H. G. PETERSON
Regional Director Pacific
R. M. DOWNING

EXHIBIT 6 ISMS Organization Chart

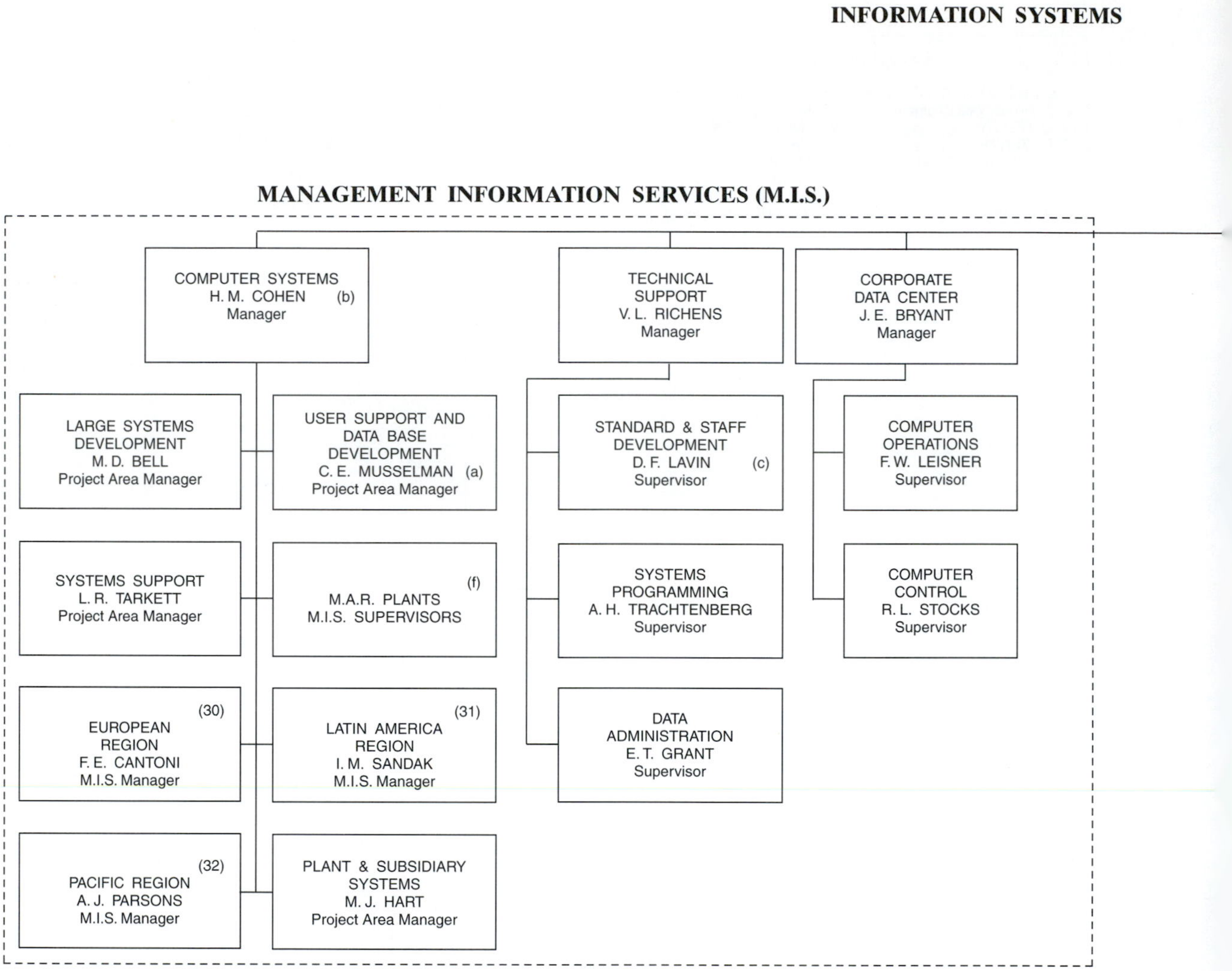

INFORMATION SYSTEMS

MANAGEMENT INFORMATION SERVICES (M.I.S.)

COMPUTER SYSTEMS
H. M. COHEN (b)
Manager

LARGE SYSTEMS DEVELOPMENT
M. D. BELL
Project Area Manager

USER SUPPORT AND DATA BASE DEVELOPMENT
C. E. MUSSELMAN (a)
Project Area Manager

SYSTEMS SUPPORT
L. R. TARKETT
Project Area Manager

(f)
M.A.R. PLANTS
M.I.S. SUPERVISORS

(30)
EUROPEAN REGION
F. E. CANTONI
M.I.S. Manager

(31)
LATIN AMERICA REGION
I. M. SANDAK
M.I.S. Manager

(32)
PACIFIC REGION
A. J. PARSONS
M.I.S. Manager

PLANT & SUBSIDIARY SYSTEMS
M. J. HART
Project Area Manager

TECHNICAL SUPPORT
V. L. RICHENS
Manager

STANDARD & STAFF DEVELOPMENT
D. F. LAVIN (c)
Supervisor

SYSTEMS PROGRAMMING
A. H. TRACHTENBERG
Supervisor

DATA ADMINISTRATION
E. T. GRANT
Supervisor

CORPORATE DATA CENTER
J. E. BRYANT
Manager

COMPUTER OPERATIONS
F. W. LEISNER
Supervisor

COMPUTER CONTROL
R. L. STOCKS
Supervisor

(a) Also serves as coordinator for Engineering and Research.
(b) Also serves as coordinator for NAR, and Other Industries.
(c) Also serves as Data Security Coordinator.
(d) Also serves as Home Office Security Officer.
(e) Also serves as coordinator for New Businesses.

AND MANAGEMENT SERVICES

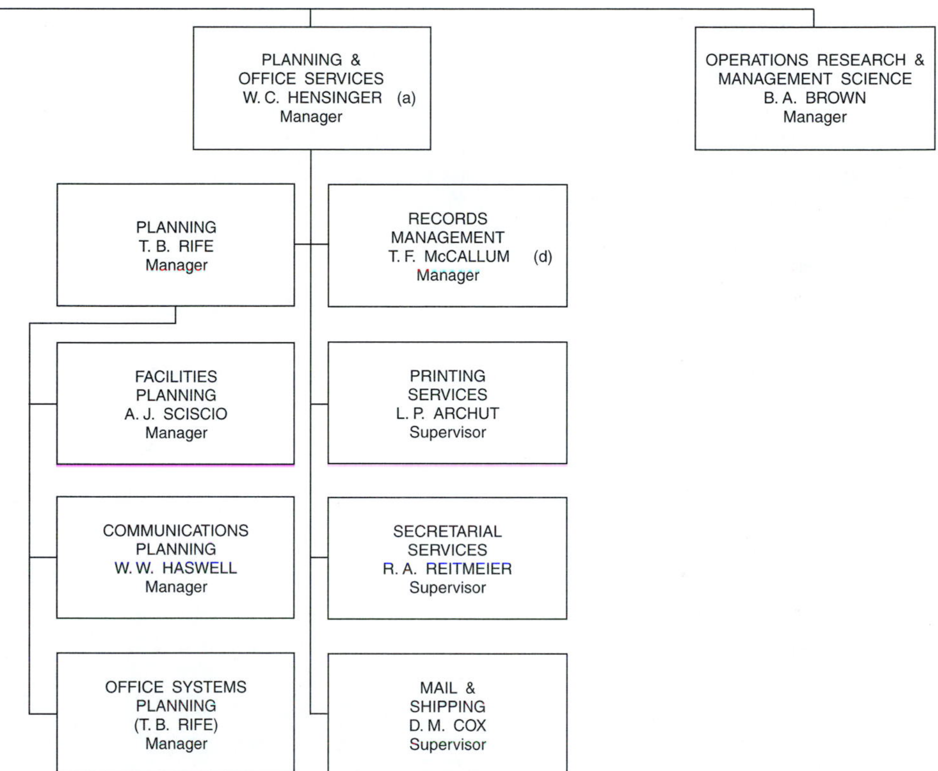

EXHIBIT 7 1985 Charge Out Rates

Category	*Total ACT Hours*	−	*CDC ACT Hours*	=	*Net ACT Hours*[a]
PRIME					
Batch	647	−	18	=	629
TSO	1,563	−	42	=	1,521
Interactive	1,078	−	13	=	1,065
NONPRIME					
Batch	1,220	−	281	=	939
TSO	360	−	30	=	330

Total TSO Hours = 1521 + 330 = 1851

Rates:		
Non-Prime Batch	(N) = 1	
Prime Batch		(P) = 1.2 * N
TSO		(T) = 1.4 * N
Interactive		(X) = 1.5 * N

$12,420,914 = $(939*N + 629*1.2N + 1851*1.4N + 1065*1.5N) * 60
$12,420,914 = $(939*N + 755N + 2591N + 1598N) * 60
$12,420,914 = $5,883N * 60
$12,420,914 = $352.980N
$35.19 = $35 = N

	1985	*1984*
NonPrime Batch	(N) = $35	$42
Prime Batch	(P) = 1.2 * N = $42	$50
TSO	(T) = 1.4 * N = $49	$59
Interactive	(X) = 1.5 * N = $53	$63

Proof:
$12,420,914 = $(939*N + 629*1.2N + 1,851*1.4N + 1,065*1.5N) * 60
$12,420,914 = $(939*35 + 629*42 + 1,851*49 + 1,065*53) * 60
$12,420,914 = $(32,865 + 26,418 + 90,699 + 56,445) * 60
$12,420,914 = $(206,427) * 60
$12,420,914 = $12,385,620

[a]Explanation: Total Actual Computer Hours − Computer Data Center Actual Hours = Net Actual Computer Hours Charged to Users

EXHIBIT 8 Cumulative User Changes by Month (Actual through June)

PROJECTED YEAR-END BUDGET = $11,669
PROJECTED OVER CHARGE = $1,596

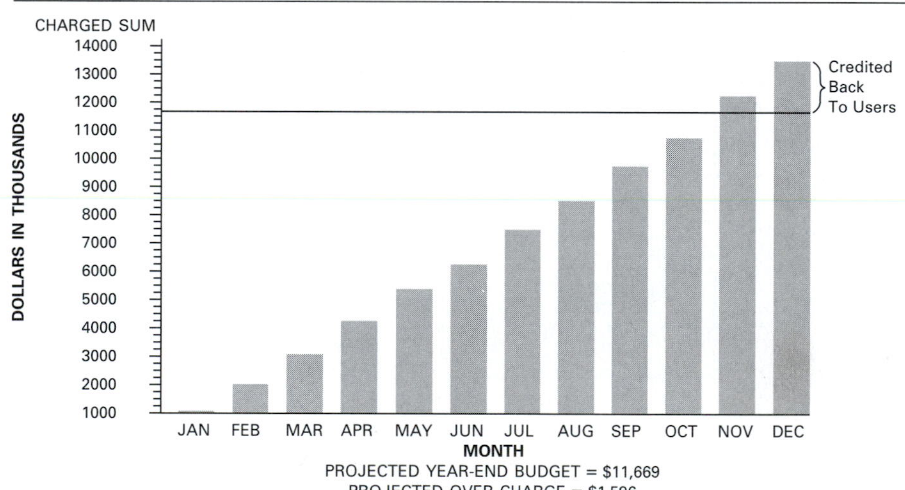

EXHIBIT 9 ISMS Expenditures

	Capital Expenditures ($ thousands)	*Operating Expenditures ($ millions)*
1985 Proposed:		
MIS Group	15700	25
Other ISMS Groups	1200	
Approved 11/84:		
MIS Group	2100	24
Other ISMS Groups	1200	
1984 Actual:		
MIS Group	2000	21
Other ISMS Groups	326	
1983 Actual:		
MIS Group	1600	18
Other ISMS Groups	53	

CHAPTER 3

Results Controls

If asked to think about devices used to influence behavior in business organizations, in the United States at least, most people would probably think first about pay-for-performance. Pay-for-performance is a prominent example of a type of control that can be called *results control* because it involves rewarding individuals (and sometimes groups of individuals) for generating good results, or punishing them for poor results. The rewards linked to results go far beyond monetary compensation, even in U.S. firms, and include, among others, job security, promotions, autonomy, and recognition.

Results controls create *meritocracies.* In meritocracies, the rewards are given to the most talented and hardest working employees, rather than those with the longest tenure or the right social connections.

The combinations of rewards linked to results inform or remind employees what result areas are important and motivate them to produce the results the organization rewards. Results controls influence actions because they cause employees to be concerned about the *consequences* of the actions they take. The employees' actions are not constrained; the employees are *empowered* to take whatever actions they believe will best produce the desired results. Results controls also encourage employees to discover and develop their talents and to get placed in jobs where they will be able to perform well. For these reasons, a well-designed results control system should help produce the desired results.

Like all other forms of controls, however, results controls cannot be used in every situation. They are effective only where the desired result areas can be controlled (to a considerable extent) by the individual(s) whose actions are being influenced and where the controllable result areas can be measured effectively.

INCIDENCE OF RESULTS CONTROLS

Results controls are in common use for employees at many organization levels. They are particularly dominant as a means of controlling the behaviors of professional employees. Reengineering guru Michael Hammer even defines a professional as "someone who is responsible for achieving a result rather than [for] performing a task."[1]

Results controls are consistent with, and even necessary for, the implementation of decentralized forms of organization with largely autonomous responsibility centers. Business pioneer Alfred P. Sloan observed that he sought a way to exercise effective control over the whole corporation, yet maintain a philosophy of decentralization.[2] At General Motors (and numerous other organizations that followed), the answer for many years under Sloan's leadership and beyond was results controls built on a return-on-investment (ROI) performance measure. By using this type of control system, upper management could review and judge the effectiveness of the various organizational entities while leaving the actual execution of operations to people responsible for the performance of those entities.

DuPont, Coca-Cola, Alcoa, and Sunrise Medical are among the many companies that have gone through the process of instituting more decentralized forms of organization with a concurrent increased emphasis on results control. In 1993, DuPont's CEO replaced a complex management hierarchy by splitting the company into twenty-one strategic business units (SBUs), each of which operates as a free-standing unit. The SBU managers were given greater responsibility and asked to be more entrepreneurial and more customer-focused. They were also asked to bear more risk, because a large portion of SBU managers' compensation is based on both SBU sales and profitability. The managers noticed the change. One SBU manager said, "When I joined DuPont [twenty-one years ago], if you kept your nose clean and worked hard, you could work as long as you wanted. [But today] job security depends on results."[3] The change was perceived as being successful. A *Business Week* article noted that, "The image of DuPont has morphed from giant sloth to gazelle."[4]

Coca-Cola's president explained his company's intent in decentralizing as follows:

> We're giving our division managers around the world a lot of authority, and we're holding them responsible. We aren't going to reward people . . . for perfect attendance. We're going to reward them for meeting objectives that they have agreed to. If they meet them, they're going to have money jingling in their pocket; if they don't, somebody else will be given that opportunity.[5]

Paul H. O'Neill, Alcoa's chairman, said,

> We cannot succeed if we persist in our use of the traditional command and control system of management where many thousands of people believe their only responsibility is to do what they are told to do.[6]

Richard H. Chandler, CEO of Sunrise Medical, a medical products company headquartered in Carlsbad, California, defended his company's decentralized organization and lucrative performance-based bonuses as an effort to "replicate the entrepreneurial model" within a multifaceted corporation. He said,

> People want to be rewarded based on their own efforts. [Without divisional accountability] you end up with a system like the U.S. Post Office. There's no incentive [for workers to excel].[7]

Indeed, many companies have found that managers will act in the entrepreneurial manner necessary to thrive in fast-moving markets only if they are subjected to the same market forces and pressures that drive independent entrepreneurs and if they are promised at least similar rewards for the risk they must bear.

At middle organization levels, results controls are often implemented under the framework of a management-by-objectives (MBO) system. In its most basic form, MBO is

> a process whereby the superior and subordinate managers of an organization jointly identify common goals, define each individual's major areas of responsibilities in terms of the results expected of them [sic], and use these measures as guides for operating the unit and assessing the contribution of each of its members.[8]

Results controls can also be emphasized down to the lowest levels in the organization, as many companies have done with good effects. In a survey of mid-sized manufacturers (with annual sales between $10 million and $500 million) sponsored by professional service firm Grant Thornton, 80 percent of the respondents reported they were working on programs to give their workers more power and responsibility on the shop floor.[9]

It is common for delivery personnel to be paid on a commission basis. At the Frito-Lay division of Pepsi Cola, deliverymen receive only a small weekly salary, but are paid a 10 percent commission on all the chips they sell. Studies have found that this system encourages them to serve the company's interest better; the drivers do not merely deliver the chips, they also "stop to talk with supermarket managers, angling for an extra foot of shelf space."[10]

Porsche, the German automobile manufacturer, and Cleveland-based Lincoln Electric Company are among the companies which use results controls down to the lowest organizational levels in their manufacturing areas. Porsche, which is known for high-quality products, enters the name of the worker who installs each major engine component in the engine's log so if a fault (a result) appears later, it can be traced back to the person responsible.[11] Lincoln Electric provides wages based solely on piecework for most factory jobs and liberal performance-related bonuses that can more than double an individual's pay.[12] This incentive system has created such high productivity that some of the industry giants have found it difficult, or even impossible, to compete in Lincoln's line of business: arc welding. Because of Lincoln's success, General Electric left the arc-welding business entirely, and Westinghouse was squeezed into a small corner of the market. A *Business Week* article observed that "in its reclusive, iconoclastic way, Lincoln Electric remains one of the best-managed companies in the United States as is probably as good as anything across the Pacific."[13]

Franchising is another approach for implementing results controls. With franchising, business ownership, with all of its risks and rewards, is passed to a franchisee. The franchisee has some decision making powers, although these are often somewhat constrained by a franchise contract. In particular, franchisees are not allowed to deviate significantly from the *concept.* MacDonald's hamburger franchisees must offer Big-Macs, which are an important element of the menu concept used around the world, but the control advantage of franchising is that franchisers can spread the use of their concept and earn fees and royalties with minimum control risk because franchisees' rewards stem directly from the profits they earn. The rewards motivate the franchisees to be hardworking, efficient, responsive to customers, and entrepreneurial.

RESULTS CONTROLS AND THE CONTROL PROBLEMS

Results controls are preventative-type controls which are effective because they address some of the problems which cause the needs for controls. They are particularly effective in addressing motivational problems. Without upper-level manager supervision or intervention, the results controls induce employees to maximize their chances of producing the results the organization desires. This desirable motivational outcome occurs because the organizations' desired results are also, not coincidentally, those that will maximize the employees' own personal rewards.

Results controls also inform employees of what is expected of them. Employees know they should do what they can to produce the desired results. In this way, the results controls alleviate the potential problem of lack of direction.

Results controls do not directly address the personal limitation problems. Results controls inform employees of what results are valued, but not how the valued results can be produced. However, results controls can have powerful indirect effects on the personal limitation problems. Results controls can encourage employees to address their limitations and to develop their talents to position themselves to earn the results-dependent rewards.

The performance measures which are a part of the results controls also provide some nonmotivational, detection-type control benefits of a cybernetic (feedback) nature, as was mentioned in Chapter 1. The results measures help managers answer questions about how various strategies, organizational entities, and employees are performing. The managers can then change the strategies or intervene in the operational processes if necessary.

ELEMENTS OF RESULTS CONTROLS

The implementation of results controls requires these four steps: (1) defining the dimension(s) on which results are desired (or not desired); such as profitability, product reliability, or customer satisfaction; (2) measuring performance on these dimensions; (3) setting performance targets for employees to strive for; and (4) providing rewards (or punishments) to encourage (or discourage) the behaviors that will lead to the desired results. Each of these steps has pitfalls.

Defining Performance Dimensions

Defining the right performance dimensions is critical because the goals which are set and the measurements that are made shape employees' views of what is important. In the terms often heard in business organizations, "What you measure is what you get."[14] What is worrisome is that employees work to improve the areas which are measured regardless of *whether or not the measurement dimensions are defined correctly.* If the measurement dimensions are not defined correctly; that is, if they are not *congruent* with the organization's objectives or agreed-upon strategies, the results controls will actually encourage employees to do the wrong things. This problem is discussed further in Chapters 6 and 12.

Measuring Performance

Measurement, which involves the assignment of numbers to objects, is a critical element of a results control system. The object of importance is the performance of an individual (or a group of individuals) in a certain time period.

Many different results measures can be linked to rewards. Many objective financial measures; such as net income, earnings per share, and return on assets, are in common use. So are some non-financial measures; such as market share, growth (in units), and the timely accomplishment of certain tasks. Some measurements involve subjective judgments. Evaluators may be asked to judge whether a manager is "being a team player" or "developing employees effectively" and to record their judgments on a measurement scale from 1 (poor) to 5 (excellent).

For most high-level line managers, most of the key results areas linked to rewards are defined in financial terms. The measures may be either market-based performance indicators (such as stock price or returns) or accounting profits or returns (such as return on equity). Lower-level managers, on the other hand, are typically evaluated in terms of operational data which are more controllable at the local level. The key result areas for a production manager might be a combination of efficiency (such as labor hours per units produced), inventory control (such as days sales on hand), quality (such as average number of defects per unit produced), delivery time, and product development time.

This discontinuity between financial and operational performance measures creates a critical pivotal point in the management hierarchy which one set of researchers called a *hinge*.[15] At some critical middle organizational level, often a lower-profit-center level, managers must translate financial goals into operational goals. These managers' goals are primarily defined in financial terms, so their communications with their superiors are primarily in financial terms. Because their subordinates' goals are primarily operational, their downward communications are primarily in operational terms.

If managers identify more than one result measure for a given employee, they must attach relative importance weightings to each measure so that the judgments about performance in each result area can be aggregated into an overall evaluation. The weightings can be additive; for example, 60 percent of the overall evaluation is based on return on assets and 40 percent is based on sales growth. The weightings can also be multiplicative; for example, Browning-Ferris Industries multiplies a score on achievement of profit and revenue goals by a score assessed based on environmental responsibility.[16] If the environmental responsibility score is less than 70 percent, the multiplier, and hence, the resulting bonus, is zero.

Sometimes, such as in the examples presented above, the organization makes the weightings of performance measures explicit to the individuals being evaluated. Often, however, particularly where performance evaluations are done somewhat subjectively, the weightings are partially or totally implicit. Leaving the weighting implicit blurs the communication from superiors to subordinates about what results are important. Employees are left to try and infer what results will most affect their overall evaluations.

Setting Performance Targets

Performance targets, or standards, are another important results control system element. In a results control system, targets should be specified for every aspect of performance dimension that is measured.

Performance targets affect behavior in two basic ways. First, they stimulate action, improve motivation, by providing conscious goals for individuals to strive for. Most people like to be given a specific target to shoot for, rather than merely being given vague statements like "do the best you can" or "work at a reasonable pace."[17] Second, performance targets allow individuals to interpret their own performance. People do not respond to feedback unless they are able to interpret it,[18] and a key part of interpretation involves comparing actual performance with the predetermined performance targets. The targets distinguish good from bad performance. Failure to achieve the targets provides managers with a signal that they should probably change their actions.

Providing Rewards or Punishments

Rewards and punishments are the final important element of a results control system. The rewards included in motivational contracts can be in the form of anything employees value; such as salary increases, bonuses, promotions, job security, job assignments, training opportunities, freedom, recognition, and power. Punishments are things employees dislike; such as demotions, supervisor disapproval, public embarrassment, failure to get rewards earned by peers, or, at the extreme, loss of job.

Organizations can derive some motivational value from their contracts if they link promises of any of these valued rewards to results measures the employees can influence. Managers can, and do, use any of a number of *extrinsic rewards* (that is, those provided by the organization). They grant successful employees additional rights and powers and increase their status within the firm by publicizing achievements of superior results. They grant additional pecuniary rewards in the form of cash, delayed payments of cash, or stock. They sometimes threaten to reduce the pleasure middle managers derive from managing their entities by refusing to fund ideas for expenditures in entities where performance is not good.

Results measures can provide a positive motivational impact even if no rewards are explicitly linked to results measures. People often derive their own internally generated *intrinsic rewards* through a sense of accomplishment for achieving the desired results. When William J. Bratton became the New York City Police Commissioner in January 1994, he gave department personnel one clear, simple goal: cut crime.[19] (Previously the thinking had been that crime was due to societal factors beyond the department's control. The police were "largely measured by how quickly they responded to 911 calls.") He also implemented a results control system. He decentralized the department by giving the seventy-six precinct commanders the authority to make most of the key decisions in their station houses, including the right to set personnel schedules, and he started collecting and reporting crime data daily. Even though Commissioner Bratton legally cannot award good performers with pay raises or merit bonuses, the system was tremendously successful. In 1994, major felonies in New York fell by 12 percent, and in the first three quarters of 1995 they fell another 18 percent below 1994 levels. The police department personnel began to focus on actions they could take to meet the goal of reducing crime.

The motivational strength of any of the extrinsic or intrinsic rewards can be understood in terms of any of the many motivational-process theories that have been developed, such as *expectancy theory*. One common formulation of expectancy theory[20] postulates that individuals' motivational force, or effort, is a function of their (1) *expectancies;* that is, their belief that certain outcomes will result from their behavior (such as, a bonus for increased effort), and (2) the *valences* of (the strength of their preference for) those outcomes. The valence of an outcome is, in turn, a function of its instrumentality for obtaining other outcomes and the valence of these other outcomes. A wage increase may have no value by itself, but it is valuable in terms of its instrumental role in securing other valued items; such as food, shelter, clothing, entertainment, and status.

Managers should promise their employees the rewards which provide the most powerful motivational effects in the most cost effective way possible. However, it is difficult to know all the motivational effects because the effects of each of the various reward forms can vary widely depending on managers' personal tastes and circumstances. Some managers are greatly interested in immediate cash awards, whereas others are more interested in increasing their retirement benefits, increasing their autonomy, or improving their promotion possibilities.

Only scattered evidence exists as to the motivational effects of the various forms of rewards for different groups of individuals, but a few systematic reward-taste patterns are apparent. First, as compared with top executives, lower-level managers are probably more interested in protecting their autonomy and in improving their prospects for promotion. They are less interested in the stability of their short-term income (after their base salaries are assured). Second, the mix of desires managers have is, on average, different from those of production-line workers. Most managers' physiological and safety requirements are largely assured, but the same is not true for production-line workers. Finally, it is apparent that reward tastes also vary systematically across countries for a number of reasons, including differences in cultures and local income tax rates.

If organizations can tailor their reward packages to their managers' individual preferences, they can provide meaningful rewards at the lowest possible costs. A tailoring of rewards to individuals or small groups within a large organization is not easy to accomplish. A tailored system will likely have to be complex and costly to administer. If it is poorly done it can easily lead to employee perceptions of unfairness.

CONDITIONS DETERMINING THE EFFECTIVENESS OF RESULTS CONTROLS

Although they are an important form of control in many organizations, results controls cannot always be used effectively. They work best only when *all* of the following conditions are present:

1. managers know what results are desired in the areas being controlled,
2. the individuals whose behaviors are being controlled have significant influence on results in the desired performance dimensions,
3. managers can measure the results effectively.

Knowledge of Desired Results

For results controls to work, managers must know what results are desired in the areas they wish to control, and they must communicate those desires effectively to the individuals working in those areas. *Results desirability* means that more of the quality represented by the results measure is preferred to less, everything else being equal, or the *optimal* or *correct* actions lead to higher measured results than do less optimal actions.

At a general level, most people agree that the primary objective of profit-making organizations is to maximize shareholder (or owner) value.[21] It does not follow, however, that because this overall objective is known, the desired results are then also known at all intermediate and lower levels in the organization. The disaggregation of overall organizational objectives into specific expectations for all individuals lower in the hierarchy is often difficult because different needs and trade-offs may be present in different parts of the organization.

Purchasing managers can create value by procuring good-quality, low-cost materials when needed. These three result areas (quality, cost, and schedule) can often be traded-off against each other, and the overall organizational objective to maximize shareholder value does not provide much help in making these trade-offs. The importance of each of these result areas may vary over time and among parts of the organization, depending on differing needs and strategies. A company short of cash may want to minimize the amount of inventory on hand, and this may make schedule the dominant consideration; a company (or SBU) with a lowest-cost-producer strategy may want to emphasize the cost considerations; and a company (or SBU) with products with a quality image may emphasize meeting or exceeding the specifications of the materials being purchased. To ensure proper purchasing manager behaviors, managers must make clear the importance orderings (or weightings) of these three result areas.

If the wrong result areas are chosen, or if the right areas are chosen but given the wrong importance weightings, the combination of results measures is not *congruent* with the organization's true objectives. Using an incongruent set of results measures will actually motivate employees to take the wrong actions.

Ability to Influence Desired Results (Controllability)

A second condition that is necessary for results controls to work is that the person whose behaviors are being controlled must be able to affect the results in a material way in a given time span. This *controllability principle* is one of the central tenets of responsibility accounting. Here are some representative expressions of that principle:

> A man should be held accountable for only that which he alone can control.[22]
>
> It is almost a self-evident proposition that, in appraising the performance of divisional management, no account should be taken of matters outside the division's control.[23]
>
> A manager is not normally held accountable for unfavorable outcomes or credited with favorable ones if they are clearly due to causes not under his control.[24]

The main rationale behind the controllability principle is that results measures are useful only to the extent they provide information about the desirability of the actions that were taken. If a results area is totally uncontrollable, the results measures tell us nothing about what actions were taken. Partial controllability makes it difficult to infer from the results measures whether or not good actions were taken.

Controllability can be illustrated graphically. Assume that the general manager of a largely autonomous division is evaluated on some congruent measure of performance (for example, net income) and that he performs exactly as the organization wishes. If everything were controllable, the measure would show that the manager was contributing to the firm at a constant rate, as shown in Figure 3-1. Income for the period would be the ending value less the starting value, or x_1 minus x_0. By looking at this performance measure, one could infer that the manager had performed appropriately.

Now, instead of everything being totally controllable, assume that two uncontrollable events occurred during the period of time shown in Figure 3-1. First,

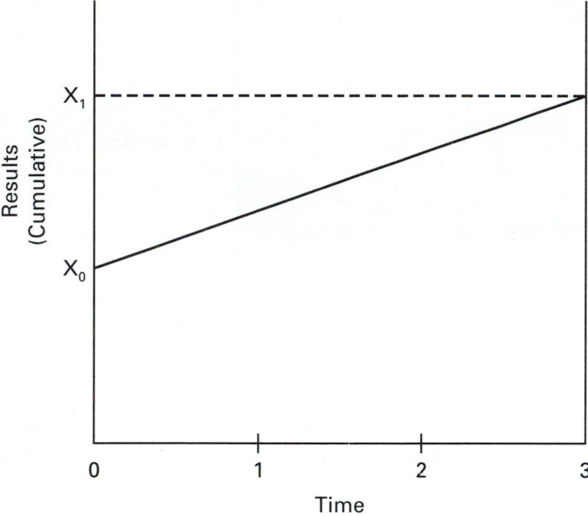

FIGURE 3-1. Measurement of Results Affected by No Uncontrollable Factors

assume that at the end of time period 1, oil is discovered on land entrusted to the manager and he immediately sells (or is otherwise given credit for) the mineral rights. This fortuitous event would provide a sudden *increase* in the results measure. Next, assume that at the end of time period 2, a country in which the manager was compelled by higher management to maintain a plant devalued its currency. This would result in a sudden *decrease* in the economic value of the entity run by the manager whose behaviors we are trying to control.

The resulting performance pattern is shown in Figure 3-2. One would have to conclude that for this period of time, at least, the results measure for which the manager was being held accountable, net income, was noisy. The fluctuations were largely uncontrollable. If, as has been assumed in Figure 3-2, the effect of the devaluation was greater than the total effect of the oil discovery and the normal value created by the controllable actions, the net income measure for this man-

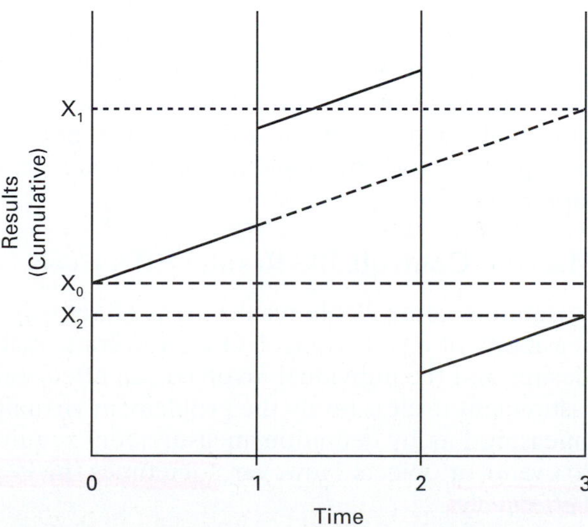

FIGURE 3-2. Measurement of Results Affected by Two Uncontrollable Factors

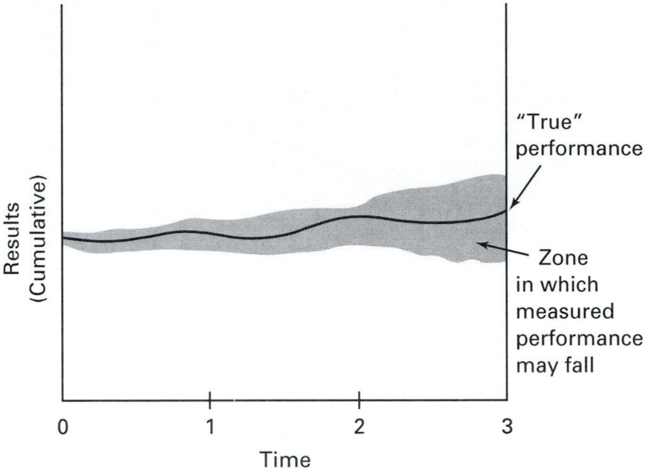

FIGURE 3-3. Measurement of Results Affected by Many Uncontrollable Factors

ager over this time period might show a loss, such as $x_0 - x_2$. Yet, this net loss would have occurred despite the fact that the manager was assumed to continue to perform exactly as the organization wished (note the upward-sloping line between the discontinuities).

In most organizational situations, of course, numerous uncontrollable, or partially uncontrollable, factors affect the measures used to evaluate managerial performance. These uncontrollable influences hinder efforts to use results measures for control purposes. If the effects of the uncontrollable factors cannot be sorted out and eliminated, often all that can be measured is a broad band within which performance probably lies, rather than a precise measure of performance, as shown in Figure 3-3. In this case, it becomes difficult to say whether the results achieved are due to the actions taken or to uncontrollable factors. Good actions will not necessarily produce good results. Bad actions may similarly be obscured.

In situations where many large uncontrollable influences affect the available results measures, results controls are not effective. Managers cannot be relieved of their responsibility to respond to relevant environmental factors. If these factors are difficult to track so that their effects can be eliminated from the results measures, results controls do not provide much information useful either for evaluating performance or for motivating good behaviors. The implication, then, should be clear; where the results that can be measured are either not controllable or are largely uncontrollable, results control will not be effective. In other words, the effectiveness of results controls is inversely related to the importance of the noncontrollable factors that affect the results reports. (The methods organizations use to cope with uncontrollable factors in results control systems are discussed in Chapter 15).

Ability to Measure Controllable Results Effectively

Ability to measure the controllable results areas effectively is the final constraint limiting the feasibility of results control. Often the controllable results the organization truly desires and the individual involved can affect cannot be measured effectively. Measurement itself is rarely the problem; in virtually all situations *something* can be measured as, by definition, measurement requires only that numbers be assigned to events or objects. However, sometimes the key results areas cannot be measured *effectively.*

The one criterion that should be used to judge the effectiveness of results measures is the ability to evoke the desired behaviors. This criterion really says nothing about the underlying *veracity* of a results measure (such as net income). If a measure evokes the right behaviors in a given situation, then it is a good control measure. If it does not, it is a bad one, even if the measure accurately reflects the quantity it purports to represent.

It is sometimes possible to use just this one criterion, ability to evoke the right behaviors, to evaluate results measures. However, evaluations are usually more reliable when this overall criterion is divided into four parts and the measures are judged in terms of each part. To evoke the right behaviors, results measures should be (1) precise, (2) objective, (3) timely, and (4) understandable. If any of these measurement qualities cannot be achieved, results control will not be effective in evoking the desired behaviors. The following sections describe the importance of each of these qualities.

Precision

Measurement *precision* refers to the amount of randomness or *white noise* in the measure. For precision to be high, the dispersion among the values placed on a given result area by multiple independent measurers must be small. If ten independent measurers conclude that the quantity being measured is exactly 120.3, the measure is precise. If they can conclude only that the quantity is between 100 and 130, the measure is not as precise. Some aspects of performance (such as, social responsibility and personnel development) are difficult, or even impossible, to measure precisely.

Precision is an important quality because without it the measure loses much of its information value. Imprecise results measures cause managers to run a higher risk of misevaluating performance. Subordinates will react negatively to the inequities that will inevitably arise when equally good performances are rated differently.

Objectivity

Objectivity, which means freedom from bias, is another desirable measurement quality. Measurement objectivity is low, meaning the possibility of biases is high, where either the choice of measurement rules or the actual measuring is done by the persons whose performances are being evaluated. Low objectivity is likely, for example, where performance is self-reported or where managers are allowed considerable discretion in the choice of measurement methods (as is true with the measurement of accounting income).

Managers have two main alternatives for increasing measurement objectivity. They can have the actual measuring done by people who are independent of the process, such as personnel on a controller's staff, or they can have the measurements verified by independent persons, such as auditors.

Timeliness

Timeliness refers to the lag between the individual's performance and the measurement of results (and provision of rewards). Timeliness is an important measurement quality for two reasons. The first is a motivational reason. Individuals need consistent, *short-term* performance pressure to perform at their best. The pressure helps ensure that people do not become lazy, sloppy, or wasteful. Measures, and thus rewards (or punishments), that are delayed for significant periods of time lose most of their motivational impact. Short-term pressure can also stimulate creativity. It increases the likelihood that people will be stimulated to search for new and better ways of improving their results. This is an application of the old adage: "Necessity is the mother of invention."

A second advantage is that timeliness increases the value of interventions that might be necessary. If significant problems exist, but the performance measures are not timely, it might not be possible to intervene to fix the problems before they cause severe harm.

Understandability

Two aspects of *understandability* are important. First, the individuals whose behaviors are being controlled must understand what they are being held accountable for. This requires communication. Training, which is a form of communication, may also be necessary if individuals are to be held accountable for achieving goals expressed in new and different terms, such as "economic value added" or "real return on capital employed."

Second, the individuals involved must understand what they must do to influence the measure, at least in broad terms. Purchasing managers who are held accountable for lowering the costs of purchased materials will not be successful until they develop strategies for accomplishing this goal; such as improving negotiations with vendors, increasing competition among vendors, or working with engineering personnel to redesign certain parts. Employees who are held accountable for customer satisfaction must understand what their customers value.

In most situations, understandability is not a limiting factor. When individuals understand what a measure represents, they will figure out what they can do to influence it. In fact, this is one of the advantages of results controls; managers can accomplish good control without knowing exactly how employees will produce the results.

Many measures cannot be classified as either clearly effective or clearly ineffective. Different trade-offs among the evaluation criteria create some advantages and disadvantages. Measures can often be made more congruent, controllable, precise, and objective if timeliness is compromised. Thus, in assessing the effectiveness of results measures, many difficult judgments are often necessary. These judgments are discussed in more detail in later chapters.

CONCLUSION

This chapter described an important form of control, results control, which is used at many organization levels in most organizations. Results controls are an indirect form of control because they do not focus explicitly on the employees' actions. This indirectness provides some important advantages. Results controls can often be effective when it is not clear what behaviors are most desirable. In addition, results controls can yield good control while allowing the people whose behaviors are being controlled high autonomy. Many people, particularly those higher in the organizational hierarchy, value high autonomy and respond well to it. High autonomy often breeds innovation.

Results controls are not effective in every situation, however. Failure to satisfy all three effectiveness conditions, knowledge of desirable results, ability to affect desirable results, and ability to measure controllable results effectively, will render the control impotent. It could also precipitate any of a number of dysfunctional side effects, many of which are discussed in later chapters.

Results controls and action controls usually form the major elements in the

MCS used in all but the smallest organizations. Results and action controls are usually supplemented by personnel and cultural controls, as discussed in Chapter 4.

Notes

1. M. Hammer, *Beyond Reengineering: How the Process-Centered Organization is Changing Our Work and Our Lives* (New York: Harper Business, 1996).
2. A. P. Sloan, Jr., *My Years with General Motors* (New York: Doubleday, 1964).
3. J. Weber, "For DuPont, Christmas in April," *Business Week* (April 24, 1995), p. 130.
4. Ibid, p. 129.
5. Don Keough quoted in J. Huey, "New Top Executives Shake Up Old Order at Soft-Drink Giant," *Wall Street Journal* (November 6, 1981), p. 17.
6. D. Milbank, "Changes at Alcoa Point Up Challenges and Benefits of Decentralized Authority," *Wall Street Journal* (November 7, 1991), p. B7.
7. Richard H. Chandler, quoted in T. Petruno, "Sunrise Scam Throws Light on Incentive Pay Programs," *Los Angeles Times* (January 15, 1996), p. D3.
8. G. Odiorne, *Management by Objectives: A System of Management Leadership* (Belmont, Calif.: Pitman Learning Inc., 1965), pp. 55–56.
9. "Employee Autonomy Results in Enhanced Profitability," *Manufacturing & Distribution Issues 7* (Summer 1996), pp. 3–4.
10. J. Guyon, "The Public Doesn't Get a Better Potato Chip without a Bit of Pain," *Wall Street Journal* (March 25, 1983), p. 1.
11. "Automaking on a Human Scale," *Fortune* (April 5, 1982), pp. 89–93.
12. N. Fast and N. Berg, "The Lincoln Electric Company," case no. 9-376-028 (Boston: HBS Case Services, 1975); and M. Mrowca, "Ohio Firm Relies on Incentive-Pay System to Motivate Workers and Maintain Products," *Wall Street Journal* (August 12, 1983), p. 23.
13. "This Is the Answer," *Business Week,* (July 5, 1982), pp. 50–52.
14. For example, R. S. Kaplan and D. P. Norton, "The Balanced Scorecard—Measures that Drive Performance," *Harvard Business Review,* 70, no. 1 (January–February 1992), p. 71.
15. K. J. Euske, M. J. Lebas, and C. J. McNair, "Performance Management in an International Setting," *Management Accounting Research,* 4, no. 4 (1993), pp. 275–299.
16. Institute of Management Accountants, *Implementing Corporate Environmental Strategies,* Statement of Management Accounting #4W (Montvale, N.J.: Institute of Management Accountants, July 31, 1995).
17. K. A. Merchant, *Rewarding Results: Motivating Profit Center Managers* (Boston: Harvard Business School Press, 1989).
18. E. A. Locke and G. P. Latham, *A Theory of Goal Setting & Task Performance* (Englewood Cliffs, N.J.: Prentice-Hall, 1990), p. 17.
19. E. Lesly, "A Safer New York City," *Business Week* (December 11, 1995), pp. 81, 84.
20. V. H. Vroom, *Work and Motivation* (New York: Wiley, 1964).
21. D. L. Wenner and R. W. LeBer, "Managing for Shareholder Value—From Top to Bottom," *Harvard Business Review,* 67, no. 6 (November–December 1989), pp. 2–8; J. L. Treynor, "The Financial Objective in the Widely Held Corporation," *Financial Analysts Journal* (March–April 1981), pp. 68–71.
22. G. W. Dalton, "Motivation and Control in Organizations," in *Motivation and Control in Organizations* G. W. Dalton and P. R. Lawrence (eds.) (Homewood, Ill.: Richard D. Irwin and the Dorsey Press, 1971), p. 27.
23. D. Solomons, *Divisional Performance: Measurement and Control* (Homewood, Ill.: Richard D. Irwin, 1965), p. 83.
24. K. J. Arrow, "Control in Large Organizations," in *Behavioral Aspects of Accounting* M. Schiff and A. Y. Lewin (eds.) (Englewood Cliffs, N.J.: Prentice-Hall, 1974), p. 284.

ARMCO, INC.: Midwestern Steel Division

In January 1991, management of the Kansas City Works of Armco's Midwestern Steel Division began implementing a new performance measurement system. Bob Nenni, Director of Finance for the Midwestern Steel Division, explained:

> With our old system, our managers spent more time explaining why changes in costs were caused by problems with our accounting system than they did fixing the problems. The new performance measurement system is designed to give us better management focus on the things that are most important for them to worry about, earlier warning of problems, and improved commitment to achieve objectives.

In the summer of 1991, the new system was still being implemented and its design refined. But Bob Nenni believed that the new system would be successful at the Kansas City Works, and he hoped that its use would spread throughout Armco.

BACKGROUND OF ARMCO AND THE KANSAS CITY WORKS

Armco, Inc. was a producer of stainless, electrical, and carbon steels and steel products. Through joint ventures the company also produced coated, high strength and low-carbon flat rolled steels and oil field machinery and equipment. In 1990, Armco was the sixth largest steel manufacturer in the United States with slightly over $1.7 billion in net sales, and operating profits of $77 million. Exhibit 1 shows a three-year history of Armco's financial results.

Armco's Midwestern Steel Division generated $550 million in sales in 1990. (A division organization chart is shown in Exhibit 2.) Within the division, the Kansas City Works was by far the largest entity, accounting for approximately $250 million in sales. Like that of most of the firms in the U.S. steel industry, business at the Kansas City Works had declined significantly in the last decade. Employment was down from 5,000 employees in 1980 to 1,000 in 1990.[1] The Works had recorded significant losses in the decade of the 1980s, but it had been marginally profitable since 1988.

The Kansas City Works produced two primary products: grinding media and carbon wire rod. Grinding media were steel balls used for crushing ore in mining operations. Carbon wire rod was used to make shopping carts, bed springs, coat hangers, and other products. In 1990 the Kansas City Works sold 700,000 tons of steel: 200,000 tons of grinding media and 500,000 tons of rods. Armco was recognized as the leading supplier of grinding media products in the U.S. Armco's balls had proven themselves to be the most durable, and Armco received fewer customer complaints about its balls than did its competitors. Carbon wire rods, on the other hand, were basically a commodity product. Armco's rod mill, which used relatively old technology, was not cost competitive, so rods were not a profitable product. But the rods did generate volume and helped cover some of the fixed costs of the plant.

The Kansas City Works was not a low cost manufacturer. Its union labor costs in Kansas City were higher than those of some of its nonunion competitors, particularly those located in the Southeastern U.S. and non-U.S. locations. And the Works had an inefficient plant infrastructure be-

[1]Over the same period, Armco Inc. decreased in size from 70,000 to 23,000 employees.

Patrick Henry, Research Assistant, and Professor Kenneth A. Merchant wrote this case as the basis for class discussion rather than to illustrate either effective or ineffective handling of an administrative situation.

cause the plant was designed to accommodate five times as many employees as were currently working there. Instead of being efficiently laid out, the buildings still being used were spread across a 900-acre plant site.

Because of the plant's cost disadvantage, the Work's managers looked for ways to differentiate their products and to develop new higher value products, and they had had some success in doing so. Each year approximately 10 percent of the shipments of the Kansas City Works were of new higher value, high carbon content products.

All salaried employees in the Works were eligible for cash incentive awards based on a performance evaluation made by their immediate superior and, ultimately, Rob Cushman, the division president. The incentive award potentials ranged from approximately 5 to 30 percent of annual salary depending on the individual's organization level. The performance evaluations were subjective but were based on, typically, three measures of performance applicable to the position. For example, Rob Cushman described the criteria he used for evaluating the performance of Charlie Bradshaw, the Works Manager, as being based approximately one-third on plant safety, one-third on hard production numbers (particularly productivity and quality), and one-third on his evaluation of Charlie's "leadership" (i.e., Do I hear good things and see good things going on?").

THE MANUFACTURING PROCESS AT THE KANSAS CITY WORKS

The manufacturing process used for making both rods and grinding media included four basic steps. First, scrap steel was melted in the ladle arc furnaces. Second, the melted steel was poured into a continuous caster that produced solid bars 30 feet in length with a 7″ by 7″ cross-section. Third, the 19″ mill pressed the steel bars between two large cylindrical rollers to give them either a square or circular shape and with either 3″ or 4″ cross sections.[2] Finally, the bars were processed into finished rods or balls. The rod mill shop worked with square cross-section bars. It reduced the bars' diameter to between ¼″ and ⅝″ and coiled them into 2,000-pound bundles for shipment to customers. The rods were further reduced in size ("cold drawn to wire") at the customers' facilities for use in their products. The grinding media shop worked with the circular cross-section bars produced by the 19″ mill. It formed them into spheres using a roll-forming machine. Finished balls ranged in size from 1″ to 5″ in diameter.

CRITICAL SUCCESS FACTORS IN THE WORKS

A. The Melt Shop

The melt shop, which included the ladle arc furnace and the continuous caster, produced molten steel in 167-ton batches known as "heats". The shop's goal was to run three "turns" (shifts) a day, seven days a week, 50 weeks a year, excluding the eight hours a week used for preventative maintenance. The other two weeks of the year were used for extensive preventative maintenance and installation of new equipment. The melt shop could theoretically produce about 110 heats/week, but the best quarter it had ever achieved was an average of 99 heats/week.

For a number of reasons, good performance in the melt shop was critical to the performance of the Kansas City Works as a whole. First, the melt shop was the "bottleneck" operation, so output from this phase of manufacturing process determined the output of the plant as a whole.

Second, the melt shop costs accounted for nearly 40 percent of the total steel conversion costs incurred in the plant. The largest expenditures in the melt shop were for labor, production materials of various types, and energy. Energy alone accounted for approximately 10 percent of the melt shop costs. Works managers were working toward computer control of energy, but in 1991 the melt shop manager still made most decisions about the heat used in the furnace, a major energy consumer. In 1988, Armco made an $8 million investment in a new ladle arc furnace that significantly changed the melting furnace technology used in the plant, and costs were declining as the melt shop managers learned how best to use the new technology.

Third, the quality of raw steel produced by the melt shop was an important component in determining whether the finished products met the re-

[2]The distance from center to center of the two pressing rolls was 19 inches. Hence the name for the process.

quired specifications. Quality was affected by the grades of scrap steel and nonmetallic materials used in the process. Nonmetallic materials were consumable items added to batches to remove contaminants from the steel. Armco managers purchased a variety of grades of scrap steel and nonmetallic materials, and they used different proportions of scrap to nonmetallic materials depending on the grades of scrap and nonmetallics being used; lower grades of scrap typically contained more contaminants. Some of the production processes were standardized, with the addition of some nonmetallics done either by automated equipment or by production employees following standardized recipes. Other processes, however, required the manufacturing manager and his technical supervisors to exercise judgment.

B. Rolling and Finishing

Personnel in the Rolling and Finishing areas were asked to make parts to specification while controlling yields and costs. Customer specifications for rods usually contained physical property requirements, such as for ductility and elasticity. One specification for balls required a two-story drop test. If the test ball cracked into two parts on impact after being dropped from two stories, then the product was rejected on quality grounds. In addition, the lives of the balls were tested in Armco's customers' actual grinding operations. Those tests had shown that Armco's balls were more than competitive; they lasted up to 15 percent longer than did its closest competitor's balls. The rolling areas were heavily capital intensive. Significant costs in the finishing areas were for labor, energy, maintenance, and yield losses.

C. Maintenance

Maintenance was also an important determinant of success in the Kansas City Works. The goal of maintenance was to maximize equipment up-time while controlling maintenance expenditures. Organizationally, the maintenance activities were divided into three groups. Teams of electrical and mechanical maintenance employees were assigned to each manufacturing cost center. A third group operated a centralized maintenance shop. The cost of maintenance was significant, as approximately 40 percent of the 700 hourly employees in the plant were maintenance workers.

THE OLD PERFORMANCE MEASUREMENT SYSTEM

The manufacturing areas of the Kansas City Works were divided into five responsibility centers: melting, casting, the 19″ mill, the rod mill department, and the grinding media department. Each responsibility center was comprised of one or more cost centers.

Before changes were made in 1991, the performances of the cost center managers and their superiors in the plant were evaluated in terms of cost control and safety. The key cost performance measure was a summary measured called "Cost Above" which included the cost added per ton of steel at each production stage and for the entire plant. Cost Above and the items that comprised it were reported to the manufacturing managers on an Operating Statistics Report that was produced on approximately the 15th day following each month end.

The Operating Statistics Reports provided a five-year history, monthly and year-to-date actuals, and monthly and year-to-date objectives and variances from objectives for each of the factors that determined total Cost Above for each cost center. Exhibit 3 shows a portion of the Operating Statistics Report for one cost center—the #2 Melt Shop.[3] (The entire report, printed on five computer pages, included detailed information about 46 separate expense categories.) The report also gave cost per net ton ($/NT) for many of the cost categories. The Total Cost Above/NT is shown in the next to last column of page 3 of Exhibit 3.

The Operating Statistics Reports used the same accounting information that was used for financial reporting and inventory valuation purposes, so the figures included allocations of indirect manufacturing costs. For example, to provide smoother cost patterns, the charge for the two-week plant maintenance shutdown was spread over the 50 weeks of operations. These costs, which included labor and material were shown on the Operating Statistics Report as "S-Order" costs.

The operating managers had become accustomed to the Operating Statistics Report and in general they liked it. For example, Gary Downey, the Melting Operations manager, said that he

[3]The #1 melt shop contained obsolete equipment and was no longer used.

looked at 95 percent of the information presented in the report, although he acknowledged that some of the items were quite small in dollar value. Paul Phillips, the Rolling and Finishing Manager liked having the monthly and annual trends and the information comparing actual costs with objectives. Paul felt that the Operating Statistics report was "the minimum amount of detail necessary." He would have preferred to have the Operating Statistics Report on a weekly basis and in his hands on Monday morning because, for example, "If we see that fuel consumption is unusually high, we can go and look for the cause."

The accounting department also provided other reports showing the detail behind the figures for some of the cost elements on request. For example, one report showed the cost for nonmetallic materials broken down by the specific materials used.

THE NEW PERFORMANCE MEASUREMENT SYSTEM

A. The Goals of the New System

Bob Nenni, the director of finance, had been working on the performance measurement system since 1989, but due to staff constraints he had been unable to design and implement the new system while keeping the old system going. On November 1, 1990, Rob Cushman was appointed as president of the Midwestern Steel Division, and Rob sponsored the implementation of a new performance measurement system. He allowed Bob Nenni to discontinue production of the Operating Statistics Report in January 1991 in order to implement the new system.

Rob Cushman observed:

> The old system wasn't working. People were relying on something that was not adequate. . . .
>
> Enough companies are using good performance measurements as building blocks to excellence. I don't want to go against the grain. I want to give my managers the information they need. And I want to have good measures that tell us how we've done. I'm not using the performance measures as a threat. I'm trying to make it fun so that when we determine we've done well we can celebrate our successes. . . .
>
> If this plant does everything right, we should be able to make $30 million per year. But we're not doing it. This system is part of a spirit of change that has to happen. We will give people more responsibility. . . . and more latitude to fail.

Bob Nenni added:

> The cost part of our old performance measurement system was built for accountants. It was designed to produce financial statements, operating reports, and product cost reports. One system can't do all these things well.

The new system was designed both as a means of providing middle- and lower-level managers with a greater understanding of how their actions related to the implementation of the division's business strategies and as an improved method for managers at all levels to assess the extent to which the desired results were being achieved. The vision and goals of the organization were to be translated into key success factors which would be disaggregated into department and individual objectives that would be compared with measures of actual results. The basic philosophy is illustrated in chart form in Exhibit 4.

Rob Cushman and Bob Nenni thought that the new system promised two major improvements. First, the new system was designed so that managers would focus on the few key objectives that largely determine the success of the Kansas City Works and not get involved in the detail until a problem existed. As Bob Nenni observed:

> When managers get too much data, they can easily get unfocused. The new system will cause them to focus on the 5 or 6 things that cause 80 percent of the costs, not the 40 that cause 100 percent.

Second, the new system was designed to provide an improved basis for evaluating operating managers and manufacturing supervisors. The system would include a balanced set of performance measures, including quality, schedule achievement, and safety, in addition to costs. And the cost reports would be improved because they would include only those costs deemed controllable by each individual operating manager. They would not be distorted by volume changes as in the old system.

B. The Design of the New System

The new system design process began early in 1990. Rob Cushman, Charlie Bradshaw, Bob Nenni, and Gil Smith (commercial director), and others defined 10 key performance measures for the Kansas City Works:

1. Heats per week
2. Tons per man hour
3. Disabling injury index
4. Total quality index
5. Spending
6. Maintenance performance
7. Cash flow
8. Product mix
9. Inventory days on hand
10. Sales price minus cost of net metal

Performance measure 1, heats per week, was only relevant to the melt shop. However, since the melt shop was the bottleneck operation, heats per week was a critical measure for the Works as a whole. Measures 2 through 6 were applicable to all manufacturing areas. Tons per man hour was a productivity measure. The disabling injury index was a safety measure. The total quality index was the product of three measures: physical yield, percentage of product meeting specification, and percentage on-time shipment. Spending was the accumulation of all expenses incurred by the people reporting directly to a manager. The maintenance performance measures had not yet been clearly defined by the middle of 1991, but maintenance labor cost and material cost were being measured. Performance measures 7 through 10 were plant-wide (not cost center) measures. Cash flow was measured monthly for the plant. Product mix was the percentage of high carbon products sold compared to low carbon. Inventory days on hand was tracked monthly. Accountability for inventory performance was shared among plant purchasing managers, manufacturing managers, and commercial managers. Sales price minus net metal, a measure of value added, was tracked monthly.

The design group discussed the components of each performance area and the ways in which each measure could be disaggregated to guide performance at lower management levels. For example, the cascading of goals relating to Total Quality is illustrated in Exhibit 5. Total quality at the Works level was affected by the proportion of products meeting customer specifications, the yields, and the percentage of on-time shipments; and each of these indicators could be disaggregated further. The intent was to measure each of these areas of performance at the lowest relevant level of the organization.

One of the most significant changes was the elimination of The Cost Above measure. Production managers were no longer held accountable for all costs incurred in or allocated to their respective areas so, in effect, they were no longer cost center managers. The cost detail in the new performance reports was reduced considerably. In the new system, the only cost figure on which managers were evaluated was the spending by the employees in their organizations. For example, in January 1991 spending on maintenance in the melt shop was $300,000, but only $30,000 of this amount was spent by people reporting in Gary Downey's organization. Thus Gary's report included only the $30,000 figure. The other $270,000 was reported to other managers, particularly those of maintenance and purchasing.

C. The Implementation Process

On January 1, 1991, Bob Nenni discontinued the Operating Statistics Report system. He believed that the new system would have had no chance if "the managers kept using the old data and never seriously considered improvements that could be made." The accounting department began the process of producing new sets of reports. As the entire task could not be accomplished immediately, they focused their attention on producing some pilot reports for a subset of the measures. They focused first on heats per week, tons per man hour, physical yield (a component of the total quality index), and spending. Exhibit 6 gives an example of a report for the Melting Operations Manager.

The operating managers' initial reaction to the sample reports they were given was dissatisfaction. The early reports did not provide the line-item expense detail to which they had become accustomed. In addition, they were no longer given Cost Above information, so they asked, "Where are my spending numbers?" In early April 1991, Charlie Bradshaw told Bob Nenni, "I've received nothing of use from your department since you discontinued the old reports." Another manager complained, "It almost seems like the operating managers finally understood the old report, so they decided to change it."

In late April, the accounting group backed off their initial implementation plan. They started to provide spending numbers for the entire cost center in addition to the spending initiated by a manager's direct reports. This change was made to give the operating managers a number that they could compare to their budgeted spending targets which had been prepared using the old measurement philosophy. Starting in 1992, however, they promised that the reports would reflect only the new cost performance philosophy. By then the performance targets would be set using that same philosophy.

In June 1991, Bob Nenni reflected on nine months since the design meetings began. He was convinced that the company was on the right track even though some of the managers were uncomfortable with the new system. And he knew that the delays in the implementation process had frustrated both the information users and his accounting staff. He noted:

> We're trying to change the way the managers think. The new system is not yet part of their mentality. Changing mindsets is ultimately more important and more challenging than the technical job of producing the reports.
>
> But we in accounting feel we will now be more useful to the organization. We were spending 60 percent of our time in accounting on the non-value-added chores of inventory valuation for financial reporting purposes. We have now reduced that to 20 percent.

REMAINING ISSUES

In 1991, two related performance evaluation/incentive issues arose in discussion. One was an issue about how to evaluate managers' performances in situations where the numbers were distorted by uncontrollable factors. For example, early in 1991 the melt shop suffered two transformer failures, apparently because of fluctuations in the line voltages provided by the local utility, Kansas City Power and Light. Such failures had happened nearly every year, but shop managers had recently upgraded some of their electrical switches to try to eliminate the problem. Nonetheless, the failures occurred again, and by April, Gary Downey knew that his goal to average 101 heats per week was impossible. The failure of the melt shop to achieve its plan would mean that the Kansas City Works as a whole would not be able to achieve its plans for 1991. Rob Cushman knew that at the end of the year he would have to decide whether or not to let this, and perhaps other similar occurrences, affect the evaluations of his operating managers.

The second was an issue as to whether to increase the proportion of total compensation that was linked to individual performance evaluations. In other words, how much of total compensation should be provided in fixed salary, and how much should be paid only to those who were good at getting things done and done well?

EXHIBIT 1 Three Year Financial History of ARMCO, Inc.[1]

(Dollars and shares in millions, except per share data)			
	1990	*1989*	*1988*
Sales[2]	1735.2	2,422.7	3,277.3
Operating profit[3]	76.9	239.8	222.3
Net income (loss)[4]	(89.5)	165.0	145.4
Net income (loss) per share—primary	(1.10)	1.78	1.57
Capital Expenditures	85.8	169.7	120.2
Number of shares of common stock outstanding	88.5	88.4	87.8
Number of employees[5]	9,800	10,500	19,500
Total domestic retirees	15,700	15,900	21,400

[1]Certain amounts in the prior periods have been reclassified to conform to the 1990 presentation.

[2]Effective May 13, 1989, Armco sold certain assets and a portion of its Eastern Steel Division's business to Kawasaki Steel Investments, Inc. in exchange for cash and a partnership interest in a joint venture. This division had annual revenues in excess of $1 billion.

[3]Includes special credits (charges) of $80.7 and $(35.0) in 1989 and 1988, respectively.

[4]Includes the cumulative effect of accounting changes in 1988 of $37.4 or $.43 per share.

[5]Excludes discontinued operations, associated companies, and Armco Financial Services Group.

EXHIBIT 2 Organization Chart

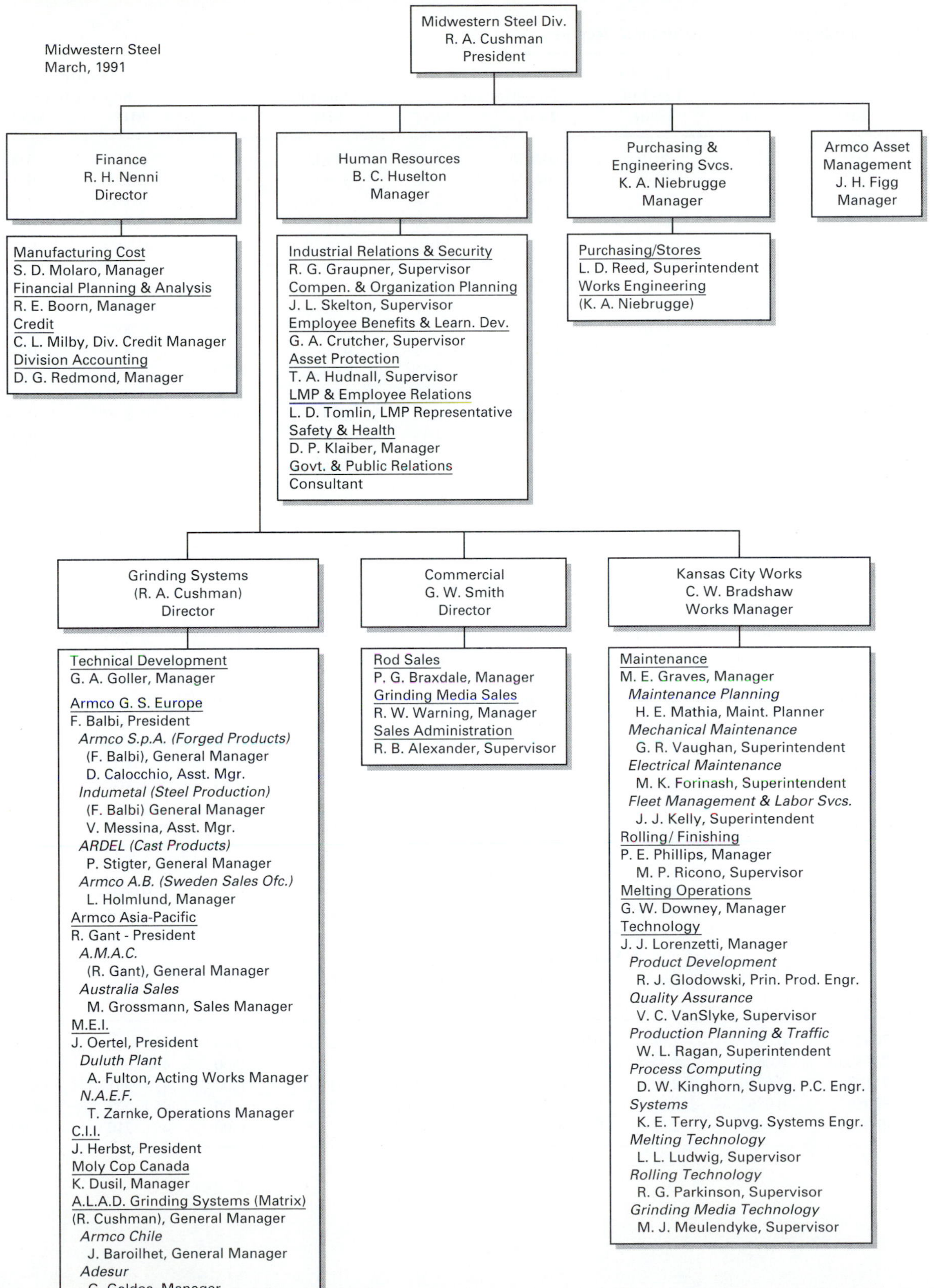
Midwestern Steel
March, 1991
Midwestern Steel Div.
R. A. Cushman
President
Finance
R. H. Nenni
Director
Manufacturing Cost
S. D. Molaro, Manager
Financial Planning & Analysis
R. E. Boorn, Manager
Credit
C. L. Milby, Div. Credit Manager
Division Accounting
D. G. Redmond, Manager
Human Resources
B. C. Huselton
Manager
Industrial Relations & Security
R. G. Graupner, Supervisor
Compen. & Organization Planning
J. L. Skelton, Supervisor
Employee Benefits & Learn. Dev.
G. A. Crutcher, Supervisor
Asset Protection
T. A. Hudnall, Supervisor
LMP & Employee Relations
L. D. Tomlin, LMP Representative
Safety & Health
D. P. Klaiber, Manager
Govt. & Public Relations
Consultant
Purchasing &
Engineering Svcs.
K. A. Niebrugge
Manager
Purchasing/Stores
L. D. Reed, Superintendent
Works Engineering
(K. A. Niebrugge)
Armco Asset
Management
J. H. Figg
Manager
Grinding Systems
(R. A. Cushman)
Director
Technical Development
G. A. Goller, Manager
Armco G. S. Europe
F. Balbi, President
Armco S.p.A. (Forged Products)
(F. Balbi), General Manager
D. Calocchio, Asst. Mgr.
Indumetal (Steel Production)
(F. Balbi) General Manager
V. Messina, Asst. Mgr.
ARDEL (Cast Products)
P. Stigter, General Manager
Armco A.B. (Sweden Sales Ofc.)
L. Holmlund, Manager
Armco Asia-Pacific
R. Gant - President
A.M.A.C.
(R. Gant), General Manager
Australia Sales
M. Grossmann, Sales Manager
M.E.I.
J. Oertel, President
Duluth Plant
A. Fulton, Acting Works Manager
N.A.E.F.
T. Zarnke, Operations Manager
C.I.I.
J. Herbst, President
Moly Cop Canada
K. Dusil, Manager
A.L.A.D. Grinding Systems (Matrix)
(R. Cushman), General Manager
Armco Chile
J. Baroilhet, General Manager
Adesur
G. Galdos, Manager
Business Development
V. Carrion, Manager
Commercial
G. W. Smith
Director
Rod Sales
P. G. Braxdale, Manager
Grinding Media Sales
R. W. Warning, Manager
Sales Administration
R. B. Alexander, Supervisor
Kansas City Works
C. W. Bradshaw
Works Manager
Maintenance
M. E. Graves, Manager
Maintenance Planning
H. E. Mathia, Maint. Planner
Mechanical Maintenance
G. R. Vaughan, Superintendent
Electrical Maintenance
M. K. Forinash, Superintendent
Fleet Management & Labor Svcs.
J. J. Kelly, Superintendent
Rolling/ Finishing
P. E. Phillips, Manager
M. P. Ricono, Supervisor
Melting Operations
G. W. Downey, Manager
Technology
J. J. Lorenzetti, Manager
Product Development
R. J. Glodowski, Prin. Prod. Engr.
Quality Assurance
V. C. VanSlyke, Supervisor
Production Planning & Traffic
W. L. Ragan, Superintendent
Process Computing
D. W. Kinghorn, Supvg. P.C. Engr.
Systems
K. E. Terry, Supvg. Systems Engr.
Melting Technology
L. L. Ludwig, Supervisor
Rolling Technology
R. G. Parkinson, Supervisor
Grinding Media Technology
M. J. Meulendyke, Supervisor

EXHIBIT 3 Excerpts from Operating Statistics Report

	Tons	Yield	Tons/ Tap/Tap Hour	Non-Metallics Tons	Non-Metallics $/NT	Salaries MH	Salaries $/NT	Hourly Supervision MH	Hourly Supervision $/NT
1985	706237	93.64	36.01	0.04056	3.43	0.0815	1.67	0.0000	0.00
1986	737380	93.38	37.40	0.04304	3.58	0.0818	1.73	0.0000	0.00
1987	741234	93.85	39.17	0.04536	3.58	0.0756	1.63	0.0013	0.03
1988	800581	92.79	41.30	0.04776	3.74	0.0822	2.06	0.0006	0.02
1989	870768	94.42	45.15	0.04224	4.58	0.0649	1.53	0.0023	0.07
MONTHLY STATISTICS									
JAN	69920	93.88	42.71	0.0411	6.50	0.0620	1.58	0.0057	0.19
FEB	68106	91.41	44.81	0.0471	7.69	0.0628	1.57	0.0047	0.15
MAR	68240	95.74	49.58	0.0512	7.75	0.0625	1.55	0.0038	0.12
APR	83797	95.30	46.33	0.0398	5.57	0.0442	1.14	0.0033	0.11
MAY	74507	95.50	46.96	0.0593	7.50	0.0433	1.30	0.0046	0.15
JUN	80190	96.18	44.44	0.0532	6.56	0.0462	1.28	0.0047	0.15
JUL	76513	94.58	44.37	0.0409	4.95	0.0486	1.27	0.0032	0.10
AUG	32489	96.32	43.84	0.0851	11.18	0.1140	3.10	0.0047	0.15
SEP	70475	95.54	51.03	0.0578	5.90	0.0525	1.34	0.0038	0.13
OCT	85128	95.21	52.66	0.0466	5.76	0.0430	1.21	0.0014	0.04
NOV	85992	96.47	54.48	0.0546	5.85	0.0426	1.13	0.0037	0.12
DEC	85945	94.15	54.48	0.0400	5.72	0.0427	1.24	0.0038	0.13
YEAR-TO-DATE STATISTICS									
FEB	138026	94.91	43.72	0.0441	7.09	0.0625	1.58	0.0052	0.17
MAR	206268	95.72	44.00	0.0464	7.30	0.0625	1.57	0.0047	0.15
APR	290065	96.10	45.48	0.0445	6.81	0.0572	1.44	0.0043	0.14
MAY	364572	96.32	45.65	0.0475	6.94	0.0543	1.41	0.0044	0.14
JUN	444761	96.57	45.88	0.0486	6.88	0.0529	1.39	0.0044	0.14
JUL	521274	96.55	45.66	0.0474	6.59	0.0523	1.37	0.0043	0.14
AUG	553763	96.63	45.59	0.0496	6.86	0.0559	1.47	0.0043	0.14
SEP	624238	96.70	45.38	0.0506	6.75	0.0554	1.46	0.0042	0.14
OCT	709366	96.73	45.99	0.0501	6.63	0.0540	1.43	0.0039	0.13
NOV	795358	96.86	46.63	0.0506	6.55	0.0528	1.40	0.0039	0.13
DEC	881303	96.79	47.30	0.0495	6.47	0.0518	1.38	0.0039	0.13
OBJECTIVES									
DEC	80910	92.75	48.10	0.0000	4.18	0.0537	0.83	0.0005	0.02
YEAR	942114	92.75	48.10	0.0000	4.18	0.0600	0.85	0.0005	0.02
VARIANCE FROM OBJECTIVES									
DEC	5035	0.41	5.38	−0.0400	−1.536	0.0111	−0.41	−0.0033	−0.11
YTD	−60811	1.24	−1.80	−0.04952	−2.288	0.0083	−0.53	−0.0034	−0.11

1985	706237	0.0671	2.06	0.0005	0.01	0.01	2.41	0.00	528.3264	20.90
1986	737380	0.0670	2.25	0.0047	0.14	0.17	2.60	0.00	494.3517	19.23
1987	741234	0.0749	2.22	0.0000	0.00	0.19	1.57	0.00	479.9061	18.41
1988	800581	0.0862	2.86	0.0000	0.00	0.61	2.53	0.00	469.7077	18.37
1989	870768	0.0685	2.32	0.0021	0.06	0.12	2.47	0.00	455.1210	18.99

EXHIBIT 3 Excerpts from Operating Statistics Report *Continued*

	Tons	Repair Labor MH	Repair Labor $/NT	S-Order Labor MH	S-Order Labor $/NT	S Order Matl	Maint Matl	Maint Outage	Electricity KWH	Electricity $/NT
MONTHLY STATISTICS										
JAN	69920	0.0848	2.97	0.0006	0.01	0.54	3.50	0.84	497.9036	19.20
FEB	68106	0.0686	2.38	0.0013	0.04	0.99	4.27	0.86	507.3894	19.82
MAR	68240	0.0722	2.48	0.0020	0.06	1.06	3.73	0.86	522.4422	18.34
APR	83797	0.0563	2.01	0.0030	0.10	0.74	2.81	0.70	491.3568	18.01
MAY	74507	0.0749	2.71	0.0035	0.11	0.83	2.89	0.79	512.6357	20.43
JUN	80190	0.0521	1.92	0.0050	0.16	0.71	2.68	0.73	516.9778	18.51
JUL	76513	0.0338	1.25	0.0061	0.20	0.72	2.92	0.77	511.5135	19.89
AUG	32489	0.3352	12.40	0.0174	0.57	1.81	8.66	−19.91	540.0536	28.03
SEP	70475	0.0472	1.76	0.0010	0.03	1.19	2.42	0.83	540.4950	21.54
OCT	85128	0.0504	1.84	0.0007	0.02	1.99	3.40	0.69	528.3277	18.66
NOV	85992	0.0526	1.96	0.0003	0.01	2.07	1.79	0.68	533.7443	19.51
DEC	85945	0.0347	1.40	0.0001	0.00	1.02	2.18	0.68	510.6142	18.95
YEAR-TO-DATE STATISTICS										
FEB	138026	0.0768	2.68	0.0009	0.03	0.76	3.89	0.85	456.8288	19.50
MAR	206268	0.0752	2.61	0.0013	0.04	0.86	3.84	0.86	462.1852	19.12
APR	290065	0.0698	2.44	0.0018	0.06	0.83	3.54	0.81	458.1932	18.80
MAY	364572	0.0708	2.50	0.0021	0.07	0.83	3.41	0.81	459.7953	19.13
JUN	444761	0.0674	2.39	0.0026	0.08	0.81	3.28	0.79	461.6315	19.02
JUL	521274	0.0625	2.22	0.0031	0.10	0.79	3.22	0.79	462.1277	19.15
AUG	553763	0.0785	2.82	0.0040	0.13	0.85	3.54	−0.42	463.7972	19.67
SEP	624238	0.0750	2.70	0.0036	0.12	0.89	3.42	−0.28	466.9283	19.88
OCT	709366	0.0720	2.60	0.0033	0.11	1.02	3.41	−0.17	468.5328	19.73
NOV	795358	0.0699	2.53	0.0030	0.10	1.14	3.24	−0.07	470.3372	19.71
DEC	881303	0.0665	2.42	0.0027	0.09	0.93	3.13	0.00	469.7382	19.64
OBJECTIVES										
DEC	80910	0.0552	1.95	0.0048	0.15	0.34	1.75	0.00	445.5000	19.15
YEAR	942114	0.0552	1.95	0.0048	0.15	0.34	1.75	0.00	445.4858	19.15
VARIANCE FROM OBJECTIVES										
DEC	5035	0.0205	0.55	0.0047	0.15	1.36	−0.43	−0.68	−18.69472	0.20
YTD	−60811	−0.0113	−0.47	0.0047	0.07	−0.59	−1.38	0.00	−24.25236	−0.48

1985	706237	0.0147	0.06	0.02	0.00	0.0000	0.00	76.06	168.70
1986	737380	0.1766	0.50	0.01	0.00	0.0000	0.00	79.38	164.20
1987	741234	0.2242	0.60	0.01	0.01	0.0000	0.00	76.30	173.78
1988	800581	0.2408	0.70	0.02	0.03	0.0003	0.03	79.03	216.37
1989	870768	0.2180	0.52	0.02	0.03	0.0002	0.02	79.40	211.40
MONTHLY STATISTICS									
JAN	69920	0.1530	0.31	0.01	0.16	0.0002	0.02	89.62	198.21
FEB	68106	0.1419	0.33	0.00	0.03	0.0001	0.01	93.82	207.92
MAR	68240	0.2234	0.81	0.00	0.12	0.0001	0.01	90.68	202.70
APR	83797	0.2002	0.54	0.01	0.00	0.0000	0.00	81.56	193.05

EXHIBIT 3 Excerpts from Operating Statistics Report *Continued*

	Tons	Natural Gas MMBTU	Natural Gas $/NT	Gas & Diesel Fuel	Lubri-cants	Loco Cranes Hrs	Loco Cranes $/NT	Total Cost Above	Total Cost
MAY	74507	0.2033	0.55	0.01	0.00	0.0000	0.00	94.82	211.44
JUN	80190	0.2094	0.57	0.01	0.21	0.0001	0.00	89.58	204.01
JUL	76513	0.2698	0.72	0.01	−0.15	0.0002	0.02	90.10	204.57
AUG	32489	0.3314	0.74	0.04	0.11	0.0005	0.04	142.82	251.19
SEP	70475	0.9326	2.06	0.00	0.04	0.0003	0.02	99.91	216.90
OCT	85128	−0.6225	−0.98	0.01	0.04	0.0000	0.00	93.99	205.63
NOV	85992	0.0847	0.20	0.02	0.05	0.0001	0.02	86.31	195.64
DEC	85945	0.0888	0.23	0.01	−0.02	0.0001	0.00	80.60	194.33
YEAR-TO-DATE STATISTICS									
FEB	138026	0.1475	0.32	0.01	0.10	0.0002	0.02	91.69	203.01
MAR	206268	0.1726	0.48	0.01	0.11	0.0001	0.02	91.35	202.91
APR	290065	0.1806	0.50	0.01	0.08	0.0001	0.01	88.53	200.06
MAY	364572	0.1852	0.51	0.01	0.06	0.0001	0.01	89.82	202.38
JUN	444761	0.1896	0.52	0.01	0.09	0.0001	0.01	89.78	202.68
JUL	521274	0.2014	0.54	0.01	0.05	0.0001	0.01	89.82	202.95
AUG	553763	0.2090	0.56	0.01	0.06	0.0001	0.01	92.92	205.79
SEP	624238	0.2907	0.73	0.01	0.05	0.0001	0.01	93.72	207.04
OCT	709366	0.1811	0.52	0.01	0.05	0.0001	0.01	93.76	206.87
NOV	795358	0.1707	0.49	0.01	0.05	0.0001	0.01	92.95	205.66
DEC	881303	0.1627	0.46	0.01	0.05	0.0001	0.01	91.74	204.57
OBJECTIVES									
DEC	80910	0.2192	0.51	0.02	0.03	0.0002	0.02	76.36	
YEAR	942114	0.2192	0.51	0.02	0.03	0.0002	0.02	76.53	
VARIANCE FROM OBJECTIVES									
DEC	5035	0.1304	0.28	0.01	0.05	0.0001	0.01	−4.24	
YTD	−60811	0.0565	0.05	0.01	−0.02	0.0001	0.01	−15.21	

EXHIBIT 4 Vision Management Process

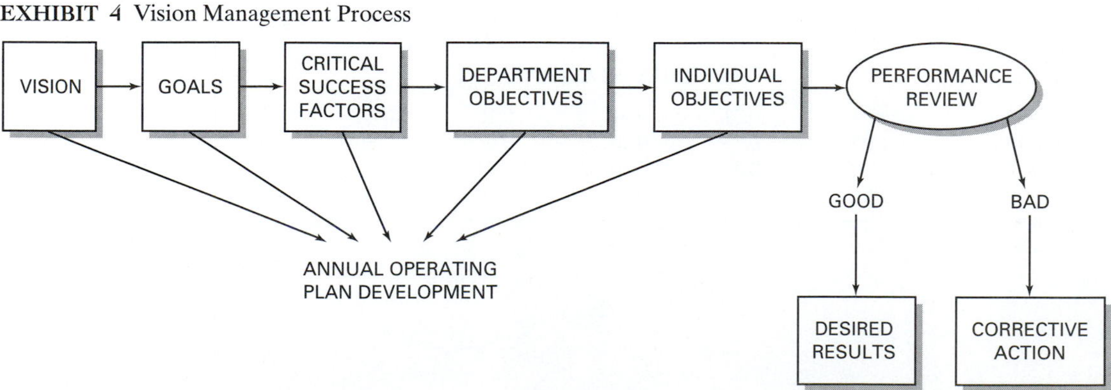

EXHIBIT 5 Cascading of Total Quality Goals

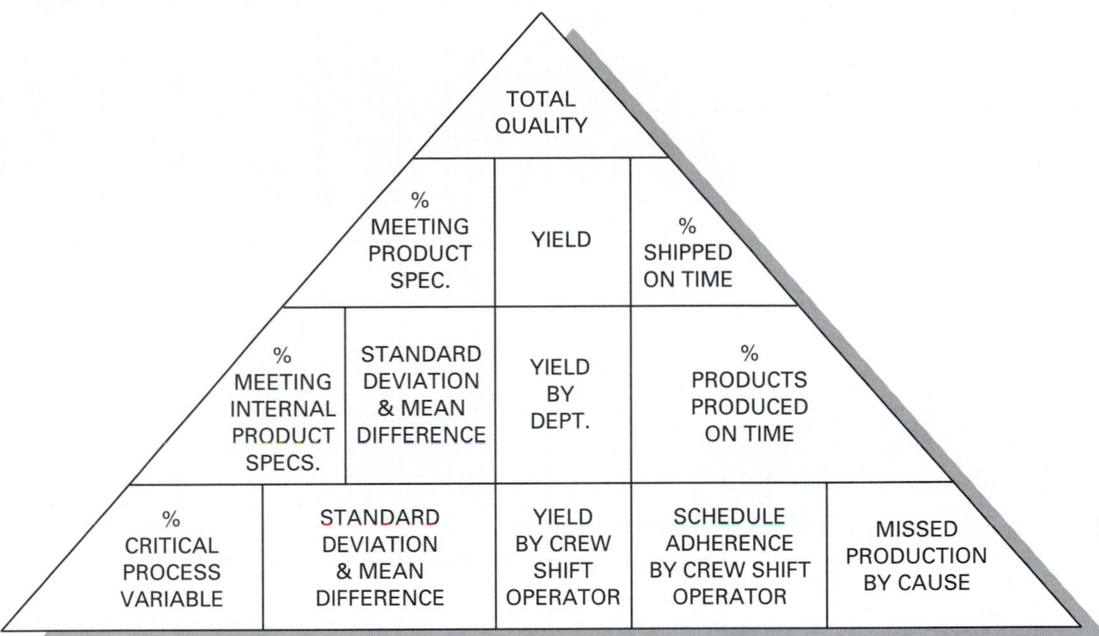

EXHIBIT 6 New System Pilot Performance Report

			Actual						*Plan*	*Var*	*YTD*	*YTD*	*YTD*
		1990	*Jan*	*Feb*	*Mar*	*Apr*	*May*	*June*	*June*	*June*	*Actual*	*Plan*	*Var*
PRODUCTIVITY													
EAF/LAR:	Tons	587,535	58,080	46,624	55,532	57,281	46,706	56,188	58,832	(3,302)	320,359	347,564	(34,007)
	Tap to Tap Hrs	12,164	1,152	982	1,133	1,149	956	1,143	1,102	(53)	6,517	6,617	100
	Tons/Hr	38.64	40.30	37.97	39.19	39.86	37.44	39.32	42.75	(4.29)	39.32	42.02	(3.37)
	Heats/Wk		79.20	70.40	75.20	78.40	61.60	77.60	81.60	(5)	73.60	80.00	(8)
	HIT Rate												
CASTER:	Tons	572,704	56,901	44,655	54,201	56,246	45,751	55,272	57,361	(2,611)	313,030	338,876	(32,310)
	Hours	6,346.40	563.20	512.00	563.20	550.40	556.80	550.40	550.40	0	3,296.00	3,308.80	12.80
	Tons/Hr	72.19	80.82	53.78	76.99	81.75	65.74	80.34	83.38	(3.80)	75.98	81.94	(7.44)
LABOR													
EAF/LAR:	Man Hours	107,307	9,837	8,929	10,236	9,806	9,806	10,000	9,514	(608)	58,632	55,629	(3,753)
	Prod Tons/Manhr	4.38	4.72	4.17	4.34	4.03	3.81	4.66	4.94	(0.56)	4.37	5.00	(0.78)
CASTER:	Man Hours	78,110	6,683	6,089	6,724	4,964	6,938	6,724	6,567	(196)	39,724	39,616	(136)
	Prod Tons/Manhr	6.01	6.81	5.86	6.45	6.86	5.27	6.58	6.98	(0.51)	6.30	6.84	(0.87)

YIELD														
EAF/LAR:	Reported	95.5%	96.4%	96.6%	97.0%	96.3%	97.9%	96.0%			96.7%			
	Applied		95.4%	95.3%	95.6%	94.3%	95.0%	95.0%	95.0%	0.0%	95.2%	95.0%	0.2%
CASTER:		97.5%	96.0%	95.6%	97.6%	96.2%	98.1%	98.4%	97.5%	0.9%	97.7%	97.5%	0.2%
SPENDING													
	EAF (Electric Arc Furnace)		1,443,067	1,243,625	1,329,800	1,499,361	1,386,807	1,421,037	1,658,740	236,102	8,325,300	9,870,859	1,545,559
	LAF (Ladle Arc Furnace)		116,149	68,427	79,751	46,168.80	136,724	92,687	115,669	22,982	539,908	693,743	153,835
	CASTER		351,824	290,937	305,132	313,962	312,456	289,136	325,392	36,255	1,863,450	1,936,292	72,842
TOTAL SPENDING													
	Total $		1,909,441	1,602,990	1,714,684	1,859,492	1,835,987	1,804,461	2,099,801	295,340	10,728,658	12,500,895	1,772,236
	$/NT		26.87	28.72	25.31	26.45	32.10	26.12	29.29	3.17	27.42	29.51	2.10
ADDITIONAL MEASURES													
EAF:	KWH/NT	3.41	342.40	353.60	344.00	331.20	353.60	342.40	332.00	(13)	344.00	332.00	(15)
	Electrodes/NT:	4.94	5.41	5.52	4.86	5.07	5.30	4.73	4.73	0.00	4.11	3.78	(0.51)
	MMBTU's/NT	0.16	0.09	0.49	0.46	0.48	0.56	0.39	0.18	(0.25)	0.40	0.19	(0.26)
LAR:	KWH/NT	28.80	20.80	23.20	25.60	27.20	28.80	25.60	28.80	3.20	25.60	29.60	4.00
	Electrodes/NT:	0.78	0.54	0.45	0.63	0.00	1.46	0.60	0.80	0.20	0.59	0.80	0.21

Merck & Co., Inc. (A)

"It's very easy to develop a rational compensation system," argues Steve Darien, Vice President of Worldwide Personnel. "The problem is that people are not always that rational."

In March 1985, newly appointed Chief Executive Officer Dr. P. Roy Vagelos formed the Employee Relations Review Committee charged with the task of reviewing and evaluating personnel policies and practices at Merck. Chaired by Steve Darien, the task force included officers from almost every division, collectively supervising over 4,500 Merck employees. The committee was chartered to:

- Examine employee policies and practices to determine if they create an environment that encourages and rewards greater productivity and employee excellence.
- Determine whether policies and practices are being adequately communicated to employees in a way they can clearly understand.
- Review the application of these policies and practices to determine whether they are being applied consistent with the objective set forth above and are achieving their intended results.

Over a period of six months, the committee reviewed Merck's policies and practices, visited other companies noted for outstanding employee relation programs, and met with 300 employees of various rank in a variety of Merck sites across the United States and Canada.

In late 1985, Mr. Darien and the other members of the task force reviewed their findings as they prepared recommendations designed to improve Merck's employee relations environment.

COMPANY HISTORY

Merck & Co., Inc., a pharmaceutical company headquartered in Rahway, New Jersey, has roots dating back to 1668 when Friedrich Jacob Merck bought a small apothecary in Darmstadt, Germany. The family business continued for centuries, expanding into full-scale drug manufacturing in 1827. Within thirty years, the German firm had achieved an international reputation as a supplier of chemicals for medicinal uses. In 1887, Merck opened a branch office in New York City to market its German-produced pharmaceuticals, and in 1903 descendant George Merck launched chemical and drug manufacturing operations at Merck's new plant in Rahway. The enterprise became incorporated in the U.S. in 1908, and within the next decade all ties with the German company were severed. Merck continued to expand throughout the century, and in 1953 merged with the Philadelphia-based pharmaceutical firm of Sharp & Dohme. Today, Merck manufactures and markets more than 80 prescription pharmaceuticals and vaccines, and is the nation's largest provider of prescription medicines.

Merck's growth over the past several decades can be traced to major new prescription drugs. In the 1960s, Merck introduced Indocin (for rheumatoid arthritis) and Aldomet (to counter high blood pressure). These two drugs together soon accounted for a quarter of Merck's total sales. In the 1970s, Merck launched Timoptic (a glaucoma treatment), Clinoril (an arthritis painkiller), and Mefoxin (an antibiotic). The 1980s saw the introduction of Pepcid (for ulcers), Mevacor (for lowering cholesterol levels) and Vasotec (which in 1988 became the first Merck product to exceed $1 billion in annual sales). Merck launched seven major new medicines in 1986 and 1987 alone. Spurred by new product innovation, Merck annual sales grew from $218 million in 1960 to $6.6 billion in 1989.

Merck enjoys a reputation for fine manage-

Associate Professor Kevin J. Murphy prepared this case as the basis for class discussion rather than to illustrate either effective or ineffective handling of an administrative situation.

Quotes and other information in this case are derived from interviews with key management and from internal documents and videotapes distributed or shown to Merck employees in connection with the revised personnel policies.

ment and was selected "America's Most Admired Corporation" by *Fortune* magazine for four straight years, 1987–1990. *Fortune's* 1990 rankings of 305 large corporations—based on a survey of nearly 8,000 senior executives, outside directors, and financial analysts—rated Merck first in innovativeness, shareholder value, product quality, and financial soundness. For the fourth year in a row, Merck received top marks for its ability to attract, develop, and keep talented people.

Merck has traditionally enjoyed a higher-than-average return on assets relative to its largest competitors (Exhibit A1). The early 1980s brought a decline in Merck's return on assets, and by 1988 Merck's performance began lagging behind the performance of other large pharmaceutical firms. Some causes of the declining performance were obvious, such as disappointing new products, inflation, and changes in foreign exchange rates. But newly appointed Chief Executive Officer Dr. P. Roy Vagelos sought to look deeper, and in March 1985 formed the Employee Relations Review Committee to review and evaluate personnel policies and practices at Merck.

PERSONNEL PRACTICES AT MERCK

From the beginning, Merck has been a global corporation—more than half of its 34,500 employees work outside the United States. Approximately 10,000 of its 18,000 domestic workforce are exempt salaried professionals employed in the human and animal health fields, including research professionals, marketing personnel, manufacturing employees, and corporate staff. Most of these employees (with the exception of about 3,000 field salespeople) are covered by the firm's Performance Appraisal and Salary Administration programs.[1] (Eight thousand hourly, unionized, and non-exempt salaried workers are not covered by the same plan, but about 1,000 overseas employees *are* covered by the plan.) Compensation for exempt salaried employees at Merck has traditionally ranked among the top 25% of large U.S. companies. Merck's progressive personnel policies and aggressive pay practices have contributed to high levels of employee loyalty as characterized by historically low turnover rates.

Performance Appraisal under the Old Plan

Merck's existing Performance Appraisal and Salary Administration program, itself a revision of an earlier program was first introduced in 1978. Under the plan, supervisors rated employees on a scale from one to five, with five designating exceptional performance and one indicating unacceptable performance. Pluses and minuses were allowed (excluding scores of 1− and 5+), thus supervisors effectively chose from thirteen different rating categories. The scale was *absolute*—the rating assigned to an individual was to reflect only that individual's performance independent of the performances of other employees.

Salary Determination under the Old Plan

Salaries for exempt employees are based on a combination of job characteristics (as measured by "Hay points") and merit. Hay points are determined by individually evaluating each position in terms of the three "Hay factors"—know how, problem solving, and accountability. Numerical scores are assigned to each factor according to guidelines provided by Hay Associates, and the sum of these scores defines the Hay points for each position in the organization.

Hay points are converted to a "control point" (roughly an average monthly salary) using a salary line formula. For example, the 1986 salary line formula was:

$$\text{Control point} = \$1502 + \$4.69 \times (\text{Hay points}).$$

Thus, a mid-level employee with 500 Hay points had a 1986 control point of $3,847 per month. The employee's actual salary can range from 80% to 125% of the control point; actual salary as a percentage of the control point is called the employee's "compa-ratio." An employee with 500 Hay points and a compa-ratio of 90, for example, would have a 1986 monthly salary of $3,462. An employee's compa-ratio goes up each time he/she gets a merit increase, and falls whenever the salary line formula is moved upward (holding salaries constant).

John Markowski, Director of U.S. Compensation, explains that Merck sets the salary line formula so that employees with compa-ratios of 100 earn roughly seven or eight percent more than av-

[1] In addition, a small number of research professionals are covered by a key innovator and key contributor stock option plan.

erage compensation (for similar Hay points) in other large firms:

> In determining Merck's overall compensation levels, Merck takes part in an extensive variety of salary surveys each year. In May 1986, 920 industrial organizations submitted data for this survey. For comparative purposes, Merck selected only those companies with sales that exceed $1 billion, since these companies tend to be the higher paying ones.

The salary line formula is revised annually on April 1 so that control points for a particular position (quantified by Hay points) approximates pay at the 75th percentile for similar positions in the sample of large firms. Salaries are not automatically adjusted when the salary line formula changes; thus, individual compa-ratios generally decline every April 1 when control points are increased.

Salary revisions are linked to both control point increases and performance ratings through guidelines established by the personnel department. Employees with higher ratings tend to get larger pay increases, while raises for a given performance rating tend to be smaller for employees who have already attained a high compa-ratio. For example, the recommended salary revision for an employee rated 4+, 4, or 4− might be 5%–7% if her compa-ratio was in the 80–95 range, but only 3%–5% if her compa-ratio was in the 120–125 range.

Mr. Markowski points out that compa-ratios considerably above 100 "should indicate that the employee's performance level is consistently above the level of his/her Merck peers." In addition, since salaries are rarely decreased, compa-ratios may be above 100 in the short run for employees *not* performing well and, therefore, *not* being promoted.

The maximum attainable compa-ratio is 125. Thus, salaries are effectively capped at 125% of the control point, and employees near the cap can only receive up to (but not surpassing) the cap. In practice, however, very few employees achieve and sustain compa-ratios exceeding 120. First, the salary line formula is adjusted prior to salary revisions. Thus even employees hitting the cap in a particular year will likely be well below the cap after the salary line changes on April 1. Second, employees with high compa-ratios are often strong candidates for internal promotions. Since it takes time to learn the skills required for a new position, the starting compa-ratio for a newly promoted employee is usually lower than his final compa-ratio in his prior position.[2]

THE EMPLOYEE RELATIONS REVIEW COMMITTEE

The Employee Relations Review Committee ultimately made more than 50 recommendations in a number of areas including management training, recruiting practices, alternate work patterns, employment stability and communications. The most difficult issues, however, related to identifying and rewarding performance.

According to task force member Joe Keating, President of the Pharmaceutical Manufacturing Division:

> The thing that really struck us was the negative feeling of some of our best performers concerning rewards. We spent more time on the issue of rewarding excellence than on any other. The appraisal system was the most difficult issue of all, but it had to be dealt with.

There was general agreement among employees that rewards for excellent performance were not adequate: outstanding performers got salary increases that were, in many cases, only marginally better than those given to average performers. In many cases, outstanding performance was not even clearly identified.

The problem was that everyone had different ideas as to how to structure a performance appraisal system. The Employee Relations Review Committee got an earful about the existing appraisal system:

> Managers are afraid to give experienced people a 1, 2, or 3 rating. It's easier to give everyone a 4 and give new people a 3.
>
> I could walk on water and spit gold quarters and my supervisor wouldn't give me a 5; he never got a 5 so why should I get one?

[2]For example, the average starting compa-ratio for all employees promoted into positions in the 400–600 Hay-point range during 1984–1985 was 87.

There is no way to get rid of the 'dead wood.' They just hang in there with 3- ratings and no one will move on them. Marginal people are draining our strength.

What's the use of killing yourself? You still get the same rating as everyone else, and you still get the same 5% increase. It's demoralizing and demotivating.

Charlie's been in that job for 20 years. He hasn't done anything creative for the last 15 years. Do you think my boss would give him a 3 rating? No way! Then, he'd have to spend the next 12 months listening to Charlie complain.

Tell me this, how in the world can 83% of the people be exceeding job expectations while the Company, as a whole, is doing just average? It just doesn't make any sense.

I'm the one who carries this department, and yet I get the same increase as everyone else. It's just not fair.

A lot of these people get to the top of the range and just sit there sucking up merit money, because the boss is afraid to give them anything less than an average increase. Where's the equity?

How can I rate my people objectively when the other directors are giving all their people 4s? A 3 isn't acceptable. I wouldn't mind if everyone played by the same rules, but they don't.

I'll be honest. It's getting to the point where some of the best people are going to walk out of here unless they get recognized and rewarded properly. Now, who do you want to do the walking? Your best people or your worst?

The committee concluded that many of the complaints raised in the employee interviews could be traced to the way employees were evaluated under the existing performance appraisal program (see Exhibit A2):

Very few employees received ratings of 5. The vast majority of our employees were rated 3 or 4. There were only a few 2s, and even fewer rated as 1 (not performing well). What we had done was homogenize our ratings by giving just about everyone the same rating. Although some divisions would assign uniformly higher ratings than others, there was very little differentiation among people within a division and, as a result, very little differentiation in the rewards they received for their contribution to the Company. Someone who had an outstanding year rarely received an outstanding reward for those results because so many other people in the division were rated the same. The Employee Relations Review Committee felt that certainly was not the way to encourage the kind of performance we need to excel as a Company.

EXHIBIT A1 Return on Assets for Merck and Merck's 10 Largest Competitors, 1970–1984

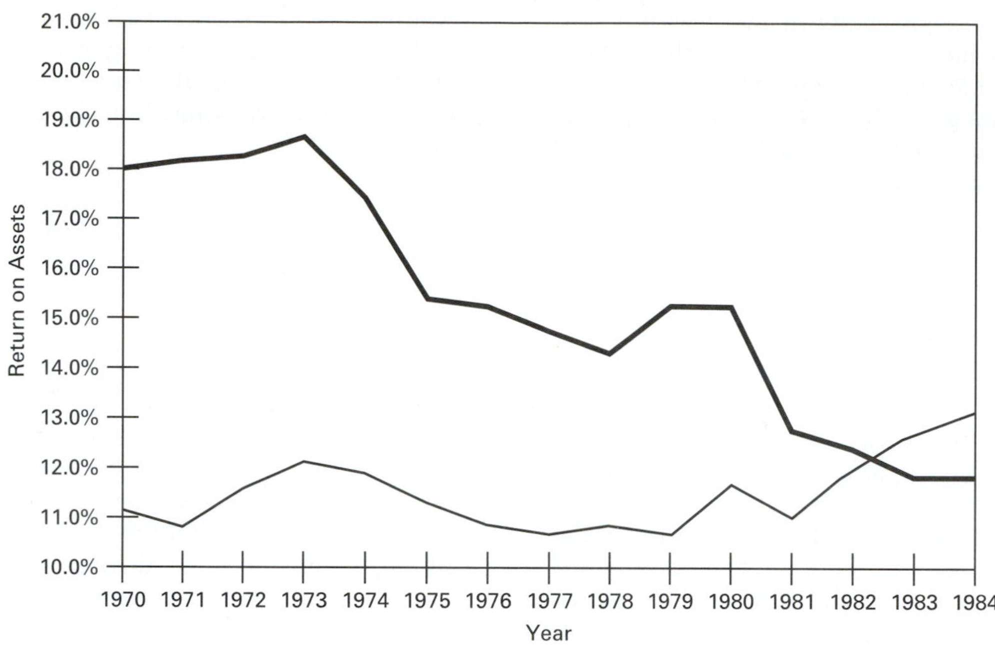

Note: Return on assets, defined as after-tax income plus interest divided by assets, obtained from *Compustat.* The list of Merck's 10 largest competitors (as measured by sales, SIC code 2834) has generally varied from year to year, due to takeovers, acquisitions, and different rates of growth. The companies depicted in the graph (and the years during which they were one of Merck's 10 largest competitors) are Abbott Laboratories (70-73, 75-84), American Home Products (70-84), Baxter International (85-84), Bristol-Myers (70-84), International Minerals & Chemicals (70, 71, 74-81), Johnson & Johnson (70-84), Eli Lilly & Co (70-84), Pfizer Inc (70-84), Schering-Plough (82), Smithkline Beckman Corp (80-84), Squibb (70-78, 84), Sterling Drugs (70-79, 83), Upjohn (72-74, 78-84), and Warner-Lambert (70-84).

EXHIBIT A2 1985 Rating Distribution and Average Pay Increases under the 1978 Performance Appraisal and Salary Administration Program

			Average 1985 Pay Increase, by Compa-Ratio			
1985 Rating	*Number of Employees*	*Percentage Distribution*	*Compa-Ratio 80.00–95.00*	*Compa-Ratio 95.01–110.00*	*Compa-Ratio 110.01–120.00*	*Compa-Ratio 120.01–125.00*
5 5–	19 77	.28% 1.14%	8.3%	8.1%	6.5%	4.4%
4+ 4 4–	709 1,849 1,427	10.53% 27.46% 21.19%	6.5%	5.5%	4.8%	4.6%
3+ 3 3–	1,607 694 200	23.86% 10.31% 2.97%	5.7%	4.0%	3.3%	3.5%
2+ 2 2–	97 44 3	1.44% .65% .04%	4.3%	1.3%	0.0%	0.0%
1+ 1	2 6	.03% .09%				

Merck & Co., Inc. (B)

"I'd be remiss if I didn't say that I recognize our Performance Appraisal Program isn't perfect," admitted Steve Darien, Vice President of Worldwide Personnel and chairman of the task force that designed the revised program. "In fact, I know of no company that feels it has a perfect program and I know of none that is totally satisfied with its approach."

The Merck Revised Performance Appraisal and Salary Administration program, in effect for two full years and covering over 7,000 employees, had just undergone its first formal evaluation. The evaluation process included focus group interviews with employees in the United States and Europe, questionnaires from members of the Executive Incentive Plan, interviews with senior executives, training program feedback, and analysis of data generated from the Human Resource Information System. Although the results were generally favorable, Steve Darien was concerned that only half of the employees interviewed believed the new Performance Appraisal Program was a clear improvement over the program it replaced.

Mr. Darien pondered the evaluation results as he prepared for his presentation to the Operating Review Committee (comprised of the nine highest-ranking Merck executives) on May 1, 1989. He planned to highlight the favorable attributes of the revised program—including the greater distinction between levels of employee performance and better rewards for outstanding performance. He would also discuss the negative attributes—the rating distribution targets, for example, were considered too inflexible and too many employees were forced into the "High Standard" category. In addition, he would note that managers were too often not using the program as it was designed. Finally, Mr. Darien planned to offer recommendations for potential changes to the program.

THE REVISED PERFORMANCE APPRAISAL AND SALARY ADMINISTRATION PROGRAM

In late 1986, as a result of the findings and recommendations of the Employee Relations Review Committee, Merck revised its performance review and pay practices.

Performance Appraisal

The revised Performance Appraisal program is summarized in *Exhibit B1*. The major revisions include:

- *Revised Rating Categories.* The old numerical 13-point scale (including pluses and minuses) is replaced by five rating descriptors:

SYMBOL	CATEGORY
EX	Exceptional within Merck
WD	Merck Standard with Distinction
HS	High Merck Standard
RI	Merck Standard with Room for Improvement
NA	Not Adequate for Merck

  There is also an optional sixth category called PR ("Progressing") designed for employees who are too new to the job to get a comprehensive evaluation.

- *Shift to Relative System.* While the old system was based on absolute measures of performance, the new system focuses on performance measured relative to Merck peers.
- *Revised Performance Categories.* The performance categories and definitions have been clarified and

Associate Professor Kevin J. Murphy prepared this case as the basis for class discussion rather than to illustrate either effective or ineffective handling of an administrative situation.

Quotes and other information in this case are derived from interviews with key management and from internal documents and videotapes distributed or shown to Merck employees in connection with the revised personnel policies.

expanded. The three major performance categories are:

- *Specific Job Measures, Ongoing Duties.* This category describes performance against both quantitative and qualitative measurements. Examples of quantitative measures include sales vs plan, operating expenses, etc. Qualitative descriptors include timeliness of work, quality, and consistency of output.
- *Performance Against Planned Objectives.* The typical focus is on the top five to seven planned objectives.
- *Management of People.* For the first time, managers and supervisors will be rated on their performance in hiring/staffing, training and development, performance feedback and recognition, employee relations, communications, and affirmative action.

- *Targeted Distribution.* Ratings (for groups of at least 100 employees) should be distributed as follows:

RATING	TARGET	CONSTRAINTS
EX	5%	Max of 8%
WD	15%	Max of 17%
HS	70%	Min of 65%
RI	8%	Min of 5%
NA	2%	No Minimum

Managers of groups of fewer than 100 employees are not expected to fit the guidelines exactly, but are expected to adhere to the basic objective: clear differentiation between employees in order to recognize those whose performance far surpasses their peers during a given year.

- *January Evaluation.* Performance appraisals under the old system were conducted throughout the year, although any given employee would always be evaluated in the same month every year. Under the target distribution system, all employee appraisals are conducted within a single month.

Salary Administration

The total dollars distributed under the revised program are the same as would have been distributed under the prior system. What has changed is *how* the dollars are allocated to employees.

- *Salary Planning Guidelines.* Each year managers will be given a new guideline showing the range of suggested merit pay increases for each rating and compa-ratio category. (The 1986 guideline is reproduced as Exhibit B2). While there is a range of suggested increases for all employees, supervisors may recommend 0% when no increases are warranted.
- *Compa-Ratio Targets.* While an employee's performance rating may change from one year to the next, the compa-ratio targets are where the employee should end up if he/she maintained the same level of performance for several years.

RATING	COMPA-RATIO TARGET
EX	115–125
WD	100–120
HS	90–110
RI	80–95
NA	None

- *Timing of Salary Revisions.* Salary revisions can occur any time during the year; HS employees with compa-ratios of 100 should receive raises every 13–15 months (Exhibit B2). Increases given at less than a twelve-month interval are possible but are considered unusual and an exception to plan.

IMPLEMENTATION

Upon recommendation from the Employee Relations Review Committee, the company's Revised Exempt Performance Appraisal and Salary Administration Program was introduced to employees in late 1986. By the end of January 1987, managers, supervisors, and all covered employees attended four-hour briefing sessions to learn about the major changes in corporate personnel policy. The briefing sessions consisted of a combination of managerial lectures, slide presentations, videotapes, and question-and-answer sessions.

In a videotaped address, Dr. Vagelos challenged Merck employees:

> For many years, Merck has been one of the top paying companies in the United States. We've been able to do so because of our historically superior results. Frankly, however, our performance as a company has slipped in recent years. We need to make certain that in the future we're getting results that match the standard we set for ourselves.
>
> Meeting the Merck Standard requires performance that is far better than average, far better than what is acceptable in other companies. Our revised Performance Review and Salary Administration programs will assure that employees who meet the Merck Standard will continue to be paid very well. Those employees who produce ex-

ceptional results during a particular year will receive exceptional rewards.

I can assure you that I will evaluate the senior managers reporting to me using the same guidelines. The Merck Standard is something special. We need to perform at that level so we can meet the goal we've set for ourselves—to be the preeminent health care company in the world.

THE DISCRETIONARY AWARD PROGRAM

After introducing the new Performance Appraisal and Salary Administration program in 1986, Merck executives quietly and informally instituted a Discretionary Award Program designed to further reward superior performers. Never announced as a formal program, the first year's cash bonuses came as a surprise to almost 2,500 recipients (representing about 40% of all eligible salaried exempt employees). Guidelines showing the targeted number of recipients by performance rating, and the suggested cash bonus payment (as a percentage of salary) by performance rating, are determined each year by top management. Discretionary awards in 1988 were given to all employees achieving EX and WD ratings, and to just under a third of employees with an HS rating. Cash bonuses for EX and WD employees in 1988 averaged about 10% and 6% of base salary, respectively, while bonuses for those HS employees who received awards averaged about 4% of their base salary.

THE TWO-YEAR REVIEW OF THE REVISED PROGRAM

In early 1989, after being in effect for two full years, the revised performance review and salary programs were evaluated by Steve Darien and his Human Resources staff.

In preparing the evaluation, the Human Resources staff reviewed the rating distribution and average pay increases for 1988 (Exhibit B3). In addition, interviews were conducted with ten senior managers and eleven "focus groups" of employees at U.S. and European sites. The staff also tabulated the results from questionnaires returned by 251 managers and 5,413 covered employees.

Survey Responses

Mr. Darien found that while 50% of the surveyed employees thought the new Performance Appraisal program was better than the one it replaced, 25% thought it was worse, and 25% saw no differences in the two plans. The revised Salary Administration program fared better—63% saw the new program as an improvement, while only 8% thought the old program was better. Almost a third (29%) were equally happy under either program.

The focus group interviews generated many specific complaints and comments regarding the new programs. Some managers in one European plant complained that the program demotivated staff. These managers felt that there were "too many objectives" and that "the salary link made discussions on performance improvement difficult."

A sampling of the comments offered by surveyed employees include:

> HS category is simply too big. No way to show an employee he's at the high end or low end.
>
> One problem is that people are used to being rated against the job and its demands and expectations rather than against each other.
>
> On the positive side, the targeted distribution has forced managers to make tough decisions. It has produced frank and interesting discussions on performance.
>
> Shouldn't force distribution at the low end or high end. If you don't have a 'true' EX, don't be forced to give one just to fit the targets.
>
> Labels are a problem. People were in the middle before, but they didn't know it. It's the discovery that they're in the middle that is disquieting to them.
>
> The old program had more gradations. You could 'move someone through with small rewards.' Can't do that as well now.
>
> Competitive approach is valid. People aren't working in a vacuum. They are competing with peers—just like in the 'outside' world.
>
> We will have a future problem if we continue to get rid of people who aren't performing well. Very soon, we'll need to begin to get rid of people who are solid performers—but

just not as good as others. This will cause a major morale problem in the workforce.

Another problem is the labels. Get rid of them and go to a full ranking of people.

Significant problem between line and staff people. When the division is doing very well in meeting its financial goals, most higher ratings are given to the line. There aren't any left over for staff people who may be performing just as well. More staff people get higher ratings during a bad year. Last year, many of staff performed superbly, but couldn't give them ratings that reflected that.

A definite plus is having all appraisals done at the same time. This gives you the opportunity to compare performance of one employee with another and help you make decisions on each employee's performance.

Forced distribution is inappropriate. Last year our group had the best year ever, but, because of the rest of the division's performance, higher ratings were 'used up.' How can you reward people in a situation like this where they deserve it, but are excluded from higher ratings because there are only so many to go around. It becomes very demotivational to people who performed extremely well.[1]

[1]Interestingly, this particular division didn't use its full 'quota' of EX ratings.

Managerial Abuses

The employee focus groups also provided an opportunity to identify common managerial abuses in the implementation of the programs:

- Insisting that "first-year" employees (new to the Company or job) must be rated PR, or cannot be rated HS or higher.
- Imposing rating targets on small groups of employees.
- The "it's her turn" syndrome—providing higher ratings in alternative years in an attempt to be perceived as "fair."
- Supervisors tell their employees "I rated you X, but they changed it upstairs."

Is the System Working?

Steve Darien reviewed the evaluation results as he prepared his presentation for the Operating Review Committee. Although concerned by the ample complaints uncovered in the evaluation, his gut instinct told him that the revised system was at least on the right track. He added, however, that,

> Performance Appraisal is one of the most difficult processes I know of. When you evaluate peoples contribution it's a very emotional issue. All of us like to think we're 'at the top.' Unfortunately not every outstanding person can be at the top each year.

EXHIBIT B1 Exempt Performance Rating Definitions and Targeted Guidelines

PERFORMANCE RATINGS			*PERFORMANCE DEFINITIONS*		
	Rating	*Distribution Target*	*Specific Job Measures Ongoing Doings*	*Planned Objectives*	*Management of People*
EX	*Exceptional Within Merck*	5%	Far above Merck peers Capitalized on unexpected events to gain superior results	Made significant breakthroughs or exceptional achievements	Outstanding leader Exceptional development and recruitment of people Superior communications
WD	*Merck Standard With Distinction*	15%	Clearly superior to Merck peers in most respects Took advantage of unexpected events to achieve unusually good results	Objectives met and many exceeded	A clear leader among Merck peers Top quality people recruited and developed
HS	*High Merck Standard*	70%	Comparable to Merck peers Made use of unexpected events to achieve very good results	Objectives met	A very good leader. Hired very good people and develops people as well as peers Very good communication
RI	*Merck Standard Room for Improvement*	8%	Work is not quite as good as Merck peers Contended with unexpected events	Most objectives met. Some shortfalls	Adequate leader Hires good people Satisfactory communication
NA	*Not Adequate for Merck*	2%	Work is not up to that of Merck peers Did not fully cope with unexpected events	Missed significant objectives	Poor leader Communications could be better
PR	*Progressing*	Not Applicable	Typically this employee is new to the company or in a significantly different assignment. Normally this rating would apply only during the first year in the new job.		

- too vague
- consequences
- plan for improvement

EXHIBIT B2 1986 Salary Planning Guideline

		Suggested Merit Increase Percentage			
	Performance Rating	*Compa-Ratio 80.00–95.00*	*Compa-Ratio 95.01–110.00*	*Compa-Ratio 110.01–120.00*	*Compa-Ratio 120.01–125.00*
EX	*Exceptional Within Merck*	13%–15%	12%–14%	9%–11%	to maximum of range
WD	*Merck Standard With Distinction*	9%–11%	8%–10%	7%–9%	—
HS	*High Merck Standard*	7%–9%	6%–8%	—	—
RI	*Merck Standard Room for Improvement*	5%–7%	—	—	—
NA	*Not Adequate for Merck*	—	—	—	—

		Suggested Timing Since Last Increase			
	Performance Rating	*Compa-Ratio 80.00–95.00*	*Compa-Ratio 95.01–110.00*	*Compa-Ratio 110.01–120.00*	*Compa-Ratio 120.01–125.00*
EX	*Exceptional Within Merck*	12–13 months	12–14 months	14–15 months	—
WD	*Merck Standard With Distinction*	12–14 months	12–14 months	14–16 months	—
HS	*High Merck Standard*	13–14 months	13–15 months	—	—
RI	*Merck Standard Room for Improvement*	13–14 months	—	—	—
NA	*Not Adequate for Merck*	—	—	—	—

EXHIBIT B3 1988 Rating Distribution and Average Pay Increases under Revised Performance Appraisal and Salary Administration Program

			Average 1988 Pay Increase, by Compa-Ratio			
1988 Rating	*Number of Employees*	*Percentage Distribution*	*Compa-Ratio 80.00–95.00*	*Compa-Ratio 95.01–110.00*	*Compa-Ratio 110.01–120.00*	*Compa-Ratio 120.01–125.00*
EX	404	6.6%	12.9%	11.3%	7.6%	maximum of range
WD	1,218	20.0%	9.1%	8.0%	6.1%	—
HS	4,267	70.0%	6.7%	5.1%	4.3%	—
RI	190	3.1%	3.5%	3.0%	—	—
NA	18	0.3%	0%	—	—	—

Roy Rogers Restaurants

It was 8:00 p.m. when Frank Martinez, vice president of franchising for Roy Rogers Restaurants, finally left for home after his second day of meetings in March 1988 with the Franchisee Advisory Council. Although the decision to hold council meetings monthly, rather than biannually, imposed many new demands on himself and his managers, Martinez was encouraged to see a strong rapport developing between the Roy Rogers staff and the franchisees. Attendance at the meetings was increasing, and franchisees were expressing enthusiasm for the company's plans to expand the Roy Rogers system. Martinez was convinced that a successful partnership of Roy Rogers and the franchisees was necessary if the division was to meet the profit growth goal set by Roy Rogers' parent, the Marriott Corporation.

As he left the office, Frank Martinez recalled his conversation with Jack Towle, a major franchisee, who had approached him after the meeting with a request to eliminate the salad-bar concept when he built his next Roy Rogers restaurant. Towle, who was Roy Rogers' third-largest franchisee, operated 16 units in major Baltimore locations. Towle was also one of a small number of franchisees who was expected to play a critical role in the company's new growth strategy; he had recently signed a development agreement to build 34 new units by the end of 1992. As Frank Martinez picked up the phone to inform Ed Bradford, Roy Rogers' vice president and general manager, of Jack's request, he wondered how the organization should respond to an issue with such major implications for both the company and the interests of the 50 other franchisees.

MARRIOTT CORPORATION

Roy Rogers Restaurants (often referred to within the company and in advertising as Roy's) was a subsidiary of the Marriott Corporation, a Washington, D.C.-based company which was founded in 1927 by J. Willard Marriott. From its beginnings as a small root beer stand, Marriott had grown to $6.5 billion dollars in sales in 1987, with operations and franchises in 50 states and 24 countries. The company was in three principal businesses: lodging, comprised of both hotel operations and lifecare retirement communities; contract food services for businesses, hospitals, educational institutions, and airlines; and restaurants, comprised of family-oriented and fast-food restaurants as well as highway travel plazas. As a corporation, Marriott was well-known for its expertise in applying creative financing strategies to its real estate development activities. Exhibits 1 and 2 contain the company's 1987 financial statements and provide sales and income data by business sector.

In its restaurant segment, Marriott operated or franchised more than 1,100 restaurants in 24 states. Its largest chain, Big Boy, was sold in 1987 to a major franchisee. The approximately 220 company-owned units operating at the time of the sale were expected to be converted to a new restaurant concept. Roy Rogers, a fast-food chain serving hamburgers, fried chicken, and roast beef sandwiches, had both franchises and company-owned facilities located primarily in the Middle Atlantic states. Marriott's smallest chain in the restaurant segment was Hot Shoppes, which operated approximately 15 units in the Washington, D.C. area.

Marriott also operated a large number of highway restaurants and merchandise outlets located in travel plazas on 14 turnpikes. The restaurant facilities at the travel plazas included Big Boy and Roy Rogers Restaurants, as well as the fast-food restaurants of competitors such as Burger King. As of 1988, all of these units, including those of the competitors, were operated by Marriott's Travel Plazas Division rather than by the specific chain of which they were a part.

Patricia J. Murray, MBA '88 prepared this case under the supervision of Professor William J. Bruns, Jr. as the basis for class discussion rather than to illustrate either effective or ineffective handling of an administrative situation.

THE FAST-FOOD INDUSTRY

The fast-food industry was comprised largely of restaurant chains, primarily franchises, that served hamburgers, chicken, pizza, sandwiches, or ethnic food such as Mexican or Chinese dishes. Franchising is explained in Appendix A. Chains serving hamburgers as their primary product offering dominated this industry, with approximately 31,511 units and $25.2 billion in sales as of 1986. Fast-food restaurants typically offered restaurant seating or takeout dining, including drive-through service. Takeout service was the most popular, with 60 to 65 percent of all fast food purchased for takeout consumption. Fast-food dining had become a habit in American life, with nine out of ten people over the age of 12 eating in a fast-food restaurant regularly.[1] Nevertheless, competition within the fast-food segment of the restaurant market had become fierce as the hamburger market matured, particularly with the entry of untraditional competitors such as supermarkets, convenience stores, and producers of prepackaged products suitable for microwave cooking. Exhibit 3 summarizes information about major competitors in the fast-food industry in 1988.

One industry analyst identified several factors that distinguish the successful restaurant ventures from the failures.[2] First, the individual restaurant or chain must have a standard of product quality that is acceptable to the consumer. Of equal importance is the restaurant's ability to standardize its concept so that customers can predict what their dining experience will be like well before they enter the restaurant. The ability to franchise successfully is also important, because franchising provides for more rapid growth than company operations typically can manage. The most successful chains tend to be marketing-driven organizations that strive to attain the critical mass of advertising needed to establish a strong presence in the target market. Finally, the caliber of a firm's management, both in the various functional areas and in the restaurant facilities themselves, greatly affects the firm's ability to respond to changing industry trends. The ability to compete on these many dimensions becomes particularly important as a market segment matures and growth opportunities become more limited.

Competitors in the hamburger segment of the fast-food industry employed a number of strategies to prepare for the anticipated decline in hamburger demand. Most diversified their offerings with breakfast and other special menus and developed new concepts such as drive-through-only units and home delivery; many attempted to develop international markets for their products. Yet several other factors exacerbated the pressures facing the industry.[3] The first was changing demographics. By the late 1980s, the aging of the baby boom generation (people born between 1945 and 1970) in the United States, and the increase in the elderly population were already having a significant impact on the industry's labor pool and the character of its customer base. Fast-food chains needed to develop product and service offerings, as well as employment opportunities, that would meet the needs of an aging society. In addition, experts pointed out that many localities had become saturated with fast-food restaurants, with the result that suitable prime real estate either was not available or was quite costly to acquire. The cost of media advertising programs had also risen dramatically, making it increasingly difficult for smaller chains without scale economies to afford this traditional tool for increasing customer awareness. Last, because American consumers remained health conscious, they would continue to demand innovative product offerings that were both convenient and nutritious.

In discussing these trends, Ed Bradford, Roy Rogers' vice president and general manager, pointed out the dilemma facing many fast-food restaurant systems:

> While we must continue to develop new product offerings in anticipation of changing consumer preferences, consumers also ex-

[1]The Naisbitt Group, *The Future of Franchising: Looking 25 Years Ahead to the Year 2010* (Washington, D.C: International Franchise Association, 1986), p. 1.

[2]Daniel R. Lee, "Why some Succeed Where Others Fail," *Cornell Hotel and Restaurant Administration Quarterly* (November 1987), pp. 33–34.

[3]Sidney J. Feltenstein, "Fast Food Businesses Must Adjust to Trends," *Marketing News,* September 25, 1987, p. 22.

> pect us to offer them a dining experience which is both enjoyable and easily replicable throughout the system. Firms in this business must balance the pressures for innovation with the need to retain the integrity of the service concept which is at the core of their strategy.

Although the many pressures facing the industry were expected to limit opportunities for new national fast-food chains to enter the market, regional competitors like Roy Rogers were expected to enjoy some competitive advantage because of their ability to react quickly to trends, exploit relationships with local real estate developers, and develop niche strategies well-suited to geographically limited markets.

ROY ROGERS RESTAURANTS

The Roy Rogers Restaurant system had a strategic mission that emphasized hamburger and chicken products, a family orientation, and a high-price/high-value perception. The system was named for Roy Rogers, a country-and-western singer in the 1950s, best known for his TV and feature-film appearances with his wife, Dale Evans, and his horse, Trigger. Although he had retired in the mid-1970s, he remained active in the entertainment industry and continued to make himself available to attend grand openings of new Roy Rogers units and other special company events.

Two of the Roy Rogers system's unique features were its salad bar and its Fixin's Bar, a condiment bar located in the middle of the store at which customers could add tomatoes, lettuce, pickles, and other condiments to their sandwiches. At the end of 1986, chicken and hamburgers were the most popular products in Roy Rogers Restaurants in terms of sales revenues, accounting for just over 45 percent of all sales. Drinks, french fries, cole slaw, and roast beef accounted for another 40 percent of sales. Salads typically accounted for about 5 percent of sales. With 345 company-owned and 214 franchised units as of 1987, Roy Rogers was thirteenth in revenues among the top fast-food franchises.[4] Following the arrival in 1986 of Ed Bradford, vice president and general manager, and Frank Martinez, vice president of franchising, the Roy Rogers management team had developed a plan to double the system within the five years. Exhibit 4 shows the organization Ed Bradford had created by 1988. The division hoped to add 100 company units and 202 franchised units by 1992; the latter objective required the addition of 45 new franchisees.

Like most franchises, Roy Rogers had a highly competitive selection process for its franchisees. Applicants, whether individuals or partnerships, were expected to complete a document summarizing their personal data, business experience, and independently verified statements of their personal assets, as well as to provide a plan for financing and managing the franchise. Prospective franchisees were expected to have a combined net worth of $500,000 or more, exclusive of their principal residences and personal property, with at least $150,000 in liquid assets available for investment. According to company statistics, 1 percent of the applicants succeeded in becoming franchisees. In addition to financial qualifications, applicants were evaluated on the basis of their previous restaurant experience, community standing, business accomplishments, and other factors such as character and motivation. Individual owners and operating partners (who were required to have at least a 50 percent equity position in their partnership) were expected to devote substantially all of their time to the franchise.

Franchisees with the resources to develop multiple sites were attractive applicants to franchisors like Roy Rogers, whose strategy emphasized rapid growth of their system. These franchisees were selected not only for their financial resources and operating experience but also for their expertise in local real estate markets and for the organizational structure they had in place to manage multiple units. Frank Martinez described the situation as follows:

> Franchisors facing pressure to increase profitability and market share constantly struggle with the question of whether they should constrain the growth of their system by adhering to the pure franchise form of single-unit ownership. While single-unit owners have strong incentives to provide the on-site supervision necessary to maintain the quality of their operations, more time and re-

[4]Andrew Kostecka, "Restaurant Franchising in the Economy," *Restaurant Business,* March 20, 1988, p. 194.

> sources may be required to integrate them into the franchise system. On the other hand, franchisees with the resources to develop multiple sites may be able to integrate new units into the system more rapidly, although they may be less effective as managers because they do not have an operating role in their units.

Since there were only a small number of franchisees with the resources and expertise required to operate multiple units, there was considerable competition within the franchisor community to secure multisite development agreements with them. The current population of 51 Roy's franchisees was comprised primarily of individual owner-operators of single or multiple units, with only eight out of the group organized as operating-investment partnerships and three organized as limited partnerships.

Franchises were awarded for a period of 20 years and could be acquired either by constructing a new restaurant or, in selected instances, by purchasing an existing company-owned or franchised facility. When matching franchisees to areas chosen for development, Roy Rogers tried to honor the geographical preferences of franchisees; however, they were expected to relocate if no local sites were available. The Franchise Agreement did not include a guarantee of territorial exclusivity. Other franchises or company-owned restaurants could be established within the same territory if Roy Rogers so desired.

The initial fee to acquire a Roy Rogers franchise was \$25,000, plus an option fee of \$5,000 for the first unit. The total investment required, and income of a typical franchised unit are summarized in Exhibits 5 and 6. Roy's received ongoing monthly royalties of 4 percent of gross sales from each franchisee as well as the franchisee's commitment to expend 5 percent of gross sales per month for advertising. Other fast-food chains charged initial franchise fees ranging from \$15,000 to \$40,000 and royalty fees ranging from 2 to 6 percent of gross sales. Some competitors also exacted fees of \$20,000 to \$50,000 for technical services related to the opening of a new unit and training of personnel. As of 1988, McDonald's, the recognized industry leader, charged an initial franchise fee of \$22,500 but did not charge any technical fee.

The Roy Rogers Franchise Agreement contained detailed provisions regarding the location, design, operation, and sale of franchised units. (A summary of the Roy Rogers Franchise Agreement is presented in Appendix B.) One of the essential elements of the contract, which was relevant to Jack Towle's request to discontinue the salad bar, was the requirement that the franchisee serve only the menu items specified by the company and follow all company specifications regarding the content, weight, preparation, and variety of products offered. Franchisees were visited approximately every two months by a Roy's franchise consultant, who inspected each operation for compliance with the system and assisted franchisees in making improvements. As of 1988, there were nine franchise consultants, each of whom had responsibility for approximately 25 restaurants. Since uniformity in both quality specifications and the variety of product offerings was considered quite important to the integrity of the system, any deviations from the standard concept were considered serious infractions deserving of close monitoring by management. Although the company tried to be constructive in helping franchisees to rectify performance deficiencies or contract violations, the Franchise Agreement could be terminated if problems were not corrected within a reasonable period of time.

While the company recognized the importance of preserving the Roy Rogers system, management also recognized the need to encourage innovation among the franchisees. As Frank Martinez explained:

> While we do have a well-funded, in-house research and development effort, we also recognize that our franchisees have a great deal to contribute to the Roy Rogers organization. After all, they are entrepreneurs, many of whom have invested a good percentage of their personal wealth and careers in the Roy Rogers system. They also tend to have a unique perspective on the business, which comes from their daily contact with the customers, the suppliers, and the work force. While we want our franchisees to challenge us, to question the status quo, we also want them to see the benefits of working through the organization to accomplish change. Our task as a franchisor is to harness their dedica-

tion, creativity, and entrepreneurial spirit in a way which can benefit both the individual franchisees and the system as a whole.

One of the programs the company had introduced to manage the testing and implementation of new ideas was its Product Testing Policy (PTP). In the past, franchisees with suggestions for new products or operational improvements had simply submitted their suggestions to Roy's management for approval to introduce the new concept at their facility. While many ideas had been rejected because they were not sufficiently well-developed or were incompatible with the company's strategy, the franchisees had not been given timely feedback about the reasons certain ideas were not selected for further evaluation. While the company viewed its role in managing the research and development (R&D) process as consistent with its mandate to preserve the integrity of the system, some confusion had existed among the franchisees as to whether Roy's was truly committed to innovation. The new PTP represented an attempt to define the roles of the franchisee and Roy Rogers management in the product development process, while providing a mechanism for objective, timely evaluation of new ideas.

To initiate the PTP, the franchisee submitted a Product Test Request describing the new product idea or proposed operational improvement. The proposal was circulated within Roy Rogers to the managers of franchising, marketing, and R&D. If the concept was deemed appropriate for further study, the company and franchisee jointly developed a plan for testing the new idea and judging its success. Although the new idea could be tested by either the company R&D department or the franchisee, the franchisee was encouraged to carry out the test whenever feasible. Franchisees received no royalties or other remuneration for ideas they proposed that subsequently were selected for commercial development. Nevertheless, franchisees were quite receptive to the PTP and felt it improved communication and forced some necessary discipline and thoughtful analysis in judging new products.

The Jack Towle Organization

With 16 Roy Rogers units operating in urban Baltimore locations, Jack Towle was the third-largest Roy Rogers franchisee. He had been a franchisee for about six years. His units were quite successful, with average sales of $1,300,000 each, 30 percent higher than the typical Roy Rogers restaurant. Jack Towle was unique among Roy Rogers franchisees in that he owned a number of restaurant franchises with multiple firms. While the Towle franchise contract with Roy Rogers prohibited him from purchasing franchises involving food offerings similar to Roy's, the various franchisors nevertheless did compete with one another for access to the Towle real estate holdings in Baltimore. The Towle organization had considerable expertise in local real estate development and based its franchise development decisions on the profitability of the franchise and the nature of the working relationship with the franchisor. In order to secure the original contract with the Towle organization, Roy Rogers had agreed to reduce the standard royalty payment from 4 to 3 percent of gross sales for all of Jack Towle's units.

The Towle organization was one of a small percentage of franchisees with whom Roy Rogers had signed franchise development agreements. In 1987, Towle had agreed to develop 34 new units by the end of five years, resulting in a total of 50 units in operation by 1992. Towle had several Roy Rogers Restaurants under construction at the time that he approached Frank Martinez with the request to discontinue the salad bar at the newest facility.

THE SALAD BAR ISSUE

When Jack Towle had approached Frank Martinez at the Franchisee Advisory Council (FAC) meeting, he had argued his case by pointing out that there were circumstances unique to his locations that warranted modification of the system. Towle had explained that the new facility being planned was going to be situated in a business district with considerable lunchtime traffic. From past experience Towle recognized that adequate seating was important to urban customers when selecting a fast-food restaurant for lunch. Since salad sales typically represented only 5 percent of a unit's business, Towle had concluded that it would be preferable to eliminate the salad bar in the unit being planned and replace it with six additional seats. With customer turnover at lunchtime occurring approximately every 12 minutes, Towle felt that the number of customers who would benefit from the additional seating capacity would outweigh those who could not order salad. Furthermore, with an average customer check estimated at $3.34, Towle felt his unit's revenues and profits would improve if the additional seating succeeded in attracting incremental lunchtime traffic. While the typical check of a salad-bar customer was higher, at $3.85, Towle estimated that only 2.5% of the salad-bar customers would be lost if the salad bar were not available.

As he contemplated possible responses to Towle's request, Frank Martinez was well aware that the Franchise Agreement was unequivocal in prohibiting individual franchisees from modifying the system. The agreement stated: "Franchisee agrees to serve the menu items specified by Franchisor, [and] to follow all specifications and formulas of Franchisor as to contents and weight of products served."[5] Yet Martinez also knew that other factors had to be considered.

A major concern was the effect of a refusal on Jack Towle's motivation to develop future Roy Rogers franchises. While Martinez felt that Towle would honor his contractual obligation to meet the established development timetable, he was far less certain whether Towle would choose his most attractive sites for the new Roy Rogers facilities. Without Jack Towle's local contacts, it would be difficult and potentially costly for Roy Rogers to gain access to the desirable locations in the Baltimore market. Since rapid franchise development was essential to the firm's strategy, Martinez did not wish to take any action that would prohibit him from becoming the franchisor of preference to this important franchisee.

Yet Frank Martinez conceded that he had an important obligation to protect the interests of the 50 other franchisees as well as the company-owned Roy Rogers operations. Uniformity of product offerings was an essential component of the franchising concept, and he wondered whether allowing Jack Towle to eliminate the salad bar from a restaurant in a major urban location would dilute the consumer's image of Roy Rogers in a way that would harm the entire system. Since the value of an individual franchise depended largely on the success of the system as a whole, Martinez knew that any action he took with respect to Jack Towle's facilities would have important implications for both the company and the individual franchisees.

Martinez also found himself concerned about the precedent that would be set by allowing a franchisee to deviate from the standard menu. Since there were several other franchisees who had signed development agreements or who owned multiple units, many of them could approach Roy Rogers for concessions if they discovered that Jack Towle had been allowed to deviate from the terms of the contract. The FAC meetings provided numerous opportunities for the franchisees to meet and share information, so it was inevitable that the company's handling of this problem would become a topic of conversation within the franchise community. Furthermore, Martinez had already made some concessions during the original contract negotiations with Jack Towle, and he did not want Towle to develop the impression that the terms of the Franchise Agreement could easily be waived.

As he dialed Ed Bradford's number from his car telephone while on the way home, Frank Martinez was far from certain what he should recommend.

APPENDIX A

Franchising

The term *franchise* refers to a contract between two entities, one of whom, the franchisor, has a product or service and a system for setting up and operating a business to sell it. The opportunity to replicate this system and to market the product, with its recognized trademarks, has some economic value for which a prospective franchisee is willing to pay a fee. This fee ordinarily consists of an initial payment plus an ongoing percentage of gross revenues or other fees based on the sale of goods or services to the franchisee. Franchise systems in which the franchisor functions as a supplier, with an independent sales relationship with the franchisee, are referred to as product or trade name franchises. Examples of this type of franchise are automobile sales dealerships or gasoline service stations. Systems in which franchisees gain access to an entire business concept, marketing and operating plans and standards, as well as to continuing assistance from the franchisor, are called business format fran-

[5]Roy Rogers Franchise Agreement, 1987, version, p. 12.

chises. It is this latter type of franchise, of which Roy Rogers is an example, that is expected to contribute most to franchising's growth in the next decades. There is also a third type of franchising, called conversion franchising, in which established businesses become franchise outlets for established companies. The conversion franchisees pay fees to the franchise organization in the form of annual fixed fees and royalties in exchange for advertising support and other services. The Century 21 real estate company is a well-known example of this type of franchise.

Franchise business now accounts for approximately one-third of all retail sales in the United States, more than $590 billion dollars, and is expected to account for half of all retail sales by the year 2000.[6] Although franchising is most prevalent in the fast-food restaurant and lodging businesses, franchises offering such diverse services as housekeeping, automobile maintenance, and videocassette rentals have also emerged and are contributing to franchising's dramatic growth. Franchise businesses are notable for dramatically low failure rates as compared with independent businesses. Approximately 97 percent of the franchises started in a given year are still in operation 12 months later, compared with 62 percent of independent businesses. After 10 years, 90 percent of the franchises remain in operation, as compared with 18 percent of the independent businesses.[7] Because of these impressive results, franchising is often described as a way of capturing many of the advantages of entrepreneurship while minimizing the risks.

In its purest form, franchising involves the purchase of a single-unit operation by an individual who invests his or her personal assets in the franchise and agrees to act as the full-time owner/manager of the facility. In addition to single-unit franchisees, franchisors also may recruit individuals and firms with substantial experience and financial resources who have an interest in developing and operating multiple units in a particular geographical area. A franchisor may also award a master franchise contract, in which he or she sells the right to develop franchises in an entire territory to a middleman, who in turn sells the individual units.

Whatever its structure, the relationship between the franchisor and franchisee is delineated in quite specific terms in the franchise contract, which is negotiated well before a unit opens for business. These agreements typically contain standards for site selection and design, operations, marketing, and sale of the facility. One of the critical factors distinguishing the franchisor-franchisee relationship from that of an employer and employee is the fact that the franchisee is considered the owner of the unit and, therefore, has the right to sell the franchise provided he or she can locate a qualified buyer. Franchise contracts typically allow the franchisor considerable latitude in approving prospective purchasers as well as terminating the franchise contracts of those operators who fail to adhere to the performance standards established for the franchise system, although this latitude is increasingly being restricted by the courts. A summary of the Roy Rogers Franchise Agreement has been included as Appendix B.

Franchise offerings must adhere to regulatory standards established by the Federal Trade Commission and various state governments. Franchisors must provide prospective franchisees with a Uniform Franchise Offering Circular (UFOC), whose purpose is to provide extensive background on the franchisor's management team, the franchise concept and contract, and the financial position of the firm. The regulatory agencies scrutinize the financial data contained in the UFOC to ensure that no guarantees of financial performance are offered. This regulatory oversight came about in response to the fraudulent practices that became public during the franchising boom in the 1960s. Many investors were lured into purchasing franchises that, in fact, were pyramid schemes in which a franchisee's income was generated not by selling a product, but rather by recruiting new franchisees.

APPENDIX B CASEWRITER'S SUMMARY OF THE FRANCHISE AGREEMENT

Franchise Option Agreement

The construction and development of a Roy Rogers facility preceded the signing of the Franchise Agreement and were governed by a sepa-

[6]Howard Reill, "Business Barometer," *Restaurant Business*, March 20, 1988, p. 2.

[7]Ibid.

rate document called the Option Agreement. Following approval of an application, the first-time franchisee paid a $5,000 option fee and submitted a written Site Approval Package that included a basic layout of the facility, aerial photographs, a marked map, a demographic analysis, a financing plan, and three-year cash flow projections. The Real Estate Department at Roy Rogers evaluated each site request and notified the franchisee of whether construction could proceed. Multiple submissions could be required before a site was finally selected.

Roy Rogers supplied the general building plans for each new facility; franchisees were expected to retain local architects who could modify the plans to comply with local building codes. Franchisees were required to submit any such changes for review as well as to provide copies of all required permits. Franchisees independently negotiated to purchase or lease the land on which the facility was to reside.

Once construction was underway, franchisees purchased the necessary equipment and provided Roy Rogers with documentation that the equipment conformed to the company's specifications. Although franchisees were free to purchase the equipment wherever they chose, Roy Rogers made available a list of qualified vendors whose products the company had already inspected.

The Franchise Agreement

The actual Franchise Agreement was typically executed within 30 days of a unit's opening, although technically it could be signed up to 180 days prior to opening. Upon opening the initial franchise fee of $25,000 was paid to the company. Typically, 12 to 18 months elapsed between the approval of a franchisee and the opening of a new facility. The facility approval process was similar for franchisees planning to renovate and convert existing restaurant buildings.

Franchisees were expected to adhere to a strict timetable in opening units for business. Those who fell behind schedule in opening their restaurant could be charged a monthly fee of $3,000 until the unit became operational or, where applicable, until the agreement could be terminated and a replacement located. Both owners and lessees were required to pay the company an ongoing royalty fee of four percent (4 percent) of gross revenues once the unit became operational.

Financing As reflected in Exhibit 5, the total cost of building and equipping a new facility ranged between $976,000 and $1,374,000. Costs were somewhat lower for conversions or leasings. Franchisees were permitted to obtain some outside financing, provided the debt to total capital ratio for the franchise project did not exceed 65 percent.

Advertising and Promotion Franchisees were expected to contribute to regional advertising and promotion campaigns as well as to devote a specific percentage of their gross receipts to local advertising efforts. The franchise agreement specified a minimum monthly contribution of 5 percent of gross sales for regional and local advertising expenditures combined. Of this total expenditure, a minimum of 1 percent of gross revenues were required to be spent on local marketing. The company could increase these spending requirements beyond the contractually established percent-ages only after obtaining the approval of two-thirds of the franchisees. Franchisees conducted local marketing programs independently; however, they were expected to secure Roy Rogers' approval of their annual plans, including any promotional materials to be used.

The regional advertising programs were directed by the Marketing Department at Roy Rogers. In designing these programs, the company was not required to ensure that a particular facility benefited directly from the funds it had contributed. The company also was not required to secure the franchisees' approval of the plans or of any materials to be used.

Roy Rogers contributed a maximum of $7,500 from the regional advertising pool for expenses associated with the Grand Opening of a franchise. Should Roy Rogers, the film star after whom the franchise system was named, attend a Grand Opening or other special event at a restaurant, the franchisee was expected to pay for any expenses associated with his visit.

Opening the Unit Roy Rogers was contractually obligated to make the services of its franchise consultant available to a franchisee opening a new unit. The franchise consultant offered guidance concerning the many tasks involved in opening a new unit and provided training for the franchisee's employees. The franchise consultant was also free to requisition the services of other Roy Rogers personnel whose assistance may be required to ensure a successful opening.

Training The manager and assistant managers of each unit were required to complete the Roy Rogers training program before beginning work. Franchisees were required to absorb the costs of any training programs that the company deemed necessary to address deficiencies in the operation of a unit. They also were required to conduct training on-site for all employees using standard programs developed by Roy Rogers.

Operations Franchisees were expected to adhere to the company's Operating Manual, which described the many performance, quality, and design standards that constituted the Roy Rogers system. Company representatives had the authority to enter the restaurant unit without notice to verify that required procedures were being followed.

The Operating Manual contained standards regarding the cleanliness and maintenance of the equipment and facility. Those who failed to operate the restaurant in a manner required to obtain the highest health classification awarded by local authorities could be required to pay the costs of remedial training for the employees. The Operating Manual specified the days and hours during which each facility was required to operate and the uniforms to be worn by the employees. Franchisees were required to renovate the restaurant building, equipment, and signs at least once every five years to comply with the current image of the system. Furthermore, they were expected to carry out any modifications to the system that the company initiated during the period of the agreement. Signs of the type specified by the company were required to be placed prominently near the unit.

Company specifications concerning the restaurant menu were quite stringent. As part of the Franchise Agreement, the franchisee agreed to serve all of the menu items specified by the company, to follow all specifications regarding the contents, weight, and preparation of the food products, and to sell only products approved by Roy Rogers. The company provided the franchisee with the names of approved suppliers whose products conformed to specifications. Although franchisees were free to purchase supplies from any vendor they chose, they were required to submit new vendors' samples or product specifications for a qualifying evaluation. Sale of alcohol and display of entertainment devices such as video games or slot machines were prohibited unless approved by the company. The agreement also contained a provision that any taxes associated with the operation of the facility were to be paid promptly so the operation of the facility would not be jeopardized.

Financial Reporting Franchisees were required to submit weekly sales reports by telephone and written sales reports to headquarters within 10 days of the end of each calendar month. Monthly written operating statements were expected to follow the preliminary reports within 25 days after the end of each month. A balance sheet and operating statements were submitted at the end of each fiscal year. Roy Rogers could require that these reports be prepared by independent auditors and could visit the franchise without notice to inspect the financial statements and supporting documentation. The Roy Rogers Operating Manual contained detailed specifications for the formats of any reports to be used.

Trademarks The trademarks owned by Roy Rogers included all "words, symbols, insignia, devices, designs, Trade Names, Service Marks, and rights in distinctive designs of buildings and signs" used to identify restaurants licensed to use the system and its products and services.[8] Franchisees were prohibited from using the trademarks, any variations, or any names confusingly similar to the trademarks, in a manner not approved by Roy Rogers. They also were prohibited from taking any steps to claim ownership of the trademarks. Trademarks of other firms could not be used at a Roy Rogers facility without the company's approval.

Noncompete Provision The franchisee and its key employees ordinarily were prohibited from taking part in any food business similar to Roy Rogers, located within a specific mile radius of their unit, for 18 months following the termination of the agreement. (Ownership of less than 1 percent of the stock of a public corporation in a similar business was allowed.) While operating the franchise, they were expected to avoid any outside activities that would prevent them from

[8]ROY ROGERS UNIT FRANCHISE AGREEMENT, Standard Form, October 28, 1987, p. 16.

devoting full-time effort, i.e., 40 hours per week, to the business.

Relationship between Franchisor and Franchisee The franchisee was prohibited from holding itself out as an agent, legal representative, partner, subsidiary, joint venturer, or employee of Roy Rogers. The franchisee had no legal authority to enter into any binding agreements on the company's behalf. No fiduciary relationship existed between the franchisee and the company.

Sale or Transfer of Interest Under the terms of the Franchise Agreement, Roy Rogers had the right to transfer or sell all or some of its rights and obligations as franchisor to another individual or entity. Because the franchisee had been selected for his or her individual business skills, financial resources, and personal character, however, he or she was not allowed to sell, transfer, or mortgage any interest in the franchise without the company's consent. Franchisees who violated this important element of the agreement could have their franchises terminated without notice.

Roy Rogers was permitted to require that a franchisee offer to sell his or her interest to the company before making it available to other interested parties. In addition, franchisees could not offer the unit for sale to another party on more favorable terms than the company received. Franchisees were prohibited from advertising for prospective purchasers unless the company permitted them to do so. Prospective acquirers were expected to undertake the application process described earlier to ensure their fitness to operate the business. Roy Rogers received $3,000 to cover any legal and training expenses associated with the transfer. In addition, the original franchisee remained secondarily liable for all obligations relating to the franchise for a period of 24 months following the sale to the new franchisee.

Franchisees could organize as corporations only under circumstances prescribed by Roy Rogers. Such corporations could not sell any of their shares in a public offering, nor could any shares be transferred without the company's approval. The operating partner of the franchise was required to retain 51 percent of the shares of the corporation holding the franchise. Violation of these requirements constituted grounds for terminating the franchise.

The Franchise Agreement also contained provisions for transferring the franchise in the event of death or permanent incapacity of the franchisee.

Termination of Franchise There were several performance-related reasons for which a franchise could be terminated without notice. Some of the more important were as follows: (1) in the event of bankruptcy or insolvency; and (2) in the event that a plan of liquidation or reorganization was filed, whether or not the plan subsequently was approved by the courts. The franchise agreement specifically noted that the franchise could not be deemed an asset in any reorganization or bankruptcy proceeding.

The franchise could be terminated following a grace period for a number of performance-related reasons as well. Franchisees who failed to perform according to the terms of the agreement were given written notice of their deficiencies. Within the next 30 days, they were required either to resolve the problems cited or to show progress in correcting them. A franchisee could be terminated following written notice if he or she was more than 10 days late in making his or her required royalty or advertising payments to Roy Rogers. Other reasons for which a franchise could be terminated with notice included significant health and safety violations, failure to satisfy a legal judgment within 30 days after it became final, falsification of reports to the company, ceasing to do business at the unit, or loss of possession or lease of the property on which the unit was located. A franchisee who received three or more notices regarding the same or similar deficiencies within a 12-month period could have his or her agreement terminated without notice.

EXHIBIT 1 Marriott Corporation's Balance Sheet, January 1, 1988 and January 2, 1987

	1987	*1986*
ASSETS		
Current assets		
Cash and temporary cash investments	$ 15.6	$ 26.7
Accounts receivable	493.6	450.7
Due from affiliates	125.8	98.2
Inventories, at lower of average cost or market	186.5	171.3
Prepaid expenses	97.6	81.0
Total current assets	$ 919.1	$ 827.9
Property and equipment	469.5	348.3
Building and improvements	323.6	402.9
Leasehold improvements	1,064.9	874.4
Furniture and equipment	680.0	591.8
Construction in progress	690.2	537.3
	$3,228.2	$2,754.7
Accumulated depreciation and amortization	(650.1)	(547.3)
	$2,578.1	$2,207.4
Investments in and advances to affiliates	495.1	484.5
Assets held for sale	501.2	386.4
Intangible assets	528.5	403.2
Other assets	348.5	269.9
	$5,370.5	$4,579.3
LIABILITIES AND SHAREHOLDERS' EQUITY		
Current liabilities		
Accounts payables	$ 508.6	$ 440.8
Accrued payroll and benefits	225.0	211.9
Other payables and accrued liabilities	342.7	331.9
Current portion of long-term debt	46.4	32.9
Total current liabilities	$1,122.7	$1,017.5
Long-term debt	2,498.8	1,662.8
Other long-term liabilities	212.1	193.7
Deferred income	289.5	316.8
Deferred income taxes	436.6	397.5
Shareholders' equity		
Common stock, 147.1 million shares issued	147.1	147.1
Additional paid-in capital	87.7	60.1
Retained earnings	1,150.2	948.9
Treasury stock, at cost, 28.3 and 16.5 million shares, respectively	(574.2)	(165.1)
Total shareholders' equity	$ 810.8	$ 991.0
	$5,370.5	$4,579.3

EXHIBIT 2 Marriott Corporation's Income Statement (Fiscal years ended January 1, 1988, January 2, 1987, and January 3, 1986)

	1987	*1986*	*1985*
	($ in millions, except per share amounts)		
Sales			
Lodging	$2,673.3	$2,233.1	$1,898.4
Contract services	2,969.0	2,236.1	1,586.3
Restaurants	879.9	797.3	757.0
Total sales	$6,522.2	$5,266.5	$4,241.7
Operating expenses			
Lodging	$2,409.4	$2,017.4	$1,712.6
Contract services	2,798.4	2,081.2	1,467.7
Restaurants	797.5	718.2	678.8
Total operating expenses	$6,005.3	$4,816.8	$3,859.1
Operating income			
Lodging	$ 263.9	$ 215.7	$ 185.8
Contract services	170.6	154.9	118.6
Restaurants	82.4	79.1	78.2
Total operating income	$ 516.9	$ 449.7	$ 382.6
Corporate expenses	$ (74.5)	$ (71.7)	$ (54.2)
Interest expense	(90.5)	(60.3)	(75.6)
Interest income	47.0	42.5	42.9
Income before income taxes	$ 398.9	$ 360.2	$ 295.7
Provision for income tax	$ 175.9	$ 168.5	$ 128.3
Net income	$ 223.0	$ 191.7	$ 167.4
Earnings per share	$ 1.67	$ 1.40	$ 1.24

EXHIBIT 3 Fast-Food Restaurant Systems—1986–1987 Systemwide Sales and Units[a]

		1987 Sales				*Units*		
Ranking by Sales	*Chain Name (Parent Company)*	*Systemwide-Sales ($ in millions)*	*Average Unit Volume*	*Company-Owned ($ in millions)*	*Franchise-Owned ($ in millions)*	*Systemwide*	*Company-Owned*	*Franchise-Owned*
1	McDonald's	$14,300	$1,433,000	4,800	9.500	9.911	3,151	6,760
2	Burger King (Pillsbury Co., Inc.)	5,179[b]	1,092,000[b]	794[b]	4,385[b]	5,179	794	4,385
3	Kentucky Fried Chicken (PepsiCo., Inc.)	4,100	659,000	1,036[b]	3,064[b]	7,522	1,901	5,621
4	Hardee (Imasco, Ltd.)	3,100	878,000[b]	1,400	1,700	2,912	963	1,949
5	Pizza Hut (PepsiCo., Inc.)	3,000	500,000	1,400	1,600	6,163	2,863	3,300
6	Wendy's	2,817[b]	767,000[b]	992[b]	1,825[b]	3,848	1,259	2,589
7	Domino's Pizza	1,906	483,000[b]	513[b]	1,393[b]	4,279	1,109	3,170
8	Taco Bell (PepsiCo., Inc.)	1,502[b]	560,000[b]	825[b]	677[b]	2,682	1,473	1,209
9	Arby's (Royal Crown Cola, Inc.)	1,000	541,000[b]	109[b]	891[b]	1,848	202	1,646
10	Dunkin' Donuts	729	437,000[b]	12[b]	717[b]	1,669	29	1,640
11	Little Ceasar's	725	464,000[b]	176[b]	549[b]	1,820	441	1,379
12	Jack in the Box (Foodmaster, Inc.)	655	750,000[b]	512	143	897	639	258
13	Roy Rogers (Marriott Corp.)	568[b]	1,000,000[b]	328[b]	240[b]	583	344	239
14	Church's	580[b]	390,000[b]	418[b]	162[b]	1,486	1,072	414
15	Popeyes (A. Copeland Interests)	460	663,000[b]	80	380	730	112	618

Source: Adapted from "Restaurant Franchising in the Economy," *Restaurant Business,* March 20, 1988, p. 194.
[a]Data include international operations.
[b]Estimated by *Restaurant Business Magazine.*

EXHIBIT 4 Organization Chart

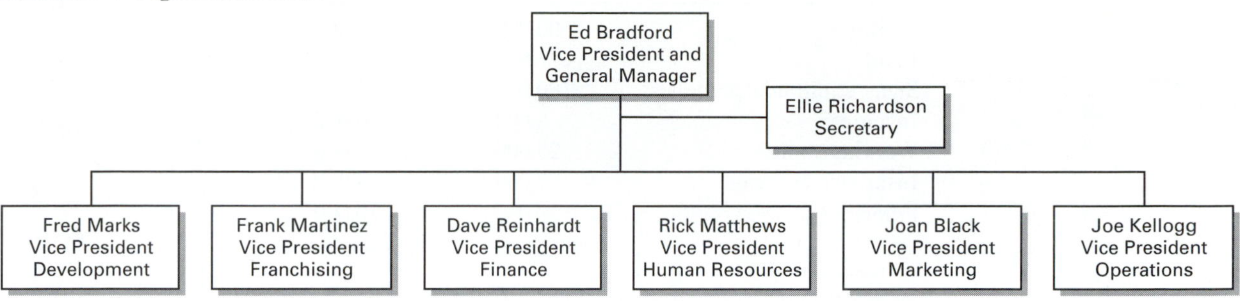

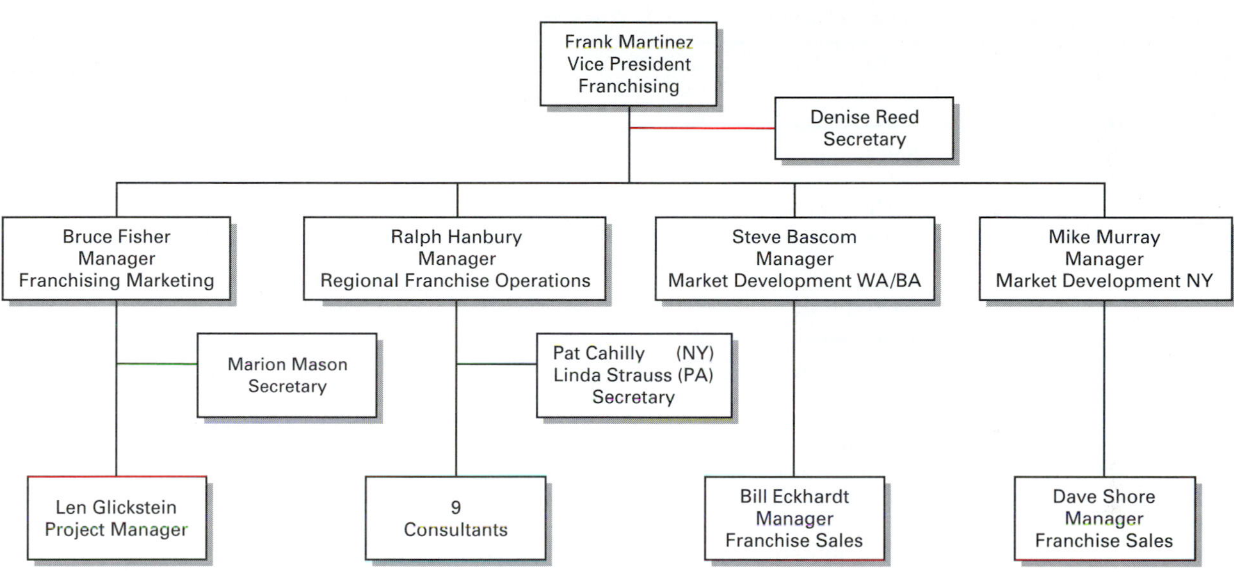

EXHIBIT 5 Cost Structure of a Franchise Unit

Capital Investment	*Estimated Cost Range*	
Facility	$500,000	$ 550,000
Land	225,000	500,000
Signs, equipment, supplies	180,000	230,000
Inventory	8,000	10,000
Working capital	25,000	40,000
Insurance coverage	8,000	14,000
Franchise fee and option	30,000	30,000
	$976,000	$1,374,000

Source: Roy Rogers, *Uniform Franchise Offering Circular,* 1987 version, p. 26.

EXHIBIT 6 Income Statement for a Typical Franchise (Leased Facility)

	Amount	*Percentage Total Sales*
Sales		
Gross sales	$1,050,000	99%
Discount/employee sales	6,300	1
Total sales	$1,056,300	100%
Cost of goods (food purchase)	311,500	29
Gross profit	$ 744,800	71%
Expenses		
Salaries and benefits	267,000	25
Rent	97,600	9
Paper supplies	46,400	5
Utilities	41,100	4
Interest expense	29,300	3
Equipment depreciation expense	24,100	2
Promotions	17,800	2
Maintenance	15,000	1
Real estate tax	4,600	
Training	4,200	
General expenses	2,200	
Trash removal	1,900	
Cleaning supplies	1,800	
Cash register contract	1,500	2
Amortization of franchise fee	1,250	
Window cleaning	1,200	
Uniforms	1,000	
Bookkeeping	800	
Office supplies	800	
Dining room plants	500	
Roy Rogers' name fee	300	
Exterminator	200	
	$ 560,850	53%
Royalties/Other Fees		
Royalties	42,000	4
National advertising	42,000	4
Total Royalties/Other fees	$ 84,000	8%
Profit before Tax	99,950	10
Income tax	49,975	5
Net income	$ 49,975	5

CHAPTER 4

Personnel and Cultural Controls

Some organizations are able to effect good control without relying much on either action or results controls. Instead, they take steps to ensure that employees will control their own behaviors or that the employees will control each others' behaviors. When they do so, these managers are using what is called *personnel* or *cultural controls.*[1]

Personnel and cultural controls are a part of virtually every management control system (MCS). Action and results control systems usually cannot be made perfect, or are prohibitively expensive to make perfect. The personnel and cultural controls help fill in the gaps. In some MCS, however, personnel and cultural controls are so important they are the dominant form of control.

PERSONNEL CONTROLS

Personnel controls help employees do a good job. They build on employees' natural tendencies to control themselves.

Personnel controls serve any of three basic purposes. First, some of them clarify expectations. They help ensure that each employee understands what the organization wants. Second, some of them help ensure that each employee is able to do a good job; that they have all the capabilities (for example, experience and intelligence) and resources (for example, information and time) needed to do a good job. And third, some of them increase the likelihood that each employee will engage in *self-monitoring.* Self-monitoring is the naturally present force that pushes most people to want to do a good job, to be naturally committed to the organization's goals. Self-monitoring is effective because most people have a conscience that leads them to do what is right and are able to derive positive feelings of self-respect and self-satisfaction when they do a good job and see their organization succeed. The phenomena underlying self-monitoring have been discussed in the management literatures under a variety of labels, including *self-control, intrinsic motivation, ethics and morality, trust and atmosphere,* and *loyalty.*

John McConnell, the chairman of Columbus, Ohio-based Worthington Industries, a superior performer in the steel processing industry, said, "You have to trust the work force. If you don't, you've done a bad job."[2] Trust can be defined as "an expectancy held by an individual or a group that the word, promise, verbal or written statement of another individual or group can be relied upon.[3] Trust is a substitute for other, more formal forms of control such as time clocks or plant supervisors.

Three major methods of implementing personnel controls are through (1) selection and placement of employees, (2) training, and (3) job design and provision of necessary resources.

Selection and Placement

Finding the right people to do a particular job and giving them both a good work environment and the necessary resources can obviously increase the probability that a job will be done properly. Firms devote considerable time and effort to selection and placement, and a huge literature has been built up to describe how these tasks should best be accomplished. Much of this literature describes possible predictors of success, such as education, experience, past successes, personality, and social skills. More exotic techniques have also been developed and used, as some firms have resorted to analyzing potential employees' handwriting or using polygraph tests to try to weed out high-risk individuals.

Whatever techniques are used, selection and placement are sometimes the single most important elements in firms' control systems. Sam Walton, the founder of the highly successful retailer Wal-Mart, attributed much of his company's prosperity to the company's success in selecting its people:

> Our philosophy is that management's role is simply to get the right people in the right places to do a job and then to encourage them to use their own inventiveness to accomplish the task at hand.[4]

Training

Training is another common way to help ensure that employees do a good job. Training can provide useful information about what results or actions are expected and how the assigned tasks can best be performed. It can also have positive motivational effects because employees can be given a greater sense of professionalism, and they are often more interested in performing well in jobs they understand better.

Many organizations use formal training programs, such as in classroom settings, to improve the skills of their personnel. The Los Angeles Unified School District wanted to decentralize and give school principals much more decision-making authority. District managers concluded, however, that the principals would not know how to use their increased authority. They decided to put the principals through a formal mini-MBA program to teach them how to improve the educational process and manage school costs. The principals attended classes over an eighteen-month period and follow-up workshops. The program was judged so successful that it has expanded to the San Francisco Bay area and the East Coast.[5]

Much training takes place informally, such as through employee mentoring. Jerry Reinsdorf, a successful entrepreneur and chairman of the Chicago White Sox baseball club, noted the importance of his role as a mentor:

> My management style is to hire good people and develop a relationship with them so that 95% of the time they'll know what decision I'd make and go ahead without asking me.[6]

His control system could be described as being dominated by selection and training.

Job Design and Provision of Necessary Resources

Another way to help individual employees act appropriately is simply to make sure that the job is designed to allow motivated and qualified employees a high probability of success. Some companies do not give all their employees a chance to succeed. Some jobs are too complex. Salespeople may be assigned too many accounts to handle effectively. Also, employees often need a particular set of resources available to them in order to do a good job. The list of resources needed is highly job specific, but it can include such items as information, equipment, supplies, staff support, decision aids, or freedom from interruption. In larger organizations, particularly, there is a strong need for much transfer of information among organizational entities so that the coordination of effort is maintained.

CULTURAL CONTROLS

Cultural controls are designed to encourage *mutual-monitoring,* an often powerful social pressure exerted by groups on individuals within the groups who deviate from the groups' norms and values. Cultural controls can both encourage good behaviors (for example, ensuring that all employees report to work on time) and discourage harmful behaviors (for example, drinking on duty).

Cultural controls are most effective when members of a group have emotional ties to one another. In some collectivist cultures, such as Japan, incentives to avoid anything that would disgrace oneself and one's family are paramount. Similarly, in many communities, such as the Hasidic Jewish community in New York City, and in many countries, notably those in Southeast Asia, many business deals are sealed by verbal agreement only. The communities' social and moral pressures are stronger than legal contracts.

However, strong cultural controls produced by mutual-monitoring processes also exist within single organizations. The pressures can be created among co-workers where nonconformers are often pressured to accept group norms. Powerful social pressures can also be created in a bottom-up direction, as superiors often feel pressure to fulfill subordinates' expectations of their role.

Cultures are built on shared traditions, norms, beliefs, values, ideologies, attitudes, and ways of behaving.[7] Organizations' cultures remain relatively fixed over time, even while their strategies, tactics, and goals necessarily adapt to changing business conditions.[8] The cultural norms are embodied in written and unwritten rules that govern employees' behaviors. To understand an organization's culture, ask long-time employees questions like: What does it take to get ahead here? How do you stay out of trouble? If a strong organizational culture exists, the vast majority of long-time employees will have consistent answers to these questions even when the answers are not written down.

At their best, strong organizational cultures cause employees to work together in an energetic, well-coordinated fashion. One author suggested that the social control forces generated by strong cultures might even be considered one of the common elements of successful organizations:

> To create an institution we rely on many techniques for infusing day-to-day behavior with long-run meaning and purpose. One of the most important of these techniques is . . . to state . . . what is distinctive about the aims and methods of the enterprise. Successful institutions are usually able to fill in the formula, "What we are proud of around here is . . ."[9]

Managers attempt to create and shape organizational cultures in many ways, both in words and by example. Five important methods of shaping culture, and thus effecting cultural controls, are (1) codes of conduct, (2) group-based rewards, (3) intraorganizational transfers, (4) physical and social arrangements, and (5) tone at the top.

Codes of Conduct

Most larger companies attempt to shape their culture through what are known, variously, as codes of conduct, codes of ethics, corporate credos, or statements of mission, vision, or management philosophy.[10] These formal, written documents provide broad, general statements of corporate values, commitments to stakeholders, and the ways in which top management would like the organization to function. Each of these codes or statements is designed to help employees understand what behaviors are expected even in the absence of a specific rule or principle. These statements may include important messages about dedication to quality or customer satisfaction, fair treatment of staff and suppliers, employee safety, innovation, risk taking, adherence to strict ethical principles, open communications, a minimum of bureaucracy, and willingness to change. For maximum effect, the messages included in these statements should be reinforced through formal training sessions, or at least through some discussions among employees and their superiors.

The various codes and statements differ considerably in form. Figure 4-1 shows what United Technologies Corporation calls its *Corporate Principles.* On this page, the corporation has identified its most important stakeholders; customers, employees, suppliers, shareowners, competitors, and communities, and has made important statements about the corporation's felt commitments and responsibilities to each of them.

Figure 4-2 shows the Code of Conduct used at the Provident Mutual Organization, which includes a general policy and guidance on specific issues. Provident's general policy statement is aimed at influencing the organization's culture, but the code goes on to provide behavioral guidance on specific issues. The detailed behavioral prescriptions provide action-accountability control because employees who violate these prescriptions will be punished.

One survey of 264 companies (70 percent from the United States, and the rest from Europe, Canada, and Mexico) found that 84 percent of the U.S. respondents and 58 percent of the non-U.S. respondents, have a code of conduct.[11] The codes are drafted, most commonly, by top management, the corporate legal department, and to a lesser extent, the board of directors. This survey shows that where codes exist, the vast majority of them define "fundamental guiding principles of the company." The only specific issues cited by 50 percent or more of the companies deal with purchasing guidelines (56 percent) and security of proprietary information (53 percent). Other statements commonly included relate to environmental, marketing, product safety, workplace safety, and confidentiality of employee records responsibilities. The survey also found that the codes are dynamic documents; 59 percent had been changed within the three years prior to the survey. The most frequent reasons for change are specific incidents, either

FIGURE 4-1. Corporate Principles of United Technologies Corporation

United Technologies is committed to the highest standards of ethics and business conduct. This encompasses our relationships with our customers, our suppliers, our shareholders, our competitors, the communities in which we operate, and with each other as employees at every organizational level. These commitments and the responsibilities they entail are summarized here.

Our Customers	**Our Employees**	**Our Suppliers**
Our primary responsibility is to those who use our products and services. We are committed to providing high quality and value, fair prices and honest transactions. We will deal both lawfully and ethically with all our customers.	We are committed to treating one another fairly, and to maintaining employment practices based on equal opportunity for all employees. We will respect each other's privacy and treat each other with dignity and respect irrespective of age, race, color, sex, religion, or nationality. We are committed to providing safe and healthy working conditions and an atmosphere of open communication for all our employees.	We are committed to dealing fairly with our suppliers. We will emphasize fair competition, without discrimination or deception, in a manner consistent with long-lasting business relationships.
Our Shareowners	**Our Competitors**	**Our Communities**
We are committed to providing a superior return to our shareowners, and to protecting and improving the value of their investment through the prudent utilization of corporate resources and by observing the highest standards of legal and ethical conduct in all our business dealings.	We are committed to competing vigorously and fairly for business, and to basing our efforts solely on the merits of our competitive offerings.	We are committed to being a responsible corporate citizen of the worldwide communities in which we reside. We will abide by all national and local laws, and we will strive to improve the well-being of our communities through the encouragement of employee participation in civic affairs and through corporate philanthropy.

within the company or the industry, that need to be addressed; a new CEO, new laws, or a change in business mix.

Most companies find the adoption of codes stimulates discussion as to what constitutes desirable behavior and forces development of a consensus. The adoption of written codes also enhances communication of expectations and the reasons for the expectations. One research study found that pressure to achieve specific financial targets was greatest in companies with formal code of conduct, perhaps indicating that performance pressures create one need for the codes.[12]

Do codes of conduct work? The evidence is equivocal. On the positive side, one survey found that employees who work for companies with codes of ethics were much more likely to rate the commitment to ethical conduct by others in their company as "about right." They were also as much as 88 percent more likely

FIGURE 4-2. Code of Conduct of the Provident Mutual Organization

General Policy
The Provident Mutual organization is committed to achieving high standards of business and personal ethics for itself and its personnel. Through performance in accordance with these standards, the Organization and all its employees will merit and enjoy the respect of the public, the business community, policyholders, customers, and regulatory authorities.

It is the personal responsibility of all employees to acquaint themselves with the legal and policy standards and restrictions applicable to their assigned duties and responsibilities, and to conduct themselves accordingly. Over and above the strictly legal aspects involved, all company personnel are expected to observe high standards of business and personal ethics in the discharge of their assigned responsibilities.

Employee Conduct
Each member of the Organization must avoid any action, relationship or situation which could jeopardize or impair the confidence or respect in which the Organization is held by its customers and the general public, or which appears to be contrary to the interests of Provident Mutual or its policyholders.

Employees shall comply fully with all applicable statutes and regulations. Willful and knowing disregard of the law may result in severe penalties to the Organization. In its many business activities, Provident Mutual and its affiliated companies engage in vigorous, fair and ethical competition. Discussions and agreements with competitors concerning pricing or other competitive policies and practices are strictly prohibited.

Conflict of Interest
Provident Mutual annually circulates a policy statement of Conflicts of Interest. The basic policy states that every employee must avoid any interest that conflicts with the interests of Provident Mutual. The document provides detailed examples and explanations of situations and types of transactions which can give rise to conflicts of interest. In order to implement the conflict of interest policy of Provident Mutual, all officers and other affected persons are required to submit annually a completed disclosure statement to the Chairman and Chief Executive Officer of Provident Mutual. Each affiliated company has a similar requirement.

Gifts to or by Employees
Employees may not give or receive anything of more than token value to or from any individual or organization with whom Provident Mutual or its affiliates does business, or who is seeking to do business with Provident Mutual or its affiliates. "Token" is defined as having a value of $50 or less.

Certain business courtesies, such as payment for a lunch or dinner in connection with a business meeting, normally would not be a gift within the context of this policy. However, such activity shall be limited in frequency. Employees shall endeavor to avoid any situation where a gift or activity might appear to influence business judgment or relationships. Any question as to whether a gift might appear to be improper or questionable shall be addressed in writing, with a statement of all relevant facts, to the office of the General Counsel.

Political Contributions
No funds or assets of the Company shall be used for federal, state or local political campaign contributions. These prohibitions cover not only direct contributions but also indirect assistance or support of candidates or political parties through purchase of tickets to special dinners or other fund raising events or the furnishing of any other goods, services or equipment to political parties or committees.

No funds or assets of the Company shall be used directly or indirectly for political contributions outside the United States, even where permitted by applicable law, without the prior written approval of the Chief Executive Officer or General Counsel.

The above prohibitions apply only to the direct or indirect use of corporate funds or assets for political purposes and are, of course, not intended to discourage employees from making personal contributions to the candidates, parties or committees of their choice, through the Company's Political Action Committee. Under no circumstances shall employees be reimbursed in any way for personal contributions.

Confidential Information and Insider Trading
Employees frequently have access to confidential information concerning the Organization's business and the businesses of present and prospective customers, policyholders and other employees. Safeguarding confidential information is essential to the conduct of our business. Caution and discretion must be exercised in the use of such information, which should be shared only with those who have a clear and legitimate need and right to know.

FIGURE 4-2. Code of Conduct of the Provident Mutual Organization *Continued*

No employee shall disclose confidential information of any type, to anyone, except persons within the employee's company who need to know. Information regarding a customer may not be released to third parties, government, or other organizations, without the consent of the customer unless required by law.

Any requests for information arising through a legal process (e.g., subpoena or court order) must first be referred to the office of the General Counsel before the release of information and before the client is contacted.

Selling or acquiring stocks, securities or other investments, on the basis of non public information is prohibited. Securities include stocks, bonds, notes, debentures, or any other interests, instruments, documents or rights which represent securities. Questions concerning the definition of non public information or a security shall be referred to the office of the General Counsel before any transactions are undertaken.

Service and Customer Concerns

The foundation of the Organization is to provide high quality service to our existing and prospective customers. Each company endeavors to give prompt, courteous and accurate response to inquiries and complaints received from customers. When appropriate adjustments are warranted, employees will make them promptly and courteously. Equally important, we seek to add or improve policies, procedures and products that contribute to customer satisfaction.

Integrity of Records and Compliance with Accounting Procedures

Accuracy and reliability in the preparation of all business records is mandated by law. It is of critical importance to the corporate decision-making process and to the proper discharge of Provident Mutual's financial, legal and reporting obligations. All business records, expense accounts, vouchers, bills, payroll and service records and other reports are to be prepared with care and honesty. False or misleading entries are not permitted in the books and records of Provident Mutual or any affiliated company. All corporate funds and assets are to be recorded in accordance with applicable corporate procedures. Compliance with accounting procedures and internal control procedures is required at all times. It is the responsibility of all employees to ensure that both the letter and the spirit of corporate accounting and internal control procedures are strictly adhered to at all times. They should advise the responsible person in their department of any shortcomings they observe in such procedures.

Administration of the Code

Employees are encouraged to seek guidance regarding application or interpretation of this Code of Conduct and are expected to cooperate fully in any investigation of a potential violation. The statements set forth in this Code of Conduct are intended as guidelines for employees. Routine questions of interpretation regarding the Code shall be directed to the employee's supervisory officer, and if necessary, referred to the office of the General Counsel. If any employee believes the code may have been violated, the matter shall promptly be reported to the Director of Internal Audit. Violations of the Code of Conduct may be disciplined by the Organization, up to and including dismissal. However, the Code of Conduct does not set forth all of the reasons or situations in which employees may be disciplined.

The Code of Conduct is not an employment contract, and the Organization may at any time modify the provisions of this Code of Conduct as it deems appropriate.

to rate their company's fulfillment of its ethical obligations as exceptional.[13] However, one research study which compared 202 manufacturing companies with codes of conduct with 104 companies without codes found that the companies with codes in place were just as likely to be convicted of illegal acts as those without them.[14] Most managers in companies without formal codes believe that codes of conduct are unnecessary, that they only duplicate the practices, policies, and corporate value systems already in place.

Some codes of conduct fail because they are not supported by strong leadership and proper "tone from the top." Top management does not always appear committed to them. A recent study found that one-fourth of the corporate codes of conduct studied were *dormant,* meaning that employees perceived the codes as simply public relations and not something to be taken seriously.[15]

Group-Based Rewards

Providing rewards based on collective achievement also encourages cultural control. Reward plan based on collective achievement come in many forms. Common examples are bonus, profit-sharing, or gain-sharing plans which provide compensation based on corporate or division performance, in terms of growth, profits, or accounting returns. Encouraging broad employee ownership of company stock also helps ensure that all employees share in the company's success, and it encourages employees to think like owners.

Group-based reward plans are discussed here as a type of cultural control rather than as a results control because they are quite different in character from rewards given for individual accomplishment. With group rewards, the link between individual efforts and the results being rewarded is weak, perhaps even zero. Thus, motivation to achieve the rewards is not among primary forces effected by group rewards; communication of expectations and mutual-monitoring (social control) are. As more than one employee has remarked after being told bonuses would now be based on the performance of a large group, "That sounds like socialism." Group-based rewards are like socialism; however, they can work, even in countries like the United States with a culture oriented towards individualism and personal accountability. Managers know their group-based rewards are working (inducing the desired mutual monitoring) when they hear hardworking employees urging on their lazy colleagues with statements like, "You're hurting my profit sharing."

Most managers understand quite clearly the difference between results controls and cultural controls. Graham Sterling, former vice-president of strategic planning at Analog Devices, observed that a primary purpose of his company's incentive plan, which is based on collective (either corporate or division) performance, was based on this approach:

> I do not like to refer to the plans as incentive plans. I visualize them as plans for communicating some important facts of life. . . . The bonus plans help deliver [these facts] and enable us to share the fruits of whatever success we accomplish as a total organization.[16]

Even though the link between individual performance and rewards is weak, typically near zero, evidence suggests that group-based rewards have a positive effect on motivation and performance.[17] At steelmaker Nucor, group incentives used in production areas encourage teamwork, which is reflected in on-the-job training of new workers by more experienced ones, and the creation of peer pressure on individual workers to exert themselves for the good of the group.[18]

Panhandle Eastern Corporation, a natural gas company, installed a gain-sharing plan which calls for all employees to receive a 2 percent bonus if the company earns $2 per share and a 3 percent bonus if the earnings are $3 per share.[19] It has created a cost-cutting culture that pervades the organization. A *Business Week* article concluded that the plan has turned "employees from top to bottom . . . into cost-cutting vigilantes."[20]

C. Michael Armstrong, the new chairman of Hughes Electronics Corporation, used group incentives to change the company's culture. Before Armstrong, Hughes' culture was a regimented, top-heavy hierarchy

> that mirrored its military clients. Managers had little accountability. And the engineers' culture rewarded those who came up with the most sophisticated inventions—whether or not the market wanted them.[21]

To change the culture, Armstrong instituted a new bonus program for all employees with payments based on the profits of the employee's business unit. He insists that managers achieve their planning targets. As Jack Shaw, the manager of Hughes' Network Systems put it, "Mike is not tolerant of not doing what you say you're going to do."[22] He required that engineers attend finance classes and he opened the company's books for all employees to see the results of their efforts. Steven Dorfman, president of Hughes' satellite unit said, "Now, everyone [is] walking the floors talking about return-on-net assets."[23]

Group-based rewards essentially delegate the monitoring of employees' activities to employees' co-workers. This is the essence of mutual-monitoring. The use of group, rather than individual, incentives also reduces measurement costs because each individual's unique contribution to overall performance does not have to be measured.

Other evidence of the success of group-based rewards comes from the literature that describes companies' experiences with a program known as *open-book management* (OBM), an important dimension of which includes group-based rewards. The goal of an OBM program is to create both a clear line of sight between each employee's actions and the corporate financial results and an incentive for the employees both to behave in the corporation's best interest and to make useful suggestions for improvement. OBM programs involve: (1) regular sharing of the company's financial information and any other information that will help the employees work together with management to help the organization's success, (2) training, so that employees understand both what that information means and how they can contribute to company profits, (3) rewards linked to company performance, and (4) if necessary, a cultural change away from a top-down culture to ensure that employee ideas are both encouraged and considered fairly. Most commonly, OBM incentives involves tying a portion of each employee's pay to key corporate financial indicators, usually in the form of an employee stock ownership plan (ESOP) or a profit-sharing plan.

The earliest program given the OBM label was that implemented at the Springfield Remanufacturing Company in the early 1980s.[24] This program was credited with turning around a near-failing company. The idea has spread and the business literature now contains a number of examples explaining how OBM programs have yielded significant improvements in productivity and profits.[25]

Intraorganizational Transfers

Another option is to transmit culture through a policy of intraorganizational transfers. Transfers tend to improve the socialization of the individuals in an organization and thereby inhibit the formation of incompatible goals and perspectives. One study of transfers of executives among divisions of multinational firms found that the transfers increased the executives' organizational (as opposed to subunit) identification and gave them a better appreciation of the problems faced by different parts of the organization.[26]

One of the keys to the success of Japanese firms seems to be their policy of moving managers frequently among functions and divisions to give the managers a better understanding of the organization as a whole.[27] This approach stands in sharp contrast to the transfer policies of most U.S. firms, where managers tend to stay primarily in a single function or single division, sometimes for an entire career.

Physical and Social Arrangements

Physical arrangements, such as office plans, architecture, and interior decor, and social arrangements, such as dress codes and vocabulary, can also shape organizational culture. Some organizations, such as technology firms in the Silicon Valley, have created informal cultures, with open office arrangements and casual dress codes, that deliver messages about the importance of innovation and employee equality.

At Disneyland, employees are called *cast members;* being on the job is being *onstage* (off the job is *offstage*); a work shift is a *performance;* and a job description is a *script.* This vocabulary, which is imparted immediately on joining the company and is reinforced through training, separates Disney employees from the rest of the world, bringing them closer together, and reminding them that they are performers whose job is to help fulfill the company's mission: to make people happy.

The largest Japanese firms find it easier to maintain a strong culture because they tend to retain their employees for long periods of time, usually a lifetime. This stability in the employee base increases the homogeneity of perspectives in the organization. The employees become socialized to their organization's values and their "way of doing things."

Tone at the Top

Finally, corporate managers can shape culture by setting the proper *tone at the top.* Their statements should be consistent with the type of culture they are trying to create and, importantly, their behaviors should be consistent with their statements. Like it or not, managers serve as role models. They cannot say one thing and do another.

TABLE 4-1 Control Problems Addressed by the Various Ways of Effecting Personnel and Cultural Controls

	Lack of Direction	*Motivational Problems*	*Personal Limitations*
Ways of Effecting Personnel Controls			
Selection and placement	x	x	x
Training	x		x
Job design and provision of necessary resources			x
Ways of Effecting Cultural Controls			
Codes of conduct	x		x
Group-based rewards	x	x	x
Intraorganizational transfers	x		x
Physical arrangements	x		
Tone at the top	x		

PERSONNEL/CULTURAL CONTROLS AND CONTROL PROBLEMS

As a group, the personnel/cultural controls are capable of addressing all of the control problems, although, as shown in Table 4-1, not each type of control is useful in addressing each type of problem. The lack-if-direction problem can be minimized by hiring only experienced personnel, by providing training programs, or by assigning new personnel to work groups that will provide good direction. The motivational problems, which may be minimal in firms with strong, beneficial cultures, can be minimized in other organizations by hiring highly motivated people or by assigning people to work groups that will tend to make them adjust to group norms. Personal limitations can also be reduced through one or more types of personnel controls; particularly selection, training, and provision of necessary resources.

EFFECTIVENESS OF PERSONNEL/ CULTURAL CONTROLS

Personnel/cultural controls are adaptable. All managers rely to some extent on their employees' guiding and motivating themselves. Even in prisons, with administrators facing general inmate hostility and, seemingly, few control options available other than physical constraints, administrators screen inmates so as not to assign dangerous personnel to high-risk jobs, such as in a machine shop.

Some corporate control systems are dominated by personnel controls. William F. Cronk, president of Dreyer's Grand Ice Cream, said, "We consider hiring the most important decision we can make. We hire the smartest, most inspired people we can find, give them the resources they need, then get out of their way."[28]

Cultural controls can also, by themselves, dominate a control system. The best chance to create a good, reliably strong culture seems to be early in an organization's life when a founder can imbue the organization with a distinctive culture.[29] To some extent, however, strong leaders and management policies added later in an organization's history can also have an impact, particularly if the organization faces a crisis, or the leader creates the impression of an impending crisis. Regardless of the difficulty in implementing them, cultural controls should serve some positive purpose in every organization. In fact, one of the distinguishing traits of strong, effective leaders is that they transmit their values throughout the organization.

Cultural controls often have the advantage of being relatively unobtrusive. The limits of acceptable behaviors may be prescribed in terms as simple as "the way we do things around here."[30] The people whose actions are being controlled may not even think of the shared norms as being part of the organizational control system, but it is clear that organizational cultures (that is, shared values) can substitute for other more formal types of controls. Consultants authors Peters and Waterman observed that "the stronger the culture . . . the less need there is for policy manuals, organization charts, or detailed procedures and rules."[31]

The degree to which personnel/cultural controls are effective can vary significantly across individuals, groups, and societies. Some people are most honest than others, and some groups and societies have stronger emotional ties among their members. In addition, some types of personnel/cultural controls may not be usable in some settings. The exactly "right" person for a job may not be available, and the available people may not be easily trainable.

CONCLUSION

This chapter has described a third major category of control alternatives, personnel/cultural controls. Managers implement personnel/cultural controls by encouraging either or both of two positive forces which are normally present in the organization: self- and mutual-monitoring. These forces can be encouraged in a number of ways, including effective personnel selection and placement, training, job design and provision of necessary resources, codes of conduct, group-based rewards, intraorganizational transfers, physical and social arrangements, and tone at the top.

Personnel and cultural controls, which are sometimes referred to as *soft* controls, have become more important in the 1990s. Organizations have become flatter and leaner. Supervisors have wider spans of control and elaborate hierarchies and systems of action controls (bureaucracies) have been dismantled and replaced with empowered lower-level workers. In this environment, shared organizational values have become a more important tool for ensuring that everyone is acting in the organization's best interest.[32]

Personnel/cultural controls have several important advantages over results and action controls. They are usable to some extent in almost every setting, their cost is often lower than more obtrusive forms of controls, and they usually produce fewer harmful side effects.

Notes

1. Control systems dominated by personnel and cultural controls have been called organic (as opposed to mechanistic) by Burns and Stalker, and a professional bureaucracy (as opposed to a machine bureaucracy) by Mintzberg. T. Burns and G. M. Stalker, *The Management of Innovation* (London: Tavistock, 1961). H. Mintzberg, *The Structuring of Organizations* (Englewood Cliffs, N.J.: Prentice-Hall, 1979).
2. H. Rudnitsky, "'You Have to Trust the Work Force,'" *Forbes* (July 19, 1993), p. 78.
3. J. B. Rotter, "A New Scale for the Measurement of Interpersonal Trust," *Journal of Personality,* 35, no. 4 (1967), p. 651.
4. "Wal-Mart: The Model Discounter," *Dun's Business Month* (December 1982), p. 60.
5. R. Wartzman, "School Inc.: Principals Taught to Act Like CEOs," *Wall Street Journal* (October 16, 1996), p. CA1.
6. "Jerry Reinsdorf Pulls a Double Play in Chicago," *Business Week* (October 10, 1983). p. 53.
7. An extensive literature exists on the benefits and methods of shaping corporate culture. See R. M. Kilmann, *Managing Beyond the Quick Fix* (San Francisco: Jossey-Bass, 1989); R. H. Kilmann and M. J. Saxton (eds.), *Gaining Control of the Corporate Culture* (San Francisco: Jossey-Bass, 1985); E. H. Schein, *Organizational Culture and Leadership: A Dynamic View* (San Francisco: Jossey-Bass, 1985); and R. E. Walton, "Toward a Strategy of Eliciting Employee Commitment Based on Policies of Mutuality, in *HRM Trends and Challenges* R. E. Walton and P. R. Lawrence (eds.) (Harvard Business School Press, 1985), pp. 35–65.
8. J. C. Collins and J. I. Porras, *Built to Last: Successful Habits of Visionary Companies* (New York: Harper Business, 1994).
9. P. Selznick, *Leadership in Administration: A Sociological Interpretation* (New York: Row, Peterson, 1957).
10. The Conference Board, *Corporate Ethics Practices* (New York: The Conference Board, Inc., 1992).
11. The Conference Board, 1992.
12. A. J. Rich, C. S. Smith, and P. H. Mihalek, "Are Corporate Codes of Conduct Effective?" *Management Accounting* (1990), pp. 34–35.

13. "Employees Say It's Hard to be Ethical in Some Organizations," *Internal Auditor* (February 1995), p. 9.
14. See R. Berenbeim, "An Outbreak of Ethics," *Across the Board* (May 1988), pp. 15–19.
15. S. Landekich, *Corporate Codes of Conduct: An Examination and Implementation Guide* (Montvale, N.J.: National Association of Accountants, 1989).
16. K. A. Merchant, "Analog Devices, Inc. (A)" case no. 9-181-001 (Boston: HBS Case Services, 1980).
17. D. L. Kruse, "Profit Sharing and Productivity: Microeconomic Evidence from the United States," *The Economic Journal* (January 1992), pp. 24–36.
18. P. Ghemawat, "Competitive Advantage and Internal Organization: A Case Study," unpublished working paper, (Harvard Business School, June 1993).
19. E. Nelson, "Gas Company's Gain-Sharing Plan Turns Employees into Cost-Cutting Vigilantes," *Wall Street Journal* (September 29, 1995), p. B1.
20. Ibid.
21. E. Schine, L. Armstrong, and K. Kerwin, "Liftoff: Michael Armstrong Has Made Hughes an Electronics and Telecom Contender," *Business Week* (April 22, 1996), p. 142.
22. Ibid.
23. Ibid.
24. J. Stack, *The Great Game of Business* (New York: Doubleday, 1992).
25. See C. Lee, "Open Book Management," *Training* (July 1994), pp. 66–80; J. Fierman, "Winning Ideas from Maverick Managers," *Fortune* (February 6, 1995), pp. 21–27; J. Case, *Open-Book Management: The Coming Business Revolution* (Harper, 1995); A. Adelson, "Casual, Worker-Friendly, and a Moneymaker, Too," *The New York Times* (June 30, 1996), p. F8; and J. P. Schuster, J. Carpenter, and M. P. Kane, *The Power of Open-Book Management* (New York: John Wiley, 1996).
26. A. Edstrom and J. R. Galbraith, "Transfer of Managers as a Coordination and Control Strategy in Multinational Organizations," *Administrative Science Quarterly,* 22 (June 1977), pp. 248–63.
27. See W. G. Ouchi and A. M. Jaeger, "Type Z Organization: Stability in the Midst of Mobility," *Academy of Management Review* 3, no 2 (April 1978), pp. 305–14.
28. Quoted in D. Ferguson, "Do Entrepreneurial Companies Lose Their Innovative Spark as They Grow Larger?" *Cal Business* (Fall 1995), p. 12.
29. E. H. Schein, "The Role of the Founder in the Creation of Organizational Culture," *Organizational Dynamics,* 12 (Summer 1983), pp. 13–28.
30. V. Faux, "Unobtrusive Controls in Organizations: An Action Research Approach to Organizational Change" (unpublished Ph.D. dissertation, Harvard University, 1981).
31. T. J. Peters and R. H. Waterman, Jr., *In Search of Excellence* (New York: Harper & Row, 1982), p. 75.
32. See H. A. David and F. Militello, *The Empowered Organization: Redefining the Roles and Practices of Finance* (Morristown, N.J.: Financial Executives Research Foundation, 1994); and S. Sherman, "How Will We Live With the Tumult?," *Fortune* (December 13, 1993), p. 125.

Alcon Laboratories, Inc. (A)

In early 1985, George Leone, senior vice president of Science and Technology at Alcon Laboratories, Inc., reflected on his concerns about the challenges his company faced in measuring the productivity of its research and development (R&D) activities:

> R&D is perhaps the most critical part of Alcon's business; the company will thrive only if we are effective at developing new breakthrough products. In managing the research function, we have to address three difficult but important issues. The first is how much to spend on R&D. The second is how to allocate the resources among the various programs and projects. The third is how to ensure that the resources are used effectively. The combination of answers to these three questions determine how productive our research activity will be.
>
> While all three questions are important, I am especially concerned about the third one—how to control the use of our resources. What causes me concern is that I don't think we do a very good job of measuring our productivity, and that can limit our managerial effectiveness. At the time we are spending our resources, both money and time, and even for some time after they have been spent, it is very difficult to tell how productive we are being and have been. We could be missing some important information about problems we might be having. I feel we should do some thinking about this issue and what we can do to improve the tracking of our R&D productivity.

THE COMPANY AND ITS PRODUCTS

Alcon Laboratories was founded in 1947 in Fort Worth, Texas by two pharmacists, William C. Conner and Robert D. Alexander, who saw a need for more accurate, sterile and stable ophthalmological drugs (that is, those used in the treatment of defects and diseases of the eye). At the time, 85 percent of all eye-care drugs were being compounded in retail drug stores.

The founders' judgments proved to be correct, and within two decades, Alcon had become an international leader in the research, development, manufacturing, and marketing of a wide range of products for the diagnosis and treatment of ophthalmic disorders. The company marketed both prescription and nonprescription drugs, a wide variety of products for use in ophthalmic surgery, products for the care of hard, soft and gas-permeable lenses, and a few dermatological products. In 1984, Alcon sold products in over 100 countries; worldwide sales totalled almost $400 million. A corporate organization chart is shown in Exhibit 1.

In 1977, Alcon was purchased by Nestlé S.A., the giant Swiss-based multinational corporation. Nestlé provided increased funding and gave Alcon management a mandate to increase new product development. The increased research fueled very rapid growth: Alcon's sales tripled over the period between 1977 and 1984, and over 25 percent of 1984 sales were from products released in the past five years.

THE R&D ORGANIZATION

Alcon's research and development facilities were located in a modern complex adjacent to the corporate headquarters on the southern edge of Fort Worth. The R&D department, headed by Dr. Dilip Raval, included 350 people: 290 scientists (80 of whom had PhD degrees), and 60 support staff.

The purpose of the R&D organization was to develop new, marketable eye care products

This case was prepared by Research Assistant Chris S. Paddison and Associate Professor Kenneth A. Merchant as a basis for class discussion rather than to illustrate either effective or ineffective handling of an administrative situation.

that would fuel the company's growth. Alcon's board of directors established broad research policies based on the long-term strategies of the marketing divisions, but the board depended heavily on Mr. Leone and Dr. Raval to provide the guidance and direction necessary to ensure effective research activities.

Mr. Leone and Dr. Raval complemented each other well in terms of knowledge and experience. Mr. Leone had an in-depth knowledge of Alcon's products and markets because he had advanced through the sales organization. He joined Alcon in 1950 and spent 21 years in sales, including eight years as national sales manager. He was made vice president of Science and Technology in 1971. Dr. Raval was a chemist. He joined Alcon in 1971 and was made vice president of Research and Development in 1976.

The R&D department was organized in matrix form (see Exhibit 2). On one dimension of the matrix were four medical specialty groups: ophthalmology, optical, dermatology, and basic research. Personnel in these groups specialized in particular types of diseases. The basic research group was distinguished from the other three medical specialty groups in that its work took place early in the drug development cycle (described later). On the other dimension of the matrix were four preclinical science departments: microbiology, chemistry, toxicology, and pharmaceutical sciences. Personnel in these departments were experts in one of these scientific fields.

The matrix form of organization was used because of the need for interactions among the people with highly specialized knowledge. Each research program and project was managed by a medical specialty expert. The preclinical science personnel were assigned to programs and projects when needed, and they often had more than one assignment at any particular time.

The personnel on the research staff had needs and characteristics that were different from those of employees in other parts of the organization, and managers in the R&D department had to be sensitive to those differences. Bill York, a senior director in the basic research group explained:

> We're not an organization comprised of conformists, and we don't want to be; the other companies can have those people. Good researchers are unique. They are creative and intelligent, and although they can be lazy, they will work their tails off when they get on a project they like. But their feelings are easily hurt. It's very easy to kill ideas. We have to be careful because if we use punishment or discouragement, we may never get another idea.

PRODUCT DEVELOPMENT CYCLE

The product development cycle in pharmaceutical companies such as Alcon was long, typically totalling up to 15 years for a totally new drug and from three to five years for a simple product. Often the cycle started with some basic research designed to provide a better understanding of the basic biochemistry of the disease processes at the molecular level. For example, in 1985 doctors treated glaucoma by reducing interocular pressure, but Alcon researchers were trying to understand the biochemical basis of lesion of glaucoma with the goal of discovery of a more effective therapy. In 1985, Alcon had five basic research programs underway, all in the area of ophthalmology: inflammation, immunology, glaucoma, diabetic retinopathy/cataracts, and drug delivery.

When a new product concept was formed, the product development cycle was said to begin. Development consisted of a number of relatively distinct steps. First was the discovery phase of development, the purpose of which was to identify compounds with potential commercial applications. Scientists designed and tested new drug compounds against the characteristics of the diseases they were studying both in test tubes and later in live animal subjects, generally rabbits, dogs and monkeys. For most new drug concepts, these screening and testing activities would last from two to five years.

When the compounds moved into the discovery phase of development, Alcon management assigned the effort a development program number, and this number identified the effort until the product entered the clinical phase of testing. In 1985, Alcon had a total of 11 development programs underway, four each in ophthalmology and optical, and three in dermatology.

A successful culmination of the discovery phase of development was marked by the identification of a compound that showed promise. Such compounds were moved into the optimization phase of development. This phase usually involved one to two years of studies of how the compound may act in the body. Scientists would study how the compound was absorbed, distributed, metabolized and excreted in animal subjects. They would do some exploratory testing of toxicity (i.e., harmful side effects) and stability (i.e., length of time the drug retains its effectiveness when stored). By the end of this phase of development, the scientists would prescribe a preliminary chemical formulation and make a preliminary packaging decision (i.e., mode of delivery and size of dosage).

Drugs continuing to show promise were moved into the preclinical phase of development. This phase involved better controlled laboratory experiments to validate the results of the exploratory tests conducted in the optimization phase of development. The preclinical phase of development usually lasted about six to twelve months. The drugs that continued to show promise were filed as IND (Investigation of a New Drug) candidates with the U.S. Food and Drug Administration (FDA). At this point, a reasonably complete composition and specification existed, and a manufacturing procedure suitable for the preparation of clinical supplies was in place.

Once the IND was filed, the project moved into the clinical phase of development. This phase involved toxicity and stability testing of a longer-term nature than had been done previously. The testing was performed on live subjects: first normal human subjects and then diseased human subjects. During this testing, the scientists would make judgments of the safety and efficacy of the drug candidates and make final decisions about the dosages and modes of delivery to be used.

The clinical phase of development generally lasted between five and eight years. When a product entered the clinical phase of development, a project number was assigned, and this number would stay with the effort until the product received FDA approval or the effort was abandoned. In 1984, Alcon had a total of 30 active projects.

A drug that passed clinical testing was filed as an NDA (New Drug Application) with the FDA. The FDA approval process took from one to three years, and approval was needed before the drug could be marketed in the U.S. The product could be sold in many countries after it had passed clinical testing.

Exhibit 3 shows an overview of the product development cycle. The times shown in the exhibit for completion of each of the phases in the cycle are for development of major drugs. For fairly simple drugs and optical devices, the times were considerably shorter; as for these products, INDs were often filed within 12 months, and clinical testing took between 12 and 18 months.

A SHIFT IN EMPHASIS

In 1985, Alcon management was contemplating a fairly significant shift in the R&D efforts to emphasize more basic research. Up to 1985, Alcon had been relying heavily on other pharmaceutical companies not involved in ophthalmic markets as sources of new product ideas. Alcon scientists would screen compounds developed from these companies, and if they showed promise, Alcon would license the compounds and introduce tailored forms of them into ophthalmic markets. Compounds screened in such a manner were entered into the product development process in the preclinical phase of development because the properties of the compounds were already understood.

Mr. Leone felt that the licensing source of new product would become less important over time. The ophthalmic markets were getting large, and as they continued to grow, it became more likely that other companies would enter some of Alcon's market segments. These companies would then be less likely to offer Alcon their newest compounds.

Alcon had already begun shifting its emphasis in recent years toward more basic research. The research focus had been evolving toward larger-scale, longer-term studies of more complex, sophisticated diseases of the eye. This is because the company already had a broad product line covering most niches in the eye care market, and to meet the company's aggressive growth targets, new breakthrough products were needed. The inevitable shift toward more basic research made Mr. Leone and Dr. Raval even more concerned about having measures of research productivity available for control purposes because the investments in basic research were longer-term and riskier.

FIGURE 1.

Phase	*Probability of Failure*
Discovery	90%
Optimization	50%
Preclinical	25%
Clinical	70%
FDA & Patent	Negligible

DRUG INVESTMENTS AND PAYOFFS

New product development involved high risk investments for potentially lucrative payoffs. Across the industry, only about one of every 10,000 compounds investigated in the early exploratory research stages eventually proved to be commercially successful. The probabilities of failure of a typical compound in each of the phases of the product development cycle were approximately as shown in Figure 1.

The payoffs from the research were highly dependent on the size and term of the competitive advantage Alcon enjoyed when the new products were developed. Some drugs were breakthrough products which provided significant advantages over the competition in large market segments. Others were either minor modifications of already existing Alcon products or were aimed at small market segments. Sometimes competing firms developed alternatives to commercially successful new drugs in periods as short as two to three years, while on other occasions, Alcon products were sold for 20 years or more with little or no competition.

To a large extent, the timing of the development efforts was critical. If the development of a particular drug was pursued too early, the company could be subject to a high probability of failure and/or significant extra development expenses, and if problems were found after introduction, possible legal liability expenses. If the development was pursued too late, the result would be a "me-too" product.

PLANNING AND BUDGETING

Alcon used a well-developed set of management systems to help manage its R&D effort. Planning and budgeting was done on an annual cycle which took place from mid-July to mid-September. Planning was an iterative process. Mr. Leone and Dr. Raval began the process by setting program and project objectives and priorities and by outlining an overall budget for the R&D department. In establishing these guidelines, Mr. Leone and Dr. Raval met with Alcon directors and top-level managers to ensure that they had a good understanding of market trends and the amount of resources the company (and Nestlé) were willing to spend on R&D. Then directors and managers in each medical specialties group and each preclinical science department determined the labor hours and resources required to satisfy project and program objectives. This process was accomplished through a multitude of meetings between directors and managers.

Plans for the basic research programs were easier to prepare than were those for the development projects in that the programs used very few resources from the preclinical science departments, so very little cross-organizational coordination was required. Most development projects required the assistance of all, or at least most, of the preclinical science groups, so many meetings between the managers of the medical specialty groups and Dr. Charles Robb, director of Preclinical Sciences, were required to ensure that resources were allocated appropriately and, if necessary, that steps were taken to procure additional resources.

After the plans were prepared, Dr. Raval reviewed them and made suggestions and adjustments as necessary. Then the plans were consolidated and compared with the overall targets, and sometimes further adjustments were necessary.

By February, all Alcon employees were required to develop, in consultation with their immediate supervisor, personal objectives for the year. The company did not require the use of a standardized form or format for documenting these objectives, but the objectives had to be written down, and this document had to be signed by both the employee and the supervisor.

During the year, budget analyses were prepared on a quad (every four months) basis consistent with the planning schedule used at Nestlé. The budget analysis process, like the annual planning processes, was very informal because, as Dr. Raval explained:

> We do not expect the scientists to act like businessmen when they plan new product activity. We want to encourage them to develop new ideas without many constraints, and they don't like a lot of paperwork.

A research program manager explained his dislike for paperwork requirements:

> We work only on programs with payoffs so large that a monkey can run the figures showing the payoff. The trick is to score, not to try to figure out that a new breakthrough therapy for glaucoma will pay off. It will!

Mr. Leone had two main concerns about the planning process. First, he wondered if too much detail was still being required. And second, he wondered if requiring numbers about the research activities made the managers and scientists conservative in presenting their ideas. Given the company's need for good ideas, he thought it was important that no administrative barriers to ideas were erected.

MEASUREMENT AND REPORTING

Accounting in the R&D department was done on a full absorption cost basis. All direct expenses, both labor and materials, were charged to specific programs and projects. Labor was charged on the basis of time sheets completed weekly by R&D personnel. Costs not specifically identifiable with a particular project or program were allocated monthly on the basis of direct labor hours.

Alcon produced an extensive set of cost reports. Many of the reports were on a project, program or medical specialty basis. They showed costs compared to budget and were available on a monthly basis (an example is shown in Exhibit 4). Another set of reports, were on a cost center basis; the R&D department was divided into 75 costs centers. Exhibit 5 shows an example of a cost center report. The cost reports were summarized at various levels of aggregation, such as by type of medical specialty and by type of project or program. The program/project cost accounting system provided the information necessary to monitor the flow of resources to medical specialty areas, research versus development, and for long-term versus short-term purposes.

The project/program and cost center reports were sent to the managers responsible for the costs. The managers reviewed the reports, but they were not required to explain variances. This was because most of the variances were caused by changes in the scope or timing of the project/program, and such changes were almost always preapproved by Mr. Leone and/or Dr. Raval.

Alcon management recognized that the cost reports were not very useful for measuring the productivity of the R&D activity. Traditional accounting measures, such as return on investment, were not very meaningful because the lag between the investment in R&D and the returns generated from those investments was usually at least several years.

To date Mr. Leone and Dr. Raval had focused their attention on the consolidated financial summary (actual vs plan) and on the major achievements of the year. In the last few years, these achievements were as follows:[1]

	1984	1983	1982
INDs filed	3	4	3
NDAs filed	6	5	3
Research publications	25	19	17
Patent applications filed	15	9	8
Patents indicated allowable	7	8	5
Patents issued	5	6	4

Mr. Leone and Dr. Raval realized, however, that none of these indicators was a totally reliable indicator of forthcoming commercial success.

INCENTIVE PLANS

Alcon used two formal incentive plans which offered cash awards for good performance, one for scientists and one for senior-level managers. The scientist incentive plan was introduced in the R&D department in 1983. Four cash awards of $5000 each were made annually for technical excellence. The awards were split between scientists doing basic research and those involved in development activities.

Candidates for the scientist award were nominated by director-level managers in the R&D department. The candidates' accomplishments were judged by a seven-person committee which included four working-level scientists,

---

[1]These numbers are disguised.

two director-level managers, and one person from outside R&D (e.g., from corporate marketing). The committee assigned the awards based on "perceptible contributions or unusual problem solving capabilities which are perceptible to fellow workers."

The management incentives were provided through a companywide program which provided stock options and bonuses to senior managers down to the director level of the firm. Each year an incentive award pool was assigned to the R&D department based on a predetermined percentage of Alcon profits. This pool was allocated by R&D management to R&D employees included in the plan in conjunction with the annual performance review.

For purposes of assigning the awards in the R&D department, R&D employees were classified into three categories of achievement: (1) distinguished performance (DP), (2) superior performance (SP), and (3) good solid performance (GSP). (A fourth category called "Needs Improvement" was also used on occasion but, as Dr. Raval observed, "Those people don't get to stay very long.") Figure 2 shows the approximate percentage of people who were classified in each category of achievement and the bonuses that could be expected in an average year in each of the categories.

The evaluations were based on a weighted average of three factors: (1) meeting the technical milestones in the annual plan, (2) discovering new product candidates, and (3) contribution provided from new products and getting new products through FDA approvals. The factors used for weighting accomplishments in each of these areas were preestablished at the beginning of the year. In general, the highest weightings were given to the accomplishments that could be measured in a tangible fashion in the next 12 months.

The weighting factors varied significantly among the various areas of the department. For example, managers in development areas (as opposed to those in basic research) were expected to have products progress through the FDA approvals, but they were not expected to generate many new product leads.

The standards used to assess performance also varied significantly among the areas, reflecting the probability of payoffs of the various activities. For example, managers of basic research activities might be expected to achieve 40 percent of their objectives for the following year to be evaluated as SP (superior performance). For managers of ophthalmology drug development activities, however, the achievement of 50 percent of their objectives might qualify only as GSP, while SP might require the achievement of 70 percent. For product development managers in optical, GSP might require achievement of 60 percent of their objectives, and SP might require achievement of 80 percent.

FIGURE 2.

Category of Achievement	*Percent so Evaluated*	*Average Award (% of Salary)*
DP	<1%	30–35%
SP	50–60%	15–20%
GSP	40–50%	10%

MANAGEMENT CONCERNS

Alcon managers felt they had an excellent research team that had produced many new products that had fueled the company's growth. They were concerned, however, that they did not have a good early warning system in place to signal potential problems on a timely basis because of the difficulty in measuring R&D productivity, and this might be particularly costly as the emphasis shifted toward more basic research.

Here are some of their observations:

Mr. Leone:

> What's important in conducting research is to keep achieving progress on a daily basis. When it takes ten years to develop a product, you can't wait until tomorrow to get the work done. The important questions are: Are we doing everything we can to ensure that we are being productive every day? And how can I tell if we're being productive?
>
> Eighty percent of the really good ideas—those that lead to breakthrough products—come from twenty percent of our people. It is important for us to hire as many of those good people as we can, and perhaps even more important not to lose any we've already employed. But it is very difficult to tell who the really good people are until their accomplishments are apparent, but that may not be for some years after they were hired.

From my perspective, it's not very important whether a product costs $30 million or $60 million to develop. When we are working on a drug that will give us a billion dollars in sales over 15 years and a 25 percent cost of goods sold, overspending a little on research doesn't matter much as long as the drug gets created.

Dr. Raval:

I think we have an excellent scientific team. In 1984 we filed more regulatory submissions [INDs and NDAs] than ever before, and we expect to surpass that record in 1985. But we still need a better way to measure our performance among other things to prove to Alcon and Nestlé management that the R&D department is very productive. It's important, however, that the measures be simple enough to assemble and use without devoting too much time away from the job at hand.

We now have 16 programs and 30 projects underway, and the growth has made coordination of the groups more difficult. It is increasingly difficult to keep up with the status of each program and project well enough to be able to decide priority issues. In the last six months, we have started an effort to try to identify a set of standard product development milestones and decision points around which a computerized information system could be built and used for control purposes. Because of the great variance among projects, however, not everybody in the organization is convinced as to the worth of trying to organize an information system around a conceptualization of a standardized process.

Even in defining what we mean by productivity, we have to be careful in how we define our terms and use the measures that could result. For example, we rarely terminate projects, but we do adjust priorities and let some of them sit in an inactive state until a solution to a particular problem surfaces. Should the inactive projects reflect negatively on our productivity?

EXHIBIT 1 ALCON LABORATORIES, INC. (A) Corporate Organization

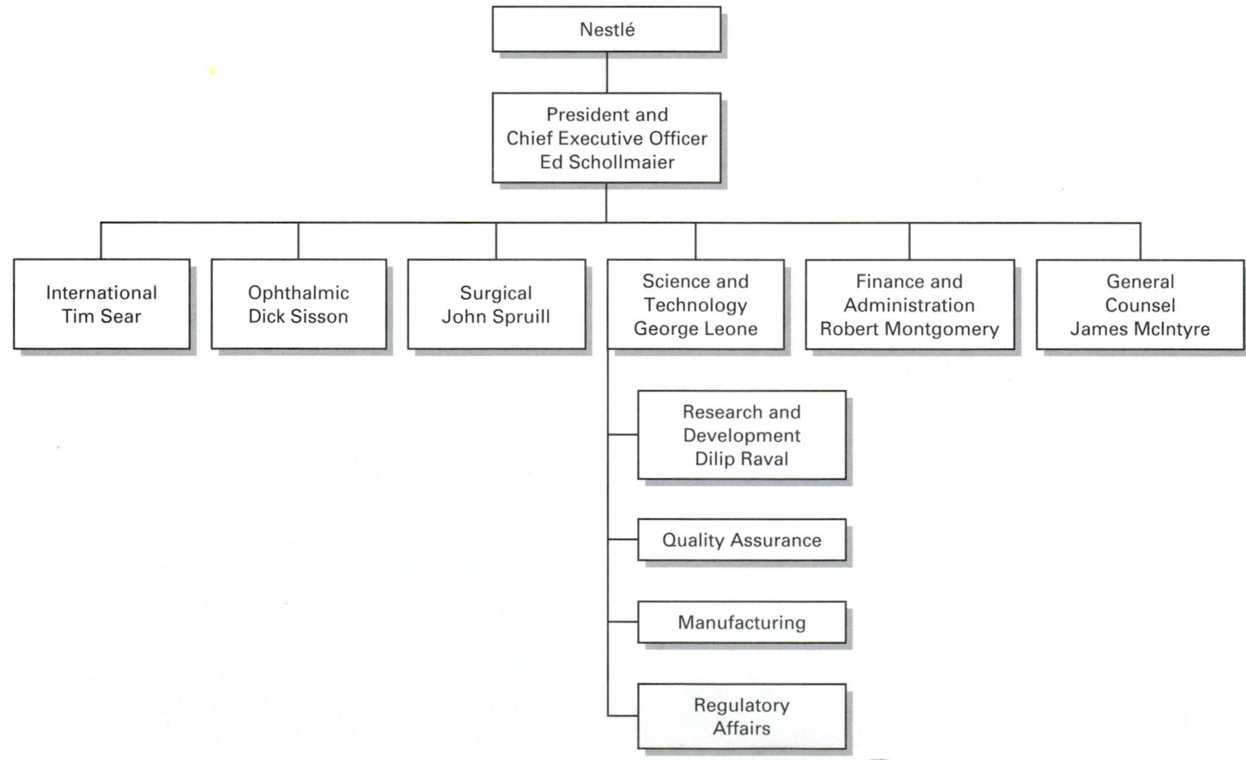

EXHIBIT 2 ALCON LABORATORIES, INC. (A) Organization of R&D Department

Dr. Dilip Raval
Vice President
Research and Development

Tom Mitchell
Controller

Henry Baldwin
Director of Administration

Sudhir Davé
Planning and Project
Management

Dr. Gerald Cagle
Ophthalmology

Dr. Kiran Randeri
Optical

Dr. Robert Adamski
Basic Research

Dr. Peter Hebborn
Dermatology

Dr. Charles Robb
Preclinical Science

Dr. Barry Schlech
Microbiology

Dr. John Mullins
Chemistry

Dr. Joseph Middeman
Toxicology

Dr. Gene Cooper
Pharmaceutical Sciences

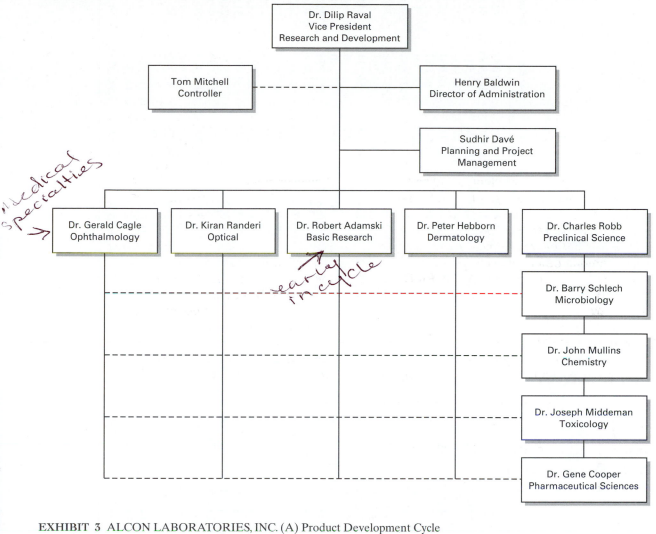

EXHIBIT 3 ALCON LABORATORIES, INC. (A) Product Development Cycle

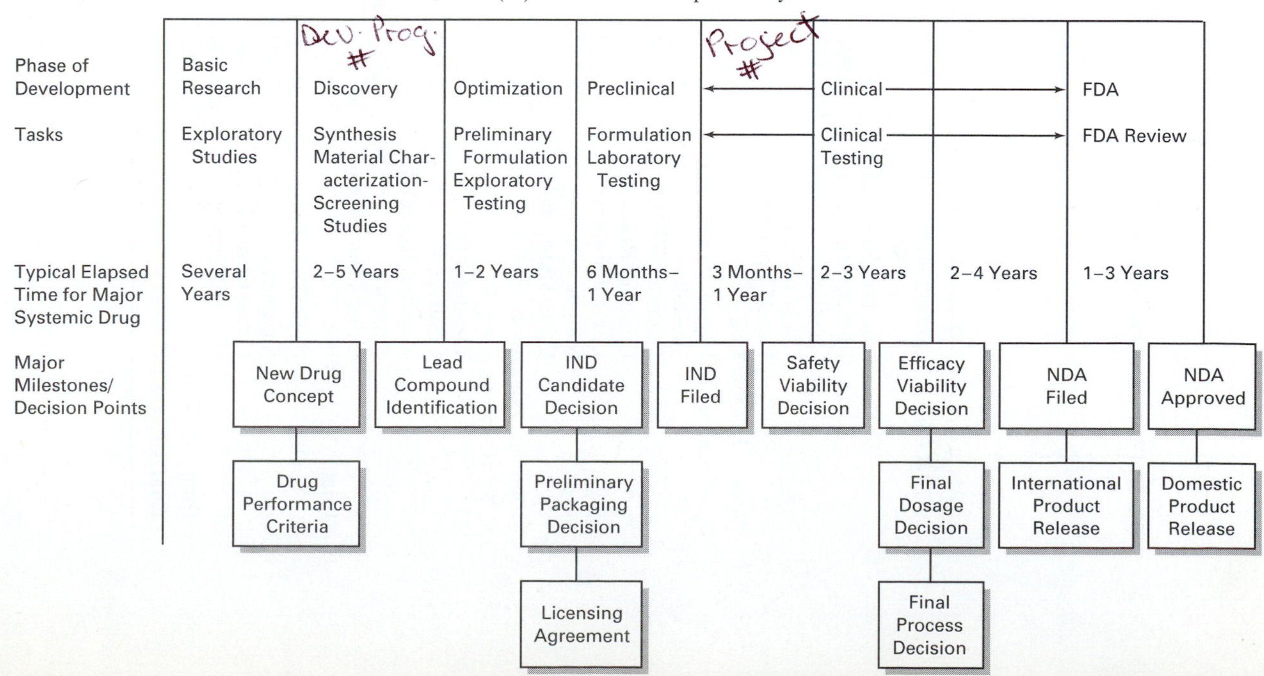

EXHIBIT 4 ALCON LABORATORIES, INC. (A) Example of Medical Specialty Cost Report

Research and Development
December 1985
220000

	Account	*Medical Specialty Ophthalmic Actual*	*Budget*	*Variance*	*Quad Act*	*Quad Bud*	*Variance*	*Year Act*	*Year Bud*	*Variance*
1. Dirct Chg	Consultants	4,929	4,900	−29	9,182	14,000	4,818	17,281	30,000	12,719
	Contract Service	43,638	32,856	−10,781	104,286	94,018	−10,268	261,657	343,500	81,843
	Contract Research	67,160	24,675	−42,485	113,410	70,500	−42,910	225,640	182,500	−43,140
	Clinical Studies	60,099	122,150	62,051	167,021	349,000	181,978	396,361	704,000	307,639
	Supplies	21,777	4,875	−16,302	119,746	19,500	−100,246	245,560	80,000	−165,560
	Other Controllable	633	8,963	8,329	14,397	35,850	21,453	56,445	97,850	41,405
	Fixed Expenses	0	0	0	0	0	0	−1,928	0	1,928
*Total 1. Dirct Chg		197,636	198,419	783	528,043	582,868	54,825	1,201,015	1,437,850	236,835
2. Allocated	Payroll	225,779	255,487	29,708	912,934	1,024,043	111,109	2,847,194	2,917,348	70,153
	Consultants	5,872	2,759	−3,114	5,872	8,555	2,682	6,213	15,205	8,991
	Contract Service	6,420	9,361	2,941	20,623	28,346	7,724	54,518	89,334	34,816
	Contract Research	0	0	0	0	0	0	182	0	−182
	Clinical Studies	0	0	0	0	0	0	857	0	−857
	Supplies	33,132	42,646	9,514	101,933	172,021	70,088	340,529	481,876	141,347
	Other Controllable	40,058	28,630	−11,427	150,263	114,606	−35,657	382,385	341,906	−40,479
*Total 2. Allocated		311,261	338,882	27,621	1,191,624	1,347,570	155,946	3,631,878	3,845,667	213,789
3. Var. O/H	Payroll	108,707	66,619	−42,088	318,091	272,892	−45,199	903,191	679,617	−223,574
	Consultants	5,231	131	−5,100	8,682	464	−8,218	16,017	2,477	−13,540
	Contract Service	9,210	4,806	−4,404	13,680	13,798	118	38,278	36,783	−1,495
	Contract Research	16	5,739	5,723	16	23,033	23,017	−72	31,916	31,989
	Supplies	8,927	4,061	−4,866	19,140	17,113	−2,027	61,655	37,590	−24,065
	Other Controllable	101,347	23,218	−78,130	178,064	93,844	−84,220	283,723	234,093	−49,629
*Total 3. Var. O/H		233,438	104,574	−128,865	537,673	421,144	−116,529	1,302,792	1,022,476	−280,315
4. Fix O/H	Contract Service	10,170	9,476	−695	30,919	27,151	−3,768	83,425	75,636	−7,789
	Supplies	7,900	3,345	−4,555	16,023	13,425	2,598	55,785	37,392	−18,392
	Other Controllable	3,481	3,062	−419	7,576	12,290	4,714	15,760	33,959	18,179
	Fixed Expenses	157,350	119,695	−37,655	469,885	480,809	10,924	1,427,039	1,349,593	−77,447
*Total 4. Fix O/H		178,902	135,578	−43,324	524,403	533,674	9,272	1,582,010	1,496,561	−85,449
*Total MEDSPEC 220000		921,236	777,453	−143,783	2,781,743	2,885,257	103,514	7,717,694	7,802,555	84,860

EXHIBIT 5 ALCON LABORATORIES, INC. (A) Example of Cost Center Expense Report

Report Number GLCP0020R07 Final | Alcon Science and Technology | Domestic | April 1985
Page Number 123 Run Date = 05/08/85 | Budget vs Actuals by Territory | Performance Ledger | 3921-3621
Variance is Budget − Actual (− = Over) | Degenerative Disease Programs | Amounts are in U.S. Dollars

Account Description	*Account Code*	*April 1985*		*Current Quad to Date*		*Current Year to Date*	
		Actual	*Variance*	*Actual*	*Variance*	*Actual*	*Variance*
Salaries	61100	17,399.63	2,042.37	72,711.56	5,056.44	72,711.56	5,056.44
Profit sharing trust	61500	1,913.96	46.96−	7,649.96	181.96−	7,649.96	181.96−
Payroll tax, group insurance	61600	2,696.94	122.06	11,090.96	185.04	11,090.96	185.04
Temporary labor costs	61800		1,250.00		5,000.00		5,000.00
Payroll costs	Total	22,010.53	3,367.47	91,452.48	10,059.52	91,452.48	10,059.52
Travel and entertainment	62000		2,175.00		8,700.00		8,700.00
Meals	62100	58.04	58.04−	1,003.88	1,003.88−	1,003.88	1,003.88−
Entertainment	62200			121.94	121.94−	121.94	121.94−
Auto mileage and rental	62300	267.75	267.75−	521.98	521.98−	521.98	521.98−
Air other transportation	62500	50.60	50.60−	6,361.10	6,361.10−	6,361.10	6,361.10−
Lodging	62600	248.14	248.14−	1,378.34	1,378.34−	1,378.34	1,378.34−
Parking and tolls	62700	31.00	31.00−	46.55	46.55−	46.55	46.55−
Misc travel & entertainment	62800	168.37	168.37−	533.25	533.25−	533.25	533.25−
Meetings, seminars, & conventions	62900	100.00	100.00−	1,041.27	1,041.27−	1,041.27	1,041.27−
Travel and entertainment	Total	923.90	1,251.10	11,008.31	2,308.31−	11,008.31	2,308.31−
Domestic consulting	63110	83.95	1,666.05	4,363.85	636.15	4,363.85	636.15
Contr SVC—general	63211	200.00	200.00−	1,688.57	1,688.57−	1,688.57	1,688.57−
Contr SVC—prof	63212	2,500.00	11,815.00	5,798.06	35,101.94	5,798.06	35,101.94
Contr SVC & labor	Total	2,700.00	11,615.00	7,486.63	33,413.37	7,486.63	33,413.37
Contr RESH—domes	63221	24,741.00	3,274.00−	58,784.00	2,549.00	58,784.00	2,549.00
Contr RESH—forgn	63222		3,500.00		10,000.00		10,000.00
Contract research	Total	24,741.00	226.00	58,784.00	12,549.00	58,784.00	12,549.00
Contract services & labor	Total	27,441.00	11,841.00	66,270.63	45,962.37	66,270.63	45,962.37
Professional & commercial SVCS	Total	27,524.95	13,507.05	70,634.48	46,598.52	70,634.48	46,598.52
Printing	64400	43.96	43.96−	115.96	115.96−	115.96	115.96−
Freight & postage	66000		250.00		1,000.00		1,000.00
Freight in	66100	481.50	481.50−	566.77	566.77−	566.77	566.77−
Freight out	66200			9.50	9.50−	9.50	9.50−
Postage	66300	51.27	51.27−	100.27	100.27−	100.27	100.27−
Freight & postage	Total	532.77	282.77−	676.54	323.46	676.54	323.46
General supplies	67100	1,036.32	536.32−	6,146.58	4,146.58−	6,146.58	4,146.58−
Supplies—lab	67410	660.68	589.32	2,512.01	2,487.99	2,512.01	2,487.99
Supplies	Total	1,697.00	53.00	8,658.59	1,658.59−	8,658.59	1,658.59−
Rental—equipment	68200	491.03	258.97	2,359.59	640.41	2,359.59	640.41
Lease—equipment	68300			1,178.33	1,178.33−	1,178.33	1,178.33−
Purchased software	68400		500.00	1,321.20	678.80	1,321.20	678.80
Rents & leases	Total	491.03	758.97	4,859.12	140.88	4,859.12	140.88
Employment expense	69100	14.49	735.51	14.49	2,985.51	14.49	2,985.51
Recruiting (excl field sales)	69111			40.00	40.00−	40.00	40.00−
Employment expense	Total	14.49	735.51	54.49	2,945.51	54.49	2,945.51
Employee relations	69200		1,625.00	1,040.00	5,460.00	1,040.00	5,460.00
Telephone & telegraph	69300	164.90	2,085.10	851.53	8,148.47	851.53	8,148.47
Repair & maintenance	69400	20.02	3,904.98	342.04	15,357.96	342.04	15,357.96
Professional dues	69500		150.00	435.00	165.00	435.00	165.00
Professional literature	69600	46.11	203.89	531.88	468.12	531.88	468.12
Miscellaneous expense	Total	245.52	8,704.48	3,254.94	32,545.06	3,254.94	32,545.06
Controllable expense	Total	53,469.66	27,315.34	190,660.42	85,584.58	190,660.42	85,584.58
Depr—lab equip & fixtures	74400	409.77	6,182.23	1,254.94	25,113.06	1,254.94	25,113.06
Depr—office furn/fixt/equip	74500		189.00	68.54	687.46	68.54	687.46
Depr—information systems	74600	70.91	1,229.09	70.91	5,129.09	70.91	5,129.09
Depr—other than bldg	Total	480.68	7,600.32	1,394.39	30,929.61	1,394.39	30,929.61
Cost center total	Total	53,950.34	34,915.66	192,054.81	116,514.19	192,054.81	116,514.19

Hewitt Associates[1]

"We have three principal objectives for our firm," noted Mr. Peter Friedes, chief executive of Hewitt Associates, a firm specializing in compensation, employee benefits and other financial/personnel functions.

"They are to provide outstanding service to our clients, to provide a satisfying work experience for associates, and to be a profitable and successful firm. I think we have a lot to be proud of. We've grown rapidly; we are a national presence with the best reputation in benefits consulting in the industry; and our partners' earnings are comparable if not higher than those of the Big 8 accounting firms and certainly among the highest in our industry (Exhibits 1 and 2). But in addition to all of this we are proud of our values. What the visitor soon recognizes is that there is something very different about the environment here. It is most evident in the absence of titles and artificial status symbols. Here, titles reflect function, not status. Everyone, from the newest hire to the oldest partner has the same size office. We have no profit centers. We work hard to maintain an environment in which people have the freedom to develop and, to some extent, control their own work lives. We do not believe in associates competing with each other: we work for an environment of mutual cooperation." The principles of Hewitt Associates' management style, widely disseminated in the organization and in its promotional literature, are shown in Exhibit 3.

"While they may sometimes conflict," continued Mr. Friedes, "we believe that in the long run our three goals of outstanding service, satisfying work experience and financial success are mutually reinforcing. However, establishing and managing a system to effect this takes constant time and effort. Each year as our firm grows, we face new challenges in management. How, for example, do we demonstrate in a large organization that we feel all jobs are important? We attract and retain people because we believe that each person is unique and has special talents. And yet, we are an organization that must operate with some procedures, make fair decisions as a group, have basic standards on such matters as hours worked, merit increases, expenses incurred, etc. How do we merge these sometimes opposing principles?"

HISTORY

Hewitt Associates was founded in 1940 by Edwin Shields Hewitt and initially provided services to assist individuals in estate planning and in the selection of insurance to fulfill estate goals. Working with company executives on their financial planning made obvious the need for an organization to assist employers in developing financial programs and retirement plans for their employees. This led to the decision to expand services into the entire employee benefits field. By 1946, work performed for individuals had been phased out, the firm no longer accepted insurance commissions, and it had become an independent management consulting firm in the employee benefits field. From a concentration on retirement benefits the services offered expanded to include, first, all forms of employee benefits, and later, direct compensation systems (both wage and salary administration and executive compensation). By the mid-1970s, the firm was describing itself as "independent consultants and actuaries in compensation, employee benefits, communication, and other related personnel functions."

Mr. Hewitt had opened his business in Lake Forest, Illinois, and moved to Chicago in 1941. In

[1]Selected financial and other numerical data in this case have been disguised.

This case was prepared as the basis for class discussion rather than to illustrate either effective or ineffective handling of an administrative situation.

1951 the firm moved to Libertyville where it remained until 1971, then moving to Deerfield. In May 1978, a final move was made to spacious new facilities in Lincolnshire, Illinois. The first regional office had been opened in Minneapolis in 1959, which marked the beginning of Hewitt Associates' steps to becoming a national organization. Additional offices were opened in New York (1964), Chicago (reopened in 1964), Milwaukee (1965), Los Angeles (1966), Dayton, Ohio (1968), San Francisco (1973), Atlanta (1975), Toronto, Canada (1975), and Houston (1979). In 1972 Management Compensation Services (MCS) was purchased to conduct research and comparative studies in the field of executive, middle management, international and sales compensation.

In the mid-1970s, Hewitt Associates had faced a major decision in its location and operating strategy. Although it had offices in many locations, it was a highly centralized consulting firm because most of its "Professional Group" people (for example, actuaries) were located at the main location in Deerfield (Illinois), the regional offices being staffed with account managers who served as primary consultants, dealt directly with clients and managed the client-company interface. However, rapid growth and market forces created a need to have Professional Group people close to clients. Rather than staff each regional office with its own professional groups, Hewitt Associates opened an Eastern Center in Stamford, Connecticut (1976) and a Western Center in Newport Beach, California (1977). The centralization of Professional Group people in these locations, it was felt, gave Hewitt Associates a strong advantage over its competitors since it helped in training and allowed people with the same interests to discuss ideas and problems. It also placed key professionals closer to the client, thus both creating a local presence and reducing travel time for Hewitt Associates' personnel.

THE COMPENSATION CONSULTING MARKET

Throughout the 1970s the total compensation field (including the planning, design, administration, financial management and communication of both benefits and pay) had taken on increasing importance in U.S. industry. It was estimated that, in 1977, U.S. industry had spent in excess of $300 billion in employee benefits alone, and one observer had noted that, by 1985, pension funds would own at least 50 to 60 percent of the equity capital of U.S. business. General Motors had asserted that the largest single expense in building a car was the Blue Cross Insurance for employees.

Because of the complexity of the field (encompassing such diverse subjects as pensions, investments, the social security system, tax laws, executive compensation, mergers and acquisitions, union relationships, national health insurance and human behavior and motivation) many U.S. corporations turned to consultants for guidance. This trend was encouraged by the rapid changes in legislation and I.R.S. rulings. Hewitt Associates had performed work for 1350 clients in the 24 months of 1978 and 1979, including 50 percent of the Fortune 500. In fiscal 1978 they served (billed) 962 clients. Most contact between Hewitt Associates and its client was at the benefit officer (or financial officer) level. However, when new clients were considering the firm's service, contact would normally be at the president, or vice president of personnel or vice president of finance level. It was rare for the Hewitt account manager not to know the client company's president.

Many assignments continued from year to year, although much of the consulting (as opposed to administrative) work was carried out in the early years of a client relationship. At one major client, Hewitt Associates' staff had been involved with the company's benefit system longer than any of the company's own staff. Significant variation existed in the nature, size and scope of the projects performed for clients. However, a "typical" project might last six months and bring in $30,000 in billings. In Fiscal 1979, 73 clients were billed over $100,000, accounting for 44 percent of total billings, and 300 clients were billed less than $5000.

In 1980, Hewitt Associates offered more than 60 to 70 distinct services or service products to its clients. These ranged from proprietary databanks and surveys compiled by Hewitt to working with clients' attorneys to ensure the compliance with relevant law of compensation systems. Hewitt developed training programs, conducted employee meetings, performed systems analysis and software installation for complex payroll systems, advised on and designed investment management systems for pension funds and provided a host of other customized services. New products and services were frequently added.

Hewitt Associates competed with a wide range of firms, including over 100 actuarial firms. However, only five or six were "true" competitors in that they could offer the range and depth of services required by major corporations. Among these major competitors were Hay-Huggins Associates; Towers, Perrin, Foster and Crosby; Wyatt; Kwasha Lipton; Buck; and A. S. Hansen. Although competitive information was hard to obtain, Hewitt Associates estimated that it ranked fourth in billings among these firms. However, since such a wide range of services were included in the "total compensation" field, it was not possible to generalize about the relative strength of individual competitors. Corporations often used different consulting firms for different components of their compensation systems. The reputation of different firms also varied by the particular component of service being considered, with different consulting companies being perceived as having different strengths and weaknesses. "We believe that we are perceived as the premier quality firm in employee benefits," noted Mr. Friedes, "but perhaps not yet across all of our services. However, that is clearly our goal." Hewitt Associates' prices were generally considered at the upper end of the scale, but comparable to the other major competitors identified above. "However," commented Mr. Friedes, "we are beginning to see some price competition develop. Some of the smaller firms are quoting prices 30 to 40 percent below ours."

Hewitt Associates attempted to distinguish itself from its competition by its consulting philosophy. Mr. Friedes commented, "We have developed many specific services which are of great value to our clients. They are, however, only a supplement of our single, most important service—helping clients solve problems. We do not have a storehouse of items on our shelves that we reach for when problem X arises. Rather, we help a client solve his problem in the best way possible for him." The emphasis on client involvement was elaborated by Mr. Tom Wood, manager of the account management group.

> Hewitt Associates' approach is entirely different—perhaps "educators," "catalysts," or "facilitators" more accurately describe Hewitt Associates consultants. The initial phase of client work often involved "objective setting." Working closely with those responsible for personnel and finance, and often the chief executive office, the Hewitt Associates consultant assists the organization in defining its objectives and philosophies. Once the objectives have been clearly defined, the consultant can then educate the client on the assumptions underlying alternative solutions as well as their strengths and weaknesses. The final decision then falls to those who know the situation better than anyone else—the client. The consultant does not become a "crutch." The client understands how and why a particular solution makes sense as well as the issues associated with the problem. Because of the close involvement through the development stage, there is a commitment to implementation often missing in less cooperative consulting relationships.

This philosophy was often illustrated by the language used in Hewitt Associates: few reports contained "recommendations"; rather, the term "suggested alternatives" was used.

ORGANIZATION

Staff at Hewitt Associates were organized into eight service groupings. These groups were Actuarial, Executive Compensation/Salary Administration, Plan Administration, Communication, Installation, Client Special Services (which included Investment Services and Research), Systems, and Account Management (which included subgroups specializing in Group Insurance Financing and International consulting, as well as the primary group of account managers). (Billings by group are shown in Exhibit 4). All of these groups, with the exception of the Account Management primary groupings, were termed "Professional Groups" and were made up of specialists in one or more of the functional components of compensation consulting.

The Actuarial Group (172 associates in 1980) analyzed and estimated the present and future costs of employee benefit plans, benefit charges, acquisitions and mergers, and plant closings. It also determined cost/value comparisons among alternative total compensation programs. *The Executive*

Compensation/Salary Administration Group (36 associates) developed total compensation programs for executives, including incentive, bonus, and capital accumulation arrangements, and consulted in salary administration, salary systems, personnel evaluation systems, and salary policies and pay procedures for client companies. *The Plan Administration Group* (23 associates) reviewed clients' personnel and financial records and procedures, and advised on administrative processes for workflow and staff size. *The Communication Group* (54 associates) designed long- and short-range employee information programs, creating, writing, and producing printed and audiovisual materials. It also conducted surveys of employees. *The Installation Group* (15 associates) worked with client attorneys to develop plans, trusts, insurance and employment contracts, and other legal instruments. It also prepared materials for filing with government agencies, and monitored day-to-day changes in government regulations. *Group Insurance Financing* (five associates) analyzed client group insurance plans and presented alternative insurance approaches. *International* (seven associates) worked with U.S. based companies with foreign divisions to develop employee benefit plans for local nationals and expatriates. *Investment Services* (seven associates) developed written policies and objectives to guide those who managed retirement fund investments for client companies. It also helped clients select investment managers. Pension, profit sharing, and savings fund investment performances were monitored and compared to those of similar funds. *Research* (16 associates) published research reports on a regular basis to inform clients of trends and developments in total compensation, and conducted special research studies and surveys on aspects of total compensation. Included among this group's activities were ongoing research projects that had been initiated and developed in-house, the results being shared with (or sold as a service to) client companies. *The Systems Group* (97 associates) designed computer systems and programs for client compensations administration, defined benefit plan accounting, and employee benefit statements. Systems could be installed on client computers or retained on Hewitt Associates' Burroughs 7700 computer.

The final group, *Account Management* (117 associates), was the group with the largest number of partners and principal consultants. While the Professional Group consultants were highly trained in their specialized areas, the account managers—in addition to being trained fully in the subject area of employee benefits and, for some, executive compensation—also were trained in the skills of maintaining client relations and broadening the relationship with the existing clients. The account managers were charged with coordinating all the firm's services for their clients, and staying current with all the client's needs. They were responsible for the total compensation policy setting, objective setting, program evaluation, and program design. This philosophy of individualized client care was developed to enhance new business development by not relying on the specialist Professional Group consultant to know all of the business areas, and to ensure continuity for each client. This system differentiated Hewitt Associates from the majority of its competitors, who tended to try to combine the account management function with the technical professional function—which resulted, Hewitt Associates believed, in failure to do the account management part of that combination.

Of the total employees at Hewitt Associates, approximately two-thirds were exempt personnel, and approximately one-third were nonexempt (primarily clerical and secretarial). *All* employees at Hewitt were called associates, including secretarial and other staff support personnel, and all were considerable billable employees, their time being credited, as appropriate, to the engagements they worked on.

MANAGEMENT OF THE FIRM

Originally a proprietorship, Hewitt Associates became a partnership in 1952. All partners were active members of the firm and were committed to the principle of internal ownership. The organization was controlled by an Executive Committee, formed from seven partners elected for three-year terms (up to a maximum of nine years). Although the Executive Committee had final authority in the operation of Hewitt Associates, the authority was exercised through their selection of a chief executive to manage the business (Peter Friedes had been chief executive since 1970). Group managers were selected by the chief executive and approved by the Executive Committee.

Each of the groups (including account managers) were divided into units with each unit having a manager. Every associate in Hewitt Associates was thus a member of a unit within a group. No particular norm existed for the size of a unit. Some consisted of one person, others more than a dozen. While the unit size and structure mirrored to some extent the nature of the work performed by the unit, it was also determined by the desires and abilities of the unit manager. Units existed to provide reporting relationships, allocate and distribute work and provide a context for the development of individual associates. Being a unit manager did not determine, and was not determined by, status in the firm. "Our structure is along functional lines," continued Mr. Friedes, "and all roles result from functions performed: they are not signs of status. We avoid as much as possible the use of titles." It was thus possible, and indeed the case, in some instances, that an associate who was a partner might be a member of a unit headed by an associate who was not a partner. Partnership was normally awarded after a period of five to eight years, and was based on a broad evaluation of the individual's "contribution to the firm," which might or might not include managerial responsibilities. (Statistics on the number of partners and associates are shown in Exhibit 5).

"We believe," noted Mr. Friedes, "that management is a function, a responsibility, not a status. We have individuals who became unit managers, found that they were not comfortable in that role, and went back to being full-time consultants. The real heart of the unit manager's job is to develop people and assist in maintaining their long-term relationships with the firm. Among the function performed are creating a team; participating in hiring, and transferring; helping people become more productive and more satisfied; helping associates have pride in their contributions; administering compensation; and evaluating performance and giving feedback. Our philosophy of management is very specific. We believe that anyone who has an individual assigned to them takes on the responsibility of seeing that an individual is appropriately managed. People expect to be managed: that doesn't mean 'bossed,' it means managed. We make a strong distinction between the concept of supervision and coaching. An essential difference is that coaching starts with the individual. A good manager adjusts to different people, treating each of them as unique. I don't believe managers have a great impact on motivating others within Hewitt Associates. People who naturally work hard do so for themselves, not for the manager. A manager can destroy the desire to work hard, but rarely within a consulting firm can a manger turn around an individual who is not naturally motivated. On the other hand, channeling motivation that is already there into productive efforts is clearly a job of the manager. People who are motivated can be stretched. A good manager knows when to require just a bit more than the individual thinks they can do. People need to rise to heights they thought they couldn't reach—that's the challenge from which satisfaction is achieved."

An important component of the unit manager's task was performance appraisal, which had four major purposes: for salary administration; to assess development needs of the individual; to judge what role the associate might be able to perform; and to be used as a basis for letting people know how they were doing. Performance was judged by unit managers on the basis of how well individuals contributed to the three goals of the firm: contribution to high quality of service, contribution of others' satisfaction, and contribution to maintaining a good level of earnings and financial stability. Not all junior associates were comfortable with this system. Commented one: "It takes a little time to get used to this place. I used to work for a large insurance company where everything was formal and you were told precisely what to do and how you were doing. I have a lot of autonomy here, and there's not enough management in my opinion. I am not closely supervised, and it's sometimes hard to get feedback, good or bad: the review process is a little unstructured. People will usually tell you how you are doing, but you sometimes have to take the initiative to ask. It is sometimes hard to know what I'm supposed to be good at and how I stack up. I need to be reassured a little more."

In both professional groups and account management, associates' salaries were determined by these performance appraisals. No bonus system existed for associates, although salary reviews were relatively frequent.

Great attention was paid to recruiting efforts by Hewitt Associates. "One of the major tools, if not *the* major tool, that we have in achieving our goals is through control of the number and quality of the people we hire. In fiscal 1980, we hired 50 new exempt personnel, and this was the result of interviewing 1,043 students at 65 schools. We brought 198 back for further interviews on our premises and made 72 offers. We try to find people who share our values: a helping orientation, someone who is not always trying to maximize personal gain; someone who is adaptable, flexible and can deal with individuals *as* individuals. Most of the people we hire are also achievers, who want to keep learning. Part of the interview process for those we bring to our premises is a half-day session with a psychologist, at a cost to us of $600 per person. We're looking for SWANs: people who are Smart, Work hard, Ambitious, and Nice."

Hewitt Associates drew its exempt personnel from a variety of backgrounds. For the actuarial group, it recruited individuals with degrees in actuarial science. For the communications group, individuals with a bachelor's or masters in journalism were commonly recruited. The systems group required people trained in computer science, while account managers had traditionally come from the actuarial group. Hewitt Associates had begun to hire MBAs to staff the research, account management, executive compensation and systems areas. Turnover of exempt personnel had been less than 10 percent per year for the last 10 years, and less than 5 percent for most years. "This is much lower than most other consulting firms," commented Mr. Friedes. "Yet there's no one here who couldn't get an offer for more money. In large part, this is a reflection of our quality. People who we might rate as average are judged as excellent by our competitors. I know of cases where someone we were paying $45,000 was lured away to a 'bigger' job by a competitor at a salary of $80,000. Our people are always being contacted, but few choose to leave us. Of course, we pay well ourselves. We participate in a variety of surveys, and we're at the top relative to our competition in our area of consulting. We do not compete for the top MBA candidates at the $40,000 to $50,000 level. Most of the MBAs we hired in 1980 were at $25,000 to $30,000."

MANAGEMENT CONTROL SYSTEMS

In common with virtually all professional service firms, Hewitt Associates employed a time accounting system for billing purposes. Time was recorded in 15-minute increments called units, an eight-hour day thus containing 32 units. Time was recorded in five categories: client chargeable time; client nonchargeable time (often, this is time worked in excess of budget); special project (time spent on nonclient projects); Hewitt Associates' time (administrative, promotional, or training activities); and time off. Time cards were due from each associate at the end of each month. From these cards the time accounting system provided a number of reports made available to managers. Among these were (1) a billings summary, available to account managers, accumulating for each client chargeable and nonchargeable time, outside supplier charges and travel expenses, by associate, billing and assignment number; (2) product reports, available to group and unit managers, which were similar to billings summaries but, summarized the time charged to the projects of the group or unit members. Group and unit managers could receive the report for their group or unit only; (3) a time-analysis-by-individual report, sent to group and unit managers, which allowed an individual's work activity to be measured against either a standard work year or the budgeted time allocation. In addition to these (and other) standard reports, a number of special reports could be requested by individual unit or group managers.

"Productivity is currently our favorite topic," noted Mr. Friedes, "and I have asked all group managers for a productivity improvement action plan. One major goal is to increase the amount of our time that is chargeable to clients. In 1976, 36 percent of all our time was chargeable (counting secretarial, printing, photocopying, and all other staff's time as potentially chargeable). This included the time of individuals and groups performing nonchargeable tasks, such as administration of the firm, support services, recruiting and the like. By 1979, the figure had dropped to 31 percent. In part this drop is attributable to our growth. We have had to do a great deal of training, and our new service offerings have forced us into more and more research needs. Each individual has a chargeable time budget, but while I want everyone to know what theirs is, I don't want them to get too concerned about it. Too vigorous a pursuit of increased personal billability could lead to declines in client service and could easily affect adversely our cooperative work climate."

Fee estimations were the responsibility of

the relevant account managers. However, since most projects involved the services of one or more Professional Groups, in practice they were a joint effort. Each professional group unit manager involved in a project would estimate, based on discussions with the account manager, a dollar and time budget for this team's component of the project. Based on these estimates, and an allowance for his or her own time in coordinating the project, a total budget would be prepared. Hewitt Associates had a policy of attempting to "establish budgets" (as in "we suggest you establish a budget of x-dollars for this project") rather than make fixed price estimates. It was left to the account manager to decide whether to estimate through a single number or through the use of ranges, depending on the type of job assignment. "The problem with ranges," noted Mr. Wood, "is that clients tend to think in terms of the low number, whereas we think in terms of the high number. Unless the estimate is properly prefaced, the client feels better if our actual billing is less than the highest number in a range estimate."

Account managers bore the responsibility of monitoring the chargeable and nonchargeable time spent on their projects. Mr. Friedes also monitored these, keeping a careful watch for write-offs (projects where the budget had been exceeded but the client not billed an additional sum). If an account manager had more than $500 write-offs in a month, he or she was required to file an explanatory form with Mr. Friedes, who received approximately 30 to 40 of these per month. There was no direct relationship between account profitability and account manager compensation. In fact, no individual could determine the overall profitability of a project. The account manager would know the budgeted time and billable rates for the people on the project, but since he would not know the salaries of the individuals involved, he was not expected to estimate the cost of the resources consumed. A project group manager could gauge his group's performance relative to the budget he had quoted, but could not determine the profitability of the overall project. "No one here," noted Mr. Friedes, "would think they were measured by profitability." The account manager monitored the amount of time spent on his or her projects by the professional group members, but in the words of one account manager, "we have no sanctions against a Professional Group charging outrageous amounts of time for their work. They have the right to delve into a given topic for a client as much as they think necessary: I cannot tell them when to stop working on a given topic. But the systems works—through cooperation."

In establishing a team to serve a client, a request would be made to a Professional Group manager, who would assign the task to one of the units under his or her direction. The unit manager would then select a member of the unit to work on a given project. There was no definite rule about who took responsibility for the day-to-day management of a project. Project leaders could be chosen from the professional group or be the account manager, depending upon who was best suited to the task.

Budgeting was performed annually at Hewitt Associates, in order to arrive at a reasonable estimate of income and expenses for the fiscal year. Two methods were used initially to estimate income for a subsequent fiscal year: (a) group managers' estimates of total chargeable time, and (b) account managers' estimates of billings to all clients. After reconciliation and the establishment of targets, each account manager was given a mutually agreed revenue target and chargeable time targets were set for group managers.

PROBLEMS OF ACCOUNT MANAGEMENT – PROFESSIONAL GROUP RELATIONS

"Fifteen years ago," noted Mr. Friedes, "Hewitt Associates had a consulting group and product groups, so named because we tried to have product fees for their services. In the minds of many of our junior people, it became clear that consulting was the place to be. By 1968, we were developing a big problem in keeping actuaries in the Actuarial Group: they all wanted to become consultants. In 1970, the consulting group became the Account Management group because we wanted to recognize that there were consultants in other client service groups too. We changed the Product Group name to Professional Groups to increase recognition of the professional nature of these responsibilities. We evolved the concept of the account manager as the generalist consultant in employee benefits and the Professional Group consultant as the specialist.

"A number of trends created a confusion of roles. First, we were asking the Professional Groups to do two sometimes conflicting things. We wanted them to be the best professionally in their specialty in the country. Yet we also wanted them to serve the account manager in a thorough, timely and accurate way. To some extent our growth exacerbated problems between the groups. Historically, our account managers were fully trained to do employee benefit plan design, and hence could deliver that portion of our services on their own. However, as we grew rapidly we were forced to create account managers whose technical skills were not fully developed. We could not afford to staff the account management function solely from graduates of an Actuarial Group. In addition, we added many new services during the 1970s, and it became difficult for the account managers to keep up, to be experts in all our fields. As a consequence, many of the new services were being sold directly by the Professional Groups. This bred the attitude that we don't need the account manager to sell, he is a burden, keep him out. In turn, the feeling then developed into one where the account manager was viewed solely as a door opener. There was an atmosphere of general resentment and lack of understanding. The problem did not really exist with the experienced people, but when a trainee account manager and a trainee Professional Group member had to interact, the conflict tended to arise. A final element in Professional Group resentment of Account Management was the fact that because Account Management problems were now ones (responding to client requests and problems) the cooperation had tended to be one way."

While many of the stress points between Account Management and the Professional Groups had been resolved, some still remained. In 1979, Tom Paine, manager of the New York office, took the initiative to review the account manager function in writing. Mr. Paine began his report by emphasizing that there was a general commitment within Hewitt Associates to maintaining the basic structure of the system: "The two types of professionals work together to serve the client better than either type of professional alone could do the job. This dual perspective helps assure the client of high-quality decisions in a complex subject area. The account manager is trained to be familiar with the entire subject area of total compensation, to identify problems and discuss broad alternatives. He is also highly skilled at following processes which lead to effective solutions. The Professional Group consultant is trained to identify and solve problems of much greater depth in a narrower subject area."

Mr. Paine noted that the account manager performed three different functions in Hewitt Associates. First, as benefits expert, he or she acted as a specialist, not normally sharing responsibility with consultants from Professional Groups. He or she may require information from actuarial or installation or research, but these were primarily tools to allow the expert function to be performed. Second, the account manager could function as a project team leader, providing coordination and leadership to a client team consisting of both Account Management and Professional Group consultants. When functioning as a team leader, the account manager was a project coordinator and leader, but the Professional Group consultants were working directly for the clients and were fully responsible for the quality of their consulting. The third role performed by the account manager was that of account executive. In this role, the account manager might not be the project leader (which function may have been assigned to a member of a Professional Group), but would act as the client relations representative, sometimes participating in the project, sometimes not.

Mr. Paine noted, "Different account managers place varying emphasis on these three roles. The degrees to which each of these component roles is performed varies so widely that it is impossible to determine a normal method of operating."

Mr. Paine identified the problems that Hewitt Associates was encountering with the account management system. He noted: "No person can perform effectively in all three functions of the account management role as defined today. Furthermore, the problem will get worse with each passing year in spite of the best efforts of an account manager to learn and grow. The problem has two dimensions. First, the benefits field has become much more complicated and a generalist restricted to the benefits field has a hard time keeping up. Second, our Professional Group services are becoming more sophisticated and the account manager cannot keep up with developments in all these disciplines.

"Another dimension of the problem is time restraints. As our billings per client rises and our scope of service rendered to the typical client increases, more time is needed for the account executive functions. However, less time is available to do them since more time is being required to perform the functions of benefit expert and project leader. Because of the lack of time and the three roles, each account manager makes practical decisions leaning towards his or her own practical bent. This produces inconsistency. Perhaps even more of a threat to the goal of a satisfying work experience, frustrations generated by the shortage of time produces among some account managers tendencies to get the job done, to be somewhat autocratic, and to perceive the Professional Group consultant as someone to whom he delegates work because he's too busy to do it all himself."

Appraisal of Account Management personnel was also considered a problematical area, since a large number of factors had to be taken into account including various measures of the quality of the work done by the individual, his or her relationships with others in the organization, the management of client relationships, project management, management of billings and collections, and other contributions to the firm, to the local office, to the professional field, and so on. Related to this problem was the issue of partnership expectations: "Our basic standard for making an associate a partner is whether that individual can effectively represent the organization in his or her particular service area. If the account manager is to be measured solely on the basis of ability to consult on issues of benefit plan design, a traditional five-year time requirement is probably pertinent. However, if he or she is to be measured on ability to be an effective project leader as well as an account executive, a time span of eight to ten years is probably required before all functions of the job can be performed up to the required standard."

The importance of partnership decisions was discussed by Susan Kaye, Mr. Friedes' assistant: "Hewitt Associates tries to meet its people's needs for belonging, esteem and autonomy. But a number of factors make it increasingly hard to do. One is partnership, which inevitably engenders feelings on the part of nonpartners that some belong more than others. Another is the lack of hierarchy and titles for those who want to look esteemed. A third is our rapid growth and geographical dispersion, which leads to feelings of belonging to the Systems Group, for example, or the New York office, instead of to Hewitt Associates as a whole. Finally, the account manager structure makes some professional group people feel that account managers have more autonomy than others (more entrepreneurial latitude). Rewards are perhaps the most problematical in our environment. Since compensation is confidential, and taking on managerial responsibilities is not necessarily viewed as a promotion, the only certain, highly visible reward is partnership."

THE FUTURE

"As I look toward the future, reflected Mr. Friedes, "I wonder what changes, if any, we will need to make in our administrative systems and procedures: whether we can continue and maintain our philosophy as we grow larger. Changes of some form will certainly be necessary: an example might be the issue of productivity. We have avoided direct links between billability, financial performance of individual projects and personal reward. We are not trying to motivate people only with money. If the only reason people work hard is to earn more, they'll end up resenting it. We do not have a direct relationship between financial performance of projects and personal rewards. The rewards for extra effort are long-term, but in the short term most people here would tell you that the monetary rewards alone are not worth the extra effort.

"We think that having no profit centers is a great advantage to us. Other organizations don't realize how much time they waste fighting over allocations of overhead, transfer charges and other mechanisms caused by a profit center mentality. Whenever there are profit centers, cooperation between groups suffers badly. Of course, we pay a price for not having them: specific accountability is hard to pin down. We often don't know precisely whose time we are writing off, or who precisely brought in that new account. But at least we don't fight over it: we get on with our work. Our people know that over time good performance will be recognized and rewarded.

"Given all of this, how do I go about introducing productivity improvement without challenging or compromising our other goals? I am planning to introduce some specific productivity measures on a group basis only. For the professional groups, I will monitor chargeable time as a percent of dollars of salary. For the regional offices (i.e., account manager groups), the measure I have chosen is billings plus four times chargeable time, all divided by dollars of salary. However, I plan to make it clear that these are *goals,* not performance measures, and that they are group, not individuals goals. I will leave it to the individual groups to determine *how* to improve productivity, and I will encourage groups to share ideas: but I won't attempt to tell them how to.

"I think this will achieve the desired effect, but it is only an example of the pressures for change. Perhaps our biggest challenge will come from below. The desire by our new people to have definitive measures of performance is greater than we can (or want to) supply. We are hearing more frequently the question, 'How precisely, am I going to be measured?' It's the sort of question that you don't like to answer. Once you establish firm, definitive measures, people tend to excel only at the things you measure. I can't think of any quantitative measure that people cannot get around. We have a system based on judgment, and judgment requires trust."

EXHIBIT 1 Statement of income, 1978 and 1979 ($000)

	1979	*1978*
Fee income	$27,589	$23,370
Expenses		
Personnel, exclusive of partners	12,379	10,255
Occupancy	2,401	1,764
Equipment	1,553	1,265
Contact and promotion	621	450
Other operating expenses	2,703	2,425
Interest, net	251	75
Total expenses	$19,908	$16,234
Net income, allocable to partners	$ 7,681	$ 7,136

EXHIBIT 2 Balance Sheet, September 30, 1978 and 1979 ($000)

	1979	*1978*
Assets		
Cash and marketable securities	$ 460	$ 1,527
Receivables	6,317	5,705
Unbilled WIP	1,131	877
Prepaid expenses	276	279
Deposits	64	931
Total current	$ 8,248	$ 9,119
Property and equipment (less depreciation)	13,160	10,783
Total assets	21,409	19,902
Liabilities		
Current liabilities	3,343	3,071
Long-term debt	9,411	9,126
Net partnership capital	8,654	7,705
Total liabilities	$21,408	$19,902

EXHIBIT 3 Principles of Hewitt Associates' Management Style

1. We believe that adaptability is a characteristic needed by the individual and the organization. An organization can do much to accommodate the needs and preferences of the individual. Similarly, the individual should accommodate the needs and preferences of the organization.
2. We try to remember to demonstrate that every job is important and each individual, in carrying out his/her function well, is an important contributor to the organization.
3. We believe most people have capabilities beyond those they are called upon to demonstrate in their jobs. When people want to grow in ways that are productive for the organization, we try to provide them with the opportunity and encouragement to do so.
4. As our organization grows, we recognize the need for our associates to develop singular and, sometimes, specialized skills. At the same time, we feel we can best serve clients and associates if each associate is given the opportunity to develop and maintain a broad outlook in our field.
5. The ideal situation is one in which manager and associate have mutual expectations about the current and immediate future role for the associate, and this role fits in well with organizational objectives. This commonness of expectations can exist only in an open environment with a constant exchange of information.
6. We try to realistically appraise the strengths and weaknesses of each associate in order to maximize strengths and work around weaknesses. We then try to work closely with associates so that they can make their greatest contribution to the organization.
7. Associates are given the opportunity to participate in the determination of their own jobs, direction of progress, areas of interest, regional location, as long as they are consistent with the objectives of the firm and the strengths of the individual. The success of this individualistic approach is dependent on feedback of work performance, development of mutual expectations and adaptability of the associate and management.
8. Competition between people in an organization tends to conflict with cooperation—and retard any natural tendency to work together toward common goals of excellence and high quality. Thus we try to avoid, to the extent possible, competition between individuals, either qualitatively or quantitively, and avoid pitting one individual against another in the process of work assignments or positions.
9. Individuals have a right to know anything (except personal matters of other associates) about Hewitt Associates that might be useful to them in their judgments about the organization and their future in it. We try to disseminate information through personal discussion, periodic bulletins, general memos, information sharing meetings, etc. (Sometimes a topic must be kept confidential in order to protect the organization, but this situation is rare.) These devices will never be sufficient to communicate effectively to a large group. We welcome and encourage associates to *ask* questions when they want to know something.
10. No matter how large we become, we want to achieve a work environment in which ideas and concepts can develop with freshness and spontaneity, uninhibited, as far as possible, by rigid "communication channels."

EXHIBIT 4 Billable Time Charges by Group ($000)

	1979	*1978*
Machines and Administration		63
Account Management	3,221	5,867
Actuarial	3,625	9,936
Plan Installation	894	1,129
Plan Administration	341	1,138
Communications	1,020	3,173
Client Special Services	193	715
Systems	764	3,179
Salary, Admin./Exec. Comp.	417	2,014
MCS	392	899
Total organization	10,867	28,113[a]

[a]Differences between this total and billings shown in Exhibit 1 may be accounted for by work in progress (work performed and not billed), deferred revenue recognition and changes in receivables reserves.

EXHIBIT 5 Personnel Statistics

	1975	*1976*	*1977*	*1978*	*1979*
Total personnel	276	384	461	510	560
Nonpartners[a]	230	331	402	444	488
Partners					
Administration	3	4	5	6	6
Account management	26	28	31	32	34
Professional group	17	21	23	28	32
	46	53	59	66	72

[a]Includes secretarial and other staff not considered, or who did not consider themselves on the "partnership track." Approximately one-third of all personnel at Hewitt Associates were in this category.

CHAPTER 5

Control Tightness (or Looseness)

As was discussed earlier, the benefit of any control (or control system) is derived from the increase in the likelihood that the organizational objectives will be achieved over what could be expected if the control were not in place. This benefit can be called the *amount of control achieved* or the *degree of certainty provided* by a control system, and it can be described in terms of how *tight* or *loose* the system is. Assuming away the problems of costs and the possibilities of harmful side effects that are often coincident with tight control (these are discussed in Chapter 6), tight control is good because it provides a high degree of certainty that people will act as the organization wishes.

Many articles and books in the practitioner-oriented management literature use the *control tightness* phrase. They describe firms as having *tight* or *loose* controls (or as having *tightened* or *loosened* their controls). When Sterling Software acquired Knowledge Ware, the two companies' MCSs were described in contrasting terms. Sterling was said to have *tight financial controls,* while Knowledge Ware was said to have *very weak or nonexistent financial controls.*[1]

How tightly to apply controls is a major management decision that has received little attention in research papers and textbooks, and there primarily in a results-control context. Tight control does not necessarily involve detailed monthly budgets and frequent, careful reviews of performance, as one management control textbook describes it,[2] although some firms have control systems with those MCS elements that do seem to product tight control. There are many other ways to effect tight control.

This chapter argues that tight control is not always feasible because too little information exists as to how the object of control; results, actions, or personnel/culture, relates to the overall organizational objectives. Where such information is in sufficient supply, differences in the use of that information can precipitate tighter or looser levels of control. In some settings, tight control can be effected by intensively using a single form of control, except, in most situations, personnel/cultural controls. Tight control can also be effected by using combinations of control types. No single control type or element is either necessary or sufficient for producing tight control.

TIGHT CONTROL AS A FUNCTION OF KNOWLEDGE

Tight control can only be effected where all (or most) of the control problems can be avoided or, more usually, where management has detailed and reasonably certain knowledge about how one or more of the control objects; results, actions, or personnel/culture, are related to the overall organizational objectives. This latter circumstance was described well in a book by Russell Stout:

> Every controlled circumstance implies a cause-effect relationship, so that a change in one causal factor will produce a predetermined change in another dependent factor. Our ability to control, therefore, is a function of our knowledge.[3]

This seems to suggest a universal rule about control, albeit one that may be difficult to use in practice: the amount of control capable of being generated in any situation is positively related to the extent and certainty of the knowledge linking the object of control and the desired outcomes. In other words, tight control is feasible only when reasonably certain, specific knowledge is available. Managers who restrict their organization's activities to its core competencies are more likely to have the knowledge necessary to effect tight control than those who do not.

While relatively certain, specific knowledge is necessary to effect tight control, it is not sufficient. The other necessary element is use of that knowledge. The following sections describe how each of the control types can be used to take advantage of the object-of-control knowledge that is available in order to generate tight control. Tight control depends on the ways in which the controls are designed and used.

TIGHT ACTION CONTROLS

Since the action control types are quite different from each another, the ways in which each type might be used to achieve tight control must be discussed separately. Overall, action control systems should be considered tight only if it is highly likely that employees will engage consistently in all of the actions critical to the operation's success and not take harmful actions.

Behavioral Constraints

Behavioral constraints, either physical or administrative, can produce tight control in some areas of an organization. Physical constraints come in many forms, ranging from simple locks on desks to elaborate software and electronic security systems. No simple rules can be provided as to the degree of control they provide, except, perhaps, that extra protection usually costs more. The controls used in most bank vault areas are a good example of a control system that is tight, largely owing to the physical constraints used.

Administrative constraints also provide widely varying degrees of control. In general, restricting decision making to higher organizational levels provide tighter control (1) if it can be assumed that higher-level personnel can be expected to make more reliable decisions than lower-level personnel, and (2) if it can be guaranteed that those who do not have authority for certain actions cannot violate the constraints that have been established. Separating sensitive duties among a larger number of people should make the accomplishment of a harmful activity less likely; therefore, control can be described as tighter.

Preaction Reviews

Preaction reviews sometimes cause control systems to be considered tight if the reviews are frequent, detailed, and performed by a diligent, knowledgeable person (or persons). Preaction reviews are typically tight in areas involving large resource allocations because many investments are not easily reversible and can, by themselves, affect the success or failure of a business or corporation. These tight preaction reviews often include thorough scrutiny of all business plans and requests for capital by staff personnel and multiple levels of managers, including top management. Some companies use tight preaction reviews before employees can spend even small amounts of money.

Examples of tight preaction reviews abound. At Irving Oil, a company that operates 3,000 gas stations throughout Eastern Canada, control is considered tight because Irving personnel "don't buy pencils before checking with [the chairman]."[4] L.A. Gear, the sport shoe manufacturer, is described as a *tight-fisted company* because senior management has to approve any expenditure greater than $2,500.[5] At most banks control is usually exercised more tightly over foreign branches than domestic branches; domestic branch managers are more frequently given the power to sign for larger loans without headquarter's approval. The control system at Amerada Hess is considered tight because the chairman "pursues his business down to its grimiest details."[6]

Tight preaction control can even be exercised at the board of directors level. Ted Turner, chairman of the huge Turner Broadcasting System ($3.4 billion in sales and $102 million in net income in 1995), and an acknowledged visionary in the communications industry, has made decisions that several times pushed his company close to insolvency. As a consequence, his board of directors will not let him spend more than $2 million, a tiny amount for such a large company, without a supermajority approval of the board.[7]

The requirement of reviews by top-level officers, committees, or even the board of directors does not, however, automatically signify that the preaction control is tight. Many busy top-level managers and even capital committees do not take the time to examine carefully all expenditure proposals, particularly smaller ones; they merely *rubber-stamp* them.

Action Accountability

The amount of control generated by action accountability controls depends on characteristics of the definitions of desirable (and undesirable) actions, the effectiveness of the action-tracking system, and the reinforcement (rewards and punishments) provided.

Definitions of Actions

To effect tight control, the definitions of actions in an action accountability control system must be congruent, specific, well communicated, and complete. *Congruence* means that the performance (or nonperformance) of the actions defined in the control system will indeed lead to the achievement of the true organizational objectives.

Tighter control can also be effected by making the definitions of acceptability more *specific*. *Specific* means defining the desirable behaviors in the form of work rules (for example, no smoking) or specific policies (for example, a purchasing policy to obtain three competing bids before releasing a purchase order); as opposed to general guidelines or vague codes of conduct (for example, act professionally).

Tight action control depends on *understanding* and *acceptance* on the part of those whose behaviors are being controlled. If the people involved do not understand the rules, the rules cannot affect them. If they do not accept the rules, they may try to find ways to avoid the whole system. Understanding and acceptance can be improved through developing effective communication processes and by allowing employees to participate in the rule-defining processes.

Finally, if the MCS relies exclusively or extensively on action accountability, the definitions of desired actions must be *complete. Completeness* means that all the important, acceptable (and unacceptable) actions are well defined. One indicative comment from someone who is working in a tight action accountability environment is, "We have procedures for everything we do." The procedures should cover things that *could* or even just *might* affect the organization.

Action Tracking

Control in an action accountability control system can also be made tighter by improving the effectiveness of the action-tracking system. Personnel who are certain that their actions will be noticed, and noticed relatively quickly, will be affected more strongly by an action accountability control system than those who feel that the chance of being observed is small. Constant direct supervision is one tight action-tracking method. Detailed audits of action reports is another. This type of tight control apparently took place at Commodore International, as the company chairman, Jack Tramiel, was said to conduct detailed reviews of expenses, sometimes down to items costing as little as $25.[8]

Rewards or Punishments

Finally, control can be made tighter by making the rewards or punishments more significant to the individuals affected. In general, significance varies directly with the size of the reward (or the severity of the punishment); however, different individuals may react differently to identical rewards or punishments.

Even the most detailed action specifications combined with excellent action-tracking systems can be undercut by the lack of link with rewards or punishments. The requirements described in company planning or capital budgeting manuals, many of which are quite explicit, will not be followed if top management does not show interest in having them followed. For action accountability to be tight, *all* of the elements of the action control system; definitions of actions, action tracking, and rewards or punishments, must be designed appropriately.

Examples of Tight Action Controls

The way commercial airlines control the actions of their pilots provides a good example of a tight action accountability control system. The pilots are given detailed checklists specifying nearly all required actions, not only for normal operations but also for all foreseeable contingencies (such as, engine failure, fire on board, wind shear, and hijacking). Intensive training helps ensure that the procedures are understood, and frequent checking and updating help ensure that they remain in the pilot's active memory. The tracking of deviant actions is precise and timely as all potential violations are thoroughly screened by objective investigators. Finally, reinforcement is significant because pilots are threatened with severe penalties, including loss of profession (and loss of life).

Some government procurement procedures, such as those for the U.S. Department of Defense, are also prototypical examples of tight action controls. The procedures require contractors to have extensive written documentation describing how all their processes (purchasing, handling, machining, assembling, fabricating, inspecting, testing, modifying, and installing) should work and how they ensure that those processes are executed properly. When government officials find noncompliance, they hold the companies liable and may assess them significant damages.

Examples of Loose Action Controls

The numerous stories of *rogue traders* in financial institutions provide good illustrations of loose action control systems. Toshihide Iguchi, a trader of U.S. Treasury Securities for Daiwa Bank of Japan, lost $1.1 billion for the bank by making about 30,000 unauthorized trades over an eleven-year period. Yasuo Hamanaka, the chief copper trader at Sumitomo Corporation, cost his employer an estimated $2.6 billion. Over a period of a decade, he lost money on trades and then attempted to cover the losses with borrowing and falsified documents.[9] Trader Nicholas Leesen similarly cost the British bank Barings $1 billion. Robert Citron, the treasurer for Orange County, California, lost $1.7 billion in public funds on highly leveraged investment gambles on interest rates. What is common in these examples is little or no preaction reviews by superiors, often because they did not understand, or did not want to understand, how the interim profits were being generated. In addition, these companies had few, if any, audits, which could have detected the illicit scheme.

Loose action controls are increasingly common in the many forward-looking companies who have engaged in the *reengineering* of their business processes. These reengineering efforts, aimed at eliminating *non-value-added* tasks, have made these companies' processes more efficient. Reengineering consultants often define preaction reviews, segregation of duties, paper trails, and reconciliations as non-value-added. While these controls might not add value, they help prevent the dissipation of value the company may have otherwise generated. The result is that the controls in reengineered business processes are often loose, or sometimes even nonexistent.

TIGHT RESULTS CONTROL

Tight results controls are effected in a manner quite similar to that for effecting tight action accountability controls. The achievement of tight results control depends on characteristics of the definitions of the desired result areas, the performance measures, and the reinforcements provided.

Definitions of Desired Results

For control to be considered tight in a results control system, the results dimensions must be congruent with true organizational objectives; the performance targets must be specific, with feedback in short time increments; the desired results must be effectively communicated and internalized by those whose behaviors are being controlled; and if results controls are used exclusively in a given performance area, the measures must be complete.

Congruence

Chapter 3 discussed congruence as one of the prime determinants of the effectiveness of results controls. Results control systems may suffer congruence problems either because managers do not understand well the organization's true objectives or because the performance dimensions on which the managers choose to measure results do not reflect the true objectives well.

For many types of organizations and for many specific areas within organizations, it is a reasonable assumption that the true objectives are well understood. It is clearly desirable for production workers to be more efficient and for sales personnel to sell more, everything else being equal. In many other organizations, however, good understanding is not a reasonable assumption. In many types of public and not-for-profit organizations, major constituents disagree as to the organization's objectives. Is the primary objective of a government entity to provide more services or reduce its costs (and tax burden)? Where objectives are not clear, congruence becomes a more limiting problem.

Choosing measurable performance dimensions that reflect an organization's true objectives is often challenging. Is number of patents granted a good indicator of a research and development organization's ability to create value, most of which comes from developing commercially successful ideas for new products? Is annual profits a good indicator of the success of a company with significant growth prospects? Is the number of visitors a good indicator of the success of a museum? If the chosen measurable performance dimensions are not good indicators of the organization's true objectives, then the results control system cannot be tight, regardless of any of the other systems characteristics.

Specificity and Timeliness

Tight results control also depends on having performance targets described in specific terms and in relatively short increments of time. Specific targets are disaggregated and quantified, $2.21 labor costs per unit of production, a 15 percent return on assets each quarter, or less than 1 percent customer complaints. Examples of less specific or vague targets include: Do a good job; Be efficient; and, Keep the customers happy.

As a loose form of control over managers' *environmental* performance, superiors might merely evaluate the global performance area subjectively or rely on government auditors' reports. The superiors could tighten control in this area by setting quantitative targets and measuring performance in multiple environmental performance areas, such as energy usage, number and size of spills, volume and type of waste generated, and extent of recycling.[10]

In some areas of most companies, detailed and specific performance targets and measures are not feasible. It is usually difficult to be specific as to how many cases a lawyer should handle in a year or what is meant by ethical behavior; however, specificity is one of the elements necessary for the implementation of tight results control.

Communication and Internalization

It is obvious that for results control to be tight, performance targets must be communicated effectively and internalized by those charged with their accomplishment. Only then can the targets influence performance. The degree to which goals are understood and internalized seems to be affected by many factors, including the qualifications of the personnel involved, the amount of participation allowed in the goal-setting processes, the perceived degree of controllability, and the reasonableness of the goals. Internalization is likely to be low where employees believe the goals are unachievable, where they consider the desired results to be uncontrollable, and, sometimes, where those whose behaviors are being controlled are simply not allowed to participate in setting the goals.

Failure to get employees to internalize goals can cause problems, as William Hartman found when he took over Interpace Corporation, a $350 million (sales) conglomerate headquartered in Parsippany, New Jersey. Hartman attempted to transform Interpace into a dynamic growth company in part by implementing a control system modeled after the system employed by ITT in the successful Harold Geneen era. The system focused on financial results and "[compelled] managers to abide by financial dicta." The results, however, were poor, apparently because the managers never understood either what their goals were or how they were to accomplish them. The managers claimed that Hartman "kept his strategic goals to himself." Hartman claims he was consistently "frustrated [because] people don't see the important factors in getting to goal."[11]

Completeness

Completeness is the final requirement for tight results control. It is important only if control is effected exclusively, or at least extensively, through results controls. Completeness means that the result defined in the control system include all the areas in which the organization desires good performance and for which the individual involved can have some impact. What is not measured becomes less visible, or perhaps even invisible.[12] Thus, when the defined result areas are incomplete, individuals often allow performance in the unmeasured areas to slip. A purchasing manager who is evaluated solely on meeting cost standards may allow quality to slip. Similarly, salespeople who are asked to meet a sales volume quota are likely to strive for volume, at the expense, possibly, of smaller but more profitable sales.

In a hybrid control system made up of some combination of results, actions, and personnel controls, the definition of results areas does not have to be complete. Managers must take care to ensure that all significant potential control problems are covered in some manner.

Measurement of Performance

Tight results control also depends on the effectiveness of the measures of performance that are generated. As discussed in Chapter 3, results control relies on measures that are precise, objective, timely, and understandable. A control system that is used to apply tight control requires excellence in all of these measurement qualities. If measures fail in any of these areas, the control system cannot be characterized as tight because behavioral problems are likely.

Rewards or Punishments

Results controls are likely to be tighter if rewards and punishments that are significant to the individuals involved are directly and definitely linked to the accomplishment (or nonaccomplishment) of the desired results. A *direct link* means that results translate automatically into rewards or punishments, with no buffers and no ambiguity. A *definite link* between results and rewards means that no excuses are tolerated. Many companies use direct and definite links in their results control systems:

- The systems used at Tenneco and at Cypress Semiconductor Corporation are actually called *no-excuses management*.[13] Managers are expected to meet short-term performance targets consistently, regardless of outside economic forces. In the words of T. J. Rodgers, Cypress's president:

> How do we measure success at Cypress? By doing what we say we are going to do. We meet sales projections within a percentage point or two every quarter. We don't go over budget—ever.[14]

- At Bausch & Lomb, a former president said, "Once you signed up for your target number, you were expected to reach it." Managers who failed to achieve annual profit targets by even a small amount received paltry bonuses, while those who exceeded them earned hefty payouts.[15]
- At Campbell Soup Company, budgets were formerly treated "more like guidelines than goals."[16] No more. Now when managers make their budgets, the CEO—"a shameless cheerleader given to hokey publicity stunts—will hire a brass band and serve you cake on a plate. Miss it [and the CEO] will serve your can on a platter."[17]

The strength of the effects of any particular reward is difficult to predict, as different individuals often react differently to identical rewards or punishments. Many employees respond to rewards such as job security, recognition, or self-satisfaction more strongly than monetary rewards. At General Mills entrepreneurs whose companies have been acquired but who stay on as division managers are motivated with sizable performance bonuses. Bonuses and threat of divestment seem to provide less motivation than does the desire to avoid embarrassment before peers. As one such entrepreneur, Thad Eure, Jr., president of the Darryl's Restaurant chain which was acquired by General Mills, noted: "Our pride makes us want to show these people what we can do."[18]

Results-related reinforcement appears to be weak at *top* management levels in most companies. Even where bonus awards appear to be large, evidence suggests the awards often have little or no relationship to company performance.[19] It is natural that most managers, being risk averse, prefer guaranteed payments (salary) rather than payments which are contingent on performance. Many companies, however, have been criticized for providing these guaranteed payments. Critics have noted that "many compensation committees [of boards of directors] are rubber stamps, unwilling to be hard-nosed about the pay of top executives."[20] The recent trend in management compensation, however, is toward making the link between compensation and performance more direct and more definite.

Examples of Tight Results Controls

The system used to control drivers at United Parcel Services (UPS) of America provides a good example of a tight results control system. UPS pays good wages but pushes its drivers hard. Management compares each driver's performance (how many miles, how many deliveries, and how many pickups) every day with a computerized projection of what performance should have been. Drivers who cannot meet the standards are assigned a supervisor to ride with them to provide suggestions for improvement, and those who do not improve can be warned, suspended, and eventually dismissed.[21]

This control system meets every characteristic of tight results control. The results measures seem to be congruent with the company's goal of maximizing shareholder value because the company has been successful; it dominates the small-package delivery market. The measures seem to be complete at the driver level. Drivers have no other significant responsibilities other than to deliver packages efficiently. The performance targets are specific; measurement is thorough and done on a frequent (daily) basis; and the rewards, which include job security and sizable amounts of money, are significant to the personnel involved.

Sony, the large Japanese electronics company, is an example of a company that took steps to tighten its results controls. When Nobuyuki Idei took over as Sony's president, he started the process of "trying to bring [Sony's U.S.] operation under tighter control."[22] Sony Pictures, particularly, had not been performing well, and the performance problems forced Sony to take a write-off in excess of $3 billion. Sony managers realized that, "They have to get in and get their hands dirty. They have to understand the business."[23] They also began to get "tougher and meaner" in "holding their international executives accountable for their financial performance."[24]

TIGHT PERSONNEL/CULTURAL CONTROLS

MCSs dominated by personnel/cultural controls can sometimes be considered tight. In voluntary organizations, personnel controls usually provide a significant amount of control, as most volunteers derive a keen sense of satisfaction just from doing a good job, and are thus motivated to do well.

Tight personnel/cultural controls also exist in some business situations. They are common in small family-run businesses where the already-present, individual personnel controls may be totally effective because of the complete, or at least extensive, overlap between the desires of the organization and those of the individuals on whom it must rely.

Some companies use multiple forms of personnel/cultural controls which, in combination, seem to effect tight control. Among the controls used in production areas of Wabash National Corporation, a truck-trailer manufacturer located in Lafayette, Indiana are[25]

- *walk and talk* interviews in which job applicants get to observe the *frenetic factory pace,*
- group incentive plans, including a profit-sharing plan that gives employees 10 percent of after-tax earnings, and a retirement plan that bases contributions on profit margins,
- required training. New employees are strongly encouraged to take two specified Wabash improvement classes on their own time and are rewarded with pay raises for doing so. Supervisors are promoted only after they take special classes and pass a test.

Performance at Wabash has been consistently outstanding since the company was founded. The company's sales grew at an annual growth rate of more than 50 percent in the company's first ten years, to $562 million in 1994; market share climbed to 15 percent in 1994, up from less than 6 percent in 1988; and sales per employee rose 18 percent in 1994 alone. An executive who recently visited Wabash remarked that, "I've never seen a work force that motivated."

In most cases, however, the degree of control provided by the personnel/cultural controls is less than tight. In most business organizations, the natural overlap between individual and organizational objectives is smaller than in family firms. It is also unstable. An impending divergence between the individual and organizational objectives is difficult to observe. What was effective for years can break down quite quickly.

Many independent oil producers had a longstanding tradition of trust in their employees that kept them from adopting strict controls. One of them, Mitchell Energy, did not audit its suppliers, rarely required sealed bids, and had a weak, poorly communicated conflict-of-interest policy. When employees were caught in a kickback scheme that had been operating for over a decade, the company's general counsel's reaction was, "We trusted the employees. We thought everyone would be too proud of the company to do something like that."[26]

Similarly, acquaintances of Bernard F. Bradstreet were shocked when Mr. Bradstreet's role in a major *cooking-the-books*-type fraud became known. Bradstreet was the president of Kurzweil Applied Intelligence, a Waltham, Massachusetts-based company which specializes in voice recognition technology. With Bradstreet's involvement, the company booked millions of dollars in phony sales in a two-year period, straddling its initial public offering in August 1993. To hide the scheme, Bradstreet and other employees created phony sales documents with forged customers' signatures, hid unsold goods from auditors, and in at least one case, retrieved an auditor's receivables confirmation letter from a customer and forged a signature on that. When the fraud was exposed, the company's stock sunk to about 2½, from a high of 21 in late 1993. Bradstreet's acquaintances were shocked because Bradstreet had never shown any signs of dishonesty. He was a graduate of Harvard College and Harvard Business School and had been a marine fighter pilot and air combat instructor during the Vietnam war. Over a successful twenty-year career as a loan officer, treasurer, CEO, and president, he was "the epitome of an honest and straightforward executive."[27] A former business school classmate remembered Bradstreet as "honorable, decent, steady, and straight as rain, not flashy at all."[28] The former chief financial officer at Prime Computer at the time when Bradstreet worked as Prime's treasurer said, "He was a highly ethical family man. Certainly, the guy I knew wouldn't knowingly perpetrate the kinds of things he has been accused of."[29] An assistant treasurer at Prime said, "Bernie was squeaky clean. He didn't even swear." Sentencing guidelines call for Bradstreet now to receive up to ten years in jail.

Like the reliability of the personnel controls, the effectiveness of the steps that might be taken to increase the strength of personnel controls is usually difficult to assess. In general, personnel control effectiveness is a function of the knowledge available to link the control mechanism with the solution of the existing control problems. Often the information about how well factors such as education, experience, and personality predict performance is not reliable.

Cultural controls, on the other hand, are often powerful and stable. Culture involves a set of shared beliefs and values that employees use to guide behavior. Some companies' cultures can be termed strong because they include quite a few deeply held and widely shared beliefs and values. Electronic Data Systems, Hewlett-Packard, Johnson & Johnson, Merck, Sony, Motorola, Nordstrom, The Walt Disney Company, Wal-Mart, Nike, and Procter & Gamble are among the companies generally considered to have a strong culture.[30] Most large companies have weak cultures because of their diversity and dispersion of people.

Except for companies with strong cultures, tight control probably cannot be effected with the use of personnel/cultural control devices alone. Most personnel controls and cultures are unstable. They can break down quickly if demands, opportunities, or needs change, and they provide little or no warning of failure.

MULTIPLE FORMS OF CONTROLS

When they wish to tighten controls, managers often use multiple forms of controls. The controls can either reinforce each other or overlap, thus filling in each others' gaps so that they, in combination, provide tight control over all of the factors critical to the entity's success.

Managers of the Continental Illinois National Bank & Trust tightened up controls in the bank's lending area by insisting on more extensive loan documentation and by having this documentation reviewed and approved by more bank officers than was required previously before a loan was authorized (preaction review). At the same time, they created a new credit-review division to analyze the loan portfolio in a more careful, more objective, more timely fashion"[31] (results control).

At the corporate level, tight control almost always involves multiple forms of control. Campbell Soup Company is an example of a company that has implemented multiple mechanisms to keep "management on a tight leash."[32] Campbell places up to 75 percent of managers' total compensation at risk (results control). The managers earn bonuses only if the company meets specific annual goals for sales, profits, and return-on-assets relative to the performance of other food companies. Seventy top executives must own stock valued at one-half to three times their base salary to help ensure that they share shareholders' perspectives. Vice chairman Bennett Dorrance's primary assignment is to exercise tight oversight of top managers by making sure the company's policies are implemented properly (preaction review and action accountability).

Under Harold Geneen, the legendary leader of ITT from the 1950s to the 1970s, ITT was considered to have a prototypical tight control system.[33] The company hired good managers (personnel control) and motivated them by paying large results-dependent bonuses that brought their total salaries to approximately 30 percent over comparable jobs in other firms (results control). The company used an extremely detailed planning, budgeting, and reporting system, and top management, with the support of a large staff organization, used it to monitor the plans, activities, and performances of all business units (preaction review and results control). It is interesting to note, however, that Geneen's successor, Rand Araskog, dismantled much of the tight control infrastructure because it did not suit his managerial style. Araskog also had serious concerns that he might be lacking some of the knowledge necessary to implement tight controls, particularly knowledge regarding the factors critical to the success of each of the company's various businesses.[34]

CONCLUSION

This chapter has focused on another major characteristic of controls and control systems: their degree of tightness. Tight control is defined here as good. It means a high degree of assurance that people will behave as the organization wishes. Managers should implement tight controls, using any of the designs discussed in this chapter, if they have good knowledge about how one or more objects of control (that is, actions, results, and personnel/culture) relate to the organization's goals *and* if they can implement the chosen form(s) of controls effectively.

All of the control types can be used to provide tight control, depending on

TABLE 5-1 A Summary of the Characteristics That Make a Control "Tight"

Type of Control	*What Makes It Tight*
Results or Action Accountability	Definition of desired results or actions: • Congruent with true organizational skills • Specific • Effectively communicated and internalized • Complete (if accountability emphasized) Measurement of results or tracking of actions: • Congruent • Precise • Objective • Timely • Understandable Rewards or punishments: • Significant to person(s) involved • Direct and definite link to results or actions
Behavioral Constraints	Reliable Restrictive
Preaction Reviews	Frequent Detailed Performed by informed person(s)
Personnel/Cultural Controls	Certainty and stability of knowledge linking personnel/cultural characteristics with desired actions

how and where they are designed and used. A summary of the characteristics of each of the control types that can be varied to produce tight (as opposed to loose), control is presented in Table 5-1.

Managers are not limited to tinkering with the characteristics of just one form of control, of course. There are many examples of situations where a particular type of control has been replaced with another type, which provides a better fit with the situation, in order to tighten controls. Observers of Varian Associates concluded that the company's managers had tightened up their controls because they replaced a "gentlemanly 'atta boy' approach" (personnel control) with results controls. The results controls included incentive plans for improved division-level financial performance and achievement of strict targets for inventory and receivables levels.[35] Alternatively, top management of Texas Instruments tightened up controls over the company's troubled consumer electronics areas by de-emphasizing results controls and emphasizing detailed preaction reviews.[36] Managers can also use multiple forms of control simultaneously to tighten up control systems.

Some managers who have concluded either that they do not have adequate knowledge about how one or more objects of control relate to the organization's objectives or that they cannot implement the chosen form(s) of controls effectively have chosen to *loosen* their company's control systems. They have done so because an inappropriate use of controls can cause any of a number of harmful side effects. It is these side effects that cause many people to have negative feelings when they hear the mere mention of tight control.

Gould loosened up its results controls by reducing the volume and specificity of the information used to monitor its divisions. Prior to the change, Gould corporate-level managers required their division managers to submit a weekly budget containing twelve pieces of information; including daily sales, order backlog, and working capital, not just a *bottom-line* number.[37] After the change, the corporate managers reviewed performance only monthly and allowed division managers to operate more autonomously. They made this change because they were concerned that the tight preaction reviews sometimes created costly operating delays. They were also concerned that the twelve pieces of information were not congruent with the company's goal to create shareholder value. In particular, they wanted division managers to focus on longer-term performance, on innovation more than weekly operating details. The costs and negative side effects associated with some control types and, particularly, with imperfect or inappropriate uses of controls are discussed in Chapter 6.

Notes

1. T. L. O'Brien, "Knowledge Ware Accounting Practices are Questioned," *Wall Street Journal* (September 7, 1994), p. B2.
2. R. N. Anthony, J. Dearden, and V. Govindarajan, *Management Control Systems* (Homewood, Ill.: Irwin, 1992).
3. R. Stout, Jr., *Management or Control?: The Organizational Challenge* (Bloomington: Indiana University Press, 1980), p. 4.
4. A. Freeman and J. Urquart, "Hard-Working Irvings Maintain Tight Control in a Canadian Province," *Wall Street Journal* (November 1, 1983), p. 1.
5. D. Darlin, "Getting Beyond a Market Niche," *Forbes* (November 22, 1993), pp. 106–107.
6. S. Mufson, "Amerada Hess Chief Keeps Controls Tight, Emphasizes Marketing," *Wall Street Journal* (January 11, 1983), p. 1.
7. R. Goldberg and G. J. Goldberg, *Citizen Turner: The Wild Rise of an American Tycoon* (Harcourt Brace, 1995).
8. S. Chace and M. W. Miller, "Commodore's Tramiel Sharpens Competition in Small Computers," *Wall Street Journal* (August 18, 1983), p. 1.
9. M. Shirouzu, S. Frank, and S. McGee, "Sumitomo Puts Its Copper Losses at $2.6 Billion, Will Sue Ex-Trader," *Wall Street Journal* (September 20, 1996), p. C1.
10. Institute of Management Accountants, *Implementing Corporate Environmental Strategies*, Statement of Management Accounting #4W (Montvale, N.J.: Institute of Management Accountants, July 31, 1995).
11. "How a Winning Formula Can Fail," *Business Week* (May 25, 1981), pp. 119–20.
12. G. Morgan and H. Willmott, "The 'New' Accounting Research: On Making Accounting More Visible," *Accounting, Auditing and Accountability Journal* (6 No. 4 (1993), pp. 3–36.
13. W. Zellner, "The Fight of His Life," *Business Week* (September 20, 1993), p. 54–64; and T. J. Rodgers, "No Excuses Management," *Harvard Business Review*, 68, no. 4 (July-August 1990), pp. 84–98.
14. Rodgers, 1990, p. 84.
15. M. Maremont, "Blind Ambition: How the Pursuit of Results Got Out of Hand at Bausch & Lomb," *Business Week* (October 23, 1995), p. 81.
16. B. Saporito, "Campbell Soup Gets Piping Hot," *Fortune* (September 9, 1991), p. 144.
17. Ibid., pp. 145–146.
18. "How to Manage Entrepreneurs," *Business Week* (September 7, 1981), p. 69.
19. See M. Jensen and K. Murphy, "Performance Pay and Top-Management Incentives," *Journal of Political Economy*, 98, no. 2 (1990), pp. 225–264.
20. See C. J. Loomis, "The Madness of Executive Compensation," *Fortune* (July 12, 1982), p. 45.
21. "Behind the UPS Mystique: Puritanism and Productivity," *Business Week* (June 6, 1983), pp. 66–73.

22. J. Osha, analyst at Merrill Lynch Japan, quoted in L. Helm, "Idei Man: Schulhof Ouster May Signal Tighter Control by New Sony Chief," *Los Angeles Times* (December 6, 1995), pp. D1, D11.
23. Helm, "Idei Man," p. D1.
24. Ibid.
25. This example taken from R. L. Rose, "Hard Driving: A Productivity Push at Wabash National Puts Firm on a Roll," *Wall Street Journal* (September 7, 1995), p. 1.
26. B. Burrough, "Oil-Field Investigators Say Fraud Flourishes From Wells to Offices," *Wall Street Journal* (January 15, 1985), p. 20.
27. M. Maremont, "Anatomy of a Fraud," *Business Week* (September 16, 1996), p. 90.
28. Ibid, p. 91.
29. Ibid, p. 90.
30. See J. C. Collins and J. I. Porras, *Built to Last: Successful Habits of Visionary Companies* (New York: Harper Business, 1994).
31. J. Helyar, "Big Continental Illinois Hopes It Will Recover as U. S. Economy Does," *Wall Street Journal* (January 5, 1983), p. 1.
32. P. Berman and A. Alger, "Reclaiming the Patrimony," *Forbes* (March 14, 1994), p. 52.
33. This example is taken from H. Geneen, *Managing* (Garden City, NY: Doubleday, 1984).
34. "ITT: Groping for a New Strategy," *Business Week* (December 15, 1980), pp. 66–80.
35. K. K. Wiegner, "It's About Time," *Forbes* (April 25, 1983), pp. 41–42.
36. D. Stipp, "Texas Instruments Seeks Comeback Trail in Consumer Electronics; Outlook Is Hazy," *Wall Street Journal* (September 12, 1983), p. 4.
37. H. Klein, "Gould Loosens Up as It Gains in High-Tech, But Some Doubt Strong Chief Will Let Go," *Wall Street Journal* (May 26, 1983), p. 33.

Controls at the Sands Hotel and Casino

In July 1983, Stephen F. Hyde, president of the Sands Hotel and Casino in Atlantic City, commented on his company's control system which, he was convinced, was a model of excellence:

> Our controls are probably as good or better than those in use in any other company. Most companies couldn't afford the controls we use, but we really have to have them. In the casino, which is our major attraction and our most lucrative business, there is a lot of money changing hands, and that provides a lot of temptation for our employees and guests to try to take that money away from us. Our controls help us ensure that we get our fair share of what is wagered.
>
> Many of *our* controls are legally required, as the state of New Jersey has an extensive list of regulations to make sure it gets its share. But we would have those controls whether they were required or not, because it makes good business sense to do so. In support of that contention, I can tell you that we used almost the same set of controls that we have here in our Las Vegas casino, even though the Nevada regulations are not nearly as stringent as those in New Jersey. Also, our controls exceed even the New Jersey requirements in some cases, because we feel that despite the expense, an outstanding system of controls is in the best interest of our shareholders.

Gambling in New Jersey

In 1976, New Jersey voters amended their state's constitution to allow casino gambling in Atlantic City. The hopes were that this once-glamorous city would be rejuvenated and that taxes on gambling would provide a lucrative source of revenue for the state.

To regulate the new gaming industry, the New Jersey Casino Control Commission (NJCCC) was established. The NJCCC's first action was to develop a comprehensive set of regulations that established minimum guidelines to be followed in all phases of the gaming operations. Every organization that wanted to build gaming establishments in Atlantic City had to prepare a detailed application that included an in-depth discussion of the casino layouts, strategies, and controls that would be used, and these had to be approved by the NJCCC.

The gaming industry moved into Atlantic City very rapidly. The first casino (Resorts International) opened in 1978, and by 1982, nine large hotel/casinos were operating under such well-known gaming names as Harrah's, Caesar's World, Bally, Playboy, Tropicana, and the Sands. In 1982, twenty million people visited Atlantic City, making it the most-visited city in the United States, and combined gambling revenue for the nine casinos was approximately $1.5 billion.

After the casinos began operations, the NJCCC continued to exercise close scrutiny over them. Full-time NJCCC inspectors were required to be present on the floor of each casino and in the count rooms (where the winnings were counted) to ensure that the regulations were being followed and that the casinos were maintaining an orderly house. In addition, NJCCC personnel had to approve all major policy decisions made by casino management, even including how they promoted their businesses.

The Sands

The Sands Hotel and Casino was the operating unit of the Great Bay Casino Corporation (GBCC). In 1982, the Sands' (and GBCC's)

Research Assistant Jeffrey M. Traynor and Professor Kenneth A. Merchant prepared this case as the basis for class discussion rather than to illustrate either effective or ineffective handling of an administrative situation.

gross revenue was $184 million, of which $144 million came from gaming (casino) operations and the rest from hotel operations, which included rooms, entertainment, and food and beverage. (GBCC's 1982 financial statements are shown in Exhibit 1.)

The casino and hotel were run as separate profit centers. The unique feature of the organization (see Exhibit 2), as compared to that in most corporations, was the relatively large size of the finance staff. Of a total of approximately 2,600 people in the organization, over 400 were in the finance organization, reporting in a direct line to the vice president-Finance, Ed Sutor (see Exhibit 3). Strict separation was maintained between operations and recordkeeping, and the finance organization was large because it had responsibility for cash control and recordkeeping, both important functions in the casino and food and beverage parts of the business, particularly. Thus, the finance organization included cashiers, casino change personnel, pit clerks, and count room personnel, in addition to people who were normally part of a finance organization, such as accounting clerks and financial analysts.

In the casino operations area, the Sands operated 1,077 coin-operated gaming devices (slot machines), 59 blackjack tables, 20 crap tables, 10 roulette wheels, 2 baccarat tables, and 2 big six wheels. The games operated on a two-shift basis—day and swing shifts—covering a total period from 10:00 A.M. to 4:00 A.M. weekdays and 10:00 A.M. to 6:00 A.M. weekends. A total of 930 people were employed in casino operations (see Exhibit 4).

CONTROLS IN THE CASINO

The controls used in the casino were intended to ensure that the Sands and the state of New Jersey each kept their fair share of the money that was wagered. In a short case, it is not possible to describe all of the many controls that were employed in the casino, but the function of many of them can be described in terms of how they enabled casino management to control: (1) cash and the movement of cash within the casino and, (2) the operation of the casino table games.

To simplify the discussion, all references will be to the table game of blackjack.[1] The following section provides a brief description of blackjack and the personnel involved in running it.

Operation of Blackjack Game at Sands Casino

Blackjack is a very popular card game where up to seven patrons play against the house. The players' object is to draw cards whose total is higher than the dealer's total without exceeding 21.

In 1983, the Sands Hotel operated 89 gaming tables, 59 (66%) of which were for blackjack. In May 1983, the blackjack drop[2] was $23 million and the win[3] total was $3.2 million. These totals were the highest for any table game or type of coin-operated gambling device in the casino except for the $.25 slot machines.

Each blackjack table was run by a dealer whose job was to sell chips to customers, deal the cards, take losing wagers, and pay winning wagers. Dealing was a skilled profession that required some training and considerable practice. Experience was valuable, as the dealer's value to the casino increased with the number of games that could be dealt within a given time period, and speed usually increased with experience. Experience was also valuable in identifying players who might be cheating.

Dealers received a 20-minute break every hour. Dealers assigned to a table worked for 40 minutes and then were replaced by a "relief dealer" during their break. Relief dealers worked at two different tables for 20 minutes each and then received their break. The frequent breaks were required because the job was mentally and physically taxing—dealers were required to be standing up while they dealt; they had to maintain intense concentration, as errors in paying off bets

[1]This is done with little loss of generality. Control over all the table games in the Sands was nearly identical. The one major exception was that one extra level of supervision (boxperson) was used at the crap tables. In the coin-operated gaming devices area, control was simpler because machines eliminated the human element (dealers). The machines did, however, have to be inspected regularly for evidence of tampering.

[2]At the gaming tables, drop refers to the total amount of cash and credit exchanged at the tables for chips. In the slot machine areas, drop refers to the total amount of money removed from the drop bucket.

[3]The term "win" refers to the difference between gaming gains and losses before deducting costs and expenses.

were not tolerated; and they had to maintain good humor under sometimes difficult conditions (e.g., dealing to players who became irritable because they were losing).

Dealers were paid well. New dealers earned approximately $23,000 to 25,000 including tips (which were shared among all dealers).

Two levels of direct supervision were used over the blackjack tables. A "floorperson" was assigned to monitor two blackjack tables. A "pit boss" supervised eight tables.

Control of Cash

Because of the casino business was conducted in terms of cash or cash equivalents (i.e., chips), it was important to have good control over the many stocks of cash and chips that were located within the casino, and to be able to move these stocks without loss. The Sands' cash control system can be described in terms of three main elements: (1) individual accountability for cash and (cash equivalent) stocks, (2) formal procedures for transfers, and (3) tight control in the count rooms.

Individual Accountability for Cash Stocks

All cash stocks—with the exception of those kept at a game table or those taken from a game or slot machine for counting—were maintained on an impress basis. This meant that most personnel who dealt directly with cash, such as change personnel, coin redemption personnel, cashiers, and chip fill bank personnel, were held individually accountable for a specific sum of money that was charged out to them. These personnel were required to turn in the exact amount of money for which they were given responsibility, and any large shortages or persistent patterns of shortages were grounds for dismissal.

Formal Procedures for Transfers

For transfers of cash or chips to or from non-imprest funds (e.g., a game table), very strict procedures had to be followed. All required the creation of formal transactions signifying the transfer of accountability for the money involved. These procedures can be illustrated by describing what was required to move cash or chips to and from a blackjack table.

When a blackjack table was opened for playing, the dealer and "floorperson" had to count the inventory of chips and complete and sign an *opener* slip which simply provided a listing of the inventory (see Exhibit 5). One copy of the opener slip was deposited in the incoming dealer's *drop box,*[4] and a second copy was delivered to the finance department for input into the computer system.

As the game was played, several different kinds of transactions would take place. One involved players buying chips from the dealer for cash or credit. Cash was deposited immediately in the drop box. Credit had to be approved by checking the customer's credit authorization limit through the use of a computer terminal located in the pit. If the credit was approved, a *counter check*[5] was prepared, signed by the customer, dealer, and pit boss, and then deposited in the drop box. (An example of a counter check is shown in Exhibit 6).

Players could not make reverse exchanges (chips for cash) at the tables. They had to take their chips to the casino cage[6] where this type of exchange was made.

When the floorperson noticed that additional chips were needed at the table, he or she prepared a "request for fill." This request for a particular mix of chips was input into the computer terminal in the pit and relayed to the fill bank cashier in the casino cage. The fill bank cashier would fill the order, have the computer print out a *fill slip* (see Exhibit 7), sign the fill slip, and have a security guard transport the chips and fill slip to the dealer. Bill Bagnell (Manager of Casino Accounting) explained a unique form of control that came into play at this point:

> The computer keeps track of the time it takes to consummate fill transactions. The security guard may be walking around the casino with $10,000 or more in chips and it should take only a few minutes to get to the table and get the transaction completed. If the whole

[4]This was a locked container affixed to the gaming table into which the drop was placed.

[5]These were also known as "markers."

[6]This was a secure work area within the casino where the casino bankroll was kept.

process takes more than X minutes,[7] a message flashes on the computer screen in the security center, and they start looking for the guard. This is just an extra control we use to make sure the chips get to the table.

When the guard arrived at the table, the dealer and floorperson both counted the chips and signed the fill slip indicating receipt, and the clerk at the computer terminal in the pit entered a code indicating that the fill transaction had been completed. The security guard made sure a copy of the fill slip was placed in the drop box and then returned the original fill slip to the fill bank cashier.[8]

When the dealer's shift was over, the dealer and the floorperson counted the table inventory, and prepared and signed a *closer* slip (see Exhibit 8) which was deposited in the outgoing dealer's drop box. In the case of a shift change, a copy of this slip would also serve as an opener for the incoming dealer. The drop box of the outgoing dealer was sealed and security personnel carried it directly to the room where the money was counted.

Exhibit 9 shows a page of a summary report of the transactions that occurred at each table. The transactions illustrated in Exhibits 5–8 occurred on Blackjack Table #40 on the swing shift of June 23, 1983, and a list of these transactions is shown in the middle of this page of the report.

Tight Security in Countrooms

Wins (or losses) on a particular game table (or slot machine) could not be determined until the money in the drop box was counted. All counting of money from table games was done in the soft count room,[9] a highly secure room located adjacent to the casino cage. NJCCC regulations required that count rooms be equipped with a metal door, alarm, closed-circuit television cameras, and audio and video taping capabilities. In the middle of the room was a "count table" constructed of clear glass or similar material.

Tight security and supervision was necessary in the count rooms to ensure that the revenues were tallied accurately and that all the money to which the casino was entitled was added to stores in the casino cage. During the actual counting processes, very strict procedures were followed. (Excerpts from the procedures required in the Sands' countrooms are described in Exhibit 10.) In order to prevent the pocketing of currency, counting personnel were required to wear jumpsuits without pockets while they were in the count room, and personal belongings had to be carried only in clear plastic bags. The counting process took place under the supervision of an NJCCC inspector, and it was filmed by the television cameras located in the room. After the money was counted, it was transferred to the casino cage.

Only after the cash and counter checks in the drop box had been counted was it possible to calculate the winnings for each table. The win for Table 40, swing shift on June 23, 1983, was calculated as shown in Figure A.

The results for all games for each shift were reported on the Master Game Report (MGR), which was produced daily and summarized by type of game. The uses of the MGR as a control report are described in a later section of this case.

Control of Games

The table games and the slot machines provided the only ways by which the casino made money. The table games were particularly difficult to control because of the need to rely on people (dealers) who might be tempted by the extremely large amounts of money that could exchange hands very quickly.

In response to this difficult control problem, multiple forms of control were required by the NJCCC and used in the Sands to help ensure that the casino kept the cash to which it was entitled.

FIGURE A Calculation of Win on Blackjack Table 40, Swing Shift, June 23, 1983

Cash in drop box		$1,640.00
Counter checks issued		500.00
Total drop		**$2,140.00**
Less: Beginning table inventory	$8,235.00	
Fills	1,580.00	
	9,815.50	
Ending table inventory	(8,793.00)	
Win		**1,022.50**
		$1,117.50

[7]The actual time programmed into the computer was kept secret.

[8]A similar procedure was followed when the dealer wished to send an overabundance of chips to the chipbank for credit.

[9]This money was mostly bills and counter checks; hence the name "soft count" room. Coins taken from the slot machines were counted in the "hard count" room.

These included: (1) licensing of casino personnel, (2) standardization of actions of personnel running the games, (3) careful supervision and surveillance of the action taking place at the table, and (4) monitoring of results. These are discussed in the following sections.

Licensing

All employees working in the casino had to be licensed by the NJCCC, even personnel such as cooks, clerks, and barmaids who were not directly involved in gaming. The intent of licensing was to eliminate from the casino, people who had been involved in crimes or violations of casino rules, or those who might be attracted because of a need for some quick cash.

In order to get a dealer's license, prospective dealers had to complete an accredited six-month course in gaming and to demonstrate their knowledge of New Jersey gaming procedures. Separate licenses were granted for each type of game (e.g., blackjack, craps). In addition, dealers had to complete a 23-page license application that requested a detailed personal and family history, the details of which were checked by NJCCC investigators.

Those personnel in supervisory and policy-making, including pit bosses, accounting supervisors, and corporate officers, had to pass an even more comprehensive background check. The application for this highest-level license was 86 pages long and required a very extensive list of information, including five years of personal financial statements and tax returns.

Standardization of Actions at the Tables

At the gaming tables, most of the dealers' physical motions were standardized in order to make supervision and surveillance easier. For example:

1. All cash and chip exchanges were to be made in the middle of the gaming table to make them easier to see by supervisory personnel.
2. Tips were to be accepted by tapping the cash or chips on the table and placing them in a clear, locked "toke" box attached to the gaming tables. This was done to distinguish these exchanges from normal wages.
3. Before dealers left their tables, they were required to place their hands in the middle of the table and to show both the palm and back of their hands. This was done to prevent them from "palming" money or chips in order to take it from the table as they left. Dealers were also required to wear large, pocketless aprons over their clothes to make it more difficult for them to pocket cash or chips.

Initial knowledge of the required actions was tested as part of the licensing procedure, and the Sands provided regular training sessions to make sure the dealers did not forget them.

Supervision and Surveillance

Front-line gaming personnel (e.g., dealers) were subjected to multiple forms of supervision and surveillance. Direct supervision was provided by the floorpeople and pit bosses. These people were highly experienced gaming people who were highly paid for their expertise.[10] One of their primary functions was to watch the gaming activity and spot events that were out of the ordinary. They had a keen sense of the activity going on around them and thus were generally good at spotting nonroutine events, such as dealers paying losing bets in blackjack or customers counting cards in blackjack or switching dice in craps.

Extra surveillance of the table games was provided through what was called the "eye in the sky" and through a system of closed-circuit cameras. The term "eye in the sky" referred to surveillance provided by security personnel who viewed the activity of the gaming tables from a set of catwalks located above the gaming floor. They could view the activity of any gaming table from directly overhead without dealer or patron knowledge.[11]

The closed-circuit camera system included over 100 cameras located throughout the casino. They were situated to provide a view of every table on the floor and had lenses powerful enough to zoom in to view objects as small as the date on a dime on the table. The pictures were viewed in a security room located on the mezzanine level of the casino. The system provided the capability to record the activities shown on videotape for later viewing, or, if necessary, as evidence (e.g., if malfeasance was suspected).

To ensure that the surveillance was done objectively, strict separation was maintained be-

---

[10]For example, pit bosses were paid an average of $55,000 per year plus overtime.

[11]In some casinos, these personnel looked through one-way mirrors.

tween the personnel working on the casino floor and those working in the surveillance areas.

The levels of casino management above the pit bosses—shift supervisors, casino manager, vice president of casino operations—did very little direct supervision of the gaming activity. They were mainly involved in keeping good customers happy, resolving special problems that arose, and improving the casino operations.

Monitoring of Results

The MGR provided three key indicators of the results of the gaming activity: drop, win, and hold percentage.

1. The *drop* was interpreted as the total amount of money the customers were willing to bet against the casino. The drop number had some limitations as an activity indicator, however, as it was biased upward when table-game players exchanged money for chips at the table but did not bet, thereby creating what was called "false drop," and it was biased downward when players gambled with chips bought at another table, perhaps on another shift or day. A better indicator of activity would have been the "handle," the total value of wagers made, but there was no way to determine this number for the table games.
2. The *win* was the casino's gross profit number. It was calculated as shown in Figure A.
3. The *hold percentage* (also called the hold ratio) was the primary measure of casino profitability. It was defined as the win divided by the drop.

A comprehensive set of reports was produced that provided these performance measures in various levels of detail, by table and shift and by time period. Exhibit 11 shows a detailed report of the performance of individual blackjack tables on each shift. Exhibit 12 shows a summary by type of game. Special analyses were also prepared using similar formats to see, for example, how much play the casino got from particular customers or junkets.[12]

Sands' management watched the drop and hold numbers carefully. The drop number was the best available measure of the volume of betting activity, and as such, it was useful as an indicator of the success of the company's marketing strategies and credit policies. It was used, for example, to determine what entertainers attracted the best betting crowd to the casino.

The old percentage was the best available measure of casino profitability. Ed Sutor (vice president-Finance) explained how Sands managers used the reports of hold percentage for control purposes:

> We look for patterns. We know that each table game should maintain a certain hold ratio; for example, the blackjack hold percentage should average 14 to 16 percent. The managers in casino operations, particularly, look at the hold generated on each shift in each pit and at each table. The dealers are not always assigned to the same tables, so we have no information to tie them to except that they always work in the same pit. But the floorpeople are always assigned to the same two tables, and the pit boss remains in the same pit. So we can go back to those people and ask them to explain why the hold was down. It may just have been a high-roller who was on a hot streak, but if we suspect something is not right, the casino operations people can call for some extra surveillance.
>
> I also watch the hold percentages. If the hold percentage is low across the casino, on all shifts and all tables, and that pattern persisted for a period of, say, several weeks, I'd have to take a hard look at our control system to see if there was a leak somewhere.

The drop, win, and hold percentage measures were standard throughout the gaming industry, and competitive analyses were facilitated because summaries were prepared and distributed by a trade association.[13] (For an example of such a report, see Exhibit 13.)

Bonuses

The results measures are figured in bonuses paid to management personnel. Managers at the Sands received an annual bonus based on the bottom-line performance of the hotel-casino. This bonus could be doubled if the personal management-by-objectives (MBO) targets that were set during the annual budgeting process were met.

---

[12]A junket was an arrangement made to induce a group to travel to a casino to gamble. Frequently, the transportation, food and/or lodging were paid directly or indirectly by the gambling establishment.

[13]Atlantic City Casino Hotel Association.

Some of the MBO objectives were based on standard annual performance measures, such as increased volume (drop), good hold percentages, and decreased costs, but as Stephen Hyde explained, these measures had to be supplemented with factors that were more difficult to quantify:

> The standard measures of performance are important indicators of our success, but we try to be careful not to place too much emphasis on them, because we don't want to be encouraging our people to sacrifice everything for bottom-line growth this year. We want them to be building the company and doing everything they can to ensure that we're going to be successful three to five years from now, and even further out. In our MBO program, we supplement the quantitative measures with factors that are usually more difficult to quantify. A good example is customer relations. If a customer has a complaint, we want our managers to make them happy, even if it costs us something today, so that they will come back. Other examples might be the successful completion of a project such as installation of a new computer system or maintenance of good employee relations.

Future Controls

In response to a request for a speculation as to what controls in the casino might look like in the future, Ed Sutor responded:

> In the gaming areas, the ultimate form of control for us would be to be able to record every transaction. Then we'd have a good record of who has done what, and we'd be able to capture a lot of information that would be very valuable for decision-making purposes.
>
> But I can't visualize how we could record every transaction. Over and above the direct costs that would be involved in such record keeping, there would be some perhaps sizeable indirect costs. We're in the entertainment business, and we can't do anything that would diminish our customers' enjoyment. Furthermore, we don't want to do anything that would slow the games down too much; the number of wagers handled per hour is a standard measure of productivity in this business. So, unless there is some technological innovation that I can't foresee right now, I don't think the controls would be much different from what we have right now.

Control improvements were always being made or contemplated, however. Stephen Hyde explained:

> We're always looking for ways to improve. This is a tough, competitive business. We continually have to make sure that the controls we've got are still working, and we have to be alert for new trends and new ruses. I'll give you a couple of examples.
>
> Right now, we are going through training programs for all of the various positions. The programs have been reinstituted, and everybody who has gone through them (some as much as two years ago) is going back through them. Theoretically, with the improved training, we will improve the controls in the casino.
>
> In the blackjack area, we are working on our shuffles. You may find this hard to believe, but we have found that some people seem able to track some cards through the shuffle and they can derive some advantage from it in their plays. So about every six months we have to change our shuffle, and that is one of the things we're looking at right now.
>
> We're also working on improving our information systems. By the end of the year, we'll have a new computer system that will provide better information for control of credit and complimentaries. If, for example, a pit boss is asked for some complimentary tickets, he or she could go to a computer terminal and get detailed information about the requestor's betting history (regularity, size of drop) and find out if that same person had just been given other "comps" by another pit boss. Then the pit boss will have the information to make the judgment as to whether the request should be filled. The key is the player's profit potential.

EXHIBIT 1A Income Statement for Great Bay Casino Corporation

	Year Ended December 31,		
	1982	*1981*	*1980*
Revenues			
Gaming	$144,236,000	$ 91,614,000	$ 27,278,000
Rooms	11,775,000	8,700,000	2,833,000
Food and beverage	20,875,000	15,686,000	5,450,000
Other	7,449,000	4,563,000	793,000
Gross revenues	**$184,335,000**	**$120,563,000**	**$ 36,354,000**
Less: promotional allowances	20,899,000	13,031,000	2,802,000
Net revenues	**$163,436,000**	**$107,532,000**	**$ 33,552,000**
Costs and expenses			
Operating	$113,178,000	$ 79,712,000	$ 34,864,000
General and administrative	17,607,000	16,131,000	9,567,000
Depreciation	6,005,000	4,773,000	1,816,000
Interest	11,402,000	12,822,000	2,754,000
	$148,192,000	**$113,438,000**	**$49,001,000**
Income (loss) before income taxes and extraordinary item	$ 15,244,000	$ (5,906,000)	$(15,449,000)
Provision for income taxes	7,783,000	—	—
Income (loss) before extraordinary item	**$7,461,000**	**$ (5,906,000)**	**$(15,449,000)**
Extraordinary item—utilization of tax loss carryforward	6,561,000	—	—
Net income (loss)	**$ 14,022,000**	**$ (5,906,000)**	**$(15,449,000)**
Net income (loss) per share of common stock			
Income (loss) before extraordinary item	$1.42	$(1.12)	$(2.93)
Extraordinary item	1.24	—	—
	$2.66	**$(1.12)**	**$(2.93)**
Average common shares outstanding	**5,279,000**	**5,279,000**	**5,279,000**

EXHIBIT 1B Balance Sheet

	December 31,	
	1982	*1981*
ASSETS		
Current assets:		
Cash and temporary investments	$ 8,243,000	$ 8,198,000
Receivables		
Gaming	$ 15,044,000	$ 8,108,000
Other	990,000	1,227,000
Less: allowance for doubtful accounts	(5,633,000)	(1,965,000)
	$ 10,401,000	**$ 7,370,000**
	$957,000	$ 656,000
Inventories		
Other current assets:		
Prepaid advertising and promotion expenses	$ 1,678,000	$ 806,000
Other prepaid expenses	2,258,000	1,463,000
	$ 3,936,000	**$ 2,269,000**
Total current assets	**$ 23,537,000**	**$ 18,493,000**
Property and Equipment		
Land	$ 5,022,000	$ 5,022,000
Buildings	60,311,000	54,036,000
Furniture, fixtures, and equipment	24,957,000	17,678,000
Less: accumulated depreciation	(12,594,000)	(6,589,000)
	$ 77,696,000	**$ 70,147,000**
Other assets	**$ 1,131,000**	**$ 349,000**
Total assets	**$102,364,000**	**$ 88,989,000**
LIABILITIES AND SHAREHOLDERS' EQUITY		
Current liabilities:		
Current portion of long-term debt	$ 11,088,000	$ 6,245,000
Accounts payable and accrued expenses:		
Trade accounts payable	$ 12,243,000	$ 6,380,000
Salaries and wages	2,303,000	1,955,000
Taxes and licenses	2,026,000	3,892,000
Progressive jackpot accrual	2,017,000	538,000
Interest	332,000	1,889,000
Other	1,200,000	700,000
	$ 20,121,000	**$ 15,354,000**
Other current liabilities	3,010,000	$ 1,241,000
Total current liabilities	**$ 34,219,000**	**$ 22,840,000**
Long-term debt	**$ 48,108,000**	**$ 60,530,000**
Other long-term liabilities	**$310,000**	—
Total liabilities	**$ 82,637,000**	**$ 83,370,000**
Commitments and contingencies		
Shareholder's equity		
Class A Common Stock, $.25 par value; authorized 10,000,000 shares; issued and outstanding 5,287,642 shares in 1982 and 1,479,017 in 1981	1,322,000	370,000
Class B Common Stock, $.25 par value; authorized 5,000,000 shares; issued and outstanding -0- in 1982 and 3,800,000 in 1981	—	950,000
Capital in excess of par value	26,913,000	26,829,000
Retained earnings (deficit)	(8,508,000)	(22,530,000)
Total shareholders' equity	**$ 19,727,000**	**$ 5,619,000**
Total liabilities and shareholders' equity	**$102,364,000**	**$(88,989,000**

EXHIBIT 2 Organization

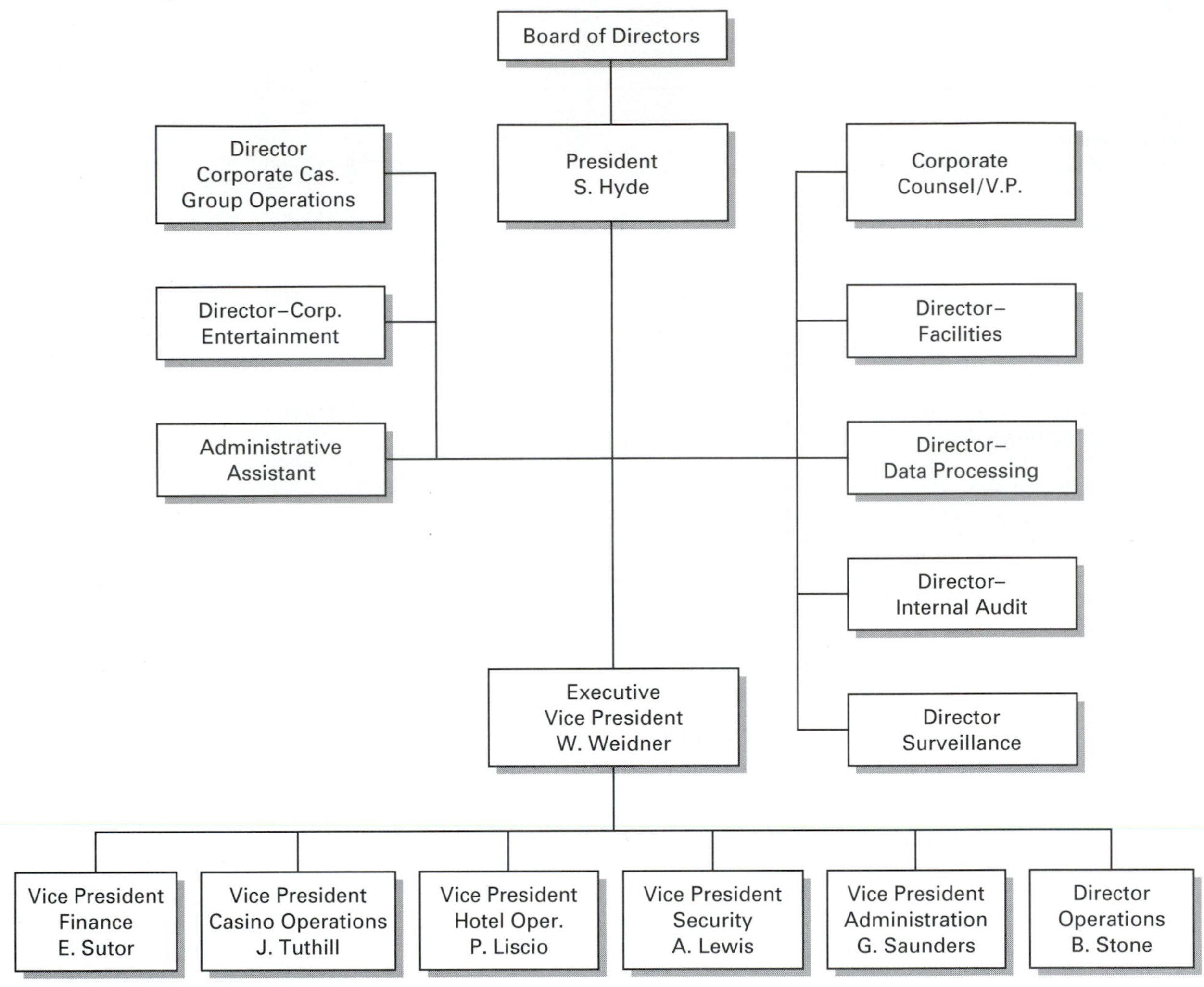

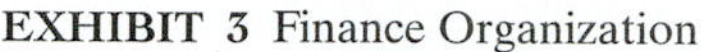

EXHIBIT 3 Finance Organization

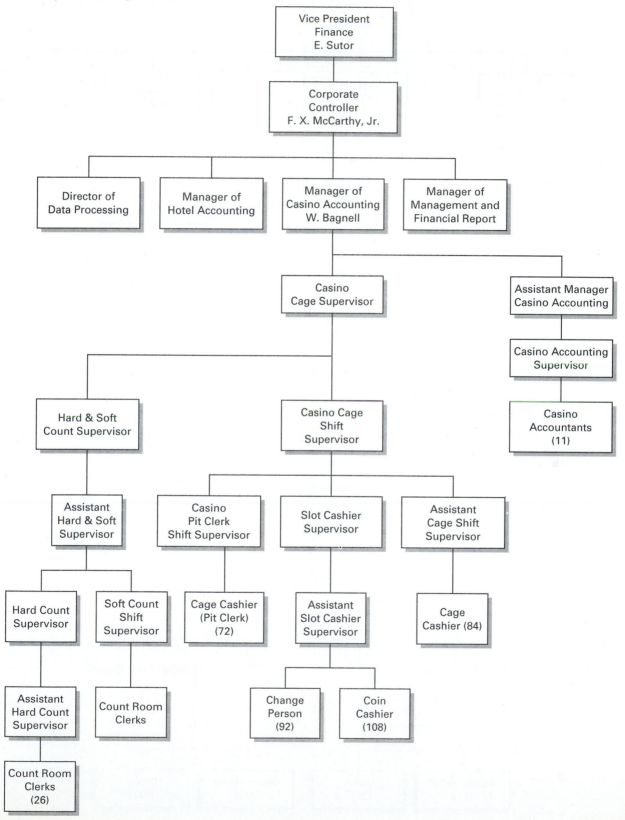

- Vice President Finance E. Sutor
  - Corporate Controller F. X. McCarthy, Jr.
    - Director of Data Processing
    - Manager of Hotel Accounting
    - Manager of Casino Accounting W. Bagnell
      - Casino Cage Supervisor
        - Hard & Soft Count Supervisor
          - Assistant Hard & Soft Supervisor
            - Hard Count Supervisor
              - Assistant Hard Count Supervisor
                - Count Room Clerks (26)
            - Soft Count Shift Supervisor
              - Count Room Clerks
        - Casino Cage Shift Supervisor
          - Casino Pit Clerk Shift Supervisor
            - Cage Cashier (Pit Clerk) (72)
          - Slot Cashier Supervisor
            - Assistant Slot Cashier Supervisor
              - Change Person (92)
              - Coin Cashier (108)
          - Assistant Cage Shift Supervisor
            - Cage Cashier (84)
      - Assistant Manager Casino Accounting
        - Casino Accounting Supervisor
          - Casino Accountants (11)
    - Manager of Management and Financial Report

EXHIBIT 4 Casino Operations Organization

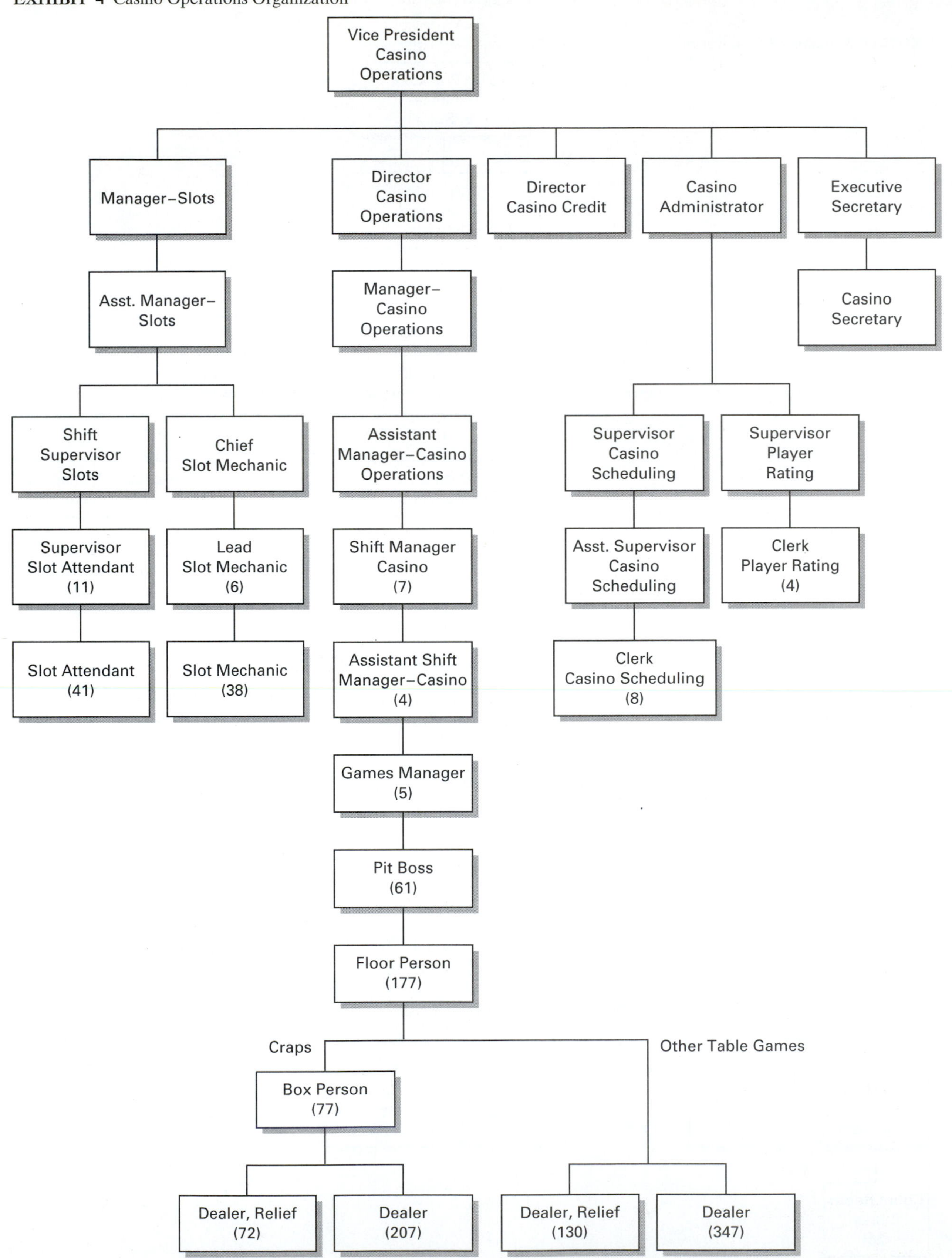

EXHIBIT 5 Opener (Blackjack Table 40, Swing Shift, June 23, 1983)

HOTEL & CASINO ATLANTIC CITY

DATE 6-23-83

OPENER	GAME BJ		TABLE 40
SHIFT	☐	DAY/SWING ☒	SWING/DAY ☐

CHIP DENOMINATION	AMOUNT	
500	$ —	.
100	4000	.—
25	3025	.—
20	—	.
5	1020	.—
2.50	90	.—
1	66	.—
.50	34	.50
.25	—	.
TOTAL	$ 8235	.50

DEALER/ BOXPERSON	K. Walters 08438-21
OUTGOING CASINO SUPERVISOR	C. Jantzen 1634-4
DEALER/ BOXPERSON	L. Clark 4842-2021
INCOMING CASINO SUPERVISOR	S. Sabatori 1634-11

OCA-7 4-81

EXHIBIT 6 Countercheck

J-40
GAME AND TABLE NO.

Polly Waltz
PIT CLERK SIGN

27100-21
LICENSE NUMBER

Merlin DiMann
DEALER BOX PERSON SIGN

28101-21
LICENSE NUMBER

Ivan O'Connell
SUPERVISOR SIGN

29102-11
LICENSE NUMBER

83174-S-0012639 23:30 06/23/83
Hazlet
United Jersey Bank
Hazlet/Holmdel

GREATE BAY HOTEL & CASINO, INC. ******500

PAY TO THE ORDER OF

**************************Five Hundred and no/100 Dollars

I REPRESENT THAT I HAVE RECEIVED CASH FOR THE ABOVE AMOUNT AND THAT SAID AMOUNT IS ON DEPOSIT IN SAID BANK OR TRUST COMPANY IN MY NAME. IT IS FREE FROM CLAIMS AND IS SUBJECT TO THIS CHECK.

William Rizzo
William Rizzo

EXHIBIT 7 Fill Slips (Blackjack Table 40, Swing Shift, June 23, 1983)

64-11

*** TABLE FILL SLIP ***

FS83174-S-0012638 6/23/83 20:32

PIT 10 J40

DENOM	UNITS	AMOUNT
500		
100		
25		
20		
5		
2 1/2		
1	80	80.00
1/2		
1/4		
**** TOTAL FILL		80.00

	SIGNATURE	LICENSE NO.
FILL CASHIER	S. Wilming	#36579-21
SECURITY	L. Newell	#21670-21
CASINO SUPER	C. Busey	#15919-21
DEALER	C. Cartwright	#15937-21

DROP COPY

WR
64-11

*** TABLE FILL SLIP ***

FS83174-S-0012640 6/23/83 23:57

PIT 10 J40

DENOM	UNITS	AMOUNT
500		
100		
25	40	1,000.00
20		
5	100	500.00
2 1/2		
1		
1/2		
1/4		
**** TOTAL FILL		1,500.00

	SIGNATURE	LICENSE NO.
FILL CASHIER	S. Wilson	#30579-21
SECURITY	L. Houpe	#42064-21
CASINO SUPER	G. Larson	#15170-21
DEALER	C. Christensen	#10931-21

DROP COPY

EXHIBIT 8 Closer (Blackjack Table 40, Swing Shift, June 23, 1983)

Sands

DATE 6-23-83

CLOSER	GAME BJ	TABLE 40
SHIFT ☐	DAY/SWING ☐	SWING/DAY ☒

CHIP DENOMINATION	AMOUNT
500	$ —
100	3,500.—
25	3,525.—
20	—
5	1,510.—
2.50	92.50
1	132.—
.50	33.50
.25	—
TOTAL	$ 8,793.00

DEALER/ BOXPERSON	Arthur J. Green 21710-21
OUTGOING CASINO SUPERVISOR	W. Rogers 64-11
DEALER/ BOXPERSON	
INCOMING CASINO SUPERVISOR	

OCA-7 4-81

EXHIBIT 9 Table Games Daily Transaction Report

Run Date June 24, 1983	*Time 8-41-33*	*Table Games Daily Transaction Report*								*BCAS 10*
			Initiated		*Acknowledge*		*Consummated*		*Cr. Acct.*	
Serial Number	*Transaction*	*Amount*	*By*	*Time*	*By*	*Time*	*By*	*Time*	*No.*	*Remarks*
83173-S-0012299	Closer-Previous Day	7,846.00	22364	02-49						
83174-D-0012300	Opener	7,846.00	45290	12-05						
83174-D-0012301	Fill	2,130.00	45290	12-19	45290	12-54	23960	12-54		
83174-D-0012302	Closer	8,565.00	18354	18-20						
83174-S-0012303	Opener	8,565.00	18354	18-21						
83174-S-0012304	Counter Check	500.00	12896	19-03					25758	Yuhl, John
83174-S-0012305	Fill	1,300.00	12896	20-43	12896	20-59	33998	21-23		
83174-S-0012306	Closer	7,328.50	22364	04-01						
Game—Blackjack	**Table 39**	**Table Open for Shifts—Day, Swing, Document Range—12426 to 12625**								
83173-S-0012533	Closer-Previous Day	6,698.00	22364	02-38						
83174-D-0012534	Opener	6,698.00	45290	12-04						
83174-D-0012535	Fill	4,110.00	45290	12-15	45290	12-35	23960	12-41		
83174-D-0012536	Counter Check	500.00	45290	14-23	14757	14-29			4179	Rosenberg, Max
83174-D-0012537	Fill	500.00	18354	16-25	18354	16-47	30579	16-51		
83174-D-0012538	Closer	9,864.00	18354	18-23						
83174-S-0012539	Opener	9,864.00	18354	18-23						
83174-S-0012540	Fill	60.00	12896	20-31	12896	20-48	33998	21-23		
83174-S-0012541	Closer	7,583.50	22364	03-42						

EXHIBIT 9 Table Games Daily Transaction Report *Continued*

Run Date June 24, 1983 *Time 8-41-33* *Table Games Daily Transaction Report* *BCAS 10*

Serial Number	*Transaction*	*Amount*	*Initiated By*	*Initiated Time*	*Acknowledge By*	*Acknowledge Time*	*Consummated By*	*Consummated Time*	*Cr. Acct. No.*	*Remarks*
Game—Blackjack	**Table 40**	**Table Open for Shifts—Day, Swing, Document Range—12626 to 12825**								
83173-S-0012632	Closer-Previous Day	12,656.00	22364	03-23						
83174-D-0012633	Opener	12,656.00	45290	12-09						
83174-D-0012634	Credit	4,500.00	45290	12-13	45290	12-53	23960	12-57		
83174-D-0012635	Fill	600.00	45290	12-14	45290	12-52	23960	12-53		
83174-D-0012636	Closer	8,235.00	18354	18-25						
83174-S-0012637	Opener	8,235.00	18354	18-25						
83174-S-0012638	Fill	80.00	12896	20-32	12896	20-58	33998	21-23		
83174-S-0012639	Counter Check	500.00	12896	23-30	29554	23-38			5406	Rizzo, William
83174-S-0012640	Fill	1,500.00	12896	23-57	27823	00-02	33998	00-03		
83174-S-0012641	Closer	8,793.00	22364	03-26						
Game—Blackjack	**Table 41**	**Table Open for Shifts—Day, Swing, Document Range—12826 to 13025**								
83173-S-0012883	Closer-Previous Day	30,680.50	22364	03-41						
83174-D-0012884	Opener	30,680.50	45290	12-07						
83174-D-0012885	Credit	20,000.00	45290	12-17	45290	12-37	23960	12-41		
83174-D-0012886	Fill	600.00	45290	12-17	45290	12-36	23960	12-41		
83174-D-0012887	Fill	1,600.00	18354	14-09	18354	14-23	23112	14-25		
83174-D-0012888	Closer	10,073.50	18354	18-33						
83174-S-0012889	Opener	10,073.50	18354	18-33						
83174-S-0012890	Counter Check	500.00	12896	20-01	15555	20-07			17217	Weiss, Melvin
83174-S-0012891	Counter Check	500.00	27823	21-53	15555	21-59			26864	Famighette, George
83174-S-0012892	Closer	6,636.50	22364	03-39						
Game—Blackjack	**Table 45**	**Table Open for Shifts—Day, Swing, Document Range—13626 to 13825**								
83173-S-0013735	Closer-Previous Day	8,066.50	30739	03-46						
83174-D-0013736	Opener	8,066.50	20806	11-03						
83174-D-0013737	Fill	1,610.00	20806	11-13	20808	11-25	23112	11-28		
83174-D-0013738	Fill	2,600.00	14750	14-36	14750	14-43	23112	14-44		

EXHIBIT 10 Excerpts from Sands Soft Count Procedures

Immediately prior to commencement of the count, one count team member will notify the person assigned to the closed circuit television monitoring station that the count is about to begin, after which such person will make an audio-video recording, with the time and date inserted thereon, of the entire counting process which will be retained by the surveillance department for at least five (5) days from the date of recordation unless otherwise directed by the Commission or the Division. The entire count will be performed in full view of the television monitor.

Concurrently, on both sides of a clear plastic count table, (both sides of the table used only during peak periods) a count team member will open the drop box, empty its contents onto the table and verbalize *in a tone of voice to be heard by all persons* the game, table number and shift, all in full view of the closed circuit television camera. After the drop box is empty, the count team member will show *the inside of the drop box* to the closed circuit camera, another member of the count team and the Commission Inspector and then the drop box will be locked in the storage area for empty drop boxes. Currency sorters on both sides of the count table will separate the denominations of currency, coin, and the forms, records and documents by type. The paperwork will be passed to the count room bookkeeper who will match the opener, closer, fills, and credits to the Drop Verification Report.[a] Upon completing the currency sort for each drop box, the sorters will attach to the currency a game/table identification card.

The currency and game/table identification card are passed to a first verifier who enters the game and table number into a currency count machine. The currency is passed through the count machine by denomination with a tape produced indicating all detail and the total of drop box currency. The currency is passed to a second verifier *in full view of the closed circuit television camera* while the supporting tape is retained for comparison to the second count.

The currency verification process described above is repeated by the second verifier with the resultant tape compared to the one retained by the first verifier. Any count discrepancies are resolved at this point to the satisfaction of both verifiers, the soft count supervisor or assistant and the Commission Inspector.

After the second currency verification, count team members located at this area of the count table bundle and consolidate currency as counted. The currency and both count tapes are forwarded to a count team member located at the end of the count table. The currency is verified in total to both count tapes and placed in a holding area near the count table.

The count tapes are passed on to the countroom bookkeeper or assistant who enters the total currency *paid coin* drop by gaming table. The countroom bookkeeper or assistant generates printing of the Master Game Report, which indicates win by table game and shift. The Master Game Report is used by the countroom bookkeeper to agree the total of openers, closers, fills, and credits to that reported on the Drop Verification Report. *Upon completion of the count for each drop box shift, a main bank cashier will be called into the countroom to verify the cash count. The main bank cashier bulk counts the cash by bundle, all loose straps and clips are individually verified. The main bank cashier then compares the total to the totals listed on the Master Game Report and resolves any differences. The main bank cashier then signs the Master Game Report attesting to the amount of cash received.*

The Master Game Report will be signed by the Commission Inspector evidencing his presence during the count and the fact that both the cashier and count team have agreed on the total amount of currency and coin counted, the soft count supervisor, all count team members and the cage representative summoned to the count room to assist in the transfer of currency to the main bank for inclusion in the overall cage accountability after it has been recounted, either manually or mechanically.

The Master Game Report, along with all supporting documents removed from the drop boxes, are forwarded to the Accounting Department for review and posting to the Gaming Income Journal.

The counting and recording of drop box contents will continue over two normal work shifts. Each shift will complete the count of one shift of drop boxes before the other count team shift begins.

The Master Game Report fills, Credits and Table Inventory Slips (Opener and Closer slips) will on a daily basis be:

- Taped and the totals agreed with the totals indicated on the Master Gaming Report;
- Reviewed on a judgmental basis for the appropriate number and propriety of signatures;
- Tested for proper summarization and recording; and
- Subsequently recorded and maintained and controlled by the Accounting Department as a permanent accounting record.

[a]A list of transactions affecting the drop box contents. It is similar in format to the transaction report shown in Exhibit 9 of this case.

EXHIBIT 11 Master Game Report—Detail

Run Date—June 24, 1983 Time-18-07
Play Date June 23, 1983—Thursday *Casino Report* *Preliminary*

Pit/Game	Table	Shift	*Today*			*Month to Date*			*Year to Date*		
			Drop	*Win*	*Hold %*	*Drop*	*Win*	*Hold %*	*Drop*	*Win*	*Hold %*
09	33	Total				47,559	6,721	14.13	504,474	62,698	12.43
Blk Jack	34	Day				16,897	2,927	17.33	166,774	26,482	15.88
	34	Swing				38,345	13,457	35.09	283,698	44,733	15.77
	34	Total				55,242	16,384	29.66	450,472	71,215	15.81
09 Blk Jack	35	Day				17,633	3,634	20.61	168,301	3,070	1.82
	35	Swing				35,324	3,011	8.53	250,123	45,217	18.08
	35	Total				52,957	6,645	12.55	418,424	48,288	11.54
09 Blk Jack	36	Day				17,386	1,501−	8.64−	189,628	9,107	4.80
	36	Swing				30,207	5,116	16.94	310,561	62,461	20.11
	36	Total				47,593	3,614	7.59	500,189	71,568	14.31
10 Blk Jack	37	Day	2,099	605	28.82	88,998	6,415	7.21	615,023	103,584	16.84
	37	Swing	5,962	91	1.53	116,715	23,316	19.98	814,801	143,076	17.56
	37	Total	8,061	696	8.63	205,713	29,732	14.45	1,429,824	246,660	17.25
10 Blk Jack	38	Day	1,890	479	25.34	66,344	10,030	15.12	493,801	57,558	11.66
	38	Swing	4,319	1,782	41.27	96,090	10,778	11.22	655,642	136,971	20.89
	38	Total	6,209	2,261	36.42	162,434	20,808	12.81	1,149,443	194,529	16.92
10 Blk Jack	39	Day	1,680	236	14.05	64,137	13,308	20.75	493,189	68,554	13.90
	39	Swing	2,447	106	4.35	96,951	19,412	20.02	642,658	119,755	18.63
	39	Total	4,127	342	8.30	161,088	32,720	20.31	1,135,847	188,310	16.58
10 Blk Jack	40	Day	1,478	957	64.78	71,599	7,529	10.52	533,117	59,239	11.11
	40	Swing	2,140	1,117	52.22	90,788	18,345	20.21	696,361	123,855	17.79
	40	Total	3,618	2,075	57.35	162,387	25,875	15.93	1,229,478	183,094	14.89
10 Blk Jack	41	Day	2,904	97	3.34	79,812	11,836	14.83	605,173	84,041	13.89
	41	Swing	3,601	164	4.55	107,602	31,754	29.51	766,816	144,548	18.85
	41	Total	6,505	261	4.01	187,414	43,590	23.26	1,371,989	228,589	16.66
10 Blk Jack	42	Day	1,091	439	40.28	74,250	8,213	11.06	524,339	98,634	18.81
	42	Swing	2,817	1,285	45.63	90,864	24,017	26.43	635,928	151,603	23.84
	42	Total	3,908	1,725	44.14	165,114	32,230	19.52	1,160,267	250,237	21.57
10 Blk Jack	43	Day	1,782	839	47.11	75,804	10,970	14.47	503,059	100,334	19.94
	43	Swing	4,047	167	4.14	88,382	15,547	17.59	609,689	106,484	17.47
	43	Total	5,829	1,007	17.28	164,186	26,517	16.15	1,112,748	206,818	18.59
10 Blk Jack	44	Day	4,204	803	19.10	79,166	9,924	12.54	585,815	110,009	18.78
	44	Swing	5,224	1,649	31.58	104,119	10,743	10.32	702,022	103,927	14.80
	44	Total	9,428	2,452	26.01	183,285	20,667	11.28	1,287,837	213,937	16.61
11 Blk Jack	45	Day	3,425	997	29.11	93,084	15,524	16.68	669,637	92,277	13.78
	45	Swing	3,394	1,363	40.17	148,392	23,242	15.66	838,985	143,274	17.08
	45	Total	6,819	2,360	34.62	241,476	38,766	16.05	1,508,622	235,551	15.61
11 Blk Jack	46	Day	3,362	402−	11.96−	74,266	2,956	3.98	502,424	63,373	12.61
	46	Swing	7,673	1,267	16.52	108,432	13,599	12.54	696,141	118,120	16.97
	46	Total	11,035	865	7.84	182,698	16,555	9.06	1,198,565	181,493	15.14
11 Blk Jack	47	Day	3,544	1,515−	42.76−	80,907	5,861	7.24	494,976	71,358	14.42
	47	Swing	2,983	606	20.32	98,051	23,637	24.11	647,812	141,205	21.80
	47	Total	6,527	909−	13.93−	178,958	29,498	16.48	1,142,788	212,563	18.60
11 Blk Jack	48	Day	6,285	2,676	42.58	71,304	5,824	8.17	521,703	84,121	16.12
	48	Swing	3,731	1,940	52.00	106,631	24,142	22.64	682,084	157,292	23.06
	48	Total	10,016	4,616	46.09	177,935	29,966	16.84	1,203,787	241,413	20.05
11 Blk Jack	49	Day	1,270	296	23.25	95,993	21,307	22.20	577,840	75,079	12.99
	49	Swing	2,025	990−	48.89−	83,185	13,887	16.69	643,847	139,857	21.72
	49	Total	3,295	693−	21.05−	179,178	35,194	19.64	1,221,687	214,936	17.59
11 Blk Jack	50	Day	4,323	2,477	57.30	73,435	12,798	17.43	506,423	92,065	18.18
	50	Swing	5,265	1,595−	30.30−	78,904	9,662	12.25	555,499	95,321	17.16
	50	Total	9,588	881	9.19	152,339	22,460	14.74	1,061,922	187,386	17.65

EXHIBIT 12 Master Game Report—Summary

Run Date—June 24, 1983 Time-18-07
Play Date June 23, 1983—Thursday *Casino Report* *Preliminary*

Final Total Page		*Today*			*Month to Date*			*Year to Date*		
Pit/Game		*Drop*	*Win*	*Hold %*	*Drop*	*Win*	*Hold %*	*Drop*	*Win*	*Hold %*
Blk Jack	Day	237,569	62,395	26.26	7,060,821	1,055,062	14.94	51,908,803	7,003,734	13.49
	Swing	346,867	158,114	45.58	8,586,885	1,779,110	20.72	62,488,716	10,716,594	17.15
	Total	584,436	220,509	37.73	15,647,706	2,834,172	18.11	114,395,519	17,720,329	15.49
Baccarat	Day	10,971	8,716−	79.45−	797,246	88,467	11.10	6,659,386	876,993	13.17
	Swing	15,014	2,453−	16.34−	1,245,670	97,566	7.83	10,359,402	1,473,800	14.23
	Total	25,985	11,169−	42.98	2,042,916	186,034	9.11	17,018,788	2,350,793	13.81
Craps	Day	254,164	11,925	4.69	7,251,450	783,554	10.81	53,409,701	5,548,571	10.39
	Swing	339,832	16,324	4.80	8,596,480	1,654,711	19.25	56,120,257	9,490,489	16.91
	Total	593,996	28,249	4.76	15,847,930	2,438,265	15.39	109,529,958	15,039,060	13.73
Roulette	Day	26,042	10,351	39.75	772,208	231,272	29.95	5,942,310	1,704,971	28.69
	Swing	39,986	15,265	38.18	988,944	228,291	23.08	6,748,677	1,559,351	23.11
	Total	66,028	25,617	38.80	1,761,152	459,563	26.09	12,690,987	3,264,322	25.72
Big Six	Day	4,553	2,291	50.33	129,600	52,843	40.77	933,157	410,771	44.02
	Swing	4,583	2,329	50.83	135,217	63,312	46.82	902,712	438,282	48.55
	Total	9,136	4,621	50.58	264,817	116,155	43.86	1,835,869	849,053	46.25
All Game	Day	533,299	78,247	14.67	16,011,325	2,211,198	13.81	118,853,357	15,545,041	13.08
	Swing	746,282	189,580	25.40	19,553,196	3,822,992	19.55	136,617,764	23,678,517	17.33
	Total	1,279,581	267,827	20.93	35,564,521	6,034,191	16.97	255,471,121	39,223,558	15.35
Credit Drop		505,500			13,324,095			92,628,515		
% of Total Drop		39.51			37.46			36.26		
Daily Average—Credit Drop and Table Win				579,308	262,356		532,348	225,423	*Daily Marker Activity*	
Daily Slot Activity										

Beginning balance	5,347,595
Less markers	
Deposited	82,560
Redemptions	490,045
Consolidations	13,500
Plus markers	
Issued	711,160
Consolidations	13,500
Ending balance	5,513,150
Returned markers outstanding	8,929,121
Total receivable	14,442,271
Safekeeping	
Beginning balance	120,535
Deposits made	20,200
Withdrawals	30,400
Ending balance	110,335

Casino Final Total	**Today**	**M-T-D**	**Y-T-D**
Total win	447,870	10,890,542	68,583,941
Daily average		473,502	394,161

Denomination		**Drop**	**Win**	**Daily Average**
Nickels	Daily	6,142.35	5,592.35	
	M-T-D	154,311.80	92,907.55	4,039
	Y-T-D	1,240,086.25	1,052,211.15	6,047
Dimes	Daily	4,115.80	3,915.80	
	M-T-D	98,539.90	93,439.90	4,063
	Y-T-D	566,698.00	435,918.00	2,505
Quarters	Daily	147,199.50	130,209.90	
	M-T-D	3,918,959.75	3,520,276.29	153,055
	Y-T-D	25,290,262.00	22,459,384.48	129,077
Halves	Daily	11,367.00	11,337.00	
	M-T-D	377,953.00	315,759.60	13,729
	Y-T-D	2,239,143.00	1,722,115.75	9,897
Dollars	Daily	31,588.00	28,988.00	
	M-T-D	912,368.00	833,968.00	36,259
	Y-T-D	5,480,027.00	3,680,753.80	21,211
Total All Denominations	Daily	200,682.65	180,043.05	
	M-T-D	5,462,132.45	4,856,351.34	211,146
	Y-T-D	34,816,216.25	29,360,383.18	168,738

EXHIBIT 13 Example of Industry Results Report

Report 91500 *00.00.00* *SANDS—ATLANTIC CITY* *RUN DATE June 14, 1983* *SCHEDULE C-5*

TABLE GAME MARKET SHARE ANALYSIS

MONTH OF MAY

	% of Blackjack Tables	*% of Blackjack Win*	*% of Craps Tables*	*% of Craps Win*	*% of Roulette Wheels*	*% of Roulette Win*	*% of Baccarat Tables*	*% of Baccarat Win*	*% of Big Six Wheels*	*% of Big Six Win*
Sands	10.4	9.2	9.3	10.5	10.6	10.0	8.3	11.7	6.7	7.7
Claridge	6.0	7.2	8.1	7.1	8.5	6.9	8.3	6.3	6.7	5.0
Bally	13.3	9.1	12.8	12.7	12.8	11.5	12.5	9.2	13.3	11.6
Caesars	10.5	12.1	16.3	16.2	11.7	12.2	16.7	24.3	10.0	8.9
Playboy	9.3	7.5	8.1	6.4	8.5	8.5	12.5	5.2	6.7	8.3
Resorts	14.7	21.6	11.6	12.5	11.7	13.0	12.5	17.5	20.0	15.8
Harrahs	11.9	8.8	12.8	10.1	12.8	10.6	8.3	6.4	10.0	11.0
Golden Nugget	10.7	13.4	10.5	14.6	10.6	15.2	8.3	24.2	13.3	18.1
Tropicana	13.2	11.2	10.5	10.0	12.8	12.0	12.5	(4.6)	13.3	13.5
Total	**100.0**	**100.0**	**100.0**	**100.0**	**100.0**	**100.0**	**100.0**	**100.0**	**100.0**	**100.0**

The Lincoln Electric Company

> We're not a marketing company, we're not an R&D company, and we're not a service company. We're a manufacturing company, and I believe that we are the best manufacturing company in the world.

With these words, George E. Willis, president of The Lincoln Electric Company, described what he saw as his company's distinctive competence. For more than 30 years, Lincoln had been the world's largest manufacturer of arc welding products (Exhibit 1). In 1974, the company was believed to have manufactured more than 40 percent of the arc welding equipment and supplies sold in the United States. In addition to its welding products, Lincoln produced a line of three-phase alternating-current industrial electric motors, but these accounted for less than 10 percent of sales and profits.

Lincoln's 1974 domestic net income was $17.5 million on sales of $237 million (Exhibit 2). Perhaps more significant than a single year's results was Lincoln's record of steady growth over the preceding four decades, as shown in Figure A.

During this period, after-tax return on equity had ranged between 10 percent and 15 percent. Lincoln's growth had been achieved without benefit of acquisition and had been financed with internally generated funds. The company's historical dividend payout policy had been to pay to the suppliers of capital a fair return each year for its use.

COMPANY HISTORY

Lincoln Electric was founded by John C. Lincoln in 1895 to manufacture electric motors and generators. James F. Lincoln, John's younger brother, joined the company in 1907. The brothers' skills and interests were complementary. John was a technical genius. During his lifetime he was awarded more than 50 patents for inventions as diverse as an apparatus for curing meat, an electric drill, a mine-door-activating mechanism, and an electric arc lamp. James's skills were in management and administration. He began as a salesman but soon took over as general manager. The Lincoln Electric Company was undeniably built in his image.

In 1911, the company introduced its first arc welding machine. Both brothers were fascinated by welding, which was then in its infancy. They recognized it as an alternative use for the motor-generator sets they were already producing to recharge the batteries for electric automobiles. The success of Ford, Buick, and others indicated that the days of the electric auto might be numbered, and the brothers were anxious to find other markets for their skills and products.

John's mechanical talents gave the company a head start in welding machines which it never relinquished. He developed a portable welding machine (a significant improvement over existing stationary models) and incorporated a transformer to allow regulation of the current. As his biographer noted, "This functional industrial development gave Lincoln Electric a lead in the field that it has always maintained, although the two giants—Westinghouse and General Electric—soon entered the market."[1]

By World War II, Lincoln Electric was the leading American manufacturer of arc welding equipment. Because of the importance of welding to the war effort, the company stopped producing electric motors and devoted its full capacity to

[1]Raymond Moley, *The American Century of John C. Lincoln* (New York: Duell, Sloan & Pearce, 1962), p. 71.

This case was prepared by Norman Fast, research assistant, under the direction of Professor Norman Berg, as the basis for class discussion rather than to illustrate either effective or ineffective handling of an administrative situation.

FIGURE A.

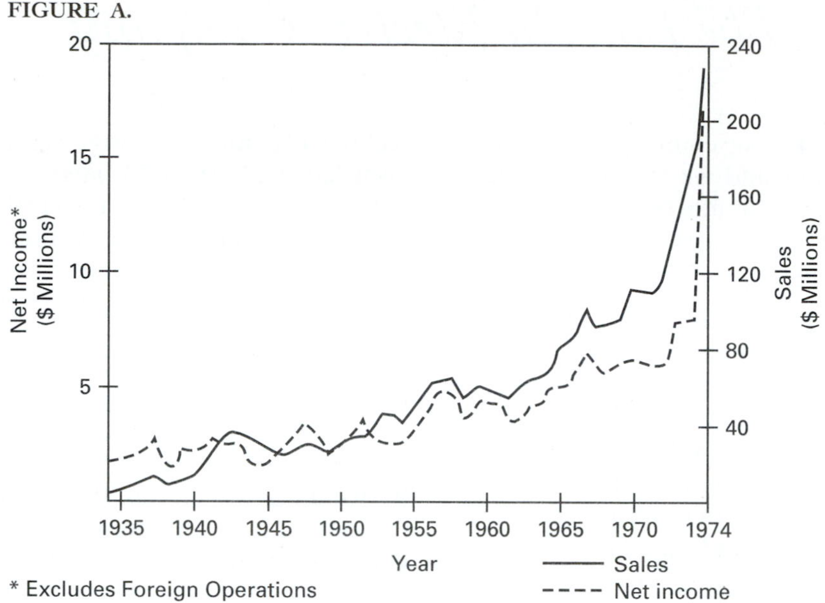

welding products. Demand continued to outpace production, and the government asked the welding equipment manufacturers to add capacity. As described by Lincoln's president, George Willis:

> Mr. Lincoln responded to the government's call by going to Washington and telling them that there was enough manufacturing capacity but it was being used inefficiently by everyone. He offered to share proprietary manufacturing methods and equipment designs with the rest of the industry. Washington took him up on it and that solved the problem. As a result of Mr. Lincoln's patriotic decision, our competitors had costs which were close to ours for a short period after the war, but we soon were outperforming them like before.

In 1955, Lincoln once again began manufacturing electric motors, and since then its position in the market had expanded steadily.

Through the years, Lincoln stock had been sold to employees and associates of the Lincoln brothers. In 1975, approximately 48 percent of employees were shareholders. About 80 percent of the outstanding stock was held by employees, the Lincoln family, and their foundations.

In its 80-year history, Lincoln had had only three board chairmen: John C. Lincoln, James F. Lincoln, and William Irrgang, who became chairman in 1972.

STRATEGY

Lincoln Electric's strategy was simple and unwavering. The company's strength was in manufacturing. Management believed that Lincoln could build quality products at a lower cost than their competitors. Their strategy was to concentrate on reducing costs and passing the savings through to the customer by continuously lowering prices. Management had adhered to this policy even when products were on allocation because of shortages in productive capacity. The result had been an expansion of both market share and primary demand for arc welding equipment and supplies over the past half century. Lincoln's strategy had also encouraged the exit of several major companies (including General Electric) from the industry and had caused others to seek more specialized market niches.

Management believed its incentive system and the climate it fostered were responsible in large part for the continual increase in productivity upon which this strategy depended. Under the Lincoln incentive system, employees were handsomely rewarded for their productivity, high quality, cost reduction ideas, and individual contributions to the company. Year-end bonuses averaged close to 100% of regular compensation, and some workers on the factory floor had earned more than $45,000 in a single year.[2]

Lincoln's strategy had remained virtually unchanged for decades. In a 1947 Harvard Business School case study on the company, James F. Lincoln described the firm's strategy as follows:

> It is the job of The Lincoln Electric Company to give its customers more and more of a better product at a lower and lower price. This will also make it possible for the company to give to the worker and the stockholder a higher and higher return.

In 1975, Chairman William Irrgang's description was remarkably similar:

> The success of The Lincoln Electric Company has been built on two basic ideas. One is producing more and more of a progressively better product at a lower and lower price for a larger and larger group of customers. The other is that an employee's earnings and promotion are in direct proportion to his individual contribution toward the company's success.[3]

Management felt it had achieved an enviable record in following this strategy faithfully and saw no need to modify it in the future. Lincoln Electric's record of increasing productivity and declining costs and prices is shown in Exhibit 3.

COMPANY PHILOSOPHY

Lincoln Electric's corporate strategy was rooted in the management philosophy of James F. Lincoln, a rugged individualist who believed that through competition and adequate incentives every person could develop to his or her fullest potential. In one of his numerous books and articles he wrote:

> Competition is the foundation of man's development. It has made the human race what it is. It is the spur that makes progress. Every nation that has eliminated it as the controlling force in its economy has disappeared, or will. We will do the same if we eliminate it by trying to give security, and for the same reason. Competition means that there will be losers as well as winners in the game. Competition will mean the disappearance of the lazy and incompetent, be they workers, industrialists, or distributors. Competition promotes progress. Competition determines who will be the leader. It is the only known way that leadership and progress can be developed if history means anything. It is a hard taskmaster. It is completely necessary for anyone, be he worker, user, distributor or boss, if he is to grow.
>
> If some way could be found so that competition could be eliminated from life, the result would be disastrous. Any nation and any people disappear if life becomes too easy. There is no danger from a hard life as all history shows. Danger is from a life that is made soft by lack of competition.[4]

Lincoln's faith in the individual was almost unbounded. His personal experience with the success of Lincoln Electric reinforced his faith in what could be accomplished under the proper conditions. In 1951 he wrote:

> Development in many directions is latent in every person. The difficulty has been that few recognize that fact. Fewer still will put themselves under the pressure or by chance are put under the pressure that will develop them greatly. Their latent abilities remain latent, hence useless. . . .
>
> It is of course obvious that the development of man, on which the success of incentive management depends, is a progressive process. Any results, no matter how good, that come from the application of incentive management cannot be considered final. There will always be greater growth of man under continued proper incentive. . . .
>
> Such increase of efficiency poses a very real problem to management. The profit that

[2]By contrast, the median income for U.S. manufacturing employees in 1974 was less than $9,200, according to Bureau of Labor Statistics data.

[3]*Employee's Handbook* (Cleveland: The Lincoln Electric Company, 1974).

[4]James F. Lincoln, *Incentive Management* (Cleveland: The Lincoln Electric Company, 1951), p. 33.

> will result from such efficiency obviously will be enormous. The output per dollar of investment will be many times that of the usual shop which practices output limitation. The labor cost per piece will be relatively small and the overhead will be still less.
>
> The profits at competitive selling prices resulting from such efficiency will be far beyond any possible need for proper return and growth of an industry. . . .
>
> How, then, should the enormous extra profit resulting from incentive management be split? The problems that are inherent in incentive dictate the answer. If the worker does not get a proper share, he does not desire to develop himself or his skill. Incentive, therefore, would not succeed. The worker must have a reward that he feels is commensurate with his contribution.
>
> If the customer does not have a part of the saving in lower prices, he will not buy the increased output. The size of the market is a decisive factor in costs of products. Therefore, the consumer must get a proper share of the saving.
>
> Management and ownership are usually considered as a unit. This is far from a fact, but in the problem here, they can be considered together. They must get a part of the saving in larger salaries and perhaps larger dividends.
>
> There is no hard and fast rule to cover this division, other than the following. The worker (which includes management), the customer, the owner, and all those involved must be satisfied that they are properly recognized or they will not cooperate, and cooperation is essential to any and all successful applications of incentives.[5]

Additional comments by James F. Lincoln are presented in Exhibit 4.

COMPENSATION POLICIES

Compensation policies were the key element of James F. Lincoln's philosophy of "incentive management." Lincoln Electric's compensation system had three components:

- wages based solely on piecework output for most factory jobs,
- a year-end bonus which could equal or exceed an individual's full annual regular pay, and
- guaranteed employment for all workers

Almost all production workers at Lincoln were paid on a straight piecework plan. They had no base salary or hourly wage but were paid a set "price" for each item they produced. William Irrgang explained:

> Wherever practical, we use the piecework system. This system can be effective, and it can be destructive. The important part of the system is that it is completely fair to the worker. When we set a piecework price, that price cannot be changed just because, in management's opinion, the worker is making too much money. Whether he earns two times or three times his normal amount makes no difference. Piecework prices can only be changed when management has made a change in the method of doing that particular job and under no other conditions. If this is not carried out 100 percent, piecework cannot work.
>
> Today piecework is confined to production operations, although at one time we also used it for work done in our stenographic pool. Each typewriter was equipped with a counter that registered the number of times the typewriter keys were operated. This seemed to work all right for a time until it was noticed that one girl was earning much more than any of the others. This was looked into, and it was found that this young lady ate her lunch at her desk, using one hand for eating purposes and the other for punching the most convenient key on the typewriter as fast as she could; which simply goes to show that no matter how good a program you may have, it still needs careful supervision.[6]

A Time Study Department established piecework prices which were guaranteed by the company, until methods were changed or a new

---

[5]Ibid., pp. 7–11.

[6]William Irrgang, "The Lincoln Incentive Management Program," Lincoln Lecture Series, Arizona State University, 1972, p. 13.

process introduced. Employees could challenge the price if they felt it was unfair. The Time Study Department would then retime the job and set a new rate. This could be higher or lower but was still open to challenge if an employee remained dissatisfied. Employees were expected to guarantee their own quality. They were not paid for defective work until it had been repaired on their own time.

Each job in the company was rated according to skill, required effort, responsibility, and so on, and a base wage rate for the job was assigned. Wage rates were comparable to those for similar jobs in the Cleveland area and were adjusted annually on the basis of Department of Labor statistics and quarterly to reflect changes in the cost of living. In this way, salaries or hourly wages were determined. For piecework jobs, the Time Study Department set piece prices so that an employee producing at a standard rate would earn the base rate for his or her job.

The second element of the compensation system was a year-end bonus, which had been paid each year since 1934. As explained in the *Employee's Handbook,* "The bonus, paid at the discretion of the company, is not a gift, but rather it is the sharing of the results of efficient operation on the basis of the contribution of each person to the success of the company for that year." In 1974, the bonus pool totaled $26 million, an average of approximately $10,700 per employee, or 90% of pre-bonus wages.

The total amount to be paid out in bonuses each year was determined by the board of directors. Lincoln's concentration on cost reduction kept costs low enough that prices could generally be set (and not upset by competition) on the basis of costs at the beginning of the year to produce a target return for stockholders and to give employees a bonus of approximately 100% of wages. The variance from the planned profits was usually added to (or subtracted from) the bonus pool to be distributed at year-end. Since 1945, the average bonus had varied from 78% to 129% of wages. In the past few years, it had been between 40% and 55% of pre-tax, pre-bonus profit, or as high as twice the net income after taxes.

An individual's share of the bonus pool was determined by a semiannual "merit rating" which measured individual performance compared to that of other members of the department or work group. Ratings for all employees had to average out to 100 on this relative scale. If, because of some unusual contribution, an individual deserved a rating above 110, he or she could be rewarded from a special corporate pool of bonus points, without any penalty to co-workers. Ratings above 110 were thus reviewed by a corporate committee or vice presidents who evaluated the individual's contribution. Merit ratings varied widely, from as low as 45 to as high as 160.

In determining an employee's merit rating, four factors were evaluated separately:

- dependability
- quality
- output
- ideas and cooperation

Foremen were responsible for the rating of all factory workers. They could request help from assistant foremen (dependability), the Production Control Department (output), the Inspection Department (quality), and the Methods Department (ideas and cooperation). In the office, supervisors rated their people on the same items. At least one executive reviewed all ratings. All employees were urged to discuss their ratings with their department heads if they were dissatisfied or unclear about them.

Lincoln complemented its rating and pay system with a Guaranteed Continuous Employment Plan. This plan provided security against layoffs and assured continuity of employment. Every full-time employee who had been with the company at least two years was guaranteed employment for at least 75% of the standard 40-hour week. In fact, the company had not had any layoffs since 1951 when initial trials for the plan were put into effect. It was formally established in 1958.

The guarantee of employment was seen by the company as an essential element in the incentive plan. Without such a guarantee, it was believed that employees would be more likely to resist improved production and efficiency for fear of losing their jobs. In accepting the guaranteed continuous employment plan, employees agreed to perform any job that was assigned as conditions required, and to work overtime during periods of high activity.

The philosophy and procedures regarding the incentive plan were the same for management and workers, except that William Irrgang and George Willis did not share in the bonus.

EMPLOYEE VIEWS

To the researchers, it appeared that employees generally liked working at Lincoln. The employee turnover rate was far below that of most other companies, and once a new employee made it through the first month or so, he rarely left for another firm (see Exhibit 5). One employee explained, "It's like trying out for a high school football team. If you make it through the first few practices, you're usually going to stay the whole season, especially after the games start."

One long-time employee who liked working at Lincoln was John "Tiny" Carrillo, an armature bander on the welding machine line, who had been with the company for 24 years. Tiny explained why:

> The thing I like here is that you're pretty much your own boss as long as you do your job. You're responsible for your own work and you even put your stencil on every machine you work on. That way if it breaks down in the field and they have to take it back, they know who's responsible.
>
> Before I came here, I worked at Cadillac as a welder. After two months there I had the top hourly rate. I wasn't allowed to tell anyone because there were guys who still had the starting rate after a year. But, I couldn't go any higher after two months.
>
> I've done well. My rating is usually around 110, but I work hard, right through the smoke breaks. The only time I stop is a half hour for lunch. I make good money. I have two houses, one which I rent out, and four cars. They're all paid for. When I get my bills, I pay them the next day. That's the main thing, I don't owe anyone.
>
> Sure, there are problems. There's sometimes a bind between the guys with low grades and the guys with high ones, like in school. And there are guys who sway everything their way so they'll get the points, but they [management] have good tabs on what's going on. . . .
>
> A lot of new guys come in and leave right away. Most of them are just mamma's boys and don't want to do the work. We had a new guy who was a produce manager at a supermarket. He worked a couple of weeks, then quit and went back to his old job.

At the end of the interview, the researcher thanked Tiny for his time. He responded by pointing out that it had cost him $7.00 in lost time, but that he was glad to be of assistance.

Another piece worker, Jorge Espinoza, a fine-wire operator in the Electrode Division, had been with the company for six years. He explained his feelings:

> I believe in being my own man. I want to use my drive for my own gain. It's worked. I built my family a house and have an acre of land, with a low mortgage. I have a car and an old truck I play around with. The money I get is because I earn it. I don't want anything given to me.
>
> The thing I don't like is having to depend on other people on the line and suppliers. We're getting bad steel occasionally. Our output is down as a result and my rating will suffer.
>
> There are men who have great drive here and can push for a job. They are not leaders and never will be, but they move up. That's a problem. . . .
>
> The first few times around, the ratings were painful for me. But now I stick near 100. You really make what you want. We just had a methods change and our base rate went from 83 to 89 coils a day. This job is tougher now and more complex. But, it's all what you want. If you want 110 coils you can get it. You just take less breaks. Today, I gambled and won. I didn't change my dies and made over a hundred coils. If I had lost, and the die plugged up, it would have cost me at least half an hour. But, today I made it.

MANAGEMENT STYLE

Lincoln's incentive scheme was reinforced by top management's attitude toward the men on the factor floor. In 1951, James Lincoln wrote:

> It becomes perfectly true to anyone who will think this thing through that there is no such thing in an industrial activity as Management and Men having different functions or

> being two different kinds of people. Why can't we think and why don't we think that all people are Management? Can you imagine any president of any factory or machine shop who can go down and manage a turret lathe as well as the machinist can? Can you imagine any manager of any organization who can go down and manage a broom—let us get down to that—who can manage a broom as well as a sweeper can? Can you imagine any secretary of any company who can go down and fire a furnace and manage that boiler as well as the man who does the job? Obviously, all are Management.[7]

Lincoln's president, George Willis, stressed the equality in the company:

> We try to avoid barriers between management and workers. We're treated equally as much as possible. When I got to work this morning at 7:30, the parking lot was three-quarters full. I parked way out there like anyone else would. I don't have a special reserved spot. The same principle holds true in our cafeteria. There's no executive dining room. We eat with everyone else.[8]

Willis felt that open and frank communication between management and workers had been a critical factor in Lincoln's success, and he believed that the company's Advisory Board, consisting of elected employee representatives, had played a very important role in achieving this. Established by James F. Lincoln in 1914, the board met twice a month, providing a forum in which employees could bring issues of concern to top management's attention, question company policies, and make suggestions for their improvement. As described in the Employee's Handbook:

> Board service is a privilege and responsibility of importance to the entire organization. In discussions or in reaching decisions Board members must be guided by the best interests of the Company. These also serve the best interests of its workers. They should seek at all times to improve the cooperative attitude of all workers and see that all realize they have an important part in our final results.

All Advisory Board meetings were chaired by either the chairman or the president of Lincoln. Usually both were present. Issues brought up at board meetings were either resolved on the spot or assigned to an executive. After each meeting, William Irrgang or George Willis would send a memo to the executive responsible for each unanswered question, no matter how trivial, and he was expected to respond by the next meeting if possible.

Minutes of all board meetings were posted on bulletin boards in each department and members explained the board's actions to the other workers in their department. The questions raised in the minutes of a given meeting were usually answered in the next set of minutes. This procedure had not changed significantly since the first meeting in 1914, and the types of issues raised had remained much the same (see Exhibit 6).

Workers felt that the Advisory Board provided a way of getting immediate attention for their problems. It was clear, however, that management still made the final decisions.[9] A former member of the Advisory Board commented:

> There are certain areas which are brought up in the meetings which Mr. Irrgang doesn't want to get into. He's adept at steering the conversation away from these. It's definitely not a negotiating meeting. But, generally, you really get action or an answer on why action isn't being taken.

In addition to the Advisory Board, there was a 12-member board of middle managers which met with Irrgang and Willis once a month. The topics discussed here were broader than those of the Advisory Board. The primary function of

[7]James F. Lincoln, *What Makes Workers Work?* (Cleveland: The Lincoln Electric Company, 1951), pp. 3–4.

[8]The cafeteria had large rectangular and round tables. In general, factory workers gravitated toward the rectangular tables. There were no strict rules, however, and management personnel often sat with factory workers. Toward the center was a square table that seated only four. This was reserved for William Irrgang, George Willis, and their guests when they were having a working lunch.

[9]In some cases, management allowed issues to be decided by a vote of employees. Recently, for example, employees had voted down a proposal that the company give them dental benefits, recognizing that the cost of the program would come directly out of their bonuses.

these meetings was to allow top management to get better acquainted with these individuals and to encourage cooperation between departments.

Lincoln's two top executives, Irrgang and Willis, continued the practice of James F. Lincoln in maintaining an open door to all employees. George Willis estimated that at least twice a week factory employees took advantage of this opportunity to talk with him.

Middle managers also felt that communication with Willis and Irrgang was open and direct. Often it bypassed intermediate levels of the organization. Most saw this as an advantage, but one commented:

> This company is run strictly by the two men at the top. Mr. Lincoln trained Mr. Irrgang in his image. It's very authoritarian and decisions flow top down. It never became a big company. There is very little delegated and top people are making too many small decisions. Mr. Irrgang and Mr. Willis work 80 hours a week, and no one I know in this company can say that his boss doesn't work harder than he does.

Willis saw management's concern for the worker as an essential ingredient in his company's formula for success. He knew at least 500 employees personally. In leading the researcher through the plant, he greeted workers by name and paused several times to tell anecdotes about them.

At one point, an older man yelled to Willis good-naturedly, "Where's my raise?" Willis explained that this man had worked for 40 years in a job requiring him to lift up to 20 tons of material a day. His earnings had been quite high because of his rapid work pace, but Willis had been afraid that as he was advancing in age he could injure himself working in that job. After months of Willis's urging, the worker switched to an easier but lower paying job. He was disappointed in taking the earnings cut and even after several years let the president know whenever he saw him.

Willis pointed out another employee, whose wife had recently died, and noted that for several weeks he had been drinking heavily and reporting to work late. Willis had earlier spent about half an hour discussing the situation with him to console him and see if the company could help in any way. He explained:

> I made a definite point of talking to him on the floor of the plant, near his work station. I wanted to make sure that other employees who knew the situation could see me with him. Speaking to him had symbolic value. It is important for employees to know that the president is interested in their welfare.

Management's philosophy was also reflected in the company's physical facilities. A no-nonsense atmosphere was firmly established at the gate to the parking lot where the only mention of the company name was in a sign reading:

> $1,000 REWARD for information leading to the arrest and conviction of persons stealing from the Lincoln Electric parking lot.

There was a single entrance to the offices and plant for workers, management, and visitors. Entering, one could not avoid being struck by the company motto, in large stainless steel letters extending 30 feet across the wall:

> THE ACTUAL IS LIMITED
> THE POSSIBLE IS IMMENSE

A flight of stairs led down to a tunnel system for pedestrian traffic which ran under the single-story plant. At the base of the stairs was a large bronze plaque on which were inscribed the names of the 8 employees who had served more than 50 years, and the more than 350 active employees with 25 or more years of service (the Quarter Century Club).

The long tunnel leading to the offices was clean and well lit. The executive offices were located in a windowless, two-story cement-block office building which sat like a box in the center of the plant. At the base of the staircase leading up to the offices, a Lincoln automatic welding machine and portraits of J. C. Lincoln and J. F. Lincoln welcomed visitors. The handrail on the staircase was welded into place, as were the ashtrays in the tunnel.

In the center of the office building was a simple, undecorated reception room. A switchboard operator/receptionist greeted visitors between filing and phone calls. Throughout the building, decor was Spartan. The reception room was furnished with a metal coat rack, a wooden bookcase, and several plain wooden tables and chairs. All of the available reading material dealt with Lincoln Electric Company or welding.

From the reception room, seven doors each led almost directly to the various offices and departments. Most of the departments were large open rooms with closely spaced desks. One manager explained that "Mr. Lincoln didn't believe in walls. He felt they interrupted the flow of communications and paperwork." Most of the desks and files were plain, old, and well worn, and there was little modern office equipment. Expenditures on equipment had to meet the same criteria in the office as in the plant: The Maintenance Department had to certify that the equipment replaced could not be repaired, and any equipment acquired for cost reduction had to have a one-year payback.[10] Even Xerox machines were nowhere to be found. Copying costs were tightly controlled and only certain individuals could use the Xerox copiers. Customer order forms which required eight copies were run on a duplicating machine, for example.

The private offices were small, uncarpeted, and separated by green metal partitions. The president's office was slightly larger than the others, but still retained a Spartan appearance. There was only one carpeted office. Willis explained: "That office was occupied by Mr. Lincoln until he died in 1965. For the next five years it was left vacant and now it is Mr. Irrgang's office and also the Board of Directors' and Advisory Board meeting room."

PERSONNEL

Lincoln Electric had a strict policy of filling all but entry level positions by promoting from within the company. Whenever an opening occurred, a notice was posted on the 25 bulletin boards in the plant and offices. Any interested employee could apply for an open position. Because of the company's sustained growth and policy of promoting from within, employees had substantial opportunity for advancement.

An outsider generally could join the company in one of two ways: either taking a factory job at an hourly or piece rate, or entering Lincoln's training programs in sales or engineering.[11] The company recruited its trainees at colleges and graduate schools, including Harvard Business School. Starting salary in 1975 for a trainee with a bachelor's degree was $5.50 an hour plus a year-end bonus at an average of 40% of the normal rate. Wages for trainees with either a master's degree or several years of relevant experience were 5% higher.

Although Lincoln's president, vice president of sales, and personnel director were all Harvard Business School graduates, the company had not hired many recent graduates. Clyde Loughridge, the personnel director, explained:

> We don't offer them fancy staff positions and we don't pretend to. Our starting pay is less than average, probably $17,000–$18,000[12] including bonus, and the work is harder than average. We start our trainees off by putting them in overalls and they spend up to seven weeks in the welding school. In a lot of ways it's like boot camp. Rather than leading them along by the hand, we like to let the self-starters show themselves.

The policy of promoting from within had rarely been violated, and then only in cases where a specialized skill was required. Loughridge commented:

> In most cases we've been able to stick to it, even where the required skills are entirely new to the company. Our employees have a lot of varied skills, and usually someone can fit the job. For example, when we recently got our first computer, we needed a programmer and systems analyst. We had twenty employees apply who had experience or training in computers. We chose two, and it really helps that they know the company and understand our business.

---

[10]Willis explained that capital projects with paybacks of up to two years were sometimes funded when they involved a product for which demand was growing.

[11]Lincoln's chairman and president both advanced through the ranks in Manufacturing. Irrgang began as a pieceworker in the Armature Winding Department, and Willis began in Plant Engineering. (See Exhibit 7 for employment history of Lincoln's top management.)

[12]In 1975, the median starting salary for Harvard Business School graduates who took positions in industrial manufacturing was $19,800.

The company did not send its employees to outside management development programs and did not provide tuition grants for educational purposes.

Lincoln Electric had no formal organization chart and management did not feel that one was necessary. (The chart in Exhibit 8 was drawn for the purposes of this case.) As explained by one executive:

> People retire and their jobs are parceled out. We are very successful in overloading our overhead departments. We make sure this way that no unnecessary work is done and jobs which are not absolutely essential are eliminated. A disadvantage is that planning may suffer, as may outside development to keep up with your field.

Lincoln's organizational hierarchy was flat, with few levels between the bottom and the top. For example, Don Hastings, the vice president of sales, had 37 regional sales managers reporting to him. He commented:

> I have to work hard, there's no question about that. There are only four of us in the home office plus two secretaries. I could easily use three more people. I work every Saturday, at least half a day. Most of our regional men do too, and they like me to know it. You should see the switchboard light up when 37 regional managers call in at five minutes to twelve on Saturday.

The president and chairman kept a tight rein over personnel matters. All changes in status of employees, even at the lowest levels, had to be approved by Willis. Irrgang also had to give his approval if salaried employees were involved. Raises or promotions had to be approved in advance. An employee could be fired by his supervisor on the spot for cause, but if the grounds were questionable, the decision had to be approved afterward by either Willis or Irrgang. Usually the supervisor was supported, but there had been cases where a firing decision was reversed.

MARKETING

Welding machines and electrodes were like razors and razor blades. A Lincoln welding machine often had a useful life of 30 years or more, while electrodes (and fluxes) were consumed immediately in the welding process. The ratio of machine cost to annual consumables cost varied widely, from perhaps 7:1 for a hand welder used in a small shop to 1:5 or more for an automatic welder used in a shipyard.

Although certain competitors might meet Lincoln's costs and quality in selected products, management believed that no company could match the line overall. Another important competitive edge for Lincoln was its sales force. Al Patnik, vice president of sales development, explained:

> Most competitors operate through distributors. We have our own top field sales force.[13] We start out with engineering graduates and put them through our seven-month training program. They learn how to weld, and we teach them everything we can about equipment, metallurgy, and design. Then they spend time on the rebuild line [where machines brought in from the field are rebuilt] and even spend time in the office seeing how orders are processed. Finally, before the trainees go out into the field, they have to go into our plant and find a better way of making something. Then they make a presentation to Mr. Irrgang, just as if he were one of our customers.
>
> Our approach to the customer is to go in and learn what he is doing and show him how to do it better. For many companies our people become their experts in welding. They go in and talk to a foreman. They might say, "Let me put on a headshield and show you what I'm talking about." That's how we sell them.

George Ward, a salesman in the San Francisco office, commented:

> The competition hires graduates with business degrees (without engineering backgrounds) and that's how they get hurt. This job is getting more technical every day. . . . A customer in California who is using our equipment to weld offshore oil rigs had a

---

[13]The sales force was supplemented in some areas by distributors. Sales abroad were handled by wholly owned subsidiaries or Armco's International Division.

problem with one of our products. I couldn't get the solution for them over the phone, so I flew in to the plant Monday morning and showed it to our engineers. Mr. Willis said to me, "Don't go back to California until this problem is solved. . . ." We use a "working together to solve your problem" approach. This, plus sticking to published prices, shows you're not interested in taking advantage of them.

I had a boss who used to say: "Once we're in, Lincoln never loses a customer except on delivery." It's basically true. The orders I lost last year were because we couldn't deliver fast enough. Lincoln gets hurt when there are shortages because of our guaranteed employment. We don't hire short-term factory workers when sales take off, and other companies beat us on delivery.

The sales force was paid a salary plus bonus. Ward believed that Lincoln's sales force was the best paid and hardest working in the industry. He said, "We're aggressive, and want to work and get paid for it. The sales force prides itself on working more hours than anyone else. . . . My wife wonders sometimes if you can work for Lincoln and have a family too."

MANUFACTURING

Lincoln's plant was unusual in several respects. It seemed crowded with materials and equipment, with surprisingly few workers. It was obvious that employees worked very fast and efficiently with few breaks. Even during the 10-minute smoke breaks in the morning and afternoon, employees often continued to work.

An innovative plant layout was partly responsible for the crowded appearance. Raw materials entered one side of the plant and finished goods came out the other side. There was no central stockroom for materials or work-in-process. Instead, everything that entered the plant was transported directly to the work station where it would be used. At a work station, a single worker or group operated in effect as a subcontractor. All required materials were piled around the station, allowing visual inventory control, and workers were paid a piece price for their production. Wherever possible, the work flow followed a straight line through the plant from the side where raw materials entered to the side where finished goods exited. Because there was no union, the company had great flexibility in deciding what could be performed at a work station. For example, foundry work and metal stamping could be carried out together by the same workers when necessary. Thus, work could flow almost directly along a line through the plant. Intermediate material handling was avoided to a great extent. The major exception arose when multiple production lines shared a large or expensive piece of machinery, and the work had to be brought to the machines.

Many of the operations in the plant were automated. Much of the manufacturing equipment was proprietary,[14] designed and built by Lincoln. In some cases, the company had modified machines built by others to run two or three times as fast as when originally delivered.

From the time a product was first conceived, close coordination was maintained between product design engineers and the Methods Department; this was seen as a key factor in reducing costs and rationalizing manufacturing. William Irrgang explained:

> After we have [an] idea . . . we start thinking about manufacturing costs, before anything leaves the Design Engineering Department. At that point, there is a complete "getting together" of manufacturing and design engineers—and plant engineers, too, if new equipment is involved.
>
> Our tooling, for instance, is going to be looked at carefully while the design of a product is still in process. Obviously, we can increase or decrease the tooling very materially by certain considerations in the design of a product, and we can go on the basis of total costs at all times. In fact, as far as total cost is concerned, we even think about such matters as shipping, warehousing, etc. All of these factors are taken into consideration when we're still at the design stage. It's very essential that this be done: otherwise, you can lock yourself out from a lot of potential economies.[15]

---

[14]Visitors were barred from the Electrode Division unless they had a pass signed by Willis or Irrgang.

[15]"Incentive Management in Action," *Assembly Engineering*, March 1967. Reprinted by permission of the publisher © 1967 by Hitchcock Publishing Co. All rights reserved.

In 1974, Lincoln's plant had reached full capacity, operating nearly around the clock. Land bordering its present location was unavailable and management was moving ahead with plans to build a second plant 15 miles away on the same freeway as the present plant.

Over the years, Lincoln had come to make rather than buy an increasing proportion of its components. For example, even though its unit volume of gasoline engines was only a fraction of its suppliers', Lincoln purchased engine blocks and components and assembled them rather than buying completed engines. Management was continually evaluating opportunities for backward integration and had not arbitrarily ruled out manufacturing any of Lincoln's components or raw materials.

ADMINISTRATIVE PRODUCTIVITY

Lincoln's high productivity was not limited to manufacturing. Clyde Loughridge pointed to the Personnel Department as an example: "Normally, for 2,300 employees you would need a personnel department of about 20, but we have only 6, and that includes the nurse, and our responsibilities go beyond those of the typical personnel department."

Once a year, Loughridge had to outline his objectives for the upcoming year to the president of the company, but as he explained, "I don't get a budget. There would be no point to it. I just spend as little as possible. I operate this just like my home. I don't spend on anything I don't need."

In the Traffic Department, workers also seemed very busy. There, a staff of 12 controlled the shipment of 2.5 million pounds of material a day. Their task was complex. Delivery was included in the price of their products. They thus could reduce the overall cost to the customer by mixing products in most loads and shipping the most efficient way possible to the company's 39 warehouses. Jim Biek, general traffic manager, explained how they accomplished this:

> For every order, we decide whether it would be cheaper by rail or truck. Then we consolidate orders so that over 90% of what goes out of here is full carload or full truckload, as compared to perhaps 50% for most companies. We also mix products so that we come in at the top of the weight brackets. For example, if a rate is for 20,000 to 40,000 pounds, we will mix orders to bring the weight right up to that 40,000 limit. All this is computed manually. In fact, my old boss used to say, "We run Traffic like a ma and pa grocery store."

As in the rest of Lincoln, the employees in the Traffic Department worked their way up from entry level positions. Jim Biek had become general traffic manager after nine years as a purchasing engineer. He had received an M.B.A. degree from Northwestern after a B.S. in mechanical engineering from Purdue, started in the engineering training program, and then spent five years in Product Development and Methods before going to Purchasing and finally to Traffic. Lack of experience in Traffic was a disadvantage, but the policy of promoting from within also had its advantages. Biek explained:

> One of my first tasks was to go to Washington and fight to get welders reclassified as motors to qualify for a lower freight rate. With my engineering experience and knowledge of welders, I was in a better position to argue this than a straight traffic man. . . .
>
> Just about everybody in here was new to Traffic. One of my assistant traffic managers had worked on the loading platform here for 10 years before he came into the department. He had to go to night school to learn about rates, but his experience is invaluable. He knows how to load trucks and rail cars backwards and forward. Who could do a better job of consolidating orders than he does? He can look at an order and think of it as rows of pallets.
>
> Some day we'll outgrow this way of operating, but right now I can't imagine a computer juggling loads like some of our employees do.

Lincoln's Order Department had recently begun computerizing its operations. It was the first time a computer had been used anywhere in the company (except in engineering and research), and according to Russell Stauffer, head of the Order Department, "It was a three-year job for me to sell this to top management." The computer was expected to replace 12 or 13 employees who would gradually be moved into new jobs. There had been some resistance to the computer, Stauffer noted:

> It's like anything new. People get scared. Not all the people affected have been here for the two years required to be eligible for guaranteed employment. and even though the others are assured a job, they don't know what it will be and will have to take what's offered.

The computer was expected to produce savings of $100,000 a year, and to allow a greater degree of control. Stauffer explained:

> We're getting information out of this that we never knew before. The job here is very complex. We're sending out more than two million pounds of consumables a day. Each order might have 30 or 40 items, and each item has a bracket price arrangement based on total order size. A clerk has to remember or determine quickly whether we are out of stock on any items and calculate whether the stock-out brings the order down into another bracket. This means they have to remember the prices and items out of stock. This way of operating was okay up to about $200 million in sales, but now we've outgrown the human capability to handle the problem.

Although he had no previous experience in computers, Stauffer had full responsibility for the conversion.

> I've been here for 35 years. The first day I started, I unloaded coal cars and painted fences. Then I went to the assembly line, first on small parts, then large ones. I've been running the Order Department for 12 years. Since I've been here, we've had studies on computers every year or two and it always came out that we couldn't save money. Finally, when it looked like we'd make the switch, I took some courses at IBM. Over the last year and a half, they've totaled eight and a half weeks, which is supposed to equal a full semester of college.

To date, the conversion had gone well, but much slower than anticipated. Order pressure had been so high that many mistakes would have been catastrophic. Management thus had emphasized assuring 100% quality operations rather than faster conversion.

LINCOLN'S FUTURE

The 1947 Harvard Business School case study of Lincoln Electric ended with a prediction by a union leader from the Cleveland area:

> The real test of Lincoln will come when the going gets tough. The thing Lincoln holds out to the men is high earnings. They work like dogs at Lincoln, but it pays off. . . .
>
> I think [Mr. Lincoln] puts too much store by monetary incentives—but then, there's no denying he has attracted people who respond to that type of incentive. But I think that very thing is a danger Lincoln faces. If the day comes when they can't offer those big bonuses, or his people decide there's more to life than killing yourself making money, I predict the Lincoln Electric Company is in for trouble.

Lincoln's president, George Willis, joined the company the year that this comment was made. Reflecting on his 28 years with the company, Willis observed:

> The company hasn't changed very much since I've been here. It's still run pretty much like Mr. Lincoln ran it. But today's workers are different. They're more outspoken and interested in why things are being done, not just how. We have nothing to hide and never did, so we can give them the answers to their questions.

Looking forward, Willis saw no need to alter Lincoln's strategy or its policies:

> My job will continue to be to have everyone in the organization recognize that a common goal all of us can and must support is to give the customer the quality he needs, when he needs it, at the lowest cost. To do this, we have to have everyone's understanding of this goal and their effort to accomplish it. In one way or another, I have to motivate the organization to meet this goal. The basic forms of the motivation have evolved over the last 40 years. However, keeping the system honed so that everyone understands it, agrees with it, and brings out disagreements so improvements can be made or thinking changed becomes my major responsibility.
>
> If our employees did not believe that

management was trustworthy, honest, and impartial, the system could not operate. We've worked out the mechanics. They are not secret. A good part of my responsibility is to make sure the mechanics are followed. This ties back to a trust and understanding between individuals at all levels of the organization.

I don't see any real limits to our size. Look at the world with a present population of just under four billion now and six and a quarter billion by the year 2000. Those people aren't going to tolerate a low standard of living. So there will be a lot of construction, cars, bridges, oil and all those things that have got to be to support a population that large.

My job will still be just the traditional things of assuring that we keep up with the technology and have sufficient profit to pay the suppliers of capital. Then, I have to make sure communication can be maintained adequately. That last task may be the biggest and most important part of my job in the years ahead as we grow larger and still more complex.

EXHIBIT 1 Arc Welding

Arc welding is a group of joining processes that utilize an electric current produced by a transformer or motor generator (electric or engine powered) to fuse various metals. The temperature at the arc is approximately 10,000 Fahrenheit.

The welding circuit consists of a welding machine, ground clamp, and electrode holder. The electrode carries electricity to the metal being welded and the heat from the arc causes the base metals to join together. The electrode may or may not act as a filler metal during the process; however, nearly 60% of all arc welding that is done in the United States utilizes a covered electrode that acts as a very high quality filler metal.

The Lincoln Electric Company manufactured a wide variety of covered electrodes, submerged arc welding wires and fluxes, and a unique self-shielded, Flux-cored electrode called Innershield. The company also manufactured welding machines, wire feeders, and other supplies that were needed for arc welding.

EXHIBIT 2 Lincoln's Status in 1974

Statement of Financial Condition (Foreign Subsidiaries Not Included) *December 31*	*1974*
ASSETS	
Current assets	
Cash and certificates of deposit	$ 5,691,120
Government securities	6,073,919
Notes and accounts receivable	29,451,161
Inventories (LIFO basis)	29,995,694
Deferred taxes and prepaid expenses	2,266,409
Total	73,478,303
Other assets	
Trustee—notes and interest receivable	1,906,871
Miscellaneous	384,572
Total	2,291,443
Intercompany	
Investment in foreign subsidiaries	4,695,610
Notes receivable	0
Total	4,695,610
Property, Plant and Equipment	
Land	825,376
Buildings[a]	9,555,562
Machinery, tools and equipment[a]	11,273,155
Total	21,654,093
Total assets	$102,119,449
LIABILITIES AND SHAREHOLDERS' EQUITY	
Current liabilities	
Accounts payable	$ 13,658,063
Accrued wages	1,554,225
Taxes, including income taxes	13,262,178
Dividends payable	3,373,524
Total	31,847,990
Shareholders' equity	
Common capital stock, stated value	281,127
Additional paid-in capital	3,374,570
Retained earnings	66,615,762
Total	70,271,459
Total liabilities and shareholders' equity	$102,119,449

[a]After depreciation

EXHIBIT 2 Lincoln's Status in 1974 *Continued*

Income and Retained Earnings *Year Ended December 31*	*1974*
Income	
Net sales	$232,771,475
Interest	1,048,561
Overhead and development charges to subsidiaries	1,452,877
Dividend income	843,533
Other income	515,034
Total	236,631,480
Costs and Expenses	
Cost of products sold	154,752,735
Selling, administrative, and general expenses and freight out	20,791,301
Year-end incentive bonus	24,707,297
Pension expense	2,186,932
Total	202,438,265
Income Before Income Taxes	34,193,215
Provision for Income Taxes	
Federal	14,800,000
State and Local	1,866,000
	16,666,000
Net Income	$ 17,527,215

EXHIBIT 3 Lincoln Electric's Record of Pricing and Productivity

A. Lincoln Prices[a] Relative to Commodity Prices[b], 1934–1971

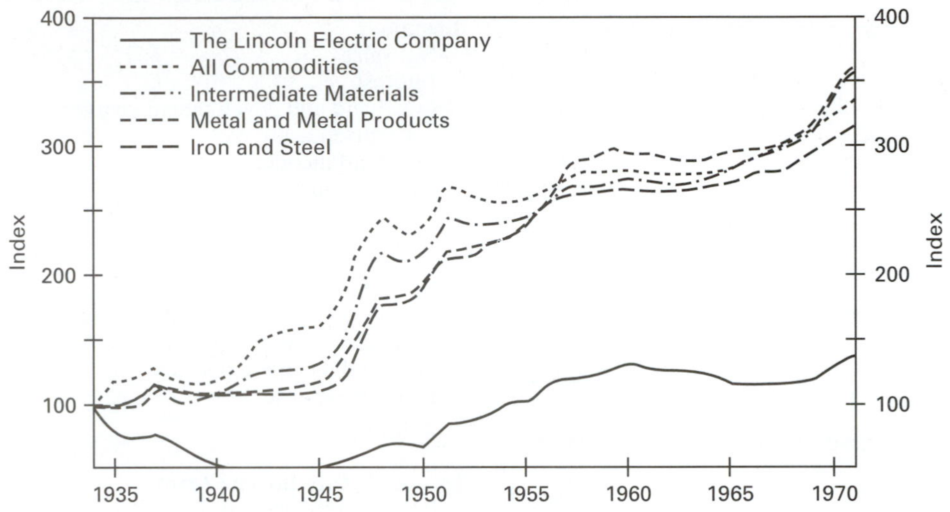

[a]Index of annual selling prices of 3⁄16-inch diameter electrode in No. 5 and No. 5P in 3,000-pound quantities

[b]Indexes of wholesale prices

B. Lincoln Prices[c] Relative to Wholesale Machinery and Equipment Prices, 1939–1971

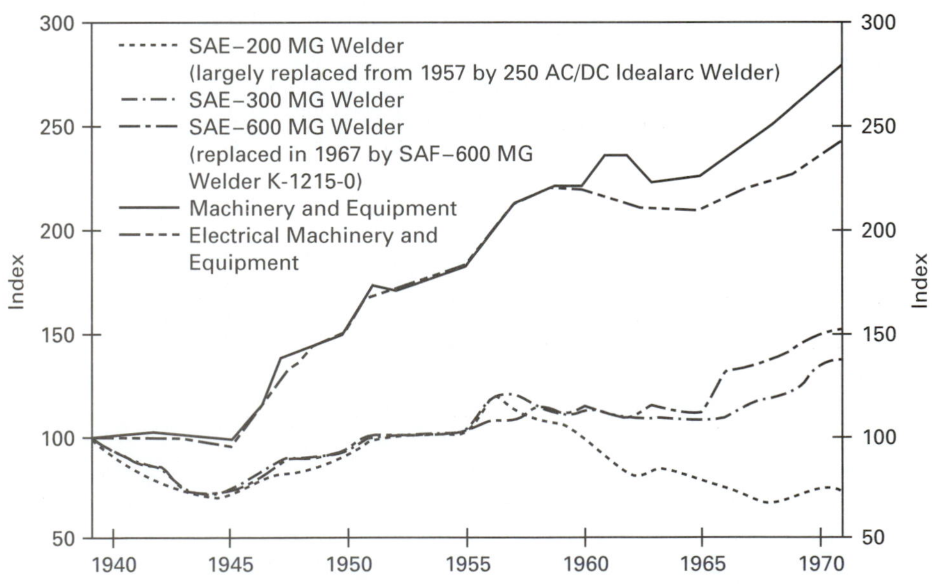

[c]Average annual prices of specific Lincoln welders

EXHIBIT 3 Lincoln Electric's Record of Pricing and Productivity *Continued*

C. Productivity of Lincoln Production Workers Relative to Workers in Manufacturing and Durable Goods Industries, 1934–1971

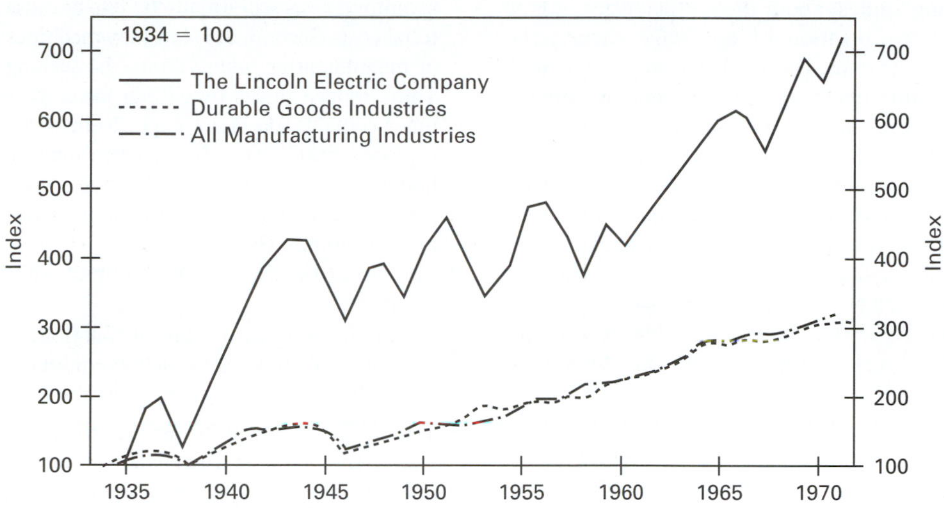

D. Lincoln Productivity Relative to Three Other Companies: Sales Value[d] of Products per Employee, 1934–1971

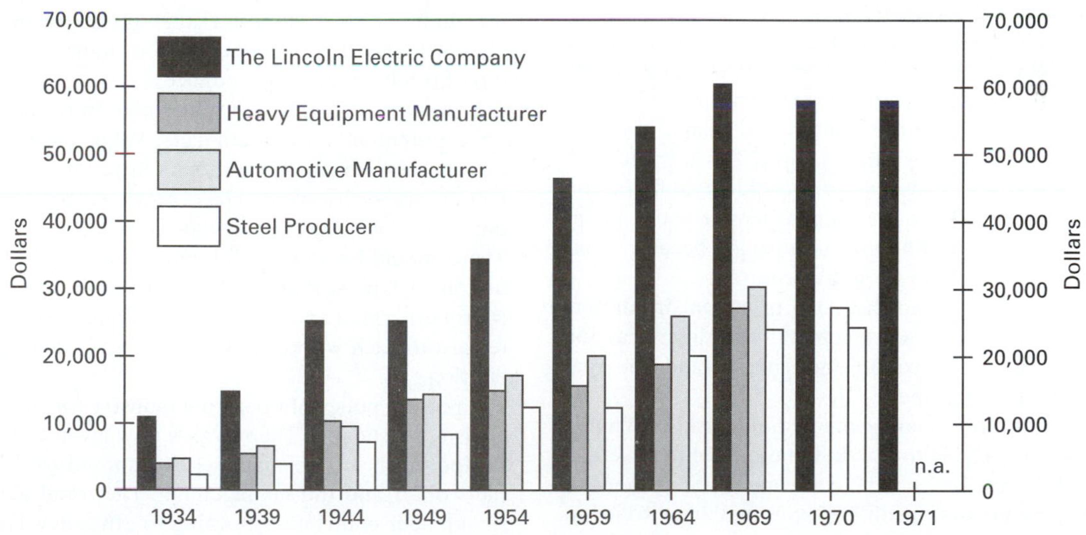

[d]At current prices

Source: Company records

EXHIBIT 4 James F. Lincoln's Observations on Management

- Some think paying a man more money will produce cooperation. Not true. Many incentives are far more effective than money. Robert MacNamara gave up millions to become Secretary of Defense. Status is a much greater incentive.
- If those crying loudest about the inefficiencies of labor were put in the position of the wage earner, they would react as he does. The worker is not a man apart. He has the same needs, aspirations, and reactions as the industrialist. A worker will not cooperate on any program that will penalize him. Does any manager?
- The industrial manager is very conscious of his company's need of uninterrupted income. He is completely oblivious, though, to the worker's same need. Management fails—i.e., profits fall off—and gets no punishment. The wage earner does not fail but is fired. Such injustice!
- Higher efficiency means fewer manhours to do a job. If the worker loses his job more quickly, he will oppose higher efficiency.
- There never will be enthusiasm for greater efficiency if the resulting profits are not properly distributed. If we continue to give it to the average stockholder, the worker will not cooperate.
- Most companies are run by hired managers, under the control of stockholders. As a result, the goal of the company has shifted from service to the customer to making larger dividends for stockholders.
- The public will not yet believe that our standard of living could be doubled immediately if labor and management would cooperate.
- The manager is dealing with expert workers far more skillful. While you can boss these experts around in the usual lofty way, their eager cooperation will not be won.
- A wage earner is no more interested than a manager in making money for other people. The worker's job doesn't depend on pleasing stockholders, so he has no interest in dividends. Neither is he interested in increasing efficiency if he may lose his job because management has failed to get more orders.
- If a manager received the same treatment in matters of income, security, advancement, and dignity as the hourly worker, he would soon understand the real problem of management.
- The first question management should ask is: What is the company trying to do? In the minds of the average worker the answer is: "The company is trying to make the largest possible profits by any method. Profits go to absentee stockholders and top management."
- There is all the difference imaginable between the grudging, distrustful, half-forced cooperation and the eager, whole-hearted, vigorous, happy cooperation of men working together for a common purpose.
- Continuous employment of workers is essential to industrial efficiency. This is a management responsibility. Laying off workers during slack times is death to efficiency. The worker thrown out is a trained man. To replace him when business picks up will cost much more than the savings of wages during the layoff. Solution? The worker must have a guarantee that if he works properly his income will be continuous.
- Continuous employment is the first step to efficiency. But how? First, during slack periods, manufacture to build up inventory; costs will usually be less because of lower material costs. Second, develop new machines and methods of manufacturing; plans should be waiting on the shelf. Third, reduce prices by getting lower costs. When slack times come, workers are eager to help cut costs. Fourth, explore markets passed over when times are good. Fifth, hours of work can be reduced if the worker is agreeable. Sixth, develop new products. In sum, management should plan for slumps. They are useful.
- The incentives that are most potent when properly offered are:

  Money in proportion to production.
  Status as a reward for achievement.
  Publicity of the worker's contributions and skill.
- The calling of the minister, the doctor, the lawyer, as well as the manager, contains incentive to excel. Excellence brings rewards, self-esteem, respect. Only the hourly worker has no reason to excel.
- Resistance to efficiency is not normal. It is present only when we are hired workers.
- Do unto others as you would have them do unto you. This is not just a Sunday school ideal, but a proper labor-management policy.
- An incentive plan should reward a man not only for the number of pieces turned out, but also for the accuracy of his work, his cooperation in improving methods of production, his attendance.
- The progress in industry so far stems from the developed potentialities of managers. Wage earners, who because of their greater numbers have far greater potential, are overlooked. Here is where the manager must look for his greatest progress.
- There should be an overall bonus based on the contribution each person makes to efficiency. If each person is properly rated and paid, there will not only be a fair reward to each worker but friendly and exciting competition.
- The present policy of operating industry for stockholders is unreasonable. The rewards now given to him are far too much. He gets income that should really go to the worker and the management. The usual absentee stockholder contributes nothing to efficiency. He buys a stock today and sells it tomorrow. He often doesn't even know what the company makes. Why should he be rewarded by large dividends?
- There are many forms and degrees of cooperation between the worker and the management. The worker's attitude can vary all the way from passivity to highly imaginative contributions to efficiency and progress.

Source: *Civil Engineering*, January 1973, p. 78. Reprinted by permission.

EXHIBIT 5 Stability of Employment

A. Lincoln and Industry Labor Turnover Rates, 1958–1970

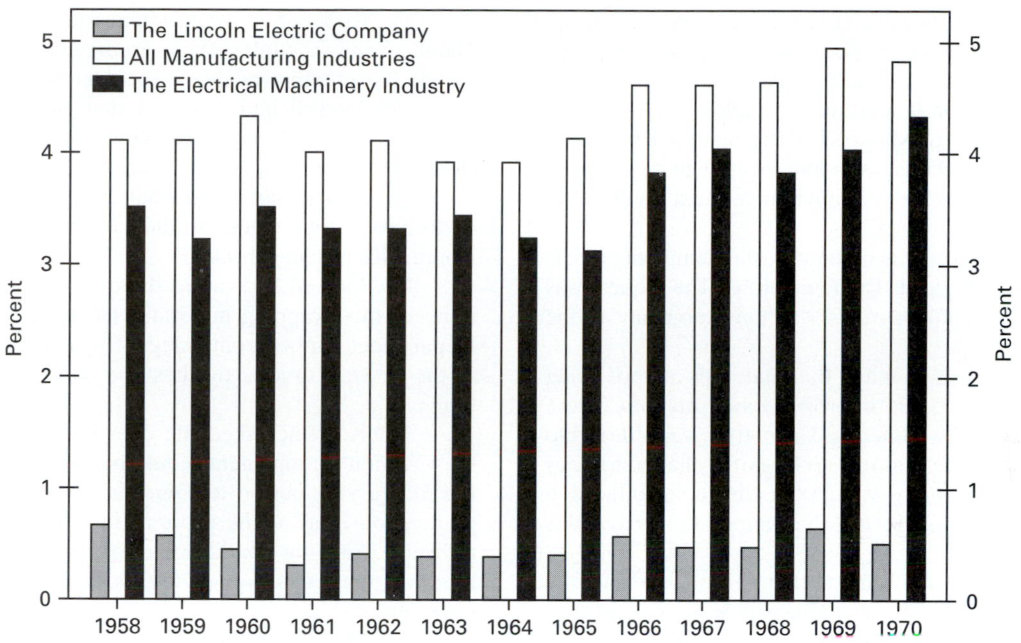

B. Employee Distribution by Years of Service, 1975

Employee's Years of Service	*Number of Employees*
Less than 1	153
1	311
2	201
3	93
4	34
5	90
6–10	545
11–20	439
21–30	274
31–40	197
41–50	27
51 or more	1
Total	2,365

EXHIBIT 6 Management Advisory Board Minutes

September 26, 1944

Absent: William Dillmuth

A discussion on piecework was again taken up. There was enough detail so it was thought best to appoint a committee to study it and bring a report into the meeting when that study is complete. That committee is composed of Messrs. Gilletly, Semko, Kneen and Steingass. Messrs. Erickson and White will be called in consultation, and the group will meet next Wednesday, October 4th.

The request was made that the members be permitted to bring guests to the meetings. The request was granted. Let's make sure we don't get too many at one time.

The point was made that materials are not being brought to the operation properly and promptly. There is no doubt of this difficulty. The matter was referred to Mr. Kneen for action. It is to be noted that conditions of deliveries from our suppliers have introduced a tremendous problem which has helped to increase this difficulty.

The request was made that over-time penalty be paid with the straight time. This will be done. There are some administrative difficulties which we will discuss at the next meeting but the over-time payment will start with the first pay in October.

Beginning October 1st employees' badges will be discontinued. Please turn them in to the watchmen.

It was requested that piecework prices be put on repair work in Dept. J. This matter was referred to Mr. Kneed for action.

A request was made that a plaque showing the names of those who died in action, separate from the present plaques, be put in the lobby. This was referred to Mr. Davis for action.

The question was asked as to what method for upgrading men is used. The ability of the individual is the sole reason for his progress. It was felt this is proper.

J. F. Lincoln
President

September 23, 1974 (Excerpts)

Members absent: Tom Borkowski, Albert Sinn

Mr. Kupetz had asked about the Christmas and Thanksgiving schedules. These are being reviewed and we will have them available at the next meeting.

Mr. Howell had reported that the time clocks and the bells do not coincide. This is still being checked.

Mr. Sharpe had asked what the possibility would be to have a time clock installed in or near the Clean Room. This is being checked.

Mr. Joosten had raised the question of the pliability of the wrapping material used in the Chemical Department for wrapping slugs. The material we use at the present time is the best we can obtain at this time. . . .

Mr. Kostelac asked the question again whether the vacation arrangements could be changed, reducing the fifteen year period to some shorter period. It was pointed out that at the present time, where we have radically changing conditions every day, it is not the time to go into this. We will review this matter at some later date. . . .

Mr. Martucci brought out the fact that there was considerable objection by the people involved to having to work on Saturday night to make up for holiday shutdowns. This was referred to Mr. Willis to be taken into consideration in schedule planning. . . .

Mr. Joosten reported that in the Chemical Department on the Saturday midnight shift they have a setup where individuals do not have sufficient work so that it is an uneconomical situation. This has been referred to Mr. Willis to be reviewed.

Mr. Joosten asked whether there would be some way to get chest x-rays for people who work in dusty areas. Mr. Loughridge was asked to check a schedule of where chest x-rays are available at various times. . . .

Mr. Robinson asked what the procedure is for merit raises. The procedure is that the foreman recommends the individual for a merit raise if by his performance he has shown that he merits the increase. . . .

Chairman

William Irrgang: MW
September 25, 1974

EXHIBIT 7 Employment History of Top Executives

William Irrgang, Board Chairman	
1929	Hired, Repair Department
1930	Final Inspection
1934	Inspection, Wire Department
1946	Director of factory engineering
1951	Executive vice president for manufacturing and engineering
1954	President and general manager
1972	Chairman of the board of directors
George E. Willis, President	
1947	Hired, Factory Engineering
1951	Superintendent, Electrode Division
1959	Vice president
1969	Executive vice president of manufacturing and associated functions
1972	President
William Miskoe, Vice President, International	
1932	Hired, Chicago sales office
1941	President of Australian plant
1969	To Cleveland as vice president, international
Edwin M. Miller, Vice President and Assistant to the President	
1923	Hired, factory worker
1925	Assistant foreman
1929	Production Department
1940	Assistant department head, Production Department
1952	Superintendent, Machine Division
1959	Vice president
1973	Vice president and assistant to the president
D. Neal Manross, Vice President, Machine and Motor Division	
1941	Hired, factory worker
1942	Welding inspector
1952	General foreman, Extruding Department and assistant plant superintendent
1953	Foreman, Special Products Department, Machine Division
1956	Superintendent, Special Products Division
1959	Superintendent, Motor Manufacturing
1966	Vice president, Motor Division
1973	Vice president in charge of Motor and Machine Divisions
Albert S. Patnik, Vice President of Sales Development	
1940	Hired, sales student
1940	Welder, New London, Conn.
1941	Junior salesman, Los Angeles office
1942	Salesman, Seattle office
1945	Military service
1945	Reinstated to Seattle
1951	Rural Dealer Manager, Cleveland sales office
1964	Assistant to the vice president of sales
1972	Vice president
Donald F. Hastings, Vice President and General Sales Manager	
1953	Hired, sales trainee
1954	Welding engineer, Emeryville, Cal.
1959	District manager, Moline office
1970	General sales manager, Cleveland
1972	Vice president and general sales manager

EXHIBIT 8 Organization

Chairman of the Board Treasurer and Chief Executive Officer

Chief Engineer Factory Engineer
Vice President Mach. & Mtr. Development
Vice President International
Specialist Foreign Operations
Secretary
Vice President Sales Development
Vice President Research
Vice President Electrode Development

President

Vice President Asst. to Pres.
Superintendent of Maintenance
Controller Gen. Acctg.
Manager Cost. Dept.
Personnel Director
Director of Purch.
Manager of Pub. & Ed. Services
Manager of Adv. & Sales Pro.
Manager App. Eng.
Service Manager

Foreman Plant Prot., Salv. Custodian Serv.
Manager Adm. Serv.
Manager Order
Gen. Mgr. Traffic
Foreman Shipping
Chief Inst. Wldg. Sch.
Parts Manager

Supervisor Gen. Serv.
Credit Manager

Vice President Mach. & Mtr. Divisions
Vice President Sales
Assistant to the President Plt. & Equip.
Chief Insp. Electrode Division
Vice President Electrode Division

Chief Insp. Mach. & Mtr. Divisions
Superintendent Mach. & Mtr. Divisions
District Managers (37)
Asst. Supt. Electrode Div.
Manager Spec. Prod.

Production Control Manager
Manager Methods Dept.
Foreman (11) Production
Sales Force
Production Control Manager
Manager Methods
Foreman (7) Production

Distributors

EXHIBIT 9 Lincoln Comment on the Case

After reading the 1975 Harvard case study, Richard S. Sabo, manager of publicity & educational services, sent the following letter to the casewriter:

July 31, 1975
To: Mr. Norman Fast
Dear Mr. Fast:

I believe that you have summarized the Incentive Management System of The Lincoln Electric Company very well; however, readers may feel that the success of the Company is due only to the psychological principles included in your presentation.

Please consider adding the efforts of our executives who devote a great deal of time to the following items that are so important to the consistent profit and long range growth of the Company.

I. Management has limited research, development and manufacturing to a standard product line designed to meet the major needs of the welding industry.
II. New products must be reviewed by manufacturing and all production costs verified before being approved by management.
III. Purchasing is challenged to not only procure materials at the lowest cost, but also to work closely with engineering and manufacturing to assure that the latest innovations are implemented.
IV. Manufacturing supervision and all personnel are held accountable for reduction of scrap, energy conservation, and maintenance of product quality.
V. Production control, material handling and methods engineering are closely supervised by top management.
VI. Material and finished goods inventory control, accurate cost accounting and attention to sales costs, credit and other financial areas have constantly reduced overhead and led to excellent profitability.
VII. Management has made cost reduction a way of life at Lincoln and definite programs are established in many areas, including traffic and shipping, where tremendous savings can result.
VIII. Management has established a sales department that is technically trained to reduce customer welding cost. This sales technique and other real customer services have eliminated non-essential frills and resulted in long term benefits to all concerned.
IX. Management has encouraged education, technical publishing and long range programs that have resulted in industry growth, thereby assuring market potential for The Lincoln Electric Company.

Richard S. Sabo

bjs

CHAPTER 6

Direct and Indirect Control System Costs

Managers incur real out-of-pocket costs by investing in systems of controls in return for one primary benefit: a higher probability that people will work hard and direct their energies to serve the organization's interests. Controls may also cause some indirect, often less obvious, costs which can be many times greater than their direct costs.[1] Some of these indirect costs are created by negative side effects which are inherent in the use of specific types of controls. Others are caused either by a poor management control system (MCS) design or by an implementation of the wrong type of control for the given situation. To make informed cost/benefit judgments, managers must understand these side effects, their costs, and their causes.

This chapter discusses both out-of-pocket costs and the costs of several of the most common and most harmful side effects produced by one or more of the control types. Chapters 12 and 13 discuss in more detail more of the harmful side effects uniquely caused by the use of financial controls, the form of results control that involves holding individuals (particularly general managers) accountable for results defined in monetary terms (such as accounting profit).

OUT-OF-POCKET COSTS

The term *out-of-pocket costs* refers to the direct, monetary costs of implementing a control. These costs should affect decisions about whether the benefits of a control justify the costs and whether one or another form of control should be implemented.

Excessive out-of-pocket costs can cause an MCS to fail. An Urban Institute study of thirteen merit-pay incentive plans for teachers implemented in the 1980s and 1990s found that eleven had been terminated by 1993. Observers attributed the major causes of the failure to the "high program costs and heavy demands on administrators."[2]

Some out-of-pocket costs of controls, such as the costs of cash bonuses, recognition plaques, and internal audit staffs, are easy to measure. Other significant costs, such as the costs of the time employees spend in planning and budgeting activities, must be estimated.

Generally, the full out-of-pocket costs of the control should be considered. In the case of a preaction review of an investment proposal by a senior management committee, the *marginal* costs of reviews may be zero, if all the committee members are employees, or only a nominal amount, if the meeting(s) require some telephone calls or travel. The *full* costs of the time consumed in reviewing and discussing the proposal may be large. If the preaction review was not necessary, the managers' times would be freed up to do other things, or the size of the management staff could be reduced.

BEHAVIORAL DISPLACEMENT

Behavioral displacement is a common, harmful control system side effect that can subject the organization to significant costs, not all of which are easy to identify and quantify. Behavioral displacement occurs wherever the control system produces, actually encourages, behaviors that are not consistent with the organization's objectives, or at least the strategy that has been selected.

Behavioral displacement is most common with accountability-type controls (either results or action accountability) where the specification of the results or actions desired is incongruent or incomplete. Some forms of personnel/cultural controls can also produce the problem.

Behavioral Displacement and Results Controls

Behavioral displacement will result everywhere an organization defines sets of results measures for which employees are rewarded that are incongruent with the organization's *true* objective. Here are some illustrations:

- When companies give their salespeople monthly sales quotas, the salespeople tend to work on the easiest sales, not the most profitable or those with the highest priority.
- When companies base part of their research scientists' rewards on the number of patents filed, which is an imperfect indicator of research effectiveness, they are likely to see an increase in the number of patents filed, but a decrease in the number of successful research projects.
- When brokerage firms reward their brokers through commissions on customer trades, many brokers respond by *churning* accounts; engaging in more transactions than are in the customers' best interests.[3]
- When companies reward their programmers for output measured in lines of code per day, the programmers tend to generate programs with lengthy code even when the company's problems can be better addressed by simpler programs or by off-the-shelf applications.

These behavioral displacement problems are caused by either a poor understanding of the desired results and/or an overreliance on easily quantified results.

Poor Understanding of Desired Results

The first major cause of displacement is an incorrect or incomplete understanding of the role of the person(s) being controlled. An *incorrect understanding* of what needs to be done might occur in a company that sets sales quotas for its *cash-cow* departments based on volume, not profitability. Volume-based quotas might be appropriate for a department in an industry with manufacturing costs declining with experience, but in a stable, cash-generating business such targets are likely to reflect merely an imperfect understanding of the appropriate strategy.

Results controls can also cause displacement if there is an *incomplete specification* of the results that are desired. Even conscientious individuals will be induced to concentrate their energy on the results monitored and emphasized by the control system and to slight other, unmeasured result areas which, in reality, may also be quite important. In other words, it becomes possible to maximize performance according to the rules of the control system without concurrently contributing optimally toward the organization's objectives. Here are some examples of behavioral displacement caused by an incomplete specification of the results desired:

- A plant manager was unwilling to modify production schedules to accommodate even highly profitable rush orders. Because he was evaluated primarily in terms of his ability to control costs, he had little incentive to make last-minute schedule changes.[4]
- A trailer company decided to monitor the number of trailers its salespeople sold. The monitoring change produced a dramatic improvement in sales, but many of the sales were to poor credit risks, and the sales lot quickly filled up with overpriced trade-ins.[5]
- A department store implemented a results control system that involved rewarding sales personnel on the volume of sales they generated. Just after the introduction of the control system, sales did increase, but this turned out to be only a short-term improvement. As the sales personnel learned how to maximize their performance according to the rules of the control system, they began to compete among themselves for customers and to neglect important activities for which they were not rewarded, such as stocking and arrangement of merchandise.[6]
- Managers of a commercial waste incinerator put intense profit pressure on their subsidiaries. The subsidiary managers were not rewarded directly for safety. Some of the managers started skimping on safety equipment (for example, gloves and respirators), shutting off their pollution monitoring equipment, and feeding toxic wastes into their incinerators at rates higher than those allowed by law. They placed phony labels on some barrels of waste so regulators would not discover their scheme. Eventually, an incinerator exploded, releasing toxic fumes.[7]
- Managers at a seventy-two-store chain of automobile repair shops implemented a system of performance incentives for their mechanics and service advisors. Fixed pay for individuals in both roles was cut. To compensate for the cut, the mechanics were paid a *productivity incentive* comparable to a piece rate paid to a factory worker. The service advisors, who were responsible for advising customers on potential repairs and parts, consulting with mechanics, and processing repair orders, were offered commission possibilities based on their achievement of specific job (for example, number of muffler replacements per shift) and sales volume quotas. A year-and-a-half after the compensation change, the California Consumer Affairs department, after a yearlong undercover investigation, accused the chain of ripping off customers by performing unnecessary repairs. The settlement cost to the company was approximately $15 million after taxes, not including the negative reputational effects and declining sales at the auto repair shops.[8] The performance incentive system was abandoned.

As these situations illustrate, relying on results control with an incomplete specification of desired results can be costly. A complete understanding of the trade-offs required of a person in the role being controlled is particularly important when multiple indicators are used to monitor different aspects of performance. A method of aggregation must be set so that the individual measures can be combined into an overall performance measure. If the relative importance of the various factors is not made explicit, employees may not allocate their effort appropriately, and the outcome will not be optimal.

Similarly, incorrect or incomplete sets of goals have been blamed as one of the causes for the common lack of success of MBO systems. Here is an example of such a criticism:

> Tying personnel performance evaluation, promotions, compensation and the like to objective-achievement is often counterproductive, because it discourages the development of innovative, high-risk, high-reward objectives.[9]

Overquantification

A second major cause of displacement in results control systems is a tendency, which is common, "to concentrate on matters that are concrete and quantifiable, rather than intangible concepts that may be even more important."[10] Peter Drucker has been among those who have commented on this problem:

> The more we can quantify the truly measurable areas, the greater the temptation to put all-out on those—the greater, therefore, the danger that what looks like better "controls" will actually mean less "control," if not a business out of control altogether.[11]

This type of criticism was leveled at Mattel, the toy company that moved into consumer electronics. An independent observer criticized the company as being "a highly structured, run-by-the-numbers type of company in a business that requires more intuitive management."[12]

Avoiding quantified indicators is not the general solution to these criticisms, because quantified indicators are not inherently bad and they do have some advantages, particularly with regard to the clarity with which performance targets and results can be communicated. One solution to the results controls-related displacement problem is to find or to develop acceptable quantified indicators of the intangible concepts that may be missing in order to alleviate the problems for which results controls are being criticized. An acceptable surrogate measure of quality might be *percent rejects,* and employee welfare might be assessed by means of attitude surveys.

However, situations do exist where quantified measures cannot be used; for example, it may not be possible to develop timely measures of success for research scientists. There also seems to be an ever-present risk that quantified measures will be overused (that is, used where they do not provide an acceptably close representation of the actual quality desired). Organizations are prone to appear to want what they can measure, rather than taking adequate care to develop reasonable measures of what they want.

Behavioral Displacement and Action Controls

Behavioral displacement can also occur where action controls are used. One form of action-related displacement is often referred to as *means-ends inversion* because employees can be induced to pay more attention to what they do (the means) and can lose sight of what they are to accomplish (the ends). Managers who are given an approval limit for capital expenditures have been known to invest in a series of small projects, each of which falls just below the ceiling of their authority. Following this procedure, they do not violate any of the terms of their organization's action accountability controls, but the resulting pattern of small, incremental investments is likely to be suboptimal.[13]

Sometimes action-related displacement occurs simply because the defined action sets are incongruent. Incongruence occurs wherever performance of the specified actions would not be the most desirable from the organization's standpoint, in the sense that optimal results could not be expected if those actions were performed. Peter Drucker observed that

> a company that tells its foremen that the job is human relations but which promotes the foreman who best does his paper work makes it very clear to even the dumbest man in the shop that it wants paper work rather than human relations. And it will get paper work.[14]

Many examples of displacement problems produced in an action accountability control system have been documented. A public employment agency controlled its interviewers by monitoring the number of interviews conducted. This caused a goal displacement problem because the interviewers were motivated to increase the number of interviews they conducted, but they were not spending enough time actually locating jobs for their clients. Eventually, the agency recognized the displacement problem, and agency management started to control both actions and results. They devised eight quantitative measures (for example, number of placements, number of referrals, ratios of placements to interviews and placements to referrals) and monitored them to control the performances of the interviewers.

Rigid, nonadaptive behaviors is a pathology commonly associated with what are called *bureaucratic* forms of organization. This is a form of displacement that is common where action controls dominate. Formal action controls, in the form of standard operating procedures and rules, can cause employees to routinize their behaviors and discourage them from thinking about how they might do their jobs better and adapt to a possibly changing environment. The standardized operating procedures and rules tend to filter away environmental inconsistencies and to encourage a complacency to environmental changes. This problem was noted by Adam Smith, well before the rise of the modern corporation:

> The man whose whole life is spent in performing a few simple operations . . . has no occasion to exert his understanding or to exercise his invention . . . He generally becomes as stupid and ignorant as it is possible for a human creature to become.[15]

As Stephen Robert, chief executive at Oppenheimer & Company, a large stock brokerage house, expressed it, "Unless you reward people as entrepreneurs, they become technocrats."[16]

Examples of rigid, nonadaptive behaviors abound. The automobile industry provides a prominent example. Not many years ago, U.S. automobile manufacturers thought they had, through extensive time-and-motion studies and heavy investments in equipment, nearly optimized the design of their assembly-line operations. Their control systems required production employees to adhere rigidly to elaborate action prescriptions. Japanese corporations then introduced new processes that proved to be more efficient. On Japanese assembly lines, the control systems were more flexible. Workers were encouraged to experiment with different ways of doing their jobs, for example, to try putting the doors on the car before the locks were installed, and then to alternate the order to see which was more efficient. Over time, the Japanese firms gained a large competitive advantage. Lately, the U.S. automobile firms, and many others in other industries, have relaxed their tight action control systems. They are giving their workers more flexibility, encouraging participation and experimentation, and are rewarding the workers for the improved productivity.

An older, widely publicized example of behavioral displacement took place at IBM Corporation. After the company suffered well-publicized production and cost problems with its System 360 computer, Thomas Watson ordered the institution of an elaborate system of checks and balances in new-product testing. The controls, however, made the IBM people so cautious that they stopped taking risks. When Frank Cary became president of IBM, one of the first things he did was to loosen the controls because he recognized that the new system would indeed prevent such an expensive problem from ever happening again, but its rigidity would also keep IBM from ever developing another major system.[17] This is a displacement problem because if the control system were designed to force individuals to think about survivability and long-term consequences, adaptability would be on their minds constantly.

Similarly, tight action controls caused problems at Gulf & Western Industries (G&W). At G&W's Consolidated Cigar division, Alexander N. Brainard, the division president, observed that G&W's dislike of any action that deviated from plans "stifled creativity."[18] In 1982, Brainard and other Consolidated managers took the company private. They immediately loosened controls over personnel such as salesmen, and in Brainard's words, "We haven't had growth like this in my thirteen years with Consolidated."[19]

Thus, while formal action control systems, which usually include elaborate repertoires of standard operating procedures and detailed plans, tend to make the behavior of individuals in the firm more consistent, they often make it difficult for those individuals to adapt to, and sometimes even to see, changing circumstances. This was the battle being faced at Campbell Soup Company when top managers at the company decided to give its managers more autonomy. As a Campbell manager noted,

> If all your life you worked for people who told you when to step and where to step, you don't quite know how to take it when suddenly somebody says, "Go to it, you're on your own."[20]

The conclusion, then, is that action controls and bureaucratization can be good in stable environments with considerable centralized knowledge about what actions are desired because they help establish good, efficient work habits. In changing environments with ill-informed top-level managers, however, they become dangerous, even to the point where they can threaten the survival of the firm.

Behavioral Displacement and Personnel/Cultural Controls

Behavioral displacement can also be produced with personnel or cultural controls. It can occur where the company is recruiting the wrong type of person for a job or providing the wrong kind of training. Strong cultures can also cause displacement where the behavioral norms that groups use to guide the behaviors of their members or the measures used to provide group-based rewards are not totally in line with what the organization desires. Many organizations rely on the fact that research scientists are highly professional and will control themselves better than the organization could by implementing formal controls. To a large extent, this is probably true, but many research scientists are motivated to acquire patents and write papers in areas that have little or no immediate commercial applications for their firm because they get a sense of personal accomplishment and a furtherance of their reputations. Doctors, too, are highly motivated by their professional standards to provide good health care, but sometimes they have little concern for financial considerations (until they establish their own practices). These are clear examples of displacement caused by a reliance on cultural controls.

One recent study of 207 major U.S. corporations found that over an eleven-year period, the corporations with healthy cultures grew their revenues four times more, profits 700 times as much, employment eight times more, and stock price gain twelve times as much as those with unhealthy cultures.[21] The unhealthy cultures did not serve all three major constituencies: stockholders, customers, and employees. They were not adaptable; they made employees highly resistant to changing macroeconomic or competitive conditions. Unhealthy cultures can cause even intelligent people in an organization to act without thinking, without benchmarking their performances externally, under the questionable assumption that their behavioral norms give them all the proper answers. Managers' attempts to shape an organization's culture can also be phrased in negative terms. They might be described as exploitation of those who do not control or own the means of production or, particularly in the United States, as exploitation by white males to maintain ideological hegemony.[22]

Solutions to the Behavioral Displacement Problems

Promptly and accurately recognizing the problems and diagnosing the causes are the keys to alleviating the behavioral displacement problems. These processes require thinking about whether there is a difference between what employees are supposed to do and what the control system motivates them to do. If a displacement problem is deemed to exist, many solutions can usually be considered.

In the department store example where the sales personnel neglected their stocking and merchandise-arrangement duties, the managers might have simply rewarded their personnel for maintaining well-stocked and neatly arranged departments. Alternatively, they might have been able to redefine the areas of responsibility (the organization structure) so that the sales areas were completely independent, and the employees would then have seen that it was to their own advantage to perform the necessary maintenance activities. A third possibility might have been to supplement the results-oriented controls with other types of controls. Action controls, in the form of work rules or direct supervision, could have been used to ensure that the stocking and arranging was performed; or personnel controls, such as training, could have been used to help the salespeople understand the need to keep the racks stocked and properly arranged.

Displacement is one of the most serious negative control system side effects. It is difficult to avoid the underlying problems of completeness and congruence. It is so difficult, in fact, that some people believe it is not worth trying to use results controls in many situations. Results controls, however, can exert powerful influences on behavior in a wide range of situations, and most managers, particularly those in the United States, believe that if you want employees to do something, then you should pay them for doing it. Results controls are not going to disappear, but if managers are considering the use of results controls, they must be aware of the potential for behavioral displacement. This problem is serious and pervasive and is not always easy to detect.

GAMESMANSHIP

The term *gamesmanship* is used here to refer generally to the actions that managers take that are intended to improve their performance indicators without producing any positive economic effects. Gamesmanship is a common harmful side effect faced in situations where accountability forms of control, either results or actions accountability, are used. Two major forms of gamesmanship are creation of slack and data manipulation.

Creation of Slack

Slack involves consumption of assets by organizational members in excess of what is required.[23] It involves tactical responses by individuals who are motivated to keep the organization's control system from hurting them. Slack sometimes causes severe dysfunctional effects; other times it is beneficial.

The research evidence that has been gathered suggests that significant amounts of slack do exist in most business organizations. The conclusion of one detailed study of three divisions of three separate *Fortune* 500 firms was that slack might be as much as 20 to 25 percent of the divisions' budgeted operating expenses.[24] Another study conducted in five firms found that 80 percent of the managers interviewed were willing to admit that they bargained for slack.[25]

Slack has some beneficial and some negative effects. On the positive side, slack can reduce manager tension, increase organizational resiliency to change, and make available some resources that can be used for innovation. On the negative side, it can cause an inefficient allocation of resources and, consequently, inferior operating performance. It can also cause information distortion. Slack adds a pathology to the information set, which can make it difficult to separate the true, underlying operating performance from the consumption of excess resources.

In most situations, slack is nearly impossible to prevent. Theoretically, slack is feasible only where superiors have less-than-complete knowledge about what can be accomplished in any given area, where measurement of results fails to satisfy the precision criterion, and where subordinates are allowed to participate in setting their performance targets. Thus, where targets can be set in a top-down manner or where it is possible to set tight and accurate standards and to develop precise measures of performance, it should be possible to prevent, or at least detect, slack easily. Unfortunately, those conditions exist only in very stable, structured situations. If accountability controls are used in other situations, slack must be considered to be almost inevitable.

Data Manipulation

Data manipulation is another form of gamesmanship that is a common side effect of accountability-type control systems. Manipulation involves an effort on the part of the individual being controlled to look good by fudging the control indicators. It comes in two basic forms: *falsification* and *data management. Falsification* involves reporting erroneous data. *Data management* involves any action designed to change the reported results; such as sales, earnings, or a debt/equity ratio, while providing no real economic advantage to the organization and, sometimes, actually causing harm. Generally, data management actions are designed to make the entity or manager look better, perhaps to achieve a budget target or to increase stock price, but some of these actions are designed to make the entity look worse. Sometimes managers *save* sales or earnings for a future period when they might be needed; sometimes they take a *bath* (put problems caused by a prior management team in the past and, in effect, create a hidden reserve); and sometimes they report abnormally poor results to try to lower the stock price to facilitate a management buyout.

Management of financial data can be accomplished through either accounting or operating means. *Accounting methods* of management involve an intervention in the measurement process. Individuals engaging in accounting methods of management sometimes violate generally accepted accounting principles (GAAP), but more frequently they use the flexibility available in both the selection of accounting methods and the application of those methods to affect accruals. They might shift from accelerated to straight-line depreciation or change their judgments about accounting estimates (reserves, allowances, and write-offs). *Operating methods* of earnings management involve the altering of operating decisions, such as the timing of discretionary expenditures or decisions to work overtime to push out additional shipments (sales) in the current accounting period. These methods often affect cash flows, as well as reported sales and earnings.

The evidence available suggests that data manipulation is common. For example, a survey of general managers in a large diversified corporation which is generally highly regarded for its management excellence showed that 46 percent of the managers admitted that they shifted funds between accounts to avoid budget overruns.[26]

Most data manipulation methods are not illegal, but some are more insidious and involve outright fraud. In the late 1980s, managers at MiniScribe Corporation, feeling pressure to achieve stringent sales targets, engaged in a series of illegal acts. Among other things, they shipped faulty disk drives, and even bricks packed in containers, to customers and recorded the shipments as sales. They also added scrapped components to inventory, thus inflating inventory values. The massive fraud led MiniScribe to file for bankruptcy.[27]

Auditors of Leslie Fay, the U.S.'s second-largest maker of women's apparel sold to department stores, concluded that the company lost $13.7 million in 1992, rather than the $23.9 million profit previously reported, and that 1991 earnings were overstated by 42 percent.[28] Managers at the firm had back-dated invoices, overstated production levels, and understated manufacturing costs.

At Phar-Mor, a privately-owned discount retailer, managers overstated the levels of inventories and some other assets, understated liabilities and expenses, and exercised stock options after their expiration date by backdating promissory notes.[29] Reported profits had been large enough to obtain more than $1 billion worth of capital from investors such as Sears Roebuck, Westinghouse Electric, and Corporate Partners (an affiliate of Lazard Freres). In reality, however, the company generated no profit in the five years before it declared bankruptcy in August 1992.

At contact lens manufacturer Bausch & Lomb, the culture was a mirror image of Daniel Gill, the company's longtime chairman and CEO: "tenacious, demanding—and very numbers-oriented."[30] Pressure to maintain double-digit annual profit growth led division managers to sell products to gray-market distributors, to force distributors to take large quantities of unwanted products, to ship goods before customers ordered them (a violation of GAAP), to run large promotions at every quarter-end, and to give customers abnormally long payment terms in exchange for large orders.[31] An operations manager at Bausch & Lomb's sunglass distribution center said, "We'd ship 70% of the month's goods in the last three days."[32]

At Sunrise Medical, four employees at one of the company's major divisions, including the division's chief financial officer, were involved in falsifying financial reports. The employees' scheme intended to disguise a deteriorating financial situation. The company's performance-based bonus plan was seen as a major cause of the fraud. The plan can pay annual cash bonuses worth 10 to 50 percent of salary; however, it pays no bonuses in divisions that fail to record an *earnings increase* for the year. Many observers were shocked that such a fraud could occur at Sunrise which "has long presented itself as a values-conscious health-care firm whose employees carry lofty corporate precepts about customers, shareholders, and social responsibility on wallet cards."[33]

These data manipulation schemes are encouraged by strong, short-term performance pressures and inadequate controls to prevent the dysfunctional side effects. A *Business Week* article on the Bausch & Lomb situation noted that "B&L's

performance-oriented ethos delivered outstanding results for many years, . . . but when the company's markets slowed at the same time that several acquisitions soured, B&L's culture was a train wreck waiting to happen."[34] In many other situations, investigators lay much of the blame on the failure of the auditors to perform their functions well. Too often, they do not sufficiently understand the company's business or its accounting methods, their procedures are deficient, and they do not pursue some of the observed improprieties far enough.

Manipulation is a serious problem because it can render an entire control system ineffective. If the data are being manipulated, it no longer becomes possible for managers to determine if a particular individual has done a good job. The effects of manipulation can also go far beyond the control system because it can destroy the accuracy of a company's entire information system.

Reports in the business press seem to indicate that manipulation is a growing problem. The growth may be caused by increasing competition that leads to added pressure for high performance and the setting of targets which are more difficult to attain. On the other hand, it is possible that advancing information technologies and information user sophistication has merely made manipulations more apparent.

OPERATING DELAYS

Operating delays are an often unavoidable consequence of the preaction review types of action controls and some of the forms of behavioral constraints. Delays such as those caused by limiting access to a stockroom or by requiring a signature check by an accounting clerk are usually minor, but other control-caused delays can be very major.

After executives of the Harley-Davidson Motor Company bought the firm from AMF, the director of marketing services boasted that a rebate program was instituted in ten days, rather than the six to eight weeks it would have taken with all the reviews necessary in the multileveled AMF hierarchy.[35] At Genesco, the retail and apparel conglomerate, required approvals were said to have *straitjacketed* operations, as delays "of only a few weeks resulted in the loss of precious selling time at the height of the season."[36] At Xerox Corporation, one manager complained that the checks and balances necessary to move from the conceptual to the detailed engineering phase of developing a new product took two years, instead of the two weeks to a month that should have been required.[37] At DuPont, the corporation's new decentralized organization structure allowed development of a new plastic bumper for Chrysler's Neon automobile in just nine months. It was estimated that in the old organization this project would have taken several years because of requirements for sending "endless memos through layers of higher-ups" and then waiting for clearances.[38] And at Hewlett-Packard, before a 1990 reorganization, a manager in the laser-printer operation needed eight signatures, including those of two executive vice presidents.[39]

Obviously, where fast action is important, delays such as these can be quite costly. Delays are a major reason for the negative connotation associated with the word bureaucracy. In the organizations that tend to place more emphasis on the action controls and, as a consequence, suffer these bureaucratic operating delays, many control system changes are motivated by a desire to reduce the burdens caused by these types of controls. When Helmut Maucher took over as the chief executive at Nestlé, the large Swiss food corporation, he diagnosed the company's major problems as "bigness—slow reaction time, a tendency to bureaucratic perfectionism, and a diffuseness of purpose." Maucher was quoted as saying that "the administrative system was somewhat 'heavy.'"[40]

A similar occurrence took place at the Honeywell Information Systems subsidiary of Honeywell. When James Renier was installed as the new president, his first action was to emphasize results controls at managerial levels in the organization. He set up new product divisions with profit-and-loss responsibility in order to allow managers "to develop and market new systems without the bureaucratic interference that has often slowed Honeywell in the past." The prior control system had "killed the entrepreneurial spirit . . . and many executives fled the slow-moving bureaucracy."[41]

Operating delays caused by controls are not an independent problem; they can cause other managerial reactions which are probably not desirable. One study of general managers in a well-run diversified corporation found that 74 percent obtained required approvals after the money was spent in order to speed up the process.[42]

NEGATIVE ATTITUDES

Even if the sets of controls being used are well designed, they can cause negative attitudinal effects, including job tension, conflict, frustration, and resistance. Such attitudes are important not only because they are indicators of employee welfare but also because they are coincident with many behaviors that can be harmful, such as gameplaying, lack of effort, absenteeism, and turnover.

The causes of negative attitudes are complex; they may be precipitated by a large number of factors, such as economic conditions, organization structure, and administrative processes, alone and in combinations. Furthermore, these factors seem to affect different types of managers differently.

Negative Attitudes Produced by Action Controls

Most people, particularly professionals, react negatively to the use of action controls. David Louks, controller at Lear Siegler, observed that over the years he and his staff had much greater opportunities to participate in preaction reviews of operations, but he acknowledged that "this chafes line managers."[43]

Preaction reviews can be particularly frustrating if the managers being reviewed do not perceive the reviews as serving a useful purpose. This was apparently the situation at Fairchild Camera and Instrument after the company was bought by Schlumlberger. A manager who left the company observed: "It got to be frustrating to get new ideas endorsed by, basically, an oil-field company that didn't have the foggiest notion of what high technology is really all about."[44]

Action controls can also annoy lower-level personnel. A junior employee at Atari, observed that

> Atari is run by telling people what to do and giving them almost no responsibility. That's why most of us just think of this as a great training ground and don't plan to stay.[45]

Similarly, Value Line uses some highly restrictive, perhaps even petty, action controls. One article said that the company's chief executive officer, Jean Bernhard Buttner, "barraged employees with memos regulating virtually every aspect of their work life.[46] For example,

- "Every employee must sign in by 9 A.M. and sign out when leaving."
- "Anyone who signs out for the day before 5 P.M. or fakes a time of arrival or departure is subject to discharge."
- "Department heads [must] file a 'clean surfaces report' at the end of each workday certifying that all desk tops in their areas are clean."
- "Unauthorized media interviews provide grounds for immediate dismissal."

The result, not surprisingly, is a demoralized, embittered workforce and high turnover.

Negative Attitudes Produced by Results Controls

Results controls can also produce negative attitudes. One cause is lack of employee commitment to the performance targets defined in the control system. Most individuals are not committed to targets they consider too difficult, not meaningful, not controllable, unwise, illegal, or unethical. In the example of a tight results control system presented in Chapter 5, the system used at UPS, commitment seems low because the targets set are perhaps too difficult. Some of the drivers compared their working conditions with those in a "Roman galley."[47] The company seems to have avoided major labor problems apparently because it provides generous salaries.

Negative attitudes may also stem from problems in the measurement system. It is common to hear managers complain that their performance evaluations are not fair because they are being held responsible for things over which they have little or no control. Here are two examples:

> We start the planning process at the beginning of the year. It takes four to five months. The 1992 plan was done in mid-1991, and that was quite a good year for us. I was forced to present an optimistic plan, because I couldn't go in with numbers that were lower than what we were doing. You always have to forecast some growth. But the recession hit us very hard in 1992, and I missed my plan by quite a large margin. That seems to reflect badly on my performance, but I don't think that's fair. I think the standard was wrong.[48]
>
> It is terribly frustrating to be evaluated as a profit center when I do not have complete control over revenues. The Export Division is responsible for over 75% of our total sales. They determine the price, the destination and the quantity of most of the milk we sell. We have no direct authority over that department, yet we are held responsible when sales are poor. If [the Export Division does] not perform up to expectations, then we cannot meet the budgeted profit target for which we are held responsible by headquarters.[49]

Other potential causes of negative attitudes may be associated with the rewards (or punishments) associated with the control system. Rewards that are not perceived to be equitable, and perhaps most forms of punishment, tend to produce negative attitudes.

Even the target-setting and evaluation processes themselves may produce negative attitudes. Many authors suggest that results controls which are applied in conjunction with a people-insensitive, nonsupportive, or negative leadership may tend to lower commitment to achieve performance targets and to cause negative attitudinal reactions. Allowing employees to participate in setting their targets often reduces negative feelings toward results-oriented control systems.

Finally, just the act of changing results controls is annoying to many people. Companies that have acquired other companies have encountered this resistance.

Xerox Corporation saw some of the managers of its two key high-technology acquisitions, Diablo Systems and Shugart Associates, resign in part because of frustration caused by the institution of new reporting procedures.

The collection of factors affecting attitudes is complex. There is some evidence that poor performers may react more negatively the better a control system is because the limitations in their abilities are easier to discover. More important are system flaws that could cause negative attitudes in potentially good performers. Attitudes are important outcomes of control systems to monitor, not only because they have their own value as indicators of employee welfare, but also because the presence of these negative attitudes may indicate the propensity to engage in any of a number of harmful behaviors, such as feeding the systems invalid data or other forms of gamesmanship, withdrawal, or even sabotage. Each of the characteristics mentioned here as a possible cause of negative attitudes has been the focus of much research and the subject of more than one whole book. One important point that is clearly true is that the design of the structure of a control system does not guarantee its success; the implementation of the system is also an important determinant.

CONCLUSION

Control system designers must be cognizant of the possibility of creating a wide variety of harmful side effects as they strive to create a good control environment. These side effects can be significant. One study of general managers found that only 26 percent of the respondents disagreed with the following statement: "Overall, the controls have done more harm than good to the long-term success of my profit center."[50]

Four general observations can be made about the occurrence of these side effects. First, as the summary shown in Table 6-1 points out, the harmful side effects are not unique to one form of control. The risk of side effects does seem to be smaller where the personnel controls are used, however.

TABLE 6-1 Control Types and Possible Harmful Side Effects

Type of Control	*Behavioral Displacement*	*Gamesmanship*	*Operating Delays*	*Negative Attitudes*
Results Controls				
Results accountability	x	x		x
Action Controls				
Behavioral constraint			x	x
Preaction review			x	x
Action accountability	x	x		x
Redundancy				x
Personnel/Cultural Controls				
Selection and placement	x			
Training	x			
Provision of necessary resources				
Creation of a strong organizational culture	x			
Group-based rewards	x			

Second, some of the control types have negative side effects that are largely unavoidable. It is difficult, or even impossible, for people to enjoy following a strict set of procedures (action accountability) for a long period of time, although the negative attitudes can probably be minimized if the reasons for them are well communicated and if the list is kept to a minimum.

Third, the likelihood of severe harmful side effects is greatest where there is either a failure to satisfy one or more of the desirable design criteria or a misfit between the choice of type(s) of control and the situation.

Fourth, where controls have design imperfections or where they are inappropriately used, the tighter the controls are applied, the greater are both the likelihood and the severity of harmful side effects.

What makes dealing with these potential side effects so difficult is that there is not always a simple one-to-one relationship between the control type and the effect. Furthermore, the existence of the side effects is often difficult to detect. A failure to make the measurement processes objective in a results or action accountability control system just presents the possibility for data manipulation; actual manipulation may not occur until an individual has a personal need for more money, poor performance creates additional pressure to perform, or a new, unfair leader creates a motivation to manipulate.

Another difficult factor to deal with is the fact that resistance to control systems is often based on misinformation. Control system changes can generate great anxiety in the individuals to be affected, and if complete and accurate information is not provided and believed, some people may make inferences based on their incomplete information set and may behave in manners that appear irrational to an outside observer.

Notes

1. Ridgway provided an early discussion of the dysfunctional effects of performance measures: V. F. Ridgway, "Dysfunctional Consequences of Performance Measurements," *Journal of Business*, 29 (September 1956), pp. 240–247.
2. "Bad Marks for Pay-by-Results: Teacher Cash Incentives Don't Work," *Business Week* (September 4, 1995), p. 28.
3. See L. N. Spiro and M. Schroeder, "Can You Trust Your Broker?" *Business Week* (February 20, 1995), pp. 70–76.
4. E. Flamholtz, "Organizational Control Systems as a Managerial Tool," *California Management Review*, 22, no. 2 (Winter 1979), pp. 50–59.
5. E. E. Lawler III and J. G. Rhode, *Information and Control in Organizations* (Pacific Palisades, Calif.: Goodyear, 1976), p. 95.
6. N. Babchuk and W. J. Goode, "Work Incentives in a Self-Determined Group," *American Social Reviewer* 16, no. 5 (1951), pp. 679–87.
7. J. Flynn, "The Ugly Mess at Waste Management," *Business Week* (April 13, 1992), pp. 76–77.
8. See K. Kelly and E. Schine, "How Did Sears Blow This Gasket?" *Business Week* (June 29, 1992), p. 38 and M. Santoro and L. S. Paine, "Sears Auto Centers (A), (B), and (C), Harvard Business School cases #9-394-009, -010, and -011, 1993.
9. C. H. Ford, "MBO: An Idea Whose Time Has Gone," *Business Horizons*, 22, no. 6 (December 1979), p. 54.
10. D. Mitchell, *Control Without Bureaucracy* (London: McGraw-Hill, 1979), p. 6.
11. P. F. Drucker, "Controls, Control and Management," in *Management Controls: New Dimen-*

sions in Basic Research C. P. Bonini, R. K. Jaedicke, and H. M. Wagner (eds.) (New York: McGraw-Hill, 1964), p. 294.

12. S. J. Sansweet, "Troubles at Mattel Seen Extending Beyond Fallout in Electronics Line," *Wall Street Journal* (December 1, 1983), p. 31.
13. See M. Ross, "Capital Budgeting Practices of Twelve Large Manufacturers," *Financial Management*, 15, no. 4 (Winter 1986), pp. 15–22.
14. Drucker, "Controls," p. 295.
15. A. Smith, *An Inquiry into the Nature and Causes of the Wealth of Nations* (1776; reprinted ed., Modern Library [Random House], 1937), p. 734.
16. "A Takeover Hasn't Cramped Oppenheimer's Freewheeling Style," *Business Week* (October 10, 1983), p. 94.
17. T. J. Peters, "Putting Excellence into Management," *Business Week* (July 21, 1980), p. 205.
18. "Conglomerate Managers Fall into Step, Too," *Business Week* (February 6, 1984), p. 50.
19. Ibid., p. 54.
20. B. Morris, "After a Long Simmer, The Pot Boils Again at Campbell Soup Co.," *Wall Street Journal* (July 16, 1982), p. 1.
21. J. P. Kotter and J. L. Heskett, *Corporate Culture and Performance* (New York: The Free Press, 1992).
22. W. G. Ouchi, *Theory Z* (Reading, Mass.: Addison-Wesley, 1981).
23. See R. M. Cyert and J. G. March, *A Behavioral Theory of the Firm* (Englewood Cliffs, N.J.: Prentice-Hall, 1963).
24. M. Schiff and A. Y. Lewin, "Where Traditional Budgeting Fails," *Financial Executive* (May 1968), pp. 50–62.
25. M. Onsi, "Factor Analysis of Behavioral Variables Affecting Budgetary Slack," *Accounting Review* (July 1973), pp. 535–548.
26. K. A. Merchant, "The Effects of Financial Controls on Data Manipulation and Management Myopia," *Accounting, Organizations and Society* 15, no. 4 (August 1990), pp. 297–313.
27. A. Zipser, "Cooking the Books: How Pressure to Raise Sales Led MiniScribe to Falsify Numbers," *Wall Street Journal* (September 11, 1989), pp. A1, A16.
28. "Who Played Dress-Up With the Books," *Business Week* (March 15, 1993), p. 34; and T. Agins, "Dressmaker Leslie Fay Is an Old-Style Firm That's in a Modern Fix," *Wall Street Journal* (February 23, 1993), p. 1.
29. G. Stern, "Chicanery and Phar-Mor Ran Deep, Close Look at Discounter Shows," *Wall Street Journal* (January 20, 1994), p. 1.
30. M. Maremont, "Blind Ambition: How the Pursuit of Results Got Out of Hand at Bausch & Lomb," *Business Week* (October 23, 1995), p. 80.
31. Ibid., pp. 78–92.
32. Ibid., p. 82.
33. T. Petruno, "Sunrise Scam Throws Light on Incentive Pay Programs," *Los Angeles Times* (January 15, 1996), p. D1.
34. M. Maremont, "Blind Ambition: How the Pursuit of Results Got Out of Hand at Bausch & Lomb," *Business Week* (October 23, 1995), p. 80.
35. H. Klein, "At Harley-Davidson, Life Without AMF Is Upbeat But Full of Financial Problems," *Wall Street Journal* (April 13, 1982), p. 37.
36. "The Controller: Inflation Gives Him More Clout with Management," *Business Week* (August 15, 1977), p. 95.
37. "The Shrinking of Middle Management," *Business Week* (April 25, 1983), p. 55.
38. J. Weber, "For DuPont, Christmas in April," *Business Week* (April 24, 1995), p. 130.
39. S. K. Yoder, "A 1990 Reorganization at Hewlett-Packard Already is Paying Off," *Wall Street Journal* (July 22, 1991), p. A5.

40. R. Ball, "A 'Shopkeeper" Shakes Up Nestlé, *Fortune* (December 27, 1982), p. 105.
41. "Honeywell's Survival Plan in Computers," *Business Week* (May 23, 1983), p. 111.
42. K. A. Merchant, "The Effects of Financial Controls on Data Manipulation and Management Myopia," *Accounting, Organizations and Society* 15, no. 4 (August 1990), pp. 297–313.
43. "The Controller: Inflation Gives Him More Clout with Management," *Business Week* (August 15, 1977), p. 86.
44. "Chip Wars: The Japanese Threat," *Business Week* (May 23, 1983), p. 85.
45. "Atari's Struggle to Stay Ahead," *Business Week* (September 13, 1982), p. 56.
46. A. Bianco, "Value Line: Too Lean, Too Mean?" *Business Week* (March 16, 1992), p. 105.
47. "Behind the UPS Mystique: Puritanism and Productivity," *Business Week* (June 6, 1983), p. 68.
48. Personal interview with a general manager in a large, diversified firm.
49. W. A. Sahlman and M. E. Barrett, "Laitier, S.A.," case no. 9-176-118 (Boston: HBS Case Services, 1975).
50. K. A. Merchant, "The Effects of Financial Controls on Data Manipulation and Management Myopia," *Accounting, Organizations and Society* 15, no. 4 (August 1990), pp. 297–313.

Hyatt Hill Health Center

"These numbers don't mean a thing," said Hank Clemens. "They don't reflect what my department does and needlessly make us look terrible."

Clemens was talking to his fellow department heads, the administrative staff, and the executive director of the Hyatt Hill Health Center (HHHC) at their weekly executive committee meeting. The subject of Hank's ire was the control system recently installed in the health center.

BACKGROUND

The Hyatt Hill Health Center was established in New York City. It was sponsored by the Fowler Hospital, widely considered to be one of the leading hospitals in the United States for the quality of its medical care, research, and teaching. The health center was established, on an experimental basis, to provide community-centered health care to the residents of the town of Bedford, in which it was located. Bedford was a lower-income area which suffered from a heavy incidence of medical, dental, and psychiatric problems; for example, over 40% of Bedford's adults needed dental plates, and a large proportion of its adult population were alcoholics and drug abusers.

Because few physicians resided in Bedford, its residents used the emergency room of the Fowler Hospital as a substitute for a family physician. As a result, they received sporadic therapeutic medical care and little preventive care in the form of yearly checkups, x-rays, and so on.

The purpose of the health center was to provide adequate preventive as well as therapeutic care and to do so by becoming an accepted force in the Bedford community. This wasn't an easy mission, for Bedford was geographically isolated from the rest of New York City; and its residents, who were largely composed of one closely knit ethnic group, were traditionally suspicious of any "outsiders." Despite the heavy incidence of emotional problems in the area, the residents of Bedford were particularly resistant to receiving the services of social workers and psychiatrists. The personnel in these departments spent a great deal of time in the community trying to break down this resistance.

ORGANIZATION AND PERSONNEL

The Hyatt Hill Health Center consists of the following departments: pediatrics, internal medicine, nursing, mental health, social work, nutrition, dental, and specialists. Most of its practitioners hold joint appointments at the Fowler Hospital, are considered to be of high professional caliber, and are incurring substantial opportunity costs by working at the health center. These effective practitioners have dedicated themselves to demonstrating that a community health center can indeed provide effective therapeutic and preventive medical care and, thus, have a significant impact on its target area.

In addition to its goal of delivering community health care, the HHHC also served as a training ground for members of the Fowler Hospital or N.Y.C. Department of Health staff who were interested in community medicine. Training activities were conducted in all of HHHC's departments but were particularly concentrated in the mental health, social work, and nutrition departments.

FUNDING

The health center, which has a yearly operating budget of nearly $1,000,000, is funded from a variety of sources, including the Fowler Hospital. The HHHC hopes it will eventually become financially self-sufficient and not require hospital funds for its operation. At the present time, the largest portion of its funds come from the federal government. In return, the health center must provide quarterly reports about the characteristics of its patients, the kinds of services they received, and the impact of

Professor Regina E. Herzlinger prepared this case as the basis for class discussion rather than to illustrate either effective or ineffective handling of an administrative situation.

the center on the community. Together these data, all practitioners complete the form displayed in Exhibit 1 immediately after every encounter with a patient. The data on the encounter form are then entered into Fowler Hospital's system.

THE CONTROL SYSTEM – BACKGROUND

Late in 1997, a researcher of the costs of ambulatory medical care facilities visited the health center. At the time, Dr. Steven Kyler, the health center's executive director, was becoming increasingly concerned over the potential for the achievement of the HHHC's financial self-sufficiency goal. Although the center had a good financial accounting system for billing and external reporting, it had no managerial accounting data. Dr. Kyler thus didn't know the total costs of his departments, of different kinds of cases, and of his practitioners. Because the only financial data available to him were the costs of the different line-items on his budget, Dr. Kyler couldn't really assess the feasibility of his center's accomplishing its financial self-sufficiency goals. He, thus, agreed to the installation of a management control system which would provide him with the data he wanted.

THE CONTROL SYSTEM – MECHANICS

The management control system was based on the existing data system and provided the following data for each of the HHHC's departments:

1. Average cost, per encounter and per hour spent in seeing patients, for each practitioner.
2. Average cost of the different kinds of encounters entered on the encounter form.
3. A comparison of actual costs to a standard cost, based on the average costs, in the past, of that department.
4. Total revenues, per practitioner, and for the department.

A sample of the cost and revenue data for the social work department is contained in Exhibit 2. The flow chart used to compute the costs is in Exhibit 3 and the total cost data are in Exhibit 4.

These data were distributed to Dr. Kyler and his department chiefs about two weeks after the end of each month. They enabled the HHHC's management to compare the efficiency of different practitioners, in performing the same kind of work. They also enabled comparison of the relative efficiency and utilization of capacity of different departments.

The key data input for the control system was the time entered by the practitioner on the encounter form for each service performed. To check on the validity of these data, a timesheet was completed by all the practitioners, on a daily basis, for a full month, once every three months. The direct patient care category on the timesheet was, by definition, identical to the time entered on the encounter form. Continuous comparisons were made on the total times derived from the two forms to ensure that the time entered was valid. The timesheet data for the social service department are in Exhibit 5.

As indicated by the timesheet categories, the HHHC's departments performed a number of activities other than that of providing direct patient care. Yet only the direct patient care activities generated revenue. If the HHHC were ever to be self-sufficient, the revenues created by the practitioners' medical care activities would have to absorb the costs of all their other activities. Thus, the financial data produced by the control system included the costs of all the time spent by the practitioners in HHHC—regardless of whether they spent it in seeing patients or in the other activities listed on the timesheets.

On the basis of these data, the social work department didn't seem to be very efficient. Its costs per encounter were higher than those of any other department, and its practitioners used less of their time for seeing patients than did those of the other departments. (See Exhibit 6.)

Dr. Kyler was quite disturbed by these data and discussed them with the head of the social work department at the executive committee meetings. "Why are your costs per encounter so high?" he asked. "Your department's average costs are twice as high as those of the medical department, and yet the social workers' salaries are half of those of the physicians. You had better shape up. You're costing all of us a lot of money."

ASSIGNMENT

1. What is the purpose of the Hyatt Hill Health Center?
2. How do you interpret the patterns in Exhibit 6?
3. Is the control system consistent with the purposes of the health center? If not, how should it be modified?

EXHIBIT 1 Mental Health Visit Form

2 Professional no.: H☐☐

1 Date: – 5 –
☐☐ mo. ☐☐ day ☐☐ year

3 Visit:
1 ○ walk-in
2 ○ visit kept
3 ○ visit broken

Date of Birth ______

Visit location:
1 ○ BHHC
2 ○ Home
3 ○ School
4 ○ Other

Unit No. ☐☐☐ ☐☐☐ ☐☐

8 Family no.: A☐ ☐☐☐☐

Name:

10 Duration of visit: ☐☐ minutes

Modification of charges:
☐ half charge
☐ no charge

12 Assessment status:
1 ○ not started
2 ○ in process
3 ○ complete this visit
4 ○ complete prior visit

Current status of treatment planned at assessment:
1 ○ not needed
2 ○ short-term, in process
3 ○ short-term, completed
4 ○ long-term

13 Activity during this contact consisted of: (check one)
60 ☐ patient-interview
61 ☐ others in family-interview
62 ☐ patient and family-interview
63 ☐ group therapy
64 ☐ psych. testing
65 ☐ other

Additional services:

14 Primary problem: (code primary problem and enter *only* code)

A. Enter CODE P☐☐☐

B. presumptive 1☐ confirmed 2☐

C. mild 1☐ moderate 2☐ severe 3☐

15	Referrals: Made To:	A in HHHC	B out-side	C Fowler Hos-pital	Received From:	D in HHHC	E out-side	F Fowler Hos-pital	Check, if current involvement:
1.	nursing				1.				☐
2.	dental health				2.				☐
3.	nutrition				3.				☐
8.	medical and specialties				8.				☐
10.	mental health				10.				☐
13.	LBJ Center				13.				☐
14.	Schools				14.				☐
15.	New York State Hospital				15.				☐
16.	Police/courts				16.				☐
17.	self/friend				17.				☐
18.	VNA/LSA				18.				☐
12.	Other agencies				12.				☐

Mental Health Visit Form

EXHIBIT 2 Cost Data Social Work Department

	Entire Department	*Practitioners* 1	2	3	4
Total hours available	400	100	100	100	100
Total hours spent in patient care	100	20	20	50	10
Hours spent/hours available	25%	20%	20%	50%	10%
Cost per hour spent in patient care	$50.00	$62.50	$62.50	$25.00	$125.00
Cost per encounter:	$50.00	$125.00	$62.50	$20.83	$125.00
Initial interview, alone		$125.00	$62.50	$20.83	$125.00
Initial interview, family		$125.00		$20.83	$62.50
Additional interviews, alone			$62.50	$10.41	$187.50
Additional interviews, family				$31.25	
Total revenues	$5,750.00	$1,400.00	$1,200.00	$2,500.00	$650.00

EXHIBIT 3

Symbol	*Meaning*	*Symbol*	*Meaning*
$x	Fixed cost of the department	Tij	Time spent on encounters of type j by physician j
$y	Salary per minute of physician j	NWj	Number of walk-in patients treated by physician j
zj	Time in minutes, that physician j was available	TWj	Time spent on walk-in encounters by physician j
		Nrj	Number of patients who made regular appointments treated by physician j
Nij	Number of encounters of type i by physician j	Trj	Time spent on regular appointment encounters by physician j

1. The total time spent in patient care by physician j: $Tj = \sum_i Tij$
2. The direct labor cost of physician j: $\$DLCj = (Tj)\ (\$Yj)$
3. The total time spent in nonpatient care activities by physician j: $Qj = Zj - Tj$
4. The direct overhead cost of physician j: $\$DOHj = (Qj)\ (\$Yj)$
5. The total time spent in nonpatient care activities by physicians in the department: $Q = \sum_j Qj$
6. The fixed overhead cost of physician j: $\$FOHj = \left(\frac{Qi}{Q}\right)(\$x)$
7. The total cost of physician j: $\$TCj = \$DLCj + \$DOHj + \$FOHj$
8. The proportion of the total cost of physician j attributable to encounters of type i: $\$TCij = \left(\frac{Tij}{Tj}\right)(\$TCj)$
9. The average cost of encounters of type i for physician j: $\$Acij = \$\frac{TCij}{Nij}$
10. The average cost per encounter for physician j: $\$ACj = \frac{\$TCj}{\sum Nij}$
11. The total costs of walk-ins and regular appointments for physician j: $\$TCwj = \left(\frac{Twj}{tj}\right)(\$TCj)$

$$\$TCrj = \left(\frac{Trj}{tj}\right)(\$TCj)$$

12. The average cost of walk-ins and regular appointments for physician j: $\$ACwj = \frac{\$TCwj}{Nwj}$

$$\$ACrj = \frac{\$TCrj}{Nrj}$$

13. The average cost for the department of walk-in and regular appointments: $\$ACw = \frac{\sum_j TCwj}{\sum_j Nwj}$

$$\$AC_r = \frac{\sum_i TCrj}{\sum_j Nnj}$$

14. The average cost for the department of an encounter: $\$ACW = \frac{\sum_i TCw + \sum_i TCrj}{\sum_j Nwj + \sum_j Njr}$
15. The total cost for the department of encounters of type i: $\$TCi = \sum_j TCij$
16. The average cost for the department of encounters of type i: $\$ACi = \sum_j \frac{\$TCi}{Nij}$

EXHIBIT 4 Total Cost Data

	Salaries			*Departmental Fixed Costs*											
	Direct Patient Care	*Direct Overhead*	*Fringe*	*Furniture and Equipment*	*Supplies*	*Rent*	*Heat and Power*	*Evaluation*	*Medical Records and Accounting*	*Administration*	*Service Reps*	*HCCC Outpatient*	*General*	*Total*	*% of Total*
Pediatrics	$ 2,400	$ 1,956	$ 610	$ 16	$ 441	$ 162	$ 20	$1,117	$ 817	$ 490	$ 220	$ 40	$ 330	$ 8,609	11.9%
Internal Medicine	3,336	1,331	653	23	467	189	33	894	1,170	533	239	43	359	9,270	12.9
Nutrition	537	260	68	4	—	42	7	381	264	189	81	15	127	1,975	2.7
Nursing	4,148	4,371	657	62	320	398	60	394	455	2,313	931	187	1,557	15,853	22.0
Dental	1,140	2,407	493	84	150	162	20	333	0	877	—	71	590	6,327	6.6
Mental Health	737	4,814	554	41	—	382	47	331	187	1,246	—	101	838	9,278	12.8
Social Work	502	4,906	421	30	—	301	40	458	258	1,720	243	139	1,158	10,176	14.1
Specialists	854	447	—	14	—	—	—	269	413	112	51	9	75	2,244	3.1
Eye Clinic	478	172	29	96	—	126	13	165	253	267	—	22	179	1,800	2.5
Laboratory	1,147	645	143	46	275	41	7	—	666	567	243	46	382	4,208	5.8
Radiology	139	392	49	189	272	68	7	—	387	189	80	15	127	1,914	2.7
Therapists	—	—	—	7	—	47	7	39	25	95	40	8	64	332	.5
Total	$15,418	$21,701	$3,677	$612	$1,925	$1,918	$261	$4,381	$4,895	$8,598	$2,128	$696	$5,786	$71,986	

EXHIBIT 5 Social Work Department Time Allocation

	Activities				
	Direct Patient Care	*Indirect Patient Care*	*Community Development*	*Training*	*Lunch, Breaks, Administrative Activities*
Time spent (hours)	100	100	80	80	40
Percent of time available	25%	25%	20%	20%	10%
Monthly costs of activity	$1,250	$1,250	$1,000	$1,000	$500

EXHIBIT 6 Source of Difference Between the Actual Cost per Visit, First Quarter

Department	*Standard Cost per Visit*	*Actual Cost per Visit*	*Difference (Variance) Between Standard and Actual Cost*	*Differential Effect of Change in Efficiency*[a]	*Differential Effect of Change in Utilization of Capacity*[b]
Social Work	$61.10	$27.31	$+33.79	$+ 5.37	$+28.42
Mental Health	53.65	27.77	+25.88	+ .23	+25.65
Dental Health	42.88	25.72	+17.16	+ .41	+16.75
Nutrition	34.97	20.45	+14.52	+ 6.04	+ 8.48
Pediatrics	25.64	22.16	+ 3.48	− .57	+ 4.05
Internal Medicine	24.72	24.00	+ .72	− .14	+ .86
Nursing	28.34	36.20	− 7.56	−11.15	+ 3.29

[a]Efficiency effects result from changes in the time spent with each patient.

[b]Utilization of capacity effects result from changes in the percentage of their available time that practitioners devote to seeing patients.

Glamour Fragrances, Inc.

In October 1984, Bob Adams president of Glamour Fragrances, was reviewing the details of his company's performance for the year 1983 and the first nine months in 1984. Overall, performance had not been good, and one of the major causes of the poor performance was that the company was missing its cost improvement targets by substantial margins. The cost improvement programs had been instituted to help the company offset inflation, and while they had once been quite successful, in recent years failure had been the norm. This year one major cost improvement program (CIP), known as the B-20 project, had not only failed to provide the projected savings, but according to Lisa Mannetti, the controller, it might even end up costing the company money. This project had been the company's major CIP program for 1984, and it was a major cause of the failure to meet the overall CIP goals.

If the B-20 project was an isolated problem, Mr. Adams would not have been particularly worried, but it really was just one example of a series of CIP failures. Mr. Adams was convinced that he had to determine the cause of the problems. "What is going wrong?" he wondered. "We've had problems with a new assembly in toiletries, the start-up on our 'just-in-time' line, and the new formulation for nail enamels, and these are just this year's headaches. Are our problems in the design, testing, and/or implementation of the CIPs? Or perhaps we should reconsider the overall cost reduction concept itself. We must do something to change this pattern of failure."

THE COMPANY

Glamour Fragrances, Inc., was an international company engaged in the beauty products industry. Its primary activities involved the manufacturing and sale of cosmetics and fragrances, but in the last several years the company had moved into a line of toiletries, in response to growth trends in the industry. In 1983, most (76 percent) of Glamour's total sales, which were $364 million in 1983, were in domestic markets (which include Canada and Puerto Rico), but the company also distributed products in Europe, through a direct sales force, and in the Middle East, through a broker network.

Up until 1974, Glamour, like many cosmetic companies, was managed by its founder, Jon Francis. Upon Mr. Francis' retirement, the management of the company changed substantially. The new president, Bob Adams had a financial background, and he formalized the organizational structure along functional lines, as shown in Exhibit 1, and brought a new focus on the "numbers."

Under the new management, Glamour's strategy broadened to focus less on top-of-the-line, or "prestige," products, and more on mid-price range, or mass-market products. The new strategy appeared to be very effective in the mid-to-late 1970s, but Mr. Adams had wondered lately if the company had owed its success over this period more to overall market expansion rather than a basic superiority of its corporate strategy.

During this period of strategic change, formal cost reduction and financial targeting procedures were introduced in order to keep the cost of goods manufactured as low as possible. This cost reduction focus had enabled the company to maintain a 35 percent cost of goods percentage (of wholesale price) in the face of rapid increases in its raw materials prices. Exhibit 2 shows summary income statements for the years 1977 to 1983. The successes of these cost and efficiency programs enabled the company to maintain its profitability in the last several years even as the actual units of shipment decreased. The "easy" reductions had disappeared, though, and this was

This case was prepared by Research Assistant C. J. McNair, under the supervision of Associate Professor Kenneth A. Merchant, as a basis for class discussion rather than to illustrate either effective or ineffective handling of an administrative situation.

particularly painful at a time when the company was suffering a profit squeeze.

INDUSTRY TRENDS

In 1984, many analysts were estimating that profits in the personal care industry, while sluggish, would improve modestly. Industry volume was expected to rise to approximately $15.5 billion, up about 5 percent from the $14.8 billion spent at retail in 1983. The 1983 total reflected activity in the major categories of: cosmetics (26 percent), women's fragrances (16 percent), women's hair products (19 percent), men's toiletries (7 percent), skin preparations (18 percent), and personal cleanliness items, such as bath soaps and deodorants (14 percent).

While the '60s and '70s had witnessed robust growth, the industry in the 1980s was characterized by a decline in real shipments (inflation-adjusted) and increasing price competition. Demand for personal care products, which were considered to the discretionary purchases, was hurt by the sluggish economic activity of the 1981–82 period, as well as by the secular changes in the product markets. With less discretionary income available, consumers had cut back on the impulse buying that had been responsible for up to two-thirds of all cosmetics and personal care purchases.

Disappointing sales in the 1981–83 period had resulted in rising manufacturers' inventories throughout the industry, which in turn had intensified competition and price discounting in many lines. This discounting at the company level was being augmented by inventory liquidation moves at the retail level, as stores combated overstocking and decreases in overall consumer demand.

The overall softening of consumer demand for cosmetics and fragrances caused a slowdown in new product activity throughout the industry. The established firms were moving to secure their market position. Many companies had implemented stringent cost reduction programs, trying to improve their operating margins. This low-cost focus was seen as one way to increase the competitive power as it provided greater pricing leverage and the ability to purchase market share through pricing policies. The transition to maturity for the industry, therefore, was being reflected in increased competition based on price, the predominant role of large firms in setting the trends in new product areas, and an overall profit squeeze. Exhibit 3 shows a retail sales analysis for the toiletries and cosmetics industry for the years 1980–83.

The main trends in the personal care industry, then, reflected a move towards the maturity phase of the life cycle, and a shift away from cosmetics to toiletries as the primary area of competition and growth. While the "prestige" products had held their own during this period, the mid-price product lines were hurt as economy-minded consumers traded down to lower priced or generic products. Glamour, having a majority of its products in this mid-price range, was particularly hurt by these trends.

PLANNING AND BUDGETING

Since he assumed the presidency, Bob Adams had taken steps to formalize some of Glamour's control processes and procedures. Long-range planning was still done informally at the top corporate level, and the company's long-range goals and strategies were not communicated to all functional managers.

The annual budgeting process, however, involved several levels of management. Budgeting began in mid-July when top management gave each functional area preliminary targets for its operating and capital budgets and other performance areas specific to the function. For example, marketing managers were given preliminary sales growth targets for each of the various categories of existing products, manufacturing managers were given preliminary cost targets by product category, and R&D managers were given cost improvement targets and timetables for introduction of new products. The functional managers and their subordinates were expected to coordinate their plans with those of the other functional managers and to prepare their plans down to the product level. A series of budget reviews were held in October and early November, and final budgets and performance targets were fixed by mid-November.

During the year, formal performance reviews were conducted monthly. Managers were asked to explain variances to a top executive committee. If significant variances were expected to continue, the budgets were revised, although it was understood by all the managers involved that the original budget would be the primary standard against which to judge managerial performance.

CAPITAL BUDGETING

Capital budgeting reviews took place in mid-September. Functional managers presented formal capital appropriation requests to a top management committee. For several years the company had published guidelines suggesting that each project being justified on economic grounds should promise a two-year payback. The short-term emphasis was emphasized even more heavily in the troubled year of 1984 as the following guidelines, taken from Glamour's 1984 budget manual, indicate:

1. Budgeted capital spending proposals must be guided by the general trends indicated in the operating budget, especially as regards unit (volume) growth and new product introduction.
2. Capacity expansion projects should be restricted to those absolutely necessary to achieve 1984 profit and sales goals and objectives while also meeting the criterion of providing the appropriate economic return.
3. Cost reduction projects should be given a high priority. However, serious consideration will be given by corporate to business constraints at the time approval is requested.
4. Spending of a replacement nature should be deferred unless there will be a serious obstruction to operations.
5. Spending for quality improvement should be considered only if the product's marketability is seriously affected.
6. All nonresearch expenditures related to the marketing of new products are to provide an economic justification and reflect approval by the appropriate senior executive.

INCENTIVE COMPENSATION

Incentive compensation was provided annually to managers down to the director level in the firm (one organization level below vice president). In January of each year, an aggregate bonus pool was established as a preestablished percentage of corporate net income. In February, just after the annual performance review meetings, a bonus committee, consisting of the top company officers, allocated this pool to individual managers. The evaluations of performance were based heavily on objective measures of performance, but the bonuses were not directly linked with the performance measures by formula. Typical bonuses for vice presidents ranged from zero to 20 percent of salary, and for directors zero to 10 percent of salary.

COST REDUCTION PROGRAM

An important part of Bob Adams' upgrading of Glamour's management systems was the implementation of a formal cost reduction program. Cost reductions were deemed to be of two basic types: cost avoidance projects (CAPs) and cost improvement projects (CIPs). Any project designed to reduce direct materials costs without concomitant changes in products or manufacturing processes was designated a CAP. The company's CAP goal was an annual 5 percent reduction in direct materials costs.

Any project designed to effect cost reductions through process or product changes, such as a reformulation of a product to incorporate less expensive ingredients was designated as a CIP. The company also had a specific CIP goal, as is clear from the following statement in the 1984 budgeting manual:

> Each manufacturing location is to develop and implement Cost Improvement programs as part of their budget, the annualized savings of which are to be equal to or greater than 5 percent of the current year's total cost of goods manufactured, adjusted for the budget year volume and mix changes. The goals should be based on total cost of goods manufactured and the action programs should encompass all factors of manufacturing, including materials, labor and overhead:
>
> - all labor cost associated with manufacturing
> - all overhead associated with manufacturing
> - only those material costs resulting from:
>   - reduced usage and improved yields.
>   - reduction in freight-in costs.
>
> Cost improvements are the result of specific actions programs directed toward a measurable reduction in existing cost levels.

Purchasing and value analysis were the two departments most directly responsible for identifying CAP projects. R&D and engineering were the departments most directly charged with identifying CIP prospects. But while these areas were charged with identifying good CIP/CAP ideas, the CIP ideas, in particular, had to be implemented by the operating manager most directly affected, in most cases, a manufacturing manager.

The CIP/CAP projects were expected to achieve a one-year payback where possible. If an individual CIP/CAP was not able to meet this payback criterion, it was subject to close scrutiny by Bob Adams' staff before approval would be granted.

When the cost reduction program was first instituted, the company realized many important cost savings. In recent years, however, the company had not been achieving its cost improvement targets. The targets and actual results of the cost reductions achieved for each of the years 1980–84 are shown in Exhibit 4.

AN EXAMPLE: THE B-20 PROJECT

Some of the major problems in the cost reduction program can be illustrated by describing one large CIP project called the B-20 project. The B-20 project involved the substitution of fluorocarbons for hydrocarbons as propellants in aerosol fragrance bottles.

Fluorocarbons had two main advantages over hydrocarbons for use as propellants. One was that fluorocarbons had much lower fill pressures when mixed with fragrance concentrate than hydrocarbons. This meant that Glamour could eliminate the use of bottles with relatively expensive plastic coatings that had been necessary with hydrocarbon propellants to ensure the bottles' integrity and to pass industry safety standards. The other advantage was that fluorocarbons were less flammable than hydrocarbons, and this provided advantages in both safety and in the production procedures that could be used.

Glamour and the other firms in the fragrance industry had used fluorocarbons as propellants almost exclusively up until the mid-1970s when fluorocarbons were banned by the U.S. government because of concerns about their destroying the ozone layer of the atmosphere. The propellant suppliers who had relied on fluorocarbons as their major sources of revenues were severely affected by the ban, and since the ban they aimed much of their research toward developing a new ozone-safe fluorocarbon propellant. B-20 was one of the first new products to be developed in this regard.

Personnel in Glamour's R&D department noted the development of B-20 and immediately saw its potential advantages. They tested the new propellant in simulated production settings and found it to be superior to the propellants being used. Based on these results, they prepared a Capital Appropriations Request, the summary page of which is shown in Exhibit 5. A summary of their investment analysis is shown in Exhibit 6.

On July 18, 1983, Glamour's capital appropriations committee met and approved the money for the B-20 project. Bob Adams' initial reaction to the project was very enthusiastic as is indicated by the memo shown in Exhibit 7. Shortly thereafter, Jake Andrews (VP-R&D) had people in his department draw up specifications for the use of B-20 on the production line. Work to convert the production lines to use the B-20 propellant started, with the switchover to take place on January 2, 1984.

But the B-20 project ran into several serious problems. One problem was a production delay; the implementation could not be effected until the end of February. More seriously, however, when B-20 was put in bottles that were not properly filled with fragrance, it became very unstable. The pressure inside the larger bottles then rose from 40 pounds per square inch (P.S.I.) to over 200 P.S.I., a level that the larger-size bottles (2 oz. and larger) without a plastic coating could not always withstand. As a consequence, the production areas had had several incidents of exploding bottles, and many bottles had to be rejected by quality control because of cracking.

REVIEW OF THE B-20 PROJECT

In November 1984, Bob Adams called a meeting with his top executives to review the problems with the B-20 project.

Allen Burns (VP-Finance) started the meeting by showing the financial picture. As he handed out the analysis, presented in Exhibit 8, he noted:

> Lisa Mannetti (controller) has been following this project very closely. She now estimates that because of the problems we are all aware of—the implementation delay, reduced volumes, higher bottle prices, the problems with the large bottles, and the lost labor efficiency—the 1984 savings will be $162,000, down from the original estimate of $550,000. But if we have to write off our inventory of

3¼ oz. bottles, we will actually lose approximately $39,000 on this project this year.

Bob Adams (president):

> This is obviously not good news. Who can explain to me why we've missed the forecast so badly, and I would like a few clarifications. First, are these labor charges noted as "additional" going to continue? And, what are we planning to do with the 3¼ oz. bottles?

Glenn Kelley (VP-Operations):

> This project has been a disaster from the beginning. I was involved in this project at the crucial point—implementation. I heard of the proposed switch from our standard hydrocarbons to B-20 from Jake (Andrews, VP-R&D). He had pinpointed it as his major cost reduction program for the year. Then when it came time to put the plan in action, research dropped the ball; it became the plant's responsibility to implement the project. Research was claiming the cost reduction but taking no leadership role in putting it in place.
>
> R&D insists that the glass bottles be handled to minimize the rubbing of one bottle on another because they say that is weakening the bottles and making them explode more easily. I've never been convinced that the rubbing has anything to do with the problem, but the new procedures they forced us to follow (Exhibit 9) have added to our problems.
>
> I think we have to continue to incur the additional labor costs until we get a new piece of equipment that will check the fill heights of bottles before they enter the gas house. We've had some exploding bottles, and I've felt the safety factor had to come first, so I've had some people visually checking the fragrance levels before we add the B-20. We estimate that equipment that would automatically eject low fills would cost approximately $15,000 per line, so for our eight lines, that would be an additional expenditure of $120,000. If we had this equipment, I think we could save most of the additional labor costs.
>
> Finally, as to the 3¼ oz. bottles, I'm afraid that we're facing a direct write-off here. While we may be able to siphon off some of the product into stronger glass, the rework, scrap, and other problems here will undoubtedly result in significant expense. We're still working on this issue, looking for the best answer.

Jake Andrews:

> Really, all this talk about dropping the ball and glass handling is not addressing what I see as our major concern. If production, namely the machine tenders and line personnel, followed our specifications, these issues would not come up. We've known that glass-handling techniques were a long-standing problem, but it wasn't critical before. All B-20 has done is to decrease our margin of error and it has pinpointed operating deficiencies as a result.

These comments brought the meeting to a boiling point, as Glenn Kelley exploded:

> Boy! It's easy for research to point to us as the reason for the glass problems. I've already altered my whole decorating and handling process. But the real problem here is the gas, not the glass-handling techniques or the way my machine operators do their job! You guys in research still don't know how sensitive this propellant is to variations in the concentrate/propellant ratio, yet you're running around changing procedures in the entire plant without first documenting the characteristics of this gas!

Bob Adams was disturbed by the conflict between his top men, and he thought it was best to adjourn the meeting until the next day. He asked each manager to consider not only the key issues of concern in his own area, but also the future prospects of the company and his role in making this current problem an exception rather than a rule. As they left, Bob sat back and wondered once again where his company was going, and why these CIP/CAP projects had begun to go sour:

> We have to stop this pattern of failure, whether it is due to implementation problems, lack of adequate testing, or the CIP/CAP concept itself. Where are we really headed? What has gone wrong with the cost reduction program?

EXHIBIT 1 Organization Chart

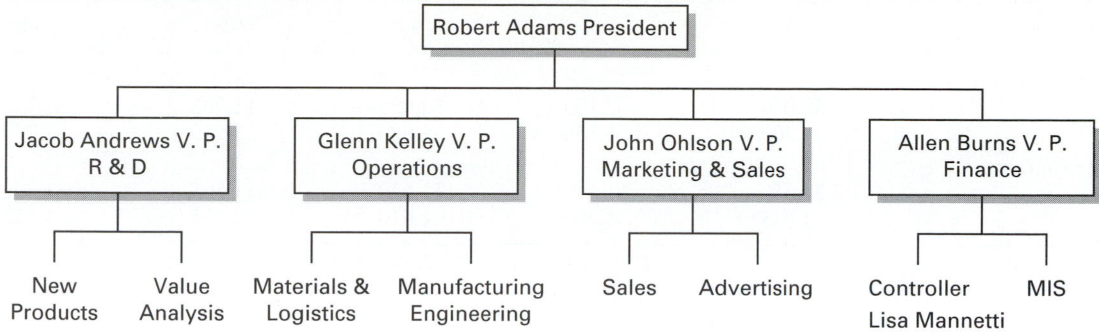

EXHIBIT 2 Summary Income Statements ($000s)

	Years Ended December 31						
	1983	*1982*	*1981*	*1980*	*1979*	*1978*	*1977*
Net sales	$364,157	$359,889	$362,178	$337,285	$266,629	$225,217	$175,020
Cost of goods sold	127,455	125,961	126,762	118,057	93,320	78,826	61,257
Selling & admin.	198,699	199,266	183,822	164,376	127,291	106,079	82,166
Profit from operations	38,003	34,662	51,594	54,852	46,018	40,312	31,597
Interest income	5,789	6,776	8,962	5,346	3,572	2,884	2,246
Total income	43,792	41,438	60,556	60,198	49,590	43,196	33,843
Interest expense	12,695	10,713	10,266	7,380	4,293	3,344	3,236
Miscellaneous	(592)	384	4,053	1,570	1,142	1,908	2,332
Income taxes	14,666	14,529	19,474	22,195	20,376	17,911	13,303
Net income	$ 17,023	$ 15,812	$ 26,763	$ 29,053	$ 23,779	$ 20,033	$ 14,972

EXHIBIT 3 Retail Sales of Selected Toiletries and Cosmetics (in $000). Excerpted from Moody's *Industrial Surveys.*

Products	*1980*	*1981*	*1982*	*1983*
Hair Products				
Shampoos	$1,116,160	$1,275,079	$1,405,940	$1,510,268
Rinses, tints, dyes	426,575	478,594	683,851	800,626
Men's aerosol & non-aerosol spray & other dressing	93,207	89,479	97,978	103,857
Women's hair sprays	411,600	437,892	493,931	511,603
Home permanent kits	111,124	114,458	125,904	137,235
Hand Products				
Lotions	222,492	244,741	267,991	288,090
Nail polish & enamel	294,911	265,034	283,586	304,855
Cosmetics				
Face creams	496,039	570,445	624,639	687,103
Makeup base	536,733	561,356	584,316	658,286
Face powder	109,851	123,033	123,648	103,000
Eye makeup	1,331,797	1,464,273	1,608,990	1,746,062
Talc & body powder	65,271	65,271	65,271	68,535
Lipsticks	894,236	965,775	1,047,866	1,131,695
Liquid facial cleansers	87,511	91,887	192,847	198,632
Fragrance Preparations				
Perfumes	129,550	134,732	141,469	160,060
Toilet water & cologne	681,019	726,062	770,658	1,001,960
Other Toiletries				
Toilet soaps	1,096,791	1,157,502	1,265,495	773,027
External personal deodorants	690,367	806,890	869,857	959,514
Shaving Products				
Shaving preparations	271,720	290,390	302,350	316,944
After-shave lotions	195,377	214,915	223,512	234,688
Men's cologne	249,125	274,038	298,702	319,611
Shaving accessories	825,169	900,710	916,143	996,531

EXHIBIT 4 Cost Reduction Program Performance 1980 to 1984 (in $000)

Cost Reductions	*1984*	*1983*	*1982*	*1981*	*1980*
Cost improvement programs:					
Target	$2,070	$2,100	$2,025	$1,905	$1,770
Actual	1,200*	1,850	1,980	1,910	1,770
Cost avoidance programs:					
Target	$1,650	$1,680	$1,620	$1,525	$1,420
Actual	1,645*	1,700	1,610	1,525	1,425

*projected

EXHIBIT 5 Capital Appropriations Request

GLAMOUR — CAPITAL APPROPRIATIONS REQUEST

AR	M01	956	K
DATE	2/16/84		

DIVISION ____________

LOCATION ____________

VARIANCE

This Project $________

Year to Date $________

1 CAPITAL CONTROL DATA

TOTAL BUDGET	PROJECTS $	CASH SPENDING
198_ LOCATION BUDGET		
THIS CAR		
CARS TO DATE		

	BUDGETED			
CAPITAL	YES	XX	NO	
P&L IMPACT	YES	XX	NO	

Exchange Rate ________ U.S. $1.00

PROJECT TITLE

2

INVESTMENT IMPACT	YEARS	1	2	3	4	5	6–10
With the Project	Sales						
	Net Income A.T.						
Without the Project	Sales						
	Net Income A.T.						
Due to the Project	Sales						
	Net Income A.T.	476.5					
Return on Invest. %		100%					

REASON: C ☒ Cost Reduction (Profit Improvement) | E ☐ Expansion Capacity | Q ☐ Quality Improvement | R ☐ Replacements | S ☐ Safety Security (Regulatory) | O ☐ Other (Specify) ____

TYPE: A ☐ Autos | B ☐ Buildings | D ☐ Data Processing Equipment | F ☐ Furniture & Office Equipment | L ☐ Land | M ☐ Machinery And Equipment | O ☐ Other (Specify) ____

3 INVESTMENT SUMMARY

	AUTHORIZATION	AUDITED ACTUAL
1. FIXED CAPITAL	272,230	
2. WORKING CAPITAL		
3. RELATED EXPENSES (Capitalized)	12,044	
4. **TOTAL CAPITAL APPROVAL**	284,274	
5. ANNUAL LEASE PAYMENTS NO. OF YEARS		
6. **TOTAL PROJECT**	392,274	

4 7. RELATED RETIREMENTS — 8. PAYBACK PERIOD 0.7 YEARS

5 Description:

Authorization for funds is requested to convert from propane to a B-20 propellant. With this conversion the first year after tax savings is estimated to be $476,500 due to bulk savings and the elimination of plastic coating on the bottle which was previously required on fills greater than 1 oz. Equipment to handle the new bottles will cost approximately $108,000 and will be purchased through contract with our Tool and Die supplier. This particular cost is not included in the fixed capital sum of this C.A.R., but it is included in the investment analysis for the return on investment calculations.

6 APPROVAL

REGIONS/DIVISIONS/COUNTRIES	Date	Group controller / Group Head	Date	CAPITAL REVIEW BOARD / Chairman	Date

EXHIBIT 6 B-20 Project Investment Analysis (annualized returns in $000s)

Material savings	$956.0
Additional depreciation	(73.5)
Net income before tax	882.5
Tax (46%)	406.0
Net income after tax	476.5
Add: depreciation	(73.5)
Net cash generated	$550.0
Total project expenditure	392.3
Payback period in years	0.7
Return on investment	140%

EXHIBIT 7 President's Initial Reaction to B-20 Project

INTEROFFICE MEMO

DATE: July 9, 1983

TO: Allen Burns (Vice President, Finance)

FROM: Bob Adams (President)

SUBJECT: Cost Reductions

I was delighted to hear from Jake that we have certain annual savings of almost $1 million as a result of a new propellant called B-20.

Glenn[a] and Jake[b] are going to make certain this occurs on a timely basis. Please put this down on our list of 1984 savings. Jake also believes that we have a prospect to reduce cost on several other products, which on a total savings basis will amount to a lot of money.

ATTENTION Jake and Glenn:

Most essential that we find this kind of savings in order to provide the money necessary to build the business in 1984. Please make certain that we take the necessary steps now in order to realize the full effects starting with the end of this year.

[a]Glenn Kelley, VP-Operations
[b]Jake Andrews, VP-R&D

EXHIBIT 8 Controller's Analysis of B-20 Project (October 1984) ($000)

Original, 1984 lab commitment	$550.0
Implementation delayed to February 23	(97.5)
Production volume reduction	(82.0)
Material savings below original projection	(35.4)
Problems with 3¼ oz., 2¾ and 2¼ oz. bottles (excluded from forecasted savings)	(191.4)
Net savings to mid-August	143.7
Subsequent findings:	
Problems with 2¾ oz. and 2¼ oz. bottles resolved (rest-of-year savings added back)	128.4
Additional labor costs	(110.0)
October revised forecast	$162.1
Memo:	
Inventory exposure (115M pieces of filled 3¼ oz. bottles on hold)	$200.9

EXHIBIT 9 Interoffice Memo

Date: August 15, 1984

To: Glenn Kelley (VP-Operations)

From: Jake Andrews (VP-R&D)

Subject: *Revised Glass Handling Techniques*

1. Incoming glass shipments from vendor to be pressure-checked by Q.C. as part of incoming inspection procedure.
2. All approved glass receipts released to Container Decorating to be handled in the following manner:
   a) All containers to be removed from corrugate nests, i.e., corrugate nests to be removed from shipping cartons only after all glass has been removed.
   b) Containers to be handled through decorating process avoiding contact with metal edges and minimizing surface contact.
   c) Decorated containers to be placed on lehr belt so as to be able to be packed at discharge end directly off lehr belt avoiding plowing off belt or eliminating need to transfer onto packing belt.
   d) Decorated glass to be spray-coated at discharge end with MYRJ 52S stearate spray being careful to spray only aerosol glass.
   e) All decorated glass to be packed back into corrugate nests, i.e., nests are to be inserted into shipping carton before glass is loaded into carton.
3. In process pressure checks will be performed by Quality Control after decorating to assure minimum pressure requirements exist in decorated glass. All decorated lots will be released to filling floor based upon those in-process audits.
4. Decorated glass to be handled on filling floor in the following manner:
   a) All containers to be removed from corrugated nests and inserted directly into pucks, i.e., corrugate nests to be removed from shipping cartons only after all glass has been removed.
   b) Containers to be handled through filling process avoiding contact with metal edges and minimizing surface contact prior to cartoning.
   c) Any eight-stage pack must be fully corrugate nested.

Disctech, Inc.

Rich O'Donnell, chairman of the Audit Committee of Disctech, Inc., had to decide what to say at the board of directors meeting on October 25, 1985. He was concerned about problems of revenue recognition and inventory management, based on the information given in this case (see Exhibit 1). He had accumulated this information from various sources. Some of the details may not have been exactly correct, but he was convinced that the general picture was as described (see Exhibit 2).

THE HARD DISK INDUSTRY

Disctech manufactured and sold disk drives. Disks are circular platters covered with magnetic material on which data are recorded in concentric circles. Although disk technology was well-established, the market was fast-growing and dynamic. Market positions changed rapidly, and disk drive manufacturers had to keep up with technological advances in order to survive. Data capacity was doubling every three years, and this trend was expected to continue.

The market for disk drives can be divided into two distinct submarkets: one for disks installed as part of large computer systems and one for those installed as part of minicomputer systems. The market for large computer disk drives was dominated by IBM, although other large mainframe manufacturers such as Sperry and Control Data also made disk drives for their own use. Independent disk drive manufacturers served this market by supplying IBM plug-compatible systems directly to end users. Independent disk drive manufacturers concentrated on replacing IBM drives because the sales volume for non-IBM models was considered too small. The mainframe disk drive market was expected to grow at about 5 percent per year.

The market for minicomputer disk drives, in which Disctech participated, was highly competitive. Some leading minicomputer manufacturers made some of their own disk drives, but most minicomputer manufacturers were part of the Original Equipment Manufacturer (OEM) market serviced by a large number of small independent disk drive manufacturers. This market was expected to grow 25 to 30 percent per year.

DISCTECH'S BEGINNINGS

Disctech was founded in 1977 by John Garvey, an executive who had left his job with a large manufacturer of minicomputers and computer disk memories. John was an electrical engineer by training, but was better known for his interest in and talent for organizing. John had felt constrained by the staid corporate environment and wanted to venture out on his own. He felt that with a good product, good marketing, and the right pitch to the capital markets, a "killing could be made." Three other talented executives left the large company to join with John in his new endeavor: Ed Steinborn (controller for the large manufacturer) became Disctech's chief financial officer, Peter Farrell (director of manufacturing) became the vice president for Design and Operations, and Mary Foley (manager of Minicomputer Marketing) became the executive vice president for Sales and Marketing. (See Exhibit 3 for an organization chart.)

The period 1977–78 was spent organizing the corporation and building prototypes of the advanced 14- and 8-inch disk drives that the company would market. Early in 1979 the corporation went public with 3.3 million shares offered at $3.00 a share. At a large party for shareholders and analysts, John announced that the corpora-

Research Assistant Joseph P. Mulloy prepared this case under the supervision of Professor Kenneth A. Merchant as the basis for class discussion rather than to illustrate either effective or ineffective handling of an administrative situation. The case is based on knowledge of actual company situations, but the facts have been disguised, and any resemblance to actual people or events is unintentional.

tion already had significant amounts of guaranteed sales for its new drives and that he expected Disctech products to become an industry standard. John also stated that the company expected to increase revenues and earnings per share (EPS) by a minimum of 30 percent per year.

Since the inception of the company, planning had been a very simple, top-down process. During the summer of each year, John met with Mary and Ed and set sales growth for the next year. This sales figure would then be rolled to the bottom line using expected margins and estimates of fixed expenses to get a net income figure and a tentative EPS. Prior to the beginning of the fiscal year in October, these goals for net income and EPS would then be passed down through the Finance and Marketing organizations where they became "law." The Design and Operations division planned production from the expected revenue and gross margin figures, while the R&D budget was negotiated separately between John and Peter.

Strategies to reach the annual plan were conceived and implemented at regularly scheduled "revenue meetings." Attendees included John, Ed, Mary, and the senior people of the marketing and sales staff. These meetings primarily sought the means of identifying and generating potential revenues.

Revenues for Disctech were derived from the sale and service of the company's equipment. Revenues were recorded at the time of shipment of products or performance of services. Customer orders were initiated by Disctech's receipt of an Equipment Order Form (EOF); this was either completed by the customer or prepared by Disctech personnel pursuant to a Master Sales Agreement signed by the customer. The EOF included a description of the equipment, the price of the equipment, and the earliest equipment delivery date that was acceptable to the customer.

BOARD OF DIRECTORS AND AUDIT COMMITTEE

Since the company's inception, Disctech's board of directors had consisted of seven members: two inside directors (the CEO and the CFO) and five outside directors. The board usually met four times a year to review the corporation's progress and plans for the future. The meetings were generally short and standardized, with John in control of the agenda. The outside directors were all impressed with the company's performance and the dedication displayed by the top officers.

The Audit Committee of the board consisted of three outside directors. The members of the Audit Committee served three-year terms on a rotating basis, although the chairman of the committee usually served for a longer period. The Audit Committee generally met twice a year, before and after the annual audit.

A number of changes came about in 1982 after Richard (Rich) O'Donnell, an outside director, was named as chairman of the Audit Committee. Rich firmly believed that an audit committee "could not be effective without being active." He increased the committee's schedule to at least four meetings a year and set up private meetings between the committee and the outside auditors. Rich tried to get the committee to look at the company's exposures and to question discretionary items in the financial statements. He suggested that the inside and outside auditors make some unannounced inspections and audits, and he wanted to strengthen the internal audit function, such as through training and improved hiring practices.

Rich admitted in 1983 that he had some concerns about serving on a board of directors and, particularly, on an Audit Committee:

> A member of an Audit Committee is always a potential victim of management and the outside auditors since you depend on them so much. To a great extent, you have to trust them. However, I try to set a tone of watchfulness by asking a lot of questions at all of our meetings; but I need to get other board members to do it or I will just look like an old crank.
>
> Perhaps my concerns are just excessive caution, however, because it appears that the top officers are very talented, and John Garvey is very dedicated to the company. He wants to make good disk drives and sell a lot of them.

INTERNAL AND EXTERNAL AUDIT

The Internal Audit division, consisting of the head auditor, Doug McAneny, and two staff members, reported to Ed Steinborn (CFO). The primary roles of Internal Audit were to ensure that corporate accounting policies were followed and that safeguards existed to ensure that the company's assets were protected. A secondary role was to be alert to opportunities for cost cutting and efficiency.

At the request of Rich O'Donnell, Doug McAneny had attended some meetings of the Audit Committee. Rich tried to establish a rapport with Doug and assured him that any misgivings that he had about anything, or anyone, in the company would be brought to the attention of the Audit Committee.

Disctech's external audit firm was Touche, Young and Andersen (TYA), a Big Eight firm. Each year in July, the auditors met with top management and the Audit Committee to lay out the schedule of the annual audit and to review changes in the company since the previous year.

1979–82

The years 1979 to 1982 were very exciting at Disctech; sales revenues grew at a compound rate of 39 percent. Every quarter the company announced record earnings, and the stockmarket reacted as John predicted, with the trading price continually reaching new highs. John made regular announcements about the company, stating how earnings were going to continue to grow at above industry rates. The total market in 1979 for minicomputer disk memories at OEM prices was $2.1 billion, so there was plenty of room for Disctech to grow.

Disctech had continued to make modest R&D expenditures but by the middle of 1982 its once "head of the pack" products were beginning to fall behind the latest technology. In response, John applied pressure to the Product Design division to come out with new products even if they were only slight improvements on existing products.

1983

The sales pattern in 1983 was a little erratic. John Garvey and Mary Foley (executive vice president—Sales and Marketing) agreed that quarterly sales (and earnings) had to continue to grow to keep the glowing image of Disctech alive. To maintain this growth record, they sometimes found it necessary to have the shipping department work round the clock during the last few days of each quarter in order to push as many orders as possible out the door so as to recognize the revenue for those transactions.

Mary also decided to take advantage of the way some OEMs ordered disk drives. Many OEMs would place a large order for 100 to 200 disks, get a discount, and then ask for delivery at a date 2 to 3 months in the future. This assured them of a supply of the disks and a delivery date that supported their computer construction and shipment schedules. Many times an order placed in one quarter would not be scheduled for delivery until the next quarter. To recognize these sales in the present period, Mary directed that as many orders as possible receive early shipment to the OEM, with the understanding that the OEMs would not be liable for payment until the previously-agreed-upon delivery dates.

The auditors from TYA questioned this early shipment program but Ed Steinborn was able to convince them that the sales met the requirements of "sales" as defined under generally accepted accounting principles: title to the disks did transfer to the OEM upon shipment; the OEM was obliged to pay Disctech for the disks; and Disctech did contact the OEM prior to shipment to get their authorization. What was not clear at the time was that some of these authorizations were verbal: the salesperson responsible for an account would get the authorization and call it back to the home office.

Some of the OEMs did not object to this early shipment policy, but many other OEMs did not have extra storage room and would not accept early delivery. In such cases, the Disctech salespeople were told to "use their imaginations" and find storage at a local Disctech distributor or another convenient location.

Although 1983 revenues were $107.1 million, $5.9 million of this was for disks originally scheduled for delivery in 1984. (Of the $5.9 million, $3.7 million were shipped without a written authorization.)

1984

The only major change at Disctech in 1984 was in marketing policy. John Garvey had long thought that the minicomputer memory industry would slowly evolve to become more like the mainframe business, with fewer sales to computer manufacturers and more sales directly to end users. This evolution did occur and was accelerated as the economy slowed. Many companies held onto the systems they already had installed. John believed that a truism of computers—"information to be stored quickly grows to fill all available memory"—would be the salvation of Disctech. Accordingly, more salespeople were hired, and the sales force was directed to approach all current users of minicomputers compatible with Disctech disk memories to attempt to generate sales in this potentially large market.

After the results of the second quarter were announced (another record high), John called Mary, Ed, and Peter together for a private meeting. John indicated that he was very proud of their results and that he knew they would continue to outperform the industry. He pointed out, however, that each quarter's goals had been harder and harder to reach, and that delays in the completion of new disk designs and prototype construction and the growing obsolescence of their inventory might level or even decrease the company's short-term earnings.

John went on to say that with his children nearing college age, he needed some money set aside that was not tied up in risky investments. As a result he had begun quietly to sell some of his Disctech stock, which had appreciated considerably since 1979. He told his staff that while he was still optimistic about the company's future, it might be wise for them also to look carefully at their own financial needs. If they chose to sell some stock, of course they should do it discreetly.

The year 1984 was another record. The marketing shift toward memory end users was a big success and significantly contributed to another record year, and early shipments continued to increase as the marketing department pressured OEMs and salespeople for early authorization. Of \$134.9 million total sales, early-shipment revenues were \$12.4 million, of which \$9.8 million was shipped without a written authorization.

INVENTORY CONTROL AND RESERVES FOR OBSOLESCENCE

In 1979, demand exceeded production capacity, so Disctech shipped units as soon as they were assembled. But efforts to improve efficiency and cleanliness raised production yields, so by 1980 production began to produce drives for inventory.

In 1981, less than 15 percent of Disctech's inventory was in raw materials; over 85 percent was in finished goods inventory. This unusual inventory mix was caused by a general shortage of raw materials in the industry. Disctech and other manufacturers, therefore, sent raw materials directly to the production line. Also, Disctech wanted as little work in process inventory as possible because partially assembled disk drives were highly susceptible to damage; even the slightest dirt or dent rendered the disk or its drive unit inoperable.

In 1982, the Design Division began to make a large number of small improvements to the disk drives to ensure that the product remained competitive. This had a large effect on inventory levels. Disassembling the finished disk drive often caused complete disk failure, and as a result very little rework on finished drives was done. Instead, new drives in production would be modified and then assembled. Thus each change or alteration created another layer of finished inventory slightly different from the last. Disctech's policy for creating reserves for obsolescence of inventory was:

- Any equipment over two years old would be reserved at 5 percent per quarter for five years so that at the end of seven years there would be a 100 percent reserve.
- Any equipment declared unmarketable would have a 100 percent reserve taken against it.

These rules resulted in small reserves. Very little equipment that was technically obsolete was actually very old. Moreover, Disctech had no corporate standards or guidelines for determining when disk drives became unmarketable. This problem was intensified by the corporate attitude that Disctech equipment was not subject to obsolescence.

In September 1982, a production controller forwarded a memo via Peter Farrell to the CFO and the executive vice president for sales and marketing that summarized a study he had done on the growing inventory problem. It listed three recommendations:

1. A study to produce a new reserve policy, since it appeared that the product life cycle was far shorter than five years.
2. An intensive effort by the Marketing department to sell the older inventory as soon as possible.
3. An increase in the reserve for obsolescence from \$800,000 to \$1.4 million.

This memo was discussed by the senior corporate officers who all felt that the problem was not that serious; they were absolutely unwilling to increase the reserve by any amount. Marketing, however, attempted to stimulate sales of the older disk drives with various specials, discounts, and promotions. The CFO also stated that he would "closely watch the inventory problem."

In 1983, the amount of obsolete inventory grew faster than the reserves, and by the end of the fiscal year the deficit was estimated by the production controller to be almost $2.4 million. The outside auditors did not see the total extent of the problem but they did question the reserve policy in their management letter:

> Continual monitoring of Disctech's FGI reserve policy is required and procedures should be implemented to develop historical experience to measure the propriety of the formula adopted. The policy should also be extended to recognize obsolescence of products no longer in production sooner than required by the present formula.

Disctech's management acknowledged the auditors' report but also informed the Audit Committee that they already had done an internal study in 1982 and were working actively to fix all problems with inventory control.

During 1984, Disctech management was aware that the exposure for inventory obsolescence was increasing, but little was done other than continuing the marketing promotions and taking reserves as calculated by the reserve formula. Disctech's management maintained that reserving for or writing off inventory made it less likely that it would be sold. They stressed that they had an obligation to the stockholders to find uses for the inventory rather than write it off.

By the time of the 1984 year-end audit, the auditors had become more agitated by the inventory situation (in addition to the aggressive revenue recognition practices) and sought written assurance from Disctech's management that a formal program existed to "significantly impact the obsolescence exposure." The CFO, Ed Steinborn, wrote to the auditors:

> Our response to the problems in the inventory area will be to outline the programs we have underway to reduce inventory levels. We will agree to study policy alternatives in the area of providing reserves for excess equipment; however, affordability considerations really preclude our ability to make any meaningful change in this area this year.

The board and the Audit Committee were informed that a problem with inventory control still existed and that efforts to rectify the situation were ongoing. They were also told that "reserves for obsolescence may have to be increased next year as the product life cycle for disk memories shortens." They were not given an exhibit to the 1984 auditors' management letter that contained the following sentence: "This [obsolescence reserve] policy results in full valuation of excess inventory, overstates inventory, and may lead to serious future financial adjustments." The board was not told that the exposure on FGI had grown to an estimated $3.9 million.

The Audit Committee asked questions about inventory valuation, but John and Ed had quick answers and were confident that the inventory situation would soon be under control. Nevertheless, the Audit Committee in a private session with the outside auditors admitted that some things, including inventory obsolescence, had begun to worry them. They also told the engagement partner that they intended to meet more often in 1985 and they wanted a senior representative from the outside auditors and Doug McAneny, the head of internal auditing, at their meetings.

1985

The year 1985 was difficult for Disctech, and tremendous pressure was placed on the sales force to achieve the planned sales goal. A combination of a soft market for the 14-inch disk drives and unexpected delays in production of the advanced 8- and the new 5¼-inch drives made sales difficult.

Some salespeople came up with ingenious ideas to stimulate sales that were often designed to take advantage of the company's aggressive revenue policies. One such scheme could occur when a customer filled out an equipment order form (EOF) with a delivery date far in the future and submitted it to Disctech for processing. Within a week or two the responsible salesperson would contact the marketing department and inform them that he had convinced the customer to accept an early delivery in the current quarter, with the understanding that payment would not be due until the date on the EOF. From the salesperson's view this made everyone happy: Disctech booked a sale; the salesperson got a commission; and the customer received a disk memory at a reasonable price with delayed payments and no finance charges.

At the same time sales were becoming more difficult, order cancellations were becoming a problem. As Disctech's competitors came out with new products, many OEMs switched disk memory suppliers; direct end-user sales were also affected because people wanted more memory and shorter access time for their dollars.

Near the end of the first quarter of 1985, a Marketing department meeting was held to discuss the order of cancellation problem. Mary chose this opportunity to announce a new policy: any order canceled within six weeks of expected delivery would still be shipped and the revenue recorded. Her staff told her that most customers would just refuse to accept delivery. She responded that on each of these deliveries the responsible salesperson would go along and ensure that "the sale stuck." All of these problems caused a lot of consternation in the sales force but they all knew better than to argue with Mary when her mind was made up.

A MID-YEAR MEETING

At mid-year, John Garvey called a meeting of the top officers to review some pressing problems. The first problem was financing. As receivables had grown, cash was getting short. Consequently $10 million in bonds would be issued for public sale early in the fourth quarter; $4 million of the cash raised would be used to retire the bonds currently outstanding, and the rest of the proceeds would go to operations.

Second, inventory problems were getting worse. An internally generated estimate of the current obsolescence exposure was $6.8 million, and this was expected to grow to over $8 million by the end of the year. The outside auditors were very worried about the obsolescence exposure. John explained he had placated them by informing them that the company was currently doing another internal study of obsolescence policies and that he expected a significant writedown, probably as early as the first quarter of 1986.

Third, the new disk memory designs still had development problems, but John expected them to be available before the end of the calendar year. Finally, there was a growing problem with returned equipment. This would probably cause a significant reversal in revenues in future periods.

Putting these all together, John admitted that the record string of growth and profits would probably be broken. John wanted the company to take all its "lumps" in the first quarter of 1986, and he wanted to take the inventory writedown at the same time as the new product announcement. He also stated that strong quarterly and annual results in 1985 would help the bond issue and would likely mitigate the impact of a loss in the first quarter of 1986. Everyone came away from the meeting clearly understanding that they had to make the 1985 budget—no matter what they had to do.

Despite heroic efforts by the sales force, fourth-quarter predictions indicated that without further action Disctech would come up short of the 1985 budget. A plan was worked out in the Marketing department to make a large shipment to a warehouse rented by Disctech under another name; this shipment (for $4.2 million) was booked as revenue in 1985. Plans were to use the equipment to help fill early 1986 orders.

In the end, the 1985 goal of $162 million in sales was achieved—total annual sales were $164.6 million. Early shipment revenues totaled $15.8 million, of which $10.6 million was equipment shipped without authorization. This $15.8 million did not include the $4.2 million shipped to the new warehouse.

THE OCTOBER 25, 1985 BOARD MEETING

The board of directors met on October 25 to review the results of FY 1985. John first went over the high points of the year and the records achieved. He next turned to the inventory problem and gave a quick summary of the events of the last few years. John then told the board that to bring inventory back in line, a one-time writedown of $8.2 million would be required.

Rich O'Donnell, chairman of the audit committee, thereupon asked for the floor.

EXHIBIT 1 Income Statements for Fiscal Years Ending September 30 ('000s omitted)
(*Source:* Annual reports.)

	1978	*1979*	*1980*	*1981*	*1982*	*1983*	*1984*	*1985*
Revenue	$5,997	$30,003	$42,004	$59,646	$81,119	$107,076	$134,916	$164,598
Cost of Sales	6,531	21,288	29,403	41,752	55,161	72,812	91,743	111,927
Gross margin	(534)	8,715	12,601	17,894	25,958	34,264	43,173	52,671
R&D expense	1,354	2,528	3,760	3,772	4,056	4,283	4,722	4,938
SG&A expense	1,990	4,138	5,220	6,561	10,545	13,920	17,539	21,398
Operating profit	(3,878)	2,049	3,621	7,561	11,357	16,061	20,912	26,335
Interest income	131	(517)	84	119	162	214	(104)	(541)
Profit before tax	(3,747)	1,532	3,705	7,680	11,519	16,275	20,808	25,794
Income tax	0	767	1,704	3,533	5,299	7,487	9,572	11,866
Profit before tax	(747)	765	2,000	4,147	6,220	8,788	11,236	13,928
Tax loss forward	0	685	1,400	0	0	0	0	0
Net income	$(3,747)	$1,450	$3,401	$4,147	$6,220	$8,788	$11,236	$13,928
Earnings per share	$(1.06)	$0.21	$0.50	$0.60	$0.90	$1.27	$1.61	$1.99

EXHIBIT 2 Consolidated Balance Sheets at September 30 ('000s omitted)
(*Source:* Annual reports.)

	1979	*1980*	*1981*	*1982*	*1983*	*1984*	*1985*
ASSETS:							
Cash and marketable securities	$10,020	$ 3,654	$ 3,778	$ 3,273	$ 2,947	$ 2,808	$ 3,920
Accounts receivable (net)	8,752	9,801	11,921	15,508	22,091	30,843	39,300
Inventories (net)	12,221	8,601	11,241	15,122	22,046	27,557	36,682
Prepaid expenses	142	375	525	746	730	750	809
Total current assets	$31,135	$22,431	$27,465	$34,649	$47,814	$63,958	$80,711
Property, plant, and equipment (net)	2,110	6,901	9,661	13,719	18,657	24,628	31,031
Other	929	120	169	239	284	321	364
Total assets	$34,174	$29,452	$37,295	$48,607	$66,755	$86,907	$112,106
LIABILITIES:							
Notes payable	$4,050	0	0	0	0	0	0
Accounts payable	5,664	3,600	5,401	9,158	12,734	16,849	23,190
Accrued liabilities	1,179	1,500	2,100	2,982	4,056	5,354	6,746
Total current liabilities	$10,893	$1,500	$7,141	$12,140	$16,790	$18,203	$29,936
Bank debt	0	0	0	0	0	2,000	0
Capital leases	1,363	4,485	6,820	8,917	12,127	16,008	18,170
Bonds	3,570	0	0	0	4,000	4,000	10,000
EQUITY:							
Common stock	3,651	3,677	3,703	3,729	3,755	3,782	3,807
Other capital	20,978	21,020	21,062	21,104	21,146	21,188	21,231
Retained earnings	(6,281)	(4,831)	(1,431)	2,717	8,937	17,726	28,962
Total liabilities and equities	$34,174	$29,452	$37,295	$48,607	$66,755	$86,907	$112,106

EXHIBIT 3 Organizational Chart

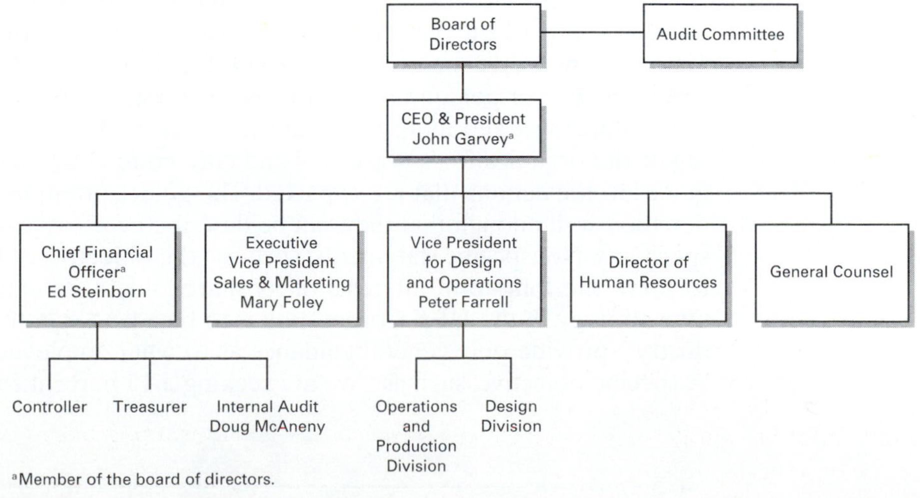

CHAPTER 7

Designing and Evaluating Control Systems

The preceding chapters have described the range of controls that can be used and how the affect behaviors. This chapter discusses a general framework that can be used by those who are interested in designing control systems or in improving existing systems.

The processes of designing and improving control systems require the addressing of two basic questions. The first question is: What is desired? Each individual's role, from that of the chief executive officer to those of the employees lowest in the hierarchy, should be analyzed to develop an understanding of the critical determinants of success. The second question is: What is likely to happen? If what is likely is different from what is desired, then managers must address the basic MCS-design questions: (1) What controls should be used? and (2) How tightly should each be applied? These questions are the core elements in an MCS evaluation framework shown in Figure 7-1. The following sections in this chapter describe how to structure the information to address each of the questions in this framework. The chapter concludes with some observations about common control issues.

UNDERSTANDING WHAT IS DESIRED AND WHAT IS LIKELY

MCSs cannot be designed or evaluated without an understanding of the demands of the roles being controlled; what it is the organization wants the individuals involved to do. Greater and more certain knowledge yields a larger set of feasible control alternatives, provides a better chance of being able to apply each alternative tightly, if so desired, and reduces the chance of creating a behavioral displacement problem. The understanding of what is desired is most valuable if it is defined in terms of the actions desired, since the purpose of controls is to influence actions. However, controls can be devised with only an understanding of some desirable results or personnel/cultural characteristics.

Objectives, and more importantly, strategies derived from a good understanding of the organization's objectives and core competencies often provide important guides to the actions that are expected. The guides are more valuable if they are understood well enough that they can be described with at least some minimal level of specificity. Nonspecific statements; such as "the objective of the ABC Corporation is to serve the long-term interests of its shareholders, its employees, and society" or "the strategy of the DEF Corporation is to be a leader in the consumer durables industry", provide only general guidance as to what employees in the firm should do. A specific objective, such as "We are seeking a 15 percent return on invested capital

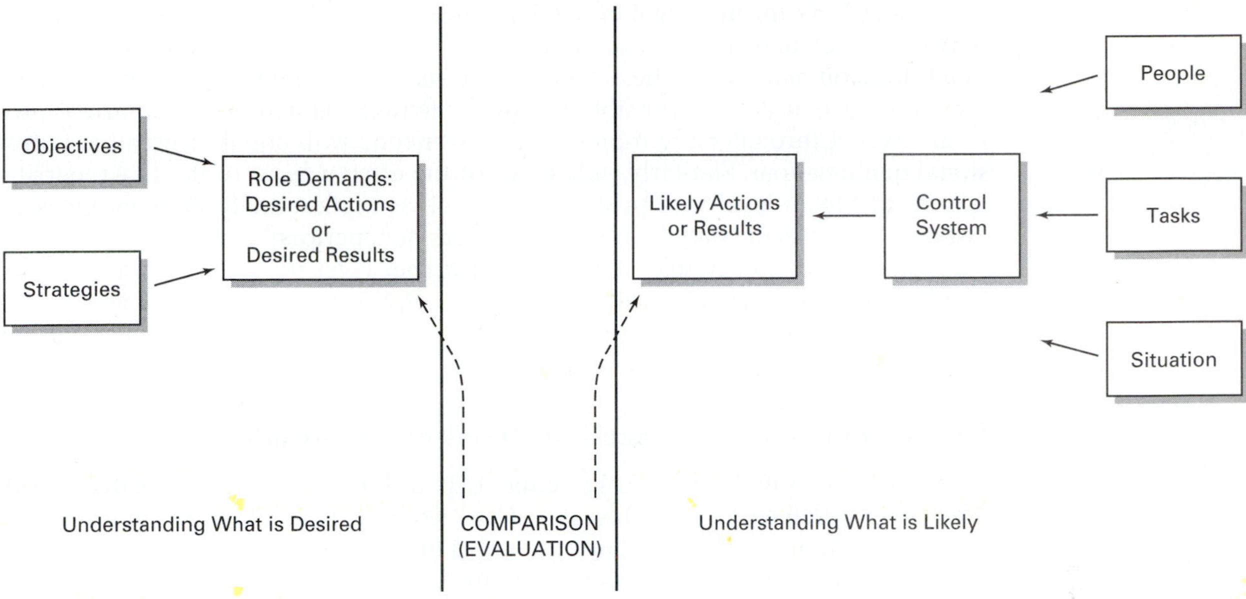

FIGURE 7-1 A Management Control System Evaluation Framework

after taxes and a 20 percent growth in sales" provides better guidance as to how decisions should be made. Similarly, having a business unit employ a *growth strategy* is less specific than detailing how the growth should be accomplished (what market segments to emphasize) and how the growth-versus-current return trade-offs should be made. It is certainly possible to determine that some actions, such as stealing, will not serve any nonspecific objectives or strategies, but that knowledge is not as useful as knowing how the trade-offs between conflicting objectives should be handled. For control purposes, more specific statements of objectives and strategies are preferable, under the important conditions that they are congruent with true organizational goals and can be updated to be kept congruent.

Knowledge of what is desirable is most useful for control purposes if it can be translated into knowledge of the specific demands on the roles of individuals (or perhaps groups) in the organization. Much of this elaboration and translation is typically done as part of the organization's planning and budgeting processes. Role demands can be specified in terms of either the actions that must be performed or the results that determine success or failure in that role.

Understanding Role Demands in Terms of Key Actions

One way to understand what must be controlled is to identify the key actions (KAs) that must be performed in order to provide the greatest probability of success. These actions differ considerably among firms and among different roles in a firm.

It is not always easy to isolate a short list of KAs, but sometimes it can be done, particularly for the oft-recurring actions, or what Drucker calls the *regular process.*[1] For lower-level personnel, such as production line workers, the KAs may be well understood because they are highly routinized and largely mechanical, such as folding a garment and placing it in a box. For a professional service firm, the KAs may be the hiring decisions. A manager in such a firm noted: "One of the major tools, if not the major tool, that we have in achieving our goals is through control of the number and quality of the people we hire."[2]

Most KAs for most higher-level *line* personnel (managers) are not well understood. They may include problem finding, personnel team building, and investment decision making. As these types of actions require considerable professional judgment, it is usually impossible to judge whether the actions taken are appropriate except through close monitoring by someone with equal or greater professional qualifications. Similarly, judgments of the effectiveness of the key recurring actions of higher-level *staff* professionals, such as market analysts, economists, or lawyers, can be made only by reviews by peers or superiors.

That is not to say that some KAs of higher-level personnel cannot be isolated for control purposes. Most companies require standard sets of actions for personnel preparing investment proposals, business plans, and justifications for new hires. These are action controls.

Understanding Role Demands in Terms of Key Results

Another way to understand role demands is in terms of the key results (KRs). KRs can be defined as "the few key areas where 'things must go right' for the business to flourish. If results in these areas are not adequate, the organization's efforts for the period will be less than desired."[3]

In most situations the number of KRs managers must consider is small, perhaps six or eight at most. The Ryder System, the largest truck-leasing and rental company in the U.S., apparently has only two KRs at the company level: utilization of assets and market share. Ryder's chairman observed that "if you put those two factors together, you end up increasing your profitability."[4] At different organization levels and within different functions with Ryder, however, the list may be longer. For the purchasing managers within Ryder to be effective, they would have to ensure the right quantity (and mix) of quality vehicles (and other items), on schedule, and at reasonable cost.

KRs may or may not be stable. For some companies and entities within a company, the KRs may be relatively constant over time; for others they may change as the environmental conditions and/or the chosen strategy change. A company pursuing a low-cost-producer strategy must monitor costs carefully, and if it is in a situation where costs are declining with cumulative experience (that is, a learning curve exists), it must maintain a strong market share position. These are KRs that are relatively constant. A switch to a different strategy; such as to market a unique, differentiated product, will change the KRs. Control of the individuals charged with carrying out this new strategy will probably require measuring product performance characteristics and comparing them with those of competitors, or implementing of action controls over the design efforts.

Understanding Likely Actions or Results

The second part of the situational analysis involves understanding what actions or results are likely. Managers should investigate the potentials for each of the control problems: lack of direction, motivational problems, or personal limitations. They should ask whether the employees understand what they are expected to do (KAs) or to accomplish (KRs), whether they are properly motivated, and whether they are able to fulfill their desired roles.

If informed judges conclude that what is desired is not greatly different from what is likely (or what has just happened), then they can conclude that the organization has an effective MCS. On the other hand, if the likely actions or results are different from the KAs or KRs, more or different controls might be called for, depending on the severity of the problems and the costs of the controls that could be used to solve the problems. Managers should then address the questions about what controls to use and how tightly to apply them.

DECISION 1: CHOICE OF CONTROLS

The different types of controls are not equally effective at addressing each of the control problems. Table 7-1 provides a summary of the control problems each of the types of controls addresses. It shows, for example, that behavioral constraints do not help solve lack-of-direction problems; so if direction is a significant problem in the area of concern, other forms of controls will have to be considered. The questions can then be addressed as to what controls should be used and how tightly they should be applied.

The specific set of control mechanisms to be selected from among the feasible alternatives should be those that will provide the greatest net benefits (that is, benefits less costs). The benefits of a control system are derived from the increased probability of success, but since controls are usually costly to implement and operate, these costs must be subtracted from the total benefits provided.

Personnel/Cultural Controls as an Initial Consideration

In deciding among the many control alternatives, managers should start by considering whether personnel or cultural controls will be sufficient. Personnel/cultural controls are worthy of first consideration because they have relatively few harmful side effects and relatively low out-of-pocket costs. In some cases, such as small organizations, personnel/cultural controls may provide completely effective control by themselves. Consider this observation by the chairman of a small high-technology start-up company in response to a question as to what control meant to his company:

TABLE 7-1 Control Types and Control Problems

	Control Problems		
Control Types	*Lack of Direction*	*Motivational Problems*	*Personal Limitations*
Results Controls			
Results accountability	x	x	
Action Controls			
Behavioral constraints		x	
Preaction reviews	x	x	x
Action accountability	x	x	x
Redundancy			x
Personnel/Cultural Controls			
Selection and placement	x	x	x
Training	x		x
Provision of necessary resources			x
Creation of a strong organizational culture	x	x	
Group-based rewards	x	x	

> We don't have a need for most of the controls that large companies have. We're still small—just three professionals and twenty people in our ordertaking, assembly, and packing areas—and we're all working as hard as we can, some of us twelve to fourteen hours a day, seven days a week. We understand what we want to do, and we're highly motivated to do it. We don't have any bonus system, and the only budget we have is a simple cash forecast. I guess you could say the most important part of our control system is the information we collect, particularly about where the market is headed and how our products stack up against those of our competitors.[5]

This company obviously has little need for results or action controls at this stage of its development.

Even in settings where personnel/cultural controls are not sufficiently reliable by themselves, it is useful to focus on them first because they will have to be relied upon to some extent no matter what other forms of controls are used. Don Johnston, chairman and chief executive of the JWT Group, parent company of the J. Walter Thompson advertising agency, was well aware of this. A control system failure at his firm led him to draw the following conclusion: "As long as business depends on human beings, we will all be vulnerable to human frailty. . . . In today's world, you are more than ever dependent on the personal integrity of the people involved."[6] Considering personnel/cultural controls first will allow managers to consider how reliable these forms of controls are and, therefore, how aggressive they should be in using other forms of controls.

Personnel/cultural controls are sufficient only if the people in the particular roles being considered (or those who might be put in the roles) understand what is required, are capable of performing well, *and* are motivated to perform well without additional rewards or punishments provided by the organization. Rarely are these conditions satisfied so completely that managers can conclude that the personnel/cultural controls are reliable by themselves. Even when people say they trust someone else, their reliability assessment is usually less than 100 percent. Further, judgments of trust are subjective and not totally reliable. One who has extreme trust that is unwarranted is called *gullible.*

Many examples are available to show the dangers of relying excessively on personnel/cultural controls. Apple Computer has traditionally prided itself on having employees who worked hard because they believed they were changing the world. As performance lagged, former CEO John Sculley saw a need to articulate clearer strategies and to impose more rigid responsibility structures to control costs and to "impose order on Apple's free-wheeling management."[7] After the changes, a *Fortune* magazine article noted, "Suddenly, instead of spouting New Age bromides that celebrate the 'empowerment of employees,' executives are tossing around words like pragmatism and accountability."[8]

In another setting, the president of a small candy distributorship relied on personnel controls while attempting to set up new businesses to diversify operations. He hired people who he thought were experienced and trustworthy to run the new businesses, which included exporting, trucking, auto leasing, computer software development, and wine distribution. He was not concerned that he did not understand those businesses well or that his company did not have good financial-reporting systems. The results were disastrous. Four years later, none of the new businesses had survived; he was stuck with considerable excess inventory and the payables for them; and his business, which had been quite profitable up until that time, was in danger of failing.[9]

While this particular executive could be faulted for his implementations of personnel controls (one of his new employees turned out to be an alcoholic), it is rare that personnel controls are, by themselves, sufficient. In most cases it is necessary to supplement them with controls over actions, results, or both. One of the most commonly cited principles of control is: "You shouldn't put all your trust in one person."[10] If you are selling your house, it is good to try to find a real estate agent you can trust. If you also have a contract that mandates certain desirable behaviors and/or aligns your interests with those of the agent, the probability that you will be pleased with the eventual outcome will be increased.

Choices among the various forms of action and results controls should depend on the particular advantages and disadvantages each has in the setting in question.

Advantages and Disadvantages of Action Controls

Perhaps the most significant advantage of action controls is that they are the most direct form of control. If it is absolutely essential that an action be performed properly the first time (for example, a significant investment decision), perhaps because the decision is not easily reversible. Action controls usually provide the best control because the control-action link is so direct. Further, if controls over the actions themselves are judged to be adequate, there is no need to monitor results. They will be as good as could be expected in the circumstances.

Action controls also provide several other advantages. One is that they direct managerial attention to the actions being used within the firm. Debates and conflicts that arise will then be focused on the right questions.

Action controls also tend to lead to documentation of the accumulation of knowledge as to what works best. The documents that are produced (policies and procedures) are an efficient way to transfer accumulations of knowledge to the people who are performing the actions. They also act as a form of organizational memory, so that the knowledge is not lost if, for example, key employees leave the organization.

Finally, action controls, particularly in the form of policies and procedures, are an efficient way to aid organizational coordination. They increase the predictability of actions and reduce the amount of interorganizational information flows required to achieve a coordinated effort. They are a key element in a bureaucratic form of organization (using this term in a positive sense) which makes the organization "capable of attaining the highest degree of efficiency and is in this the most rational known means of carrying out the imperative of control over human beings."[11]

Action controls have a number of significant disadvantages. First is a severe feasibility limitation. As was discussed earlier, excellent knowledge of what actions are desirable exists only for highly routinized jobs.

Second, most action control forms discourage creativity, innovation, and adaptation. Employees often react to action controls by becoming passive. They develop their work habits based on the work rules they are given. This adaptation may be so complete that they begin to depend on the rules, cease to think how the processes could be improved, and become resistant to change. In some cases this discouragement is not a significant disadvantage; for example, creativity from pilots in the air is not normally desirable. In other cases, action controls cause significant opportunities for improvements to be foregone.

Third, action accountability, in particular, can cause sloppiness. Employees who are accustomed to operating with a stable set of work rules are prone to cut corners. Several recent airplane disasters have been traced to checklist errors, meaning that the pilots have carelessly rushed through their pre-takeoff and pre-landing procedures. One United Airlines crash on takeoff was traced to the crew's failure to properly set the stabilizer trim.[12]

Fourth, action controls often cause negative attitudes. Some, perhaps even most, people are not happy operating under them. Some people, especially the more independent, creative people, may leave to find other jobs that allow more opportunity for achievement and self-actualization.

Fifth, action accountability in particular, often leads to behavioral displacement. It is easy to focus on actions of lesser importance that are easy to monitor. Furthermore, it is difficult and costly to adapt procedures to changing environments. As one author noted:

> It has long since become a familiar observation that generals regularly spend their time preparing to fight the previous war. Managers often do the same. Whether from the force of habit or from the appeal of comfortable modes of thought and action, they often fail to see how the problems that beset them are unlike those with which they have become familiar. Or they fail to make the painful effort to determine what from the past continues to apply, what does not, and that what is new must be learned.[13]

Indeed, most companies have difficulty in modifying their procedures as situations change, and communicating changes that are made can be expensive. Several of the problems that were discussed in Chapter 6 (for example, the tendency toward bureaucratization of behavior) were caused by procedures that did not adapt to changing conditions.

Finally, some action controls, particularly those which require preaction or evaluative reviews, are costly. The reviews must usually be performed by individuals who are as well or more qualified than those who are taking the original actions. Thus, the reviewers must be highly knowledgeable, and their services are costly.

Advantages and Disadvantages of Results Controls

Results controls also have several significant advantages and disadvantages. One common advantage is feasibility. Results controls can provide effective control even where knowledge as to what actions are desirable is lacking. This situation is typical of many (even most) of the important roles in many organizations.

Another advantage of results controls is that peoples' behaviors can be influenced even while they are allowed significant autonomy. This is particularly desirable where creativity is required because autonomy allows room for new and innovative ways of thinking. Even where creativity is not important, allowing autonomy has some advantages. It usually yields greater employee commitment and motivation because higher-level personal needs (such as, personal accomplishment) are brought into play. Results controls can provide on-the-job training. People learn by doing and by making mistakes. It also allows room for idiosyncratic styles of behavior (such as, a unique sales approach), which can provide better results than standardization of one approach.

A final advantage of results controls is that, as compared to some forms of action controls, they are often inexpensive. Performance measures are often collected for reasons not directly related to management control; for financial reporting, tax reporting, or strategy formulation, and if these measures can be used or easily adapted for results controls, the incremental expense of the control can be relatively small.

Results controls, however, have three major disadvantages. First, results measures usually provide less than perfect indications of whether good actions had been taken because the measures failed to meet one or more of the qualities of good measure: congruence, precision, objectivity, timeliness, or understandability. As discussed earlier, it is often difficult to fix, or even recognize, these measurement problems.

Marshall Industries, one of the largest electronic component distributors in the United States ($1.2 billion in sales in 1996) faced some of these measurement problems. In response, the company abandoned individual results controls for one important employee group, its sales force, substituting instead personnel/cultural controls. Marshall's results control system was based on full-commission compensation linked to sales. Sales was a flawed measure which made the sales people excessively short-term oriented and created many conflicts. Some salespeople hoarded inventory in their cars in case they needed it. They created a shipping rush at the end of every month as they generated last-minute orders to try to achieve monthly quotas, and some of these orders were shipped before customers needed them, thus harming customer relationships. The sales people were frequently arguing about who was responsible for sales which were really produced as a result of a team effort. Top management had to get involved to resolve these disputes.

Because of these problems, Marshall discontinued all of its sales commissions, incentives, and contests. All sales people were put on salary, although they were included in a company profit-sharing plan. Gordon Marshall, Marshall's chairman and CEO explained, "People don't work for money. They work hard because they want to work hard, because they have something important to do and they are part of something worthwhile. . . . Sure there are some lazy people. But we find out who they are and get rid of them."[14] These organizational elements, selection and creation of shared values, are defining elements of personnel/cultural control.

A second disadvantage of results controls is that when results are affected by anything other than an employee's own skill and effort, as they almost always are, results controls shift risk from owners to employees. This risk is caused by measurement noise created by any of the many *uncontrollable* factors, including environmental factors, organizational interdependencies, and *bad luck*.

Subjecting employees to this risk is bad because the vast majority of employees do not like risk (they are *risk averse*). When organizations force their employees to bear risk, they find they must offer these employees a higher expected level of compensation than if the employees were not subjected to the risk. This extra compensation is generally referred to as a *risk premium*. Failure to offer the premium makes it difficult for the organization to hire and retain employees.

Regardless of whether the risk premium is provided, the corporation will have to guard against employee's tendencies to take some risk-reducing, rather than value-maximizing, actions. Allowing employees to bear these forms of risk is inefficient; elaborate capital markets exist for just that purpose. Business owners are better able to bear these forms of risk because they can diversify their portfolios.

A third disadvantage is that results targets are often asked to perform two important, but competing, control functions. The first is motivation to achieve. For this function it is best for the targets to be challenging but achievable. The other function is communication. Plans are often treated as commitments and passed among the various entities in an organization so that each entity knows what to expect from the other entities. For this function the targets should be a best guess, or maybe even slightly conservative, to make sure they are achieved. Obviously, one set of plans cannot serve both purposes optimally; one purpose (or both) must be sacrificed if results controls are used.

DECISION 2: CHOICE OF CONTROL TIGHTNESS

The decision as to whether controls should be tight or loose in any particular company, or area within the company, depends on the answers to three questions: (1) What are the potential benefits of tight controls? (2) What are the costs? and (3) Are any harmful side effects likely?

In any organization, tight control is most beneficial over the areas most critical to the organization's success. These critical success factors can vary widely across businesses. A *Business Week* article focused on the trend toward superstores in many retail categories noted, correctly, that "Carrying heavy inventories without tight controls is, of course, a recipe for bankruptcy."[15] Tight inventory control can be implemented by focusing on either KRs, if employees can be trusted to figure out how to keep inventory near the optimal levels, or KAs, if managers want to dictate a set of inventory processes and decision rules. On the other hand, inventory control is of only minor importance in capital intensive service businesses. In airlines, for example, seat capacity is one of the critical success factors. Most airlines effect tight control in this area through extensive, careful preaction reviews over the airplane acquisition and replacement decisions.

In most businesses, the KAs or KRs and, hence, the benefits of tight controls are not stable. They can vary over time. Controlling purchases tightly may be essential in times of financial distress, but the costs of restricting employees' abilities to make some purchases may exceed the benefits when the company's financial situation improves.

Second, what are the costs involved in implementing tight controls? Some forms of control are costly to implement in tight form. Tight action controls in the form of preaction reviews can require considerable top management time. Tight results controls might require extensive studies to gather useful performance standards, or they might require new information systems or measuring equipment.

Third, are any harmful side effects likely? All the conditions necessary to make a type of control feasible, such as knowledge about how the control object relates to the desired ends, may not be present. If so, harmful side effects are likely if the control is implemented, particularly if the control is implemented in tight form. If the environment is unpredictable and the need for creativity is high, such as is the case for high-technology firms, good knowledge does not exist about either the actions that are needed or the results that should be accomplished. Therefore, neither action nor results control can be said to be clearly effective, and the implementation of either in tight form is likely to cause problems. Tight action controls would likely cause behavioral displacement and tend to stifle creativity. Tight results controls would limit adaptability, as results standards are often difficult to adjust to the changing environmental conditions.

Simultaneous Tight-Loose Controls

In a dated but oft-cited management book, *In Search of Excellence,* Peters and Waterman observed that a number of companies they defined as *excellent* employ what they call *simultaneous tight-loose controls.* They observed that the control systems used in these companies can be considered loose in that they allow, and even encourage, autonomy, entrepreneurship, and innovation, but that these same control systems can also be called tight because the people in the company share a set of rigid values (such as, focus on customers' needs). Peters and Waterman observed that policies and procedures and other types of controls are not necessary in these companies because "people way down the line know what they are supposed to do in most situations because the handful of guiding values is crystal clear"[17] and "culture regulates rigorously the few variables that do count."[18] In other words, the control systems in these companies are dominated by personnel/cultural control.

It sounds like nirvana: Let culture provide a high degree of reliance that the firms' employees are acting in their best interests and avoid most of the harmful side effects. This desirable state is difficult to achieve, and Peters and Waterman's observations do not provide much useful advice for managers of companies whose employees do not share a single set of values. Companies without strong cultures seem to be far in the majority. What do managers of the companies without strong cultures do?

It may be possible to approach a similar type of simultaneous tight-loose control even where a strong culture does not exist. This can be accomplished by using tight controls over the few key factors, either actions or results, that have the greatest potential impact on the success of the organization. More control should be exercised over strategically important areas than over minor areas, regardless of how easy it is to control each. Every KA or KR should be controlled as tightly as possible, because failure in one of these areas is, by definition, costly. None of the controls that might be substituted for culture can be assumed to be free of harmful side effects, but selective use of tight controls may limit these effects. Most individuals can tolerate a few restrictions if they are allowed some freedom of action in other areas.

ADAPTING TO CHANGE

Most firms emphasize one form of control for each given role, but they often change their emphasis from one form to another as their needs and capabilities change. As has been noted often, small companies can often be controlled adequately through the supervisory ability of a strong owner-manager, but as the companies grow, this form of action control has to be replaced. Here is an observation about that point, specifically referring to control in developing chains of restaurants:

> Energetic entrepreneurs are often very successful competitors because of their ability to control operations through intensive personal supervision of all the details of the restaurant. As the firm expands and the volume of business and number of locations increase, the task of control quickly exceeds the abilities of even the best entrepreneurial manager.[19]

As a consequence, as firms grow their controls evolve, usually toward increased formalization of procedures for action accountability purposes and/or development of more elaborate information systems for results control purposes.

This progression away from centralization and action control can be observed in many companies. From 1963 to 1974, the control system at the Massachusetts Port Authority (Massport) was dominated by personnel and action controls. The executive director, Ed King, was a strong leader who developed a staff of loyal employees, but he also centralized many key decisions and involved himself personally in detailed reviews of budgets and expenditures. King's successor, David Davis, instead chose to implement a formal decentralized control system with the emphasis on "clear responsibility and accountability at the operational levels."[20]

Had he remained in the organization as it grew, King might also have had to implement more formal controls, but much of the shift in controls must be attributed to differences in management style. The important point is that it is not possible to say that one control system worked better for Massport than the other. They were both effective for their respective times.

KEEPING A BEHAVIORAL FOCUS

What makes the analysis of controls so difficult is that their individual benefits and side effects are dependent on how people will react to the controls that are being considered. Predicting behaviors is far from an exact science. Significant behavioral differences exist among people in different countries, in different parts of a single country, in different firms, and in different areas of the same firm, and managers must be aware of such differences because the effectiveness of the controls used will vary depending on the reactions of the people involved. *Creative types,* such as advertising executives and design engineers, tend to react more negatively to action controls than do persons working in accounting or personnel. Some employees, particularly those at lower organizational levels, seem to be relatively highly interested in money as a reward, whereas others are more interested in stimulating work, autonomy, and challenge.

These differences make the application of controls particularly challenging, and it is crucial to emphasize that there is no one best form of control; what works best in one company, or area within a company, may not work in another. However, it is still important to keep the focus on the people involved because it is their responses that will determine the success or failure of the control system. The benefits of controls are derived only from their impacts on behaviors.

MAINTAINING GOOD CONTROL

What causes control problems so serious that a company is *out-of-control?* Actually, this condition is not rare. In addition to the many companies that no longer exist because their control systems failed them, the list of surviving companies that have been criticized for poor (or lax) controls is long and includes: Warner Communications,[21] Verbatim,[22] Rockwell International,[23] Mattel,[24] Chemical Investors,[25] Tandem,[26] Kidder Peabody,[27] and Apple Computer.[28]

The causes of the problems these companies have had can probably all be described in terms of either an imperfect understanding of the setting and/or the effect of the controls in that setting or an unwillingness to implement good controls. An imperfect understanding of the situation is often associated with rapid growth. Rapid growth often precipitates control problems because it causes the key factors that need to be controlled tightly to change. Growth sometimes also causes managers to delay the development of adequate controls, usually while they choose to emphasize marketing.

Personal style also makes some managers unwilling to implement proper controls, at least on a timely basis. Entrepreneurs, particularly, often find it difficult to relinquish the centralized control they exerted when their firm was small in order to adopt a more appropriate set of controls. This appeared to be the case at Warner Communications. Warner's former chairman, Steven Ross, seemed "uninterested in building formal structures to protect Warner from repeating past mistakes."[29]

Criticisms, however, should be made carefully. While many companies, probably including most of those mentioned in the list above, had control system weaknesses of various magnitudes, knowing what should be criticized is not easy. Control systems that do not look *neat* and *efficient* might not be deserving of criticism. It is not easy to keep a finely tuned set of controls in place, particularly when the company or function is operating in rapidly changing environments. Further, it may actually be desirable to implement control systems that are seemingly sloppy because these systems can minimize some of the harmful control system side effects. In its glory years of the 1970s and 1980s, Digital Equipment Corporation had what could be described as a rather loose control system. It used a four-dimensional matrix organization structure with unclear and overlapping lines of authority. Digital's management saw their company's *controlled chaos* as a virtue and, indeed, it probably contributed to the company's considerable success.

The explication of the advantages of control systems that are not too tidy has been presented several times recently in the research literature. One of the major conclusions coming out of Richard Vancil's large empirical study was that allowing *ambiguity* in the roles of profit center managers in decentralized firms is natural and not necessarily undesirable.[30] Bo Hedberg and Sten Jonsson suggest that *semi-confusing* information systems might be better than well-defined, well-established systems, especially in changing environments, because they can help keep the people in the organization alert for changes and receptive to them.[31]

Criticisms of control systems must be made with great caution. Controls that seem sloppy may have some unseen benefits, in terms of high creativity, a healthy spirit of cooperation, or low cost. Even the suffering of ill effects due to the occurrence of one or more of the control problems does not necessarily mean that a poor control system was in place. Control systems only reduce the probability of poor performance; they do not eliminate it.

The important point is that most criticisms should be leveled only after a thorough investigation of the situation. Control is a complex part of the management function. There is no perfect control system. There is no one best way to accomplish good control. There are many control benefits and costs that are not apparent at first glance.

Notes

1. P. F. Drucker, *Management: Tasks, Responsibilities, Practices* (New York: Harper & Row, 1974), p. 220.
2. D. H. Maister, "Hewitt Associates," case no. 2-681-063 (Boston: HBS Case Services, 1981).
3. J. F. Rockart, "Chief Executives Define Their Own Data Needs," *Harvard Business Review,* 57, no. 2 (March-April 1979), pp. 81–93.
4. J. Cook, "How to Beat the Recession—Any Recession," *Forbes* (December 20, 1982), p. 55.
5. Personal interview with the chairman of a small start-up company.

6. "JWT's 'Irregularities' Top $30 Million," *New York Times* (March 31, 1982), p. D2.
7. B. R. Schlender, "Yet Another Strategy for Apple," *Fortune* (October 22, 1990), p. 82.
8. Ibid., p. 87.
9. K. A. Merchant, "MIKO Corporation," case no. 9-181-068 (Boston: HBS Case Services, 1980).
10. Quotation from Regan Rockhill, a white-collar crime specialist with the accounting firm of Laventhol & Horwath, in "How to Prevent an Employee from Ripping Off the Firm," *Wall Street Journal* (May 5, 1982), p. 33.
11. M. Weber, *The Theory of Social and Economic Organizations,* trans. A. M. Henderson and T. Parsons (New York: Free Press, 1947), p. 337.
12. R. L. Sullivan, "Don't Count Your Chickens," *Forbes* (February 27, 1995), p. 102.
13. W. J. Abernathy, K. B. Clark, and A. M. Kantrow, *Industrial Renaissance: Producing a Competitive Future for America* (New York: Basic Books, 1983), p. 128.
14. Private conversations with Gordon Marhsall.
15. E. W. Book, "Here Comes a Cat Killer," *Business Week* (April 22, 1996), p. 52.
16. T. J. Peters and R. H. Waterman, Jr., *In Search of Excellence* (New York: Harper & Row, 1982).
17. Ibid., p. 76.
18. Ibid., p. 105.
19. D. D. Wyckoff and W. E. Sasser, *The Chain-Restaurant Industry* (Lexington, Mass.: Lexington Books [D. C. Heath], 1978), p. 1xv.
20. F. Jones and R. Herzlinger, "Massport," case no. 9-179-169 (Boston: HBS Case Services, 1979).
21. "How Steve Ross's Hands-Off Approach is Backfiring at Warner," *Business Week* (August 8, 1983), pp. 70–71.
22. K. K. Wiegner, "The One That Almost Got Away," *Forbes* (January 31, 1983), pp. 46–47.
23. D. P. Levin, "Poor Controls at Rockwell Helped Make It a Fraud Victim, Report Says," *Wall Street Journal* (August 18, 1983), p. 25.
24. S. J. Sansweet, "Troubles at Mattel Seen Extending Beyond Fallout in Electronics Line," *Wall Street Journal* (December 1, 1983), p. 1.
25. H. Klein, "Fast-Growing Company's Fall Attributed to Flawed Accounting and Risky Buyouts," *Wall Street Journal* (August 2, 1983), p. 31.
26. H. Klein, "Zooming Firms of 1980 Find That Fast Growth Can Turn into a Curse," *Wall Street Journal* (August 24, 1983), p. 1.
27. M. Siconolfi, "With Scandal Report Due Today, Kidder Ousts Another Official," *Wall Street Journal* (August 4, 1994), p. 1.
28. K. Rebello, P. Burrows, and I. Sager, "The Fall of an American Icon," *Business Week* (February 5, 1996), p. 39.
29. "How Steve Ross's Hands-Off Approach is Backfiring at Warner," *Business Week* (August 8, 1983), p. 70.
30. R. F. Vancil, *Decentralization: Managerial Ambiguity by Design* (Homewood, Ill.: Dow Jones-Irwin, 1979).
31. B. Hedberg and S. Jönsson, "Designing Semi-Confusing Information Systems for Organizations in Changing Environments," *Accounting, Organizations and Society,* 3, no. 1 (1978), pp. 47–64.

Rabobank Nederland

In May 1983, Hugo Steensma, general manager of the New York branch of Rabobank Nederland, reflected on the difficult challenges he faced in controlling the account management (lending) side of his branch:

> There is, I think, something of a conflict between the motivation to send our people out marketing and the control aspect of: "Yes, but I really want to make sure that our assets are of the highest quality." The competitive aspects of banking are tremendous in this country. There are over 14,000 domestic commercial banks, plus 337 foreign banks in this city alone, and there are also the savings and loans and other forms of financial institutions. We're all dealing with a commodity product—their money is just as green as ours. So marketing is very important to us.
>
> However, asset control is critical, too. If you figure out how many good loans it takes to make up for one bad loan, you'll see how important control over asset quality is. In addition to quality, we also have to be selective about where we find our quality accounts. We are a large retail bank (for example, we have 42 percent of the savings deposits in the Netherlands), and we are very sensitive to public opinion. We can't become involved in deals like financing unfriendly takeovers or arms shipments, no matter how profitable they might be.
>
> So, there is a very difficult trade-off here between entrepreneurship (marketing) and control, and just how to accomplish the proper balance is the toughest question for any corporation, I think. This may be particularly true for banks.
>
> As a large corporation, we tend to put in an incredible array of controls to make sure that our assets are of the highest quality and that they are serving good causes, and there is no doubt that these controls can diminish the entrepreneurial spirit of our account officers and take the edge off their performance. How do we strike the proper balance? I don't have the answer except that we want our officers to specialize and in the process become so good at the area they've specialized in that they develop a high level of credibility. Then we can let them exercise their entrepreneurial flair.

HISTORY OF RABOBANK NEDERLAND

Coöperatieve Centrale Raiffeisen-Boerenleenbank B.A., generally known as "Rabobank Nederland," was the central bank for a group of cooperative banks in the Netherlands known as the Rabobank Group. The Rabobank Group was the result of a merger between Coöperatieve Centrale Raiffeisen-Bank of Utrecht and Coöperatieve Centrale Boerenleenbank of Eindhoven in 1972. In 1983, the group included: (1) 964 local banks, all of them cooperative companies and having between them over 3,000 branches throughout the Netherlands and approximately 910,000 members; (2) Rabobank Nederland, the central bank for the local banks, which also functioned as a full-line commercial bank; and (3) special finance subsidiaries, including Rabohypotheebank N.V., a mortgage bank, and De Lage Landen N.V., which was active in consumer finance and leasing. All the Rabobank Group entities were financially and legally interlinked through a mutual guarantee system.

Rabobank Nederland was the liquidity manager for the local banks. The local banks had to place all deposits with Rabobank Nederland, and in return they were paid a nominal interest rate

Professor Kenneth A. Merchant of the University of Southern California prepared this case as the basis for class discussion rather than to illustrate either effective or ineffective handling of an administrative situation.

and were provided almost all of the services required for retail banking (e.g., check clearing, data processing, employee training). Rabobank Nederland also provided all funding that was obtained from outside the Group, participated in some of the larger loans made by the local banks, and provided a full range of services (e.g., lending, letters of credit, foreign exchange) for large customers.

Rabobank's strength in its home market, the Netherlands, made it among the 50 largest banks in the world, with total assets in 1983 of the equivalent of over $42 billion. (See financial statements in Exhibits 1 and 2). Rabobank had savings deposits from 8 million savers (in a country with a population of 14 million) and a total deposit base market share of approximately 40 percent. In terms of lending market share in the Netherlands, Rabobank had approximately 40 percent of the residential real estate loan base, of the commercial and industrial loan base, and, reflecting its focus on agriculture, approximately 90 percent of the agricultural loan base.

Hugo Steensma felt very good about the Rabobank organization:

> I think Rabobank is widely regarded as a top quality bank. There are many good reasons for our top financial ratings [AAA for bonds and A1/P1 for commercial paper]. We have high net worth, a good earnings record, low leverage, high quality assets, and none of the "typical" international problems, such as a lot of less-developed country debt and too many branches. We focus our activities on a single industry—agribusiness—in which we have a good track record. But we're willing to innovate; we're doing some new, exciting things.

THE NEW YORK BRANCH

In April 1981, Rabobank Nederland opened its first foreign branch—in New York. Hugo Steensma explained the rationale behind this move:

> We had three reasons for opening a New York branch. First, our physical presence in New York will help us serve our customers better and fulfill our corporate mission of being an international bank. Second, we will have a presence in the clearing/foreign exchange/ money and capital market center for U.S. dollars. Third, we will be better informed about the trends affecting profit opportunities and risks in the agribusiness industry on a worldwide basis.

The New York branch was primarily a wholesale operation. It made loans to U.S. or multinational companies, and, except for a $15 million capital contribution from Utrecht, it raised all its money in the U.S. money markets. Retail accounts were not encouraged; only about 15 demand accounts were established, all for Dutch traders who wanted to keep their money management business with Rabobank. Clearing services were contracted out to Irving Trust. No special services, such as cash management accounts, were offered to build the retail side of the business.

The total organization was small, as could be expected in a start-up mode. In April 1981, the branch included only 25 people (see Exhibit 3). The responsibilities of the account managers were differentiated by their area(s) of specialization which included, production agriculture, commodity trading, agricultural products processing and marketing, and coordination with corporations involved in Dutch-U.S. trade or investment.

The New York branch had direct authority to make loans. Rabobank delegated lending authority to Hugo Steensma. Hugo's approval limit was $5 million. This limit was relatively high for a foreign branch of a bank, but lower than what was typically given to the managers of domestic branches (e.g., the N.Y. branches of U.S.-based banks). Hugo in turn delegated lending authority for $1 million to each of his account officers. Hugo also established a credit Committee, consisting of himself and two account officers—Roger Barr and Joe Beresford—to review all loan proposals and to make decisions or recommendations on proposals over $1 million. For loans up to $5 million, the committee operated under Hugo's authority, and it was said that "the credit committee concurs that Hugo approves."

Proposals for loans greater than $5 million had to be approved by the Credit Committee in Utrecht. Mr. Steensma described the committee's role:

> The role of the Credit Committee in Utrecht is to make sure that the $30+ billion in loans

the bank has on the books are of the right quality so that hopefully we can continue to be in business for quite a while. In terms of the New York branch, they are taking a closer look right now because we're new, and the idea of a foreign branch is still a bit unfamiliar. They want to be very sure that the corporate perception of what's going on in New York remains healthy.

THE NORTH AMERICAN STRATEGY

The Rabobank strategy in the United States was to compete by building on its experience and contacts in agribusiness. One of the first actions Hugo Steensma took was to assemble a prioritized list of potential clients. The list included companies involved in all aspects of agribusiness—production, processing, and/or marketing of farm products of all types. The list was also divided into A (high) and B (lower) priority targets based on the size and type of business. For example, cooperatives were given higher priority because it was felt that Rabobank would have a comparative advantage in getting an entree with these organizations. Small organizations were given lower priority because of their relatively small needs for cash.

Another aspect of the Rabobank strategy was to become involved, hopefully on a partnership basis, with other agribusiness cooperative banks. These included international banks, such as France's Credit Agricole and West Germany's DG Bank, and those which were part of the U.S. Farm Credit System. Involvement in lending activities with these banks would serve to further the bankers understanding of the world agriculture industry. They would also provide a way of diversifying the lending risk, something that would be particularly helpful in the branch's early years.

THE ACCOUNT MANAGER'S ROLE

Some banks used account managers as salesmen who went out for loan prospects, and used another person to analyze and decide whether the deal should be made. Others, including Rabobank, left the prospect-generating and analysis functions together. According to Hugo Steensma, the goal of a Rabobank's account manager is to book good deals, period. While there was a lot of opportunity, the account manager had to manage his or her time productively. Hugo explained:

> As long as there are $10 million term[1] deals out there, we should not be spending time on $25 million, 90-day deals because the work involved in getting any prospect analyzed and approved is substantial. We also want to make a comfortable spread. It's a lot better to work a long time on a deal on which you make a 3 percent margin than an hour on one on which you only make 1/16 percent. Figuring out what to do requires self-initiative—entrepreneurship—and a lot of professional judgment.

In contrast to many large banks, Rabobank did not have an elaborate set of procedures that account officers needed to follow in identifying and analyzing prospects or in making presentations. This was partly due to the fact that Rabobank hired only experienced account managers who needed little guidance. Another reason was to avoid the administrative burden that formal communications would impose. The account managers had presumably established responsible work routines in their previous job, and standardization of new Rabobank routines costly for them to learn and uncomfortable for them to use. Hugo recognized that the organization was small, and informal, face-to-face communications could be used in place of formal communications.

Account managers were allowed considerable autonomy. Within the confines of the branch's charter and their own specialties, they were free to identify potential clients and to conduct discussion with them. When the account manager identified a loan prospect, he or she prepared a credit application. If the loan exceeded his or her individual lending limit ($1 million), the application had to be approved by the New York Credit Committee. If the loan was greater than $5 million, the Credit Committee in Utrecht had to approve it as well. There was no specific format required for credit applications, but they generally included a description of the client and its business, the proposed loan terms (e.g., payments, fees, interest, security, covenants) and an analysis

[1]Term loans are of medium length in duration. Seven or eight years is typical.

EXHIBIT 1 Rabobank Group—Consolidated Balance Sheet

As of December 31	*1982*	*1981*
ASSETS		
Cash and money at call	f 1,111,327,000	f 1,025,564,000
Treasury paper	4,665,561,000	4,026,946,000
Due from banks	17,058,594,000	18,742,314,000
Securities	3,965,971,000	3,293,724,000
Advances against Treasury paper and/or securities	232,904,000	82,805,000
Bills	189,153,000	93,578,000
Advances to or guaranteed by public authorities	12,671,819,000	12,591,949,000
Debtors	67,100,494,000	66,743,840,000
Equity investments and amounts due therefrom	337,299,000	320,165,000
Premises and equipment	2,825,036,000	2,560,022,000
TOTAL	f 110,158,158,000	f 109,481,007,000
LIABILITIES		
Own funds	f 5,220,721,000	f 4,694,416,000
Capital debentures	70,000,000	80,000,000
	f 5,290,721,000	f 4,774,416,000
Negotiable paper and loans not subordinated	13,619,097,000	14,775,313,000
Savings deposits	54,759,365,000	52,005,594,000
Time deposits	6,293,427,000	6,692,453,000
Creditors	16,268,923,000	14,242,104,000
Due to banks	13,312,156,000	14,809,712,000
Borrowed funds	614,469,000	2,181,415,000
TOTAL	f 110,158,158,000	f 109,481,007,000
Contingent liabilities on account of:		
Guarantees	1,158,884,000	910,066,000
Irrevocable letters of credit	109,971,000	73,256,000
Bills discounted with recourse	18,177,000	9,635,000

Note: 1.00 guilder (f) = US$0.381.

EXHIBIT 2 Rabobank Group—Consolidated Statement of Income

For the year ended December 31	*1982*	*1981*
INCOME		
Net interest	f 3,232,160,000	f 2,956,499,000
Commission	366,550,000	343,793,000
Other income	103,672,000	60,445,000
TOTAL INCOME	f 3,702,382,000	f 3,360,737,000
EXPENSES		
Personnel	1,607,548,000	1,404,079,000
General expenses	590,402,000	515,344,000
Depreciation	173,344,000	154,701,000
TOTAL EXPENSES	f 2,371,294,000	f 2,074,124,000
Income before provision and taxes	1,331,088,000	1,286,613,000
Addition to provision for general contingencies	580,437,000	472,456,000
Income before taxes	f 750,651,000	f 814,157,000
Taxes	261,632,000	286,119,000
NET INCOME	f 489,019,000	f 528,038,000

Note: 1.00 guilder (f) = US$0.381.

EXHIBIT 3 1981 Organization

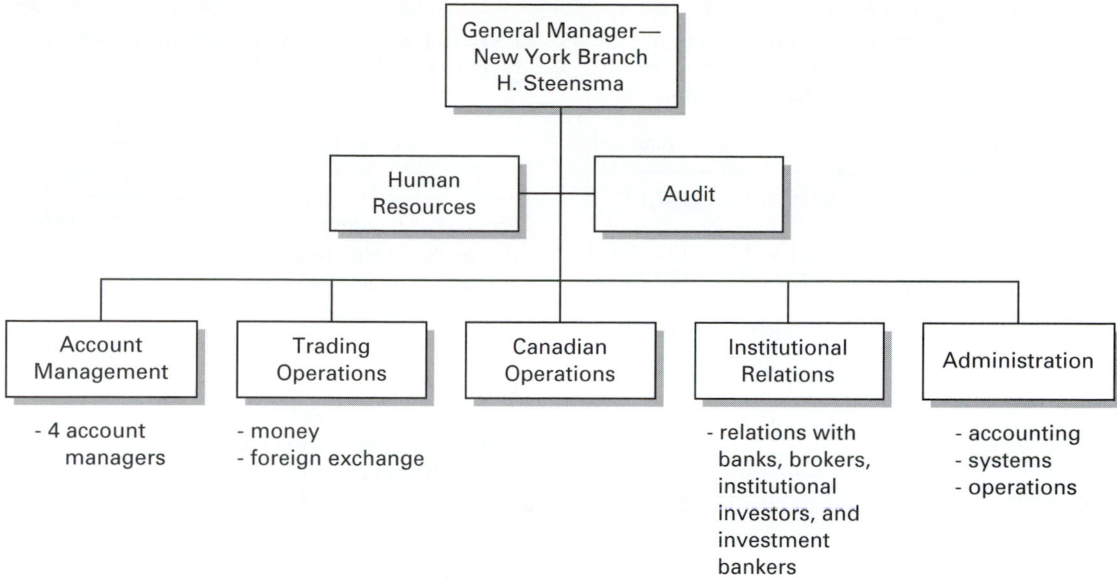

EXHIBIT 4 NTCC—Balance Sheets ($000s)

	1981	*1982*
CURRENT ASSETS		
Cash	$ 487	$ 1,074
Receivables	22,248	26,530
Due from members	13,785	1,815
Inventories	85,335	59,439
Prepaid expenses	7,577	5,432
TOTAL CURRENT ASSETS	$129,432	$ 94,290
OTHER ASSETS		
Land	3,122	3,102
Buildings and leasehold improvements	25,631	23,705
Machinery and equipment	60,840	56,019
Construction in progress	3,920	3,109
	$ 93,513	$ 85,935
Less accumulated depreciation	46,591	42,238
	$ 46,922	$ 43,697
INVESTMENTS	16,535	10,202
TOTAL ASSETS	$192,889	$148,189
Current Liabilities:		
Notes payable to banks	$ 85,300	$ 58,558
Accounts payable and accrued expenses	21,826	17,385
Current installments on long-term debt	2,993	556
TOTAL CURRENT LIABILITIES	$110,119	$ 76,499
Long term debt	45,073	39,849
Deferred income taxes	—	196
Members equity:		
Allocated equities	48,648	43,076
Unallocated impairment	(10,951)	(11,431)
	$ 72,770	$ 71,690
TOTAL LIABILITIES AND MEMBERS' EQUITY	$192,889	$148,189

EXHIBIT 5 NTCC—Statements of Operations ($000s)

	Year Ended May 31	
	1981	*1980*
NET SALES	$210,477	$197,137
Costs and expenses:		
Cost of sales	181,657	173,190
Interest	17,014	10,745
Selling, administrative and general	19,810	18,897
	$218,481	$202,832
Proceeds (loss) before income taxes (credits)	$ (8,004)	$ (5,695)
Income taxes (credits)	(626)	152
Net proceeds (loss)	$ (7,378)	$ (5,543)
Distributed as follows:		
Amounts payable to members	—	$780
Members' equity:		
Allocated credits	—	—
Unallocated impairments	480	270
Charged to members	7,858	4,493
	$ (7,378)	$ (5,543)

EXHIBIT 6 NTCC—Statements of Amounts Due to (from) Members ($000s)

	Year Ended May 31	
	1981	*1980*
Balance of beginning of year	$ (1,815)	$ 3,533
Established value of members' raw product delivered	45,432	36,720
Net proceeds (loss)	(7,378)	(5,543)
	$36,239	$34,710
Less:		
Investment retains	4,543	—
Acreage contribution receivable	508	—
Net proceeds credited to members' equity:		
Allocated credits	—	—
Unallocated impairment	—	270
Payments to members	44,973	36,255
	50,024	$36,525
Balance at end of year	($13,785)	($ 1,815)

EXHIBIT 7 NTCC—Statements of Members' Equity ($000s)

	Allocated Equities				Impairment			
	Credits	*New Acreage Contributions*	*Investment Retains*	*Total*	*Restricted Allocated Equities*	*Unallocated*	*Total*	*Total Equity*
Balance as of June 1, 1979	$42,713	$ 293	—	$43,006	$2,242	($13,943)	($11,701)	$31,305
Contributions	—	70	—	70	—	—	—	70
Credit to unallocated impairment	—	—	—	—	—	−270	270	270
Balance at May 31, 1980	$42,713	$ 363	—	$43,076	$2,242	($13,673)	($11,431)	$31,645
Contributions	—	2,044	—	2,044	—	—	—	2,044
Less contributions receivable	—	(1,015)	—	(1,015)	—	—	—	(1,015)
Credit to unallocated impairment	—	—	—	—	—	480	480	480
Investment retains	—	—	4,543	4,543	—	—	—	4,543
Balance at May 31, 1981	$42,713	$1,392	$4,543	$48,648	$2,242	($13,193)	($10,951)	$37,697

EXHIBIT 8 Outline of Formal Credit Application Package

1. Description of size and terms of loan, including pricing, collateral, and covenants—3 pages.
2. Narrative description of need for loan—2 pages.
3. Background information on cooperative—5 pages.
4. Financial analysis. Three pages of narrative supported by 7 pages of schedules, including:
    - Balance sheets and income statements—actuals for 1978–1981, projections for 1982–1985.
    - Statement of Changes in Working Capital—actuals for 1980–1981, projections for 1982–1985.
    - Analysis of Due From (To) Members—actuals for 1979–1981, projections through 1985.
    - Trade Analysis (Margins on Sales to Different Types of Customers)—for six months ended November 30, 1981.
    - Analysis of how ETCC could adjust member raw product payments to assure interest coverage during a difficult year.
    - Analysis of Profit and Cash Flow Impact of Purchasing Additional Processing Facilities—by year through 1987.

EXHIBIT 9 Summary Section of Credit Application

Positive

- A cooperative borrower with strong grower-members support and experienced management.
- Significant control over the cash paid to members and, hence, cash available to service debt.
- Opportunity to work with the Texas Bank for Cooperatives and Credit Agricole.
- Additional short-term loans will follow if we desire.

Negative

- Cotton industry is subject to supply fluctuations that significantly influence net proceeds.
- NTCC is negotiating for purchase of a fairly large cotton gin company. If acquired, this will cause high financial leverage for several years.
- NTCC is interest rate sensitive due to large floating rate borrowing requirements.

EXHIBIT 10 1983 Organization

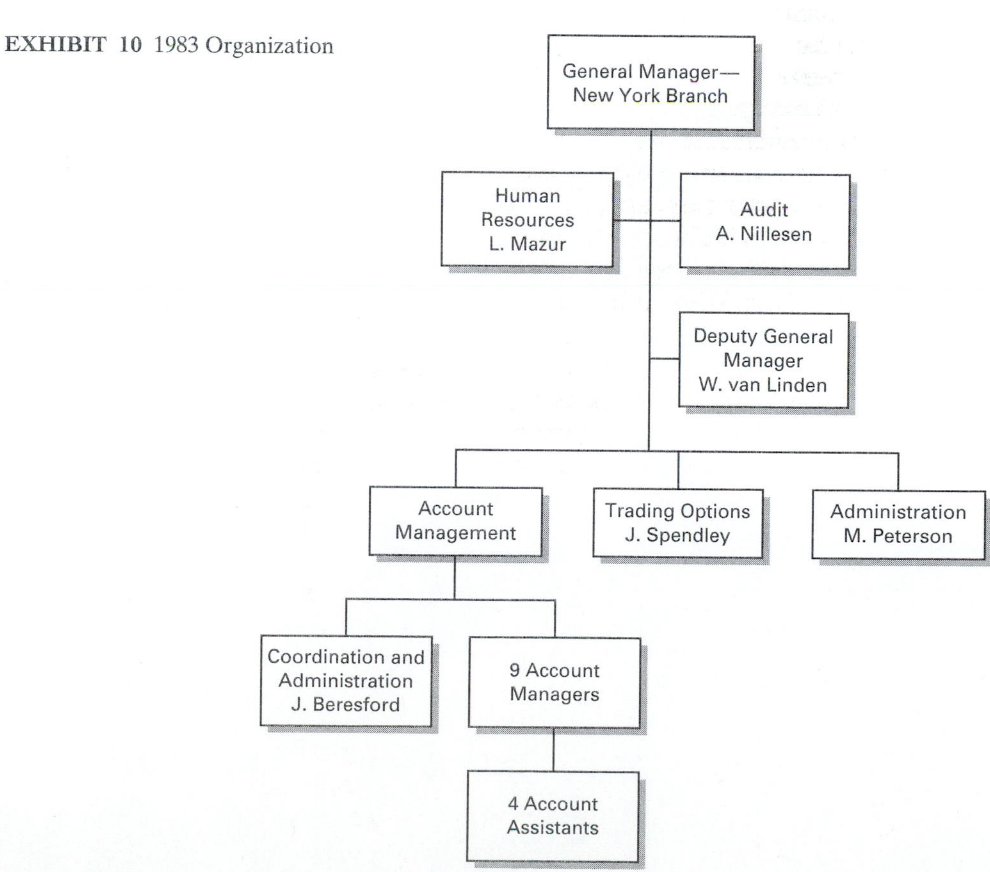

EXHIBIT 11 Four Reports Directly Related to Lending Activities Available on the Existing Information Systems

1. **Loan Portfolio Sheet (daily)**—This report listed the outstanding loans (which totaled approximately 60) by borrower and provided information such as loan amount, date of initiation, interest rate, and maturation date. Each month this report was used as a key input to the preparation (by hand) of the Loan Commitment Report which listed the loans outstanding, new commitments made during the month, and commitment transactions under negotiation. This Loan Commitment report was reviewed by the New York Loan Committee, and a copy was sent to the Credit Committee in Utrecht along with the minutes of the New York committee meeting.
2. **Balance Sheet and Income Statement**—As in most banks, these were prepared daily.
3. **Account Manager Status Report (monthly)**—This report provided a prioritized listing of all accounts or prospects, sorted by the account manager to whom they were assigned. The priorities were: (1) current borrowing relationship, (2) nonborrowing relationship (depositor), (3) high priority prospect, (4) lower priority prospect, and (5) other (not a current prospect, but want to record the company's existence). This report was not being used because the master account responsibility list needed updating: some account managers had changed their responsibilities without reporting the changes to the information coordinator.
4. **Account Manager Activity Report (monthly)**—This report listed the deals made and in progress for each account manager. It had been printed for a few months when the branch first opened and this discontinued because the information was not being used.

Assuming Control at Altex Aviation (A)

We closed on Altex Aviation in the late evening of December 29, 1971. Frank flew back to Los Angeles that night and I went up to Dallas immediately thereafter to pick up some papers and to resign from McKenzie & Booze. I took a check for $100,000, which represented all the cash we had, gave it to Bill Dickerson, who no longer owned the company, and said, "Would you give this to Sarah and have her deposit it." He said, "Fine"; he gave it to Sarah and she deposited it the next day. I went down to M&B, resigned, and then about lunch time, after saying goodbye to folks, I picked up the phone and called Sarah. With the $100,000 we gave her, Altex had $102,000 in the bank. I said, "Hello, Sarah, this is Ted Edwards," "Oh, Mr. Edwards," she said, "I am so glad you called. When will you be in?" I said, "I will be in shortly." She said, "Oh good, I have a few checks for you to sign." I said, "That's wonderful. What are the checks for?" She said, "I have written checks only for our most pressing bills. I tried very hard to make sure that only those that are most important be paid." I said, "That's fine. What's the total of the checks you have written?" She said, "$92,000." I said, "We'll discuss it."

I drove very calmly down to Altex Aviation to have my first confrontation with Sarah Arthur. Now I had envisioned, as every business school graduate does, that when I bought my company, I would walk in the front door the next morning; everyone would bow down; and there would be a brass band. Instead, I'm walking in through the back door (a) realizing that I have a crisis on my hands; (b) hoping no one is going to see me so I can deal with this crisis; and (c) of course, I don't really know how I am going to deal with it. What I did was, I said to Sarah, "We are *not* going to pay these bills." And she said, "Oh, but you *must.*" And I said, "No, *I* will decide what bills we are going to pay." She said, "Okay." And then sat back to watch this idiot make a fool of himself—that was my first day.

Thus did Ted Edwards describe the beginning of Frank Richards' and his ownership of Altex Aviation.

THE PURCHASE

Theodore Edwards and Frank Richards met in 1968 as graduate students at the Harvard Business School. Although planning on working initially for large companies, they decided they eventually wanted to own their own business. Upon graduation in 1970, Frank took a job in the corporate finance department with an electronics firm in Los Angeles, and Ted went with a New York consulting firm's Dallas office doing market planning.

After six months, Frank transferred to the marketing support group for the Southwest operations, and Ted and Frank saw each other frequently. In the process, they evolved the idea of going into business together, "In good business school fashion," said Frank, "we established some criteria, which were:

1. The company couldn't cost anything since we didn't have any money;
2. The company had to need what we had to offer—which we thought at that time were managerial skills;
3. The industry had to be fragmented and nonoligopolistic. We didn't want to be a small fish in a big pond;
4. We needed to be able to see our way clear to have the company grow at a rate of 20 percent per year the first five-year period."

This case was prepared by Professors Neil C. Churchill of SMU, Edmund M. Goodhue of MIT, and Kenneth A. Merchant of HBS as a basis for class discussion rather than to illustrate either effective or ineffective handling of an administrative situation.

Ted and Frank looked at a number of businesses over the next year and a half and in early fall of 1971, located a "fixed-base operation"[1] at San Miguel Airport in Texas that was losing money and looking for a buyer. After four months of negotiation, on December 29, 1971, Ted, age 26, and Frank, age 28, purchased the stock of the company for $10,000 each, assumed the lease on the building (and all the assets and liabilities) and were in business.

The lease on the facilities had a purchase option at a price considerably less than the market value. By exercising the option and then selling and leasing back the building, Ted and Frank were able to raise the $100,000 for working capital referred to above.

Ted and Frank had discussed the organization structure at Altex and agreed to decentralize its operations by making each operating activity a profit center and grouping them by departments. Each departmental manager would be given authority over his operations, including granting of credit, purchasing to a predetermined limit, setting policies, and collecting receivables. He would also be held responsible for its results. Frank was concerned, however:

> I agree with our decision to decentralize this authority, but I am concerned whether now is the time to do it. We will have a tough time when we first walk in the door and I don't know if the departmental managers can be taught some of these management techniques fast enough. After all, some have never finished high school. Maybe we should begin by making all these decisions ourselves for a month or two. I realize that we don't know the aviation business yet but even though neither of us has been a line manager, maybe we can learn the aviation business faster than some of our managers can learn formal management skills. Either way, we're putting the company on the line and the two-minute warning whistle has already blown.

During the four months they were negotiating the deal, Frank and Ted spent virtually every weekend together. Of this period, Ted commented:

> We spent something on the order of ten hours a week, of which maybe two or three hours would be trying to understand Sarah Arthur's accounting system and accounting statements, and another two or three on discussing pro forma financial projections and the rest on what we would do when we acquired it. Frank basically did the financial projections and I designed the accounting system. Actually, I dreamt it up one afternoon at McKenzie & Booze. I sat down at the IBM composer and designed the forms, using their artwork. Frank's projections, by profit center for the next ten years, showed that things were really tight. Even with the $100,000 from the sale and leaseback of the facilities, Frank projected that we were going to run out of money near the end of the first year. We knew this when we were negotiating for the company, and it made us a bit nervous.
>
> Well, three days before the closing, Frank came to me, white as a sheet, and confessed that we had made, not an arithmetic error, but a structural error in the projections. He was computing accounts payable on the wrong basis, and we were going to run out of money in three months. We had a little discussion as to whether we should blow the whole deal out of the water right there—knowing that we couldn't survive. He basically turned to me and said, "I will do whatever you want to do." I said, "Let's do it anyway." So we did it, but I have to say we were a bit shaken. We knew it would be an impossible job no matter how we sliced it but we were prepared to do it, and I must say we leaned on each other for support a great deal in the first few months.

Altex Aviation Prior to Purchase

Altex Aviation was one of eight fixed-base operations at San Miguel Airport which served Center County, Texas—one of the most rapidly growing communities in the nation. Altex had a loss of $100,000 on sales of $2,000,000 in fiscal year 1971, and this left the company with a negative net worth (see Exhibit 1). The company con-

[1]Fixed-based operations (FBO) are companies located on an airport that service the nonairline aviation market. They generally sell, fuel and maintain aircraft as well as provide flight instruction and charter services. These companies can range from small family operations to multiple-location companies with sales exceeding $100 million.

ducted activities through six informal departments, described below (see Exhibit 2). Altex's location on the airport is shown in Exhibit 3A.

FUEL (LINE) ACTIVITY

This activity employed some twelve unskilled fueling people, with an average tenure with the company of eight months, and three dispatchers who coordinated their activities via two-way radio. It was managed by Will Leonard, a man in his mid-30s, who had been the construction foreman for Bill Dickerson when Bill was a real estate developer. When Dickerson bought Altex in 1964, he brought Will Leonard with him to manage the line crew. Will was enthusiastic about his job, extremely loyal to Dickerson, and well liked by his employees. Although lacking in any theory of management (he had a high school diploma and some junior college credits), Will was a good first line manager who was instinctively people-conscious while holding them in line.

The fuel activity encompassed five operations:

Retail Fueling—A Phillips Petroleum franchise of underground storage of 60,000 gallons of jet fuel, 20,000 gallons of AV-Gas, and five fuel trucks to serve locally based and transient aircraft.

Wholesale Fueling—Service of a fuel farm for Tex Air, a regional airline, connecting San Miguel with cities in Texas, Louisiana, Arkansas, and Oklahoma. Altex charged a gallon-variable fee for this service. Tex Air bought its own fuel separately.

Fuel Hauling—An over-the-road fuel truck and a Texas Public Utilities permit to haul fuel on public roads. The truck, in essence, served Phillips, at a price, by delivering its fuel to Altex.

Rental Cars—An agency of a local automobile rental company. Basically, this was a service to transient pilots.

Tie-Downs—Storage of transient and San Miguel-based aircraft in six hangars and fifty open tie-downs.[2]

The fuel activity was open 18 hours a day, seven days a week, 365 days a year.

SERVICE AND PARTS

The service activity repaired, maintained, and overhauled piston-engined aircraft. It employed six mechanics and a departmental secretary. The parts activity, a separate accounting entity, employed one person and was managed by the head of service, as sales went almost entirely to the service activity.

The manager of these operations was Carl Green, a man in his 60s, who had been chief mechanic for Dove Aircraft at Love Field in Dallas prior to his moving to Altex. Before that, he was the mechanic/co-pilot for a Dallas oil executive. Carl had a high school diploma, aircraft and power plant licenses, and multi-engine and commercial pilot certificates. He knew airplanes, engines, and aircraft mechanics. He was, in Ted's words, "not a self-starter, had a bit of retirement mentality, and avoided conflict except when it came to quality: You would never worry about anything he rolled out of his shop."

FLIGHT TRAINING

The flight training activity was managed by Roy Douglas whose pilot's license was signed by one of the Wright Brothers. Roy had held several world records in aviation's early days and was highly respected by the aviation community. He spent a lot of time "hangar flying" with old cronies and, while he didn't manage the department in any real day-to-day sense, he hired the seven instructor pilots and three dispatchers, gave check rides[3] to students prior to their Federal Aviation Administration flight examination, and set safety policies. He and his chief dispatcher, who now had been with him for over ten years, were intensely loyal to both Altex Aviation and the flying community. They had, however, "seen everything and were surprised by nothing," and they were very resistant to change, be it new aircraft technology, aviation teaching methodology, or accounting systems.

---

[2]A tie-down is an area of asphalt or concrete with ropes where an aircraft is parked by tying it down to prevent it from rolling away or from sustaining wind damage. It is the aviation equivalent of a parking lot.

[3]FAA regulations require a certified instructor to check each student's competence prior to recommendation for the FAA flight examination.

The flight training activity, which had lost money each year, had two types of operations:

> *Flight School*—Flight training in 18 single-engine light aircraft from eight flight instructors coordinated by three dispatchers. Flight ratings were offered from private pilot through air transport ratings.
>
> *Pilot Shop*—Sales of flight supplies, such as logbooks, navigational charts, and personal and training flight supplies. Sales were made from three display counters by the flight school dispatchers.

AVIONICS

Avionics was a single-person activity conducted by Leon Praxis. Leon was a college-trained electronics technician whose interests were in repairing radios, and electronic navigational equipment from eight until five. Every day, however, he left promptly at five for his non-job-related activities.

AIRCRAFT SALES

Altex had been a Piper Aircraft dealer until two months before its sale. The owner, Bill Dickerson, was unable to finance the number of aircraft Piper required to be carried in inventory so he lost the franchise, fired his two salespeople, and closed down the department.

ACCOUNTING

The Accounting Department was central to the company in two ways. First, it was located in a glass-enclosed office in the center of the building (see Exhibit 3B) where it could be seen by everyone and everyone could be seen from it.[4] The second part of its centrality was the role that its manager, Sarah Arthur, played in Altex. Sarah had worked for Bill Dickerson for some twenty years. Indeed, in his absence, which was frequent, Sarah managed the company. While her title was accountant, she had no accounting training of any kind and her idea of running the company was to be the central repository of all information. She received and opened all the mail—not just accounting kind of mail—and she would distribute it to the department heads as she saw fit. What she distributed, in Ted's words, "was typically nothing—bills would come and she would keep them; checks would appear and she would keep them; and at the end of the day, she would collect cash from all the departments and keep it." Sarah managed all the receivables and payables.

All accounting information was Sarah's and nothing left her office. The department managers knew nothing about the profitability of their operations. All they knew was that airplanes would fly and that Sarah Arthur would come around at the end of each day and collect their money. Then occasionally she would berate the department managers for their high receivables. Of course, they had no idea how big their receivables were or who they represented; they would just be beaten over the head. Other times, mysteriously, suppliers would put the company COD and somebody would go to Sarah and say, "I want COD money, I can't get janitorial supplies" or "I need cash because I can't get aircraft parts," and she would say, "Okay," and mysteriously, a week later they would go off COD.

As Ted described it:

> The management system that was in place when we bought the company was one woman who magically kept everything in her head. There was a limited and almost incomprehensible formal system. There were basic financial statements and a set of reports that were produced for and according to Piper Aircraft's specifications each month but they helped Piper, not the management. We may have negotiated with Bill Dickerson but we were going to take over the management of the company from Sarah Arthur.

ASSUMING MANAGEMENT RESPONSIBILITIES

The Roles of Ted and Frank

Frank and Ted took over the business not only as full and equal partners but as best friends who understood each other very well. Frank assumed the chairmanship, and turned his attention to specific and critical projects, the first being the reestablishment of aircraft sales—potentially a major profit area. Ted took the title of president

[4]By contrast, the Aircraft Sales Department was located, according to Ted, "in an old dark office far away from the action."

and chief operating officer and began to manage the rest of the business. As Ted said later:

> I knew Frank wouldn't be at my right side at every decision but I made sure that four times a day I could walk into his office and say, "Frank, I don't really know what I am doing," and he would pat me on the back—symbolically—and put my head in order.

Frank, in turn, depended on Ted for operational inputs and intellectual support. They both worked 12-hour days, five days a week, with Ted, a bachelor, putting in 10–12 hours each day on weekends, and Frank, a family man, three or four hours on Saturdays and often on Sundays as well.

MANAGEMENT AND CONTROL

Beyond the immediate cash crisis, Ted viewed his three most important tasks as:

1. Revamping the management of Altex Aviation;
2. Installing a control system that would:
   a. support the management, and
   b. provide information needed in order to make the decisions. (Although the company wasn't large, it was rather complicated in terms of the businesses it was in.)
3. Wresting *de facto* control of the company from Sarah Arthur promptly.

Frank and Ted believed that it was very important to provide an environment where the departmental managers made correct decisions on their own since they had decided they could not make all the decisions themselves—they had neither the time nor the technical knowledge. As Ted put it:

> One of the things I was very concerned about was how to manage by providing an environment that encouraged the managers to make decisions the way I would want them made. That was very, very important to me. I wanted to provide a framework that didn't limit their actions but certainly provided very fast feedback as to how they were doing and made it personally worthwhile for them to do the right things. I spent a lot of time thinking about how to do that and it occurred to me that there were really two ways to do that. I recognize that there has to be the black hat and the white hat in any of these situations and so I decided to make the control system represent reality and my personal role would then be that of an emotional leader as opposed to a task leader. I would let the control system be the task leader, and then I could exert more avuncular personal leadership.
>
> I also realized that I didn't have the time to train everyone in the management approach we wanted to use at Altex. Nor did I have the guts to fire everyone and bring in new talent, and that wouldn't have been a good idea anyway. I also realized that unless I changed the basic attitudes in the company, we would never survive. In order to do that, we needed to do a lot of educating, and that would be my personal role. But, if I was going to do that successfully, I couldn't at the same time be berating them about the receivables, so it was necessary to take the nitty-gritty daily tasks of banging people over the head and put them somewhere else. I didn't really feel that Frank should do that and so to provide this environment for decentralized decision making was very, very important.

Ted began to implement a management control structure incorporating the following policies:

1. Profit centers would be established for each major activity. These profit centers would be combined where appropriate into departments;
2. Revenues and expenses would be identified by profit center and communicated to the profit center manager;
3. Departmental managers would be responsible for their profit centers and receive a bonus of 10 percent of their profit center profits after administrative allocation;
4. The profit center managers would have pricing authority for their products or services, both internally and externally; the fuel department manager could, and did, charge the Flight School retail price for the fuel they used whereas he charged the Service Department his cost for its oil;
5. The profit center managers could buy products externally rather than internally if it was in their best interests to do so. The Flight School manager could, and did, have his aircraft repaired outside Altex's shop when it was unable to fulfill his service needs;

6. The profit center managers could buy needed capital equipment and operating supplies on their own authority within established purchase order limits. Ted recalled one of the first times this decentralized authority was tested:

> When we bought the company, it had a mimeograph machine and an old, rotten, obsolete copier. They were under the control of Sarah Arthur and everyone who wanted a copy of anything had to go to Sarah, the Witch of the North, and plead—which was really an awful thing to do. I remember one day, Will Leonard, the manager of the Fuel Department, said, "Can I get a Xerox machine?" I said, "Will, you can do anything you want within limitations of the PO." So he acquired the smallest Xerox machine made, and he let everyone in the company make copies, charging them 10¢ a copy. At the end of the month, he would present bills to every department for the copies they used. He made money on his Xerox machine because everyone else was scared to death to walk into the Accounting Department and face the Witch of the North. Here was a classic entrepreneurial example, and it became almost a *cause celebre.* People were saying, "How did he get a Xerox machine? What right does he have to charge me for the Xerox machine?" I would say, "If you want a Xerox machine, go get one." But with one here at 10¢ a copy, they realized they couldn't really afford one themselves so they grumbled that Leonard had stolen the march on them.

7. The profit center managers had the authority to hire, fire, and administer the salary schedule in their departments quite independent of the rest of the company.

CASH MANAGEMENT

Cash and Accounts Payable

When Ted arrived at Altex on the first day of his ownership, he gathered up the checks Sarah had written and the accounts payable ledger cards, called in his departmental managers one by one and said, "Who are your most important suppliers?" Then he looked at the ledger cards to see how old the balances were and called up each of the suppliers saying, "I'm the new owner of Altex Aviation and I would like to come down and talk to you about our credit arrangements." Ted stated:

> Over the next six months, I got on good terms with the suppliers. I talked to them, took them out to lunch, and let them take me out to lunch. We paid them a little bit here and a little bit there and we stayed out of serious trouble.

A direct result of Ted's assumption of the accounts payable decision was that Sarah Arthur began to view her stay at Altex Aviation as being limited to the four months agreed upon. As it became clear that Ted was not going to let her make the management decisions anymore, she limited her work for the company strictly to the four-month transition period agreed upon in the purchase agreement. As Ted put it:

> She effectively said, "I will work from 11:00 a.m. to 2:00 p.m. every day. I will answer your questions and that is all." That was fine with me. I hired a new accounting clerk to be Sarah's assistant. She worked from 8 in the morning until 7 at night. I hired her; she worked for *me*; and when Sarah Arthur quietly packed up and left, after four months, the departure was easy.

CASH AND ACCOUNTS RECEIVABLE

With the accounts payable crisis on the road to a solution, Ted turned his attention to cash inflow. In his words:

> My biggest worry was how we were going to control cash, or rather, how I was going to provide a system that would motivate the departments to manage cash. The solution I came up with was to take the receivables and give them back to the departments. That was very controversial: everybody in the whole company fought me on that. Frank didn't like it—I was totally alone. The reason they didn't like it was severalfold. First of all, the managers didn't understand it. They had never seen receivables, they didn't know what they were. They felt as though they were playing with dynamite. "Here they are but what am I to do with them?" Frank, on the other hand, was concerned that things would get totally out of control because our

most important asset—our incoming cash flow—had suddenly been handed out to amateurs. Sarah Arthur may not have been perfect but she had a lot of experience.

In the Fuel Department, I handed the receivables to the dispatcher, a 20-year old surfer who had dropped out of college after two years. In the Flight School, I also gave them to the dispatcher, a 55-year-old, loyal employee. These were the only two departments with significant accounts receivables. In Service and Avionics, I gave them to the managers, but these were not significant.

Literally, one Saturday morning, I went to a stationery store and bought a metal folder and some ledger cards, and I sat down in the Accounting Office while Sarah was not there. I transferred all the balances over to the ledger cards and physically presented them to these two women—the de facto departmental heads. Then I sat down and showed them how to use the forms using the current week's transactions. So we started to collect data on the accounts receivable.

To motivate the department heads to manage their accounts receivables, Ted gave them the credit-granting authority and the responsibility for collections. He also established the following monthly charges against their departmental profits:

Receivables	60 days old or less	1% of the balance
Receivables	60–90 days old	3% of the balance
Receivables	90–120 days old	6% of the balance
Receivables	over 120 days old	Charged the unpaid balance to the profit center

CASH AND THE BANKS

When Frank and Ted acquired Altex, they also acquired short-term bank notes payable of $60,000 from the Center National Bank which had been outstanding for several years. Ted was concerned since if Center National Bank called the notes, it would put the company into bankruptcy. As Ted recalled:

One of the people I called just before we bought the company was Harold Lattimer, the manager of the branch we did business with. I took him out to dinner, and over dinner and a glass of wine, I told him about myself, what I was doing, my thoughts and I said, "We have this problem of the $60,000 I owe you." He replied, "What do you want to do with it?" I said, "I would love to convert it to a 24-month note to get it out of the short-term category so as to increase our working capital to make us more attractive to our suppliers. That way we can get better terms from them." He looked at me and said, "Fine, I'll do it."

He had made a gut decision based upon some vibrations, and I was shocked since I was prepared to negotiate with him, I thought to myself, "The basis upon which business is done, at least with this man, is total candor and honesty." So I started this program of giving the bank our internal financial reports every month along with a cover letter summarizing what I was doing. Hal's reaction was superb. He thought it was the greatest thing he'd seen. No customer had ever done that to him before, ever! The result was that whenever I went to him—we paid off the loan ahead of time—and said, "Hal, it looks as if I'm going to need $100,000 for 60 days," he would say, "Yes, I've been following it, I've been watching your receivables growing because of your extra business. I know a growing business needs this money from time to time. It's no problem and I'll put the money in your account this afternoon."

The Accounting System

By the end of the second month, Altex was producing a profit and loss statement on the activities of each department. (Appedix A shows the August 1972 reports for the fuel department.) Each department kept account of its own sales, receivables, inventories, expenses and, through the PO system, expenses initiated by the department.

In order to provide a predictable and simple method of cost allocation which still would be understood and managed by the department heads, Ted established an Administration Profit Center which paid taxes, borrowed money, paid interest, utilities, bills, and other general administrative expenses. The Administrative Department in turn levied a series of monthly charges to each department as follows:

I wanted to be basically independent. The reports weren't all that onerous. It might have been childish, but it was partly, "I own this place and no one is going to tell me what to do." It was also partly a feeling that I wanted to establish an equal relationship with Piper. I did not want to come to them as a supplicant. For the past several years, Altex had always been begging Daddy Piper for handouts. I wanted to establish a relationship with them that was one of equals. "We have different jobs to do. You help me. I help you." So it was psychological but also I didn't want to waste the time of my people on something that I did not think would be productive. I told them they could have access to any of our reports that they wanted. I said, "Here are our forms. If there is any information that you would like that is not here, we would be happy to supply it, and if you want to transfer this information to a Piper form, go ahead. But we think all the information is here." They didn't like it but they bought it. I think Frank worked pretty hard on that one.

After obtaining the Piper franchise, Frank rehired the old salesmen but personally shepherded the first aircraft sales through. The first one was, in Frank's word, "memorable." He continued:

Our first sale was to a local Chevrolet dealer. He wanted to buy the aircraft, but he wouldn't pay for it until it arrived at San Miguel saying, "In my business, you don't pay for a car until you see it." Now we had to pay for it when we picked it up at the factory, so I asked Ted how we stood. He said, "We have enough money although if he doesn't pay for it, we won't make the next payroll, and we will be out $40,000 for however long it takes to get the airplane from Vero Beach to here. But I'm willing to do it. Go do whatever you have to do." So we did. I engaged the son of the aircraft salesman to fly the airplane. Unfortunately, there was horrible weather that grounded him in Tuscaloosa, Alabama for a week—thunderstorms and everything. I nearly lost my mind. I had committed every last cent the company had, and it was sitting in Tuscaloosa. That's how tight things were.

Profitability of the aircraft sales activity proved to be highly variable between months. For example, while losses were shown in May and August 1972 (see Exhibits 7 and 8), several very high-margin sales, accounting for nearly $100,000 in operating profit, were made in the June–July 1972 period.

Personnel Management

In the second month of Ted and Frank's ownership, Will Leonard, the manager of the Fuel Department resigned. There were two reasons: First, a local newspaper had written up Altex Aviation and the new boy wonder owners in a way that seemed to disparage the former owner, a close friend of Will's. The second involved Ted and Frank's philosophy of management. As Ted related it:

One of the fuel drivers came to us about two weeks after we bought the company and said, "The former owner never let us wear mustaches or beards or anything like that. How do you guys feel about mustaches or beards?"

Now there was a lot of feeling about facial hair and long hair during that period and the fuel drivers were in contact with the public. Frank and I wanted to say, "We agree with the former owners." But we were consistent Harvard Business School people and we said, "As long as it does not affect your work performance, you can do anything you want." As a result, beards started cropping up all over the place. The manager of the Fuel Department rightly felt that he had been undercut, and he quit. We really blew that. We were dumb—just from pure inexperience, naivete. He was not that valuable, but that is not the way to get rid of a man—forcing him to quit in a huff.

MANAGEMENT STYLE

In running the company, Ted took an active role both through long hours of planning and managing and also through learning and doing. He learned to fly and got a multi-engine commercial license, changed the oil in the shop, and worked on the engines. It was as Ted said:

. . . a part of the process of being an avuncular, emotional leader. In the first couple of years, I deliberately set out to make my role a teacher. The first thing I did in my office was to put up a blackboard and arrange the furniture so that there was a sofa facing the blackboard and a sidechair canted towards the blackboard. My desk was at right angles to the blackboard—all of us could see it. When departmental managers would come to me with problems, rather than focusing on the problem, we would talk about the process. I would say, "Where is your accounting data? Where are your profit center reports? What do your profit center reports tell you about this problem? What thought processes did you go through to extract information from the profit center reports that would help you solve this problem? What alternatives did you consider?" And I did this in a typical Socratic teaching process. Through Frank's and my personal involvement in the company and through this teaching approach, we could not only obviate Frank's forecast of bankruptcy in three months, but we could rely on our managers and build for the future.

EXHIBIT 1 Balance Sheets (000's)

Assets	*8/26/71*[a]	*1/1/72*[b]	*Liabilities and Net Worth*	*8/26/71*	*1/1/72*
Cash and Marketable Securities	$ 8	$ 88	Accounts Payable–Trade	$ 62	$ 50
Accounts Receivable	25	49	Accounts Payable–Phillips Oil	112	116
Contracts Receivable–current	51[c]	15	Contracts Payable–Current	31	33
Financing Commissions Due	20	20	Customer Deposits	—	2
Receivables from Officers & Employees	68	—	Notes Payable	88	31
Other Receivables	14	—	Accrued Expenses	32	35
Inventory:			Deferred Block Time	5	4
Aircraft	33	103	Other Current Liabilities	2	2
Parts and Flight Supplies	50	45	Total Current Liabilities	332	273
Fuel	13	25			
Work in Process	7	2	Contracts Payable–long-term	41	90
Prepaid Expenses	7	30	Long-term debt	424	34
Total Current Assets	296	377	Total Liabilities	797	397
Fixed Assets (net)	437	27	Net Worth	(17)	62
Contracts Receivable–long-term	—	26	Total Liabilities and Net Worth	$780	$459
Investments	29	29			
Other	18	—			
Total Assets	$780	$459			

[a]Fiscal year-end before purchase
[b]Just after purchase
[c]Not split out between current and long-term
No room on Piper aircraft form to do so.

EXHIBIT 2 Pre-Purchase Organizational Chart

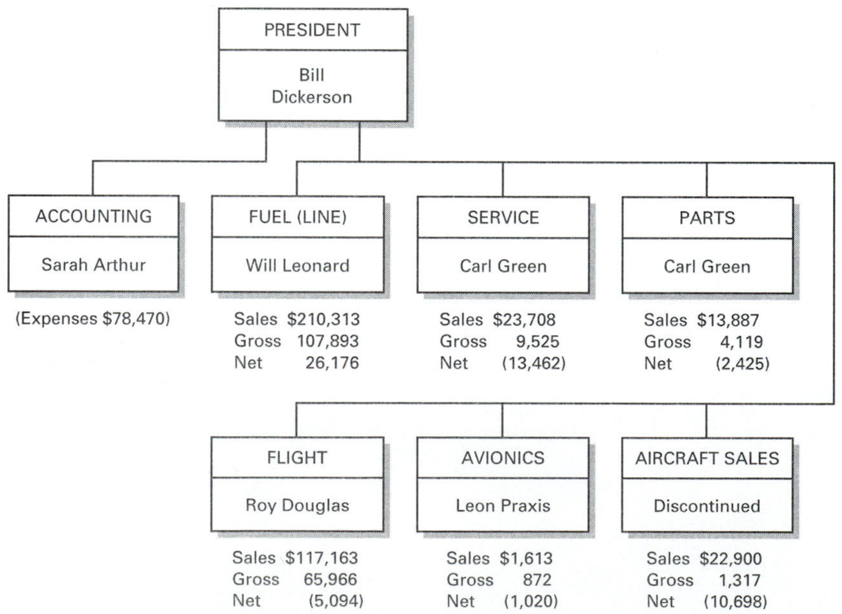

Sales, Gross Profit Margin, and Net Income were for the four months preceding purchase — September–December, 1971. Profit was calculated from the extant accounting system which fully allocated administrative costs. Comparable figures for the August 31, 1970 fiscal year were Sales $2,073,000, Gross $657,000, Net ($109,000).

EXHIBIT 3A Physical Facilities
29 December 1971

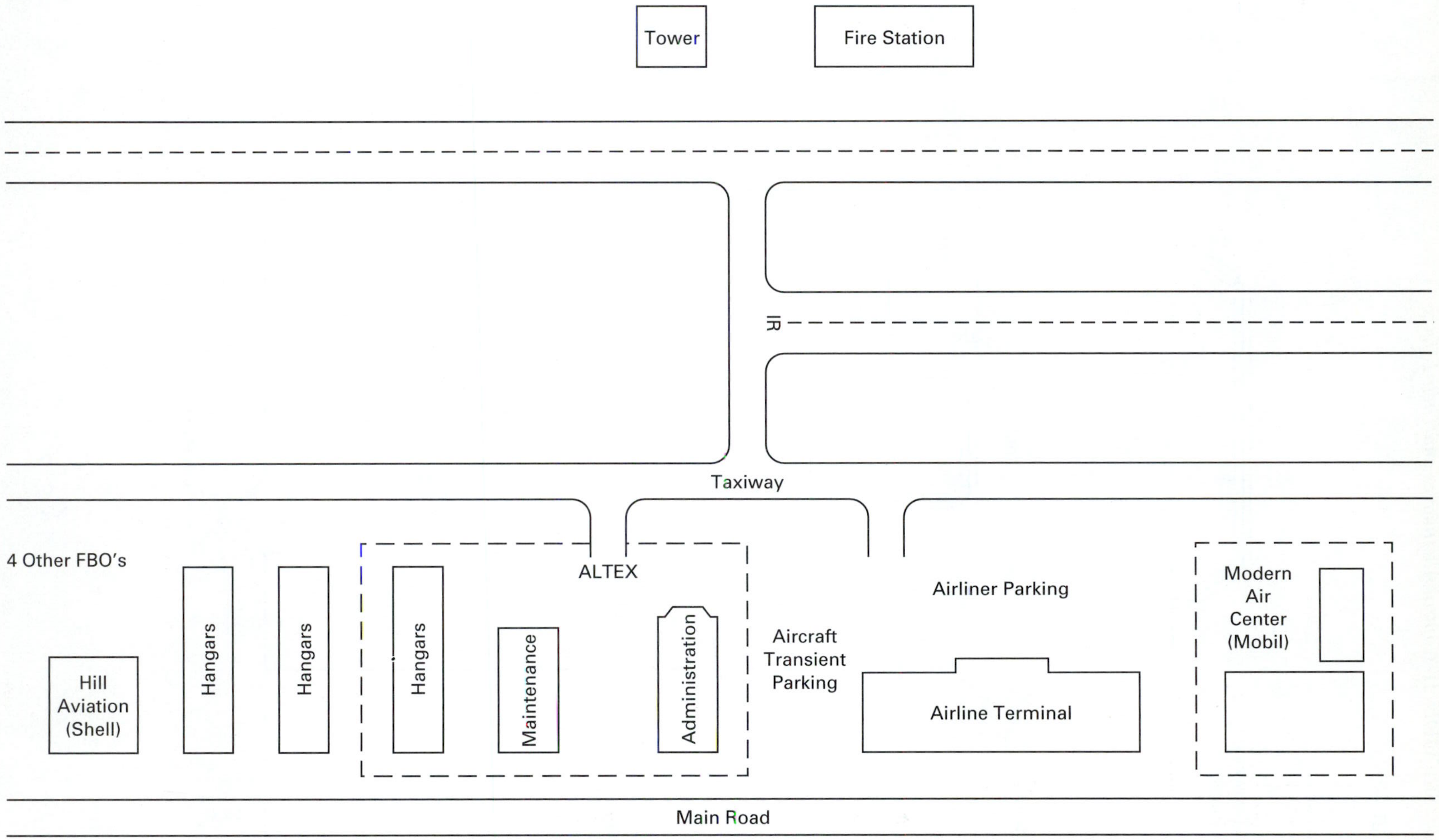

EXHIBIT 3B

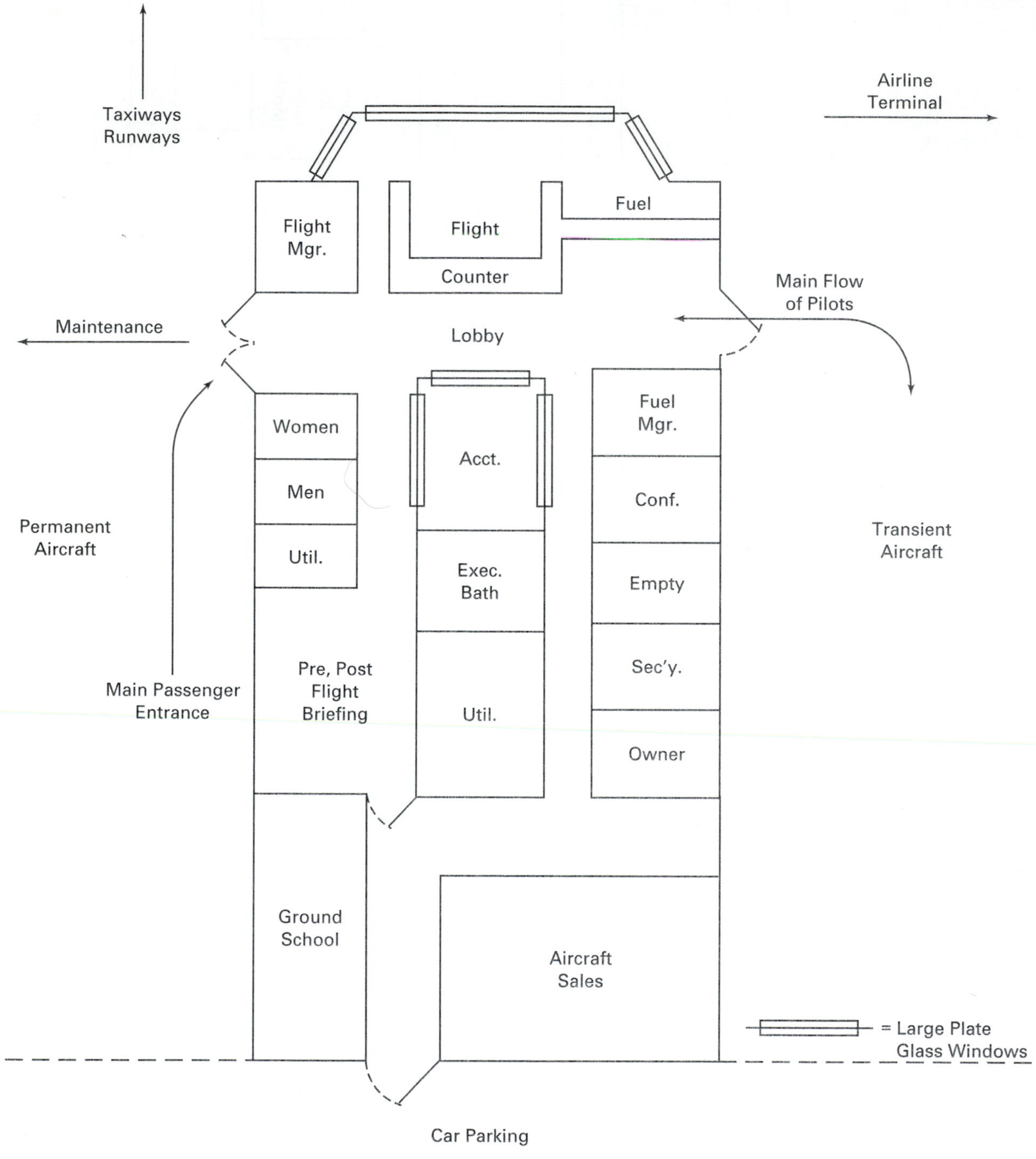

Taxiways
Runways

Airline
Terminal

Flight
Mgr.

Flight
Counter

Fuel

Main Flow
of Pilots

Maintenance

Lobby

Women

Men

Util.

Acct.

Exec.
Bath

Util.

Fuel
Mgr.

Conf.

Empty

Sec'y.

Owner

Permanent
Aircraft

Transient
Aircraft

Main Passenger
Entrance

Pre, Post
Flight
Briefing

Ground
School

Aircraft
Sales

= Large Plate
Glass Windows

Car Parking

EXHIBIT 4 Summary Balance Sheets (at end of month indicated) (000's)

Assets	*Feb. 1972*	*May 1972*	*Aug. 1972*	*Liabilities and Net Worth*	*Feb. 1972*	*May 1972*	*Aug. 1972*
Cash and Marketable Securities	$ 67	$112	$129	Accounts Payable–Trade	$ 39	$ 38	$ 47
Accounts Receivable	52	73	91	Accounts Payable–Phillips Oil	103	102	52
Contracts Receivable–current	35	4	4	Contracts Payable–Current	34	33	46
Finance Accounts Receivable	12	12	12	Customer Deposits	1	4	1
Inventory:				Notes Payable	29	28	27
Aircraft	103	144	183	Accrued Expenses	30	35	14
Parts	52	52	53	Deferred Block Time	14	21	20
Fuel	20	19	15	Total Current Liabilities	250	261	207
Work in process and other	0	2	8	Contracts Payable–long-term	85	85	104
Prepaid Expenses	30	32	39	Long-term debt	34	104	104
Total Current Assets	371	450	534	Total Liabilities	369	450	415
Contracts Receivable–long-term	5	4	3				
Fixed Assets (net)	28	27	28	Net worth	64	63	187
Investments and Other	29	32	37	Total Liabilities and Net Worth	$433	$513	$602
Total Assets	$433	$513	$602				

EXHIBIT 5 Summary Monthly Income and Operating Statements (for period indicated) (000's)

Corporate Summary	*Jan.–Feb. 1972*	*May 1972*	*August 1972*
Sales	$181	$164	$162
Cost of Sales	146	133	113
Gross Margin	35	31	49
Total Expenses	24	28	29
Operating Profit (Loss)	$ 11	$ 3	$ 20
Profit (Loss) by Activity			
Parts	$ (1)	$ (2)	$ 1
Radio[a]	(2)	—	—
Service	0	(2)	4
Flight School	3	4	3
Flight Supplies	1	(1)	0
Tie-Downs and Hangars	(1)	0	0
Fuel Hauling	(1)	1	2
Retail Avgas	0	(2)	2
Retail Jet Fuel		4	3
Wholesale Fuel	4	7	11
Aircraft Sales	3	(4)	(6)
Car Rentals	(1)	—	—
Charter	—	0	2
Unrecovered Admin. Costs (+ = gain)	6	(2)	(2)
Total Operating Profit	$ 11	$ 3	$ 20
Other Income	0	1	1
Extraordinary Items	(22)	(8)	(2)
TOTAL INCOME	$(11)	$ (4)	$ 19

[a]Merged with Service Dpt. in March 1972.

EXHIBIT 6 Summary Income Statements by Activity—January–February 1972 ($000's)

	Parts	*Radio*	*Service*	*Flight School*	*Flight Supplies*	*Tie-Downs & Hangars*	*Fuel Hauling*	*Retail Fuel**	*Wholesale Fuel*	*Aircraft Sales*	*Car Rentals***
Sales	4.7	-0-	11.0	23.4	1.7	3.8	2.7	50.0	5.4	87.9	.7
Cost of Product	3.4	1.4	2.3	10.4	***	1.2	1.6	37.5		76.4	.6
Salaries & Commissions	.5		3.0	5.7	.3	.6	.6	5.8	.5	.5	.3
Payroll-related Exp.	.1		.6	1.1		.3	.1	.6			
	4.0	1.4	5.9	17.2	.3	2.1	2.3	43.9	.5	76.9	.9
Gross Margin	.7	(1.4)	5.1	6.2	1.4	1.7	.4	6.1	4.9	11.0	(.2)
Other Expenses	1.6	.1	5.2	3.7	.8	2.7	1.6	6.0	.5	7.9	.2
Operating Profit	(.9)	(1.5)	(.1)	2.5	.6	(1.0)	(1.2)	.1	4.4	3.1	(.4)

*Avgas and jet fuel

**Discontinued in April

***Could not be captured in January–February because inventory control system not yet in place

EXHIBIT 7 Summary Income Statements by Activity—May 1972 ($000's)

	Parts	*Service*	*Flight School*	*Flight Supplies*	*Tie-Downs & Hangars*	*Fuel Hauling*	*Retail Avgas.*	*Retail Jet Fuel*	*Wholesale Fuel*	*Aircraft Sales*	*Charter**
Sales	4.8	8.2	39.4	2.0	4.4	3.8	26.4	18.9	9.6	45.1	1.6
Cost of Product	3.8	.1	20.5	1.4	1.3	.8	18.0	13.2		42.9**	1.4
Direct Payroll	.7	4.3	8.9	.4	.4	.8	4.8	1.3	1.0		
Commissions							1.0				
Payroll-related Exp.	.1	.7	1.1		.2	.6	.8	.2	.1		
	4.6	5.1	30.5	1.8	1.9	2.2	24.6	14.7	1.1	42.9	1.4
Gross Margin	.2	3.1	8.9	.2	2.5	1.6	1.8	4.2	8.5	2.2	.2
Other Expenses	1.7	4.8	5.8	.8	2.7	.5	4.4	.6	1.6	6.2	.1
Operating Profit	(1.5)	(1.7)	4.1	(.6)	(.2)	1.1	(2.6)	3.6	6.9	(4.0)	.1

*Charter activity started in May

**Costs not broken out after March

EXHIBIT 8 Summary Income Statements by Activity – August 1972 ($000's)

	Parts	*Service*	*Flight School*	*Flight Supplies*	*Tie-Downs & Hangars*	*Fuel Hauling*	*Retail Avgas.*	*Retail Jet Fuel*	*Wholesale Fuel*	*Aircraft Sales*	*Charter*
Sales	10.1	16.4	33.4	2.0	4.9	4.3	28.6	13.7	14.0	22.3	12.3
Cost of Product	6.3	3.0	17.4	1.2	1.0	.8	20.2	11.7		19.9	6.8
Salaries & Commissions	.6	4.0	7.5	.3	.6	.7	4.6	.8	1.0		.6
Payroll-related Exp.	.1	.8	.8	.1	.2	.7	1.8				
	7.0	7.8	25.7	1.6	1.8	2.2	26.6	12.5	1.0	19.9	7.4
Gross Margin	3.1	8.6	7.7	.4	3.1	2.1	2.0	1.2	13.0	2.4	4.9
Other Expenses	2.0	4.7	5.2	.8	2.8	.4	(.2)*	(1.7)*	1.5	8.6	2.5
Operating Profit	1.1	3.9	2.5	(.4)	.3	1.7	2.2	2.9	11.5	(6.2)	2.4

*Includes Inventory Adjustment (end of year)

EXHIBIT 9 Flight Department Daily Report

DATE: ______________

SALES
Primary Ground School . . . . ______________
Flight Instruction (Wait, Ground Training, Pre-Post) . . . . ______________
Leaseback Owner's Rental + Employees Rental . . . . (______________) . . . . ______________
+ Cost of Sales
Rental (Solo) . . . . ______________
Flight Supplies and Over Counter Sale-Retail Sales . . . . ______________
Sales Tax Collected . . . . ______________
Check Rides . . . . ______________
Waiver . . . . ______________
Mexican Insurance . . . . ______________
Car Wash and Aircraft Wash + Tie-downs . . . . ______________
Student Tuition Refund Fee . . . . ______________
Enrollment Fee + X-C Dues . . . . ______________
Interest Service Charges . . . . ______________

RECEIPTS TOTAL $______________ (1)
Cash or Checks . . . . ______________
Credit Card Payment . . . (Phillips ____________) . . . . . . (AX ____________) ______________
Block Accounts and Block Account Supplies . . . . ______________
Altex Charges and Altex Charge Supplies . . . . ______________
Master Charge and Visa . . . . ______________
Leaseback Refunds . . . . ______________

DIRECT COST OF SALES TOTAL $______________ (2)
Leaseback Expenses . . . . ______________
Instructor Wages . . . . ______________
Cost of Supplies Sold Today . . . . ______________
TOTAL $______________ (3)

APPENDIX A

Profit Center Reports
Fuel Department
August 31, 1972

Profit Center Report

	Retail Jet Fuel, August 1972					
	This Month			*2/1/72 to Date*		
	Actual	*Budget*	*Variance*	*Actual*	*Budget*	*Variance*
Sales	13,686			69,527		
Direct Payroll	797			4,502		
Commissions		N/A				
Overtime & Vacations						
Fringe at %	12			160		
Payroll Taxes				290		
Cost of Product	11,688			51,659		
Gross Margin	1,189			12,916		
Expenses						
Supervisory Payroll	341			1,796		
Commissions						
Fringe at %	10			54		
Payroll Taxes						
Administrative	547			3,339		
Use of Assets	41			41		
Advertising						
Demonstration Flights[1]						
Bad Debts						
Telephone, etc.						
Donations, Dues, etc.						
Freight, Postage, etc.						
Insurance						
Inventory Adjustment	(3,079)			(5,125)		
Maintenance						
Professional Services						
Rent	200			800		
Supplies						
Tie-Downs[2]						
Travel, Entertainment						
Utilities						
Vehicles	215			860		
Warranty						
Adjustments						
Cash O/S				20		
Miscellaneous	7			7		
Total Expenses	(1,718)			1,792		
Total Profit (Loss)	2,907			11,124		

Cost of Product Detail
Primary Cost[3]
Freight, Delivery[4]
Taxes[5]
Other Costs
____
____
____

Less Breakdown[6]
____
____
____
____

Breakdown of Administrative Charges

	Retail Jet Fuel, August 1972		
		Rate	*Charge*
Total Direct Payroll (incl. comm., overtime, etc.)	$______	___% =	$______
Total Supervisory Payroll	$______	___% =	$______
	Total		$______

Breakdown of Charges for Use of Assets

Item	*Amount*	*Rate*	*Charge*
Accounts Receivable (less than 60 days)	$______	1.0% =	$______
Accounts Receivable (60–90 days)	$______	3.0% =	$______
Accounts Receivable (over 90 days)	$______	6.0% =	$______
Inventory	$ 2,752	1.5% =	$ 41
Market Value of Physical Assets Used			
________________	$______	1.5% =	$______
________________	$______	1.5% =	$______
________________	$______	1.5% =	$______
________________	$______	1.5% =	$______
________________	$______	1.5% =	$______
________________	$______	1.5% =	$______
Total			$ 41

[1] For any use by any department that uses flight school planes for demonstration or promotion purposes. This amount is the same as if a customer rented one of our aircraft and is credited to flight school sales.

[2] This is a charge for aircraft under your control that used tie-down space and appears as part of the revenue of the tie-down department.

[3] Primary cost is:

Parts: invoice cost of parts sold
Service: transfer cost of parts used or installed
Flight: cost of leasebacks
Fuel: cost of fuel and oil
Sales: cost of aircraft

[4] All freight and delivery charges are added to the inventory cost of products and become an expense when the product is sold. For the fuel department, PUC rates are used.

[5] This includes all taxes that we must pay for the products used, primarily excise taxes. These taxes are carried in inventory and are expensed when the product is sold.

[6] Each department head can specify how he wants his sales broken down. This subcategory should be used for different activities that are not sufficiently separable to warrant becoming a separate profit center. For example, service might be subdivided into flat rate sales versus time and material sales. The flight school department might wish to separate instruction from charter.

Profit Center Report

	Retail AVGAS, August 1972					
	This Month			*2/1/72 to Date*		
	Actual	*Budget*	*Variance*	*Actual*	*Budget*	*Variance*
Sales	28,623	N/A	N/A	105,132		
Direct Payroll	4,605			18,610		
Commissions	910			3,596		
Overtime & Vacations	229			481		
Fringe at %	252			921		
Payroll Taxes	403			1,814		
Cost of Product	20,234			72,142		
Gross Margin	1,990			7,568		
Expenses						
Supervisory Payroll	340			1,813		
Commissions						
Fringe at %	10			55		
Payroll Taxes						
Administrative	1,145			4,971		
Use of Assets	376			1,562		
Advertising						
Demonstration Flights						
Bad Debts						
Telephone, etc.						
Donations, Dues, etc.						
Freight, Postage, etc.				13		
Insurance	200			401		
Inventory Adjustment	(3,935)			(2,042)		
Maintenance	278			1,064		
Professional Services						
Rent	239			596		
Supplies	182			977		
Tie-Downs						
Travel, Entertainment						
Utilities						
Vehicles	865			3,999		
Warranty						
Adjustments						
Cash O/S						
Miscellaneous	68			96		
Total Expenses	(232)			13,505		
Total Profit (Loss)	2,222			(5,937)		
Cost of Product Detail						
Primary Cost						
Freight, Delivery						
Taxes						
Other Costs						
__________						
__________						
__________						

Less Breakdown

____
____
____
____

Breakdown of Administrative Charges

	Retail AVGAS, August 1972		
		Rate	*Charge*
Total Direct Payroll (incl. comm., overtime, etc.)	$______	___% =	$_____
Total Supervisory Payroll	$______	___% =	$_____
	Total	....	$_____

Breakdown of Charges for Use of Assets

Item	*Amount*	*Rate*	*Charge*
Accounts Receivable (less than 60 days)	$ 6,111	1.0% =	$ 61
Accounts Receivable (60–90 days)	$ 1,903	3.0% =	$ 57
Accounts Receivable (over 90 days)	$ 1,032	6.0% =	$ 62
Inventory	$ 9,187	1.5% =	$ 138
Market Value of Physical Assets Used			
____________________	$ 3,902	1.5% =	$ 58
____________________	$______	1.5% =	$_____
____________________	$______	1.5% =	$_____
____________________	$______	1.5% =	$_____
____________________	$______	1.5% =	$_____
____________________	$______	1.5% =	$_____
Total			$ 376

Profit Center Report

	Wholesale Fuel, August 1972					
	This Month			*2/1/72 to Date*		
	Actual	*Budget*	*Variance*	*Actual*	*Budget*	*Variance*
Sales	13,977	8,200	(5,777)	66,746		
Direct Payroll	981			6,716		
Commissions						
Overtime & Vacations						
Fringe at %	39			275		
Payroll Taxes						
Cost of Product				173		
Gross Margin	12,957	6,900	6,507	59,582		
Expenses						
Supervisory Payroll	84			882		
Commissions						
Fringe at %	3			28		
Payroll Taxes						
Administrative	559			3,278		
Use of Assets	124			622		
Advertising						
Demonstration Flights						
Bad Debts						
Telephone, etc.						
Donations, Dues, etc.						
Freight, Postage, etc.						
Insurance						
Inventory Adjustment				(231)		
Maintenance						
Professional Services						
Rent	159			1,113		
Supplies						
Tie-Downs						
Travel, Entertainment						
Utilities						
Vehicles	575			2,875		
Warranty						
Adjustments						
Cash O/S						
Miscellaneous						
Total Expenses	1,504	1,500	(4)	(8,567)		
Total Profit (Loss)	11,453	5,400	6,053	51,015		
Cost of Product Detail						
Primary Cost						
Freight, Delivery						
Taxes						
Other Costs						
____________						
____________						
____________						

Less Breakdown

____
____
____
____

Breakdown of Administrative Charges

	Wholesale Fuel, August 1972		
		Rate	*Charge*
Total Direct Payroll (incl. comm., overtime, etc.)	$ ______	___% =	$ ______
Total Supervisory Payroll	$ ______	___% =	$ ______
	Total		$ ______

Breakdown of Charges for Use of Assets

Item	*Amount*	*Rate*	*Charge*
Accounts Receivable (less than 60 days)	$ ______	1.0% =	$ ______
Accounts Receivable (60–90 days)	$ ______	3.0% =	$ ______
Accounts Receivable (over 90 days)	$ ______	6.0% =	$ ______
Inventory	$ 8,257	1.5% =	$ 124
Market Value of Physical Assets Used			
____________________	$ ______	1.5% =	$ ______
____________________	$ ______	1.5% =	$ ______
____________________	$ ______	1.5% =	$ ______
____________________	$ ______	1.5% =	$ ______
____________________	$ ______	1.5% =	$ ______
____________________	$ ______	1.5% =	$ ______
Total			$ ______

Profit Center Report

	Fuel Hauling, August 1972					
	This Month			*2/1/72 to Date*		
	Actual	*Budget*	*Variance*	*Actual*	*Budget*	*Variance*
Sales	4,335`	3,700	635	24,994		
Direct Payroll	736			5,037		
Commissions						
Overtime & Vacations	568			2,286		
Fringe at %	52			307		
Payroll Taxes	67			568		
Cost of Product	775			6,470		
Gross Margin	2,137	1,600	537	10,326		
Expenses						
Supervisory Payroll						
Commissions						
Fringe at %						
Payroll Taxes						
Administrative	173			1,197		
Use of Assets						
Advertising						
Demonstration Flights						
Bad Debts						
Telephone, etc.						
Donations, Dues, etc.						
Freight, Postage, etc.				397		
Insurance				35		
Inventory Adjustment						
Maintenance	139			1,339		
Professional Services						
Rent	80			559		
Supplies				711		
Tie-Downs						
Travel, Entertainment						
Utilities						
Vehicles						
Warranty						
Adjustments						
Cash O/S				45		
Miscellaneous						
Total Expenses	392	700	308	4,283		
Total Profit (Loss)	1,745	900	845	6,043		
Cost of Product Detail						
Primary Cost						
Freight, Delivery						
Taxes						
Other Costs						
____________						
____________						
____________						
Less Breakdown						
____________						
____________						
____________						
____________						

Profit Center Report

	Tie-Downs and Hangars, August 1972					
	This Month			*2/1/72 to Date*		
	Actual	*Budget*	*Variance*	*Actual*	*Budget*	*Variance*
Sales	4,923	4,800	(123)	31,984		
Direct Payroll	649			3,220		
Commissions						
Overtime & Vacations	134			964		
Fringe at %	31			175		
Payroll Taxes	26			297		
Cost of Product	1,000			8,259		
Gross Margin	3,083	3,000	83	19,069		
Expenses						
Supervisory Payroll	85			534		
Commissions						
Fringe at %	3			17		
Payroll Taxes						
Administrative	197			1,587		
Use of Assets						
Advertising						
Demonstration Flights						
Expenses						
Bad Debts						
Telephone, etc.						
Donations, Dues, etc.						
Freight, Postage, etc.						
Insurance						
Inventory Adjustment						
Maintenance						
Professional Services						
Rent	2,467			17,269		
Supplies						
Tie-Downs						
Travel, Entertainment						
Utilities						
Vehicles						
Warranty						
Adjustments						
Cash O/S						
Miscellaneous						
Total Expenses	2,752	2,800	48	19,407		
Total Profit (Loss)	331	200	131	(338)		
Cost of Product Detail						
Primary Cost						
Freight, Delivery						
Taxes						
Other Costs						
________________						
________________						
________________						
Less Breakdown						
________________						
________________						
________________						
________________						

Section III: Financial Results Control Systems

CHAPTER 8

Financial Responsibility Centers

The vast majority of organizations control the behaviors of many of their employees, particularly their managers, through *financial results control systems.* In financial results control systems, results are defined in monetary terms, most commonly in terms of accounting measures such as revenues, costs, profits, and returns (on assets, capital, or equity). Financial results control systems are powerful systems with wide applicability.

Financial results control systems have three core elements: (1) financial responsibility centers (which define the apportioning of accountability for financial results within the organization), (2) formal management processes, such as planning and budgeting (which are used for defining performance expectations and standards for evaluating performance), and (3) motivational contracts (which define the links between results and various organizational rewards and punishments). Financial results control systems also rely on what are commonly referred to as *internal controls* which ensure the reliability of the organization's information. These were discussed in Chapter 3.

This chapter lists the advantages of financial results control systems and discusses in depth one important element of these systems: financial responsibility centers. The other financial results control system elements and common system problems are discussed in later chapters.

ADVANTAGES OF FINANCIAL RESULTS CONTROL SYSTEMS

Several good reasons explain the ubiquity of financial results control systems in business organizations. First, financial objectives are paramount for profit-making firms.[1] Profits and cash flows ensure the organizations' survival. They also provide returns to investors and are among the primary measures outsiders use to evaluate the organizations' performances. Thus, it is natural that managers of profit-making organizations monitor their success in financial terms and use the financial measures to direct their employees' actions toward important organizational ends. Managers of not-for-profit organizations must also monitor finances closely because cash flows usually create significant constraints for their organizations.

Second, financial measures provide a comprehensive, summary measure of performance. They aggregate the effects of a broad range of operating qualities or characteristics into a single measure, thus reducing the possibility of conflicting signals about the importance of the various operating indicators. They provide a useful way of aggregating across different categories of activities, products, or services. They remind employees that the various operating improvements they may bring about; such as in units of production, response times, defect rates, delivery reliability, or product capabilities, benefit the organization only if they result in improved financial performance.

Because they are a comprehensive summary measure of performance, financial measures provide a relatively easy and inexpensive way for upper-level managers to ensure that everything is working as they had hoped. Their simplicity is particularly valuable for top managers of complex, diversified firms. The top-level managers can usually set corporate goals in financial terms, decompose the corporate goals into multiple financial responsibility centers, and then monitor only one (or just a few) results measures; that is, accounting profits or returns and their components (revenues, costs, assets, and liabilities), which provide a good summary of the effects of most of the actions needing to be controlled. The managers then do not need to track either the actions that are affecting financial performance (for example, how time was spent, how specific expenditures were made) or the specific line items that comprise the summary measures of performance until performance problems (such as, declining profits or failures to achieve targets) appear in the summary measures. As a consequence, the amount of information that managers need to assimilate is reduced. This process of getting involved only when problems appear is often referred to as *management-by-exception*.

Third, most financial measures are relatively precise and objective. They generally provide significant measurement advantages over *soft* qualitative and subjective information and over many other quantifiable alternatives (for example, quality or customer satisfaction). Cash flows (the financial measure primitive) are easy to observe and measure; and accounting rules, on which many financial measures are built, are described in writing in great detail. This detail limits the financial measurement possibilities (management discretion) and facilitates the verification of the resulting measures, thus minimizing the potential for disputes.

Fourth, financial results controls can provide a relatively subtle or unobtrusive form of control. They provide control while allowing those being controlled considerable autonomy. This freedom of action allows managers to adapt their operations to fit their managerial styles, and it may stimulate creative thinking.

Fifth, financial results controls have wide applicability. They can be effective even when management does not know what specific actions are best, as is often the case in uncertain environments and with jobs that require considerable professional judgment.

Finally, the cost of implementing financial results controls is often small relative to that of other forms of control. This is because the core financial results control measurement elements are largely in place. Organizations already routinely prepare and transmit through formally defined channels elaborate sets of accounting information that must be sent to government agencies, creditors, shareholders, and/or potential investors. This information can readily and inexpensively be adapted for control uses.

TYPES OF FINANCIAL RESPONSIBILITY CENTERS

All but the smallest organizations use financial results control systems as at least a part of their overall control systems. Financial responsibility centers are a central part of these systems. The term *responsibility center* denotes the apportioning of responsibility (or accountability) for a particular set of outputs and/or inputs to an individual (or a group of individuals). Responsibilities can be expressed in terms of physical units of output, particular characteristics of the services provided (such as defects, schedule attainment, or overall customer satisfaction), quantities of inputs consumed, or financial indicators of sets of performance in these areas. *Financial responsibility centers* are responsibility centers in which the individuals' responsibilities are defined at least partially in financial terms. Where the financial responsibility is defined in accounting terms, as is common at managerial levels in most organizations, the organization is said to use *responsibility accounting*. Responsibility accounting is a reporting system that classifies accounting (and often other) information about an organization's activities according to the managers responsible for them.

Four basic types of financial responsibility centers can be distinguished: investment centers, profit centers, revenue centers, and cost centers. These centers are distinguishable by the financial statement line items which the managers are held accountable for in each type of center, as shown in Table 8-1.

Investment Centers

Investment centers are responsibility centers whose managers are held accountable for the accounting returns (profits) on the investment made to generate those returns. A corporation is an investment center, so top-level corporate managers, such as the chairman, president, and chief operating officer, are investment

TABLE 8-1 Typical Examples of Financial Responsibility Centers

Selected Financial Statement Line Items	*Revenue Center*	*Cost Center*	*Profit Center*	*Investment Center*
INCOME STATEMENT				
Revenue	x		x	x
Cost of Goods Sold		x	x	x
Gross Margin			x	x
Advertising and Promotion		x	x	x
Research and Development		x	x	x
Profit Before Tax			x	x
Income Tax			x	x
Profit After Tax			x	x
BALANCE SHEET				
Accounts Receivable				x
Inventory				x
Fixed Assets				x
Accounts Payable				x
Debt				x

(x signifies that the responsibility center manager is (or could be) held accountable for some elements included in that financial statement line item) center managers; as are the managers of many corporate subsidiaries, operating groups, and divisions.[2]

Accounting returns can be defined in many ways, but they typically involve a ratio of the profits earned to the investment dollars used. The varying definitions cause many different labels to be put on the investment centers' *bottom line,* such as return-on-investment (ROI), return-on-equity (ROE), return-on-capital-employed (ROCE), return-on-net-assets (RONA), and return-on-total-capital (ROTC). Differences between these investment center variations follow.

Profit Centers

Profit centers are responsibility centers whose managers are held accountable for profit, which is a measure of the difference between the revenues generated and the costs of generating those revenues. Organizational terminology is not precise, and many corporations call their investment center managers profit center managers, although a conceptual distinction can be made between investment centers and profit centers.

Profit centers (some of which are investment centers) are an important control element of the vast majority of companies above minimal size. In a survey conducted in the late 1970s of 684 manufacturing companies whose financial officers were members of the Financial Executives Institute, 83 percent of the firms reporting had two or more profit (or investment) centers.[3] Another survey conducted at about the same time, this of the Fortune 100 industrial companies, showed that 96 percent of the 620 firms responding comprised multiple profit centers.[4]

Profit centers come in many different forms, some of which are considerably more limited in scope of operations than others. In deciding whether or not a responsibility center manager truly has profit center responsibility, the critical question to ask is whether the manager has significant influence over both revenues and costs.

One limited form of profit center is created when sales-focused entities are made into profit centers by charging the responsible managers the standard cost of the products sold, thus making them accountable for gross margin. As narrow as this form of profit center is, this assignment of costs provides the manager with useful information because decisions about marketing direction and intensity will be made based on the incremental contribution to the firm, gross margins, not gross revenues.

Another limited form of profit center is created where cost-focused entities are assigned revenues based on a simple function of costs. A typical example exists where manufacturing and administrative departments supply unique products or services for which external market prices cannot be determined to internal customers only. Revenues for these entities might be calculated as cost plus a 20 percent markup. Thus, the revenues are not affected by changes in short-term market conditions.

Are these cost-focused entities profit centers? It depends on the extent to which the employees in these entities influence the revenue figure. If their customers can outsource their purchases, then the employees in these entities probably do have considerable influence over the revenue that will be assigned to them. They can produce quality products or services; they can provide superior delivery schedules; and they can provide friendly, hassle-free customer service. The entity managers make multiple decisions requiring revenue/cost trade-offs. If the employees do not have significant control over the revenues assigned, however, these entities are merely *pseudo* profit centers. Assigning revenues to these entities, and thus allowing a *profit* figure to be shown, is merely a way to charge the buying entities a full cost-plus approximation of a market price so that their profits are not overstated and so their returns can be compared more easily with entities which source externally.

In deciding whether an entity is a profit center, it is *not* important to consider whether the entity's goal is to maximize profits or whether any revenues are generated from outside the organization. The financial goal of many profit centers, such as most of those in not-for-profit organizations, is to break-even, or perhaps even incur limited losses and, significantly, it is normally *not considered desirable* to generate higher profits than was budgeted. The goal of these organizations is to provide maximum services to constituencies within the constraint applied by the profit budgeted. Still, these entities should be considered profit centers because their managers make trade-offs between revenues and expenses.

Similarly, it is not necessary that a profit center generate any revenue from outside the organization. Many profit centers derive most, or even all, of their revenues by selling their products or services to other entities within the same organization. These sales are made at what are called *transfer prices* and are discussed in detail in Chapter 15.

Revenue Centers

Revenue centers are responsibility centers whose managers are held accountable for generating revenues, which is a financial measure of output. Common examples are sales managers and, in not-for-profit organizations, fundraising managers.

Revenue, rather than profit, provides a simple and effective way to encourage sales and marketing managers to attract and retain customers. It will encourage them to make profitable sales, however, if and only if it can be ascertained that all sales are approximately equally profitable. If all revenues are not equally endowed, controlling with a revenue center structure can encourage personnel to make easy sales, rather than those that most benefit the company.

Most revenue center managers are also held accountable for some expenses. For example, many sales managers are accountable for their salespeople's salaries and commissions and perhaps some advertising expenses. While these managers are held accountable for both revenues and costs, they should not be considered profit center managers because no profit calculation relating outputs to inputs is calculated. The difference between the revenues and expenses for which revenue center managers are held accountable is not meaningful because the expenses are typically a tiny fraction of the revenues generated; revenue centers are not charged for the costs of the goods or services that they sell. These managers should be considered to manage both a revenue center and a cost center, or a *net revenue* center.

Cost or Expense Centers

Cost or expense centers are responsibility centers whose managers are held accountable for some elements of cost or expense. Costs and expenses are financial measures of the inputs to or resources consumed by the responsibility center.[5] In standard *cost centers,* such as manufacturing departments, the outputs are relatively easy to measure. Further, the causal relationship between inputs and outputs is direct and relatively stable. Thus, control can be exercised by comparing a standard cost (the cost of the inputs that *should have been* consumed in producing the output) with the cost that was *actually incurred.*

In discretionary *expense centers* (sometimes called managed cost centers), such as research and development departments and administrative departments (for example, personnel, purchasing, accounting, and facilities), the outputs produced are difficult to value in monetary terms. In addition, the relationship between inputs and outputs is not well known. Evaluations of expense center managers' performances often have a large subjective component to them. Control is usually exercised by ensuring that the expense center organization adheres to a budgeted level of expenditures while successfully accomplishing the tasks assigned to it.

VARIETY WITHIN EACH FINANCIAL RESPONSIBILITY CENTER TYPE

While the four categories of financial responsibility centers can be distinguished, there is considerable variety within each financial responsibility type. Table 8-2 shows four responsibility centers, each of which is a profit center even though the breadth of responsibility, as reflected in the number of income statement line items for which the managers are held accountable, varies considerably. *Gross margin* managers may be quite low-level salespeople who happen to sell products of varying margins. The *profit* measure gives them an incentive to sell higher margin products, rather than merely generating additional, possibly unprofitable, revenues. The *incomplete* profit center managers may be managers of product divisions, but without authority for all of the functions that affect the success of their products, such as research and development or sales. *Complete* profit center managers may be senior vice presidents who are accountable for all aspects of the worldwide performance of major business segments. Similar variety among the other responsibility center types is also common as the managers are held accountable for more or fewer financial statement line items.

HIERARCHY OF FINANCIAL RESPONSIBILITY CENTERS

The four financial responsibility center types can be contrasted in a hierarchy reflecting the breadth of financial responsibility, or the number of financial statement line items for which the manager is held accountable, as was shown in Table

TABLE 8-2 Four Types of Profit Centers

Selected Financial Statement Line Items	*Gross Margin Center*	*Incomplete Profit Center*	*Before-Tax Profit Center*	*Complete Profit Center*
INCOME STATEMENT				
Revenue	x	x	x	x
Cost of Goods Sold	x	x	x	x
Gross Margin	x	x	x	x
Advertising and Promotion		x	x	x
Research and Development			x	x
Profit Before Tax			x	x
Income Tax				x
Profit After Tax				x

(x signifies that the responsibility center manager is held accountable for that financial statement line item)

TABLE 8-3 Subtle Distinctions Between Profit Centers and Investment Centers

Items for Which Manager is Held Accountable	*A* Profit Center	*B* Investment Profit Center	*C* Not Quite an Investment Center
Profit	x		x
Return on Assets		x	
Days' Receivables			x
Inventory Turnover			x
Asset Turnover			x

(x signifies that the responsibility center manager is held accountable for that financial statement line item)

8-1. Revenue and cost center managers are held accountable for only one, or sometimes a few, income statement line items. Profit center managers are held accountable for some revenue and some expense line items. Investment center managers are held accountable for a measure of profit which is related directly to performance in areas reflected on the balance sheet.

One important point to keep in mind is that the lines between the financial responsibility center types are not always easy to discern, so responsibility center labels may not be particularly informative. In actual practice, financial responsibility centers can be arrayed on an almost seamless continuum from cost or revenue centers to investment centers. One possible subtle distinction between profit centers and investment centers is illustrated in Table 8-3. The manager of the entity described in Column C is held accountable for profit and, perhaps through a formal management-by-objectives (MBO) system, indicators of performance in three significant balance sheet areas: receivables, inventories, and fixed assets. Even though this manager is held accountable for performance in exactly the same areas as is the investment center manager (Column B), the manager of the Column C entity would rightly be called a profit center manager, not an investment center manager.

The lines between the other entity types can also be blurred. Consider the cause of manufacturing managers who are held accountable for meeting customer specifications, production quality standards, and customer delivery schedules, in addition to costs. In combination, these noncost factors may largely determine the company's success in generating revenues, and these managers clearly have to make trade-offs between costs and factors that affect revenues. Technically, these managers are cost center managers.

WHAT TYPE OF FINANCIAL RESPONSIBILITY CENTER SHOULD BE USED?

Much more important than the labeling of financial responsibility centers is the class of decisions that have to be made in designing financial responsibility structure. The important question to answer is: When should managers be held accountable for specific financial statement line items? These choices are obviously important because they affect behavior; managers pay attention to the measures for which they are held accountable. Fortunately, the basic answer to the financial responsibility center question is relatively straightforward: Hold managers accountable for the line items you want them to pay attention to.

To a large extent, financial responsibility center structures are coincident with the managers' areas of authority. Areas of authority are defined by organization structures and policies which define managers' rights and obligations to make certain decisions. In a typical functional organization (see Figure 8-1), none of the managers has significant decision making authority over generation of revenue and consumption of costs, so revenues and costs (including the costs of investments) are brought together in a return measure only at the corporate level. The manufacturing, engineering, and administrative functions are typically cost centers, and the marketing function is a revenue center. In a typical divisionalized organization (see Figure 8-2), division managers are given authority to make decisions in all, or at least many, of the functions that affect the success of their division. Consistent with this broad authority, each division is a profit center (or investment center) which comprises multiple cost and revenue centers.

Decisions about an organization's structure do not necessarily precede decisions about the type of responsibility centers that should be used; the responsibility structure decision may come first. For example, the desire to have managers make trade-offs between revenues and costs may lead to the choice of a divisionalized organization structure. All that can be said is that there is a close relationship between organization structures and responsibility centers.

The desire to have managers pay attention to a particular line item does not necessarily mean that they have direct and complete control over the item; although it should mean that the managers have (or should have) some influence over it. Some managers are held accountable for line items over which they have no direct control, such as corporate administrative expenses, to empower them to influence the behaviors of the managers with direct control.[6]

Specific strategic concerns sometimes affect the choice of responsibility center structure. A strategy relying on superior customer service may dictate that the managers of responsibility centers interfacing directly with customers (such as customer support) should be held accountable for revenue or profit because having these managers just focus on costs could cause behaviors that conflict with the company's strategy. Alternatively, these managers could be held accountable for costs plus a measure of customer satisfactions.

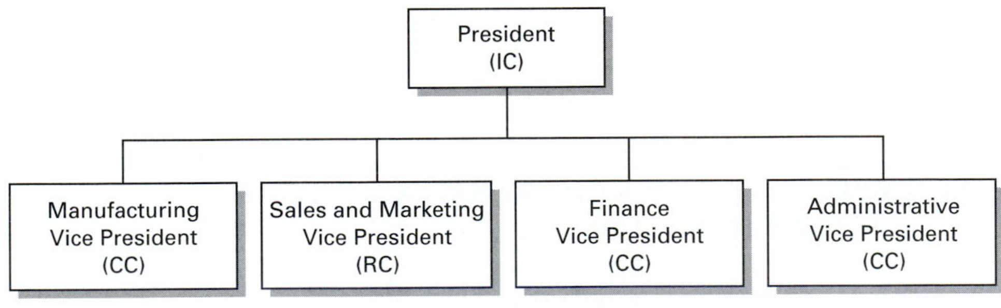

FIGURE 8-1 Typical Financial Responsibility Centers in a Functional Organization

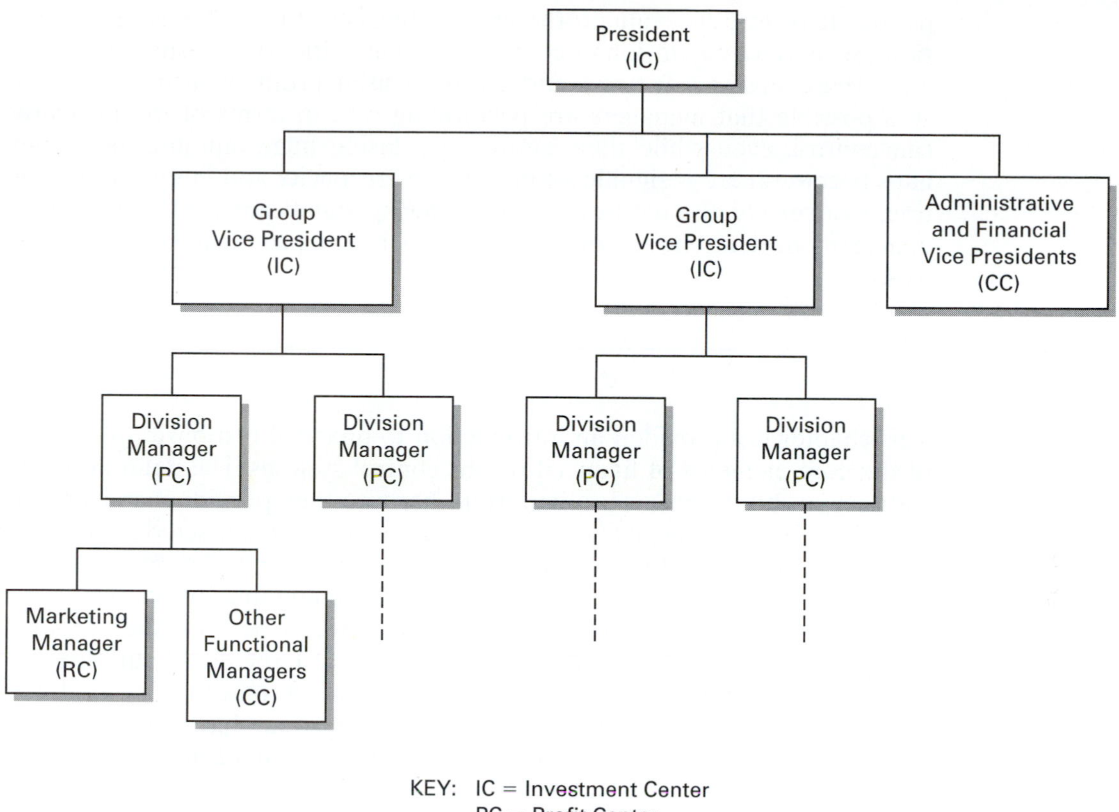

FIGURE 8-2 Typical Financial Responsibility Centers in a Divisionalized Organization

Some strategies might even suggest that some managers not be held accountable for line items over which they clearly have some influence. It may be desirable *not* to charge business unit managers for the costs of certain activities in order to stimulate greater use of the activity. A corporation might not want to charge certain business units with research and development costs. If the unit's strategy depends on technological leadership, its success may depend on spending money on every worthwhile research project. Corporate managers might not want the unit manager to make cost-benefit trade-offs on every expenditure.

PERFORMANCE MEASUREMENT OF ENTITIES VERSUS MANAGERS

In many corporations, two different profit and return-on-investment measures are computed for two distinct purposes. One measure, of the performance of the manager of the entity, emphasizes the elements of performance that the manager can influence. It is used to motivate the proper behaviors and to evaluate the manager's performance. The second measure is of the economic performance of the entity. This measure includes many items the manager cannot influence, such as interest expense, taxes, and full allocations of central administrative staff expenses. It is used to evaluate the entity's business for purposes of making decisions, such as for expansion or contraction of activities or divestment.

These manager-focused and entity-focused profit measures often diverge. It is possible that managers are performing well in terms of the measures they can control, even while their entities are losing huge amounts of money, perhaps because there is significant industry overcapacity and intense price competition. Conversely, the entities may be showing significant profits but, because of management deficiencies, still lagging the performance of most of their competitors.

CONCLUSION

This chapter has provided an introduction to financial responsibility centers, one of the core elements of financial results control systems. The definitions of financial responsibility centers are important because they provide managers with signals about what financial statement line items they are expected to pay attention to. Generally, financial responsibilities are congruent with the managers' decision rights, although sometimes managers are held accountable for financial statement line items over which they have no direct authority because the accountability empowers them to influence the actions of those with the direct authority.

Chapter 9 discusses planning and budgeting systems, the second core element of financial responsibility centers. These systems have many control purposes, one of the most important of which is the setting of financial performance targets.

Notes

1. For example, "Profit must be the prime motivation for all companies, except those who are formed as a charity or similar purpose," D. E. Hussey, *Introducing Corporate Planning* (Oxford, U.K.: Pergamon Press, 1991), p. 42.
2. The terminology distinction between investment centers and profit centers is included in virtually every management accounting textbook, but it is rarely used in business practice. In the many companies in which managers of business entities, such as divisions, are held accountable for RONA-type ratios, the managers are typically referred to as profit center managers.
3. R. F. Vancil, *Decentralization: Managerial Ambiguity by Design* (Homewood, Ill.: Dow Jones-Irwin, 1979).
4. J. S. Reece and W. R. Cool, "Measuring Investment Center Performance," *Harvard Business Review*, 56, no. 3 (May–June 1978), pp. 28–49.
5. The term cost center has a cost accounting meaning that is different from that of responsibility accounting. Most organizations comprise many cost centers set up for cost accounting purposes, for collecting like types of costs and assigning them to products and services, that are not responsibility centers because they do not have a manager accountable for those costs alone. Organizations typically use many more cost centers for cost accounting purposes than for responsibility center-control purposes.
6. R. F. Vancil, *Decentralization*: Managerial Ambiguity by Design (Homewood, Ill.: Dow Jones-Irwin, 1979).

Shuman Automobiles Inc.

Clark Shuman, the part owner and manager of an automobile dealership, was nearing retirement, and wanted to begin relinquishing his personal control over the business's operations. (See Exhibit 1 for current financial statements).The reputation he had established in the community led him to believe that the recent growth in his business would continue. His longstanding policy of emphasizing new car sales as the principal business of the dealership had paid off, in Shuman's opinion. This, combined with close attention to customer relations so that a substantial amount of repeat business was available, had increased the company's sales to a new high level. Therefore, he wanted to make organizational changes to cope with the new situation, especially given his desire to withdraw from any day-to-day managerial responsibilities. Shuman's three silent partners agreed to this decision.

Accordingly, Shuman divided up the business into three departments: new car sales, used car sales, and the service department (which was also responsible for selling parts and accessories). He then appointed three of his most trusted employees managers of the new departments: Jean Moyer, new car sales; Paul Fiedler, used car sales; and Nate Bianci, service department. All of these people had been with the dealership for several years.

Each of the managers was told to run his department as if it were an independent business. In order to give the new managers an incentive, their remuneration was to be calculated as a straight percentage of their department's gross profit.

Soon after taking over as manager of new car sales, Jean Moyer had to settle upon the amount to offer a particular customer who wanted to trade his old car as a part of the purchase price of a new one with a list price of $6,400. Before closing the sale, Moyer had to decide the amount he would offer the customer for the trade-in value of the old car. He knew that if no trade-in were involved, he would deduct about 15 percent from the list price of this model new car to be competitive with several other dealers in the area. However, he also wanted to make sure that he did not lose out on the sale by offering too low a trade-in allowance.

During his conversation with the customer, it had become apparent that the customer had an inflated view of the worth of his old car, a far from uncommon event. In this case, it probably meant that Moyer had to be prepared to make some sacrifices to close the sale. The new car had been in stock for some time, and the model was not selling very well, so he was rather anxious to make the sale if this could be done profitably.

In order to establish the trade-in value of the car, the used car manager, Fiedler, accompanied Moyer and the customer out to the parking lot to examine the car. In the course of his appraisal, Fiedler estimated the car would require reconditioning work costing about $350, after which the car would retail for about $1,850. On a wholesale basis, he could either buy or sell such a car, after reconditioning, for about $1,600. The wholesale price of a car was subject to much greater fluctuation than the retail price, depending on color, trim, model, etc. Fortunately, the car being traded in was a very popular shade. The retail automobile dealer's handbook of used car prices, the "Blue Book," gave a cash buying price range of $1,375 to $1,465 for the trade-in model in good condition. This range represented the distribution of cash prices paid by automobile dealers for that model of car in the area in the past week. Fiedler estimated that he could get about $1,100 for the car "as-is" (that is, without any work being done to it) at next week's auction.

The new car department manager had the right to buy any trade-in at any price he thought appropriate, but then it was his responsibility to dispose of the car. He had the alternative of either trying to persuade the used car manager to take over the car and accepting the used car manager's appraisal price, or he himself could sell the car

This case was prepared as a basis for class discussion rather than to illustrate either effective or ineffective handling of an administrative situation.

through wholesale channels or at auction. Whatever course Moyer adopted, it was his primary responsibility to make a profit for the dealership on the new cars he sold, without affecting his performance through excessive allowances on trade-ins. This primary goal, Moyer said, had to be "balanced against the need to satisfy the customers and move the new cars out of inventory—and there was only a narrow line between allowing enough on a used car and allowing too much."

After weighing all these factors, with particular emphasis on the personality of the customer, Moyer decided he would allow $2,135 for the used car, provided the customer agreed to pay the list price for the new car. After a certain amount of haggling, during which the customer came down from a higher figure and Moyer came up from a lower one, the $2,135 allowance was agreed upon. The necessary papers were signed, and the customer drove off.

Moyer returned to the office and explained the situation to Joanne Brunner, who had recently joined the dealership as accountant. After listening with interest to Moyer's explanation of the sale, Brunner set about recording the sale in the accounting records of the business. As soon as she saw the new car had been purchased from the manufacturer for $4,445, she was uncertain as to the value she should place on the trade-in vehicle. Since the new car's list price was $6,400 and it had cost $4,445, Brunner reasoned the gross margin on the new car sale was $1,955. Yet Moyer had allowed $2,135 for the old car, which needed $350 repairs and could be sold retail for $1,850 or wholesale for $1,600. Did this mean that the new car sale involved a loss? Brunner was not at all sure she knew the answer to this question. Also, she was uncertain about the value she should place on the used car for inventory valuation purposes. Brunner decided that she would put down a valuation of $2,135, and then await instructions from her superiors.

When Fiedler, manager of the used car department, found out what Brunner had done, he went to the office and stated forcefully that he would not accept $2,135 as the valuation of the used car. His comment went as follows:

> "My used car department has to get rid of that used car, unless Jean (Moyer) agrees to take it over himself. I would certainly never have allowed the customer $2,135 for that old tub. I would never have given any more than $1,250, which is the wholesale price less the cost of repairs. My department has to make a profit too, you know. My own income is dependent on the gross profit I show on the sale of used cars, and I will not stand for having my income hurt because Jean is too generous towards his customers."

Brunner replied that she had not meant to cause trouble, but had simply recorded the car at what seemed to be its cost of acquisition, because she had been taught that this was the best accounting practice. Whatever response Fiedler was about to make to this comment was cut off by the arrival of Clark Shuman, the general manager, and Nate Bianci, the service department manager. Shuman picked up the phone and called Jean Moyer, asking him to come over right away.

"All right, Nate," said Shuman, "now that we are all here, would you tell them what you just told me?"

Bianci, who was obviously very worried, said: "Thanks Clark; the trouble is with this trade-in. Jean and Paul were right in thinking that the repairs they thought necessary would cost about $350. Unfortunately, they failed to notice that the rear axle is cracked, which will have to be replaced before we can sell the car. This will probably use up parts and labor costing about $265."

"Besides this," Bianci continued, "there is another thing which is bothering me a good deal more. Under the accounting system we've been using, I can't charge as much on an internal job as I would for the same job performed for an outside customer. As you can see from my department statement (Exhibit 2), I lost almost eight thousand bucks on internal work last year. On a reconditioning job like this which costs out at $615, I don't even break even. If I did work costing $615 for an outside customer, I would be able to charge him about $830 for the job. The Blue Book[1] gives a range of $810 to $850 for the work this car needs, and I have always aimed for about the mid-

[1]In addition to the Blue Book for used car prices, there was a Blue Book which gave the range of charges for various classes of repair work. Like the used car book, it was issued weekly, and was based on the actual charges made and reported by vehicle repair shops in the area.

dle of the Blue Book range. That would give my department a gross profit of $215, and my own income is based on that gross profit. Since it looks as if a high proportion of the work of my department is going to be the reconditioning of trade-ins for resale, I figure that I should be able to make the same charge for repairing a trade-in as I would get for an outside repair job."

Messrs. Fiedler and Moyer both started to talk at once at this point. Fiedler, the more forceful of the two, managed to edge out Moyer: "This axle business is unfortunate, all right; but it is very hard to spot a cracked axle. Nate is likely to be just as lucky the other way next time. He has to take the rough with the smooth. It is up to him to get the cars ready for me to sell."

Moyer after agreeing that the failure to spot the axle was unfortunate, added: "This error is hardly my fault, however. Anyway, it is ridiculous that the service department should make a profit out of jobs it does for the rest of the dealership. The company can't make money when its left hand sells to its right."

At this point, Clark Shuman was getting a little confused about the situation. He thought there was a little truth in everything that had been said, but he was not sure how much. It was evident to him that some action was called for, both to sort out the present problem and to prevent its recurrence. He instructed Ms. Brunner, the accountant, to "work out how much we are really going to make on this whole deal," and then retired to his office to consider how best to get his managers to make a profit for the company.

A week after the events described above, Clark Shuman was still far from sure what action to take to motivate his managers to make a profit for the business. During the week, Bianci, the service manager, had reported to him that the repairs to the used car had cost $688, of which $320 represented the cost of those repairs which had been spotted at the time of purchase, and the remaining $368 was the cost of supplying and fitting a replacement for the cracked axle. To support his own case for a higher allowance on reconditioning jobs, Bianci had looked through the duplicate invoices over the last few months, and had found examples of work that was similar (but not identical) to the work that had been done on the trade-in car. The amounts of these invoices averaged $455, which the customers had paid without question, and the average of the costs assigned to these jobs was $596. (General overhead was not assigned to dual jobs.) In addition, Bianci had obtained from Ms. Brunner, the accountant, the cost analysis shown in Exhibit 2. Bianci told Shuman that this was a fairly typical distribution of the service department expense.

QUESTIONS

1. Suppose the new car deal is consummated, with the repaired used car being retailed for $1,850, the repairs costing Shuman $688. Assume that all sales personnel are on salary (no commissions), and that departmental overheads are fixed. What is the dealership contribution on the total transaction (i.e., new and repaired-used cars sold)?
2. Assume each department (new, used, service) is treated as a profit center, as described in the case. Also assume in a–c that it is known with certainty beforehand that the repairs will cost $688.
   a. In your opinion, at what value should this trade-in (unrepaired) be transferred from the new car department to the used car department? Why?
   b. In your opinion, how much should the service department be able to charge the used car department for the repairs on this trade-in? Why?
   c. Given your responses to a and b, what will be each of the three departments' contributions on this deal?
3. Is there a strategy in this instance that would give the dealership more contribution than the one assumed above (i.e., repairing and retailing this trade-in used car)? Explain. In answering this question, assume the service department operates at capacity.
4. Do you feel the three profit center approach is appropriate for Shuman? If so, explain why, including an explanation of how this is better than other specific alternatives. If not, propose a better alternative and explain why it is better than three profit centers and any other alternatives you have considered.

EXHIBIT 1 Income Statement for the Year Ended December 31

Sales of new cars			$3,821,873
Cost of new car sales*		$3,156,401	
Sales remuneration		162,372	
			3,318,773
			$ 503,100
Allowances on trade**			116,112
New cars gross profit			$ 386,988
Sales of used cars		$2,395,696	
Cost of used car sales*	$1,907,277		
Sales remuneration	91,564		
		1,998,841	
		$ 396,855	
Allowances on trade*		61,118	
Used cars gross profit			335,737
			$ 722,725
Service sales to customers		$ 347,511	
Cost of work*		256,984	
		$ 90,527	
Service work on reconditioning			
Charge	$ 236,580		
Cost*	244,312	(7,732)	
Service work gross profit			82,795
			$ 805,520
General and administrative expenses			491,710
INCOME BEFORE TAXES			$ 313,810

*These amounts include overhead assignable directly to the department, but exclude allocated general dealership overhead.

**Allowances on trade represent the excess of amounts allowed on cars taken in trade over their appraised value.

EXHIBIT 2 Analysis of Service Department Expenses for the Year Ended December 31

	Customer Jobs	*Reconditioning Jobs*	*Total*
Number of Jobs	2780	1051	3831
Direct labor	$106,930	$ 98,820	$205,750
Supplies	37,062	32,755	69,817
Department overhead (fixed)	31,558	26,067	57,625
	$175,550	$157,642	$333,192
Parts	81,434	86,670	168,104
	$256,984	$244,312	$501,296
Charges made for jobs to customers or other departments	347,511	236,580	584,091
Gross profit (loss)	$ 90,527	($ 7,732)	$ 82,795
General overhead proportion			57,080
Departmental profit for the year			$ 25,715

Pinnacle Mutual Life Insurance Company

Grumbling is the only weapon we have as managers in these newly formed profit centers. When the Executive Committee decided to institute this new concept at Pinnacle, the members made it clear *what* they wanted, but not *how* it was to be accomplished. For example, as vice president, Individual Equity and Pension Products, I continue to manage that area and do the work I've always done in that function; with the creation of profit centers, I also have responsibility for the new Institutional Pension Products and Services: Nonparticipating profit center, but I have no additional staff! It's difficult to take advantage of the company's support systems, especially the accounting group, because none of these groups have ever had to think in terms of profit before. There's really a paucity of numbers to help us do our jobs.

All of us who were appointed as profit center managers (PCMs) to get this idea off the ground are very visible. The process of converting to profit centers and changing the attitudes of employees is turning out to be a lot more difficult than we thought.

These words were spoken by Elizabeth Duncan, vice president, Individual Equity and Pension Products, and Profit Center manager for Institutional Pension Products and Services: Nonparticipating. She and the other seven PCMs had been in their new positions for seven months and they were discovering that their uncharted road posed challenges at almost every turn. One of the biggest problems they faced was the lack of financial information to help them forecast and budget; they complained that when they finally did get financial reports, the numbers were often out of date and not useful. Pinnacle management looked ahead to addressing these and other problems, and to putting a great deal of time and effort into making the profit centers successful.

RATIONALE FOR DEVELOPING PROFIT CENTERS AT PINNACLE

The profit center concept was introduced at Pinnacle in May 1985 and the first profit center managers were identified and appointed. By creating profit centers, the Management Committee (composed of the chairman, president, and heads of Marketing, Product Services, Law, Corporate Operations, and Investment Operations) hoped to provide greater focus to product development and marketing around the expanding set of financial service products offered by the company; in addition to life insurance, these included annuities, consumer banking, securities, real estate, equipment leasing, and home mortgage financing. Profit center managers would become the promoters of their products inside the company, thereby giving greater vitality to the competitiveness of the company.

The concept of profit centers seemed very new to many at Pinnacle. The mutual company form of organization emphasized the idea of service to customers who would benefit because they became part of the organization. (A mutual life insurance company is owned by its policy holders and differs from a stock insurance company which is owned by anyone who buys stock in that company.) The mutual form and its regulated accounting procedures emphasizing reserves and safety had led to little concern or emphasis on profit. Volume of revenues and preservation and growth of assets were much more familiar performance criteria than profits. Only recently, as the company's range of financial services expanded, had efforts begun to convert accounting reports to a generally accepted accounting principles basis.

This case was prepared by Associate for Case Development Karen E. Hansen, under the supervision of Professor William J. Bruns, Jr., as the basis for class discussion rather than to illustrate either effective or ineffective handling of an administrative situation. This case was made possible by a firm which chooses to remain anonymous. All of the data have been disguised.

Most life insurance companies used Statutory Accounting Principles (SAP) rather than GAAP. SAP was a set of principles required by statute which had to be followed by an insurance company when submitting its financial statements to the state insurance department. Such principles differed from GAAP in some important aspects; one was that SAP required that expenses be recorded immediately and not be deferred to be matched with premiums as they were earned and taken into revenue. The adoption of GAAP was intended to produce financial results consistent with those of other industries and to assure consistency in financial reporting.

When Pinnacle decided to emphasize profit, it switched to GAAP for internal purposes, to gain the benefits of that reporting basis. GAAP helped match benefits and expenses to premium income, which resulted in earnings emerging as a more nearly level percent of the premiums collected. To accomplish this matching, natural reserves were developed based on actuarial assumptions appropriate at the date of issue. Natural reserves included benefit, acquisition, and maintenance expense reserves. The reserve assumptions included provisions for adverse deviation from that assumed for ratemaking. GAAP also allowed profits to emerge in proportion to the release from the risk for adverse deviation.

The profit center concept was also at odds with the way Pinnacle had always been organized. At various times, the company's organization had emphasized type of customer (individual vs group, for example) or functions (sales, investments, or customer service). The creation of profit centers focused attention on how products and services could be developed and sold for the good of the company as a whole. Inevitably, some profit centers would compete with each other as they developed and sold products; this competition was a radical idea in a mutual company.

Despite both anticipated and unanticipated problems and resistance from corporate culture, top management was committed to the profit center form of organization. If Pinnacle was to be customer-driven, a stated management goal, then the company had to be able to respond quickly to customer demands and competitor threats. The industry was changing rapidly as more companies offered financial services outside their traditional businesses. A profit center organization seemed necessary for Pinnacle to maintain a leadership position in the areas of insurance, and financial and administrative services for individuals and groups.

THE PINNACLE COMPANIES

Pinnacle Mutual Life Insurance Company had been chartered in Connecticut and was nearly 100 years old. This strong, stable company had long been known for its product line of various types of life insurance. Through the years, Pinnacle had grown steadily to become an industry leader; among its competitors in the life insurance business were Connecticut Mutual, Prudential, John Hancock, Aetna, Hartford Life, Massachusetts Mutual, Metropolitan Life, Allstate, and New York Life. But Pinnacle's competition wasn't limited to insurance companies. Any company offering financial services or administrative services was really vying for the same customers as Pinnacle. This included companies which offered banking products, brokerage services, institutional investment, and management of data systems.

In the 1970s and 1980s, Pinnacle had expanded the number and type of financial services it offered to its customers in an attempt to satisfy consumers who were looking for more profitable ways to invest in times of higher inflation. Not only were new types of insurance and annuities added, such as a disability income insurance and single premium deferred annuities, new services were developed for individual, institutional, and corporate clients. As a result, the company found itself offering a broad range of products and services in real estate; home mortgage financing; data processing; farming; commercial development; equipment financing and leasing; medical and dental preferred provider organizations; and financial services in brokerage, banking, and mutual funds. Management expected that much of the company's future growth would be in areas and activities outside its traditional insurance areas.

Until 1984, the company organization reflected its emphasis on the distinction between products and services sold to individuals and those sold to groups (Exhibit 1). In 1984, the company reorganized to emphasize functions (Exhibit 2). Under the new structure, products would be sold or serviced by one part of the organization, regardless of the nature of the customer, to minimize duplication of functional efforts across product or customer lines.

Pinnacle management felt that the reorganization contributed to stronger performance in 1984 (Exhibit 3). The company's mission that year was to emphasize those products and services which would provide an attractive return on investment, competitive product value to their clients, and opportunities for growth by providing additional products and services for existing customers or attracting new customers to their expanded array of financial services. Pinnacle began to change its image, and to examine not only the range of investment opportunities it could offer its clients, but how the company could manage those investment areas most profitably.

Prior to the reorganization, Pinnacle management had not thought in terms of competitive stance or aggressively seeking new customers; the company had always been proud of its concern for existing customers and their life insurance needs. Elizabeth Duncan commented:

> A mutual life insurance company environment is about as uncompetitive as you can get. Because our participating policy holders are our owners and the company is run for their benefit, the best thing for them, financially speaking, is for Pinnacle to stop selling new life insurance! Every new policy sold actually diminishes the amount of funds that can be returned to current policy holders in dividends because the cost of both the agent's commission and issuing the new policy usually exceeds the first year premium.

But Pinnacle's aggressive plans for the future did not include the alternative of dropping out of the life insurance business. As Pinnacle continued to expand into noninsurance products and services, it competed directly with other financial service institutions. Managers focused on this new competition and began to develop ways to manage change while continuing to meet client needs.

THE PROCESS OF CREATING PROFIT CENTERS

The Executive Committee favored profit centers organized around existing products and services as the way to focus managers on profit, cost, and competition. But its members were unsure how to make the transition to this new form of management. Therefore, the Committee appointed Stephen Cooper, vice president, Corporate Analysis, to coordinate the creation and staffing of profit centers.

In a memorandum to the Executive Committee on January 23, 1985 (Exhibit 4), Cooper summarized the beginning of this process and reviewed reasons to have profit centers. He was eager to ensure agreement on rationale and goals. The memo also established the agenda for a meeting two days later to discuss how many profit centers to create, how to select their managers, and how to measure their performance.

At that meeting, the Executive Committee decided to create eight profit centers to handle current products and services. However, no one was sure how to change the roles of the functional groups and then coordinate interaction between the two groups to maximize company earnings. The meeting emphasized the company's emerging needs, which members decided could be best served by creating value centers out of the existing functional groups (Marketing, Product Services, Financial Operations, Law and Corporate Secretary, and Corporate Operations). Value centers, for a fee or at least an allocation of cost, would provide services including market research and data on competition, information on pricing products, accounting information and suggestions, and tax and legal advice. For example, if a PCM needed legal counselling from the Law and Corporate Secretary value center, that value center would charge the PCM for the lawyer's time to research and answer the PCM's questions. In the future, other services might be created as needed and offered to PCMs by Value Center managers (VCMs).

In order to give the new structures time to develop and a fair chance at success, profit centers would be required to use the services of the value centers for two to three years. During this start-up phase, PCMs and VCMs would work together to negotiate services and fees and establish quality measures which could be used by the PCMs to help them determine the value of the services for which they would be paying. The VCMs' Incentive Compensation would eventually be influenced by how well expense and quality measures were attained. At the end of this time, PCMs would be allowed to go outside the company to contract for these and other services if they discovered sources which would give them better service, reduce their costs of doing business, or improve their profit centers' performance.

Allowing PCMs to go to outside vendors for services which were offered internally was unusual; management hoped this competition from external sources would inspire each VCM to operate efficiently and to try to win the business of the profit centers by competing against other service providers. PCMs would be required to state their intentions to seek outside services and the reasons for doing so. This would give the value center a chance to respond and to try to meet the PCMs' needs, if possible, so that value centers would continue to provide necessary service. But if PCMs could prove that continuing to use the value center, rather than an external supplier, would result in failure to meet profit goals, then PCMs could seek outside resources. While not wanting to limit PCMs' freedom, management wanted to avoid having them focus on short-term profit at the expense of long-term growth goals. Consequently, certain restrictions, in the areas of use of outside vendors, personnel policies, management development programs, and community relations programs would be placed on PCM actions.

The January 25 meeting also covered performance measures and incentive compensation for PCMs and VCMs. The Management Committee decided that PCMs would be measured on three criteria: GAAP profits, Return on Surplus Needs (ROSN), and Product and Service Income (PSI). "Surplus needs" was a calculation, for internal purposes only, of the appropriate amount of equity for a profit center, given its liabilities. In a mutual company, ROSN was similar to return on equity. Insurance companies usually maintained a "policyholders' surplus," which was an amount in addition to liabilities, available to meet future obligations to its policyholders; for a mutual insurer, this was the whole equity section of the balance sheet. PSI was similar to gross operating revenue and was earned by selling new products and accruing revenue each year from those sales. In order to protect PCMs during the start-up phases in 1985, their compensation would not be tied to their profit center's performance. In 1986, however, they would be measured against their profit goals, but not on their profit center's growth.

During the first two weeks of February, the Committee for the Measurement of Corporate Performance (CMCP), chaired by Stephen Cooper, worked on the creation of profit centers. Even though the Executive Committee had decided that eight profit centers should be created, the CMCP felt that 10 or 12 would encourage better focus of sales efforts as well as allow for the creation of future products and services. The Management Committee approved the CMCP's list of 10 profit centers, but decided to appoint only eight PCMs; two of the eight PCMs would each manage two similar profit centers. They discussed which senior managers to appoint to these positions. Exhibit 5 shows a grid of the profit centers and value centers; the X's indicate the intended interactions between the two groups.

As Elizabeth Duncan had mentioned, management was clear about what they wanted the PCMs to do. Within six weeks of the approval of the 10 profit centers, the CMCP had developed a lengthy description of the PCMs' responsibilities and relationships (Exhibit 6). On April 1, 1985, Stephen Cooper sent a memo to the Chairman of the Board and to the president of Pinnacle containing this description and the list of 10 recommended profit centers.

The announcement of the creation of profit centers was somewhat out of character for this stately, old mutual life insurance company. At an annual management meeting in May, attended by about 100 officers of Pinnacle, the eight senior managers who were appointed PCMs were introduced and given Captains' hats and megaphones as symbols of their new responsibilities and authority. Many of the PCMs were actuaries, some had experience in the areas they would now manage, and all had successful track records at Pinnacle. They were congratulated and told that they would be responsible for making the profit centers viable, for working out the bugs inherent in new systems, for establishing strategic plans, and for creating budgets. At the same time, they would continue to do their current jobs, and they would be given no additional staff to do their new jobs.

The new PCMs had many questions for top management about their new roles. To help answer initial and future questions, Stephen Cooper remained in his role as coordinator of the profit center project and served as organizer and advocate to address the needs and concerns of the PCMs.

In initial meetings with the PCMs, Cooper noted that their major complaints centered on two items: the PCMs had enormous goals but no staff, and they had difficulty getting accurate financial information about their products and services. To help address these problems, Cooper asked PCMs in November 1985 to submit *wish lists of tools* which would make their new jobs easier. Seven PCMs responded; Elizabeth Duncan's list (Exhibit 7) was representative of the kinds of tools many PCMs wanted. She went one step further and listed tools the Management Committee needed to help make profit centers work and sent these in a separate memo to Cooper (Exhibit 8).

Three items appeared consistently on the wish lists: 1) rules on the allocation of expenses to new products, 2) rules on deferring the expenses of Developmental Funds Programs (DFPs), and 3) earlier and more extensive involvement in the planning, evaluation, and approval of DFPs. DFPs were essentially R&D expenditures that were budgeted independently of regular operational budgets and were approved on a program by program basis. A decision on how DFPs would be treated was important because DFPs could be costly and out of proportion to the benefit received by some profit centers; other profit centers might not even be allocated a share of DFP projects under the current system. Cooper agreed that the CMCP would act on the first two items. For resolution of the third issue, he sent two memos (Exhibit 9) to George Steiner in his capacity as senior vice president and controller and as chairman of the DFP Steering Committee.

"Although I think we're making progress, it will be an on-going process for the PCMs to figure out what they need and how to get it," said Stephen Cooper. "I think it would be enlightening to talk to some of them. They are in the planning and budgeting cycle now and have some pretty strong feelings about the implementation of the profit center concept here at Pinnacle."

INTERVIEWS WITH PROFIT CENTER MANAGERS

Elizabeth Duncan: Vice president, Individual Equity and Pension Products; Profit Center Manager for Institutional Pension Products and Services: Nonparticipating

Creating profit centers has been a lot more difficult than any of us thought it would be. Our past culture of not thinking competitively has been hard to overcome; no one had ever asked which products were winners and which were losers.

Pinnacle needs a mechanism for deciding which profit centers will get resources. We've never had to pick and choose before. Right now, I'm having to fight for resources in the legal department and this takes a lot of my time. I can only spend about 25 percent or 35 percent of my time managing my profit center. My current job of managing Individual Equity and Pension Products keeps me pretty busy; in addition, I'm a director of two subsidiaries, and I serve on the Surplus Committee, and Demutualization Committee, and the Asset Allocation Committee.

As a profit center manager, I'm fairly unique. I have the least relationship naturally to my profit center in terms of other work I do. In the beginning, this compounded my difficulties because I wasn't already in the channels of distribution for information about my products and services. In some instances, it was a case of not even knowing what I didn't know!

All of the PCMs are still learning and discovering what they need. Upper management is grappling with understanding this process, too. It's like the story of the blind men and the elephant; the problems look different to the executive vice presidents and the PCMs because they are standing in different places. In some cases, no one is sure where the authority lies to make decisions when the viewpoints are so different.

Benjamin Field: Vice president and Group Actuary; Profit Center Manager for Individual Annuity Products and Services

The problem is that we all have different ideas of how things should be done and there are no tools in place to either direct our efforts or provide information. A big part of achieving our goals will be attributable to our ability to negotiate with the value centers to get good information on which to base decisions. But in the fall of 1985, the Controllers didn't want to make the move to the profit center system because it would change the way they would have to compile reports.

Pinnacle has operated for nearly 100 years without worrying about profit; it's a slow process to change our orientation. We're experiencing problems with levels of authority on some decisions and with communicating. For example, the CEO occasionally disagrees with what PCMs think is the right thing to do to keep costs down. Who really makes the final decisions? It's also been hard to convince value centers that we need accurate information and we need it in a hurry, even when that information has never been compiled before.

The profit center managers don't have much time to devote to pressuring value centers for what we need. Some weeks I spend 40 percent of my time being a profit center manager, and other weeks I don't spend any time on it at all. I'm also a value center manager which puts me in an interesting situation; I was already in the information flow, unlike Elizabeth Duncan, which made my life easier. But the two hats I wear as PCM and VCM will probably create some conflicting situations in the future. What's good for the profit center may not be good for the value center.

Peter Wright: Vice president, Policyholder Services; Profit Center Manager for Individual Life Insurance Products and Services: Nontraditional

I see the role of the profit center manager more as a catalyst than a coordinator, more entrepreneurial in nature. But the corporate culture has often avoided change and confrontation. This makes it difficult to switch to profit-oriented thinking.

I have an advantage over some of the other PCMs in that I was already familiar with the products and services of my profit center. I also have value center departments which report to me, so I have established working relationships.

One problem we're all facing is that we wear too many hats to be able to get deeply immersed in some profit center issues. For example, the Controller sent a memo to some of the PCMs saying that they would be charged for a new accounting system, but the memo didn't mention a dollar amount. No one complained, partly because they couldn't find out the cost because the tools aren't in place to do that, and partly because they couldn't focus on this issue and do the 60 other things they were trying to do in their regular jobs. There's a lot of confusion now; the system is still evolving.

EXHIBIT 1 Pinnacle Mutual Life Insurance Company Organization Prior to 1984

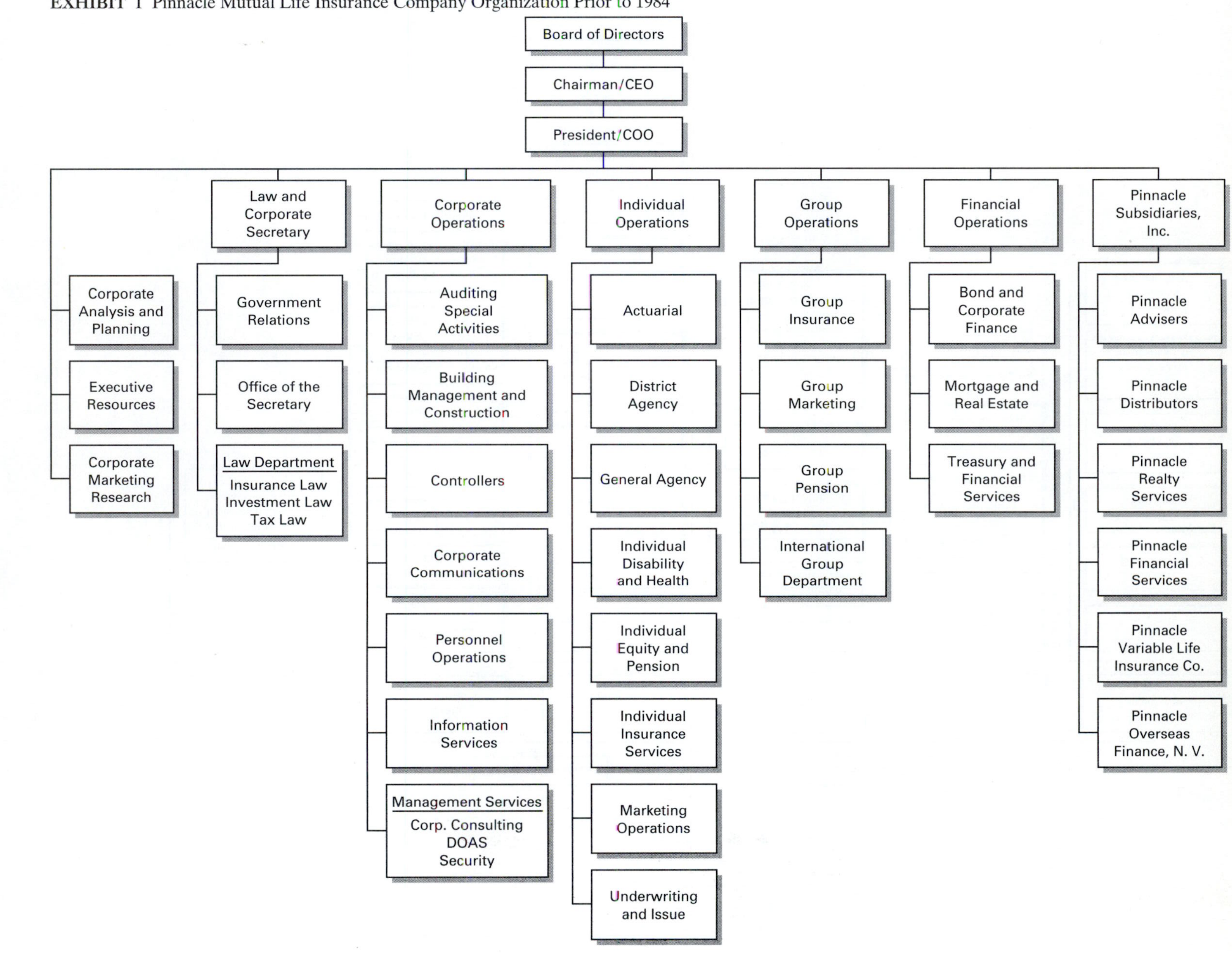

EXHIBIT 2 Pinnacle Mutual Life Insurance Company Organization After Reorganization in 1984

- Board of Directors
  - Chairman/CEO
    - President/COO
      - Executive Resources
      - Strategic Planning
      - Law and Corporate Secretary
        - Corporate Secretary: Office of the Secretary; Government Relations
        - Law Department: Administration; Insurance Law; Investment Law; Tax Law
      - Corporate Operations
        - Auditing/OSA: Auditing; OSA
        - Controllers
        - Corporate Analysis
        - Corporate Communications
        - Information Services
        - Management Services: Corp. Consulting; DOAS; Security
          - Building Management and Construction
        - Corporate Personnel
      - Product Services
        - Staff
        - International IGP
        - Group Insurance: Health Policy; Admin. Intl. Assn.; Claims & Systems; Financial (ACI); Group Creditor; Contract Services
        - Group Pension: Customer Service; Actuarial Services; Systems
        - Individual Ins. Ser.: Policy Admin.; Policy & Field Admin. Systems
        - Underwriting & Issue: Und. Pol. & Research; Medical; New Business
        - Actuarial
        - Ind. Equity & Pension
        - Do. Dis. & Health
      - Marketing
        - Staff
        - Market Research
        - Marketing Services: Group Marketing; Ind. Marketing; Product Development
        - Relationship Officers
        - Sales: District Agency; General Agency; Group Pension; Group Insurance; Direct Response; Indp. 3rd Party & Network
      - Investment Operations
        - Bond and Corporate Finance: Capital Growth; Venture Capital
        - Mortgage and Real Estate: City Mortgage; Agricultural Inv.; Equity Real Estate
        - Treasury and Financial Services
        - Investment Marketing Services
      - Pinnacle Subsidiaries, Inc.
        - Pinnacle Advisers
        - Pinnacle Distributors
        - Pinnacle Realty Services
        - Pinnacle Financial Services
        - Pinnacle Variable Life Insurance Co.
        - Pinnacle Overseas Finance, N. V.

EXHIBIT 3 Pinnacle Mutual Life Insurance Company

Consolidated Statement of Financial Position *Year ended December 31 (in millions)*	*1984*	*1983*
Assets:		
Bonds	$ 6,198.8	$ 6,355.0
Stocks	793.9	935.5
Mortgage loans on real estate	6,190.0	6,345.7
Real estate	957.5	773.7
Policy loans and liens	2,097.8	1,980.0
Cash	549.4	580.8
Other assets	7,307.7	5,863.3
Total Assets	$24,095.1	$22,834.0
Obligations:		
Policy reserves	11,418.5	11,303.3
Policyholders' and beneficiaries' funds	4,117.0	4,465.1
Other payables	1,529.8	1,454.8
Obligations related to separate account business	6,016.7	4,672.9
Total Obligations	$23,082.0	$21,896.1
Policyholders' Contingency Reserves:		
Total contingency reserves	1,013.2	937.9
Total Obligations and Contingency Reserves	$24,095.2	$22,834.0

Consolidated Summary of Operations and Changes in Policyholders' Contingency Reserves *Year ended December 31 (in millions)*	*1984*	*1983*	*1982*
Income	$ 4,203.1	$3,957.5	$ 3,697.4
Benefits and Expenses:			
Payments to policyholders and beneficiaries	1,559.2	1,342.7	987.7
Additions to reserves to provide for future payments to policyholders and beneficiaries	1,319.9	1,513.4	1,551.3
Expenses of providing service to policyholders and obtaining new insurance	668.2	600.9	554.4
Taxes	61.0	56.4	55.7
	3,608.3	3,513.4	3,149.1
Net gain before dividends to policyholders and federal income taxes	594.8	444.1	548.3
Dividends to policyholders	376.2	378.8	316.9
Federal income taxes	65.9	34.9	70.0
	442.1	413.7	387.0
Net Gain	$152.7	$ 30.4	$161.3

(Continued)

EXHIBIT 3 Pinnacle Mututal Life Insurance Company *Continued*

Consolidated Statement of Changes in Financial Position Year ended December 31 (in millions)	*1984*	*1983*	*1982*
Additions:			
From operations	$1,421.8	$1,561.7	$1,641.2
Proceeds from indebtedness to affiliate			70.5
Proceeds from commercial paper		70.3	
Net carrying value of long-term investments upon disposal	2,120.6	1,682.0	1,275.1
Net capital gains (losses realized for general account upon disposal of long-term investments)	(57.5)	3.2	(7.2)
	3,484.9	3,317.2	2,979.6
Deductions:			
Acquisition of long-term investments	1,997.3	1,943.7	1,141.2
Other—net	1,519.0	1,570.8	1,267.9
	3,516.3	3,514.5	2,409.1
Increase (decrease) in cash and temporary cash investments	(31.4)	(197.3)	570.5
Cash and temporary cash investments at beginning of year	580.8	778.1	207.6
Cash and temporary cash investments at end of year	$ 549.4	$ 580.8	$ 778.1

EXHIBIT 4 Pinnacle Mutual Life Insurance Company

M E M O R A N D U M

TO:	Executive Committee	DATE:	January 23, 1985
FROM:	Stephen Cooper Vice President Corporate Analysis	CC:	CMCP

The purpose of this memorandum is to briefly review what transpired on January 4, describe what I hope we'll address and accomplish on January 25, and enumerate the tasks to be worked on over the next few months, and into the future.

I. Review of January 4 meeting:

I delineated what I felt were the two primary reasons for having profit centers:

1. To define meaningful units within the company whose results (e.g., profits) can be measured in a satisfactory manner. This will help the company determine which of its "parts" are doing well, and which need improvement (or should be discarded).
2. To more precisely define areas of responsibility for company managers; to measure how well those managers are performing and to provide a valid basis for determining incentive reward based on a manager's performance within his/her area of responsibility.

Clarification added to the above by Executive Committee members included the following:

1. Changing attitudes of the business community, management, and the public dictate a greater emphasis on profitable operations.

* * *

(Continued)

EXHIBIT 4 Pinnacle Mutual Life Insurance Company *Continued*

Memorandum to Executive Committee
January 23, 1985
Page 2

The next area of discussion concerned what "units" should be defined as profit centers. I expressed a predilection for a primary profit center level based on our functional organization, with secondary and tertiary levels being product based. However, most discussion indicated an inclination for product-based profit centers. It was felt that the organization was susceptible to change or, alternatively, may be adjusted to support agreed-upon profit center structures. Product performance measures were felt to be the primary concern, and thus the driving force behind profit centers.

Final discussion involved appropriate measures for profit center results. ROSN (Return on Surplus Needs), GAAP (Generally Accepted Accounting Principles) net income (before and after dividends), and PSI (Product and Service Income) were all suggested, and the pros and cons of each were touched upon briefly.

II. January 25 Agenda

I'll commence with a review of the information obtained thus far on profit center techniques and problems of other companies. I'd then want to confirm what the basic profit center unit should be (opinions expressed favored product segments), explore the ramifications of that decision (organization coordination requirements, etc.), determine an *initial* number of profit centers to be measured, decide on *specific* profit centers as a result of the foregoing, and decide on the method to be used to select profit center managers (i.e., who will name them and when). Further discussion would consider whether the above structure is complete or whether it should be supplemented by any "cost centers" measured on fees for services less actual expenses.

I'd then like to continue our previous discussion on profit center measures. . . .

Finally, I'd be interested in the Executive Committee's opinion on the time period they envision to implement the various aspects of profit center measurement and organization. . . .

* * *

I look forward to a fruitful session on the 25th.

EXHIBIT 5 Profit Center/Value Centers Grid

	Profit Centers[a]									
Value Centers	*1 Ind Life Trad*	*2 Ind Life NonT*	*3 Ind Ann*	*4 Ind Hlth*	*5 Inst Ins*	*6 Inst Pen NonP*	*7 Inst Pen Par*	*8 Inv Prod Trad*	*9 Inv Prod Spec*	*10 Int Nat'l Ins*
Law & Corp Secty	X	X	X	X	X	X	X	X	X	X
Corporate Ops										
Info Services	X	X	X	X	X	X	X	X	X	X
Other Corp Ops	X	X	X	X	X	X	X	X	X	X
Product Services										
Group Servs					X	X	X	X	X	X
Under & Pol Serv	X	X	X	X						X
International					X	X	X	X	X	X
Other Prod Serv	X	X	X	X	X					X
Marketing										
Dist Agency	X	X	X	X	X					
Gen Agency	X	X	X	X	X					
Gr Pens Sales						X	X	X	X	
Group Ins.					X					
Other Mktg	X	X	X	X	X	X	X			X
Investment Ops										
Bond & Corp Fin	X	X	X	X	X	X	X	X	X	X
Mort & R E	X	X	X	X	X	X	X	X	X	X
Inv Mktg									X	
Other Inv Ops	X	X	X	X	X	X	X	X	X	X
Executive	X	X	X	X	X	X	X	X	X	X

[a]Complete names of profit centers shown above:

1. Individual Life Insurance Products and Services: Traditional
2. Individual Life Insurance Products and Services: Nontraditional
3. Individual Annuity Products and Services
4. Individual Health Products and Services
5. Institutional Insurance Products and Services
6. Institutional Annuity Products and Services: Nonparticipating
7. Institutional Annuity Products and Services: Participating
8. Investment Products and Related Services: Traditional
9. Investment Products and Related Services: Specialty
10. International Insurance Operations

EXHIBIT 6 Profit Center Managers Responsibilities and Relationships

The primary responsibility of the profit center manager (PCM) is to achieve maximum profitability and growth as measured by the following:

—Return on Surplus Needs (ROSN)—definition and requirements established by the Surplus Committee.
—Profitability—bottom line as produced by Product Profitability Accounting and Reporting System (PPARS)—definitions established by the Committee for the Measurement of Corporate Performance (CMCP).
—Product and Service Income (PSI)—measures determined by the CMCP.

As straightforward as this definition of responsibilities appears to be, it raises a number of questions and poses a number of problems which must be addressed. One such problem arises from the fact that many PCMs will actually be responsible for a number of products rather than a single product.

* * *

A second complication affecting the PCM's job results from the need to coordinate activities of people within different functional areas. Because the company is not organized by product lines, the PCM must work within a management team crossing several organizational lines.

* * *

The PCM will negotiate with value center managers (VCMs) for services at certain expense and quality levels. It is important to note that this process of negotiation will not initially take place in a "free market" setting, in that the PCM will be required, for the time being, to obtain services from sources available in the Pinnacle companies rather than immediately going outside for them. It is highly likely, of course, that PCMs will quickly become aware of competing sources which may provide the required services more inexpensively and will use this information in their negotiations. The availability of such data will no doubt place considerable pressure on each VCM to operate as efficiently as possible.

Since this kind of pressure may not suffice, however, we contemplate a policy under which the PCM will be able to give advance notice of his/her intention to use non-Pinnacle resources with reasons for doing so. If the Pinnacle department cannot provide the service at the stated cost within that time period (e.g., 2–3 years), the restrictions on utilizing outside resources will be eased, particularly if the PCM can demonstrate that failure to do so will prevent the attainment of his/her profitability goals which otherwise could be met.

* * *

(Continued)

EXHIBIT 6 Profit Center Managers Responsibilities and Relationships *Continued*

An important aspect of the negotiation process may prove to be the determination by the PCM, in conjunction with VCMs, of acceptable trade-offs between quality and cost. Inappropriate resolution of such questions could easily result in sacrificing long-term goals for short-term profits.

Relationships

In many cases, the PCM will have a dual reporting relationship. First, as a functional manager, he/she will continue to report, directly or indirectly, to an executive area head. As a PCM, however, he/she will report to the Management Committee as a whole. In addition, there will be a third relationship resulting from the need for teamwork referred to above. These third relationships will be rather extensive. Most PCMs will be negotiating and contracting for such services as:

Pricing—for both new and existing products
Marketing—including sales, training, etc.
Market research
Underwriting
Claims processing
Systems development, testing and maintenance
Data processing programming and production
Accounting services
Legal services
Personnel services, such as hiring, salary administration

As long as this list may at first appear to be, it is undoubtedly not complete; but it does serve to drive home the point that the PCM will have many relationships which he/she will have to manage (or at least coordinate) in order to operate profitably.

* * *

PCM as Entrepreneur

While the PCM clearly has the responsibility for managing his/her product portfolio profitably, the nature of the PCM's responsibility to demonstrate a truly entrepreneurial approach to the job may be less evident. In addition to doing everything possible to see that he/she receives the best possible services from VCMs or others at the best possible price, the PCM should continually be on the watch for opportunities to introduce new products, expand existing products to meet new market needs, etc. A truly entrepreneurial PCM will not sit back and let others uncover opportunities to perform more efficiently or to develop new products and markets. He/she should therefore consider the identification and development of such opportunities as a major responsibility and should, through the compensation system, be rewarded accordingly.

EXHIBIT 7 Pinnacle Mutual Life Insurance Company

MEMORANDUM

TO:	Stephen Cooper Vice President	DATE:	November 15, 1985
FROM:	Elizabeth Duncan Vice President		
SUBJECT:	Tools Necessary for My Profit Center to Work Right		

1. Clear definitions of which costs are fixed and which are variable, including as part of the exercise:
   a) Expenses which are agreed upon in advance going into the year and change only with activity measures and/or a value center's failure to meet its budget with me—not with someone else's failure to meet an activity measure.
   b) An understanding of how change in an activity measure, such as Single Premium Deferred Annuity (SPDA) sales, will affect expenses by value center.
   c) A clear grasp of how expenses for a new product will be treated. (Allocations are not now made until more than 1 year after a new annuity product is introduced. Heaven knows who pays them in the meantime.)
2. A thorough analysis of how costs compare with the competition's, in areas such as distribution, overhead, marketing, etc. The competition includes other large insurance companies, companies selling through general agencies, brokers, direct response, etc.
3. Detailed expense and revenue data by product for all my products with some understanding of why the numbers were derived that way.
4. GAAP profit data for my profit center (if prospective sales look as though it can be cost-justified).
5. An understanding of how Product and Service Income (PSI) is defined for each of my products and what a hurdle Return on Surplus Needs (ROSN) really means in terms of a profit margin for each. (This is undoubtedly available somewhere, once I make the effort to track it down.)

EXHIBIT 8 Pinnacle Mutual Life Insurance Company

MEMORANDUM

TO:	Stephen Cooper Vice President	DATE:	November 15, 1985
FROM:	Elizabeth Duncan Vice President		
SUBJECT:	Tools the Management Committee Needs to Make Profit Centers Work		

1. A capital budget for the whole company (including subsidiaries) that would set limits for both true investment and development expenses affecting the corporation.
2. A list of potential capital and development projects which might surface over the next five years with associated price tag estimates and a probability of occurrence in each of the years.
3. A way to tie target Return on Surplus Needs (ROSN) hurdle rates to the capital budget on the theory that exceeding the capital budget will force up our cost of capital and should therefore drive up the hurdle rate.
4. A method to force every profit center manager and subsidiary CEO to implicitly pay back his/her cash flow each year and then to compete with everyone else for it. This will be necessary to free up resources for new projects and shifts in priorities.

EXHIBIT 9 Pinnacle Mutual Insurance Company

MEMORANDUM

TO:	George Steiner Senior Vice President and Controller Controller's Department	DATE:	January 9, 1986
FROM:	Stephen Cooper Vice President Corporate Analysis	CC:	Profit Center Managers
SUBJECT:	Profit Center Data		

The profit center managers recently enumerated a list of the "tools" (primarily data and information) they need to do their jobs. A compilation of these lists indicates some consensus on areas where controllers could help the profit centers acquire those tools. The following is a summary of their requests:

A. Expenses
All expense data is needed in the following configuration:
—three years historical and one year projected, on an annual basis
—one year historical and one year projected, on a quarterly basis
—direct and indirect expense components separated wherever possible

1. General Expense Information
   —profit center expenses, broken down by cost center and grouped by value center
   —cost center expenses and value center groupings, broken down by the Committee for the Measurement of Corporate Peformance (CMCP) product segment
   —the function performed by each cost center should be indicated
   —the present allocation assumptions and methods should be briefly explained

2. Indirect Expense Analysis
   —a definition of the various components of indirect expense is required
   —indirect expense components, broken down by such items as: personnel, health clinic, food services, advertising, legislative activities, library, and institute
   —the profit center allocation assumptions and methods should be briefly explained
   —a comparison of competitors' indirect expenses (to help judge the reasonableness of such expenses)
   —ratios of indirect expenses to direct expenses (to help judge the reasonableness of indirect expenses)

3. Developmental Funds Program (DFP) Expense Analysis
   —for each DFP project, budgeted expenses broken down by cost center
   —profit center allocation assumptions and methods for budgeted DFPs should be briefly explained
   —an analysis of actual DFP expenses and allocations compared to budgeted values is required

4. Unit Functional Expense Analysis
   —profit center expenses, broken down by Life Office Management Association (LOMA) functional expense category such as: cost for underwriting, issue, maintenance, acquisition, and marketing
   —a comparison of competitors' functional expenses (to judge the reasonableness of such expenses)

5. Field Expense Analysis
   —profit center field expenses, broken down by such activities as: sales compensation, supervisory costs, training costs, and employee benefit costs

(Continued)

EXHIBIT 9 Pinnacle Mutual Life Insurance Company *Continued*

—a comparison of competitors' field expenses (to judge the reasonableness of such expenses)

6. Investment Expense Analysis
   —profit center investment expenses, broken down by type of investment (e.g., bond, mortgage) and shown as a percentage of that investment's asset value
   —each of the above expense categories should be split into acquisition and maintenance components and shown as a percentage of the appropriate asset values

B. Income Statement
1. income statements by CMCP product segment are needed on a Statutory Accounting Principles (SAP) and GAAP basis
2. after-tax GAAP results require a deferred tax analysis by segment
3. surplus reconciliations should be included with income statements
4. provide three years historical and one year projected, on an annual basis
5. provide one year historical and one year projected, on a quarterly basis
6. resource personnel are needed for answering questions, performing active tax planning, and providing other analyses

C. Balance Sheet
1. balance sheets by CMCP product segment are needed on a SAP and GAAP basis
2. provide three years historical and one year projected, on an annual basis
3. provide one year historical and one year projected, on a quarterly basis

D. Cash Flow Analysis
1. cash flow data, developed at the CMCP product segment level
2. detailed data on sales and in-force premium income should be included
3. provide three years historical and one year projected, on an annual basis
4. provide one year historical and one year projected, on a quarterly basis

As all of this information would be useful to all profit centers, I assume your department would prepare it for each profit center, and forward it directly to them. What would be helpful at this time is a proposed timetable as to when each item would be available.

Corporate Analysis is available to coordinate this process, and provide any other help we can, so please feel free to call on us.

Last month, I asked the profit center managers to provide me with lists of items which would allow them to more effectively do their jobs. One item that was generally agreed upon was an earlier and more extensive involvement in the planning, evaluation, and approval of DFP projects.

I realize your committee has stated its desire to involve the profit center managers in the DFP approval process, and you intend to invite PCMs to the 1986 meetings involving discussion of DFP project memorandums. Therefore, the purpose of this memo is simply to apprise you of the PCMs concurrence with such involvement, and to suggest that when planning for the 1987 DFP cycle, you consider participation of the PCMs at the earliest stage possible.

CHAPTER 9

Planning and Budgeting Systems

Planning and budgeting systems are another important element of financial results control systems. These systems, which are combinations of information flows and administrative processes, organize and coordinate the decisions and activities of the organization's employees. Planning and budgeting systems produce only one form of tangible output, written plans, which clarify where the organization wishes to go, how it intends to get there, and what results should be expected. Many of the organizational benefits of planning and budgeting come from the processes of developing the plans. The processes force people to think about the future, prepare their ideas and plans carefully, discuss their ideas and plans with others in the organization, and be committed to achieve goals that will serve the organization's interests.

The issue is not whether to prepare a plan of budget, but rather how to do it. Research evidence has shown that most firms (the most notable exception being small firms) benefit from engaging in planning in a quite formal way.[1] Companies which plan outperform those which do not, on average, and companies that introduce formal planning improve their performance.

Companies planning and budgeting systems vary considerably. Some are more formal than others. Some are more elaborate and time-consuming. Some involve considerable top management involvement, while others operate more on a bottom-up, management-by-exception basis. Certainly there are many ways to design an effective planning and budgeting system, but not all systems are equally effective, and some systems work better in certain settings than do others. This chapter discusses the multiple purposes of planning and budgeting systems, some of the most important characteristics of the systems, and some of the factors that lead corporations to use systems with differing characteristics.

PURPOSES OF PLANNING AND BUDGETING SYSTEMS

The purposes which planning and budgeting systems serve can be classified into four main categories. One purpose is *planning.* Planning is decision making in advance. Most people tend to become preoccupied with their seemingly urgent, day-to-day problems. Unless they are encouraged to do so, they fail to engage in more strategic, often more important longer-term thinking. Planning and budgeting systems provide the needed encouragement. They serve as a powerful form of action control which forces managers to think about the future and to make decisions in advance. They give managers a list of future-oriented tasks, link them to a series of enforced deadlines, and force managers to think about the future. In doing the forward thinking, the managers come to understand better the company's market opportunities and threats, its strengths and weaknesses, and the effects of possible strategic and operational decisions.

This future-oriented thinking and decision making process sharpens the organization's responses and reduces risk. It also shortens the response time, as management decisions regarding strategies, staffing, and operational tactics can be adjusted based on predictions of outcomes before the organization suffers major problems. Effective planning processes make the control system *proactive,* not just *reactive.* They help managers shape the future, not just respond to the conditions they face and measured performance they observe.

A second purpose is *coordination.* The planning and budgeting processes force the sharing of information across the organization. The processes involve a top-down communication of organizational goals and priorities and bottom-up communication of opportunities, resource needs, constraints, and risks. They also involve sideways communication that enhances the abilities of organizational subunits (that is, business units, functions, and administrative units) working together toward common purposes, as necessary. Everyone involved becomes more informed, so the process is more likely to result in decisions that consider all perspectives. The sales plan is coordinated with the production plan so that shortages or surpluses of inventory, space, and personnel are less likely. The production plans are coordinated so that the potentials for bottleneck constraints are minimized. Plans for growth, investments, and divestments are communicated to the finance function, which takes steps to ensure that the organization is able to pay its bills.

A third purpose is direct *top management control.* This control occurs in the form of preaction reviews, as plans are examined, discussed, and approved before actions are taken at successively higher levels in the hierarchy. Top management also uses plans as the performance standards used to implement the *management-by-exception* form of control. The planning and budgeting processes provide a forum that allows the organization to arrive at challenging but realistic performance targets by balancing top managers' wishes for higher performance with lower-level managers' information about possibilities. Negative variances, measured performance below targeted levels, provide top-level managers with an early warning of potential problems and justification for either reconsidering the organization's strategy or for interfering in the operating affairs of lower-level managers.

The final purpose is *motivation.* The plans and budgets become targets that affect manager motivation because the targets are linked to performance evaluations and, in turn, many organizational rewards and punishments. The impact of various forms of performance targets and rewards on motivation are discussed in more detail in Chapters 10 and 11.

PLANNING CYCLES

The critical planning question is: What should we do? Detailed answers to that question are best developed by breaking it into a series of more specific questions that are dealt with in sequence. Large, divisionalized organizations often use three formal, distinguishable, sequenced planning cycles called *strategic planning, programming,* and *operational budgeting.*[2] Each of these cycles involves a series of steps and the involvement of managers at multiple organization levels, as shown in Figure 9-1.

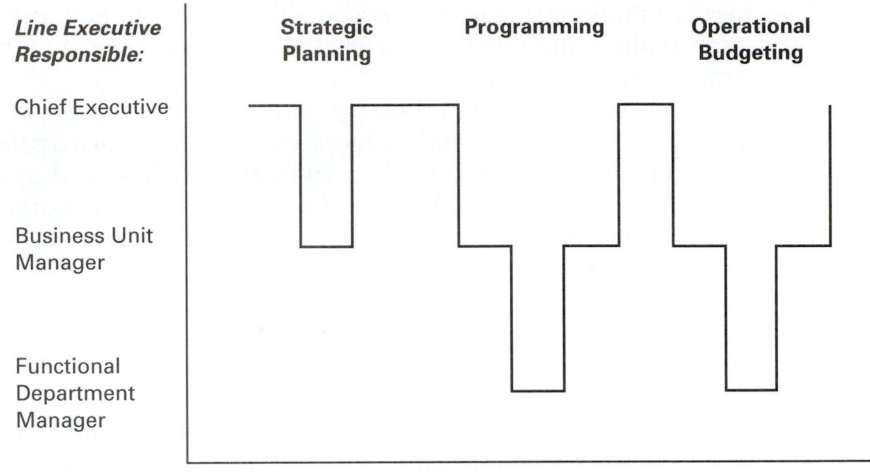

FIGURE 9-1 Formal Planning and Budgeting: Three Cycles

Adapted from: R. F. Vancil and P. Lorange, "Strategic Planning in Diversified Companies," *Harvard Business Review* (January–February 1975), pp. 84–85.

Strategic Planning

Strategic planning, sometimes called long-range planning, includes the relatively broad processes of thinking about the organization's missions, objectives, and the means by which the missions and objectives can best be achieved (that is, the strategies). Strategic planning involves both analyses of the past; using data on known quantities, costs, and revenues, and forecasts of the future. It leads to the creation of hypotheses about how the company and each of its businesses will perform within an uncertain macroeconomic and competitive environment.

Strategic planning is the essence of a general manager's job. It is normally a top management process which involves mostly top corporate and, to a lesser extent, division (business unit) managers. Top-level managers are the most broadly informed; limiting the processes to relatively few people simplifies the needed communication processes.

Strategic planning processes include five main steps which normally take place in an iterative (not linear) process[3]:

1. Develop the corporate vision, mission, and objectives,
2. Understand the company's present position, its strengths and weaknesses, and its opportunities and risks,
3. Decide on a strategy or strategies for moving from the present position to one that leads to achievement of the corporate objectives,
4. Prepare the strategic plan, which is a qualitative and quantitative representation of the strategic actions to be taken and the likely outcomes,
5. Monitor performance and update the strategic plan as necessary.

A complete, formal strategic planning process leads to definition of the corporate diversification strategy and all business strategies, identification of resource requirements, and statement of tentative performance goals. Strategic planning provides a framework for the more detailed planning that takes places in the following cycles. By the end of the cycle, business unit's managers should have reached agreement with top-level managers about their unit's charter, strategy, and objectives.

Programming

Programming involves the identification of specific action programs to be implemented over the next few years and specification of the resources each will consume. Programs should translate each business unit's externally oriented business strategy into an internally focused, well-coordinated set of activities designed to implement the strategy and, in turn, to lead to the achievement of the units' goals.

Programs can focus on the activities of any functional area (marketing, production, facilities, information systems) or any related combination of functional areas. Programs may be developed at various levels of detail, ranging from a purchase of a single new machine for a production line to a program covering all the activities necessary to allow a business unit to sell its products in a new geographical territory.

Programming is constrained in that the program options considered must be consistent with the tentative agreements reached during the strategic planning process. Programming is a complicated process because it involves many more people than does strategic planning, and it requires substantially more detailed plans.

The programming process usually starts with discussions between division managers and their subordinates about the action programs needed in the near future. As part of this process, managers must inevitably review ongoing programs to judge whether they are fulfilling their intended purposes and whether they should be modified or discontinued. Scarce resources are then allocated to specific programs. Much of the existing theory of resource allocation focuses on allocation of *capital* funds, and it is true that some of the screening and comparisons of potential investments is structured in financial terms using discounted cash flow analyses; however, rarely is resource allocation a mechanical process dependent solely on the financial calculations. Other resources which may be scarce in the time period being considered and which are more difficult to quantify in financial terms (space, engineers, capacity of a bottleneck machine), often also influence the final allocation decisions. Resource allocation is almost always heavily dependent on the track record, preparation and evidence, arguing skill, and political power of the managers concerned. Managers have to compete for resources and persuade those making the allocations that their requests should be supported.

Some top-level managers are usually involved in reviewing larger program proposals, often as part of a review committee. These reviews allow the top-level managers another opportunity to communicate corporate priorities to lower-level managers and to exercise another preaction review-type control. They also serve to help lower-level managers, particularly functional managers, understand how their activities fit into the larger corporate picture and influence other organizational units and initiatives. The reviews also have an important bottom-up communication function; they serve as a forum for lower-level managers to communicate opportunities, threats, and requests for upcoming cash outflows to the top-level managers. If programming is done well, the programs receiving resources are individually consistent with corporate objectives and strategies and mutually consistent with other related programs.

Budgeting

Budgeting involves short-term financial planning. Budgets are structured to match the organization's responsibility structure, with as much revenue, expense, asset and liability line item detail as is appropriate. Budgets are so important in providing day-to-day decision-making guidance for managers that it might be said that the primary purpose of the other planning cycles (strategic planning and programming) is merely to develop a *smart* budget.

Consistent with its importance, budgeting is a near universal organizational process. In the most recent survey, the vast majority (97 percent) of respondents reported that their company had a formal budgeting process. Of these, 91 percent reported that their budget was for a one-year period; 3 percent for a six-month period; and 1 percent for a three-month period.[4] In budgeting, quantitative data are emphasized: Only 11 percent of the firms stated that they placed more emphasis on qualitative data than quantitative data.[5]

Every effectively-run organization performs the functions of each of the three planning cycles; strategic planning, programming, and budgeting, although the formality and distinguishability of the cycles vary greatly from one company to the next. In smaller organizations, particularly, one or more of these cycles are usually relatively informal, and many organizations combine two, or sometimes all, of these cycles.

Evidence suggests that there is a fairly systematic planning process development cycle. As companies mature, a more elaborate and formal planning process evolves; one closer to a full three-cycle system.[6] Young companies start with a simple, largely top-down budgeting system and often make heavy use of outside consultants. Gradually, and at varying paces of change, they phase out the consultants and involve more of their own managers. They also place more emphasis on forecasting and more elaborate planning thought processes. The planning process becomes much more than production of just a single numerical plan.

CONTINGENCY PLANNING

Many companies engage in what is called *contingency, scenario,* or *what-if* planning exercises in one or more of their planning cycles. These exercises define how the company's resource requirements, risks, and performance will vary if the macroeconomic and competitive forecasts prove to be inaccurate.

The Royal Dutch/Shell Group, the giant oil company, is long renowned for its contingency planning approach called *War Gaming.*[7] Shell managers prepare for the unexpected by developing strategies to safeguard the company against a broad range of possible risks defined in terms of scenarios. Two recent Shell scenarios, prepared out to a twenty-year horizon, were called *Sustainable World* and *Global Mercantilism.* The first scenario assumed solutions were found to the major international economic disputes and thus greater attention was devoted to environmental issues; such as global warming trends, conservation, recycling, and emissions controls. The major implication for Shell was an energy industry mix change toward more use of natural gas and less use of oil. The Global Mercantilism scenario assumed a gloomier future with numerous regional conflicts, a destabilized world, an increase in protectionism, and world recession. This scenario implied less regulation, less focus on environmental issues, and greater oil consumption.

Similarly, Southern California Edison (SCE), looking ahead ten years, prepares plans under twelve different scenarios.[8] Each scenario carries implications for how much power SCE would need to supply. SCE managers believe contingency planning has improved the company's ability to cope with radical variations in demand.

Asking managers to prepare plans for each of a series of scenarios stretches their minds and helps condition them to think. It also helps them prepare for the unexpected without having to think in a rushed, sometimes adverse (even panicked), mode. When the Gulf War disrupted the supply of several hundred thousand barrels of crude oil per day from Kuwait and Iraq, Shell managers quickly implemented procedures that had been developed for just this contingency and replaced the supply.

PERFORMANCE REVIEW PROCESSES

Reviews comparing actual performance with plans and budgets are also an important planning and budgeting system element. These reviews are necessary to produce much of the system benefits. The review discussions, which tend to focus on variances between actual performance and targets, can lead to improved understanding of what is and what is not working well. The reviews improve organizational coordination by providing another forum for intraorganizational communication. They also provide an important part of the motivation produced by financial results control systems. Most managers are highly motivated to achieve their performance targets if for no other reason than to avoid having to explain in a public forum why the budget targets were not achieved.

VARIATIONS IN PRACTICE

The ways in which planning and budgeting systems are used reflect the outcome of literally hundreds of management design and implementation decisions. There is no universally superior, off-the-shelf planning and budgeting system, so it is not surprising that companies' systems are often quite different from each other. Managers make different system design or implementation decisions because they are emphasizing different mixes of the purposes which these systems serve or because they face different constraints or different benefit/cost trade-offs.

It is theoretically possible to address the varying contingencies at the business-unit level of the firm, or even lower, by varying the organizational planning and budgeting processes to adapt them to the different units' concerns. A recent survey showed that few corporations make this adaptation: 70 percent of the respondents reported that their budget policies and procedures allowed for no, or only slight, variation across business units.[9]

The following sections describe some major planning and budgeting system decision variables, firms' practices (where survey data are available), and some of the factors that can affect managers' choices.

Planning Horizon

The planning horizon reflects the longest period of time for which formal plans are prepared. Most firms' planning horizons are short: 1 year or less (34 percent), 2–3 years (20 percent), 4–5 years (38 percent), over 5 years (7 percent).[10] Some firms, however, such as those in the power utility industry, have to plan quite far in the future, often twenty-five years or more.

The key contingent factor affecting firms' planning horizons is the length of the normal business cycle, the lag between firms' investments, and their investment payoffs. Firms' planning horizons should be equal to, or perhaps slightly longer than, the cycle of their longest business decisions, not significantly longer. There is no need for a fast-food chain to prepare a twenty-five year plan because the long-range forecasts and plans will not affect decisions that have to be made anytime soon.

Content of Plans

Firms' planning and budgeting systems can vary significantly in the content and type (quantitative versus qualitative) of information that is considered, in the level of aggregation of the information, and the formats in which that information is displayed. Relatively formal systems usually specify elaborate, standardized sets of forms to be filled out. Many of these forms are in standard financial statement format (pro forma income statements and balance sheets), but many others are not. Top-level managers often want to see considerable nonfinancial information presented to them in planning and budgeting reviews. Table 9-1 shows survey data indicating the proportion of firms that "establish specific nonfinancial budgetary targets for its managers" in a number of common performance areas.

Usually the information portrayed in budgets is much more detailed than that in the strategic plans. Almost invariably, only annualized numbers are included in companies' long-range plans, but the survey of practice showed that the vast majority of firms break their annual budget into either months (88 percent) or quarters (12 percent). Rounding of numbers is almost always greater in strategic plans also. It is common to portray budget data to the nearest thousand dollars while showing strategic plan financial data only in millions.

Length and Timing of Processes

Firms' planning processes vary considerably both in total length of time and the time devoted to each cycle. The practice survey showed that nearly half of the firms began their *long-range* planning process five to seven months before the end

TABLE 9-1 Use of Non-Financial Performance Targets

Does your company usually establish specific nonfinancial budgetary targets for its managers in any of the following areas?

	Nonfinancial targets are used	
	Yes	*No*
New Product/Service Development	59%	41%
Quality of Product/Service	67	33
Market Share	51	49
Customer Relations	55	45
Relationships with Suppliers	32	68
Productivity	73	27
Human Resources Development	61	39
Employee Attitudes	39	61
Public Responsibility	40	60
Balance Between Short- and Long-Range Goals	52	48

Adapted from: S. Umapathy, *Current Budgeting Practices in U.S. Industry: The State of the Art,* (New York, Quorum, 1987), p. 138.

of the fiscal year, although the range was great; from two to eighteen months before the end of the year.[11] A majority of the firms take five months or less to complete their long-range plans, and approximately 65 percent complete their long-range plans three months or less before the end of the fiscal year. Most firms start their *budgeting* process four to six months before the end of the fiscal year and complete it in the last two months of the year.[12] The budgeting process takes about four months in most firms. These data show that planning processes in most firms span a considerable portion of the year and that the long-range and budgeting processes overlap.[13]

No universal prescriptions about length or timing of planning and budgeting processes can be provided. Planning activities are costly, particularly in terms of management time, and it is not uncommon to hear managers complain that they spend so much time planning that they have little time to do any work. Where planning provides benefits that exceed its costs, it should be done. The benefits are greater, hence more planning is necessary, in organizations with complex reporting structures (which have a higher need for coordination), those operating in rapidly changing environments (which need to make more frequent environmental adaptation decisions), and those just starting into new business areas (which must consider all decision areas).[14] Managers in these types of firms should design their processes with longer, more intense planning cycles; with a slower, more deliberate narrowing of strategic options, as shown in Figure 9-2.

At the extreme, some firms have some planning activities; strategic planning, programming, and/or budgeting, underway throughout the year. They never stop planning! Conversely, smaller firms whose managers are familiar with the firms's business prospects and possibilities can hasten the narrowing of strategic options and proceed directly to the development of action programs and budgets. These processes are obviously less costly.

The three planning cycles represent an orderly, gradual process of commitment to specific actions. Ideally, each step in each cycle should be linked to those preceding it. When significant lags exist between the timing of the cycles, the linkages are weakened. Survey data show that the numbers in the first year of the long-range plan and those in the corresponding year's annual budget were identical or almost the same in only 62 percent of the respondent firms. They were slightly different in 31 percent and very different in 7 percent.[15] Undoubtedly, in

FIGURE 9–2 Slow versus Rapid Narrowing of Strategic Options.

Adapted from: P. Lorange, and R. F. Vancil, "How to Design a Strategic Planning System," *Harvard Business Review* (September–October 1976), p. 80.

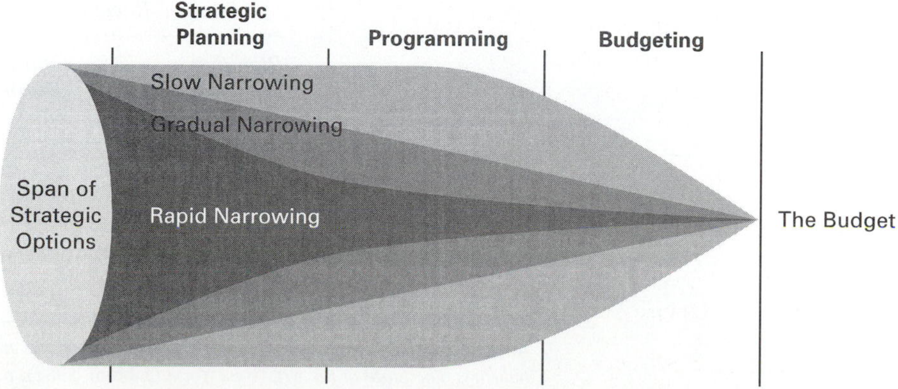

most of the firms in which these numbers were different, the long-range plan was finalized many months earlier than the budget. These lags reduce the likelihood of direct correspondence between the cycles.

Plan Updates

The practice survey showed that the vast majority (84 percent) of firms update their long-range plans annually. Others update them every three years (4 percent), every five years (2 percent), or on an as-needed basis (11 percent).[16] The recent trend seems to be toward the latter category (as-needed updating), which is, in an increasingly dynamic world, more frequent than annual.

Most companies update their plans on a rolling basis. That is, every time an update is prepared, a new plan is prepared out to the end of the planning horizon (for example, five years).

Most firms update their budgets more frequently than their long-range plans, as shown in Table 9-2. This table shows that firms make a distinction between two prominent purposes of budgeting: planning and evaluation. They are more likely to leave the budget unchanged for evaluation purposes than for planning purposes. They ask their managers to achieve their original budget targets, no matter what business conditions are faced. They use the updated budgets as inputs into decisions about investments, hiring, and financing.

Planning Guidance Provided

The amount of planning guidance provided to lower-level managers is another important design issue. Guidance can be provided through a planning manual or the equivalent, such as a series of memoranda. The practice survey showed that 64 percent of the respondent companies used a "budget manual or its equivalent;" 36 percent did not.

A planning manual is a written description of the more permanent elements of the planning process. Ideally it gives managers an overview of the process, describes the calendar of activities, and provides some planning guidelines and as-

TABLE 9-2 Frequency of Budget Reviews

How frequently do you review your annual budget for possible revision of goals, either for planning or evaluation purposes?

	Budget Reviewed for	
Reviewed	*Planning Purposes (n = 380)*	*Evaluation Purposes (n = 365)*
Monthly	32%	34%
Quarterly	42	29
Semi-annually	13	12
As-needed	7	9
Never	7	16

Adapted from: S. Umapathy, *Current Budgeting Practices in U.S. Industry: The State of the Art,* (New York, Quorum, 1987), p. 139.

sumptions, such as forecasts of economic activity and pay scale increases. A good manual saves managers time and ensures that the process proceeds in a coordinated manner. A manual should not be stifling. It should give managers some freedom to adapt their planning process to their personal style and their organization's culture. It should also avoid petty detail.

Roles of Planners and Controllers

Line managers are almost always actively involved in their firm's planning and budgeting processes, but staff roles in the processes can vary significantly. Staff who may or may not be deeply involved in planning and budgeting processes include planners and controllers.

Planners can be used in either analyst or coordinator roles, and either role can be made extensive or limited, weak or powerful. Planners in *analyst* roles are extensions of the line manager's office. They are actively involved in suggesting or elaborating ideas or in analyzing and reviewing others' ideas and plans. They are valuable because they can provide an objective review of plans prepared by others and because they often have some unique industry or technical expertise to add to the planning discussions. Analyst-type planners can have such diverse backgrounds as economics, statistics, chemistry, market research, or law; but they almost invariably have expertise in strategic management.

Planners in *coordinator* roles design and facilitate the planning processes. They define the roles, design the forms, prepare the schedules of activities, and communicate all of this to the involved parties. Coordinators help ensure that those doing the planning are capable, that they perform their tasks, and that their efforts are coordinated.

Many companies make good use of planners, but planners can easily be overused. General Electric is one company that has cut back on the use of analyst-type planners. GE used to have a 350-member planning staff that "churned out voluminous reports, meticulously detailed and exquisitely packaged."[17] Now the company has only approximately twenty full-time planners, called business development specialists, whose role is to advise line managers, not formulate strategy.

The planning role of controllers, both at corporate and business unit levels, can be similarly varied. Controllers' measurement expertise can be valuable in preparing well-analyzed plans. On the other hand, high controller involvement causes some managers concern that the focus will become extensively quantitative, that the emphasis on the numbers will squeeze all the creative, strategic thinking out of the process.

CONCLUSION

Planning and budgeting systems are potentially powerful management tools which serve multiple purposes. They provide a way of converting managers' visions into an organized set of tactics that are employed throughout their organizations. They provide a standard that can be used to judge organizational success or progress. They have many behavioral implications, such as regarding the effort invested in thinking about the future and commitment to achieve budget targets.

While some commonalities exist among companies' planning and budgeting systems, there are many more differences. No single system is optimal in a broad range of settings. The systems must be judged in terms of the purposes which they are intended to serve.

Just because a company prepares a plan does not mean that it is engaging in useful planning. Frequent criticisms are voiced that, "At too many companies strategic planning has become overly bureaucratic, absurdly quantitative, and largely irrelevant."[18] Often plans are prepared but not used; they just take up shelf space. Similarly, just because a company has a mission statement does not mean that the statement has an effect.

For plans and mission statements to have a significant effect, they must be used as a near-constant guide for the employee actions and, in fact, converted into action. They must be linked to individual or group responsibilities for performance that force them to be used in running the company.

Notes

1. S. S. Thune and R. J. House, "Where Long-Range Planning Pays Off," *Business Horizons*, 13, no. 4 (August 1970), pp. 81–87; H. I. Ansoff, et al., "Does Planning Pay? The Effect of Planning on Success of Acquisition in American Firms," *Long Range Planning*, 3, no. 2 (December 1970), pp. 2–7; D. Herold, "Long-Range Planning and Organizational Performance: A Cross Validation Study," *Academy of Management Journal*, 15, no. 1 (March 1972), pp. 91–102.
2. R. F. Vancil and P. Lorange, "Strategic Planning in Diversified Companies," *Harvard Business Review* (January–February 1975), pp. 81–90.
3. G. A. Pogue, "Strategic Management Accounting," *Management Accounting* (UK) (January 1990), pp. 44–47; G. A. Pogue, "Strategic Management Accounting and the Corporate Objective," *Management Accounting* (UK) (January 1990), pp. 46–49; G. A. Pogue, "Strategic Management Accounting and Marketing Strategy," *Management Accounting* (UK) (January 1990), pp. 52–54; and G. A. Pogue, "Strategic Management Accounting and Production Strategy," *Management Accounting* (UK) (January 1990), pp. 58–60.
4. S. Umapathy, *Current Budgeting Practices in U.S. Industry: The State of the Art* (New York: Quorum, 1987), p. 137.
5. Ibid., p. 140.
6. See S. W. Wheelright and R. L. Banks, "Involving Operating Managers in Planning Process Evolution," *Sloan Management Review* (Summer 1979), pp. 43–59; and F. Gluck, S. Kaufman, and A. S. Walleck, "The Four Phases of Strategic Management," *Journal of Business Strategy* (Winter 1982), pp. 9–21.
7. C. Knowlton, "Shell Gets Rich by Beating Risk," *Fortune* (August 26, 1991), pp. 79–82.
8. R. Hentkoff, "How to Plan for 1995," *Fortune* (December 31, 1990), p. 75.
9. S. Umapathy, *Current Budgeting Practices in U.S. Industry: The State of the Art* (New York, Quorum, 1987), p. 143.
10. Ibid., p. 145.
11. Ibid., pp. 59–60.
12. Ibid., p. 73.
13. Programming was not considered as a separate category in Umapathy's survey.
14. P. Lorange and R. F. Vancil, "How to Design a Strategic Planning System," *Harvard Business Review* (September–October 1976), pp. 75–81.
15. S. Umapathy, *Current Budgeting Practices in U.S. Industry: The State of the Art* (New York, Quorum, 1987), p. 146.
16. Ibid., p. 145.
17. R. Hentkoff, "How to Plan for 1995," *Fortune* (December 31, 1990), p. 72.
18. Ibid., p. 71.

G. A. Kleissler Co.

Ed Kleissler, president of the G. A. Kleissler Co. (GAK), a small engineering company and manufacturer of dust control systems and equipment, explained the problem:

> We have a considerable amount of tension present in our professional staff now, with most of the dissatisfaction focused on the project budgeting system. Everybody has strong feelings on the subject. The project leaders and operations people feel that the original estimates made by the sales engineers are not very realistic and, therefore, not very useful for planning workloads and schedules. The sales engineers, on the other hand, feel that a lot of the budget changes are motivated only to produce a zero variance, and that there is not enough thought or effort invested to try to meet the budget.

THE COMPANY

GAK, located in Edison, New Jersey, was founded in 1916 by Ed Kleissler's grandfather. The company was privately held, with the Kleissler family controlling nearly all the stock. By 1980, annual revenues were approximately $4 million, and the company had just under 100 full-time employees located in two buildings approximately one mile apart. In the early 1970s, GAK's financial position was weak, but under Ed Kleissler's leadership the finances had strengthened to the point where the company had no long-term debt and was earning modest profits.

GAK had a background in providing dust control systems for general industrial applications, but in the past 15 years it had specialized in systems for the paper industry. The systems filtered the air from machines which generated dust or particulate air pollution and passed the clean air back into the plant.

The separator (see Exhibit 1) and the manifold core components of a dust control system were more or less standardized products, although they varied somewhat depending on the type of dust generated, the size of the application, and the desired methods of emptying the dust bags. The other components, such as main and branch pipes, hoods and conveyers, had to be custom-designed to fit the customer's equipment and plant layout.

GAK preferred to sell entire systems and handle the job all the way from design to installation and test. It was the dominant supplier of such systems to the paper industry, but company managers were beginning to consider diversifying both into other industries and into other products which would utilize their engineering expertise.

PROJECT MANAGEMENT

Because a large proportion of the company's revenues were derived from a limited number of large-scale projects, project management was very important to GAK. Organizationally, two key roles were specifically project-oriented—sales engineers and project leaders (see organization chart in Exhibit 2). The sales engineers were responsible for the initial customer contact, analysis of the problem, definition of the system concept, selling, original job cost estimating, and pricing. The project leaders were responsible for the detailed technical development (design) of the project and the management of the job from time of order entry to completion. Throughout the remainder of this case, Project 79145 will be used to illustrate the functioning of these roles and the company's management systems.

Professor Kenneth A. Merchant prepared this case with the assistance of Research Assistant Howard Koo as the basis for class discussion rather than to illustrate either effective or ineffective handling of an administrative situation. Certain facts in the case have been changed to avoid the disclosure of confidential information, but they do not materially lessen the value of the case for educational purposes.

PROJECT 79145

In 1978, GAK was asked by the Great Western Paper Corporation (GWP) to submit a proposal for a complete dust control system for the converting area of a toilet-paper processing plant. The machines in the converting area took tissue paper from the mill, rolled it into logs 96 inches wide, slit it into widths of $4\frac{1}{2}$ inches, and packaged it for sale. GWP was interested in a dust control system because it would reduce maintenance on the converting machines, make a less dusty product, and keep the plant safely within federal safety standards.

GAK submitted an estimate for the entire job, but for their own internal reasons, GWP asked that the project be broken into two phases. Thus, GAK submitted a phase I proposal for part of the job. This proposal was accepted and GAK began the work. The request for a proposal for phase II, a job which eventually was assigned number 79145, followed as expected. Background information on the GAK personnel most heavily involved in this project is shown in Exhibit 3.

PROPOSAL

For all potential jobs where the customer was considered serious about adding equipment, the sales engineer prepared formal estimating sheets. These required detailed estimates for each element of direct cost, built up by pounds of material and hours of labor for each system component. These units were converted to dollars by multiplying by standard costs, which were updated every six months by accounting, and by getting quotes for special materials or service.

To get to a *full-cost* estimate, overhead was applied on pounds of material or hours of labor. Accounting personnel updated the 16 overhead rates, eight each for variable and fixed overhead categories once a year. Exhibits 4 through 6 show examples of Estimating Sheets. Exhibit 4 was used for estimating the Main Pipe component of a system. Exhibit 5 was for General Job Costs, and Exhibit 6 was a job summary.

The price was determined by adding a profit percent onto the full cost estimate. The company's goal was to maintain a 10 to 15 percent net profit margin on sales (before tax).

Because time was often limited, Gary McCarthy, sales engineer, used a rough rule-of-thumb based on dollars per required volume of air (cubic feet per minute) to estimate the total cost and price for Project 79145. For the breakdown in costs, Gary compared this job with a similar, large job completed the year before.

Carl Honecker, proposals manager, explained:

> First of all, you have to realize that these estimates involve a lot of guesses. This project is now being installed, but portions of the new GWP building are not finished even yet, and their equipment is not in location. So with this as with many other jobs, we had to estimate it based on their drawings. For more or less standardized components, such as separators, those do not cause a big problem. But for customized components, such as branch lines, the estimates become only guesses.

To protect the company against these project uncertainties, sales engineers typically added an unspecified element of cost, called a contingency, to the estimate. The contingency was done on an entire job and not on an individual component unless the risk was high on a particular section of the job, perhaps because there was little information about it. The contingency was intended to protect GAK from cost uncertainties. It was not affected by what the market would bear. However, some extra revenue dollars might be added if GAK managers felt the company was in a strong competitive position. These were shown on the bottom right of the Estimating Sheet Summary (Exhibit 6).

The proposed price of $1,279,056 for the Phase I work was presented to GWP. It was accepted on November 26, 1979, and the project was assigned number 79145.

PROJECT KICK-OFF

On November 27, the project kick-off meeting was held. The primary purpose of this meeting was to transfer the responsibility for the job from the sales engineer, Gary McCarthy, to the project leader assigned to the job, Harry Johantgen. Also in attendance at the meeting were Carl Honecker (Proposals Manager), Bob Kleissler (Design Manager), Les Owen (Operations Manager),

Charlie Clayton (Plant Manager), Norm Potter (a separator specialist), and Grace Calandruccio (Job Cost Accountant). Most of the discussion at the two-hour meeting was on technical subjects, such as about what filter media and fan size were required, and the expert team provided their inputs.

After this meeting, Harry, the project leader, planned the project, broke the tasks into work orders, starting with the design work, established the schedule, as well as coordinating manpower and material needs.

PROJECT CONTROL

Control of the project was an ongoing process, with frequent communications required between Harry the project leader and both GWP and the various GAK work areas: design, operations, and installation. Each month, Harry was required to assemble a Job Status Report which showed the percent physical completion at the end of the month and the predicted dollar variance to completion for each element of cost. This was built up from the work order level and summarized by the project leader to the level of detail provided in the original project budget (see Exhibit 7).

The estimates of percent complete were an important part of the control process because they directly affected the percent of the budget used for comparison with actual expenditures to date and, therefore, the variances. In estimating the percent complete in the design area, Harry used drawings as his gauge. Drawings were a much smaller element of work than in other areas and did not normally stretch out several reporting periods. It was not difficult to estimate how long a drawing should take or to judge whether a drawing was done.

In the fab area, Harry relied on inputs from the fabrication department. Based on their experience and accumulated records, the fabrication department broke down the work orders into individual operations and established standard hours for each operation to come up with a total standard for each work order. Then they looked at how much they've accomplished and calculated the total percent complete on each work order. Harry believed their estimates were generally quite good, better than he could make, but he noted that errors could occur on occasion:

> For instance, they may say their fabrication is so many percent complete on a given work order, but I know we have already shipped all of it. Or the records may show only 50 percent of the material on a job has been withdrawn, but they are indicating 100 percent fabrication.

Field installation was a bigger problem, since GAK was only beginning the establishment of standards for installation. Harry had to rely on the estimates of installation foremen who were generally optimistic. For example, a foreman might say that he was 99 percent complete with a work order when it was more like 85 percent. Since Harry often worked with new foremen, it was impossible for him to judge which were optimistic and which were pessimistic. But the foremen were able to tell Harry which items on a work order were complete, so Harry had some information on which to apply judgments on the estimates.

The Job Status estimates were input to the computer, and the portion of the budget determined by the percent complete was compared with actual costs to date. Three monthly reports were produced. The Detailed Job Cost Report (Exhibit 8) showed a comparison of actual costs (and labor hours) with fraction of budget (total budget multiplied by percent complete) for variable cost categories only. The Summary Job Cost Report (Exhibit 9) summarized variable costs by component and showed variance-to-date and forecast-to-completion. The Job Cost Fully Accounted Summary (Exhibit 10) summarized variances by component and showed variances to date for variable cost, full cost and net profit.

The projects were monitored by accounting staff. Shortly after the reports were produced, Grace Calandruccio, job cost accountant, asked the project leaders for explanations of cost category variances greater than $1,000 appearing during the month and of any obvious errors (e.g., expenses incurred but showing zero percent completion). She was trying to determine whether an actual problem existed or whether, for example, the variance was merely a timing problem. Any large input errors were corrected before the financial statements were produced.

Around the tenth working day of each

month, a company-level financial review meeting was held with the key managers in attendance: Ed and Bob Kleissler, Bill Leist, Les Owen, Susan Jaskula and Carl Honecker. About one-half hour of this meeting was devoted to a review of the top six to ten projects, which typically covered about 80 percent of the costs incurred during the month. Grace Calandruccio would present a summary of the project variances with the explanations provided by the project leaders, and the discussion would focus mostly on overall performance, not the specifics of the jobs.

BUDGET ADJUSTMENTS

A number of budget adjustments were made in Project 79145. Appendix A explains the rationale and general procedure for budget adjustments. The following are two illustrative examples of budget adjustments for Project 79145:

A. Blow-back Dampers

In December and January, work proceeded on Project 79145, mostly on project design. On January 23, Harry Johantgen, submitted a budget adjustment for $3,045 for the inclusion of three blow-back dampers. Normally, the blow-back dampers had to be specifically called out in the budget, since they were unique and required a certain amount of time to be fabricated. However, sales engineering allocated the dollars for the blow-back dampers to M (Main Line), instead of separating them under V (Valves) or some other designation. But because the blow-back dampers were shown in the drawing as part of A (manifold), Harry released them on an A work order. (He later admitted that he should have gone back to sales engineering and requested that the blow-back dampers be shown as part of the manifold.) On the job cost report, these choices made A look bad and M look unnaturally good.

Harry observed, however, that "Even with these dollars allocated to the manifold, the sales engineering estimate was extremely low." It did not include enough pounds for the three blow-back valves. Based on actual drawings, Harry submitted the budget adjustment.

Even after the budget revision, however, when fab actually built the dampers, they were way off budget. Harry guessed that the material requirement calculation done in design from actual drawings failed to include scrap, or it may have been based on metal cuttings of sizes of sheets that did not exist. These differences between estimate, design and fab showed up as budget variances because a budget adjustment could not be made after work was started.

Gary McCarthy, the sales engineer, commented:

> I agree that in comparison with what was actually built, the material estimate was low. However, it's my contention that the manifold was over-designed and thus over-built for this application. Before this happened, design should have met with sales engineering to discuss the anticipated variances to attempt to develop corrective action.

B. Platforms

On June 16, a second formal meeting was held. Design had progressed to the point where it was possible to tell operations that they could look for specific work orders on a specific schedule. In attendance at this meeting were Harry Johantgen, Bob Kleissler, and Les Owen. The next day, because of what he learned at the meeting, Harry submitted an adjustment which increased the budget by $14,351, the details of which are shown in Exhibit 11. Harry elaborated on the largest item which individually caused a $15,964 increase:

> In order to estimate accurately, we can't extrapolate directly from past data. We need to look more closely at what's required from the current job. Last year we built a very similar collector and used that as a gauge for estimating. But this collector required a minimum of four platforms that weren't in the estimate. . . . I think sales engineering basically took their estimate from their old estimate. But not only did they overlook the platforms, we overran their original estimate. They should have looked at the *actuals* on that job and not reproduced a bad estimate.

Gary McCarthy explained from his perspective:

> We have to use last year's job as a guide. They are both 18 hoppers of collector, with a slightly different configuration, but the size of the GWP collector is actually *smaller.* I checked against the actuals on last year's job

when that job was about 98 percent complete, and the separators were 100 percent complete at that time. Based on that check I estimated we should come in at about 135,000 pounds of material. Allowing for some additional bracing and reinforcing, I forecast the actuals would come in closer to 140,000 pounds. But we are predicting this job will come in at about 165,000 pounds. Not only is the material way off, but installation on last year's job took 2,300 hours, and we're now forecasting 2,800 on this job. The platform will make a difference, but not 500 hours.

We did include some hours for the platforms in the original estimate, although I admit we didn't have anything specific in mind, and that's an obvious shortcoming. We certainly didn't think in the grand scale that was eventually drawn up. I don't know how to explain the extra 25,000 pounds of material. There must be some overdesigning. But our original estimate for fab hours was 3,864, and on the latest cost sheets we're running at about 3,000 hours. That's obviously to the good, and it's not consistent with the material overrun.

SCOPE CHANGES

When a scope change requires the customer price to be renegotiated, a budget revision was required. Appendix B describes this price renegotiation and budget revision process in general and the rationale for involving the sales engineer in it. The following are two examples of scope changes on Project 79145.

A. Move Collectors

In February, after the manifold was released for fabrication, Harry, the project leader, provided GWP some additional information about where the collectors would be located on the roof and the static and wind loads that would be imposed on the roof. GWP decided that these loads were unacceptable and asked that the collector be shifted 150 feet north and to the grade level of the building. Even though GAK was well into production at that point, an acceptable alternative for the collectors could not be found. Substantial modifications were required to incorporate the existing manifold in with some additional piping that had to be installed. This necessitated a reestimate of the job, agreement on a new price and revision of the budget.

Gary McCarthy, the Sales Engineer, was responsible for negotiating the price change. The customer accepted the proposed price increase of $81,400, and Gary revised the budget to reflect his estimate of the savings and additional costs that would be incurred.

A short time later, Harry submitted two adjustments which increased the budget by just under $19,000, because the final drawings showed the job had expanded beyond where sales engineering had figured. Since this occurred after GAK had received the additional money from the customer, Harry had to adjust the budget. Harry explained:

> One of the problems we had with this change, and it happens on occasion, is a definitional problem of where the manifold left off and where the main pipe began. I may report the costs against the manifold while the sales engineer had figured the budget for the main. The sum total for the manifold and main may be the same, but we would show a variance for each.
>
> We also had a problem with the total dollars budgeted. This is only speculation, but what may have happened here is that sales engineering figured we couldn't ask the customer for all of the dollars for the change and they decided that GAK would absorb part of the cost.

Gary McCarthy was not aware of this budget adjustment at the time but he commented on it several months later:

> I wish Harry had let me know what was happening. There is nothing worse than knowing after the fact that, for example, your manifold is 10,000 pounds over budget. It may have ended up that way anyway, but we can't provide suggestions or learn from problems if we don't know about them.

B. Pipework Supports

On June 24, another budget revision was input. GWP insisted that the pipework did not meet their standard, even though GAK protested that it met the industry standard. GWP also felt that the change should be made at no cost to them, since they gave GAK the total package without competition. GAK protested and finally settled on a price increase of just $6,000. The total cost estimate, however, which went through as a budget revision, was around $17,000.

Harry Johantgen commented:

> This revision is a good example of a major problem we have with sales—their budget changes are often painfully slow. In this case, we had known for months that the budget needed revising, and I had to keep prodding them to make the change. These expected changes can often span several reporting periods, and it creates confusion as to whether we should be reporting against the budget or what we expect the budget will be. Sometimes the revision takes so long that the work is done before the revision comes through.

STATUS AT AUGUST 1980

From the beginning, Project 79145 had had its share of problems as reflected by the numerous budget adjustments, as well as budget revisions. The Summary Job Cost Report for 79145 at July 31, shown in Exhibit 10 showed a small unfavorable total variance versus the budget at the estimated 43 percent complete, caused mainly because of the problems in the collector part of the separator component. Harry Johantgen described the current problems and his remaining concerns:

> A gross estimation error has just recently surfaced. The budget for Material-Sundry in the S (separator) component is $16,746. We have already spent over $18,000, and our forecast to complete is in excess of $27,000. It could be argued that we should have recognized this problem earlier, but this is also a notable example of poor estimating. I'm going to have to adjust the budget upwards in this area.
>
> We could also have more trouble with the budget for management hours. Each addition to project scope or extension of the project schedule extends the number of reporting periods and increases management time. Since the company has grown, we have progressed from *doing* a project to *managing* a project, but the budgets haven't reflected this. On a large project, management time can be 20 to 22 percent of the total design budget, but the original budget for 79145 allowed only 4 to 5 percent.
>
> In addition, I'm a little worried about the estimates for getting painting and pneumatic piping done on this particular project. We're not as good as we could or should be at estimating other trades, such as printing, plumbing and electrical, and I'm not sure there are enough dollars in there to get the job done. . . . And finally, we could always run into some problems in installation.

Since the budget changes had increased the planned costs much faster than the price had been negotiated upward, the project's planned profit margin had slipped from an original 11 percent to less than 6 percent, a level considered below the desired range of between 10 percent and 15 percent (see Exhibit 12). The margin would slip even lower if the budget was adjusted upward any further, and Harry seemed to think it would have to be.

Carl Honecker looked back at the job and summarized his feelings:

> I don't think this was a particularly difficult job. I still feel that in an overall sense our original estimate was accurate, although I will agree that there were numerous discrepancies in the components. At this point, however, it's even hard to tell that. We may be seeing variances because conservative estimates of percent complete are making the jobs look worse than they really are. Design and fabrication seem to like to hold back a few percent as a hedge against something going wrong or because they are nervous about what might come up next.
>
> But more importantly, what seems to be missing is a commitment to bring a job in at the minimum cost possible. If we involved the various groups in setting the budgets, the numbers would be so super-conservative that they would be meaningless, and we'd either be planning projects at a loss or we'd be pricing ourselves out of the market. Not all of the budgets set by sales engineering are tight. They should be a target to shoot for; an

incentive for superior performance, so we are motivated to search for creative solutions to our problems. We've got to get this commitment internalized because standards of performance aren't available for everything we do. We're not trying to punish anybody, but the company does have to exist, after all.

APPENDIX A

Budget Adjustments

Over time, many changes were likely to be made to the system as it was originally planned and estimated. More information would be gathered as to the precise customer requirements, such as for the layout of the exhaust piping, and as company personnel reviewed the technical design, suggestions would be made to improve performance or cut costs.

In addition, while the sales engineers were considered excellent at estimating the total cost of a job, very often their estimates for specific phases of a job (e.g., main, exhausters) were very inaccurate, overestimated for some parts and underestimated for others, and the dollars in the budget would have to be moved between components. The custom elements of the systems, such as branch piping, presented the greatest estimating uncertainty. Some definitional problems also existed, as the boundary between components was not clear. A project leader might build on a branch line work order what a sales engineer estimated as part of the main piping.

The job budgets were intended to reflect the company's best estimate of what it should cost to do the work described. This was because while the projects were in process, the budgets were important tools for planning and control, and after a job was completed, budgets which proved to be accurate were useful as an aid for estimating future similar jobs. As the project unfolded, the detailed breakdown in original budget was likely to become less and less realistic. Thus, the company instituted a budget adjustment procedure to allow the project leader to change the budget to reflect a realistic standard, but with the following constraints:

1. No budget adjustments were allowed once work within a labor category (e.g., design, fabrication, installation) was started within a job section (e.g., separators, main, exhausters), with the exception of general job costs.
2. No budget adjustments were allowed unless the adjustment totaled at least eight hours and 10 percent of the total hours in the work order.
3. All budget adjustments had to be approved by the Operations Manager.

APPENDIX B

Budget Revisions

If for any reason the customer price had to be renegotiated, such as for a scope change or customer-caused cost overruns (e.g., schedule delay), the sales engineer was notified to prepare a budget revision. This involved a reestimate of costs, using the same Estimating Sheets used when the project was proposed, and a renegotiation of price. When the price change was agreed upon, the new cost estimate was entered as the revised project budget.

Even though at the time of most of these budget revisions, the project leader's detailed knowledge far exceeded that of the sales engineer on the job, because they had been following progress daily, it was seen as desirable to involve the sales engineer in the budget revision because:

1. More realistic estimates were likely. The sales engineers had been exposed to a broader range of jobs, and they had begun to accumulate a data base of standards for recurring operations that could facilitate the estimating process. They were also more skilled at preparing estimates at the concept stage; i.e., before detailed drawings and specification sheets were available.
2. It was a good opportunity to develop the sales engineer/customer relationship because it was a chance to meet without a new sale being the explicit intent. In addition, it would provide a relationship continuity for the customer, as the sales engineer may have made agreements regarding the specifications of the system that were not put explicitly in the written agreement.
3. It was a good learning opportunity for the sales engineers. By getting out in the field and seeing how the project was progressing, they could learn, both technically and in their estimating.

EXHIBIT 1 Schematic of Separator

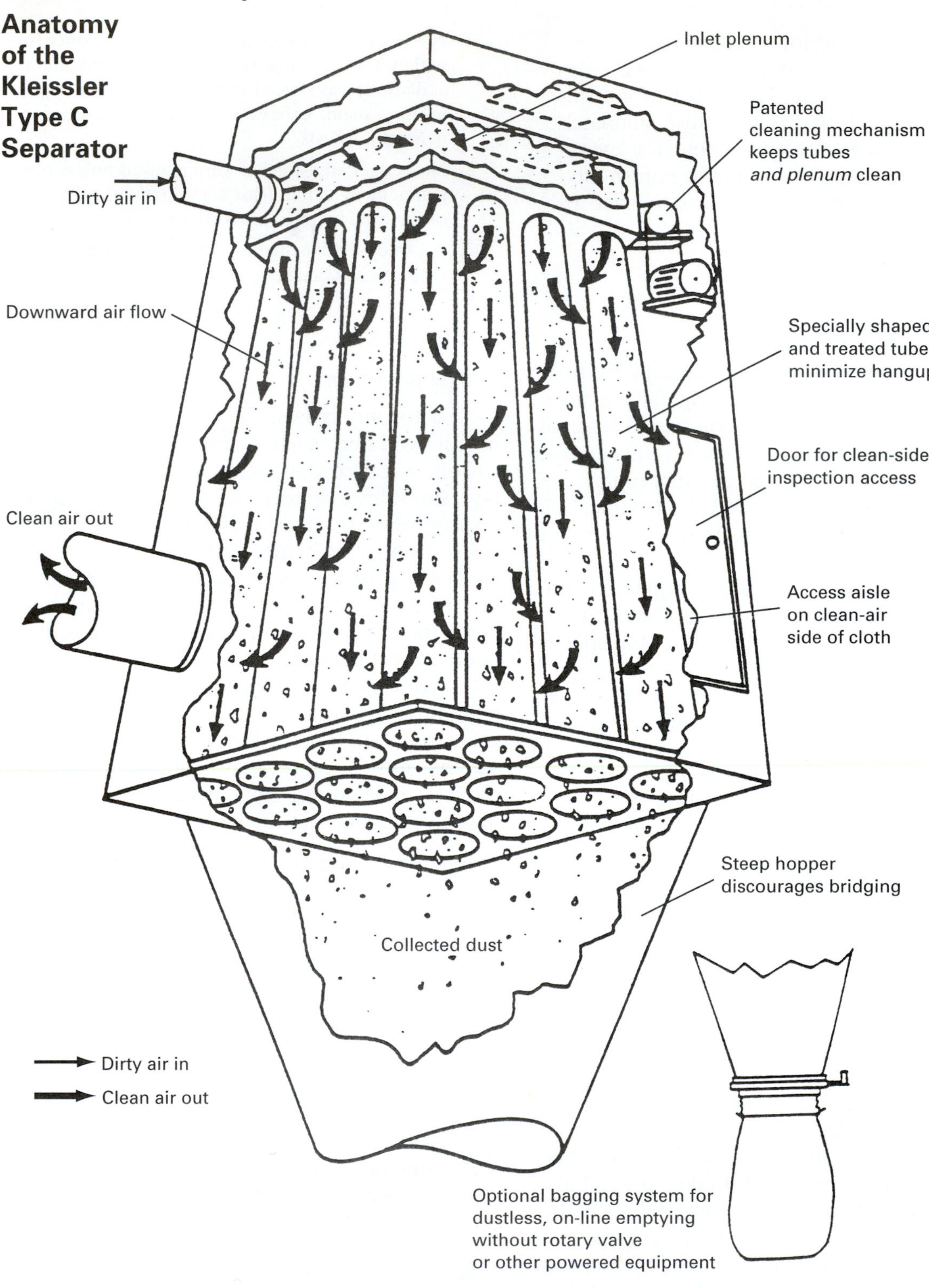
Anatomy of the Kleissler Type C Separator
Inlet plenum
Patented cleaning mechanism keeps tubes *and plenum* clean
Dirty air in
Downward air flow
Specially shaped and treated tubes minimize hangup
Door for clean-side inspection access
Clean air out
Access aisle on clean-air side of cloth
Steep hopper discourages bridging
Collected dust
Dirty air in
Clean air out
Optional bagging system for dustless, on-line emptying without rotary valve or other powered equipment

EXHIBIT 2 Organization Structure

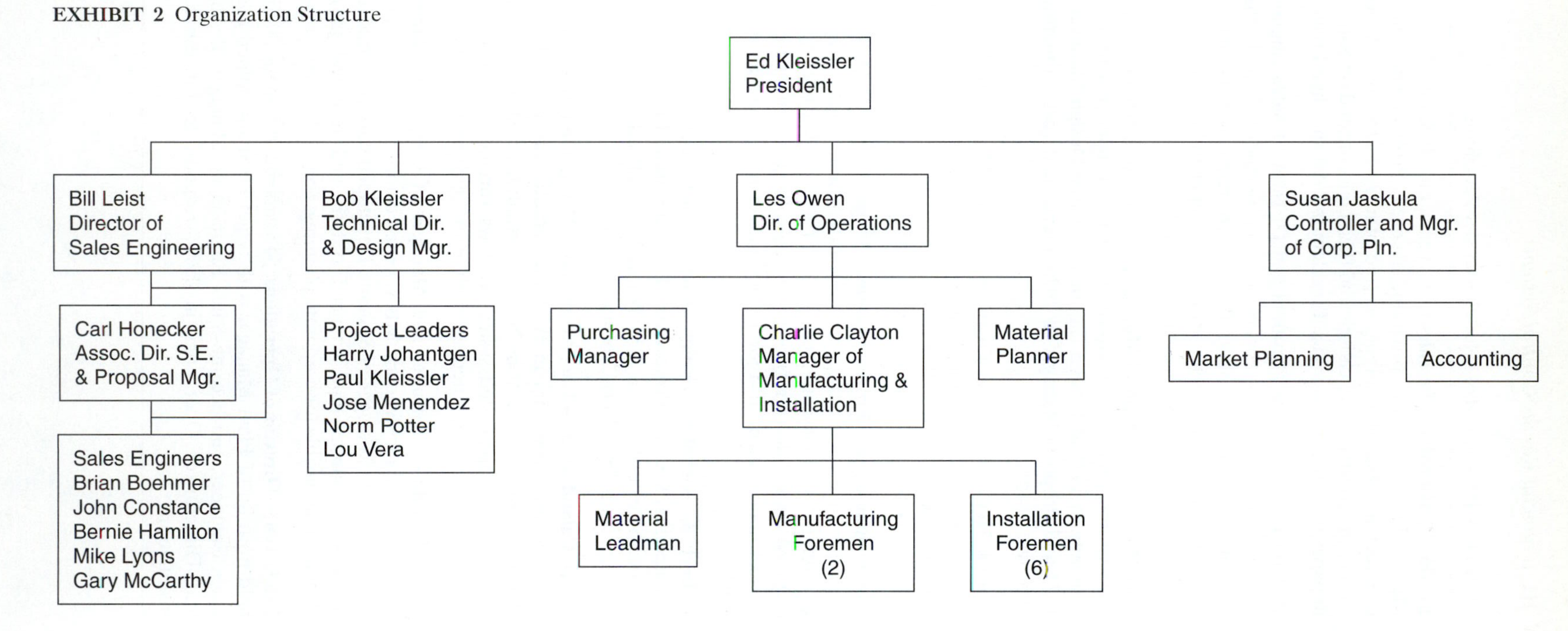

EXHIBIT 3 Background of Selected Kleissler Personnel

Edwin A. Kleissler—President, 52 years old: B.S. and M.S. in mechanical engineering, MBA, Harvard SCMP program, licensed Professional Engineer: joined company as engineer in 1952 after serving as line officer in U.S. Navy. Worked on system design in a variety of industrial applications and then concentrated on Sales Engineering effort in 1960s in paper industry. Became Vice President in 1996 and then President in 1972.

William L. Leist—Vice President and Director of Sales Engineering, 52 years old: B.S. in political science and two years of engineering studies. Joined company as a student, working part time in fabrication shop. Because Designer then Design Manager in 1966. Assumed Sales engineering role, concentrating on paper industry, in 1971. Became Vice President in 1971 and Director of Sales engineering in 1978.

Carl Honecker—Proposal Manager, 44 years old: B.S. in mechanical engineering, licensed Professional Engineer: previously was Chief Engineer with a large dryer company, joined company in 1971 as Design Engineer, became Design Manager in 1972, Sales Engineer in 1974 and Proposal Manager in 1978. Developed cost estimating procedures and proposal approval system.

Gary T. McCarthy—Sales Engineer, 34 years old: A.S. and B.S. in aerospace and mechanical engineering, M.B.A.: joined company in 1976 as a Project Leader. Transferred to Sales Engineering position in 1978. As a Sales Engineer he is responsible for analysis of customer problem, cost estimate and proposal, and sale of job. Tracks jobs through startup.

Harry Johantgen—Project Leader, 35 years old: B.S.E.T. in mechanical engineering, presently in masters program in Environmental Engineering: joined company in 1969 as Drafter. Became Designer, then Design Engineer; became Project Leader in 1974. Has been engaged on a wide variety of projects. As Project Leader he is responsible for design and project management of a job after turnover from Sales Engineer and follows job through startup.

Robert J. Kleissler—Design Manager, 44 years old: B.S. and M.S. in mechanical engineering, licensed Professional Engineer, joined company in 1963 as Design Engineer, became Sales Engineer in 1965. Worked on applications in varied industries. Became Design Manager in 1975 and Vice President in 1978.

Grace Calandruccio—Cost Accountant, 24 years old: B.S. in accounting: joined company as Administrative Assistant in 1978 after graduation. Worked on procedures and personnel. Became Cost Accountant in July 1979. Analyzes costs of standard production items, enters budgets to computerized system, reviews variance on all jobs monthly and at close, and routes annotated computerized analysis to appropriate persons.

Susan Jaskula—Controller and Manager of Corporate Planning, 27 years old: B.A. in English and Library Science, MBA: joined company in 1974 as Administrative Assistant and shortly became Manager of Systems. Developed corporate budgeting system, computerized job cost accounting and financial system, and technical information retrieval system. Became responsible for corporate planning, accounting and marketing services in 1977.

Les Owen—Director of Operations, 54 years old: B.S. in mechanical engineering: previously held position of Plant Manager with larger company: joined company in 1968. Worked as Sales Engineer, and became Sales Engineering Manager. Became Vice President in 1976 and Director of Operations in 1978; responsible for purchasing, manufacturing and installation.

EXHIBIT 4

G. A. KLEISSLER CO.

G. A. KLEISSLER CO. ESTIMATING SHEET MAIN PIPE

CUSTOMER: ______ Proposal # ______ SHEET # ______

LOCATION: ______ DATE ______

ENGINEER: ______ PREPARED BY ______

MATERIALS OF CONSTRUCTION: ______	HOURS					
______	183	280	340	430		
1 #AS GA.	D	T	F	I		
183 DRAFT X HRS/#						
265 TEAMSTER X HRS/#						
340 FABRICATION X HRS/#						
430 INSTALLATION X HRS/#						
430 INSTALLATION ADJ.						
SUBTOTAL						

DESCRIPTION	EQUIP.	MATERIAL #		SUNDRY							
	575	525	550	555							
	$	STAND.	SPEC.	$							
525 ACTUAL POUNDS											
555 FLANGES #@ $/@											
ADDED PIPE SUPPORTS											
CLEAN OUTS											
DAMPERS											
HOLES & FLASHINGS											
605 FREIGHT IN											
610 EQUIPMENT RENTAL											
615 SUBCONTRACTS											
OTHER											
APPLIED PREMIUM HRS											
		@	@								
										@	
										@	
										@	
										@	
										@	
DUST. ______					@	@	@	@	@	VARIABLE	
CFM: ______										FIXED	

FULLY ACCOUNTED COST	
999 CONTINGENCY	
SUB TOTAL	
PROFIT @ %	
S.P. TOTAL	

S/CFM (SP) ______

S/CFM (F. A. COST): ______

FORM XXXX 4/90

EXHIBIT 5

G. A. KLEISSLER CO.

G. A. KLEISSLER CO. | ESTIMATING SHEET | GENERAL JOB COSTS

CUSTOMER: ____________ | Proposal # ____________ | SHEET # ____________

LOCATION: ____________ | DATE ____________

ENGINEER: ____________ | PREPARED BY: ____________

DESCRIPTION	$	HOURS					
		102	183	280	425		
		E	D	T	I		
SALES ENGINEERING AND DESIGN							
102 ENGINEERING TIME							
104 S.E. TRAVEL EXPENSE # OF TRIPS							
MILEAGE AIRFARE							
R & S DAYS @$ /DAY (INCLUDING CAR)							
104 DESIGN TRAVEL # TRIPS HRS/TRIP							
116 DESIGN MEASURING HRS.							
124 PROJECT MANAGEMENT HRS.							
132 SERVICE & START UP (INCLUDE TIME FOR MANUALS) HRS.							
140 DESIGN TRAVEL EXP. # OF TRIPS							
MILEAGE AIRFARE							
R & S DAYS @$ /DAY (INCLUDING CAR)							
SHIPPING:							
205 TRUCK LOADING HRS.							
220 TRUCK DRIVING HRS.							
230 TRUCK OURS— @$ /MILEAGE @$ /MILE							
235 CRATING—SHIPPING SUPPLIES CF @$ /CF							
243 FREIGHT OUT #LOADS @$ /LOAD							
250 RETURNS—FREIGHT IN							
INSTALLATION:							
435 INSTALLATION MANAGEMENT HRS.							
445 TRUCK UNLOADING AND/OR MOVING MATERIAL HRS.							
455 INSTALLATION TRAVEL #TRIPS HRS/TRIP							
465 TRAVEL—R/S EXPENSES							
MILEAGE AIRFARE							
R & S DAYS @$ /DAY (INCLUDING CAR)							
470 LOCAL TRAVEL:							
# DAYS @ $/DAY							
MILEAGE @ $/MILE							
OTHER:							
610 RENTALS							
615 SUB CONTRACTS						@	
619 SUNDRY CHARGES—(CLOTHING ALLOWANCE)						@	
PREMIUM TIME APPLIED O HRS. T HRS.						@	
F HRS. I HRS.						@	
						@	
	@	@	@	@	@	VARIABLE	
						FIXED	
DUST: ____________				FULLY ACCOUNTED COST			
CFM: ____________				999 CONTINGENCY			
				SUB TOTAL			
____________ % OF JOB SELLING PRICE				PROFIT @ %			
____________ % OF JOB COSTS				S.P. TOTAL			

FORM XXXX-02 4/90

EXHIBIT 6

G. A. KLEISSLER CO. | ESTIMATING SHEET | SUMMARY
CUSTOMER: ____________ | Proposal #: ____________ | SHEET # ____________
LOCATION: ____________ | INDUSTRY CODE: ____________ | DATE ____________
ENGINEER: ____________ | MIS CODES: ____________ | PREPARED BY ____________

COMPONENT	TOTAL VARIABLE COST $	TOTAL FIXED COST $	FULLY ACCOUNTED COST $	CONTINGENCY $	PROFIT $	SELLING PRICE $
SEPARATOR						
AUXILIARY EQUIP.						
MANIFOLDING						
EXHAUSTER						
MAIN						
BRANCH LINES						
HOODS						
OTHER						
GENERAL JOB						
TOTAL						

FULLY ACCOUNTED	
999 CONTINGENCY	
SUB TOTAL	
PROFIT @ %	
TOTAL S.P.	

ADDED REV	
TOTAL SP	

DUST: ____________
CFM: ____________

S/CFM (SP) ____________
S/CFM (F. A. COST) ____________
FORM APP-01 4/80

EXHIBIT 7

G. A. KLEISSLER COMPANY
JOB STATUS REPORT
JOB NUMBER: F79-145

G. A. KLEISSLER CO.
CUSTOMER NAME: GWP

PROJECT LEADER: H. L. JOHANTGEN
DATE July 31, 1980
EFF. DATE % COMPLETE 7/31/80

		70/175		145/386		22/92		57/80		72/86	
	COMPONENT DESCRIPTION:	B-Branch		H-Hoods		P-Papertraps		Z-Conveyors		A-Manifold	
183	DESIGN	.40	225	.38	277	.52	0	.71	0	.84	0
280	MH-FINISHING	0	0	.01	0	1.0	0	0	0	.46	0
340	FABRICATION	0	0	.03	0	1.0	0	0	0	.46	0
430	INSTALLATION	0	0	0	0	0	0	0	0	0	0
	APP. PREM.	—	—	—	—	—	—	—	—	—	—
525	STD. SHEET & STRUC.					1.0	0	0	0	.95	0
550	SPEC. SHEET & STRUC.	—	—	—	—	1.0	0	0	0	—	—
555	MAT'L SUNDRY					1.0	0	0	0	.95	0
565	EXHAUSTERS	—	—	—	—	—	—	—	—	—	—
570	MOTORS	—	—	—	—	—	—	—	—	—	—
575	AUX. EQUIPMENT	—	—			.89	214	.32	0	—	—
605	FREIGHT IN	—	—	—	—	—	—	.25	0	—	—
610	EQUIP. RENTALS	—	—	—	—	—	—	—	—	—	—
615	SUBCONTRACTS	—	—	—	—	—	—	—	—	—	—
999	CONTINGENCY	—	—	—	—	—	—	—	—	—	—
399	GAK FAB LABOR	—	—	—	—	—	—	—	—	—	—

FOR EACH COLUMN ALONG THE COMPONENT LINE FILL IN THE COMPONENT LETTER. THE LEFT HAND BOX FOR EACH LINE ITEM FOR EACH COMPONENT IS TO SHOW THE DECIMAL PERCENT (TWO PLACES) PHYSICAL COMPLETION. THE RIGHT HAND BOX IS TO SHOW IN DOLLARS OF COST ANY PREDICTED VARIANCE FROM THE DATE SHOWN TO COMPLETION OF WORK - ( ) IS OVERRUN OR LOSS VARIANCE

EXHIBIT 8

G. A. KLEISSLER CO.

G. A. KLEISSLER COMPANY
CONFIDENTIAL INFORMATION
JOB #: 79145

CAB-2 DETAILED JOB COST REPORT (INT/CUR)

DATE ISSUED: 07/31/80 10:32
DATE LAST ETC: 07/31/80 PM
LAST TRX: 07/31/80

		UNITS					COST				
	% CMP	TOTAL BDGTD UNTS	BDGTD UNITS AT % COMP.	ACTUAL UNITS	FAV. (UNFAV) VARIANCE UNITS	%	TOTAL BDGTD COST	BDGTD COST AT % COMP	ACTUAL COST	FAV. (UNFAV) VARIANCE DOLLARS	%
TOTAL VARIABLE O/H							4043	41	14	27	65
TOTAL VARIABLE COSTS	0						82781	190	118	72	38
M—MAIN		MATERIAL:									
DESIGN P. L.—SYSTEM				129					2275		
DESIGN—SYSTEM				261					3190		
SUBTOTAL DEB. LABOR SYST.		332	312	390	78–	25–	4714	4431	5465	1034–	23
MAT'L MNQT-FINISHING SYST.	60	403	242	175	67	28	3833	2300	1712	588	26
FABRICATION—SYSTEM	70	3012	2108	1973	136	6	40240	28168	26827	1341	5
INSTALLATION FOREMAN—SYST.				238					4946		
INST. CREW—LOCAL—SYST.				764					10536		
SUBTOTAL INSTALL.—SYST.		2443	1099	1002	97	9	46657	20995	15481	5514	26
INSTALLATION MANAGEMENT	0	0	0	6	6–	**	0	0	120	120–	**
TOTAL LABOR & BENEFITS		6190	3762	3546	216	6	95444	55894	49605	6289	11

EXHIBIT 9

G. A. KLEISSLER CO.

G. A. KLEISSLER COMPANY
CONFIDENTIAL INFORMATION

SUMMARY JOB COST REPORT (J)

DATE ISSUED: 07/31/80 10:10
DATE LAST ETC: 07/31/80
DATE LAST TRX: 07/31/80

JOB NUMBER: F79145
CUSTOMER: GREAT WESTERN PAPER
LOCATION: RACINE, WISCONSIN

SALES ENGINEER: W. LEIST/C. HONECKER
PROJECT LEADER: H. JOHANTGEN/N. POTTER
FIELD FOREMAN:

		JOB REVIEW						JOB FORECAST				
COMPONENT DESCRIPTOR	% CMP	TOTAL BUDGETED COST	BUDGETED COST AT % COMP	ACTUAL COST	FAV (UNFAV) VARIANCE DOLLARS	%	VAR CHNG PRIOR PER'D	BDGT TO COMP	EST COST TO COMP	EXPECTED VARIANCE $	EXPECTED VARIANCE %	EXPECTED VARIANCE AT COMP
# GENERAL JOB COSTS	21	177,594	36,886	36,761	125	0	+	140,707	138,961	1,746	1	1,871
# SEPARATOR	63	226,361	141,815	151,193	(9,378)	(7)	+	84,546	94,342	(9,796)	(12)	(19,174)
# (3) EXHAUSTERS	0	82,781	190	118	72	38	–	82,591	64,419	18,172	22	18,245
# MAIN LINE	65	188,513	123,360	113,394	9,969	8	–	65,150	53,815	11,335	17	21,304
# BRANCH LINES	6	25,578	1,414	1,155	259	18	+	24,164	23,939	225	1	404
# HOODS	7	52,801	3,569	5,497	(1,927)	(54)	–	49,232	48,955	277	1	(1,650)
# INLET MANIFOLDS	75	43,684	32,567	29,850	2,717	8	+	11,118	11,118	0	0	2,717
# 4 BLF-CLNING P/T/DIVERTER	91	19,273	17,502	18,479	(977)	(6)	–	1,771	1,557	214	12	(763)
# SCREW CONVEYOR & ROT. VALV	23	33,687	7,718	10,896	(3,178)	(41)	–	25,969	22,706	3,263	13	85
TOTAL JOB COST	43		365,025		(2,318)		+		459,811		5	
		850,272		367,343		(1)		485,247		25,436		23,118

EXHIBIT 10

G. A. KLEISSLER CO.

G. A. KLEISSLER COMPANY
CONFIDENTIAL INFORMATION
JOB #: F79145

JOB COST FULLY ACCOUNTED SUMMARY (INT/CUR)

DATE ISSUED: 07/31/80 11:40
PAGE: 1
DATE LAST ETC: 07/31/80
DATE LAST TRX: 07/31/80
W. LEIST/C. HONECKER

		UNITS					COST				
	% CMP	TOTAL BDGTD UNTS	BDGTD UNITS AT % COMP.	ACTUAL UNITS	FAV. (UNFAV) VARIANCE UNITS	%	TOTAL BDGTD COST	BDGTD COST AT % COMP	ACTUAL COST	FAV. (UNFAV) VARIANCE DOLLARS	%
O—GENERAL JOB COSTS		MATERIAL:		% CPLT:	21						
TOTAL VARIABLE COSTS							177594	36894	36761	133	0
FIXED OH							46914	8684	8684	0	0
FULLY ACCT'D COSTS							224508	45579	45445	133	0
SELLING PRICE							209490	43511	43511	0	0
MARGINAL CONTRIBUTION							31896	6617	6750	133	2
MARGINAL CONTRIB. %							15.23	15.21	15.51	0.30	2
NET PROFIT							−15018	−2068	−1934	133	6
NET PROFIT %							−7.17	−4.75	−4.45	0.30	6
S—SEPARATOR		MATERIAL:		% CPLT:	63						
TOTAL VARIABLE COSTS							226361	141808	151193	−9385	−7
FIXED OH							121173	90526	90526	0	0
FULLY ACCT'D COSTS							347534	232335	241720	−9385	−4
SELLING PRICE							370017	231816	231816	0	0
MARGINAL CONTRIBUTION							143656	90008	80622	9385	10
MARGINAL CONTRIB. %							38.82	38.83	34.78	4.05	10
NET PROFIT							22483	−519	−9904	9385	−999
NET PROFIT %							6.08	−0.22	−4.27	4.05	−999
E—(3) EXHAUSTERS		MATERIAL:		% CPLT:	0						
TOTAL VARIABLE COSTS							82781	190	118	72	38
FIXED OH							48856	1212	1212	0	0
FULLY ACCT'D COSTS							131637	1402	1330	72	5
SELLING PRICE							153921	354	354	0	0
MARGINAL CONTRIBUTION							71140	164	236	72	−44

EXHIBIT 11 June 17, 1980 Budget Adjustment—Project 79143

Component	*Increase (Decrease) in Budget*	*Reason*
S	$15,964	Sales had not included enough for access platforms. Fab time estimates were based on performance on 79017 collector which was very similar.
E	(1,417)	Design decided that fan adjustments would be made by fan supplier.
E	(2,536)	Design felt sales had overestimated fabrication time.
B	7,817	Design felt sales had underestimated fabrication time.
A	2,265	Input from the field.
Z	(7,210)	Design reevaluation based on improvement in method of fabricating and installing.
	$14,351	

EXHIBIT 12 Project Plan—Project 79145

	Original Plan	*Forecast at 7/31/80*
Selling price	$1,279,048	$1,370,499
Variable costs	764,115	850,272
Marginal contribution	$ 514,933	$ 520,227
Allocated fixed overhead	373,441	441,159
Net profit	$ 141,492	$ 79,068
Marginal contribution %	40.25	37.96
Net profit %	11.06	5.77

Codman & Shurtleff, Inc.: Planning and Control System

This revision combines our results from January to April with the preliminary estimates supplied by each department for the remainder of the year. Of course, there are still a lot of unknown factors to weigh in, but this will give you some idea of our preliminary updated forecast.

As the Board members reviewed the document provided to them by Gus Fleites, vice president of Information and Control at Codman & Shurtleff, Roy Black, president, addressed the six men sitting at the conference table, "This revised forecast leaves us with a big stretch. We are almost two million dollars short of our profit objective for the year. As we discussed last week, we are estimating sales to be $1.1 million above original forecast. This is due in part to the early introduction of the new Chest Drainage Unit. However, three major factors that we didn't foresee last September will affect our profit plan estimates for the remainder of the year.

"First, there's the currency issue: our hedging has partially protected us, but the continued rapid deterioration of the dollar has pushed our costs up on European specialty instruments. Although this has improved Codman's competitive market position in Europe, those profits accrue to the European company and are not reflected in this forecast. Second, we have an unfavorable mix variance; and finally, we will have to absorb inventory variances due to higher than anticipated start up costs of our recently combined manufacturing operations.

"When do we have to take the figures to Corporate?" asked Chuck Dunn, vice president of Business Development.

"Wednesday of next week," replied Black, "so we have to settle this by Monday. That gives us only tomorrow and the weekend to wrap up the June budget revision. I know that each of you has worked on these estimates, but I think that the next look will be critical to achieving our profit objective."

"Bob, do you have anything you can give us?"

Bob Dick, vice president of Marketing, shook his head, "I've been working with my people looking at price and mix. At the moment, we can't realistically get more price. Most of the mix variance for the balance of the year will be due to increased sales of products that we are handling under the new distribution agreement. The mix for the remainder of the year may change, but with 2,700 active products in the catalogue, I don't want to move too far from our original projections. My expenses are cut right to the bone. Further cuts will mean letting staff go."

Black nodded his head in agreement. "Chuck, you and I should meet to review our Research and Development priorities. I know that Herb Stolzer will want to spend time reviewing the status of our programs. I think we should be sure that we have cut back to reflect our spending to date. I wouldn't be surprised if we could find another $400,000 without jeopardizing our long-term programs."

"Well, it seems our work is cut out for us. The rest of you keep working on this. Excluding R&D, we need at least another $500,000 before we start drawing down our contingency fund. Let's meet here tomorrow at two o'clock and see where we stand."

This case was prepared by Professor Robert Simons as the basis for class discussion rather than to illustrate either effective or ineffective handling of an administrative situation.

CODMAN & SHURTLEFF, INC.

Codman & Shurtleff, Inc., a subsidiary of Johnson & Johnson, was established in 1838 in Boston by Thomas Codman to design and fashion surgical instruments. The company developed surgical instrument kits for use in Army field hospitals during the Civil War and issued its first catalogue in 1860. After the turn of the century, Codman & Shurtleff specialized in working with orthopaedic surgeons and with pioneers in the field of neurosurgery.

In 1986, Codman & Shurtleff supplied hospitals and surgeons worldwide with over 2,700 products for surgery including instruments, equipment, implants, surgical disposables, fiberoptic light sources and cables, surgical head lamps, surgical microscopes, coagulators, and electronic pain control simulators and electrodes. These products involved advanced technologies from the fields of metallurgy, electronics, and optics.

Codman & Shurtleff operated three manufacturing locations in Randolph, New Bedford, and Southbridge, Massachusetts, and a distribution facility in Avon, Massachusetts. The company employed 800 people in the United States.

In 1964, Codman & Shurtleff was acquired by Johnson & Johnson, Inc. as an addition to its professional products business. Johnson & Johnson operated manufacturing subsidiaries in 46 countries, sold its products in most countries of the world, and employed 75,000 people worldwide. 1985 sales were $6.4 billion with before tax profits of $900 million (Exhibit 1).

Roy Black had been president of Codman & Shurtleff since 1983. In his 25 years with Johnson & Johnson, Black had spent 18 years with Codman, primarily in the Marketing Department. He had also worked at Ethicon and Surgikos. He described his job,

> This is a tough business to manage because it is so complex. We rely heavily on the neurosurgeons for ideas in product generation and for the testing and ultimate acceptance of our products. We have to stay in close contact with the leading neurosurgeons around the world. For example, last week I returned from a tour of the Pacific rim. During the trip, I visited eight Johnson & Johnson/Codman affiliates and 25 neurosurgeons.
>
> At the same time, we are forced to push technological innovation to reduce costs. This is a matter of survival. In the past, we concentrated on producing superior quality goods, and the market was willing to pay whatever it took to get the best. But the environment has changed; the shift has been massive. We are trying to adapt to a situation where doctors and hospitals are under severe pressure to be more efficient and cost-effective.
>
> We compete in 12 major product groups. Since our markets are so competitive, the business is very price sensitive. The only way we can take price is to offer unique products with cost-in-use benefits to the professional user.
>
> Since the introduction of DRG costing[1] by hospitals in 1983, industry volume has been off approximately 20 percent. We have condensed 14 locations to four and have reduced staff levels by over 20 percent. There have also been some cuts in R&D, although our goal is to maintain research spending at near double the historical Codman level.

Chuck Dunn, vice president of Business Development, had moved three years earlier from Johnson & Johnson Products to join Codman as vice president for Information and Control. During his 24 years with Johnson & Johnson, he had worked with four different marketing divisions as well as the Corporate office. He recalled the process of establishing a new mission statement at Codman,

> When I arrived there, Codman was in the process of defining a more clearly focused mission. Our mission was product oriented, but Johnson & Johnson was oriented by medical specialty. On a matrix, this resulted in missed product opportunities as well as turf problems with other Johnson & Johnson companies.

[1]On October 1, 1983, Medicare reimbursement to hospitals changed from a cost-plus system to a fixed-rate system as called for in the 1983 Social Security refinancing legislation. The new system was called *prospective payment* because rates were set in advance of treatment according to which of 467 *diagnostic-related groups* (or DRGs) a patient was deemed to fall into. This change in reimbursement philosophy caused major cost-control problems for the nation's 5,800 acute-care hospitals which received an average of 36 percent of their revenues from Medicare and Medicaid.

It took several years of hard work to arrive at a new worldwide mission statement oriented to medical specialty, but this process was very useful in obtaining group consensus. Our worldwide mission is now defined in terms of a primary focus in the neuro-spinal surgery business. This turns out to be a large market and allows better positioning of our products.

In addition to clarifying our planning, we use the mission statement as a screening device. We look carefully at any new R&D project to see if it fits our mission. The same is true for acquisitions.

REPORTING RELATIONSHIPS AT JOHNSON & JOHNSON

In 1985, Johnson & Johnson comprised 155 autonomous subsidiaries operating in three health care markets: consumer products, pharmaceutical products, and professional products. Exhibit 2 provides details of the business operations of the company.

Johnson & Johnson was managed on a decentralized basis as described in the following excerpt from the 1985 Annual Report,

> The Company is organized on the principles of decentralized management and conducts its business through operating subsidiaries which are themselves, for the most part, integral, autonomous operations. Direct responsibility for each company lies with its operating management, headed by the president, general manager or managing director who reports directly or through a Company group chairman to a member of the Executive Committee. In line with this policy of decentralization, each internal subsidiary is, with some exceptions, managed by citizens of the country where it is located.

Roy Black at Codman & Shurtleff reported directly to Herbert Stolzer at Johnson & Johnson headquarters in New Brunswick, New Jersey. Mr. Stolzer, 59, was a member of the Executive Committee of Johnson & Johnson with responsibility for 16 operating companies in addition to Codman & Shurtleff (Exhibit 3). Stolzer had worked for Johnson & Johnson for 35 years with engineering, manufacturing, and senior management experience in Johnson & Johnson Products and at the Corporate office.

The senior policy and decision-making group at Johnson & Johnson was the Executive Committee comprising the chairman, president, chief financial officer, vice president of administration, and eight Executive Committee members with responsibilities for company sectors. The 155 business units of the Company were organized in sectors based primarily on products (e.g., consumer, pharmaceutical, professional) and secondarily on geographic markets.

FIVE- AND TEN-YEAR PLANS AT JOHNSON & JOHNSON

Each operating company within Johnson & Johnson was responsible for preparing its own plans and strategies. David Clare, president of Johnson & Johnson, believed that this was one of the key elements in their success. "Our success is due to three basic tenets: a basic belief in decentralized management, a sense of responsibility to our key constituents, and a desire to manage for the long term. We have no corporate strategic planning function nor one strategic plan. Our strategic plan is the sum of the strategic plans to each of our 155 business units."

Each operating company prepared annually a five- and ten-year plan. Financial estimates in these plans were limited to only four numbers: estimated unit sales volume, estimated sales revenue, estimated net income, and estimated return on investment. Accompanying these financial estimates was a narrative description of how these targets would be achieved.

To ensure that managers were committed to the plan that they developed, Johnson & Johnson required that the planning horizon focus on two years only and remain fixed over a five-year period. Thus, in 1983, a budget and second-year forecast was developed for 1984 and 1985 and a strategic plan was developed for the years 1990 and 1995. In each of the years 1984 through 1987, the five- and ten-year plan was redrawn in respect of only years 1990 and 1995. Only in year 1988 would the strategic planning horizon shift five years forward to cover years 1995 and 2000. These two years will then remain the focus of subsequent five- and ten-year plans for the succeeding four years, and so on.

At Codman & Shurtleff, work on the annual

five- and ten-year plan commenced each January and took approximately six months to complete. Based on the mission statement, a business plan was developed for each significant segment of the business. For each competitor, the marketing plan included an estimated *pro forma* income statement (volume, sales, profit) as well as a one-page narrative description of their strategy.

Based on the tentative marketing plan, draft plans were prepared by the other departments including research and development, production, finance, and personnel. The tentative plan was assembled in a binder with sections describing mission, strategies, opportunities and threats, environment, and financial forecasts. This plan was debated, adjusted, and approved over the course of several meetings in May by the Codman Board of Directors (see Exhibit 4), comprising the president and seven key subordinates.

In June, Herb Stolzer travelled to Boston to preside over the annual review of the five- and ten-year plan. Codman executives considered this a key meeting that could last up to three days. During the meeting Stolzer reviewed the plan, aired his concerns, and challenged the Codman Board on assumptions, strategies, and forecasts. A recurring question during the session was, "If your new projection for 1990 is below what you predicted last year, how do you intend to make up the shortfall?"

After this meeting, Roy Black summarized the plan that had been approved by Stolzer in a two-page memorandum that he sent directly to Jim Burke, chairman and chief executive officer of Johnson & Johnson.

Based on the two-page "Burke letters," the five- and ten-year plans for all operating companies were presented by Executive Committee members and debated and approved at the September meeting of the Executive Committee in New Brunswick. Company presidents, including Roy Black, were often invited to prepare formal presentations. The discussion in these meetings was described by those in attendance as, "very frank," "extremely challenging," and "grilling."

FINANCIAL PLANNING AT JOHNSON & JOHNSON

Financial planning at Johnson & Johnson comprised annual budgets (i.e., profit plans) for the upcoming operating year and a second-year forecast. Budgets were detailed financial documents prepared down to the expense center level for each operating company. The second-year forecast was in a similar format but contained less detail than the budget for the upcoming year.

Revenues and expenses were budgeted by month. Selected balance sheet items, e.g., accounts receivable and inventory, were also budgeted to reflect year-end targets.

Profit plan targets were developed on a bottom-up basis by each operating company by reference to two documents: (1) the approved five- and ten-year plan and (2) the second-year forecast prepared the previous year.

Chuck Dunn described the budgeting process at Codman & Shurtleff,

> We wrote the initial draft of our 1987 profit plan in the Summer of 1986 based on the revision of our five- and ten-year plan. By August, the profit plan is starting to crystallize; we have brought in the support areas such as accounting, quality assurance, R&D, and engineering, to ensure that they *buy in* to the new 1987 profit and marketing plans.
>
> The first year of the strategic plan is used as a basis for the departments to prepare their own one-year plans for both capital and expense items. The production budget is based on standard costs and nonstandard costs such as development programs and plant consolidations. As for the R&D budget, the project list is always too long, so we are forced to rank the projects. For each project, we look at returns, costs, time expended, sales projections, expected profit, and gross profit percentages as well as support to be supplied to the plants.
>
> The individual budgets are then consolidated by the Information and Control Department. We look very carefully at how this budget compares with our previous forecasts. For example, the first consolidation of the 1986 profit plan revealed a $2.4 million profit shortfall against the second-year forecast that was developed in 1984 and updated in June 1985. To reconcile this, it was necessary to put on special budget presentations by each department to remove all slack and ensure that our earlier target could be met if possible. The commitment to this process is very strong.

> We are paying more and more attention to our second-year forecast since it forces us to re-examine strategic plans. The second-year forecast is also used as a benchmark for next year's profit plan and, as such, it is used as hindsight to evaluate the forecasting ability and performance of managers.

The procedure for approving the annual profit plan and second-year forecast followed closely the procedures described earlier for the review of the five- and ten-year plans. During the early fall, Herbert Stolzer reviewed the proposed budget with Roy Black and the Codman & Shurtleff Board of Directors. Changes in profit commitments from previous forecasts and the overall profitability and tactics of the Company were discussed in detail.

After all anticipated revenues and expenses were budgeted, a separate contingency expense line item was added to the budget; the amount of the contingency changed from year to year and was negotiated between Stolzer and Black based on the perceived uncertainty in achieving budget targets. In 1986, the Codman & Shurtleff contingency was set at $1.1 million.

Stolzer presented the budget for approval at the November meeting of the Johnson & Johnson Executive Committee.

BUDGET REVISIONS AND REVIEWS

During the year, budget performance was monitored closely. Each week, sales revenue performance figures were sent to Herb Stolzer. In addition, Roy Black sent a monthly management report to Stolzer that included income statement highlights and a summary of key balance sheet figures and ratios. All information was provided with reference to (1) position last month (2) position this month (3) budgeted position. All variances that Black considered significant were explained in a narrative summary.

The accuracy of budget projections was also monitored during the year and formally revised on three occasions. The first of these occasions occurred at the March meeting of the Executive Committee. Going around the table, each Executive Committee member was asked to update the Committee on his most recent estimates of sales and profits for each operating company for the current year. Herb Stolzer relied on Roy Black to provide this information for Stolzer's review prior to the March meeting.

The *June Revision* referred to the revised budget for the current year that was presented to the Executive Committee in June. The preparation of this revised budget required managers at Codman & Shurtleff and all other Johnson & Johnson companies to re-budget in May for the remainder of the fiscal year. This revision involved re-checking all budget estimates starting with the lowest level expense center as well as revising the second-year forecast when necessary.

The third review of budget projections was the *November update* which was presented to the Executive Committee at the November meeting concurrently with their consideration of the budget and second-year forecast for the upcoming budget year. The November update focused on results for the 10 months just completed and revised projections for the remaining two months. At Codman & Shurtleff, preparation of the November update involved performance estimates from all departments but was not conducted to the same level of detail as the June revision.

CORPORATE VIEW OF THE PLANNING AND CONTROL PROCESS

David Clare, president of Johnson & Johnson:

> The sales and profit forecasts are always optimistic in the five- and ten-year plans, but this is O.K. We want people to stretch their imagination and think expansively. In these plans we don't anticipate failure; they are a device to open up thinking. There is no penalty for inaccuracies.
>
> The profit plan and second-year forecast are used to run the business and evaluate managers on planning, forecasts, and achievements.
>
> We ask our managers to always include in their plans an account of how and why their estimates have changed over time. That is why we use the five- and ten-year planning concept rather than a moving planning horizon. This allows us to revise our thinking over time and allows for retrospective learning.
>
> If a manager insists on a course of action and we (the Executive Committee) have misgivings, nine times out of ten we will

let him go ahead. If we say, 'No,' and the answer should have been, 'Yes,' we say, 'Don't blame us, it was your job to sell us on the idea and you didn't do that.'

Johnson & Johnson is extremely decentralized, but that does not mean that managers are free from challenge as to what they are doing. In the final analysis, managing conflict is what management is all about. Healthy conflict is about *what* is right, not *who* is right.

Our Company philosophy is to manage for the long term. We do not use short term bonus plans. Salary and bonus reviews are entirely subjective and qualitative and are intended to reward effort and give special recognition to those who have performed uniquely. The Executive Committee reviews salary recommendations for all managers above a certain salary level, but Company presidents, such as Roy Black, have full discretion as to how they remunerate their employees.

Herbert Stolzer, Executive Committee member,

The planning and control systems used in Johnson & Johnson provide real benefits. These systems allow us to find problems and run the business. This is true not only for us at Corporate, but also at the operating companies where they are a tremendous tool. Once a year, managers are forced to review their businesses in depth for costs, trends, manufacturing efficiency, marketing plans, and their competitive situation. Programs and action plans result.

You have to force busy people to do this. Otherwise, they will be caught up in day-to-day activities—account visits, riding with salesmen, standing on the manufacturing floor.

Our long-term plans are not meant to be a financial forecast; rather, they are meant to be an objective way of setting aspirations. We never make those numbers—who can forecast sales five or ten years out with unforeseen markets, products, and competitors? Even the accuracy of our two-year forecast is bad. The inaccuracy is an indication of how fast our markets are changing. Our businesses are so diverse, with so many competitors, that it is difficult to forecast out two years.

I visit at least twice a year with each operating company board. We usually spend the better part of a week going over results, planning issues, strategic plans, and short and long term problems. The Executive Committee, to the best of my knowledge, never issues quantitative performance targets before the bottom-up process begins.

At the Executive Committee meetings, a lot of argument takes place around strategic planning issues. How fast can we get a business up to higher returns? Are the returns in some businesses too high? Are we moving too fast? However, the outcome is never to go back to the operating company and say we need 8 percent rather than 6 percent. The challenge has already taken place between the Executive Committee member and the Company Board. If the EC member is satisfied with the answers provided by the Board, that's the end of it.

It happens very rarely that the consolidated budget is unacceptable. Occasionally, we might say, 'We really could use some more money.' However, in the second review, this may not turn up any extra. If so, that's O.K.

Our systems are not used to punish. They are used to try and find and correct problems. Bonuses are not tied to achieving budget targets. They are subjectively determined, although we use whatever objective indicators are available—for example, sales and new product introductions for a marketing vice president.

The key to our whole system is the operating Company presidents. We are so decentralized that they define their own destiny. A successful Company president needs to be able to stand up to pressure from above. He needs to have the courage to say, 'I have spent hours and hours on that forecast and for the long term health of the Company, we have to spend that budget.'

Clark Johnson, corporate controller,

At the Executive Committee review meetings, we always review the past five years before starting on the forecast. We look at volume growth rates—sales growth adjusted for inflation—and discuss problems. Then, we compare growth rate against GNP growth. We keep currency translation out of it. We evaluate foreign subsidiaries in their own currency and compare growth against a country specific GNP. We are looking for market share by country. On almost any topic, we start with forecast versus past track record.

The Committee never dictates or changes proposals—only challenges ideas. If it becomes clear to the individual presenting that the forecast is not good enough, only that person decides whether a revision is necessary. These discussions can be very frank and sometimes acrimonious. The result of the review may be agreement to present a revision at the next meeting, specific action items to be addressed, or personal feedback to David Clare.

This process cascades down the organization. Executive Committee members review and challenge the proposals of Company presidents. Company presidents review and challenge the proposals of their vice presidents.

Thursday, May 8, 1986—8:00 P.M.

Following the Codman & Shurtleff Board meeting to discuss the June budget revision on the afternoon of Thursday, May 8 (described at the beginning of the case), Roy Black, Chuck Dunn, Bob Dick, and Gus Fleites worked into the evening going over the list of active R&D projects. Their review focused on R&D projects that had been included in the original 1986 budget. They searched for projects that could be eliminated due to changed market conditions or deferred to 1987 because of unplanned slowdowns. After discussing the progress and priority of each major project, Roy Black asked Chuck Dunn to have his staff work the next morning to go over the 40 active projects in detail and look for any savings that could be reflected in the June revision of the budget.

Friday, May 9, 1986—7:45 A.M.

In addition to Chuck Dunn, four people were seated around the table in the small conference room. Bob Sullivan and Gino Lombardo were program managers who reported to Bill Bailey, vice president of Research. John Smith was manager, Technical Development, of the research facility in Southbridge that specialized in microscopes, fiberoptics, and light scopes. Gordon Thompson was the research accountant representing the Finance Department.

After coffee was delivered, Chuck closed the door and turned to the others,

> Here's the situation. We are approximately two million short of the June Revision pretax profit target. As you know, our sales volume this year has been good—better than budget, in fact—but a few recent unpredictable events, including unfavorable product mix, and that large variance in the cost of specialty European products, are hurting our profit projection.
>
> This morning, I want the four of you to look at our original spending projections to see where we stand. For example, we know that R&D underspent $200,000 in the first quarter. Therefore, I think we should take it as a starting point that R&D has $200,000 to give up from its 1986 budget. I know that you can argue that this is just a timing difference, but you know as well as I do that, given the record of the R&D department, this money will probably not be spent this year.
>
> It's time to get the hopes and dreams out of the R&D list. If we roll up our sleeves, we can probably find $400,000 without sacrificing either our 1986 objectives or our long term growth.
>
> We worked late last night looking at the project list and I think it can be done. I have to meet again today at 2:00 with the Board and I want to be able to tell them that we can do it. That leaves it up to you to sift through these projects and find that money. We're looking for projects that have stalled and can be put on hold, and some belt-tightening on ongoing work.

After Chuck Dunn had left the group to its work, Gordon led the group through the list of projects. For each project, the group discussed spending to date, problems with the project, and spending needed for the remainder of the year. For each project, Gordon asked if anything could be cut and occasionally asked for points of clarification. On a separate sheet of paper, he kept track of the cuts to which the R&D managers had agreed. He turned to Project 23,

> How about 23? You were planning on a pilot run of 100 prototypes this year. Should that still be included in the schedule?
>
> Yes, the project is on track and looks promising. I suppose we could cut the run to 50 without sacrificing our objective. Would anyone have a problem with that?
>
> It's a bad idea. That item has a very high material component and we have a devil of a time getting it at a reasonable price, even for a run of 100. If we cut the volume any more, the unit material cost will double.
>
> O.K., we'll stick with 100. How about the salesmen's samples? Is there anything there?
>
> If we reduced the number of samples by a third, we could save $20,000. I suppose I could live with that, but I don't know how that will impact the marketing plan. Let me call Bob Dick and see what he thinks.

Gordon kept a running total of the expense reductions as the morning progressed. Dunn stopped in approximately once an hour to ask how the work was coming.

Friday, May 9—2:00 P.M.

Roy Black opened the meeting, "Gus, do you have the revised budget with the changes we've made? What does it look like?"

As Gus Fleites distributed copies of the budget document to the Codman & Shurtleff Board, Chuck Dunn interjected, "Roy, at the moment, we have found $300,000 in R&D. That reflects adjusting our priority list for the rest of the year and cutting the fat out of ongoing projects. As for the last $100,000, we are still working on recasting the numbers to reflect what I call our 'project experience factor.' In other words, I think we can find that $100,000 by recognizing that our projects always take longer than originally planned. My people say that we've cut right to the bone on ongoing programs. The next round of cuts will have to be programs themselves, and we know we don't want to do that."

"We've discussed this before," responded Black, "and I think we all agree on the answer. In the past, we have authorized more projects than we can handle and have drawn the work out over too long a time. The way to go is fewer projects, sooner. It's the only thing that makes sense. Our mission is more focused now and should result in fewer projects. It's unfortunate that Bill Bailey is unavailable this week, but we are going to have to go ahead and make those decisions."

As Fleites briefed the Board on the revised budget, Roy Black turned to Bob Dick to discuss inventory carrying costs. "Bob, don't you think that our inventory level is too high on some of our low turnover products? Wouldn't we be better to cut our inventory position and take a higher back order level? With 2,700 products, does it make sense to carry such a large inventory?"

Bob Dick nodded his head in agreement, "You're right, of course, our stocking charges are substantial and we could recover part of our shortfall if we could cut those expenses. But our first concern has to be our level of service to customers."

"Agreed. But perhaps there is room here to provide fast turnaround on a core of critical products and risk back orders on the high-specialty items. The 80/20 rule applies to most of our business. For example, say we offered top service for all our disposables and implants and flagged setup products for new hospital construction in our catalogue as '90 day delivery' or 'made to order.' We could then concentrate on the fastest possible turnaround for products where that is important and a slower delivery for products that are usually ordered well in advance in any case."

"I think that may be a good tactic. It won't help us for the June revision, but I'll have our market research people look at it and report back next month."

"Good," responded Black, "that just leaves our commercial expenses. We need some donations from each of you. What I am suggesting is that each of you go back to your departments and think in terms of giving up two percent of your commercial expenses. If everyone gives up two percent, this will give us $500,000. In my opinion, we have to bring the shortfall down to $900,000 before we can draw down part of our contingency fund. We're a long way from the end of the year and it's too early to start drawing down a major portion of the contingency."

Black turned to Bob Marlatt, vice president of Human Resources. "Bob, where do we stand on headcount projections?"

"The early retirement program is set to clear our Corporate Compensation Department next month. That should yield 14 headcount reductions. Otherwise, no changes have been made in our projections through the end of the year. I think that we could all benefit from thinking about opportunities to reduce staff and pay overtime on an as-needed basis to compensate."

Black summed up the discussion,

> Well, I think we all know what is needed. Chuck, keep working on that last $100,000. All of you should think in terms of giving up two percent on commercial expenses and reducing non-critical headcount. That means that you will have to rank your activities and see what you can lose at the bottom end. Bob, I think that we should go back and look at our marketing plan again to see if we can make any changes to boost revenues.
>
> We need to take a revised budget to Stolzer that is short by no more than $250,000. If necessary, I think we can live with drawing down the contingency to make up the difference.
>
> So, your work is cut out for you. See you back here on Monday. Have a nice weekend! (laughter all around.)

After the meeting, Roy Black reflected on what had transpired, and his role as an operating manager in Johnson & Johnson.

> These meetings are very important. We should always be thinking about such issues, but it is tough when you are constantly fighting fires. The Johnson & Johnson system forces us to stop and really look at where we have been and where we are going.
>
> We know where the problems are. We face them every day. But these meetings force us to think about how we should respond and to look at both the upside and downside of changes in the business. They really get our creative juices flowing.
>
> Some of our managers complain. They say that we are planning and budgeting all the time and that every little change means that they have to go back and rebudget the year and the second-year forecasts. There is also some concern that the financial focus may make us less innovative. But we try to manage this business for the long term. We avoid at all costs actions that will hurt us long term. I believe that Herb Stolzer is in complete agreement on that issue.
>
> It is important to understand what decentralized management is all about. It is unequivocal accountability for what you do. And the Johnson & Johnson system provides that very well.

EXHIBIT 1 Johnson & Johnson and Subsidiaries, Consolidated Statement of Earnings and Retained Earnings

Dollars in Millions Except Per Share Figures (Note 1)	*1985*	*1984*	*1983*
Revenues			
Sales to customers	$6,421.3	$6,124.5	$5,972.9
Other revenues			
Interest income	107.3	84.5	82.9
Royalties and miscellaneous	48.1	38.0	49.4
Total revenues	$6,576.7	$6,247.0	$6,105.2
Costs and expenses			
Cost of products sold	2,594.2	2,469.4	2,471.8
Selling, distribution and administrative expenses	2,516.0	2,488.4	2,352.9
Research expense	471.1	421.2	405.1
Interest expense	74.8	86.1	88.3
Interest expense capitalized	(28.9)	(35.0)	(36.9)
Other expenses including nonrecurring charges (Note 2)	50.3	61.8	99.9
Total costs and expenses	$5,677.5	$5,491.9	$5,381.1
Earnings before provision for taxes on income	$ 899.2	$ 755.1	$ 724.1
Provision for taxes on income (Note 8)	285.5	240.6	235.1
Net earnings	$ 613.7	$ 514.5	$ 489.0
Retained earnings at beginning of period	$3,119.1	$2,814.5	$2,540.1
Cash dividends paid (per share: 1985, $2.175; 1984, $1.175; 1983, $1.075)	(233.2)	(219.9)	(204.6)
Retained earnings at end of period	$3,499.6	$3,119.1	$2,824.5
Net earnings per share	$ 3.36	2.75	2.57

Segments of Business *(Dollars in Millions)*		*1985*	*1984*	*1983*	*Percent Increase (Decreased)* *1985 vs. 1984*	*1984 vs. 1983*
Sales to customers (2)						
Consumer—	Domestic	$1,656.0	$1,588.3	$1,502.5	4.3%	5.7%
	International	1,118.5	1,161.4	1,185.3	(3.7)	(2.0)
	Total	2,774.5	$1,749.7	$2,687.8	.9%	2.3%
Professional—	Domestic	$1,553.9	1,429.3	1,465.5	8.7	(2.5)
	International	653.1	626.1	620.3	4.3	.9
	Total	$2,207.0	$2,055.4	$2,085.8	7.4	(1.5)
Pharmaceutical—	Domestic	$ 780.0	$718.3	$ 642.5	8.6	11.8
	International	659.8	601.1	556.8	9.8	8.0
	Total	$1,439.8	$1,319.4	$1,199.3	9.1	10.0
Worldwide total		$6,421.3	$6,124.5	$5,972.9	4.8%	2.5%
Operating profit						
Consumer		$ 408.7	$ 323.4	$ 422.7	26.4%	(23.5)%
Professional		149.2	118.7	120.0	25.7	(1.1)
Pharmaceutical		461.1	440.4	358.4	4.7	22.9
Segments total		$1,019.0	$ 882.5	$ 901.1	15.5	(2.1)
Expense not allocated to segments (3)		(119.8)	(127.4)	(177.0)	—	—
Earnings before taxes on income		$ 899.2	$ 755.1	$ 724.1	19.1%	4.3%
Identifiable assets at year-end						
Consumer		$1,616.2	$1,560.1	$1,535.9	3.6%	1.6%
Professional		1,876.1	1,717.6	1,673.5	9.2	2.6
Pharmaceutical		1,343.8	1,024.3	996.2	31.2	2.8
Segments total		$4,836.1	$4,302.0	$4,205.6	12.4	2.3
General corporate		259.0	239.4	255.9	—	—
Worldwide total		$5,095.1	$4,541.4	$4,461.5	12.2%	1.8%

EXHIBIT 2

CHICOPEE

Chicopee develops and manufactures products for use by other Johnson & Johnson affiliates, in addition to a wide variety of fabrics that are sold to a broad range of commercial and industrial customers. Chicopee's consumer products include disposable diapers for the private-label market segment.

CODMAN

Codman & Shurtleff, Inc. supplies hospitals and surgeons worldwide with a broad line of products including instruments, equipment, implants, surgical disposables, fiberoptic light sources and cables, surgical head lamps, surgical microscopes and electronic pain control stimulators and electrodes.

CRITIKON

Critikon, Inc. provides products used in the operating room and other critical care areas of the hospital. Intravenous catheters, infusion pumps and controllers, I.V. sets, filters and devices for monitoring blood pressure, cardiac output and oxygen are among its products.

DEVRO

Edible natural protein sausage casings made by Devro companies in the United States, Canada, Scotland and Australia are used by food processors throughout the world to produce pure, uniform, high-quality sausages and meat snacks.

ETHICON

Ethicon, Inc. provides products for precise wound closure, including sutures, ligatures, mechanical wound closure instruments and related products. Ethicon makes its own surgical needles and provides thousands of needle-suture combinations to the surgeon.

IOLAB

Iolab Corporation manufactures intraocular lenses for implantation in the eye to replace the natural lens after cataract surgery, as well as instruments and other products used in ophthalmic microsurgery.

JANSSEN PHARMACEUTICA

Janssen Pharmaceutica Inc. facilitates availability in the U.S. of original research developments of Janssen Pharmaceutica N.V. of Belgium. Its products include SUFENTA, INNOVAR, SUBLIMAZE and INAPSINE, injectable products used in anesthesiology; NIZORAL and MONISTAT i.v. for systemic fungal pathogens; NIZORAL Cream 2% topical antifungal; VERMOX, an anthelmintic, and IMODIUM, an anti-diarrheal.

JOHNSON & JOHNSON
BABY PRODUCTS COMPANY

The Johnson & Johnson Baby Products Company produces the familiar line of consumer baby products, including powder, shampoo, oil, wash cloths, lotion and others. Additional products include educational materials and toys to aid in infant development, SUNDOWN Sunscreen and AFFINITY Shampoo and Conditioner.

JOHNSON & JOHNSON
CARDIOVASCULAR

Johnson & Johnson Cardiovascular manufactures and markets cardiovascular products used in open heart surgery that include HANCOCK Heart Valves, Vascular Grafts, MAXIMA Hollow Fiber Oxygenators, INTER-SEPT Blood Filters and Cardiotomy Reservoirs.

JOHNSON & JOHNSON
DENTAL PRODUCTS COMPANY

The Dental Products Company serves dental practitioners throughout the world with an extensive line of orthodontic, preventive and restorative products. The company also provides dental laboratories with a broad line of crown and bridge materials, including the high-strength ceramic CERESTORE system.

JOHNSON & JOHNSON
HOSPITAL SERVICES

Johnson & Johnson Hospital Services Company develops and implements corporate marketing programs on behalf of Johnson & Johnson professional companies. These programs make it easier to do business with Johnson & Johnson and respond to the needs of hospitals, multihospital systems, alternative sites and distributors to reduce costs. Programs include Corporate Contracts and the COACT On-Line Procurement System.

JOHNSON & JOHNSON
PRODUCTS INC

Johnson & Johnson Products' Health Care Division provides consumers with wound care and oral care products. Its Patient Care Division offers hospitals and physicians a complete line of wound care products. Its Orthopaedic Division markets surgical implants and fracture immobilization products. The company also provides products to the athletic market.

(Continued)

EXHIBIT 2 *Continued*

JOHNSON & JOHNSON

ULTRASOUND

Johnson & Johnson Ultrasound specializes in ultrasound diagnostic imaging equipment. This equipment is used in a wide range of medical diagnoses, including abdominal, cardiovascular, gynecologic, obstetric, pediatric, surgical, neonatal and veterinary applications.

McNEIL

McNEIL CONSUMER PRODUCTS COMPANY

McNeil Consumer Products Company's line of TYLENOL acetaminophen products includes regular and extra-strength tablets, caplets, and liquid; children's elixir, chewable tablets, drops and junior strength tablets. Other products include various forms of COTYLENOL Cold Formula, PEDIACARE cough/cold preparations, SINE-AID, Maximum-Strength TYLENOL Sinus Medication and DELSYM cough relief medicine.

McNEIL PHARMACEUTICAL

McNeil Pharmaceutical provides the medical profession with prescription drugs, including analgesics, short and long-acting tranquilizers, an anti-inflammatory agent, a muscle relaxant and a digestive enzyme supplement.

ORTHO DIAGNOSTIC SYSTEMS, INC.

Ortho Diagnostic Systems Inc. provides diagnostic systems for the clinical and research laboratory community. Products include instrument and reagent systems for the blood bank, coagulation and hematology laboratories as well as immunology systems and infectious disease testing kits.

ORTHO PHARMACEUTICAL CORPORATION

Ortho Pharmaceutical Corporation's prescription products for family planning are oral contraceptives and diaphragms. Other products include vaginal antibacterial and anti-fungal agents. The Advanced Care Products Division markets non-prescription vaginal spermicides for fertility control, in-home pregnancy and ovulation test kits and an athlete's foot remedy. The Dermatological Division provides dermatologists with products for professional skin treatment.

PERSONAL PRODUCTS

Products for feminine hygiene—STAYFREE Thin Maxi's, Maxi-Pads and Mini-Pads, STAYFREE SILHOUETTES BODY-SHAPE Maxi's, ASSURE & NATURAL Breathable Panty Liners, CAREFREE PANTY SHIELDS, SURE & NATURAL Maxishields, MODESS Sanitary Napkins, 'o.b.' Tampons and related products—are the specialty of Personal Products Company. Other consumer products include COETS Cosmetic Squares, TAKE-OFF Make-up Remover Cloths and SHOWER TO SHOWER Body Powder.

PITMAN-MOORE

Pitman-Moore, Inc. manufactures and sells an extensive line of biological, diagnostic, and pharmaceutical products for use by veterinarians in treating various disease entities in the pet animal segment of the animal health market. Most notable is IMRAB, the only rabies vaccine approved for use in five animal species. Pitman-Moore also supplies vaccines and pharmaceuticals for use in food-producing animals and it markets surgical products of Johnson & Johnson affiliates applicable to animal health.

SURGIKOS

Surgikos, Inc. markets an extensive line of BARRIER Disposable Surgical Packs and Gowns and surgical specialty products for use in major operative procedures. Other major products include CIDEX Sterilizing and Disinfecting Solutions for medical equipment, SURGINE Face Masks and Head Coverings, MICRO-TOUCH Latex Surgical Gloves and NEUTRALON Brown Surgical Gloves for sensitive skin.

TECHNICARE

Technicare Corporation offers physicians products in four of the most important diagnostic imaging fields—computed tomography (CT) scanning, nuclear medicine systems, digital X-ray and the new field of magnetic resonance (MR).

VISTAKON

Vistakon, Inc. develops, manufactures and distributes soft contact lenses. The company provides contact lens dispensing professionals with daily wear and extended wear lenses for nearsighted and farsighted persons. It also is a major supplier of specialty toric lenses for the correction of astigmatism.

XANAR

Xanar, Inc. specializes in products for laser surgery. Laser surgical devices can be used in general surgery and other surgical specialties to provide an effective, less invasive alternative to traditional techniques. Xanar's products include surgical lasers for gynecology, otolaryngology, dermatology and podiatry.

EXHIBIT 3 JOHNSON & JOHNSON Partial Organization Chart

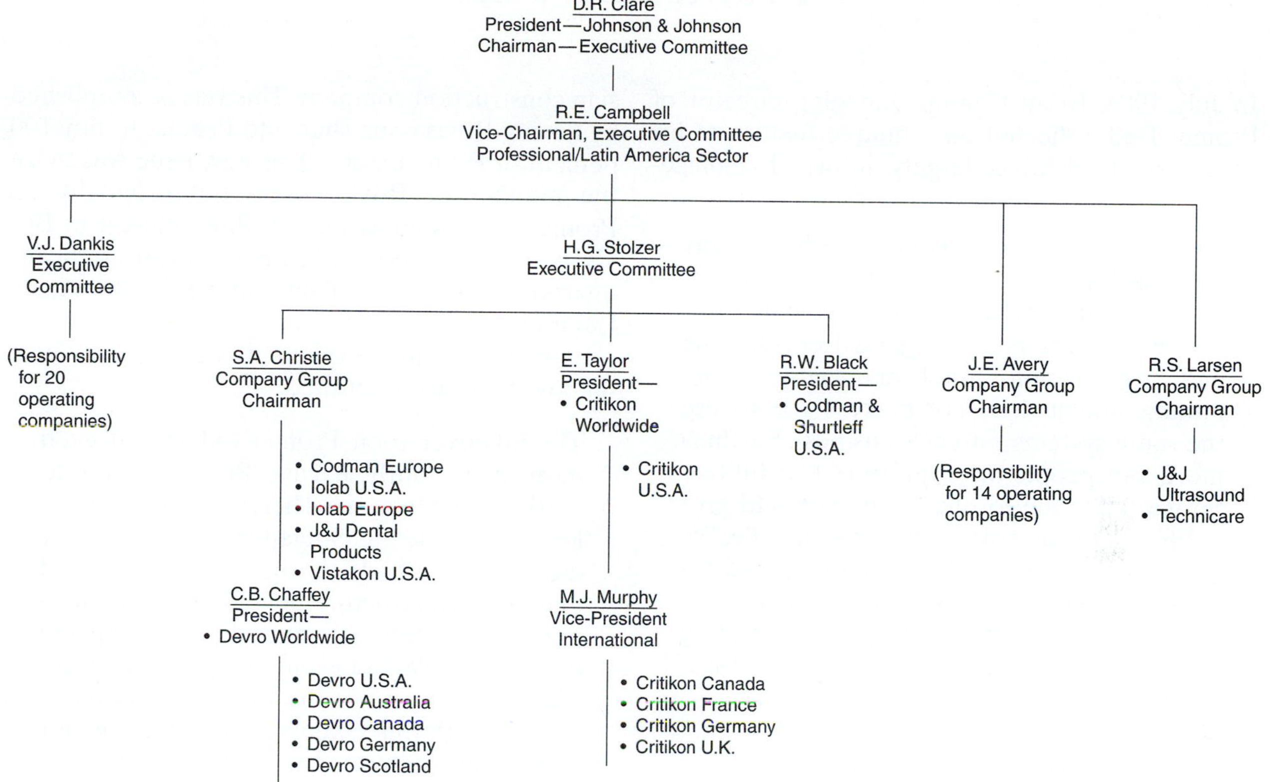

EXHIBIT 4 Board of Directors

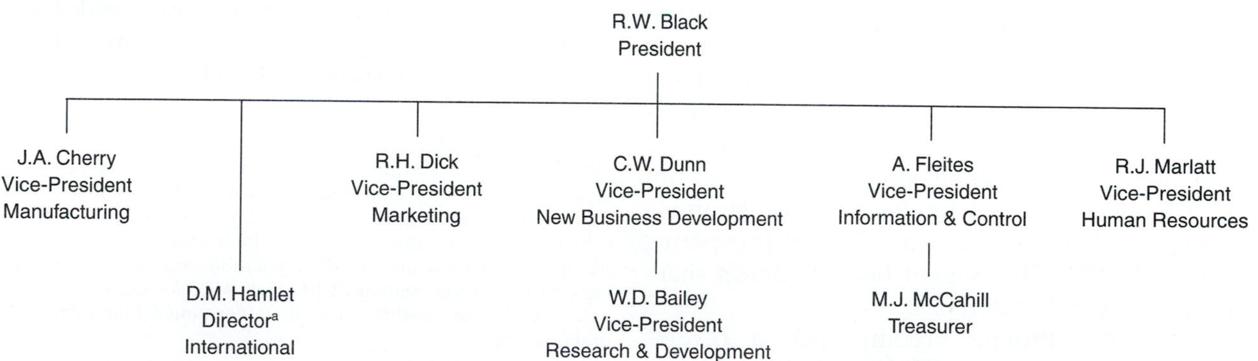

[a]Not a board member

Promet Berhad

In July 1984, Brian Chang, managing director of Promet Bhd, reflected on a unique feature of his company: its flexible, largely informal management systems.

> We do not have one system—we have many systems. We are in many businesses, including steel fabrication, marine contracting, vessel owning and chartering, civil engineering and construction, hotel management and mining, and it does not make sense to use the same systems for each business. Furthermore, our people have different capabilities. So we tailor the job to the person and give people as much work as they can handle. We also operate informally; we look to end results and try not to burden our managers with a lot of systems. This way of operating has been one of the key elements of our success.

COMPANY HISTORY

Brian Chang founded Promet in 1970 in Singapore with an original investment of about U.S. $10,000. The company's original business involved supplying labor, materials and equipment to support the offshore oil industry.

To finance expansion, Mr. Chang sold 40 percent of the equity in the early 1970s to Jardine Matheson (Southeast Asia), part of the large Hong Kong-based trading conglomerate. Operations were expanded into construction of offshore oil exploration equipment and shipbuilding. But Mr. Chang felt stifled by Jardine's constraining management policies, so with Promet prospering in the late 1970s, he bought back Jardine's share of the equity in installments.

In 1981, Promet accomplished a reverse takeover of Bovis SEA Bhd, a troubled Malaysian construction company. This was accomplished by having Bovis issue shares to Promet to buy 100 percent of Promet stock. This new issue was twice the number of Bovis shares out originally, so Promet owners gained controlling interest in Bovis. After the takeover, Promet's corporate headquarters was moved from Singapore to Kuala Lumpur.

Brian Chang explained why the reverse takeover was accomplished:

> The takeover took Promet public, but even more importantly, it gave Promet access to markets in Malaysia. There's no home market for Promet in Singapore; it's export or die. Malaysia had its own oil industry and massive infrastructure development requirements, and there was nobody there capable of doing it. We had always stayed away from Malaysia because of the Bumiputra requirements.[1] With this takeover, we made a major Malaysian commitment, and the government had a stake in how we did.

Over the period 1970–1983, Promet was very successful, growing at 35 percent compounded in both earnings and sales. Promet's total 1983 revenue was M$373 million,[2] profit after tax was M$65 million, and the company employed 4,000 people. (Summary profit and loss accounts for the years 1980–83 are shown in Exhibit 1.)

[1]The Malaysian government had strict regulations limiting the amount of nonMalay labor and equity investment that could be used by companies operating in Malaysia; these were the so-called Bumiputra requirements. Bumiputra meant, literally, *people of the land.* How limiting the regulations were varied depending on whether the company's products were for export or home use, and whether production of them consumed Malaysian natural resources.

[2]One Malaysian ringgit was worth approximately U.S. $.43.

This case was prepared by Assistant Professor Kenneth A. Merchant as a basis for class discussion rather than to illustrate either effective or ineffective handling of an administrative situation.

Promet Bhd was actually a holding company for a large number of operating companies. Exhibit 2 shows the Promet legal structure for all companies in which ownership was greater than 20 percent. The companies in the left two columns of Exhibit 2 were Malaysian companies; those in the middle two columns were Singapore companies; and those in the right two columns were incorporated in other countries. In 1984, Promet operated in 25 countries in South East Asia, the Middle East and South America.

There were two basic reasons for the multitude of legal entities. The ability to limit liability was one reason: Promet borrowing tended to be through each of the smaller companies, with no parent-company guarantees. Business custom was another reason, as Tony Shackel, Promet's finance director, explained:

> In Southeast Asia, people don't believe they have any security if they don't have a written agreement with you that says you are a participant with them in a certain profit center or legal entity. They want to have script.

PRESENT LINES OF BUSINESS

It was difficult to match Promet's legal structure with its lines of businesses. For the most part, Promet did not design its organization or management reports by lines of business, for reasons discussed later in this case. Nonetheless, Promet can be said to have been operating in four major lines of business—steel fabrication, marine-related activities, civil construction, and properties—and three smaller lines of business: mining, hotel management, and oil exploration. Here is a brief description of each:

Steel fabrication. Steel fabrication was Promet's original, and still largest, line of business. The company was one of the region's largest marine contractors and fabricators. Products included oil rigs, offshore platforms, marine pipelines, small offshore vessels (e.g., tug and supply boats). Despite the depressed condition of the oil rig construction industry in the early 1980s, this line of business still contributed over half of Promet's revenues and profits, although it was expected that by the end of the decade, rig fabrication would amount to less than 10 percent of the company's total business.

Marine-Related Activities. Promet was involved in the ownership and operation of specialized vessels and equipment, such as cranes, tugs and barges. It also undertook the marketing and sale of marine equipment, dredging contracts, offshore contraction of harbors, jetties, shotblasting and engineering design.

Civil Construction. Promet's civil construction business, which used concrete as a primary building material, was acquired in the takeover of Bovis. Recent emphasis was on larger and more profitable contracts, including bridge, road and building construction in Malaysia. Promet also had a consulting subsidiary which provided consulting services for civil engineering works and building construction.

Properties. Promet built some properties on a speculative basis, usually limiting risk by selling equity in the property before construction was complete or, if possible, even before it started. Properties being worked on in 1984 included a 237-unit housing estate with shops in Kuala Lumpur, a shopping center/office complex in Kota Kinabalu, Sabah, and a shopping complex/bus terminal/entertainment center in Kuching, Sarawak. Largest of all was a M$4 billion resort project on the northern Malaysian island of Langkawi which was given to Promet by the Malaysian government in exchange for a promise to develop it as a major tourist destination. Plans for the Langkawi project were announced in November 1983. The first phase, due to be completed in 1986, was to include five hotels, a town center, 2000 condominiums, a golf course, and an airport which would accommodate wide-bodied aircraft. Promet was trying to limit its investment in the Langkawi project to M$100 million, or less. The company had already convinced investors from Malaysia, Singapore, Indonesia, Japan and Sweden to provide most of the capital for the Langkawi developments.

Hotel. Promet owned and operated the 104-room Aurora Hotel in Bintulu, Sarawak. This hotel catered mostly to personnel attached to the oil industry located in that area of Malaysia.

Mining. Promet operated a bauxite mine in Malaysia, and it had a 50 percent stake in an Indonesia granite quarry, the largest in the region.

Oil Exploration. In 1982, Promet began a thrust into oil and gas exploration. A new energy subsidiary was formed, with Promet providing 100 percent financing, and U.S. oil consultants Gaffney-Cline & Associates providing expertise in exchange for 20 percent of the equity. Contracts were signed for exploration in Malaysia, Indonesia, and China, and early drilling had located some oil and gas reserves.

ORGANIZATION STRUCTURE

The top of the Promet organization consisted of five men with quite different backgrounds and skills who operated as a general management team:

- Tan Sri Datuk Haji Ibrahim Mohamed.[3] 41, Promet's executive chairman, was a lawyer and close associate of Brian Chang since their days together at London University. Tan Sri Ibrahim was almost exclusively concerned with long-term planning and senior governmental and commercial relations. He had a close relationship with the prime minister of Malaysia and had entree to the highest levels of government and civil service. He was not concerned with day-to-day company operations.
- Dato' Brian Chang, 41, managing director, was an engineer who had previously worked for Mobil Oil and for a Singapore shipbuilding company. He founded Promet when he was age 28. His present responsibilities were primarily in medium- and long-term planning and solving major operating problems.
- Dr. Benety Chang, 36, a medical doctor and Brian's brother, was primarily involved in day-to-day management of Singapore operations.
- Dato' Abdullah Mohamed, 38, a lawyer and Tan Sri Ibrahim's brother, was primarily involved in day-to-day management of Malaysian operations.
- A.J. Shackel, 37, a British expatriate, was responsible for all financial operations. All finance personnel, approximately 80 in number, reported on a solid line to Tony Shackel. A chart of the finance organization is shown in Exhibit 3. The financial controllers located in Singapore and Malaysia were responsible for reporting and monitoring day-to-day operations in their respective countries. The group financial controller was responsible for preparing cash flow and profit projections and company consolidated financial reports. The head of group costing was responsible for project reporting.

[3]Tan Sri, Datuk, and Dato' were Malaysian titles conferring honor akin to a British knighthood.

From 1971 to 1981 Promet had operated with a three-man executive board (the Chang brothers and Tony Shackel). The Mohamed brothers joined the board at the time of the Bovis takeover; Tan Sri Ibrahim had been Bovis' chairman. Neither of the Mohamed brothers was able to devote full time to Promet, as each was involved in some outside ventures.

The five-man executive committee rarely met formally as a group, but there were many of what Dato' Abdullah called *corridor board meetings.*

Reporting directly to the executive committee were about 20 managers responsible for various pieces of the business. The managers in the larger lines of business were functional managers. For example, T. K. Ong was responsible for all offshore oil-rig construction and fabrication activities, including project management, engineering, production and quality control, but Vincent Lum was responsible for marketing and selling these projects. In some smaller areas of business, such as bauxite mining and shot-blasting, managers were responsible for both marketing and operations. Some functions, most notably accounting, purchasing and personnel, were centralized at the group level.

In describing the organization, Brian Chang cautioned that Promet's managers' responsibilities were not fixed.

> You can't portray our organization in boxes. Different persons from among our five-man executive committee will come in and do different things according to their abilities and the time they have available at that moment. The only person who has full control of his portfolio is Tony Shackel, our financial guy.
>
> Similarly, the next level of organization under the board is quite gray. We don't have vice presidents who have total responsibility for divisions, like in America. We do a lot of cross-control, and it's very complex because it's all personalities. We have the tendency to bring someone up from within the organization, someone we know, and we upgrade him as necessary. We think that is preferable to bringing someone in from outside the organization and seeing in about six months if it was a good decision. We aren't looking for an ideal manager. We take a trustworthy

> manager, build the job around him, and beef him up where necessary. There's no way we can mold a person into a job; we have to mold the job to the person.

PLANNING AND BUDGETING

Promet's financial plan was built from the bottom up. In September/October of each year, the manager of each project or business prepared projections for the following three-year period. The first year was broken out by month, and the subsequent two years were shown only in total. Finance personnel from Tony Shackel's organization helped the managers portray their projections in financial terms. During the year, these projections were updated each month.

The consolidation of the project and operating business plans became the company plan, as Brian Chang explained:

> We don't have a formal company planning process. We don't say we are going to have, say, 15 percent growth next year and have everybody sharpen their pencils and write down how they're going to accomplish that. We take the elements of our business—the projects—and project them out, and we see what other projects we can get, and that becomes our plan. We don't have a long-term profit objective. The world is not like that. First you have to understand the market, and then you see what you can do with the market.
>
> Do we get into oil exploration, resorts, aviation, marine transport? Do we get out of fabrication? These are the questions that I answer. I thrash it out with my fellow directors, and we come to a conclusion. We may decide that we want to get into a certain business but that we can't until we get the right person or the right partner to work with.
>
> I also talk with people lower in the organization. We don't have any formal way of communicating. I don't require a five-page report on what they'd like to do. We have discussions with them.

Brian also felt that Promet's high tolerance for making changes in plans distinguished Promet's planning approach from that used in many companies:

> A typical company has a board composed of people who are involved in many companies. So they delegate all the responsibility for the company to a general manager who prepares plans and is charged with accomplishing those plans. The problem is that the general manager gets locked in. When he changes direction, he is criticized very badly by the board and, in fact, a board member gets a feather in his cap when he finds some details that differ from plan. This makes the general manager very defensive. He starts saying that the plan will be achieved only if the assumptions behind it prove to be correct. But he becomes unable to respond positively to market changes. His mind operates to protect himself at the board meetings.
>
> Promet does not operate this way. We are not critical of our managers when they make a change.

Brian Chang had been almost unerringly accurate in forecasting future trends. For example, in 1979 he correctly predicted the decline in the oil rig-building business and persuaded reluctant Promet managers to reposition the company in anticipation of this decline; and the Bovis takeover had been a great success. The company's latest thrusts were in the areas of oil exploration and Malaysian resort development.

REPORTING AND CONTROL

Operating reports were prepared monthly on each project and operating unit. A sample page of a project cost summary is shown in Exhibit 4. The reports were prepared and consolidated by personnel in Tony Shackel's organization. Exhibit 5 shows the format of the monthly Promet Group's consolidated profit and loss statement. The managers were also required to submit a short written report summarizing the problems being experienced and/or the plans being made. There was no set content requirement or format for this report.

The monthly reports were reviewed by both operating managers and personnel in the finance organization. Follow-up discussions were held as necessary with the managers involved on an informal basis.

Tony Shackel explained which numbers in the monthly reports received the most attention:

Our monthly profit numbers are largely irrelevant because for projects we take profit at stages. We take no profit up to 50 percent complete, 25 percent at 50 percent complete, and another 25 percent at 65 percent complete. So if the guy on-site says a project is 51 percent complete but my guy says it's 49 percent complete and concludes that we should not take any profit on it, I don't get worried. It will sort itself out in the next month.

But we do monitor some monthly numbers closely, particularly cash flows. We look at general and administrative overheads to see that they haven't risen above budget. We look at receivables. We look at debt ratios. We also look at the revised projections: are we going to finish the jobs on time and within cost? Different companies have different sensitivities that must be monitored.

The executive committee members were careful to devote most of their attention to the larger-impact companies, as Brian Chang explained:

We have companies that have only M$2 million in sales and others with M$100 million sales. We can't treat the managers the same. For some companies we say simply: "Go make a profit." For example, we started a company that does corrosion protection. Shipyards deliver steel to it. They shotblast it to remove all the rust, put a primer coat on it, and return the steel. The manager of this business does everything—debtors, creditors, management of the plant, everything. She returns 1 million profit every year on turnover of 2 million. I haven't seen her for eight months and haven't talked about her business for over two years.

Tony Shackel and Benety Chang also talked about control of the shotblasting business:

TONY: We check up on the shotblasting lady (and others like her) through the monthly financial statements. I'll ring her up every once in a while and say something like: "Hey Ann, your receivables are getting a bit out of hand." We don't spend a lot of time on it, but Benety and I are watching her business.

BENETY: I haven't seen her for two months, but I'm not worried because I see her financials. I don't care where she goes, and whether or not she comes to work today is not important. I see from the marketing figures that she's still selling well. When we see each other, it's more social than anything. We don't have formal marketing meetings or the like.

For the larger-impact businesses, the executive committee took a very active part in the management. Brian explained:

We give people as much responsibility as they can handle, but we have backstops to prevent major errors from occurring. People do not take major decisions without checking in with the center; my door is always open. For some of our larger projects, I keep up with a running projection that changes monthly, weekly, even daily. In our businesses—fabrication, construction, energy—we can't afford to have people learn from mistakes; they're too expensive. We'd rather the mistakes weren't made. And we haven't had that many slip-ups; we haven't been stuck with any rigs, and we haven't had any outstanding debt from anyone who had us build a rig.

THE IMPACT OF MANAGEMENT SYSTEMS ON PROMET'S SUCCESS

Company managers felt that the company's informal management systems were an important part of Promet's success over the years. For example, T. K. Ong (director of steel fabrication operations):

People fit in with the way things are being done in a company. Promet has a very well-established informal mode of operation. It is efficient, and it works. Our turnover is very low, and morale is high. And look at our achievement! Informality does not mean we are not serious about business; we make hard-nosed decisions. But we are also very flexible. We jump into anything we feel has potential. I am also appreciative of the fact that we don't have to write reports. I wouldn't feel comfortable in a company with heavy requirements for communicating in writing.

BENETY CHANG: Our people like our way of doing business. We have built up a very stable team which performs very well. There is always a danger of cross communication, such as where Brian and I give conflicting orders. But we avoid problems because the person receiving the conflicting orders knows to speak up, and then we straighten it out. Anybody can talk to anybody. People down in the organization don't have to communicate through their immediate superiors. They can talk right to Brian, Dato' Abdullah or me. Our doors are always open.

In response to a question as to how much of Promet's success was due to its management system and philosophies as opposed to a perhaps superior ability to predict the future and/or good business and government connections, Brian Chang responded:

> I don't know. I think it's a combination of everything. You might have a good forecast, but if you can't divert the company in that direction to take advantage of it, the gain is zero. Similarly, if you have good government connections but can't use them, you've got nothing. On the other hand if you have a superb management team but are in the wrong business, such as the present hotel business in Singapore, you might not even be able to break even.

CONCERN FOR THE FUTURE

One of the executive committee's primary concerns was about how Promet's management systems would evolve as the company's growth continued. Brian Chang was working 16-hour days and wanted to reduce, not increase, his workload, and Tony Shackel was concerned that it was becoming more and more difficult to find the time for holidays. They were considering questions such as: Should the company change its management systems? Or should a move be made into businesses that did not require the company to be so nimble?

EXHIBIT 1 Profit and Loss Accounts of Promet Group (for years ended December 31) (M$000)

	1983	*1982*	*1981*	*1980*
Turnover	373,472	307,187	369,754	261,656
Operating profit	111,465	56,962	35,520	8,701
Share of profits of associated companies	4,086	8,789	6,361	2,049
Profit before taxation	115,551	65,751	41,881	10,750
Taxation	(50,365)	(19,594)	(13,386)	(2,312)
Profit after taxation	65,186	46,157	28,495	8,438

EXHIBIT 2 PROMET BERHAD, The Promet Berhad Group Structure

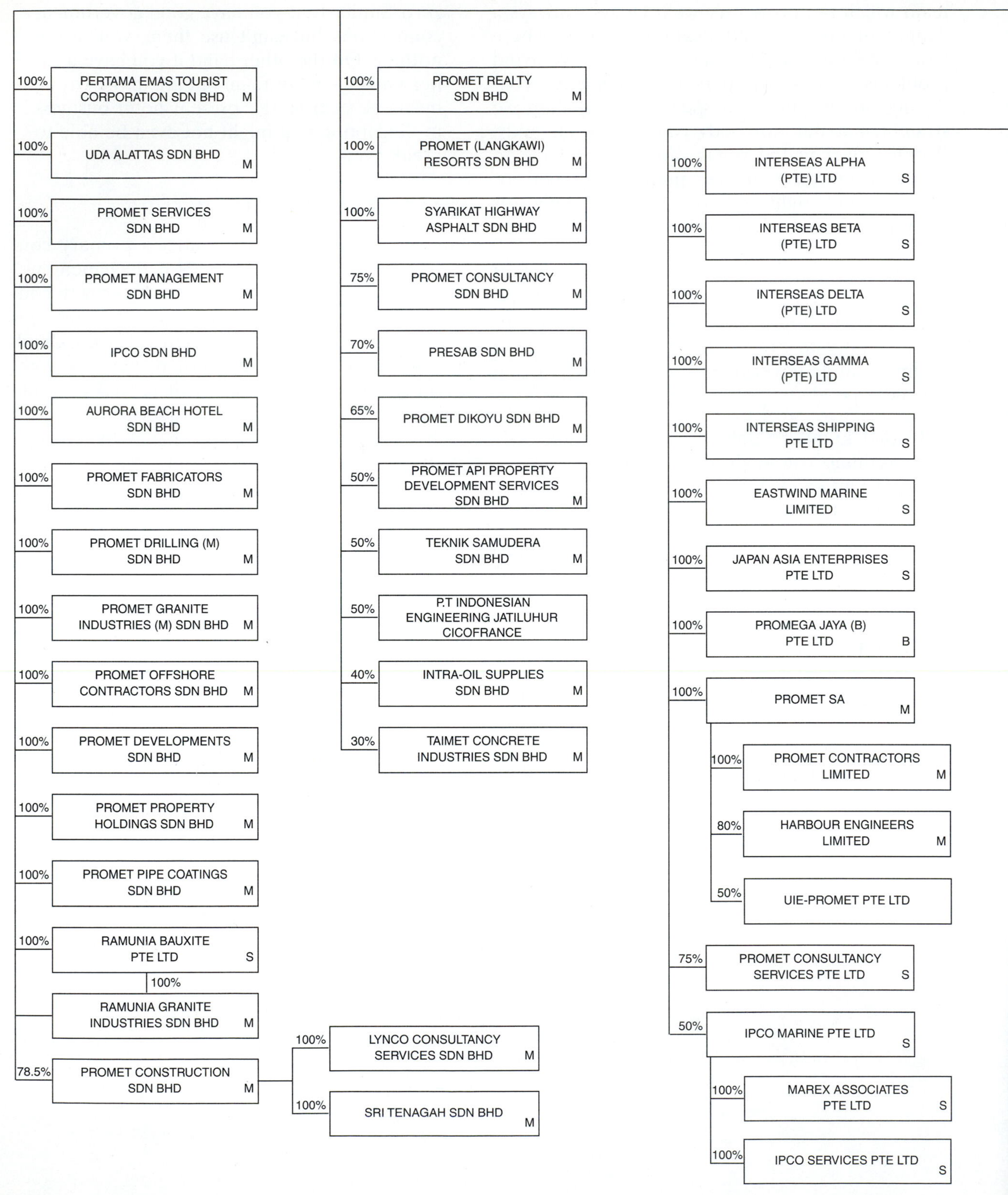

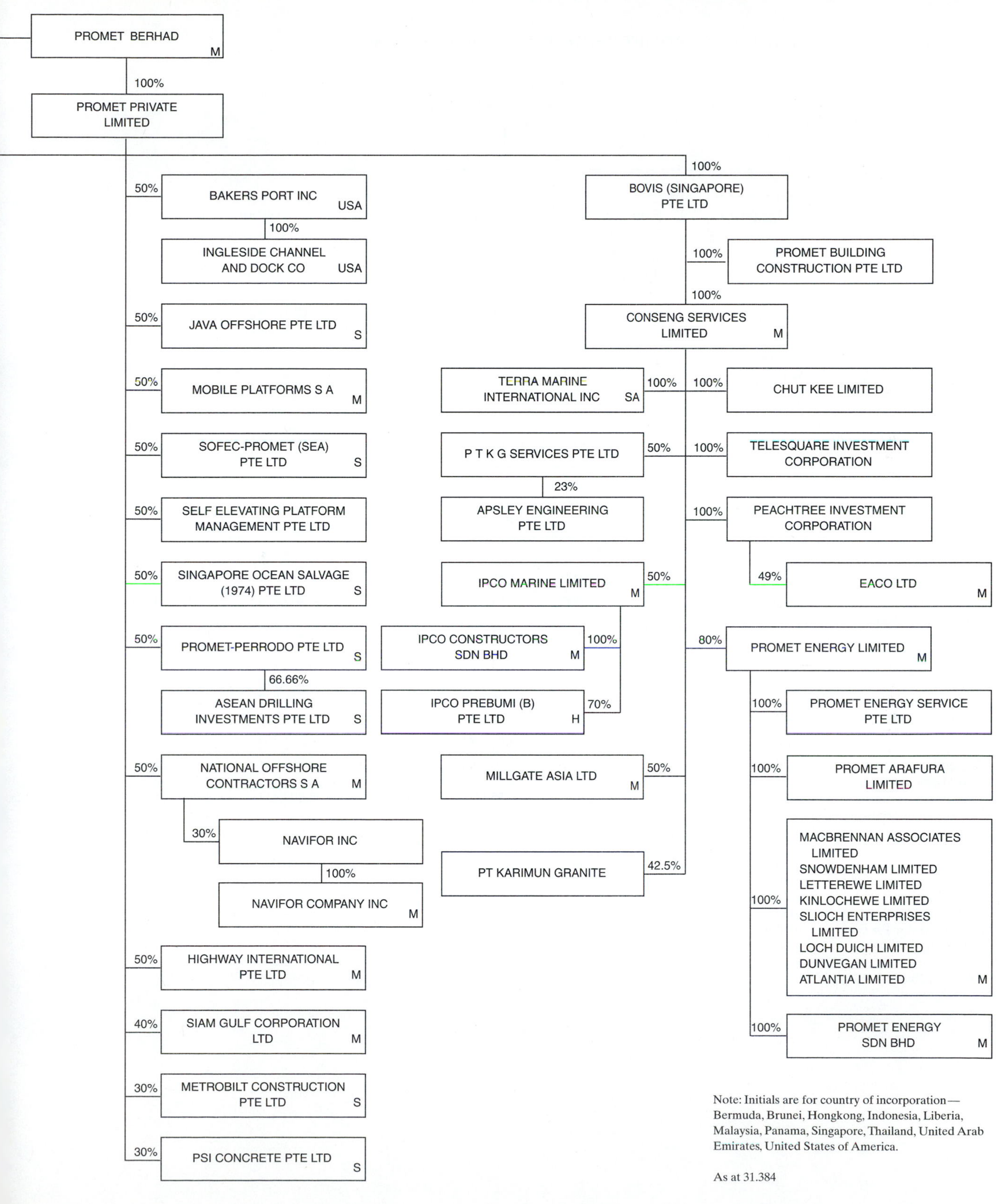

Note: Initials are for country of incorporation— Bermuda, Brunei, Hongkong, Indonesia, Liberia, Malaysia, Panama, Singapore, Thailand, United Arab Emirates, United States of America.

As at 31.384

EXHIBIT 3 PROMET BERHAD, Financial Organization

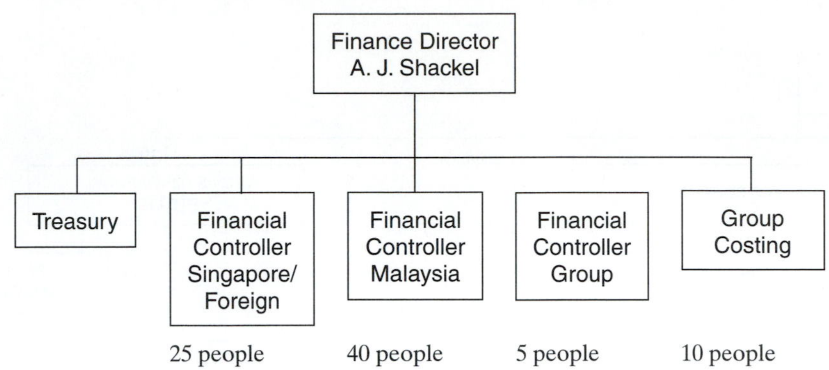

EXHIBIT 4 PROMET BERHAD, Cost Summary for Menara Beluran[a]

	Cost Code	*Previous Projections*	*Current Projections*	*Budgeted*	*Variance*	*Committed as at May 31st*	*Actual 1984*
		M$	M$	M$	M$	M$	M$
A. *Preliminaries*	0100	7,741,000	7,159,800	7,159,800	—	4,843,367	3,405,914
Mobilization	0101	375,000	571,000	571,000	—	300,470	245,184
Admin. Overhead	0102	900,000	—	—	—	—	—
Site Overhead	0103	2,510,000	3,513,800	3,513,800	—	1,412,693	1,387,032
Setting Up of Site Ofc.	0104	150,000	30,000	30,000	—	130,771	130,431
Facilities for Site Ofc.	0105	120,000	245,000	245,000	—	44,781	44,781
Plant Hire	0106	3,128,000	—	—	—	2,677,910	1,325,555
Plant and Machinery	0107	458,000	2,750,000	2,750,000	—	276,742	272,931
Demobilization	0108	100,000	50,000	50,000	—	—	—
B. *Foundation*	0200	5,720,000	5,295,305	4,850,000	(445,305)	5,295,305	5,295,305
Drive/Sheet/Bored or H-Piles	0201	320,000	301,894	300,000	(1,894)	301,894	301,894
Strip Foundation/ Trench Foundation	0202	5,400,000	4,993,411	4,550,000	(443,411)	4,993,411	4,993,411
C. *Substructure*	0300	150,000	96,005	50,000	(46,005)	96,005	94,945
Pile Cap	0301	100,000	96,005	—	(96,005)	96,005	94,945
Column Stump	0302	—	—	—	—	—	—
Ground Beam	0303	—	—	—	—	—	—
Basement Slab	0304	—	—	—	—	—	—
Lift/ Escalator Pit Base	0305	—	—	—	—	—	—
Retaining Wall	0306	—	—	—	—	—	—

[a]Disguised name.

EXHIBIT 5 PROMET BERHAD

PROMET GROUP

MONTHLY OPERATING SUMMARY

PROFIT & LOSS STATEMENT

SCHEDULE 2
COMPANY ____________________
CURRENCY ____________________
__________________________ 19__

		CURRENT MONTH		YEAR TO DATE			ANNUAL BUDGET	LATEST FORECAST	PROJECTION 19__
		BUDGET	ACTUAL	BUDGET	ACTUAL	PRIOR YEAR			
1.	SALES —Customer								
2.	Intercompany								
3.	TOTAL								
4.	COST OF SALES—Customer								
5.	Intercompany								
6.	TOTAL								
7.	GROSS PROFIT —Customer								
8.	Intercompany								
9.	TOTAL								
10.	% of line 3								
11.	Production O/H Over/(Under)								
12.	NET OPERATING PROFIT								
13.									
14.	Fees and Commission Received								
15.	Dividends Received								
16.	Interest Received								
17.	Other Income/(Expenses)								
18.	TOTAL INCOME (Lines 12, 14 to 17)								
19.	OVERHEADS								
20.	Staff								
21.	Premises								
22.	Administration								
23.	Selling & Distribution								
24.	Interest Paid								
25.	Exchange Losses/(Gains)								
26.	Management Fees								
27.	Vessel Depreciation								
28.	TOTAL								
29.	PROFIT BEFORE TAX								
30.	TAXATION								
31.	PROFIT AFTER TAX								
32.	% of line 3								
33.									
34.									
35.	PROFIT FORECASTS								
36.	(S$' 000)								
37.	PROFIT/(LOSS)								
38.	TAXATION								
39.	MINORITY INTERESTS								
40.	NET PROFIT/(LOSS)								

CHAPTER 10

Financial Performance Targets

Financial performance targets, most of which are set as part of the organization's planning and budgeting processes, are an important part of a financial results control system. They form a basis for performance evaluations, and they are critical to motivation. As was mentioned briefly in Chapters 2 and 9, while it would be nice merely to be able to tell people to "do their best" and have them do so, such vague exhortations are not optimally motivating. People perform better if they are asked to achieve specific, short-term performance targets that are neither too easy nor too difficult. The targets improve performance by providing the individuals with specific goals to strive for, information about how they should direct their efforts, and standards by which they can interpret feedback about their actual performances.

While all performance targets can provide these benefits, this chapter focuses on financial performance targets, those used as part of a financial results control system. Financial performance targets can be set for the corporation as a whole, or they can be tailored to specific lower-level responsibility centers. Financial targets for profit center managers are defined in terms of profit or merely in terms of selected line items of revenues and expenses. Financial targets for cost center managers are defined in terms of cost.

This chapter describes the different type of financial performance targets that companies use and then discusses three important target-related issues: (1) Should a relatively fixed corporate financial objective be established? (2) How challenging should financial performance targets be? and (3) Should financial target-setting processes be predominately top-down or bottom-up? That is, how much influence should subordinates have in setting their financial targets?

TYPES OF FINANCIAL PERFORMANCE TARGETS

Financial performance targets can be distinguished in a number of ways. Three important ways are in terms of whether the targets are (1) model-based, historical, or negotiated, (2) internal or external, or (3) fixed or flexible.

Model-Based versus Historical versus Negotiated Targets

Performance targets can be derived directly from a quantitative model of what performance should be; they can be based on historical performance; or they can be derived from a process of negotiation between subordinates and their superiors. *Model-based targets* provide a prediction of the performance which should ensue in the upcoming measurement periods. When model-based targets are used in areas where activities are *programmable* (where there is a direct and relatively stable, deterministic causal relationship between outputs and inputs) they are said to be *engineered* targets. On production lines material input/output relationships can often be derived directly from the product specifications. Every computer manufactured should have a mother board, a power supply, a disk drive, and so on, and those physical quantities can be made into financial standards by multiplying the quantities by the standard unit costs. For some operations, models of labor input/output relationships can also be specified quite accurately through *time-and-motion studies.*

Some other targets are model-based but not engineered because they require forecasts or assumptions about one or more unknown variables. Profit plans are built on a financial accounting model, but they require many important forecasts, such as information about the total available market, competitors' actions, and factor prices.

Historical targets are derived directly from performance in prior periods. A manager may be told to increase revenues or profits by 10 percent each year.

Finally, some performance targets are *negotiated* between superiors and subordinates. Negotiation is common where there is a significant *information asymmetry* gap between superiors and subordinates. This gap is common because superiors generally are more knowledgeable about the overall organization's preferences and resource constraints. Subordinates generally have superior knowledge about the links between outputs and inputs, opportunities, and constraints at the operating level. Negotiations about performance targets can induce superiors and subordinates to share at least some of their information.

Tight results control is easiest to implement when targets are engineered because the link between effort and results is direct. Consumption of inputs greater than an engineered target indicates, with high probability, a performance problem. Managers can also use historical targets to effect tight results control if the processes being controlled are stable over time. Tight results control is more difficult when important assumptions about the future are necessary or if negotiation is used, unless the negotiation is tightly constrained by good performance models or good historical performance data. In these latter situations, performance variances from the target might indicate a performance problem, but they might indicate only that the original assumptions were wrong or that the negotiation process was biased.

Internally versus Externally Derived Targets

Targets can also be described as being either *internally* or *externally* derived. Some performance target models, such as time-and-motion studies, are totally *internally* focused on what is possible within the organization being considered.

Two types of *externally* focused target-setting practices which have become more common in recent years are target costing and benchmarking. With *target costing,* cost targets are price-driven. They are set so that when the product (or service) is sold, the company will earn its desired profit margin. Companies use the resulting cost targets to motivate employees to act in ways that will make the company profitable in the competitive global marketplace.[1] The message to employees is, "If we cannot produce this product at the target cost, we cannot be competitive in the world market." The cost targets may not be explicitly linked to monetary rewards, but they influence behavior because employees know if they fail to achieve the cost targets, their business will not be viable and their jobs will be at risk.

Target costing is not a new idea. Henry Ford had target costing in mind when he developed the first mass-produced automobile, the Model T, in 1908. Many companies seemed to lose sight of the concept until some of the largest and most successful Japanese companies, including Toyota, Nissan, and NEC, began applying it in a comprehensive and intensive manner in the 1980s. A recent survey found that over 80 percent of Japan's largest assembly manufacturing firms have adopted target costing.[2] Interest in both the concept and the techniques that facilitate its successful implementation has exploded in recent years.[3]

Internally-focused target setting approaches seem to be good because they ask employees to focus on important variables, such as cutting costs, and to do better than they had in the past. Target costing, however, is often better. In companies which compete on low cost bases, target costing appears often to lead to products with lower costs. It is effective because designing to a specific low cost which is necessary for product viability creates a more intense pressure to reduce costs than does designing to an unspecified minimum cost.[4] Target cost-setting processes also encourage, or force, useful communications between the marketing, production, purchasing, and engineering departments.

Benchmarking is a process in which an organization studies other organizations' best practices, and implements processes and systems to enhance its own performance.[5] Benchmarking can involve comparing the organization's performance on critical aspects of its operation against the best-in-industry (direct competitors) or best-in-class (companies recognized for superior performance of certain functions). Many aspects of performance can be benchmarked, including specific product or service characteristics (functions or costs), specific activities or processes (production, inventory management, or customer service), the strategies being followed, or overall organizational outcomes (return-on-assets). The theory behind benchmarking is that one's performance must be compared with the best if one aspires to become the best.

Informally, companies have benchmarked their operations to a greater or lesser extent for many years, but the term *benchmarking* is relatively new, as are most attempts to study the conditions and processes that affect its success. In recent years, the use of benchmarking has grown markedly. It is one response to the increased competition many companies faced in recent years and its inclusion as a prerequisite for many important quality awards and certifications, including the U.S. Malcolm Baldridge National Quality Award, the Japanese Deming Award, the European ISO 9000 Quality Certification, and the Canadian Award for Business Excellence.

Xerox Corporation has been one of the leaders in benchmarking in the United States. Xerox started benchmarking in 1979 as a response to the company's loss of market leadership in the copier business. It started with a study of unit manufacturing costs and found that competitors were selling comparable machines at Xerox's manufacturing cost. The success of that first study lead Xerox to implement benchmarking processes in all of its functional areas throughout the world. Benchmarking has become a widespread practice only since the late 1980s, as many other U.S. companies, including AT&T, DuPont, Ford, IBM, Kodak, and Mellon Bank, have followed Xerox's lead.

The most common form of benchmarking is *unilateral.* Companies independently gather information about one or more companies that excel in the product or function of interest. Some examples of *cooperative* benchmarking exist. Cooperative benchmarking requires that firms share information with others through mutual agreements designed to identify and share best practices. These agreements have grown as companies have found it is easier to share the sometimes sensitive data with companies that are not direct competitors.

Cooperative information sharing partnerships are often built around independent organizations which use either surveys or studies by third-party consultants to build a shared database. The American Productivity and Quality Center in Houston established the International Benchmarking Clearinghouse with nearly 200 members,[6] and the Strategic Planning Institute (SPI) established the SPI Council on Benchmarking with about 50 members.[7] The partners in these associations share data, conferences, and courses which provide information about numerous product and functional areas. Computer-Aided Manufacturing-International (CAM-I) is an example of a highly specialized industry consortium designed to facilitate the sharing of information about manufacturing cost systems. Participating companies hope to gain a better understanding of the competitiveness of their own operations and, if they are lagging, the processes other companies use to reach leadership positions in performing the same function. A 1992 survey, conducted by the American Quality Foundation and Ernst & Young, of 580 U.S. firms in four industries; computers, autos, hospitals, and banks, found that 31 percent of the firms regularly benchmarked their products and services, and only 7 percent reported that they did not engage in any form of benchmarking.[8]

As compared to unilateral benchmarking, cooperative benchmarking is potentially more efficient. Once the sharing agreements are set, information is more readily available. The information is presumably more accurate since the information is provided by willing participants. Typically firms engaging in cooperative benchmarking abide by a code of conduct which they agree upon prior to the beginning of the study. One example is the International Benchmarking Clearinghouse's code of conduct which specifically addresses principles to be used in exchanging information.

Fixed versus Flexible Targets

Another way to distinguish targets is in terms of whether they are *fixed* or *flexible.* Fixed targets do not vary over a given time period, while flexible targets are changed according to the conditions faced during the period as reflected by the volume of activity, interest rates, or currency exchange rates.

At the highest managerial levels in most firms, financial targets are usually *fixed.* The managers are held accountable for achieving their plans regardless of the business conditions they face. If they fail to do so, they lose some important forms of rewards; such as bonuses, autonomy, and sense of satisfaction.

Targets for some other managers, however, are made *flexible.* Many manufacturing managers are not held accountable for achieving a fixed total cost budget. They are asked to achieve flexible budgets. The flexible budget can be a total cost budget that varies with the volume of production (for example, $100,000 for production of 100,000 units), or it can involve the use of unit cost standards (for example, $1.00 per unit). The effect is identical; however, the recent survey of budgeting practices showed that only a minority of firms (28 percent) report using flexible budgets,[9] and indeed flexible standards are difficult to implement in many industries (oil and gas exploration or insurance) either because there is no dominant volume of activity indicator or because total costs are not highly correlated with the activity indicator (few costs are variable).

Targets can also be made flexible by stating them in terms of *relative performance;* that is, relative to the performance of others facing identical, or at least similar, business conditions. Evaluation in relative performance terms means that employees' performances are evaluated not in terms of the absolute levels of their performance, but relative to the performance of others. The others may be other employees in the organization performing similar tasks or managing like entities, or they may be the closest outside competitors.

Relative performance evaluations can be done objectively or subjectively. Evaluators can rank employees or business entities based on objective performance measures (parts assembled per hour or return-on-investment) or combinations of measures. Often, however, evaluators add to the objective rankings their own judgment based on some other, nonquantified factors. It is usually for outsiders, and even the employees being evaluated, to identify all the factors the evaluator considers or the weighting of those factors. Often the evaluators themselves are not aware of all the factors that affect their subjective evaluations.

MAJOR FINANCIAL PERFORMANCE TARGET ISSUES

The effects of any results control system can be undermined if the wrong targets are set or if the targets are not set in the proper way. Three of the most important financial performance target-related issues are discussed in the following sections.

Should a Corporate Performance Target Be Established?

Some corporations develop an explicit, timeless corporate financial performance target, such as 15 percent return-on-equity at top management levels, and communicate this target both to employees and to outside parties, such as investors. Other corporations' financial targets, however, emerge at the end of the formal planning and budgeting processes as, more or less, the sum of the business units' targets.

The establishment of formal corporate financial performance targets during or before the beginning of the planning and budgeting process has some advantages. The corporate targets provide a performance benchmark which reminds top-level managers of what the stakeholders want (or in extreme situations what the corporation needs to survive). They provide a target to strive for and they provide a standard that is useful for judging success or progress and for enhancing interpretations of feedback about actual performance.

The communication of corporate targets to lower-level organizational participants before they are involved in their own planning processes can serve to narrow the common *planning gap* between corporate performance as envisioned by top-level managers and that forecast by business-unit managers. Business-unit managers can use preset corporate goals as guidelines to keep in mind while preparing their plans, knowing that their plans will likely receive extra scrutiny if their business-unit plans promise performance below the corporate standard. Ways in which the gap can be reduced can be the focus of the planning reviews. In this way, the corporate goals can have a positive effect on both top-level manager motivation and their conduct of the planning review processes.

The formulation and communication of corporate goals can cause problems, however. If the wrong goals are set, managers are likely to make poor decisions. They might seek high returns instead of growth. If the goals are not set at the right level, if they are too easy or too difficult, they might not be optimally challenging; they might lead managers to take imprudent risks; and they probably will not provide good feedback as to whether management has been taking the proper actions. Even properly set goals can easily become obsolete if, as is common, economic or competitive conditions or the company's product offerings change significantly. Inflation is a prominent, sometimes volatile, factor that affects corporate returns, as Paul Volcker (former chairman of the Federal Reserve Bank and more recently chairman of the New York investment banking firm of James D. Wolfensohn) noted

> Corporations always seem to aim for 15% rates of return. That's going to have to change. Those numbers are not in this world for a large number of companies. You can't expect inflationary rates of return in noninflationary times.[10]

Financial performance targets that *flex* with changing factors such as inflation, or those that express desired performance relative to that of a company's closest competitors, can minimize this obsolescence potential.

Communication of corporate goals to lower-level managers can also cause game-playing. They can cause the managers of below-average-performing business units to forecast performance at levels higher than is desirable, and thus create demotivation or tendencies to take imprudent risks or to manipulate performance reports. They can cause the managers of above-average-performing business units to *satisfice;* to forecast performance at or above the corporate guideline, but below maximally possible levels. To preserve some of the benefits of having corporate goals without suffering the game-playing costs of dysfunctional actions from lower-level managers, some companies set corporate goals for use by top management but do not communicate them to lower-level participants in the organization.

How Challenging Should Financial Performance Targets Be?

Another major financial performance target issue is about how difficult, or challenging, to make the targets. For planning purposes, the budget target should equal expected performance; that is, it should have a 50 percent probability of achievement.[11] For motivational purposes, however, the optimal target is often quite different. The budgeting survey found that more than 75 percent of companies use the same budget for planning and motivational purposes,[12] so the budget system designer's problem is how to choose a target which either suits the primary purpose of budgeting or provides a reasonable compromise between the planning and motivational purposes.

The theory regarding the effects of performance targets on motivation is complex. Clearly if managers do not set high performance expectations, the people in their organizations will not produce superior results, but performance targets can be set too high. Findings from psychological research have shown a fairly consistent, *non-linear* relationship between target difficulty and motivation (and hence performance) as shown in Figure 10-1. If the targets are perceived as quite easy to achieve, there is virtually no relationship between target difficulty and motivation. People's levels of aspiration (and hence motivation and performance) are low because they are able to achieve their targets with a minimum of effort, persistence, and creativity. Above a threshold level of difficulty, motivation seems to increase with target difficulty up to the point where people approach the perceived limits of their ability.[13] After that, the relationship levels off and eventually turns down. At high levels of difficulty, most people get discouraged, lose their commitment to achieve the target, and exert less effort. Motivation is highest

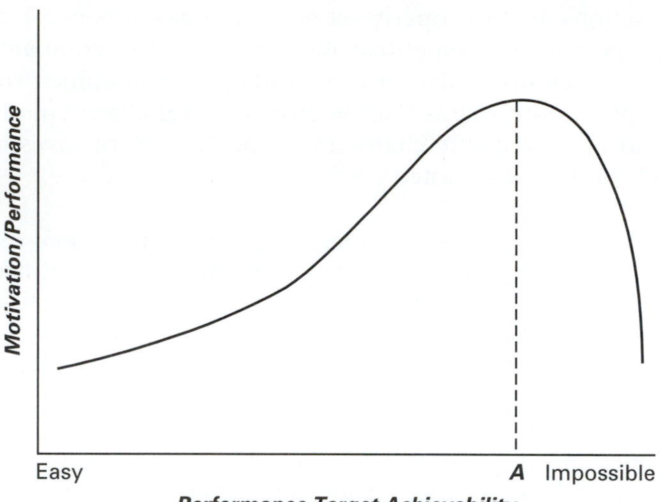

FIGURE 10-1 Relationship Between Performance Target Achievability and Motivation/Performance

when performance targets are set at an intermediate level of difficulty (point A in Figure 10-1), that can be called *challenging, but achievable.*

Where, specifically, is the point of optimum motivation; the inflection point in the target difficulty/performance relationship? That is, where do perceptions of excessive difficulty and, hence, lack of commitment to achieve the target, set in? The point varies depending on the maturity, experience, and self assurance of the individuals involved. Many authors suggest that on average the highest performance seems to be induced when targets are highly challenging; when individuals perceive less, perhaps significantly less, than a 50 percent chance of target achievement.[14] One author put the optimum somewhere between a 25 and 40 percent chance of achievement.[15]

These psychological findings provide useful guidelines for setting targets for many people at low organizational levels, but they do not seem to apply to the most important corporate financial targets, *annual profit budgets.* Most companies set their annual profit budget targets, at both corporate and profit center levels, at levels that are highly achievable.[16] Their budgets are set to be challenging but achievable 80 to 90 percent of the time by an effective management team working at a consistently high level of effort. Because they require competence and consistent effort, these targets should not be described as *easy,* even though they are highly likely to be achieved. Combined with other MCS elements, these highly achievable budget targets have many motivation, planning, and control advantages.

Manager Commitment

Highly achievable budget targets increase managers' commitment to achieve the targets. Most managers operate in conditions of considerable uncertainty; their performance is affected by many unforeseen circumstances. Relatively highly achievable targets protect the managers to a considerable extent from the effects of unfavorable, unforeseen circumstances and allows them few, if any, rationalizations for failing to achieve their targets. They have no choice but to commit themselves to achieve their targets, regardless of the business conditions faced. This increased commitment causes the managers to prepare their budget plans more carefully and to spend more of their time managing, rather than preparing rationalizations to explain away their failures.

Because of the lengthy budget performance period, typically one year in most corporations, the costs of a lack of commitment to achieve budget targets are high. If highly challenging targets are set and something negative occurs early in the year, the loss of commitment and decreased motivation may persist for many months. If the budget targets are highly achievable, managers can withstand even considerable bad luck.

Corporate managers have other possibilities for insuring managers against the effects of unforeseen, negative circumstances. They could shorten the planning horizon and set targets for periods shorter than a year, but budget target-setting processes are expensive, and profit measures for short time periods require many interperiod revenue and expense allocations, so they are not highly congruent with the corporate objective. (This is discussed further in Chapter 12.) Another possibility is to *flex* the budget when unforeseen effects are encountered. This budget flexing approach is difficult because organizational entities, such as profit centers and sometimes cost centers, are affected by many unforeseen events, some positive and some negative. It is costly to have someone analyze the effects of each unforeseen effect and make a judgment as to how the manager should have reacted to it, if at all.

Protection Against Optimistic Projections

Highly achievable budget targets protect the corporation against the costs of optimistic revenue projections. The first step in budgeting is usually preparation of sales forecasts. Production (or service) levels are then geared to the forecasted level of sales. If the budgets have optimistic revenue projections, managers will be induced to acquire resources in anticipation of revenue (activity) levels that may not be forthcoming. Some of these acquisition decisions are at least partially irreversible. It is often difficult and expensive to shed people and specialized fixed-asset resources. It is usually safer to forecast sales (and hence profits) relatively conservatively and acquire additional resources when their need is assured. This conservatism leads to highly achievable budget targets.

Manager Achievement

Highly achievable budget targets make most managers feel like winners. In the minds of most managers, budget achievement defines the line between success and failure. Managers who achieve their budgets are given a package of rewards; bonuses, autonomy, and higher probability of promotion, and their self-esteem is given a boost. Organizations derive advantages when their managers have good self-esteem and feel like winners. Managers who feel good about themselves and their abilities are more likely to be eager to go to work, take prudent risks, and increase their levels of aspiration for the future.[17] Unlike subjects in a psychological experiment or workers on a production line, when managers fail to achieve their budget targets, they live with that failure for an entire year, not for a matter of minutes or hours. The prolonged period of discouragement and depression can be quite costly to the organization.

Cost Reduction

Highly achievable budget targets reduce the costs of organizational interventions. Most corporations use a management-by-exception philosophy. Superiors intervene in the affairs of their subordinates when unfavorable variances from

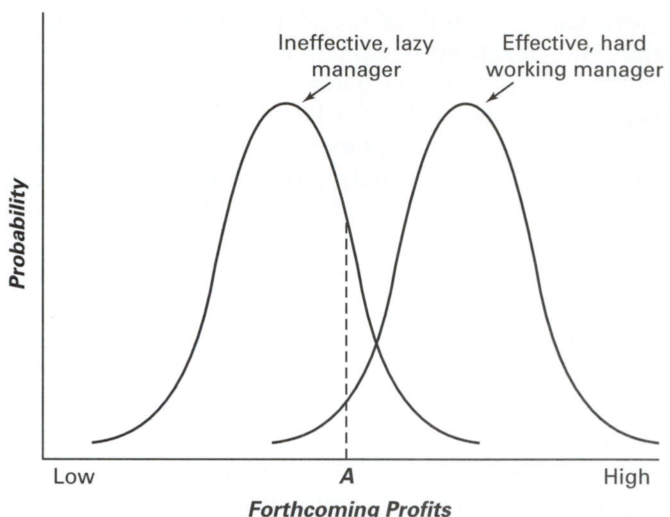

FIGURE 10-2 Probability Distributions of Forthcoming Profits for Effective and Ineffective Managers

budget signal the need. When 80 to 90 percent of the managers are achieving their budgets, top management attention is directed to the relatively few situations where the operating problems are most likely and most severe.

This point is illustrated in Figure 10-2. The figure shows two probability distributions of forthcoming profits, one for an effective, hardworking manager and one for an ineffective, lazy manager. Because the scaling shows better performance to the right, the distribution for the ineffective manager is to the left of that for the effective manager. If the budget target is set at point A, the vast majority, perhaps 90 percent, of effective, hardworking managers will achieve their targets. A much smaller proportion of ineffective managers, perhaps only 20 percent, will get lucky enough to achieve their targets. Top-level managers will spend relatively little time intervening in the affairs of effective managers; most of their intervention efforts will be directed at ineffective managers.

Game-playing Reduction

Highly achievable budget targets reduce the risk of game-playing. The stakes associated with budget achievement in most firms; which include bonuses, promotions, and job security, are so significant that managers who are in danger of failing to achieve their budget targets have powerful motivations to play "games" with the numbers. As was discussed in Chapter 6, games are actions managers take to make their performance indicators look more favorable while knowing the actions are having no positive effects on real performance, and might actually be harming it. This game-playing may involve deceptive accounting practices (altering judgments about reserves or changing accounting methods) or costly operating decisions (working overtime to boost sales and profits at year-end or delaying preventative maintenance). The games can be designed to boost current period's performance or, if the targets are considered impossible to achieve, to reduce current period's performance to position the entity for better performance in the subsequent measurement period.

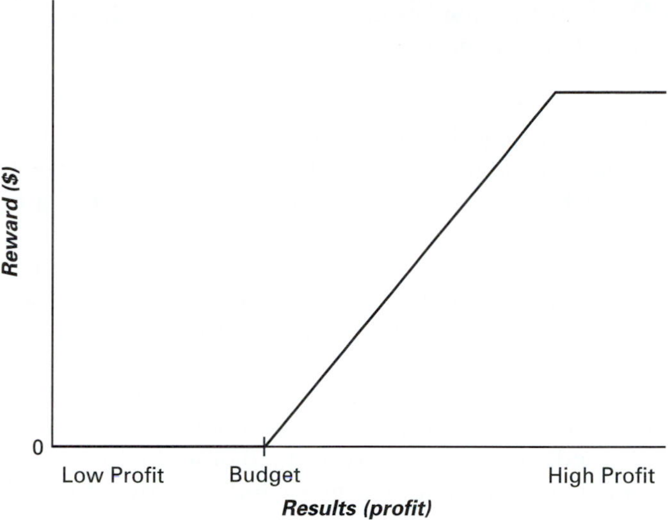

FIGURE 10-3 Typical Rewards/Results Function for a Profit Center Manager

The primary risk organizations face by setting highly achievable budget targets is that managers' aspirations, and hence motivation and performance, might be lower than they should be. The managers might not be inspired to perform at their maximum ability. This is a potentially serious risk; however, organizations can protect themselves from this risk by giving managers incentives to *exceed* their budget targets. Figure 10-3 shows a typical rewards/results function for the profit (and investment) center managers. This figure shows that managers earn all (or sometimes most) of their bonuses by exceeding their budget targets (up to a prespecified maximum). If the rewards given for exceeding budget targets are sufficiently high relative to those given merely for achieving the budget targets, managers will have incentives not to slack off after the achievement of their budget targets is assured.

While the use of highly achievable budget targets is the typical corporate practice, not all budget targets should be set to be highly achievable. If the corporation is in danger of failing or defaulting on a significant loan, top managers may set highly challenging profit targets to signal to operating managers the short-term exigency. Top managers sometimes also set high profit targets to limit managers' discretionary investments, both as a way to provide a signal to business unit managers that the unit's strategy has changed (that is, that short-term profits now have priority over growth) and to enforce that change. They sometimes set high targets because they suspect organizational "fat" or because they want to set up a rationale to replace a manager. They may also set high targets to penalize managers for earning high bonuses in prior periods based solely on luck, not their own efforts.

Another budget target-setting possibility is to set multiple levels of targets; such as optimistic, realistic, and worst case, each designed to serve a different budget purpose (motivation, planning, or control). This is a budget-focused approach to contingency planning; however, the practice survey indicated that only 7 percent of the respondent firms use different budgets to serve multiple budgeting purposes better.[18]

How Much Influence Should Subordinates Have in Setting Their Financial Targets?

A third important issue to be faced in designing a financial results control system when targets are negotiated is the extent to which subordinates should be allowed to participate in and influence the target-setting processes. This issue is sometimes phrased as whether plans and budgets should be set in a *top-down* versus a *bottom-up* manner.

Few companies' processes can be described as either totally top-down or totally bottom-up, but there are significant differences in companies' practices regarding the authority for setting financial targets. Most, but not all, companies' target-setting processes tend toward bottom-up for managers. A broad survey of U.S. firms' planning and budgeting practices conducted in the late 1980s found that most firms set managerial goals in a bottom-up fashion. Seventy-two percent of the respondents chose this wording to describe their process: "Subordinate levels of management submit their goals and objectives for review and final approval by higher levels of management."[19]

Allowing employees to participate in and to have influence on the process of setting their performance targets can provide any of several benefits. One is *commitment to achieve the targets.* Employees who are actively involved in the process of setting their performance targets are more likely to understand why the targets were set at the levels they were, so they are more likely to accept the targets and be committed to achieve them.

A second benefit is *information sharing.* In most companies, target setting involves a process of sharing information about business possibilities and corporate preferences and resources. Managers who are closest to the business, or employees who are closest to operations, can provide useful information to superiors about business or operational potentials and risks. Top-level managers can provide information about corporate priorities and constraints.

A third benefit is *cognitive.* Including people in target-setting processes has the beneficial effect of clarifying expectations and starting the employees thinking about how best to achieve the targets. This thinking often involves learning, which can lead to process improvements and, perhaps, innovation.

A final benefit is *organizational commitment.* Employees who are given top-down performance targets often become alienated from their organizations. This demotivation leads to poorer performance which, in turn, often causes managers to employ stronger sanctions to attempt to motivate the employees to achieve the targets. This leads to greater alienation, and so on. At the extreme, this destructive escalating cycle leads to absenteeism, turnover, carelessness, and even sabotage.

An example that illustrates several of these benefits is that of the New United Motor Manufacturing (NUMMI), a Fremont, California-based joint venture between General Motors (GM) and Toyota.[20] Before the joint venture's formation, one manager called Fremont "the worst plant in the world."[21] It then ranked among the worst GM plants in productivity, quality, absenteeism, and labor militancy. The GM production control system used industrial engineers to set the work standards, but the NUMMI joint venture system allowed the workers to set their own standards. Within the first couple of years, with 85 percent of the workers hired from GM's employee lists, NUMMI's productivity was ranked first among GM plants, absenteeism had dropped from between 20–25 percent to 3–4 percent, and workers described themselves as substantially more satisfied with their job.

The bottom-up setting of work standards does not account for all of the improvement at the Fremont plant. A new production system, fear of plant closure, employee selection, and socialization all played a part; but empowering the employees to set their own work standards undoubtedly accounted for a substantial amount of the improvement because it provided employees a strong signal that they are a vital part of a team, that the company is not just management's to run. They responded by working harder and smarter.

Not all employees, and not even all managers, should be highly involved in companies' planning and budgeting processes and, in particular, the setting of performance targets. Among the situations where target-setting processes can be set in a predominantly top-down manner with good results are the following.

First, targets can effectively stem from a top-down process when top-management has knowledge of the operating business and operational prospects that is either sufficient for setting properly challenging performance targets or that essentially subsumes the knowledge possessed by the subordinate. Superiors have the required knowledge to set top-down targets in quite a few situations. This occurs most commonly when a given activity or operation is programmable; where targets can be engineered or set exclusively by projecting historical trends. In these cases, there is no need to negotiate targets through some form of bottom-up process.

Another situation where top management knowledge is sufficient for setting performance targets occurs where superiors have an excellent understanding, perhaps because they formerly ran the business and conditions have not changed much. Even when budgets are prepared in a seemingly bottom-up process, when superiors have this knowledge they exert greater influence on the final decisions about performance targets. They are less prone to listen to subordinates' arguments as to why performance targets cannot be raised.

A second situation that can lead to top-down target setting is where top-level managers have the information available for evaluating performance on a relative basis. They may be managing a large number of relatively homogenous entities operating in a stable environment. These situations exist in some industries, such as where firms manage large numbers of like-concept retailing outlets, but relative performance evaluation is less feasible when products are differentiated.

A third situation where top-down target-setting is effective, and should even be preferred, is where lower-level managers are not good at budgeting. Top-down target-setting is common in small businesses for just this reason. Small business operating managers are often technically skilled, but their management and financial education and experience is quite limited.

Fourth, top-down target-setting should be preferred where lower-level managers' thinking is dysfunctionally bound by historical achievements. Top management may know how to set standards according to a learning curve model that has proven accurate in the past or they may know that a new technology will cause structural changes in the way things are done and dramatically different business prospects, thus obsoleting historical performance standards.

Finally, top-down target-setting processes should be used where lower-level managers are prone to impart biases into the budgets that cannot be controlled. Biases can lead the organization to set performance targets either higher or lower than is optimum. Most operating managers have a *conservative* bias. They use the opportunity involvement in the target-setting processes allows them to set lower targets. Lower targets increase the probability of target achievement, enhance the managers' reward potentials, and make it possible for them to achieve their targets with less effort. Some operating managers, particularly entrepreneurial and sales-oriented managers, have an *optimistic* bias. Some of these managers want a challenge that will give them a feeling of accomplishment. Some are so committed to improvement of their entity's performance that they ignore their own self-interests. Some want to signal to top management that they are aggressive, perhaps to compete for additional resources.

Sometimes top managers can control these biases. They can select for managerial positions people who have a greater reputation for truth-telling, or they can implement some form of truth-inducing incentive system. Truth-inducing systems reward both the setting of high performance targets *and* the achievement of those targets, thus overcoming the common tendency toward conservatism in target-setting.[22]

While top-down target-setting has advantages in some settings, managers who use this type of process must be careful not to forego too many of the benefits of a bottom-up process so as not to risk losing their subordinates' commitment to achieve the targets. Top-level managers may set targets that a reasonably smart, consistently hardworking management should be able to achieve with high probability, but if the operating managers do not share that perception of achievability, they may be discouraged. The resulting lack of motivation may lead to a low probability of achievement. In this case, perception becomes reality.

CONCLUSION

Performance targets are an important part of a financial results control system. They can have significant effects on employee motivation and the reliability of performance evaluations. Financial performance targets can be distinguished in a number of ways. They can be model-based, historical, or negotiated; internally or externally derived; and fixed or flexible. Only a few simple prescriptions as to which form of target should be used can be provided. One prescription is that engineered standards should be used where it is possible to do so; that is, where activities are programmable.

Most target-related decisions, however, depend on the setting. This chapter has discussed three important financial performance target issues related to the desirability of communicating a corporate performance target, the optimal amount of challenge in a target, and the proper amount of influence to allow subordinates in setting targets. These discussions show that multiple alternatives and trade-offs must be considered in making these decisions.

Notes

1. T. Hiromoto, "Another Hidden Edge: Japanese Management Accounting," *Harvard Business Review*, 88, no. 4 (July–August 1988), pp. 22–26.
2. M. Sakurai, "Target Costing and How to Use It," *Journal of Cost Management* (Summer 1989), pp. 39–50.
3. See T. Tanaka, "Target Costing at Toyota," *Journal of Cost Management* (Spring 1993), pp. 4–11; P. Horvath, "Target-Costing: State of the Art Report," (Arlington, Tex.: Computer Aided Manufacturing-International, 1993); Y. Monden and K. Hamada, "Target Costing and Kaizen Costing in Japanese Automobile Companies," *Journal of Management Accounting Research*, 3 (Fall 1991), pp. 16–34.

4. R. Cooper, *The Confrontation Strategy: When Lean Enterprises Collide* (Boston: Harvard Business School Press, 1995).
5. See D. Elnathan, T. W. Lin, and S. M. Young, "Benchmarking and Management Accounting: A Framework for Research," *Journal of Management Accounting Research*, 8 (1996), pp. 37–54.
6. J. Main, "How to Steal the Best Ideas Around," *Fortune* (October 19, 1992), pp. 102–106.
7. M. Kharbanda, "Benchmarking: Making It Work," *CMA Magazine* (March 1993), pp. 30–33.
8. J. Main, "How to Steal the Best Ideas Around," *Fortune* (October 19, 1992), pp. 102–106.
9. S. Umapathy, *Current Budgeting Practices in U.S. Industry: The State of the Art* (New York, Quorum, 1987), p. 149.
10. "Brave New World," *Forbes* (May 10, 1993), p. 184.
11. C. Chow, J. Cooper, and W. Waller, "Participative Budgeting: Effects of a Truth-Inducing Pay Scheme and Information Asymmetry on Slack and Performance," *The Accounting Review* (January 1988), pp. 111–122.
12. S. Umapathy, *Current Budgeting Practices in U.S. Industry: The State of the Art* (New York, Quorum, 1987), p. 149.
13. Locke and Latham provide a summary of the many experimental studies that have found this linear relationship. E. A. Locke and G. P. Latham, *A Theory of Goal Setting & Task Performance* (Englewood Cliffs, N.J.: Prentice-Hall, 1990), pp. 27–29.
14. For example, D. T. Otley, *Accounting Control and Organizational Behavior* (London: William Heinemann Ltd, 1987); R. L. M. Dunbar, "Budgeting for Control," *Administrative Science Quarterly* (March 1971), pp. 88–96; G. Shillinglaw, *Managerial Cost Accounting*, Fifth edition (Irwin, 1982).
15. R. L. M. Dunbar, "Budgeting for Control," *Administrative Science Quarterly* (March 1971), pp. 88–96.
16. Most of this discussion is taken from K. A. Merchant, *Rewarding Results: Motivating Profit Center Managers* (Boston: Harvard Business School Press, 1989) and K. A. Merchant, "How Challenging Should Profit Budget Targets Be?" *Management Accounting* (November 1990), pp. 46–48.
17. Locke and Latham provide a summary of the many experimental studies that have found this linear relationship. E. A. Locke and G. P. Latham, *A Theory of Goal Setting & Task Performance* (Englewood Cliffs, N.J.: Prentice-Hall, 1990), pp. 110–114.
18. S. Umapathy, *Current Budgeting Practices in U.S. Industry: The State of the Art* (New York, Quorum, 1987), p. 139.
19. Ibid., p. 138.
20. This example is taken from P. Adler, "Time-and-Motion Regained," *Harvard Business Review*, 71, no. 1 (January–February 1993), pp. 97–108.
21. Ibid., p. 98.
22. An analytically-derived truth-inducing incentive system is discussed by A. Kirby, S. Reichelstein, P. Sen, and T. Paik, "Participation, Slack, and Budget-Based Performance Evaluation," *Journal of Accounting Research*, 29, no. 1 (Spring 1991), pp. 109–127. For laboratory evidence of the effects of such a system, see C. Chow, M. Hirst, and M. Shields, "Motivating Truthful Subordinate Reporting: An Experimental Investigation in A Two-Subordinate Context," *Contemporary Accounting Research* (Spring 1994), pp. 699–720; and W. Walker, "Slack in Participative Budgeting: The Joint Effect of a Truth-Inducing Pay Scheme and Risk Preferences," *Accounting, Organizations and Society*, 13, no. 1 (January 1988), pp. 87–98. For a practical example of the use of a truth-inducing incentive system, see J. Gonik, "Tie Salesmen's Bonuses to Their Forecasts," *Harvard Business Review*, 56, no. 3 (May–June 1978), pp. 116–23.

Citibank Indonesia

In November 1983, Mehli Mistri, Citibank's country manager for Indonesia, was faced with a difficult situation. He had just received a memorandum from his immediate superior, David Gibson, the division head for Southeast Asia, informing him that during their just-completed review of the operating budgets, Citibank managers at corporate had raised the SE-Asia division's 1984 after-tax profit goal by $4 million. Mr. Gibson, in turn, had decided that Indonesia's share of this increased goal should be between $500,000 and $1,000,000. Mr. Mistri was concerned because he knew that the budget he had submitted was already very aggressive; it included some growth in revenues and only a slight drop in profits, even though the short-term outlook for the Indonesian economy, which was highly dependent on oil revenues, was pessimistic.

Mr. Mistri knew that to have any realistic expectation of producing profits for 1984 higher than those already included in the budget, he would probably have to take one or more actions that he had wanted to avoid. One possibility was to eliminate (or reduce) Citibank's participation in loans to prime government or private enterprises, as these loans provided much lower returns than was earned on the rest of the portfolio. However, Citibank was the largest foreign bank operating in Indonesia, and failing to participate in these loans could have significant costs in terms of relations with the government and prime customers in Indonesia and elsewhere. The other possibility was to increase the total amount of money lent in Indonesia, with all of the increase going to commercial enterprises. But with the deteriorating conditions in the Indonesian economy, Mr. Mistri knew that it was probably not a good time for Citibank to increase its exposure. Also, the government did not want significant increases in such offshore loans to the private sector at this time because of their adverse impact on the country's balance of payments and services account.

So, Mr. Mistri was contemplating what he should do at an upcoming meeting with Mr. Gibson. Should he agree to take one or both of the actions described earlier in order to increase 1984 profits? Should he accept the profit increase and hope that the economy turned around and/or that he was able to develop some new, hitherto unidentified sources of income? Or should he resist including any of the division's required profit increase in his budget?

CITIBANK

Citibank, the principal operating subsidiary of Citicorp, was one of the leading financial institutions in the world. The bank was founded in 1812 as a small commercial in New York City, and over the years it had grown to a large, global financial services intermediary. In 1983, the bank had revenues of almost $5.9 billion and employed over 63,000 people in almost 2600 locations in 95 countries.

Citibank's activities were organized into three principal business units: institutional banking, individual banking, and the capital markets group. The Institutional Banking units provided commercial loans and other financial services, such as electronic banking, asset-based financing, and foreign exchange, to corporations and governmental agencies around the world. The Individual Banking units, which operated in the U.S. and 18 other countries, provided transactional, savings, and lending services to consumers. The Capital Markets Group served as an intermediary in flows of funds from providers to users. With a staff of 3500, this group was one of the largest investment banks in the world. (Exhibit 1 shows the relative size of these activities, and Exhibit 2 shows a summary corporate organization chart.)

This case was prepared by Assistant Professor Kenneth A. Merchant as a basis for class discussion rather than to illustrate either effective or ineffective handling of an administrative situation.

MEHLI MISTRI

Mehli Mistri, Citibank's country corporate officer for Indonesia, joined Citibank as a management trainee in the Bombay office in 1960, just after finishing a B.A. degree in Economics from the University of Bombay. Between 1960 and 1964, Mehli gained experience in a number of assignments in the Bombay office, and in 1965 he transferred to New York to work in the credit analysis division. He returned to Bombay in 1966, and then became manager of Citibank branches in Madras (1968), Calcutta (1969–71), New Delhi (1972), and Beirut (1973). In 1974, he was promoted to regional manager with responsibility for five countries in the Middle East (Turkey, Syria, Iraq, Jordan, Lebanon), and he held that position until 1979 when he was appointed the country head of Indonesia. He remained in that position up until the time of this case. In 1982, Mehli attended the Advanced management Program at the Harvard Business School.

CONTROL OF INTERNATIONAL BRANCHES

Citibank managers used two formal management processes to direct and control the activities of the corporation's international branches: reviews of sovereign risk limits for each location and reviews of operating budgets and accomplishments.

Sovereign Risk Limits

Each year Citibank management set sovereign risk limits for its international branches based on country risk analyses. The term sovereign risk actually refers to a wide spectrum of concerns that would impair the bank's ability to recapture the capital it invested in foreign countries. These included macroeconomic risk, foreign exchange controls that the government of the host country might employ that would make it difficult for clients to pay their obligations, or, in the extreme, expropriation of assets. Once Citibank had opened a given branch, however, it intended to keep it open, so the reviews of sovereign risk were concerned only with setting limits of the amount of money a branch could lend in foreign currency.

The sovereign risk review process started in mid-year with the country manager proposing a sovereign risk limit. This limit was discussed with division and group managers and was finally approved, on a staggered time schedule, by a senior international specialist on the corporate staff. The foreign currency lending limit for Indonesia had grown substantially as the branch had grown.

The sovereign risk limit set during these reviews was an upper guideline. When the economic conditions in a country changed in the period between sovereign risk reviews, country managers sometimes chose to operate their branches with self-imposed sovereign risk limits that were below the limits set by management in New York. Corporate managers encouraged this behavior because they knew that the managers on site often had a better appreciation of the risks in the local environment.

Budgeting

Budgeting at Citibank was a bottom-up process which started in July when headquarters sent out instructions to the operating units describing the timing and format of the submissions and the issues that needed to be addressed. The instructions did not include specific targets to be included in the budget, although it was widely recognized that the corporation's combined long-term goals were approximately as follows:

Growth: 12 to 15 percent per annum
Return on Assets: 1.25 percent (125 basis points)
Return on Equity: 20 percent

The above norms were established for Citibank as a whole, but a number of international branches, including Indonesia, traditionally exceeded these norms, and these entities often established their own targets at higher levels.

At the time the operating managers received the budget instructions, they would have the results for half the year (through the end of June), and in the period from July until the end of September, they would prepare a forecast for the remainder of the current year and a budget for the following year. The starting point for the preparation of the budget was projections about each of the major account relationships, and discussions continued until the summation of the account relationship projections could be reconciled with the desired profit center bottom line. Then costs were considered. The budget submission form included all the line items shown in Exhibit 3. In some past years, the bank had prepared two- and five-year projections, but the numbers were seen to be very soft and not very useful.

Formal reviews of the annual budgets were held according to the following schedule:

LEVEL OF REVIEW	TIMING
Division	end of September
Group	mid-October
Institutional Bank	end of October

If the sovereign risk review for a particular entity had not yet been held, the budgets were submitted with the assumption that the risk limits would be approved as submitted. If this assumption proved to be incorrect, the budget had to be revised before it was incorporated in the corporate consolidated budget.

Performance was monitored and compared against budget each month during the year. Every quarter a new forecast for the remainder of the year was made. Whether these were reviewed formally by division managers varied widely, depending on the division manager's style. Some managers held relatively formal on-site reviews of performance and budget revisions, and others communicated only by mail or by telephone.

Mr. Mistri was very comfortable with the review processes:

> Every level of management has a role to play, and there is a lot of horsetrading and give and take in the budget review processes. Usually there is more revision of the numbers at lower management levels, but revisions do not necessarily mean increased profit goals. I have seen cases where the division head thought the country head was being too aggressive and he asked for the budget to be lowered. The managers sitting further away are more objective, and the review processes are consultative, collegial, and constructive.

Budgets were taken very seriously at Citibank, not only because they were thought to include the most important measures of success, and also because incentive compensation for managers at Citibank was linked to budget-related performance. For a country manager, incentive compensation could range up to approximately 70 percent of base salary, although awards of 30 to 35 percent were more typical. Assignment of bonuses were based approximately 30 percent on corporate performance and 70 percent on individual performance, primarily performance related to forecast. The key measures for assessing both corporate and international-branch performance were growth, profits, return on assets, and return on equity. However, in the analyses of individual performance for the purposes of assigning incentive compensation, considerable care was taken to differentiate base earnings from extraordinary earnings (or losses) for which the manager should not be held accountable.

CITIBANK IN INDONESIA

Indonesia was a relatively young country; it achieved independence only in 1949 after many years of being a Dutch colony. Citibank had operated in Indonesia only since 1968 when President Suharto allowed eight foreign banks to set up operations in Jakarta. From the point of view of the Indonesia government, the role of the foreign banks was to help develop a young economy by transferring capital into the country, establishing a modern banking infrastructure, attracting foreign investment, and developing trained people.

The foreign banking community operated in Indonesia with some important restrictions. The most serious constraints were that foreign banks were not allowed to open branches outside the Jakarta city limits, and local currency loans could be made only to corporations with headquarters and principal operations within the Jakarta city limits. But, on the other hand, the Indonesian government did not require any local ownership of equity, it set no lending quotas for the banks (e.g., requirements to lend certain amounts of money to certain types of businesses at favorable rates), and it valued and maintained a free foreign exchange system.

In explaining the goals of the government with respect to the foreign banks, Mr. Mistri commented:

> We consider ourselves privileged to be in Indonesia. We realize that the country wants to develop economically, and we know that the government sees us in the role of a development and change agent, attracting and developing not only capital, but also new financial products, services and techniques and trained managers and professionals for the financial services industry. The govern-

ment also expects us and other international banks to participate in extensions of credit to both the public and private sectors.

Citibank and the other foreign banks were interested in operating in Indonesia for several reasons: (1) to serve their international and local customers, (2) to assist in the economic development of the country, and (3) to share in the potential for profits and growth the Indonesian economy offered. The Indonesian economy had tremendous potential: the country was the fifth largest in the world in terms of population, and the economy had shown excellent growth for many years, as the figures shown in Exhibit 4 illustrate. The country was rich in raw materials, particularly oil and tin, and the Indonesian government was very interested in developing the country's industrial activities.

In 1983, Citibank's Indonesian operation included activities in each of the three major lines of business—institutional, individual and capital markets. Mehli Mistri was the Country Corporate Officer, and as such, he was the primary spokesman for all of Citibank's activities in Indonesia. His prime line responsibility, however, was the Institutional Banking activity which provided by far the greatest proportion of revenues and profits. Other individuals headed the Individual Banking and Capital Markets activities in Indonesia, and they reported through separate management channels (see Exhibit 5).

Since its inception, Citibank's Indonesian operation had been very successful. Its growth paralleled that of the Indonesian economy.

THE SITUATION IN 1983

In 1983, Mr. Mistri was concerned about the risk-return ratio in his branch. He felt comfortable with Indonesia's long-term prospects, but the country, which was highly dependent on oil revenues, had slipped into a recession when oil prices decreased significantly. His concern was as to whether the government would take strong enough steps to correct its balance-of-payments problem.

Inside the bank, Mr. Mistri was faced with a problem of high staff turnover. High turnover had been a problem for Citibank for many years because the bank provided its people with training that was recognized as probably the best in Indonesia, and local financial institutions had lured many Citibank people away with generous offers. This had happened so often that Citibank had been given labels such as "Citi-university" and "Harvard-on-wheels," and the government often held Citibank up as an example of how foreign banks could (and should) supply trained professionals to the country. To attempt to retain more of its trained people, Citibank had recently increased its compensation levels, but some people in the branch felt that the bank could not compete on the basis of salary because of its desire to be profitable, its limited domestic branch network, and significant career opportunities elsewhere.

The year 1983 was particularly difficult from a staff turnover standpoint, as the losses included Mr. Mistri's chief of staff and two senior officers. In mid-1983, the average account manager experience was under two years, and there were three unfilled slots at management levels. Mr. Mistri knew that the inexperience and people shortages in the branch were also serious constraints to growth.

Given these significant problems, Mr. Mistri thought that the budget he submitted, which projected modest growth, should be considered as aggressive. He wanted to submit an aggressive budget because

> . . .we are an aggressive organization. We like to stretch because we feel the culture of our corporation and the will and desire of our people to succeed and excel can make up the difference.

In reflection of the fast-changing uncertainties in the economy and the personnel problems, however, Mr. Mistri decided to operate with a self-imposed sovereign risk limit that was somewhat lower than that which had been formally approved by management in New York. He knew that his responsibility was as much to manage risk as to generate profits.

In late October, 1983, however, the budget for the whole Institutional Bank was reviewed at headquarters, and the consolidated set of numbers did not show the growth that top management desired. This led management to suggest some budget increases, and these increases presented Mr. Mistri with the dilemma described in the introduction to this case.

EXHIBIT 1 Selected Citicorp Financial Data—1983 (dollars in millions)

	Citicorp Consolidated	*Institutional Bank*	*Individual Bank*	*Capital Markets Group*
Revenues	$5,883	$2,896	$2,380	$587
Net Income	$ 860	$ 758	$ 202	$128
Return on Shareholders Equity	16.5%	22.0%	17.7%	32.2%
Return on Assets	.64%	.87%	.69%	1.26%

Source: 1983 Citicorp Annual Report

EXHIBIT 2 Partial Citibank Organization Chart

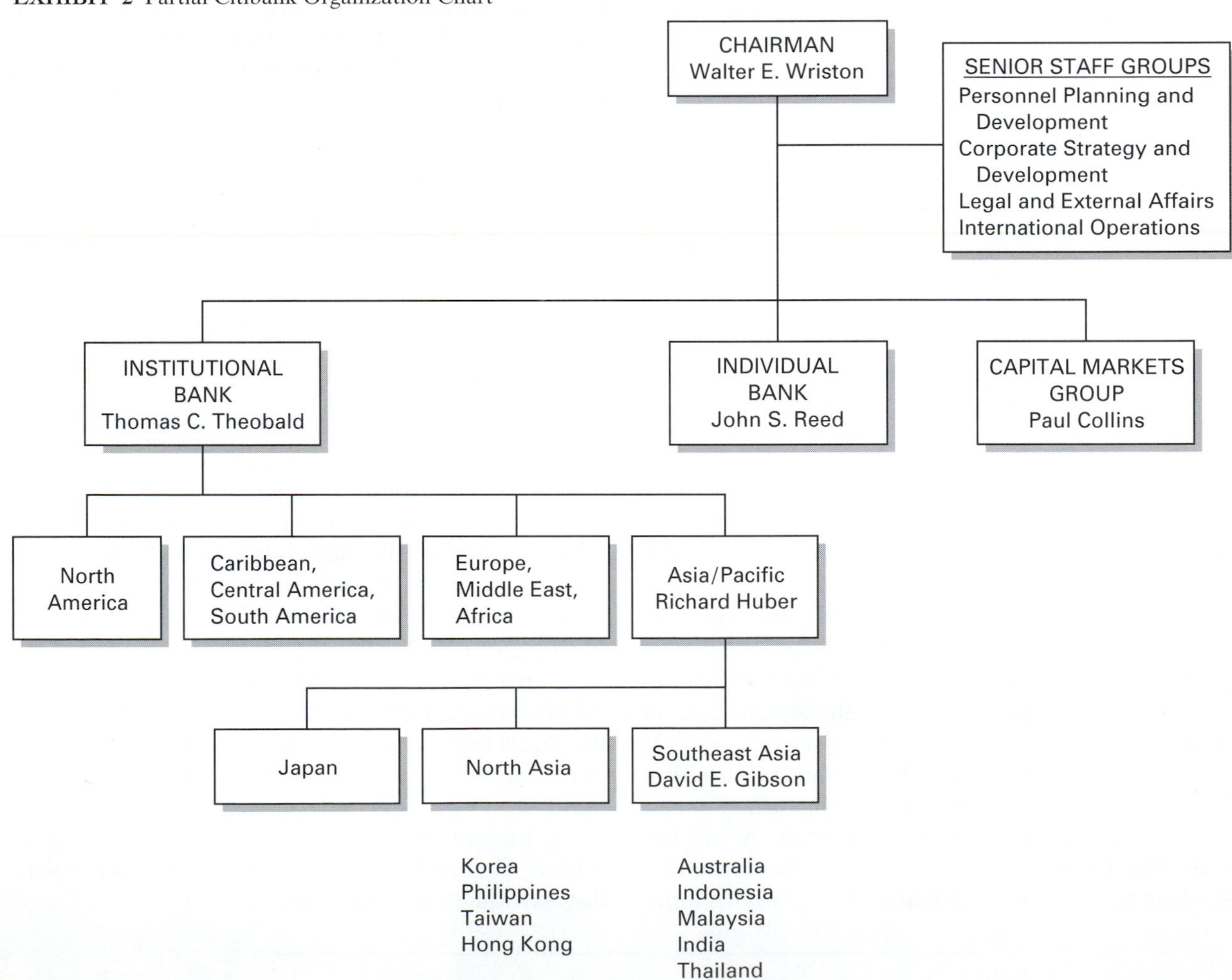

EXHIBIT 3 Line Items on Budget Submission Form

REVENUE/EXPENSE	PROFIT CENTER EARNINGS
Local Currency NRFF	Equity Adj.—Translations
Foreign Currency NRFF	Placements (AVG.)
Allocated Equity NRFF	Total Staff (EOP)
BAD DEBT RESERVE EARNINGS	Total Non-Performing Loans-EOP
NET REVENUE FROM FUNDS	Rev./Non-Performing Loans
Exchange	Avg. Total Assets—Lcl Curr.
Translation Gains/Losses	Avg. Total Assets—Fgn Curr.
Trading Account Profits	Allocated Equity
Trade Financing Fees	LOCAL CURRENCY—AVG. VOL.
Securities Gains/Losses	Loans
Fees, Commissions & Other. Rev.	Sources—Non-Interest Bearing
Affiliate Earnings	Sources—Interest Bearing
Gross Write-Offs	FOREIGN CURRENCY—AVG. VOL.
Gross Recoveries	Loans
Loan Provision Excess	Sources—Non-Interest Bearing
Direct Staff Expenses	Sources—Interest Bearing
Direct Charges	END OF PERIOD (EOP)
Other Direct Expenses	Past Due Obligations
Allocated Processing Costs	Interest Earned Not Collected
Minority Interest	Loans
Other Allocated Costs	Assets
Matrix Earnings	
EBIT	
Foreign Taxes	
U.S. Taxes	

EXHIBIT 4 Indonesia Gross Domestic Product (billions of rupiahs)

Year	*Gross Domestic Product*	*Gross Domestic Product (1980 Prices)*
1968	2,097	18,493
1969	2,718	20,188
1970	3,340	21,499
1971	3,672	22,561
1972	4,564	24,686
1973	6,753	27,479
1974	10,708	29,576
1975	12,643	31,049
1976	15,467	33,187
1977	19,011	36,094
1978	22,746	38,925
1979	32,025	41,359
1980	45,446	45,446
1981	54,027	49,048
1982	59,633	50,150
1983	72,111	52,674

Source: International Financial Statistics Yearbook, 1984

EXHIBIT 5 Organization Chart—Citibank Indonesia

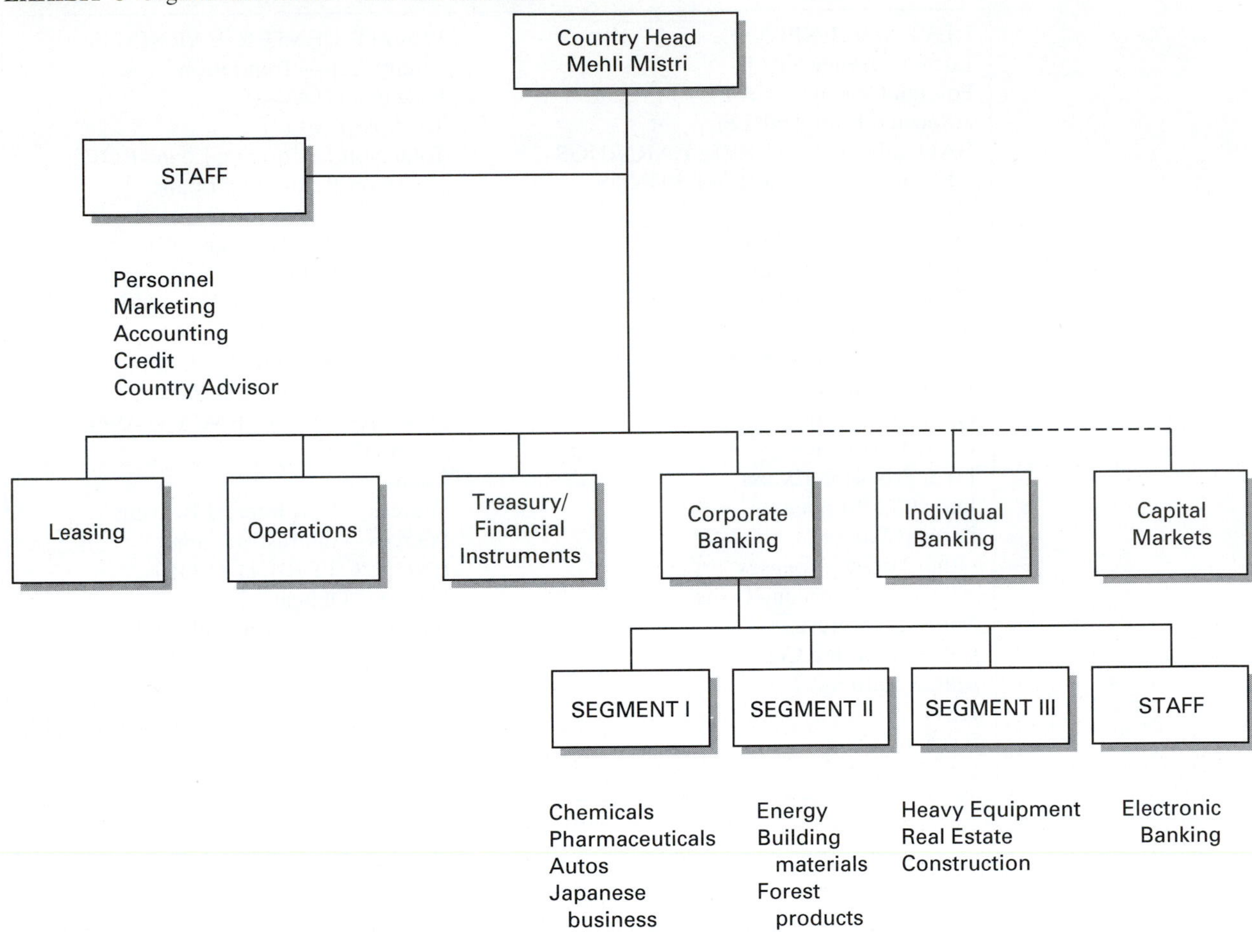

HCC Industries

Until 1987, HCC Industries, a manufacturer of hermetically sealed electronic connection devices and microelectronic packages, operated with a philosophy of having *stretch* performance targets for its operating managers. This philosophy was based on the belief that aggressive targets would motivate the managers to perform at their highest possible levels. In planning for fiscal year 1988, however, this philosophy was changed. Andy Goldfarb, HCC's CEO explained:

> [A large consulting firm] designed our old budgeting philosophy and the incentive compensation plan associated with it, but I'm not sure they understand companies smaller than the *Fortune 500.* They gave us "the great incentive plan of 1982," but it hasn't worked very well.
>
> The problem is that if you're forecasting for stretch targets, you must be thinking optimistically. This concept might work well at some companies of a certain size that understand their markets well enough and are in a position to influence it. But we haven't been in that position. We have just been taking orders, not doing marketing. In the meantime, the corporation has been missing its plans. For four years now we have had some divisions do well and some do poorly, but the corporation never achieved its targets. As a public company, we need that to happen. Also, people at corporate haven't earned any bonuses.
>
> Now we've changed our philosophy. We want to judge people first on whether they are hitting a "minimum performance standard." Only then can they start earning extra rewards. We've asked our managers to submit budgets with targets that are realistic and achievable, and to make sure the managers have gotten the message about the change, we made it clear to them that missing budget now could cost them their jobs.
>
> Most of our general managers didn't like the change when we announced it. They worried that bonuses aren't automatic and that the amounts they could earn weren't large enough. They might be right, and we may make some changes. And as I look at the actual results for the first quarter of FY 1988, I'm concerned that we haven't yet implemented the new concept quite as we intended. Some of our divisions have missed their minimum performance standards by large margins.

THE COMPANY

HCC was a small publicly held corporation, headquartered in Encino, California, that designed, manufactured and marketed hermetically sealed electronic connection devices and microelectronic packages. Revenues totalled $36 million in fiscal year 1987 (ended March 28, 1987). (A five-year summary of financial data is presented in Exhibit 1.)

HCC was an industry leader in electronic connectors requiring glass-to-metal and ceramic-to-metal seals, and particularly those requiring unusual or close tolerance machining and the sealing of exotic metals. Many of the company's products were used for aerospace and military applications requiring high reliability or operation in adverse conditions (such as high temperatures or pressures).

The company was organized into four primary operating divisions, each run by a general manager (see Exhibit 2). The general managers were each responsible for all the division's busi-

Research Assistant Lourdes Ferreira and Professor Kenneth A. Merchant prepared this case as the basis for class discussion rather than to illustrate either effective or ineffective handling of an administrative situation.

ness functions except that the division controllers reported on a solid line to Chris Bateman, HCC's chief financial officer. Andy Goldfarb explained:

> The division controllers are paid to be controllers. We don't want them to be motivated to *cook the books.* That is danger because we base bonuses on division results and because they work at quite a distance from headquarters and naturally develop an emotional attachment to the people with whom they work. The solid-line reporting to corporate helps remind them that their primary job is to protect the corporation's assets.

Three of the divisions—Hermetic Seal, Glasseal, and Sealtron—produced connectors of various types. Hermetite produced custom-designed, microelectronic packages. Exhibit 3 shows some typical products. Exhibit 4 provides some summary information about each division.

The three connector divisions were similar in that they were profitable but growing slowly. Their industry was highly fragmented. The number of potential customers was huge because many products used electrical connectors. Many small competitors served some portions of the market. The connector divisions did not have a solid base of knowledge about their competitors' strengths and weaknesses, their market shares, and forthcoming business possibilities because of the dearth of readily available marketing information and limited size of their marketing staffs. Thus it was difficult for them to make accurate sales forecasts.

The primary difference among the connector divisions was in the degree of standardization of their product lines. Sealtron was at one extreme, as it produced standardized connectors in relatively large volumes. Hermetic Seal, on the other hand, operated primarily as a job shop which designed and produced small batches of custom connectors, predominantly for military customers. Glasseal's operations were between the two extremes.

Hermetite, which produced microelectronic packages, was different from the connector divisions in several important ways. First, its market and competitors were relatively well defined. Customer contacts were typically made at trade shows, and most customers and competitors were well known. There were five main competitors in the industry, and Hermetite's market share was third or fourth in rank. Second, Hermetite's potential for growth was great. In contrast with the connector market, which was stable, the packaging market was growing at 20 to 30 percent per year. Third, it faced tremendous price competition. A new competitor had entered the market in 1985 and had lowered prices to buy market share. The existing competitors responded by lowering their prices to attempt to fill their production capacity. Fourth, Hermetite faced significant production technology and control problems. The production processes were complex, and the division had had instability in its engineering and production organizations. This had resulted in half of its $3 million backlog being delinquent, even though on-time delivery was an important competitive factor. Because of the price competition and the production problems, Hermetite had been operating at a loss since before it was acquired in August 1985.

The divisions were all largely self-contained and independent of each other. They served different customers and had different part number systems, product standards, and accounting and information systems. Corporate management had never tried to force, or even encourage, synergy between the divisions. As Chris Bateman, HCC's CFO, explained it:

> We want to let the managers be managers. They will do the best for you that way. Decentralization is a sound business concept.

Corporate staff had always monitored nonoperating decisions closely (for example, corporate authorization was necessary for any capital acquisition in excess of $500). But they had been providing few direct services to the divisions, however. This was starting to change. In 1987, a corporate marketing function was created to assist the divisions with market research, advertising and promotions. And a corporate engineering service function was started to develop new product designs that might be used by any or all of the connector divisions. Chris Bateman observed that the division managers were generally not receptive to receiving this support: "Some of them say that corporate is now dictating when they should brush their teeth."

STANDARDS FOR EVALUATING THE DIVISIONS' PEFORMANCES

The divisions' performances were evaluated in terms of seven performance areas: (1) profit before tax, (2) bookings, (3) shipments, (4) returns (as percent of total dollars shipped), (5) rework aging (number of jobs and percent less than 30 days), (6) efficiency (net sales/number of employees), and (7) delinquencies (dollar volume and percent of delinquent orders outstanding). Profit was generally the most important evaluation criterion, but good performance in all of these performance areas was considered necessary for achievement of the profit targets.

Division and corporate management negotiated performance standards in each of these areas during HCC's formal planning process—an annual budgeting cycle. This process began in December (or early January) and concluded in mid-March, just before the start of the new fiscal year.

The process started with the division managers' preparation of sales forecasts. To prepare these numbers, they typically contacted their largest customers directly. Then they worked with their operating managers to prepare budgets for expenses, capital expenditures and cash flow. They summarized the numbers into thirteen-week quarters that were broken into *monthly* periods of four, four and five weeks.

In February, corporate officers visited the divisions and conducted thorough reviews of these preliminary targets. They looked at the detailed numbers, such as sales by customer and by product, and challenged the general managers' assumptions and numbers by account. Chris Bateman explained why they conducted such a thorough review:

> There are a couple of reasons. First, most of our managers are not very good at budgeting. They are engineers and generally do not have a lot of business training. Second, they tend not to play it straight with us. Some will submit conservative targets. Others will submit numbers they have little chance to make.

After this review, the revised targets were 95 percent ready. Typically the divisions just needed to work out a few details before their budgets were presented to the board of directors. The board formally approved the budget in March.

After the budget was approved, it became a fixed evaluation standard for purposes of awarding incentive compensation. The division managers were asked to send updated forecasts to corporate monthly, but these forecasts were used for planning purposes only.

HCC managers did some planning for periods greater than one year, but these processes were handled almost exclusively at corporate. Al Berger explained:

> The general managers are not in a position to do what needs to be done two years down the road. They compete day-to-day. The corporation needs to do some long-term things, such as improving our marketing and consolidating some of our efforts. We involve the general managers in some of those discussions only occasionally because they are not leading those efforts.

MONITORING OF PERFORMANCE

Corporate managers, particularly Al Berger, who was hired as COO in March 1987, monitored division performances closely. He was in frequent contact with the division managers and reviewed performance reports in detail when they were produced. Al was even monitoring quality reports from Hermetite on a daily basis because of the significance of that division's known production problems.

The division managers were acutely aware of the emphasis placed on quarterly results. Each quarter they had to write a commentary explaining their division's results as input to a formal budget review. Considerably less explanation was necessary if they exceeded their performance targets. For example, Mike Pelta, manager of Hermetic Seal noted that:

> If I miss a monthly target, I can always explain that something happened at the last minute, and they accept that explanation. If I miss a quarterly target, that's a big thing.

And Lou Palamara, manager of Sealtron, explained that:

> If I miss a quarterly budget, Al Berger will visit me immediately asking what I am doing about the problem.

PERFORMANCE TARGETS AND INCENTIVES UNDER THE *STRETCH* BUDGETING CONCEPT

Until 1987, HCC's philosophy was to have *stretch* performance targets based on the belief that aggressive targets would push managers to strive to do their best. These targets were "not unreachable, just tough." The intended probability of achievement was 75 to 80 percent.

The budget targets directly affected bonuses paid to those included in the bonus plan. Each person included in the plan was assigned a bonus potential which, for most division managers, was 30 percent of base salary. The bonuses paid were based half on profit before taxes (PBT) and half on a subjective rating of performance (which was also influenced by profit performance).The objective portion of the award was paid according to the following schedule:

ACTUAL DIVISION PBT (% BUDGET)	BONUS PAID (% BONUS POTENTIAL)
<60%	0
60	80
100	100
140	150

The subjective portion of the evaluation was based primarily on top management's judgment of the degree of accomplishment of the targets in all seven performance areas. For example, if a division manager met the standards for five out of the seven performance criteria mentioned earlier, top management would have to judge that importance of the targets that were not met. If the two targets that were not met were judged to be critical, the manager might earn no subjective bonus.

Bonuses were paid based on annual performance, but payments were made quarterly. The interim (quarterly) payments were made only at 80 percent of the earned rate to protect the company from paying bonuses that might not eventually be earned.

DISSATISFACTION WITH THE STRETCH BUDGETING CONCEPT

Gradually corporate managers became dissatisfied with the stretch budgeting concept. Most important, they felt it was causing the corporation not to achieve its plans. Each year some divisions achieved their targets and some did not, but the corporation was consistently missing its targets. Chris Bateman explained:

> Since everybody knew that the *stretch* targets were too optimistic, it became "OK to miss budget." For example, from the time when I joined HCC in September 1986 until March 1987 I had to prepare eight budget reviews because the corporation was not achieving its plans. The problem was that at 60 percent of budget, the managers were still in bonus territory, so they didn't have to worry much about meeting budget. Their budgets were like a wish. They were too easily blown off.

There was also dissatisfaction with the bonus plan associated with the stretch budgets. The division managers, in particular, considered it to be too subjective and complex to communicate to their middle managers. Communication of the details of the plan was also hampered at two divisions because the division managers did not want to disclose division-level financial information to their personnel because they feared that the information might be leaked to competitors. As a consequence, most of the division personnel included in the plan never knew their bonus potential nor the bases on which the bonus awards were made.

Most managers were also dissatisfied with the plan because the awards were typically not made until three to four months after the end of the quarter. The delay was caused by the several levels of approvals that were necessary before the payments could be made.

THE CHANGE TO MINIMUM PERFORMANCE STANDARDS

In October 1986, Andy Goldfarb met with his division managers and corporate staff and announced that from then on the company would operate with a *minimum performance standard* (MPS) budgeting philosophy. MPS budgets were to be set so that the felt probability of achievement was 100 percent. In addition to the MPS, the managers were asked to set *targets* that reflected a performance level considered to be beyond normal capability. Al Berger explained that these targets might involve a 25 to 30 percent increase in something, rather than 5 to 10 percent. They represent a level that might be said to have only a 50 percent probability of achievement.

The change in level of difficulty of standards was coincident with a change in the incentive compensation plan. Under the new plan, a division bonus pool was created based on 20 percent of the amount by which actual division PBT exceeded the MPS, plus 25 percent of the amount by which it exceeded the target.

The most important performance measure for bonus purposes was still PBT, but bonuses could be affected by results in the other six performance areas. Al Berger explained:

> If they make all their targets, they will be paid the full bonus pool. If they miss only a couple of targets, they may earn 100% or close to 100 percent of the pool. If they make only half their targets, they may earn only 60 percent of the pool. I left the details of the plan vague because the importance of particular targets varies over time—for example, this year delinquencies and quality are even more important than profit—and some targets are more important in some divisions than in others. I did not want to quantify the relationships.

The division managers were given the discretion to decide (before the year started) which of their subordinates would share in the bonus pool and how the pool would be allocated among themselves and the others included. Corporate guidelines suggested that they reserve between 30 percent and 40 percent of the pool for themselves. At targeted performance levels, the division managers were expected to earn bonuses of approximately 20 to 25 percent of base salary.

Bonuses were still paid quarterly at a level of 90 percent of that earned. The remaining 10 percent was accrued to be paid at the end of the year contingent on annual performance.

THE 1988 BUDGET NEGOTIATION PROCESSES AND REACTIONS TO THE CHANGE IN BUDGETING PHILOSOPHY IN THE FOUR DIVISIONS

Hermetic Seal

Mike Pelta, general manager of Hermetic Seal, was a cofounder (with Jack Goldfarb, the current chairman) of HCC. Mike was a major HCC stockholder, owning 15 percent of the corporation's stock. He had been managing Hermetic Seal since January 1987, after having served a stint as general manager of Hermetite. Mike was known as an effective, hard-working manager, but one who had a tendency to be autocratic and ineffective at developing his subordinates. This limitation was becoming a more serious problem because Mike was nearing retirement age.

Mike's philosophy in setting performance targets was to be conservative:

> Knock on wood, in my 33 years as a manager, I've never missed a budget. I'm not really sandbagging; I'm an upbeat person. When I get a target to meet, I go for it. I do have to be careful with the optimism of my subordinates, however. I often have to lower their estimates when putting together my budgets.

Mike's reasoning for wanting to achieve budget targets consistently:

> If you keep missing budget, how do you feel? You feel like a failure. If you exceed a budget, you feel proud. You're going to project higher the next year. You can't keep beating down on people. You've got to build them up. Stretch budgets don't make me work harder. They can't make me do something I can't do. If the bookings are not there, the profit targets are impossible.

Consistent with his philosophy, Mike submitted a conservative budget for fiscal year 1988. Al Berger explained from his point of view:

> Mike was looking for a large bonus. He had good reasons for pessimism, bookings were terrible and the bookings rate had declined in the last three months of the year; they were shipping 25 percent more than they were booking; delinquencies were numerous, as production was inefficient. But he didn't explain his numbers in terms of these problems. He just said he was new in the job and was in the process of rebuilding. I listened to what he had to say and then we went through the customer list a number of times. We finally agreed on sales and bookings numbers, and then quality, delinquencies and profit targets.

After the revisions were approved, Mike felt between 95 percent and 98 percent confident that he would achieve his sales target. And even if he missed the sales target, he expected to meet the profit goal. He explained:

> It would simply be a matter of digging into my backlog and cutting costs here and there. I know this business inside out, so I know what I have to do to make budget. I wouldn't do anything that could hurt the company in the long run, though.

He noticed the change in budgeting philosophy. He recalled that in the past he used to have only an 85 to 90 percent chance of making the *stretch* profit targets.

Glasseal

Carl Kalish was the manager of Glasseal. Carl had been vice president, marketing for Glasseal at the time it was acquired by HCC. He was appointed general manager of Glasseal soon after the acquisition.

Carl considered it very important to prepare realistic forecasts:

> It's easy to sit in a staff position and be optimistic, but as a general manager, I have to be right. In the past four years I have been tremendously accurate in my market projections. You can't anticipate everything, though. For instance, in fiscal year 1987, we exceeded our profit budget by 12 percent primarily because of unusual gains in sales volume. A major competitor was going through some crises, and we were able to pick up part of their share. We exceeded budget during each of the first three quarters, but in the last quarter our customers started deferring shipments to use up their inventory, and our sales decreased sharply. We expected our volume to go back to normal in 1988.

Carl's first budget projected $7.4 million in bookings and $7.2 million in shipments. Corporate managers told him to increase both targets by $200,000, based on their interpretation of market trends. They also increased his PBT target by almost 2 percent, up to $1.1 million.

Carl's reaction to these changes:

> Personally, I think that my initial forecast was right, but I'm committed to the new budget. It's a number that I'm trying to live with . . .
>
> [Under the old system] I used to feel 90 percent sure that I'd make budget in a given year. Now I'm still only 90 percent sure, but the difference is that my job depends on it . . .
>
> The old plan allowed for bonus payments if you missed budget, so we had something to shoot for even if we knew we would come out short, and the rewards were also greater than they are now. Furthermore, corporate was not so dictatorial when setting the targets. But I'm trying to stay open-minded and see how it goes. I consider this first year as an experiment.

Sealtron

Lou Palamara, Sealtron's general manager, was recruited from outside HCC in January 1986. His background was as a ceramic engineer and engineering manager.

Lou's initial 1988 budget submission was for sales of $6.4 million and PBT of $900,000. This budget was rejected. Lou explained:

> Andy Goldfarb told me, "Your charter is to make $1 million in PBT next year. Show me a plan to make that much profit."

Lou then prepared a budget that increased the projected sales and reduced costs of advertising, promotions and other discretionary spending. He discussed this new budget with Chris Bateman (CFO). Neither Lou nor Chris were confident that the $1 million target would be achieved, so Chris agreed to propose the $900,000 PBT target again to Andy. Andy would not budge. He sent Lou a letter stating that "Sealtron's target for 1988 must be $1 million."

Lou felt that while he had perhaps a 95 percent chance to achieve the $900,000 profit budget, his chance to achieve the $1 million MPS budget was only 60 to 65 percent. His PBT target was $1.1 million, a level that he considered impossible to achieve. Lou was somewhat discouraged:

> Mine is a strange plan. If I make budget, which is an 18 percent increase from our last

year actuals, I get no bonus. I really feel that if you put together a plan and don't hide anything and plan capital investments and expenditures for the future, and you feel comfortable with it, then that's the best plan. The plan must be realistic. My plan is a threat. I may even have to lay off some people that we will likely need later. But if I don't do it and I miss my minimum performance standards, I may get fired.

Lou was concerned because nobody at Sealtron expected a bonus in 1988. Missing budget also prevented salary increases. In fiscal year 1987, for example, nobody at Sealtron got a salary increase, because the division did not make budget. This situation made him worry about employee retention:

If this salary freeze persists for two more years, I may lose some of my key employees. We missed our profit target last year mainly because I had to hire a new industrial engineer and a production control manager to get our manufacturing operations in shape. Now I know of a local company that wants to hire the industrial engineer, and he is just starting to put our systems in order. I think we should keep people happy if we want them to stay. They should be compensated for their effort.

Corporate managers' perspectives about the situation at Sealtron were somewhat different. Al Berger thought that the $1 million PBT budget was necessary to change the aspiration levels of Sealtron personnel. He explained that Sealtron's efficiency, measured in terms of sales per employee, was 50 percent below that of the other connector divisions even though its production processes were simpler. And Al was particularly annoyed that even though Sealtron had missed its budget by 30 percent in 1987, the number of employees in the division had actually grown. Al felt that with good management, Sealtron would be certain to achieve its $1 million PBT budget, but this would probably require cutting staff and shipping more product.

Chris Bateman rated the probability of Sealtron achieving the $1 million target at only 90 percent:

Because of the people. The people in that division have historically not been thinking much about costs. Their perspective has always been that they need sales to make money. We're trying to get the message to them that we can't afford any fat in the organization, and I'm not sure how fast they will learn to adjust.

Lou felt that personnel at Sealtron truly were concerned about costs:

I recognize that some good comes out of budget pressures. Everybody becomes conscious of overhead costs, and the pressures force expense cuts and productivity improvements faster. But I still feel that hiring the people I did was in the best long-term interest of the company.

HERMITITE

Alan Wong, the general manager at Hermetite, was an MBA/CPA/lawyer who worked for a major public accounting firm before joining HCC as CFO. He accepted the job as general manager of Hermetite in August 1986, only four months before he had to submit his initial budget for 1988.

Alan's first budget showed projections of $13 million in sales, and PBT of $130,000. These figures compared with 1987 actual sales of $7 million and a loss of $2.8 million. Although he knew these were aggressive targets, Alan felt that it was important for him to be optimistic:

You have to be an optimist in a turnaround situation. If you don't set high standards, you'll never achieve high performance.

Alan thought that the pressure to make budget every year would encourage him and his personnel to become more efficient:

We may have to postpone maintenance or purchases of supplies in a tough quarter. If the profit is not there, you shouldn't spend the money. It is my job to provide the profits this quarter. And it is up to corporate to think long term.

Alan's initial budget submission was also based on a belief that corporate managers would not accept a budget that projected a loss. It had

EXHIBIT 3 Typical Products

Hermetically Sealed Connectors

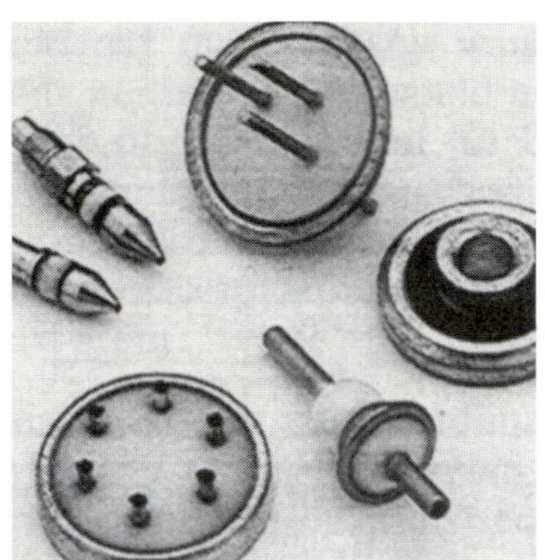

Hermetically sealed headers and terminals and ceramic-to-metal seals used in high temperature and pressure requirements such as jet fuel nozzles.

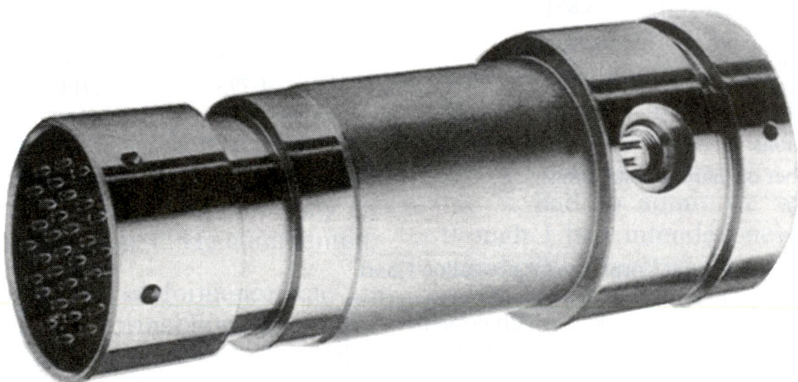

Connector used in deep-hole oil exploration.

Custom-designed Microelectronic Packages

Kovar fiberoptics package with precisely dimensioned tube designed for telecommunications.

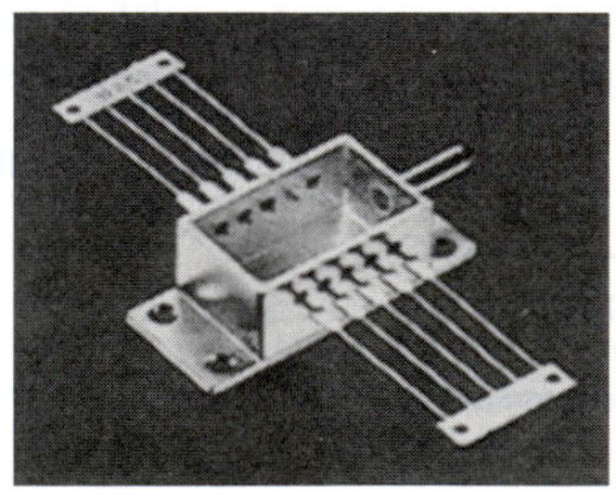

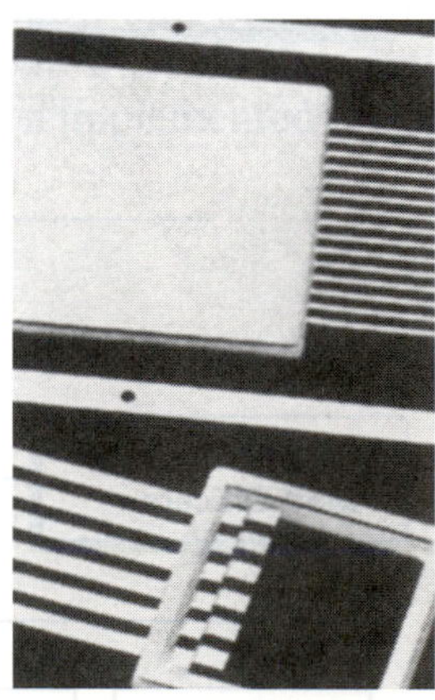

Microelectronic packages for hermetically sealed hybrid integrated semi-conductor applications such as in MX missiles.

EXHIBIT 4 Summary Information about Divisions

Division	*Products*	*1987 Revenues ($ millions)*	*Location*	*Other*
Hermetic Seal	Connectors	12	Rosemead, California	The original HCC business
Glasseal	Connectors	6	Lakewood, New Jersey	Acquired in June 1983
Sealtron	Connectors	6	Cincinnati, Ohio	Was wholly owned subsidiary of Glasseal when acquired
Hermetite	Microelectronic packages	10	Avon, Massachusetts	Acquired in August 1985

EXHIBIT 5 Felt Probability of Budget Achievement at Time Target was Set (March 1987)

	Al	*Estimate from:*	
Division	*Al Berger (COO)*	*Chris Bateman (CFO)*	*General Manager*
Hermetic Seal	100%	100%	95%–98%
Glasseal	100	100	90
Sealtron	100	90	60–65
Hermetite	100	70	80

EXHIBIT 6 First Quarter Results—1988

	Hermetic Seal			Glasseal			Sealtron			Hermetite		
Criteria	MPS	Target	Actual	MPS	Target	Actual	MPS	Target	Actual	MPS	Target	Actual
Sales												
Bookings	2,600	2,800	2,844	2,020	NA	1,645	1,500	1,600	1,513	1,811	2,000	1,234
Shipments	2,600	2,900	2,843	1,815	NA	1,742	1,400	1,450	1,442	2,351	2,200	2,323
Quality												
Returns (% of shipment)	10%	7%	14.4%	3%	NA	3.5%	3%	2%	1.3%	10%	5%	6.3%
Rework: number of jobs/ percent less than 30 days	60/ 85	40/ 92	62/ 30	10/ 80	NA	10/ 80	6/ 70	4/ 75	9/ 67	25/ 50	12/ 80	10/ 82
Productivity												
Profit (before tax)	650	800	843	283	300	192	167	175	195	(410)	(300)	(188)
Efficiency (sales/employee)	60	62	60	57	59	67	38	40	38.7	52	59	53
Delinquency ($.%)	220K 6%	0	460K 10.4%	80K	0	48K	70K	0	151K	250K	150K	368K

Key: ◯ Below MPS ▭ Exceed target

Provigo Inc.

In 1986, Pierre Lortie, newly elected chairman, CEO, and president of Provigo Inc., made public a set of corporate goals, a first for the company (see Exhibit 1). In order to produce the superior performance the new objectives called for, Mr. Lortie believed that the company's informal annual bonus plan had to be modified to provide senior managers with more incentives. Consequently, the company introduced two new incentive plans: an annual bonus plan and a performance stock plan with a three-year performance cycle. These new plans, designed with the help of a major compensation consulting firm, promised higher potential awards that were tied more closely to performance. Mr. Lortie explained:

> The compensation policy for senior executives has been set such that total rewards, including cash and equity incentives, will reach top quartile for comparable companies if the goals are met. The strategy calls for salary levels set at the market average, to be supplemented by variable compensation in the form of an *annual* bonus, based on the attainment of budget and other agreed-upon objectives, and *long-term* equity incentives based on attainment of the Strategic Plan.

While most Provigo managers agreed with the intent of the new incentive plans, some were not happy with the ways in which the plans were administered. Indeed, Provigo's experience with the plans in the first couple of years showed that plan administration presented some significant challenges. Henri Roy, Provigo's executive vice president, explained:

> Incentive plans involve more than just establishing formulas. You have to agree on targets, which isn't easy, especially when these targets come from budgets or strategic plans. Then, at the end of the year, you have to decide whether or not to exercise discretion in attributing bonuses, and you'll be damned if you do and damned if you don't.

THE COMPANY

Provigo was a publicly held holding company headquartered in Montreal, Quebec. Primarily involved in the wholesale and retail distribution of consumer goods, Provigo had grown rapidly since its creation in 1969 (the result of a merger of three small Quebec companies) to become the tenth largest company in Canada. Consolidated sales in fiscal year 1987 were $5.4 billion.[1] (See Exhibit 2 for a five-year summary of financial data.)

Provigo consisted of nine operating companies that were organized into five operating groups. (Exhibit 3 shows an organization chart. Exhibit 4 presents summary financial data for each group.) The largest group, the Food Group, included four operating companies with combined sales in 1987 of $3.7 billion. These sales ranked Provigo as the second-largest food distributor in Canada.

Annually, each operating company presented a budget and a three-year strategic plan to the Management Committee, which included the top five managers of Provigo Inc. Proposals for projects requiring large amounts of resources also had to be submitted to the committee. Henri Roy explained:

> We're a growth company. If you want your capital to bring returns, you've got to show growth numbers and commit yourself to them. Spending capital that's in the operat-

[1]All the financial data appearing in this case are in Canadian dollars. At the time the case was written, one Canadian dollar was worth about US$ 0.80.

Professor Kenneth A. Merchant of the University of Southern California prepared this case as the basis for class discussion rather than to illustrate either effective or ineffective handling of an administrative situation.

ing company's budget is easy selling. If it's outside of their budget, that's tougher to get.

The numbers in these budgets and strategic plans were used to calibrate the awards made from Provigo's annual and long-term incentive compensation plans.

ANNUAL BONUS PLAN

Provigo's annual bonus plan offered managers a cash bonus based on a comparison between actual and budgeted performance of the relevant administrative unit. The annual bonus award was calculated according to the following formula:

$$\text{Bonus} = \text{TB} \times \text{PF}$$

where:

TB was the manager's *target bonus.* The target bonus ranged from 10 percent of base salary for a first-level manager in an operating company up to 25 percent of salary for an operating company president.

PF was the *payout factor.* The payout factor varied between 0 and 2 and was a function of R. R was defined as actual performance income (defined as operating profit before interest and any allocation of corporate overhead, but after taxes), less a 6 percent penalty for net working capital in excess of budget, divided by the budgeted performance income. The bonus payout function is shown in Table A.

The relevant administrative unit for Provigo Inc. *corporate* managers was the entire corporation.[2] For *operating company* managers, the relevant unit generally varied with their position, as follows:

TABLE A

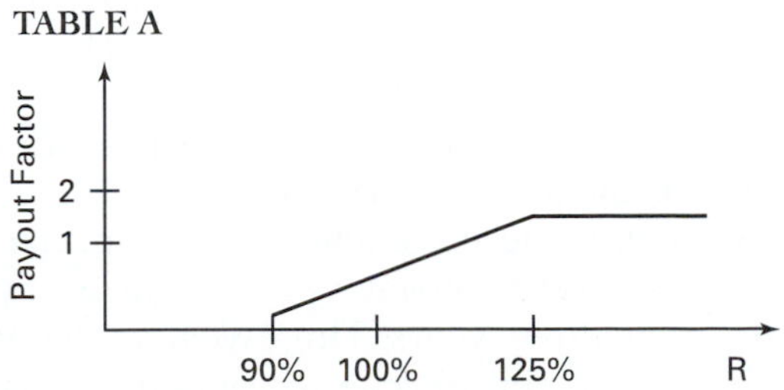

Operating company president:	100% operating company
Profit center (division) managers within an operating company and their direct report:	50% operating company 50% own division
Lower level managers:	100% own division

In a few operating companies without homogeneous administrative subunits, the bonus for all managers was a function of the operating company's performance.

Henri Roy explained the rationale for several of the features of the plan:

> For most operating companies, the importance of global performance increases as one moves up the hierarchy. This reflects the necessity for senior managers to think about the impact of their unit on the whole company. It also reinforces the image of the management group as a team. . . .
>
> Performance income is a better measure of operations company managers' performance than is net earnings because issues of capital structure and tax planning are handled at corporate and are thus out of the operating managers' control. . . .
>
> Capital expenditures must be submitted to corporate and are thus easy to monitor. Also, we are not imposing any charge on long-term assets within the annual bonus plan so as not to discourage investments that take more than a year to cover their cost of financing. Working capital, however, is really under the responsibility of operating company managers. The 6 percent penalty on net working capital in excess of budget is designed to prevent managers from attempting to increase profit by overinvesting in working capital.

PROVIGO PERFORMANCE STOCK PLAN

The Provigo Performance Stock Plan (PPSP) provided senior operating company executives awards based on their company's performance as compared to plan, typically over three-year performance cycles. The plan was designed as a performance stock plan for tax reasons, even though such plans were inevitably complex. The

[2]Some Provigo Inc. corporate executives also received options to purchase company stock. But almost all of the operating companies were wholly owned subsidiaries of Provigo Inc., so they had no publicly-traded shares.

managers included in the plan were allowed to purchase a specific number of performance shares at the beginning of the cycle at a price set at the level required by Canadian tax authorities to qualify the award for capital gains treatment. The number of shares offered to each manager was a function of the manager's salary and target bonus. At the end of the cycle, the performance shares were converted to Provigo common stock at the then-prevailing market rate. Managers could then hold the stock, or sell it immediately to capture the gain, which was taxed at a lower rate than ordinary income.[3] A new cycle started each year, resulting in a potential yearly conversion.

The shares appreciated in value over the cycle depending on the operating company's performance as indicated by a measure called Contribution to Shareholders' Wealth (CSW), calculated as:

$$CSW = \frac{\text{Actual Value Added}}{\text{Planned Value Added}}$$

Value was said to be added when a company's average *residual income* (performance income less a capital charge for net assets employed) over a cycle exceeded that of the base year, the year immediately preceding the beginning of the cycle. Henri Roy explained why a *value-added* concept was used, instead of a measure like return on assets;

> ROA does not encourage growth of earnings. Once the assets are in place, one can repeat an ROA ratio from year to year without increasing earnings. Further, one can even *increase* this ROA by disinvesting, which is exactly the opposite of what we expect managers to do. We want managers to keep investing in projects that earn at least the 12 percent return that represents our long-term cost of capital.

Exhibit 5 shows an example of a PPSP award calculation.

Like for the annual bonus plan, the Target Bonus for the PPSP varied between 10% and 25% of salary depending on the individual's position and responsibility, as follows:

OPERATING COMPANY ROLE	TARGET BONUS CSW = 100% (% OF SALARY)	MAXIMUM BONUS CSW = 150% (% OF SALARY)
President	25%	50%
Vice president	10%–20%	20%–40%

The PPSP officially started with fiscal year 1988 (beginning February 1, 1987). Given a three-year strategic planning cycle, no series would have become due before February 1990. To give managers an immediate and ongoing incentive, three series or shares were offered the first year. The 87-1 series was to be based on fiscal 1988 budget, and series 87-2 and 87-3 were to be based on the 1988–1990 strategic plan:

SERIES	YEAR OFFERED	CONVERSION DATE
87-1	Immediate (January 31, 1987)	January 31, 1988
87-2	Immediate (January 31, 1987)	January 31, 1989
87-3	Immediate (January 31, 1987)	January 31, 1990
88	January 31, 1988	January 31, 1991
89	January 31, 1989	January 31, 1992
etc.		

Following discussions among Provigo managers, two other PPSP start-up decisions were made. First, some operating companies' objectives were revised downward. The 1988–1990 strategic plan had been submitted before the PPSP was introduced. The plans of a few operating companies featured very aggressive growth forecasts, well in excess of Provigo's objectives for operating companies (18 percent growth in performance income and 15 percent return on capital). In order to give managers of these companies a fair chance to reach their targets, these targets were reset to equal Provigo's objectives. (This was hereafter referred to as the *transition rule.*)

Second, some companies facing special circumstances were given performance cycles shorter than three years. Three-year cycles were perceived to be appropriate for operating companies with sound strategies facing reasonably stable environmental circumstances. But, for example, Medis, a pharmaceutical distributor, was facing a turnaround situation, so its managers' annual bonus and PPSP were both based on a one-year measurement period.

---

[3]The first cumulative $100,000 of capital gains was tax-free. When that once-in-a-lifetime exemption was used up, further amounts were taxed at half the normal rate. This percentage was raised to two-thirds the normal rate in 1988 and to 75 percent in 1989.

DISCRETION IN AWARDING BONUSES

Corporate managers were empowered to use discretion in assigning both annual and long-term incentive awards. They were reluctant to use that discretion, however. Henri Roy explained the reasons for this reluctance:

> Provigo is a decentralized corporation, and that puts the performance onus on operating company presidents. Shareholders entrust us with their money, and they expect returns. For our operating companies, we have a minimum acceptable financial performance—the cost of money—and a longer-term target of 15 percent return on our investment. But these plans are not based on *absolute* numbers, but rather on *relative* performance by taking into account budgeted results. So if a budget reflects forthcoming investments and returns, a manager will not be penalized for inheriting a low-performing unit, but rather will be rewarded for improving its performance. . . .
>
> These plans are designed to pay out the target bonus. If a company doesn't reach it, there must be something wrong with either the people, the strategy, or the execution of the strategy. . . .
>
> We all have to manage within evolving industry dynamics and need to react quickly. You have to understand that the distribution business is based on execution, and things are supposed to fall into place quickly. The operating company managers have all the autonomy required to run their businesses. Our compensation policy is set up accordingly, with a large upside potential for superior results. We are sympathetic to special situations, and we have the flexibility to adapt our programs. But we feel very strongly that operating company management is responsible for delivering the results to which they committed in their budget. . . .
>
> We follow the operating companies' performances very closely throughout the year. We will help them as much as possible to achieve their targets, through monthly and quarterly discussions of results and reviews of possible actions. The targets, however, come from their plans. If subsequent information shows that the budget was set too high, it is mostly their problem. We will have some empathy for them, but they are responsible for producing their planned results.

OPERATING COMPANY MANAGERS' REACTIONS TO THE PLANS

Provigo's operating company managers had mixed reactions to the new incentive plans. These reactions will be illustrated in two operating companies, one that was performing well (Loeb Inc.) and another that was struggling (Medis Inc.):

A. Loeb Inc.

Established in Ontario and Western Quebec, Loeb was part of the Food Group. The leading food distributor in the Ottawa area, it operated 5 distribution centers and 22 self-service warehouses and served a large, diversified clientele that included more than one hundred affiliated supermarkets.

Loeb was a very solid and steady performer. Its profits had been increasing year after year through both increases in sales and improvements in productivity. After a few years of stability in terms of the number of stores served, Loeb was planning a significant expansion. Its latest strategic plan called for the addition of almost 75 new supermarket customers over the next three years.

William Kipp, president and COO of Loeb Inc., headed the company's management team, which was comprised of long-time employees. Mr. Kipp felt that Loeb managers had always operated with a mid-term and long-term view. While they had some mid-term targets before the introduction of the PPSP, the PPSP had helped them focus on these targets, and forced them to plan more specifically on how to achieve their targets. Kipp also had the following to say about the incentive plans:

> I am a 95 percent supporter of the PPSP. Its greatest quality is that it exists. My team and I really appreciate the company's willingness to share the long-term growth with its key executives. It is also rich, tax effective, and ongoing. On the other hand, it is complex; we were not involved in its elaboration; and it would be unachievable if not for the transition rule. . . .

Three years is a good horizon. I have difficulty thinking past three years. . . .

With the annual bonus plan, any given year is included in four incentive plans at the same time. But it would be too time consuming to try to game this aspect of the system. Besides, the long-term incentive plan is not important enough in our culture that we would do anything foolish. . . .

So far I have no feeling of increasing centralization following the introduction of a strategic planning process and of PPSP. But we will soon present our second strategic plan, and we will be monitoring corporate's attitude toward the change in estimates for the first two years of this new plan (the last two years of the previous plan). If energy has to be focused to explain why they changed from last year's plan, we will resist strongly. As a matter of fact, we won't be bringing any explanations except for *because that was last year.* If we are not careful, analysts could build a lifetime job for themselves. . . .

Mr. Kipp explained that while he was confident that Loeb would be able to report a 20 percent increase in earnings for next year, he would budget an increase of only 12 percent.

Why not budget 20 percent from the start? Because if I do so, I'm telling all my people that a 150 percent bonus requires 30 percent. And if we make 18 percent, we're losers! Performance is emotional; we want to be winners, and winners are people who make their targets. . . .

I discuss my targets with Pierre Lortie. He would give me a hard time if he thought my target was soft. But we are self-demanding, and I don't sandbag him. It is a matter of integrity. . . .

The fact that we make our target every year does not mean it is soft. We make it because we keep increasing the efficiency of our operations, and we outperform the competition.

Mr. Kipp believed that discretion should not be used in assigning bonuses because bonuses are for achievement, not effort:

You have to accept life. Some things in life are out of your control. Some will help; some will hurt the results. But if you don't make the plan, you don't get the bonus. It comes down to the question of "Do you want your God to be fair or generous?" Fair implies that the plan is the plan; generous implies that if something happens, you will compensate for it.

For the plan to be successful, you need to be objective or on the *fair* side so that people know that you and they must live by the contract. If you don't, subjectivity will permeate your entire system and it will eventually drive you to statements like, "But this time, I really mean it!" Energy is a scarce resource, and you want your managers to focus it on *achieving* the plan, not on influencing you as to what you should or should not compensate for. Plus, with subjectivity come problems of measurement.

As for myself, I don't want to owe a gift, and I don't want a feudal lord system. Plus receiving a discretionary bonus is not as nice as making it on your own. I can't convince my people that we made it if we didn't. That's not winning.

B. Medis Inc.

As the only national distributor of pharmaceutical products in Canada, Medis was responsible for about 55 percent of the drug wholesale business in Canada. Its customers were predominantly retail pharmacies. The company's return on capital employed (ROCE)[4] was about 16 percent in 1986.

The pharmaceutical distribution business was characterized by high fixed costs and low margins. A competitive advantage could be secured through investments in technology, information systems, efficient distribution centers, information systems, and capable people. But Medis had been operated largely as a cash cow for several years, and its infrastructure was weak.

Many of Medis's senior management team were replaced in 1986, largely by managers from outside the company. William Brown was appointed as president.

---

[4]Return on Capital Employed (ROCE) was defined as the ratio of after-tax income (excluding interest expense) to the net capital employed (total assets less noninterest-bearing liabilities).

Provigo management supported a turnaround strategy for Medis that called for increased investments in fixed assets and working capital. Everyone realized that during the turnaround period, it would be impossible for Medis to deliver anywhere near a 15 percent ROCE and concurrent high growth in operating income. But in a few years, the strategy was expected to yield a business with greatly enhanced operating income.

At the end of fiscal year 1988, however, Medis was well off its targets, with a performance income of only 30 percent of original budget and working capital levels significantly in excess of budget. Because of the poor results, Medis managers received no short-term or long-term bonus payments. The major event at the company was the integration of a major new client in the Ontario Division calling for a huge increase in sales ($200 million of sales in the first year), at a time when the company's infrastructure did not support even the prior level of business. Mr. Brown attributed the performance shortfall both to a *strive budgeting mentality*—a new, dynamic management team setting difficult goals for itself—and some managerial inexperience at planning in a highly dynamic environment.

Mr. Brown felt that while Provigo's incentive plans could be very lucrative they were not favorable to a company like Medis. He pointed out that in Medis's dynamic operating environment, it was very difficult to budget accurately even six months ahead. Furthermore, Medis required significant investments to sustain its growth. Mr. Brown elaborated:

> Our sustained growth requires significant investments, which penalizes us in the PPSP. First, Provigo expects a high ROI from us. Second, the plan affects us twice on assets: once through depreciation and once through the 12 percent capital charge, and both are calculated based on a high book value, as our assets are in a high state of renewal. Third, the three-year horizon discourages investments that take longer to harvest, and in the case of Medis, most investments today have a long payoff horizon. . . .
>
> Clearly, companies that start with a low ROI and enjoy steady, predictable growth have an easier time than Medis. I don't know what the solution is. We could think of measures other than ROI, a shorter budgeting horizon or a renegotiation of budgets during the year, but Provigo has difficulty with all these ideas. It is a closely-held public company,[5] and as our chairman (Henri Roy) often says, "At Provigo, you're elected every quarter." That doesn't encourage long-term thinking.

Medis's situation was not greatly improved in fiscal year 1989. Even though Medis's management team had endeavored to submit a budget they thought they had a 75 percent chance to achieve, the company's first quarter operating results were significantly below budget. In May 1988, Mr. Brown said that:

> Unforeseeable and uncontrollable circumstances have affected our markets to a point where it would take a miracle for us to make the budget. When the first signs of trouble appeared, I informed Provigo that it would be impossible for us to reach our budget of $6.2 million and that $5 million would likely be as much as we could deliver. They said that for bonus purposes, they would be sympathetic to lowering the budget. But it is now clear that we won't even come close to $5 million.
>
> Based on first quarter results and taking into account the postponement of some investment projects that we had planned to make, I would say there is only a 30 percent chance that performance income will reach $4.6 million. If the current strategic direction is maintained, we would need a target of about $3 million to have a 75 percent probability of achievement.
>
> My team and I have worked extremely hard over the past two years, and if the targets are not adjusted, this will mean no bonus for the management team for the second year in a row. With salaries at market average, a number of senior managers accepted a compensation reduction when they joined the company in 1986 in expectation of major upside through the incentive plans. If this problem is not resolved within the next

[5]The three largest shareholders hold more than 50 percent of the company's stock.

30 days, we will probably have some senior management resignations.

The prospect of another year without bonuses will also have serious effects on morale. Coming from a bad year and knowing, one quarter into the game, that we have no chance to achieve our targets is very difficult. As a motivating influence, the incentive plans will become null and void. Decreasing the target slightly will not be enough; it could actually be even more frustrating. Provigo *must* make sure the target is reachable this time. Failure to come to grips with this issue would almost ensure the breakdown of our human assets.

EXHIBIT 1 Corporate Goals

HUMAN RESOURCES

Our objective is to ensure that each employee attains his or her full potential, thus enabling Provigo Inc. to develop teams of individuals confident in their own abilities to generate and adapt to change; motivated by a commitment to remain at the forefront of the distribution industry by attaining high levels of quality in every aspect of their work, within one of the best-performing Canadian companies.

RETURN ON AVERAGE EQUITY
before extraordinary items

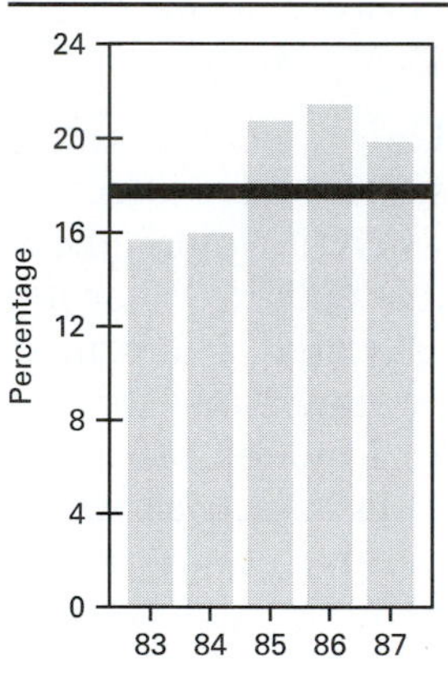

Rank among the best performers in the industry with an 18% return on average equity.

EARNINGS PER SHARE GROWTH
before extraordinary items

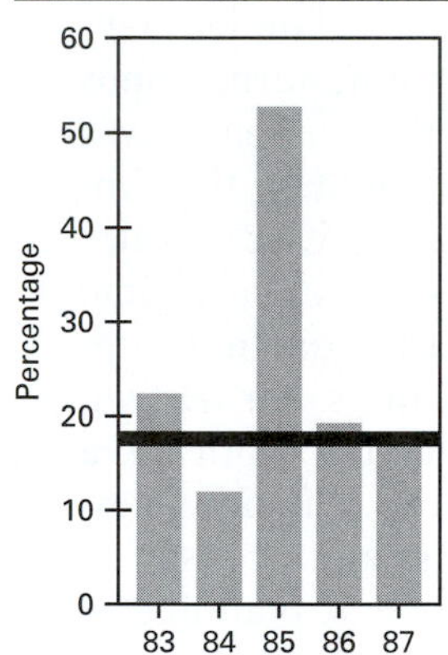

Achieve and maintain a superior growth rate of 18% per year.

TECHNOLOGY

To maximize the benefits stemming from the latest information technologies and the mastery of their applications to the distribution industry, so as to reinforce the Company's competitiveness and leadership position in the North American market.

PAY-OUT RATIO

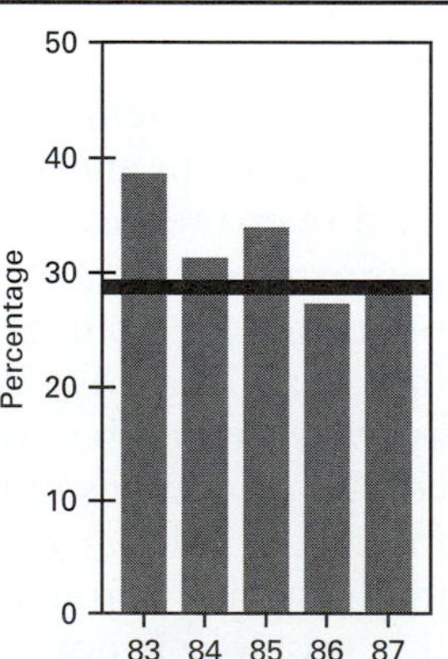

Pay shareholders dividends amounting to 30% of the previous year's income before extraordinary items.

EQUITY: TOTAL DEBT RATIO

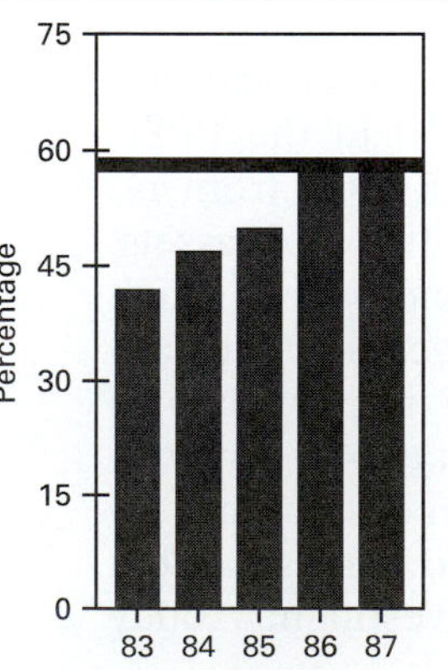

Maintain an A credit rating.

EXHIBIT 2 Summary Financial Data

	1987	*1986*	*1985*	*1984*	*1983*
Operations ($ millions)					
Net sales	5,401.6	4,746.1	4,367.4	3,891.2	3,683.0
Operating income	156.6	131.9	110.4	88.4	91.6
Depreciation and amortization	25.7	24.4	21.8	20.6	21.3
Interest—net	16.6	19.0	18.6	19.6	30.0
Income taxes	54.8	39.4	29.6	21.5	16.5
Income before extraordinary items	60.3	48.3	40.3	26.5	24.1
Net income	65.2	34.5	40.3	26.5	22.5
Changes in Financial Position ($ millions)					
Funds from operations	95.4	82.9	58.5	43.9	43.5
Capital expenditures	86.2	64.2	47.9	19.4	26.1
Dividends	14.9	12.0	10.2	9.0	9.7
Financial Position ($ millions)					
Current assets	625.4	535.3	453.0	404.4	358.2
Current liabilities	509.9	424.7	369.2	331.4	312.2
Working capital	115.5	110.6	83.8	73.4	46.0
Fixed asets	262.3	230.8	2198.7	202.4	217.3
Total assets	1,002.9	863.9	728.9	660.8	624.2
Total debt	206.7	202.5	206.5	195.2	213.5
Shareholder's equity	316.1	278.3	211.7	180.9	163.7
Financial Ratios					
Return on average equity	20.5%	22.0%	21.6%	16.4%	16.2%
Total debt : equity	40:60	42:58	49:51	42:48	57:43
Current ratio	1.23x	1.26x	1.23x	1.22x	1.15x
Interest coverage ratio	7.9x	6.5x	4.7x	3.4x	2.4x
Per share					
Income before extraordinary items	1.43	1.21	1.01	0.655	0.58
1st quarter	0.25	0.26	0.25	0.075	0.09
2nd quarter	0.41	0.40	0.29	0.175	0.18
3rd quarter	0.30	0.29	0.21	0.21	0.15
4th quarter	0.47	0.26	0.26	0.195	0.16
Net income	1.54	0.86	0.01	0.655	0.535
Fully diluted:					
Income before extraordinary items	1.36	1.15	10.98	0.655	0.58
Net income	1.46	0.82	0.98	0.655	0.535
Dividends	0.346	0.288	0.238	0.20	0.20
Funds from operations	2.27	2.10	1.50	1.13	1.13
Capital expenditures	2.05	1.63	1.23	0.50	0.68
Shareholders' equity	7.51	6.42	5.10	4.25	3.73
Market value					
High	2.25	17.00	9.56	9.81	6.88
Low	15.25	8.81	7.31	5.75	3.00
Common shares outstanding	42,077,208	41,907,030	39,031,612	38,936,474	38,839,392
Average number of shares traded weekly[a]	243,967	218,597	233,684	138,458	98,618
Shareholders of record	7,346	6,515	5,537	7,153	8,911
Effective income tax rate	47.7%	44.6%	42.3%	44.6%	40.7%

[a]Montreal and Toronto Stock Exchange

EXHIBIT 3 Organization Chart

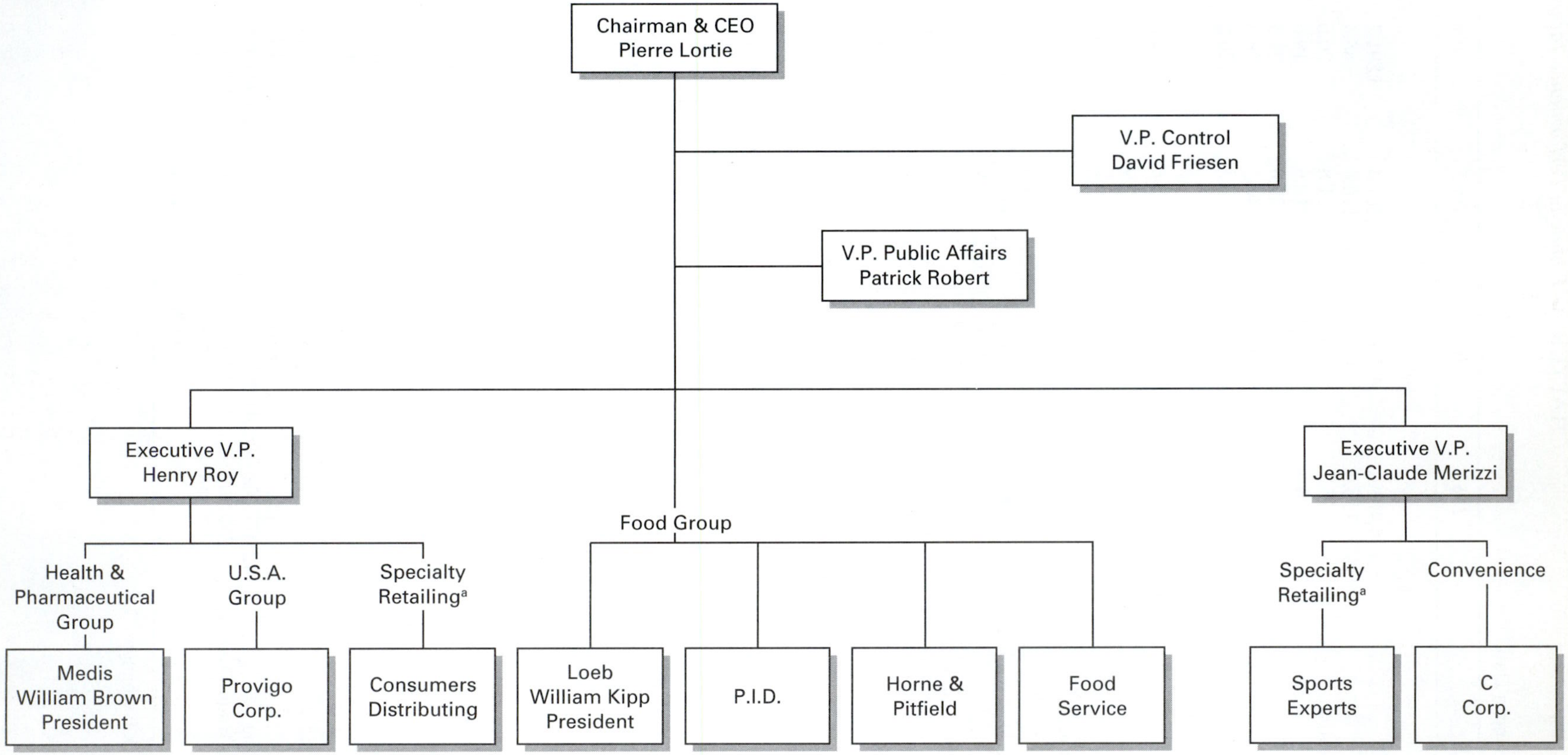

Chairman & CEO
Pierre Lortie

V.P. Control
David Friesen

V.P. Public Affairs
Patrick Robert

Executive V.P.
Henry Roy

Health & Pharmaceutical Group
Medis
William Brown
President

U.S.A. Group
Provigo Corp.

Specialty Retailing[a]
Consumers Distributing

Food Group
Loeb
William Kipp
President

P.I.D.

Horne & Pitfield

Food Service

Executive V.P.
Jean-Claude Merizzi

Specialty Retailing[a]
Sports Experts

Convenience
C Corp.

[a]Specialty retailing includes both Consumer Distributing and Sports Experts (Provigo acquired 23.5% of Consumers Distributing's ownership in 1985. Effective November 6, 1987, the company acquired the remaining issues and outstanding voting shares of Consumers Distributing).

EXHIBIT 4 Business Segment Information (Fiscal Year Ended January 31, 1987)

		Sales			*Performance Income*[a]			*Net Assets Employed*[c]			*Capital Expenditures*	
Group	*Operating Company*	*Net ($ millions)*	*%*	*Growth*[b] *(%)*	*Net ($ millions)*	*%*	*Growth*[b] *(%)*	*Net ($ millions)*	*%*	*Growth*[b] *(%)*	*($ millions)*	*%*
Food	P.D.I. Loeb Horne & Pitfield Food Service	3,692	68%	13%	43.8	67%	30%	247.9	53%	1%	55.6	64%
Health & Pharmaceutical (H&P)	MEDIS	792	15	35	8.0	11	3	89.4	19	94	9.9	11.5
U.S.A.	Provigo Corp.	446	8	1	6.2	9	(6)	40.6	9	(17)	1.5	2
Convenience	C Corp.	319	6	0	8.7	12	19	40.2	9	28	9.1	10.5
Specialty Retailing	Sport Experts	152	3	9	0.8	1	(77)	46.0	10	83	10	12
		5,401	100%		72	100%		464.1	100%		86.1	100%

Source: Annual report

[a]Operating profit before interest expense, after taxes.

[b]1986 to 1987.

[c]Basically noncash identifiable cash, net of "free financing" (e.g., Accounts Payable).

EXHIBIT 5 PPSP Awards: An Illustration

	Actual	Strategic Plan		
	19-0	19-1	19-2	19-3
Performance income (PI) (millions)	$13.5	$17.0	$24.0	$32.0
Net assets employed[a] (NAE) (millions)	30.6	60.0	83.0	103.0

From these, the performance benchmarks could be calculated.

	Base Year (19-0)	19-1	19-2	19-3
PI ($ million)	$13.50	$17.00	$24.00	$32.00
NAE ($ million)	30.60	60.00	83.00	103.00
Residual income (RI)[b] (PI - 12% of NAE)	9.83	9.80	14.04	19.28
Improvement over base year		−0.03	4.21	9.45
Planned Value Added			13.63	

[a]Net Assets Employed was defined as average noncash identifiable assets net of "free financing" (e.g., accounts payable.)
[b]For the first years of the plan, the capital charge was set at 12%. This percentage could be changed in future years to reflect Provigo's cost of capital.

At the end of 19-3, the actual results for the cycle became available:

	Base Year (19-0)	19-1	19-2	19-3
PI ($ million)	$13.50	$17.50	$22.00	$35.00
NAE ($ million)	30.60	58.00	80.00	101.00
Residual income (RI)[b] (PI - 12% of NAE)	9.83	10.54	12.40	22.88
Improvement over base year		0.71	2.57	13.05
Actual Value Added			16.33	

Accordingly:

$$\text{CSW} = \frac{\text{Actual Residual Income} - (3 \times \text{base year's residual income})}{\text{Planned Residual Income} - (3 \times \text{base year's residual income})}$$

$$= \frac{\text{Actual Value Added}}{\text{Planned Value Added}}$$

$$= \frac{16.33}{13.63} = 120$$

CHAPTER 11

Performance-Dependent Rewards (and Punishments)

The final major element of financial results control systems is the system of rewards and punishments which are linked to the performance evaluations. Rewards are important because they inform or remind employees what result areas are desired and motivate them to achieve and exceed the performance targets. Punishments are negative rewards or, sometimes, the absence of positive rewards.

Hereafter the term *rewards* will be used to refer both to things employees value and those they would like to avoid, but it must be remembered that some rewards are quite negative. Public humiliation, as it is used at Black & Decker, is one example. At Black & Decker's semiannual meeting of division heads, Nolan Archibald, the company's chairman, president, and chief executive officer requires the managers who have met their profitability and cash flow targets to sit on the left side of the room. Those who have missed their targets must sit on the right and, during the meeting, explain to the others why they have not met their targets. Mr. Archibald explained, proudly,

> They hate being over on the right. We think this kind of peer competition is motivational.[1]

This chapter describes the benefits of performance-dependent rewards. It then identifies the many forms of rewards that can be and are promised as part of motivational contracts and provides a set of criteria for evaluating the rewards and punishments. Finally, the chapter focuses on one common form of reward, monetary rewards, and describes how to make decisions about important aspects of the contracts linking performance with rewards, including the shape and explicitness of the function linking rewards with performance measures and the size of the results-dependent monetary rewards.

THE BENEFITS OF PERFORMANCE-DEPENDENT REWARDS

Performance-dependent rewards provide the impetus for the aligning of employees' natural self-interest with the organization's objectives. They provide two types of control benefits.[2] The first control benefit is *informational.* The rewards attract the employees' attention and inform or remind them of the relative importance of often-competing results areas; such as costs, quality, customer service, asset management, and future growth. The rewards add impetus to the measurement signal that helps employees decide how to allocate their time and effort. Merely telling employees that quality is important might have some effect on their behavior, however, telling them that the quality measures will be an important factor in determining their raises, bonuses, and promotions is more likely to convince them to emphasize quality in their work.

The second control benefit is *motivational.* Some employees need incentives to exert the extra effort required to perform tasks well (for example, working late or on a weekend). Sometimes even hardworking employees need incentives to overcome their natural aversion to some difficult or tedious actions that are in their organization's best interest, such as laying off personnel, making a sales cold call, preparing paperwork, or cleaning the warehouse.

Performance-dependent rewards are often chosen to serve a number of noncontrol purposes as detailed below.

1. Performance-dependent rewards are an important part of many employees' total compensation package. Some rewards are promised because the organization wants to improve employee recruitment and retention either by offering a package that is comparable or superior to those offered by their competitors or by linking payments to an employee's continued employment.
2. Properly structured rewards can sometimes reduce the corporation's after-tax compensation expense or increase the employee's after-tax income. Some reward system choices are affected by tax considerations, such as whether the monetary payments are taxable to the employee and at what tax rate, and whether the corporation can deduct the expense.
3. Some reward choices are made to get common stock in managers' (and other employees') hands as part of a defense against a hostile takeover.
4. Some performance-dependent awards are designed primarily to make compensation more variable with firm performance, thus decreasing the cash outlays required when performance is poor and reducing the company's operating leverage.

While this chapter focuses on the control benefits of the various forms of rewards, it must be recognized that the control and noncontrol purposes of reward systems can sometimes be traded-off against each other. Observing organizations' reward practices does not necessarily provide definitive clues as to which rewards the organizations have found to be most effective for control purposes.

FORMS OF REWARDS AND PUNISHMENTS

Anything employees like or dislike can be linked with any action indicator or any performance measure or combinations of measures that can be used to distinguish good from mediocre or poor performance. A recent best-selling book described "1001 ways to reward employees."[3] Table 11-1 lists some of the major forms of rewards that companies use.

Managers typically do not rely on just a single form of rewards. Corporate managers can, and do, threaten to reduce the pleasure middle managers derive from managing their entity without interference by refusing to fund ideas for expenditures in entities where performance is not good. They grant managers additional power and increase their recognition within the firm by publicizing their good results. They provide additional pecuniary rewards in the form of cash, stock, country club memberships, cars, and trips. They grant benefits in many perquisite forms, such as titles, parking spots, and sizes and locations of offices.

TABLE 11-1 Examples of Positive and Negative Rewards

Positive Rewards	*Negative Rewards (Punishments)*
autonomy	interference in job from superior(s)
power	loss of job
opportunities to participate in important decision-making processes	zero salary increase
salary increases	assignment to unimportant tasks
bonuses	chastisement (public or private)
stock options	no promotion
restricted stock	demotion
praise	public humiliation
recognition	
promotions	
titles	
job assignments	
office assignments	
preferred parking places	
country club memberships	
job security	
merchandise prizes	
vacation trips	
participation in executive development programs	
time off	

TYPES OF PERFORMANCE-DEPENDENT MONETARY REWARDS

Money is an important form of reward which is often linked to performance, particularly at managerial levels of organizations. It is certainly not the only form of reward, and it is not necessarily always the best one (as will be discussed below), but its use is so common that it deserves special mention. Performance-dependent monetary reward systems can be classified into three main categories: performance-based salary increases, short-term incentive awards, and long-term incentive awards.

Performance-Based Salary Increases

All organizations give salary increases to employees at all organizational levels. A portion of these salary increases are cost-of-living adjustments. The remainder are merit-based increases. Merit can be demonstrated through performance or the acquisition of skills that promise improved performance in future periods.

Salary increases are typically a small proportion of an employee's salary, but they have considerable value because they are not just a one-time payment. They provide an annuity that typically persists for many years because rarely are employees' salaries reduced.

Short-Term Incentive Awards

Nearly all U.S. firms above minimal size, and increasingly larger firms in many other countries, use short-term incentive awards, which include bonuses, commissions, and piece-rate payments. Short-term awards provide cash payments based on performance measured over periods of one year or less. The awards can be based on the performance of a single individual or that of a group of which an individual is a member, such as a workteam, a profit center, or the corporation as a whole.

Some short-term incentive awards are calculated directly by formula, such as 2 percent of sales or 10 percent of net profits. Some are assigned in two steps. First a *bonus pool* is funded, often based on corporate performance. Then the pool is assigned to individuals, usually through a process of ranking or rating individuals that provides higher awards to better performers.

Incentive awards account for a large proportion of the total annual compensation of some employees, particularly higher-level managers and sales personnel. Survey data from Sibson & Company showed that 1994 annual bonuses averaged 41 and 35 percent of base salary for chief executive officers and chief operating officers, respectively.[4] The bonus proportions of compensation generally decrease at lower organization levels. Data from Wyatt Data Services showed that 1995 annual bonuses for CEOs averaged 40 percent of base salary, but for middle managers they were only 11 percent.[5]

The compensation consultants' surveys also show that bonus proportions of compensation are increasing. CEO bonuses have been growing at an annual compounded rate of 8.3 percent in the 1990s, while base salaries have been increasingly only at a 5.3 percent rate.[6]

Long-Term Incentive Awards

Long-term incentive awards are based on performance measured over periods greater than one year. Such awards are usually restricted to relatively high management levels.

The use of long-term awards has been growing. Survey data from the consulting firm TPF&C show that long-term incentive compensation was 46 percent of total compensation in 1994, and long-term compensation has been increasing at a compound rate of 24 percent in the 1990s, while total compensation has been increasing at only a 10 percent rate.[7]

Long-term incentive awards come in multiple forms. Some long-term incentive plans measure performance in terms of accounting variables, most commonly earnings per share growth, return-on-equity, assets, or investment, measured over a period that generally ranges from three to six years. These types of plans are commonly referred to as *performance plans.*

Two variations of performance plans are in common use. With *performance unit* plans, each manager is allocated a specific number of units of a fixed dollar value at the beginning of the award period. At the end of the award period, the value of the award is calculated as the number of units earned times the fixed predetermined dollar value per unit. The number of units earned depends on the extent to which the accounting performance goal is achieved. *Performance share* plans are similar to performance unit plans in that the earnings are based on achievement of accounting performance goals. The difference between these plans is that the performance share awards are shares of stock, not units of fixed dollar value. Performance share plans are not strictly accounting-based because the value of the award depends on the change in the company's stock price over the award period.

Some other long-term incentive awards are *stock-based*. They provide rewards based on changes in the value of the company's stock. Stock-based plans come in many forms, including the following:

Stock Option Plans

Stock option plans give an employee a contractual right to purchase stock from the employer at a fixed price during a specified period of time. When the stock price is above the option exercise price, the employee can exercise the option and sell the stock at a profit. Stock option plans are the most prevalent stock-based incentive plan by far. One survey found that they were used by 84 percent of large manufacturing firms. They are also probably the fastest growing form of long-term incentives. One study of 356 large publicly-held companies found that stock option grants grew by 42.1 percent in 1994 (as compared with 1993) and by another 31.5 percent in 1995.[8]

Stock Appreciation Rights (SARs)

SARs are similar to options in that the employee benefits from appreciation in the company's stock price. They are different in that the employee does not have to spend cash to acquire the stock directly. When the SAR is exercised, the employer pays the employee cash, stock, or a combination of both, in an amount equal to the stock's appreciation since the date of grant.

Phantom Stock Plans

With a phantom stock plan, the firm assigns a stated number of stock units to the employee for a specified period of time. Each unit has the fair market value of an outstanding share of stock, the book value of a share of stock, or a formula price value (for example, ten times earnings). During the award period, the firm might pay the employee amounts equal to the dividends paid on outstanding shares. At the end of the award period, the firm pays the employee an amount equal to the appreciation in the value of the units. The payments are sometimes made in a lump sum or in installments, or they may be deferred to a future time, such as retirement or other separation from service.

Several of the forms of rewards listed in Table 11-1 are associated with one or more of these forms of monetary payments. Promotions typically involve a salary increase and, at managerial levels of the organization, inclusion in more incentive-compensation plans and inclusion in the plans at higher award levels. Recognition awards, too, can involve a monetary payment or the granting of a cash equivalent, such as a pleasure trip.

GROUP REWARDS

In an era increasingly requiring the cooperation of people from across the corporation, many consultants have called for increased use of group rewards in place of those based on the performance of individual achievement. A *Fortune* magazine article about the conditions that enhance corporations' readiness for change stated bluntly, "Team-based rewards are better than rewards based solely on individual achievement."[9] Team-based rewards certainly have their advantages; they were discussed in Chapter 4 as one of the methods by which personnel/cultural controls can be implemented.

Team- or group-based rewards have a significant disadvantage, though; they rarely provide a direct incentive effect. The group-based rewards provide a direct incentive only if the individuals to whom the rewards are promised perceive that they can influence the performance on which the rewards are based to a considerable extent. When the measurements are of the performance of a large group, no individual except, perhaps, the group's leader is likely to have a material effect on the performance measures. Stock-based plans provide direct incentives only for the small number of managers at the very top of publicly-held corporations who can influence the company's stock price in a meaningful way. When lower-level employees are included in stock-based plans, their compensation is made more volatile, but their motivation is not affected. With only rare exceptions, such as a research scientist who makes a breakthrough discovery, even if the lower-level employees perform heroically, their efforts will not have a significant influence on stock price.

Large, group-based rewards can produce a beneficial form of cultural control, however. Group members may monitor and sanction each others' behaviors and produce improved results. Comments like, "Get to work; you're hurting my profit sharing" are evidence that cultural control (mutual monitoring) is working. It is the benefit, and the avoidance of some dysfunctional effects of individual rewards in cases where measurements are flawed, such as suboptimization and conflict, that group-based rewards can provide.

LINKS BETWEEN REWARDS AND RESULTS

For most organizations the link between rewards and results, however defined, is linear. This was illustrated in a budget setting in Chapter 10 (see Figure 10-3). Most profit center managers do not earn any bonus until they achieve all (or a substantial portion) of their budget target. Their bonus then increases linearly with performance. This linear function is the simplest to communicate and administer.

Rewards are typically promised only over a restricted performance range, however. The function has lower and upper reward cutoffs, and it is linear in shape between the cutoff extremes. At profit center organization levels, most firms set a lower cutoff in their short-term incentive compensation contract. Below some significant fraction (such as, 80 percent) of targeted annual performance (which is typically the budget), managers are promised no incentive compensation for financial performance. These corporations set this lower cutoff because they do not want to pay any bonuses for performance they considered mediocre. The fraction of the target set as the lower limit varies with the predictability of the target; it is a lower fraction where the predictability is lower.[10]

Most firms also set an upper cutoff on incentive payments for middle-level managers, although payout functions for higher-level managers are less likely to have an upper cutoff. An upper cutoff means that no extra rewards are provided for results above the cutoff. The cutoffs are set at a broad range of results but are typically also set at a percentage of the annual performance target, such as 150 percent of budget. Upper cutoffs are set for any of a number of reasons, including

1. fear that the high bonuses that would be paid might not be deserved because of a windfall gain (unforeseen good luck);

2. fear that managers will be unduly motivated to take actions to increase current period reported profits at the expense of the long-term. This could produce results, especially in the areas of growth and profitability, which are unsustainably high and inconsistent with the typical corporate desire to show steady performance improvement;
3. fear of a faulty plan design, the risk of which is greatest when the plan is new;
4. desire not to pay lower-level managers more than upper-level managers earn, thus maintaining vertical compensation equity;
5. desire to keep total compensation somewhat consistent over time so that managers are able to sustain their lifestyle;
6. desire to adhere to standard corporate and industry practices.

CRITERIA FOR EVALUATING REWARD SYSTEMS

For ideal motivation, a system of performance-dependent rewards should satisfy the following criteria.

First, the rewards should be *valued.* Rewards that have no value do not provide motivation. Only scattered evidence exists as to the motivational effects of the various forms of rewards, but it seems clear that reward tastes vary across individuals.[11] As compared with top executives, lower-level managers are probably more interested in protecting their autonomy and in improving their prospects for promotion, and less interested in the stability of their short-term income (after their base salaries are assured).[12] Highly-educated workers are often driven more by pride in accomplishment than money.

Reward tastes vary systematically across citizens of different countries due to many factors; including culture, socio-economic status, and local income tax rates. If organizations can tailor their reward packages to their employees' individual preferences, they can provide the control benefits at the lowest possible costs. Unfortunately, this tailoring is not easy to accomplish, as it is easier to administer a single organization-wide reward system (or at most just a few systems).

Second, the rewards should be large enough to have *impact.* If rewards that are valued are provided in trivial amounts, the effect can be counterproductive. Employees can be insulted and react with such emotions as contempt and anger. A recent editor of the *Harvard Business Review* often gave staff members gifts, such as wine and restaurant gift certificates. These gifts had value but not much impact. One associate editor reported that, "While we wanted professional recognition, compensation and career development, the gifts, bonuses and parties made us feel like a McDonald's Employee of the Month."[13] Reward visibility can also affect impact. If rewards are visible to others, the motivational effect is enhanced by a sense of pride and recognition.

Third, rewards should be *understandable.* Employees should understand both the reasons for their earning a given reward and the value of their reward. Companies can incur considerable expense providing potentially valuable rewards, but if employees do not understand them well, their expense will not generate the desired motivational effects.

Fourth, rewards should be *timely.* They must be provided soon after the performance that is to be rewarded or they will lose much of their motivational effect. Evidence has shown that rewards provided soon after actions are taken have a far stronger motivational effect than do rewards that are delayed; prompt rewards increase the speed and permanence of any learning that takes place.[14] The discount rate employees apply to delayed rewards seems to be far greater than the time value of money.[15]

Fifth, the effects of the rewards should be *durable.* Rewards have greater value if the good feelings generated by the granting of a reward are long-lasting; that is, if employees remember them.

Sixth, rewards should be *reversible.* Performance evaluators often make mistakes, and some reward decisions are more difficult to correct than others. People decisions, such as promotions, are difficult to reverse.

Finally, rewards should be *cost efficient.* Some rewards are expensive, and others are not. It is obviously best for the company if the desired motivation can be achieved at minimal cost, but this is not easy to do because the effects of each of the various reward forms vary depending on managers' personal tastes and circumstances. Some managers are greatly interested in immediate cash awards, whereas others are more interested in recognition, in preserving or increasing their autonomy, or in improving their promotion possibilities.

MONETARY REWARDS AND THEIR EVALUATION CRITERIA

Monetary rewards can have powerful impacts on employees' behaviors because virtually everyone values money. Money can be used to purchase goods and services that can satisfy many desires. Money also has important symbolic values. It reflects achievement and success, and sometimes accords people with prestige and power. Some people even seem to use monetary rewards as a measure of their own self-worth.

Many of the monetary rewards that most U.S. companies, and increasingly those in other countries give, and in fact emphasize, fail to satisfy most of the criteria described above. Some monetary awards fail to attract attention. One common failure occurs when companies which are not performing well flatten their reward payments; that is, lower the rewards they give to superior performers. The situation is exacerbated when inflation is low. Because it is difficult to cut an employee's nominal pay, managers are limited simply to giving poor performers no bonuses or raises. The penalty to these employees is low because they are only losing a small amount of purchasing power, perhaps 3 percent inflation. These companies economize (save cash) by lowering the payments to their top performers, even though these employees may be responsible for producing the bulk of the profits that are earned. The result is an employee perception of inequity, demotivation, and often, loss of the most marketable employees.

Some monetary rewards fail to satisfy the understandability criterion. Because agreements with superiors are ambiguous and because performance-related feedback is incomplete or biased, employees often fail to understand the reasons why they are given their rewards. If reward plans are complex, as is the case with many long-term incentive plans (such as, stock option plans), employees often fail to understand the value of some of the rewards they are given.

Many monetary rewards fail the impact criterion. Performance-dependent raises are typically quite small in times of low inflation and lagging company performance, so they do not have much behavioral impact. Monetary rewards, both salaries and bonus awards, are typically kept confidential, except for the required public disclosures of rewards paid to a handful of the very top management. This lack of visibility limits employees' feelings of pride and recognition.

Most monetary rewards are not timely. The most common period for performance reviews is annually. These reviews are used to announce salary increases and bonuses, but these reviews are not timely. If an employee does something good in January, there is no reward for twelve months (or sometimes longer). Long-term incentive awards, those based on multi-year performance, are even less timely. One good example of a timely reward are the piece-rate incentive plans used in many production operations.

Most monetary rewards are not durable. Salary increases are lost in the paycheck, and employees' spending patterns quickly adjust to the new income level. Soon employees have no idea how they made ends meet before they got the raise. Similarly, bonuses are quickly spent. Durability can perhaps be improved if the award is given but restricted for a period of time, such as with an award of restricted stock, because the employee can see the reward and can value it, but cannot spent it. No monetary award is as durable as some other forms of reward, such as a recognition plaque on a wall, a larger office, a promotion, or a trip that provides lasting memories.

Some monetary rewards are reversible, but others are not. Bonus awards are reversible because they are typically given for only a single period. Salary increases, on the other hand, provide an almost permanent annuity to the employee. They are more attractive to the employee, but less attractive to the company. Promotions are often difficult to reverse.

Finally, monetary rewards tend to be expensive. The value provided to the employees is a direct cost to the company. Some other forms of rewards, such as titles, recognition, preferred parking spaces, and interesting job assignments, are much less expensive.

Although monetary rewards do not always satisfy the set of evaluation criteria well, they are in common use because they tend to satisfy the criteria better, on balance, than do the reward alternatives in a broad range of settings. The criteria are not all equally important, and monetary rewards are most effective in satisfying the most important criteria. In particular, money is highly valued, so monetary awards attract most employees' attention. That is not to say, however, that monetary rewards are not sometimes overused or that they could not be better designed.

IMPORTANT ISSUES IN DESIGNING MONETARY REWARD SYSTEMS

How should monetary rewards be designed? The following sections describe some of the most important design choices and their critical parameters.

What Proportion of Rewards Should Be Performance-Dependent?

Since employees, almost without exception, value money, the larger the proportion of compensation based on performance, the greater are the employees' incentives to achieve the performance goals. Taken to an extreme, this argument suggests that employees should not be given any fixed salary, that all of their compensation should be performance-dependent. Corporations use few motivational contracts of this type.

The most significant impediment to the high use of performance-dependent rewards is that, if such performance is not totally controllable by the employees, the reward system forces the employees to bear business risks. Typically, the business owners are in a better position to bear these risks than are employees because their rewards come from a diversified portfolio. Employees, being risk averse, must be compensated for bearing risk, and the additional compensation raises the firm's employee expense. If the firm fails to provide the additional compensation, it will find itself unable to compete for talent in the labor markets. This issue is discussed in greater detail in Chapter 14.

How Explicit Should the Reward Promises Be?

Another potentially important feature of motivational contracts is the explicitness of the reward promise. Sometimes the forms of the rewards promised and the bases on which the awards will be given are communicated to the managers explicitly. Some of them are described in writing in great detail.

Other, often quite important, contracts are left mostly implicit. The implicit, unwritten understandings between managers are implemented on a case-by-case basis and used to fill the gaps left either intentionally or unintentionally in the written contracts. The bases on which the rewards are assigned may be left vague because the evaluations are done subjectively. Managers may be told that the corporation will try to protect them from the harmful effects of selected adverse economic factors beyond their control if the corporation turns out to have a good year. The important promotion-prospects contract is almost invariably implicit. Managers have to infer the factors that are used to determine promotions by observing over time the skills, personal qualities, and accomplishments of those who are promoted.

Superiors sometimes purposely leave contract terms implicit for any of several reasons. They may not know how to describe the bases for the rewards or the weightings of importance of each of the individual items in the set of evaluation criteria prior to the performance period. They may want to keep the contract flexible to avoid motivating managers in directions that turn out to be no longer appropriate as environmental or competitive conditions change. The superiors may want to encourage managers to "do their best" and not give up in the face of an impossible performance target or coast after target achievement. They may want to reduce managers' propensities to engage in short-term manipulations of the performance measures.

Lack of explicitness about the contract terms increases the employees' risk. They must bear the risk that their superiors will evaluate them on different bases than they were assuming when they made their decisions. Again, because the employees are risk averse, the organization must compensate them for bearing this risk.

The fact that a contract (or contract element) is unwritten does not necessarily mean that it is implicit, however. Some contract terms are communicated in ways that are so clear that the employees immediately understand their terms, such as in direct face-to-face meetings. A simple verbal order that the manager will be fired if the budget targets are not achieved this year is quite explicit. Explicitness depends on the clarity of the communication between the managers and their evaluators. Clear communication is desirable unless a chance exists that the contract terms will quickly become obsolete.

CONCLUSION

Performance-dependent rewards are an important part of the results-control contracts used to control employees' behaviors. Rewards that can be linked to measures of performance or subjective performance evaluations come in many forms. It is widely, but not universally, believed that monetary rewards are important for motivation. However, a wide range of other forms of rewards, such as praise, recognition, promotions, titles, preferred parking spaces, offices, and club memberships can also be powerful motivators and often have advantages both in terms of satisfying the evaluation criteria and in their cost efficiency.

Motivational contract design presents problems that are far larger than just the choice of rewards. It seems to be cost effective to tailor rewards to managers' individual reward preferences. Contract costs can be borne in many forms, and the tailoring of reward promises to individual managers' taste is not necessarily an optimal control design choice because it increases the potential for managers' perceptions of contract inequities and the costs of contract administration. Similarly, it is well-recognized that organizations' total compensation package must be competitive to attract and retain qualified employees. If a portion of the compensation package, such as base salaries, is not competitive, perhaps because a salary cut or freeze was applied during a difficult operating period, then the results-dependent reward function may have to be adapted to compensate.

The most solid advice that can be provided is that performance-dependent rewards should be sufficiently meaningful to offset other incentives employees have to act in ways that are contrary to their organization's best interest, but the rewards should not be greater than those necessary to provide the needed motivation. Solid evidence as to the positive and negative effects of most of the specific reward choices is only just emerging.

Notes

1. M. Schifrin, "Cut-and-Build Archibald," *Forbes* (September 23, 1996), p. 46.
2. They also provide other benefits, such as to help attract and retain effective employees.
3. B. Nelson, *1001 Ways to Reward Employees* (New York: Workman, 1994).
4. Sibson & Company, *1994 Management Compensation Survey* (Princeton, N.J.: Sibson & Company), August 1994.
5. Wyatt Data Services, *Top Management Report* and *Middle Management Report* (Fort Lee, N.J.: Wyatt Data Services) April 1995.
6. Sibon & Company, *1994 Management Compensation Survey* (Princeton, N.J.: Sibson & Company), August 1994.
7. TPF&C, *Executive Compensation Survey* (New York: TPF&C), 1994.
8. G. Crystal, "Average U.S. CEO Boosted Pay 21% in '95, to $4.5 Million," *Los Angeles Times* (May 26, 1996), pp. D4, D6.
9. T. A. Stewart, : "Rate Your Readiness to Change," *Fortune* (February 7, 1994), p. 106.
10. K. A. Merchant, *Rewarding Results: Motivating Profit Center Managers* (Boston: Harvard Business School Press, 1989).
11. For example, a review article by Ehrenberg and Milkovich concluded that: "While a variety of theories exists about the effects of various [management] compensation policies, surprisingly little evidence exists on the extent to which compensation policies vary across firms and more importantly on the effects of pursuing alternative compensation strategies." R. G. Ehrenberg and G. T. Milkovich, "Compensation and Firm Performance," in *Human Re-*

sources and the Performance of the Firm, edited by M. Kleiner, et al. (Madison, Wis.: Industrial Relations Research Association, University of Wisconsin, 1987), pp. 87–122.

12. J. Eaton and H. S. Rosen, "Agency, Delayed Compensation, and the Structure of Executive Remuneration," *Journal of Finance,* XXXVIII (1983), pp. 1489–1505.
13. P. Hemp, "Shake-Up at the Harvard Business Review," *Boston Globe* (June 2, 1992), p. 41.
14. T. W. Costello and S. S. Zalkind, *Psychology in Administration* (Englewood Cliffs, N.J.: Prentice-Hall, 1963).
15. K. A. Merchant, *Rewarding Results: Motivating Profit Center Managers* (Boston: Harvard Business School Press, 1989).

Loctite Company de México, S.A. de C.V.

Corporate managers of the Loctite Company, a U.S.-based specialty chemical company, allowed the general managers of their foreign subsidiaries to tailor their employees' compensation packages to the local environments. José Monteiro, general manager of Mexico, values this autonomy, but he admitted that performance evaluations and compensation structures caused him considerable concern:

> One of the most difficult management areas in Mexico is compensation. When the [Mexican] borders opened, every company found itself in a special situation, and usually worse off. The lowering of tariffs, an important part of President Salinas's plan to bring down inflation and bring investment to the country to enable Mexico to compete globally, has caused a notable increase in foreign competition. For example, the tariff on cianoacrylate adhesives, a product we manufacture in Mexico, has been lowered from 37 percent to 15 percent.
>
> Everybody needs good people to compete effectively in this environment, so we have seen a tremendous increase in the competition for labor. The demand for skilled employees and executives far outstrips the supply. Bilingual employees, in particular, are being tempted by other companies, mostly U.S. companies expanding their operations in the Mexican market. So I pay a lot of attention to how much we pay out employees as well as the bases for and the forms and timing of the payments. Loctite is a young company in Mexico, and if you want to grow, you must compensate your people appropriately.

In 1992, José faced a special compensation problem. Faced with a sales slowdown, some of the salespeople in the Mexico City area were working with distributors within their territories to capture sales, and hence commissions, from outside their territories. José had to decide whether to tolerate this intracompany competition or to take steps to eliminate either the salespeople's prerogatives to cross territory boundaries or their incentives to do so.

LOCTITE CORPORATION

Loctite Corporation was founded as American Sealants Co. in 1953 in Hartford, Connecticut by Dr. Vernon Krieble, a retired Trinity College chemistry professor. Its first product was an anerobic[1] sealant called Loctite. Over the years the company maintained a dominant (85 percent in 1992) market share in the world market for anerobic sealants, and it grew both internally and by acquisition. In 1992, Loctite was a worldwide company specializing in a broad range of sealant and adhesive products. Among the applications for Loctite's sealant products were to seal porosity in metal castings to stop leak paths, to seal bolts and nuts so that they would not come loose, and to seal transmissions to prevent oil leakage (i.e., liquid gaskets). Loctite's adhesives (e.g., gasket eliminator, *super* glue) were used for both manufacturing and repairs.

Loctite's 1991 sales ranked it 477th on the *Fortune* 500 list of the largest U.S. industrial corporations, and it employed 3,500 people. The company's 10-year annual earnings-per-share growth rate of 22.4 percent was the 18th highest among the *Fortune* 500. (See financial highlights in Exhibit 1.) Company managers were proud that the company's *diversity without diversification* had allowed it to continue to grow through difficult economic times. They identified four elements to the diversity:

[1]Anerobic sealants cure without air.

Professor Kenneth A. Merchant of USC and Professors Francisco Arenas and Pedro Suärez of IPADE wrote this case as the basis for class discussion rather than to illustrate either effective or ineffective handling of an administrative situation.

1. **Geographic.** Loctite had operating units in 33 countries around the world, and representative offices and joint ventures in many other countries, so its risk was spread across a range of national economic environments.
2. **End use markets.** Company managers recognized six major market areas: original equipment manufacturing (OEM), industrial maintenance, repair and overhaul (MRO), automobile manufacture, auto repair, auto body repair, and consumer.
3. **Product usage.** Many of Loctite's products could be used for multiple purposes and, in fact, the company had relatively high expense-to-sales ratio because Loctite engineers developed solutions tailored to individual industrial customer needs.
4. **Product diversity.** Loctite's R&D efforts had resulted in new technologies (e.g., specialty silicones) that broadened and expanded the company's sales offerings.

The company was organized into four geographical groups: North America, Europe, Latin America, and Asia/Pacific. North America and Europe were the largest groups by far, accounting for 46 percent and 39 percent of Loctite's total sales, respectively. José Monteiro, general manager of Loctite's Mexican subsidiary, reported to Gerry Briels, president of the North American Group.

In vast majority of its markets, Loctite completed on the basis of the superiority of its products. In the U.S., competitors often undercut Loctite prices by 20 to 40 percent, and Loctite's price disadvantage was even more pronounced in many other countries, including Mexico.

LOCTITE'S MEXICAN SUBSIDIARY

Loctite's Mexican subsidiary, headquartered in Mexico City, was founded in 1958 by a U.S. engineer formerly employed by Ford Motor Company. He imported a sealant product from a U.S. company, Permatex, Inc., bottled it in Mexico, and sold it to the local Ford manufacturing plant. Permatex bought this Mexican distributor in 1964, and it became part of Loctite in 1973 when Loctite acquired Permatex.

In 1992, Loctite's Mexican subsidiary was still small but was growing rapidly. Sales had grown from $3.1 million in 1987 to a level expected to be slightly below $9 million in 1992. In the near term, growth was expected to continue in the Mexican market, which was less mature than that of the U.S., at the annual rate of 15 percent in sales and 20 percent in profits.

Loctite operated two small manufacturing facilities in Mexico which, in 1992, employed a total of 45 people. The company started manufacturing anerobics in 1978 and cianoacrylate (instant) adhesives in 1980, both for the Mexican market only. But José Monteiro expected that eventually Loctite would not do any manufacturing in Mexico because costs were increasing four to five times faster than the peso's devaluation relative to the dollar, and the small size of the subsidiary's manufacturing operations precluded economies of scale.

The subsidiary was organized functionally (see Exhibit 2). All but two of the 119 employees were Mexican nationals. The two exceptions were Luis Riquelme, the controller, who was from Argentina, and José Monteiro, the general manager, who was from Portugal. José had worked for Loctite for several years in the U.S. as a consolidation accountant; he had been the comptroller in both the Brazilian and Mexican subsidiaries; and he had been the general manager of the Mexican subsidiary since 1988.

The sales function was divided into two areas: Industrial and Permatex. The Industrial sales force, reporting to Larry Goldsmith,[2] was comprised of two separate groups, one which sold products direct to OEMs, mostly in the automotive industry, and the other which sold through distributors to MRO users. The Permatex salesforce, reporting to Victor Moreno, sold products directly to distributors and retailers (e.g., hardware stores). In all cases, the salespeople were assigned to territories designed to be approximately equal in sales potential. (In some remote territories, industrial salespeople sold both OEM and MRO products.) Prices were set by José Monteiro; the salespeople had no pricing authority.

Because the product markets and distribution networks were quite different, the appropriate sales approach were also quite different. All of the industrial salespeople worked both directly with users and through distributors, but the mix of their activities varied. OEM salespeople spent most (60 to 70 percent) of their time working directly with users;

[2]Larry Goldsmith had five American and three Mexican sales managers reporting to him. He was based in Dallas, Texas, and reported on a dotted-line basis only to Jose Monteiro.

MRO salespeople split their time working with distributors and giving in-plant maintenance seminars. The sales cycle for large OEM sales was relatively long, often six months or more. MRO and Permatex sales, on the other hand, were made almost immediately, Most MRO sales were made at in-plant sales seminars given to corporate audiences. Permatex products were sold primarily through direct calls to retailers and wholesalers.

The best OEM salespeople sold their products by inventing new applications for existing Loctite products. They studied customers' products and production processes and suggested ways in which Loctite products could help. As Javier Marron, OEM sales manager, emphasized, "We don't sell products. We sell solutions."

Specification of Loctite products could be influenced by engineering, production, or maintenance managers. The salespeople sometimes approached these people directly; sometimes they worked through the purchasing department; and sometimes they worked through the training function, usually located in human resources department, and gave product seminars. The salespeople's inventiveness, however, only helped generate the first few sales. After a new application had been developed, it was easy for competitors to suggest that their products, which were usually cheaper, be substituted. So to retain their customers, the salespeople had to continue to provider superior service.

PERFORMANCE DEPENDENT COMPENSATION

Compensation of Loctite de México employees dependent on performance in three ways.[3] All employees were eligible for both company profit sharing and semi-annual salary increases. Salespeople and manager-level personnel were eligible for commissions or bonuses based on individual performances.[4]

[3]Manufacturing line employees were given small bonuses (one day's pay) for coming to work on time every day for an entire month, but they were promised no production incentives. Studies have shown that piece rates are not very successful in Mexico because of adverse effects on the quality of the work done.

[4]The fringe benefit package was the same for all employees, with one exception: Plant employees were provided with free lunches. They considered this an important benefit, and the company received a direct benefit in that the employees were healthier, in particular less likely to become ill from parasites.

1. Profit sharing.

All Mexican companies were required by law to distribute 10 percent of their pretax income to employees based on days worked and earnings (up to a maximum approximately equal to a salesman's base salary). José considered the profit sharing payments to be incentive compensation, but he admitted that he had had less than complete success in convincing his employees that these payments provided an incentive for superior performance. He said, "They take (the payments) for granted."

2. Salary increases.

Employee salaries were increased semi-annually.[5] José Monteiro wanted to offer excellent compensation packages to enhance his ability to attract and retain good people, but he found that it was not easy to judge the competition because every Mexican company's compensation package was somewhat unique. For sales personnel, for example, some companies paid salary only; some paid salary plus commission; some based their sales commissions on growth while others based them on the absolute level of sales; some provided a car while others did not; and the fringe benefit packages also varied considerably. But with the help of a compensation consulting firm, José conducted a study to identify a comparison group of Mexican companies which were considered *aggressive* in their compensation practices, and he set his salary and total compensation scales to be competitive with this group. As a result, Loctite's recent salary increases had been far above inflation.

The bases for the salary increases were determined subjectively by each employee's immediate superior. It was generally felt that the bases for which salary increases were given were quite similar to those that determined incentive compensation (described later).

Despite the high compensation levels, Loctite de México had still experienced considerable turnover. Loctite employees were seen as having received good training and experience, so they had many job opportunities presented to them. Turnover was particularly high in industrial sales—78 percent in 18 months—and in each of

[5]When inflation in Mexico was high (greater than 70 percent), Loctite gave its employees quarterly salary increases.

the last two years, the top salesperson had left the company to take more lucrative positions.

INCENTIVE COMPENSATION PLANS

Loctite de México offered different incentive compensation plans for salespeople, sales managers, first-line managers (i.e., those reporting directly to the general manager), and the general manager:

A. Salespeople

The company's sales commission plan was designed to encourage the salespeople to work hard and to spend their time where the company's profit potential was greatest. About salespeople in general, José Monteiro said: "The tendency of most salespeople is to talk to people, to be liked, to do what they are comfortable with. The company needs to encourage them to have perseverance and to do tough things, such as to make the high value-added sales."

The plan paid a commission based on sales growth, as measured in liters/kilograms of product sales. José did not believe in paying a commission based on the absolute level of sales: "The biggest nonsense practiced in Mexican companies is to pay a straight commission on sales. That's a royalty, not a commission for performance." Payments were made on a bimonthly basis. The standard for each bimonthly period was the total prior year sales divided by six. No adjustments were made for seasonality because it was not considered to be an important factor.

Table 1 shows the commission chart for OEM salespeople. This chart shows that higher commission rates were earned for higher levels of growth and that the amount of growth needed for each level of commission varied depending on whether or not an MRO salesman was assigned to the same territory.

The salespeople were paid commissions bimonthly, rather than on an annual basis as was done in Loctite's U.S. locations. José chose a shorter evaluation period because: "Mexico is a less mature market (than the U.S.). If you want to grow at the rate we do, you need to look at very short periods of time. You get more focus and more rapid feedback." To reduce the incidence of gameplaying, sales in any bimonthly period below the base were added to the base for the following bimonthly period (except in the last period of the year).

Although Loctite product gross margins varied significantly, from approximately 30 percent for equipment sales to 95 percent for some product sales (the average for industrial products was approximately 70 percent), commissions were based on sales, not gross margins, as was done in Loctite's U.S. locations starting in 1992, because the subsidiary did not yet have a good cost accounting system. One problem was that the Mexican production process were relatively new, so the production standards were not yet accurate. A second problem was that for many sales the Mexican subsidiary paid product transfer prices to Loctite's U.S. subsidiaries that had a profit margin built into them. This intercompany profit was rebated to Mexico only in a lump sum that was not disaggregated to the product level.

Salespeople were also eligible for four other forms of incentive payments:

1. **Commission on house account sales.** House accounts were large OEM accounts (mostly automotive), the product specifications for which were set at corporate headquarters. Commissions on house account sales were paid at a lower rate, reflecting the salesperson's lack of control over those sales.

TABLE 1 OEM Salesperson Commission Chart

Volume[a] growth in territory without MRO salesman	*Volume[a] growth in territory including MRO salesperson*	*Commission (% revenue growth)*
1–30	1–50	5
31–65	51–95	6
66–110	96–140	7
>111	>141	8

[a]Measured in liters/kilograms.

The house account commission rate was set at 1 percent on sales below the base (last year's levels); 4.5 percent commission up to 14 percent growth over base; and higher commissions (up to 6 percent) for higher growth.

2. **New Orders.** Permatex salespeople were paid an extra 2 percent commission on the first order from a new customer, defined as one to which there were no sales in the last six months.
3. **Achievement of SOP targets.** Salesmen could earn up to one month salary each year for achievement of SOP (standards of performance) targets set in 13 performance areas (importance weighting shown in parentheses):
   - in-plant seminars (15 percent)
   - out-plant seminars (15 percent)
   - new product ideas (10 percent)
   - distributor visits (10 percent)
   - sales (8 percent)
   - special attention to major customers (8 percent)
   - new prospects (8 percent)
   - mailings (7 percent)
   - new customers to data base (7 percent)
   - on-time monthly reports (4 percent)
   - preparation of budget (3 percent)
   - expenses within budget (3 percent)
   - quarterly reports (2 percent)

   SOP performances were evaluated quarterly, and up to ¼ of one month salary was paid at that time. In a typical year, SOP ratings averaged 75 to 80 percent of maximum, and an average salesperson SOP bonus was approximately ⅔ of one month salary.
4. **Top performance.** Each year the top OEM and MRO salespeople were each given a vacation trip and a ring.

There was no limit to the amount of compensation a salesperson could earn, and the top salespeople earned quite handsome commissions. For example, in one 1992 bimonthly period, one salesman earned a commission of 19 million pesos.[6] Because of the economic slowdown, however, which caused the slowest period of growth ever for Loctite de México, about 75 percent of the salespeople earned no commission in the first half of 1992. Commission payments were not adjusted to offset bad (or good) luck because José believed, "Luck always seems to accompany those who are good."

B. Sales Managers

The commission and SOP bonus plans for sales manager was quite similar to that for salespeople. Commission payments were based on sales growth over the preceding year, but the marginal rates for payment were lower than those provided to salespeople, as is shown in the representative schedule shown in Table 2. Also, payments were made quarterly, rather than bimonthly. There was no limit to what could be earned, but successful sales managers typically earned commissions totalling approximately 60 to 80 percent of salary.

Like the salespeople, sales managers could earn up to one month salary for SOP performance. The list of SOP areas was quite similar to that for salespeople except that some targets were for activities unique to the sale manager role, such as conduct of SOP reviews of salespeople and conduct of regional sales meetings. The average SOP rating for the sales managers was typically above 90 percent.

[6]In 1992, a typical bimonthly commission for a salesperson was slightly less than 3 million pesos.

TABLE 2 Representative Bonus Function for an OEM Sales Manager

% Growth over Last Year Base (in liters/kilograms)	*Commission paid (% revenue growth)*
1–10	2.0
11–20	2.5
21+	3.0

C. First-line managers

Incentive payments made to the managers reporting directly to the general manager were based on performance in SOP areas specific to their areas of responsibility. For example, Larry Goldsmith (manager of industrial sales) had 23 SOP objectives which were weighted approximately equally in importance. Some of the first-line managers also received small grants of restricted stock.

D. General manager

José Monteiro was included in a general manager's plan administration from the U.S. José's annual bonus was based on sales and profit performance as compared with annual plan, both measured in terms of U.S. dollars (not pesos), and performance in a few key areas (including days receivables, cash self sufficiency, implementation of statistical process control, use of participative management style). If the Mexican subsidiary achieved its annual profit and sales plan, José would earn a cash bonus of 40 percent of salary. If the plan was not achieved, no bonus was given, regardless of performance in the other areas. If the financial plans were achieved but some or all of the performance targets were not achieved, up to 25 percent of the bonus amount could be forfeited.

If the subsidiary's performance was *exceptional* (i.e., the plan was exceeded by a substantial margin), José would also be given some stock options to be exercised within a 5–10 year window. This had happened in two of the four years José had been in the general manager's job. The value of the options, of course, depended on the performance of Loctite stock. In recent years, Loctite stock had performed quite well, and José expected that each of the two options awards he had been given would be worth significantly more than an annual bonus award in a successful year.

COMPETITION AMONG SALESPEOPLE IN MEXICO CITY TERRITORIES

In 1992, a problem arose in the Mexico City area, an area which was divided into four relatively small geographic territories. The sales slowdown was causing the integrity of the territorial system to break down. The most common problem was that some salespeople began to travel into territories other than that to which they were assigned to sell products to users serviced by distributors located within their territories. Loctite used 12 major distributors in the Mexico City area, and the distributors were free to sell wherever they wanted. But out-of-territory selling activity by salespeople was not good for Loctite because the salespeople spent time and money traveling outside their territories, and Loctite's sales efforts were sometimes duplicated. Another, relatively infrequent, violation of territories involved salespeople who were having a bad year *give* sales to another salesperson or distributor in return for a sharing of the commission.

Daniel Rivera, an OEM salesman in a Mexico City territory, expressed some representative concerns:

> Right now the situation is very tough, and the bonus system does not give us any motivation. The product almost sells by itself, but I am the fourth salesman who has been assigned to this territory in a very short period of time. We could sell a lot more if we didn't have as much turnover of salesmen.
>
> I have to accomplish a 3,300 Lt/Kg base before I earn my first bonus. The growth commission is a doubly sharp knife. It is particularly tough because our competitors sell at lower prices, and our distributors compete against us to make their quotas. They don't have any territories as we, Loctite salesmen, do.
>
> In my territory there are big companies, such as Black & Decker, Hewlett-Packard, and General Electric. I have to serve them, and there are at least 40 more prospects to whom we could sell, but at times like this, you have to follow-up with your clients to make the sale.
>
> It's not fair that at times like this, when customers are reducing their purchases, competitors are lowering their prices, and our distributors are competing with us unloyally, that I have to sell at increased prices and generate sales growth in order to make a bonus. Other companies' salesmen, like the ones from 3M, earn as much as three times my paycheck.

Comments from Javier Marron, OEM sales manager in Mexico City:

> I really don't know how many customers we are serving. Neither the distributors nor the salesmen will tell me honestly because they fear I will keep some of the customers as house accounts. But my estimate is that within the Mexico City area, we have at least 3,000 potential customers.
>
> I think our incentive system is good. It motivates the salespeople to sell and to serve old customers, because if you don't, our competitors will take them from you. But it is true that we have lost some salesmen with high sales bases who concluded that growth from that level is difficult.
>
> One idea we had to eliminate the piracy problems between territories is to establish one joint territory within the Mexico City area. Then the bonus pool would depend on performance within the entire area, and we would allocate the pool to each individual based on SOP performance.

EXHIBIT 1 Loctite Corporation–Ten Year Financial Highlights

	Net Sales		*Net Earnings*	
Year Ended	*$millions*	*% incr.*	*$millions*	*% incr.*
1991	$561.2	1%	$71.9	7%
1990	555.2	17	67.4	16
1989	473.9	8	58.2	22
1988	438.9	14	47.6	30
1987	383.4	31	36.7	45
1986	292.4	22	25.3	32
1985	239.9	(2)	19.1	(26)
1984	243.8	7	25.7	16
1983	228.1	7	22.2	63
1982	212.6	(3)	13.6	(9)

EXHIBIT 2 Loctite de México Organization

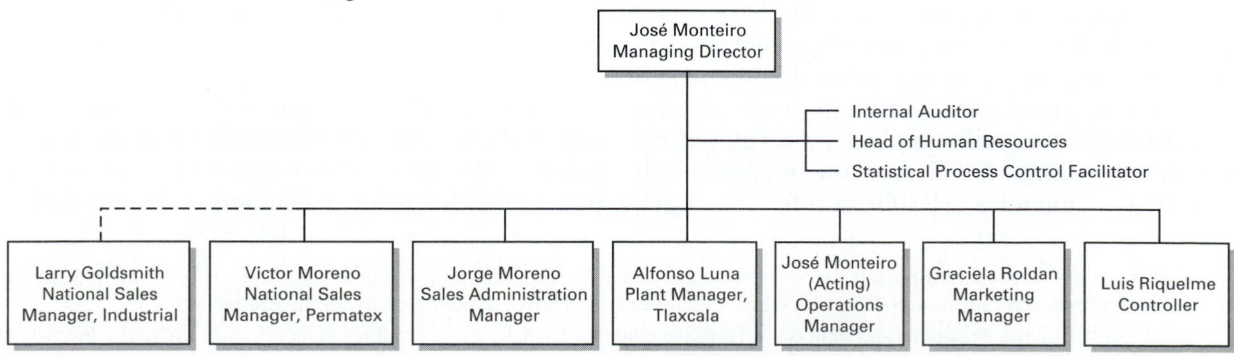

GTE Corporation: Long-term Incentive Plan

In May 1990, the Corporate Compensation Department at GTE Corporation was given the task of evaluating the company's long-term incentive compensation plan. The three major objectives for which the plan was originally implemented were as follows:

- It should motivate managers to think long-term.
- It should promote teamwork among GTE's top executives.
- It should link upper management's compensation with the returns realized by GTE stockholders.

The task was to evaluate the plan, study its current competitiveness, and recommend changes if any were warranted. The plan had been in place for four years and would be up for renewal by the company's stockholders next year.

THE COMPANY

GTE Corporation was a large communications company headquartered in Stamford, Connecticut. (Summary financial figures are shown in Exhibits 1 and 2.) GTE's three main businesses were local telephone service (72 percent of total 1989 revenues of $17.4 billion), telecommunications products and services (16 percent), and lighting and electrical products (12 percent). These three main businesses were organized into seven business groups. The largest business group, Telephone Operations, provided local phone service in parts of Texas, Southern California, Hawaii, the Midwest, Southeast, and Northwest regions of the United States, and in Canada and the Dominican Republic. Unlike long-distance telephone service, which had largely been deregulated and opened up to competition in the United States, local telephone service was still supplied by regulated regional monopolies. GTE, and the regional Bell operating companies (RBOCs)—for example, Ameritech, Bell Atlantic, Nynex, Pacific Telesis, and Southwestern Bell—were the major suppliers of local telephone service in the United States.

While good growth was still expected in the local telephone service market, the Telephone Operations group was also expanding into faster growing, less regulated markets for data communications, high speed digital networks, and large corporate communications systems. It also had an interest in moving into cable television and information services as government regulation of those businesses began to change.

GTE's next largest business group, Electrical Products, manufactured lighting products, including household light bulbs, auto headlamps, and specialized commercial and industrial lighting. The group also contained GTE's Precision Materials unit which made materials for GTE's lighting and communications products as well as specialized materials for the metal cutting, automotive and electronics industries.

In addition to these two major groups, GTE produced a variety of telecommunications products and services in five other smaller operating groups:

OPERATING GROUP	PRODUCT
Mobile Communications	cellular phone service
Government Systems	military communications
Information Services	Yellow Pages and software
Spacenet	satellite services
AG Communications Systems	new switching technologies

The cellular communications industry was one of the fastest growing industries in the United States, and GTE Mobile Communications was experiencing that growth. (Summary financial infor-

Research Associate Eric D. Beinhocker prepared this case under the supervision of Professor Kenneth A. Merchant as the basis for class discussion rather than to illustrate either effective or ineffective handling of an administrative situation.

mation about the business groups is shown in Exhibit 2.)

GTE has 155,000 employees and operated subsidiaries in 41 countries. However, all of its major operating groups were headquartered in the United States, and domestic sales accounted for 83 percent of the company's total sales in 1989.

INCENTIVE COMPENSATION PACKAGE FOR MANAGERS

GTE offered some of its managers one or both of two major incentive plans: a short-term plan called the Executive Incentive Plan (EIP), and a long-term plan called the Long-Term Incentive Plan (LTIP). The company's top 1,107 managers were eligible for the EIP, and the top 34 executives were eligible for both the EIP and the LTIP.

Eligibility for the incentive compensation plans was determined both by an individual's organization level and type of responsibilities. People with line responsibilities who had a clear impact on performance were more likely to be included in an incentive plan than were their staff peers. Thus a manager of a small manufacturing plant might be eligible for the EIP, while a mid-level member of corporate staff might not be. The 34 managers included in the LTIP were business group presidents, major staff heads, or "other employees of outstanding abilities and specialized skills" who were judged to have a significant effect on long-term corporate performance.

Base salaries of the managers included in the incentive compensation plans were generally below competitive levels. However, GTE's management believed that its total compensation packages, salaries plus incentives, were competitive.

EXECUTIVE INCENTIVE PLAN (EIP)

The EIP provided an annual award which could be comprised of cash, GTE common stock, or both, although to date the company had only given cash awards. The normal annual incentive value varied with the mid-point salary of each manager's job grade. The normal incentive value for the lowest-level included in the EIP (the manager of a small plant) was 20 percent of mid-point salary; it was 43 percent for an upper level operating unit executive, and 66 percent for the chief executive officer. This relationship between job grades and award sizes is illustrated in Exhibit 3.

The EIP awards were based on the accomplishment of annual objectives set at the beginning of the year through discussions with each manager's two immediate supervisors. Objectives could be either quantitative (e.g., sales, profits) or qualitative (e.g., accomplishment of a development program milestone), but each objective was intended to be precisely stated, with clear indicators as to whether it was achieved. (Exhibit 4 presents some examples of good objective statements.)

Generally the objectives were for performances in areas for which the individual was both directly responsible and had measurable impact. But some managers who were members of various groups which had to work together shared some common objectives, such as regional sales targets or accomplishment of a project requiring cross-organizational cooperation.

Evaluations were made on a scale from 50 to 150 percent of normal performance at the end of the year by each individual's two immediate superiors. (Starting in 1990 the range was expanded to a maximum of 200 percent of norm.) Normal performance was the level where all objectives were satisfactorily met, although objectives were generally stretched in nature.

In a typical year, operating under the former 50 to 150 percent range, the average achievement level of EIP objectives across GTE was 120 percent of norm. In a good year the average performance could be fairly high: it was 130 percent in 1989, for example. A corporate manager noted that:

> The goals are set such that doing 100 percent represents an acceptable job, so if you are below 100 percent some significant objectives have not been achieved, and if you're above 100 percent you're doing well. I think that an average performance level above 100 percent is evidence that the plan is working. It is pushing people to do more than just what is acceptable.

Individual performances prior to 1990 spanned the entire range from below 50 to 150 percent. Business unit averages, however, tended to be concentrated between 110 percent and 140 percent. The EIP awards were directly linked to the performance rating, as is shown in the example presented in Exhibit 5.

The Executive Compensation Committee of the Board of Directors had the final responsibility for allocating EIP incentive awards. Generally no incentives would be authorized if GTE's overall return on equity (ROE) failed to exceed 8 percent, and the total incentive pool was not allowed to exceed 5 percent of the company's consolidated net income. The committee was allowed to make adjustments for any unusual or exogenous factors affecting performance, however.

HISTORY OF LONG-TERM INCENTIVES AT GTE

GTE's current LTIP was the third form of a long-term incentive plan the company had used. From the early 1960s to 1972, GTE offered a few senior managers a stock option plan that was typical for plans at that time—it only included a few top-level managers and the awards were small.

In 1972 the company replaced the stock option plan with a Performance Share Plan which included 300 managers (down to the group staff level). Incentive awards were *phantom GTE shares.* The shares were assigned based on performance over three-year performance cycles. But this plan was judged not to be successful because few managers understood the plan. It was dropped after 1978, with the final award cycle paying out in 1981.

The current LTIP was established in 1981 as one response to changes in the domestic communications market—deregulation and increased competition. The plan was intended to encourage a select group of upper level executives—the top 34 managers in the company—to make decisions that would have a favorable long-term impact on overall company performance. The LTIP awards were designed to be distinct from the EIP in that they were based on meeting long-term (multi-year) *corporate* objectives, rather than short-term (annual) *individual* objectives.

To prevent a gap between plans where participants would go two years without an award until the first cycle was complete, the new plan initially paid out awards for two shortened performance cycles: 1987 was paid at 40 percent of a full-three year award, and 1987–88 was paid at 70 percent. The first full three-year cycle was 1987–1989.

THE LTIP IN 1990

The LTIP had two components: a stock option plan to encourage stock ownership by senior managers, and a performance bonus program to reward participants based on long-term overall corporate performance.

Stock options were granted annually at the beginning of an award cycle to LTIP participants. The number of options to be granted was calculated by multiplying the mid-point of the salary range for an individual's job grade times a multiple set by the Board's Compensation Committee and then dividing by GTE's average stock price for the prior week. (Exhibit 6 shows a sample calculation.)

The multiples used in the above calculation were reviewed annually by the Board's Compensation Committee. The recommended multiples for 1990 ranged from 1.20 for the lowest level participants in the plan (a vice president in one of the two main operating groups) to 2.75 for the company's chief executive officer. These multiples were based on an analysis of comparable company stock option plans. In 1988 GTE hired two well-known compensation consulting firms to analyze competitive practices and report back to help it in planning for the cycle starting in 1990. The study compared GTE's option awards for senior managers against 45 similar sized (as measured by number of employees) companies, and against GTE's five major competitors (the RBOCs). The study concluded that GTE substantially needed to raise its level of option awards for 1990, particularly for the company's most senior LTIP participants.

The options vested at the end of the three-year cycle and expired at the end of the tenth year. The exercise price of the option was the average of the high and low of GTE's stock price on the day of grant.

One traditional problem with stock options is that recipients often need to commit substantial personal capital to exercise them. Despite an increase in the value of the underlying stock and a guaranteed profit by exercising, recipients often have to sell assets or borrow to purchase the stock. To alleviate the cash squeeze, GTE offered its executives two ways to realize the profit in their options without paying for the stock in cash. One was a *stock swap* procedure which allowed participants to pay for their new shares with previously owned shares of GTE stock (without first selling them and thus incurring capital gains taxes). The second was a *Stock Appreciation Right* (SAR) which was given with each option and allowed participants to simply surrender the option and receive payment for the gain in the value of GTE stock during the period. Normally, half the payment would be made in GTE stock and the other half in cash. (Exhibit 7 shows examples of how each of these methods was implemented).

PERFORMANCE BONUS

The second component of the LTIP was a Performance Bonus which provided cash awards based on achievement of targets for corporate ROE and shareholder returns (changes in stock price plus dividends). On the same day that options were granted at the beginning of each three-year award cycle, each participant was granted a *maximum performance bonus opportunity* for the coming three-year period. This *maximum performance bonus opportunity* was a multiple of the mid-point of each participant's salary range.

The Board would then set performance criteria for the award cycle consisting of maximum and minimum average return on equity targets. If the maximum ROE target was achieved, 100 percent of the *maximum performance bonus opportunity* would be awarded. If the minimum was achieved, 20 percent would be awarded. Below the minimum no award was made.

In addition, if the maximum target was exceeded, an *over-achievement* award was granted of 2 to 3 percent of the maximum performance bonus opportunity was added for each .1 percent by which actual ROE exceeded the maximum target. (This function is illustrated in Exhibit 8).

The corporate ROE targets set for the LTIP were based on several factors. The company began with the ROE forecast in its strategic plan, and then looked to outside measures to insure that the target, if achieved, would make GTE a top-performing company as compared with the ROEs of its competitors, the S&P 500, and a group of companies that GTE management believed were viewed by the public and the media as *world class.* For the 1989–1991 cycle the ROE target range was from 12.5 to 16.5 percent, but GTE's performance had improved so much that actual performance promised to exceed the upper end of the range. Actual 1989 ROE was 17.0 percent and GTE's Chairman, James L. (Rocky) Johnson, had publicly stated that he expected the company to be able to raise its ROE to 20 percent within the next few years.

Performance Bonus awards were made in the form of *stock equivalent units.* Awards were determined on completion of an award cycle as follows: a dollar figure would be determined by multiplying the *maximum award bonus opportunity* percentage times the midpoint of the individual's base salary range at the start of the three-year award cycle. This dollar figure would then be multiplied by a percentage reflecting the position of the actual average ROE within the maximum/minimum range. The result would then be divided by the price of GTE common stock at the start of the cycle. This would determine the *initial grant* of stock equivalent units (a number of fictitious GTE shares), and then additional units would be added to the initial grant to reflect dividend payments over the three-year cycle. Finally, at the end of the three-year period the total accumulated units (initial grant plus dividends) would be converted to cash at the then current GTE stock price. (Exhibit 9 shows a sample calculation.)

According to the corporate executives, this system effectively tied long-term bonus compensation to changes in shareholder value. Executives could both benefit from and be penalized for changes in ROE, dividend payments, and stock price appreciation (or depreciation).

The Executive Compensation Committee was given some discretionary power to adjust LTIP awards for changes in ROE that were not necessarily connected to long-term changes in shareholder value. For example, in 1990 the company instituted a large employee stock ownership plan (ESOP) that had a significant positive impact on ROE. The committee adjusted the LTIP ROE target to offset the effect of this nonoperating effect.

When the LTIP was first implemented, awards were based on five-year cumulative earnings per share (EPS). Subsequently, the Compensation Committee of the Board of Directors decided that for plans starting after 1987 LTIP awards would be based on three-year average return on equity (ROE), rather than five-year cumulative EPS. GTE's controller described why this substitution was made.

> Over a multiyear period, ROE is the best measure of company performance—it is most highly correlated with stock price performance. If you're generating a good ROE, you must be doing a lot of things right; getting customers, maintaining quality, making sure the business is healthy. EPS is a more short-term measure. If your EPS exceeds analysts' expectations, your stock price rises, but you may not have changed the fundamentals of the business.

The LTIP was intended to provide expected rewards that were slightly larger than those provided by the EIP. But the values of stock- and option-based rewards are difficult to estimate. GTE had conducted two seminars in the prior seven years to teach managers how to value and exercise options in hopes they would understand how lucrative the LTIP could be.

Exhibit 10 shows a comparison of rewards provided to GTE's five most highly compensated executives. This exhibit is prepared using one common option-pricing method—the Black-Scholes model.

A REVIEW OF THE PROBLEM

It was important that the company have a successful long-term incentive plan. GTE's president and chief operating officer, a strong supporter of the LTIP, was concerned that the plan was perhaps not having the effect it should have. He had noted that:

> I know people are driven by that short-term [EIP] bonus payment. I can hear its effects, as people mention it in about one out of three phone calls I get during the day from people who work here. I have seen people run through walls to make their targets on that plan. But I don't hear that the long-term plan is having that kind of effect.

The review would have to consider both whether the LTIP was designed correctly and whether its effects were being swamped by the strong short-term incentives provided by the EIP. The corporate compensation group performing the review knew, however, that the correct conclusions might not be supportable with the data existing at the time a recommendation had to be made.

EXHIBIT 1 Summary Consolidated Financial Information ($ millions)

Years Ended December 31	*1989*	*1988*	*1987*	*1986*	*1985*
Revenues and sales	17,424	16,460	15,421	15,112	14,372
Operating income	3,189	3,052	3,153	3,238	3,201
Net income applicable to common stock	1,370	1,177	1,082	1,153	(198)
Earnings per common share	$4.16	$3.58	$3.29	$3.53	$(.63)
Dividends per common share	2.80	2.60	2.48	2.20	2.08
Return on common equity	17.0%	14.8%	14.0%	15.9%	(2.6)%
Common stock price:					
High	71½	45⅞	44¾	44½	30⅞
Low	42⅞	33¾	29⅜	30⅛	25⅜

Source: GTE Corporation 1989 Annual Report

EXHIBIT 2 Summary Financial Information for Major Business Groups ($ millions)

Years Ended December 31	*1989*	*1988*	*1987*	*CAGR*[a] *1984–89*
Telephone Operations				
Revenues	12,459	11,686	11,158	6.2%
Operating income	2,839	2,718	2,879	2.0
Identifiable assets	25,346	24,252	22,946	4.8
Electrical Products				
Sales	2,184	2,237	2,129	3.3%
Operating income	222	228	222	1.0
Identifiable assets	2,209	2,075	2,090	12.6
Telecommunications Products and Services[b]				
Revenues	2,838	2,597	2,210	4.6%
Operating income	128	196	52	18.8
Identifiable assets	3,368	3,228	2,749	3.0

Source: GTE Corporation 1990 Annual Report

[a]Compound annual growth rate

[b]Consolidated results for A G Communications, Government Systems, Mobile Communications, Information Services, and Spacenet

EXHIBIT 3 Normal EIP Award as a Percentage of Mid-Point Salary

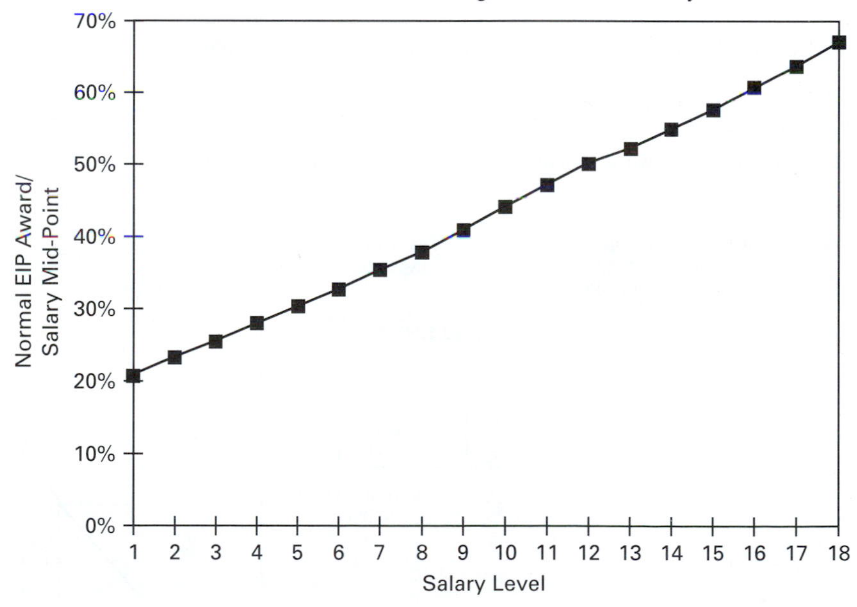

EXHIBIT 4 Examples of Well-Written EIP Objectives

Statement	Measure of Achievement
1. Reduce annual budgeted (specific project or department) cost by at least $1 million by December, 199_.	Year end expense statement
2. Ensure continuity of capable management by establishment of a program to identify, motivate and train superior executive talent. In place by October, 199_.	Program set up and participants identified
3. Restructure organization to reduce executives proposed reporting to (specific unit head) to six by July, 199_.	New organization structure functioning as intended
4. Have (specific) manufacturing facility in production by June 199_.	Plant operating
5. Increase sales of (specific product) through revamped advertising approach implemented by April, 199_.	Sales increase by X% by December, 199_
6. Implement (specific development program) responding to future energy conservation requirements by August, 199_.	Program in place
7. Reduce (specific) product reject rate to X% in 199_.	Documented at year end
8. Complete integration of management systems of newly acquired subsidiary into (specific) management structure by end of year.	Documented integration
9. Complete franchise agreements with (specific) target organizations by December, 199_.	Agreements completed
10. Hire five MBA's for managerial training program by December, 199_.	Quota hired

EXHIBIT 5 Sample EIP Award Calculation for a Senior Group Manager

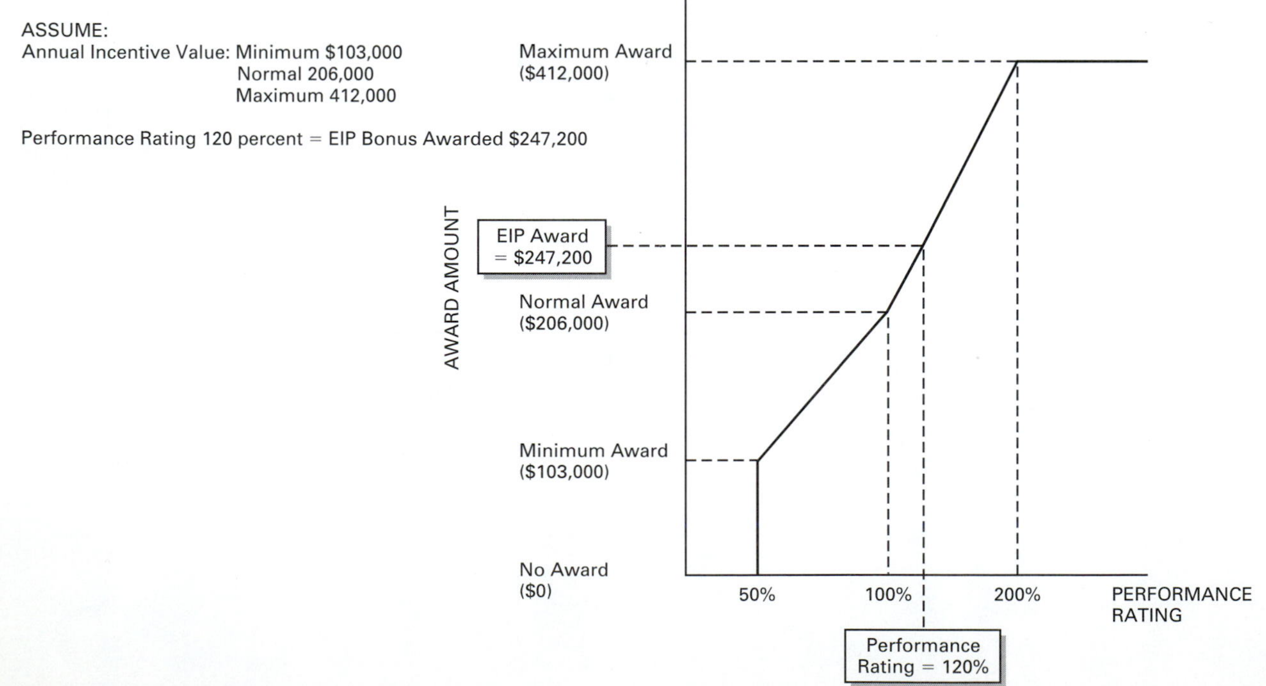

EXHIBIT 6 Sample Calculation of LTIP Stock Option Award for Chief Executive Officer

Mid-point of salary range: $740,000
Award multiple set by Board of Directors Executive Compensation Committee: 2.75
$740,000 × 2.75 = $2,035,000
Average of prior week high and low of GTE common stock price: $64.625
Size of grant = 2,035,000 + 64.625 = 31,489 option shares
Exercise price = last day average price of GTE stock = $66.25

EXHIBIT 7 Example of Stock Swap and Use of Stock Appreciation Right (SAR)

Stock Swap

Participant already owns a number of GTE shares at a current market price $70 per share. In addition, the participant has vested options for 5,700 shares at an exercise price of $33.2083 per share. In order to exercise the 5,700 options, the participant surrenders (or "swaps") 2,704 of the shares he or she already owns:

Option price		No. of options being exercised		Total payment required
$33.2083	×	5,700	=	$189,287.50
Payment amount		GTE stock price		Shares surrendered
$189,287.50	+	$70	=	2,704

Shares received from exercise of options = 5,700

The stock swap allows the participants to receive shares from the option without incurring capital gains taxes or transaction fees from the sale of previously owned stock.

Stock Appreciation Right (SAR)

Initial grant: 4,900 option shares
Exercise price: $46 per share
Stock price at vesting (end of third year): $54.48 per share
Stock appreciation: $8.48 per share
SAR value: 4,900 shares × $8.48 per share = $41,500

Award given upon exercise of SAR:

$41,500 + 2 = $20,750 in cash

plus

$20,750 + current stock price $54.48 = 381 shares of GTE stock

EXHIBIT 8 LTIP Over-Achiever Award

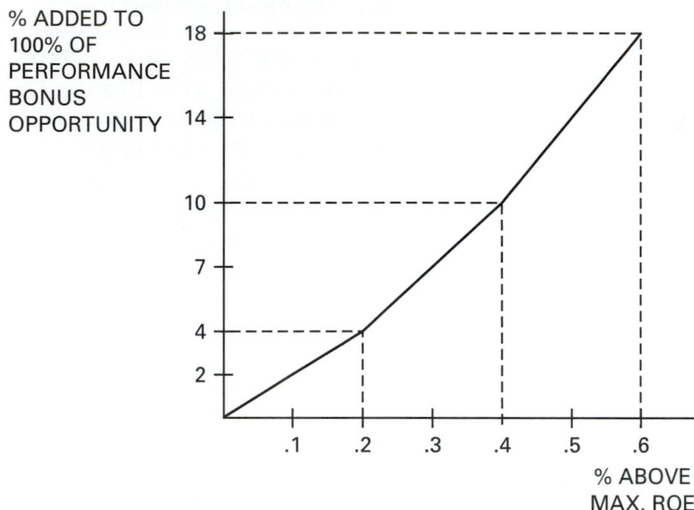

EXHIBIT 9 Sample Calculation of LTIP Performance Bonus for a Senior Staff Executive

"Maximum Award Bonus Opportunity" percentage set by the Board of Directors Executive Compensation Committee: 25%

Mid-point of salary range: $195,000

.25 × 195,000 = $48,750 = "Maximum Award Bonus Opportunity"

Three-year average ROE targets:
- Maximum: 16.5% (100% of maximum award)
- Minimum: 12.5% (20% of maximum award)

Actual average ROE achieved during cycle: 15.5% (80% of maximum award)

48,750 × .80 = $39,000

The award is then converted into stock equivalent units at the price of GTE common stock at the beginning of the three-year cycle:

Stock price at beginning of cycle: $48.75

39,000 ÷ 48.75 = 800 stock eqivalent units granted

Additional units purchased over the three-year cycle with dividends = 172.2

800 + 172.2 = 972.2 total accumulated units

The stock equivalent units are then converted back into cash at the GTE common stock price at the end of the cycle:

Stock price at the end of the cycle: $54.50

972.2 units × $54.50 = cash Performance Bonus awarded to participant

EXHIBIT 10 Actual LTIP Awards: GTE's Five Most Highly Compensated Executives

	1989	%	*1988*	%	*1987*	%
James L. Johnson, Chairman and CEO						
Salary plus EIP bonus	$1,410,503	66.4	$1,113,523	75.4	$790,239	86.6
Stock options granted	42,400		35,500		18,200	
Estimated value of options[a]	$474,244	22.3	$215,308	14.6	$58,386	6.4
Performance bonus[b]	239,000	11.3	148,300	10.0	63,900	7.0
Total Compensation	**$2,123,747**	**100.0**	**$1,477,131**	**100.0**	**$912,525**	**100.0**
Charles R. Lee, President and COO						
Salary plus EIP bonus	$934,035	66.3	$540,512	76.6	[c]	na
Stock options granted	30,300		15,500		10,300	
Estimated value of options[a]	$338,906	24.0	$94,008	13.3	$33,042	na
Performance bonus[b]	136,800	9.7	71,000	10.1	34,100	na
Total Compensation	**$1,409,741**	**100.0**	**$705,520**	**100.0**	**na**	**na**
Edward C. Schmults, Senior VP, External Affairs, General Counsel						
Salary plus EIP bonus	$593, 184	68.6	$533,950	76.4	$488,269	87.9
Stock options granted	14,700		15,500		10,300	
Estimated value of options[a]	$164,420	19.0	$94,008	13.4	$33,042	5.9
Performance bonus[b]	106,500	12.3	71,000	10.2	34,100	6.1
Total Compensation	**$864,104**	**100.0**	**$698,958**	**100.0**	**$555,411**	**100.0**
Bruce Carswell, Senior VP, Human Resources and Administration						
Salary plus EIP bonus	$559,923	68.0	[c]	na	[c]	na
Stock options granted	14,700		13,300		8,800	
Estimated value of options[a]	$164,420	20.0	$80,665	na	$28,230	na
Performance bonus[b]	98,800	12.0	63,000	na	30,200	na
Total Compensation	**$823,143**	**100.0**	**na**	**na**	**na**	**na**
Nicholas L. Trivisonno, Senior VP, Finance						
Salary plus EIP bonus	$565,054	77.5	[c]	na	[d]	na
Stock options granted	14,700		11,600		[d]	
Estimated value of options[a]	$164,420	22.5	$70,354	na	na	na
Performance bonus[b]	[d]	0.0	[d]	na	[d]	na
Total Compensation	**$729,474**	**100.0**	**na**	**na**	**na**	**na**

Source: All data, with the exception of the option value estimates, are from GTE Corporation proxy statements, 1988–1989.

[a]Estimated values are for the day of grant, which is assumed to be the last business day of February following the year for which the shares are granted. Calculated using the Black-Scholes option pricing model with the following assumptions: 1. Option price is the stock price on the date of grant; 2. The risk-free rate is the ten-year U.S. Treasury yield on the date of grant; 3. The instantaneous variance is .061, which was estimated using publicly traded GTE call option prices; 4. Dividends are accounted for by subtracting the present value of estimated future dividends from the stock price on the date of grant.

[b]Performance bonuses are for the cycles 1987–89, 1984–88, 1983–87.

[c]Not available from proxy statements.

[d]Mr. Trivisonno joined GTE in 1988.

Section IV: Common Problem Areas in Financial-Results Control

CHAPTER 12

Accounting Performance Measures and the Myopia Problem

The primary objective of profit-making organizations is to maximize shareholder (or owner) value. Thus, the results-control ideal would be to measure the value created by each employee. Because direct measurement of value creation is rarely possible, most firms base their managerial-level results controls on accounting measures of performance; that is, accounting profits and returns and their components (revenues, costs, assets, and liabilities). Earlier chapters (particularly Chapter 8) have discussed the reasons why accounting measures of performance are in such common use. It must be recognized, though, that even the best accounting measures are not perfect; they are only surrogate indicators of changes in shareholder values.

The use of accounting performance measures as surrogate indicators of changes in values creates some significant control problems. Most corporate managers are well aware of these problems, but they choose to use the accounting measures anyway because of the advantages these measures provide. This chapter and the following chapters describe four of the most significant problems and how they can be solved, or at least alleviated. The first problem discussed in this chapter is a potentially severe behavioral displacement problem; a tendency for accounting performance measures to make managers excessively short-term oriented, or myopic. The second problem, discussed in Chapter 13, is suboptimization, another form of behavioral displacement caused particularly by the use of ROI-type measures. The third, discussed in Chapter 14, is the problem of dealing with the effects on performance measures of events which managers cannot completely control. The final problem, discussed in Chapter 15, is that of pricing goods and services transferred internally.

VALUE CREATION: THE PRIMARY GOAL OF FOR-PROFIT ORGANIZATIONS

It is generally agreed that the primary objective of for-profit organizations is to *maximize the value of the firm* (or ownership wealth), subject to some constraints, such as compliance with laws and adequate concern for employees, customers, and other stakeholders.[1] Value is a basic economic concept which is calculated by discounting future cash flows:

$$\text{Value} = \frac{C_1}{(1 + r_1)} + \frac{C_2}{(1 + r_2)^2} + \frac{C_3}{(1 + r_3)^3} + \cdots$$

The *C*s represent cash flows in future periods, out to an infinite horizon. The *r* (discount factor) should reflect the time value of money (generally considered to be approximately 3 percent per year), the changing size of the monetary unit (inflation), and risk. For any entity, these three factors combined should equal the cost of capital the entity would face if it were free-standing (that is, not part of the larger organization). For entities with greater business risks (uncertain environments) and greater financial risks (greater proportion of debt financing), *r* should be higher.

Participants in virtually all financial markets use the value formula in pricing the assets in which they trade. A basic premise in finance, which is supported by considerable evidence, is that the total value of any publicly-held corporation's common stock is equal to the discounted value of that portion of the corporation's expected future cash flows which will be paid to the owners of the existing stock outstanding.[2]

The value formula is important for management control purposes because it indicates that employees can increase the value of the entity in which they work by increasing the size of the future cash flows, by accelerating the receipt of those cash flows, or by making them more certain (less risky). The change in value over any given period is called *economic income.* An alternative way of phrasing the basic corporate financial objective is *maximization of economic income,* not *accounting income* (revenues less expenses, both as defined by accountants).

Managers in profit-seeking organizations should act to maximize value. Those who do not will cause their firms to lag behind their effectively run competitors and, in competitive markets, to fail. Sometimes shareholders have filed lawsuits to force managers to consider value maximization more centrally in making decisions. Time Warner withdrew a rights offering after shareholders sued the company. After the deal, a senior vice president of a fiduciary for one million Time Warner shares, commented, "We hope this is the first step of management recognizing that the company has to be run with an eye to shareholder value."[3]

NEAR-PERFECT INDICATORS OF VALUE CREATION

Many people believe the results-control ideal is to hold all employees accountable for the wealth they individually create (or destroy) for the owners of the entities in which they work. John Rutledge, chairman of Rutledge & Company, a Greenwich Connecticut-based merchant bank, wrote:

> Shareholders get paid when managers create equity value, not when managers check off items on to-do lists. To align manager interests with owner interests, pay managers the same way shareholders are paid.[4]

Similarly, Sanford I. Weill, CEO of Travelers Group, a diversified financial services company said,

> We've been working for years to get the majority of our employees to hold company stock. [The idea is to get all the employees] to think like owners and build our wealth beyond what we would get in cash compensation.[5]

Many employees are, in fact, held accountable for shareholder returns, or at least its most significant component, changes in the value of the common stock. As was discussed in Chapter 10, corporations employ a variety of compensation plans that link incentive payments to stock price. Stock option and stock performance plans have been in common use for top-level managers for many years. In 1989, PepsiCo became the first company to grant stock options to every employee; the grants were equal to 10 percent of the employee's base salary. By 1996, an estimated 2,000 companies had instituted broad-based stock options plans, those designed to get options into the hands of even lower-level employees.[6]

Stock performance-based rewards should work reasonably well for top management of many publicly traded corporations. For these organizations, the wealth created (returns to shareholders) can be measured directly for any period (yearly, quarterly, or monthly) as the sum of the dividends granted to shareholders in the measurement period plus (or minus) the change in the market value of the stock. Both dividends and stock price changes can be measured precisely and objectively on a timely basis.

Are stock performance-based measures useful indicators of the performances of lower-level employees? Do they have useful motivational value at lower organization levels? In most cases, the answer to both these questions is probably no. Individually, the efforts of virtually all employees below the very top level of management have an infinitesimally small impact on stock prices. As Bob G. Gower, CEO of Houston-based Lyonell Petrochemical Company, a company which once gave all its employees stock options equal to 20 percent of their salary, said:

> So many things can affect stock-price performance that have nothing to do with the individual employee. Employees may actually be de-motivated upon realizing that it can be like a lottery . . . We should only ask employees to control things they can influence, like earnings.[7]

If employees cannot influence stock market valuations, then basing rewards on those valuations will have no affect on the employees' behaviors.

Stock market performance often does not provide a near-perfect measure even of top-level managers' performances. Markets are not always well informed about companies' plans and prospects and, hence, their future cash flows and risks. One reason for this is that companies rightly treat information about R&D productivity, pricing and sourcing strategies, product and process quality, customer satisfaction, and layoff intentions as confidential. If sizable rewards are linked to market valuations, however, managers might be tempted to disclose this information publicly to affect valuations, even if the early disclosures could be harmful to their company. Market measures also contain significant *noise* that makes it difficult to perceive their *signal* regarding managerial performance. Stock market valuations are affected by many factors the managers cannot control (recessions, interest rate changes, rumors) that obscure the information they provide about corporations' and managers' performances. (Methods of making adjustments for the effects of some of these uncontrollable factors are discussed in Chapter 14).

Sometimes other (nonstock market-based) near-perfect indicators of value creation can be found and used for result control purposes at organization levels below that of top managers. The value created by individuals in any given role may be largely derived from a single performance element (or just a few elements). For employees assembling units on a production line, the volume of good units assembled may be an excellent indicator of (highly correlated with) the value these employees create for the organization (if quality can be assumed to be constant). For sales personnel, sales generated may be a good measure of value created (in those situations where all monetary units of sales are approximately equally profitable).

For most employees below the very top management levels it is not possible to measure directly the values they create in any given measurement period. Measuring directly the value created by middle-level managers would require estimates of uncertain and distant future cash flows; therefore, these measures would be far from precise. Direct measures of economic income are also not always objective because the individual most knowledgeable about the setting, and thus in the best position to make the cash flow estimates, is usually the individual whose performance is being evaluated. These significant failures on the precision and objectivity measurement criteria cause organizations to look for surrogate measures of performance. At middle, general management levels, accounting measures, specifically accounting profits and returns, are the most important surrogates used.

ACCOUNTING PROFIT MEASURES AS SURROGATE INDICATORS OF VALUE CREATION

Accounting profits and returns are in widespread use as summary, surrogate indicators of value creation for several important reasons. First, accounting profits and returns can be measured on a timely basis (in short time periods) relatively precisely and objectively.

Timeliness, precision, and objectivity are all important critical measurement qualities. Virtually every individual responds better to specific, predetermined, short-range targets and prompt performance feedback than to vague exhortations such as "do your best" and to feedback that is delayed by months, and even years. Short-term performance pressure helps ensure that managers do not become sloppy or wasteful, and it stimulates them to be creative because "necessity is the mother of invention."[8] As Charles Knight, the chairman and CEO of Emerson Electric, says, "The 'long term' consists of a sequence of 'short terms'"[9] In other words, poor short-term performance, as indicated by low profits, margins, or returns, is likely to be indicative of poor long-term performance.

Accounting rules for assigning cash inflows and outflows even to very short measurement periods have been set and described in great detail by accounting rule-makers, such as the U.S. Financial Accounting Standards Board (FASB). It is possible to measure accounting profits in short time periods, such as a month, with considerable precision. Because accounting rules exist, different people assigned to measure the profit of an entity for any given period will arrive at approximately the same number. Further, independent auditors provide an objectivity check of the accounting calculations. Objectivity is important when rewards are linked to measures because it eliminates, or at least sharply reduces, the potential for arguments about measurement methods.

Second, as compared with other quantities that can be measured precisely and objectively on a timely basis; such as cash flows, shipments, or sales, accounting measures are relatively *congruent* with the true firm goal of maximization of shareholder value. Accounting profits provide an advantage over cash flows because accounting accruals are designed to provide a better matching of cash inflows and outflows.

The best evidence about the congruence of accounting performance measures is at the corporate level of analysis because actively-traded stock markets with many informed traders, such as the large U.S. stock markets, provide objective assessments of corporate value which can be compared with accounting performance measures. Research studies have consistently shown that the correlations between accounting profits and changes in stock prices are positive.[10]

Third, usually accounting measures can be largely *controlled* by the managers whose performances are being evaluated. The profit performance of a middle-level entity (division or group) is almost certainly more controllable by, and therefore more indicative of the performance of, a middle-level general manager than is the change in the company's stock price. The manager's actions materially affect their entity's profit, but they rarely have a material effect on the overall company's performance and its stock price. Furthermore, accounting profits are not buffeted by some of the uncontrollable factors (for example, interest rates) that make stock prices volatile.[11]

Fourth, accounting measures are *understandable*. Accounting is a standard course in every business school, and managers have used the measures for so long that they are well familiar with what the measures represent and how they can be influenced.

Finally, accounting measures of performance are *inexpensive*. Corporations have to measure and report financial results to outside users, most notably shareholders and creditors. Most managers have followed the advice of pioneer manager Alfred P. Sloan who said, "No other financial principle with which I am acquainted serves better than [accounting] rate of return as an objective aid to business management."[12]

LIMITATIONS OF ACCOUNTING PERFORMANCE MEASURES

Accounting performance measures are far from perfect indicators of value. While the research studies have shown that the correlations between annual profits and stock price changes are positive, the correlations are small. They are far from the 1.0 correlation which would signify a perfect surrogate. The correlations are usually in the range of .20 to .30, depending on the sample of firms being studied."[13] Thus, annual accounting profit measures must be said to be only imperfect surrogates for economic income.

Measurement congruence, the correlations between accounting profits and entity value changes, does increase with the length of the measurement period. One large-sample study found that the correlations between profits and market values for periods of one, two, five, and ten years were, respectively, .22, .39, .57, and .79.[14] These increasingly higher correlations with increasingly longer measurement windows occur primarily because, in general, accounting profits provide a lagged indicator of economic income.[15] When economic income changes, those changes are often reflected only sometime later in the profit measures. How much later depends on both what caused the economic income change and what type of accounting measurement rules are being used.

It is easy to explain why accounting profit measures do not reflect economic income perfectly. Many things affect accounting profits but not economic profits, and vice versa. First, accounting systems are *transactions oriented.* Accounting profit is primarily a summation of the effects of the transactions that took place during a given period. Most changes in value that do not result in a transaction are not recognized in income.

Second, accounting profit (and measures derived from it) is highly dependent on the *choice of measurement method.* Multiple measurement methods are often available to account for identical economic events. Depreciation accounting options, straight-line versus sum-of-the-years digits versus double-declining balance, are one example.

Third, accounting profit is derived from measurement rules that are often *conservatively biased.* Accounting rules require slow recognition of gains and revenues, but quick recognition of expenses and losses.

Fourth, profit calculations *ignore some economic values and value changes* that accountants feel cannot be measured accurately and objectively. Investments in major categories of companies' intangible assets; such as research in progress, human resources, information systems, and customer goodwill, are expensed immediately. These types of assets do not appear on the balance sheet. The omission of intangible assets occurs even though for many companies these types of assets are much more important than the old industrial-era type assets of plant, equipment, and land. The physical assets of Microsoft Corporation are only approximately 10 percent of the company's total market value. Another oft-discussed example of ignored value changes occurs in U.S. firms where profit does not reflect the cost of compensation given in the form of stock options, even though most people agree that the companies granting options bear a real economic cost.

Fifth, profit *ignores the costs of investments in working capital.* Managers sometimes increase their sales and profits by making bad investments in extra inventory, the costs of which do not appear on the income statement.

Sixth, profit reflects the cost of borrowed capital, but *ignores the cost of equity capital.* Firms earn real income only when the returns on capital are greater than the cost of that capital, and ignoring the cost of equity capital overstates the difference between returns and costs (profit). This omission is serious because equity capital is typically more expensive than borrowed capital. In the United States, stock returns have historically been approximately six percentage points higher than returns on long-term government bonds, and the cost of equity capital is even higher for companies with risky (volatile) stocks. Failure to reflect the cost of equity capital also hinders comparisons of the results of companies with different proportions of debt and equity in their capital structures.

Seventh, accounting profit *ignores risk and changes in risk.* Entities that have not changed the pattern or timing of their expected future cash flows but have made the cash flows more certain have increased their economic value. This value change is not reflected in accounting profits.

Finally, profit *focuses on the past.* Economic value is derived from future cash flows, and there is no guarantee that past performance is a reliable indicator of future performance.

The multiple reasons why accounting income and economic income diverge, the lack of congruence of the measures, have caused some critics to make strong statements arguing against the use of accounting performance measures. One stated that, "Paper profits, the yardstick by which stockholders and boards of directors often measure the performance of managements, make no contribution to the material well-being of people anywhere."[16]

Most managers, however, have found that the advantages of accounting profit measures outweigh their limitations, and they continue to use them. They must be aware that motivating general managers to maximize, or at least produce, accounting profits, rather than economic income, can create a number of behavioral displacement problems. *Myopia* is probably the most potentially damaging. Managers whose focus is on accounting profits measured in short periods (months or quarters) tend to be highly concerned with increasing (or maintaining) monthly or quarterly profits (or returns). When managers' orientations to the short-term become excessive, when the managers are more concerned with short-term profits than entity value, the managers are said to be myopic.[17]

INVESTMENT AND OPERATING DECISION MYOPIA

Accounting earnings measures can cause managers to act myopically in making either investing or operating decisions. Holding managers accountable for short-term earnings or returns induces managers to reduce or postpone investments that promise payoffs in future measurement periods, even when those investments clearly have a positive net present value. This is *investment myopia.*

Investment myopia stems directly from two of the problems on the list of problems with accounting performance measures described earlier: accounting numbers' conservative bias and their ignoring of changes in the values of intangible assets. Accounting rules do not allow firms to recognize gains until they are realized, meaning the critical income-producing activities (such as a "sale") have taken place and the earnings can be measured in an objective, verifiable way. The rules require firms to begin recognizing costs when the investments are made. The understatement of earnings in early measurement periods is magnified because accounting rules are purposely conservative. Projects with uncertain returns and little liquidation value, such as research and development projects and employee training, must be expensed as the costs are incurred, and capital investments must be expensed over periods that are typically shorter than those in which returns will be realized.

The motivational effect of these measurement rules is perverse because managers who are motivated to produce accounting earnings can (in the short term) do so by *not* making investments, even clearly excellent ones. By not making the investments, they reduce expenses in the current period and do not suffer the lost revenue until future periods.

Managers can also boost period earnings by destroying goodwill that has been built up with customers, suppliers, employees, or society at large. They can force employees to work excessive overtime at the end of a measurement period to finish production so that the product can be shipped and revenues and profit can be reported. If the product is of lower quality, customer satisfaction (and future sales) may diminish; the costs of field repairs or customer returns may have to be borne; and some employees may be demotivated and tempted to leave. This is an example of *operating decision myopia.*

Every business has a potential myopia problem. Investment myopia occurs only in businesses where investments are being made in the future, but operating decision myopia is a potential problem for all businesses, even those with seemingly short operating horizons. Managers of hamburger stands who are focused on short-term accounting profits may be tempted to scrimp on the meat they put in their hamburgers. Scrimping in this way will improve the current month's profits because food expenses will be lower, but future profits may well be lower because at least some customers will notice the reduced product quality and will not return. Similarly, newspaper publishers can increase short-term profits by cutting reporting and editorial expenses, but if the cuts affect newspaper quality significantly, the readership base (and profits over the longer term) will shrink. Any business can treat customers in an insensitive manner, such as by refusing to refund money when the product sold does not meet expectations. Such actions, however, will harm future performance if these customers shift their business to a competitor.

ADDRESSING THE MYOPIA PROBLEMS

Two steps must be taken to address the myopia problems effectively. First, managers, particularly top-level managers, must be made to understand how the stock market reacts to earnings announcements. Many managers believe that the stock market reacts forcefully to every public earnings announcement, even quarterly disclosures. A survey of 100 chief executive officers of major corporations found that 89 agreed that America's competitive edge has been dulled by its failure to emphasize long-term investments, and 92 percent of this group believed that the stock market's preoccupation with quarterly earnings was the cause.[18] Because of this belief, the managers take steps to try to maintain a smooth, steady earnings growth pattern.

Most research studies, however, show that the stock market is not short-term oriented. Its valuations are based to a large extent on investors' collective judgments of the company's future cash flows and risk, on to an infinite horizon. One recent study found that typically 80 to 90 percent of stock values were attributable to expected cash flows paid out in the form of dividends beyond a five-year horizon.[19] Another study of 634 strategic announcements, including investments in research and development and future joint ventures, found that the market rewards such long-term initiatives.[20] Stock increased in value when the investments were made public.

Easy-to-understand interpretations of these results are finding their way into the popular business press. Here are some representative quotations from authors who have examined the empirical evidence. The first, by an accounting professor, appeared in *the New York Times;* the second and third, from management consultants, appeared in popular business publications; the fourth, written by one of its writers, appeared in *Fortune* magazine:

- If management announces the right decisions, the market tends to reward it based on what the long-term impacts on earnings will be, even though the short-run effects on profits may be poor.[21]
- The stock market sends a clear message that earnings per share is not the most important measure . . . What matters is long-term cash generation. That's what drives long-term stock performance . . .[22]
- Stock market prices . . . are driven by a company's long-term prospects, not its short-term outlook.[23]
- It's pretty clear that investors evaluate companies—big, small, old, new—not on the basis of reported earnings but on expected cash flows.[24]

These writings may be changing managers' beliefs about the lack of value of *managing* short-term earnings.

To have the will to address the myopia problem, top-level managers, particularly, must understand that the stock market is not myopic. Without that understanding, they will actually encourage their subordinates to act myopically, in the mistaken belief that the higher short-term earnings will prop up the company's stock price.

When managers learn that the stock market's horizon is relatively long, then they can consider implementing one or more devices that can offset the tendencies of the accounting-profit measures they use to cause myopia. Critics have been writing about the myopia problem and problems with accounting measures of performance for many years.[25] Leading companies have developed and implemented any of six major approaches to reduce the myopia problem. The following sections describe these approaches. None of them is a panacea; each has its advantages and disadvantages, and the advantages and disadvantages vary significantly across situations.

Measure Changes in Shareholder Value Directly

One possibility is to try to measure economic income itself by estimating future cash flow and discounting them to a present value. This calculation can be made for an entity at the beginning and end of a measurement period. The difference in the beginning and ending values is a direct estimate of economic income.

Most people have a negative first reaction to the idea of measuring economic income directly and then using it in a financial results control system to motivate managers' behaviors. Who knows if the cash flow forecasts will prove to be accurate? As Henry Ford once said, "You can't build a reputation on what you are *going* to do" [emphasis in original].[26] Certainly some measurement difficulties need to be faced, but there are those who believe that measuring changes in shareholder values directly might be workable within usable levels of accuracy in some situations.

Estimating future cash flows and discounting them to a present value is not a new management concept. Most companies have considerable experience in preparing estimates of future cash flows and in reviewing the estimates for reasonableness. Potential cash flows are a standard part of investment and acquisition proposals, and some companies are also experimenting with using discounted cash flow methods for strategic planning of business units.[27] The discounting of cash flow estimates is also an important part of many accounting rules despite the importance accountants place on measurement precision and verifiability. Discounted cash flow concepts are part of the accounting rules for long-term receivables, leases, impairment of long-term assets, and retiree pensions and health care benefits. One of the significant trends in accounting actually seems to be a greater tolerance for this so-called soft, but more relevant, data.

At this point, however, measurement precision and objectivity are still significant stumbling blocks to the use of direct measures of economic income. When rewards are linked to the cash flow estimates, it is likely that managers will be tempted to bias their estimates. These biases could perhaps be controlled by having the estimates prepared, or at least reviewed, by an independent third party, perhaps a consulting firm. To have their work be useful, these outsiders would have to be given access to considerable amounts of information the organization considers sensitive (competitive analyses and marketing plans). The process would undoubtedly be expensive. Nonetheless, if these problems can be overcome, direct estimates of economic income (changes in cash flow potentials) could be given practical use in the MCS.

Use Financial Results Controls for Short-Term Performance; Control Investments with Preaction Reviews

To control investment myopia, some companies (for example, Texas Instruments) find it useful to use financial results controls to control short-term operating performance only. The costs of longer-term investments are considered *below* the income statement line for which the managers are held accountable.

This approach is shown in Table 12-1. Panel A of the figure shows the aggre-

TABLE 12-1 Separating Developmental Investments from Short-Term Operating Performance

Panel A. Standard Income Statement	
Revenues	$100
Expenses	90
Net Income	$ 10
Panel B. Income Statement with Short-Term Operating Performance Isolated	
Revenues	$100
Operating expenses	50
Operating margin	50
Developmental investments	40
Net income	$ 10

gated income statement, perhaps for a profit center. Panel B shows the segregation of short-term (or operating) income from total income. The key to implementing this approach is to distinguish between *operating expenses,* which are necessary to produce the current period's revenue, and *developmental expenses,* which are incurred in order to generate revenues in future periods. If this distinction can be made, the profit center managers are asked to maximize operating income, which provides a good indicator of short-term performance: current period sales and operating efficiency. The managers are asked to propose ideas for developmental investments, those that will produce revenues and profits in future operating periods. The successes from the development expenditures can be monitored with other forms of control, such as preaction reviews of expenditure proposals and monitoring of accomplishments against predefined milestones.

Some companies use variations of this approach. Many, including Corning Glass, General Electric, and Emerson Electric, do not charge some operating units at all for some development expenses that benefit them. They fund some types of business development at high (such as corporate or division) organization levels until the investments begin to generate revenues in order to cushion lower-level entities' earnings from the impact of the expense. Some corporations have split themselves into what can be called *today* businesses and *tomorrow* businesses. In the today companies, managers are charged with making their businesses lean, efficient, and profitable, while they defend it against competitors. Managers of tomorrow companies are charged with inventing new businesses that will augment or replace the existing today companies. Today companies (operating businesses) are controlled through financial results controls. Tomorrow companies are controlled with a combination of nonfinancial performance indicators and action controls.

This approach of separating and protecting development expenditures has two major limitations. The first is that no clear distinction exists between operating expenditures and development expenditures. Manufacturing process improvements and market development programs will probably provide benefits (cost reductions or additional revenues) in the current and following periods. Consequently, managers have some latitude to incur expenses either above or below the operating margin line, and they can use this latitude to *game* the system. When their entity is performing well in comparison with budget targets, they can choose to fund development expenditures within their operating budget.

Another limitation of this approach to addressing the myopia problem is that it passes final decisions about which development expenditures to fund to a senior management committee. These committee members are almost inevitably less well informed about a specific business's prospects and the desired type and level of funding than is the business unit manager, and the quality of these key resource allocation decisions may be harmed.

Improve the Accounting Profit Measures

Another approach for reducing investment myopia involves changing the measurement rules to make the accounting income measures better, meaning more congruent with economic income. These improvements address one or more of the deviations between accounting income and economic income listed earlier.

Some measurement improvements provide a better matching of revenues and expenses. Companies can choose depreciable lives for fixed assets which are close to the useful economic lives of the assets, not conservatively short, as is typical.[28] Similarly, companies can capitalize all, or at least more, categories of expenditures made for the express purpose of bringing in cash flows (revenues or cost savings) in *future* periods. Capitalization of investments, such as for research and development, advertising and sales promotion, and employee development will provide a better matching of revenues and expenses if the future cash flows (revenues) are forthcoming from these investments (as they should be if the investments are good ones).

Some measurement improvements recognize profits (and losses) more quickly; as soon as they can be measured or estimated, rather than waiting for completion of a transaction. Enron Corporation, which sells or transports 20 percent of the United States' natural gas supply, accelerates its revenue and profit recognition process by booking the discounted present value of future profits from fixed-price gas contracts as soon as the contracts are signed.[29] *Mark-to-market accounting,* which U.S. banks must use to record financial assets held for trading on the balance sheet at their market value rather than their historical cost, causes profits and losses to be recorded when the changes in value are observed, not just when the assets are sold.

Some companies use a form of *current-value accounting* which reflects current (or replacement) values on the balance sheet and current-value depreciation on the income statement. This form of accounting is designed to improve the company's ability to maintain its *productive capacity,* not just its *monetary capital.* In periods of rising prices, companies cannot maintain their productive capacity by paying out their entire GAAP income in dividends. Current-value accounting provides an estimate of the income the company can report after funds have been set aside to maintain productive capacity.

In a variation of market-value accounting, some companies charge depreciation for older assets that, for financial reporting purposes, are considered fully depreciated. These companies' financial measures recognize that these assets, which are in use, still have market values that should be protected and that managers should be given an incentive to replace the assets when the decline in the assets' service potentials warrants the replacement.

Some improvements are designed to reflect the company's entire cost of capital. Companies concerned about this problem include an imputed cost of equity capital on their income statements.

Some accounting-measure improvements are designed primarily to improve the denominator of return-on-investment measures. Some companies put all of their entities' leases on the balance sheet, regardless of whether they qualify under accounting rules as capital leases.

Some of these improvements are consistent with GAAP, and others are not. If the measurement improvements deviate from GAAP, their adoption will cause the performance reports used for control purposes to be different from those prepared for financial reporting purposes, causing an extra expense. The improvements require a third set of financial records, in addition to the financial reporting and tax sets of books, and the added processing cost and possible costs of confusion might not be inconsequential.

Extend the Measurement Horizon (Long-Term Incentive Plans)

Lengthening the period of measurement is another alternative for improving the congruence of the accounting measures of performance. The longer the period of measurement, the more congruent are the accounting measures of performance with economic income (changes in shareholder returns).[30] Annual accounting income is, on average, a better indicator of annual economic income than quarterly accounting income is of quarterly economic income, and three-year accounting income is a better indicator than annual accounting income.

As was discussed in Chapter 11, long-term incentive plans are common, and their use is increasing. These plans come in a variety of forms, but they usually provide rewards either for stock appreciation or for the attainment of three- to six-year performance targets, expressed in terms such as earnings per share or accounting return-on-equity, sales, or assets.

Basing incentives on stock market valuations can lengthen managers' decision-making horizons *if* managers believe that the stock market is forward looking; that it considers performance beyond a quarter or a year, as the evidence surveyed above suggests. Evidence about managers' beliefs is mixed. One study found that basing incentives on stock prices reduced managers' tendencies to cut R&D investment to maintain short-term earnings performance.[31] Another study found that investments in R&D and property, plant, and equipment actually declined for firms adopting stock option plans.[32] Several studies have failed to show that the concentration of stock ownership, in either management or groups that can directly influence management (for example, a family), positively affects capital investment.[33]

The overall performance effects of accounting measure-based long-term incentive plans is also mixed. One study compared a sample of twenty-five firms that had adopted a long-term performance plan between 1971 and 1978 with a matched sample of firms that had not adopted such a plan and found that a significant increase in capital investment followed the plan adoption and that security markets reacted favorably when the adoption of the plan was disclosed publicly.[34] These findings are consistent with the interpretation that implementation of the plans has the desirable effect of lengthening managerial horizons and, hence, of combating management myopia. The findings are also consistent with the interpretation that firms which are performing relatively well and able to make greater capital investments are more likely to implement a long-term incentive plan. A larger sample (204-firm) study of firms that adopted performance plans between 1971 and 1980 found little evidence that capital spending increased following the adoption of a performance plan.[35]

It seems clear that extending the period of measurement can avoid some of the congruence problems of accounting performance measures. To have noticeable positive motivational effects, however, the payoffs must be potentially quite lucrative for the individual, and expensive to the company. Managers' rates for discounting the value of their future, potential rewards tend to be quite high; far in excess of the time value of money. An equal weighting in monetary units (for example, dollars) between the potential payoffs of the long-term and short-term rewards, which many firms' plans seem to approximate, will provide motivational effects that are heavily weighted toward the short-term. To reduce a myopia problem, the rewards based on long-term performance must be much larger than those based on short-term performance.

Another issue to be addressed in designing accounting-based long-term incentive plans is the performance standard. Firms commonly use the numbers included in the long-term strategic plan as the standard, but this practice may drive much of the creative thinking out of strategic planning. It will tend to make managers conservative in their thoughts and aspirations. On the other hand, using a fixed long-term target, such as 30 percent return-on-investment, is not necessarily the answer. Such targets can easily become obsolete and not optimally challenging as economic conditions change.

Measure a Set of *Value Drivers*

Many firms have found it useful to measure a set of *value drivers*. At higher organization levels, the value-driver set typically includes some financial measures of performance and some additional measures of *leading indicators* of value changes. Leading indicators are timely indicators of value changes or measures of the few key aspects of performance which will lead reliably to profits and cash flows in subsequent accounting periods. At lower organization levels, the value driver set may include only nonfinancial performance measures. If the organization tracks the right set of leading indicators and gives them proper importance weightings, then profits do not really have to be measured (for results control purposes). The profits will inevitably follow.

Many measures, most of which are nonfinancial measures, can serve as leading indicators in certain settings. Common examples are market share, backlog (or book-to-bill ratio), growth, new product introductions, new product development lead times, product quality, customer satisfaction, employee morale, personnel development, inventory turnover, bad debt ratios, safety, or the achievement of specific, technical milestones in a development project. New product development is critical at 3M Corporation. Consequently, all 3M divisions are required to have new products account for at least 30 percent of their sales. At Emerson Electric, 10 percent of division (profit-center) managers' bonuses are tied to keeping their plants union-free.[36]

AT&T Corporation distinguishes three categories of value drivers. *Operating value drivers* influence profitability. Examples are indicators of changes in price, product mix, operating efficiency, and tax management. *Investment value drivers* influence invested capital. Examples are days sales outstanding, capacity utilization, inventory turnover, capital expenditures, and investments/divestments. *Financing value drivers* influence the cost of capital. Examples are the company's debt rating and the debt/equity mix. At AT&T, the operating and investment value drivers are controlled by the business units; the financing value drivers are controlled by the corporate treasury.[37]

The value driver sets reflect the economic effects on shareholder value of specific management accomplishments and failures more quickly than do accounting measures. Holding managers accountable for some combination of leading indicators shifts the balance of incentives toward longer-term concerns because it forces the managers to make trade-offs between short-term profits and future profits. To make the value-driver sets effective, managers must carefully consider which leading indicators to use and how the chosen indicators should be weighted, individually and in total.

Kaplan and Norton suggest that at business-unit levels a combination of short-term measures and leading indicators, what they call a *balanced scorecard,* must address four perspectives.[38]

- Customer perspective (How do our customers see us?) (on-time delivery, percent of sales from new products.)
- Internal perspective (What must we excel at?) (cycle time, yield, efficiency.)
- Innovation and learning perspective (Can we continue to improve and create value?) (time to develop next generation, new product introduction versus competition.)
- Financial perspective (How do we look to shareholders?) (operating income, ROE).

The last perspective is primarily short-term oriented, while the first three are leading indicators of future financial performance.

Basing results controls on a set of value drivers can have several advantages. It provides short-term performance pressure, yet reduces the risk of myopia. It links performance measures at all levels of the organization with the organization's overall objectives and strategies. It also limits the number of measures that must be tracked, if a few good measures are chosen to address each of the critical performance dimensions or perspectives.

Value driver sets can also create problems and costs. If the wrong indicators are chosen or if they are not weighted properly in importance, congruence will not improve, and it may actually deteriorate. It is value that managers should be providing, and some organizations' value-driver choices indicators have turned out not to be reliable indicators of future cash flows and profits. A large electronics firm made huge improvements in quality and on-time delivery performance over a three-year period from 1987 to 1990. The outgoing defect rate dropped from 500 to 50 parts per million; yield increased from 26 to 51 percent; and on-time delivery improved from 70 to 96 percent.[39] During the same three-year period, however, the company's financial results showed little improvement, and its stock price at the end of 1990 was approximately one-third of its July 1987 value. The huge operating improvements did not yield improved financial performance, perhaps because customers did not greatly value the improvements, because what the organizational resources consumed was greater than the value of the improvements, and/or because company managers diverted their focus from other, more important, aspects of performance. It is important for managers to understand explicitly and reliably the linkages between each value driver and organizational value to make sure each chosen measure truly is a value driver.

Other problems are also possible. If the same measures are not used in all organizational entities, then the mere choice of measures can lead to perceptions of bias. Undoubtedly performance in some areas will be, or more importantly will be perceived as being, inherently more difficult than in others. Further, if too many indicators are chosen, and some companies evaluate their managers in terms of twenty or more performance measures, the managers can become distracted by the complexity. The attention they devote to any one aspect of performance, including the most important ones, may be lost or diffused. Limiting the number of measures that must be tracked is the primary advantage of the balanced scorecard approach. Balanced scorecards summarize organizations' performances from multiple perspectives in relatively simple, summary reports.

Some measures are also quite expensive to use, particularly if they involve tracking a number of difficult-to-measure quantities. It is expensive to administer customer satisfaction surveys, to employ secret shoppers to evaluate operations from a customer perspective, and to conduct safety audits.

Reduce Pressure for Short-Term Profit

Sometimes the best myopia-avoidance solution seems to be to relax the pressure for short-term profit. Telling certain managers not to worry about short-term profits (or, in many cases, losses) allows the managers to make long-term discretionary investments and reduces their need to take short-term actions which have long-term costs.

The reductions in pressure can be communicated in either of two basic ways. The weighting placed on the annual (or quarterly) profit target can be reduced, perhaps even to zero, while other, longer-term performance indicators, such as market share or technical breakthroughs, are emphasized. At Johnson & Johnson, the large and successful U.S. pharmaceutical company, profits are not directly linked with rewards. David Clare, J&J's president explained:

> Our Company philosophy is to manage for the long term. We do not use short term bonus plans. Salary and bonus reviews are entirely subjective and qualitative and are intended to reward effort and give special recognition to those who have performed uniquely.[40]

Alternatively, the short-term profit targets can be made easier to achieve. Profit targets that are more highly achievable create operating slack which can be used to fund longer-term projects. The danger here is that managers who relax short-term profit pressure risk sloppiness, a loss of concentration on short-term results, without, necessarily, a sharper long-term focus. They must either trust the managers whose pressure is being relaxed or impart the pressure in other ways, such as through timely nonfinancial performance indicators. The advantages of financial control systems are foregone because the cost of the myopia dysfunction is higher than the benefits.

CONCLUSION

The primary goal of managers of for-profit corporations should be to maximize shareholder value, and value is a long-term concept. Short-term accounting profit and return measures provide imperfect, surrogate indicators of value changes. Management myopia, an excessive focus on short-term performance, is an almost inevitable side-effect of the use of financial results control systems built on accounting performance measures.

Myopia can be avoided at top management levels by holding these managers accountable for increasing market valuations. Since corporations have indefinite lives, shares of stock are priced based on the corporation's future cash streams, not just on current-period results. When markets are informed and efficient, managers attempting to maximize long-term cash flows (or earnings) are simultaneously maximizing short-term stock prices.

The task of reducing myopia is more difficult at middle management levels. This chapter described six alternatives which can be used individually or in combination to eliminate or reduce myopia. None of the alternatives is a panacea. Each has advantages and disadvantages, and those advantages and disadvantages vary across settings.

Notes

1. D. L. Wenner and R. W. LeBer, "Managing for Shareholder Value—From Top to Bottom," *Harvard Business Review,* 67, no. 6 (November–December 1989), pp. 2–8; J. L. Treynor, "The Financial Objective in the Widely Held Corporation," *Financial Analysts Journal* (March–April 1981), pp. 68–71.
2. R. Brealey and S. Myers, *Principles of Corporate Finance* (New York: McGraw-Hill, 1984), p. 48.
3. "Time Warner Feels the Force of Shareholder Power," *Business Week* (July 29, 1991), pp. 58–59.
4. J. Rutledge, "Making Managers Think Like Owners," *Business Week* (April 22, 1996), p. 131. This point has also been made by many other authors, including M. C. Jensen and K. J. Murphy, "CEO Incentives—It's Not How Much You Pay But How," *Harvard Business Review* (May/June 1990), pp. 138–153, and G. B. Stewart, "Performance Measurement and Management Incentive Compensation," in J. Stern, G. B. Stewart, and D. Chew, *Corporate Restructuring and Executive Compensation* (Cambridge, Mass.: Ballinger, 1989), pp. 339–346.
5. K. Capell, "Options for Everyone," *Business Week* (July 22, 1996), p. 81.
6. Ibid., p. 80.
7. Ibid., p. 84.
8. K. A. Merchant, *Rewarding Results: Motivating Profit Center Managers* (Boston: Harvard Business School Press, 1989), pp. 52–53.
9. C. F. Knight, "Emerson Electric: Consistent Profits, Consistently," *Harvard Business Review,* 70, no. 1 (January–February 1992), pp. 57–70.
10. B. Lev, "On the Usefulness of Earnings: Lessons and Directions from Two Decades of Empirical Research," *Journal of Accounting Research* (Supplement 1989), pp. 153–192.
11. This point was made by Lambert and Larcker, "An Analysis"; and R. G. Sloan, "Accounting Earnings and Top Executive Compensation," *Journal of Accounting and Economics* 16 (1993) pp. 55–100.
12. A. P. Sloan, Jr., *My Years with General Motors* (Garden City, N.Y.: Doubleday, 1964), p. 140.
13. B. Lev, "On the Usefulness of Earnings: Lessons and Directions from Two Decades of Empirical Research," *Journal of Accounting Research* (Supplement 1989), pp. 153–192.
14. P. D. Easton, T. S. Harris, and J. A. Ohlson, "Accounting Earnings Can Explain Most of Security Returns: The Case of Long Return Intervals," *Journal of Accounting and Economics,* 15, no. 2–3 (June/September, 1992), pp. 119–142.
15. See S. P. Kothari and R. Sloan, "Price-Earnings Lead-Lag Relation and Earnings Response Coefficients," *Journal of Accounting and Economics,* 15, no. 2–3 (June/September 1992), pp. 143–171.
16. G. A. Pall, *Quality Process Management* (Englewood Cliffs, N.J.: Prentice-Hall), p. 44.
17. Many critics have cited evidence of U.S. managers, in particular, acting myopically. For example, R. Jacobsen and D. Aaker, "Myopic Management Behavior with Efficient, but Imperfect, Financial Markets," *Journal of Accounting and Economics,* 16, no. 4 (1993), pp. 383–405; J. C. Stein, "Efficient Capital Markets, Inefficient Firms: A Model of Myopic Investment Behavior," *Quarterly Journal of Economics,* 104, no. 4 (1989), pp. 655–669; M. L. Dertouzous, R. K. Lester, and R. L. Solow, *Made in America: Regaining the Productive Edge* (Cambridge, Mass.: MIT Press, 1988); A. Morita, with E. Reingold and M. Shimonura, *Made in Japan* (New York: Dutton Press, 1986). A survey of U.K. managers also found sig-

nificant evidence of management myopia: M. Ezzamel, S. Lilley and H. Willmott, *Major Survey of Management Practices* (London: CIMA Research Foundation, 1995).

18. Business Bulletin, *Wall Street Journal* (June 12, 1986), p. 1.
19. A. Rappaport, "CFOs and Strategists: Forging a Common Framework," *Harvard Business Review,* 70, no. 3 (May–June 1992), p. 84–91.
20. J. R. Woolridge, "Competitive Decline and Corporate Restructuring: Is A Myopia Stock Market to Blame?" *Journal of Applied Corporate Finance,* 1, no. 1 (Spring 1988), pp. 26–36.
21. William Beaver, accounting professor at Stanford Business School, quoted in S. Greenhouse, "The Folly of Inflating Quarterly Profits," The *New York Times* (March 2, 1986), p. 3–8.
22. D. L. Wenner and R. W. LeBer, "Managing for Shareholder Value—From Top to Bottom," *Harvard Business Review,* 67, no. 6 (November–December 1989), p. 8; J. L. Treynor, "The Financial Objective in the Widely Held Corporation," *Financial Analysts Journal* (March–April 1981), pp. 68–71.
23. A. Rappaport, "CFOs and Strategists: Forging a Common Framework," *Harvard Business Review,* 70, no. 3 (May–June 1992), p. 88.
24. G. Colvin, "Stock Options: For CEO Eyes Only . . . ," *Fortune* (April 4, 1994), p. 16.
25. One of the sharpest, and most widely publicized, critiques of U.S. managers' myopia was by R. H. Hayes and W. J. Abernathy, "Managing Our Way to Economic Decline," *Harvard Business Review,* 58, no. 4 (July–August 1980), pp. 67–77. But many critics had recognized problems with accounting measures of performance well before that. For example, in 1969 J. Dearden ("The Case Against ROI Control," *Harvard Business Review,* 47, no. 3 (May–June 1969), pp. 124–135) observed that "the major problem with setting profit objectives and evaluating performance against those objectives is that one year is often too short a period to evaluate a task as complex as managing a profit center" (p. 133).
26. "Thoughts on the Business of Life." *Forbes* (February 28, 1994), p. 140.
27. A. Rappaport, *Creating Shareholder Value: The New Standard for Business Performance* (New York: The Free Press, 1986).
28. If it is disclosed to the tax authorities, this option can jeopardize the tax deductibility of the depreciation expense, particularly in some non-U.S. jurisdictions.
29. T. Mack, "Hidden Risks," *Forbes* (May 24, 1993), p. 54.
30. For example, F. J. Fabozzi and R. Fonfeder, "Have You Seen Any Good Quarterly Statements Lately?" *Journal of Portfolio Management* (Winter 1983), pp. 71–74.
31. P. Dechow and R. Sloan, "Executive Incentives and the Horizon Problem," *Journal of Accounting and Economics,* 14, no. 1 (1991), pp. 51–89.
32. R. DeFusco, T. Zorn, and R. Johnson, "The Association Between Executive Stock Option Plan Changes and Managerial Decision Making," *Financial Management Review* (Spring 1991), pp. 26–43.
33. C. Hill and S. Snell, "Effects of Ownership Structure and Control on Corporate Productivity," *Academy of Management Journal,* 32, no. 1 (March 1989), pp. 25–46; J. Elliott, "Control, Size, Growth, and Financial Performance in the Firm," *Journal of Financial and Quantitative Analysis,* 7, no. 1 (January 1972), pp. 1309–1320.
34. D. F. Larcker, "The Association between Performance Plan Adoption and Corporate Capital Investment," *Journal of Accounting and Economics,* 5 (1983), pp. 3–30.
35. J. J. Gaver and K. M. Gaver, "The Association Between Performance Plan Adoption and Corporate Capital Investment: A Note," *Journal of Management Accounting Research* 5 (Fall 1993), pp. 145–158.
36. L. Therrien, "A Knight with Thick Armor for IBM," *Business Week* (1993).
37. Presentation by Maureen Tart, AT&T vice president and controller, at The Conference Board 1996 Executive Compensation Seminar called "Successfully Implementing Economic Value Concepts," New York, June 4, 1996.

38. R. S. Kaplan and D. P. Norton, "The Balanced Scorecard—Measures that Drive Performance," *Harvard Business Review* 70, no. 1 (January–February 1992), pp. 71–79; R. S. Kaplan and D. P. Norton, "Putting the Balanced Scorecard to Work," *Harvard Business Review,* 71, no. 5 (September–October 1993), pp. 134–142.
39. R. S. Kaplan and D. P. Norton, "The Balanced Scorecard—Measures that Drive Performance," *Harvard Business Review* 70, no. 1 (January–February 1992), p. 77; R. S. Kaplan and D. P. Norton, "Putting the Balanced Scorecard to Work," *Harvard Business Review,* 71, no. 5 (September–October 1993), pp. 134–142.
40. R. Simons, "Codman & Shurtleff, Inc.: Planning and Control System," Harvard Business School case # 9-187-081, p. 8.

ES, Inc.

In 1982, ES, Inc. (ESI) was starting a process which could lead to major changes in its planning and measurement systems. Cliff Jamieson, Vice-president—Planning and Services, explained:

> The basic thrust of what we are starting to do is very simple, but it has potentially major ramifications. We are changing the basic decision rules by which we evaluate our plans and our accomplishments. We have become convinced, that for ESI, at least, the traditional accounting measures such as net earnings or return on net assets, are neither good criteria on which to base decisions, nor reliable indicators of performance.
>
> The primary objective of our company is to create value for our shareholders. We believe that stock values, like the values of all economic resources, depend on investor's expectations of future cash flows, discounted for time and risk. Consequently, we think that in evaluating possible actions, it is more important to focus on the possible impacts on future cash flows and risk, rather than estimating the impact on the accounting indicators. In addition, we think that it makes sense to judge our performance based on what we accomplish for our shareholders—meaning the amount of value we generate for them.

THE COMPANY

ESI was a large, diversified corporation with headquarters in New York City. The company's 1981 sales of $2.2 billion ranked it among the largest 300 corporations in the U.S. ESI had experienced excellent growth in both revenues and earnings for many years (see Exhibit 1).

ESI was organized into four main business groups: Semiconductor, Electrical Products, Industrial Products, and Consumer Products (see Exhibit 2). The Semiconductor Group (SG) designed, manufactured and marketed a broad line of semiconductor devices, including electronic sensors (e.g., photodiodes), memory devices, microprocessors, and transmission devices (e.g., fiber optics, speech synthesis chips). The Electrical Products Group (EPG) produced such varied products as generators and motors (fractional horsepower only), circuit breakers, and electrical connectors. Also included in EPG was the Electrical Supply Division which sold the products of approximately 100 of the leading U.S. electronics and electrical component manufacturers to over 25,000 customers worldwide. The Industrial Products Group (IPG) sold a wide range of products, including custom engineered ball, roller and slider bearings, precision engine parts, mechanical seals, industrial laminates, nonwoven materials, and some industrial chemicals. The Consumer Products Group (CPG) designed, manufactured, and distributed products which used in-house technologies, including electronic watches and calculators, small garden tractors and mowers, luggage, footwear, and health and beauty products. A financial comparison of these groups is presented in Exhibit 3.

The groups were divided into a total of 19 divisions which were, in turn, divided into 70 product departments each with profit-center responsibility.

In 1982, the compensation of a typical manager was expected to be approximately 60 percent salary and 40 percent performance incentives. The performance incentives were based 75 percent on operating income less a capital change (i.e., residual income), and 25 percent on the accomplishment of specific MBO (management-by-objectives) targets.

This case was prepared by Assistant Professor Kenneth A. Merchant as a basis for class discussion rather than to illustrate either effective or ineffective handling of an administrative situation.

ESI was a growth-oriented company with relatively young management. Most general managers had an engineering education and either technical or marketing experience, or both. The average age of the division managers was approximately 41. Brian Kinney, the Chairman of the Board, was only 51. Top management was interested in maintaining at least moderate levels of overall internal growth and was also interested in acquiring companies with operations that would complement present ESI activities.

PLANNING PROCESSES

Planning at ESI was intended to be a bottom-up process. In March, the strategic planning process was started with headquarters sending general planning guidelines to the business units. These guidelines included an economic forecast and some preliminary estimates of the resources the company would make available to each business unit. The department managers (and lower-level managers where appropriate) were expected to propose their own goals and strategies. They were asked to prepare three-year plans with the emphasis on market analysis and identification of strategic alternatives. Quantitative data (including financial) were required in only summary form.

These plans were then reviewed at successively higher organizational levels. The Corporate Management Committee (CMC) reviewed the plans and evaluated the total portfolio of businesses early in September. The CMC rarely made material changes to the strategic plans at this time; changes were usually made only if the resource-availability situation changed or if an acquisition or divestment was imminent.

After CMC approval of the strategic plan, the department managers prepared detailed operating plans (budgets) for the next year. The operating plans included targets for sales growth, profit margins, and operating earnings and were intended to be consistent with the strategic plans. The operating plans were also reviewed at successively increasing organizational levels, usually with only minor modifications being made.

THE SHAREHOLDER VALUE MODEL

In the late 1970's corporate staff had begun to use a model called VALUmod as an aid in evaluating strategic plans. VALUmod was developed by Bourne and McIntosh, a Chicago-based management consulting firm, with the help of several leading academics in the fields of finance, accounting, and strategic planning. At the heart of VALUmod was a discounted cash flow model which, with the input of estimates of future cash flows and factors for discounting time and risk, could be used to place a value on any business entity at any point in time. For strategic planning purposes, VALUmod could be used to value an entity given the assumptions behind any of a number of different strategic alternatives.

A particular strategy was considered to generate a positive value for shareholders only if it increased the business entity's cash flows in a manner sufficient to more than offset new investments that might be required. Cash flows (and value) might be generated by, for example, increasing the volume of sales, increasing the contribution generated by each incremental sale, or reducing the amount of investment tied up in working capital as compared to the levels in the base period.

In addition to providing the basic value calculations, VALUmod helped in the preparation of the cash flow forecasts themselves by allowing easy manipulation of the parameters affecting future cash flows. This made it easy to ask the *what-if* questions necessary for performing sensitivity analyses.

In concept, VALUmod was identical to capital-investment-analysis models based on the net present value method. But with VALUmod, *all* cash outlays required to implement a strategy were considered, not just capital investments which typically comprised only a small fraction of the total.

HISTORY OF USE OF THE SHAREHOLDER VALUE MODEL

Diane Avery, Director of Corporate Planning, described how ESI came to use a shareholder-value model in strategic planning:

> By all the traditional accounting measures, our performance over the decade of the 1970s was excellent. Take any measure you want—sales growth, earnings growth, return on equity, return on assets, earnings per employee—they all indicate we had done very well. Our shareholders, however, hadn't really derived any benefit from this *success.* In

Let me make one qualification, however, I am not suggesting that impact on shareholders value should be the only criterion we should look at when we make our strategic resource allocation decision. What I am suggesting is that impact on shareholder value should be an important financially oriented criterion and that it is far superior to looking at projections expressed in traditional accounting terms.

CHANGE IN STATEMENT OF OBJECTIVES

At the end of 1981, the wording of ESI's primary statement of objectives was changed to read as follows:

> The primary objective of ES, Inc., is to increase shareholder value. This will be accomplished by focusing on markets where the Company has or can capture a major share, by developing a higher-than-average flow of successful new products, and by continuing to emphasize productivity of Company personnel and assets.

Formerly, the primary objective had been "to grow and to improve profitability." This change in the wording of the statement of company objectives was not brought about the VALUmod directly, but it was motivated by the same logic that the model used.

THE FUTURE OF THE SHAREHOLDER VALUE MODEL

ESI planned to work with and to refine the shareholder value model and eventually to spread its use throughout the organization. Brian Kinney (Chairman) promised to use VALUmod and related models "more intensively and extensively."

A number of important issues remained to be solved, however. One issue was the planning horizon. In making the value calculations, all cash flows, no matter how far into the future, had to be considered, but the ESI operating plans only included three years of data. To work around this limitation, the planning staff had been making the assumption that the operating cash flows in the last year of the plan would remain constant in perpetuity, in the absence of information to the contrary. While the most immediate cash flows had the largest value impact because of discounting, this assumption was subject to obvious criticisms, particularly for those divisions with products with relatively short product life cycles. Thus, to improve the accuracy of VALUmod's calculations, one possibility that had to be considered was an extension of the planning horizon, from three years to five, or perhaps even longer.

A second issue was whether the plans should reflect a single point estimate of future results or whether they should reflect a range of possible outcomes and an assessment of the likelihood of each. VALUmod's value calculations were intended to reflect the *expected value* of the future cash flows, and the model could easily accommodate probabilistic cash flow estimates. However, several senior ESI managers thought that single-point estimates were necessary for control purposes, so that managers could be held responsible for achieving a specific plan.

Risk presented another problem. ESI's early uses of the model used the same discount factor—the corporate average cost of capital—in all analyses. If ESI had been highly vertically integrated and in a single market, this might have been acceptable, but the Corporate Planning staff felt that the various ESI business units did bear quite different levels of risk. Quantifying the amounts of risk faced in order to reflect them in the discount rates used in the value calculations was not straightforward, however, and more thought would have to be given to this issue before use of the model was made more widespread.

A fourth issue was the speed of implementation, meaning how fast to involve managers at each organization level in the use of the model. Because they were convinced of its worth, top management was inclined to use the *impact of shareholder value* criterion for evaluating plans immediately. This might, however, cause frustration and conflict if the lower-level managers did not understand the bases on which the decisions were being made. All managers were familiar with the net present value concept because they were required to use it in preparing their capital investment proposals, but it was not clear whether they could easily transfer their knowledge of this basic concept to the preparation of whole operating plans.

Finally, if impact on shareholder value became an important criterion in strategic decision making, another issue would arise; that is whether or not to link a value-related performance criterion—impact on shareholder value—to the management reward system. To reinforce the shareholder value concept, some portion of management compensation could be made contingent on value increases—either of the corporation as a whole or of specific business units. The question was: should this be done, and if so, how soon?

EXHIBIT 1 Financial Comparison 1970–1981 ($ millions)

	1981	*1980*	*1979*	*1978*	*1977*	*1976*	*1975*	*1974*	*1973*	*1972*	*1971*	*1970*
Net sales	2,152	1,841	1,577	1,334	1,139	1,025	883	762	647	533	458	399
Net earnings	110	96	84	71	61	50	44	38	33	28	23	20
Capital expenditures	98	86	57	59	59	35	40	45	36	19	16	25
Market value (ave.)	755	769	544	526	551	619	581	563	625	662	574	541
Ratios (%)												
Increase in sales	16.9	16.7	18.2	17.1	11.1	16.1	15.8	17.8	21.3	16.5	14.8	14.3
Increase in net earn.	14.6	14.2	18.3	16.4	21.9	13.6	15.8	15.2	17.8	21.7	15.1	3.6
Net earn as % of sales	5.1	5.2	5.3	5.3	5.3	4.9	5.0	4.9	5.1	5.3	5.1	5.0
Dividends as % of net earnings	29.7	27.4	25.7	26.2	24.1	20.7	19.2	21.8	22.5	24.9	28.3	31.5
Return on average shareholder equity	15%	14.6%	14.6%	13.5%	12.9%	12.0%	12.2%	11.9%	11.6%	11.1%	10.2%	9.4%

EXHIBIT 2 Organization

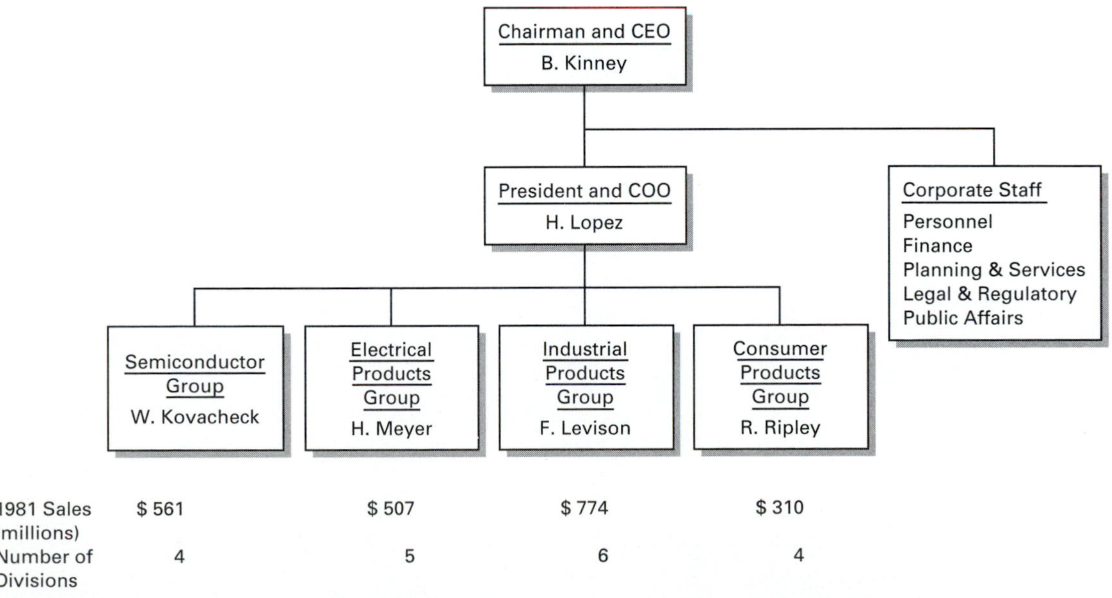

EXHIBIT 3 Financial Comparison of Major Business Groups ($ in millions)

	1981	*1980*	*% Increased*
Semiconductor			
Net sales	$ 561	$ 428	31.1
Net earnings	6	5	20.0
Electrical Products			
Net sales	$ 507	$ 469	8.1
Net earnings	28	27	3.7
Industrial Products			
Net sales	$ 774	$ 701	10.4
Net earnings	63	56	12.5
Consumer Products			
Net sales	$ 310	$ 243	27.6
Net earnings	13	8	62.5
ESI Total			
Net sales	$2,152	$1,841	16.9
Net earnings	110	96	14.6

EXHIBIT 4 Planning Division Organization

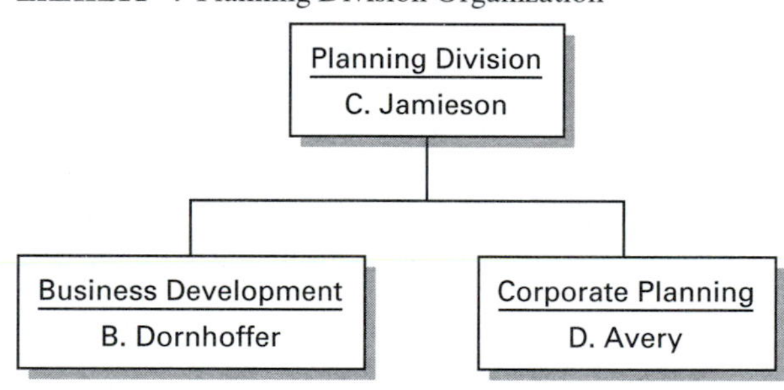

- Merger & Acquisitions
- Divestitures

- Market Planning
- Portfolio Analysis

EXHIBIT 5 Example Showing Discouragement of a Good Investment ($ in millions)

SCHEDULE 1: Projected Income Statements, Division A, Strategy 1 ("Base case")

	Actual	←	*Forecast*	→
	1981	*1982*	*1983*	*1984*
Sales	$200	$220	$242	$266
Variable operating expenses	160	176	194	213
Depreciation	10	11	11	12
Discretionary expenses	20	22	24	27
Total expenses	190	209	229	251
Profit before tax	10	12	13	15
Income tax (40%)	4	5	5	6
Profit after tax	$ 6	$ 7	$ 8	$ 9

SCHEDULE 2: Projected Income Statements, Division A, Strategy 2 (Real growth)

	Actual	←	*Forecast*	→
	1981	*1982*	*1983*	*1984*
Sales	$200	$220	$253	$291
Variable operating expenses	160	176	202	233
Depreciation	10	11	11	12
Discretionary expenses	20	27	29	32
Total expenses	190	214	243	276
Profit before tax	10	7	10	15
Income tax (40%)	4	3	4	6
Profit after tax	$ 6	$ 4	$ 6	$ 9

SCHEDULE 3: Value Calculations

Annual Cash Flows	*1982*	*1983*	*1984*	*1985 and beyond*
Strategy 1	$18	$19	$21	$21
Strategy 2	15	17	21	24

Value of Division A on December 31, 1981 at 18% (ignoring liabilities)

Strategy 1	$112.3 million
Strategy 2	$116.3 million

EXHIBIT 6 Example Showing Encouragement of a Bad Investment ($ million)

SCHEDULE 1: Projected Income Statements, Division A, Strategy 1 ("Base case")

	Actual	◁——	*Forecast*	——▷
	1981	*1982*	*1983*	*1984*
Sales	$200	$220	$242	$266
Variable operating expenses	160	176	194	213
Depreciation	10	11	11	12
Discretionary expenses	20	22	24	27
Total expenses	190	209	229	251
Profit before tax	10	12	13	15
Income tax (40%)	4	5	5	6
Profit after tax	$ 6	$ 7	$ 8	$ 9

SCHEDULE 2: Projected Income Statements, Division A, Strategy 3 (Improve operating margins)

	Actual	◁——	*Forecast*	——▷
	1981	*1982*	*1983*	*1984*
Sales	$200	$220	$242	$266
Variable operating expenses	160	172	189	208
Depreciation	10	12	13	14
Discretionary expenses	20	22	24	27
Total expenses	190	205	226	248
Profit before tax	10	15	16	18
Income tax (40%)	4	6	6	7
Profit after tax	$ 6	$ 9	$ 10	$ 11

SCHEDULE 3: Value Calculations

Annual Cash Flows	*Investment*	*1982*	*1983*	*1984*	*1985 and beyond*
Strategy 1		$18	$19	$21	$21
Strategy 3	$ (25)	21	23	25	25

Value of Division A on December 31, 1981 at 18% (ignoring liabilities)

Strategy 1	$112.3 million
Strategy 3	$108.6 million

EXHIBIT 7 Division A, Strategy X Projected Income Statements ($ in millions)

	1982	*1983*	*1984*
Sales	$74	$89	$106
Expenses	70	84	99
Profit before taxes	4	5	7
Income taxes	2	2	3
Profit after taxes	$ 2	$ 3	$ 4

EXHIBIT 8 Division A, Strategy X Shareholder Value Calculations ($ in millions)

Present value of earning assets at end of implementation of strategy	$16.8
Less: Present value of investment required	(7.9)
Less: Market value of debt (net of monetary assets)	(10.1)
Present value of division if strategy is implemented	(1.2)
Less: Pre-strategy value of division	.5
Shareholder value contribution of strategy	$(1.7)

Natomas North America

In June 1983, Mick Seidl, president of Natomas North America (NNA), described his thoughts about his company's bonus plans. Mick was pleased with a new bonus plan, called the Discovery Award Plan (DAP), which provided performance-based rewards for the explorationists who were working to find oil and gas reserves. But he was not satisfied with the company's Management Incentive Bonus Plan (MIBP). Most importantly, Mick thought that like the DAP, the MIBP should include as a key performance measure the net present value (NPV) of new oil and gas reserves added. He explained:

> The DAP is an incentive plan that is also a significant part of our compensation package. I think it's a good plan. It helps us recruit good people, and it helps us motivate the ones we've got. The DAP rewards are based on the NPV of new reserves found which, I think, is the best number we can use as the basis for rewarding our explorationists. NPV of new reserves represents real value added to the company, so it seems reasonable to have the shareholders share a portion of this value increase with the people who did the most to create it as a reward for their good work.
>
> But the MIBP is based on net income alone. This tends to screw up the incentives because there are all kinds of ways to maximize income which are not in the best interests of the shareholders. One obvious example is by deferring investments that won't pay off until future periods.

Mick proposed to Natomas corporate management a new set of business-unit performance criteria for the MIBP. In this set, Mick de-emphasized net income and added the NPV of new reserves.

NATOMAS COMPANY

Natomas Company was a San Francisco-based company with operations carried on through three principal subsidiaries. The Natomas Energy Company (NEC) directed the company's petroleum, geothermal and coal activities, with the petroleum and gas operations predominantly located in the U.S., Canada and Indonesia. The Natomas Transportation Company provided cargo transportation in the Pacific through American President Lines, Ltd. The Natomas Real Estate Company was involved in the development of residential and commercial properties, primarily in northern California.

Natomas's 1982 revenues of $1.66 billion (see Exhibit 1) ranked it 214th on the *Fortune* 500 list. Net income, calculated on a full cost basis for the energy parts of the business, was $44 million. In 1982, approximately 50 percent of total revenues and 56 percent of total operating income was derived from petroleum production and marketing (see Exhibit 2).

NATOMAS NORTH AMERICA

Natomas North America (NNA) was the Houston-based subsidiary of NEC responsible for oil and gas operations in the U.S., Canada, and the Gulf of Mexico. In 1982, NNA owned interests in oil- and gas-producing properties in 14 states and three Canadian provinces.

NNA's major activity was the exploration for and development of oil and gas reserves, both onshore and off-shore. This involved analyzing potential drilling sites, securing leasehold interests in properties to be drilled (performed by landmen), and supervising the work of contract crews hired to drill the wells and produce the reserves discovered.

This case was prepared by Professor Kenneth A. Merchant, University of Southern California, as the basis of class discussion, rather than to illustrate either the effective or ineffective handling of an administrative situation.

In 1981, to increase local initiative and accountability, NNA was decentralized into four regions: Northern, Central, Southern, and Canada (see Exhibit 3). The general managers of each region were responsible for all exploration, development, and production activity in their region (see Exhibit 4), but they worked closely with headquarters staff support personnel (e.g., geologists, geophysicists, engineering). Meanwhile, NNA sought to strengthen its domestic operations by greatly increasing the number of technical personnel in each region and at headquarters (Houston).

THE WORK OF EXPLORATIONISTS AT NNA

The explorationists at NNA, who were predominantly geologists and geophysicists, performed the vital function of recommending where to drill for oil and gas. They had to find reserve prospects, called *plays,* estimate the quantities and quality of reserves that might be present, and determine the accessibility.

Almost all of these explorationists were college educated and had field experience, usually with one of the major oil companies, prior to joining NNA. To help them determine whether the conditions suggested a reasonably high probability of the presence of hydrocarbon reserves, geologists analyzed core samples, and geophysicists analyzed seismic charts. However, even with sophisticated technology, finding oil and gas was generally considered part science, part art, and part luck.

An important task of the explorationists was to sell their plays to NNA management. Capital was allocated to the plays considered most promising. The explorationists usually sought the advice of other company personnel in the region or at corporate before formally presenting their plays to regional management. The regional plays that met certain specifications (i.e., NNA-set hurdles for minimum reserve quantity, crude quality, production costs) were proposed by regional personnel, including management and explorationists, to NNA management for funding.

The estimation of the quantity of new reserves was a particularly difficult task. Predrilling estimates of reserve quantities were based on information the explorationists could gather from samples, seismic charts, and *analog wells.* After drilling, additional information was available to improve estimates of reserve quantities (e.g., volume, flows, pressure), but even the estimates at this point were considered crude. Bill Monroe, vice president of exploitation, explained:

> I would say that 85 percent of the time the estimates made at the time of the first drilling are off 50 percent. The errors can be in either direction, but there is a tendency for the first estimate to be optimistic. As a general rule, fairly accurate reserves estimates (that is, those that are within 25 percent of the actual) are not available until after one to two years of well production. We can still be misled by the early volume and pressure indications.

All estimates of reserves considered "proved"[1] were audited by NNA's independent reserve auditors, Keplinger & Associates.

THE EXPLORATION BUDGET PROCESS

The amount of capital allocated to exploration fluctuated widely. For example, the amounts allocated by NNA for exploration and development of oil reserves were $150 million in 1978, $225 million in 1980, and $110 million in 1982. The allocation depended on a number of factors, including the total corporate cash flow available, exploration prospects, alternative investment opportunities, and prices of oil and gas.

Like all Natomas subsidiaries, NNA prepared an annual budget for approval by the parent company. This budget, called the Exploration and Production Plan, included financial forecasts in traditional income statement and balance sheet formats with considerable back-up detail, such as planned capital expenditures for exploration, development and production, and expected reserve additions. It also included a summary of well economics in terms of changes in net present values; this required assumptions about prices of oil and gas, production costs, and production schedules.

[1]Proved reserves are those quantities of crude oil and natural gas which appear, with reasonable certainty, to be recoverable in the future from known oil and gas reserves.

The budget served two purposes. First, it showed NNA's one-year forecasted results in financial statement (i.e., income statement, balance sheet) terms. Second, and perhaps more important, the budget served as NNA's request for capital to explore for and develop new reserves. NNA had to compete with the other Natomas subsidiaries for the pool of available capital from the parent. The budget represented the sum of each region's most viable prospects for new discoveries. If the parent company accepted the budget, NNA would receive the capital to fund its exploration activities. If a lesser amount was granted, NNA had to allocate money to fewer prospects.

THE DISCOVERY AWARD PLAN

The Discovery Award Plan provided cash incentives for exploration and land personnel involved in finding new energy reserves. NNA initiated the DAP in August 1980 in response to fierce industry competition over the hiring of good technical people, stemming from the oil boom of the late 1970s. The battle was mainly between the large oil companies and the rising number of independent oil companies. The large oil companies had large geologist-geophysicist staffs, good training programs, and huge resources. To entice technical people away from the large companies, some independents began offering *overrides*[2] to recruit geologists and geophysicists. The large companies refused to offer overrides.

NNA, an intermediate-sized oil company, needed a device to attract and retain these people who were critical to its success. The DAP was developed as a supplement to what was already a liberal salary and fringe benefit package. The DAP offered the same type of incentives for discoveries as overrides, and it was considerably less costly. It also helped retain employees because DAP awards were only paid to *employees,* while overrides were vested with the *individual.* If the discoveries left NNA, they would earn no further awards.

[2]An override is a vested percentage payment of the oil or gas taken from a developed well, much like a commission. It is usually a percentage (typically around 1 to 2 percent) of gross revenues, before production costs are subtracted. The payment could be made either in cash or petroleum. For very large finds, the discoverer could earn overrides totaling hundreds of thousands of dollars.

The DAP provided cash awards in the amount of one percent of the calculated net profit of the NNA reserves resulting from a discovery. Calculated net profit was defined as the net present value of total *proven* reserves after subtracting all current and future exploration, development, and production costs. Only new discoveries qualified for DAP awards (see Exhibit 5).

The net present value of new reserves was calculated by the reserve economics coordinator reporting to Bill Monroe (vice president of exploitation). Based on information obtained from the production personnel (who were not eligible for DAP awards) and the independent reserve auditors, the coordinator estimated the cash flows expected from the well. These were based on estimates of exploration costs, current and future well development and production expenses, and the expected revenue stream. The net present value of the discovery was calculated using a 10 percent discount factor.

The awards were divided into two levels of participation. Category A contributors, most likely geologists or geophysicists, were directly responsible for the conception and development of a prospect to discovery. Category B recognized all exploration and land professionals who contributed to a discovery but were not included in Category A. For a particular discovery, Category A employees shared 66.6 percent of the award, while Category B employees shared 33.3 percent of the award.

At the time of discovery, or as soon as possible thereafter, 20 percent of the calculated Discovery Award was distributed. The remaining 80 percent was distributed in four equal, or as nearly equal payments as possible, in the four consecutive calendar years after the first payment. Spreading the payments out in this way allowed for adjustments in the estimates of reserve amounts, production schedules, prices and costs. To receive any of these distributions, an individual had to be an active employee of NNA on the date the reserves were booked or amended on the specific prospect (except in the case of normal retirement or death).

Before payments were made, the Discovery Award Committee, which consisted of top NNA technical personnel, had to approve the well as qualifying as a discovery and the individuals who were entitled to receive either Category A or Category B awards.

Exhibit 6 shows an example of a calculation of a Discovery Award. The example is for a find of 3 billion cubic feet (BCF) of gas, a small, relatively common find. NNA management considered a find of around 6 BCF of gas to be *decent-sized,* a large find would be 20–30 BCF, or even larger. (Three BCF of gas was approximately equivalent to ½ BCF of oil.)

In the first two years of the plan (as of September 1982), approximately $46,000 in DAP payments had been made to 60 people, as a result of eight new reserve finds in the U.S. and two in Canada. These awards ranged from $70 to $5,000. The total amount of the awards was considerably less than had been expected when the DAP was established because the company had cut back significantly in its exploration expenditures. The cutbacks were caused by industry recession and a deterioration in the company's financial position.

Reactions to the Discovery Award Plan

Most NNA personnel agreed with Mick Seidl that NPV was a good financial measure of success and that the DAP was a good plan. Exhibit 7 presents excerpts from an interview with two explorationists in the plan. However, some NNA managers thought the DAP had caused the explorationists to be optimistic in their estimates to increase the potential that their prospects would be drilled. Bill Moffat (senior vice president-finance) explained:

> The DAP provides rewards for success, but not charge for failure. This results in a lopsided incentive system that may motivate the explorationists to move in directions that are not in the company's best interest, and I'm not convinced that we have effective controls over them. There is a lot of judgment involved in boiling the raw data down into the interpretations that are made, and because of time constraints, it is physically impossible for the managers to analyze the tremendous amounts of data that are available and to understand fully the assumptions the explorationists have incorporated into their projections.

Other managers felt that management and staff personnel could indeed guard against unwarranted optimism on the part of the explorationists. Bill Monroe (vice president-exploitation) was one of them:

> We go over damn near every number involved in their projections and, if you will, second-guess it. We try to make sure that what we have in the final plan is something we can all live with. We have to be ready to argue that these are well-founded numbers, backed up by the best information that is available.

Mick Seidl commented:

> We have talked about how to straighten out the incentives. One argument is that management personnel (exploration managers and above) provide an effective check on the explorationists. The managers don't participate in this plan; they are evaluated not only on NPV of reserves discovered, but also net income. As a consequence, they are, in effect, charged for *dry holes* because these costs are eventually subtracted in the calculation of net income. That's the check in the system. Whether it's a totally effective check is a difficult question to answer.

THE MANAGEMENT INCENTIVE BONUS PLAN

In addition to regular salary increases and a company thrift plan, Natomas Company offered management personnel, down to middle management levels, an annual incentive bonus plan called the Management Incentive Bonus Plan (MIBP). The objectives of the MIBP were: (1) to attract and retain key personnel; (2) to enable the company to maintain a competitive total compensation program; (3) to provide levels of economic incentive that reflect the varying levels of impact incumbents have upon the company's direction and success; and (4) to stimulate performance which results in the attainment or surpassing of company goals and objectives.

The amount of the MIBP bonus depended on three factors:

1. *Natomas Company performance.* The corporatewide *target* bonus pool was the sum of the business units' target bonus pools (see #2 below). But the *actual* bonus pool was subject to how well consolidated Natomas earnings compared to budgeted earnings. Recent policy had been to limit the corporate budget pool to a maximum of 3 to 4 percent of consolidated earnings after taxes and dividends.

2. *Business unit (e.g., NNA) performance.* A target bonus pool was set for each business unit during the planning process by summing the *bonus opportunities* of all individual participants in that unit. Individuals' bonus opportunities ranged from 10 to 50 percent of base salary, with higher level personnel given the opportunity for larger bonuses. A business unit's actual earned share of its target bonus pool was determined at the end of the year depending on its profit performance compared to plan, according to the following schedule:

PERCENT OF PROFIT PLAN OBJECTIVES ACHIEVED	PERCENT OF TARGET BONUS PAYABLE
Above 150	Up to 200
135–150	Up to 175
120–135	Up to 150
110–120	Up to 125
100–110	Up to 110
90–100	Up to 100
75–90	Up to 75
Below 75	0

Total awards were, however, subject to the corporate constraints described in #1 above.

3. *Individual performance.* When the corporate and business unit factors were determined, a pool of bonus money was distributed to each business unit. Business unit presidents then distributed their unit's bonus pool to their managers, after a review by headquarters. Company documentation of the MIBP suggested the following guidelines:

PERFORMANCE RATING	PERCENT OF TARGET BONUS PAYABLE
Far exceeded goals	125–150
Generally exceeded goals	101–125
Generally achieved goals	90–100
Met some but not most goals	50–89
Did not meet goals	0

The following caution was included in the documentation of the plan:

> In making the decision about performance ratings for bonus payments, the rater should not eliminate judgment factors. To do so would make the performance review under the bonus plan purely mechanical, based solely on attainment of quantitative objectives. The range for each rating category allows the rater to make distinctions by taking into consideration less tangible behaviors which cannot always be measured quantitatively. The rater, moreover, may find that the previous written performance ratings do not fit all situations. Then the rater's judgment must be applied. For instance, a participant could receive a grade below 90 percent when the rater believed the participant had *generally achieved goals* but did not exhibit other qualities expected of top managers such as the ability to plan properly, coordinate with others, lead and motivate subordinates, etc.

NNA PROPOSAL FOR CHANGE OF THE MIBP

Mick Seidl believed that the MIBP could be an important tool for communicating company expectations to individuals in key positions and for providing incentives for achievement, but he felt that significant changes were necessary. Historically, evaluations of business units' performances had been based on only one criterion: full-cost accounting net income as compared to plan. Mick realized that top management faced intense pressure for quarterly earnings, but he did not think that net income was the only measure on which to judge NNA's performance:

> It is nutty to expect quarterly earnings increases in businesses with long-lived assets, such as ours. We're investing in projects that will not pay off for years, and it doesn't make sense to respond to every perturbation in the economy by cutting back these investments just so we can show an earnings increase.

In July 1982, Mick proposed to Natomas management a new set of business-unit performance criteria for determining NNA's annual bonus pool:

PERFORMANCE CRITERIA	WEIGHT
Net present value of new oil and gas reserves added during the year, compared to budget	45 percent
Earnings compared to budget, taking into account controllable and uncontrollable factors	45 percent
Organizational development factors, defined as ability to set and achieve key management goals in a timely manner	10 percent

The *NPV-of-new-reserves-added* factor was included because reserves represented the company's major asset, and increases in this asset clearly represented successes. Finding reserves added shareholder value as the reserves could either be sold in the ground or developed and marketed at a later date. Mick considered the value of reserves added to be the primary measure of the success of NNA's exploration and development program. The reserves were necessary to ensure maintenance of NNA's earnings and growth.

Current *earnings* was a measure of how well NNA derived revenues and controlled costs. Mick included this measure for several reasons: (1) it measured aspects of performances not captured by the NPV-of-reserves-added measure, particularly cost control; (2) it was easy to apply because the measures were already a regular part of the organizational information system; and (3) managers were familiar with it.

He recognized that earnings had several significant limitations as a measure of performance, however. One limitation was that it did not recognize the longer term performance value of discovering new reserves. Another was that it could be distorted by uncontrollable factors, such as market price fluctuations and demand shocks (e.g., gas rationing), although he felt that variance analyses could be used to identify the amounts due to factors within and outside NNA managers' control.

The *organizational development* factors were measures of important managerial activities that would enhance company performance, particularly those that would provide longer term payoffs but would not be entirely captured by accounting measures. Examples were reducing personnel turnover, improving information systems, and improving purchasing procedures.

Mick believed that this combination of measures represented a clearer, more well-rounded picture of NNA's productive activity and better aligned bonus incentives with corporate goals. He defended it:

> Use of net income alone in an incentive system tends to cause an overemphasis on the short-term. In my view, the new present value of the reserves discovered is the single most important measure of our success. It's a tough concept to sell, however. Some people think it's nutty. They say: "Look at how you can manipulate those numbers." I reply: "Of course you can. But you can't manipulate NPV any more than you can manipulate many accounting numbers. As long as you can trace the assumptions and origins of the numbers, anyone can figure out if you're lying, cheating or stealing, by and large."

MANAGEMENT BONUSES IN 1982

In 1982, management bonuses at Natomas were determined as in the past, by evaluating performance in terms of net income vs. budget for both Natomas Company and the business units. One process change was made, however: Each business unit president had to submit a written assessment of his unit's results with his judgment as to the bonus pool award his unit had earned. Based on this analysis and input from the Executive Management Committee, Dorman Commons (Natomas Company president) would make the final 1982 bonus awards to the business units.

The year 1982 was very painful for NNA. Net income was below budget by approximately $110 million. Of this total, $75 million was caused by a downward revision in estimates of NNA petroleum reserves thought to have been discovered in prior years and the impairment of Gulf of Mexico leases on which no reserves were discovered.

In January 1983, Mick Seidl prepared his recommendation to Mr. Commons. Exhibit 8 shows part of his analysis which separates the budget variances into controllable and noncontrollable categories. Mick concluded that NNA had performed poorly in 1982, and he could not attribute a significant portion of the negative variances to uncontrollable factors, so he did not anticipate a large bonus pool. But he thought some parts of the organization had done very well and should be rewarded for their performance. He prepared a case for the Canadian region:

> I knew that the Canadian region discovered a lot of oil in 1982; they found 3.4 million barrels more than was planned, and this is worth over $20 million to the company. This number dwarfs any controllable profit shortfall that might be attributed to them. Thus I had to conclude that they did a good job in 1982. (This is a good example of why I think

it is important to move to multiple criteria for evaluating performance in NNA, instead of relying strictly on net income.) Based on these numbers, my recommendation was that the management personnel in the Canadian region should receive 100 percent of their target bonus and that no bonuses should be given to the rest of the managers in my organization.

Headquarter's Response

Natomas Company also had a very disappointing year in 1982, due to a number of factors, including recession in the U.S. and worldwide, high interest rates, declining energy demand, lower oil prices and a major Indonesia settlement. Net income dropped from $233 million ($4.29 per share) in 1981 to $44 million ($.65 per share) in 1982 (See Exhibit 1). Many of these problems were recognized early in the year, and strong steps had been taken, including major cuts in expenses, capital expenditures, and oil and gas exploration.

Because of these poor results, Mr. Commons decided that no management bonuses would be paid in 1982. While it was a difficult decision, he concluded that the company on a consolidated basis should achieve a *reasonable level* of income (perhaps 25 percent of budget), before management received bonuses. He felt it would be difficult to justify to shareholders that bonuses were paid when corporate earnings were so bad that dividends would likely have to be cut.

Reaction by NNA Managers

Managers in NNA were understandably disturbed by the decision not to give bonuses, particularly those in Canada. Skip Jackson, one of the regional general managers in NNA Canada, commented:

> We had our best year ever in 1982. When we did not get a bonus, I felt cheated. In 1979 the reverse happened—the company did well, but we in Canada did not—and we didn't get any bonuses. I can understand that. But in 1982 this bonus system broke down, and it shouldn't have. In my view, the directors saved face because the company as a whole had a bad year; they could then tell the shareholders that no bonuses were paid. The whole idea of a bonus incentive scheme went out the window when that happened. They lost a lot of credibility with my staff who had worked very hard. I, and my staff, can only influence the results of my unit. This makes it a lot harder for me to keep the people in my unit motivated.

EXHIBIT 1 Natomas Company Consolidated Statement of Income

Year ended December 31	*1982*	*1981*	*1980*
	(in thousands, except per share amounts)		
Revenues			
Energy			
Petroleum producing	$ 714,341	$ 677,306	$ 501,063
Petroleum marketing	113,384	106,125	89,303
Geothermal	53,005	42,580	16,860
Coal mining	81,008	73,260	66,110
Transporation	646,731	632,141	569,910
Real Estate	8,731	6,080	2,104
Interest and other	38,586	44,904	40,754
	1,655,786	1,582,396	1,286,104
Expenses			
Costs and operating	890,638	780,544	646,341
Depletion, depreciation and amortization	424,226	249,236	177,172
Taxes on income	116,940	189,053	139,826
Other taxes	12,196	7,558	5,706
Selling, general and administrative	87,247	79,988	74,307
Interest	80,539	43,490	34,382
	1,611,786	1,349,869	1,077,734
Net Income	**$ 44,000**	**$ 232,527**	**$ 208,370**
Per Share	**$ 0.65**	**$ 4.29**	**$ 4.02**

See notes to consolidated financial statements.

(in millions)	*1982*	*1981*	*1980*	*1979*	*1978*
Cash Flow from Operations					
Energy					
Petroleum producing					
International	$441	$339	$219	$122	$ 93
North America	100	82	78	48	36
Petroleum marketing	5	5	4	3	3
Geothermal	42	36	13	11	10
Coal mining	7	6	13	6	7
Interest and other	(35)	(1)	1	(13)	(12)
	560	467	328	177	137
Transportation	79	71	77	77	71
Real Estate	9	6	1	1	3
Corporate interest, expenses and taxes	(38)	(17)	(23)	(13)	(11)
	$610	**$527**	**$383**	**$242**	**$200**

Source: Natomas Company 1982 Annual Report

EXHIBIT 2 Business Segment Information Natomas Company

(in millions)	Consolidated			United States			Canada			Indonesia			Other		
	1982	*1981*	*1980*	*1982*	*1981*	*1980*	*1982*	*1981*	*1980*	*1982*	*1981*	*1980*	*1982*	*1981*	*1980*
Energy															
Petroleum producing															
Revenues	$ 714	$ 677	$ 501	$ 100	$ 97	$ 90	$ 11	$ 7	$ 8	$567	$544	$403	$36	$29	
Operating income	46	194	169	(71)	18	19	4	2	3	107	164	147	6	10	
Identifiable assets	1,345	1,153	770	535	553	374	65	50	34	670	459	291	75	91	$71
Depletion, depreciation and amortization	361	204	141												
Capital additions	598	484	308												
Petroleum Marketing															
Revenues	113	106	89			1	113	105	88						
Operating income	4	5	3				4	5	3						
Identifiable assets	35	33	33			2	35	33	31						
Depreciation and amortization	1	1	1												
Capital additions	2	1	1												
Geothermal															
Revenues	53	43	17	53	43	17									
Operating income	31	28	11	31	28	11									
Identifiable assets	575	543	76	575	543	76									
Depletion, depreciation and amortization	10	8	2												
Capital additions	67	39	11												
Coal Mining															
Revenues	81	73	66	81	73	66									
Operating income	(9)	(1)	8	(9)	(1)	8									
Identifiable assets	75	98	72	75	98	72									
Depletion, depreciation and amortization	21	6	5												
Capital additions	5	6	5												
Other															
Revenues	8	22	29	8	22	29									
Operating income	(35)	(7)	(3)	(35)	(7)	(3)									
Identifiable assets	66	73	189	66	73	189									

EXHIBIT 2 Business Segment Information Natomas Company *Continued*

	Consolidated			*United States*			*Canada*			*Indonesia*			*Other*		
(in millions)	*1982*	*1981*	*1980*	*1982*	*1981*	*1980*	*1982*	*1981*	*1980*	*1982*	*1981*	*1980*	*1982*	*1981*	*1980*
Transportation*															
Revenues	647	632	570	647	632	570									
Net income	43	38	43	43	38	43									
Identifiable assets	681	654	571	681	654	571									
Depreciation and amortization	30	29	27												
Capital additions	126	122	102												
Real Estate															
Revenues	9	6	2	9	6	2									
Net income	9	5	1	9	5	1									
Identifiable assets	38	30	51	38	30	51									
Capital additions	4	7	6												
Total segment revenues	1,625	1,559	1,274	$ 898	$ 873	$ 775	$124	$112	$96	$567	$544	$403	$36	$30	
Interest and other income	31	23	12												
Total consolidated revenues	$1,656	$1,582	$1,286												
Total segment operating income	89	262	232	$ (32)	$ 81	$ 79	$ 8	$ 7	$ 6	$107	$164	$147	$ 6	$10	
Corporate interest, expenses and taxes	(45)	(29)	(24)												
Total consolidated net income	$ 44	$ 233	$ 208												
Total segment identifiable assets	2,815	2,584	1,762	$1,970	$1,951	$1,335	$100	$ 83	$65	$670	$459	$291	$75	$91	$71
Corporate assets	18	27	36												
Total assets	$2,833	$2,611	$1,798												

*The transportation subsidiary has operations in the United States and the Far East. However, the Company is unable to allocate revenues, net income and identifiable assets on a geographic basis due to the nature of the business.

Source: Natomas Company 1982 Annual Report

EXHIBIT 3 Organization Chart

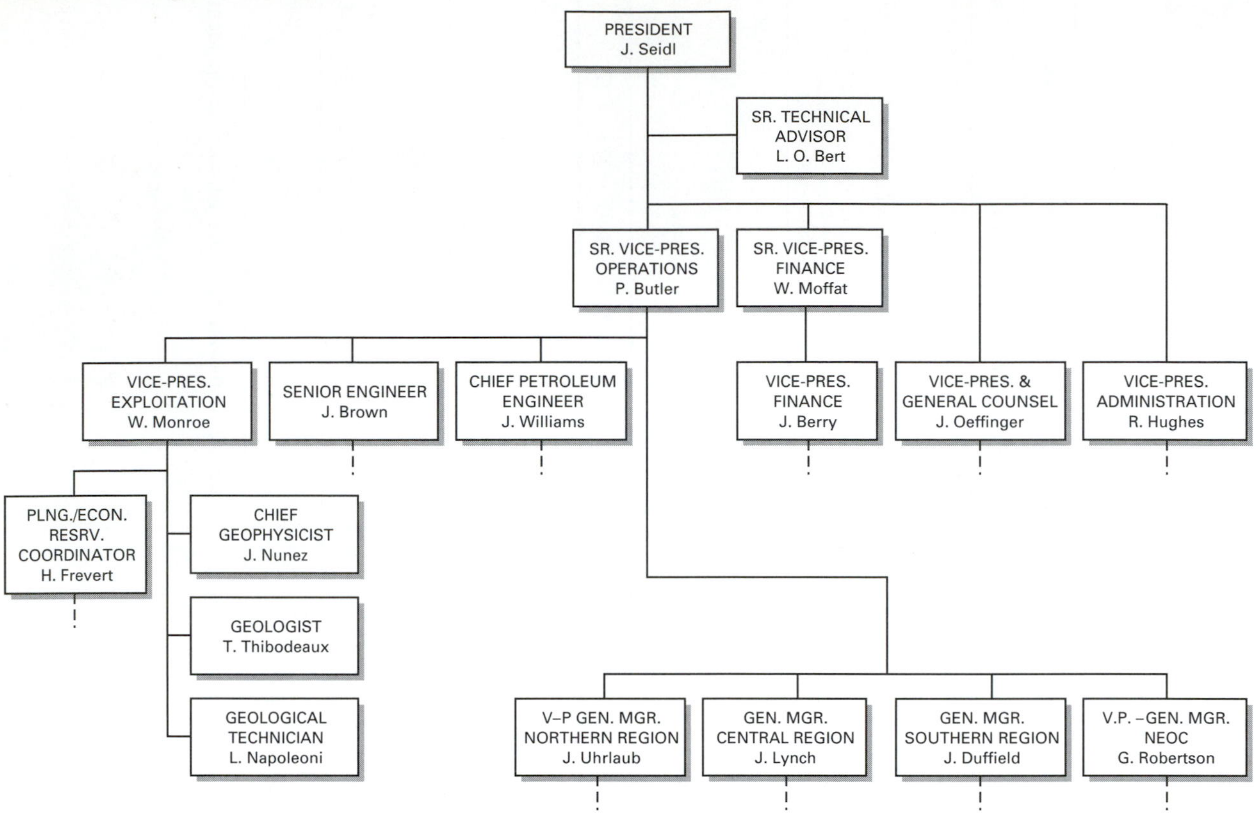

EXHIBIT 4 Regional Organization Chart

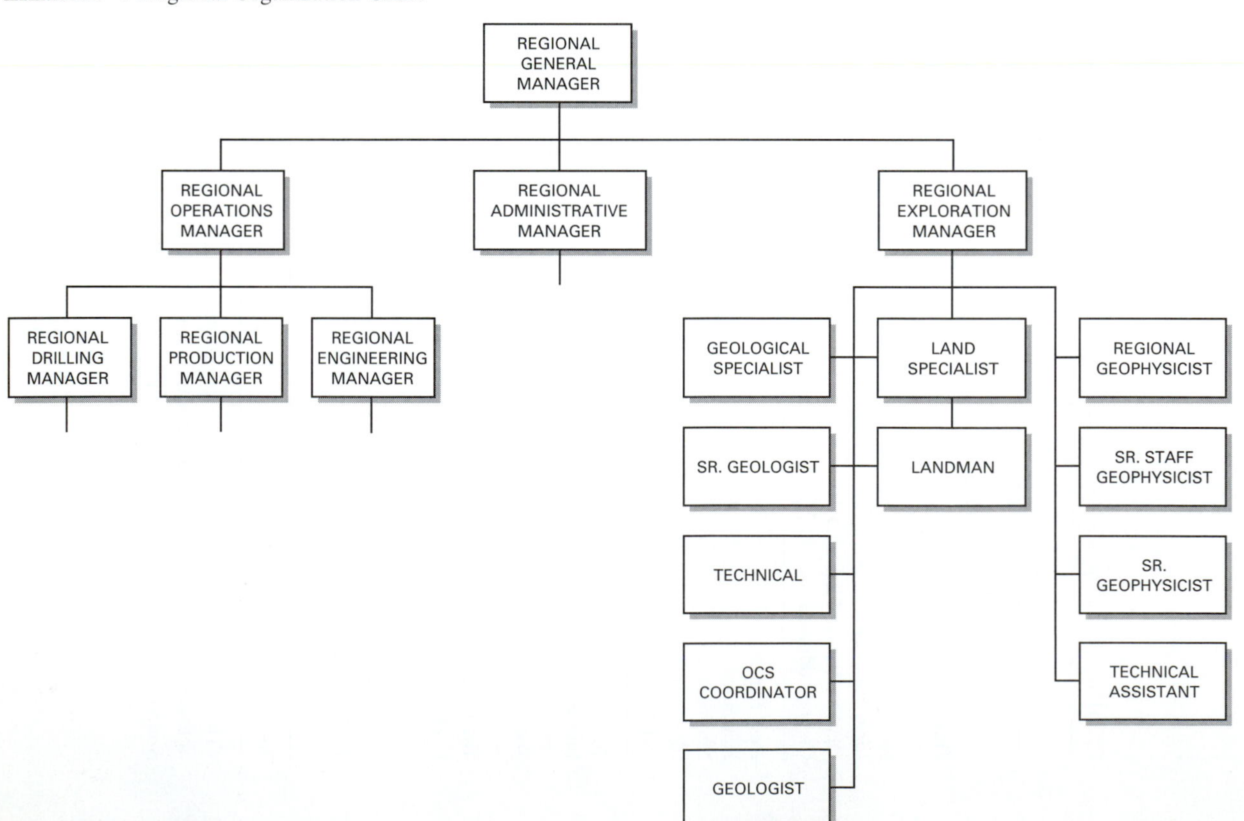

EXHIBIT 5 Discoveries Qualifying for Award

Wildcat	Well located on a structural feature or stratigraphic trap which previously has not been proven productive of oil or gas. These wells are generally at least two miles from the nearest productive area, although distance may not be the only determining factor.
New Horizon Wildcat	An exploratory test located within the productive area of a field partially or completely developed. It is drilled below the deepest production zone to explore for deeper unknown prospects or develops shallower horizons not previously recognized by industry as potentially productive in that field.
New Pool Wildcat	A well located to explore for a new pool (reservoir) on a structural feature or stratigraphic trap already producing oil or gas but outside the known limits of the producing area.
Outpost Well	Well located and drilled for the purpose of extending the productive area of a partly developed pool. It is generally two or more spacing locations distant from the nearest productive sites but distance is not the sole criterion for designating a well as an outpost. Timing and production history of the partly developed pool are also considerations.

EXHIBIT 6 Example of a Discovery Award Plan Calculation

Assumptions:

1) A wildcat is drilled based on a concept originated by an explorationist at a cost of $400,000, including acreage and seismic costs. Production facilities cost an additional $100,000.
2) Initial well discovers 3 BCF* of net proven gas reserves to NNA as determined by outside consultants.
3) Present worth of the 3 BCF discounted at 10 percent is $8 million (value of gas less operating expenses).
4) Total award for the discovery is $75,000 (one percent of $8 million present value of reserves less $500,000 investment).
5) Total Award: Category A—$50,000 (66.7% of 75,000)
   Category B—$25,000 (33.3% of 75,000)
   $75,000
6) Payment recap:

	To Category A Participant(s)	*To Category B Participant(s)*
At time of discovery	$10,000	$5000
2nd year	10,000	5000
3rd year	10,000	5000
4th year	10,000	5000
5th year	4,000**	2000**

*Billion cubic feet.

**In 5th year reserve estimate is adjusted downward reducing the total award to $66,000. If at any time during the Discovery Award base period the reserves are adjusted upward, then the award will be adjusted upward accordingly.

EXHIBIT 7 Excerpts from Interview with Regional Explorationists

Code: CW = Casewriter
BG = Barry Gidman (geologist)
JM = "Diamond" Jim Murphy (geophysicist)

CW: How long have each of you been with NNA?

BG: One and a half years.

JM: A little over two years.

CW: Did both of you come from major oil companies?

BG: I came from Amoco.

JM: Mobil.

CW: Did the DAP affect your decision to come to NNA?

BG: Definitely. It was my number one consideration. I turned down a lot of other offers that included stock options and other incentives. I didn't want to talk with anyone unless they mentioned overrides.

CW: But this isn't an override, is it?

JM: It's a type of override. It's close. Most of the other companies of Natomas's size, which offer mid-range security, at best just have a bonus plan which has nothing to do with the finds made. The DAP is better than a bonus, but it's not as good as a vested override.

CW: Has the DAP affected the way you do your job?

BG: Yes, definitely! It's a terrific incentive. There's upside potential for reward. It's a chance to make a lot of money, and it's a great incentive to work hard.

CW: You've both been on the plan for approximately 2 years. Can you give me a rough idea of how much you earned on this plan?

BG: About as much as everyone else—nothing! I haven't been involved in any wells that have been drilled. In my two years, I think we've only drilled five wells in this region, with only one being a marginal producer.

CW: Well, you have a chance to get rich if they start drilling wells again. Does that make you work harder?

BG: Definitely. I think so.

JM: Up to a point. A lot of it depends on the number of wells that are being drilled. It's more meaningful if you're drilling a lot of wells. But nobody's drilling wells now.

CW: What does that do to your work now?

BG: Most of the work we're doing has a two- or three-year lead time from the time of the idea until the preliminary drilling is done. Who knows what the situation will be at that time? We're working on lots of projects, and they aren't all going to mature. You have to be optimistic. The DAP is definitely a long-term incentive plan.

CW: From your perspective, is the DAP in the best interests of NNA?

JM: I'd have to say yes. It encourages individual effort and teamwork, and that should be what management should be trying to accomplish.

CW: How about the cost? Is it worth it?

BG: Absolutely! They're only paying off for success, so it doesn't really cost them anything. If someone makes you $100, why not give them $1?

CW: Some people might argue that you don't deserve to share in the rewards. You're getting a salary for your efforts. It's the shareholders who are bearing all the risk; they're not charging you for dry holes.

BG: The whole idea is to find a successful place to drill. It costs about $3 million per well to drill, and with a 90% failure rate, why not give the guy who is very successful a little more incentive? It only costs if you're successful, and even then it only costs about 1%.

CW: If they raised the incentive a couple of percentage points, would that give you greater incentive?

BG: Definitely. I think I would start bringing work home and working weekends . . . probably.

EXHIBIT 8 Income Variance Analysis 1982 Actual vs. 1982 Plan* (000)

				Non-controllable				*Controllable*				
	1982 Actual	*1982 Plan*	*Better (Worse)*	*Price*	*G&A*	*Other*	*Total*	*Full Cost Rate*	*Production*	*G&A*	*Other*	*Total*
Oil & Gas Sales	$115,500	$188,600	$(73,100)	$(14,900)	$—	$ —	$(14,900)	$ —	$ 59,700	$—	$1,500	$(58,200)
Expenses												
Lease Operating	$ 10,100	$ 8,700	$ (1,400)	—	—	$(3,400)	$ (3,400)	$ —	$ 1,500	$—	$ 500	$ 2,000
General & Administrative	19,300	19,700	400	—	—	—	—	—	—	400	—	400
Depreciation	2,500	1,500	(1,000)	—	—	(1,000)	(1,000)	—	—	—	—	—
Full Cost Amortization	154,500	$119,600	(34,900)	8,000	—	—	8,000	(75,100)	32,200	—	—	(42,900)
Total Expenses	$186,400	$149,500	$ (36,900)	$ 8,000	—	$(4,400)	$ 3,600	$(75,100)	$ 33,700	$400	$ 500	$(40,500)
Net Income	$(70,900)	$ 39,100	$(110,000)	$ (6,900)	—	$(4,400)	$(11,300)	$(75,100)	$(26,000)	$400	$2,000	$(98,700)

*All data are disguised.

Wertheimer-Betz, A.G.

LONG-TERM INCENTIVE PLAN

In February 1983, Wertheimer-Betz, A.G. (WB) instituted a long-term incentive plan in its U.S. subsidiary which provided cash awards for key managers whose business units were able to accomplish the targets set in their long-term strategic plans. Martin (Marty) Hayes (Senior VP-U.S. Finance and Administration) explained why the plan was established and what he saw as the major risk:

> The new long-term incentive plan is designed as an integral part of our compensation package, and we also hope it will have some positive motivational effects. In particular, we are hoping that it will reinforce the message that we are interested in managerial thinking that extends beyond just quarterly or annual earnings increases.
>
> I am worried, however, that the new plan won't accomplish what we want, and it may even be counter-productive. We are a highly decentralized firm, and the instructions we send to our division presidents about how they are to do strategic planning emphasize the fact that we want it to be a creative process. We say: "We want you to *blue-sky* and theorize. You tell us, as an entrepreneur, where you want to take the business. Assume the money is there." But we haven't always been consistent. When the divisions come in with their plans, we are prone to say: "This is ridiculous. There's no way your business will quadruple in four years. Go back and be more realistic." And now we are saying that the managers' long-term compensation is based on the strategic planning numbers. We may be eliminating any chance of getting the blue-sky thinking the company wants and really does need.

THE COMPANY

WB was a large, privately held conglomerate based on Cologne, West Germany. The company consisted of a collection of manufacturing and service businesses in eight industry groups as varied as, for example, packaging products (e.g., glass containers), pumps, farm machinery, metal products, shipping, and information services. In 1982, consolidated sales totalled $1.6 billion. (Summary financial figures are shown in Exhibit 1.)

WB was managed by a three-member Executive Committee consisting of the controlling stockholder and his representatives and a five-member Board of Management (Exhibit 2). Each Board of Management member had both line and staff responsibility; he was responsible for one or more of the eight industry groups and one or more staff functions (Exhibit 3). The industry groups were each run by a group president who was responsible for from three to seven product divisions. The divisions of which there were a total of 44 in WB, were largely self-contained businesses which were organized on a functional basis (Exhibit 4).

Although WB had operating facilities in 14 countries, a significant proportion of the company's business was in the U.S. In 1982, five of the eight industry groups and 19 of the 44 divisions were headquartered in the U.S., and the U.S. legal entity accounted for approximately 50 percent of the consolidated WB sales and 70 percent of the net income. Most of the U.S. operations had been part of a publicly held company that was acquired in 1976.

PLANNING PROCESSES

The company's planning processes were divided into two distinct cycles: strategic planning and operating planning (Exhibit 5). Strategic planning

This case was prepared by Assistant Professor Kenneth A. Merchant as the basis for class discussion rather than to illustrate either effective or ineffective handling of an administrative situation.

was a relatively new process at WB; the 1983 process was only the company's fourth cycle.

Strategic planning was intended to involve creative thinking about opportunities and strategies, with a long (5 year) horizon. Most of the strategic planning was done at the division level, with very few guidelines provided to the divisions by top management. The division presidents were expected to analyze their businesses' strengths, weaknesses, and opportunities and to present proposals to top management as to what they wanted to do. The plans might involve, for example, investments, acquisitions, and/or divestments.

The strategic plan was not required to be submitted in any particular set format, but it was expected that it would be in narrative form, backed up by a small number (perhaps 3–5) of supporting numerical schedules. (Exhibit 6 provides an outline summary of the planning package submitted by one of the Metals divisions in 1982.) Presentations of the strategic plans were made to the group presidents and the board of management on a staggered basis in the early part of the year, generally at a rate of about one group per month starting in January.

After the strategic plans had been approved, the divisions began working on their operating plans. The operating plans were expressed in terms of income statements and balance sheets for the coming year by month. The operating plans were reviewed by the group president, the board of management and headquarters staff personnel in late September or early October.

The operating plans were intended to be detailed expressions of the first year of the strategic plans, but that did not always happen. Marty Hayes explained:

> A casual observer might conclude that the operating plans bear no relation to the first year of the strategic plan. But anywhere from 3–6 months have passed between the time the strategic plan is put together and the time when the operating plan is prepared, and a lot can change over that period. The operating plans reflect the new information. I would also say that it is generally true that the operating plans are more conservative—or realistic if you prefer—than the strategic plans, sometimes significantly so.

THE COMPENSATION PACKAGE

The compensation package that WB offered its management personnel varied significantly by location. For personnel in the industry groups based on Cologne, compensation consisted almost entirely of salary. For managers in the U.S.-based groups, however, WB offered its management personnel a base salary that was competitive, but not on the high side, and relied on performance-based incentives to help retain its key personnel. The company offered two incentive plans which paid cash awards for business unit performance—a short-term plan and a long-term plan.

Short-Term Incentive Plan

The short-term incentive plan provided annual cash awards based on the level of return on investment (ROI) achieved by the profit center to which the individual was assigned (division or above). ROI was defined as pretax, preinterest operating income divided by book values of assets less current liabilities. About 150 managers were included in the short-term plan, including most managers down to one or two levels below division presidents.

As part of the operating planning process, the board of management member responsible for each division or group established a range of ROI performance that would qualify for the short-term incentive awards. Performance below the lower (threshold) level would qualify for no awards; in company terminology, the *payout factor* would be 0.0. Performance at the upper (maximum) level, would qualify for twice the normal award (payout factor of 2.0), but no extra awards would be paid for ROI above this level. The payout factor increased linearly with ROI between the threshold and maximum levels. The ROI target in the operating plan was generally near the middle of the range. This is illustrated in Exhibit 7.

At normal performance levels (payout factor of 1.0), the short-term incentive plan was designed to pay the following percentages of salary:

ORGANIZATIONAL LEVEL	EXPECTED PAYOUT (% OF SALARY)
Group President	65
Division President	50
Functional Manager	35

The Long-Term Incentive Plan

The long-term incentive plan provided cash awards to approximately 60 high-level general and staff managers. Payouts were based on sales growth and ROI performance over a longer period, generally four years, again as compared to the targets established during the planning processes. Further details on the long-term incentive plan are provided later in the case.

The Weighting Between the Elements of Compensation

The payouts were set to provide compensation in approximately the following proportions for a division president:

Salary	50%
Short-term incentive	25%
Long-term incentive	25%

For higher management (e.g., group presidents), salary was a lower proportion of total compensation, and for lower management it was a higher proportion.

HISTORY OF LONG-TERM INCENTIVES

WB's U.S. businesses had had a long-term management incentive plan since the early 1970s (before the acquisition by WB). Up until 1976, the long-term incentive plan was a performance share plan. Under this plan, participants, who included personnel down to division presidents and key staff personnel, were assigned a number of hypothetical shares of company stock and were paid biannually for growth in the value of the stock over the prior four-year period. Typical two-year awards were 100 to 150 percent of annual salary.

After WB acquired the public company, the performance share plan was continued, except that the payoffs had to be based on total corporate earnings instead of stock price because the shares were no longer publicly traded. The payouts were calculated with the assumption that the WB price-earnings ratio would be equal to, and remain equal to, that of the public company at the point in time when the shares ceased to be traded.

In 1980–81, however, the performance share plan fell on hard times. The worldwide shipping business collapsed, and business was so bad for WB's Shipping and Transport Services Group that the entire 1979 and 1981 share issues were wiped out, despite the fact the other groups were holding their own. This led WB management to replace the performance share plan with another form of long-term incentive plan. The new plan was announced in February 1983.

THE NEW LONG-TERM INCENTIVE PLAN

The new long-term incentive plan was designed to:

1. The motivation and rewards to the achievement of long-term strategic goals at the group and division levels.
2. Provide long-term incomes which, when combined with base salary, annual incentives, benefits and perquisites, would provide competitive total compensation opportunities required to attract and retain quality executives.

The following sections describe the details of the plan.

Participants and Payout Levels

Participants included the Group and Division managers and key headquarters staff managers. In addition, group managers could nominate other individuals for inclusion in the plan. These would be people who had made important contributions, who had significant responsibilities, and/or who had high potential. These nominations were subject to the approval of the Compensation Committee of the Board of Directors. In 1983, the total number of participants in the plan was about 60 (2 percent of the exempt work force in the U.S.).

The payouts varied by level in the organization. The maximum payouts were as follows:

ORGANIZATIONAL LEVEL OF PARTICIPANT	MAXIMUM PAYOUT (%)
Group management	65
Division management/ Headquarters staff	50
Functional management	35 or 25

Performance Measures

Payouts were based on: (1) real growth in sales, and (2) return on investment (ROI) in the business unit to which the individual was assigned over the performance cycle (generally four years). Real sales growth was measured on a cumulative, compound basis over the length of the performance cycle. The real growth was measured either in terms of numbers of units sold, where those numbers existed, or nominal dollars deflated by a price index which best reflected the price increases in the industry. ROI was averaged over the years in the performance cycle.

Definition of Business Units

Each profit center was not defined as a unique business unit for purposes of assigning long-term incentive awards. Some divisions were grouped together into what were called *natural complementary work units.* For example, one work unit called *Glass Containers* included four glass container-related divisions. Barry Charton (President-Packaging Products Group) explained why this was done:

> Our glass container divisions are essentially in the same business; they just operate in different regions of the country. One of our objectives in combining them in the long-term incentive plan was to get the managers to think in terms of a national glass business, rather than as a regional business. More of that kind of thinking would help us improve our facility and equipment utilization and our service to national accounts.

At the time the plan was started (February 1983), 13 business units were identified. These included 12 operating units plus New York staff. These are shown in Exhibit 8.

Performance Cycle

Despite the fact that the strategic plans were prepared with a five-year horizon, the long-term incentives were generally based on a four-year performance cycle. Pam Widdett (Director-U.S. Personnel) explained the rationale for this choice:

> There are two reasons for the four-year performance cycle. First, a four-year performance cycle keeps us in line with industrial practice. The surveys we have gathered show that most companies with long-term incentive plans have used a three- or four-year cycle. And second, the performance share plan we were replacing had a four-year performance cycle, and we didn't see any need to change.

In addition to the first normal four-year performance cycle (1983–86), two *special* cycles were started in 1983 for shorter periods, one covering 1983–84 and the other 1983–85 (Exhibit 9). This was done to help retain key personnel who had not gotten payments from the discontinued performance plan. Marty Hays remarked about the special cycles:

> We were really able to add the special cycles to replace the awards we had lost only because we're privately held. If we were a public company, we'd have had to go to a proxy statement, and it would have been a difficult thing to explain.

Payout Factors

The method of determining the long-term incentive payout factors was very similar to that used for determining the factor for the short-term awards. During the planning process, a payout range was established for each performance measure, and the extreme points on this range determined the line from which the payout factors would be calculated. (This was shown in Exhibit 7).

In general, payout factors of 1.0 were promised if the sales growth and ROI targets in the strategic plan were achieved, but the responsible board of management member was allowed room for judgment. He could decide that the plan was either tough or easy and recommend to the Corporate Compensation Committee that the payout factor be skewed in one direction or another. Pam Widdett explained:

> Assume a business unit planned a ROI of 20 percent. A normal payout range might be 14 to 26 percent because the threshold is generally set about 30 percent below plan and the maximum is set about 30 percent above. But it is very rare that targets are set below 15 percent, which is what we assume as our cost of money (12 percent)[1] plus a 3 percent risk factor, so the range would probably be set at 15 to 26 percent.[2]
>
> Further assume, however, that the responsible Board of Management member judged this plan to be optimistic or particu-

---

[1]The cost of money assumed for purposes of the long-term incentive plan could be changed annually. In 1983 it was set conservatively high. Marty Hayes estimated that in 1983 the company's marginal cost of capital was approximately 9½ percent.

[2]For the sales growth measure, it was rare that the threshold was set below zero.

larly challenging. He might then choose to skew the payout range downward, perhaps to 15 to 22 percent. He would be saying: "This is really a tough plan. If they make 20 percent ROI, I would be very pleased." Then if this unit actually achieved the 20 percent ROI, the payout factor would be approximately 1.4, or 70 percent of maximum.[3] (This example is shown in graphical form in Exhibit 10.) The opposite would also be true, as if he thought the plan was conservative, the range might be set from 17 to 29 percent.

There are different ways to skin a cat. We could keep rejecting a plan because it's too loose, or too tough, or we can make this type of adjustment to the incentive plan to take care of the problem. We have been making the same kind of adjustments to the targets for the short-term incentive plan for years.

The Award Calculation

The actual cash award was determined by multiplying the individual's award potential (i.e., assigned percentage of salary) by a weighted average of the payout factors achieved in sales growth and ROI. Exhibit 11 shows a sample calculation.

The weighting between sales growth and ROI was set differently in different business units to reflect the relative importance of each, given the unit's business strategy. Growth-oriented units had a higher weighting on sales growth, while mature units had a higher weighting on ROI. For example, the following chart shows how the weightings were set for the rapidly growing Information Technology Group and the more stable Fluid Products Group:

GROUP	SALES WEIGHTING	ROI WEIGHTING
Information Technology	60%	40%
Fluid Products	30%	70%

One final feature was included in the award calculation. In the event that a unit's actual ROI was below the cost of money, penalties were assessed according to the following schedule:

AMOUNT ROI BELOW COST OF MONEY	REDUCTION IN AWARD
1 percentage point	25%
2 percentage points	50%
3 percentage points	75%
4 percentage points	100%

It was expected that the assessment of penalties would be a rare occurrence.

Long-Term Incentives for Headquarters Personnel

For headquarters personnel (i.e., Board of Management, staff personnel), the long-term incentive awards were based on a payout factor calculated as follows:

- 90 percent was based on a simple average of the payout factors of the five groups, with no upper limit to the performance range considered.
- 10 percent was based on control of headquarters expense. Performance was rated at 1.0 at the budgeted level, 0.0 at 110 percent of budget, and 2.0 at 90 percent of budget.

Controllability Judgment Allowed

Provision was made for applying managerial judgment if it was felt that the actual performance as indicated by either measure was distorted by extraordinary circumstances. Marty Hayes explained why this after-the-fact judgment was allowed:

> We always have to keep in mind what we are trying to do—we are trying to motivate operating managers to make good business judgments. But uncontrollable factors can distort the measures so much that we can lose the motivational value.
>
> For example, one of our groups does a significant amount of business in Mexico. The Mexican devaluation has had a tremendous negative effect on that business, and if we didn't adjust the numbers, personnel in that division would lose the awards of several four-year cycles in addition to their annual incentive. We're trying to be fair, and there are always going to be judgments that will have to be made.

Recommendations for judgments were to be made by the group president of the affected business unit to the Board of Management and the Compensation Committee.

[3]The formula for the payout line would be $PF = 2/7\ ROI - 30/7$; where PF is the payout factor and ROI is the ROI percentage.

MANAGEMENT REACTIONS TO THE PLAN

The reactions of the WB managers to the new long-term incentive plan were generally favorable, particularly from those who had been part of the old performance share plan. Most had some suggestions for improvement, however. Excerpts from interviews with managers included in the plan are shown in Exhibits 12 to 15.

CONCLUSION

Long-term incentive plans based on multiyear performance were a relatively recent development in the U.S., and because the concept was new, WB management expected that the plan might have to be refined over time. Marty Hayes explained:

> We had to do something. A high proportion of our compensation is based on incentives, and our package was not really competitive when the old performance share plan zeroed out.
>
> This plan has a number of things to recommend it. The measures should be reasonably good indicators of our success. The plan is relatively easy to explain to those who are affected by it. And it involves enough money that the managers will pay attention to it. As a consequence, we should get increased attention to the long term.
>
> But there are a number of unanswered questions, and we can't look elsewhere for answers because none of the companies that have implemented similar plans did it far enough back to have had executives go through a full cycle. Here are some of the questions in my mind:
>
> - As I mentioned before, are we going to cause managers to become more conservative? Are we going to discourage really creative long-range thinking?
> - Are we providing enough emphasis on the long range? There is still a tremendous proportion (30 to 40 percent) of compensation based on annual ROI performance.
> - Are we providing too high a percentage of our management compensation on incentive pay? Some of our managers may have personally contracted for fixed payments (e.g., mortgage) at or close to the level of compensation they have come to expect. What if some of our businesses fall apart, for reasons that may or may not be under the managers' control? We might inadvertently cause some of our people to go into bankruptcy, and we can't allow that, can we?
> - How do we encourage a manager to transfer from a healthy division to one that needs to be turned around? We have tried to get around this problem by offering a guarantee (good for two years only) that their long-term awards will be no less than what they would have been if they had stayed in the other division. Will that be enough?
> - Do we have good control over our performance measures? We don't have an internal audit function, and the compensation of the most senior people who should be performing this control function is based on the same measures used to reward the managers. Is this a case of putting the *fox in the chickenhouse?* Do we have a significant risk of bias without the necessary controls?
>
> As I say, I don't have the answers to these questions, as the plan has been in place less than one year. I expect we will be in the process of evaluating this plan for many years to come.

EXHIBIT 1 Summary Financial Information ($ millions)

	1982	*1981*
Consolidated Sales	1,567	1,597
Net Income	55	107
Cash Flow	95	145

EXHIBIT 2 Organization Structure

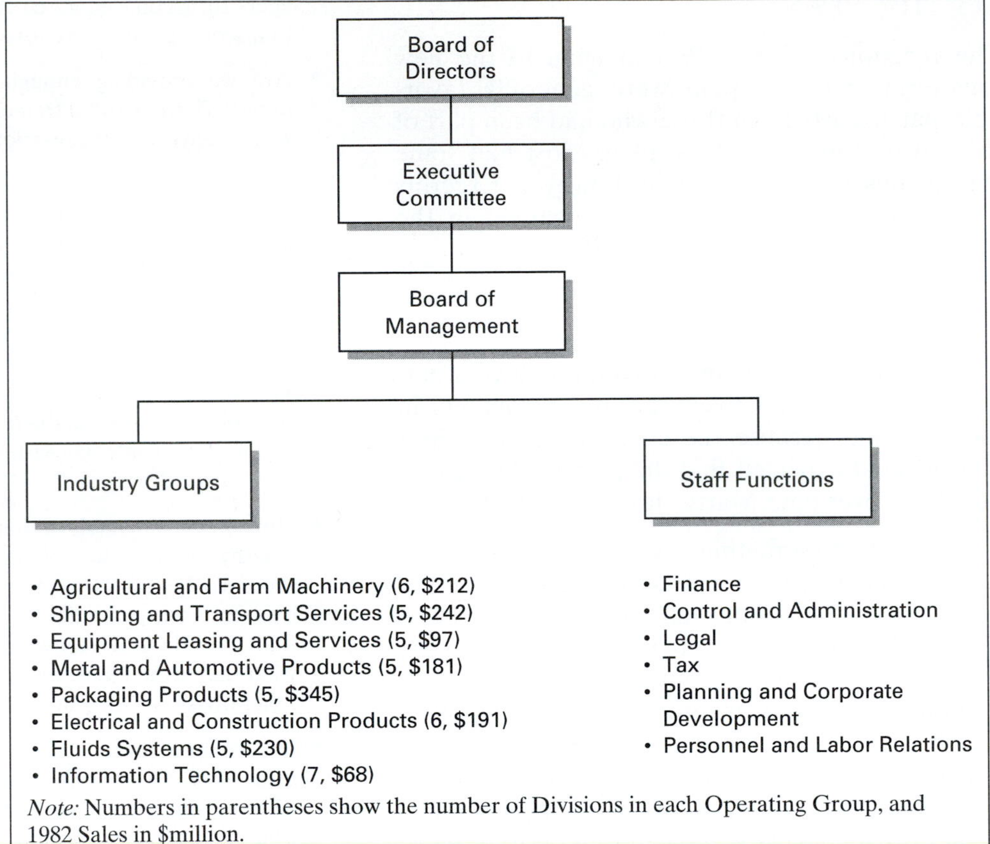

Note: Numbers in parentheses show the number of Divisions in each Operating Group, and 1982 Sales in $million.

EXHIBIT 3 Responsibilities of Board of Management Members

Board of Management Member	*Responsible for:* *Industry Groups*	*Staff Functions*
Rolf Meyer	Agricultural and Farm Machinery	Finance Control
Rudolf Burger	Shipping and Transport Services	Legal Tax
Kurt Weber	Equipment Leasing and Services	Planning and Corporate Development
Ronald Whittington*	Metal and Automotive Products	U.S. Personnel and Labor Relations
	Packaging Products	
	Electrical and Construction Products	
Daniel Smith*	Fluids Systems	U. S. Headquarters Staff
	Information Technology	

*Based in New York

EXHIBIT 4 Typical Group Organization

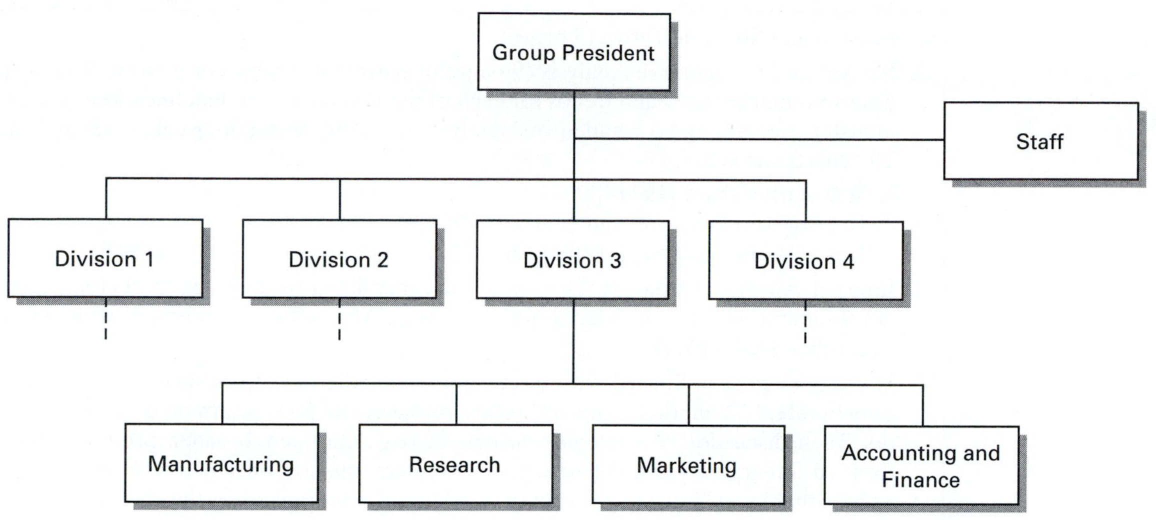

EXHIBIT 5 Timing of Strategic and Operating Planning Processes

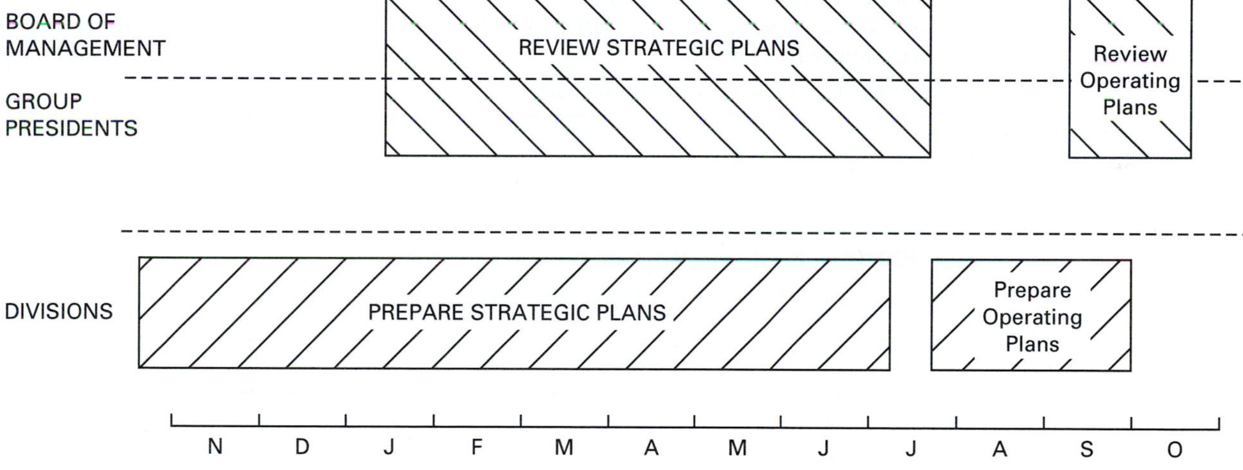

EXHIBIT 6 Outline of Strategic Plan Submitted by a Metals Division

1. Mission and Strategic Thrust (3 pages).
2. Market and Competitive Analysis (9 pages of narrative, 3 tables of figures). This section discussed market sizes and trends for each of the two major product lines, key customers, industry capacity, and a competitors' analysis, including strengths, weaknesses and plans. The charts showed:
   1. WB market share (1970–88).
   2. Industry capacity by manufacturer (1979, 1982, 1985).
   3. Key customer analysis—volume and WB market share (1981, 1982, 1988).
3. Internal Analysis (4 pages). Discussion of capabilities in areas of marketing, product development, production, and human resources. Also section on degrees of integration with other areas of WB.
4. Strategy (5 pages). Started with discussion of specific objectives, including 8% average growth rate, 15% market share, 8% return on sales, and 50% return on investment before tax. Then discussion of strategic alternatives (e.g., maintain, broaden product offerings, forward integration) and the selection of strategy made. Concluded with list of specific actions that would have to be accomplished in order to implement the chosen strategy.
5. Financial Summary (5 schedules with 3 page-up pages).
   1. Sales, Profit, Return on Investment, Cash Sources and Uses, and Employee Count (1979–1988)
   2. Summary Balance Sheet (1983–1988)
   3. Sales and Profit Comparison (1982 vs. 1983)
   4. Capital Expenditure Summary (1982–1988)
   5. Market and Sales Forecast (1982–1988)—market size, market share, competitor assumptions.
6. Organization (1 page organization chart)

EXHIBIT 7 Typical Short-Term Payout Factor Range

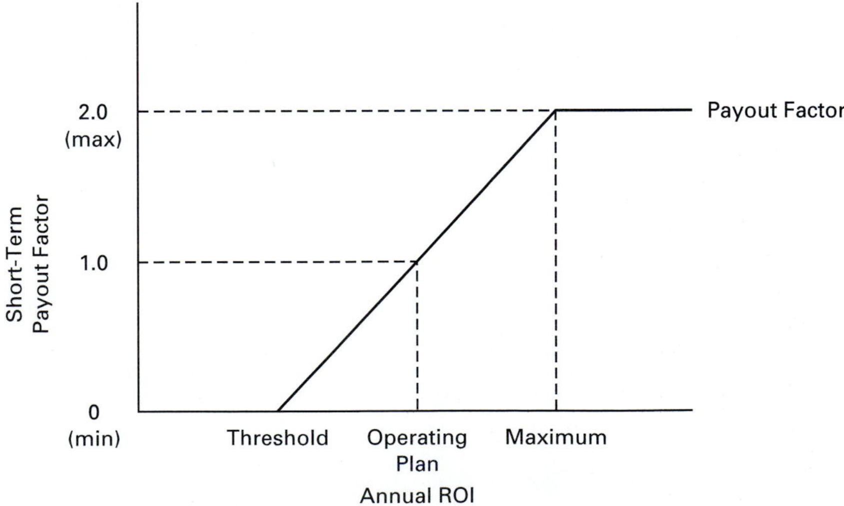

EXHIBIT 8 Business Units for Long-Term Incentive Plan

PACKAGING PRODUCTS GROUP
- Glass Containers (4 Divisions)
- Corrugated Containers (1 Division)

ELECTRICAL AND CONSTRUCTION PRODUCTS GROUP
- Plastic and Foam Products (2 Divisions)
- Electrical Products (2 Divisions)

FLUID PRODUCTS GROUP

METAL AND AUTOMOTIVE PRODUCTS GROUP
- Automotive Products (2 Divisions)
- Metal Products (2 Divisions)
- Commercial Vehicles (1 Division)

INFORMATION TECHNOLOGY GROUP

NEW YORK STAFF

EXHIBIT 9 Performance Periods and Award Cycles

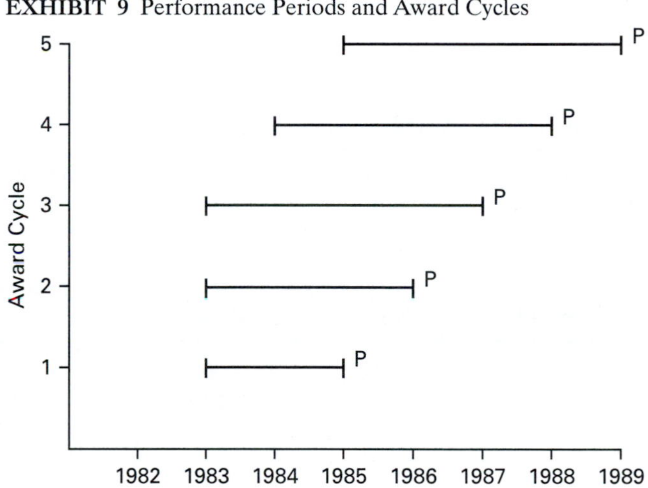

EXHIBIT 10 Determining Long-Term Payout Factors—Example

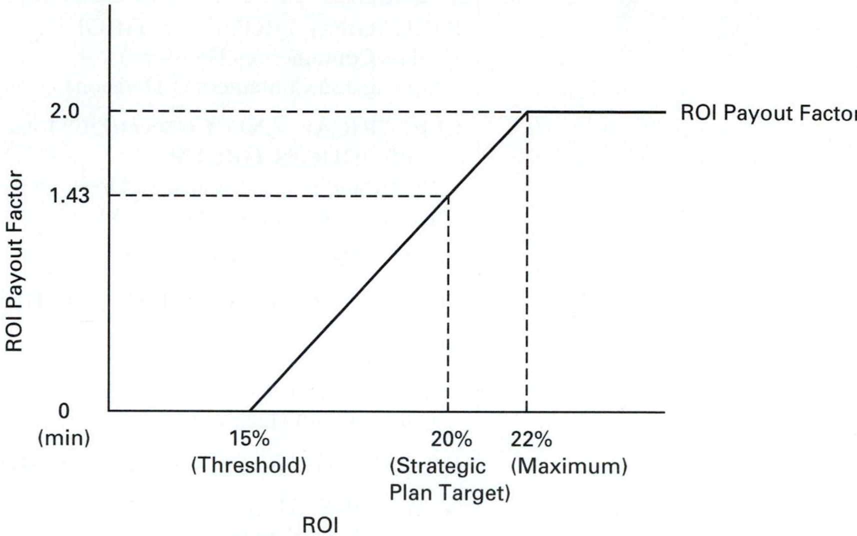

Formula: PF = 2/7 ROI − 30/7
At 20% ROI: PF = 1.43

EXHIBIT 11 Long-Term Incentive Award—Sample Calculation

Assume: Individual Assigned 100% to Business Unit with Performance Weighted 30% Sales, Growth 70% ROI
Award Potential: 50% of Salary = $40,000

Performance Factor	*Target Award*	*Target*	*Maximum*	*Actual Achieved (over 4 yr.)*	*Rating Achieved*	*Amount Payable*
Sales growth	$12,000	2%	6%	4%	1.5	$18,000
ROI	$28,000	18%	23%	18%	1.0	28,000
						$46,000

EXHIBIT 12 Excerpts from Interview with Barry Charton, Group President, Packaging Products Group

I think it's a good plan. In my opinion, the old performance share plan was designed more for retention than motivation. This is a positive change. Now people think they can see what they're contributing to and what it means. For example, they can see the effect of cutting out a couple of thousand dollars of expense.

.....

Even though the plan does create a better environment for long-term thinking, I don't think it will cause me to do any more of it. Long-term thinking is part of what a good manager must do, and I think I was already doing what had to be done. But it may cause me to look a little harder at the numbers in the plan, and that's good.

.....

The major suggestion I have is that I think some criteria other than sales growth and ROI are required. For example, sales growth is not part of the mission of this group. We're in a decline, and the forecast is for continued decline. Some other measure, such as cash flow would be a better indicator of how we're fulfilling our mission than sales growth.

.....

When there is a cutoff, such as in this plan, it is natural for managers to look for ways to defer income or accelerate some expenses to build up a bank for going into the next year. But that is more a problem with a short-term plan, and I don't think we've had a significant problem in that area. Money is not the only motivating factor. I think we have created an ethical environment within this company, and we have some controls to back it up.

EXHIBIT 13 Excerpts from Interview with Walt Abrams, Division President, Glass Containers-Western Region (Packaging Products Group)

I think the new plan is infinitely better than the old plan from the standpoint that I have a chance to help in the end result. Before I had no control over what I earned.

.....

I think it makes sense to base the awards on performance of the consolidated glass container business. It's becoming increasingly important that we work together, as some large customers are looking at dealing with a smaller number of vendors who can serve them in all their locations across the U.S. I think this plan will make us take a look at ways we might help each other. I think it would also make sense to base the short-term incentive awards on consolidated performance.

.....

Although this business is mature, and we're really in a defensive posture of trying to hold market share, I like the idea of basing the plan somewhat on sales growth, instead of just on profitability. I am a marketing person, and I've got some ideas about how to increase sales, and I like to get rewarded for what we achieve. For example, I spent some money last year and came out with two new colors which had never been produced commercially before. The expense hurt my profitability last year, but we gained some market share, and this plan gives me a chance to get credit for that growth.

.....

There's no question in anybody's mind where the emphasis is—it's still on the short term. It comes up in every meeting I attend.

.....

Our profitability has not been good. Our competitors have slashed prices, and we had to match the cuts to hold market share. But it's hard to justify not paying bonuses to people who worked hard and did everything they were asked to just because something they didn't have control over went wrong.

EXHIBIT 14 Excerpts from Interview with Steve Haley, Division President, Pump Division (Fluid Products Group)

I'm not terribly excited about the plan. The payoffs are very generous, but they aren't really based on the efforts of the individual. Our awards are based on group performance, and I don't have any control over the performance of the other two divisions. I understand the purpose of putting the fluid products divisions together is to develop some cooperation, some synergies, but there aren't many things I can do with the other fluid divisions. In my opinion, this is an expensive way to try to get cooperation.

. . . . .

I may sound a bit bitter, but there is a reason. I've missed out on the last two long-term payouts, even though my division won the award for the best performance of any division in the company.

. . . . .

I don't think this plan will change the way I prepare my plans. I've always tried to set conservative targets; I like to have a 70% chance of making them. I'm not trying to sandbag management. I just want to be able to meet my plan.

EXHIBIT 15 Excerpts from Interview with Bob Vautran, Division President, Information Handling Division (Information Technology Group)

Overall I think the concept is good, and the dollars involved are meaningful. But I have some problems with the plan. First, our awards are based on the results of the entire group, and that's frustrating because there's a lot I obviously have no control over. The divisions they've lumped together are in related but different businesses, and I don't think there's much cooperation required. People tend to work together if the interests of the company are at stake. I'm not sure this will encourage any more teamwork.

Second, I still don't understand how they're going to compute real growth for my business which is basically involved in providing computer services. Let's say my sales go from $50 million to $60 million. They're going to discount my sales by some factor, maybe an inflation index or a wholesale price index. That could either be good news or bad news. We were in a very competitive market this year, and my prices probably went up about 3%. So if they use a wholesale price index number, say 6–7%, they haven't been fair to us. On the other hand, if my prices had gone up 15% and they use a number like that, then they've been too fair. There really isn't any government index they can use that accurately reflects what's going on in this business, so we may be kidding ourselves that we can measure real growth. If you're going to have a plan that is a real effective motivator, you've got to spell it all out in the beginning.

. . . . .

What happens if early on in the plan, say 1984, we have a bad year. It's likely to kill off several years of payoffs. So if the company is looking at it as a golden handcuff, I don't think it will work.

. . . . .

The numbers managers present in their strategic plans are likely to be much more conservative now. Is that bad? In one sense you could say it is, but in another sense, it keeps you from having people who go off the deep end with a lot of crazy ideas. I think the company has had a lot of those "off-the-deep-end" situations in the past. I would hope that we'd still do the creative thinking but be more inclined to say that instead of that market bringing us $10 million in year 3, we'll say it will bring $5 million in year 3.

. . . . .

I think there is a great short-term orientation in this company. Annual compensation is based anywhere from a third to 40% on this year's ROI. Given that so much of the compensation is based on annual results, it's pretty tough to get away from thinking short term.

Duckworth Industries, Inc. — Incentive Compensation Programs

In early 1992, Mr. John Duckworth, president and controlling shareholder of Duckworth Industries was considering a change in Duckworth Industries' management incentive compensation systems. If implemented the new plan for Duckworth management would, it was hoped, align more closely the interests of management and shareholders. Several industrial firms which were pioneers in value-based management had recently adopted similar management compensation systems. Adopting the new system would keep Duckworth in the vanguard of management incentive compensation planning.

Background

Mr. Duckworth was a strong believer in the power of incentives to guide management action. When he was first promoted to a plant management job in the 1950s, Mr. Duckworth took over a plant which had an operating loss of $2.7 million on sales of $9.0 million. He implemented what was then a *state-of-the-art* plan for factory incentives. The plan applied to all supervisors. Achievement of specified goals earned a 15 percent premium over an individual's base rate of pay. As noted by Mr. Duckworth:

> The more sobering side of the plan consisted of docking supervisors 12 percent of their base rate when goals were not achieved. Paychecks having a 12 percent deduction for failure were distributed in bright red envelopes. At that time I was plant manager of the operation, and I got several red pay envelopes. Some 15–18 months after the 12% Club was profitably and smoothly functioning, the National Labor Relations Board issued a cease and desist order predicated on the fact you cannot tamper with an individual's base pay. Naturally, I complied, but the results were already in—the division was profitable.

Mr. Duckworth founded his own business in 1971. Sales grew from $400,000 in that year to almost $125 million in 1992 (Exhibit 1). In 1986, a holding company (Duckworth Industries) was established. It included the original business, Worth Corp., which was a highly profitable producer of proprietary fasteners and adhesives. In 1986, Hospitality Equipment Service was acquired at a purchase price of $5.5 million. In 1988, Hotel Telecom Services was acquired for about $15.0 million. The two newer acquisitions were service businesses rather than manufacturers, and to date had not yet generated satisfactory levels of profitability. In 1992, Duckworth Industries employed 755 people. The structure of the organization is shown in Exhibit 2.

The Six Duckworth Incentive Plans

Pay for performance was firmly embedded in the corporate culture at Duckworth Industries. In the words of one senior executive, "we put incentives, within reason, behind everything we can."

For plant-level employees, Duckworth had an *attendance* bonus. A 60 cents per hour pay incentive was earned for each pay period during which an employee was never more than 2 minutes late for work.

For plant-level employees up to the shift supervisory level, there was also a *quality* incentive plan (Exhibits 3 and 4). Quality measures included many variables such as meeting promised shipment dates and reducing customer complaints of any nature. The quality incentive payment target equaled $100 per employee per month. Performance was often a team effort, and the average employee working under this incentive plan received about $600 per year from it. Employees re-

This case was prepared as the basis for class discussion rather than to illustrate either effective or ineffective handling of an administrative situation.

ceived a separate check each month for the quality bonus to highlight the importance of quality in the company culture.

All Duckworth employees were participating in a *profit-sharing* plan. At the level of each business unit a profit-sharing pool was created. The pool was equal in size to 15 percent of pretax profits after a deduction equal to 10 percent of the beginning-of-year net worth allocated to the business unit. At the end of each year the profit-sharing pool was allocated to employees, pro rata, based on their individual share of total wages and salaries in the business unit. At the Worth business unit profit sharing had grown from about 2 percent of pay to about 15 percent of pay in recent years. A plant worker earning $15,000 per year would get $2,250. Information sharing with plant personnel as to profit and margin levels was common at Duckworth, so an estimate of the size of their individual profit sharing allocation could be made by employees as the year progressed.

For all sales and supervisory personnel the company had *individual* incentive plans. These typically afforded an employee the opportunity to earn incentives ranging from 10 to 40 percent of base pay. The incentive plan targets for a typical customer service representative are included as Exhibit 5.

THE EXISTING SENIOR MANAGEMENT INCENTIVE PLANS

The more senior managers at Duckworth (a group comprised of up to 40 people) all participated in an *annual* incentive compensation plan. A smaller subset of this group also participated in a *long-term* incentive program.

The incentive plans (both annual and long-term) for the senior managers had undergone considerable change in the 1983–1992 decade. Prior to 1990, the *annual* incentive plan would target for each manager a bonus of 20 to 50 percent of base salary if certain target levels of performance at the business unit level were reached during the year. Typical measures of performance (depending on the manager's area of responsibility) included at least three of the following:

1. Cash flow
2. Sales growth of proprietary products
3. Direct labor variances
4. Inventory turns
5. Accounts receivable (days sales outstanding)
6. Gross margins (less purchase price variances)
7. Special individual projects

In 1990 Duckworth abandoned the narrowly defined annual targets and opted to tie the annual bonus to a matrix built around sales growth and profitability goals. Annually goals for each business unit were set for both sales growth and profitability (Exhibit 6). These were determined with reference to the performance levels achieved by various peer group companies (Exhibit 7). Individual managers were assigned bonus targets (generally ranging from 25 to 50 percent of base compensation). Depending on the level of sales growth and profitability achieved, a manager could read directly from the matrix the factor by which his/her target bonus would be multiplied to determine the actual bonus he/she would receive. The incentive compensation matrix for the Worth business unit (Exhibit 6) indicated the following: If, in fiscal 1992, a manager working at the Worth business unit had a target bonus of 40 percent, and the business unit provided a 20 percent return on assets and 10 percent sales growth, the manager would receive 1.00 times his/her 40 percent target bonus. In fact, in 1991 and 1992, business unit managers at Duckworth received the following percentages of their target bonuses from the annual incentive plan.

	1991	*1992*
Worth Corp.	170%	0%
Hotel Telecom	0	24
Hospitality Equipment	0	0
Duckworth Industries	90	0

While Duckworth's annual incentive plan for senior managers covered several dozen employees by 1992, the long-term incentive plan covered fewer participants, particularly in the early part of the decade 1983–1992. In 1983 Duckworth implemented a five-year, long-term management incentive plan. The plan covered only two employees, the then vice president and general manager at Worth (now retired) and the then vice president, sales and marketing at Worth (now president of the Hotel Telecom Services operation). The plan made one payment at the end of five years. It was a phantom stock plan tied to the increase in book value per share multiplied by a performance factor (Exhibit 8). The performance factor was determined by several measures including a) the spread separating annual ROE from the sum of the bank prime rate plus two percentage points, b) the annual growth in net book value/share.

According to one of the participants the plan was a horror in complexity, but an attractive feature was that you could have one or two bad years and still get a payment. Because the plan paid only once at the end of five years, it was somewhat like a forced savings plan. "The size of the payment at the end made a meaningful difference in what you could do 'lifestyle'-wise. A check for $150,000 is quite significant when you bring it home. You are willing to make significant personal sacrifices along the way to make it happen."

In 1986 a new long-term management incentive plan was put in place at Duckworth. This plan was broadened to include more managers (15 by 1989) and was designed to begin payments in 1989 after the expiration of the previously described five-year plan. At the start of each year, beginning in 1986, new targets would be established so that incentive payments could be received annually. The business unit management participants in this plan would be awarded a specified percentage of base salary (generally from 25 to 40 percent) if a Challenge Earnings level of cumulative earnings before interest and taxes (approved by Duckworth's board of directors) was achieved by their business unit during the period. Lesser levels of earnings achievement would produce a proportionately reduced level of award (as shown in Exhibit 9 for the Worth business unit).

The incentive system established in 1986 continued for four years. The last update was put in place in 1989, and covered the three-year period ending in 1992.

In fact, between 1989–1992, business unit managers received the following percentages of their target bonuses from the long-term incentive plan.

	1989	*1990*	*1991*	*1992*
Worth Corp.	112%	97%	92%	91%
Hotel Telecom	—	40	20	0
Hospitality Equipment	—	—	40	45
Duckworth Industries	85	80	75	73

For the top management team at Duckworth the target and actual bonus payments (measured as a percentage of base salary) are presented as Exhibit 10.

A PROPOSED NEW EVA INCENTIVE SYSTEM

As fiscal 1992 unfolded, both management and Mr. Duckworth (the controlling shareholder) were looking for ways to more closely align the interests of management and shareholders through the incentive plan for senior management. A number of factors had contributed to dissatisfaction with the existing plans. One major factor had to do with operation of the annual incentive plan of Worth in 1992. In many ways Worth's performance in 1992 was improved over that of 1991.

	Worth Corp.	
	1991	*1992*
Return on gross performing assets	23.6%	23.9%
Sales growth	13.9	(2.3)

The return on gross performing assets had increased, but sales had declined slightly (versus a 10 percent goal and a minimum 5 percent sales growth requirement to achieve any annual incentive plan payment). The sales decline was caused by the loss of a very large customer buying a product with commodity-type profit margins. Most of the lost sales in 1992 had been replaced by new customers purchasing proprietary products at higher margins. The change in customer mix was good for enhancing long-run shareholder value, but Worth's management failed to achieve any annual incentive bonus as a result of the change given the structure of the existing annual incentive plan (Exhibit 6).

Near the close of fiscal 1992 Mr. John Duckworth began reading a book entitled *The Quest for Value* by G. Bennett Stewart. The Stewart book outlined a management incentive plan that promised to link management pay directly to the creation of long-run economic value for shareholders. Implementation of the plan required the services of Stern Stewart & Co., a financial consulting firm.

The economic value-added (EVA) compensation system developed by Stern Stewart would require (1) considerable data analysis and (2) some reorienting in thinking about how to approach the business going forward for Duckworth's senior management. The EVA system was predicated on the following logic.

1. Economic value for shareholders is created when a firm earns a rate of return on invested capital which exceeds the cost of capital. The economic value-added in a particular year should equal the product of:
   i) The average capital employed during the year multiplied by
   ii) The spread separating the cost of capital from the return on capital earned during the year.
2. The economic value-added during a year can be calculated for each business unit. The management of each unit can be directly compensated for their success in adding economic value via a compensation formula that automatically adjusts the baseline for calculating next year's bonus to reflect the actual performance of the prior year.

The Key Drivers of Economic Value-Added

Exhibit 11 shows a calculation of the economic value-added by the Worth division of Duckworth Industries from 1988 through 1992. It also shows the *forecasted* economic value-added for the period 1993–1997.

The key variables in determining the economic value-added by a business unit were:

1. Net operating profit after taxes (NOPAT)—Exhibit 11, Line 9.
   This excludes corporate overhead, and capitalizes R&D expenses and then amortizes them over three years. NOPAT excludes noneconomic noncash charges.[1]
2. Average capital—Exhibit 11, Line 19.
   This excludes construction in progress, and assumes FIFO inventory valuation and the add-back of bad debt reserves. Noneconomic noncash writeoffs are added back to average capital.[2]
3. Cost of capital—Exhibit 11, Line 17.
   This is determined annually for each business unit by using an assumed capital structure and riskiness factor (β value) for peer group firms comparable to each business unit. The formula for calculating capital cost was tied to the yield on 30-year Treasury obligations plus a risk premium.

The Mechanism for Calculating Incentive Compensation

Stern Stewart recommended a mechanism for linking economic value-added in a business unit during a given year to the incentive compensation paid to management in that year.

First, a bonus target was established. At Worth this might equal 37 percent of base pay (Exhibit 12, Line 1). Bonus units (like phantom stock) would be assigned to each manager in an amount such that if the bonus unit was valued at $1.00, the desired level of bonus would be earned by the manager (Exhibit 12, Line 3).

Second, a baseline EVA level was established (Exhibit 12, Line 4). At the end of each year the baseline EVA for the *following* year would change by one-half of the difference between the actual EVA achieved and the baseline EVA for the prior year (Exhibit 12, Lines 8–10). This made the system *self-adjusting.* If EVA performance improved each year, the new base would click up by one-half the amount of the improvement. If EVA performance deteriorated for several years, the base level would decline so that the targets would not be so far away as to be unreachable in ensuing years.

Third, a base unit value was established for each ensuing year (Exhibit 12, Lines 6 and 14). This base unit value defined, to a large degree, how much of the target bonus could be earned by just maintaining the existing level of business performance. If EVA hit exactly the baseline EVA each year, and the base unit value was set at $1.00, then exactly the target bonus would be earned each year. In the case of Worth, after the first year the base unit value dropped to $.80. This meant that simply repeating the EVA baseline performance after 1993 would produce only 80 percent of the targeted bonus.

Fourth, a bonus sensitivity factor (Exhibit 12, Lines 7 and 11) was established which could either add to or subtract from the base unit value to create a total unit value. In the Worth example, the bonus sensitivity factor was set at $1,625,000.

[1]Items such as the one-time writeoff of a divested business would be a noneconomic non-cash charge. Items such as depreciation or the amortization of debt discount would be economic noncash charges.

[2]This was designed to prevent managers from escaping responsibility for poor prior investment decisions by simply divesting the poor performing assets.

In any year that EVA varied from the baseline EVA, the amount of the gap was divided by $1,625,000, and the resulting amount (called the *performance* unit value, Exhibit 12, Lines 12 and 13) was added to the base unit value to determine the *total* unit value (Exhibit 12, Line 15). In order to earn one times the target bonus *solely* from the performance unit factor, management of the business unit had to beat the baseline EVA by the amount of the bonus sensitivity factor.

As indicated in Exhibit 12, if Worth hit the forecasted level of EVA in each year, Worth's management would earn the following percentage of their target bonus in each of the next five years.

	% of Target Bonus Earned
1993	100%
1994	51
1995	122
1996	170
1997	211[3]

As indicated in Exhibits 13–16, if the Hotel Telecom Services and Hospitality Equipment Services business units hit their forecasted level of EVA in each year, Hotel Telecom's and Hospitality Equipment's managements would earn the following percentage of their targeted bonus in each of the next five years (Exhibits 14 and 16, Line 15).

	% of Target Bonus Earned	
	Hotel Telecom	*Hospitality Equipment*
1993	45%	79%
1994	99	85
1995	69	71
1996	66	65
1997	62	66

According to Bennett Stewart, the beauty of the EVA incentive compensation system was that it was "A self-motivated, self-adjusting corporate governance system that linked capital budgeting and strategic investment decisions to the compensation system."

From John Duckworth's perspective, not only were the interests of management and shareholders aligned, but in addition the bogeys for determining bonus compensation would not have to be renegotiated each year. What had been two plans (one annual plan and a long-term plan) could be combined into *one* plan that paid on annual results but was designed to build long-term shareholder value. The system was like a self-winding watch. You set it once and it might keep going, all by itself, for quite some time.

[3]Bonuses up to two times the target bonus were paid immediately. One-third of the amount over this maximum was also paid in cash. Remaining amounts were allocated to a *bonus bank* to be paid out in the future. Negative charges for deteriorating performance reduced the bonus bank. Negative charges could even create a negative balance in the bonus bank which would have to be overcome in order to resume bonus payments in future years.

EXHIBIT 1 Consolidated Financial Statements 1975–1992, Fiscal Years Ended 5/31 ($000)

	1975	*1980*	*1985*	*1990*	*1991*	*1992*
Net sales	5,811	15,109	40,793	116,220	123,545	122,570
Cost of goods sold	4,294	11,164	30,142	85,875	89,865	86,720
Selling, gen'l & admin.	1,231	3,199	8,638	24,610	25,080	28,800
Operating income	287	746	2,013	5,735	8,595	7,050
Investment income	68	177	479	1,365	1,375	1,545
Interest expense	129	334	902	2,570	2,390	1,635
Profit sharing expense	55	142	383	1,090	1,595	1,850
Income before taxes	172	447	1,207	3,440	5,985	5,105
Taxes	50	130	351	1,000	1,850	1,565
Net income	122	317	856	2,440	4,135	3,540
Cash & marketable securities[a]	1,067	2,775	7,492	21,345	24,790	26,085
Accounts receivable	578	1,502	4,056	11,555	12,760	13,210
Inventory	572	1,487	4,014	11,435	11,380	12,995
Less: Lifo reserves	51	131	355	1,010	1,111	1,125
Net inventories	522	1,356	3,661	10,430	10,270	11,870
Other current assets	46	119	321	915	960	990
Total current assets	2,212	5,752	15,530	44,245	48,780	52,155
Construction in progress	25	65	176	500	485	3,105
Other net PP&E	799	2,076	5,605	15,970	15,450	14,330
Other assets[b]	290	753	2,032	5,790	5,735	5,685
Total assets	3,325	8,646	23,343	66,505	70,450	75,275
Short term debt	734	1,909	5,154	14,685	17,390	15,910
Other current liabilities	1,048	2,724	7,355	20,955	19,790	23,700
Total current liabilities	1,782	4,633	12,510	35,640	37,180	39,610
Long term borrowings	496	1,290	3,482	9,920	8,355	7,175
Other liabilities	63	164	444	1,265	1,105	1,140
Net worth	984	2,558	6,908	19,680	23,810	27,350
Total liab. & net worth	3,325	8,646	23,343	66,505	70,450	75,275

[a]Marketable securities were carried at the lower of cost or market. Market exceeded cost by $4,090 in 1990, $7,870 in 1991, and $10,940 in 1992.

[b]Other assets included goodwill of $5,130 in 1990, $4,995 in 1991, and $4,855 in 1992.

EXHIBIT 2 Organization Chart, Duckworth Industries, Inc., June 1, 1992

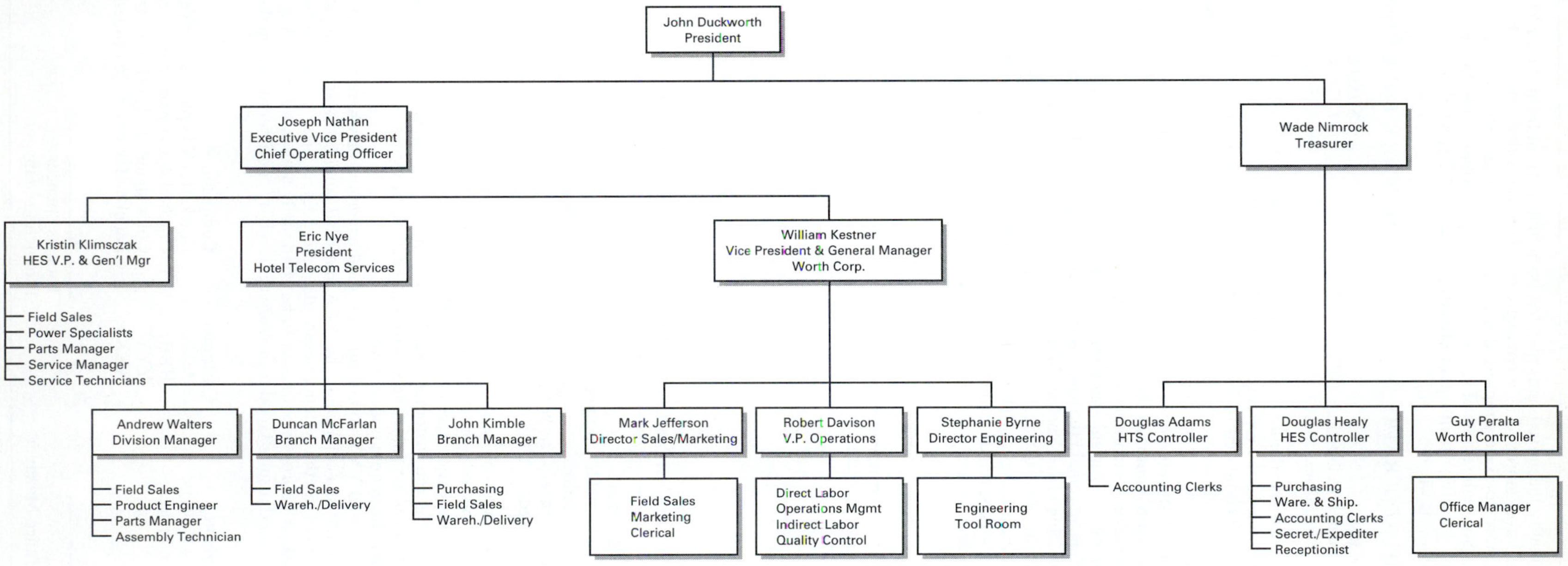

John Duckworth
President

Joseph Nathan
Executive Vice President
Chief Operating Officer

Wade Nimrock
Treasurer

Kristin Klimsczak
HES V.P. & Gen'l Mgr

- Field Sales
- Power Specialists
- Parts Manager
- Service Manager
- Service Technicians

Eric Nye
President
Hotel Telecom Services

William Kestner
Vice President & General Manager
Worth Corp.

Andrew Walters
Division Manager

- Field Sales
- Product Engineer
- Parts Manager
- Assembly Technician

Duncan McFarlan
Branch Manager

- Field Sales
- Wareh./Delivery

John Kimble
Branch Manager

- Purchasing
- Field Sales
- Wareh./Delivery

Mark Jefferson
Director Sales/Marketing

Field Sales
Marketing
Clerical

Robert Davison
V.P. Operations

Direct Labor
Operations Mgmt
Indirect Labor
Quality Control

Stephanie Byrne
Director Engineering

Engineering
Tool Room

Douglas Adams
HTS Controller

- Accounting Clerks

Douglas Healy
HES Controller

- Purchasing
- Ware. & Ship.
- Accounting Clerks
- Secret./Expediter
- Receptionist

Guy Peralta
Worth Controller

Office Manager
Clerical

	Headcount		
Fiscal Year	1993	1992	1991
Duckworth Industries	10	10	12
Worth Corp.	500	485	410
HES	135	155	170
Hotel Telecom	110	95	95
Total	755	745	687

EXHIBIT 3 Duckworth Corporation, Quality Incentive Bonus Plan, Fiscal Year 1993

The Quality Incentive bonus plan has been in its current form since FY90 (June of 1989).

As we have improved as a company it is important that our plan be modified to reflect these changes and more accurately represent what the "real world" reflects in terms of total quality performance. After a thorough review of this years' quality performance the following changes are being made to the Quality Incentive bonus plan effective June 1, 1992 (FY93). The monthly complaint ratio and bonus payout levels will be:

COMPLAINT RATIO	MONTHLY BONUS PAYOUT
.6% or less	$100.00
More than .6%, less than 2.0%	$ 75.00
More than 2.0, less than 3.5%	$ 50.00

As you can see, the lower limits have been changed and the bottom payout of $25 eliminated, but we have increased the top level payout by $25 to $100.00. The total potential maximum yearly payout is now $1,200 compared to $900 with the old plan. This year through the first 11 months we have paid $800 in incentives to each participant. As you can see from the above, superior performance will be rewarded with high-level bonus payouts.

Duckworth quality performance in FY91 improved dramatically to an average **2.7%** complaint ratio with the **last 6 months** of the year averaging **2%.** The revised plan is designed to build on this success and increase our performance to "world class" levels.

The procedure for analyzing, charging responsibility, and tallying total number of complaints by Richard Sterling all remain the same as in the past. The only additional reporting will be a new category recording invoicing errors, such as billing errors or wrong prices on orders. Complete quality is a total system—from the first customer inquiry to billing of parts and all processes in between.

With constant dedication to teamwork, continuous quality improvement and satisfying our **customers requirements,** we are confident that our new goals will be achieved and even surpassed. You are doing it now and we are counting on you to make Duckworth—**Your Company**—The best quality company possible!

William Kestner
Vice President and General Manager

cc: John Duckworth
Joseph Nathan

EXHIBIT 4 Worth Corporation, Quality Incentive Program, FY93 October Results

No. of Shipments	207
No. of Chargeable Complaints	4
Complaint Ratio	1.9%
Quality Bonus—October	$ 75
Quality Bonus—YTD	$300

With a record number of shipments, this month had the potential of being a **great quality month,** but we fell short because preventable errors were not caught. Without the large shipment level, the monthly payout would not have been $75.00.

If you look at the customer complaints listed below, you will see that these problems could have been detected by our systems. The key to continued improvement is your using the systems and informing others when the system does not work.

The XXX and YYY complaints are good examples of where the system in place was not followed and resulted in a complaint. The AAA and BBB complaints are examples of where people could have come forth to say the system doesn't adequately detect these kinds of defects.

The task of improvement needs to be continually addressed by all. We cannot just let things go on and expect good results. Good results are achieved by good people doing the right things at the right time.

Type of Complaint	**Customer**	**Complaint**
Manufacturing Process	AAA	Cracked AX47 parts and inventory not rotated.
Manufacturing Process	BBB	Cracked AX47 parts and inventory not rotated.
Color	YYY	Color significantly off standard (yellow).
Label	XXX	Label had wrong code printed.

Joy Meadow
Quality Assurance Manager

Thomas Spencer
Production Manager

EXHIBIT 5 Worth Corporation, FY93 Incentive Plan for Customer Service Representative
Maximum Award = 10% of average base salary.

	Item Results	*% of Bonus*	*% of Salary*
I. Order Accuracy:			
4% maximum potential			
Accuracy equals percentage of acceptance of orders that have correct pricing and other critical information. This accuracy is tracked by Director of Sales with bonus being paid based on overall FY93 results.	98.0% or higher	40.00%	4.00%
	96.5%	30.00%	3.00%
	95.0%	20.00%	2.00%
	<95.0%	0.00%	0.00%
II. Order Acknowledgment/Turnaround:			
3% maximum potential			
(effective 9/1/92–9 month period)			
Average number of days (excluding holidays & weekends) from order placement until printing of order acknowledgement for all orders received (except those requiring new part numbers). Results to be tracked weekly on late shipments report.	2 days or less	30.00%	3.00%
	3 days	15.00%	1.50%
	4 days	5.00%	0.50%
	>4 days	0.00%	0.00%
III. Sales Growth:			
3% maximum potential			
Total net company sales growth over FY92 net sales of $63.5 million	$7,000M	30.00%	3.00%
	$6,000M	15.00%	1.50%
	$3,000M	5.00%	0.50%
	<$3,000M	0.00	0.00

EXHIBIT 6 Duckworth Industries, Inc., Fiscal 1992 Incentive Compensation

Worth Corporation,

ANNUAL SALES GROWTH %

RETURN ON GROSS ASSETS %		4.90	5.00	7.50	10.00	12.50	15.00
					GOAL		
25.0		0	1.74	1.81	1.88	1.95	2.03
24.0		0	1.55	1.61	1.67	1.74	1.81
23.0		0	1.37	1.42	1.48	1.55	1.61
22.0		0	1.20	1.25	1.31	1.37	1.42
21.0		0	1.05	1.10	1.15	1.20	1.25
20.0	GOAL	0	0.91	0.95	1.00	1.05	1.10
19.0		0	0.78	0.82	0.87	0.91	0.95
18.0		0	0.67	0.71	0.74	0.78	0.82
17.0		0	0.57	0.60	0.63	0.67	0.71
16.0		0	0.48	0.51	0.54	0.57	0.60
15.0		0	0.40	0.42	0.45	0.48	0.51
14.9		0	0	0	0	0	0

Return on Gross Performing Assets will be determined by dividing Operational Cash Flow Earnings (OCFE) into Average Gross Performing Assets (AGPA).

OCFE is net profit adjusted to add depreciation and to eliminate (a) interest expense, (b) acquisition expenses, (c) net investment income, (d) expense or profit relating to LIFO, and (e) gains or losses from the disposition of depreciable assets. All adjustments will be made on an after-tax basis, using Worth Corporation's effective tax rate.

AGPA is a 13-month average of the company's gross book assets, with cumulative depreciation and the LIFO reserve added back, but investment securities and intercompany receivables eliminated.

The Board of Directors reserves the right to adjust the formula and its components, even after the fact, in any way it determines to be appropriate in order to better effectuate the plan and its purposes.

EXHIBIT 7 ROA/Growth Matrix for Worth Peer Group

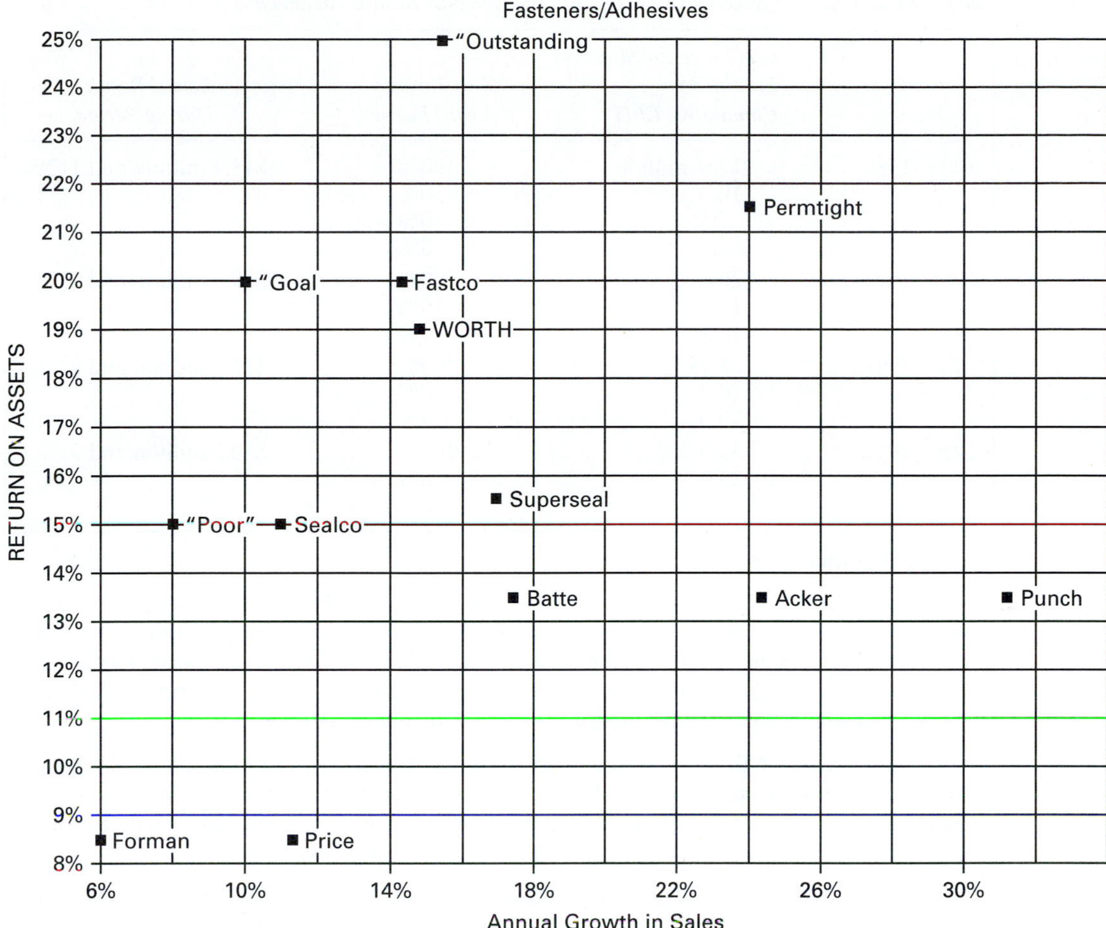

EXHIBIT 8 Worth Corporation, Inc., Executive Long-Term Incentive Plan

Summary		*31-May-83*	*31-May-88*	*5-yr Change*
Total shareholder's equity at year end		$8,616,500	$16,379,000	
Per share, using standard of 500,000 shares		$ 17.23	$ 32.76	
Value weighting "Performance Factor"		0.50	1.70	
Weighted share price		$ 8.62	$ 55.69	$47.07
(= Equity per share × performance factor)				
Per participant	$47.07 × 300 shares	= $141,210		
In total	× 2 participants	= $282,420		

EXHIBIT 9 Worth Division of Duckworth Industries—Management Long-Term Plan
Targets Established for Successive Three Year Plans versus *Results Achieved*

Plan Years	*Challenge Earnings Levels (3 yr Cumulative EBIT)*	*% of Target Award Earned*	*Actual Results During Period*
1986–1989	$12.0 million	100%	$13.4 million and 112%
	10.0	50%	
	7.5	10%	
	<7.5	0%	
1987–1990	$20.0	100%	$19.3 million and 97%
	12.5	10%	
	<12.5	0%	
1988–1991	28.75	100%	$26.1 million and 92%
	20.0	10%	
	<20.0	0%	
1989–1992	33.0	100%	$30.1 million and 91%
	25.0	10%	
	<25.0	0%	

Award Determination

Each Participant will, at the start of a Performance Period, be assigned a Target Award expressed as a percentage of the participant's average annual base salary to be paid during the Performance Period. The percent of the Target Award earned by each Participant will be based upon the relationship of Performance Period Earnings to various Challenge Earnings Levels specified by the Board for such Performance Period.

The percent of Target Award earned will be awarded on a pro rata basis if the actual results fall between specified Challenge Earnings Levels. If a Participant significantly changes responsibility or positions during the Performance Period, the Board will consider the propriety of an equitable adjustment in the Target Award assigned.

A Participant's award is subjec to organizational and environmental constraints affecting Performance Period Earnings. Unforeseen problems (other than those referred to in the next paragraph) or opportunities, as well as peer group performance, will be taken into account during the evaluation process. As soon as practicable after the end of a Performance Period, the Board will determine how successfully objectives were met. The Board will evaluate how unforeseen difficulties, as well as unexpected opportunities, were addressed. To allow recognition for quality of results and level of effort, award amounts may be adjusted (to a maximum of plus or minus 25% of the award) by the Board.

The Plan also recognizes that actions of Participants may be negated or overstated due to the occurrence of certain extraordinary events. Examples of extraordinary events include, but are not limited to, "Acts of God," financial difficulty of a major supplier or customer, unexpected tax law changes and acquisitions, divestitures, mergers or significant structural changes. Should such extraordinary occurrences take place, the Board may adjust the incentive awards (or the various formula components thereof) in any manner reasonably intended to reflect the impact of the extraordinary occurrence.

EXHIBIT 10 Target and Actual Payments (as a % of base salary) for Annual and Long-Term Incentive Compensation Plans

			1990		*1991*		*1992*	
			Target	*Actual*	*Target*	*Actual*	*Target*	*Actual*
Manager	A	Annual bonus	—	—	40[a]	68	40[a]	0
		L.T. Incentive	—	—	35[a]	32	35[a]	32
Manager	B	Annual bonus	—	—	25[a]	35	25[a]	0
		L.T. Incentive	—	—	25[a]	23	25[a]	23
Manager	C	Annual bonus	50[a]	50	50[a]	85	50[b]	0
		L.T. Incentive	40[a]	39	40[a]	37	40[b]	0
Manager	D	Annual bonus	25[a]	25	40[a]	35	25[a]	0
		L.T. Incentive	25[a]	24	40[a]	37	40[a]	36
Manager	E	Annual bonus	40[a]	40	40[a]	68	40[a]	0
		L.T. Incentive	40[a]	39	35[a]	32	35[a]	32
Manager	F	Annual bonus	—	—	25[b]	0	25[b]	6
		L.T. Incentive	—	—	25[b]	5	25[b]	0
Manager	G	Annual bonus	40[a]	40	50[b]	0	50[b]	12
		L.T. Incentive	40[a]	39	40[b]	8	40[b]	0
Manager	H	Annual bonus	—	—	25[b]	0	25[b]	6
		L.T. Incentive	—	—	25[b]	5	25[b]	0
Manager	I	Annual bonus	25[a]	25	50[d]	46	50[d]	0
		L.T. Incentive	25[a]	25	25[c]	10	60[d]	44
Manager	J	Annual bonus	—	—	—	—	25[c]	0
		L.T. Incentive	—	—	—	—	—	—
Manager	K	Annual bonus	30[c]	0	30[c]	0	30[c]	0
		L.T. Incentive	30[c]	0	30[c]	12	30[c]	14
Manager	L	Annual bonus	40[c]	0	40[c]	0	50[c]	0
		L.T. Incentive	35[c]	0	35[c]	14	35[c]	16
Manager	M	Annual bonus	50[c]	0	50[c]	0	50[c]	0
		L.T. Incentive	50[c]	0	50[c]	20	50[c]	46
Manager	N	Annual bonus	—	—	35[a]	60	35[a]	0
		L.T. Incentive	40[a]	39	40[a]	37	40[a]	36
Manager	O	Annual bonus	40[a]	40	40[a]	68	40[a]	0
		L.T. Incentive	25[a]	24	25[a]	23	25[a]	23
Manager	P	Annual bonus	20[a]	20	20[a]	34	20[a]	0
		L.T. Incentive	20[a]	19	20[a]	18	20[a]	18

[a]Worth SBU
[b]Hotel Telecom Services SBU
[c]Hospitality Equipment Services SBU
[d]Duckworth Industries SBU

EXHIBIT 11 Worth Corporation Summary of Historical and Projected Operating Performance ($000's)

		History					*Forecast*				
Line #		*1988*	*1989*	*1990*	*1991*	*1992*	*1993*	*1994*	*1995*	*1996*	*1997*
	Operating Results										
1	Revenue	$47,255	$54,615	$57,125	$65,035	$63,565	$69,500	$76,100	$83,330	$91,250	$99,915
2	% Growth	15.0%	15.6%	4.6%	13.9%	(2.3%)	9.3%	9.5%	9.5%	9.5%	9.5%
3	—Cost of Sales	34,985	40,305	41,760	46,020	42,025	47,355	51,950	56,915	62,415	68,445
4	% Sales	74.0%	73.8%	73.1%	70.8%	66.1%	68.1%	68.3%	68.3%	68.4%	68.5%
5	—SG&A	6,620	6,700	6,905	6,905	8,585	9,695	10,865	11,715	12,680	13,585
6	% Sales	14.0%	12.3%	12.1%	10.6%	13.5%	13.9%	14.3%	14.1%	13.9%	13.6%
7	—Cash Taxes	$2,280	$1,965	$2,615	$3,500	$3,650	$4,225	$4,855	$5,310	$5,785	$6,215
8	% Operating Income	40.4%	25.8%	30.9%	28.9%	28.2%	33.9%	36.5%	36.1%	35.8%	34.8%
9	**NOPAT**	**$3,370**	**$5,645**	**$5,840**	**$8,615**	**$9,305**	**$8,225**	**$8,430**	**$9,390**	**$10,370**	**$11,670**
	Capital										
10	Net Accounts Receivable	$5,310	$4,855	$ 5,460	$5,525	$ 6,060	$ 6,185	$ 6,760	$ 7,395	$ 8,090	$8,850
11	Inventory	2,865	2,965	3,360	3,865	4,020	4,030	4,260	4,585	4,945	5,325
12	PP&E	5,540	9,415	13,775	13,505	12,180	19,465	21,555	21,825	20,915	21,200
13	Other Assets	620	350	1,455	1,565	3,765	3,210	2,450	1,800	1,245	1,185
14	—NIBCL's[a]	(10,775)	(9,790)	(11,545)	(10,025)	(13,125)	(9,940)	(10,860)	(12,040)	(13,360)	(14,725)
15	**Capital**	**$3,555**	**$7,795**	**$12,505**	**$14,440**	**$12,900**	**$22,945**	**$24,165**	**$23,560**	**$21,830**	**$21,835**
	Operating Analysis										
16	NOPAT/Avg Cap (r)	51.4%	99.5%	57.5%	63.9%	68.1%	45.9%	35.8%	39.3%	45.7%	53.5%
17	—Cost of Capital (c)	13.0%	12.6%	12.7%	12.4%	12.2%	12.2%	12.2%	12.2%	12.2%	12.2%
18	Spread (r-c)	38.4%	86.9%	44.8%	51.5%	55.9%	33.7%	23.6%	27.2%	33.5%	41.3%
19	X Average Capital	$6,550	$5,675	$10,150	$13,470	$13,670	$17,925	$23,555	$23,865	$22,695	$21,830
20	**Economic Value Added**	**$2,515**	**$4,935**	**$4,550**	**$6,945**	**$7,640**	**$6,045**	**$5,565**	**$6,485**	**$7,605**	**$9,010**

[a]Noninterest-bearing current liabilities.

EXHIBIT 12 Worth Corporation

Input Table

Line #		*1993*	*1994*	*1995*	*1996*	*1997*
	Bonus Pool Characteristics					
1	Target Bonus	37%	37%	37%	37%	37%
2	Base Salary (000)	$1,710	$1,795	$1,885	$1,980	$2,075
3	# of Units (000)	630	660	695	730	765
	Bonus Calculation Framework					
4	Baseline EVA (0000)	$6,045				
5	Annual Target Adjustment Factor	50%				
6	Base Unit Value	$1.00	$0.80	$0.80	$0.80	$0.80
	EVA Bonus Sensitivity Factor					
7	EVA Bonus Sensitivity Factor (000)	$1,625				

Current Bonus Calculation

Line #		*1993*	*1994*	*1995*	*1996*	*1997*	*Average*
	Performance Unit Value						
8	EVA (000)	$6,045	$5,565	$6,485	$7,605	$9,010	$6,940
9	− Baseline EVA (000)	$6,045	$6,045	$5,805	$6,145	$6,875	$6,180
10	= EVA vs Baseline EVA (000)	$0	($480)	$680	$1,460	$2,135	$760
11	/ EVA Bonus Sensitivity Factor (000)	$1,625	$1,625	$1,625	$1,625	$1,625	$1,625
12	= Performance Unit Value	$0.00	($0.29)	$0.42	$0.90	$1.31	$0.47
	Total Unit Value						
13	Performance Unit Value	$0.00	($0.29)	$0.42	$0.90	$1.31	$0.47
14	+ Base Unit Value	$1.00	$0.80	$0.80	$0.80	$0.80	$0.84
15	= Total Unit Value	$1.00	$0.51	$1.22	$1.70	$2.11	$1.31
	Current Bonus						
16	Total Unit Value	$1.00	$0.51	$1.22	$1.70	$2.11	$1.31
17	# of Units (000)	630	660	695	730	765	695
18	Current Bonus Earned (000)	$630	$335	$850	$1,240	$1,620	$935

Past Bonus If System Had Been In Place Prior 5 Years

Line #		*1988*	*1989*	*1990*	*1991*	*1992*	*Average*
	Current Bonus						
19	Total Unit Value	$1.00	$2.29	$1.31	$2.53	$2.09	$1.84
20	# of Units	695	720	720	740	530	680
21	Current Bonus Earned (000)	$695	$1,645	$945	$1,875	$1,115	$1,255

EXHIBIT 13 Hotel Telecom Services, Summary of Historical and Projected Operating Performance ($000s)

		History				*Forecast*				
Line #		*1989*	*1990*	*1991*	*1992*	*1993*	*1994*	*1995*	*1996*	*1997*
	Operating Results									
1	Revenue	$29,115	$32,540	$29,980	$32,285	$46,600	$55,920	$60,115	$64,625	$69,470
2	% Growth	NMF	11.8%	(7.9%)	7.7%	44.3%	20.0%	7.5%	7.5%	7.5%
3	—Cost of Sales	20,750	24,120	22,395	24,730	36,150	43,435	46,735	50,205	54,005
4	% of Sales	71.3%	74.1%	74.7%	76.6%	77.6%	77.7%	77.7%	77.7%	77.7%
5	—SG&A	5,610	5,475	5,560	5,820	7,935	9,150	9,820	10,550	11,320
6	% of Sales	19.3%	16.8%	18.5%	18.0%	17.0%	16.4%	16.3%	16.3%	16.3%
7	—Cash Taxes	$455	$1,000	$700	$500	$815	$1,060	$1,135	$1,235	$1,325
8	% Operating Income	16.5%	33.9%	34.5%	28.9%	32.4%	31.8%	31.8%	31.9%	31.9%
9	**NOPAT**	**$2,300**	**$1,950**	**$1,325**	**$1,230**	**$1,700**	**$2,275**	**$2,425**	**$2,640**	**$2,825**
	Capital									
10	Net Accounts Receivable	$3,370	$3,240	$3,935	$4,365	$6,115	$7,265	$7,805	$8,385	$9,010
11	Inventory	4,525	4,145	4,570	6,245	7,120	8,520	9,150	9,820	10,550
12	PP&E	1,365	1,250	1,355	1,525	1,520	1,405	1,395	1,255	1,085
13	Goodwill	4,395	4,395	4,395	4,400	4,400	4,400	4,400	4,400	4,400
14	Other Assets	230	715	1,260	1,935	290	320	330	345	360
15	—NIBCL's[a]	(4,720)	(3,860)	(4,630)	(5,490)	(5,575)	(6,985)	(7,505)	(8,085)	(8,685)
16	**Capital**	**9,170**	**9,890**	**10,891**	**12,975**	**13,870**	**14,920**	**15,570**	**16,115**	**16,710**
	Operating Analysis									
17	NOPAT/Avg Cap (r)	22.3%	20.5%	12.8%	10.3%	12.7%	15.8%	15.9%	16.7%	17.2%
18	—Cost of Capital (c)	13.1%	13.2%	12.9%	12.7%	12.7%	12.7%	12.7%	12.7%	12.7%
19	Spread (r-c)	9.2%	7.3%	(0.1%)	(2.4%)	0.0%	3.1%	3.2%	4.0%	4.5%
20	x Average Capital	$10,345	$9,530	$10,390	$11,935	$13,420	$14,395	$15,245	$15,840	$16,410
21	**Economic Value Added**	**$950**	**$695**	**($10)**	**($280)**	**$0**	**$450**	**$495**	**$630**	**$745**

[a]Noninterest-bearing current liabilities.

EXHIBIT 14 Hotel Telecom Services

Input Table

Line #		*1993*	*1994*	*1995*	*1996*	*1997*
	Bonus Pool Characteristics					
1	Target Bonus	38%	38%	38%	38%	38%
2	Base Salary (000)	$905	$950	$1,000	$1,050	$1,100
3	# of Units (000)	345	360	380	400	420
	Bonus Calculation Framework					
4	Baseline EVA (000)	($140)				
5	Annual Target Adjustment Factor	50%				
6	Base Unit Value	$0.25	$0.25	$0.25	$0.25	$0.25
	EVA Bonus Sensitivity Factor					
7	= EVA Bonus Sensitivity Factor (000)	$700				

Current Bonus Calculation

Line #		*1993*	*1994*	*1995*	*1996*	*1997*	*Average*
	Performance Unit Value						
8	EVA (000)	$0	$450	$495	$630	$745	$465
9	− Baseline EVA (000)	($140)	($70)	$190	$340	$485	$160
10	= EVA vs Baseline EVA (000)	$140	$520	$305	$290	$255	$300
11	/ EVA Bonus Sensitivity Factor (000)	$700	$700	$700	$700	$700	$700
12	= Performance Unit Value	$0.20	$0.74	$0.44	$0.41	$0.37	$0.43
	Total Unit Value						
13	Performance Unit Value	$0.20	$0.74	$0.44	$0.41	$0.37	$0.43
14	+ Base Unit Value	$0.25	$0.25	$0.25	$0.25	$0.25	$0.25
15	= Total Unit Value	$0.45	$0.99	$0.69	$0.66	$0.62	$0.68
	Current Bonus						
16	Total Unit Value	$0.45	$0.99	$0.69	$0.66	$0.62	$0.68
17	# of Units (000)	345	360	380	400	420	380
18	Current Bonus Earned (000)	$155	$360	$260	$265	$260	$260

Past Bonus If System Had Been In Place Prior 4 Years

Line #		*1989*	*1990*	*1991*	*1992*	*Average*
	Current Bonus					
19	Total Unit Value	$1.27	$0.39	($0.68)	($.60)	$0.08
20	# of Units (000)	50	150	325	340	215
21	Current Bonus Earned (000)	$60	$60	($225)	($205)	($78)

EXHIBIT 15 Hospitality Equipment Service Co., Summary of Historical and Projected Operating Performance ($000s)

		History					*Forecast*				
Line #		*1988*	*1989*	*1990*	*1991*	*1992*	*1993*	*1994*	*1995*	*1996*	*1997*
	Operating Results										
1	Revenue	$24,770	$28,670	$26,555	$28,525	$26,720	$29,220	$31,410	$33,765	$36,300	$39,020
2	% Growth	49.2%	15.8%	(7.4%)	7.4%	(6.3%)	9.4%	7.5%	7.5%	7.5%	7.5%
3	—Cost of Sales	18,560	21,545	19,545	20,955	14,305	21,190	22,500	24,170	25,965	27,895
4	% of Sales	74.9%	75.1%	73.6%	73.5%	72.2%	72.5%	71.6%	71.6%	71.5%	71.5%
5	—SG&A	5,765	6,100	7,240	6,495	7,135	7,065	7,480	7,950	8,455	8,985
6	% of Sales	23.3%	21.3%	27.3%	22.8%	26.7%	24.2%	23.8%	23.5%	23.3%	23.0%
7	—Cash Taxes	$275	$440	$55	$420	$320	$420	$545	$615	$690	$780
8	% Operating Income	62.0%	43.0%	(23.7%)	38.8%	113.3%	43.6%	38.0%	37.2%	36.7%	36.4%
9	**NOPAT**	**$170**	**$585**	**($290)**	**$660**	**($35)**	**$545**	**$885**	**$1,035**	**$1,190**	**$1,365**
	Capital										
10	Net Accounts Receivable	$2,655	$3,775	$3,075	$3,525	$3,010	$3,660	$6,288	$4,220	$4,530	$4,865
11	Inventory	2,830	3,420	4,115	3,205	3,105	3,365	3,560	3,815	4,085	4,380
12	PP&E	545	965	815	515	360	950	1,160	1,370	1,580	1,790
13	Other Assets	535	355	335	835	850	675	770	805	805	810
14	—NIBCL's	(4,295)	(4,845)	(4,095)	(3,250)	(4,045)	(3,295)	(3,520)	(3,805)	(4,110)	(4,440)
15	**Capital**	**$2,270**	**$3,675**	**$4,250**	**$4,825**	**$3,280**	**$5,355**	**$5,900**	**$6,405**	**$6,890**	**$7,400**
	Operating Analysis										
16	NOPAT/Avg Cap (r)	7.8%	19.7%	(7.3%)	14.5%	(0.9%)	12.6%	15.7%	16.8%	17.9%	19.1%
17	—Cost of Capital (c)	13.4%	13.4%	13.4%	13.4%	13.4%	13.5%	13.5%	13.5%	13.5%	13.5%
18	Spread (r-c)	(5.6%)	6.3%	(20.7%)	1.1%	(14.3%)	(1.0%)	2.2%	3.3%	4.4%	5.5%
19	X Average Capital	$2,155	$2,970	$3,960	$4,535	$4,055	$4,315	$5,625	$6,150	$6,645	$7,145
20	**Economic Value Added**	**($120)**	**$185**	**($820)**	**$50**	**($580)**	**($40)**	**$125**	**$205**	**$290**	**$395**

EXHIBIT 16 Hospitality Equipment Service Co.

Input Table

Line #		*1993*	*1994*	*1995*	*1996*	*1997*
	Bonus Pool Characteristics					
1	Target Bonus	42%	42%	42%	42%	42%
2	Base Salary (000)	$705	$740	$775	$815	$855
3	# of Units (000)	300	315	330	345	365
	Bonus Calculation Framework					
4	Baseline EVA (000)	($310)				
5	Annual Target Adjustment Factor	50%				
6	Base Unit Value	$0.25	$0.25	$0.25	$0.25	$0.25
	EVA Bonus Sensitivity Factor					
7	= EVA Bonus Sensitivity Factor (000)	$500				

Current Bonus Calculation

Line #		*1993*	*1994*	*1995*	*1996*	*1997*	*Average*
	Performance Unit Value						
8	EVA (000)	($40)	$125	$205	$290	$395	$195
9	− Baseline EVA (000)	($310)	($175)	($25)	$90	$190	($45)
10	= EVA vs Baseline EVA (000)	$270	$300	$230	$200	$205	$240
11	/ EVA Bonus Sensitivity Factor (000)	$500	$500	$500	$500	$500	$500
12	= Performance Unit Value	$0.54	$0.60	$0.46	$0.40	$0.41	$0.48
	Total Unit Value						
13	Performance Unit Value	$0.54	$0.60	$0.46	$0.40	$0.41	$0.48
14	+ Base Unit Value	$0.25	$0.25	$0.25	$0.25	$0.25	$0.25
15	= Total Unit Value	$0.79	$0.85	$0.71	$0.65	$0.66	$0.73
	Current Bonus						
16	Total Unit Value	$0.79	$0.85	$0.71	$0.65	$0.66	$0.73
17	# of Units (000)	300	315	330	345	365	330
18	Current Bonus Earned (000)	$235	$265	$235	$225	$240	$240

Past Bonus If System Had Been In Place Prior 5 Years

Line #		*1988*	*1989*	*1990*	*1991*	*1992*	*Average*
	Current Bonus						
19	Total Unit Value	$0.71	$1.10	($1.34)	$1.20	($0.54)	$0.22
20	# of Units (000)	285	525	315	335	255	345
21	Current Bonus Earned (000)	$205	$575	($425)	$405	($140)	$125

Chemical Bank: Implementing the Balanced Scorecard[1]

In early 1995, Michael Hegarty, Head of the Retail Bank of Chemical Banking Corporation, was overseeing a transformation in his organization. The process had begun with the merger of Chemical and the Manufacturers Hanover Corporation at year-end 1991. The new, larger banking company was better positioned to compete in a marketplace characterized by intense pricing competition, an outflow of deposits to mutual funds, rapidly evolving technology, and increased customer demand for value. Hegarty commented on just one indicator of the future competitive environment for retail banking:

> At the time of the merger, the old Chemical Banking Corporation with assets of $75 billion, had a market capitalization of $2 billion. Less than four years later, Microsoft has offered to buy Intuit, a personal financial software company with $223 million in sales for $1.5 billion. What do you think Bill Gates is buying for all that money?

Historically retail banking had emphasized efficient collection and processing of deposits. Hegarty wanted to transform the bank into a market-focused organization that would be the financial service provider of choice to targeted customer groups. To implement this strategy, Hegarty knew that the bank had to make major investments to understand customer needs and to identify attractive customer segments. The bank also had to develop and tailor new products such as annuities, investment products, and technology-based payment services to meet customer needs in the targeted segments. With a broader product and service line, and excellent knowledge of its customer base, the bank would then be able to find ways to develop new relationships with its most desirable customers, and expand the bank's business with them—increasing its share of its customer's financial transactions (or *share of wallet* as it was described in the bank).

When asked how he expected to implement such dramatic and extensive strategic change, Hegarty said:

> My biggest problem is communicating and reinforcing strategy. The Balanced Scorecard is one of a set of tools we are using—along with Mission and Vision Statements, Gap Analysis, Strategy Consensus, and Brand Positioning—for strategy formulation and communication. The Balanced Scorecard can't win without a good mission statement and vision, an excellent strategy, and good execution. But it is certainly part of the architecture of success. It is an element in a major communications program to 15,000 individuals.
>
> No one owns a process end-to-end (most do just a small snippet). But every individual should understand how they fit in; what their role is for helping the company achieve its strategy. The scorecard gives us the measures we need to stay focused on performance, while at the same time enabling us to clarify and communicate our vision, and focus our energies for change. The measurement allows learning, and the learning renews the vision and refuels our energy for change.

[1] This case is meant to be taught in conjunction with two reprints by Robert S. Kaplan and David P. Norton: "The Balanced Scorecard-Measures That Drive Performance," *Harvard Business Review* Reprint #92105, and "Putting the Balanced Scorecard to Work," *Harvard Business Review* Reprint #93505.

This case was prepared by Norman Klein and Professor Robert S. Kaplan as the basis for class discussion rather than to illustrate either effective or ineffective handling of an administrative situation.

RETAIL BANKING IN THE 1990s

Experts predicted that the 1990s would prove to be an intensely competitive decade in retail banking. In the past ten years, the approximately 14,000 banks in the United States had shrunk to 10,000, and there were predictions of as few as 4,000 to 5,000 banks by early in the next century.

Customers were demanding new investment and insurance products, and far more convenient ways to do their banking. They were asking banks for new telephone options, and for improved access to ATMs with enhanced functionality. These changes meant that branch personnel would be doing fewer deposit, withdrawal, and check-cashing transactions and would have to become more involved with higher-value interactions with customers, including sales of new products. But even with the move to higher-value services, banks anticipated operating fewer branches at the turn of the decade.

Research indicated that 61 percent of retail banking customers between the ages of 18 and 24 actively used ATMs, while only 27 percent of customers 55 to 64 did so. The trend lines were clear. The banks that would survive and prosper would be deploying superior technology, offering new products, and delivering service through new channels. Further, technology would be the key to new partnerships, especially with insurance companies and brokerage firms, and new strategies to identify, attract, and retain more profitable customers.

Ted Francavilla, Managing Director of Strategic Planning and Finance, noted that the traditional retail deposit business had become very tough. Revenue growth was slow due to lower interest rates and outflows of deposits to nonbanking service providers, such as mutual funds. Growth in core operating expenses and the need to invest in new delivery systems added to the challenge.

Currently we have over $800 million in operating expenses and 8,000 employees in our New York Markets division. Landlords expect rental increases on their properties and employees expect raises. These factors, coupled with low revenue growth, produce a real profitability squeeze for retail banking. We need to demonstrate to our corporate parent that we can earn good returns on the $800 million we spend each year and free up funds for future investment.

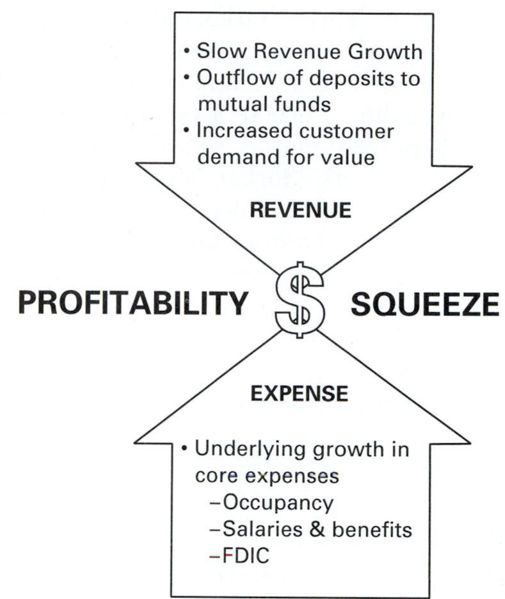

CHEMICAL BANK'S STRATEGY

After the merger had been completed in 1992, the Retail Bank's New York Markets division had identified the following six critical success factors:

1. Commit to Business Processes Driven by Service Quality
2. Implement Continuous Process for Understanding Markets, Segments, and Individual Customers
3. Develop a Rapid, Customer-Focused Product Management and Development Process
4. Insure Flexible and Market-Responsive Delivery Channels
5. Develop Information Management Processes and Platforms Driven by Business Needs
6. Implement Expense Management Process to Streamline the Cost Base

In 1994, New York Markets was responsible for managing $27 billion in consumer and small business deposits, as well as over 300 branches, over 800 proprietary ATM's, a state-of-the-art telephone service center, and other related distribution channels. The division also acted as a distributor and referral source for Chemical's mortgages, credit cards, home equity loans and other consumer credit products, which were managed by Hegarty as national business lines. Mutual funds were also sold through a branch-based brokerage operation.

The New York Markets division had the number one market share among small commercial companies (under $1 million in sales) with a total of roughly 150,000 accounts. This represented a 24 percent market share in the metropolitan area. New York Markets also claimed a 16 to 17 percent share of the consumer market, with 1.5 million customers holding approximately 3 million accounts. Net income of $15.3 million for 1993 was planned to improve to $28.6 million in 1994. Exhibit 1 shows summary financial information for New York Markets division, and Exhibit 2 shows the organization chart of the Retail Bank.

DEVELOPING THE BALANCED SCORECARD

Francavilla had been introduced to the BSC concept in mid-1992 while attending a one-week business school executive program. He had immediately sensed that the BSC insistence on clear specification of strategic objectives and appropriate measures in four areas—financial, customer, internal business, and learning and growth—would be a useful way to create change at Chemical Bank.

Francavilla asked Tony LoFrumento, Vice President-Retail Bank Strategic Planning and Finance, to chair a middle-management task force to build a Balanced Scorecard for the New York Markets division. LoFrumento recalled the task force experience:

> The group worked hard and generated good ideas and analysis. But we soon realized that a mid-level group would find it difficult to push performance measures up to senior management. If the BSC was going to have an impact, Mike Hegarty had to be committed to the concept.

In May 1993, Hegarty attended a presentation introducing the BSC and was convinced that this approach could help create the cultural change he desired at the Retail Bank. Other senior managers at the bank, however, remained skeptical. David Norton, one of the co-authors of the initial BSC article, was brought in for a presentation to the senior management group. After the presentation, the group became committed to moving ahead with a Scorecard project.

THE RETAIL BANK'S BALANCED SCORECARD

Francavilla, as head of Strategic Planning and Finance, functioned as the internal champion for the BSC. LoFrumento led the day-to-day functioning of BSC activities, and Norton was retained for consulting support. They divided the senior management group into four subgroups, each one responsible for developing objectives for one of the BSC perspectives. By October 1993, strategic objectives had been identified for each of the four BSC perspectives (see Exhibits 3A–3D).

The subgroups, with assistance from lower-level managers, then developed measures for the objectives in their assigned BSC perspective. By the end of 1993, the entire group had reached consensus on a complete scorecard for the New York Markets division (see Exhibit 4).

Francavilla noted that an immediate impact of the BSC project was to simplify the bank's strategy statements:

> Formerly, we communicated our strategy to the 8,000 people in the organization using the five dimensions on the left of the list shown later. We found we could boil it down to three core strategic themes which aligned well with three of the perspectives of the BSC. The scorecard focused our thinking in this way, and Mike (Hegarty) now communicates these three themes continually to all 8,000 people. It's been branded into their minds so that they know that if they're doing something that doesn't fit into one of these three themes, they probably shouldn't be doing it. And as we were building the scorecard, we found that we could relate each measure to one of those three themes.

ORIGINAL STATEMENTS	CORE STRATEGIC THEMES	BALANCED SCORECARD PERSPECTIVE
Focus on Attractive Markets	Shifts the Customer/	Customer
Increase Fee Revenue	Profit Mix	
Improve Service Quality	Improve Productivity	Internal
Improve Operating Efficiency		
Promote Continuous Learning & Improvement	Create an Enabled Organization	Learning and Growth

In addition to aligning the scorecard measures to the three strategic themes, the team developed causal links across the objectives and measures. For example, two of the financial objectives—Revenue Growth and Reduce Risk—were expected to be outcomes from the theme—Shift the Customer/Profit Mix. The BSC group linked the Revenue Growth and Reduce Risk outcome objectives back to objectives in, respectively, the customer, internal, and learning and growth perspectives that were the performance drivers of these outcomes (see Exhibit 5). This chain of cause and effect relationships illustrated that if the bank was to broaden and increase the set of financial products that retail customers transacted with the bank, then it must shift its image from a provider of a narrow set of banking services to becoming a financial advisor and service provider for targeted customer groups—an objective to *increase customer confidence in our financial advice.*

Having specified the link from financial objectives to customer objectives for the Broaden Revenue Mix objectives, the BSC team then linked to three of the internal objectives that its people must excel at if the bank were to create its new image as a broad provider of financial services:

Understand Customer Segments
Develop New Products
Cross-Sell the Product Line

These internal processes were now identified as vital to implementing the bank's Broaden Revenue Mix strategy. Previously, performance measurement had focused on continuous improvement of existing processes like check processing and teller transactions. Thus the BSC process, starting from identifying financial and customer objectives, had highlighted several new internal processes for the organization to develop best-in-class delivery capabilities.

The three internal perspective objectives led naturally to objectives in the learning & growth perspective. The bank's customer representatives would have to expand their skills, so that they could serve as a customer's financial counselor, and communicate credibly and knowledgeably about an expanded set of financial products. The customer representatives also would need ready access to information on all the bank's relationships with each customer. The incentive system for the bank's employees would also have to be changed to encourage the new behavior and skill acquisition. These three enablers—new skills, access to strategic information, and aligned incentives—would contribute to more capable and skilled employees who, in turn, would drive the internal process objectives. Each objective in the Retail Bank's BSC was similarly linked in a series of cause-and-effect relationships that told the story of how the bank's strategy would be accomplished.

Francavilla commented on the benefits from establishing the linkages in BSC objectives and measures:

> In the past, we found it hard to get and maintain focus on our infrastructure—things like MIS and employee training and skills. We talked about their importance, but when financial pressure was applied, these were among the first spending programs to go. Now with measures of Strategic Information Availability and Strategic Job Coverage on the BSC, people can see the linkages between improving these capabilities and achieving our long-term financial goals. The BSC kept these issues front and center for their senior management group, so that a focus on these infrastructure investments could be sustained even in a highly constrained environment for corporate spending.

Lee Wilson, Chief of Staff for the Retail Bank, concurred with this view:

> The process has increased learning in the organization. Everybody agrees on the overall objectives, but it takes time to align 8,000 people and make appropriate infrastructure investments and commitments. If we stay the course, the BSC's learning perspective will enable Chemical Bank to really deliver superior service sooner than other banks.

By the end of 1993, measures for each of the objectives had been selected and a senior manager had been designated for collecting the information and reporting on each measure. For example, the owner of the three measures, under *Market & Sell* was Dave Mooney, manager of the Manhattan branch network, who reported to Jack Stack, the Managing Director of Sales & Service (see Exhibit 2). Mooney met frequently with branch marketing and selling managers and with Jack Stack to discuss progress along these three measures.

IMPACT OF THE BALANCED SCORECARD

Lee Wilson had not come to the bank until April 1994. While he had missed the 1993 process that led to the BSC, he could offer observations from his somewhat independent perspective:

> I see the BSC as a very valuable tool for the management team, but one that needs to keep evolving. To begin to appreciate the value of BSC at Chemical, you have to understand that its primary benefit was to pull together the two management teams. At Manufacturers Hanover, company-wide policies had been handed down by a strong central staff. Chemical, on the other hand, relied on a more decentralized approach. Given the two cultures, there were inevitable tugs-of-war between them after the merger.
>
> In early and mid-1993, the BSC meetings provided a mechanism for the senior people to focus on a common objective: devise a new strategy for the Retail Bank. Those meetings allowed people to come together and overcome their differences in assumptions and styles. A powerful shared sense emerged in these meetings about how the combined bank could capitalize on the potential from its new scale of operation. The BSC gave the senior executive group a positive perspective, focused on serving customers in a learning environment.

Francavilla concurred, recalling the frustration of attempting to develop a consensus on strategy in 1992, shortly after the merger:

> Everyone had agreed to the strategy—"Provide superior service to target customers." But we couldn't agree on how to implement this strategy since everyone had a different opinion about what superior service really meant, and who our targeted customers should be. The BSC process gave us specific and operational definitions of superior service and targeted customers.

But the glow of consensus-building gave way to frustration in late 1993 as work teams began to struggle with implementation. Several of the measures were difficult to obtain. People debated whether to use substitute measures or leave the measures blank until improved data systems could be developed.

Senior managers also noted that the BSC was quite visible only in the lives of 27 top-level managers in the Retail Bank. It was not yet being used to drive change throughout the organization. Some of the BSC themes had been communicated to employees through the monthly newsletter, *News & Views* (see Exhibit 6) and at the annual Branch Managers meeting. But the BSC had not been communicated to rank and file employees as a new management tool. LoFrumento explained:

> We got delayed by gaps in our measurement system. We had most of the information on customer satisfaction and customer profitability, but we didn't have the requisite data on customer share and retention by segment. The data for some of the new measures, like Strategic Job Coverage and Strategic Resource Alignment, did not exist at all and had to be created and developed by the responsible department. Even when we had some data, such as the mix of transactions in different channels, we had problems bringing together the information from diverse systems. As a result, we haven't built a credible base yet. The measures are just now on board. The tracking has just begun.

Wilson felt that some of the BSC measures were not critical for customer satisfaction goals, nor actionable. He explained:

> We have an internal measure called *Trailway to Trolls* (Trolls are unhappy customers). This index aggregates over a hundred different measures of customer complaints and degrees of dissatisfaction, but it isn't actionable. If the Trailway to Troll Index starts to deteriorate, I don't know if it's been caused by performance that valued customers consider critical, or whether it's a minor matter. When it was first developed, it was quite valuable in focusing management's attention on service quality. But we can't do quality for quality's sake. We need to focus on those dimensions most critical for meeting or ex-

ceeding customer expectations of service quality. And to do that we need measures that are actionable.

MEASURING CUSTOMER PROFITABILITY

William Jordan, Managing Director, had market management responsibility for the consumer and small business activities in New York Markets. When asked for his perspective on the BSC, he immediately voiced his support, and expressed, in strategic terms, the fundamental importance of BSC:

> We tend to focus on the short term and the month-by-month financials. This makes us excellent at tactics, but sometimes we find it difficult to think strategically about where we should be three to five years out. The Balanced Scorecard provided a forum for senior management to have active discussions about both the present performance and future targets we must achieve. I like the way it forced us to think about revenue opportunity and potential, and how we should measure our progress down the path that will insure our future.
>
> The BSC reinforces the need for a new focus on the customer, especially the need to get to a more profitable mix of customers, and to retain and deepen our relationship with our best customers.

Jordan for years had believed that most of the Retail Bank's small business accounts were profitable. Recently an activity-based cost study had matched *costs to serve* with *revenues earned* down to individual customers. The study showed that only 55 percent of small business accounts were profitable on a fully loaded basis. This information prompted Jordan to launch several new initiatives to enhance small-business customer profitability. He wanted to know the defining characteristics of profitable and unprofitable customers so that he could begin thinking about how unprofitable accounts could be made profitable by changing earnings credit, or minimum balance, or perhaps introducing fees and better control over fee waivers.

Jordan, however, emphasized:

> Although we have raised our consciousness about strategic measures, the measures are not yet integrated. For 1995, I would like the BSC teams to identify a number of top-of-mind measures, perhaps as few as two or three, that reflect our strategic themes and priorities. I want to see a graphical presentation of the BSC that gives us a five-year view of the journey, and to be able to view short-term performance in terms of progress towards our five-year targets.

TAKING SALES MEASURES TO THE BRANCHES

Dave Mooney was implementing one of the first BSC measures—"Selling Contacts per Salesperson"—in the Manhattan branches. He recalled his first impressions of the BSC:

> I remember thinking, as we were going through it, how valuable the process was. It forced us to specify and understand the simple causal linkages from high-level financial objectives to operational measures. The BSC was well accepted because it was very consistent with our management philosophy to focus on activities, process, and components that, according to our theory of linkages, must be accomplished to produce the outcomes we desire.
>
> But as simple as that sounds, we weren't working the fundamental processes. Like most other banks, we had been managing by hammering on outcomes. We kept telling people, 'Get more deposits'!
>
> In the summer of 1993, we started to focus on a measure at the beginning of the casual chain—how to make more sales contacts with customers. We now realized that a necessary condition to produce new sales was for our sales-people to have more customer contacts. So my first step was to ask for 10 *completed* contacts per sales person every week. The sales people responded, 'We can't do that. We're too busy.' But we dug in and told them that we were serious about this objective. Selling was no longer to be an optional or discretionary activity, to be done if time allowed. Selling must become something that you find time to do.

Mooney emphasized the importance of taking hold and managing the problem at that point.

"There is an important lesson here," he said. "Measures don't manage. The BSC gave us an engine, but it was management that had to put the vehicle in motion." Mooney was asked why the Balanced Scorecard was required to encourage sales people to do more selling. He replied:

> A lot of ideas were converging at the same time. We were just putting into place a more formal, highly structured customer calling process that produced the customer-contact measure. But then this measure had to survive a highly-competitive debate that the senior management team put all prospective measures through to create the BSC. My confidence increased about the importance of that measure and of the selling activity. The great value of the BSC was that it articulated the key levers of performance and reduced these to a few important drivers.

He recalled that implementation became easier when the first results of increasing sales contacts with customers were known:

> We started to see phenomenal results, two and a half to three product sales for every 10 contacts. That helped. But there was something else going on as well. People learned that the senior executives at the bank were not going to stop caring about this measure. The four or five people who ran the branch districts knew I was going to have to report out on the measure to Jack Stack and Mike Hegarty. That's one of the powerful features of the BSC: it's both motivating and obligating. The BSC forced us to stay on track and to follow up.

LOOKING AHEAD

When asked to assess the current status of BSC, Francavilla stressed that the work was well under way but nowhere near complete.

> The Scorecard has been very useful in helping us better understand the key drivers of our business. Our monthly financial review meetings have now become strategic review sessions with some excellent learning and idea generation.
>
> But the BSC is still a senior- and middle-management tool, a work in progress that we are not yet ready to introduce to the entire organization. If you were to walk into any branch in Manhattan today and ask how things are going with the BSC, they wouldn't know what you're talking about.

He and LoFrumento were intent on refining the BSC for 1995, hoping to identify fewer and better measures. They continued to live with the frustration of finding that certain measures were harder to get than they had anticipated. In 1994, they had contracted with an outside vendor to track customer retention data. After months of reported *progress,* the vendor finally admitted that it could not deliver the data. The implementation team had therefore assigned this task to an in-house expert.

At the same time, LoFrumento felt that they had come a long way:

> There's a lot we know we have to do, things like being able to track customer acquisition and retention. But we're probably ahead of the competition. Most banks are working with aggregate bottom-line information. They may know that 20 percent of their customers are generating most of their profits, but they don't know who those customers are. They are still living in a world where a marketing program would be hailed as a success for bringing 10,000 checking accounts into a bank—and the bank would never know that 9,000 of those accounts were going to lose money.
>
> We are well beyond that point. We now have three million accounts in our data base, and we can do any number of cross cuts on those accounts. We can look at deposits, credit cards, and very soon loans, and know just how profitable each account and each customer is.

Francavilla added that knowledge of customer segments and customer profitability was already driving the pricing of some products, and was allowing the bank to be far more sophisticated in designing new products and marketing programs.

In summing up, Francavilla said that there was more to be done on the infrastructure. "We've just scratched the surface on the power of Lotus Notes, for instance. Not just for E-mail but the database side," he said. And, of course, BSC itself is a tool that we will apply increasingly more rigorously as it improves." Then we went on to describe a future that would find performance goals, and performance reviews, aligned to the BSC. And once that happened he and LoFrumento expected that results would follow.

Lee Wilson concurred that for the BSC to truly drive behavior, it would have to be linked to compensation of senior executives:

> In 1994, the size of the compensation pool was tied to financial measures and BSC measures, such as customer satisfaction and customer retention. In 1995, we are making linkages much more explicit between BSC measures and the compensation to Top-20 executives. In future years, we will drive this process down through the organization.

Mike Hegarty summarized his views on the BSC:

> I like the BSC because it is both a forward-thinking tool and one that will supply the measures that will drive improved performance in our branches. And while BSC is not promoted in the branches under the name "BSC," it is visible in the branches. For example, if an ATM at a given branch isn't serviced, a computerized monitoring system will make a phone call to a branch manager and tell her that ATM #3 will go down in ten minutes. And if a branch manager should, say, decide to let three ATMs go down, the computer will call Dave Mooney and give him a status report.
>
> The team that made that kind of monitoring possible understands how that all fits with BSC, but the branch manager probably doesn't think of it that way. The 2,000 tellers in our branches will be able to tell you the dozens of things we are tracking—from customer satisfaction data to cleanliness in the ATM areas—but they won't know it by the name BSC.
>
> By the end of the year, branch managers will not only tell you what we are tracking but also tell you how they are performing on key measures. They will know, because they will be evaluated on how they perform on designated measures. We will even have bonuses determined by multiple measures that are weighted by revenue contribution to the bank.
>
> I'm not saying we have done it all. One major problem right now is that I have no idea how good my sales force is. That evaluation is not happening. We're also just beginning to rethink training, and we will have to find new measures to evaluate that training. But again, that's the virtue of the BSC. It is a tool that can get us to new goals and measures, and then to a process that will take us beyond those measures.
>
> We always had communication. That part isn't new. But the communication was by anecdotes, and not a basis for setting priorities for programs or for resource allocation. The BSC came along in the resource-constrained environment of the 1990s, where excellence in revenue, expense, and investment management would be decisive. The BSC will help us to take the *noise* out of the anecdotes, it will tell us whether we have the right priorities for our activities and whether our activities are in synch with our strategy.
>
> And finally, it provides us with feedback on our strategies, whether they are working and whether we have set our targets high enough. The scorecard is helping us all to learn and to enable change.

EXHIBIT 1 New York Markets

(Dollars in Millions) *Income Statement Item*	*Actual 1993*	*Plan 1994*
Net Interest Income	$693.3	$666.8
Total Noninterest Income	209.8	245.1
Total Revenue	$903.1	$911.9
Noninterest Expense:		
Total Salaries and Benefits	$345.7	$354.7
Occupancy & Equipment	171.3	175.0
FDIC	73.0	61.0
Other	105.4	108.6
Total Direct Expense	$695.4	$699.3
Total Indirect	177.5	159.1
Total Noninterest Expense	$872.9	$858.4
Operating Margin	$30.2	$53.5
Provision for Loan Loss	2.9	2.4
INCOME BEFORE TAXES	$27.3	$51.1
Income Taxes	12.0	22.5
NET INCOME	$15.3	$28.6
Avg Gross Deposits ($Billions):		
Consumer	$24.3	$23.4
Commercial	4.1	4.0
Total NY Markets	$28.4	$27.4

EXHIBIT 2 Retail Bank August 1994

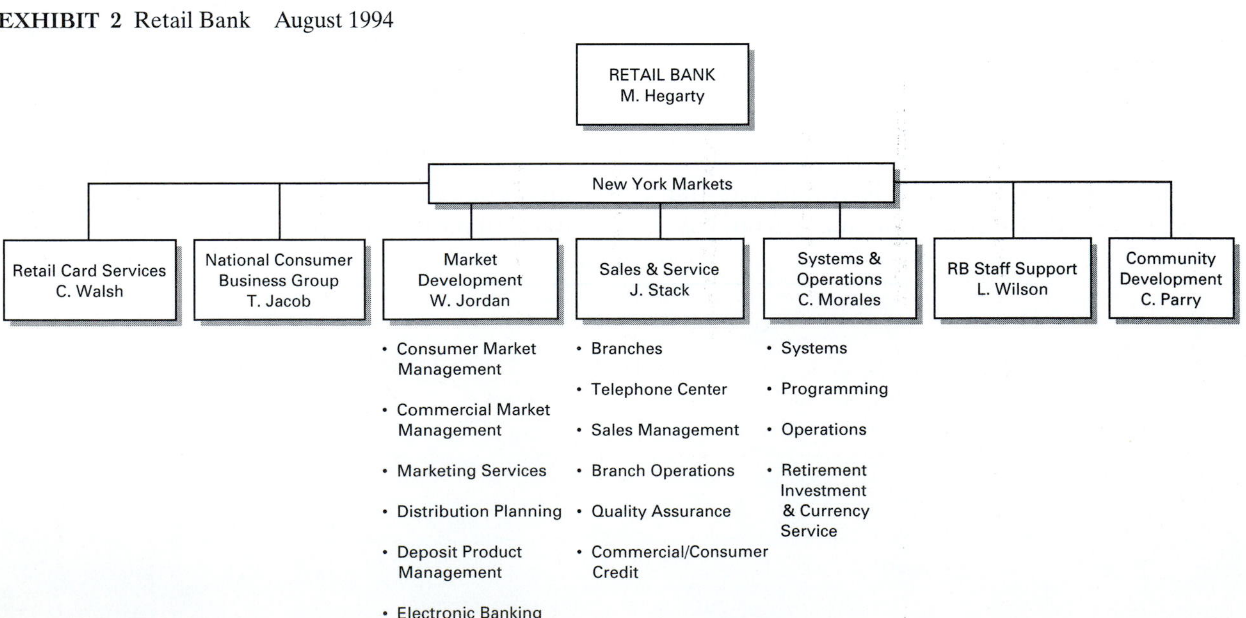

EXHIBIT 3A Strategic Financial Objectives for BSC

I. FINANCIAL (SHAREHOLDER)

Improve Return on Spending:

Return on spending reflects our ability to create wealth with the Corporation's funds. ROS is the appropriate objective because the business is assigned a low level of capital by the Corporation due to its low credit risk. ROS will align our expense outlays with the revenue generated. By aligning our spending with high value and high return activities, we will increase the return we achieve on dollars spent.

Reduce Costs:

By becoming more streamlined and efficient, we will focus resources and help to achieve acceptable profitability over the 3–5 year span. We will accomplish this by eliminating expenses that do not lead to revenue generation, by improving productivity, and by streamlining and redesigning key business processes.

Increase Revenues:

To achieve our financial vision, we need to grow our revenue streams. We need to redefine our core businesses and increase the number of valuable customers. We will achieve this by retaining and acquiring valuable customers, and broadening valuable customer relationships through the cross-sell of existing products and the sale of new products.

Reduce Risk:

We plan to move away from a dependence on net interest income by broadening and selling our portfolio of fee-based products to cover a greater portion of our expense base. Changing our mix toward more fee-based business will cushion Chemical from the risks of the interest rate cycle.

EXHIBIT 3B Strategic Customer Objectives for BSC

II. CUSTOMER

Differentiators

Offer customized value propositions to targeted customer segments:

i. Define propositions that different customers value
ii. Understand the economics of fulfilling various propositions
iii. Target those customers whose value propositions can be fulfilled profitably.

Differentiate ourselves through employees capable of recognizing customer needs and possessing the knowledge to proactively satisfy them:

A greater knowledge of Chemical's product and service offerings will help our customers better fulfill their banking needs. This knowledge, along with cross selling, consultative skills, and a supporting operating structure will satisfy a greater proportion of our customer's financial needs.

Give customers access to banking services or information 24 hours a day, consistent with the appropriate value proposition for the segment they represent.

Essentials

Perform consistently and seamlessly in the eyes of the customer

Service customers expediently: the timeliness of the response should meet or exceed the customer's perceived sense of urgency

Eliminate mistakes in all customer service encounters

EXHIBIT 3C Strategic Internal Objectives for BSC

III. INTERNAL

A. Innovation

Make the Market: Identify the needs of customer segments who represent high current profitability and their underlying economic potential. Understand the risk of each and how Chemical Bank can sustain differentiation with these target customers in the market by exploiting its key competencies.

Create the Product: Create profitable, innovative financial service products which are among the first to market, easy to use, and convenient to our targeted customers, yielding perceived superior value by the customer, and cost effective for Chemical Bank.

B. Delivery

Market & Sell: Cross-sell our products and services through organized, knowledgeable, consultative and proactive employees. We must listen to our customers, proactively educate them about our products and communicate to them how our products can meet their financial needs. To perform these activities, our salespeople must have a high level of systematic and regular contact with our customers and employ professional sales management practices.

Distribute & Service: Achieve service excellence based on our people and systems providing customers with the best reliability/availability, responsiveness, and no defects/errors. Quality delivery of our products and services is not an area of differentiation, but it is critical to our survival. Service excellence is the key to maintaining existing relationships and prerequisite to entering the battle for new customers. Without excellent performance on the "hygiene factors," we cannot move off square one.

EXHIBIT 3D Strategic Learning and Growth Objectives for BSC

IV. LEARNING & GROWTH

Strategic Information Assets

The ability to extract, manipulate, and use information holds the key to competitive advantage in our industry. First, we must recognize, harvest, and disseminate the considerable amount of information we have today. Second, business units and decision makers need to understand what and how much data are required to make a decision with a reasonably high degree of confidence. Third, we must improve the utility, access, ease of use and timeliness of information.

Reskilling: Strategic Jobs & Competencies

Build our marketing, sales, and customer service competencies to accomplish our aggressive revenue generation targets. First, our people need the competency to cross-sell our products and services. This demands a customer-focused orientation, the ability to recognize customer needs, the initiative to proactively solicit business, and superior consultative selling skills. Second, our people need a broader knowledge of our product portfolio and financial markets to support their cross-selling activities.

Accountability & Reward Linkage

Performance management systems are the pivotal points used to communicate, motivate, and reward employees for behavior that supports the Balanced Scorecard business objectives. We will align incentive plans to BSC business objectives to encourage behavior toward our business vision.

Focus our Resources

We will focus our resources to align our capital, expense, and personnel decisions with strategic priorities. Allocating resources where the return is the highest, setting priorities on competing expenditures based on that criterion, and remaining focused will enable us to operate more predictably and profitably.

EXHIBIT 4 Retail Bank's Balanced Scorecard

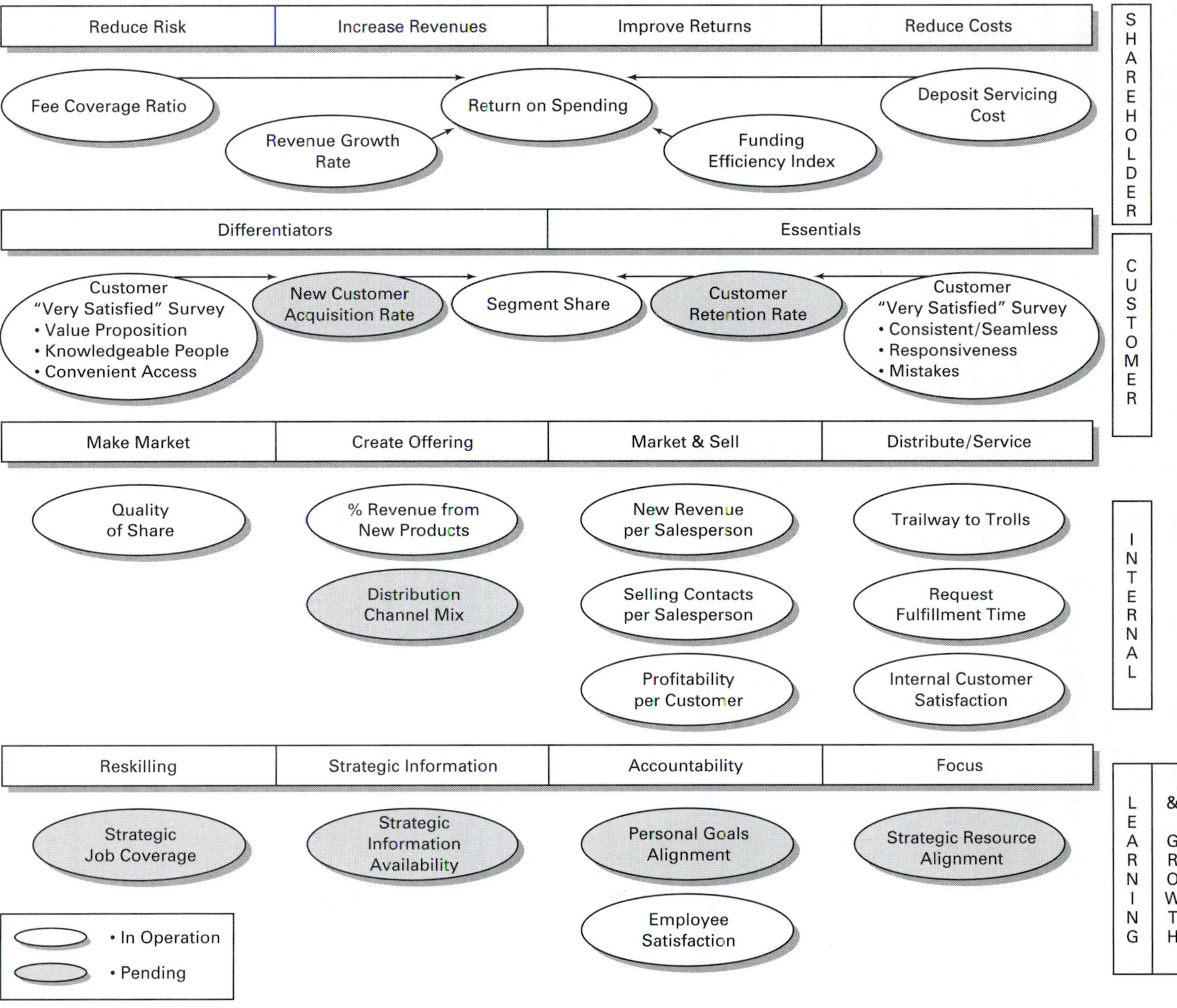

EXHIBIT 5 Strategic Objectives for Revenue Growth Strategy

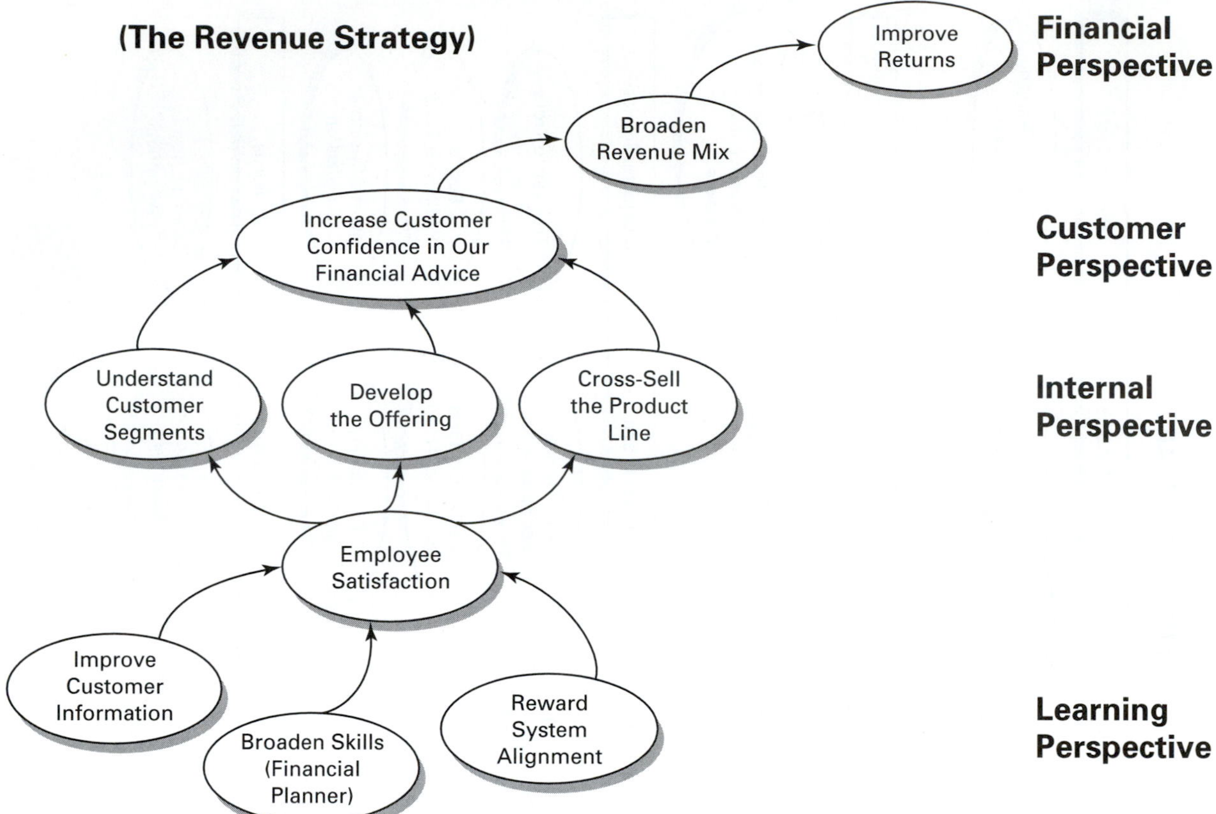

EXHIBIT 6 Retail Bank News & Views (Fall 1994)

Customer Focus (page 3, excerpts)

Segmentation: A Way To Get To Know Our Customers Better

Consumer Market Management recently completed analysis of the files of all 1.2 million deposit households of the Retail Bank and has assigned each household two scores: one indicating current relationship profitability and the second indicating the customer's Financial Personality segment—a strong indicator of potential profitability. The availability of this information is critical progress towards putting segmentation data into action.

Shifting the Customer/Profit Mix in New York Markets

One of our strategic goals is to increase the number of profitable customers. There are two related ways to develop and maintain a more profitable customer base. One is to provide exceptional service with targeted offerings to those customers who are currently highly profitable in order to strengthen the relationship and retain them longer. The other is to encourage customers who are most likely to become profitable to do more business with Chemical. The profit scores and segment codes can help us achieve these ends by helping us identify those customers.

The Segment Coding Process

The data gathering process began with a comprehensive study involving 2,000 customers and non-customers who were asked over 200 questions about how they handled money, their attitudes toward banks, and many other subjects. This initial study resulted in the identification of five financial segments. After establishing the Financial Segmentation framework, Consumer Market Management administered a much shorter questionnaire to more than 25,000 customers.

Measuring Customer Profitability

In addition to the segment codes which have been assigned to all retail deposit customers, actual profitability scores were assigned to customers of record as of December 1993. The profit score incorporates both the revenues and expenses associated with deposits, consumer and shelter loans, and revolving products for each individual household. There are four profitability levels:

Premier: the most profitable customers.

High: profitable because the revenues from fees and spreads more than cover the costs of the products and services we provide them.

Medium: the bulk of our customers yield a small profit on the products and services we provide them.

Low: generate little or no profit for the Retail Bank. In many cases, the revenues generated by their accounts do not cover the costs of providing the services.

How We Will Utilize This Information

During the first quarter of 1995, profitability and segment information will be available on-line. With information provided in a workbook, a video, and an interactive training disk, branch staff will be able to improve their sales efforts by customer segment and profit score. The ability to identify the most profitable customers for superior service will be made possible with this information. This should ultimately result in more business from our most profitable customers and more profitability for the Bank.

CHAPTER 13

Limitations of ROI-Type Performance Measures

Divisionalized *organizations* are composed of multiple responsibility centers, the managers of which are held primarily accountable for profit or some form of accounting return-on-investment (ROI). The divisionalized form of organization dates back to the 1920s when it was introduced in the DuPont Company, but its use spread quickly after World War II as one response to increased organizational size and complexity. The surveys of practice cited earlier (in Chapter 8) show that the divisionalized form of organization is now used by a high proportion of firms above minimal size. This form of organization has proved to be so useful that one prominent author called it "American capitalism's most important single innovation of the 20th Century."[1]

Divisionalization and decentralization are related, but the two words are not synonymous. An organization is said to be *decentralized* when authority for making decisions is pushed down to lower levels in the organization. All divisionalized organizations decentralize authority, at least to some extent, in specified areas of operations, notably a line of business and/or a geographical area. The converse is not true; not all decentralized organizations are divisionalized. When decentralization is effected along functional lines of authority (marketing, production, and finance), the responsibility centers are usually cost and revenue centers, not profit or investment centers.

Divisionalization provides some tremendous advantages. Large, complex organizations are not able to control behaviors effectively with action-dominated control systems involving the direct guidance of a wise, central leader or the enforcement of standard operating policies and procedures by a central administrative and support staff. No central management group can know everything about a complex organization's many product markets and operational capabilities and constraints. Even if it could, it would take time for the group to direct its attention to each issue that arose, become informed about the details, and then reach a decision. Decision making would be quite slow.

When an organization is divisionalized, local managers become experts in their specialized markets, and they are able to make good decisions more quickly. Because they control their own success to a significant extent, the local managers are likely to be more highly motivated and entrepreneurial. Their involvement in decision making helps them acquire experience that will benefit them as they move to higher organization levels. The time of the top management is freed so that they can focus on major strategic decisions.

Divisionalization is not without its problems and challenges; many relate to the problems created by the measurement of performance in terms of ROI.

RETURN-ON-INVESTMENT (ROI) PERFORMANCE MEASURES

ROI is a ratio of the accounting profits earned by the division divided by the investment assigned to the division. The vast majority of divisionalized corporations use some form of ROI measure for evaluating division performance. One survey found that 80 percent of the respondents use ROI measures[2]; another found the proportion to be 93%.[3] ROI is measured periodically, typically quarterly or monthly, and actual ROI is compared with a planned objective.

Variances from plans can be analyzed using formula charts (or ROI trees) such as the one shown in Figure 13-1. Such analyses might show that a division's actual ROI performance of 15 percent was below the planned level of 20 percent even though sales profitability (profit as a percent of sales) was on plan because asset turnover (sales divided by total investment) was worse than forecast:

Planned ROI (20%) = profit as percent of sales (20%) × asset turnover (1.0)
Actual ROI (15%) = profit as percent of sales (20%) × asset turnover (.75)

An analyst can further decompose the measures to understand whether the variance was due primarily to a sales decline or an increase in a specific kind of assets.

ROI formula charts are also useful for linking performance at all organization levels. The chart can be expanded out to the right to show specific measures that can be used for control purposes right down to the lowest levels of the organization. Sales performance can be disaggregated into sales volume and pricing factors. These factors can be further disaggregated by product, by geographical region, by customer segment, and by salesperson.

The actual forms of ROI-type ratios that companies employ vary widely, as do the labels companies put on their bottom-line investment center measures. Among the most common are return-on-investment (ROI), return-on-equity (ROE), return-on-capital-employed (ROCE), and return-on-net-assets (RONA).

FIGURE 13-1 Formula Chart Showing Relationship of Factors Affecting ROI

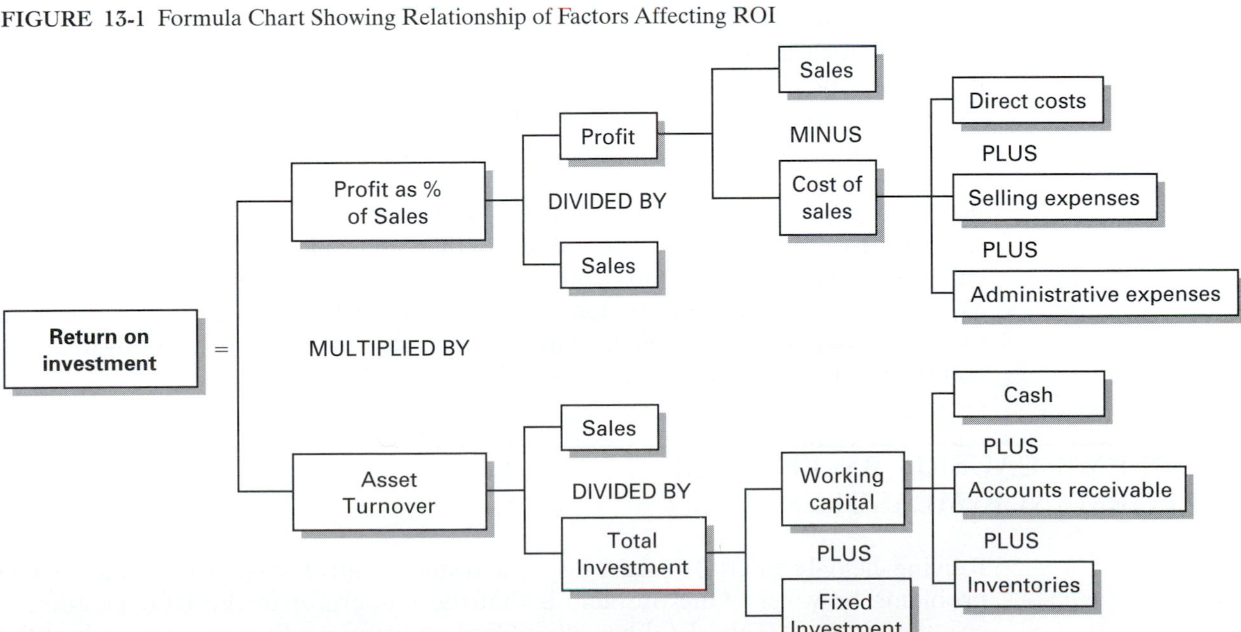

TABLE 13-1 Deviations Between ROI Measures of Corporations versus Investment Centers

Not Assigned to Investment Centers	*Percentage of 351 Companies*
Income Statement Items	
Taxes	71%
Interest Charges on Corporate Debt	64
Balance Sheet Items	
Pro-rata Share of Land and Buildings Used by Two or More Investment Centers	55
Pro-rata Share of Equipment Used by Two or More Investment Centers	59
Corporate Assets (Headquarters)	84
Intracompany Current Payables	70
Other Current Liabilities	55
Noncurrent Liabilities	80

Source: J. S. Reece and W. R. Cool, "Measuring Investment Center Performance," *Harvard Business Review* (May-June 1978), pp. 28–49.

In these ratios, both the numerator and denominator can include all or just a subset of the line items reflected on the corporate financial statements. The profit measure in the ROI calculation can be a fully allocated, after-tax profit measure, or it can be a before-tax operating income measure. Similarly, the denominator can include all the line items of assets and liabilities, including allocations of assets and liabilities not directly controlled by the division manager, or it can include only controllable assets, which generally include, at a minimum, receivables and inventories. Table 13-1 shows the deviations between measurement of corporate and division ROI that are employed by a majority of the firms responding to a survey of practice. These deviations and the reasons for them are discussed in more detail in Chapter 14.

ROI measures are in widespread use because they provide some significant advantages. First, they provide a single, comprehensive measure which reflects the trade-offs managers must make between revenues, costs, and investments. Second, they provide a common denominator that can be used for comparing returns on dissimilar businesses, such as divisions and outside competitors, or types of investments. Third, because they are expressed in percent terms, they give the impression that ROI returns are comparable to other financial returns, such as that calculated for stocks and bonds, although this impression is sometimes false (as explained in the following section). Finally, because ROI measures have been in use for so long in so many places, virtually all managers understand both what the measures reflect and how they can be influenced.

PROBLEMS CAUSED BY ROI-TYPE PERFORMANCE MEASURES

Relying heavily on ROI measures in a results control system can cause some problems, however.[4] One problem is that the numerator in the ROI measure is accounting profit. Thus, ROI has all the limitations of profit measures, such as the tendency to produce management myopia, the common form of behavioral displacement that was discussed in Chapter 12. A second limitation is a tendency for the measures to induce *suboptimization.* A narrow focus on ROI can lead division managers to make decisions that improve division ROI even though the decisions are not in the corporation's best interest. Finally, ROI measures sometimes provide misleading signals about the investment centers' performance because of difficulties in measuring the fixed asset portion of the denominator. These misleading signals can cause poor investment and performance evaluation decisions. Suboptimization and misleading performance signals are discussed in the following section.

Suboptimization

ROI measures can create a suboptimization problem by encouraging managers to make investments that make their divisions look good even though those investments are not in the best interest of the corporation. Managers of highly successful divisions are not likely to propose capital investments promising ROI returns below their division objectives, even if those investments are good ones from the company perspective. Table 13-2 shows a simplified suboptimization example of this type. Assume the corporate cost of capital is 15 percent. If an investment opportunity arises promising a 20 percent return, the investment should be made (assuming the opportunity is consistent with the corporate strategy and not too risky). The manager of Division A, whose performance targets probably reflect the historical performance of 10 percent, would be willing to make this investment, but the manager of Division B, operating at 40 percent, would not. Since most new investments that will eventually provide satisfactory returns earn a low return at the outset, this form of ROI measure-induced suboptimization is highly likely.

Conversely, ROI measures can cause managers of unsuccessful divisions to invest in capital investments promising ROI returns below the corporate cost of capital. This problem is illustrated in Table 13-3, which changes the Table 13-2 example only slightly by assuming the corporate cost of capital is 25 percent. In this situation, Division A would be willing to make this investment promising a 20 percent return, even though this investment does not cover the corporation's cost of capital.

TABLE 13-2 Example of Suboptimization: Failure to Invest in a Worthwhile Project

Assume: Corporate Cost of Capital = 15%

	Division A	*Division B*
Base Situation		
Profit Before Tax	$ 100,000	$ 400,000
Investment	$1,000,000	$1,000,000
Return on Investment	10%	40%

Assume an investment opportunity that is good for the company: Invest $100,000 to earn $20,000/year.

	Division A	*Division B*
New Situation		
Profit Before Tax	$ 120,000	$ 420,000
Investment	$1,100,000	$1,100,000
Return on Investment	10.9%	38.2%

TABLE 13-3 Example of Suboptimization: Investment in a Project That is *Not* Worthwhile

Assume: Corporate Cost of Capital = 25%

	Division A	*Division B*
Base Situation		
Profit Before Tax	$ 100,000	$ 400,000
Investment	$1,000,000	$1,000,000
Return on Investment	10%	40%
Assume an investment opportunity that is *not* good for the company: Invest $100,000 to earn $20,000/year.		
New Situation		
Profit Before Tax	$ 120,000	$ 420,000
Investment	$1,100,000	$1,100,000
Return on Investment	10.9%	38.2%

Where division managers have the authority to make financing decisions, ROI-type measures can also lead to suboptimization in that area. Return-on-equity (ROE) measures induce managers to use debt financing. They have motivations to push their entity's leverage to levels initially far in excess of the desired corporate leverage. Doing so increases their entities' ROE by decreasing the measure's denominator.

Misleading Performance Signals

Difficulties in measuring the denominator of the ROI measure, particularly that pertaining to fixed assets, can provide misleading signals about the performance of an investment center. The assets values reflected on companies' balance sheets do not represent the real value of the assets available to managers for earning current returns. The assets were added to the business at various times in the past, under varying market conditions and varying sizes of the purchasing power of the monetary unit. The accumulation of unlike amounts says little about the value of the assets; that is, their ability to generate future cash flows.

A survey of practice found that 85 percent of the firms using ROI to measure their investment centers measured their fixed assets at their *net* book values (NBV).[5] When NBV is used, ROI is usually overstated. The overstatement is larger if the entity includes a relatively large number of older assets. The NBV of older assets are far below their replacement values because they were bought in a period of lower prices (assuming inflation) and because they have been depreciated longer.

This ROI-overstatement problem is illustrated in Table 13-4. Assume that Divisions C and D are identical operating units except that Division C purchased most of its fixed assets many years ago and Division D has nearly new assets. For the sake of simplicity, assume there have been no technological advancements; the old assets perform the same tasks as efficiently as the new assets. Profit before depreciation is identical, but Division D's depreciation is twice that of Division C, so C's profit after depreciation is slightly higher. C's ROI is dramatically higher than D's, mostly because its assets have a much lower NBV. The difference between 20 percent and 3 percent ROI is not real; it is just an artifact of the measurement system.

TABLE 13-4 Example Showing ROI Overstatement When Denominator Is Measured in Terms of Net Book Value

	Division C	*Division D*
Profit Before Depreciation	$110,000	$ 110,000
Depreciation	$ 10,000	$ 20,000
Profit After Depreciation	$100,000	$ 90,000
Assets (Net Book Value)	$500,000	$3,000,000
ROI	20%	3%

Another quirk of ROI measures is that ROI calculated using NBV increases over time if no further investments are made. This is shown in Table 13-5. Assume that Division E is operating in a steady state, earning in year 1 an ROI of 12 percent. Because the assets are being depreciated, the ROI increases to 13.3 percent in year 2 and 15 percent in year 3. This ROI increase is not real either.

These measurement quirks can cause managers who are using the ROI measures to make bad decisions:

- They encourage division managers to retain assets beyond their optimal life and not to invest in new assets which would increase the denominator of the ROI calculation. This dysfunctional motivational effect is particularly strong if the managers expect their job tenures to be short. (This situation is another example of the myopia problem discussed in Chapter 12.)
- They can cause corporate managers to overallocate resources to divisions with older assets because they appear to be relatively highly profitable.
- They can contribute to the problem shown in Table 13-2, the tendency for ROI to make managers of highly profitable divisions reluctant to invest in projects which are in the company's best interest but which would lower the division's ROI.
- They can lead to different inventory policies and decisions in different divisions, even for identical items of inventory.
- If corporate managers are not aware of these distortions or do not adjust for them, they can cause errors in evaluating division managers' performances.

Measuring fixed assets at *gross* (undepreciated) book value (GBV) minimizes some of these problems because GBV is closer to replacement value than NBV, but it does not solve them. In periods of inflation, as is almost always the case, old assets valued at gross book value are still expressed at lower values than new assets, so ROI is still overstated. Valuing assets at gross book value adds another risk; that division managers will scrap equipment which is

TABLE 13-5 Example Showing Increase in ROI Due Merely to Passage of Time

		Division E	
	Year 1	*Year 2*	*Year 3*
Profit Before Depreciation	$110,000	$110,000	$110,000
Depreciation	50,000	50,000	50,000
Profit After Depreciation	$ 60,000	$ 60,000	$ 60,000
Assets (Net Book Value)	$500,000	$450,000	$400,000
ROI	12%	13.3%	15%

temporarily idle or underemployed in the short run in order to increase their ROI.

Another problem is that ROI measures create incentives for managers to lease assets, rather than buying them. Leased assets accounted for on an operating-lease basis are not recognized on the corporation's balance sheet, so they are not included in the ROI denominator. Managers can increase their division's ROI by gaming the system in this way. The survey of practice found that 34 percent of the respondent companies included the capitalized value of assets employed in division ROI calculations even when those leases were not required to be capitalized. This accounting adjustment avoids this potential behavioral problem, but the adjustments themselves are costly.

RESIDUAL INCOME MEASURES AS A POSSIBLE SOLUTION TO THE ROI MEASUREMENT PROBLEMS

A number of researchers and consultants have argued that the use of a *residual income* (RI) measure overcomes the suboptimization limitation of ROI.[6] Residual income is calculated by subtracting from profit a capital charge for the net assets tied up in the investment center. The capital is charged at a rate equal to the weighted average corporation's cost of capital. Conceptually, an argument can be made to adjust the capital charge rate for the investment center's risk, thus making the performance measurement system consistent with the capital budgeting system; however, this adjustment is made by only 19 percent of the firms which use residual income.[7]

Residual income measures do indeed solve the suboptimization problem. The residual income charge can be made equal to the corporation's investment cut-off rate of return. Residual income measures give all investment center managers an identical incentive to invest. Regardless of the prevailing levels of return in their responsibility centers, they are motivated to invest in all projects that promise internal rates of return higher than, or at least equal to, the cost of capi-

TABLE 13-6 Example of Suboptimization with Residual Income: Failure to Invest in a Worthwhile Project

Assume: Corporate Cost of Capital = 15%

	Division A	*Division B*
Base Situation		
Profit Before Tax	$ 100,000	$ 400,000
Investment	$1,000,000	$1,000,000
Return on Investment	10%	40%
Residual Income	$ (50,000)	$ 250,000
Assume an investment opportunity that is good for the company: Invest $100,000 to earn $20,000/year.		
New Situation		
Profit Before Tax	$ 120,000	$ 420,000
Investment	$1,100,000	$1,100,000
Return on Investment	10.9%	38.2%
Residual Income	$ (45,000)	$ 255,000

tal. This is shown in Table 13-6 which shows a modified version of Table 13-2 with a row added for residual income. In both divisions, residual income is increased if the desirable investment is made.

Residual income also addresses the financing-type suboptimization problem. By considering the cost of both debt and equity financing, residual income removes the managers' temptations to increase their entity's leverage to excessive levels.

Residual income does not address the distortions often caused when managers make new investments in fixed assets. Many desirable investments initially reduce residual income, but then the residual income increases over time as the fixed assets get older.

One consulting firm, Stern Stewart & Company, recommends a measure called economic value added (EVA), which combines several of the modifications to the standard accounting model in a residual income-type measure.[8] The EVA formula is:

$$\text{EVA} = \text{Modified after-tax operating profit} - (\text{total capital} \times \text{weighted average cost of capital})$$

Modified after-tax operating profit is different from that defined by accountants in that it reflects the capitalization and subsequent amortization of intangible investments; such as for research and development, employee training, and advertising. *Total capital* includes fixed assets, working capital, and the capitalized intangibles. The *weighted average cost of capital* reflects the weighted average cost of debt and equity financing.

Because it addresses some of the known weaknesses of accounting profitability measures of performance, EVA should provide better reflections of economic income than accounting income in many settings. It should mitigate the investment myopia problem discussed in Chapter 12 because it involves capitalization of the most important types of discretionary expenditures managers might try to cut if they were pressured for profits. It also has the advantages of a residual income-type measure.

It must be recognized, however, that EVA is *not* economic income. It does not address all of the problems which differentiate accounting income from economic income. In particular, EVA still reflects primarily the results of a summation of transactions completed during the period, and, importantly, EVA still focuses on the past, while economic income reflects changes in *future* cash flow potentials. EVA will be particularly poor indicator of value changes for organizations which derive a significant proportion of their value from future growth.

Academic researchers are only beginning to focus on the EVA measure of performance. Interestingly, the first complete study *did not find* the EVA measure to be superior to accounting income as an indicator of changes in shareholder value.[9] The reasons for this study's conclusion are not yet well understood.

CONCLUSION

Although the arguments in favor of residual income have been in print for many years now, surveys have shown that only a relatively small minority of firms use residual income for evaluating investment centers and their managers. A survey found that only 2 percent of companies using investment centers use residual income exclusively. Another 28 percent of the respondents reported using residual income in conjunction with ROI.[10]

Managers who still rely on ROI-type measures argue that the conceptual weaknesses of ROI are well understood, and the potential suboptimization problems can be monitored through the company's capital budgeting and strategic planning processes. Managers of highly profitable divisions can be encouraged to make more investments, and proposed investments from less profitable divisions can be scrutinized carefully. They also argue that ROI data are easier to compare across investment centers and across companies than are residual income data; that residual income is difficult for some operating managers to understand; and that there is a natural resistance to change something that has been used for so long without causing obvious problems.

It is true that the suboptimization problems can be avoided or mitigated to some extent through the investment review processes. By using these processes, companies can use ROI with some degree of effectiveness. Critics would still argue: Why use a measurement system that requires bureaucratic, administrative actions to prevent managers from taking undesirable actions?

Notes

1. Williamson, Oliver E., *Corporate Control and Business Behavior* (Englewood Cliffs, N.J.: Prentice-Hall, 1970), p. 175.
2. R. F. Vancil, *Decentralization: Managerial Ambiguity by Design* (Homewood, Ill.: Dow Jones-Irwin, 1979).
3. Reece, J. S. and W. R. Cool, "Measuring Investment Center Performance," *Harvard Business Review*, 56, no. 3 (May–June 1978), p. 30.
4. The arguments in this section are taken from J. Dearden, "The Case Against ROI Control," *Harvard Business Review*, 47, no. 3 (May–June 1969), pp. 124–135; and S. Henrici, "The Peril, Perversity and Pathos of ROI," *Financial Analysts Journal*, 39, no. 5 (September–October 1983), pp. 79–80.
5. Reece, J. S. and W. R. Cool, "Measuring Investment Center Performance," *Harvard Business Review*, 56, no. 3 (May–June 1978), p. 33.
6. The arguments in this section are taken from J. Dearden, "The Case Against ROI Control," *Harvard Business Review*, 47, no. 3 (May–June 1969), pp. 124–135; and S. Henrici, "The Peril, Perversity and Pathos of ROI," *Financial Analysts Journal*, 39, no. 5 (September–October 1983), pp. 79–80.
7. Reece, J. S. and W. R. Cool, "Measuring Investment Center Performance," *Harvard Business Review*, 56, no. 3 (May–June 1978), p. 34.
8. B. Stewart, *Quest for Value*; and S. Tully, "The Real Key to Creating Wealth," *Fortune* (September 20, 1993), pp. 38–50.
9. G. C. Biddle, R. M. Bowen, and J. S. Wallace, "Evidence on the Relative and Incremental Information Content of EVA™, Residual Income, Earnings, and Operating Cash Flow," unpublished working paper, University of Washington, August 12, 1996.
10. Reece, J. S. and W. R. Cool, "Measuring Investment Center Performance," *Harvard Business Review*, 56, no. 3 (May–June 1978), p. 30.

Pullen Lumber Company

John Pullen, founder and president of Pullen Lumber Company, was considering an incentive compensation plan for his managers which had been prepared at his request. Currently, the 700 Pullen employees were paid a straight salary (plus overtime when applicable). They were also paid an annual bonus equal to two weeks' salary. The proposed plan would apply only to the 43 managers of lumber yards, the 5 district managers, and 5 senior managers at headquarters. Instead of the annual bonus, these managers would be eligible for a bonus according to a proposal described later in the case.

THE COMPANY

Pullen Lumber Company operated 43 lumber yards located in four mid-western states. Few interdependencies existed among the yards and each carried a line of lumber, plywood, roofing materials, doors, windows, tools, paint, flooring, and builders' supplies. Sales were made to contractors, homebuilders, and to individual homeowners and hobbyists. The lumber yards were supervised by 5 district offices. Each district office also had a sales force that solicited business from large contractors. As a service, the district offices sometimes aided contractors in preparing the material components in bids and gave informal advice on the material best suited to a job. Yard managers also gave this advice to smaller contractors.

There was a fixed budget for each yard and each district, showing planned revenues and expenses. Actual revenues and expenses were reported annually. Data on the company's financial condition and performance for the year are provided in Exhibits 1 and 2.

The company had enjoyed profits the past few years which were considerably greater than those of most of its competition, for whom the average after-tax return on investment in total assets was approximately 6 percent. Although the company as a whole had done well in the opinion of the company president, some of its yards and districts had incurred operating losses. Meanwhile, competitive pressures had been growing and the differences in profits among Pullen Co. and its competitors had narrowed significantly. Because of this, the individual differences in the performances of the yards, and Mr. Pullen's often expressed desire to gain a larger market share in each of the company's lines of business, the proposed bonus plan assumed added significance.

BACKGROUND OF THE PLAN

At an Executive Committee meeting in September, Mr. Pullen introduced the idea of a bonus plan, and it seemed to be favorably received. At the end of this meeting he appointed a committee to draft a bonus plan. It consisted of the controller, who was to serve as chairman, the general sales manager, and the director of purchases. The first problem they tackled was identification of the persons to whom the plan should apply. Three groups were initially considered: (1) district salesmen, (2) buyers, and (3) managers.

The sales manager foresaw great difficulties in identifying improved sales volume with individual salesmen. Many of the company's best customers had dealt with the company for years, and no substantial selling effort was required. Furthermore, personal friendships existed between the top officers of some companies which were good customers and the top officers of Pullen Lumber Company. These conditions made it relatively unimportant which salesman called upon and serviced the account. The volume of business from these customers would remain virtually unchanged, regardless of the salemen's efforts.

This case was prepared by Assistant Professor Cornelius J. Casey, Jr. as the basis for class discussion rather than to illustrate either effective or ineffective handling of an administrative situation.

The director of purchases also foresaw problems in attempting to recognize and reward individual buyers. The discounts obtained on an order related to factors over which the buyer had so little control as not to be a valid basis for a bonus award.

The committee therefore decided that the bonus plan should be limited to managers—the managers of individual lumber yards, the district managers, and the senior management group at headquarters.

In considering the managers' responsibility for profit performance, the committee agreed generally on the following points:

1. The yard manager is the primary factor in influencing customers' loyalty toward Pullen, by giving good service, by having the goods on hand when the customer wants them, and by his supervision of yard personnel.
2. Although standard selling prices are set by the central purchasing department, the yard manager has latitude in reducing prices to meet competition and in the markdowns he allows for defective or old merchandise.
3. The yard manager is responsible for inventory, both to replenish stocked items and to decide what items should be added to or deleted from inventory within limits specified by headquarters.
4. The yard manager has major responsibility for bad debts, although for large accounts he is expected to ask headquarters for a credit check.
5. An aggressive yard manager will generate new business by calling on prospective customers.
6. The yard manager has considerable discretion in advertising, although the art work and much of the copy of space advertising is prepared at headquarters. Catalogues and direct mail pieces are also prepared at headquarters.
7. The yard manager is responsible for expense control.
8. The district manager is generally responsible for the yards in his district.
9. The district office also helps profitability by the services it renders to large customers. Orders from these customers are shipped from the yard nearest to the job.
10. Sales volume varies with construction activity in the territory served by the yard.

Most of the yard managers had only a high school education; in the opinion of the controller, they understood very little of the relationship between their performance and the profitability of their yards. It was the controller's view that a concentrated management training program for managers, supplemented by a bonus plan, would make them conscious of the necessity of increasing profits through better management and would furnish them the incentive to put better practices into effect.

When the committee reported back to the president, it was their consensus that the controller should devise a bonus plan along the lines outlined previously. Shortly thereafter, the controller submitted the following proposed bonus plan:

GENERAL STATEMENT OF PLAN

This bonus plan is designed to provide company managers with an opportunity to earn additional compensation for improved performance as reflected by an increased return on the company's investment at the yards under their management.

DEFINITION OF TERMS

A. *Investment* at each location will include the annual average of the following:
   1. Month-end cash balances.
   2. Month-end inventory, at cost, excluding central stocks placed at a given location by the Purchasing Department.
   3. Month-end accounts receivables associated with bonusable sales.
   4. Investment in automobiles and trucks assigned to the location, at depreciated cost.
   5. Investment in equipment, furniture, and fixtures assigned to the location at depreciated cost.
   6. Land and buildings at depreciated cost assigned to the location (if property is rented, the rent will show up as an expense).

B. *Bonusable Sales* are all shipments made from the location except sales orders written by district or headquarters sales personnel. These orders will be coded as written and deducted from the gross sales of the yard.

C. *Expenses* include:
   1. Cost of goods sold on bonusable sales.
   2. Operating expenses of the yard, including rental and depreciation.
   3. Actual cost of services provided by district offices to the yard and to customers of the yard. (If the customer cannot be identified with a specific

yard, these costs will be included in district office cost.)

4. Actual cost of credit investigations and collection efforts for the benefit of the yard.
5. Advertising material, catalogues, and other material supplied to the yard at actual cost.
   Note: Costs of district advertising (space and TV) for items not carried in a given yard will not be charged to that yard.
6. Pro rata share of office expenses for purchasing. This will be determined on the basis of the yard's receipts into inventory as a proportion of total company receipts into inventory.
7. Pro rata share of district office and headquarters expenses not charged directly to a yard. This will be determined on the basis of each yard's gross sales as a proportion of total company sales.
8. The following operating losses will be charged to the yard when the district manager determines that these are the responsibility of the yard manager:
   (a) Inventory shortages.
   (b) Cost of repairing damaged property.
   (c) Loss on sale of fixed assets.
   (d) Bad debt losses.

D. *Bonusable profit* is bonusable sales minus expenses.

E. *Return on investment* is bonusable profit divided by investment in total assets.

CALCULATION OF THE BONUS

A. The total bonus pool will be $90,000 plus 5 percent of the corporation's income in excess of $2,000,000 before income taxes.

B. The total bonus pool will be divided as follows:

Yard managers	– 65%
District managers	– 15%
Senior management	– 20%

C. The yard managers' bonus pool will be divided among yard managers on the basis of the number of bonus units that they earn. The manager of a yard whose return on investment is 5 percent will earn one bonus unit. For each full percentage point above 5, the manager will earn an additional bonus unit, up to a maximum of six bonus units. The monetary value of one bonus unit is found by dividing the total dollar amount in the yard managers' pool by the total number of bonus units earned by all yard managers.

D. The bonus units awarded by any yard manager who has been in that position for less than one year will be decided by his district manager, applying the previous principle as closely as is feasible.

E. The district managers' bonus pool will be divided among district managers in relation to the total bonus units earned by the yards in their district as a proportion of the total bonus units earned by all yards.

F. The headquarters' bonus pool will be divided as decided by the president.

G. Bonuses will be paid in cash as soon after the end of the year as they can be calculated.

Mr. Pullen looked over the plan quickly and observed that it was drawn to include only managers. He said, "You can bet your bottom dollar that the district salesmen aren't going to be happy when they hear about a bonus plan for yard managers. What does the sales manager have to say about the proposed plan?"

The sales manager explained that the committee recognized the role of the district sales and sales service personnel but that there was no practical way of measuring their contribution to profitability because actual sales were booked through the yards that made delivery.

The controller also explained the rationale behind the recommended size of the bonus pool. The elimination of the annual bonus for the 53 managers in the plan would create $40,000 of available funds. In addition, the usual annual salary increase to these managers of about $50,000 would not be given. Thus, at the current level of profits, a bonus of $90,000 would not affect costs. If the plan resulted in profits greater than $2,000,000 before taxes, the bonus would be correspondingly higher.

Questions

1. Evaluate the proposed bonus plan which Mr. Pullen is considering. Does your evaluation suggest any generalization for exercising management control through payment schemes?
2. How, if at all, would you modify the proposed plan?

EXHIBIT 1 Balance Sheet as of 12/31/77

Assets		
Current		
Cash and Short-Term Investments		$ 1,346,000
Accounts Receivable	5,386,000	
Less: Allowance for Doubtful Accounts	56,000	5,330,000
Inventory		11,260,000
Total Current Assets		17,936,000
Fixed		
Trucks, Automobiles and Equipment	3,450,000	
Less: Accumulated Depreciation	1,260,000	2,190,000
Land and Buildings	10,040,000	
Less: Accumulated Depreciation	4,020,000	6,020,000
Total Fixed Assets		8,210,000
Other Assets		2,900,000
TOTAL ASSETS		$29,046,000
Equities		
Liabilities		
Current Payables		$ 5,478,000
Long-Term Note Payable, 8%		5,000,000
Total Liabilities		10,478,000
Owners' Equity		
Capital Stock ($40 par; 250,000 shares issued and outstanding)		10,000,000
Retained Earnings		8,568,000
Total Owners' Equity		18,568,000
TOTAL EQUITIES		$29,046,000

EXHIBIT 2 Income Statement for 1977

Sales (Net)		56,127,000
Service Revenue		2,148,000
		58,275,000
Less Cost of Sales		41,458,000
Gross Margin		16,817,000
Operating Expenses		
Payroll	6,705,000	
Property Expense[a]	1,688,000	
Advertising	1,312,000	
Bad Debt Expense	836,000	
Equipment Expense[b]	1,127,000	
Other Expenses	1,529,000	
Total Operating Expenses		13,197,000
Operating Income		3,620,000
Non-Operating Items		
Interest Expense	400,000	
Loss on Sale of Equipment	32,000	432,000
Income before Taxes		3,188,000
Provision for Income Taxes		1,476,000
Net Income		$ 1,712,000

[a]Property expense includes real estate taxes, rentals, depreciation and utilities expense.

[b]Equipment expense includes depreciation, maintenance and repairs, and routine operating expenses.

American Standard Inc. — The Inflation Accounting System

In the fall of 1981, Kenneth R. Todd, Jr., vice president and controller, was reviewing the inflation-adjusted accounting system that was used at American Standard. American Standard was committed to inflation-adjusted accounting as the primary measurement system for the company. Todd realized that this differed from the approach taken by most U.S. firms, which either provided inflation-adjusted accounting data to managers as supplementary information or did not provide these data at all, and even though American Standard had gone further than most firms in integrating inflation-adjusted accounting data into management systems, Todd was not satisfied with the company's accomplishments. In particular, he wondered whether it would be useful to restate prior years' current cost data in constant dollars and whether changes should be made to the long-term incentive compensation plan.

AMERICAN STANDARD'S BUSINESS

American Standard was a major international manufacturing firm, with 1980 sales of $2,674 million (see Exhibits 1 and 2 for primary financial statements). The company manufactured products in 150 plants, which were located in 22 countries on five continents, and marketed these products in nearly every country in the world.

American Standard's products fell into four general categories: transportation products (braking systems for heavy trucks and systems for train monitoring and control); building products (plumbing fixtures and fittings); security and graphic products (bank safes, vaults, electronic alarms, bank checks, and business forms); and construction and mining equipment (off-highway, heavy construction trucks).

These businesses were managed through a decentralized management system, which was organized in a hierarchical structure that comprised global groups, groups, and companies and product lines (see Exhibit 3 for an organization chart). The many companies and product lines varied significantly in size, and a primary vehicle of communication among the diverse businesses within American Standard was the financial control system.

THE FINANCIAL CONTROL SYSTEM

The overall corporate objective was to attain real, inflation-adjusted, rates of return on assets that were sufficient to finance the businesses (including growth) and to offer above-average, real returns to shareholders. The financial control system was designed to help achieve the corporate objectives. Todd explained its purpose as follows:

> A key assumption is that we're going to stay in these businesses. Therefore, American Standard has adopted the concept related to maintenance of productive capacity as the basic premise of its financial control system—in other words, staying in business. We define operating income as the funds left over and available for expansion of the business after maintaining the productive capacity of our unit and providing a minimum return to security holders.

To further the corporate goals, the financial control system had to encourage maximum asset utilization by managers and to provide them with the right tools for the best economic decisions. American Standard adopted an inflation-adjusted

Julie H. Hertenstein, research assistant, prepared this case under the supervision of Professor William J. Bruns, Jr., as the basis for class discussion rather than to illustrate either effective or ineffective handling of an administrative situation.

method of accounting to help accomplish these goals. The recent financial experiences of the firm were a significant factor in the decision to adopt this accounting method.

Top management traced the impetus for American Standard's use of an inflation-adjusted method of accounting back to the latter part of the 1960s. During that period, American Standard aggressively expanded, with major acquisitions, such as Mosler Safe in 1967 and Westinghouse Air Brake Company (WABCO) in 1968, as well as numerous smaller acquisitions. From 1966 to 1969 the total assets of the company tripled; to finance this growth, American Standard borrowed heavily, significantly increasing its leverage.

The recession of 1969–1970 kept American Standard from achieving the growth that it had projected; and in 1970, as the seriousness of the situation became evident, the company began to retrench. It closed some plants and sold or phased out other operations. In 1971 William A. Marquard, who had previously been president of American Standard's subsidiary, the Mosler Safe Company, was named president and chief executive officer of American Standard, Inc. In the same year he announced to shareholders a program of asset redeployment, characterized by a philosophy of consolidation, that was in sharp contrast to the previous policy of rapid expansion. In 1971 American Standard took a writedown of $97 million (after a $25 million tax benefit) to provide for the costs to be incurred on sales or other dispositions of certain businesses and facilities; this resulted in a net loss for the year of $83.8 million. American Standard's executives thus began the steps necessary to turn the company around.

American Standard's executives were particularly aware of the need for information that reflected economic reality during this turnaround and realized that the management accounting system had to reflect their best understanding of economic reality. When American Standard's executives believed that external reporting requirements differed from economic reality, they were willing to modify their internal management accounting systems so that the data available to executives and their subordinates were as realistic as possible. Richard H. Francis, vice president and treasurer, provided an example that explained their willingness to diverge from the external reporting requirements.

> Past accounting practice did not require leased assets to be reported on the balance sheet, nor did it require the amount due to the lessor to be reported as a liability. But by following an accounting practice such as off-balance sheet leasing internally, you may forget what you were doing, or some managers may not have known. You could wind up misleading yourself, and that could cause problems.

This philosophy led to the eventual implementation of an inflation-adjusted accounting system. American Standard's managers generally agreed that the first steps toward inflation accounting occurred in the mid-1970s with the worldwide adoption of the LIFO method of accounting for cost of goods sold and inventory that led to a closer matching of the current cost of production with current revenues. In the fall of 1981 further modifications and extensions of the inflation accounting system were under consideration.

THE INFLATION-ADJUSTED ACCOUNTING SYSTEM

American Standard's inflation-adjusted accounting system can best be understood by first considering the four basic accounting elements which differed from conventional historical cost accounting elements and then considering its two composite measures of performance, in which some or all of these four basic elements appear. The four basic elements are fixed assets, depreciation, inventories, and cost of goods sold, and the two composite measures are operating income and return on net assets (RONA).

Fixed assets and depreciation Accounting for fixed assets was based on the estimated cost of replacing the assets. Replacement costs were computed by restating each asset, or category of assets, through the use of local, replacement-cost indices for each industry and country in which American Standard operated.

Exhibit 4-A illustrates the computation of replacement costs for the buildings in the Keller Crescent Company; first, the year of the acquisition of the existing buildings was determined, and then the replacement cost was calculated for each year's acquisitions. Local management selected various producer-price indices or construction-price indices that they considered to be representative of the particular assets.[1] These published indices were also acceptable for the required supplementary public reporting of inflation-adjusted data. Although this method did not incorporate technological change in the replacement cost, American Standard believed that the additional costs of a more elaborate method of calculating replacement cost would exceed the benefit to be gained, particularly since technologies were not changing rapidly in American Standard's industries. The published specific price indices were considered to be objective, and their use removed opportunities for optimism or manipulation to affect the data.

Under the basic purpose of the financial control system—to maintain productive capacity—depreciation was considered a provision for replacing productive assets used in the business; hence, depreciation was based on the replacement cost of the assets. Replacement depreciation was further based on management's realistic estimates of the economic lives of the assets involved (as shown in Exhibit 4-B). American Standard believed that to stay in business, the company should retain profits at a rate sufficient to have funds on hand for functionally replacing manufacturing equipment and facilities at the end of their useful lives. According to Todd:

> It does not matter that a replacement machine may have commensurate benefits in terms of lower production costs. Those reductions will take place after the investment has taken place. What is important is that a company retain from current operations sufficient funds to replace its fixed assets; charging income for realistic depreciation is how this is accomplished.

One indication of the extent to which the policy of replacement depreciation had been implemented was that a manager's operating income was charged replacement depreciation for all depreciable assets used, including those assets that had already been fully depreciated. Management reasoned that such assets were only considered fully depreciated because of a past error in estimating asset life, whereas, in fact, the manager was still using the assets, and therefore they ought to be providing a return. Further, charging depreciation on these assets might motivate managers to consider whether the assets should be disposed of; it would provide an incentive for managers at lower levels, who had the real knowledge of the assets' utilization and condition, to reevaluate the decision to keep the assets.

There were a few conditions, however, when replacement depreciation was not used; these occurred when an entire business was to be abandoned, or a unit's asset utilization was to be decreased substantially (and then only after concrete action had been taken to dispose of the assets). In these instances, two other changes occurred in the financial control system: first, the rate of historical cost depreciation was adjusted to reflect the remaining expected useful life, and second, any capital expenditures made in this business were expensed immediately.

The overall effect of using replacement costs as the basis for accounting for fixed assets and depreciation was significant; in 1981 these costs were each about 45% higher than they would have been under conventional historical cost accounting.

Inventory and cost of goods sold On the balance sheet, inventories were carried at current standard costs; each year, when the new current standard costs were determined, the inventory on the balance sheet was revalued to the new current standard cost. For example, if standard costs had increased by 10%, the inventory on the balance sheet would be revalued upward by 10%. This annual revaluation to current standards created an offsetting credit entry that was considered a corporate item and was not reflected in the operating income for the divisions.

American Standard determined the cost of goods sold by using current standard costs with immediate recognition of any variances from standard. It believed that this use of current standards, combined with any variance from standard that might have occurred during the period, provided an accurate estimate of the current cost of production.

The company also believed that the various historical cost methods of accounting for inventories and cost of goods sold did not match the current cost of production with current sales. Histori-

[1]Two examples of sources of such indices are the *Producer Prices and Price Indexes,* which is published by the U.S. Bureau of Labor Statistics and contains detailed categories, such as metal-cutting machine tools, metal-forming machine tools, and pumps and compressors, and *Construction Review,* which contains numerous composite construction-cost indices for commercial and factory buildings as well as indices for producers' prices of selected groups of materials and items used in construction.

cal cost income included an element of *inventory profit,* which arose from matching current revenues with the lower costs of production in earlier periods. American Standard believed that such paper inventory profits did not represent management performance, nor did they represent amounts that could be used by other divisions or distributed to security holders. The paper profits that resulted from higher inventory values had to be retained just to maintain the business at its current level; therefore, the company believed that it was beneficial for both executives and operating management to keep these paper profits out of the division's operating income.

Since American Standard had implemented LIFO for inventories and cost of goods sold, virtually no change to cost of goods sold was required to adjust for inflation. Since LIFO seriously understated the inventories on the balance sheet, however, the current cost of inventories ($551 million in 1981) represented a 61 percent increase above the conventional LIFO inventory cost of $342 million.

Operating income Operating income was the primary performance measurement at American Standard; it was calculated before the provision for taxes and contained provisions for three charges: replacement depreciation for pro-rata share of the productive capacity used, the current cost of inventory sold, and the minimum return required for security holders, known as the capital charge. (The capital charge is discussed in more detail in the next section.) The following is a simplified statement of operating income:

Revenues
Less: Current cost of good sold
Replacement depreciation
Other expenses
Capital charge

Operating income (before tax)

Operating income was defined as the funds left over and available for expansion of the business, after maintenance of the productive capacity of the unit and after a minimum return to security holders had been provided. In other words, a unit at break-even had no funds left over for expanding its own business or for distributing to other units; break-even represented the minimal level of sustainable performance.

The *capital charge* represented (1) the recovery of corporate overhead not charged to the field and (2) the inflation-adjusted (or real) cost of capital for the corporation, including both debt and equity elements. In 1981 a capital charge rate of 12 percent was charged for use of the division's net assets (net assets are discussed in the following section); since the cost of capital was stated in real terms, and hence would not vary with changes in the rate of inflation, American Standard's executives expected the capital charge to remain at 12 percent of net assets.

Net assets were defined as all assets of operations less current liabilities that were without financing cost; the assets of operations were those assets for which line managers were held responsible, such as inventories at current standard cost and fixed assets at replacement cost net of depreciation. Excluded were assets for which division managers were not held accountable, such as cash, marketable securities, and future income tax benefits; these were corporate responsibilities over which line managers had little, if any, influence. For example, American Standard had one central cash fund for all U.S. operations; it did not have separate cash funds managed by individual groups or companies.

In summary, net assets were defined as follows:

Total inflation-adjusted assets
Less: Cash
Marketable securities
Future income tax benefits
Accounts payable and accrued liabilities

Net Assets

Return on net assets (RONA) Whereas operating income was a stand-alone figure used to plan and control operations, RONA measured the long-term profitability of each operation. RONA was calculated as follows:

$$\text{RONA} = \frac{\text{Operating Income} + \text{Capital Charge}}{\text{Net Assets}}$$

American Standard believed that RONA could be directly related to the growth potential of a unit, and it developed a chart to illustrate this point (see Figure A). The chart contains two plotted lines: one shows the relationship of RONA to growth potential, assuming the dividend payout is

FIGURE A. Growth Potential

GROWTH POTENTIAL IS A FUNCTION OF

- Rate of Return
  —After-Tax Return on Assets (Debt + Equity)
- Dividends Paid
- Debt/Equity Ratio
- Interest Paid on Debt

Relationship of RONA to Growth Potential (with a debt/equity ratio of 20/80)

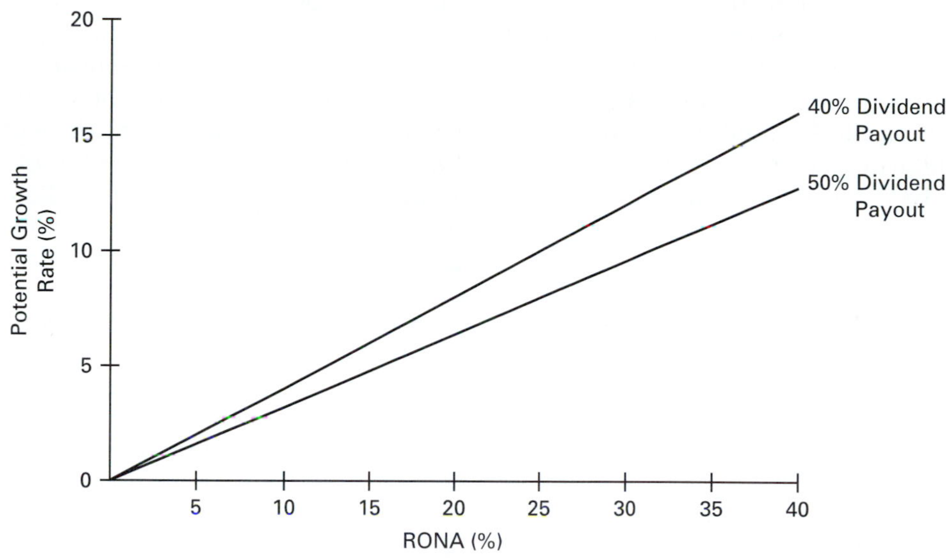

Note: Although RONA shown on this chart is a pretax figure, in order to relate RONA to growth potential, it was assumed that taxes paid would be 45% of operating income.

40 percent of inflation-adjusted earnings, and the other assumes a 50 percent dividend payout, given the assumptions in the footnotes. The chart demonstrates that a RONA of 20 percent will provide an 8 percent growth potential if the dividend payout is 40 percent and a 6 percent growth potential if the dividend payout is 50 percent.

IMPLEMENTATION

As previously mentioned, the inflation-adjusted accounting system was gradually implemented over an extended period. There were a number of reasons for this: the changes being implemented had to be explained to a large number of people; operating groups provided suggestions for improvement, which led to further changes, after initial elements of the system had been implemented; and some of the concepts on which the system was based continued to evolve as American Standard gained experience in using the system. For example, the capital charge, introduced in the early 1970s, originally reflected actual interest expense; later, it evolved into a *real cost of capital* concept (that is, an inflation-free cost of debt and equity). In 1981 the system reflected several important decisions that had been made in the implementation process.

Gathering and reporting current cost information The first decision was to use the General Electric Information Services Company's worldwide time-sharing system to gather data and generate reports. As stated previously, American Standard's companies were diverse in size, location, and nature of business. Using GE's time-sharing system, American Standard developed its own computer programs which gathered data from these diverse companies, performed financial calculations, and printed financial reports. This enabled local companies to enter data in local currencies at their own locations; for example, data on fixed assets included the acquisition date, historical cost, and the appropriate local, specific price indices. Local companies could print their own reports in local currency or U.S. dollars. Other programs consolidated data from the local companies; the consolidated data were accessible on the time-sharing system to the local companies' group and global group and to the corporate staff. Flexibility and simplicity were key objectives in designing this system, since it had to be used in the smallest to the largest companies, and in very different types of businesses. Todd reflected on the importance of this design.

> The time-sharing system gets the inflation adjustment down to the lowest levels of management. It provides the same data throughout the company and gives the plant manager the same vision as top management.

Primary measurement system A second important decision was that the inflation accounting system was to be the primary measurement system for the company; these measurements were incorporated into management systems such as budgeting and performance measurement. Historical cost data were still available and were frequently presented as supplementary information that enabled results to be reconciled with primary public financial statements; the emphasis, however, was on inflation-adjusted accounting results, as shown by the standard monthly performance reports in Exhibit 5.

Two points should be noted about these reports. First, since conventional historical cost depreciation is already incorporated in other items, the amount reported as *replacement depreciation* reflects the amount by which replacement depreciation exceeds conventional historical cost depreciation; e.g., if total replacement cost depreciation is $252 million, and historical cost depreciation is $134 million, then the amount reported on the line labeled *Replacement depreciation* will be $118 million.

The second point that should be noted about these reports is their computation of budgeted replacement depreciation, as appears in the middle column, labeled *Plan* (see Exhibit 5). When American Standard incorporated inflation-adjusted accounting into the budgeting system, it discovered an interesting problem. Budgets are forecasts or forward projections; that is, a manager preparing a budget for 1983 generally prepares it during 1982. At the time of preparation, however, the most recent specific price indices available reflect replacement costs as of the end of the prior year, e.g., 1981. The problem, then, was how to estimate a reasonable, budgeted, replacement depreciation. Since the replacement cost data available reflected the replacement costs as of the end of 1981, American Standard used the expected *general* rate of inflation for each country, from the end of 1981 through 1983, to estimate the 1983 replacement cost. Hence, for Keller Crescent's On-Going Buildings, which were originally presented in Exhibit 4, the budgeted additional replacement depreciation was calculated as shown in Exhibit 6. Accounting managers noted that there was some inaccuracy involved in using the expected general rate of inflation to forecast the replacement cost of specific assets in 1983, based on their known 1981 replacement costs. The complexity of the alternative, however—estimating the expected changes in the price indices for each of the various groups of assets in each country—was unworkable; further, it might not necessarily be more accurate. By using the current cost of an asset as of the end of 1981, and restating it by the expected general rate of inflation in that country through the end of 1983, management felt that it had captured most of the expected current cost of that asset.

APPLICATIONS

Managers at American Standard believed that inflation accounting was useful in various management applications, from strategic planning and resource allocation to performance measurement and to such operating decisions as pricing and the disposition of assets.

Strategic planning and resource allocation In the areas of strategic planning and resource allocation, there were two primary views on the usefulness of the inflation-adjusted accounting system; first, it provided the necessary information on real economic returns, and second, it satisfied the need for financial data that were comparable across diverse business units. These views appear in the statements of Kenneth R. Todd, Jr., vice president and controller, and Richard H. Francis, vice president and treasurer, presented below. Todd was concerned about the deficiencies of measures based on acquisition costs:

> Strategic decisions, resource allocation, these are the things corporate managers are supposed to worry about. But how do you know which businesses to be in or not? There's a big problem with comparability of different business units.
>
> The return on investment that a business is able to earn is one factor considered in allocating capital resources. A considerable amount of the difference in returns on book assets between units, when historical cost accounting is used, can just be a reflection of when a unit acquired its fixed assets. The unit that acquired its assets some time ago at deflated dollars in today's terms can look very good compared with a unit that acquired its fixed assets recently. It may be that the converse relation is actually true in terms of economic returns on new investments. The internal accounting system should have correct incentives for management to make economic capital investment decisions. New capital expenditures are evaluated using discounted cash flows incrementally, but overall profitability, RONA, of a unit, is a consideration in the capital investment decision.

Francis stressed that an accurate comparison of business performance was of paramount importance:

> An advantage to using inflation-adjusted accounting internally in a multiple business environment is that it puts the businesses on a common basis and allows for comparison.
>
> The inflation-adjusted accounting system is most helpful in giving senior managers, especially those who are in effect portfolio managers, another basis on which to assess the long-term viability of various businesses. It provides a more accurate assessment of the present, which is an important element in forming judgments about the future. It is also important in assessing a business over time—what has really been happening to the business? The issue is, *over time,* can you earn a sufficient rate of return to stay in business?

Performance measurement American Standard believed that the inflation-adjusted accounting system more accurately presented the performance of the operating managers. Todd commented:

> The financial control system must be designed to meet the essential roles of corporate management, which include the assessment of performance of operating units and operating management.
>
> Management must evaluate a unit's performance, both in comparison to its own goals and in comparison with other units in the corporation. Because of the differing impact of inflation on units, it becomes difficult to compare operations using just historical cost information. The conventional accounting definitions of *income* must be modified when trying to measure the operating units to assure fair comparisons between units and *not* to reward management for inflationary effects.

When inflation-adjusted operating income had been implemented, the operating income for most businesses was less than it had been on an historical cost basis; some businesses that had shown a profit on an historical cost basis had a loss on an inflation-adjusted basis. American Standard believed that *being in the red* would motivate and not discourage a manager. It believed this despite its managers' initial concern about whether an inflation-adjusted profit was achievable; in fact, many of those managers eventually improved earnings and earned an inflation-adjusted operating profit.

One operating manager stated:

> You're kidding yourself if you don't use replacement depreciation. It makes the profits look a lot less, but that's just what inflation is doing.

Francis commented:

> Most managers would say that they are simply conforming to a performance standard, not that they are taking special steps to beat inflation. But with this system, they know if they break even, they can fund their business and earn a fair return. Whether or not they fully

> understand inflation accounting, it's healthy to have a faith in the system, knowing that if you meet this standard, you are maintaining the business in an inflationary environment and earning a satisfactory return.

Operating income was also an important determinant of incentives under the short-term incentive compensation plan. The pool of funds available for distribution under the short-term incentive plan was largely determined by the company's overall operating-income performance. Individual incentive awards depended on various factors, but one that was considered to be very important was performance in meeting operating-income objectives.

Pricing Many managers felt that the inflation-adjusted accounting data influenced pricing decisions. Todd believed that this was very positive:

> There are many factors influencing the pricing decision, but one key consideration is the cost of production. If the marketing department considers as cost the historic inventory cost, it can be deceived on the current profits generated from its pricing decisions. Operating management has to have an incentive to keep its pricing in line with current cost, and one incentive is to measure results using only the current cost of production.
>
> Business is becoming more competitive. There is not enough to go around. You are facing new competitors with very different cost structures or cost advantages. In order to be effective, you'd better have a good understanding of what your costs really are.

Francis added that inflation-adjusted accounting data may be useful even if prices cannot be raised:

> Some managers ask, particularly when confronting inflation-adjusted accounting for the first time, "Once I have all of this new information, can I do anything differently? In a market environment, will the market actually let me raise my prices?" This is a very real problem. Even with the information, you may not be able to raise prices. But you're better off knowing you have a problem and understanding the nature of the problem than not knowing it. There may be other opportunities to improve your profitability.

Roy Satchell, senior vice president, Security and Graphics Products, concurred:

> Prices are set by the market, but with the inflation-adjusted data, at least you know where you're at. The person doing the selling does not *want* to raise prices—that just makes the selling job more difficult. But with this system, you can't kid yourself.

Satchell believed that once results were adjusted for inflation, some managers found that they were not doing as well as they had previously thought, and this led to their being much more aggressive in pricing. He recalled the example of an American Standard subsidiary that participated in a market dominated by a large competitor. Facing increasing costs and low inflation-adjusted earnings, the American Standard subsidiary became more aggressive in its pricing strategy. Satchell felt that the availability of inflation-adjusted accounting data that quantified the magnitude and severity of the problem had encouraged managers to take actions that they otherwise might not have taken, or at least might not have taken so soon. In addition, Satchell stated that the data were used to clean up product lines and identify items that did not have a future.

Disposing of assets Todd believed that a lot of unutilized or underutilized assets had been disposed of; he felt that besides providing cash and freeing up space, this also encouraged managers to move to new technologies, since the managers were already being charged for the cost of "new" assets. Satchell concurred with this viewpoint.

> The system places a tremendous amount of heat on managing assets. There are situations I know about where managers in my group have fixed assets that are not fully utilized. Those managers are trying like heck to get them out, because the system hits them where it hurts.

A business manager echoed this view, stating that replacement depreciation was a consideration in his evaluation of old equipment in this business. He cited some 20-year-old equipment that had experienced a significant writeup when it was appraised; the equipment was only partially utilized, and the manager was currently evaluating whether or not it was worth retaining since it represented such a large expense.

AGENDAS FOR THE FUTURE

In Todd's opinion, the inflation-adjusted accounting system at American Standard was working well and was accepted by managers. A senior line executive agreed:

> It's the job of the operating manager to decide what to make and how to make it. They should not be left to their own devices to account for inflation and its implications for working capital, capital expenditures, and pricing. The operating manager may not know how to account for inflation, or may not be willing to spend the time.
>
> Given that American Standard has implemented inflation accounting, as a practical matter, it's impossible not to use the data. It's in all the reports; the inflation adjustments are already cranked in. One of the reasons American Standard is so successful during tough economic times is that these data are part of the management system; they are not outside the system. The inflation-adjusted accounting system provides a description that is directionally correct. It is not perfect; but it is better than assuming inflation is equal to zero.

Todd felt, however, that opportunities remained to further improve the system; one area was long-term incentive compensation. Although inflation-adjusted operating income was used in the measurement of short-term performance and the determination of short-term incentive compensation, the long-term incentive compensation plan had not yet been modified to incorporate inflation adjustments. As of the end of 1981 the eligible employees under the long-term plan were executive officers of the company and other key executives of the company or its subsidiaries. Cash awards were distributed after five-year periods, and they depended upon the performance of the company in meeting certain publicly reported, historical cost earnings objectives over the applicable period. Each objective related to a cumulative growth of earnings per share over an earnings base established by the board of directors. If the earnings objective was not reached, but cumulative earnings per share still exceeded the earnings base, the cash payment was proportionately less. No payments were made, however, unless cumulative earnings per share for the period exceeded the earnings base by an average of 5 percent (compounded annually) over the period. The amount of the individual's cash award was generally based on salary level.

Despite American Standard's commitment to the use of inflation-adjusted accounting, concerns arose regarding its application to the long-term incentive program. First, some managers wondered about how to set an appropriate target; they had very little inflation-adjusted data from prior years and, therefore, they did not have a track record that might suggest what would be a good return versus a poor one, and it would be very expensive to go back and produce such data for the years preceding American Standard's use of inflation-accounting data. Second, the managers did not have comparative data from other firms in their industries, and these data had been important in setting targets in the past. Finally, they were concerned about the experimental stage of the inflation-accounting rules for public reporting purposes. Under the current procedures of stating objectives according to publicly reported primary earnings per share, there was considerable stability in primary earnings per share calculations. Since the rules for inflation accounting were much less firm, however, and since companies were encouraged by Financial Accounting Standard No. 33 to experiment and discover better ways of preparing inflation-accounting data, the method of preparing the publicly reported, inflation-adjusted data might vary from year to year. Some members of the controller's department questioned whether changes in method alone might determine who received a bonus and who did not.

In addition, Todd was considering restating all prior years' accounting data on a constant dollar basis. Each year American Standard incorporated the effects of inflation in its financial statements, but when managers went to compare data for prior years, they felt that these data were not fully comparable since the dollar, the unit of measure, had changed in purchasing power. Some of the controller's staff believed that if managers were trying to use prior years' data as a benchmark to determine trends, then to the extent that the change in the data was a function of inflation, and not volume or real price changes, the managers might be misled. According to one employee:

> There are several different ways of assessing performance. One is, "What has growth

been?" But with inflation, maybe there hasn't been any real growth at all. You could look at physical units, but it's hard to get your hands on physical units for a business which is not just in one product line. You can be misled as to which business in your portfolio you're the most excited about.

Another issue centered on whether any further changes to the system should be made at this time. Since the process of implementing the system had been an evolutionary one, managers had adapted to frequent changes over the years. This had resulted, at times, in the incomparability of prior years' data; that is, the data for the last year may not have been prepared on the same basis as the current year's data, and prior years' statements were not restated on the new basis. Were the benefits of the proposed changes sufficient to justify modifying the system again?

EXHIBIT 1 Statement of Income and Retained Earnings ($ thousands except per share amounts)

Year Ended December 31	*1980*	*1979*	*1978*
Sales	$ 2,673,589	$ 2,431,557	$ 2,110,860
Costs and expenses			
Cost of sales	2,039,715	1,849,217	1,597,343
Selling and administrative expenses	370,949	325,860	294,454
Net foreign exchange (gain) loss	(6,802)	10,219	12,906
Other (income) expense	(20,200)	(19,305)	(11,559)
Interest expense	32,679	33,057	28,791
	2,416,341	2,199,048	1,921,935
Income before taxes on income	257,248	232,509	188,925
Taxes on income	100,355	100,354	87,587
Net income	156,893	132,155	101,338
Retained earnings, beginning of year	419,009	334,157	265,238
Cash dividends:			
$4.75 convertible preference stock	—	(398)	(1,856)
Preferred stock	(105)	(111)	(116)
Common stock	(54,803)	(41,487)	(30,262)
Purchase of shares of stock in excess of par value	—	(5,307)	(185)
Retained earnings, end of year	$ 520,994	$419,009	$ 334,157
Average outstanding common shares and equivalents[a,b]	27,576,765	27,734,878	28,008,086
Net income per common share[b]	$ 5.69	$ 4.76	$ 3.61
Dividends per common share[b]	$2.00	$ 1.525	$ 1.175

[a]Per-share amounts are presented as though all the $4.75 cumulative convertible preference stock, series A, had been converted into common stock until its redemption effective April 3, 1979, and all relevant stock options had been exercised.

[b]Restated to reflect two-for-one split of the common stock in December 1980.

EXHIBIT 2 Balance Sheet ($ thousands)

At December 31	*1980*	*1979*	*1978*
Current assets			
Cash	$ 20,203	$ 42,028	$ 22,105
Certificates of deposit—1978 includes other marketable securities of $1,277	26,788	25,687	15,037
Accounts receivable, less allowance for doubtful accounts—1980, $17,230; 1979, $12,058; 1978, $10,956	405,885	348,520	294,790
Inventories, at current cost	594,561	588,612	470,672
Less: LIFO reserve	212,662	192,545	148,510
Inventories, at LIFO cost	381,899	396,067	322,162
Future income tax benefits	49,183	45,457	40,618
Other current assets	66,533	17,123	13,263
Total current assets	950,491	874,882	707,975
Facilities, at cost			
Land	20,363	22,147	21,172
Buildings	272,207	262,094	243,068
Machinery and equipment	618,015	559,917	474,743
Improvements in progress	50,246	30,512	27,161
Gross facilities	960,831	874,670	766,144
Less: Accumulated depreciation	469,622	442,452	406,251
Net facilities	491,209	432,218	359,893
Other assets			
Investment in associated companies	31,599	31,130	31,103
Excess of cost over net assets of businesses purchased	70,316	71,475	71,475
Other	34,756	13,058	14,549
Total assets	$1,578,371	$1,422,763	$1,184,995
Current liabilities			
Loans payable to banks	$ 16,944	$ 34,593	$ 31,633
Commercial paper	—	21,236	—
Current maturities of long-term debt	13,585	14,803	16,777
Accounts payable	190,039	201,300	153,664
Accrued payrolls	115,743	99,350	82,005
Other accrued liabilities	130,327	104,978	96,242
Taxes on income	57,820	85,522	38,002
Total current liabilities	524,458	561,782	418,323
Long-term debt	279,982	193,466	198,568
Other credits			
Reserve for foreign pensions and termination indemnities	79,392	79,380	67,250
Deferred taxes on income	52,129	32,691	24,056
Minority interests in subsidiaries	6,363	6,289	9,679
Stockholders' equity			
7% preferred stock, 14,583 shares outstanding in 1980; 15,447 in 1979; and 16,617 in 1978	1,458	1,545	1,662
$4.75 cumulative convertible preference stock, 337,762 shares outstanding in 1978	—	—	6,755
Common stock, 27,082,920 shares outstanding in 1980; 13,751,110 in 1979; and 13,029,172 in 1978	27,083	13,751	65,146
Capital surplus	86,512	114,850	59,399
Retained earnings	520,994	419,009	334,157
Total stockholders' equity	636,047	549,155	467,119
Total liabilities and stockholders' equity	$1,578,371	$1,422,763	$1,184,995

EXHIBIT 3 Organization Chart

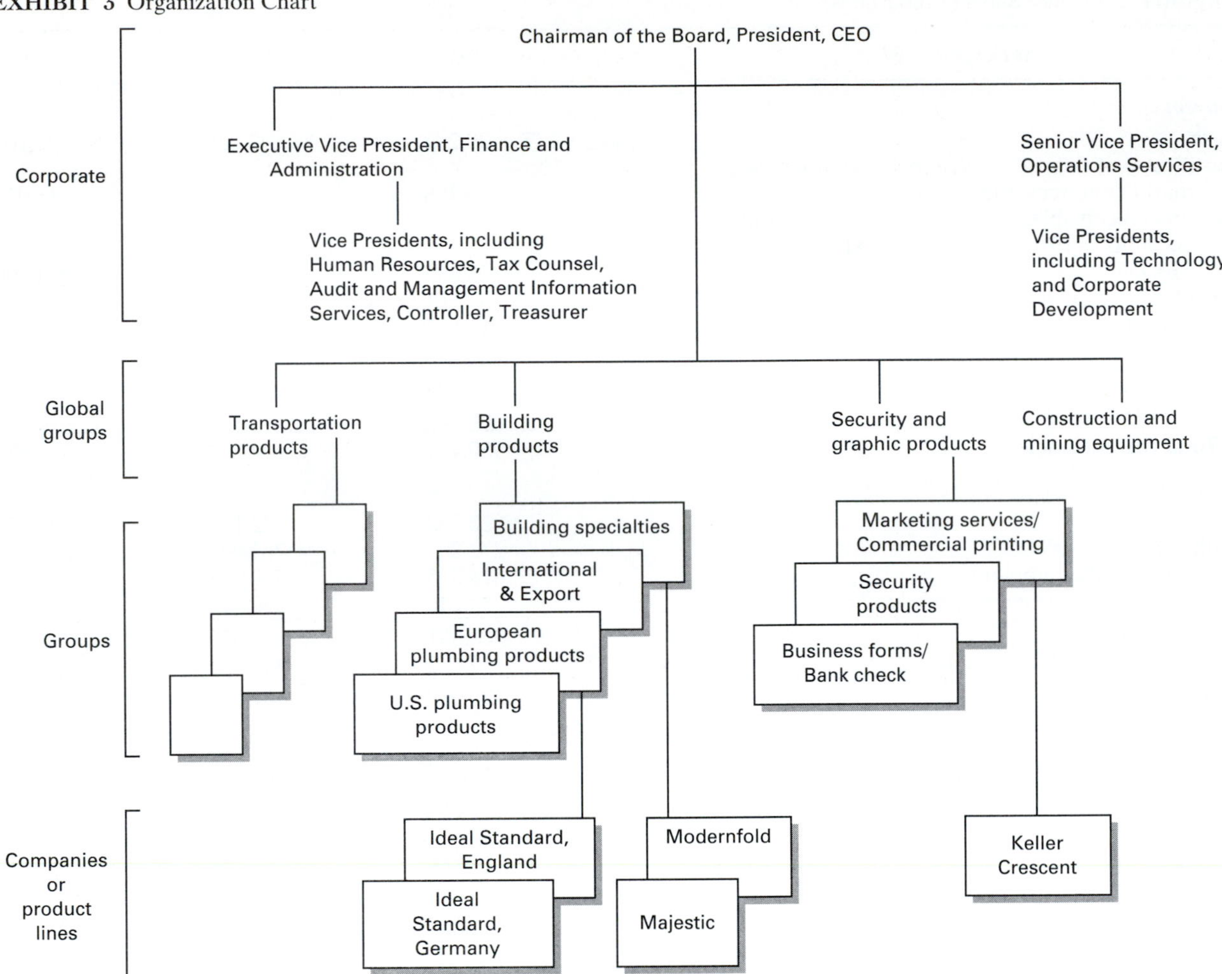

EXHIBIT 4 Facility Analysis Keller Crescent 1981 Ongoing Assets: Buildings in U.S. Dollars

A. Calculation of Replacement Costs

Year of Acquisition	*Ending Gross Facilities (historical cost)*	*Local Index* Year-end	*Local Index* Average	*Ending Gross Facilities (replacement cost)*[a]
1968	$1,343	1.0500	1.05	$3,594
1969	8	1.1300	1.09	21
1970	30	1.2000	1.165	72
1971	503	1.3100	1.255	1,126
1972	55	1.4200	1.365	113
1973	42	1.5300	1.475	80
1974	46	1.6900	1.61	80
1975	28	1.8600	1.775	44
1976	633	1.9700	1.915	929
1977	67	2.0700	2.02	93
1978	131	2.2700	2.17	170
1979	118	2.4700	2.37	140
1980	50	2.6500	2.56	55
1981	870	2.8100	2.73	895
Total	$3,924			$7,412

[a]Computation of Ending Gross Facilities (replacement cost):

$$\text{Ending Gross Facilities at Historical Cost} \times \frac{\text{Local Index} - \text{Year-End} - 1981}{\text{Local Index} - \text{Average} - \text{Year of Acquisition}}$$

B. Calculation of Replacement Depreciation

Total Ongoing Buildings (historical cost)	*Amount*	*Life*	*Annual Depreciation*	*Average Life*
Buildings	$2,501	40	$62.53	
Building Appurtenances	1,423	20	71.15	
Total Ongoing Buildings	$3,924		$133.68	29.354

Replacement Depreciation

Ending Gross Facilities 12/31/81 (replacement cost)	*Average Life*	*Total Depreciation (replacement cost)*
$7,412	29.354	$252.5

EXHIBIT 5 Standard Monthly Performance Report

				Statement of Income *April 1982*	*Form No: 1 (Page 1)* *Date: 05/07/82 15:12 GMT*		
	Month			*U.S. Dollar*	*Year to Date*		
Year	*Plan*	*Actual*		*000's Omitted*	*Actual*	*Plan*	*Last Year*
4646	4440	3798	5010	Orders Received	17978	18949	21203
4725	5047	3478	5020	Order Backlog	3478	5047	4725
4859	4590	3903	5030	Gross Sales	17676	19584	20911
179	149	150	5040	Returns & Allowances	632	634	703
				Net Sales			
4584	4339	3675	5050	Customer	16813	18578	19869
96	102	78	5060	Intercompany	231	372	339
4680	4441	3753	5070	Total Net Sales	17044	18950	20208
				Cost of Sales			
2836	2466	2147	5080	Standard Cost	9883	10443	12274
352	612	480	5090	Std. Cost Variances	2060	2385	1512
204	232	182	5100	Distribution Cost	846	941	879
0	0	10	5110	Exch. (G)L-Oper Trans	12	0	8
72	138	127	5120	Replacement Deprec.	564	592	329
115	166	141	5130	Other Costs	589	703	868
3579	3614	3087	5140	Total Cost of Sales	13954	15064	15870
1101	827	666	5150	Gross Profit	3090	3886	4338
				Operating Expense			
135	140	103	5160	Administrative	440	521	518
296	286	255	5170	Selling	1027	1116	1160
103	113	128	5180	Advertising	459	454	433
0	0	0	5190	Research & Development	0	0	0
534	539	486	5200	Total Bef. Allocation	1926	2091	2111
0	0	0	5210	Intragroup Allocation	0	0	0
534	539	486	5220	Total Oper. Expense	1926	2091	2111
567	288	180	5230	Income Bef. Other Items	1164	1795	2227
−5	−6	0	5240	Other Oper. Inc/Exp	−12	−23	−79
−438	−448	−402	5250	Capital Charge	−1629	−1746	−1817
124	−166	−222	5260	Operating Income	−477	26	331
−74	71	84	5270	Other Non-Oper. Inc/Exp	−266	−199	−226
−510	−586	−529	5280	Reversal-Line 5120 + 5250	−2193	−2338	−2146
708	349	223	5290	Pretax Income	1982	2563	2703
368	180	116	5300	Taxes on Income	1031	1330	1406
340	169	107	5310	Income Bef. Extr. Items	951	1233	1297
0	0	0	5320	Extr. Items-Net (DR)CR	0	0	0
340	169	107	5330	Net Income After Extr.	951	1233	1297
				Percent to Net Sales			
39.4	44.5	42.8	5335	Std. Gross Margin	42.0	44.9	39.3
23.5	18.6	17.7	5340	Gross Profit	18.1	20.5	21.5
11.4	12.1	12.9	5350	Operating Expense	11.3	11.0	10.4
2.6	−3.7	−5.9	5360	Operating Income	−2.8	0.1	1.6

(continued)

EXHIBIT 5 Standard Monthly Performance Report *Continued*

Financial Summary—Actual
April 1982

Form No: 13
Date: 05/07/82 15:12 GMT

U.S. Dollar			*Variance from L.F. Fav(Unfav) Due to:*			*Variance from Plan Fav(Unfav) Due to:*		
000's Omitted	*Actual*	*Last Forecast*	*Perform.*	*Currency*	*Plan*	*Perform.*	*Currency*	*Last Year*
Month								
Orders received—customer	3720	3980	−236	−24	4338	−318	−300	4550
Net Sales	3753	4047	−271	−23	4441	−385	−303	4680
Gross Profit	666	704	−35	−3	827	−107	−54	1101
% of Sales	17.75	17.40			18.62			23.53
Operating Expense	486	471	−19	4	539	14	39	534
% of Sales	12.95	11.64			12.14			11.41
Operating Income	−222	−181	−45	4	−166	−74	18	124
% of Sales	−5.92	−4.47			−3.74			2.65
Capital Expenditures	42	81			151	108	1	73
Cash Flow from Operations	−631	−1403	862	−90	759	−1340	−50	−343
Replacement Depreciation	127	128	0	1	138	0	11	72
Capital Charge	−402	−414	9	3	−448	13	33	−438
Orders Received—Interco	78	68	10	0	102	−18	−6	96
Average Employees—Hourly	749	760			798			
Average Employees—Non-Hourly	365	365			368			
Average Employees—Total	1114	1125			1166			
Year to Date								
Orders received—customer	17747	18007	−236	−24	18577	30	−860	20864
Order backlog—customer	3478	3881	−461	58	5047	−1374	−195	4725
Net Sales	17044	17338	−271	−23	18950	−1069	−837	20208
Gross Profit	3090	3128	−35	−3	3886	−649	−147	4338
% of Sales	18.13	18.04			20.51			21.47
Operating Expense	1926	1911	−19	4	2091	71	94	2111
% of Sales	11.30	11.02			11.03			10.45
Operating Income	−477	−436	−45	4	26	−529	26	331
% of Sales	−2.80	−2.51			0.14			1.64
Gross Trade Receivables	11262	11788	712	−186	12859	964	633	12910
Days Sales in Receivables	65	65			73			60
Gross FIFO Inventory	8863	8730	14	−147	9224	−137	498	9791
Inventory Turnover	3.39	3.47			3.35			3.69
Payables & Accruals	7084	6276	691	117	6788	693	−397	7228
Net FIFO Working Capital	12992	13859	1083	−216	14658	935	731	14870
Cents Per Net Sales	26.28	27.87			28.55			26.58
Capital Expenditures	140	179	42	−3	590	442	8	355
Cash Flow from Operations	−2897	−3669			−4059	873	289	1082
Net Assets	41187	41412	906	−681	44907	1403	2317	43107
R.O.N.A.	11.60	11.73			12.85			11.52
Replacement Depreciation	564	565	0	1	592	0	28	329
Capital Charge	−1629	−1641	9	3	−1746	38	79	−1817
Orders Received—Interco	231	221	10	0	372	−129	−12	339
Order Backlog—Interco	0	0	0	0	0	0	0	0
Average Employees—Hourly	756	756			797			
Average Employees—Non-Hourly	376	376			368			
Average Employees—Total	1132	1132			1165			

EXHIBIT 6 Budgeted Replacement Depreciation

Inflation Rates—Forecast

1982	*1983*	*Half-Year 1983*	*End of 1981 through mid-1983*
6.6%	5.0%	2.44%	1.066 × 1.0244 = 9.2%

Replacement Depreciation

Ending Gross Facilities 12/31/81 (replacement cost)	*Ending Gross Facilities 12/31/81 (replacement cost—inflated by 9.2%)*	*Replacement Cost Depreciation*[a]	*Book Depreciation*	*Additional Replacement Depreciation*
$7,412	$8,094	$276	$107	$169

[a]Using average life of 29.345 years; see *Exhibit 4-B.*

CHAPTER 14

Using Financial-Results Controls in the Presence of Uncontrollable Factors

Consider the following case: A division manager was asked to achieve an annual profit target of $1 million. After the budget was prepared, however, the employees of a major supplier went on a prolonged strike, and the manager could not line up acceptable alternate suppliers quickly. Production was slowed considerably, and the division was barely able to break even for the year. Virtually everyone familiar with the situation agreed that the strike could not have been foreseen and that it was not the division manager's fault that the budget target was not achieved. Despite the poor performance, would you forgive this division manager and allow him to keep his job? Give him a nice salary increase? A sizable bonus?

If you implement the *controllability principle* in a strict sense, you would give the manager in the situation described above all of these rewards mentioned. This principle, which was introduced in Chapter 3, states that people should be held accountable only for what they can control. A measure is totally controllable by an employee if it is affected only by his or her actions. The logic behind the controllability principle is obvious: Managers should not be penalized for bad luck, nor should they be given extra rewards for mere good luck.

To implement the controllability principle, performance evaluators can reduce, and sometimes even eliminate, some of the distorting effects of uncontrollable factors. They can eliminate uncontrollable performance areas from the definitions of the results measures or, as in the case described above, calculate (or estimate) and adjust for the effects of any remaining uncontrollable risk factors. Managers can use these procedures across-the-board to affect the assignment of all rewards (and punishments), or they can use different methods for different forms of reward (for example, job retention, salary increases, and bonuses).

Use of these distortion-elimination procedures is not always straightforward, however. Many important result measures, particularly at managerial organization levels, are only *partially* uncontrollable. Even though the measures are affected by occurrences outside the employee's control; such as supply shortages, changing cost factors, competitors' actions, and business calamities, managers can take actions to react to these factors and have *positive influence* on the results measures. If managers are totally protected against the uncontrollables, they might not be motivated to wield the influence they have. In addition, even when it is clear that a given factor is totally uncontrollable, the extent of the distortion of the results measures is often difficult to measure or estimate.

A number of errors are possible when dealing with the effects of uncontrollable factors. It is possible to avoid protecting managers from the effects of uncontrollable factors when they should be protected. Conversely, it is possible to protect managers from the effects of uncontrollable factors when they should *not* be protected. Sometimes the protections that are provided are ill-conceived and incorrect. If judgments about how to deal with uncontrollables are not made correctly, the advantages of results controls will be diminished, and potentially serious motivational, evaluation, and morale problems can result.

This chapter provides a more thorough discussion of the problem of evaluating performance when measures are affected by uncontrollable influences. It presents the complete rationale for the controllability principle and describes the types of uncontrollable factors that can be faced. It then discusses the various methods managers can use to implement the controllability principle and the applicability, advantages, and disadvantages of each of the methods.[1]

THE COMPLETE RATIONALE FOR THE CONTROLLABILITY PRINCIPLE

Several related arguments explain why employees should not be asked to bear uncontrollable business risks. Corporations that hold employees accountable for uncontrollable influences must bear some costs of doing so because the vast majority of employees are *risk averse.* This means the employees like their performance-dependent rewards to stem directly from their efforts and not be affected by the vagaries of uncontrollable shocks.

To illustrate risk aversion, assume a corporation has made you an offer of employment, and you are allowed to choose either of two compensation contracts. The first provides a fixed salary of $100,000 per year. The second provides an opportunity to earn $200,000 if you achieve a performance target which both you and others within your firm agree that you are 50 percent likely to achieve. If you fail to achieve this target, however, you earn *nothing.* The expected value of both contracts is $100,000. The vast majority of people, probably in excess of 90 percent, will choose the fixed salary with the guarantee of $100,000. They do not want to bear the risk of earning nothing.[2] This is risk aversion.

Risk aversion varies with some personal characteristics. Corporate executives believe that sales and marketing personnel are relatively more risk tolerant than are accounting and finance personnel. Working on commission, rather than salary, probably is a good indicator of risk tolerance. Corporate executives also believe that most personnel near retirement are more risk averse than are younger people.

The extent of a person's risk aversion can be assessed by varying the parameters in the example above. If the amount of the salary guarantee was lowered to $90,000, some relatively risk tolerant (less risk averse) people would be tempted enough by the higher expected value of compensation that they would be willing to take the 50 percent risk of earning nothing. If the salary guarantee was lowered to $80,000, another group of slightly less risk tolerant people would be willing to take the risk. The key point is: the vast majority of employees are risk averse.

Risk aversion is the basis for the primary argument supporting the controllability principle. Firms that hold risk averse employees accountable for the effects of factors they cannot completely control will bear some costs of doing so. First, to compensate for the risk, the firms will have to provide employees a higher expected reward value. If they fail to do so, they will bear some costs in alternate forms, such as an inability to hire talented employees, a loss of motivation from the employees they have, and, probably eventually, turnover.

Second, the firms will bear the costs of some employee behaviors designed to lower their exposures to uncontrollable factors, but at the expense of corporate value. The managers may fail to develop or implement ideas for investments that are in the corporation's best interest, but that involve some risk. They may also engage in some game-playing behaviors, such as managing earnings or creating budgetary slack, to protect themselves against the effects of the uncontrollable factors.

Third, the firms may bear the cost of lost time, as employees whose performances are evaluated in terms of measures that are distorted by uncontrollable influences whose effects cannot be measured definitely are prone to develop excuses. They will spend time arguing about the extent of the distortions, at the expense of doing their jobs.

Business risks should be left with the business's owners. Owners are better able to bear the risk. They are risk neutral because, unlike employees, they can diversify their portfolios through elaborate financial markets set up for exactly that purpose. The owners' rewards stem directly from the riskbearing function they perform.

TYPES OF UNCONTROLLABLE INFLUENCES

Before describing the methods managers can use to control the distorting effects of uncontrollable factors, it is useful to categorize the types of factors that can be, to a greater or lesser extent, uncontrollable. They include (1) economic and competitive factors, (2) acts of nature, and (3) interdependence.

The first uncontrollable influence includes a broad range of *economic and competitive factors* that affect one or more results measures. One important results measure, profits, is affected by many factors that change either the demand and/or prices of the company's products/services or the costs of doing business. Among the factors that affect consumer demand and prices are business cycles, competitors' actions, changing customer tastes, customer boycotts, changing laws and regulations and foreign exchange rates. Among the factors that affect costs are the supply and demand of raw materials, labor, and capital; foreign exchange rates, regulations, and taxes.

Virtually every results measure can be affected by multiple, uncontrollable economic and competitive factors. Company stock prices are affected by market cycles, rumors, and investor tastes. On-time delivery measures can be adversely affected by supply shortages and changing customer demands. Customer satisfaction measures are influenced by competitors' actions, changing costs, and changing customer demands.

Changes in the economic and competitive factors are difficult for performance evaluators to deal with because, while most of these factors appear to be uncontrollable, managers can usually make responses to these changes to positively influence the results measures. When raw material prices increase, managers can sometimes substitute alternate materials. When the cost of capital increases, they can sometimes delay capital investments and reduce inventories. When exchange rates change, they can sometimes source or sell in different countries. When customer tastes change, they can alter their product design or change their strategy. Responses such as these are a key part of being a manager. As a consequence, most evaluators do not buffer managers completely from changes in economic and competitive factors, although they might take steps to have the organization share the risk.

A second type of uncontrollable influence includes *acts of nature.* Acts of nature are large, unexpected, one-time, totally uncontrollable events; such as tornadoes, volcanic eruptions, earthquakes, floods, riots, key executive deaths and, if they are not caused by negligence (at least of the current managers), fires, accidents, machine breakdowns, thefts, vandalism, and toxic torts. Even unexpectedly good weather can cause problems for some businesses; for example, ski areas and manufacturers and retailers of winter coats and snowblowers. Most acts of nature involve negative surprises, but positive surprises sometimes occur. Oil might be uncovered on company property, or serendipity in a laboratory might result in a valuable discovery.

Many organizations are prone to protect employees from the downside risks caused by acts of nature, but only if the events are deemed to be clearly uncontrollable and if steps are taken to motivate those responsible to recover from the disaster as expeditiously as possible. Controllability is sometimes an issue, as controversy can develop over the causes of fire, accidents, breakdowns, and thefts. Also potentially controversial is the extent to which a manager should, by not purchasing insurance protection, have had the organization bear the risk of exposure to the acts of nature.

A third type of uncontrollable influence is caused by *interdependence.* Interdependence is the opposite of independence. Interdependence signifies that an organization's or an individual's area is not completely self-contained. The measured results are affected by others within the organization.

Interdependencies in production or service-providing areas can be classified into three types: pooled, sequential, and reciprocal.[3] *Pooled interdependencies* exist where a firm's entities use common firm resources or resource pools, such as shared staffs (for example, administrative or sales), or shared facilities (for example, manufacturing or research). Pooled interdependence is low when entities are relatively self-contained. Self-contained entities include all or most of the functions affecting their success and do not have to use shared resource pools.

What kinds of control questions are raised by pooled interdependencies? One common question is: Should lower-level managers be at risk for bad (or good) performance of shared resource pools, such as corporate staff activities, on which they must rely? In many large firms, these managers are protected from cost increases by the terms of an annual contract, negotiated during the annual planning process, which details the services to be provided and the costs to be paid. The expected costs are impounded in a fixed allocation rate and unexpected increases cannot be passed to customers until the next contract negotiation. If the service activity is unable to provide the negotiated-for level of service, however, the customers will have to find alternate sources of supply.

What if a disaster, such as a major trading loss on financial derivatives, strikes in mid-year? Financial trading losses are unusual charges from an activity that is unrelated to most companies' basic businesses, and such charges are rarely charged back to the operating units. In companies that use a corporate bonus-pool system, such charges often diminish the size of the bonus pool. In this sense, employees' (or perhaps just mangers') bonuses are affected by mistakes that were, to them, uncontrollable. Companies deviate from the controllability principle in this way to reduce the corporate risk; bonuses are reduced in periods when the company is less able to pay them.

Sequential interdependencies exist when the outputs of one entity are the inputs of another entity. Organizations which are high in sequential interdependence are vertically integrated firms, such as paper and steel companies. *Reciprocal inter-*

dependencies are bi-directional sequential interdependencies; organizational entities both produce outputs used by other entities and use inputs from them. Reciprocal interdependencies are high in some diversified organizations.

Most corporations deal with both sequential and reciprocal interdependencies by setting up internal *transfer price* systems that try to approximate the conditions found in external product markets. These systems, which are discussed in Chapter 15, make these interdependencies act much like the economic and competitive uncontrollables described previously, and evaluators then can deal with them in much the same way.

Another type of interdependency stems from interventions from higher-level management. Higher-level managers can force a decision on a lower-level manager and in so doing significantly affect a results measure linked to one or more forms of reward. A superior may order a subordinate to hire a particular employee or sell to a particular customer at a given, money-losing price. Superiors can also affect results measures simply by not approving decisions initiated by a lower-level manager. They might not allow the hiring or firing of an employee, a new expenditure, or a production schedule change. If these decisions are clearly forced on the lower-level manager, some organizations will make an adjustment for this uncontrollable event. Others, however, argue that these interventions are not totally uncontrollable, that the lower-level managers are usually involved in the discussions leading up to the decision and are, therefore, responsible for selling their ideas.

CONTROLLING THE DISTORTING EFFECTS OF UNCONTROLLABLE FACTORS

Managers can reduce (and sometimes even eliminate) some of the distorting effects of some uncontrollable factors by using either or both of two complementary approaches. Before the measurement period begins, they can define the results measures to include only those items the employees can control or at least significantly influence. After the measurement period has ended, they can calculate (or estimate) and adjust for the effects of any remaining uncontrollable risk factors using techniques such as variance analysis, flexible budgeting, or subjective performance assessment.

Both of these methods of controlling for the effects of the uncontrollable factors have costs. These costs must be balanced against the benefits of reducing the risks employees must bear. Agency theoreticians define this as the problem of designing *efficient* incentive contracts. The methods of controlling for uncontrollable factors and the costs of using the methods are discussed in detail in the following sections.

CONTROLLING FOR THE EFFECTS OF UNCONTROLLABLE FACTORS *BEFORE* THE MEASUREMENT PERIOD

Two methods can be employed to control for the effects of uncontrollable factors before the measurement period: purchases of insurance and design of responsibility structures.

Insurance

Many uncontrollable events, such as physical damage to company assets, employee-caused damage, product liability suits, employee errors and defalcations, riots, and vandalism, are insurable. Insurance transfers risk from the purchaser to the insurance company. Company stockholders generally can diversify away the kinds of risks that are insurable.[4] The company's employees' managers are rarely able to diversify insurable risks, so they derive benefits from purchases of insurance. The company also benefits because it does not have to pay the employees a premium for bearing this risk. Insurance purchases are often a useful solution to some uncontrollability problems.

Design of Responsibility Structures

The controllability principle underlies most of the logic guiding the design of responsibility structures. In Chapter 8, which focused on financial responsibility structures, a basic rule, which is but a slight modification of the controllability principle, was presented: Hold managers accountable for the line items you want them to pay attention to. This rule can be generalized to all employees: Hold employees accountable for the performance areas you want them to pay attention to.

This general rule is widely applied. Organizations do not hold salespeople or production managers accountable for the results of corporate financing or computer acquisition decisions. There is no need for these managers to pay attention to these decisions which are clearly outside their control.

Performance reports often segregate controllable from uncontrollable items. Table 14-1 shows such a segregated performance report with four profit measures. A control system built on this report would hold this profit center manager responsible for Controllable Profit. Everything below the Controllable Profit line is deemed to be uncontrollable. In a recent survey of budgeting practices, a majority (54 percent) of the respondents reported that they "usually classify expenses into controllable and noncontrollable categories while preparing performance reports."[5]

Are the items below the Controllable Profit line really uncontrollable? Usually the answer for some items is: not totally. One important issue is: When should managers be expected to pay attention to things over which they have less than complete control?

TABLE 14-1 Divisional Income Statement Segregating Controllable and Noncontrollable Items

	$
Sales	xxx
Less: Variable Costs	(xxx)
Sales Margin	xxx
Less: Controllable Division Expenses	(xxx)
Controllable Profit	xxx
Less: Noncontrollable Division Fixed Costs	(xxx)
Contribution Margin	xxx
Less: Allocations of Central Expenses	(xxx)
NET PROFIT	xxx

Should lower-level cost- and profit-center managers be charged with the effects of decisions about corporate financial structure or the use of corporate image-type advertising? Assigning them the costs would, in effect, hold them accountable for that line item. If these managers are not involved in these decisions and if there is no need for them to be aware of how much the corporation is spending on interest expense or image advertising, then there is no need to assign them a share of those costs.

Should lower-level managers be assigned a share of corporate administrative costs, such as those incurred in the personnel and data processing departments? Here the answer may be yes. Charging these costs can empower the lower-level managers to complain about the size of the costs or the quantity or quality of the services rendered in exchange for the costs. Charging provides a useful method of controlling these difficult-to-control costs.[6] A survey conducted for the National Association of Accountants (now called the Institute of Management Accountants) found that 46 percent of the respondents allocated indirect costs to business units explicitly to stimulate the business unit managers to put pressure on central managers to control service costs.[7] These charges violate the strict controllability principle, but they are consistent with the rule presented earlier: Hold managers accountable for the performance areas you want them to pay attention to.

When employees are held accountable for many performance areas over which they have little influence, however, the organization will bear the increased costs of making the employees bear the risk. These were discussed previously in the discussion of the rationale for the controllability principle. At some point, these costs outweigh the benefits. Thus, a second rule to consider in deciding how to implement the controllability principle before the measurement period is: Do not hold employees accountable for too many things over which they have little influence.

CONTROLLING FOR THE EFFECTS OF UNCONTROLLABLE FACTORS AFTER THE MEASUREMENT PERIOD

Sometimes the distorting effects of uncontrollable factors can be removed from the results measures after the measurement period (but before the rewards are assigned). This removal can sometimes be done *objectively* (through numerical calculation) using variance analyses, flexible performance standards, or relative performance evaluations. Alternatively, the effects of uncontrollables can sometimes be removed *subjectively,* through the exercise of personal judgment.

Variance Analyses

Variance analysis is a technique developed to, most generally, explain why two numbers are different. In control applications, it is useful for explaining why actual results are different from predetermined standards, budgets, or expectations. It can help segregate controllable from uncontrollable variances and help explain whom should be held accountable for the controllable variances, which may be either positive or negative.

Variance analysis techniques as applied to manufacturing operations are described in great detail in every cost accounting textbook. To explain why actual manufacturing costs are different from standards; materials, labor, and overhead variances are segregated and further broken down into price (or rate) variances, mix variances, yield (or usage) variances, and volume variances. Explanations of these variances and the formulas for calculating each of them typically span several textbook chapters, and they will not be repeated here.

The variance analysis technique can be usefully applied to many settings other than production. Variance analysis is a systematic method that involves varying one performance factor at a time from expected to actual levels within a computational model to see what caused overall actual performance to be different from that expected. It is like a sensitivity analysis.

Table 14-2 shows how variance analysis can be applied to a sales territory in a foreign country. Assume managers have determined that sales are largely dependent on four factors: industry volume, market share, price (in local currency), and the foreign exchange rate. They prepare a sales plan (a model) based on estimates of each of these factors. At the end of the measurement period, almost inevitably, actual sales will be different from the plan. To understand the causes of the sales variance, they can prepare an analysis such as that shown in Table 14-2.

The original sales plan is reflected in the left-hand column of Table 14-2, which shows the planned value for each of the key factors. The managers' first analysis involves changing one of the factors from the planned to the actual value. Table 14-2 segregates the effect of industry volume first.[8] The difference between the sales plan and the amount shown in Analysis #1 is the *industry volume variance.* The second analysis changes a second factor, here market share, from the planned to the actual value, while holding the previously changed value (industry volume) at actual. This identifies a *market share variance.* This process continues for each of the other two factors, identifying a *sales price variance* and an *exchange rate variance.* The sum of the four variances will equal the total *sales variance* (the amount by which actual sales are different from the sales plan). This situation is illustrated with numbers in Table 14-3.

Variance analyses such as these have two purposes. One is to segregate some uncontrollable factors from the controllable factors, causing actual results to be different from the plan. In this example, the industry volume variance would probably be considered completely uncontrollable. These analyses provide insights into the viability and riskiness of the business. The other purpose of variance analyses is to isolate certain controllable performance factors from others so

TABLE 14-2 Application of Variance Analysis to a Marketing and Sales Setting

Sales Plan	*Analysis #1*	*Analysis #2*	*Analysis #3*	*Actual Sales*
Expected Industry Volume (IV_P)	IV_A	IV_A	IV_A	IV_A
Planned Market Share (MS_P)	MS_P	MS_A	MS_A	MS_A
Planned Price (Local Currency) (PLC_P)	PLC_P	PLC_P	PLC_A	PLC_A
Planned Foreign Exchange Rate (FX_P)	FX_P	FX_P	FX_P	FX_A
	Industry Volume Variance	Market Share Variance	Sales Price Variance	Exchange Rate Variance

$_P$ = planned

$_A$ = actual

TABLE 14-3 Illustrating the Table 14-2 Example with a Set of Numbers

Assume:

IV_p = 1 million
IV_a = 1.4 million
MS_p = 10%
MS_a = 5%
PLC_P = 1.00
PLC_a = 1.10
FX_P = 1 home currency : 1 foreign currency
FX_a = 2 home currency : 1 foreign currency

Sales (in home currency)

Planned = 100,000
Actual = 154,000
Total Sales Variance = 54,000 favorable

Variances (in home currency)

Industry Volume Variance = 40,000 favorable
Market Share Variance = 70,000 unfavorable
Price Variance = 7,000 favorable
Foreign Exchange Variance = 77,000 favorable

that specific individuals (or groups of individuals) can be held accountable for them. In the previous example, it is likely that managers would deem the market share and price variances to be primarily the responsibility of the marketing and sales department; however, further analyses might show that some of the accountability for these variances should be shared with other departments, such as engineering (product design) or production (production quality and schedule attainment). The exchange rate variance might be the responsibility of the corporate finance function if personnel in this department were charged with currency hedging. If not, this variance might be considered uncontrollable.

Flexible Performance Standards

Flexible performance standards, which were discussed in Chapter 10, can also be used to protect managers from the effects of some uncontrollable factors. Flexible standards define the performance that employees are expected to achieve given the actual conditions faced during the measurement period. Flexible performance standards might be made to vary with any of a number of uncontrollable factors; industry sales volumes, plant production volumes, or the levels of interest or exchange rates.

Flexible budgets, which are flexible performance standards expressed in financial terms, are usable only where there is a dominant volume-of-activity indicator *and* when many of the costs are associated with this activity indicator (where costs are variable). These requirements are limiting conditions in many industries (for example, oil and gas exploration or insurance). The limiting conditions account for the survey finding which showed only a minority of firms (28 percent) use flexible budgets.[9]

Scenario planning, as discussed in Chapter 9, provides another way to apply flexible performance standards at corporate and business unit organization levels. At the beginning of the measurement period, managers prepare plans for each possible scenario in the future. Managers are then held accountable for achieving the plan associated with the scenario that actually unfolds.

Scenario planning linked directly with rewards is quite rare in practice because it is expensive. It is also most difficult to implement in the situations where flexible performance standards are most needed, where there is considerable uncertainty about the future.

Another method to make performance standards more flexible is simply to update them more frequently. Any time a performance standard is set, there is a chance that the conditions under which it was prepared will change, rendering the standard obsolete. Obsolete standards subject managers to uncontrollable risks.

Potential obsolescence is easy to see in a budget setting. Budgets are prepared under the assumption of a given set of planning parameters, such as economic forecasts. The budget targets then remain fixed for the duration of the planning horizon (typically one year for general managers). The managers are at risk for all the *forecasting errors.* They are asked to achieve their budget targets regardless of the conditions actually faced. Forecasting errors, and hence managers' exposure to uncontrollable risk, can be minimized if the planning horizon is shortened. Firms might evaluate managers' performances quarterly (rather than annually) and then prepare an updated, hopefully more realistic, budget for the next quarter.

Updating standards more frequently is not a panacea. It takes time and money to update standards. Preparing budgets quarterly rather than annually can be quite expensive depending on how elaborate the budget preparation process is. Measuring results in short time periods creates some other potential problems. It is not possible to determine in a short time period whether the results generated by some individuals, such as managers or research scientists, are good or bad. The short time horizon can also lead to or exacerbate a myopia problem.

Relative Performance Evaluations

Another method of protecting employees from the distorting effects of uncontrollable factors is *relative performance evaluation* (RPE). RPE means that employees' performances are evaluated not in terms of the absolute levels of the results they generate, but in terms of their results relative to each other or relative to those of their closest outside competitors.

For RPE to be effective, all parties in the comparison group must be performing roughly the same tasks and must face the same sets of opportunities and constraints. Production workers evaluated using RPE should be performing the same tasks and facing the same environmental conditions, and general managers should be operating like units in one industry and facing the same business conditions.

Because of the great variety of tasks performed and situations faced in organizations, these necessary similarity conditions are rarely satisfied, however. Relative performance evaluation is not in widespread use, at least in a formal objective sense, although they do influence subjective performance evaluations.

Subjective Performance Evaluations

Many *subjective performance evaluations* take into consideration all the logic embodied in the objective methods of adjusting for uncontrollables. Instead of making a formal, numerical calculation, the subjective evaluator makes a judgment as to whether the results generated reflect good or bad performance.

Well done subjective evaluations have undeniable advantages. Most importantly, they can correct for flaws in the results measures. Results measures rarely reflect controllable performance completely and accurately. Compensation expert Edward Lawler argued,

> In most cases, there are simply no hard, objective measures that would allow the [performance] appraisal to be based on objective data. Thus, a judgment call is necessarily involved.[10]

In other words, a rigid linking of evaluations to results measures will probably mean rewarding employees for good luck (and penalizing them for bad luck). Evaluators can use both the results measures and their knowledge of the situations faced and subjectively make judgments as to whether the employees performed well in any given period. Subjective evaluations are also popular with superiors because they provide a significant source of power over their subordinates.

Subjectivity in evaluations creates its own problems, however. First, subjective evaluations are likely to be biased. One bias is known as the *outcome effect.* An experimental study in this area found that making results known to evaluators significantly influenced performance evaluations even when the results measures were set up *not* to be informative of the individuals' performance.[11] Another related bias is known as the *hindsight effect.* Hindsight effect studies show that evaluators with knowledge of results tend to assume information about the preresult circumstances that was not available to those being evaluated. These assumptions bias their judgments of preresult probabilities and their overall evaluations.[12] While subjectivity is intended to lower employees' reward-related risks, it can sometimes raise the risk of performance evaluations that are unfair, inconsistent, or biased.

Second, subjectivity often leads to inadequate, or perhaps even no, feedback about how performance was evaluated. This lack of feedback inhibits learning and limits motivation in subsequent performance periods.

Third, even when the evaluations are fair, employees often do not understand or trust them. A mere perception of bias, whether accurate or not, can create morale and motivational problems. At the extreme, the superiors can renege on promises which were made but not documented in writing. Employees' lack of trust in evaluators, while widespread, seems to vary significantly across organizations and across evaluators within a single organization.

Fourth, subjectivity often leads to creation of an *excuse culture.* Humans seem to have an inherent trait that causes them to make excuses for poor performance. This trait has been studied often under the rubric of a psychological theory called *attribution theory.* Attribution theory states that individuals have a need to understand and explain events in their organizations, so they ascribe attributions that they can plausibly derive from proposed causes. Evidence has shown that individuals tend to attribute their success to their own efforts, abilities, skills, knowledge, or competence, while they attribute their failures to bad luck, task difficulty, or a variety of other environmental or situational factors at least partially out of their control.[13] In other words, they tend to make excuses when things are not going well.

An article in the *Wall Street Journal* noted that managers in many companies blamed their poor performance in late 1990 and early 1991 on the Persian Gulf

War.[14] Managers of Eastman Kodak Company said earnings were down because travel was down, so not as many tourist-related pictures were taken. BeautiControl Cosmetics, a Dallas-based company which employs independent contractors to sell its products door to door and through clinics in the clients' own homes, claimed sales were down because many of their contractors stayed at home "glued to their television sets" and cancelled their clinics. Wang Laboratories, a large supplier to the U.S. State Department, claimed that diplomats were focused on Mideast developments and were not placing orders for new equipment. The war was a convenient excuse.

Totally objective performance evaluations, those based strictly on the results, allow no room for excuses. In an excuse culture, instead of focusing on generating good results and being committed to achieving their targets, employees spend considerable amounts of time making excuses and lobbying their evaluators for forgiveness of poor or mediocre results. They aim to beat the evaluation system rather than to work within it. In other words, they perceive that begging is easier than working. The negotiation and, potentially, appeal processes distract employees from the real tasks at hand.

Finally, subjective evaluations are expensive in management time. Evaluators must often spend considerable time informing themselves about the circumstances each employee faced during the evaluation period. If performance targets were not reached, the evaluators must often sift through considerable information that will enable them to separate the legitimate from the illegitimate excuses. If performance exceeded targets, they must search for evidence of good, but uncontrollable luck which might have accounted for the high performance. In this latter circumstance, they are unlikely to get much, if any, help from the employees being evaluated.

OTHER UNCONTROLLABLE FACTOR ISSUES

Managers must consider other issues when considering adjustments for the effects of uncontrollable factors. One issue is the *purpose* for which the adjustments are being made. Most managers do not treat uncontrollables identically for all reward purposes. They are likely to be forgiving when considering job retention decisions; rarely is an employee fired for being unlucky. They are much less forgiving when considering compensation, particularly bonus, issues. If performance is down, organizations are less likely to have the financial resources to pay the additional compensation, so managers ask their employees to share the organization's burden.

Another controllability-related issue is exactly who the *decision maker* is within the organization. Typically, decisions about adjustments for uncontrollables are made by the employee's immediate superior. Sometimes, however, evaluations are done by or appealed to a higher-level executive or a committee which might be as high as the compensation committee of the board of directors. Having the decisions made by a higher-level executive or committee can reduce the problems of inconsistency and bias if the higher-ups take the time to inform themselves.

A third issue is regarding the *direction of the adjustments.* Most managers seem to adjust for uncontrollables after the measurement period asymmetrically. They make their adjustments in only one direction: to protect the employees from suffering from bad luck, but not to protect the owners (shareholders) from paying out undeserved, "lucky" rewards.[15] The evaluators find it difficult to deny rewards, particularly bonuses, to employees when the organization has done well. The managers face no pressure to make downward adjustments in rewards for good luck because the employees do not raise the issue. The owners (stockholders) or their representatives are probably not even aware of the issue. Even if they are aware, they are already benefiting from the good performance, so who is to complain?

Aside from the discomfort involved in denying employees rewards, no good reason exists as to why the adjustments should not be symmetric. Managers should represent the owners' interests, and owners should not have to reward employees for uncontrollable windfall gains. If employees cannot control the events, then the rewards buy no motivational benefit.

CHOOSING WHETHER AND HOW TO ADJUST FOR UNCONTROLLABLE FACTORS

The controllability principle, holding people accountable only for that they can control, seems so simple, yet implementation of the principle is far from simple. There are many complications. As mentioned earlier, most results measures are only partially uncontrollable. Top-level managers want employees to respond properly to many factors that influence the measures even if the factors are partially or totally uncontrollable. The managers cannot protect the employees completely from the effects of influences to which the employees should be responding.

Even when decisions are made to protect employees from the effects of uncontrollables, the methods for implementing those decisions are not clear. Each of the methods of protecting employees from uncontrollables involves some costs and trade-offs. If the adjustments are made after the performance period has ended, some of the advantages of having preset performance standards will be lost. Employees will not know exactly what they are aiming for. Adjustments that involve subjective judgments or crude estimates of the effects of uncontrollable factors can create bias and inconsistency. If complex procedures are implemented to deal with the many types of possible uncontrollable factors, simplicity is lost, raising the possibility that some employees will fail to understand what they are being asked to achieve.

Regardless of the complexity, the stakes are high. Significant problems can arise if uncontrollables are not dealt with properly. Managers must continue to struggle with these issues.

Notes

1. Much of the material in this chapter is adapted from K. A. Merchant, *Rewarding Results: Motivating Profit Center Managers* (Boston: Harvard Business School Press), 1989, Chapters 5 and 6.
2. The others are either "risk lovers" or "risk neutral." Some people want to take risks. They enjoy the excitement of the challenge, or the $100,000 is not sufficient to meet their needs, so they are willing to take a chance to earn more. Risk neutral employees are probably financially self-sufficient. They do not need the $100,000 to meet current expenses, so they evaluate every investment proposal of this size or smaller based only on expected values.
3. J. D. Thompson, *Organizations in Action* (New York, McGraw-Hill, 1967). See also J. Fisher,

"Technological Interdependence, Labor Production Functions, and Control Systems, *Accounting, Organizations and Society* 19, No. 6 (1994), pp. 493–505.

4. See N. A. Doherty and C. W. Smith, Jr., "Corporate Insurance Strategy: The Case of British Petroleum," *Journal of Applied Corporate Finance* (Fall 1993), pp. 4–15.
5. Umapathy, *Current Budgeting Practices in U.S. Industry: The State of the Art* (New York: Quorum Books, 1987).
6. R. F. Vancil, *Decentralization: Managerial Ambiguity by Design* (Dow Jones-Irwin, 1978).
7. J. M. Fremgen and S. S. Liao, *The Allocation of Corporate Indirect Costs* (New York: National Association of Accountants), 1981.
8. The order in which the factors are analyzed is unimportant. The actual variance amounts will be slightly different because of the placement of what is referred to in many textbooks as the "joint variance." Regardless of the ordering, the total variance will be explained and the magnitude of each of the variances will be indicative of the effect of that factor on the total.
9. Umapathy, *Current Budgeting Practices in U.S. Industry: The State of the Art* (New York: Quorum Books, 1987).
10. E. E. Lawler, *Strategic Pay* (San Francisco: Jossey-Bass, 1990), p. 90.
11. T. Mitchell and L. Kalb, "Effects of Outcome Knowledge and Outcome Valence on Supervisors' Evaluations," *Journal of Applied Psychology,* 66 (1981), pp. 604–612.
12. For a review of hindsight bias findings, see S. Hawkins and R. Hastie, "Hindsight: Biased Judgments of Past Events After the Outcomes Are Known," *Psychological Bulletin,* 107, no. 3 (May 1990), pp. 311–327.
13. Heider is the name most often associated with attribution theory. Discussions of attribution theory-related findings are provided in, for example, F. Heider, *The Psychology of Interpersonal Relations* (New York, Wiley, 1958); B. M. Staw, "Attribution of the "Causes" of Performance: A General Alternative Interpretation of Cross-Sectional Research on Organizations," *Organizational Behavior and Human Performance,* 13 (1975), pp. 414–32; R. M. Arkin and G. M. Maruyama, "Attribution, Affect and College Exam Performance," *Journal of Educational Psychology,* 71, no. 1 (1979), pp. 85–93; M. D. Shields, J. G. Birnberg, and I. H. Frieze, "Attributions, Cognitive Processes and Control Systems," *Accounting, Organizations and Society,* 6, no. 1 (1981), pp. 69–93; and B. Weiner, "An Attributional Theory of Achievement Motivation and Emotion," *Psychological Review,* 92, no. 4 (1985), pp. 548–573.
14. W. M. Buckley, "Companies' Favorite Reason for Poor Results: Gulf War," *Wall Street Journal* (April 2, 1991), p. B1.
15. Much of the material in this chapter is adapted from K. A. Merchant, *Rewarding Results: Motivating Profit Center Managers* (Boston: Harvard Business School Press), 1989, Chapters 5 and 6.

McMullen and Worby (A) (Abridged)

One morning John Worby, president of McMullen and Worby, sat down with Anne McMullen, the executive vice president, to discuss year-end performance evaluations of the management group. These discussions were important because the company had traditionally given managers a sizeable bonus based on their evaluation. To the extent that it was possible, John and Anne preferred to base their evaluation on objective measures of performance with an emphasis on achievement of budgeted goals.

The budget process began in late August and, by mid-November the management team supplied the board of directors with a complete budget outlining monthly sales estimates, production cost estimates and capital spending requirements. The directors then discussed the implications of the budget and upon acceptance, authorized it. The firm's progress throughout the year was monitored against this budget every six months, at the board meetings which were held on the January and July 15 each year. At the January meeting, the board also voted on the management bonuses for the prior year.

McMullen and Worby was a Boston-based company which manufactured a very successful line of foam rubber toys called "Uncle Grumps." These were cuddly Hobbit-like dolls with large noses, a discerning smile and enormous feet which sold for $20 wholesale. From the moment of introduction they had been a runaway success. Plans to expand the line were on the drawing board and a smaller baby version was to be introduced in the spring of 1979.

The business was highly seasonal with over half of the sales occurring from mid-August to early November. This was followed by a two-month trough, before birthday and occasional gift sales picked up again. Sales were then fairly static until the next Christmas rush began (1978 expected sales are shown in Exhibit 1). Budgeted sales for 1978 were $40 million with a standard gross margin on full cost, of 33 percent.

Management had decided that even though sales were highly seasonal, production would be level throughout the year. This enabled McMullen and Worby to stabilize employment and to sell a greater number of toys during the Christmas period than would have been possible if a shift approach had been used. Current production was at full capacity using one shift a day, five days a week. The production level was only changed if production had fallen behind in earlier months or, if the sales forecast was altered during the year. In 1977 sales were considerably greater than expectation and had almost resulted in orders being rejected due to a lack of inventory. In fact by the end of the year only 44,000 toys were left in stock.

John and Anne decided to discuss the production manager's performance first. The production manager, Holly Frost, had been with the firm for just over a year and this was to be her first bonus. John and Anne admired Holly and felt she had been very innovative and had substantially improved the production process. One improvement, which was introduced at the beginning of the third quarter, resulted in the average material content of each toy being reduced from 5 lbs. to 4.5 lbs., a substantial savings.

In measuring Holly's managerial performance, John and Anne decided to analyze the results by quarters. A quarterly analysis would, they felt, give a more balanced view of her performance across the year than that given by an aggregate view because the year 1978 had been rather turbulent. The factory had been closed from February 5 to March 3 (20 working days) due to *The Great Blizzard of '78.* Massachusetts Governor Dukakis had issued a citywide edict prohibiting

Instructor Robin Cooper and Professor Kenneth Merchant prepared this case as the basis for class discussion rather than to illustrate either effective or ineffective handling of an administrative situation.

commerce for five days, and then the factory roof collapsed under the weight of three feet of snow. During this period employees did not work but were given half pay.

To make up for lost production, a four-hour Saturday morning shift was introduced from March 3 until the end of the year. Employees were paid time and a half for this work. Additional overtime was required in the fourth quarter when the sales department managed to gain an order from a catalogue sales company for an extra 50,000 toys. The order was placed in the middle of October and, along with other orders, required that overtime be increased to 16 hours per weekend, at time and a half, for six weekends (this includes the Saturday morning time already planned).

John and Anne started with the quarterly (13-week) budget and production reports (Exhibits 2 and 3). McMullen and Worby had not implemented a standard cost system. Because unit costs were relatively stable, direct materials were tracked in pounds and direct labor in hours and actual usage was compared with budget. Before they could adequately judge Holly's performance, however, John and Anne decided they needed additional information. John spoke with the raw material inventory clerk and came back with an inventory listing (Exhibit 4), and a reminder that McMullen and Worby used FIFO inventory costing. Anne spoke with the payroll clerk and was given a summary of monthly payroll listings (Exhibit 5). In addition, Anne collected from the sales department the sales data for the four quarters (Exhibit 6).

Looking at the pile of information they had collected, John and Anne settled down to the process of evaluating Holly's performance. After several hours John and Anne took a break. They felt they had made progress but still were not certain that they knew how Holly had performed.

Over coffee Anne remarked to John, "Well now we have a lot of facts, but it's not clear to me how we can use these figures to analyze Holly's performance."

"I have the same concern," replied John. "There are so many numbers and only some are relevant to Holly."

"I know, but which ones? That's the question."

"That's first on the agenda, when we finish coffee, but there is something else that is bothering me and that is a comment Holly made about those catalogue sales," said John.

"What was that?" asked Anne.

"Well Holly thinks we lost out on the deal because we sold them below cost."

"Didn't you explain to her about contribution analysis?" asked Anne.

"Well yes, but she said she understood that, and we were still losing out. Unfortunately she was called away before she could explain to me what she meant."

"Then you're right," said Anne. "We must try and find out what she meant. At least we have the sales figures (Exhibit 6) and finished inventory figures (Exhibit 7) calculated so that should help."

On that comment, John and Anne walked slowly back into the office to complete their analysis.

EXHIBIT 1 Budgeted Sales 1978

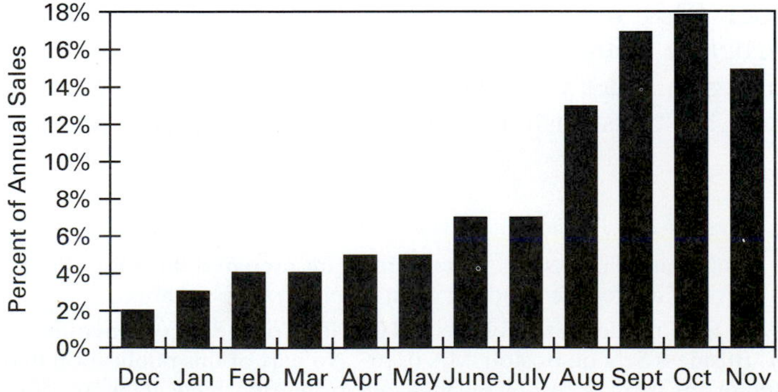

EXHIBIT 2 Quarterly Budget

Budgeted Production Units	500	
Budgeted Direct Expenses		
Raw Materials	$1,800	(5 lbs. per toy @ $.72 per lb.)
Direct Labor	$3,848	(.962 hrs per toy @ $8 per hr.)
Budgeted Indirect Expenses		
Indirect Labor	$300	($.60 per toy)
Supplies	$75	($.15 per toy)
Power	$375	($.75 per toy)
Budgeted Fixed Factory Overhead		
Repairs and Maintenance	$300	
Depreciation	$700	
Insurance	$250	
Total	$7,648	

EXHIBIT 3 Quarterly Production Report (All figures in thousands)

	1Q78	*2Q78*	*3Q78*	*4Q78*	*Tot. 1978*
Budget Production Units	500	500	500	500	2000
Actual Production Units	350	550	550	600	2050
Direct Expenses					
Raw Materials	$1,410	$1,775	$2,190	$1,880	7,255
Direct Labor	3,205	4,406	4,466	5,453	17,530
Indirect Expenses					
Indirect Labor	250	350	356	410	1,366
Supplies	50	100	50	90	290
Power	270	420	410	450	1,550
Fixed Factory Overhead					
Repairs and Maintenance	130	120	500	280	1,030
Depreciation	700	700	700	700	2,800
Insurance	252	231	260	260	1,003
	$6,267	$8,102	$8,932	$9,523	$32,824

EXHIBIT 4 Summary of Raw Materials Movements (All figures in thousands)

	1977/1978	
	lbs.	*$*
Opening Balance (Dec. 1, 1977)	718	$500
Purchases (Dec. 1–March 3)	2,000	1,410
Usage (December 1–March 3)	(1,770)	(1,237)
Purchases (March 4–June 2)	2,500	1,775
Usage (March 4–June 2)	(2,710)	(1,923)
Purchases (June 3–Sept. 1)	3,000	2,190
Usage (June 1–Sept. 1)	(2,460)	(1,781)
Purchases (Sept. 1–Dec. 1)	2,500	1,880
Usage (Sept. 1–Dec. 1)	(2,630)	(1,950)
Closing Balance (Dec. 1, 1978)	1,148	$ 864

EXHIBIT 5 Summary of Direct Labor Expenses[a]

	Average Number of Employees	*Regular Hours*[b]	*Overtime Hours*[b]	*Cost*[c]
1st Quarter (ending 3/8)	960	494[b]	0	3,205
2nd Quarter (ending 6/2)	970	500	52	4,406
3rd Quarter (ending 9/1)	980	505	54	4,466
4th Quarter (ending 12/1)	990	510	135	5,453

[a]Holly is responsible for negotiating all labor contracts.

[b]Includes 153,000 hours when factory was closed for which half pay was given.

[c]All figures in thousands

EXHIBIT 6 Summary of Sales Performance[a]

	Units			*$*		
	Budget	*Actual*	—	*Budget*	*Actual*	—
1st Quarter	180	165	(15)	3,600	3,300	(300)
2nd Quarter	280	283	3	5,600	5,660	60
3rd Quarter	540	516	(24)	10,800	10,320	(480)
4th Quarter	1,000	1,130	130	20,000	22,350[b]	2,350
	2,000	2,094	94	$40,000	$41,630	$1,630

[a]All figures in thousands

[b]Includes the special order for 50,000 toys at $15.00 each

EXHIBIT 7 Finished Goods Inventory Available for Sale (thousands of units)

	Quarter			
	1	*2*	*3*	*4*
Opening Inventory	44	229	496	530
Production	350	550	50	600
Available for Sale in Qtr.	394	779	1046	1,130
Sold in Qtr.	(165)	(283)	(516)	(1,130)
Closing Inventory	229	496	530	0

Hoffman Discount Drugs, Inc.

In January 1996, a small fire broke out in the backroom of a drugstore in Downey, California owned and operated by Hoffman Discount Drugs, Inc. The fire department concluded that the fire was started by a fault in the store's electrical system. Luckily, the sprinkler system worked, and fire damage was held to a minimum. However, the water from the sprinklers damaged some of the inventory. Jane Firstenberg, the store's general manager, completed a Damage Report which described the situation and calculated the resulting losses. The losses were calculated as follows:

Total losses incurred
= value of inventory lost
+ cleaning expenses
+ payroll used in clean-up process

The losses incurred were not charged to their ordinary line-item (for example, payroll). Instead, they were charged to an account called *Non-insured Losses*. In this case, the loss totalled $9,720.

Jane was discouraged when she saw the amount of the loss. If the loss had been greater than $10,000, a corporate adjustment would have been made to offset the effects of this *uncontrollable event* for net income bonus purposes. But since the loss was less than $10,000, no adjustment would be made. Jane commented:

> This really hurts. My store is having a great year in sales, but our margins have been down. Now this. This loss might cause us not to achieve our net income objective for the year. We were right on the edge as it was. It takes a lot of sales to make up for a nearly $10,000 loss. I was looking forward to a nice bonus check. Even worse, if our bonuses are cut, I'm worried I may lose part of my management team. A couple of them have already been considering offers from competitors.

THE COMPANY

Hoffman Discount Drugs, Inc. (HDDI) was a large retail drug store chain which operated over 400 stores located throughout the Western United States. It operated over 180 stores in the Southwest region which included Southern California, Arizona, and Nevada. HDDI stores were typically located in large shopping centers which also included a supermarket chain store.

HDDI's recent performance had been mixed. For the last few years, sales levels had been increasing and were currently the highest in the company's history. However, because of intense competition in the company's major markets, operating earnings were barely above break-even. In late 1995, HDDI's president was fired, after only two years on the job, and Matt LeGeyt was appointed president.

Matt immediately started negotiating with several major insurance carriers to have HDDI be the sole distributor of prescriptions to individuals who hold policies with those carriers. By obtaining those prescription distribution rights, Matt believed HDDI stores would benefit from increased customer traffic. But Matt believed HDDI's real key to success was to improve operations at the store level. He thought the company needed more effective local marketing, better customer service, and more efficient operations. He did not want to change the company's decentralized mode of operation, however. He believed it was potentially one of HDDI's advantages over its more centralized competitors.

STORE OPERATIONS

A typical large HDDI store carried $1 million of inventory, served nearly 800,000 customers per year, and generated annual sales of approximately $10 million and net income of $500,000. In com-

Professor Kenneth A. Merchant wrote this case as a basis for class discussion rather than to illustrate either effective or ineffective handling of an administrative situation.

puting net income, all corporate expenses except interest and income taxes were traced or allocated to the stores. In addition, the stores were charged a carrying cost on their inventory based on an annual approximation of the corporation's marginal cost of capital.

HDDI stores offered a wide range of products. The average percentage of total store sales was as follows:

CATEGORY	% OF SALES
General merchandise	64%
Pharmacy	29
Liquor	7
Total	100%

General merchandise items included health and beauty aids, detergent and soap products, baby supplies, greeting cards, toys, and seasonal items.

Many functions, such as purchasing, human resources, investor relations, and real estate, were centralized within HDDI, and inventory was shipped to the stores from one of three regional warehouses. Each store had the same basic look, and each store was required to carry a basic set of pharmacy-related inventory.

Other than these constraints, however, the stores were relatively autonomous. Store managers were allowed to adapt their merchandise offerings to their local market. Therefore, stores located near the beach stocked many sun- and water-related items, such as sunscreen, beach towels, and boogie boards. Those located near retirement communities carried large stocks of age-related items, such as pain killers, laxatives, and blood pressure monitors. And those in neighborhoods dominated by upper-income professionals with young families carried large stocks of baby- and child-related products, as well as videocassette recorders, stereos, and cameras.

The store managers were also allowed to make decisions about local advertising. That is, they selected the amount and type of local advertising (newspaper, radio, and television), although newer managers typically asked for and received considerable guidance in this area from corporate specialists and their district managers. A typical large store spent nearly $400,000 per year on local advertising.

STORE MANAGEMENT BONUS PLAN

HDDI's policy was to pay store-level managers salaries that were slightly below market levels but to provide bonus opportunities that made the total compensation package competitive. The bonuses were intended to motivate the managers to work hard and to act in the company's best interest.

The HDDI Store Management Bonus Plan was based on achievement of predetermined objectives for sales and net income for each store.[1] These objectives were set in a *top-down* fashion. In a series of discussions which considered historical performance, demographic and competitive trends, and corporate initiatives, corporate and regional managers established sales and profit objectives for the corporation. They then broke these objectives down into objectives for the three regions. The regional managers, in consultation with the district managers, disaggregated the objectives into districts. And the district managers then had the responsibility to set objectives for the individual stores in their districts.

Because the company was constantly adding some new stores and improving some store locations, the corporate, regional, and district objectives were usually increased, typically by an average of 4–7 percent annually. But the growth objectives for individual stores were generally more modest. Sometimes store objectives would even be lowered as would be the case, for example, if the major supermarket store in the HDDI store's shopping center was closed.

The objectives for each store were disaggregated into monthly periods using historical seasonality patterns and, if necessary, some management judgment. Each month during the year, store managers received reports comparing their store's sales, net income, and inventory performance with their objectives for the month and the year-to-date. Line-item detail was also provided for analysis purposes.

[1]The only other compensation plan offered to store- and lower-level employees was a stock purchase plan. Employees could have a portion of their check withheld for the purpose of purchasing stock. The stock was sold to the employees at the current market price, but the employees would not have to pay any commission fees on their purchases.

HDDI's fiscal year ended March 31. In early March, at the end of the company's annual planning process, each member of each store management team was presented with a Store Management Compensation Letter (see example in Exhibit 1). Managers had to signify receipt and understanding of this letter by signing a copy of the letter and returning it to the corporate Human Resources Department.

The Management Compensation Letters listed the individual's base salary, bonus objective, and total compensation objective. The bonus objective were set as follows:

ROLE	BONUS OBJECTIVE (% BASE SALARY)
general manager	15–20%
assistant general manager	7–10%
assistant manager	3– 5%

The managers would earn their bonus objective if they exactly achieved their predetermined sales and net income objectives.

The bonus objective was broken down into a net income (before bonus) objective and a sales objective. Reflecting HDDI's belief in the importance of high profits, the net income objective was given three times the weight of the sales objective. That is, 75 percent of the bonus was based on achievement of net income objectives. The other 25 percent was based on achievement of sales objectives.

Exhibit 2 shows the description of the bonus plan as provided annually to participants. The bonus earned based on net income performance was calculated by adding/subtracting a percentage of the variance to/from the net income bonus objective according to the following formula:

$$B_N = O_N + A = O_N + (V \times S) = A$$

where:

B_N = bonus earned based on net income performance
O_N = net income objective
A = adjustment to net income bonus objective
V = net income variance = actual net income minus net income objective
S = sharing percentage (see the following)

The sharing percentage depended on the manager's level in the store, as follows: general manager (10 percent), assistant general manager (3 percent), assistant manager (1.5 percent). These percentages were set to reflect the different levels of responsibility associated with each job.

The effect of this net income bonus formula was that for every dollar of income the store earned above its predetermined objective, the general manager earned in bonus 10 cents more than his/her bonus objective. Conversely, for every dollar actual income fell below the objective, the general manager earned 10 cents less than his/her bonus objective.

The sales portion of the bonus was based on the percent of annual sales objective achieved. The effect on the bonus objective was determined by using one of the charts shown on the bottom of Exhibit 2. The chart on the left was used if net income before bonus was above budget; the chart on the right was used if net income before bonus was below budget. These two charts differ only when sales exceed budget. If sales exceeded the objective but net income was below budget, then the managers' sales bonuses were set at lower limits.

Exhibit 3 shows a bonus calculation example.

Shortly after the mid-point of the appraisal period (that is, at the end of the 26th week of the year), HDDI gave each manager a bonus check equal to one-half of the expected year-end bonus. This was done to provide the managers more timely reinforcement in hopes that they would stay focused throughout the entire year. This aspect of the plan seemed to work. Managers who received a large interim check were excited and were motivated to earn another large check at year end. Those who received a small check were motivated to make up the difference in the second half of the year.

ADJUSTMENTS FOR UNCONTROLLABLE EVENTS

HDDI corporate managers reserved the right to make subjective adjustments to bonuses earned in case actual performance was distorted by uncontrollable events. They considered only three types of uncontrollable events: natural disasters (for example, fires, floods, earthquakes), robberies, and rioting and looting. In large (AAA classification) stores, adjustments were considered only if the damage resulting from the uncontrollable event exceeded $10,000. Events causing less than $10,000 damage were considered to be *immaterial*. Losses were considered only individually, not cumulatively, but in any case it was quite rare that an individual store would experience more than one or two uncontrollable events in a single year.

One example of an uncontrollable event was described in the introduction to this case. Here are three others:

1. In February 1996, heavy rains and a stopped-up sewer drain caused flooding around the HDDI store in Van Nuys, California. The store suffered approximately $8,000 in inventory damage as water came into the stockroom, and clean-up expenses totalled $2,000 more. A more serious problem, however, was that a sinkhole developed in the major street artery in front of the store, and the street was closed for three days for repairs. The store manager argued that customers' difficulties in getting to the store caused sales for the month to be down more than $100,000, costing the store approximately $25,000 in net income. Corporate managers readily agreed to an adjustment for the inventory damage, but their opinions were mixed as to whether to make the adjustment for the *lost profits* because they thought the estimates were *soft*. However, they eventually did agree to an adjustment totalling $35,000.
2. In December 1995, an armed robbery occurred in an HDDI store in Glendale, Arizona. Since only $190 was stolen, no adjustment was made for bonus purposes.[2]
3. In the April 1993 riots in Los Angeles, looters stole nearly $200,000 worth of merchandise from HDDI's Watts store and caused another $100,000 in structural damage to the building. Corporate managers awarded managers of this store their full bonus objectives as was their policy when stores suffered *heavy* damage.

MANAGEMENT CONCERNS

Matt LeGeyt, the new president, who believed the company's key to success was in improving store operations, had already expressed interest in having a thorough evaluation done of the Store Management Compensation Plan. When Jane Firstenberg complained to her superiors about unfairness of the situation described in the introduction to this case, HDDI managers agreed to move this task up on the agenda. The corporate Human Resources Department was asked to conduct a thorough analysis of the plan and to present their recommendations at the July management meeting.

---

[2]The losses associated with robberies average between $100 and $200. Store managers are generally able to limit the amount of robbery losses by following the company policy of collecting money from the cash registers at regular intervals.

EXHIBIT 1 Store Management Compensation Letter

Ralph Williams
General Manager
Store #142
Store Classification: AAA

PERSONAL AND CONFIDENTIAL

The following pertains to your assignment for fiscal year 1996 as of 03/31/96

BASE PAY:	$44,400
BONUS OBJECTIVE:	$ 7,900
TOTAL COMPENSATION OBJECTIVE:	$52,300
THE PERFORMANCE RATING USED FOR PAY REVIEW PURPOSES WAS:	08

25% OF YOUR BONUS OBJECTIVE IS BASED ON STORE SALES AND 75% IS BASED ON BUDGETED NET INCOME BEFORE BONUS.

YOUR STORE IS CURRENTLY ON THE REGULAR PLAN (Refer to your 1996 Store Management Compensation Booklet for Plan details)

MINIMUM % OF BONUS OBJECTIVE PAYABLE:	0%
MAXIMUM % OF BONUS OBJECTIVE PAYABLE:	500%

The following information pertains to your Store Management assignments for fiscal 1996 to date and your most recent salary history:

EFFECTIVE DATE	STORE	DIST	POSI.	* ANNUAL COMPENSATION OBJECTIVE * BASE	BONUS OBJECTIVE	TOTAL *	STORE CLASSIFICATION	NIBB[3] BUDGET / SALES BUDGET	PLAN
03/31/96	142	LO2	GM	44,400	7,900	52,300	AAA	872,777 10,700,143	REG.
02/03/95	142	LO2	GM	42,600	7,900	50,500	AAA	872,777 10,700,143	REG.

PRIOR COMPENSATION HISTORY:

02/04/95	142	GM	42,600	6,800	49,400
04/23/94	89	AGM	31,100	2,400	33,500
03/26/94	111	AGM	31,100	2,400	33,500
01/29/94	111	AGM	28,200	2,400	30,600
03/27/94	111	AGM	28,200	2,000	30,400
01/31/94	111	AGM	27,400	2,000	29,400
12/06/93	111	AGM	27,400	1,500	28,900
03/29/93	89	AM	26,000	1,000	27,000

These are the facts according to our records as of this date. Changes after this date will be sent to you in a separate carrier. No other considerations or adjustments will be made at any time unless stated and authorized in writing by the Regional Vice President of Operations.

If any of this information varies from what you understand your compensation plan to be, please contact your District Manager immediately for an explanation. Otherwise, please confirm your understanding of this information (including Appendix A, which is attached to your Store Management compensation letter, and the bonus payment table) by promptly signing one page of this letter and returning it to the Corporate Human Resources Department within two weeks.

I understand the compensation program explained above and have received a copy of Appendix A and understand the contents.

Signed: ______________________ Date: ______________

[3]net income before bonus

EXHIBIT 2 Net Income/Bonus Function for Regular Plan

This plan is broken down into two pieces—NET INCOME BEFORE BONUS and SALES. The minimum payout is 0 and the maximum is 500% of your bonus objective for the combined pieces.

NET INCOME BEFORE BONUS (NIBB) PORTION OF BONUS OBJECTIVE:

Bonus calculations are based on variance from budget. Your NIBB bonus objective will be adjusted by the amount of the variance multiplied by the sharing rates as follows:

GENERAL MANAGERS	+ or − 10.0% OF VARIANCE
ASSISTANT GENERAL MANAGERS & SENIOR MERCHANDISE ASSISTANTS	+ or − 3.0% OF VARIANCE
ASSISTANT MANAGERS, MERCHANDISE ASSISTANTS & SERVICE MANAGERS	+ or − 1.5% OF VARIANCE

SALES PORTION OF BONUS OBJECTIVE

Bonus calculations are based on the percent of Sales budget achieved using the following charts:

If Net Income before Bonus is Above Budget:		If Net Income before Bonus is Below Budget:	
% of Sales Budget Achieved	% of Sales Objective Earned	% of Sales Budget Achieved	% of Sales Objective Earned
90.0%	0.0%	90.0%	0.0%
91.0	10.0	91.0	10.0
92.0	20.0	92.0	20.0
93.0	30.0	93.0	30.0
94.0	40.0	94.0	40.0
95.0	50.0	95.0	50.0
96.0	60.0	96.0	60.0
97.0	70.0	97.0	70.0
98.0	80.0	98.0	80.0
99.0	90.0	99.0	90.0
100.0	100.0	100.0	100.0
101.0	120.0	101.0	110.0
102.0	140.0	102.0	120.0
103.0	160.0	103.0	130.0
104.0	180.0	104.0	140.0
105.0	200.0	105.0	150.0
106.0	220.0	106.0	160.0
107.0	240.0	107.0	170.0
108.0	260.0	108.0	180.0
109.0	280.0	109.0	190.0
Max. 110.0	300.0	Max. 110.0	200.0

In the event a person transfers into a store, earnings are referred as the higher of the person's adjusted earnings after a transfer of the store's adjusted earnings.

DEDUCT 5% FROM THE PAYOUT ON SALES FOR EACH 1% STORE EARNINGS ARE BELOW 97%; DEDUCT 5% FROM THE PAYOUT ON STORE EARNINGS FOR EACH 1% ACTUAL SALES ARE BELOW 100%.

EXHIBIT 3 Bonus Calculation Example

Assume:

General manager			
Base salary	$45,000	Bonus objective break-down:	
Bonus objective	8,200	Net income	$6,150
Total compensation objective	$53,200	Sales	2,050

Net income portion of bonus:

actual 1995 net income	$995,041
—1995 net income objective	758,936
variance	236,105
sharing percentage	10%
adjustment to NI bonus objective	$23,610.50

net income bonus objective + adjustment = net income bonus earned
$6,150 + 23,610.50 = $29,760.50

Sales portion of bonus:

actual 1995 sales	$9,642,910
1995 sales objective	9,304,473
actual % objective	103.6%

Since the store achieved its net income objective, use the left-side chart in Exhibit 2. Interpolating on the chart, the percent objective earned is 172%.

sales bonus objective × percent objective earned = sales bonus earned
$2,050 × 172% = $3,526

Total compensation earned:

Base salary	$45,000.00
Net income bonus earned	29,760.50
Sales bonus earned	3,526.00
Total compensation	$78,286.50

Polysar Limited

As soon as Pierre Choquette received the September Report of Operations for NASA Rubber [Exhibits 1 and 2], he called Alf Devereux, Controller, and Ron Britton, Sales Manager, into his office to discuss the year-to-date results. Next week, he would make his presentation to the Board of Directors and the results for his division for the first nine months of the year were not as good as expected. Pierre knew that the NASA management team had performed well. Sales volume was up and feedstock costs were down resulting in a gross margin that was better than budget. Why did the bottom line look so bad?

As the three men worked through the numbers, their discussion kept coming back to the fixed costs of the butyl rubber plant. Fixed costs were high. The plant had yet to reach capacity. The European Division had taken less output than projected.

Still, Choquette felt that these factors were outside his control. His Division had performed well—it just didn't show in the profit results.

Choquette knew that Henderson, his counterpart in Europe, did not face these problems. The European rubber profits would be compared to those of NASA. How would the Board react to the numbers he had to work with? He would need to educate them in his presentation, especially concerning the volume variance. He knew that many of the Board members would not understand what that number represented or that it was due in part to the actions of Henderson's group.

Pierre Choquette, Alf Devereux, and Ron Britton decided to meet the next day to work on a strategy for the Board presentation.

POLYSAR LIMITED

In 1986, Polysar Limited was Canada's largest chemical company with $1.8 billion in annual sales. Based in Sarnia, Ontario, Polysar was the world's largest producer of synthetic rubber and latex and a major producer of basic petrochemicals and fuel products.

Polysar was established in 1942 to meet wartime needs for a synthetic substitute for natural rubber. The supply of natural rubber to the Allied forces had been interrupted by the declaration of war against the United States by Japan in December 1941. During 1942 and 1943, ten synthetic rubber plants were built by the Governments of the United States and Canada including the Polysar plant in Sarnia.

After the war, the supply of natural rubber was again secure and the nine U.S. plants were sold to private industry or closed. Polysar remained in operation as a Crown Corporation, wholly owned by the Government of Canada. In 1972, by an Act of Parliament, the Canada Development Corporation (CDC) was created as a government-owned, venture capital company to encourage Canadian business development; at that time, the equity shares of Polysar were transferred to the Canada Development Corporation. In 1986, Polysar remained wholly-owned by the CDC; however, in a government sponsored move to privatization, the majority of the shares of the CDC were sold to the Canadian public in the period 1982 to 1985.

Through acquisition and internal growth, Polysar had grown considerably from its original single plant. Polysar now employed 6,650 people

This case was prepared by Professor Robert Simons as the basis for class discussion rather than to illustrate either effective or ineffective handling of an administrative situation. The financial data have been developed to illustrate the issues involved and are not representative of the true financial results of the company.

including 3,100 in Canada, 1,050 in the U.S., and 2,500 in Europe and elsewhere. The company operated 20 manufacturing plants in Canada, United States, Belgium, France, The Netherlands, and West Germany.

STRUCTURE

The operations of the company were structured into three groups: basic petrochemicals, rubber, and diversified products (Exhibit 3).

Basic Petrochemicals

Firman Bentley, 51, was Group Vice-President of Basic Petrochemicals. This business unit produced primary petrochemicals such as ethylene as well as intermediate products such as propylene, butadiene, and styrene monomers. Group sales in 1985 were approximately $800 million of which $500 million was sold to outside customers and the remainder was sold as intermediate feedstock to Polysar's downstream operations.

Rubber

The Rubber Group was headed by Charles Ambridge, 61, Group Vice-President. Polysar held 9 percent of the world synthetic rubber market (excluding communist bloc countries). As the largest Group in the company, Rubber Group produced 46 percent of Polysar sales. Major competitors included Goodyear, Bayer, Exxon, and Dupont.

Rubber products, such as butyl and halobutyl, were sold primarily to manufacturers of automobile tires (six of the world's largest tire companies[1] accounted for 70 percent of the world butyl and halobutyl demand); other uses included belting, footwear, adhesives, hose, seals, plastics modification, and chewing gum.

The Rubber Group was split into two operating divisions that were managed as profit centers: NASA (North and South America) and EROW (Europe and rest of world). In addition to the two operating profit centers, the Rubber Group included a Global Marketing Department and a Research Division. The costs of these departments were not charged to the two operating profit centers, but instead were charged against Group profits.

Diversified Products

John Beaton, 48, was Vice-President of Diversified Products, a group that consisted of the Latex, Plastics, and Specialty Products Divisions. This group was composed of high technology product categories that were expected to double sales within five years. In 1985, the group provided 27 percent of Polysar's sales revenue.

Bentley, Ambridge, and Beaton reported to Robert Dudley, 60, President and Chief Executive Officer.

RUBBER GROUP

A key component of Polysar's strategy was to be a leader in high margin, specialty rubbers. The leading products in this category were the butyl and halobutyl rubbers. Attributes of butyl rubber include low permeability to gas and moisture, resistance to steam and weathering, high energy absorption, and chemical resistance. Butyl rubber was traditionally used in inner tubes and general purpose applications. Halobutyl rubber, a modified derivative, possesses the same attributes as regular butyl with additional properties that allow bonding to other materials. Thus, halobutyls were used extensively as liners and sidewalls in tubeless tires.

Butyl and halobutyl rubber were manufactured from feedstocks such as crude oil, naphtha, butane, propane, and ethane (Exhibit 4). Polysar manufactured butyl rubbers at two locations: NASA Division's Sarnia plant and EROW Division's Antwerp plant.

NASA Butyl Plant

The original Sarnia plant, built in 1942, manufactured regular butyl until 1972. At that time, market studies predicted rapid growth in the demand for high-quality radial tires manufactured with halobutyl. Demand for regular butyl was predicted to remain steady since poor road conditions in many countries of the world necessitated the use of tires with inner tubes. In 1972, the Sarnia plant was converted to allow production of halobutyls as well as regular butyl.

---

[1]Michelin, Goodyear, Bridgestone, Firestone, Pirelli, and Dunlop.

By the 1980s, demand for halobutyl had increased to the point that Polysar forecast capacity constraints. During 1983 and 1984, the company built a second plant at Sarnia, known as Sarnia 2, to produce regular butyl. The original plant, Sarnia 1, was then dedicated solely to the production of halobutyl.

Sarnia 2, with a capital cost of $550 million, began full operations late in 1984. Its annual nameplate (i.e., design) production capacity for regular butyl was 95,000 tonnes. During 1985, the plant produced 65,000 tonnes.

EROW Butyl Plant

The EROW Division's butyl plant was located in Antwerp, Belgium. Built in 1964 as a regular butyl unit, the plant was modified in 1979/80 to allow it to produce halobutyl as well as regular butyl.

The annual nameplate production capacity of the Antwerp plant was 90,000 tonnes. In 1985, as in previous years, the plant operated near or at its nameplate capacity. The Antwerp plant was operated to meet fully the halobutyl demand of EROW customers; the remainder of capacity was used to produce regular butyl.

In 1981, the plant's output was 75 percent regular butyl and 25 percent halobutyl; by 1985, halobutyl represented 50 percent of the plant's production. Since regular butyl demand outpaced the plant's remaining capacity, EROW took its regular butyl shortfall from the Sarnia 2 plant; in 1985, 21,000 tonnes of regular butyl were shipped from NASA to EROW.

PRODUCT SCHEDULING

Although NASA served customers in North and South America and EROW serviced customers in Europe and the rest of the world, regular butyl could be shipped from either the Sarnia 2 or Antwerp plant. NASA shipped approximately one-third of its regular butyl output to EROW. Also, customers located in distant locations could receive shipments from either plant due to certain cost or logistical advantages. For example, Antwerp sometimes shipped to Brazil and Sarnia sometimes shipped to the Far East.

A Global Marketing Department worked with Regional Directors of Marketing and Regional Product Managers to coordinate product flows. Three sets of factors influenced these analyses. First, certain customers demanded products from a specific plant due to slight product differences resulting from the type of feedstock used and the plant configuration. Second, costs varied between Sarnia and Antwerp due to differences in variable costs (primarily feedstock and energy), shipping, and currency rates. Finally, inventory levels, production interruptions, and planned shutdowns were considered.

In September and October of each year, NASA and EROW divisions prepared production estimates for the upcoming year. These estimates were based on estimated sales volumes and plant loadings (i.e., capacity utilization). Since the Antwerp plant operated at capacity, the planning exercise was largely for the benefit of the managers of the Sarnia 2 plant who needed to know how much regular butyl Antwerp would need from the Sarnia 2 plant.

Product Costing and Transfer Prices

Butyl rubbers were costed using standard rates for variable and fixed costs.

Variable costs included feedstocks, chemicals, and energy. Standard variable cost per tonne of butyl was calculated by multiplying a standard utilization factor (i.e., the standard quantity of inputs used) by a standard price established for each unit of input. Since feedstock prices varied with worldwide market conditions and represented the largest component of costs, it was impossible to establish standard input prices that remained valid for extended periods. Therefore, the company reset feedstock standard costs each month to a price that reflected market prices. Chemical and energy standard costs were established annually.

A purchase price variance (were input prices above or below standard prices?) and an efficiency variance (did production require more or less inputs than standard?) were calculated for variable costs each accounting period.

Fixed costs comprised three categories of cost. Direct costs included direct labor, maintenance, chemicals required to keep the plant bubbling, and fixed utilities. Allocated cash costs included plant management, purchasing department costs, engineering, planning, and accounting. Allocated non-cash costs represented primarily depreciation.

Fixed costs were allocated to production based on a plant's *demonstrated capacity* using the following formula,

$$\text{Standard Fixed Cost Per Tonne} = \frac{\text{Estimated Annual Total Fixed Costs}}{\text{Annual Demonstrated Plant Capacity}}$$

To apply the formula, production estimates were established each fall for the upcoming year. Then, the amount of total fixed costs applicable to this level of production was estimated. The amount of total fixed cost to be allocated to each tonne of output was calculated by dividing total fixed cost by the plant's demonstrated capacity. Exhibit 5 reproduces a section of the Controller's Guide that defines demonstrated capacity.

Each accounting period, two variances were calculated for fixed costs. The first was a spending variance calculated as the simple difference between actual total fixed costs and estimated total fixed costs. The second variance was a volume variance calculated using the formula:

$$\text{Volume Variance} = \left(\text{Standard Fixed Cost Per Tonne}\right) \times \left[\left(\text{Actual Tonnes Produced}\right] - \left[\text{Demonstrated Capacity}\right]\right)$$

Product transfers between divisions for performance accounting purposes were made at standard full cost, representing, for each tonne, the sum of standard variable cost and standard fixed cost.

Compensation

Employees at Polysar had in the past been paid by fixed salary with little use of bonuses except at the executive level of the company. In 1984, a bonus system was instituted throughout the company to link pay with performance and strengthen the profit center orientation.

Non-management employees

The bonus system varied by employee group but was developed with the intention of paying salaries that were approximately five percent less than those paid by a reference group of 25 major Canadian manufacturing companies. To augment salaries, annual bonuses were awarded, in amounts up to 12 percent of salary, based on corporate and Divisional performance. Hourly workers could receive annual bonuses in similar proportions based on performance.

All bonuses were based on achieving or exceeding budgeted profit targets. For salaried workers, for example, meeting the 1985 corporate profit objectives would result in a 5 percent bonus; an additional $25 million in profits would provide an additional 4 percent bonus. Meeting and exceeding Division profit targets could provide an additional 3 percent bonus.

Using periodic accounting information, Divisional Vice-Presidents met in quarterly communication meetings with salaried and wage employees to discuss divisional and corporate performance levels.

Management

For managers, the percent of remuneration received through annual bonuses was greater than 12 percent and increased with responsibility levels.

The bonuses of top Division management in 1985 were calculated by a formula that awarded 50 percent of bonus potential to meeting and exceeding Divisional profit targets and 50 percent to meeting or exceeding corporate profit targets.

INTERVIEWS WITH RUBBER GROUP VICE PRESIDENTS[2]

Pierre Choquette

Pierre Choquette, 43, was Vice-President[3] of the NASA Rubber Division. A professional engineer, Choquette had begun his career with Polysar in plant management. Over the years, he had assumed responsibilities for product management in the U.S., managed a small subsidiary, managed a European plant, and directed European sales.

> This business is managed on price and margin. Quality, service, and technology are also important, but it is difficult to differentiate ourselves from other competitors on these dimensions.

[2]Pierre Choquette was interviewed at Harvard Business School in 1985; Doug Henderson was interviewed at Harvard in 1986. Both men were attending the thirteen-week Advanced Management Program that was developed to strengthen the management skills of individuals with potential to become chief executive officers of their companies. In addition to Choquette and Henderson, Polysar had sent Firman Bentley to the program in 1984.

[3]Due to its relatively large size, Rubber Group was the only group with regional vice presidents. Regional responsibilities of the Basic Petrochemicals group and the Diversified Products group were managed by lower-ranking general managers.

When the price of oil took off, this affected our feedstock prices drastically, and Polysar's worldwide business suffered. Now that prices are back down, we are trying to regroup our efforts and bring the business back to long term health. Polysar will break even in 1985 and show a normal profit again in 1986. Of course, the Rubber Division will, as in the past, be the major producer of profit for the company.

As you know, this is a continuous process industry. The plant is computerized so that we need the same number of people and incur most of the same overhead costs whether the plant is running fast or slow.

The regular butyl plant, Sarnia 2, is running at less than capacity. Although the plant should be able to produce 95,000 tonnes, its demonstrated capacity is 85,000. Last year, we produced 65,000. This leaves us sitting with a lot of unabsorbed fixed costs, especially when you consider depreciation charges.

Still, NASA Rubber has been growing nicely. I think that this is in part due to our strong commitment to run the Divisions as profit centers. We have been pushing hard to build both volume and efficiency and I am pleased that our programs and incentives are paying off.

Our transfers to EROW are still a problem. Since the transfers are at standard cost and are not recorded as revenue, these transfers do nothing for our profit. Also, if they cut back on orders, our profit is hurt through the volume variance. Few of our senior managers truly understand the volume variance and why profit results are so different in the two regions. The accounting is not a problem, but having to continuously explain it to very senior-level managers is. It always comes down to the huge asset that we carry whether the plant is at capacity or not.

We run our businesses on return on net assets which looks ridiculous for NASA. I worry that if I am not around to explain it, people will form the wrong conclusion about the health of the business. Also, you sometimes wonder if people ascribe results to factors that are outside your control.

Doug Henderson

Doug Henderson, 46, Vice-President of EROW Rubber Division, was also a professional engineer. His career included management responsibilities in plant operations, market research, venture analysis and corporate planning, running a small regional business in Canada, and Director of European Sales.

The Antwerp plant produces about 45,000 tonnes of halobutyl and 45,000 tonnes of regular butyl each year. In addition, we import approximately 15,000 to 20,000 tonnes of regular butyl from Sarnia each year [Exhibit 6].

We inform Sarnia each fall of our estimated regular butyl needs. These estimates are based on our predictions of butyl and halobutyl sales and how hard we can load our plant. The overall sales estimates are usually within ten percent, say plus or minus 8,000 tonnes, unless an unexpected crisis occurs.

The EROW business has been extremely successful since I arrived here in 1982. We have increased our share in the high growth halobutyl market; the plant is running well; and we have kept the operation simple and compact.

Looking at our Statement of Net Contribution (Exhibit 7), our margins are better than NASA's. For one thing, there is a great surplus of feedstock in Europe and we benefit from lower prices. Also, market dynamics are substantially different.

We pay a lot of attention to plant capacity. For example, we budgeted to produce 250 tonnes per day this year and we have got it up to 275. We are also working hard to reduce our *off-spec* material as a way of pushing up our yield. If we can produce more, it's free—other than variable cost, it goes right to the bottom line.

Given these factors, Pierre loves it when I tell him jokingly that our success at EROW is attributable to superb management.

EXHIBIT 1 Regular Butyl Rubber Statistics and Analyses

	September 1986		
	9 Months ended September 30, 1986		
Volume-Tonnes	*Actual ($000's)*	*Budget ($000's)*	*Deviation ($000's)*
Sales	35.8	33.0	2.8
Production	47.5	55.0	−7.5
Transfers			
to EROW	12.2	19.5	−7.3
from EROW	2.1	1.0	1.1
Production Costs	*($'000's)*	*($'000's)*	*($'000's)*
Fixed Cost—Direct	−21,466	−21,900	434
—Allocated Cash	− 7,036	− 7,125	89
—Allocated Non-Cash	−15,625	−15,600	− 25
Fixed Cost to Production	−44,127	−44,625	498
Transfers to/from FG Inventory	1,120	2,450	−1,330
Transfers to EROW	8,540	13,650	−5,110
Transfers from EROW	− 1,302	− 620	− 682
Fixed Cost of Sales	−35,769	−29,145	−6,624

Note: As indicated on the first page of the case, financial data have been disguised and do not represent the true financial results of the company.

EXHIBIT 2 Regular Butyl Rubber Statement of Net Contribution

September 1986

	9 Months ended September 30, 1986		
	Actual ($000)	*Budget ($000)*	*Deviation ($000)*
Sales Revenue—Third Party	65,872	61,050	4,822
—Diversified Products Group	160	210	− 50
—Total	66,032	61,260	4,722
Delivery Cost	− 2,793	− 2,600	− 193
Net Sales Revenue	63,239	58,660	4,579
Variable Costs			
Standard	−22,589	−21,450	−1,139
Cost Adjustments	54	—	54
Efficiency Variance	241	—	241
Total	−22,294	−21,450	− 844
Gross Margin—$	40,945	37,210	3,735
Fixed Costs			
Standard	−25,060	−23,100	−1,960
Cost Adjustments	168	80	88
Spending Variance	498	—	498
Volume Variance	−11,375	− 6,125	−5,250
Total	−35,769	−29,145	−6,624
Gross Profit—$	5,176	8,065	−2,889
—% of NSR	8.2%	13.7%	− 5.5%
Period Costs			
Administration, Selling, Distribution	− 4,163	− 4,000	− 163
Technical Service	− 222	− 210	− 12
Other Income/Expense	208	50	158
Total	− 4,177	− 4,160	− 17
Business Contribution	999	3,905	−2,906
Interest on Working Capital	− 1,875	− 1,900	25
Net Contribution	− 876	2,005	−2,881

Note: As indicated on the first page of the case, financial data have been disguised and do not represent the true financial results of the company.

EXHIBIT 3 Partial Organization Chart

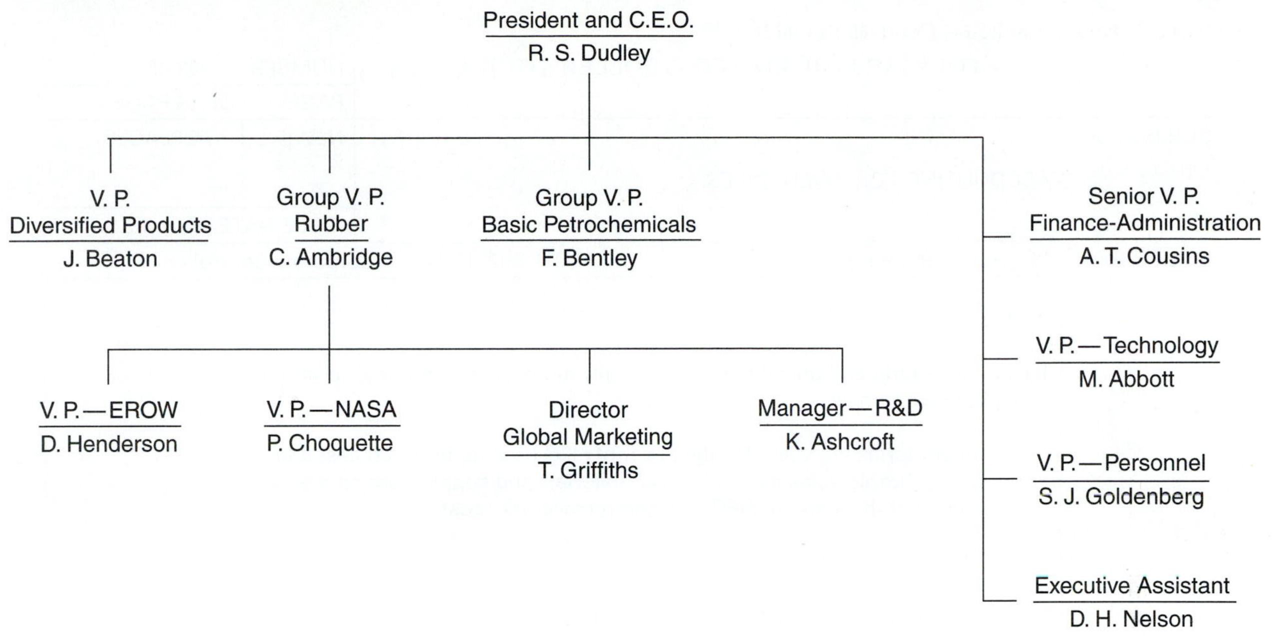

EXHIBIT 4 Rubber Production Process

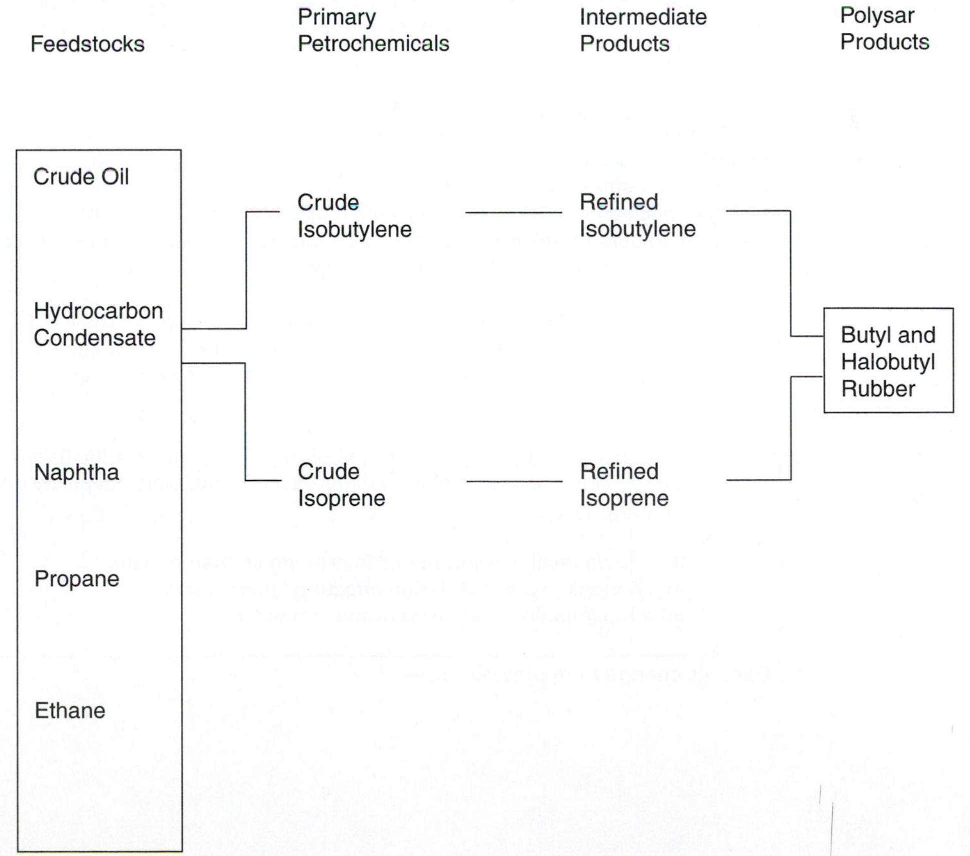

EXHIBIT 5 Polysar Limited—Controller's Guide

POLYSAR LIMITED—CONTROLLER'S GUIDE		NUMBER: 03:02	
		PAGE 1 OF 14 PAGES	
SUBJECT	ACCOUNTING FOR INVENTORIES	NEW: X	REPLACES:
		ISSUE DATE Jan. 1/81	
ISSUED BY: Director Accounting		AUTHORIZED BY: Corporate Controller	

PURPOSE

To set out criteria and guidelines for the application of the Company's accounting policy for inventories:

> "Inventories are valued at the lower of FIFO (first-in, first-out) cost and net realizable value except for raw materials and supplies which are valued at the lower of FIFO cost and replacement cost."

SPECIFIC EXCLUSION

This release does not apply to SWAP transactions.

DEFINITIONS

By-products — one or more products of relatively small per unit market value that emerge from the production process of a product or products of greater value.

Cost system — a system to facilitate the classification, recording, analysis and interpretation of data pertaining to the production and distribution of products and services.

Demonstrated capacity is the actual annualized production of a plant which was required to run full out within the last fiscal year for a sufficiently long period to assess production capability after adjusting for abnormally low or high unscheduled shutdowns, scheduled shutdowns, and unusual or annualized items which impacted either favourably or unfavourably on the period's production. The resulting adjusted historical base should be further modified for changes planned to be implemented within the current fiscal year.

a) Where a plant has not been required to run full out within the last fiscal year, production data may be used for a past period after adjusting for changes (debottleneckings/inefficiencies) since that time affecting production.

b) Where a plant has never been required to run full out, demonstrated capacity could be reasonably considered as "name plate" capacity after adjusting for,

   i) known invalid assumptions in arriving at "name plate"
   ii) changes to original design affecting "name plate"
   iii) a reasonable negative allowance for error.

* Denotes change from previous issue

EXHIBIT 6 Schedule of Regular Butyl Shipments from NASA to EROW

	Actual Tonnes	*Budget Tonnes*
1985	21,710	23,500
1984	12,831	13,700
1983	1,432	4,000
1982	792	600
1981	1,069	700

EXHIBIT 7 Regular Butyl Rubber Condensed Statement of Net Contribution

September 1986

	9 Months Ended September 30, 1986
Sales Volume—Tonnes	*47,850* *($'000's)*
Sales Revenue	94,504
Delivery Cost	− 4,584
Net Sales Revenue	89,920
Variable Cost	
Standard	−28,662
Purchase Price Variance	203
Inventory Revaluation	−46
Efficiency Variance	32
Total	−28,473
Gross Margin—$	61,447
Fixed Cost to Production	
Depreciation	− 4,900
Other	−16,390
	−21,290
Transfers to/from F. G. Inventory	− 775
Transfers to/from NASA	− 7,238
	−29,303
Gross Profit—$	32,144
Period Costs	− 7,560
Business Contribution	24,584
Interest on W/C	− 1,923
Net Contribution	22,661

Notes: 1. Fixed costs are allocated between regular butyl production (above) and halobutyl production (reported separately).

2. As indicated on p. 1 of the case, financial data have been disguised and do not represent the true financial results of the company.

Formosa Plastics Group

For many years, managers at Formosa Plastics Group (FPG) used a management control system with an element that was somewhat unique for a large corporation—all employees were evaluated subjectively. In making their judgments, evaluators looked at objective performance measures but subjectively made many adjustments for factors they deemed to be beyond the employee's control. One effect of this system was that bottom-line profit was not even considered in the evaluations of some profit center managers: These managers were evaluated only in terms of the controllable factors driving profit, such as meeting production schedules, efficiency, cost control, inventory control, and quality.

The FPG system seemed to work; the company had grown and thrived over the years. A sample of FPG managers who were interviewed in November 1991 were virtually unanimous in their praise of the company's control system. For example, Mr. C. T. Lee (senior vice president and general manager of the Plastics Division) said, "We are as close to perfect today as we can be. If we have good ideas, we implement them. We are continually refining our system."

COMPANY HISTORY, ORGANIZATION AND STRATEGY

FPG was a diversified chemical company headquartered in Taipei, Taiwan (R.O.C.). It produced and sold a broad range of products, including high density polyethylene (HDPE), chlorofluorocarbons, finished plastic products (e.g., shopping bags, garbage bags), intermediate raw materials for plastics production (e.g., polyvinyl chloride, caustic soda), carbon fiber, acrylic acids and esters, processed PVC products (e.g., flexible and rigid film, pipes, window frames), processed polyester products (e.g., polyester staple fiber, polyester chips, polyester preoriented yarn), electronic products (e.g., cooper-clad laminate, printed circuit boards), plasticizer, and textile products (e.g., rayon staple fiber, rayon and blended yarn and cloth, nylon tire cord yarn). It also ran a 6000-bed hospital, a medical college (500 students), a nursing school (1,333 students), and a technical college (1,700 students).

Founded in 1954 with a capitalization of NT$5 million, FPG had grown over the years into the largest private company in Taiwan, with over 47,000 employees. Exhibit 1, which presents operating highlights for 1992, shows that 1992 revenues for the total FPG group exceeded US$ 6.7 billion. Mr. Y. C. Wang (FPG's current chairman) still owned a significant portion of FPG's stock.

FPG management was projecting relatively difficult times in the early 1990s because of "the shortage of quality labor, rising wages, and the radicalization of the environmental movement." But the company had earned a profit for 30 consecutive years, even through some difficult periods, such as the 1973 oil embargo which had a major negative effect on FPG and other petrochemical producers.

FPG was organized into three main corporations—Formosa Plastics, Nan Ya Plastics, and Formosa Chemicals & Fibre Corp.—and more than a dozen other affiliated companies located in Taiwan and abroad (notably the U.S.). The major corporations were composed of multiple divisions (see Exhibit 2), each responsible for one product line. The divisions, which were organized functionally, were reasonably autonomous; their managers were able to make their own plans and arrange all production and marketing aspects of their business within the scope of their approved authorizations. The division managers, who ranged in age from 40–60 years, were invariably career FPG employees (as were most other employees).

Many administrative functions, including engineering and construction management, technol-

Professor Kenneth A. Merchant wrote this case with the assistance of Professor Anne Wu (National Chengchi University, Taiwan R.O.C.) as a basis for class discussion rather than to illustrate either effective or ineffective handling of an administrative situation.

ogy (research and development), accounting, finance, procurement, data processing, legal, public relations, and personnel were centralized to take advantage of economies of scale. A unique feature of the corporate organization was a large (340-person) *president's office* comprising 15 *teams* of specialists whose function was to help division management. The president's office form of organization began when the corporation was small. The central staff personnel set up procedures, trained management, monitored performance, and facilitated the spreading of effective practices from one division to others. At times, some of the central staff/division dealings had been confrontational; some division managers had referred to the staffs as *the Red Guard.* But more recently, with increased management professionalization, the staff teams placed greater emphasis on cooperating with division management. They still ensured that the division's operating systems (e.g., accounting, procurement, construction, warehousing) conformed to corporate standards. But they allowed the divisions to operate with production systems that were different in virtually every plant, and they left division management alone if no significant negative performance variances existed.

Most of FPG's chemical divisions sold commodity products, so their strategy was to be the low cost producer in their market segment(s). It was important for them to produce at full capacity because most production costs were fixed; the only significant variable costs were for raw material and selling. On average, labor costs were only 20 percent of the total production cost, but since Taiwanese labor costs were rising along with the country's higher standard of living, FPG managers were constantly looking for ways to automate production processes to improve productivity. More than 80 percent of their products were exported.

FPG was making sizable investments to improve existing products, product quality, and production efficiency, and to prevent pollution. It was also increasing its investments to develop new products. Over the years, FPG had developed some new, lower volume, but higher value-added, products (e.g., carbon fiber), but these products still accounted for a very small proportion of total company sales. FPG employed 600 people in its central technology department, and its expenditures for new product development accounted for 3.6 percent of its total sales.

FINANCIAL CONTROL SYSTEM

Within FPG, companies and divisions were measured on a return-on-investment (ROI) basis. The profit element of the ROI measure (the numerator) included allocations of all corporate expenses including interest, but profit was measured before taxes. The investment element of the ROI measure (the denominator) included only the investments that could be traced to the divisions (e.g., equipment, buildings, inventory, working capital). No corporate assets were allocated to the divisions. Within the divisions, plants and product groups were considered as profit centers; distinct production processes and group of machines were cost centers; and nonproduction-oriented units (e.g., sales, technology, management) were expense centers.

A key element of FPG's financial control system was a detailed cost accounting and reporting system. Standard costs were set for every aspect of manufacturing (e.g., labor, raw material, steam, packing, waste). The manufacturing processes tended to be stable, so the company had extensive historical records, and the cost standards were highly refined and accurate. Indirect costs were allocated to entities and products using a variety of allocation bases (e.g., number of people, production quantity). Where necessary, transfer prices for products sold internally were set either at market price less costs not incurred on internal transfers (e.g., selling costs, duties), or at full standard cost (less costs not incurred) plus a markup.

The cost standards were revised promptly when conditions warranted, and they were used to motivate continuous improvement. For example, if an investment project aimed at improving productivity was scheduled to be completed in July, the cost standards were changed in July. If the project was delayed or improvement was not as expected, the problem would show on an irregularities (variance) report. The company produced an extensive set of performance reports on a monthly basis (see Exhibit 3). These reports allowed management to attack problems quickly.

FPG's president monitored performance closely. Each month, he met with 30 senior managers (including division managers) in a detailed performance review meeting that typically lasted

2–3 hours. Every business was discussed at this meeting, and the president asked questions about sales, the competitive situation, future trends, and future products. About this meeting, one division manager said, "The president learns the details of our businesses. Sometimes we get new ideas from one or more of the managers at the meeting. Sometimes we get yelled at."

Performance-related bonus plans were also an important part of FPG's control system. All personnel in the company were included in one or more plans, and the plans were structured the same in all countries in which FPG operated. These were the major plans being used:

1. Year-end bonuses were given to everybody in the corporation based on the performance of the corporation. These bonuses were usually in the range of 3–5 months of base salary; the recent average was 4.2 months. About this plan, one corporate manager said, "This form of payment is typical in the Chinese culture. It is used by all companies in Taiwan. Most give a bonus of 1 or 2 months of *total compensation,* which is roughly equivalent to what we do, although we base the payments on *base salary.*"
2. All people under section chief level (one level below a functional manager in a division) were included in a performance bonus program. Under this program, their bonus was calculated based both on their position and the percentage of their performance targets reached. Staff and personnel in service departments were given either the same amount of bonus as those in direct departments or the average amount of bonuses given to direct departments. The purpose of this bonus program was to increase employee morale and efficiency. The bonuses awarded averaged approximately 20 to 26 percent of the employees' salaries.
3. All employees at section chief level and above were evaluated annually. A portion of these employees' salaries were reserved to create Management's Special Bonus Fund which was used to award a special bonus immediately after the close of the year. The special bonus was calculated based both on the individual's performance and on the performance of the employee's corporation. Different bonus potentials were set for different levels of management, such as section chief, plant manager, and division manager.
4. FPG also provided incentive awards for employees, such as R&D staff, who generated good ideas that increased company value.

In all cases, top management decided subjectively the sizes of the awards and the bases on which to give the awards. The factors considered in making the performance evaluations and their relative weightings varied across roles and divisions. Among the performance-related factors considered in evaluating division managers were profit as compared to plan, production efficiency, quality, new product development, production quantity, production cost, and safety and environmental factors. Evaluators often also considered the person's ability and potential for the future, years in the company, teamwork, cooperation, and the situation faced. The evaluations were done subjectively because, as one manager explained, "Some factors are not easy to evaluate because it's hard to separate the controllable factors from the uncontrollable. It's certainly not easy to put all these items in a formula."

The total bonus amounts paid did not vary much over time. A corporate manager explained that:

> These (total) amounts are put in the budget at a fixed number and are not varied by the actual profit for the year. If the corporation earns a big profit, corporate managers take a portion of the bonus and reserve it for another year. If this year is no good and next year is no good, then maybe we will consider a lower bonus. It makes the situation more steady.

PERFORMANCE STANDARDS AND EVALUATIONS

One-year profit, revenue, and cost targets were set during a bottom-up planning process that started in September and ended in December.[1] The process began with division-level functional managers producing a sales plan and then a production plan. Labor cost parameters were sent to the divisions from corporate, and division managers were involved early in the planning process to make some key planning assumptions (e.g., selling price, key raw material costs). Generally every section in every plant was expected to reduce its costs every year (continuous improvement), which was not unreasonable because each was

[1]FPG managers did not use the word budget because "That is a term used by the government. It gives the impression that you will have less budget each year."

supported with improvement-project monies. The functional plans were reviewed and approved by division managers, the corporate accounting department, and corporate management.

Corporate managers wanted the division targets to have an 80 to 90 percent probability of achievement. The divisions' first plan submission was rarely accepted because, as one corporate manager expressed it, "While the division managers understand their businesses better than does top management, they have a tendency to be very conservative about the figures." Thus in the review process, top management generally asked the division managers to raise their profit targets. (Sometimes, however, typically in recessionary periods, they asked for the targets to be lowered.) Often the division managers had to revise their plans several times before top management approved them. However, even at the end of the discussions, the division managers did not always share corporate managers' perceptions of target achievability; for example, in 1991 one manager said he believed his chances of achieving his profit target were only 30 to 40 percent; he said, "The president squeezed very hard this year."

At the corporate level, the annual plans had proved to be quite accurate, with usually less than a 3 percent deviation between budgeted and actual expenses. If necessary, the performance targets could be revised during the year, monthly at the plant level and semiannually at division level.

Annually, the corporate accounting department performed a detailed analysis of each division's performance to understand where the profit came from and to know if the profit produced was reasonable given the circumstances faced. Among the items normally factored out as uncontrollable:

- prices of products sold (in commodity product divisions only). In some divisions, the market price was treated as controllable because the division managers set their products' prices.
- raw material prices;
- effects of raw material (e.g., oil, power) supply problems;
- major problems deemed to be outside the manager's control (e.g., a fire caused by lightning);
- expenditures approved by top management after the plan was finalized. A corporate manager explained, "If it's approved, we don't care about the financial problems it causes to the budget. We want to encourage new ideas."

Because selling prices and raw material prices were considered uncontrollable in commodity product divisions, managers of these divisions were evaluated basically on quantity of product sold, product quality, consumption of materials, and production efficiency. This is well illustrated by describing the situation in 1991 in the Polyolefin Division.

1991 AT THE POLYOLEFIN DIVISION

The Polyolefin Division produced polyethylene, a commodity petrochemical used in a broad range of products, including plastic packing materials (e.g., shopping bags, bottles), rope and fishing nets, and toys and athletic equipment. Because Taiwan's polyethylene import duty of 2.5 percent was the lowest in the world, the division had to compete, primarily on the basis of price, with competitors from all over the world and especially Korea. Division sales were not growing because the high density polyethylene output of the division was limited due to a shortage of ethylene supply from CPC, the only local ethylene supplier.

Ethylene was the only raw material used in polyethylene production, and it was *the* major cost item for the division, accounting for 60 to 65 percent of the total production cost. (Direct labor accounted for less than 3 percent of total production cost.) There was only one local ethylene supplier, CPC, a government corporation, and importing was difficult and expensive because ethylene had to be stored at high pressure and at $-104°C$. Freight for importing ethylene to Taiwan was approximately US$60–80 per ton from Japan or Korea, and approximately US$120 per ton from the U.S. The Taiwanese government set ethylene prices at the average of the U.S. and European prices. In 1991, FPG was paying ethylene prices that averaged 4 to 5 percent higher than U.S. prices.

Ethylene caused the Polyolefin Division supply problems because a severe shortage existed in Taiwan. FPG had been trying for many years to secure permission to build its own ethylene plant, but the government had not given the permission because of worries about overcapacity. CPC (the government firm) was permitted to build another ethylene plant, but construction had been delayed because of environmental concerns, and FPG managers knew that a supply shortage would still exist even when this plant was completed.

Ethylene also caused financial planning problems because the Taiwanese ethylene prices fluctuated significantly, as is shown in Exhibits 4 and 5. Furthermore, the ethylene and polyethylene prices did not fluctuate together; both prices varied with market supply conditions. Lags of varying lengths existed before changes in ethylene prices were reflected in polyethylene prices. Thus division profits also fluctuated significantly.

Mr. Hsiao Chi-Hsiung, the division general manager, described his thinking in setting the plan for 1991:

> The Gulf War had just started when we began to prepare our plan, and we knew that would have a major effect on our business because ethylene is a petrochemical. We had to assess how long the war would last and what it would do to our selling prices and our ethylene costs. We thought the Gulf War would not last very long, so we forecast that the average ethylene price would be around US$500 for the year. We concluded that our customers would worry about supply, so we forecast a higher selling price in January and then assumed a decrease. Starting this year, material from our Korean competitor should be very competitive.
>
> I did the work to forecast our selling prices and ethylene costs. We had to revise our production and sales plan several times according to the current market situation before we reported it to our top management for approval.

Mr. Hsiao knew, however, that he would also be evaluated in terms of each of the items on a list of controllable factors, not solely on achievement of the profit plan. He recalled that, "Sometimes we earn a nice profit, but it's not only from our endeavor. It's mainly influenced by the market prices." Mr. Hsiao could not explain exactly the bases on which his performance rating would be based, but he guessed they would be similar to the controllable factor list which he used to evaluate his plant manager:

- production efficiency (output/input);
- quality (proportion of output meeting customer specifications);
- unit consumption of important elements of cost (e.g., ethylene, solvents, labor[2]);
- cost of maintenance;
- leadership (including union relations, responses to employee suggestions, management of the monthly plant employee meeting, maintenance of hard work).

When pressed as to how these factors were weighted in relative importance, Mr. Hsiao said the first factor would be weighted about 40 percent, the second about 30 percent, and the other three about 30 percent in total. But he emphasized, "The weightings are not made very clear to anybody." It was clear to Mr. Hsiao, however, that achievement of his division's profit plan was certainly not the only factor on which he was evaluated.

[2]Labor was considered to be almost fixed in the short-run, so controlling labor costs primarily meant controlling overtime.

EXHIBIT 1 1992 Operating Highlights

1992 Operating Highlights

Unit: US$ 1,000

Company	Capital	Total Assets	Operating Revenue	Net Income Before Tax	Profit Ratio(%)	Return on Capital(%)	Number of Employees
Formosa Plastics Corp.	623,932	1,377,876	1,219,993	154,396	12.66	24.75	3,979
Nan Ya Plastics Corp.	701,437	1,931,335	2,512,532	229,114	9.12	32.66	14,803
Formosa Chemicals & Fibre Corp.	776,459	1,855,087	1,025,227	202,029	19.71	26.02	7,446
Others	1,914,697	6,207,220	1,955,440	163,265	8.35	8.53	21,093
Total	4,016,525	11,371,518	6,713,192	748,804	11.15	18.64	47,321

The Operating Revenue Comparison

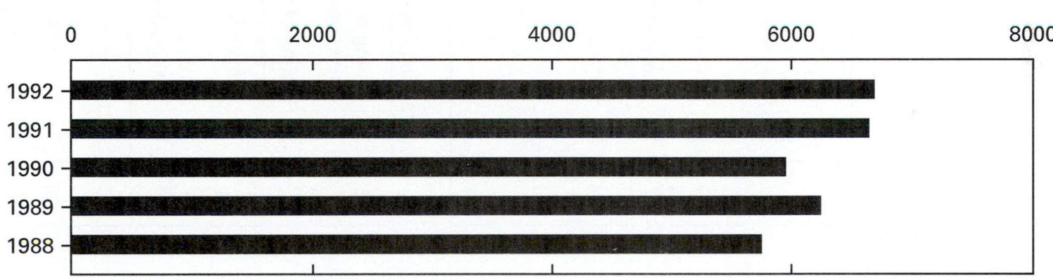

EXHIBIT 2 Formosa Plastics Group Organizational Chart—1991

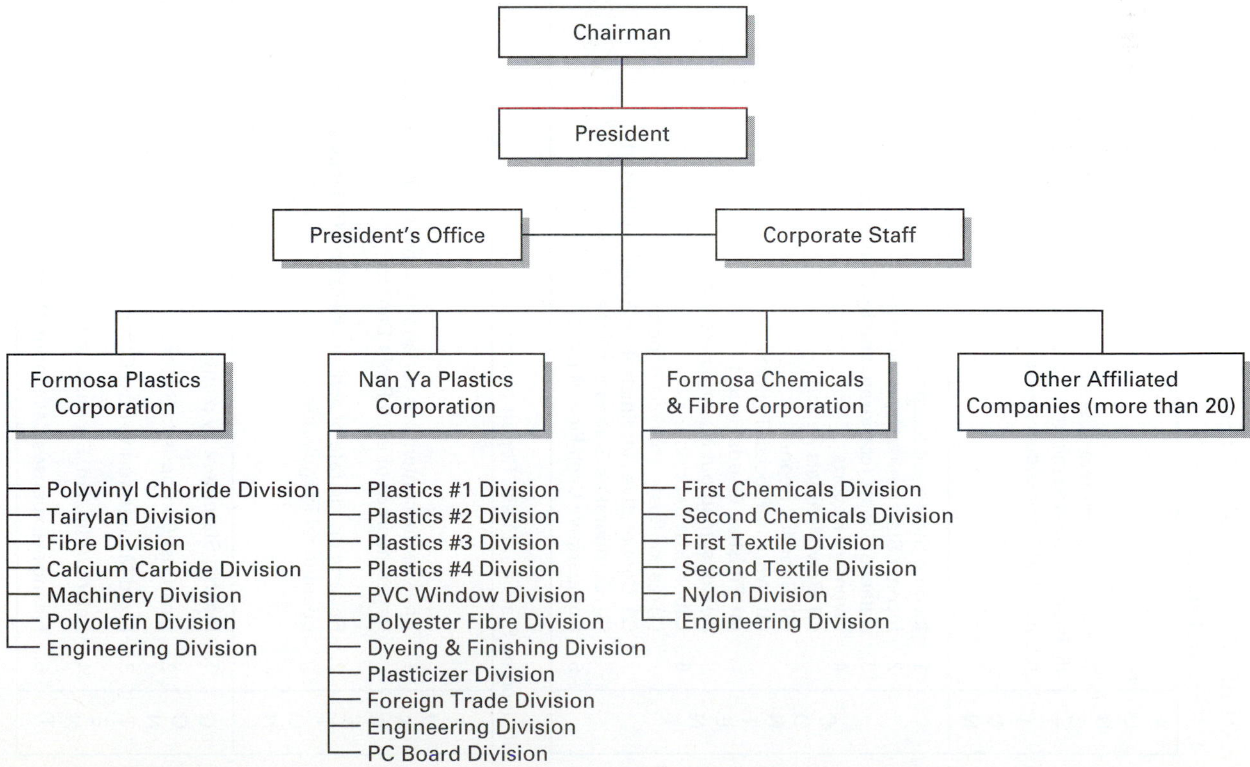

EXHIBIT 3 Operational Performance Reports

I. Financial Reports

FUNCTION	To show the complete operational conditions of a company and its divisions, including income statements, balance sheets, inventory reports, and labor costs reports.
CONTENT	1. Income Statement (corporate) 2. Income Statements (by divisions) 3. Balance Sheets (corporate and by divisions) 4. Inventory Reports (1) Raw Materials Report (2) Supplies Report (3) Work-in-Process Report (4) Finished Goods Report (5) Consigned-out Materials Report 5. Labor Cost Reports (1) Labor Costs Analysis Report (2) Cooperative Administrative Expenses Report (3) Comparative Selling Expenses Report 6. Comparative Cash Flow Report

II. Income Statement/Cash Report by Plants

FUNCTION	1. Analyze the contents of variations between the actual and target incomes of each Profit Center. 2. Reports on the rate of achievement on efficiency and on the operational irregularities.
CONTENT	1. Income Statement by plants 2. Unit Cost Comparison Report 3. Fixed Manufacturing Cost Comparison Report 4. Selling/Adm./Fin. Expenses Allocation Report 5. Financial Expenses Calculation Report

III. Income Statements and Efficiency Variation Reports by Plant

FUNCTION	1. Analyze the contents of variations between the actual and target incomes of each Profit Center. 2. Reports on the rate of achievement on efficiency and on the operational irregularities.
CONTENT	1. Sum-up reports on income variations. 2. Analytical Reports on income variations. 3. Sum-up reports on efficiency evaluation of plants.

IV. Irregularities Report

FUNCTION	1. Listing of the efficiency items which have been achieved for three consecutive months for revision of targets. 2. Listing of the efficiency items which exceed the control standards for the analysts of the President's Office and Divisional Manager's Offices to investigate and follow up. 3. Listing of the cost items which exceed the control standards for the departments concerned to investigate and improve.
CONTENT	1. Efficiency Achievement Report 2. Efficiency Loss Report 3. Cost Variations Report

EXHIBIT 4 Sampling of Ethylene Prices in Taiwan

Year	*Month*	*Price per ton ($US)*
1990	November	781[1]
	July	494
	January	501
1989	July	678
	January	701
1988	July	612
	January	436

[1]Gulf War started.

EXHIBIT 5 1991 Ethylene Prices in Taiwan

Month	*Price per ton (US$)*
January	695
February	658
March	589
April	508
May	462
June	443
July	415
August	422
September	427
October	462

CHAPTER 15

The Transfer Pricing Problem

Profit (or investment) centers often supply products or services to other profit or investment centers within the same corporation. When that happens, some mechanism for determining the prices of the transfers must be established.[1] These *transfer prices* directly affect the revenues of the producing profit center, the costs of the buying profit center and, consequently, the profits of both entities. The impact of these transfer prices depends largely on the amount of internal transfers relative to the size of each entity. When the amount of transfers is significant, failure to set the right transfer prices can have significant negative effects on a number of important decisions; including those regarding production quantities, sourcing, resource allocations, and evaluations of the managers of both the selling and buying profit centers.

PURPOSES OF TRANSFER PRICING

Transfer pricing can cause complex organizational problems. Transfer prices may have up to three organizational purposes, depending on the situation, and these purposes usually conflict.

The first purpose of transfer prices is to provide the proper economic signals so that the managers affected will make good economic decisions. In particular, the prices should properly influence both the selling profit center managers' decisions about how much product to supply and the buying profit center managers' decisions about how much product to buy.

Second, the transfer prices and subsequent profit measurements should provide information that is useful for evaluating the performances of both the profit centers and their managers. Transfer prices directly affect the profits and returns of both the selling and buying entities. Ideally, the transfer prices should not cause the performance of either entity to appear either better or worse than what actually occurred. Misleading profitability signals can adversely affect allocations of resources within the firm. They can also severely undercut profit center managers' motivations because the managers will rightly feel they are not being treated fairly.

Third, transfer prices can be set to purposely move profits between company entities or locations. Several factors can motivate managers to use transfer prices in this way. When corporations are operating in multiple tax jurisdictions (countries or states), their managers might be motivated to use transfer prices to move profits between jurisdictions to minimize taxes. Corporate income tax rates differ significantly across countries and states, and managers can set transfer prices to earn profits in relatively low-tax localities to maximize the company's after-tax worldwide profits. Managers may also be motivated by *ad valorem* import duties to under-price some intracompany transactions.

Profit repatriation limitations provide a motivation for using transfer prices to move profits between company entities. For a number of reasons, including balance of payments problems and a scarcity of foreign currency reserves, many governments prohibit repatriation of profits, either directly or indirectly. Indirect forms of restrictions include the maintenance of distorted exchange rates, high withholding tax rates, or barter trade agreements. When managers are unable to repatriate foreign profits earned, they are motivated to set transfer prices to minimize profits in those countries.

Some managers are motivated to set transfer prices so that profits are earned in wholly owned subsidiaries, rather than those in which the returns are shared with other owners of joint venture partners. Managers may also be motivated to set transfer prices to move profits to an entity which is being positioned for divestment in hopes of increasing the selling price.

This chapter is titled *The Transfer Pricing Problem* because these three transfer pricing purposes often conflict. Except in rare circumstances, managers are forced to make trade-offs because no single transfer pricing method serves all the purposes well. Almost inevitably, transfer pricing causes managers problems.

The usual desire to have transfer pricing mechanisms operate automatically, without frequent interventions from higher-level management, provides another transfer pricing complication. Transfer-pricing interventions undermine the benefits of decentralization. They reduce profit center autonomy and cause decision making complexity and delay. They also increase organizational costs, particularly in terms of the management time to review the facts of the situation. Organizations seek to set transfer pricing policies that work without producing any, or at least few, exceptions and disputes.

TRANSFER PRICING ALTERNATIVES

Most corporations use any of five primary types of transfer prices. First, transfer prices can be based on *market prices.* The market price used for internal transfers may be the listed price of an identical (or similar) product or service, the actual price the selling division charges external customers (perhaps less a discount which reflects lower selling costs for internal customers), or the price a competitor is offering. Second, transfer prices can be based on *marginal costs,* with marginal costs approximated as the variable or direct cost of production. Third, transfer prices can be based on the *full costs* of providing the product or service. Both marginal and full cost-based transfer prices can reflect either standard or actual costs. Fourth, transfer prices can be set at *full cost plus a markup* over cost. Fifth, transfer prices can be *negotiated* between the managers of the selling and buying profit centers. Information about market prices and either marginal or full production costs often provide input into these negotiations, but there is no requirement that they do so.

Tables 15-1 and 15-2 shows the results of two large-scale surveys of the primary[2] transfer pricing practices used in large U.S. corporations.[3] (Other surveys suggest that transfer pricing methods do not vary significantly across countries.[4])

TABLE 15-1 Vancil (1979) Survey of Transfer Price Practices in Large U.S. Corporations

Number of Companies Participating		291
Percentage Using Transfer Prices		85%
PERCENTAGE USING TRANSFERS ON FOLLOWING BASES		
Market Price		31.0
Competitor's Price	11.7	
List Price	17.2	
Most Recent Bid	2.1	
Variable or Direct Cost		4.6
Standard	2.9	
Actual	1.7	
Full Cost		25.5
Standard	12.5	
Actual	13.0	
Full Cost Plus		16.7
A Return on Sales	2.9	
A Return on Investment	2.9	
A Markup	10.9	
Negotiated		22.2
TOTAL		100.00

Source: R. F. Vancil, *Decentralization: Managerial Ambiguity by Design* (New York: Dow Jones-Irwin, 1979).

These data show that transfer prices are used by a vast majority (nearly 90 percent) of the firms surveyed. A small minority (less than 5 percent) of firms transfer at marginal cost. Significant proportions of firms use each of the other methods. The largest proportions transfer goods or services at either market prices or variations of full costs or full costs plus a markup.

The range of transfer pricing practices is high because situations differ and because managers make different trade-offs among the transfer pricing purposes. The objective of the transfer pricing system is one important consideration. One survey of transfer pricing practices which reported results similar to those reported in Tables 15-1 and 15-2 asked respondents to name the dominant objective of their transfer pricing system. Almost half said it was performance evaluation, and just over a third said it was decision making for profit maximization of the consolidated firm.[5]

Research theory and evidence about other factors that do and should lead companies to choose one transfer pricing method over another is not yet unequivocal. One researcher surveyed the literature, identified thirteen potentially relevant environmental and organizational variables, and in a large sample study used them to try to predict transfer pricing methods.[6] The results were weak. The most significant variable was firm size: Larger firms were more likely to use market, and then negotiated, rather than cost-based transfer pricing methods.

Enough theory and evidence does exist, however, to suggest that in given situations, each of the five primary methods has its merits, as do combinations of the methods. The following sections describe when each of the transfer pricing methods is appropriate.

TABLE 15-2 Borkowski (1990) Survey of Transfer Price Practices in Large U.S. Corporations

Number of Companies Participating		215
Percentage Using Transfer Prices		89.6%
PERCENTAGE USING TRANSFERS ON FOLLOWING BASES		
Market Price		32.7
Full Market Price	20.2	
Adjusted Market Price	12.5	
Negotiated		22.6
To External Price	13.6	
To Manufacturing Costs	3.0	
With No Restrictions	6.0	
Full Cost		41.1
Standard	14.3	
Actual	7.1	
Plus Profit Based on Cost	14.9	
Plus Fixed Profit	2.4	
Other	2.4	
Variable Cost		3.6
Standard	2.4	
Actual	0.6	
Plus Contribution Based on Cost	0.6	
Plus Fixed Contribution	0.0	
Plus Opportunity Cost	0.0	
Marginal (Incremental) Cost		0.0
Mathematical/Programming Models		0.0
Dual Pricing		0.0
TOTAL		100.00

Source: S. C. Borkowski, "Environmental and Organizational Factors Affecting Transfer Pricing: A Survey." *Journal of Management Accounting* Research 2 (Fall 1990), p. 87.

MARKET-BASED TRANSFER PRICES

In the relatively rare situation where a perfectly competitive external market exists for the internally traded good or service, it is optimal for both decision making and performance evaluation purposes to set transfer prices at the competitive market prices. A perfectly competitive market exists where the product is homogenous and no individual buyer or seller can unilaterally affect the market prices.

The case for using market-based transfer prices in perfectly competitive markets is straightforward. If transfer prices are set at competitive market prices, managers of both the selling and buying decisions will make decisions which are optimal from the corporation's perspective, and reports of their performances will provide good information for evaluation purposes. If the selling profit center cannot earn fair profits by selling at the external market price, then the corporation is better off shutting that profit center and buying from an outside supplier. Similarly, if the buying profit center cannot earn fair profits by buying at the external market price, then the corporation should shut that profit center and have its selling profit center sell all its output to outsiders.

Situations where perfectly competitive market prices provide the optimal transfer pricing policy are rare. Few products and services are sold in perfectly competitive markets. In any case, if perfectly competitive market prices dictated optimal decision making and performance evaluations, there would be little economic reason to have the entity within the corporate structure. No synergies would be produced except, perhaps, a reliable source of supply.

Many firms use market-based transfer prices where competition is not perfect by allowing deviations from the observed market prices. The deviations allow for adjustments that reflect differences between internal and external sales. These differences can reflect the savings of marketing, selling, and collecting costs; the costs of special terms (for example, warranties) offered only to external customers; or the value of special features, special services provided, or differences in quality standards. Adjustments in market prices may reflect the belief that the price quoted by an external supplier is not a sustainable long-term price. The price quoted might just be a low-ball bid designed merely to get the first order. The greater the number and size of these adjustments, however, the more the market-based transfer prices are like cost-based prices and the more difficult the transfer pricing trade-offs become.

MARGINAL-COST TRANSFER PRICES

The great strength of marginal-cost transfer prices is that in situations where external markets for the product or service being transferred are not perfectly competitive, they motivate both the selling and buying profit center managers to reach a transfer-volume decision that maximizes corporate profits regardless of whether the selling profit center has excess capacity.

The ideal goal congruence produced by this transfer pricing method can be illustrated in classical economic terms.[7] Figure 15-1 shows marginal cost and rev-

FIGURE 15-1 The Case for Marginal Cost Transfer Prices

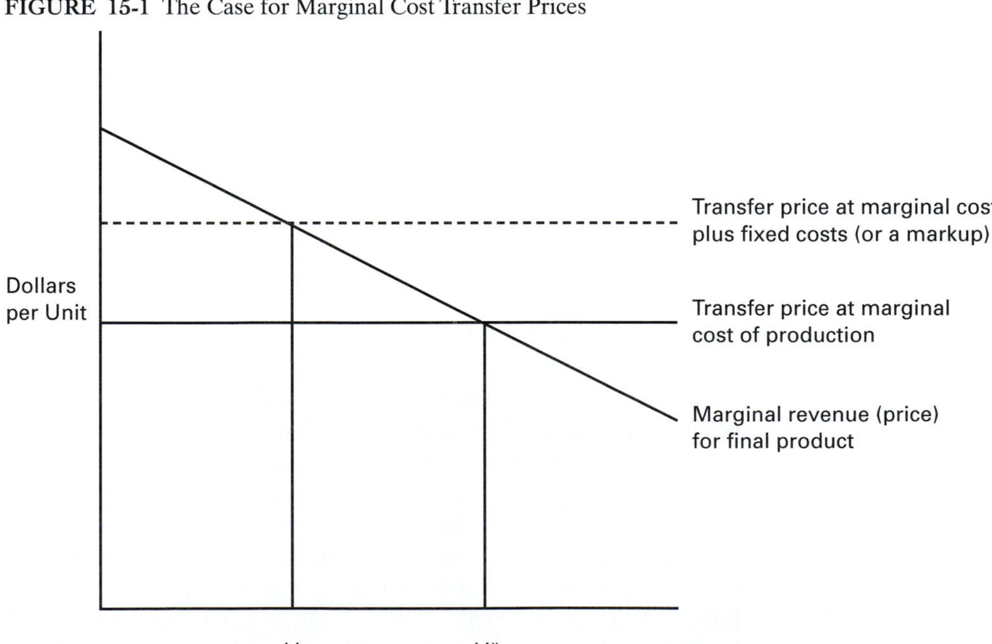

enue curves for the product or service being transferred from the perspective of the entire corporation. As is characteristic of imperfectly competitive markets, the marginal revenue curve is shown to be falling; to sell more, the price must be lowered. The graphs are drawn with two simplifications that do not greatly limit the generality of the argument: The marginal cost is shown to be constant over the relevant range, and the buying profit center is assumed merely to buy the product from the producing profit center and transfer it to the customer without incurring additional costs. The buying profit center (the one that deals directly with external customers) will buy products up to the point where marginal revenue equals marginal costs. It will buy the optimal volume from the company's perspective (V^*) only if the transfer price is set at marginal cost of producing the good or service. If the transfer price includes a premium over marginal costs (the dotted line), perhaps a share of fixed costs or a markup, then a lesser, suboptimal volume (V_1) will be ordered.

The survey data shown in Tables 15-1 and 15-2 reveal, however, that less than 5 percent of companies use marginal cost transfers, as approximated by variable or direct costs. The rarity of use of this method is primarily due to the fact that marginal cost transfers provide poor information for evaluating the economic performance of either the selling or buying profit centers or managers. The selling profit center will typically have to record losses because it bears the full cost of production while receiving in revenue only the marginal costs. Conversely, the profits of the buying profit center will be overstated because it does not have to pay for even the full cost of the transferred production.

Marginal cost transfer prices are also sometimes difficult to implement. Relatively few companies can measure marginal costs accurately. Direct costs (direct material and direct labor) are not the problem; indirect costs are. Companies that use marginal cost transfer pricing usually define marginal costs as standard variable costs, but there is no clean break between variable and fixed indirect costs. The conditions over which the costs are fixed or variable must be specified. If marginal costs are defined to mean short-run variable costs, then they are calculated as direct costs plus variable indirect costs. If marginal costs are defined to mean long-run variable costs, then they are calculated as the full incremental costs of production.

Another problem is that marginal costs are not always constant over the range of output. Sharp increases in incremental costs may occur if the selling profit center is operating near a capacity constraint.

A final problem is that marginal cost transfer prices can be distorted because the managers of the selling profit centers have an incentive to overstate their variable costs to increase their revenues. Unless a complaint is voiced (usually by a buying division) and a potentially costly investigation is launched, these distortions will not be found.

FULL-COST TRANSFER PRICES

Tables 15-1 and 15-2 show that transfers at full cost or full cost plus a markup are popular; they are used by over 40 percent of the firms who responded to these surveys. Full-cost transfer prices offer several advantages. First, they provide a measure of long-run marginal cost. If product line decisions are long-run, meaning that the firm will offer the product even in high-cost periods, then managers' product-related decisions should be based on long-run, not short-run, marginal cost. Second, full-cost transfers are relatively easy to implement because every firm has systems to calculate the full costs of production. Finally, full-cost transfers are not as distorting for evaluation purposes since the selling profit center is allowed to recover the full cost of production.

Full-cost transfer prices are not a panacea, however. The full costs rarely reflect the actual, current costs of producing the products being transferred. Standard financial accounting conventions (for example, historical depreciation and failure to recognize the cost of equity capital) cause some of the distortions. Others are caused by poor cost accounting systems which involve arbitrary allocations of shared overhead costs. In addition, full-cost transfer prices do not provide an incentive for the selling profit center to transfer internally since they include no profit margin. If internal transfers are a significant part of the selling profit center's business, they understate that entity's profit.

FULL-COST-PLUS-A-MARKUP TRANSFER PRICES

Transfers at full costs plus a markup do allow the selling profit centers to earn a profit on internally transferred products and services. They also provide a crude approximation of market price that can be used in situations where no competitive external market price exists, although such transfer prices are not responsive to changes in market conditions. Because they include a premium over marginal cost, they will cause the quantity of transfers from selling to buying profit centers to be less than is optimal from the company's standpoint if the entity managers are allowed the discretion to make decisions about the quantity to be transferred.

NEGOTIATED TRANSFER PRICES

Another popular transfer pricing alternative, used by 22 percent of the firms responding to the survey (see Table 15-1), is to allow the selling and buying profit center managers to negotiate between themselves. This policy can be effective if both profit centers have some bargaining power; that is, the selling profit center has some possibilities to sell its product outside the company and the buying profit center has some outside sources of supply.

Negotiated transfer prices can cause any of several problems. First, negotiation of the prices of a potentially large number of transactions is costly because it can require considerable management time. Second, negotiation often accentuates conflicts between profit center managers. The conflicts can cause wasted time and morale problems, and resolution of the conflicts often requires mediation from top management. Third, the outcome often depends on the negotiating skills and bargaining power of the managers involved, and the final outcome may not be close to being economically optimal. If one of the entities has reasonably good outside selling or sourcing possibilities, but the other does not, the bargaining power will be unequal. The unequal bargaining power will be magnified if the transaction is a relatively small proportion of the business of one of the entities and a relatively large proportion of the business of the other. The managers of the small-proportion entity will have considerable bargaining power because they can walk away from the transaction without bearing serious consequences. Also, managers' egos can sometimes lead them to try to gain an upper hand in the negotiations over peers with whom they compete for recognition awards, bonuses, and promotions, even at the expense of the corporation's best interest.

OTHER VARIATIONS

Researchers have proposed several variations of one or more of the primary transfer pricing methods. All of these variations have some merit, so they are worth mentioning; although their actual usage appears to be rare. One possibility is to transfer at *marginal costs plus a fixed lump-sum fee.* The lump-sum fee is designed to compensate the selling profit center for tying up some of its fixed capacity for producing products that are transferred internally. This method has some obvious appeal. It preserves goal congruence because additional unit transfers are made at marginal cost. It preserves information for evaluation purposes because the selling division can recover its fixed costs and a profit margin through the lump-sum fee. It also stimulates planning and intrafirm communications because the selling and buying entities must discuss the bases for the lump-sum fee.

The major problem with this marginal cost plus lump-sum method is that the managers involved must predetermine the lump-sum fee based on an estimate of the capacity (for example, 10 percent) that each internal customer will use in the forthcoming period. If these estimates are incorrect, then the charges will not be accurate, and the capacity will not be assigned to the most profitable uses. If the selling entity changes all the lump-sum charges after the fact to reflect each customer's actual use of capacity, then the result will be nearly identical to transferring at the full cost of production.

Dual-rate transfer prices are another variation.[8] In this variation, the selling profit center is credited with the market price (or an approximation of it), but the buying profit center pays only the marginal costs of production (plus the opportunity costs of foregoing outside sales, if any). This scheme double counts the profits the corporation earns on each transaction. The accounting entries are balanced by putting the difference in a holding account at a higher (corporate or group) organization level, which is eliminated at the time of financial statement consolidation.

Dual-rate transfer prices have two basic advantages. First, the managers of both the selling and buying profit centers receive the proper economic signals for their decision making. The seller receives the market price and is motivated to transfer product internally. The buyer pays the marginal cost (plus opportunity cost) and is motivated to buy the amount of product that is optimal from the corporation's overall perspective. Second, the dual-rate transfer pricing method almost ensures that internal transactions will take place, making it possible to maintain a more highly vertically integrated production process.

Dual-rate transfer prices are not in common use for several reasons. First, dual-rate transfer pricing can destroy the internal entities' incentives. Because the buying profit centers pay only marginal costs, they have little incentive to negotiate with outside suppliers for more favorable prices. The selling profit centers find it easy to generate internal sales because the transfer pricing policy shields them from competition and gives them little incentive to improve their productivity. Second, the top-level managers of most corporations do not like to double count profits at profit center levels because double counting gives profit center managers an inflated sense of self-worth. The profits of some individual profit centers can exceed those of the whole corporation. It is often difficult to explain to the profit center managers how the double counting has overstated their profit centers' profits, yet those overstated profits sometimes cause those profit center managers to demand commensurate compensation (salary increases or bonuses).

SIMULTANEOUS USE OF MULTIPLE TRANSFER PRICING METHODS

One potential response to the need to serve multiple transfer pricing purposes is to use multiple transfer pricing methods, one to serve each purpose. However, it is virtually impossible to use two different transfer pricing methods and simultaneously serve both the decision making and evaluation purposes because managers make decisions to produce the numbers for which they are being evaluated. Trade-offs here are usually inevitable.

When firms do use multiple transfer pricing methods, they are usually using one method for internal purposes, both decision making and evaluation, and another method to move profits between tax jurisdictions. It is often difficult to use multiple methods for these purposes because detailed laws in force in many countries constrain firms' options. The countries or states in which multiple-location corporations operate have incentives not to allow the corporate managers to manipulate reported profits through transfer prices. In particular, they will suffer tax losses if profits are moved out of their jurisdiction to another company location. They may suffer decreased market competitiveness if the corporation manipulates its transfer prices to maintain a monopoly position as a supplier. Laws are often written to require a fair transfer price. This "arm's length price" is a price that should be charged to the associated entity as the one between unrelated parties for the same transactions under the same circumstances. In the United States there are no restrictions on domestic transfer pricing methods, but Internal Revenue Code Section 482(e) prevents the shifting of income from or to an international subsidiary to avoid U.S. taxes.

It is easier for managers to claim that they are not manipulating reported income to evade taxes if they use the same transfer pricing method for tax purposes as is used for internal purposes. For this reason, and for reasons of system simplicity, multinational companies tend not to use different transfer pricing methods for domestic and international transfers.[9]

CONCLUSION

The pricing of goods or services which are transferred from one organizational entity to another often causes problems in the measurement of entity financial performance. Except in the rare situation where there is a perfectly competitive external market for the internally traded good or service, no transfer pricing approach can guide profit center managers to make decisions which are optimal from the corporation's perspective and simultaneously provide good information for evaluation. Incentives to move profits between company jurisdictions cause additional transfer pricing considerations.

Four transfer pricing methods, those based on market prices, marginal costs, full costs, or full cost plus a markup, are in common use. Some companies' employ the policy of asking profit center managers to negotiate prices with one another. No method is superior in all settings; each has it advantages and disadvantages.

Notes

1. Transfer pricing also applies to transfers involving cost centers. Transfers can be made, for example, at actual or standard cost or at full or variable cost. Because most transfer pricing problems involve profit (or investment) centers, however, this chapter will, for reasons of simplicity, refer to both the supplying and buying entities as profit centers.

2. Tang found that 56 percent of the 133 firms he studied used only one transfer pricing method and that in the other firms one dominant transfer pricing method could be identified. R. Tang, *Transfer Pricing in the United States and Japan* (New York, Praeger, 1979).
3. Other transfer pricing surveys have also revealed approximately the same pattern of practices, although they are difficult to compare because they use slightly different categories of responses. For example, some do not break out either negotiation or cost-plus transfer prices as separate categories. The discussion is organized around the Vancil survey because it is the largest, most recent study.
4. Surveys by Tang, published in 1979 and 1980, did not show significant cross-national differences among the transfer pricing policies used in U.S., Japanese, and Canadian firms. R. Y. W. Tang, *Transfer Pricing Practices in the United States and Japan* (New York: Praeger, 1979) and R. Y. W. Tang, "Canadian Transfer Pricing Practices," *CA Magazine* (Can.) (March 1980), pp. 32–38.
5. R. Y. W. Tang, "Canadian Transfer Pricing Practices," *CA Magazine* (Can.) (March 1980), pp. 32–38.
6. S. C. Borkowski, "Environmental and Organizational Factors Affecting Transfer Pricing: A Survey," *Journal of Management Accounting Research* 2 (Fall 1990), pp. 78–99.
7. These arguments were first expressed by J. Hirshleifer, "On the Economics of Transfer Pricing," *Journal of Business,* 29 (July 1956), pp. 172–184. Numerous authors have extended the Hirshleifer analysis to incorporate, for example, uncertainty, cost non-linearities, and risk-sharing between divisional and top management.
8. Multiple, or dual-rate, methods to serve the multiple purposes have been proposed by, among others, R. L. Benke and A. B. Caster, "Information Systems and Fixed Costs in Multi-divisional Companies," *Cost and Management* (March–April 1983), pp. 21–25; and P. Wraith, "Taking a Bitter Medicine," *Accountant* (January 6, 1983), pp. 16–17.
9. S. C. Borkowski, "Choosing a Transfer Pricing Method: A Study of the Domestic and International Decision-Making Process," *Journal of International Accounting, Auditing & Taxation* (1992), pp. 33–49.

Del Norte Paper Company (A)

"If I had purchased the kraft linerboard for the African box sale from one of our mills, I would have paid $360 per ton, $140 per ton higher than the price I actually paid by purchasing the linerboard in the spot market," said Frank Duffy, Managing Director of Del Norte Paper's Italian subsidiary (DNP-Italia). "I can't possibly make a profit for Del Norte if I have to pay so much for my principal raw material."

Del Norte Paper Company was a large, fully-integrated paper manufacturer. 1974 sales were about $2.8 billion, making Del Norte Paper one of the 75 largest industrial companies in the United States. The company's product line ranged from raw pulp to a large variety of converted paper products, including corrugated boxes.

DNP-Italia purchased kraft linerboard from outside suppliers and converted it into corrugated boxes. These boxes were sold primarily within Italy, though occasional sales were made outside of Italy. DNP-Italia had six plants, each of which represented a separate profit center.

THE AFRICAN BID

In mid-1975, an African firm asked a number of paper companies to submit bids on a large quantity of corrugated boxes. In total, 22 companies submitted bids, including DNP-Italia and another Del Norte subsidiary, DNP-Deutschland. The bids were said to have ranged from approximately $340 per ton to over $550 per ton, with most of them within 5 percent of $400 per ton. Del Norte-Italia won the contract by submitting the lowest bid from a firm viewed as being capable of meeting the customer's desired delivery and quality standards.

The price quoted by DNP-Italia had been substantially below that quoted by DNP-Deutschland. The primary difference between the two bids was the raw material (kraft linerboard) cost calculation embedded in each. DNP-Deutschland had formed its estimate using a per ton price for kraft linerboard of $360 while DNP-Italia had used $220. The $360/ton figure was the price (inclusive of freight) quoted for export by a Del Norte Paper Mill located in the Eastern United States. The $220 figure was the price for kraft linerboard of comparable quality in the European *Spot* market.

There were basically two reasons why the Del Norte Paper Mill price was so much higher than the European spot price. First, Del Norte Paper was a member of the Kraft Export Association (KEA), a group of kraft linerboard manufacturers which was responsible for setting and stabilizing linerboard prices for the export market. The Del Norte Paper Company mill could not, as a member of the KEA, offer a lower price to its own converting plant than to any other external customer.

The second reason for the large price differential was the extremely weak economic conditions present in mid-1975. The paper and container industries were suffering from a worldwide slump. As a result of this slump, many nonKEA producers of kraft linerboard were selling their product at very low prices. This was the exact opposite situation as had existed in 1973, a year in which there was a worldwide paper and container economic boom, when the spot price for kraft linerboard had actually exceeded by a small amount the KEA set price.

DEL NORTE'S TRANSFER PRICING SYSTEM

Prices on domestic (U.S.) intracompany sales of linerboard at Del Norte Paper were set at the *market* level. That is, the transfer price was the price at which the linerboard could be bought or sold in the market place. However, on interna-

This case was prepared with the cooperation of a firm which chooses to remain anonymous. All numbers and names have been disguised and certain other aspects have been altered. It was written by William Sahlman, Research Assistant, under the supervision of Associate Professor M. Edgar Barrett as a basis for class discussion rather than to illustrate either effective or ineffective handling of an administrative situation.

tional intracompany sales, the product price was set at a level determined by the Kraft Export Association. The KEA price could vary according to market conditions, but tended to fluctuate less than the so-called spot price. Officials of Del Norte Paper in San Francisco estimated that, even if all foreign subsidiary managers agreed to take all of the KEA-priced Del Norte Paper linerboard available, some 60 to 65 percent of their linerboard would have to come from other sources.[1]

When a Del Norte Paper converting plant located in the United States purchased its linerboard from a company mill, the profit made by the mill on the transaction was included as part of one of the reported profit figures of the converting plant. The method employed for allocating the profit was rather complex. At the time of preparing the annual budget, the converting plant made a commitment to purchase a specific amount of kraft linerboard from a specific mill. The income statement of the converting plant was then credited with the actual mill profit resulting from delivery of actual orders placed against the commitment.

The figure used for the *mill profit* was determined by taking the mill profit applicable to the specific shipment after a full allocation of both fixed and variable costs and amending it for two specific items. First, any manufacturing variances were added to or subtracted from the mill profit. Second, in the event that the converting plant did not take as much of the mill's production as expected, the proportional cost of the resulting mill down time was charged to the converting plant.

In Del Norte's international operations, the profit allocation process was similar. The foreign converting plant entered into a commitment for his U.S. produced requirements. The *mill profit,* as defined above, was credited to the converting plant and its manager. However, in contrast to domestic operations, the set of financial statements in which this amount was credited were not made freely available to the foreign subsidiary's managing director and other management personnel. The reason for this was to maintain a legal, armslength business relationship. Such statements of *integrated profit* were, however, available upon request to the managing director of each foreign subsidiary.

THE AFRICAN SALE

The bid submitted by DNP-Italia to the African customer was $400 per ton of corrugated boxes. DNP-Italia's direct costs (variable costs) were approximately $325 per ton of which 72 percent or $235[2] represented the cost of kraft linerboard.

The bid submitted by DNP-Deutschland was $550 per ton of corrugated boxes. DNP-Deutschland's direct costs on the transaction were approximately $460 of which $385 represented the cost of kraft linerboard.

The average Del Norte Paper mill had a direct cost per ton of linerboard of $190.[3] Thus, the contribution per ton at the mill was approximately $170, given the KEA selling prices of $360 per ton. The $170 contribution figure minus the actual freight costs from the U.S. to Germany (approximately $45 per ton) and the allocated overhead at the mill level would have been credited to the DNP-Deutschland converting mill had Germany won the contract.

AN INFORMAL DISCUSSION

Late one afternoon in July 1975, Frank Duffy, Managing Director of DNP-Italia held a discussion with John Powell, General Manager—International Operations of Del Norte Paper's Container Division. The specific topic of the discussion was the African container sale, but the conversation also touched on the transfer pricing system used by Del Norte Paper.

DUFFY: John, you know I would prefer to buy all my linerboard from a Del Norte Paper mill, but I just cannot compete if I have to pay $360 per ton. The price competition in the box market has been absolutely fierce this year. If I paid that much for

[1]This 60 to 65 percent was basically in grade lines not produced by DNP mills in the United States. In addition, it generally consisted of lower quality material than was normally found in the American market.

[2]Editor's Note: This figure represents the linerboard cost per ton of corrugated box sold. The actual cost per ton of linerboard used was $220.

[3]The direct cost figure of $190 per ton at the linerboard mill included the cost of raw wood going into the mill. Approximately 30 to 40 percent of the raw wood used by the mill was purchased from the Del Norte Paper Company Woodlands Division at a market determined transfer price.

linerboard, I would have to price my corrugated boxes below cost in order to win any contracts. If I am supposed to be a profit center, you can't expect me to report a loss on every sale I make—which is exactly what I would do using $360 per ton linerboard.

POWELL: But you would get credited with the mill profit in the transaction—you wouldn't have to report a loss.

DUFFY: Maybe on your books I wouldn't show a loss, but on my books I sure would. We never see that profit here in Italy. The transaction is noted in some secret little book back in San Francisco. How am I supposed to convince my plant managers and sales people they are being credited with the mill profit when they never see it?

Furthermore, from a financial point of view, the transfer pricing system doesn't make sense. Even if the mill profit were put directly into our profit and loss statement, our cash flow would not benefit. As you know, John, this is a completely self-financed operation in Italy. If I have to borrow more money than I need to, then I incur extra interest costs. There is no offsetting credit for these expenses.

POWELL: I sympathize with you, Frank, but we also have a responsibility to keep our mills operating. Further, by not purchasing Del Norte Paper linerboard when times are bad, you run the risk of not being able to buy linerboard from our U.S. mills when there is a shortage like there was two years ago. As you know, we're moving increasingly toward long-term commitments for delivery by our kraft linerboard mills. You also don't help maintain the pricing stability we've been working so hard to establish through the KEA.

DUFFY: I appreciate the problem, but I also have the responsibility to keep my plants running. Unlike the U.S., I can't fire any of my laborers in Italy—the unions just won't allow it. Any orders I can get to keep those laborers busy is pure contribution to me.

POWELL: I still think you're making a mistake by not purchasing Del Norte Paper linerboard. However, we're not going to resolve the issue today. If it were not for this damn recession, the problem probably wouldn't even exist. If it's O.K. with you, Frank, I'd like to have a chance to give the problem some more thought.

Chemical Bank: Allocation of Profits

In March 1983, Kenneth LaVine, senior vice president of Chemical Bank's Finance Division, was faced with a difficult problem: the profitability of Due Bills,[1] a lucrative product for the bank, had declined considerably. The retail branches had little incentive to sell the product actively since they received no credit for the revenues generated by Due Bills. The Treasury Group, however, which earned substantial profits on this product, felt strongly that Due Bills should be marketed aggressively. Since the Finance Division had the ultimate authority to legislate cost allocations and transfer prices, Ken had to decide what could be done to raise Due Bill volume and yet satisfy both divisions. He commented:

> This is one of those profit measurement conflicts that arise from time to time. We've got to iron out a solution which is fair to all the parties involved and, perhaps more important, which will cause the people involved to make the decisions that are in the bank's best interest.

BACKGROUND OF CHEMICAL BANK

Chemical Bank with 20,000 employees and $46.9 billion in assets, was the sixth largest U.S. commercial bank in 1983 (Exhibit 1). As a major commercial bank, Chemical offered a broad range of financial services throughout the world.

In 1982, Chemical Bank reorganized into three major profit centers: Personal and Banking Services Group, World Banking Group, and Treasury Group (Exhibit 2). The three groups were further divided into divisions, most of which were also evaluated as profit centers. Four areas at Chemical were involved in the Due Bill controversy:

1. Government trading segment of the *Treasury Group* which used Due Bills to generate revenue in the money markets.
2. *Metropolitan Division* of the Personal and Banking Services Group which sold Due Bills.
3. *Trust and Investment Division* of the Personal and Banking Services Group which administered Due Bills.
4. *Finance Division* which arbitrated the revenue and cost allocations of Due Bills.

TREASURY GROUP

In 1983, Chemical Bank had a continual funding need of roughly $25 billion. The Treasury Group was responsible for raising these funds at the lowest possible cost. Treasury also managed the bond-trading, foreign exchange trading, bond investments and all other short-term money market activities.

Treasury was organized into four business segments, each a profit center: Government Trading, Money Market Trading, Municipal Trading and Foreign Exchange. Treasury Group's incentive system was very closely tied to profit performance. For each segment, a bonus pool was calculated as a fixed percentage (usually 10 to 15 percent) of Net Earnings before Taxes, less direct and allocated expenses. This was then allocated among the traders and salespeople according to profits earned. The bonus opportunity for a trader

[1]Due Bills were receipts issued to customers that represented ownership in a security, in this case, Treasury Bills. They were issued to customers who had purchased Treasury Bills but did not need to hold the actual bills. The Due Bill promised that the bank would pay a specified rate of interest and upon maturity would remit principal and interest. (Further explanation of Due Bills is provided later in the case.)

This case was prepared by Carolyn M. Bitetti, Research Assistant, under the supervision of Professor Kenneth A. Merchant, as the basis for class discussion rather than to illustrate either effective or ineffective handling of an administrative situation.

could be as high as 200 to 300 percent of salary and therefore represented an important part of the compensation package. Due Bills were handled by the Government Trading segment of Treasury and represented about 25 percent of its 1982 revenues and profits. Since Due Bills were a major contributor to the bonus pool, the government traders were very sensitive to any decline in the profitability of this product.

METROPOLITAN DIVISION

The Metropolitan Division (Metro) included the retail branch network, VISA and MasterCard operations, and Chemical's consumer finance company. Metro provided services for individuals and small- and medium-sized New York businesses. One of Metro's strategic goals was to become a *one-stop* financial center for its customers. As part of this strategy, Metro priced deposit products very competitively and offered a broad range of financial products such as money market accounts and discount brokerage services.

Senior managers of Metropolitan were evaluated on a profit-center basis but the branch managers were rewarded on the basis of a goal system. The aim of the goal system was to evaluate branch managers on those factors which they could control. One bank manager explained the background of the goal system at Chemical Bank:

> Back in 1976, when Bob Lipp[2] took over Metro, he moved from a bottom-line evaluation of the Metropolitan branch system to a goal system. A major source of revenue for the branch system is interest earned on demand deposit balances, but the amount of revenue they generate is uncontrollable. When interest rates were up, they got a big credit for it and when interest rates came down, their earnings came down. Bob said, "This is silly—let's focus on the controllables." So he set up the goal system and evaluated people on that basis—how well do they do against the goals that have been set.

Under the goal system, certain quantitative business objectives were established on a negotiated basis between the branch manager and senior Metro managers. Dick Orr, Chief Administrative Officer for Metro, commented on this process:

> The branch manager prepares budgeted objectives for his branch based on current performance, with an eye towards whether the market is growing or declining. This is reviewed by and negotiated with the district head who also understands the marketplace. All the branch objectives are then aggregated for Metro Division as a whole. If the aggregate is too low, we go back to the branches to renegotiate. It's really a very fair process and we achieve a strong commitment to the goals from the managers.

Each objective was assigned a certain number of points which could be earned by the branch manager when the objective was achieved. The maximum number of points that could be earned was 100 (see Exhibit 3). Three levels of goal difficulty were set for each objective:

1. *Budget* was the expected performance level. Half of the points assigned to each objective could be earned by achieving the budgeted level for that objective.
2. *Base Accountability Level (BAL)* was the minimum performance level that had to be attained for each objective before points could be earned. This was set at 10 percent below budget.
3. *Goal* was the target level for which the maximum possible points could be earned. This was set 10 percent above budget.

A portion of the maximum number of points set for each objective could be earned for performance levels between the BAL and the goal. The branch manager's aim was to earn as many points as possible towards the 100-point maximum. Bonuses and raises were 95 percent determined by performance under the goal system.

Dick Orr commented on the effectiveness of the system:

> The system really has teeth because it's so closely tied to financial rewards. In addition, there's a monthly rendering of the goal system so each branch manager sees where he stands versus all the other branches. There's

[2]As of 1983, Mr. Robert Lipp was senior executive vice president in charge of the Personal and Banking Services Group.

a report listing the 10 branches which performed best under the goal system and the 10 worst. The branch managers of the 10 worst get a phone call from the Big Boss (head of Metro) at the end of the month. Believe me, it's a very powerful system.

The division head had the discretion to change the point weighting of each goal in order to tailor objectives to the geographic and economic environments faced by different branches. In 1983, the sale of Due Bills was not an objective under the goal system.

TRUST AND INVESTMENT DIVISION

Like the Metropolitan Division, Trust and Investment (T&I) was a unit of the Personal and Banking Services Group. T&I provided money management services to a range of clients including individual and institutional clients. Its traditional function was as custodian or trustee and as general investment counselor. In addition, T&I offered international banking services such as the administration of investments in precious metals or foreign securities.

T&I was involved in the Due Bills controversy because it performed the administration functions. T&I set up the Due Bills accounts and provided the data processing services.

FINANCE DIVISION

The Finance Division was the strategy and corporate planning arm of the bank. It had broad responsibilities for strategic planning, corporate finance and accounting and control.

Ken LaVine ran one of the four major parts of the Finance Division—Management Accounting and Taxes—which, among other things, managed bankwide profit planning and monitored management information such as organizational, product and customer profitability. Ken was responsible for resolving all transfer pricing issues and had ultimate decision-making authority in this area.

EXPLANATION OF DUE BILLS

A Due Bill was an acknowledgment that the bank had sold securities to a customer, that his account had been charged, and that, if requested, the securities would be delivered when they became available. The Due Bill also acknowledged that upon maturity Chemical would pay principal plus interest at a specified rate. Due Bills were issued to customers who had purchased Treasury Bills[3] through one of Chemical's branches, but who did not request actual possession of the T-Bill. The Federal Reserve Bank required that this transaction be collateralized with a similar security three days after the initial purchase.

The bank earned profits on Due Bills in three ways: a funding spread (net interest income), trading profits and fees.

1. Net interest income (NII) was earned when Treasury invested Due Bill funds to earn a higher rate than it had to pay the customer. The difference between the rate paid the customer and the rate earned on the investment was called a *spread* or net interest income.

   To illustrate, assume a customer purchased a 30-day, $10,000 Treasury Bill with an interest rate of 8 percent. If the customer did not insist on receiving the actual T-Bill, he would be issued a Due Bill which stated that Chemical Bank owed him $10,000 at the end of 30 days, plus interest at 8 percent. Meanwhile, Treasury might invest those funds for 30 days at 9.5 percent, thus earning a 150 basis point spread (1 percent = 100 basis points). Rather than match the term of the investment with the term of the deposit, Treasury also had the option of investing the funds for a shorter or longer period than the term of the deposit. This was known as mismatching, and since it resulted in interest rate risk, it required skill on the part of the traders in anticipating interest rates and reacting quickly to any changes in the market. In 1982, Treasury's average funding spread on Due Bills was roughly 150–175 basis points.
2. *Trading Profits:* Since Due Bill transactions had to be collateralized after three days, Treasury held a pool of T-Bills in inventory for this purpose. This pool gave Treasury flexibility to trade (buy and sell) T-Bills in the secondary market thus earning a trading profit (for example, by selling a particular T-Bill for a slightly higher price than it paid for it). The trading operation also required skill since there was always the risk of losing money in a trade (i.e., selling a T-Bill for a lower price than was paid for it).
3. *Fees:* The customer was charged a $25 fee for each transaction.

[3]*Treasury Bills* (commonly called "T-Bills") are short-term obligations of the United States government which are issued for three-month, six-month, or one-year periods.

BACKGROUND OF CONTROVERSY OVER DUE BILLS

The Due Bill issue first arose in early 1981. Metro Division had reviewed the profitability of Due Bills and calculated that they were losing $26.50 on a typical transaction (see Exhibit 4). This was because T&I was charging Metro for the cost of processing Due Bills but Metro was receiving no credit for Due Bill revenue. Dick Orr, chief administrator of Metropolitan Division, explained Metro's position:

> It was essentially a nuisance product for us. Selling a T-Bill required at least 20 minutes of branch personnel time—explaining the features of T-Bills versus other investments, obtaining recent interest rate quotes, filling out forms, notifying Treasury, etc. Branch personnel time is a scarce resource for us and here they were spending 20 minutes for a transaction for which Metro received *zero* credit.

Metro suggested that the transaction fee for Due Bills be increased with the additional fee allocated to Metro to cover the related expenses. Treasury, however, which was credited with all Due Bill revenue, was opposed to raising the $25 fee. In a memorandum written in February 1981, Bill Staples (Manager-Treasury Control) argued that for competitive reasons Chemical should not raise the fee:

> Treasury feels that they have developed a strong customer base in the odd-lot market.[4] Even with this strong base, we believe that there is an untapped source of customers that we have not reached. If our fee is higher than competitive rates, we feel it would be extremely difficult to expand our existing customer base.

The memo went on to conclude:

> The selling of odd-lot (Due Bill) transactions has been very profitable to Chemical Bank over the years. Treasury Group feels strongly that any increase in the fee at this time will have adverse effects on our bottom line. Additionally, we are making a reputation for the bank as a leader in the odd-lot market. If we were to increase our fee, customers may go to other commercial banks with the possibility that the entire account relationship will transfer. It is for the preceding reasons that Treasury Division feels that the bank should not increase the present fee of $25.

Treasury also steadfastly refused to give up any revenues to Metro. Petros Sabatacakis, senior vice president in Treasury, summarized their position:

> The government traders in Treasury felt Metro's demands were unjustified. The traders felt they were the ones generating the revenue by playing the market. Besides, metro was simply reacting to customers' requests for this product, they weren't actively pushing it. As far as the traders were concerned, they were doing Metro a favor by providing its customers with this service. So the traders were saying "Why should we share any revenue with Metro?" We were also taking a defensive approach. We were in a powerful position—receiving all of the revenues and incurring only relatively small direct expenses. Any change would be to our detriment.

Metro Division, however, was becoming increasingly impatient about Due Bills as reflected in an excerpt from a memo written by two Metro staff people in early 1982:

> On December 31st, we received a phone call from a Metro Division head demanding to know why we in Metro weren't unilaterally increasing the T-Bill transaction fee. The activity was clogging his branches, his employees had a hard time in general getting through to Treasury, and Metropolitan was losing money on the transactions. Pressure is mounting within Metropolitan to do something about Treasury Bill transactions.

DECEMBER 1982

The issue remained unresolved through 1982, but the conflict came to a head towards year end. At that time, two events occurred which caused a de-

[4]The *odd-lot market* included all government securities transactions under $100,000.

cline in the total profits generated by Due Bills: a drop in interest rates and the advent of bank-offered money market accounts.

The decline in interest rates reduced Treasury's funding spread and trading profits from Due Bills. Lower interest rates also reduced the attractiveness of T-Bills as investments, and this negatively affected the volume of Due Bills sold.

The bank-offered money market accounts came into being because of a December 1982 mandate from the Depository Institutions Deregulation Committee of the United States Congress. Commercial banks could now offer interest-bearing money market accounts to their customers. The Metro Division saw this as an opportunity to attract deposits back into the banking system and to further its strategy of becoming a *one-stop* financial center. In an effort to capture a share of this market, Metro offered to pay branch officers an incentive of 10 basis points on all new deposits brought into the bank.[5] The proceeds of the new accounts, however, could not be from an existing Chemical checking or savings account; they have to come from another source, such as a Merrill Lynch account. Proceeds diverted from T-Bills (or Due Bills), even those purchased through Chemical, were also allowed under this scheme. Dick Orr commented on this move:

> In retrospect we should have checked with Treasury before we went ahead and offered that incentive. Treasury thought our action was outrageous, but we had little idea how profitable Due Bills were for them—in fact, Treasury was always complaining about how expensive it was for them to handle Due Bills. Anyway, we weren't expecting the negative reaction we got from them—they went bananas.

The Metro incentive system and the decline in interest rates combined caused Treasury's level of profits from Due Bills to drop—a fact which affected the government traders directly, given Treasury's incentive system. Petros Sabatacakis commented:

> The traders were putting pressure on me to get Metro to rectify the situation by raising the *volume* of Due Bills to compensate for the drop in profitability of each transaction. But what was Metro's incentive to sell the product? I knew we'd have to give something up if we wanted to get something in return.

FINANCE DIVISION REVIEW

In light of Metro's continuing complaints and Treasury's concern over their decline, the Finance Division undertook a detailed review of the situation. It quickly became clear that for the bank as a whole, Due Bills were very lucrative. According to Finance Division estimates, 1982 contribution from Due Bills was $9.9 million (see Exhibit 5 for Finance Group calculations). The Finance Division also determined that Due Bills were more profitable for the bank than the new Super-Saver (money market) accounts (see Exhibit 6), but because of the profits were allocated, this same profit picture was not true for Metro.

A memorandum written by a Finance Division analyst concluded that the main problem was that Metro had little incentive to sell Due Bills:

> The absence of an incentive in the Metropolitan Division to stimulate T-Bill sales seems to result in counterproductive behavior. This is especially true when branch managers are motivated to offer instruments that may not be as profitable to the bank (e.g., money market accounts and savings certificates). Possible incentives include the following:
>
> - Fee sharing on all *sales*—all or part of $25 fee.
> - Fee sharing on *new* sales—all or part of $25 fee.
> - Include Due Bills in Metro goal system.
> - Others?

A second issue that was related to the Due Bill controversy was: who should be performing the administrative duties associated with maintenance of Due Bill Accounts? The administrative functions included setting up the customer accounts, keeping track of the principal and interest payments, monitoring maturity schedules and performing other related functions. All these functions were being performed by T&I, but the Trea-

[5]For example, a new $50,000 account would pay an incentive of $50 (.001 × 50,000 = $50).

sury Division maintained they could perform these functions at a considerably lower cost to the bank. For 1982, T&I charged Metro $1.3 million for processing costs, which included both fixed and variable costs, as follows:

Variable processing costs	$ 290,000
Overhead	1,010,000
Total	$1,300,000

Treasury Division had the capability to perform the same processing functions as T&I, and the Finance Division learned that Treasury could process the existing volume of Due Bills for a variable cost of $90,000. This cost would be in addition to direct expenses of $1 million that Treasury was already incurring in connection with Due Bills (see Exhibit 5).

DUE BILL MEETING

In order to get the Due Bills issue resolved as quickly as possible, Ken LaVine scheduled a meeting of the senior officials in all of the areas of the bank affected by the Due Bill controversy. The meeting was to be held on March 31, 1983.

Prior to the meeting, both Treasury and Metro suggested solutions to the problem. Treasury's recommendation was to share 50 percent of the $25 fee with metro on all sales that exceeded the 1981 Average Due Bill Balance plus 10 percent. The rationale was that Metro should be rewarded only for bringing Due Bill volume above past levels.

Metro's recommendation (shown in Exhibit 7) involved sharing the fee (which would be raised to $30) *and* the cost of processing. But Metro was open to suggestions, as Dick Orr explained:

> We in Metro decided that being intransigent and refusing to sell T-Bills was not the best way to go. We made an effort to take a more positive approach to the whole thing. First of all, it is in the best interest of the bank to resolve the Due Bill issue. Second, we are working hard to develop a package of products that will make us a one-stop financial department store. With Treasury's products and our strong distribution system, it makes sense for us to develop a spirit of cooperation, and we hope to show that our branches could be used effectively to sell other Treasury products.

Ken LaVine hoped that getting the key people together would end the controversy. He explained:

> We have to get this issue resolved. The level of Due Bills has dropped sharply, and this is having an adverse effect on the bank's earnings. We need to find a solution on which all parties can agree and get it implemented as quickly as possible. I called the meeting because I think we can best resolve this issue by getting the senior personnel—the people who have the authority to make decisions—together in the same room. If I can't get agreement at the meeting, I may just have to make the decision myself.

EXHIBIT 1 Financial Highlights

	1982	*1981*	*% Change*
For the Year (in thousands)			
Net Interest Income	$1,251,087	$1,014,187	+23.4
Income Before Securities Gains (Losses) and Extraordinary Gain	269,103	215,231	+25.0
Net Income	240,560	215,039	+11.9
Per Share			
Income Before Securities Gains (Losses) and Extraordinary Gain	$ 9.55	$ 8.71	+ 9.6
Net Income	8.41	8.70	− 3.3
Cash Dividends Declared	2.88	2.56	+12.5
Book Value	62.55	58.46	+ 7.0
Profitability Ratios (Balance Sheet Averages)			
Income Before Securities Gains (Losses) and Extraordinary Gain to:			
Stockholders' Equity	15.31%	14.99%	
Common Stockholders' Equity	15.80	15.52	
Net Income to:			
Stockholders' Equity	13.67	14.98	
Common Stockholders' Equity	13.91	15.51	
Return on Assets	0.60	0.51	
At Year-End (in millions)			
Total Assets	$ 48,275	$ 44,917	+ 7.5
Loans	30,916	29,175	+ 6.0
Deposits	27,998	29,430	− 4.9
Investment Securities	3,802	2,911	+30.6
Stockholders' Equity	1,945	1,502	+29.5

Per share results in 1982 reflected the issuance of adjustable rate preferred stock and additional conversions of convertible notes, debentures and preferred stock. Per share amounts for 1981 were restated for the 50 percent stock dividend paid in April 1982.

EXHIBIT 2 Organization Chart

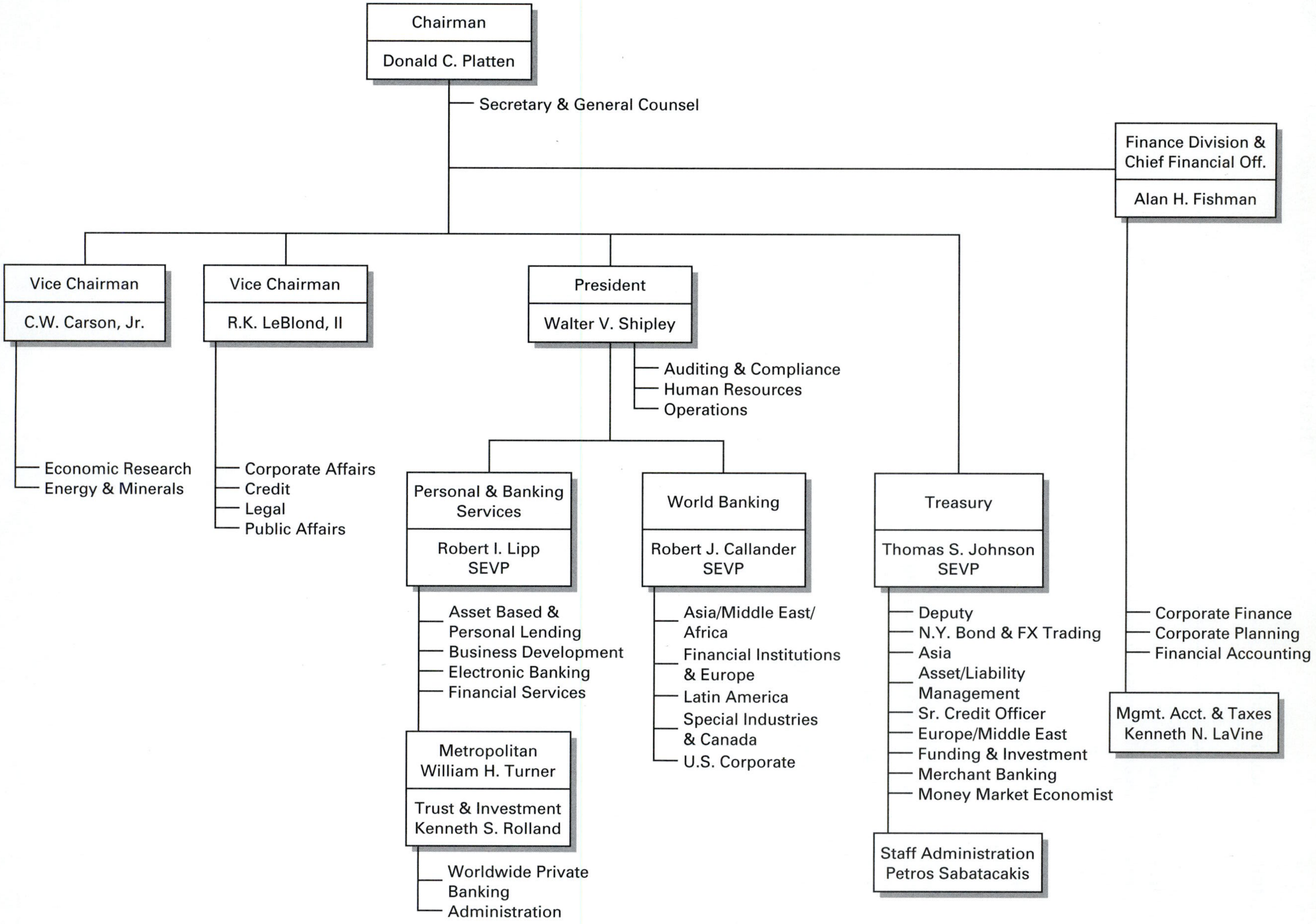

Chairman
Donald C. Platten
- Secretary & General Counsel

Finance Division & Chief Financial Off.
Alan H. Fishman
- Corporate Finance
- Corporate Planning
- Financial Accounting

Mgmt. Acct. & Taxes
Kenneth N. LaVine

Vice Chairman
C.W. Carson, Jr.
- Economic Research
- Energy & Minerals

Vice Chairman
R.K. LeBlond, II
- Corporate Affairs
- Credit
- Legal
- Public Affairs

President
Walter V. Shipley
- Auditing & Compliance
- Human Resources
- Operations

Personal & Banking Services
Robert I. Lipp
SEVP
- Asset Based & Personal Lending
- Business Development
- Electronic Banking
- Financial Services

Metropolitan
William H. Turner

Trust & Investment
Kenneth S. Rolland
- Worldwide Private Banking
- Administration

World Banking
Robert J. Callander
SEVP
- Asia/Middle East/ Africa
- Financial Institutions & Europe
- Latin America
- Special Industries & Canada
- U.S. Corporate

Treasury
Thomas S. Johnson
SEVP
- Deputy
- N.Y. Bond & FX Trading
- Asia
- Asset/Liability Management
- Sr. Credit Officer
- Europe/Middle East
- Funding & Investment
- Merchant Banking
- Money Market Economist

Staff Administration
Petros Sabatacakis

EXHIBIT 3 Typical Point Assignment Under Metropolitan Division Goal System

Summary:	
1. Deposits	55 Points
2. Loans	16 Points
3. Revenues	10 Points
4. Expenses	19 Points
	100 Points
Detailed Level:	
1. Deposits	
Business Deposits	25 Points
Personal Deposits	15 Points
Savings Accounts	5 Points
Other Time Accounts	10 Points
	55 Points
2. Loans	
Installment Loans	7 Points
Revolving Credits	3 Points
Commercial Loans	6 Points
	16 Points
3. Revenue	
Direct Fees	10 Points
4. Expenses*	19 Points

*Includes only those expenses which are directly controllable at the branch level. Points are determined by comparing actual expenses to budgeted expenses.

EXHIBIT 4 Metropolitan Division Analysis

DATE: January 12, 1982
TO: J. R. Spressert (Vice President and Division Controller—Metro)
FROM: J. D. Furber (Metro Control Analyst)
RE: Odd-Lot T-Bill Transactions

The Treasury Division performs the "trading" of all odd-lot (defined as securities under $100m) government securities within the bank. The actual purchase of the securities, however, is handled in the line areas of the bank, principally the Metropolitan Division branches, while Trust & Investment (T&I) handles the operational aspects. Metropolitan is the major contributor to the Treasury's odd-lot business, with a sampling in January 1981 indicating that the Metropolitan Division accounts for up to 85% of total odd-lot volume in the bank. It is largely due to our extensive branch system that Chemical Bank is the largest issuer of T-Bills of all the major NYC banks.

The following is a profit and loss analysis of a T-Bill sale in the branch system: Assume $10,000 principal—180 day maturity.

Revenues	*Metropolitan*	*T&I*	*Treasury*	*Total Bank*
NII–Due Bills	—	—	$54.00	$54.00*
Trading Profit	—	—	17.97	17.97**
Fee Revenue	—	—	25.00	25.00†
	—	—	$96.97	$96.97
Less				
Processing Expenses	$ 4.50‡	$22.00§	$11.43‖	$37.93
Allocation of T&I Expense to Metro	22.00	(22.00)	—	—
Pretax Profit (loss)	$(26.50)	—	$85.54	$59.04

In addition to absorbing our own director expenses ($4.38/transaction) incurred in handling the T-Bill transaction, Metro is being charged for the operational expenses ($22.00/transaction) of the T&I bank. Yet, all revenues from the odd-lot transactions are being credited to the Treasury Division alone. Thus, on the internal financial statements, Treasury's profits are somewhat overstated while Metro is bearing the bulk (70%) of the expenses associated with the transactions.

*The $54.00 is an estimate based on 1980 figures of net interest income earned per transaction.

**An estimate made by government traders of average profit achieved per trade in the secondary market.

†This is the $25.00 charged per transaction.

††Direct Metro processing, a handling expense calculated to be $4.50 per transaction.

§Calculations based on 1980 figures. A total T&I processing expense of $1,210,000 allocated over 55,000 Metro transactions ($1,210,000 ÷ 55,000 = 22.00).

‖Estimates of Treasury's 1980 T-Bill expense associated with each transaction.

Note: Numbers are disguised.

EXHIBIT 5 Finance Group Due Bill Contribution Analysis (in millions)

	1982	*Projected 1983*
Revenues		
Net Interest Income	$ 7.5	$3.0–$5.0
Trading Profits	2.4	1.5
Fees	.5	.2
Balances*	.9	.2
Total Revenue	$11.2	$4.9–$6.9
Incremental Expenses (variable)		
Treasury	1.0	$ .7
T&I Processing	.3	.2
Total Incremental Expenses	$ 1.3	$ .9
Total Contribution	$ 9.9	$4.0–$6.0

*Additional balances were often gained because some customers prefunded their accounts before purchasing a T-Bill and/or did not withdraw the funds immediately upon maturity. Interest was earned on these balances.

Note: Numbers are disguised.

EXHIBIT 6 Finance Group Analysis of Super-Saver Account and Treasury Bill Profitability

This compares the profit generated by a Super-Saver Account with a Due Bill transaction. The example assumes a $10,000 principal, a 180 day maturity, and a 13.25% interest rate.

	Super Saver	*Due Bill*
Interest Income	$725.00	$54.00
Trading Profit	—	17.97
Fee Revenue	—	25.00
Total Revenues	$725.00	$96.97
Interest Cost	$664.00	—
FDIC Assessment*	4.13	—
Processing Costs	10.60	31.11**
Total Costs	$678.73	$31.11
Pre-Tax Profit	$ 46.27†	$65.86

*Federal Deposit Insurance Corporation insurance was required for all Super Saver Accounts. FDIC charged a fee for this insurance.

**This differs slightly from the processing cost figures in Exhibit 4 due to a different allocation of indirect costs.

†This total was credited entirely to the Metropolitan Division.

Note: Numbers are disguised.

EXHIBIT 7 Metro Recommendations for Solution

1. The fee for odd-lot Treasury Bill Transactions should be increased by at least $5.00. Our market research indicates attrition in transaction volume will be a minor risk.
2. Revenues associated with this product should be shared by the Treasury and Metropolitan Divisions. Since Metro has contact with 80% of T-Bill customers, perhaps revenue could be earned by Metro in terms of a finder's fee of $20 per transaction, which is sufficiently large to cover expenses incurred in processing purchases and to provide a margin of fee revenue to the Branch. Metro is the marketing and selling agent of this product, and, as such, should have an incentive for doing the job well. Further, under this scenario of "fee splitting," the T&I cost should be shared as well. A revised income statement on a single transaction with the fee set at $30 might look like this:

Revenues	*Metro*	*T & I*	*Treasury*	*Total Chemical*
NII	—	—	$ 54.00	$ 54.00
Trading Profit	—	—	17.97	17.97
Fee Revenue	20.00	—	10.00	30.00
Total	$20.00	—	$ 81.97	$101.97
Expenses				
Processing	$ 4.50	$22.00	$ 11.43	$ 37.93
Charge back	11.00	(22.00)	11.00	—
Total	$15.50	0	$ 22.43	$ 37.93
NEBT—Proposed	$ 4.50	0	$ 59.54	$ 64.04
—Current	(26.50)	0	$ 85.54	59.04
Variance	$31.00	0	$(26.00)	$ 5.00

Based on Metro's 80% share of 78,000 transactions, the Division would expect to earn $280,800.

Note: Numbers are disguised.

Section V: Important Control Roles and Ethical Issues

CHAPTER 16

Controllers, Auditors, and Boards of Directors

Maintaining good control is an important function of management; however, many others in every organization, particularly controllers and internal auditors, have significant control responsibilities. These control-specialist positions are particularly challenging because the individuals filling them have two roles which can, and often do, conflict. One role is *management service,* which involves helping managers with their decision making and control functions. The other role is *oversight,* which involves ensuring that the actions of everyone in the organization, especially the managers, are legal, ethical, and in the best interest of the organization and its owners. This chapter discusses this conflict and some other issues faced in making individuals in these roles effective. The chapter also discusses the control-related roles of some individuals from outside the firm, notably external auditors and members of the board of directors, and the board's audit committee.

CONTROLLERS

In larger firms, financial management functions are typically divided between two roles, controller and treasurer, as illustrated in Figure 16-1. (In smaller firms, these roles may be combined.) The treasurer's function deals primarily with raising and managing capital. The controller's function deals primarily with financial reporting and control. The treasurer's function is generally highly centralized. The controller's function may be centralized; however, it is often decentralized in larger corporations, as divisionalized corporations usually have controllers in most or all of their profit centers and some of their larger cost centers (such as, plants).

Controllers play key roles in line management and in the design and operation of a management control system (MCS). They are the financial measurement experts within their firm (or their business unit) and are key members of the management team. As such, they are involved in preparing plans and budgets, challenging operating managers' plans and actions, and participating in a broad range of management decisions; including allocating resources, pricing, setting policies regarding receivables and payables, making acquisitions and divestments, and raising money. Controllers are also their organization's chief accountant. They

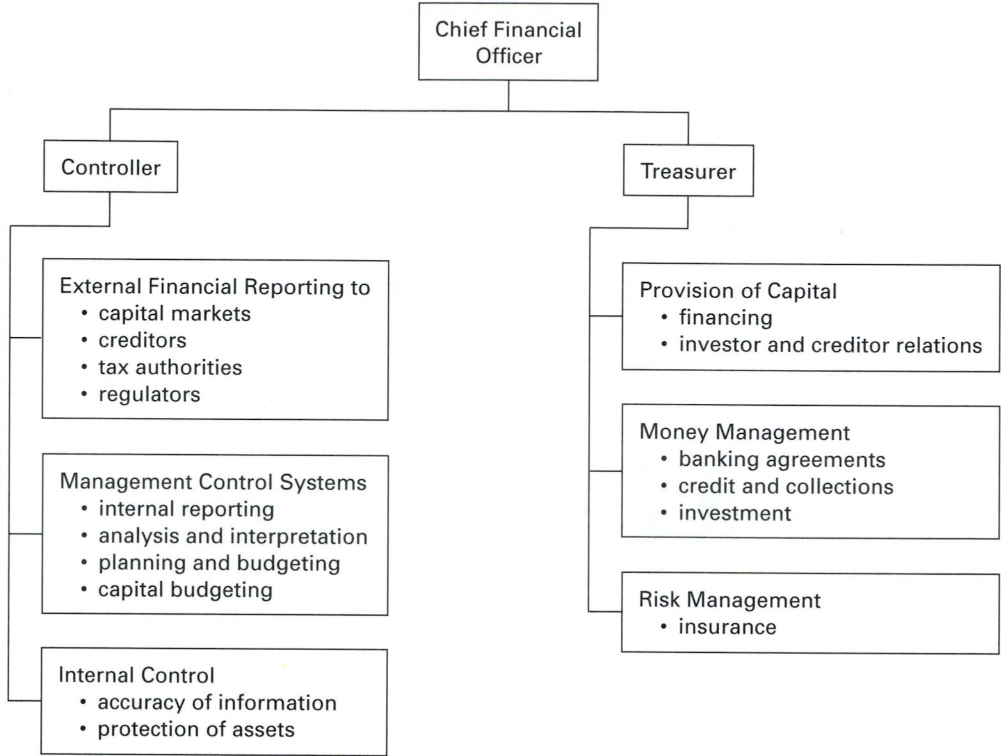

FIGURE 16-1 Corporate Financial Management Roles

prepare performance reports and fulfill financial, tax, and government reporting obligations. They establish and maintain internal control systems that help ensure the reliability of information and the protection of the company's assets. Depending on the organization, the corporate controller may supervise the internal audit and/or management information system functions.

How important are controllers in a MCS? One expert made a guesstimate that the difference between an outstanding and a merely adequate controllership function could, by itself, result in a bottom-line impact of 5 to 25 percent of net income.[1]

While controllers can and should play important management service roles in their entity, they must also stay somewhat independent of their entity's managers. They have a *fiduciary* responsibility to ensure that the information reported from their operating unit, particularly that of a financial nature, is accurate and that the unit's internal control systems are adequate.[2] They have an *oversight* responsibility to inform others in the organization if individuals in their organization are violating laws or ethical norms.

Can controllers who are highly involved as part of the management team maintain the requisite degree of independence to fulfill their fiduciary and management oversight responsibilities effectively? In other words, can controllers wear two hats, one of a team member and confidant, and the other of a watchdog or police officer? Controllers' fiduciary responsibilities are quite consistent with their management oversight responsibilities; both sets of responsibilities require a sense of independence from management. However, many people believe that the fiduciary and management oversight responsibilities often conflict with the controllers' management service responsibilities.

It is true that corporate controllers usually identify more with their corporation and its management team than they do with the stockholders and potential investors. Similarly, business-unit controllers located in the field can easily develop an emotional attachment to their organization and the people they work with. They want to be part of the team. Certainly, controllers who are included in a performance-based incentive compensation plan based on measures for which they are responsible have strong motivations to play games with the results measures, especially in times of financial stress.

These entity-identification and compensation-based temptation problems do not automatically mean that the controllers' fiduciary and management oversight roles will be compromised, but they raise warning flags. Several organizational features can be implemented to ensure that controllers fulfill their management oversight and fiduciary duties effectively. First, internal auditors and audit committees of boards of directors can be used to oversee the controller function.

Second, personnel/cultural control, through selection and training of controllers, can be used. Some controllers have better judgment, a better sense of ethical integrity, and are better able to function effectively in situations with strong role conflict than others.[3] Individuals who must follow strong and relevant professional ethics responsibilities may be good choices for controller positions. In 1993, the American Institute of Certified Public Accountants bolstered its professional code of ethics by requiring CPAs who work in corporations (rather than in public accounting) to report material misstatements of their company's financial statements to their superiors. If the superiors fail to respond, then the CPA should report the misstatements to the company's outside auditors or to regulators, such as the Securities and Exchange Commission. This code adds weight behind the fiduciary responsibility of controllers who are also CPAs, at least for material misstatements. (There is a loophole: Few business-unit misstatements are material to the corporation taken as a whole.) Finally, training programs can also be used to remind controllers of their multiple responsibilities and to give them the interpersonal skills useful in maintaining the proper balance.

Designing incentive systems that do not create temptation is a third way of ensuring that controllers fulfill their management oversight and fiduciary duties effectively. Controllers probably should not be rewarded for performance defined by measures they can manipulate.

Some firms have found that *solid-line reporting* in the controller's organization is effective for controlling business unit controllers' activities. Solid-line reporting means that the business unit controller's primary reporting relationship is to the corporate controller (or in the case of a lower-level business unit, a higher-level business unit controller). (See Figure 16-2.) The corporate controllers, not the business unit managers, define the business unit controllers' tasks and priorities and evaluate their performances.

Solid-line reporting is designed to reduce the emotional attachment between business unit controllers and the operating units to which they are assigned. It signals to the controllers that their most important roles are to protect the corporation's assets and to ensure that financial reports are accurate. This reminder is perhaps more important if the business unit is located a great distance from headquarters. For all business unit controllers, it provides a heightened emphasis on the management oversight and fiduciary responsibilities of controllership and a reduced tendency to "cook the books." Evidence has shown that changing the controllers' reporting relationships does alter business unit controllers' job priorities and loyalties.[4]

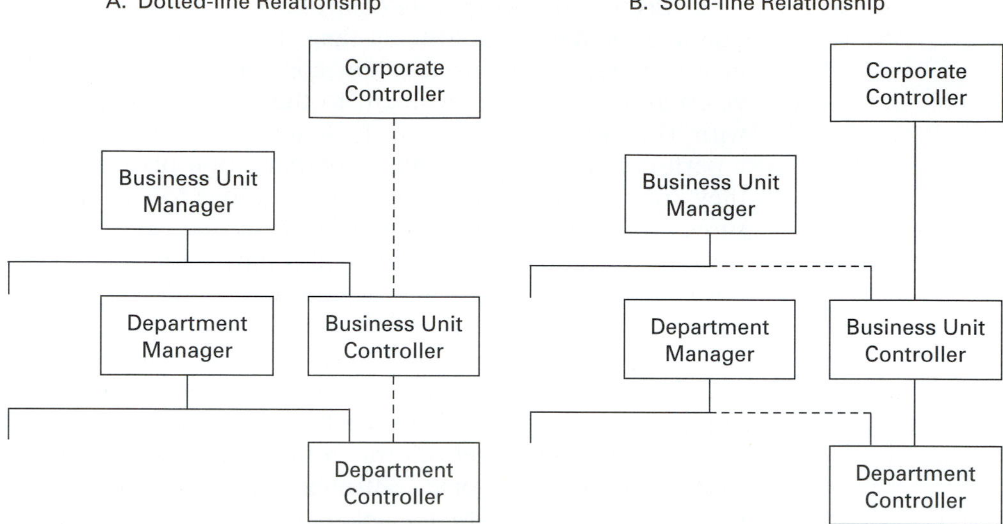

FIGURE 16-2 Possible Reporting Relationships in the Controller's Organization

The primary cost of solid-line reporting is a potential reduction in the quality of the controller's management service function. The business unit controllers can come to be viewed as outcasts, as spies from corporate. Evidence from the only survey available suggests that this cost is perceived as significant in many organizations. Only a small fraction of firms (15 percent) have solid-line reporting, although the trend at the time the survey was made (1978) seemed to be toward greater central control of the controller function.[5]

AUDITORS

When the word *audit* is mentioned, most people think first of either a financial audit, in which a public accounting firm expresses an opinion about the fairness of presentation of a company's financial statements, or a tax audit, in which government auditors test to see if taxpayers have followed the laws. These common audit forms, however, usually play only limited roles in MCSs, while other types of audits; such as internal audits, operational audits, and performance audits are often critical control-system elements.

Audits

An audit may be defined as

> a *systematic process* of (1) *objectively obtaining and evaluating evidence* regarding *objects of importance,* (2) *judging* the degree of correspondence between those objects and certain *criteria,* and (3) *communicating* the results to interested users.

This definition is broad so as to cover all types of audits. It is useful to elaborate on the meaning of the key (italicized) terms.

The phrase *systematic process* is used to connote the fact that audits are not done randomly. They involve an orderly sequence of interrelated steps, all designed with one or more audit objectives in mind. Every audit starts with what is commonly called a planning phase. The planning phase involves developing an understanding of the established criteria of the groups who will use the audit report, the required scope of concern, and the functioning of the operations of concern. It is used to design an audit program which identifies the specific tasks to be performed and, if appropriate, the schedule for starting and completing each task and the persons assigned to each task.

The second phase of the audit process, which is typically the most time consuming, involves *obtaining and evaluating evidence.* This process is *objective* because auditors are, by definition, independent of those being audited. Nonindependent reviews, such as superiors inspecting the work of the subordinates for which they are also held responsible, are *not* audits, despite the obvious similarities. Depending on the focus and scope of the audit, the evidence-gathering may involve some or all of the following: observation, interviews, reviews of reports, recomputations, confirmations, and analyses. As evidence is gathered, alterations to the original audit program may be necessary.

Differences in the *objects of importance* provide the major reason for the varied labels being put on different types of audits. Compliance audits are designed to test for compliance with rules about behavior or results; such as specific company policies, laws, or loan covenants. Marketing audits focus on the effectiveness and efficiency of the marketing function. Financial audits provide a basis for the auditors to express an opinion as to whether the financial statements fairly present the financial status and performance of the entity involved.

The third phase of an audit requires a *judgment,* based on the evidence, as to whether or not (or to what extent) the criteria have been met. These judgments are fallible, as in all but the simplest situations, some probability exists that the judgments will subsequently be proven to be incorrect. All of the evidence necessary to make an infallible judgment may not be available, or the judgment may involve an assessment about an uncertain future.

The *criteria* for comparison can vary widely between audit types. They may be very narrow and specific, such as those used in procedure-related compliance audits (requirement of two signatures on checks), or they may be no more specific than a vague definition of a desired characteristic, such as "efficiency."

The audit process is concluded by *communicating* the results to interested users. The audit report is the primary tangible product of the audit. At a minimum, the audit report describes the evidence examined and presents an opinion as to whether the established criteria were met. In issuing the report with stated opinion, the auditor is, in essence, assuming responsibility for the opinion, with the risk of economic and/or reputation losses if the opinion is subsequently determined to be less than totally correct. Sometimes the report highlights areas where improvements can be made, and it may go as far as to make specific recommendations.

External and Internal Auditors

Auditors can be classified as either external or internal. *External auditors* are independent of management because they are employed by professional service firms. Those performing financial audits (described as follows) are generally accountants employed by a public accounting firm. They have professional training and experience and are licensed by a professional association. Those executing performance audits (also described as follows) are employed by a public accounting or consulting firm. These auditors can have any of a variety of backgrounds; including general management, engineering, finance, or computer science.

Internal auditors are employees of the company they are auditing, but most of them also have ties to a professional association. In the U.S., the Institute of Internal Auditors, a professional association with more than 50,000 members, has defined professional standards and responsibilities, a code of ethics, and a common body of knowledge for internal auditors. It has also instituted a certification program (Certified Internal Auditor).

The size of firms' internal audit staffs vary widely. Small firms often have no internal auditors. Large firms may have a small or a large staff. A survey of the 500 U.S. companies with the largest sales found that internal audit functions ranged in size from one to over 600 professional auditors, with the median size being twenty-four.[6]

Internal audit staffs can operate with either narrow or broad charters, and the breadth of the charter is one of the major determinants of the size of the staff. A narrow charter, which would necessitate a relatively small internal audit staff, leads to mostly compliance audits and performance of some functions for the external auditors (preparation of audit schedules) to reduce audit fees. At the other extreme, some staffs operate with a broad charter which can include many forms of performance auditing, involvement in the design and improvement of business processes and internal control systems, and other forms of what would usually be classified as management consulting.

Internal auditor backgrounds vary with their staff's charter. Historically, most internal auditors have been accountants. As internal audit chargers have broadened, however, many firms' audit staffs have become more diverse and include, among others, engineers, computer experts, experienced managers, and liberal arts graduates.

Organizationally, the internal audit function operates in a staff capacity and almost always reports high in the organization, at least to the controller or financial vice-president. The internal audit survey found that over half of the internal audit departments of large corporations report to the chief financial officer, 20 percent report to the chairman of the board of directors, and 18 percent report to the corporate controller.[7] Many experts have recommended that the internal audit staff report directly to the audit committee of the board of directors to enhance the staff's independence and visibility.

Common Audit Types

While the mechanics and techniques are basically the same among all types of audits, the motivations and end results are different. This section briefly describes some of the most common types of audits which can serve control purposes.

Financial Audits

In a financial audit, external auditors are asked to express an opinion as to whether the financial statements prepared by management are fairly presented in accordance with generally accepted accounting principles. The guidelines that external auditors must follow in performing an audit in the U.S. are known as generally accepted auditing standards. These guidelines are established by the Auditing Standards Board of the American Institute of Certified Public Accountants (AICPA). Financial audits provide a tool by which outside regulators (stock exchanges or government bodies) can enforce standards for the preparation and presentation of accounting information to interested parties who are outside the organization.

Compliance Audits

Organizations and specific individuals are responsible for complying with many laws, rules, procedures, and administrative policies set down by higher authorities. In a compliance audit, the auditors are asked to express an opinion only as to whether actual activities or results are in compliance with the established standards. Both external and internal auditors perform compliance-type audits.

Many frauds and irregularities are uncovered by compliance audits. In early 1996 a compliance audit uncovered an accounting scandal in the radiology center of the medical center at the University of California, Davis.[8] About $330,000 was deposited into authorized bank accounts and used for extravagant purposes, such as lavish parties, banquets, and golf and tennis tournaments, which had nothing to do with the medical center's mission.

Compliance audits generally involve a narrower scope of investigation than do other types of audits, but compliance audits vary widely in the amount of evidence to be gathered and the auditor expertise needed. Audits for compliance with more complex rules, such as some tax laws, may require considerable specialized knowledge and a large amount of professional judgment. As a general rule, the need for more qualified auditors increases as the complexity of the comparison criteria and evidence-gathering procedures increases.

Performance Audits

Performance audits, which are sometimes referred to as operations audits, management audits, or comprehensive audits, are used to provide an overall evaluation of the general performance, or some specific aspect of the performance of an activity, department, or company, and its management. Performance audits can be performed by broad-scope internal auditors or external auditors functioning in a consulting role. The criteria for comparison are vague in many performance audits, perhaps consisting of nothing more specific than "good performance." Accordingly, an important part of performance audits often involves defining the criteria in more specific terms. In addition to making a judgment as to whether or not performance is good, performance auditors usually also produce an important by-product by identifying areas where improvement may enable the operation or organization to do a more effective and efficient job.

The term *performance auditing* suggests that the full range of management's responsibility is potentially within the scope of the auditor's assignment. This means that the evaluation may be not only on whether the right decisions are being made, but also whether the organization has the right information and techniques available to develop and evaluate alternatives rationally. In many cases, however, the scope is limited by focusing on a specific organization, a specific activity, or one or more specific performance dimensions (for example, quality or efficiency).

Performance auditors generally must have broader training and experience than other types of auditors. Not only must they have the ability to find and evaluate evidence to reach an opinion, but in many cases they must also be able to perform in a highly technical, specialized environment and develop their own criteria for comparison as part of the audit. Depending on the situation, performance auditors can be employees of the organization (internal consulting staff) or outsiders (government agency employees, independent auditors, or consultants). They may have expertise in accounting, law, engineering, general management, or other areas that are needed to be able to express a professional opinion. The audit reports may be directed to management, government regulatory agencies (Environmental Protection Agency or Public Utility Commission), or even a potential acquiring firm. No standard audit programs or report formats can be applied to all performance audits.

The Value of Audits

Audits create value in two primary ways. First, the audit report adds credibility to information provided to user groups. The auditors are providing an independent check against criteria presumably reflecting users' needs and desires, and the knowledge as whether, or to what extent, the criteria have been met can be extremely valuable. As a by-product of this evaluation process, the auditors often provide what can be an equally valuable benefit by identifying areas where improvements can be made and, perhaps, by providing specific recommendations. These recommendations can deal with minor procedural changes or major management policy changes. It should be noted, however, that some experts argue that recommendations should not be part of the audit function. These critics argue that recommendations compromise audit independence, if not in the first audit, certainly in all audits performed by the same auditors after the recommendations are (or are not) implemented.[9]

The second benefit of audits is provided by the anticipation of the audit, not the audit itself. Knowing that an audit might take place can have a strong motivating effect on the individuals involved to conform to the standards they think the auditors will use in their evaluation. In 1995, an embezzlement of more than $900,000 was discovered at the University of California. Investigators discovered that auditors had not visited that office in more than a decade. Gray Davis, lieutenant governor of California and a university regent, reacted as follows: "Everyone performs better if they know someone is looking over their shoulder. When you put out the word that no one is looking, it's an invitation to disaster."[10]

Situational Factors Affecting the Value of Audits

Audits are not equally valuable in all situations. One factor that affects the potential value of an audit is the importance of the area to be audited. The greater the potential consequences (the higher the stakes), the greater the potential value of the audit. Audits are also potentially more valuable if the probability is high that either the established criteria are not being met or would not be met in the absence of the audit. The criteria may not be met for intentional reasons, caused by lack of goal congruence between the individuals involved and the organization, or for unintentional reasons, such as carelessness or incompetence. Finally, audits are potentially more valuable where other control mechanisms are not feasible. Reviews by independent auditors are necessary where the user group is not able to satisfy itself directly as to whether the established criteria have been or are being met. This inability may be caused by the complexity of the subject matter, physical remoteness, or institutional barriers preventing access to some of the evidence needed (as in a joint venture).

Even where audits would seem to have a high potential value as a practical matter, their *realizable* value may be low. Audits cannot be used at all where the phenomenon to be audited cannot be measured or otherwise assessed, and the value of audits is low where the assessments are not reliable. The qualifications of the auditors are obviously also important. The realized value of an audit will depend on the degree to which the auditor qualifications meet the requirements of the job. Audits can assess only the past, so audits of truly one-time occurrences have value only if they provide some useful reinforcement of the reward system.

Audits can be extremely valuable tools in many control situations. Auditors can serve as the "eyes and ears" of management in assessing what is happening within the organization, and they can also share their expertise by providing recommendations for improvement. For management purposes, the potential value of an audit is greatest if the criteria to be used for comparison are those set by management. Audits commissioned by outsiders, such as financial status, are designed to serve the interests of those outsiders, although financial auditors may provide some observations of use to management.

Where audits are feasible, they can be an important alternative or supplement to other control mechanisms, such as direct supervision and incentives. Audits can test whether the desired behaviors were taken, and they often have powerful influences on behavior with relatively small costs. Auditors can usually reach an informed judgment by examining just a small proportion of the relevant evidence, and in many situations just the threat of an audit can be a powerful deterrent against undesirable behavior.

Audits do have some limitations and disadvantages. One is that they are done only on a periodic basis and provide little protection against problems occurring in the interim, except to the extent there is a deterrent effect. This exposure may be unacceptably high in situations where something must be done properly the first, or every, time. Audits can also create negative psychological reactions, such as defensiveness or aggression, when individuals feel their integrity is being questioned or their autonomy is being limited.

BOARDS OF DIRECTORS

In publicly-traded corporations, boards of directors receive their authority from the shareholders. Shareholders, however, typically diversify their risks and own a portfolio of numerous firms, and individual shareholders rarely have an incentive large enough to devote resources to ensure that company management is acting in the shareholders' best interest. The common solution is for shareholders to collectively delegate their authority for internal control to a board of directors. The boards are given ultimate control over management. They can monitor and approve management decisions, and they have the power to choose, dismiss, and reward managers.

Corporate boards of directors have two main control responsibilities. First, they safeguard the equity investors' interests, particularly by ensuring that management seeks to maximize the value of the shareholders' (or owners') stake in the corporation. Second, they protect the interests of other corporate stakeholders (employees, suppliers, customers, competitors, and society) by ensuring that the employees in the corporation act in a legally and socially responsible manner. Among other things, they help ensure fair financial reporting, fair compensation, fair competition, protection of the environment, and lack of undue interference in political processes.

Some independence from management is necessary for boards to fulfill these responsibilities effectively. Research evidence has shown that on average investors value outside directors because stock prices rise when outside directors are added to boards of directors.[11]

Many boards are not effective for any of a variety of reasons, which include lack of independence, competence, diligence and/or proactivity. *Interlocking direc-*

torates, situations where board members serve on each others' boards, is one problem many have pointed to. One study of the 788 largest U.S. firms found that in thirty-nine instances (nearly 5 percent of the cases), heads of companies sit on each others' boards.[12] These interlocking directorates can compromise independence. Even if they do not, they at least cause many to be concerned.

Douglas Austin, a Toledo, Ohio-based consultant described a more serious situation,

> My worst board was five people strong, and two of them had to be brought in on stretchers. One was 87 [years old] and one was 83. They just laid them on a table in the back of the room, and that's how they got their quorum.[13]

The many failures of boards of directors has led to a burgeoning literature on the functioning of boards and, more generally, *corporate governance* (the ways in which companies are directed and controlled). Part of that literature deals specifically with the board committee that is charged directly with monitoring and preventing control-related problems: audit committees.

AUDIT COMMITTEES

The boards of most publicly-held corporations have created a standing oversight committee, called an *audit committee,* made up solely of outside (nonemployee) directors, to help them fulfill their control responsibilities.[14] Audit committees enhance a board's ability to focus intensively and relatively inexpensively (without involving the full board) on the corporation's financial statements and other financial information disclosed.

While the U.S. Securities and Exchange Commission (SEC) has recommended the creation of nonemployee audit committees since 1940,[15] few companies had them until quite recently. Much of the recent growth in audit committees is attributable to a recommendation of the National Commission on Fraudulent Financial Reporting (often referred to as the Treadway Commission, after its chairman, James C. Treadway, Jr.). This commission was formed by the private sector in 1985 in response to heightened concerns about unreliable financial reporting and lax internal controls. It recommended that the SEC mandate the establishment of an audit committee made up solely of independent directors (nonemployees) in all public companies. The AICPA's Public Oversight Board has also issued numerous recommendations regarding audit committees.[16]

Audit committees are not legally required of all companies in the U.S. Only one state in the U.S., Connecticut, legally requires the appointment of an audit committee; however, a company must have an audit committee in order to be listed by the New York Stock Exchange (NYSE), the American Stock Exchange, or the National Association of Securities Dealers (NASDAQ). In June 1978, the NYSE established a requirement that firms must have audit committees and that those committees be made up solely of outside directors. The American Stock Exchange established this requirement in 1992. In 1987, NASDAQ required audit committees that are made up only of at least a majority of independent directors. In addition, to have their deposits insured by the Federal Deposit Insurance Corporation, U.S. banking institutions must have an audit committee which includes outside directors with banking or financial expertise.

Corporations in some other countries also have audit committee requirements. Canada has legal requirements for audit committees. In the United Kingdom, the report of the 1992 Committee on Financial Aspects of Corporate Government (the Cadbury Commission) mandated some audit committee functions for listing on the London Stock Exchange.[17]

Audit committees are intended to be informed, vigilant, and effective overseers of the company's financial reporting process and its internal control system. Audit committees generally assume the board's responsibilities relating to the organization's financial reporting, corporate governance, and corporate control practices. In the financial reporting area, audit committees provide assurance that the company's financial disclosures are reasonable and accurate. In the corporate governance area, audit committees provide assurance that the corporation is in compliance with pertinent laws and regulations, is conducting its affairs ethically, and is maintaining effective controls against fraud and employee conflicts of interest. In the corporate control area, audit committees monitor the company's management and internal control systems, which are designed to safeguard assets and employ them to achieve established goals and objectives. In fulfilling these responsibilities, audit committees hire the company's external auditors and monitor their performances. They maintain lines of communication between the board and the company's external auditors, internal auditors, financial management, and inside and outside counsel. Because they have limited resources directly available to them, audit committees must rely on the resources and support of other groups within the organization, particularly internal auditing.

Where audit committees exist, audit committee members are appointed by the board chairperson and approved by the full board. The median size of an audit committee in large U.S. corporations is five,[18] but the number varies with the size of the board of directors and the size of the organization. Three surveys have found that the audit committees hold an average of approximately four meetings per year.[19] The meetings last an average of 1.7 hours (range: one-half to six hours).[20] On average, an audit committee chairperson spends 24 hours per year on committee matters, exclusive of normal board of director activities (range: 7 to 80 hours).[21] In 1993, audit committee members were paid, on average, a retainer fee of $7,506 and a per meeting fee of $969.[22]

Research evidence has shown that audit committees have at least some effectiveness. One study found that public companies which overstated annual earnings were less likely to have audit committees.[23] Another study found that firms with audit committees have, on average, fewer shareholder lawsuits alleging fraud, fewer quarterly earnings restatements, fewer SEC enforcement actions, fewer illegal acts, and fewer instances of auditor turnover when there is an auditor-client accounting disagreement.[24]

Audit committees are not always effective. Independence from management, in both fact and appearance, is one essential characteristic of an audit committee. In some cases, company chief executive officers have been known to select the audit committee members, determine their rotation policies, define their duties, routinely attend their meetings, and review and approve reports given to the committee. When independence is lacking, managers and auditors will be reluctant to bring serious problems to the committee's attention, and the committee's effectiveness will be severely undermined.

Here are some other suggestions made by one or more experts.[25] Audit committees should:

- Gain support and direction from the entire board of directors.
- Adopt a written charter, use agendas, and follow formal work programs.

- Have at least three members, but not too many more so that all members can be active participants.
- Define the members' responsibilities and expect members who no longer contribute appropriately to step down.
- Meet at least four times per year, including a pre-audit meeting and a post-audit meeting. (Many people consider the frequency and duration of meetings to be highly reliable indicators of audit committee effectiveness.)
- Send a clear instruction to the independent auditor that the board of directors, as the shareholder's representative, is the auditor's client. (Management is not).
- Keep minutes of meetings and distribute them to the full board of directors.
- Review interim, as well as annual, financial reports.
- Schedule meetings in advance so participants have time to prepare.
- Review all financial information.
- Discuss with the independent auditor their qualitative judgments about the appropriateness, not just the acceptability, of the organization's accounting principles and financial disclosure practices.
- Be proactive. Participate in setting policies. Review reports. Monitor the corporate code of conduct and compliance with it. Ensure that the internal auditing involvement in the entire financial process is appropriate and properly coordinated with the independent public accountant.

CONCLUSION

This chapter has discussed three important control-related organizational roles: controllers, auditors, and members of the board of directors (particularly the board's audit committee). These control-related roles are challenging to fill because they involve an inherent conflict of interest. Individuals in these roles are asked to serve their organization and its management while at the same time providing a management oversight role on behalf of the organization's owners and other shareholders (creditors, the government, or society as a whole). Their role may require them to take actions that are quite costly to their organization in the short run, such as exposing a fraudulent financial reporting scheme. It takes strong, courageous individuals with excellent interpersonal skills to perform effectively in these roles.

Notes

1. V. Sathe, *Controllership in Divisionalized Firms: Structure, Evaluation, and Development* (New York: AMACOM, 1978).
2. V. Sathe, *Controller Involvement in Management* (Englewood Cliffs, N.J.: Prentice-Hall, 1982).
3. Ibid.
4. V. Sathe, "Who Should Control Division Controllers," *Harvard Business Review*, 56, no. 5 (September–October, 1978), pp. 99–104.
5. Ibid.
6. C. C. Verschoor, *The Interactions of Audit Committees with Internal Auditing* (Chicago: The Institute of Internal Auditors, Chicago Chapter, 1991).
7. Ibid.
8. "New UC Davis Audit Shows Need for Reform," *San Francisco Chronicle* (July 31, 1996), p. A18.

9. See R. A. Lindberg and T. Cohn, *Operations Auditing* (New York: American Management Association, Inc., 1972), p. 11.
10. A. Wallace, "UC Sues Official Over Alleged Embezzlement," *Los Angeles Times* (August 25, 1995), p. A3.
11. S. Rosenstein and J. G. Wyatt, "Outside Directors, Board Independence, and Shareholder Wealth," *Journal of Financial Economics* 26, no. 2 (August 1990), pp. 175–191.
12. Study conducted by Directorship, a Westport, Conn.-based consulting company, cited in A. L. Cowan, "Board Road Back-Scratching?" *The New York Times* (June 2, 1992), pp. Ca, C5.
13. D. Austin, quoted in "Now Hear This," *Fortune* (May 2, 1994), p. 16.
14. Much of this section was adapted from The Institute of Internal Auditors, *The Audit Committee: A Briefing on Roles and Responsibilities* (Altamont Springs, Fla. IIA, 1994); C. C. Verschoor, *Audit Committee Guidance for the 1990s* (Washington, D. C.: National Association of Corporate Directors, 1994); and M. L. Lovdal, "Making the Audit Committee Work," *Harvard Business Review*, 55, no. 2 (March–April 1977), pp. 108–114.
15. SEC Accounting Series Release No. 19.
16. For example, American Institute of Certified Public Accountants, The Public Oversight Board, *Special Report: Issues Confronting the Accounting Profession* (Stamford, Conn.: AICPA, 1993).
17. Committee on the Cadbury Report, *Financial Aspects of Corporate Governance* (London, 1992).
18. C. C. Verschoor, *The Interactions of Audit Committees with Internal Auditing* (Chicago: The Institute of Internal Auditors, Chicago Chapter, 1991).
19. Verschoor, *Interactions*, 1991; I. Bull, "Board of Director Acceptance of Treadway Responsibilities," *Journal of Accountancy* (February 1991), pp. 67–73; and W. W. Ecton and A. Reinstein, "Audit Committees: Can They Be More Effective?" *Financial Executive* (November 1982), pp. 32–37.
20. Ibid.
21. I. Bull, "Board of Director Acceptance of Treadway Responsibilities," *Journal of Accountancy* (February 1991), p. 71.
22. Korn/Ferry International, *Board of Directors Twentieth Annual Study* (New York: Korn/Ferry International, 1993, p. 17).
23. M. L. DeFond and J. Jiambalvo, "Incidence and Circumstances of Accounting Errors," *The Accounting Review* 66 (July 1991) pp. 643–55.
24. D. A. McMullen, "Audit Committee Performance: An Investigation of the Consequences Associated with Audit Committees," *Auditing: A Journal of Practice & Theory* 15, no. 1 (Spring 1996), pp. 87–103.
25. These suggestions were taken from Public Oversight Board, *Directors, Management and Auditors: Allies in Protecting Shareholder Interests* (Stamford, Conn.: Public Oversight Board, 1995); BDO Seidman, LLP, *Guide to Forming and Running An Effective Audit Committee* (New York: BDO Seidman, LLP, 1995); and Price Waterhouse, *Improving Audit Committee Performance: What Works Best* (Altamonte Springs, Fla.: The Institute of Internal Auditors, 1993).

ITT Corporation: Control of the Controllership Function, 1977 vs. 1991

Between 1960 and 1991, ITT Corporation experienced tremendous change. In an acquisition period under the leadership of Harold Geneen, it grew from a telecommunications base into the world's largest conglomerate. Then after Geneen retired (in 1980), the new chairman, Rand Araskog, divested many of ITT's businesses and restructured the corporation into nine operating groups.

As ITT's organization and management style changed, the functions of its controllership organization also changed. In the Geneen era of strong central management, ITT's controllership staff filled important information-providing and oversight roles. In the Araskog era, both the line and controllership organizations were more decentralized. Policy manuals were simplified; reporting requirements were reduced; and corporate staff groups were reduced in size. The operating controllers still played data preparation and control roles, but now many of them more actively involved in their units' decision making processes.

Ray Alleman, senior vice president and controller, was confident that ITT's controllership organization had adapted its operations and performed well throughout this 30-year period. But he also recognized the challenges of maintaining good control of his organization in the current decentralized operating era. He said, "For control to work, the correct instructions and mind-set must get down to the lowest level of responsibility, and that is continuing challenge." For this reason, he worked hard to ensure that the solid-line reporting relationships within the controller's organization not be weakened, and he decided that an elaborate controllership rating manual that had fallen into disuse in the early 1980s should be updated and rejuvenated.

ITT AND ITS COMPTROLLERSHIP FUNCTION IN THE 1960s AND 1970s

The Corporation and Its Control System

When Harold Geneen took over as chief executive in 1959, ITT was primarily involved in running telecommunications companies outside the United States. Under Geneen and his management team, ITT diversified and grew rapidly, assisted by hundreds of acquisitions, into the ninth-largest company on the *Fortune* 500 list. During this period, annual revenues grew from under $1 billion to $22 billion, and annual profits grew from $29 million to $301 million. At its peak in 1977, the company had 250 separate business units in diverse businesses such as telecommunications, insurance, baking, and car rentals, and employed approximately 400,000 people worldwide.

In the Geneen era, ITT relied primarily on an elaborate financial reporting system to control its operating units. Early in his career, Geneen became upset with operating forecasts that were fluctuating wildly, and he decided to involve his controllers actively in the business processes. Tom Krauter, a long-time ITT employee and currently vice president/assistant controller, remembered that, "Geneen's philosophy was that if you had a good general manager and a good controller, you would get a great company."

Geneen implemented an extensive, numbers-oriented control system. The system required each operating unit head to negotiate with headquarters personnel a detailed Business Plan containing up to 100 pages. This plan described in detail how the operating unit intended to achieve its objectives for each of the following two years and also contained a forecast, in less detail, for the third to fifth years out. Then each month each business unit submitted a set of 13 operating re-

Research Assistant Patrick Henry and Professor Kenneth A. Merchant wrote this case as the basis for class discussion rather than to illustrate either effective or ineffective handling of an administrative situation.

ports to regional and corporate headquarters. These reports included an income statement, a balance sheet, a cash flow statement, and a variety of operating statistics and analyses (e.g., employment statistics, analysis of inventories, analysis of receivables, status of capital projects). One of the reports was a detailed operating and financial review, written by the controller, which was often 20 pages or more in length. The operating units also submitted about a dozen other reports on a less frequent basis, either quarterly, semiannually, or annually.

The plans were a detailed expression of each manager's commitment to the corporation, and the operating reports measured the degree to which that commitment was fulfilled. Both the plans and reports were scrutinized by a large headquarters staff and managers in the line organization, including Geneen himself, to ensure that the managers' thinking was correct, the facts were accurate and up-do-date, and performance was running according to plan. When actual results fell below the plan, operating managers were invariably asked both for more detail about the problems and for explanations of how they were getting things back on track. The managers were often given *suggestions* for fixing the problems. When disagreements arose over policies or actions, the facts were available for experts to hash them out. This system of checks and balances, with tension between line and staff designed into it, was intended to keep managers on their toes and to get on top of problems early, before they created a crisis.

The Controllership Organization

ITT's controllership organization in the Geneen era was large because of both the need to prepare and communicate massive amounts of data and the philosophy of imposing multiple levels of more experienced managers on top of every manager. In 1977 the controller's organization was comprised of about 23,000 employees, 325 of whom were located at the New York headquarters. (Exhibit 1 shows a chart of the headquarters control organization in 1977.)

ITT maintained a *solid-line* reporting relationship throughout its controllership organization. The solid line relationship represented authorities for hiring, firing, setting salary levels, assigning bonuses, and setting staffing levels, although these decisions were usually made in consultation with line managers. The solid line reporting was designed to enhance the controllers' professionalism, neutrality, objectivity, integrity, and loyalty to the total corporation and its shareholders, not the individual operating entities to which they were assigned.

Ten directors of financial control (DFCs), seven located in New York and three in Brussels, played a key role in ITT's centralized control organization. The DFCs and their staffs traveled extensively, solving problems and monitoring and evaluating the performances of the 20 to 30 field unit controllers for whom each of them was responsible. The DFCs also had responsibility for headquarters analysis and reporting for their assigned units.

The Controllership Rating Manual

In 1968, Herb Knortz, then ITT's corporate controller, appointed a committee to develop a procedure for evaluating the effectiveness of each controllership activity. The committee developed a Controllership Rating Manual which described how to rate the controllership function of each operating unit in each of the 32 areas of responsibility shown in Exhibit 2. For each of these areas, the unit controllers answered between 30 and 60 specific *yes/no* questions aimed as assessing how well they and their staffs performed activities in each of these areas. For the 32 areas combined, the unit controller answered about 1700 questions. These detailed lists of questions, which evolved over the years, were known within ITT as *the rating grids.*

The DFCs computed effectiveness scores for each of the operating units under their jurisdiction. The controller's self-evaluation accounted for 75 percent of the scores assigned to the unit. The DFC responsible for the unit determined the other 25 percent by answering five questions for each of the 32 areas. Thus, the DFC answered 160 questions for each of the 20 to 30 field units under his jurisdiction.

Exhibit 3 shows an example of one of the 32 questionnaires, for the budgets and forecasts area. The first 60 questions are for the unit controller. The last page shows the five questions for the DFC. Exhibit 4 shows a hypothetical unit's numerical score for one area of responsibility (one questionnaire).

The ratings achieved for each of the 32 areas evaluated for controllership effectiveness formed the basis for establishing a re-rating timetable and for initiating action programs. A perfect evaluation score (100) was possible only if the unit controller answered *Yes* to every question and the DFC gave a Satisfactory score ("5") for each of the five items, but overall scores of 90 or above were considered satisfactory. The ratings were interpreted as follows:

RATING	EVALUATION AND ACTION	NEXT RATING IN	COLOR CODE
>89	Satisfactory	2 years	Blue
80–89	Acceptable	1 year	Green
70–79	Requires improvement, action program should be initiated	6 months	Yellow
<70	Unacceptable, action program must be initiated	3 months	Red

As a convenient overview, ITT managers constructed a color-coded *controllership grid* to show quickly how effectively each of the 250 units within the ITT system were performing in each of the 32 specific areas of controllership responsibility. Exhibit 5 shows a representation of this grid. The DFCs had the responsibility to initiate the required action programs and to provide each unit controller under their jurisdiction with the proper questionnaires according to the re-rating timetable.

The grid scores did not necessarily reflect the performance of the unit's controller. For example, it was not unusual for the controllership activity in a newly acquired unit to have an initial yellow or red rating in several areas. These lower ratings did not automatically imply that the unit's controller was ineffective because it could sometimes take even an outstanding controller a year or two to make the necessary improvements.

The evaluations of controllers as individuals were done subjectively. The controller's unit's effectiveness scores affected, but did not determine, the individual evaluations. For example, one measure of the effectiveness of controllers newly assigned to acquired business units was often the time it took them to bring the function *up to speed,* given the complexity of the situation they faced. Complexity might be increased by, for example, new production technologies, high planning uncertainty, multiple operating locations, and lack of properly trained staff.

CHANGES IN THE 1980s AND 1990s

The Corporation

In the 1980s, ITT went through a number of major structural changes. Harold Geneen retired as chief executive officer in 1977 and as chairman on January 1, 1980. Rand Araskog took over in mid-1979. Araskog simplified the corporation by divesting many of its companies and decentralized the operations. In 1986, he divested ITT's telecommunications business and reorganized the company into nine operating groups (see organization chart in Exhibit 6). By 1991, the nine operating groups included 73 separate business units employing approximately 114,000 people worldwide. In 1990, the company produced revenues of $20.6 billion and net income of $958 million.

The decentralized operating style brought a significant reduction in the business units' reporting requirements. On a monthly basis, they were asked to produce only income statements, cash flow statements, and a number of variance reports, along with the controller's report which was now typically only a few pages in length (rather than 20 pages as before). And, significantly, corporate personnel saw the financial detail only of the nine group entities, not the 73 individual operating units.

The Controllership Organization and the Group Controller Role

Many of the functions of the controllership organization were also decentralized, and the organization was reduced significantly in size. In 1991, total worldwide controllership personnel were 8,000, and the headquarters controllership staff was 134. (The organization of the corporate controller's staff in 1991 is shown in Exhibit 7.)

The headquarters DFC role was eliminated in 1986, and the unit controllers reported instead to one of the nine group controllers located in the field, not at corporate headquarters. The group controllers were considered more a part of the management team than were the DFCs. The DFCs, who were located in New York and Brussels, had to have a headquarters orientation. The group controllers, who were located at group headquarters, usually took part in developing solutions.

Larry Burns, group controller for ITT's Defense Group, and a former DFC, explained the change from his perspective:

> When I was in New York, there were strong tugs from two directions: (1) headquarters reporting and analysis, and (2) field problem solving—plus my group was one that had a group controller between the unit controllers and me. The unit controllers rarely called me, so I had to contact them to get any information. Now I talk to the unit controllers regularly. The communication intensity has increased tenfold. Technology, such as E-mail, makes communications easier, but the basic cause of the increase is that the organization is different.
>
> The nature of the communications is also different. The dialogue is more open. It's no longer an *us and them* situation. The controllers tell me their problems, and we work on solving them together. Plus, general managers often call to get my perspective on ideas or problems, and I brief the unit controllers. So we have another line of communication that we didn't have when I was in New York.

The group controllers also believed that the control environment had improved because they were more knowledgeable about both the operating entities and the personnel in them. Larry Burns noted that he visited every operating unit at least once a month. And Gerry Gendron, group controller for the Electronic Components Group said, "It's easier to communicate with the unit controllers because my focus is strictly on them and their units."

Staff support for the controllers was reduced significantly, however. Senior management transferred many controllership activities to the nine group headquarters offices, but they eliminated the large staffs that the DFCs had at their disposal. Ray Alleman explained that "This diminishment of staff reflected management's view that the staffs were too costly, too large in terms of usefulness, and at the wrong place to participate fully in the activities of the operations." Gerry Gendron worried that the company's control system might now be less effective because of the reduction in staff resources, but he concluded that, "I don't think we are to the point where our controls are weak."

One exception to the pattern of decentralization was internal audit. The internal audit function was centralized and placed under the direct responsibility of ITT's chief financial officer. Formerly large staffs of field auditors had reported to the unit controllers.

Solid Line Reporting

The controller's organization continued solid line reporting from corporate headquarters down to the lowest element of the financial organization in the field. But the general managers of the operating groups were playing a larger role in the controllers' annual evaluations that determined their bonuses, which could range up to 30 percent of salary, and this weakening of the solid-line reporting relationship concerned Ray Alleman. He noted that:

> In a couple of instances the general manager has filled out a controller's performance appraisal form. I don't like that. The general manager should sign off, but the form should be filled out by the unit controller's boss [the group controller].

Ray insisted that he and the group controllers approve all unit controllers' bonuses. He said, "I want my people to be treated fairly, and I want them to know that I approved their bonus."

Confidence in the Organization

In assessing the performance of his controllership organizations, Ray Alleman listed the areas of performance he considered critical. He explained that it was imperative that his controllers perform their routine tasks well. For example, they needed to keep their books, pay their bills, and maintain their payroll records properly. They needed to communicate contingencies and risks (e.g., potential for a strike or tax increase) promptly and accurately. They must stay on top of business conditions because "Frequent surprises reflect badly on a controller." They must interface well with the line managers. And they must develop their people.

Ray knew that ITT, like all other large corporations, had had some control problems. For example, operating managers had not always made the proper communications to corporate; they had occasionally failed to comply with the corporate approval levels for capital addition expenditures; and they had made some commitments and expenditures before securing the proper approvals. But overall, Ray was confident that ITT's controllership function was performing well. Part of his confidence stemmed from the trust he had in his people, particularly his group controllers. He had placed all of them in their positions, and he knew all were experienced controllers who had proved themselves over a number of years.

Larry Burns, one of the group controllers, agreed that control effectiveness depends to a large extent on people and that the quality of ITT's control staffs had improved as the organization had stabilized. He noted:

> The data being sent to corporate are now better because the information receives a better level of review. Plus most of our controllers now have at least 10–15 years experience. In the Geneen years we had a lot of new people in the company, and many controllers had only 5–6 years experience. . . .
>
> People are very important, and a lot of control is interpersonal. If I'm not getting answers, or if I'm getting surprises, then I know I have to step up my monitoring activity. For example, I visit one of my seven units for two days every two weeks, plus I talk with the controller at least three to four hours a week. It's a tough unit to manage, and the controller is a good accountant, but there is a lot to handle in the unit, and he needs help from me. So it's risky. On the other hand, I think about one of my other units relatively few hours in a typical month.

Despite his confidence in the control organization, Ray Alleman regretted that the controllership rating manual (*the rating grids*) had fallen into disuse. He wanted to retain it as a control tool, and he started a project to rejuvenate the grids.

Revised Controllership Rating Manual

The grids had started to fall into disuse in the early 1980s. They were seen by many managers as being out-of-date, too wordy, and requiring both too much work in a period of staff cutbacks and too much headquarters involvement during a period in which the company was decentralizing. They no longer served one of their original purposes—facilitation of bringing newly acquired companies *into the fold*—because ITT's acquisition activities had diminished significantly. The grids were seen as less manageable because the group controllers had less staff support than did the DFCs. And they were seen as not applying well to some of ITT's significant remaining businesses, such as insurance, hotels, and financial services, because they had been heavily oriented to ITT's telecommunications and heavy manufacturing businesses. Some of the groups had tried to modify some of the grids to make them more suitable for their businesses, but they found that the cost of developing and maintaining the grids was sizable.

Still, Ray Alleman believed that the grids were a valuable tool. He wanted them to be used for training purposes, to fills gaps in the controllers' backgrounds; for diagnostic purposes, to remind the controllers of things that they might have forgotten; and for control purposes, as "the first warning that something is awry." Ray explained, "A bust is usually caused by failure to pay attention to fundamentals, like not reconciling bank balances at the end of the month. The grids help to identify the little things."

In 1987, Ray assigned Lee Dobbins, corporate director of professional development activities, the task of revising the grids. Lee organized a series of meetings with operating personnel and recorded and integrated the suggestions he heard. Lee reduced the number of grids by eliminating two of them and by combining several others. By July 1990, he had revised 15 of the 27 grids that would be used (down from a maximum of 32) and planned to release the remaining 12 by the end of 1992. Lee also simplified the grids by reducing the number of questions aimed at the unit controllers significantly. For example, Exhibit 8 shows that the rating grid for Operating Plans/Budgets and Forecasts included only 33 questions, down from 60 (see Exhibit 3). And he eliminated the questions formerly answered by the DFCs. Lee acknowledged, however, that revision of the grids was not a one-time task. He expected that the grids would undergo an ongoing evolution, and he and Ray Alleman encouraged the operating entities to tailor the grids to their own operations.

The new grids were designed primarily for unit controllers to administer their own activities. Headquarters control staffs were not routinely provided access to the responses. The unit controllers were to prepare the grids and submit their responses to the group controllers, not corporate staff.

The group controllers used the scores for identifying weak areas of control and, to a lesser extent, for evaluating their units' functions and personnel. While the summary ratings set the rerating timetable, as had been done before, Ray Alleman emphasized that "The great value of the grids is in the individual questions and answers. A single 'no' may raise an important issue, even within an overall score that is over 90 percent." Internal audit teams also reviewed the questionnaire responses as a routine part of their audits and corporate managers examined the grids when visiting operating units.

EXHIBIT 1 Corporate Controller's Organization—1977

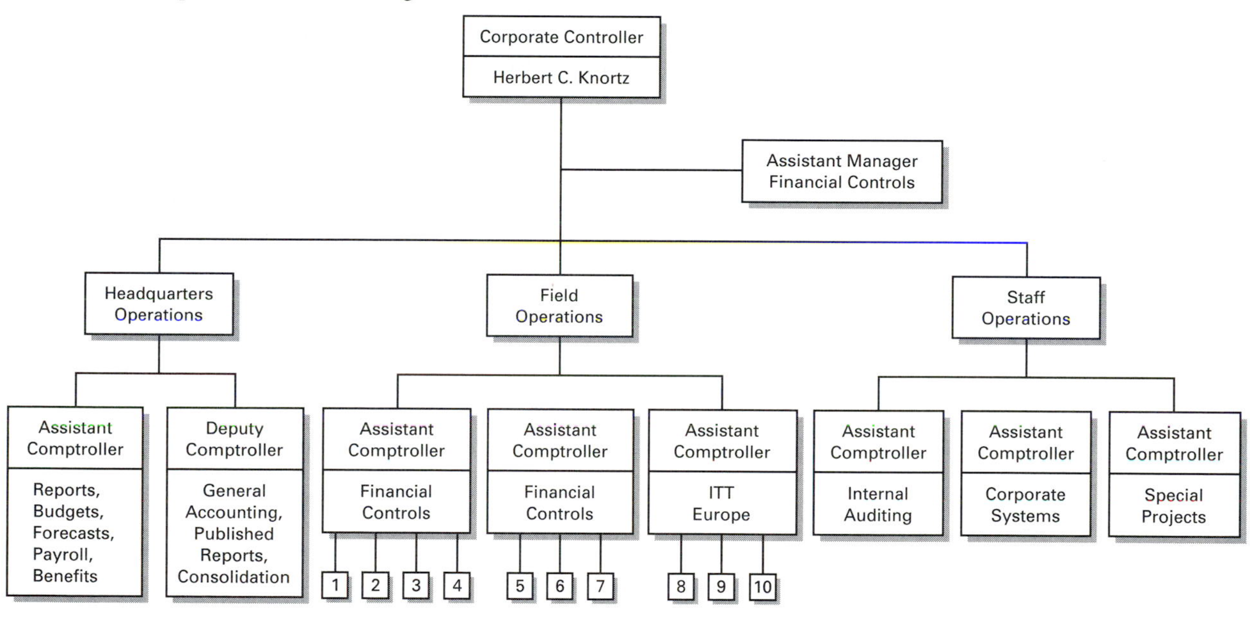

EXHIBIT 3 *Continued*

SUBJECT: BUDGETS AND FORECASTS	QUESTIONNAIRE NO. 3
	PAGE 2 of 5

		YES	NO
17.	Do you test all departmental budgets for reasonableness to insure that they are in harmony with other affected departments, and that appropriate balance and relationship exits between them (e.g. Marketing and Production)?	___	___
18.	Is each department head responsible for the development of his department's budget and does he accept the budget as realistic and attainable?	___	___
19.	Is each department head responsible for the General Manager for the attainment of his budget?	___	___
20.	Do the department heads project current year latest forecast levels as a basis for the budget year?	___	___
21.	Do you provide all department heads with copies of the budget procedures and forms applicable to their area of responsibility?	___	___
22.	Do you issue local procedures to supplement the ITT Headquarters corporate budget policies and procedures?	___	___
23.	Are firm due dates established for completion of each phase of the budget preparation and are appropriate responsibilities assigned?	___	___
24.	Are budget changes halted when the budget is finalized?	___	___
25.	Are budgets prepared down to the level of detail in the chart of accounts?	___	___
26.	Is enough information available in the budget workpapers for you to identify, analyze and explain variances?	___	___
27.	Are any aspects peculiar of business planning of budgeting computerized or prepared mechanically?	___	___
28.	Are final budget schedules identified by the unit number per Comptroller's Procedure B.O.O.?	___	___
29.	Are budget schedules reviewed for footing accuracy and internal consistency prior to submission to ITT Headquarters?	___	___
30.	Do you regularly discuss your budgeting problems, techniques, etc. with your colleagues in other units and/or the Director of Financial Controls?	___	___
31.	Are the same basic working papers used both in the preparation of business plans and for the final budget?	___	___
32.	To assist in the budget preparation, do you provide appropriate historical data to department heads and/or others with profit or cost responsibility?	___	___
33.	Do you assist department heads in developing and preparing their budgets by suggesting realistic expense levels and cost ratios?	___	___
34.	Do you personally discuss budget preparation and subsequent forecast revisions with department heads concerned?	___	___

EXHIBIT 3 *Continued*

SUBJECT: BUDGETS AND FORECASTS	QUESTIONNAIRE NO. 3
	PAGE 3 of 5

		YES	NO
35.	Have you furnished or suggested to department heads special techniques for the budgetary control of expenses?	____	____
36.	Do the department heads seek your opinions and judgements regarding their budget plans?	____	____
37.	Do you review preliminary departmental budgets and furnish department heads with your judgements and recommendations?	____	____
38.	Are major forecast revisions discussed promptly with area or group management (prior to official release to ITT Headquarters)?	____	____
39.	Have you insured that corrective action (relating to anticipated budget shortfalls) is attempted prior to recognizing the shortfall in a revised forecast?	____	____
40.	Is every department covered by a monthly internal report comparing actual performance to budget?	____	____
41.	Are these budget reports analyzed by you and do you explain the analysis to the department heads?	____	____
42.	Are department heads required to furnish explanations and corrective action planned for each significant budget variance?	____	____
43.	Are planning and budget working papers and notes filed for subsequent review and follow up?	____	____
44.	Do you identify, in writing, the weaknesses or errors in current year and prior years budgets to avoid their recurrence in new budget plans?	____	____
45.	Do you maintain budget controls over A&G manpower and compensation?	____	____
46.	Do you question costs or expenses in the narrative section of the budget presentation?	____	____
47.	Do you highlight such costs or expenses in the narrative section of the budget presentation?	____	____
48.	Have you introduced or suggested specific innovations to reduce A&G manpower requirements?	____	____
49.	Are historical cost trends and asset level changes shown in the budget as a correlation to percentage increases or decreases in sales levels?	____	____
50.	Are manpower levels budgeted (in other departments) in relationship to anticipated workload requirements and guidelines, if any, established by World and Group Headquarters?	____	____
51.	Do you or any member of your staff belong to any professional financial or budget societies or groups?	____	____
52.	Is the income benefit or cost savings on planned new capital expenditures included in units operating budget?	____	____

EXHIBIT 3 *Continued*

SUBJECT: BUDGETS AND FORECASTS	QUESTIONNAIRE NO. 3
	PAGE 4 of 5

		YES	NO
53.	Are provision for depreciation and financing costs for new capital expenditures included in the budget?	____	____
54.	Does a procedure exist whereby the Comptroller is kept informed of all significant changes anticipated in the current year to insure that the forecasts are revised as needed?	____	____
55.	Does the operating budget include the anticipated benefits of all significant work simplification programs?	____	____
56.	Does the operating budget include planned savings resulting from manpower control programs?	____	____
57.	Are forecast revisions discussed by the budget committee or by the assembly of key unit management personnel?	____	____
58.	Have you established controls to assure that an approved revision to the budget is reflected consistently in all unit financial data and projections?	____	____
59.	Are approved budget goals communicated to key department personnel in the organization?	____	____
60.	Is the applicable INCOS documentation complete and up-to-date?	____	____

Unit ________________________

Controller's Signature ________________________

Date Submitted ________________________

* * * * * * * * * * * * * * * * * * *

TO BE ANSWERED BY THE DIRECTORS OF FINANCIAL CONTROLS:

To assess the qualitative performance of the function being rated by this questionnaire, the Director of Financial Controls is requested to score the unit Comptrollership function to the following:

		Score[1]		
		0	2	5
1.	Budget committee.			
2.	Interface budgeting procedures and controls.			
3.	Interface of Comptroller with department heads in budget preparation.			
4.	Budget reports and analyses.			
5.	Forecasting techniques.			

[1]0 = Not acceptable, 2 = Minimum acceptable, 5 = Satisfactory.

EXHIBIT 4 Hypothetical Numerical Score Computation in One Area of Responsibility

QUESTIONNAIRE NO. 3

UNIT NUMBER ______________

Part I—Responses from Unit Controllers

Number of "No" Responses or Responses Rejected by Directors of Financial Controls (A)	Total Applicable Questions in Questionnaire[1] (B)	Score $\frac{B - A}{B} \times 75 =$
7	60	66

Part II—Responses from Directors of Financial Controls

Question	*Point Value Assigned*[2]
1. ______	2
2. ______	5
3. ______	5
4. ______	5
5. ______	2

Total 19

Total Rating (Part I and Part II 85

Comments (Use additional pages if required):

Signed ______________________
Director of Financial Controls

Notes:

[1]If certain questions were not applicable to the unit, they could be deleted with the DFC's concurrence.

[2]0 = Not acceptable, 2 = Minimum acceptable, 5 = Satisfactory.

EXHIBIT 5 Representation of Comptrollership Grid

Areas of comptrollership activity[1]

Field units within the ITT System	1	2	3		32
1	Green		Yellow		
2		Red			
3					Green
250			Red		

Color Codes

Blue	90 and above
Green	80–89
Yellow	70–79
Red	under 70

[1]See Exhibit 2 for a listing of the areas.

EXHIBIT 6 ITT Organization—1991

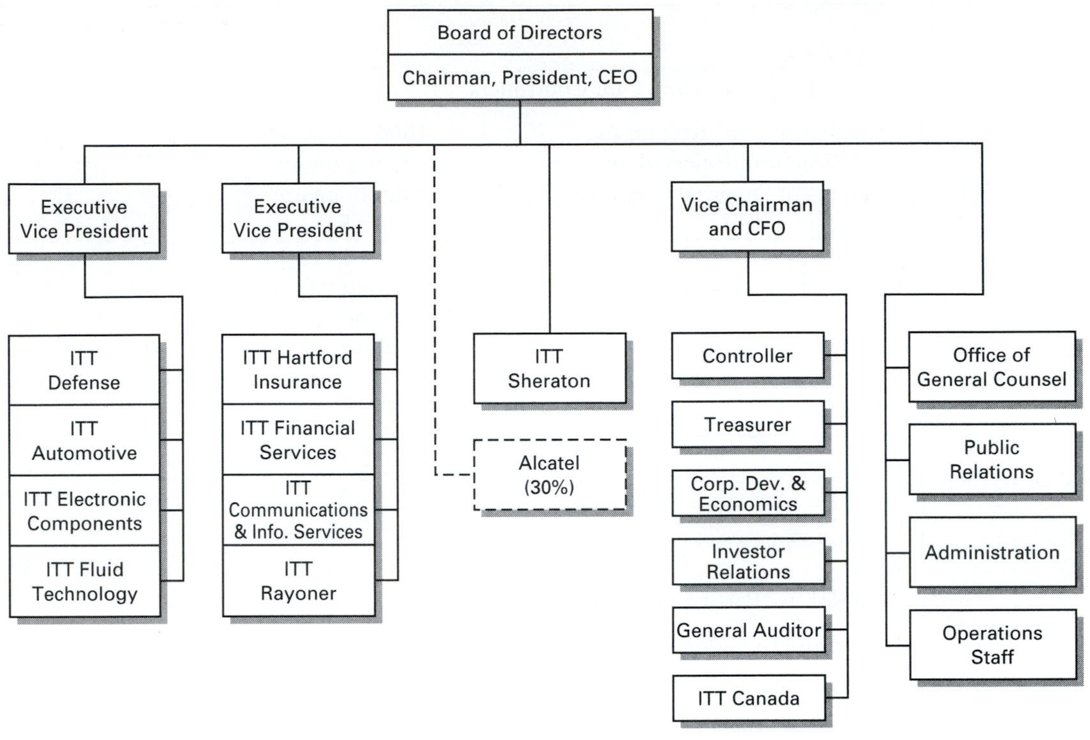

EXHIBIT 7 Corporate Controller's Organization—1991

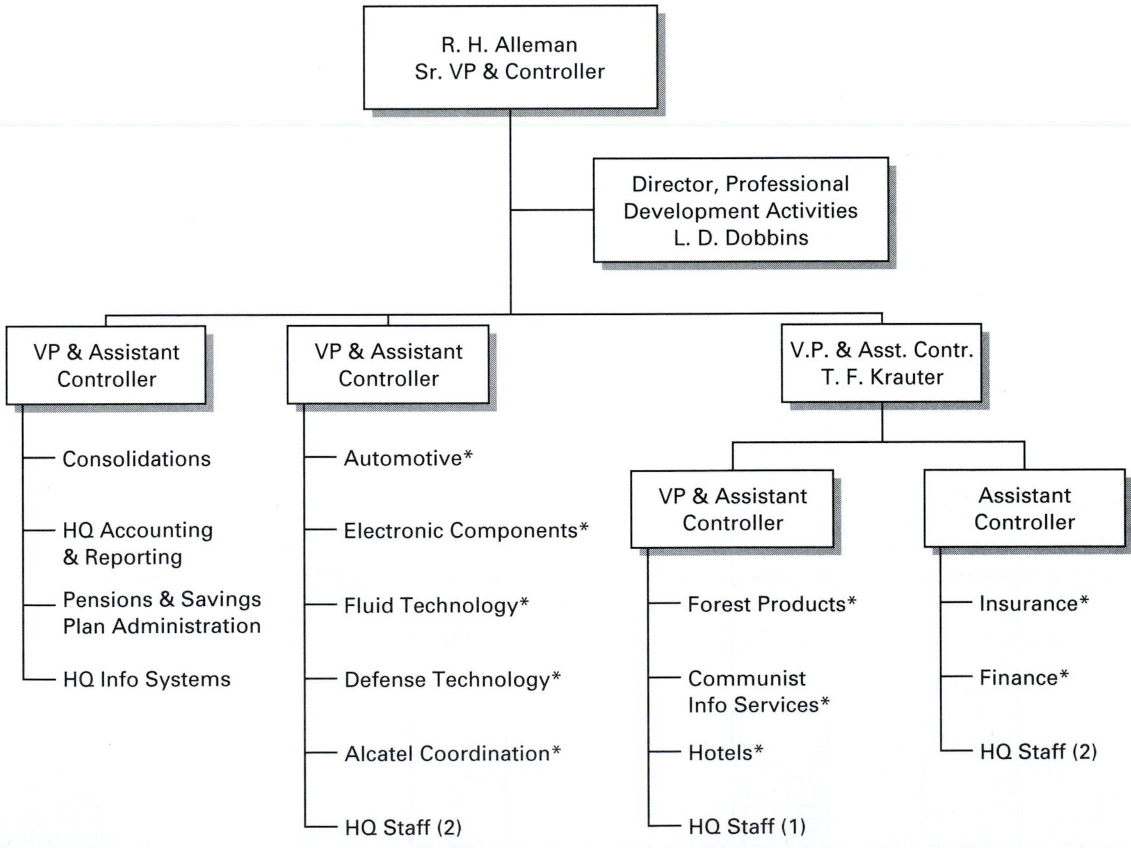

EXHIBIT 8 Sample Revised Rating Grid

ITT Controller Rating Grids	Operating Plans/ Budgets and Forecasts	Questionnaire 3 Issued 7/15/90 Page 1 of 3

NOTE: Budget commitments essentially are established in the operating plan, with selective updates for the final budget. For development of the budget, the term "budget" in Grid No. 3 refers to the combination of operating plan and budget.

		YES	NO
	★ ★ ★		
	Does the entity have a well-defined internal budget process that:		
1.	Begins with discussions of budget goals among senior management?	☐	☐
2.	Establishes budget objectives before the budget work is begun?	☐	☐
3.	Provides for budget preparation by each responsible manager?	☐	☐
4.	Includes review by entity management, with controllership participation?	☐	☐
5.	Includes firm due dates for completion of each phase?	☐	☐
	★ ★ ★		
6.	Does the entity go through a formal reforecast to use as the basis for the budget?	☐	☐
7.	Is there a clear assignment to an individual or function for the preparation, coordination, and maintenance of entity budgets?	☐	☐
8.	Does the controller review the budget assumptions and express professional judgement on the reasonableness of the assumptions?	☐	☐
9.	Does the budget process ensure that there is consistency across all budgets? (For example, are new costs and projected benefits from the capital expenditure budget reflected in cost and income budgets, or, is a revision to one budget reflected correctly in all related budgets?)	☐	☐
10.	Do details for sales budgets and forecasts come from the marketing/sales organization?	☐	☐
11.	Does the controller's office use industry or trade data on sales trends, or other appropriate sources, to evaluate independently sales budgets and sales forecasts?	☐	☐
12.	Is the entity's sales budget supported by detailed work papers identifying the customers, products, models, quantities to be marked, areas or markets covered, prices, and discount or credit terms?	☐	☐
13.	Is the production budget consistent with the order input/sales budget?	☐	☐
14.	Does the entity use the latest available manufacturing cost standards in its budget?	☐	☐

EXHIBIT 8 *Continued*

ITT Controller Rating Grids	Operating Plans/ Budgets and Forecasts	Questionnaire 3 Issued 7/15/90 Page 2 of 3

	YES	NO
★ ★ ★		
Does the entity have a well-defined internal budget process that:		
15. As part of the entity's review and approval process, are all departments' budgets tested for reasonable balance and relationship with each other and with the budget assumptions?	☐	☐
16. Do the entity's work papers from the operating plan provide details and data necessary for budget preparation?	☐	☐
17. Is the controller involved personally in discussions with other department heads in budget and forecast preparation?	☐	☐
18. Is there a budget *postmortem* to identify weaknesses or errors, to avoid recurrence in subsequent budgets?	☐	☐
19. Are marketing quotas assigned to salespersons or sales managers?	☐	☐
★ ★ ★		
Is there enough information in the budget process and work papers to:		
20. Identify cost and revenue responsibility?	☐	☐
21. Measure performance internally and externally, down to the account levels or data groupings that will be reported during the budget year?	☐	☐
22. Analyze and explain variances?	☐	☐
★ ★ ★		
23. Is each department manager held accountable for attainment of his/her budget?	☐	☐
24. Does the controller's department have active involvement with the department managers and with the entity general manager suggesting techniques for budgetary control and profit improvement?	☐	☐
25. Is every department/cost center covered by a monthly internal report that compares actual performance with budget, with an identification of the factors in budget variances?	☐	☐
26. Does the controller ensure that budget or forecast variances are surfaced for prompt recognition in forecasts and/or outlooks?	☐	☐
27. Does the entity have controls to ensure that A&G/marketing headcount and cost overruns receive prior approval in accordance with established authorities.	☐	☐

EXHIBIT 8 *Continued*

ITT Controller Rating Grids	Operating Plans/ Budgets and Forecasts	Questionnaire 3 Issued 7/15/90 Page 3 of 3

	YES	NO
★ ★ ★		
Does the entity have a well-defined internal budget process that:		
28. Are forecast assumptions reviewed at least monthly, and updated when appropriate?	☐	☐
29. Are forecast revisions discussed fully among key management personnel?	☐	☐
30. Does the entity general manager or president review and approve sales forecasts and product plans/forecasts?	☐	☐
31. Are the sales forecasts supported by appropriate level of details, such as sales by customers, sales in specific market areas and/or product grouping, prices, etc.?	☐	☐
32. Does the forecast process ensure that the financial forecast is not unknowingly inconsistent with sales projections and production plans of responsible operating managers?	☐	☐
33. Are the controls for the operating plans, budgets, and forecasts documented to the controller's satisfaction?	☐	☐

Evaluation Summary

A. Total questions	33	
B. Less: Not applicable	(____)	
C. Questions applicable	____	
D. Questions answered "yes"	____	
E. Percent of applicable (D ÷ C)	____ %	

____
Entity

____
Entity Controller's Signature

____
Date Rated

Scovill Inc.: NuTone Housing Group

In January 1982, in his first month with the company, Bob Hager, Scovill's new treasurer/controller, faced a difficult issue. He discovered that one of the major operating groups of the company, the NuTone Housing Group, was using direct labor time standards that were purposely overstated. The overstated standards caused large, favorable labor-efficiency variances, overstated product costs, and, until year-end, a substantial understatement of inventory values. Accounting adjustments had to be made at year-end to total cost of sales and inventories. For the year 1981, this adjustment totaled $2.8 million.

After studying the situation, Hager decided to approach Jim Rankin, executive vice president in charge of the Housing and Security Products Groups, with a request to make the labor standards more realistic. Rankin was against making the change:

> This issue has come up before, and I feel strongly that making the change would not be in NuTone's best interest. We make a lot of special quotes, and sometimes the pressures to squeeze margins on these quotes are too strong. That's where our inflated standards play an important role; they give us a cushion to protect our margins when we are making price decisions. This business has been very successful over the years, and I would go as far as to say that the way we've used the standards to protect our margins has been the single most important management practice that has contributed to our success.
>
> The overstated costs also make our monthly financial reports conservative because we do not capture the favorable efficiency variances until year-end, and I like that. I love to take inventory at year-end and find that we've got some extra in there. It's like Santa Claus has arrived. The extra profit takes care of a lot of little costs that occur at year-end.

Hager, however, still thought it was important that NuTone's labor standards be made realistic:

> I realize that NuTone has been operating the way it has for many years; this problem has been mentioned in the auditors' management letter for each of the last six years, and I'm sure it goes back before that. But the distortions are getting larger and larger. The 1981 end-of-year adjustment was more than a month's income for NuTone. It's not just that this is bad accounting; I'm really concerned that we may not know our real product costs, and as a consequence, we may be making some bad decisions. I'm also disturbed that Rankin has no interest in fixing an obvious problem.

Scovill's operating groups had considerable autonomy, so Hager's primary option if he wanted to pursue this issue was whether to raise it with the audit committee of the board of directors. He did not take this step lightly. He had had to make such an appeal only three times in his career for issues of major importance, and he did not wish to force a confrontation with a line manager, particularly since he had just joined the company. The issues he had to confront included how important was it to have realistic cost standards, and how much merit did Rankin's arguments have.

SCOVILL INC.

Background

Scovill Inc., was a leading producer of quality consumer and industrial products. The company had started operations in 1802 in Waterbury,

Research Assistant Lourdes Ferreira and Professor Kenneth A. Merchant prepared this case as the basis for class discussion rather than to illustrate either effective or ineffective handling of an administrative situation.

Connecticut, as a brass works, and over the years, it had grown both internally and through acquisition. By 1981, Scovill had become a diversified international company with total annual revenues in excess of $800 million. (Exhibit 1 shows a financial summary for the years 1978–1981). Scovill had been paying dividends for 126 consecutive years, longer than any other industrial company on the New York Stock Exchange.

The corporation was organized into six groups (see organizational chart in Exhibit 2). Exhibit 3 describes the groups' major product lines and shows their 1981 sales and operating income numbers. All of the groups benefited from well-known product trademarks, and most of their products were leaders in their market segments.

Scovill was operated in a highly decentralized fashion. The product groups were allowed considerable discretion in establishing and implementing the strategies appropriate to their areas of business. The primary control mechanism employed by headquarters were annual reviews of the budgets submitted from each of the groups and quarterly reviews of actual results compared with the budgets.

Scovill did not have a single unified accounting system that was used in all of its operating units. This was due to the fact that Scovill had acquired many companies over the years, and the acquired companies were allowed to continue with most of the elements of their accounting systems even after they became a part of Scovill. The accounting policies set at corporate tended to describe minimum reporting requirements and very general accounting policies rather than detailed instructions that had to be followed. For example, the accounting policy manual specified that the operating units were to follow the full absorption method of accounting "whereby most fixed and variable costs are recognized in inventory and cost of sales accounting," but it did not provide further description as to how the full absorption method was to be accomplished.

Bob Hager joined Scovill in January 1982. Bob had a solid accounting background and substantial experience. He had earned an MBA with a concentration in production and was a certified management accountant. While employed at General Electric Company early in his career, he completed that company's well-regarded financial training program. Later, he served as a divisional controller at Pennwalt Chemical and Bristol-Myers and as corporate controller of Marine Midland Bank and Loctite Corporation.

NUTONE HOUSING GROUP

Background

NuTone was founded in 1936 in Cincinnati, Ohio, as a manufacturer of door chimes. After World War II, the company extended its product lines to include auxiliary heaters, kitchen and bathroom fans, intercoms, and range hoods. NuTone merged with and became an operating group of Scovill Inc., on September 15, 1967.

The acquisition proved to be a great success. NuTone had consistently been the company's most profitable group, and it was often referred to as the *jewel* of Scovill. In 1981, NuTone had total annual sales of just over $200 million, and the group's gross margin percentage was still hovering near its historical average of about 40 percent. Exhibit 4 shows summary group financial data.

Products and Production

NuTone competed in two broad markets: the new housing and remodeling market and the consumer durables market. It manufactured and sold approximately 5,000 products in 11 product lines, including exhaust fans, heaters, range hoods, door chimes, bath cabinets, radio intercoms, paddle fans, lighting fixtures, and security systems. Exhibit 5 presents data on the size and profitability of NuTone's major product lines.

NuTone had been very successful in maintaining a market leadership position in most of the market segments in which it competed. It had good products with well-known trademarks, an experienced sales force, long-standing relationships with distributors, and an extensive service and technical support network. It also made the highest expenditures in the industry for promotional items such as catalogues, displays, and cooperative advertising. NuTone products were generally sold at premium prices because they offered superior designs, more features, and higher quality.

NuTone manufactured for stock according to demand forecasts by product line. The sales of many of the product lines were cyclical and/or seasonal, but the variations in demand were smoothed out to some extent by NuTone's broad product line. The broad product line also had an advantage in attracting large distributors who preferred to deal with manufacturers who could supply products in multiple product categories.

Each product had to go through a number of different manufacturing operations such as punch pressing, welding, painting, and assembly. Because of the cyclical demand and capacity constraints, NuTone kept multiple buffers of work-in-process inventory. If necessary, most products could be expedited through the factory from raw materials to finished goods in two days.

Organization

NuTone was organized functionally, as shown in Exhibit 6. Most of the NuTone employees had been with the company for over 10 years. All of NuTone's top management group had been with NuTone before the merger with Scovill, with the exception of Pat Dionne, director of finance, who had just recently joined the company.

The group's main manufacturing facilities were in Cincinnati, Ohio, adjacent to the group's headquarters. The experienced labor force, which was not unionized, was paid higher wages than the industry average.

Jim Rankin, executive vice president, had been with NuTone for 27 years. He had worked his way up through marketing, having served as a product manager, vice president of sales and marketing, and general manager of NuTone. Rankin was an outgoing, people-oriented manager who was well-liked by employees at all levels at NuTone. Rankin was appointed to his present position as executive vice president of the Housing and Security Groups of Scovill in 1980. Even after assuming the executive vice president position, Rankin maintained hands-on responsibility in the areas of marketing and strategic planning at NuTone. NuTone's president, J. William Cahill, was primarily involved in operations.

Pricing

Prices for NuTone products were set in three different ways: catalogue pricing, quantity-quote pricing, and special-quote pricing. The prices in the catalogues were set at NuTone headquarters to yield gross margins of between 50 percent and 60 percent. NuTone's direct sales force of over 200 (the largest in the industry) could sell at the catalogue prices without consultation with management. Management was constantly alert for conditions that might warrant price changes, particularly material cost increases. The catalogue prices were updated as necessary, usually from one to three times per year. Changes usually took about two months to take effect.

If a customer wanted a discounted price, the salesperson would have to consult with a regional sales manager, who could offer quantity discounts off a quantity-quote pricing (QQP) list. This list, also prepared at NuTone headquarters, offered discounts of up to 20 percent depending on the types of products the customers wanted and the quantities to which they were willing to commit. Historically, the discounts offered on the QQP lists had not been changed frequently.

Special-quote prices were offered for very large sales, generally to large builders and distributors. Requests for special quotes went to sales administrators at group headquarters, who prepared the quotations in close consultation with Jim Rankin (executive vice president). The first step in developing a special quote price was to apply the standard gross margin rule. Then the price was shaved depending on a number of factors, including what levels of stock were on hand; whether sales and profits were needed to meet the group's monthly budget; and whether strategic considerations were involved, such as penetrating a new market, using a new distributor, or meeting the competition.

These special quotes were an important part of NuTone's business, at times comprising up to 50 percent of total sales. On average, 15 to 20 requests for quotes were received each day and, as Jim Rankin observed, "The tighter the business, the more quotes there are out there." Rankin took care to review each of the special quotes personally. He even called in each day when he was out of town to review them.

Product Line Decisions

NuTone management was constantly refining the product line offerings. In recent years, on average, approximately 60 new products were offered each year, and 100 products were discontinued. The product lines were reviewed formally twice a year, in April and November, to identify products that should be discontinued. The reasons that could cause a product to be discontinued included low sales volume, low profitability, problems in producing the necessary volumes, or problems in sourcing the necessary production materials.

NuTone management continued to produce some products that could not be sold profitably, however, because they considered it desirable to offer a full product line. Unprofitable items that the company continued to produce tended to be relatively simple, commodity-type products that could be produced more cheaply by smaller competitors with lower labor costs but which complemented other products in the NuTone product line.

Market Trends

In the early 1980s, NuTone's traditional market leadership position was being threatened by three major changes in the housing market. First, demand for new houses was dropping because of high interest rates, and price pressures were pushing builders to use fewer and cheaper add-on products. Second, the market was shifting toward the Southern and Western regions of the United States, where 75 percent of the building in the country was taking place, instead of the Northeast, where NuTone had traditionally dominated. NuTone executives were wont to observe wryly, "The market has gone South on us." Third, competition was increasing. Some smaller competitors had entered some of NuTone's markets, and as John Cruikshank, NuTone's manager of sales and marketing, observed:

> We're the high-cost producer in many of our markets. Some of our competitors have labor rates of $4.50 compared to our $10.50 plus liberal fringe benefits, and they're willing to operate with profit margins of only 6 percent of sales. Scovill wants 14 to 16 percent.

To reduce manufacturing costs, NuTone shifted some of its production, starting in 1979, from in-house to offshore purchasing. But this shift caused a much longer production cycle and larger inventories, as the shipment time from the Far East to Cincinnati was approximately four months.

Incentive Compensation

Personnel at most levels of NuTone were given incentive compensation. The top-level managers were provided annual bonuses based on the performance of the entire corporation. If Scovill met its annual earnings per share (EPS) goal, bonuses of 50 percent of salary were provided. No extra awards were provided if actual EPS exceeded the target. If actual EPS was 10 percent or more under the target, no bonuses were provided. The bonuses were scaled linearly with actual EPS within these two extremes.

Middle-level NuTone managers were primarily rewarded based on achievement of goals specific to their own functional areas, but they were also rewarded depending on the group's profit performance compared with plan on a basis very similar to that done at the corporate level. For example, regional sales managers could earn an annual bonus of up to 50 percent of salary. Eighty percent of this bonus could be earned by meeting a total regional sales quota and certain sales targets set for some of the major product categories. The other 20 percent of the bonus was provided if NuTone met its profit targets.

Personnel in the direct sales force were paid a straight commission on sales volume, with no reimbursement of expenses. The commission rate was scaled down depending on the amount of discount off catalogue prices the customer received. For example, the commission rate was 50 percent higher if the sale was made at catalogue prices instead of at QQP pricing.

Cost Accounting

Cost accounting at NuTone dated back to 1954 when time studies were done to establish labor standards for incentive purposes. At that time, the standards were set very leniently, at approximately one-third of the level an experienced worker could achieve, so that bonuses were virtually assured. For those production employees whose output was determined by their work pace, not the speed of a machine (approximately 50 percent of the total force), the bonus was computed as the basis of $1.00 per hour times the difference between actual efficiency and the lenient standard, with no maximum imposed on the total bonus paid. For example, workers who performed at 300 percent efficiency (the average level) would be paid as follows:

Base pay (per hour)	$2.00	
Bonus for achieving 300% of standard	2.00	(= $1 × [300% − 100%])
Total expected hourly wage	$4.00	

Over the years, the cost system evolved, and by the late 1970s, NuTone's system was fairly typical for a manufacturing company. *Direct materials* were costed at standard costs plus an allowance for material overheads that were estimated for 22 categories of materials (e.g., raw materials, purchased products, motors, and mirrors) to cover freight-in, scrap, and materials variances. The material overhead rates ranged from 3 to 7 percent.

Direct labor costs were calculated by extending the time standard for an operation by the departmental labor rate. Time standards were established by the manufacturing department on each of the approximately 50,000 operations being performed in the plants; an operation was defined as somebody doing something to a particular product. Departmental labor rates, including fringe benefits, were calculated for each of 26 departments in the group.

Overhead costs, such as personnel, maintenance, utilities, and taxes, were allocated to departments based on *the most rational means* available. For example, payroll insurance and taxes were allocated on the basis of the number of employees per department; routine maintenance expenses were allocated on the basis of square footage used; and inventory, insurance, and taxes were allocated on the basis of material costs. Overhead costs were then charged to inventory as a percentage of direct labor dollars, with the overall average departmental overhead rate slightly less than 150 percent. By product line, the average overhead rates varied from 100 to 300 percent, depending on the mix of departments the products went through.

Special tooling was charged directly to the particular model or models being produced. Depreciation was taken over a four-year period from the date of installation.

Variances were recognized as follows: material price variances were recorded when the materials were entered into inventory; material efficiency and labor and overhead variances were recognized in the month incurred, with the exception of the *conversion cost adjustment,* described as follows.

Routine reviews of the standards were conducted annually. The material standards were updated based on the price paid on the latest purchase order. The labor rate standards were updated based on the new departmental labor rates. The labor efficiency standards, being tied to compensation, were changed relatively infrequently. They were revised only if a change had been made to the production process, if an employee requested a review of a labor standard, or if they looked grossly out-of-line. The overhead standards were recalculated based on the forthcoming year's budget.

The Conversion Cost Adjustment

The one major feature of the NuTone cost accounting system that was unusual was that the labor standards were still set so that the workers would achieve average efficiency rates of around 300 percent, not 100 percent, when they were working at a normal pace. Most of the actual efficiency rates for performing the various operations in the plan varied from 240 to 360 percent of standard. The $1.00 bonuses for achieving each additional 100 percent efficiency over standard were still being provided, although the incentives were now a much lower percentage of total compensation because the base pay had risen from the old average of about $2.00 per hour to a higher average of about $8.50 per hour.

Monthly, actual labor costs (regular payroll, including bonuses and fringe benefits) and the overhead applied on them were debited to inventory, with the corresponding credit to cash or a liability account. As units were sold, inventory was credited and cost of goods sold debited by an amount calculated according to standard. The variances between actual and standard caused inventory to be understated, and cost of goods sold to be overstated, during the year. At year end, these favorable variances were used to cover unfavorable variances that could be determined only after the physical inventory had been taken at year end. The unfavorable variances included losses due to scrap (which was not tracked well during the year), shrinkage, misreporting (such as overreporting of labor hours or rework reported as direct labor), employee thefts, direct labor overtime, differences in day work rates, components purchased abroad (that just required assembling), and differences across plants. Historically, these unfavorable variances totaled approximately 30 percent of the total favorable variances. At year end, the unused portion of the favorable variances was then credited to cost of goods sold as a *conversion cost adjustment* (CCA) and debited to inventory.

Year	*Amount*
1977	$ 772
1978	1,108
1979	1,499
1980	1,912
1981	2,778

FIGURE A Conversion Cost Adjustment ($000)

The CCA variance had existed since the institution of inflated labor standards at NuTone in 1954, but the size of the variance had been growing much larger in recent years, as shown in Figure A:

The CCA increases were caused by NuTone's sales growth, which caused a concomitant growth in inventories and increases in labor rates that had been running at an annual rate of over 10 percent per year in the recent inflationary period. Because of the size of the end-of-year accounting adjustments being made in NuTone's books, it was noted by some people at Scovill headquarters that "at NuTone, the 13th close is the most important." Headquarters personnel could easily see the favorable variances that were building up, but they could not estimate accurately how much would be left after the unfavorable variances were subtracted at year end.

Even harder to estimate was the impact of inflated labor costs on the profitability of each individual product line. Average product costs were approximately 55 percent material, 20 percent direct labor, and 25 percent overhead, but the cost proportions varied considerably across product lines. Exhibit 7 presents some examples of the distortions caused by the inflated labor standards. The last two columns on the right reflect actual labor and actual overhead (allocated on the basis of actual labor) costs by product line. The actual data could be estimated from information maintained by the cost accounting staff at NuTone.

THE CONFLICT

Bob Hager knew that to be able to implement more realistic labor standards, he needed the cooperation of NuTone management. The NuTone accounting personnel all reported to group management, not to Scovill headquarters, and in any case, the NuTone manufacturing department, not accounting, was responsible for setting and maintaining the labor standards.

Most people at headquarters who had thought about the issue were convinced that the standards should be made more realistic, but NuTone personnel, even those in the accounting department, were not convinced. Here are some representative views:

BOB HAGER: I know that NuTone has been a very profitable group for many years, and that's why it has been allowed to run so independently. The NuTone group uses the distorted labor standards to manage earnings over the year; they have ways of capturing some of that favorable variance if they need it to achieve monthly earnings targets. My predecessor, who was nearing retirement, allowed the situation to exist; he endorsed the philosophy of understating income in the first three quarters and then pulling it out at year end.

This is not a technical or systems problem; it is a philosophical problem. I worry about whether we really know what is happening to margins on specific line items of business because the labor and overhead content varies significantly in products of different types. I also worry that we don't have good monthly and quarterly profit numbers that should be providing us early warning indicators.

PAUL BAUER: (director of corporate planning at Scovill headquarters): The NuTone labor standards just provide a way of salting profit away until the end of the year. Scovill's primary objective is to meet or exceed the chairman's stated annual EPS target, and the NuTone managers have been the heroes because they have been producing it at year end. I don't think that's sound business because we've distorted all the product costs. Without special analyses of both labor and overhead allocations, they can't tell which products are dogs and which are earning us money. On a macro basis, their game is to generate an extra profit at the end of the year.

JIM RANKIN: I have run six different companies, and to be honest with you, I haven't had a lot of good experiences with standard cost systems. Manufacturing in this business consists of a lot of short runs with changeovers requiring setups. A standard cost system works best with long runs. A smart manufacturing manager can appear to make a lot of money just by making long runs.

If this group were run by an engineer or a manufacturing person, I'm sure we would have a typical standard cost system. But this group has been run by marketing people for many years, and this system has worked for us. If corporate forces us to go to a typical standard cost system, I am sure it will cost us margin.

You might say, "Why not put in the system and price at, say, 70 percent margin rather than 50 percent?" That sounds logical but I don't think it would work. The higher cost numbers are a crutch. Even though I know the costs are overstated, when I do my pricing calculations, I unconsciously believe those figures are the real costs. It's just like the crutch some people use of setting their clocks 10 minutes fast to ensure that they won't be late for their appointments. Overstating the costs causes us to keep our actual margins up. I like the fact that we have a little extra in there.

Would the rankings of products by margins change if the labor standards were accurate? Sure they would. But I know this business inside and out—I've been running it since 1967—and I know what our products cost. If corporate makes us go to accurate labor standards, we'd have to run with two sets of books because I don't want to change what we've been doing. It has worked well for many years. We have pride in being the high earning group at Scovill.

I like to have the monthly financials be conservative. There are a lot of things that can go wrong at year end, particularly in the inventory areas, and I don't want any of those unpleasant surprises that can occur at year end. In fact, I've told my financial people, "If there's ever an inventory loss at year end, don't even bother to stop in the office on your way out."

BILL HANKS: (manager of cost accounting and payroll at NuTone): I'm not sure that the people at corporate realize what a monumental job it would be to change these standards. We have 26 manufacturing departments and 50,000 operations. Our cost accounting group consists of only six people, and manufacturing has only two industrial engineers. Doing the whole job could take years to complete.

EXHIBIT 1 Financial and Statistical Highlights (1978–1981) ($ millions)

Selected Scovill Data	*1978*	*1979*	*1980*	*1981*
Net sales from continuing operations	$633.4	$788.1	$793.0	$817.9
Earnings from continuing operations	29.9	35.3	27.4	30.0
Earnings (loss) from discontinued operations	.8	(3.3)	(3.4)	(34.5)
Net earnings (loss)	$ 30.7	$ 32.0	$ 24.0	$ (4.5)
Per share of common stock:				
—Net earnings (loss)	3.35	3.46	2.56	(.50)
—Cash dividends	1.40	1.43	1.52	1.52
—Price range	24⅞–17¼	21½–17	19⅞–13⅞	21⅝–15⅛
Number of employees	15,918	20,396	18,416	17,526

Source: Scovill Annual Reports.

EXHIBIT 2 Organizational Chart

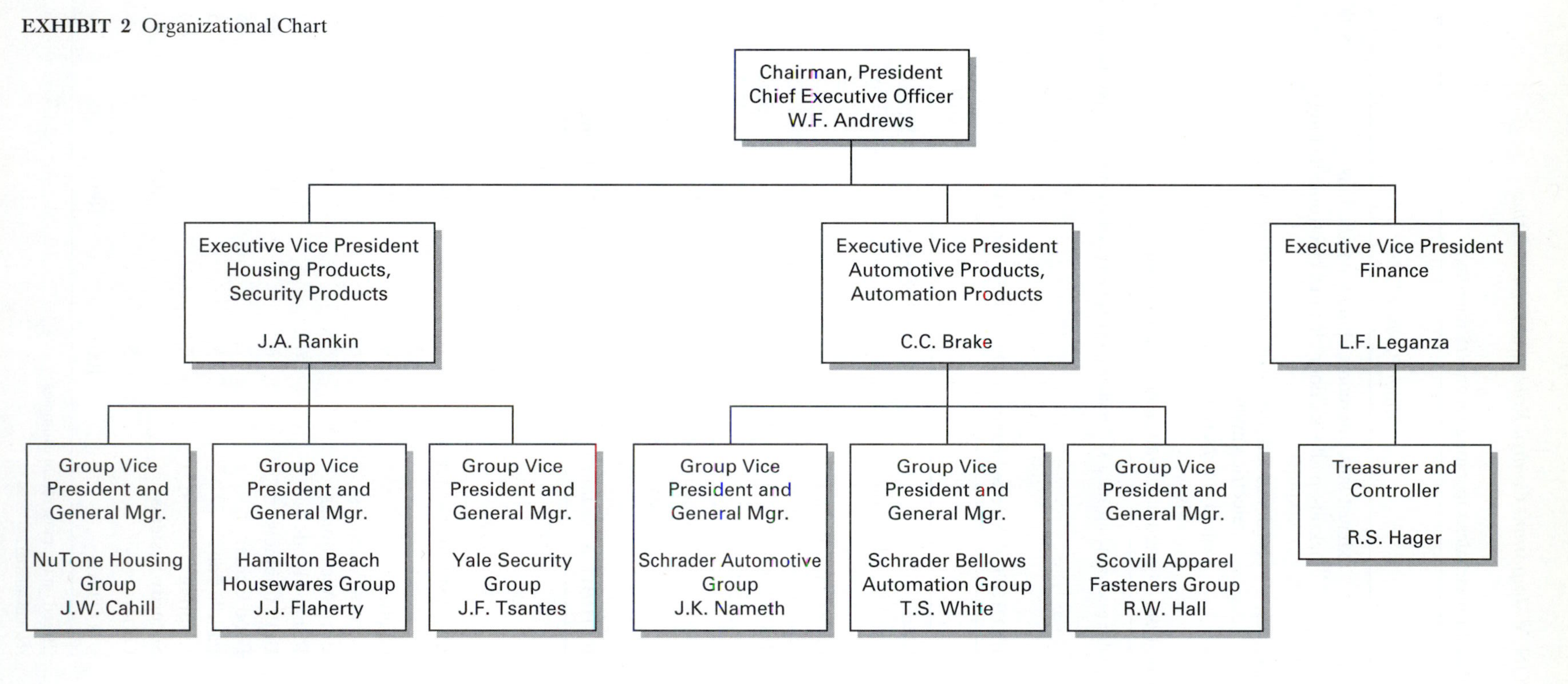

EXHIBIT 3 Group Product Lines, Sales, Operating Income ($ millions)

Group	*Major Product Lines*	*1981 Sales*	*1981 Operating Income*
NuTone Housing	exhaust fans, intercoms, chimes, paddle fans	$200.5	$31.8
Yale Security	locksets, padlocks, door closures electronic locking systems	112.6	12.3
Hamilton Beach Housewares	blenders, food processors, irons, coffee makers, electric knives	149.3	4.4[a]
Scovill Apparel Fasteners	snap fasteners, rivets, burrs, brass zippers	149.1	21.7
Schrader Automotive	tire valves	83.2	4.3
Schrader Bellows Automation	pneumatic valves, cylinders, regulators	123.2	12.0

[a]Includes a $2.4 million intangible asset write-off and a $2.5 million provision for plant shutdown and product discontinuance.

EXHIBIT 4 Selected Financial Data for NuTone (1978–1981) ($ millions)

	1978	*1979*	*1980*	*1981*
Sales	$207.3	$197.1	$183.9	$200.5
Total Standard Variable Costs	118.2	117.9	120.5	121.7
Gross Margin	89.1	79.2	63.4	78.8
Gross Margin (%)	43.0	40.2	34.5	39.3
Operating Income	27.0	28.5	21.1	31.8
Total Assets	57.6	56.3	59.1	77.9
Inventories	26.3	27.2	30.1	36.7

Source: Scovill Annual Reports. Nonpublicly available numbers were disguised.

EXHIBIT 5 NuTone Product Lines: Financial and Marketing Highlights[a]

Product Line	*% of NuTone 1981 Sales*	*% of NuTone 1981 Contribution*	*Market Share (%)*	*Relative Position in the Market*
Exhaust Fans/Heaters	25.3	29.0	34	1st
Intercoms	12.2	18.1	65	1st
Chimes	9.3	12.7	55	1st
Central Vacuums	6.0	8.6	40	1st
Bath Accessories	6.8	5.9	20	1st
Range Hoods	6.5	5.1	10	2nd
Bath Cabinets	6.3	4.8	18	2nd
Food Centers	2.5	3.1	95	1st
Paddle Fans	13.8	8.5	5	4th
Lighting	4.5	3.2	N/A[b]	N/A[b]
Security Systems	1.2	0.9	20	N/A[b]
Others	5.6	0.1	—	—
TOTAL	100.0	100.0	—	—

[a]Based on the most recent estimates.

[b]Not available.

EXHIBIT 6 NuTone's Organizational Chart

- Executive Vice President, Housing and Security Products, J.A. Rankin
  - Group Vice President & General Manager, J.W. Cahill
    - General Sales and Marketing Manager, J.T. Cruickshank
      - National Sales
      - Advertising
      - Service and Repair
      - Special Products
      - Product Managers
      - Sales Administrators (quotes)
      - Exports
    - Operations Manager, V. Buecher
      - Sales Forecaster
      - Materials Manager
      - Product Reliability and Safety
      - Purchasing
      - Manufacturing Engineering
      - Traffic
      - Plant Managers
      - Warehouse Manager
    - Director of Finance, P. Dionne
      - Assistant Secretary and Controller
      - Credit Manager
      - Data Processing and Order Dept.
      - Cost Accounting and Payroll (W. Hanks)
    - Director of Industrial Relations, M. MacFadden
    - Director of R&D and Engineering, R. Vance

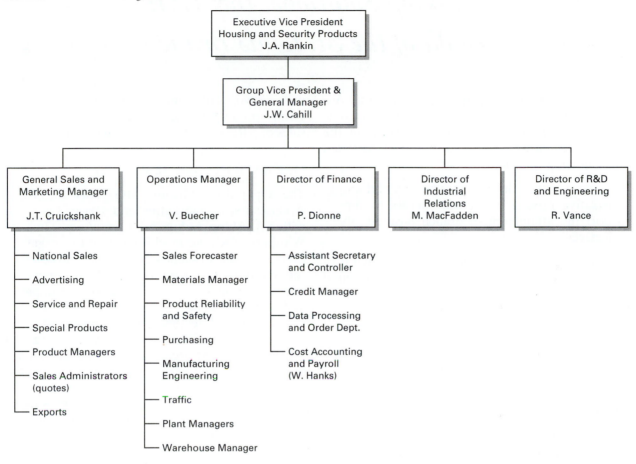

EXHIBIT 7 Examples of Product Costs and Profitability Levels

Products	Selling Price	*Standard Costs Per Unit*				*Actual Costs Per Unit*	
		Material	*Labor*	*Overhead*	*Total*	*Labor*	*Overhead*
Bathroom Exhaust Fan (Model 40)	$ 26.69	$ 8.40	$ 4.20	$ 5.35	$17.95	$2.47	$ 3.71
Door Chime (Model 15)	3.40	1.25	1.21	1.27	3.73	.67	.82
Kitchen Range Hood (Regular)	64.45	21.84	8.75	11.88	42.47	5.95	8.88
Kitchen Range Hood (Deluxe)	108.69	35.98	10.08	14.80	60.86	7.32	11.86

Desktop Solutions, Inc. (A): Audit of the St. Louis Branch

In 1995, a team of auditors from the Internal Audit staff of Desktop Solutions Inc., an electronic distributor, audited the St. Louis branch of the Operations Group. Their audit report included the following overall judgment:

> In our opinion, the St. Louis branch's administrative process was *unsatisfactory* to support the attainment of branch business objectives.

The auditors noted that many of the branch procedures were working effectively, but they found major deficiencies existed in the branch's equipment control and order entry processes.

This case focuses on the areas of the audit that led to the Unsatisfactory audit judgment. It describes what the auditors did, what they found, and how management responded.

DESKTOP SOLUTIONS INC.

Desktop Solutions produced a broad line of printing and scanning systems for desktop printing/publishing applications. In 1995, the company's revenues were over $400 million (see Exhibit 1). The company's printers and scanners were available for rental or purchase. All rental plans in the United States included maintenance, service and parts. For equipment purchase, Desktop Solutions offered financing plans over two- to five-year periods with competitive interest rates. Some equipment was sold with trade-in privileges. The company also sold supplies, such as toner, developer, and paper.

Desktop Solutions' worldwide marketing and sales organization marketed directly to end-user customers. The company also used some alternate channels, including retail stores, direct mail and sales agents. It also maintained worldwide networks of regional service centers (for servicing products) and distribution centers (for sales of parts and consumable supplies).

OPERATIONS GROUP

The Operations Group (OG) was the North American sales, marketing and service operation within Desktop Solutions' Operations Division. Within the OG, the most important line organizations were the branches. They represented Desktop Solutions' direct interface with customers and were responsible for fulfilling all their equipment and servicing needs.

Until the late 1980s, the management of the branches in OG had been highly decentralized. The decentralized organization was abandoned in the late 1980s and early 1990s in favor of a functional type of organization, which allowed for more direct control over branch functions by regional headquarters. Under the functional organization, each branch was run by three parallel functional managers—a branch sales manager, a branch control manager (or branch controller), and a branch technical service manager—each of whom reported directly to the respective functional manager at the regional level (see Exhibit 2). The sales manager was responsible for all sales and leasing of Desktop Solutions products in the branch territory. The control manager was in charge of all the internal operating, administrative, and financial reporting systems, such as order entry, accounts receivable, equipment control, and personnel. The technical service manager was responsible for the installation, servicing, and removal of sold and leased equipment.

The most difficult challenge with the new functional organization was maintaining good communication between personnel in the differ-

Professor Kenneth A. Merchant wrote this case with the assistance of Research Assistant Howard Koo as a basis for class discussion rather than to illustrate either effective or ineffective handling of an administrative situation.

ent functions of the branch. Frequent and effective communications were also important for achieving customer satisfaction, which was the most important branch success factor. Good communications were required to ensure that equipment would be installed promptly, that billings would be accurate, and that problems would be resolved with a minimum of hassle.

INTERNAL AUDIT

Internal audit had been a centralized function at Desktop Solutions since 1980. The function was centralized in order to increase auditor independence and to improve the professionalism of the staff. In 1995, the internal organization consisted of 15 people, headed by Steve Kruse, who reported to the chief financial officer, Scott Pepper.

Two features of the Desktop Solutions' Internal Audit (IA) organization were unique as compared with the internal audit groups in most corporations. First, the IA personnel had diverse backgrounds, and internal audit was not considered a career objective for most of them. The accounting/auditing personnel, who predominated on many corporate internal audit staffs, were in the minority; only three of the IA personnel were CPAs. The others were trained in a variety of disciplines, including engineering, marketing, computer science and liberal arts. Nine of the staff came into IA from outside Desktop Solutions. An initial assignment in IA was perceived as a good introduction to the company and a good training ground for moving into line operations. Most staff auditors did, in fact, move into the operations side of the company after gaining a few years' IA experience.

Second, the IA charter was very broad. The listing of IA functions (see Exhibit 3) showed that IA was expected to be involved in the development, not just the testing, of operational and internal controls. Exhibit 4 describes the different types of audits the IA staff performed and the allocation of audit resources among them in 1995.

Most of the audits were planned at headquarters, as part of the review of the company's controls. However, IA also received requests for services from line managers. In recent years, the number of such requests had exceeded IA's capacity. Balancing the needs for regular audit cycles with the needs for special services requested was the difficult part in preparing the IA plan. Audit plans were approved by the audit committee of the board of directors, which was given regular progress reports throughout the year on each audit.

After executing an audit, IA staff gave formal presentations to senior line management detailing their results and recommendations. They also followed up at a later date to see if the deficiencies had been corrected and the recommendations had been implemented.

AUDIT OF THE ST. LOUIS BRANCH

The St. Louis branch was selected for audit in 1995 for three reasons. First, the 1995 Master Audit Plan called for a number of large branch audits. The St. Louis branch, which served customers in Missouri, Illinois, and Kansas, was one of the largest of OG's 52 branches. In 1995, it earned revenue of $7.6 million and had a sale/lease equipment inventory of 7,710 machines. Second, a 1993 audit of the St. Louis branch had uncovered deficiencies in branch equipment control, and IA management thought this would be a good time to verify if improvements had been implemented. And third, a new branch control manager (branch controller) was recently hired, and the audit would give the new control manager a chance to work with the auditors and learn about the branch's systems and problems. The IA audit team and the new controller arrived at the St. Louis branch on the same day.

The objective of the audit was to determine whether the branch administrative/control processes were well defined, executed, and managed to ensure: (1) controlled and documented equipment movement and tracking; (2) timely and accurate order entry; (3) proper customer billing and adjustment; and (4) effective collections activity.

On the St. Louis audit, like most branch audits, the auditors focused most of their attention on equipment inventory and accounts receivable. These were the two largest branch balance sheet items, and both were under the direct control of the branch managers.

EQUIPMENT CONTROL/BILLING

Equipment control (EC) involved the tracking of equipment movements in and out of the branch's physical inventory and the simultaneous triggering of changes in customer billings. EC was critical to the branch's ability to schedule, deliver and install machines for Desktop Solutions customers, and to be paid for the equipment the customers used.

The key control personnel in EC were the order administrators (OAs), the equipment administrator (EA), and the schedulers. The OAs were responsible for editing incoming orders, entering the orders into the computer system, keeping track of the orders after they were sent to scheduling, and processing the install transactions (install date, serial number, meter reads).

The EA was responsible for the accuracy of inventory records, and the timely resolution of equipment discrepancies that delayed orders (thus billing) from being completed. The EA maintained the Non-Revenue Report (NRR), a computer-generated inventory listing (by equipment serial number) of all branch equipment not installed at a customer location. The NRR was updated daily with information about new installations and cancellations. At the beginning of each month, the EA took a physical inventory of all equipment at the warehouse, matched it with the NRR, and reconciled the differences. Equipment on the NRR not found at the warehouse was reclassified as uninventoriable (lost). If it was not found within 90 days, the branch was charged for the net book value of the lost equipment. The process for cancellation and deinstallation of equipment was very similar.

The Schedulers matched the orders with the equipment shown as available on the NRR. A target delivery date (ideally two days) was transmitted to the rigger who delivered the equipment (by serial number indicated).

Exhibit 5 shows a simplified flowchart of the process used in the St. Louis branch for order-entry and installation of the high-end printing and scanning systems. Personnel in the control function of the branch played a central communication role, transmitting the order information from the sales representatives to the rigger (warehouse) personnel and branch technical service personnel. They also processed the information about installations so as to trigger the customer billing.

Some low-end systems were delivered and installed by the sales representatives (reps). When this was done, the equipment control process was simplified because the rep was responsible for delivering the order paperwork and the printer serial number to the OA for entry into the computer system.

While their operations were quite similar, the branches used slightly different administrative processes and personnel roles. OG management elected not to use a detailed, centralized set of administrative process for all branches. They preferred allowing the branch managers to tailor their branch's processes to the local conditions.

AUDIT PROCEDURES

The audit fieldwork at the St. Louis branch took a team of six auditors approximately two months to complete. Exhibit 6 describes the tests performed on the equipment control process. About 40 percent of the audit time was devoted to equipment control procedures. Initially the IA personnel conducted background interviews with key branch personnel. They also reviewed organization charts and prepared detailed flow charts of the order entry, scheduling and equipment control processes. This was done to understand how the branch operated, to determine the degree of compliance with company procedures, and to determine the efficiency of branch personnel. Potential problem areas were noted for special attention during the audit fieldwork.

In addition to equipment control, they also tested several other areas, including customer billings for equipment, supplies and servicing (for accuracy and timeliness), price plan conversion (for compliance with company procedures), order entry and cancellation processes (for accuracy and efficiency), credit and collections, and order-to-installation time lag. Each of these areas represented a cycle or process activity which was important to the operation of a branch.

FINDINGS-EQUIPMENT CONTROL

The auditors found that management failed to define responsibilities clearly or hold the EA accountable for his performance. Branch management was not involved in the monitoring and maintenance of the equipment control process. And control management did not maintain effective contact with marketing and service management to ensure that the equipment control process was operating properly. Exhibit 7 describes some of the deficiencies found.

However, the branch was rated very good in other areas, and the auditors noted that the negative impacts from the deficiencies in the equipment control area seemed to be effectively minimized:

> Although the delayed equipment transaction processing contributed to incorrect billings and an increased rate of costly billing adjustments, overall the billing function was sufficiently well organized and controlled to be able to absorb the pressures generated. The billing adjustments reviewed were highly accurate, and resolution of customer inquiries was satisfactory. The credit and collection program was well administered; performance budgets were consistently met, and adjustment and write-off activity was well controlled.

RECOMMENDATIONS AND FOLLOW-UP

On July 14, 1995, the audit team presented a final listing of the recommendations to the branch managers. Shortly thereafter, they prepared a formal audit report to all OG management responsible for the St. Louis branch operations.

In the audit report, the auditors presented a list of 46 recommendations. Most of the recommendations were directed to the new branch control manager, and generally related to one or more of the following:

1. The reconciliation between the physical inventory and the inventory records (NRR) should be completed;
2. The deficient equipment processes should be studied, refined, and documented; and
3. The individuals involved in equipment control should be given clearly defined responsibilities, and be held accountable for the accuracy of the equipment reports and billings.

Ultimate responsibility for correcting deficiencies rested with line management (branch managers), not with IA. Company policy required the branch managers to prepare an action plan to address each of the deficiencies and recommendations made in the audit report. The last written response to the auditors' recommendations came from the St. Louis branch control manager on December 15, 1996. He addressed each of the auditor's recommendations and noted that most of them had already been implemented.

Company policy also required that someone independent of both IA and branch management be assigned to monitor progress in implementing the audit recommendations. In OG, this was usually someone from the headquarters finance staff.

REACTIONS

Martha Sorensen (IA manager) reflected on the audit:

> The St. Louis branch had been recognized for some time as a problem branch. In most of the branches, many of the systems and administrative procedures go back to the days when the branches were run by a single branch manager, and the branches that were not well run in those days tended not to get going well when we switched to the functional organization. So going into this audit, we had a good idea we would find some problems, and the results of the audit confirmed this judgment. I hope we're now well on the way to getting the problems ironed out.

Phil Phillips, Region 3 manager, responded to the disclosure of the St. Louis branch's ongoing equipment control problem:

> We can't blame these problems on the system because it works well in other branches. The problems occur for a combination of reasons including people, management, the sheer volume of work that was handled, and the fact that St. Louis is larger and has a more diverse organization structure than most of the other branches. These all create problems. We believe the problems are manageable but it will take time to whittle away at them. We're making progress, but at this point we have not given the St. Louis branch a specific time deadline to clear up all their problems.

EXHIBIT 1 Summary Income Statements, Desktop Solutions Inc. (in millions)

	Year Ended December 31	
	1994	*1995*
Operating Revenues		
Rentals and services	$228.1	$262.2
Sales	156.6	176.3
Total operating revenues	387.7	438.5
Cost and Expenses		
Cost of rentals and services	101.6	116.2
Cost of sales	77.9	80.6
Research and development expenses	25.9	30.1
Selling, administrative and general expenses	144.6	159.8
Total cost and expenses	350.0	386.7
Operating Income	37.6	51.8
Other Income (Deductions), Net	(9.4)	(2.4)
Income before Income Taxes	28.2	49.4
Income Taxes	7.8	13.6
Income before Outside Shareholder's Interests	20.4	35.8
Outside Shareholder's Interests	3.5	5.9
Income from Continuing Operations	16.9	29.9
Discontinued Operations	2.6	1.2
Net Income	$19.5	$31.1

EXHIBIT 2 Operations Group Organization

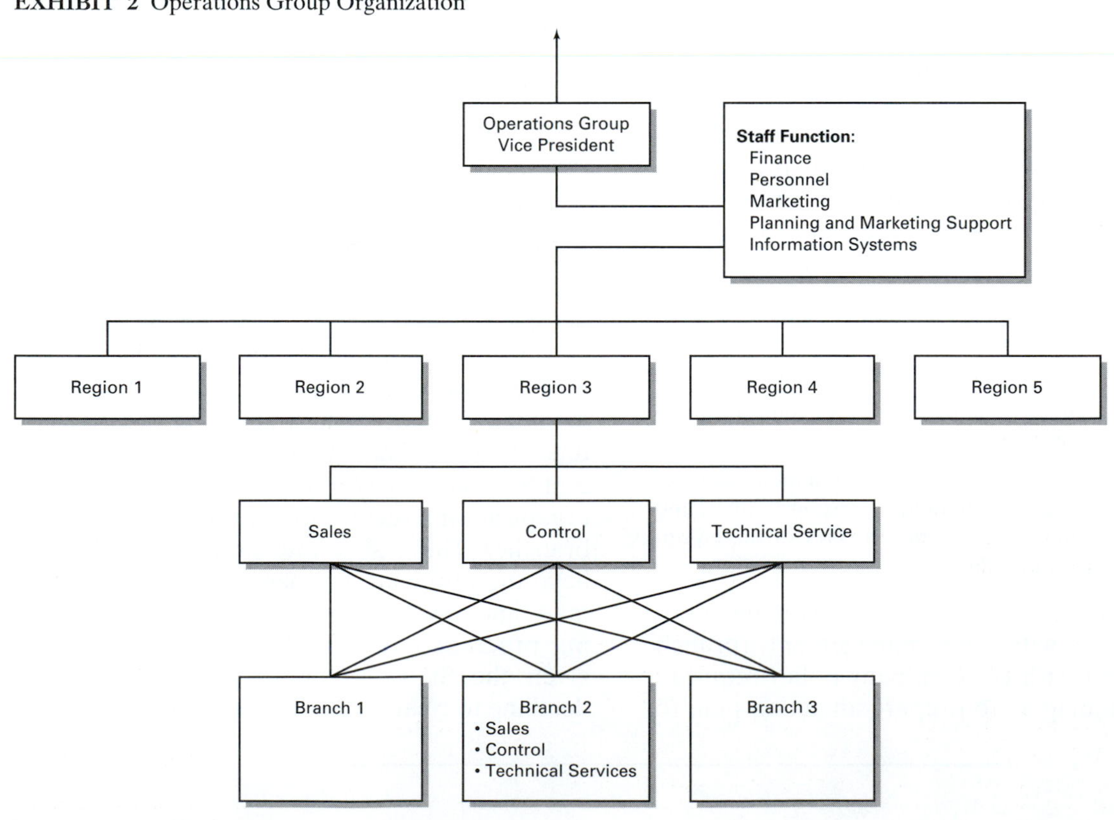

EXHIBIT 3 Internal Audit Functions

1. Develop and implement a program of operational, financial, and information systems audits that best meet the requirements of the corporation; assure the integrity of operational and internal controls in protecting the assets of the company and improve operational effectiveness.
2. Assist corporate and operating unit management in identifying and developing operational, financial, and systems policies and procedures necessary to accomplish the goals and objectives of the corporation; evaluate activities through audit report findings and recommend actions to eliminate problems uncovered during audits.
3. Perform special audits in any functional area and for all levels of management as required.
4. Present the audit plan and related audit findings to the Audit Committee of the Board of Directors and corporate management.
5. Coordinate external audit activities and control-related audit fees. Ensure an optimum balance between internal and external audit work in fulfilling the basic audit objectives and obtaining annual certification of Desktop Solutions' consolidated financial statements.
6. Develop new concepts of auditing responsive to the changing business and technological environment within Desktop Solutions and maintain a professional staff skilled in the required disciplines.

EXHIBIT 4 Audit Types and 1995 Plan for Allocation of Resources

Control Environment Audits (24% of resources in 1995)

Control Environment audits evaluate the organizational arrangements; financial planning and analysis; personnel policies and practices; and policy definition and communication within operating organizations. The objective is to assess the basis on which responsibility is assigned, accountability is determined, performance is measured, and overall specific controls are established.

Business Entity Audits (39%)

These are reviews of specific business cycle controls in a business entity such as a branch or small to medium subsidiary.

Business Cycle Audits (17%)

These are reviews of the seven business cycle as set forth in the Desktop Solutions Compendium of Internal Controls to determine if the overall and individual cycle control objectives stated there are being met. The overall objectives tested are: authorization; accounting transaction processing; and safeguarding of corporate assets. The cycle reviews will also include reviews of applicable control environment functions and tests of supporting computer controls.

Financial Audits (11%)

Financial audits, unless otherwise indicated, are in direct support of the annual audit by our external auditors and represent independent evaluation for the purpose of attesting to the fairness, and reliability of the financial data.

Systems Audits (8%)

System audits are pre-implementation and post-implementation reviews and data center audits. Pre-implementation audits consider the integrity, control, performance, security and conformance with policies and standards of each system reviewed during the design and development process. Post-implementation audits determine whether cost and performance objectives are met and test the system's integrity, including controls, in its live environment. Audits of data centers assess overall performance and the data control function and address security, scheduling and utilization, control, documentation, organization, training and cost effectiveness.

EXHIBIT 5 Simplified Flowchart of Order Entry and Installation Process for High-End Systems.

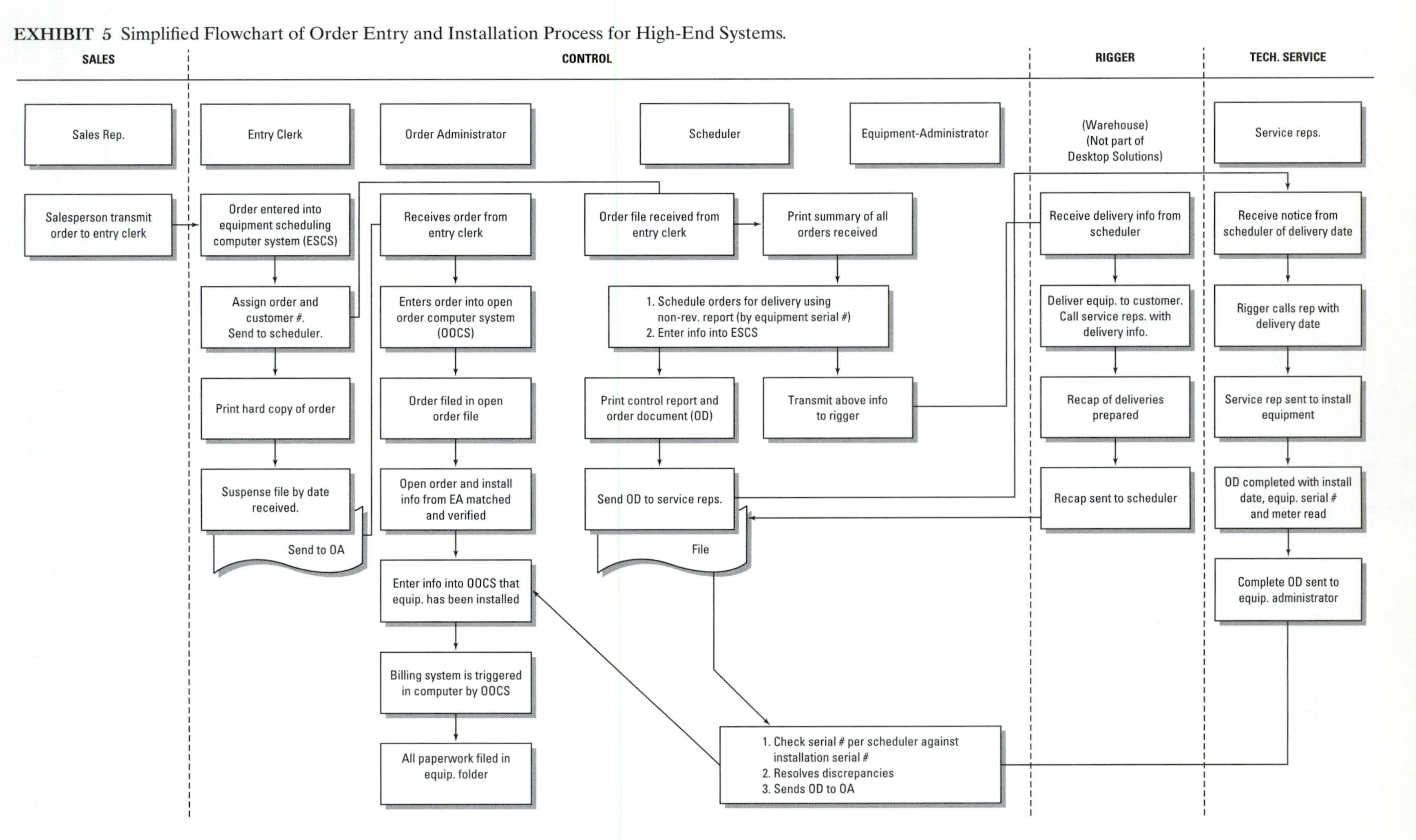

EXHIBIT 6 Audit Tests Performed on Equipment Control at the St. Louis Branch

1. *Physical inventory.* A total sample of 1387 equipment units was examined, including a complete (100%) examination of the units of one single product. The audit team recorded all the serial numbers of the sample units found at the rigger (warehouse) and matched the numbers with those shown on the NRR. Serial numbers not matching up were given to the equipment administrator for reconciliation.
2. *Scheduling process.* The auditors examined the paperwork for a sample of 243 installations to see how the schedulers notified the riggers about what equipment to install.
3. *Install lag test.* A sample of 46 machines was examined for the timeliness of the steps in the order-to-install process, including how long the sales reps held on to orders before submitting them, how long the OAs took to enter the order correctly, how long it took the schedulers to get the machine out to the customer site and then the delay before the technical service reps installed the machine; and how long the OAs take to enter the final install information correctly into the system to trigger the billing process.
4. *Cancel lag test.* A sample of 33 cancellations was examined for proper adherence to contract terms and cancellation policies. The auditors were looking to see if the customer cancellation notification policy was followed, if the stop billing date was appropriate, if the removal charges were correctly billed, and if the processing was done on a timely basis.
5. *Low-volume copier installations.* A sample of 23 low-volume copier installations was examined to see if transmission of information from the sales reps to the OAs was adequate.
6. *Trials.* A sample of 22 machines out for customer trial was tested for adherence to company duration guidelines and approval procedures.

EXHIBIT 7 Partial List of Internal Audit Findings at the St. Louis Branch

1. The responsibilities of branch personnel were found to be slightly unusual in order entry and scheduling/equipment control. Some special order transactions (e.g., maintenance agreements, price plan conversions) were processed by customer service assistants, not OAs. The OAs did not track orders through the order-to-install process. And the information about installations and status changes went to the EA, instead of the scheduler, as at most other branches.
2. The physical inventory of 1387 mainframe and sorter units showed over 633 discrepancies when compared to the NRR. Seven weeks after the audit results were turned over to the branch, the EA had only reconciled 382 of these items, leaving 251 items unreconciled—76 units potentially lost, 15 units potentially found, and 160 location and/or status discrepancies. At other branches, 95–100% of the inventory discrepancies were typically reconciled within the first two weeks.
3. The schedulers had learned they could not rely on the NRR, so they kept their own equipment inventory records. They manually assigned serial numbers to incoming orders. To move equipment quickly, they sometimes directed the rigger to deliver products directly from the receiving dock before the serial numbers had been recorded in the branch's inventory by the EA. They kept track of movements in or out of the inventory based on information received from service personnel, but the auditors found that this listing was also inaccurate.
4. It took seven days on average from the date a machine was installed to the time the system recognized it as a valid install so that billing could begin. In addition, some documentation were missing: three of the 46 sampled had no credit approval; two had no service agreement; four had no valid installation date stamp.
5. The cancellation procedure was not working effectively. One hundred machines that had been returned by the customer and sent to the refurbishing center had not been noted as canceled by the OAs, and this number had increased sharply in the prior three months.
6. The low-end printing equipment was not well controlled. Units to be delivered by the sales reps were taken from regular inventory, rather than from a special pool of machines in "consignment to sales" status. In nine cases (39%), the sales reps did not send the serial numbers of the equipment to the OAs. In one case, the rigger tried to deliver a machine to a customer who had received his a week before from the sales rep.
7. Of the machines out for customer trial, only three of the 22 tested complied with company policy, and five had no approval signature. For four successful trials (i.e., the customer wanted to keep the machine), the ending date was recorded improperly, resulting in 29 days of unbilled rental revenue. For eight unsuccessful trials, the removal was scheduled two days past the trial expiration. Four trials were extended without approval. The average length past the normal trial duration was 17 days, while the average length past the extension deadline was 9.5 days.
8. Management failed to define responsibilities clearly or hold the EA accountable for his performance. Management did not get involved in the monitoring and maintenance of the equipment control process. Finally, control management did not maintain effective contact with marketing and service management to ensure that the equipment control process was operating properly as it affected those areas.

Desktop Solutions, Inc. (B): Audit of Operations Group Systems

In September 1995, Don Lindsay, the newly appointed manager of the Systems department of the Operations Group (OG) of Desktop Solutions, Inc., believed that some deep-rooted problems were hindering his unit's operational effectiveness. Systems had a long-standing reputation as being expensive and resistant to change, and systems planning in OG was generally recognized as deficient. As one manager put it:

> Don's predecessor tended to allow the user organizations to tell him what to do. The Systems personnel work closely with the various users, so closely, in fact, that it really became a direct-line relationship to the user managers and a dotted line relationship to the Systems managers. That does not allow for a very effective operation because you really don't have control of the organization. All the users had their own parochial demands. They built their own data bases, and there was very little sharing of files even between individuals in the same branch. The result was that the number of Systems personnel needed to meet the increasing number of user needs ballooned. People became resistant to change, and they were protective of what they had created. Virtually no planning or coordination was occurring.

Don thought that personnel from Desktop Solutions's corporate Internal Audit (IA) staff could help him by providing an independent opinion as to how well Systems was performing, identifying problems that might have gone unnoticed, and making suggestions for improvement. He also thought that an audit with recommendations for change would increase the support he would get from upper-level OG management and user organizations for implementing changes. He therefore requested a special audit from the IA organization. The purpose was to assess OG-Systems' ability in performing its centralized system support functions.

OG-SYSTEMS

Systems was a centralized systems support organization charged with two primary tasks: (1) maintaining and enhancing existing OG information systems; and (2) planning and implementing replacement systems. Because of OG's diversity, these tasks were formidable. OG had ten regional offices responsible for a total of 52 branch offices. Each region and branch operated their own unique information systems with different procedures and data bases. Requests for system maintenance and development could come from any of several management levels in the user (i.e., branch or regional offices) organizations, and they were allowed to go directly to the first-line (lowest level) Systems managers responsible for their particular systems.

In 1995, System's budget was $15.8 million, of which about 60 percent was to be spent on systems maintenance, planning and development, and the rest was to be spent on data processing operations. All work was fully charged back to the user organizations. Systems employed 155 people, 93 of whom were directly involved in code-creation activity (i.e., programmers, analysts).

The Systems organization, which reported directly to the OG vice president, was divided into three parts: Operations, Planning and Systems Architecture, and Control and Administration (see Exhibit 1). The Operations organization was responsible for creating new software and running three regional data processing centers. The Planning and Systems Architecture organiza-

Professor Kenneth A. Merchant wrote this case with the assistance of Research Assistant Howard Koo as a basis for class discussion rather than to illustrate either effective or ineffective handling of an administrative situation.

tion was responsible for long-range planning of both software and hardware. It also provided technical expertise to user-organizations and reviewed all new system designs for hardware compatibility. The Control and Administration organization was responsible for financial planning, analysis and reporting.

AUDIT PROCEDURES AND FINDINGS

The OG-Systems audit was planned and executed by two auditors who spent approximately 1600 hours each on the entire project. One of the auditors had an extensive systems background, and was familiar with the operation and history of the Systems organization. Exhibit 1 describes the audit steps performed and the percent of time spent on each.

The auditors confirmed that systems planning and coordination in the OG organization were inadequate. They observed that many systems implementation decisions were being made at lower levels of management of the user organizations, without reference to related decisions in other areas. They found that Systems did not guide and coordinate the systems and programming personnel in the user organizations in the development of long-range or annual work plans, but they concluded that this problem was partly beyond the control of the Systems organization. One of the comments in their report was, "Generally, the current OG group-level business planning process does not result in formal management-approved output that is sufficiently integrated and detailed to direct a long-range systems development process."

To improve systems planning, the auditors suggested that OG senior management should:

1. Designate an information controller in each functional area to be responsible for providing an interface between strategic business planning and strategic systems planning. This person would also be responsible for integrating information needs within the function and between functions and for ensuring that all systems development activities flowed through OG-Systems. Once senior OG management had decided on a strategic business direction and the information needs, Systems personnel could develop compatible systems within each user organization to satisfy those needs.
2. Establish a process of recording and reporting of systems benefits to improve systems investment appraisal decisions and performance evaluations.

They suggested that the vice president of OG-Systems (Don Lindsay) should:

1. Establish and document responsibilities and procedures to ensure that the systems/user interface took place as needed and at the appropriate managerial levels within each organization.
2. Prepare detailed descriptions of the automated portions of the existing OG information processing cycles to support OG function and group-level business process planning. These documents should also be analyzed in order to identify opportunities to integrate existing processes and resources and to reduce costs.
3. Develop and maintain a description of the OG Systems Architecture, including hardware, software, databases, and networks which is sufficiently detailed to guide Systems planners in the development of the Long Range Systems Plan, as well as to direct operations managers in the development of application systems.
4. Establish and document responsibilities and procedures to ensure that Systems planners develop a Long Range Systems Plan based on an understanding of the OG Long Range Business Process Plan, the OG Systems Architecture, current OG information cycles, and future business requirements.
5. To ensure the promotion of the Long Range Systems Plan, ensure that the first year of the Long Range Systems Plan be sufficiently detailed to serve as the next year's Annual Work Plan; assign accountability for the execution of the Annual Work Plan to management in the user organizations; establish and document procedures to ensure the review and approval by the Systems planning staff of adjustments to the Annual Work Plan; and assign specific responsibility within the planning function for review of all new applications systems for adherence to the Long Range Systems Plan.

In the area of line operations, the auditors concluded that a diversity of operational practices existed within Systems, due to "a general lack of discipline and definition in operational practices within user first line operations, as well as the absence of common operational procedures, measures and tools at the group level." This diversity restricted management's ability to monitor and assess the quality and efficiency of software production activities, hindered the realization of economies of scale.

The auditors also concluded that key elements of the software creation process were not sufficiently controlled to ensure the efficient production of high quality software products. To remedy these deficiencies, they presented a long list of specific recommendations. These included suggestions for developing and implementing procedures for job requests and authorizations, scheduling jobs, ensuring better software security, and evaluating and documenting changes.

MANAGEMENT REACTIONS

The reactions to the audit were generally favorable. Larry Parton, manager of OG Planning and Systems Architecture, expressed his feelings:

> You can treat auditors either as outsiders or as a resource for management. Desktop Solutions has a very strong audit staff, and we like to take advantage of their expertise. We have some problems, and we have an awful lot to gain by asking them to come in and do an audit. That is the way we treated it and that is the way it turned out. We needed an independent look at what we were doing, and the audit group gave us that.

Don Lindsay was also satisfied:

> The reason I invited corporate audit to come in and do this audit was relatively straightforward. I had my own diagnosis of the problems in the Systems Department and an action plan for solving them. I just needed to get someone else's perception of the problems and their recommendations. IA is really the only group we have to do this kind of work. They are not a Gestapo organization; they are a support group that has the ability to get into this kind of work.
>
> I feel very good about the audit report. I agree with their base identification of the issues. They confirmed my analysis. I don't feel they came up with a lot of strong recommendations, however. I think the solution to many of our problems is a better focus on systems planning within the entire OG, and that is something that I, by myself, cannot solve. That is probably the single most important issue in OG, and the audit report dealt with it only superficially. It discussed planning but seemed to place more emphasis on day-to-day operating issues.
>
> It was not my original intention to use the audit report as additional leverage to plead my case, but that has certainly turned out to be an important benefit. After we realized how deeply ingrained our problems were, we realized that we had to use every means available to get the message across. The audit report was one such forum.

EXHIBIT 1 Audit Steps Performed and the Percent of Time Spent on Each on the OG-Systems Audit

1. *Scoping* (30%). Conducted preliminary independent interviews with users and Systems managers about their systems procedures and working relationships.
2. *Planning* (15%). Reviewed the results of the scoping phase and discussed them with Don Lindsay. Formulated a model of how the operations work and developed a set of problem hypotheses. Developed fieldwork questionnaires.
3. *Fieldwork* (25%). Sent questionnaires to a sample of involved or affected personnel, including 11 first-line managers and 10 analysts and programmers, all in the Systems organization, and 12 first-line user managers. Followed up the questionnaires with personal interviews and prepared a summary of responses. Interviewed five second-line and three third-line Systems managers and prepared a summary of these responses.
4. *Clearing and Summarizing* (15%). Verified interview responses where necessary. Developed conclusions drawn from fieldwork summaries and proposed recommendations. Presented conclusions and recommendations to OG-Systems management.
5. *Formal Report to Systems Management* (15%). Prepared formal written audit report with conclusions and recommendations for Systems management (Don Lindsay).

Vector Aeromotive Corporation

John Pope, a member of the board of directors of Vector Aeromotive Corporation, had a lot on his mind as he drove to his office. It was March 22, 1993, the day Vector's board had agreed to ask formally for the resignation of the company's president and founder, Gerald A. (Gerry) Weigert. Gerry had already been informed that if he did not resign, he would be fired. John hoped that Gerry would step down gracefully and not provoke a confrontation. Gerry had been the mastermind of the company for many years, but now John believed the board had little choice but to remove him because Vector was in a crisis. It was not able to pay either its employees or its payroll taxes; checks were bouncing; and outstanding accounts payable were being ignored. John and the other board members were convinced that the crisis was the result of Gerry's management style and excessive spending and that it was the board's moral and legal obligation to the shareholders to remove Gerry as president.

When John reached Vector headquarters, however, he was greeted by armed guards barring entry to the building. His efforts to enter the building through a rear entrance were futile because all the locks had been changed. Gerry had barricaded himself inside the building. Clearly this was not going to be an amicable management succession process. Gerry Weigert had declared war.

VECTOR AND THE EXOTIC SPORTS CAR INDUSTRY

Vector Aeromotive Corporation (hereafter Vector) designed, manufactured, and sold exotic sports cars. Cars are defined as exotic by their price range ($150,000–$500,000), their speed (in excess of 160 mph), their driving performance, their technology superior, high performance components, their extensive use of hand manufacturing, and their appearance. Exotic sports cars are offered to a select, wealthy clientele. Vector management estimated the total worldwide market for exotic sports cars was approximately 5,500 vehicles per year. The company's major competitors were Ferrari and Lamborghini, who together held a 75 percent market share.

Vector, located in Wilmington, California, was the only U.S.-based manufacturer of exotic sports cars. Gerry Weigert's vision was to design an automobile using the finest technology in America—aerospace technology. Indeed, the company's motto was "Aerospace Technology for the Road." In designing cars, performance was paramount; cost was no object.

Vector's standard model, the W8 Twin Turbo *luxury supercar,* priced at $448,000, had received considerable critical acclaim in automotive magazines such as *Road & Track.* The W8 was powered by a 6.0 liter, all-aluminum engine with twin turbochargers which generated over 600 horsepower at 5700 rpm. It could accelerate from 0 to 60 mph in 3.9 seconds and reach speeds of 260 mph. The car made considerable use of aerospace technology, including advanced composite materials for body panels, military specification electrical systems, and advanced tactical fighter instrumentation and displays. It also contained numerous safety and luxury features, such as an integrated rollcage, energy-absorbing crush zones, a spacious, *high tech, jet-aircraft-like leather cockpit,* and a custom, 10-disk compact disk changer.

From 1978 to 1987, the company operated as Vector Car, a privately-funded limited partnership founded by Gerry Weigert. Vector Aeromotive Corporation was formed in September 1987. It completed its Initial Public Offering in November, 1988, selling approximately 35 percent of the company's stock for $6 million. Vector delivered its first car to a paying customer in September 1990, and as of March, 1993, it had sold a total of

Research Assistant Michelle Wright wrote this case under the supervision of Professor Kenneth A. Merchant as a basis for class discussion rather than to illustrate either effective or ineffective handling of an administrative situation.

13 cars, to an international clientele. In its peak month, the company employed 45 people.

Because of its low sales volumes, Vector had reported substantial financial losses since its inception (see statements of operations in Exhibit 1). In an attempt to build volume, Vector was developing two other models, the Avtech WX3-R roadster and WX3-C coupe. Gerry Weigert wanted to price these models in the $700,000–$800,000 range, but some of the members of the board of directors thought the new models should be more modestly priced, at perhaps around $200,000.

THE BOARD OF DIRECTORS

At its incorporation in 1987, Vector Aeromotive had three members on its board of directors. Gerry Weigert was the board chairman. The two other directors, John Pope and Barry Rosengrant, had been consultants to Vector Car and business associates of Gerry for many years. Barry's background was in real estate. John was a financial consultant who acted as Vector's chief financial officer from 1988–1990 on a part-time basis.

The Board's primary role was to act as a fiduciary body, to oversee management decisions and protect shareholders' interests. The board was not involved in the formation of company strategy, but it did ratify major financial and policy decisions, such as advertising and promotion budgets. When actual expenses were greater than budgeted expenses (as they often were), Gerry Weigert, in his role as president, had to explain the variances to the other board members. Although the outside board members recognized that Gerry's effectiveness as president would probably decline as the company grew in size, they did not identify or train possible successors, partly because the company was so small and partly because Weigert would be strongly opposed to such actions.

The board of directors met quarterly on a regular basis, and additional special meetings were called occasionally to deal with specific issues, such as the signing of corporate documents. Vector management rarely provided information to board members prior to the meetings, but they shared considerable data and progress reports during the meetings. The atmosphere of the board meetings was generally congenial.

In 1991, Dan Harnett was added to the Board of Directors. Dan was an attorney and another long time associate of Gerry Weigert's. According to John Pope:

> Gerry wanted to shift the balance of power on the board. By 1991 Barry and I were not agreeing with him on some of the things that he wanted to do. He was getting voted down in some situations, and he wasn't particularly happy about that. I think he felt bringing Dan in would help shift the balance in his favor a little bit.

EARLY SIGNS OF TROUBLE

In June 1990, Don Johnson was hired as vice-president, finance. Don quickly began to feel uncomfortable with Gerry's management style. Don said, "Gerry hires good people who think they will be able to make a difference. But after about six months I realized that he doesn't give anyone the freedom to be effective." Don thought Gerry was excessively focused on raising money and promoting the company while neglecting attention to engineering and production. He also believed that Gerry's management style, which was shaped by "a compulsive, obsessive personality and a foul mouth," imposed undue stress on employees. Don confronted Gerry about his concerns, but was not able to change either Gerry's priorities or management style. Don also informed the board members of his concerns, but he received no support. For many months Don felt he was the sole voice of dissent, noting that "obviously the board was pretty much hand-picked."

Until 1992 the outside board members were not seriously concerned about Gerry Weigert's management style, although they considered him eccentric. John Pope explained that:

> At some point in his schooling, Gerry must have stayed up all night preparing for an exam or a presentation and received an 'A' for his effort. Since then he has decided that's the way life works, that if you let everything wait until the last minute and cram all your preparation into two days, you get better performance than if you spread it out over the month beforehand. That's how he functioned.

In retrospect, John attributed much of the

outside board members' support of Weigert to the fact that most of the information they received was designed to elicit agreement. He said:

> Gerry Weigert was, and is, literally a master of giving everybody, including the board, just enough information to support the conclusion he wants them to reach. The boardroom presenters were well coached, and we never received all of the relevant information.

The board finally took serious issue with some of Gerry's management actions early in 1992. Within three months of joining the board, Dan Harnett became a strong adversary of Gerry because of some issues brought to his attention by Vector employees. In a board meeting, he charged that Gerry was misusing expense reports, using company funds for personal home improvements, and participating in other forms of self-dealing at the company's expense. The board asked Don Johnson to look into these issues. Three weeks later a board meeting was called to formally discuss the charges and to decide on a course of action. Dan Harnett called for Gerry's immediate approval.

But Dan did not get the board's support. The outside board members did not think the charges of illegal activity could be substantiated. Don Johnson did a study but found no evidence that Gerry had diverted any company assets to his home. He did question approximately $17,000 of items charged on Gerry's American Express card because he had provided inadequate documentation. But Gerry explained that all the expenses were legitimate because, as the president of an exotic car company, he *had an image to maintain.*

The board did conclude that Gerry had participated in some questionable business deals. For example, Gerry lent an associate $25,000 of company money which was secured by a personal note made payable to himself. He also negotiated a lease at a below-market price and attempted to re-lease the property to Vector at the market price. The board insisted that Gerry charge Vector the lower price for the lease, arguing that he should not realize personal gain at the expense of the company. Gerry reluctantly succumbed to the board's wishes on the lease issue. Since the loan was repaid and neither of these deals ended up hurting Vector, the directors felt they did not warrant Gerry's termination. John Pope said:

> By this time I think that the Board was concerned about Gerry's management style, how he ran things and his excessive spending, but he hadn't done anything illegal. He also had an employment contract (see excerpts in Exhibit 2) which says he's allowed to be a bad manager. He just isn't allowed to do anything illegal.

The outside directors also believed it was not in the company's best interest for them to agree with Dan Harnett's call for firing Gerry because there was no obvious successor. In the words of John Pope:

> One of the concerns at that time too was that Dan had no Act II. Act I was 'get rid of Weigert.' Act II was, 'What do we do now?' There had to be something in place as far as I was concerned. You don't just throw the guy out. You have to have a plan to move forward.

One outcome of this board meeting was an agreement to change the process for reimbursing Gerry for personal expenses. Previously, Vector had paid Gerry's entire credit card bill. After the meeting, Gerry was required to submit formal expense reports to the accounting department.

Later that year, Dan Harnett resigned from the board and later died. He was replaced on the board by George Fencl, a self-employed consultant and businessman, and another long-time associate of Gerry Weigert.

AN INDONESIAN INVESTOR

In June 1992, Vector obtained $2 million in financing from Setiwan Djody, an Indonesian investor. Djody bought 4 million shares at $.50 and also paid $118,000 for an option to buy an additional 6 million shares at $.50. Mr. Djody advanced the money to Vector before completing a due diligence review. The board members perceived this quick advance as unusual and not very businesslike, but they later discovered that Djody customarily did business on the basis of trust. Included in Djody's purchase agreement was the right to appoint a director to the board. Thus a fifth director, Baduraman Dorpi, was added to protect Mr. Djody's interests in the company. Barry Rosengrant resigned shortly afterwards to make room for Mr. Dorpi, leaving the board still comprised of four members. Gerry had said that Mr. Djody insisted that the board not be increased in size, thus leaving him only a 20 percent vote. But the remaining board members later found out that this was not true; Gerry and Mr. Djody had never discussed the board-size issue.

In September of 1992, Gerry Weigert negotiated a new employment contract. It included an option to buy 1 million shares of stock at $.21875, the market price on the date the option was issued.

By December 1992, Vector was out of money again, and some employees had to be laid off. Mr. Djody was unwilling to exercise his stock purchase option, but he agreed to exercise Gerry's stock option if Gerry would transfer that option to him. Mr. Djody sent $220,000 to Vector in accordance with this agreement. But then, despite an agreement signed to the contrary, Gerry tried to renege on this deal, claiming that he had not intended that his option be transferred but just used as collateral for a loan. This disagreement breached the Indonesians' trust in Gerry. After this point, they had no interest in making additional investments in Vector, but they did keep Mr. Dorpi on as a director to protect the money they had already invested.

EVENTS LEADING TO GERRY WEIGERT'S TERMINATION

As Vector's financial position worsened, tension between Gerry and the board of directors increased. The company's payroll taxes for the period September through December 1992 were not paid on time. This caused a debate over disclosures in the company's 10-K report for the fiscal year ended September 30, 1992. According to John Pope:

> Although the 10-K report is required to be filed within 90 days of the fiscal year-end, Gerry would not allow it to be filed with the required disclosure that we hadn't paid our payroll taxes. But I would not allow it to be filed without that disclosure. So Gerry and I compromised. We had a sales prospect who was expected any day to give us a $100,000 check as a deposit on a car. That money could be used to pay the payroll taxes. We decided to let the 10-K be late.

In February 1993, John Pope was invited to Gerry Weigert's house for a baby shower for the accounting manager who was preparing to go on maternity leave. This was his first visit to the house, and when he arrived, he was shocked to find the house was decorated in *modern Vector.* Cabinets, floor tiles, and wall tiles were all identical to those used in Vector headquarters. John recalled:

> When I went into the house, I couldn't believe it. I looked around and saw what looked like a mirror image of our office. On Monday morning, I said to Don Johnson, I know you've examined all of the company invoices, but I have now been in Gerry's house and you're never going to convince me that company money wasn't used in that house. I don't know how we're going to prove it, but I will guarantee you that he had diverted company assets.

That same month, Don Johnson informed the board that the business plan Gerry was showing potential investors was, in the opinion of the heads of the marketing, finance, and production departments, wildly optimistic. He believed that Gerry's continued use of the business plan to solicit funds was fraudulent.

By March, Vector's financial position was critical. Employees weren't being paid; the 10-K still had not been issued because the payroll taxes had not been paid; $14,000 in checks had bounced; and remaining accounts payable were being ignored. But Gerry Weigert was focused on other things: He and some of his managers were out of the country, at the Geneva car show.

John Pope was ready to take action. He was convinced that with Gerry Weigert at the stern, Vector was heading for disaster. But before John could take any action against Gerry, he needed George Fencl's support. George had also become increasingly disenchanted with Gerry. George's primary charge was to assist Vector in obtaining financing, but he was finding it difficult to do so because the potential investors he had contacted did not trust Gerry. John brought up the issue over lunch. He explained:

> George talked about his inability to raise any money because of Gerry's management style. I told him about my concerns regarding the probable diversion of funds. I also

explained that I had pulled out a couple of Gerry's American Express bills and found out that the procedure we thought had been put into place had not been implemented. Gerry instead told the accounting department that they were now to pay off from only the face page of the bill. They were no longer going to get the individual tickets.

John Pope and George Fencl agreed to call the company's SEC counsel for advice. The lawyers acknowledged that the board did have authority to terminate Gerry for cause, and they further acknowledged that there appeared to be sufficient cause, most particularly the fraudulent business plan and diversion of company assets. John called Mr. Dorpi, and he agreed to support the other outside board members in their decision to terminate Gerry.

John hand-delivered to Gerry notice of a special board meeting to be held on Friday, March 19, 1993. This notice, which contained no explanation of the purpose of the meeting, was given 24 hours in advance of the meeting, as was required by company by-laws. After receiving this notice, Gerry called Mr. Dorpi, and Dorpi told him that the purpose of the meeting was to terminate Gerry as president. Gerry immediately called George Fencl and demanded an explanation.

George and Gerry met for the entire day on Thursday the 18th. John Pope was there for part of the day. At this meeting George confirmed what Mr. Dorpi had said and added that the board planned to give him the opportunity to resign in the best interests of the shareholders. If Gerry chose to resign, the board would send out a press release explaining that Gerry "wanted to devote himself to creative aspects of the business." If Gerry chose not to resign, the board would terminate him and sue him for conversion of funds.

Gerry questioned both why this was happening and why now. He said he needed to go to New Jersey for the opening of a new dealership, and he had a financing meeting set up in New York. But George and John did not want him to make the trip. They did not think he should act as president when he was soon to be fired, and they did not want him to raise money by using the fraudulent business plan.

Finally, Gerry asked that the special board meeting be postponed 30 days. The board members refused this request, but they did agree to postpone until Monday to give Gerry the weekend to decide if he would *resign* or be terminated. The meeting was scheduled for Monday, March 22, at 5:00 P.M. On Monday morning, Gerry responded by moving into the headquarters' building and barring all outsiders, including the board members, from the building. A newspaper account the next day labeled the affair *Wall Street Waco,* as it occurred at the same time as the Branch Davidians cult members' stand-off with the federal agents in Waco, Texas.

EXHIBIT 1 Statements of Operations

	Years ended September 30			*September 12, 1987 (Inception) to September 30, 1992*
	1992	*1991*	*1990*	*(Cumulative)*
Sales, net (Note 15)	**$ 1,287,866**	$ 754,800	$ 20,000	$ 2,062,666
Costs of sales	**974,966**	579,800	20,000	1,574,766
Gross profit	**312,900**	175,000	—	487,900
Costs and Expenses				
Salaries and wages (Note 3)	**917,350**	1,533,199	1,253,554	4,251,037
Rental expense (Note 3)	**96,358**	112,972	128,558	529,088
Utilities expense	**91,793**	116,578	64,264	316,575
Research and development	**1,275,841**	718,346	2,340,818	4,878,034
Depreciation and amortization	**429,394**	466,316	241,437	1,266,813
Advertising and promotion	**566,121**	535,023	655,194	1,890,137
Professional fees	**613,015**	324,411	580,852	1,833,288
General and administrative	**528,275**	917,726	427,820	2,153,405
Warranty expense	**27,564**	31,157	—	58,721
Provision for loss contingency (Note 7)	—	633,167	—	633,167
Abandonment of property and equipment	—	234,911	—	234,911
Total costs and expenses	**4,545,711**	5,623,806	5,692,497	18,045,176
Other income (expense)				
Other income	**231,299**	88,489	214,179	836,211
Other expense	**(35,400)**	(15,862)	(26,373)	(119,523)
	195,899	72,627	187,806	716,688
Net loss	**$ (4,036,912)**	$(5,376,179)	$(5,504,691)	$(16,840,588)
Net loss per share (Note 12)	**$ (0.39)**	$ (1.11)	$ (1.90)	
Weighted average common shares outstanding (Note 12)	**10,245,056**	4,832,556	2,890,329	

EXHIBIT 2 Excerpts from Gerry Weigert's Employee Contract

EMPLOYMENT AGREEMENT

EMPLOYMENT AGREEMENT, effective July 1, 1992, by and between VECTOR AEROMOTIVE CORPORATION, a Nevada corporation (the "Company") and GERALD A. WEIGERT (the "Employee").

WHEREAS, the Company has, prior to the date of this Agreement, employed the Employee as the Company's President, and

WHEREAS, the Company desires to continue to employ the Employee on a full-time basis, and the Employee desires to be so employed by the Company, from and after the date of this agreement.

NOW THEREFORE, in consideration of the mutual covenants contained herein, the parties agree as follows:

Article I

EMPLOYMENT DUTIES AND BENEFITS

Section 1.5 Expenses. The Employee is authorized to incur reasonable expenses for promoting the domestic and international business of the Company in all respects, including expenses for entertainment, travel and similar items. The Company will reimburse the Employee for all such expenses upon the presentation by the Employee, from time-to-time, of an itemized account of such expenditures.

Section 1.6 Employee's Other Business. Employee shall be allowed to participate in outside business activities provided (i) such activities do not interfere with Employee's performance of his duties as a full-time employee of the Company; and (ii) the outside business is not a Business Opportunity of the Company, as defined herein. A Business Opportunity of the Company shall be a product, service, investment, venture or other opportunity which is either:

(a) directly related to or within the scope of the existing business of the Company; or

(b) within the logical scope of the business of the Company, as such scope may be expanded or altered from time-to-time by the Board of Directors.

The Employee's current outside business activities, which activities are hereby irrevocably approved by the Company, include investments in Ram Wing and the Wet Bike.

Article II

COMPENSATION

Section 2.1 Base Salary. The Company shall pay to the Employee a base salary of not less than the amount specified on Schedule 1. This amount may be adjusted for raises in salary by action of the Board of Directors.

Section 2.2 Bonus. The Employee shall be entitled to receive a bonus at such time or times as may be determined by the Board of Directors of the Company.

Article III

TERM OF EMPLOYMENT AND TERMINATION

Section 3.1 Term. This Agreement shall be for a term which is specified on Schedule 1, commencing on its effective date, subject, however, to termination during such period as provided in this Article. This Agreement shall be renewed automatically for succeeding periods of one year on the same terms and conditions as contained in this Agreement unless either the Company of the Employee shall, at least 30 days prior to the expiration of the initial term or of any renewal term, give written notice of the intention not to renew this Agreement. Such renewals shall be effective in subsequent years on the same day of the same month as the original effective date of this Agreement.

Section 3.2 Termination by the Employee Without Cause. The Employee, without cause, may terminate this Agreement upon 90 days' written notice to the Company. In such event, the Employee shall not be required to render the services required under this Agreement. Compensation for vacation time not taken by Employee shall be paid to the Employee at the date of termination.

Section 3.3 Termination by the Company With Cause. The Company may terminate the Employee, at any time, upon 90 days' written notice and opportunity for Employee to remedy any con-compliance with the terms of this Agreement, by reason of the willful misconduct of the Employee which is contrary to the best interests of the Company. Upon the date of such termination, the Company's obligation to pay compensation shall terminate. No compensation for vacation time not taken by Employee shall be paid to the Employee.

EXHIBIT 2B Excerpts from Gerry Weigert's Employee Contract

Schedule 1

Duties and Compensation

Employee: Gerald A. Wiegert

Position: President

Base Salary: $275,000 per year, payable bi-weekly and quarterly performance payment equal to 10% of improvements over annual budget as approved by Board from time to time

Bonus: As determined by the Board of Directors

Term: December 31, 1997

Duties and Responsibilities: Supervision and coordination of all operations of the Company; supervision of all other operating officers of the Company.

APPROVED:

THE COMPANY:	EMPLOYEE:
By: ______________________	*Gerald A. Wiegert*
John Pope, Compensation Committee	Gerald A. Wiegert
Date: ______________, 1992	Date: *May 1*, 1992

CHAPTER 17

Management Control-Related Ethical Issues and Analyses

Managers involved in designing and using management control systems (MCSs) should have a basic understanding of *ethics.* Ethics is the field of study which is used to prescribe morally acceptable behavior. It provides methods of distinguishing between right and wrong and of systematically determining the rules that provide guidance as to how individuals and groups of individuals *should* behave. Its systematic nature goes beyond what even thoughtful people do in making sense of their own and others' moral experiences. Ethics is important for managers involved with an MCS because ethical principles can provide a useful guide for defining how employers should behave. Further, employees' ethics are an important component of personnel controls. If good ethics can be encouraged, they can substitute for, or augment, actions or results controls.

Ethics is a difficult subject for many managers to understand. One important reason for this is that most managers' basic discipline training is in economics. Two common assumptions in economics are that rational people should act to maximize their own self-interest and that the primary purpose of employees in for-profit organizations is to maximize shareholder value. Ethics, however, provides alternative assumptions about how people should and do behave. It assumes that ethical individuals must consider the impact of their actions on other stakeholders; those affected by their actions. (Table 17-1 shows a list of corporations' most common stakeholders.) While the commonly-cited aphorism, "Good ethics is good business," is usually true, it is not always true. Good ethics does *not* always pay either for the individuals or organizations involved. This is definitely true in the short-run, and it is also often true in the long-run. Ethical individuals sometimes must take actions that are not in their own self-interest or their organization's owners' best interest because of some legitimate interests of other stakeholders.[1] They are accountable to these nonownership stakeholders as well, and no group, not even owners, automatically has priority over the other stakeholders.[2]

This potential for personal sacrifice is reflected in many codes of professional conduct. The preamble of the Code of Professional Conduct of the American Institute of Certified Public Accountants states, "The Principles call for an unswerving commitment to honorable behavior, even at the sacrifice of personal advantage."[3] When are the ethical principles so important that one must consider actions contrary to self-interest or one's organization's best interest? That is a core ethical question.

This chapter provides an introduction to the complex subject of ethics. It starts with a discussion about the importance of good ethical analyses, then it describes how to identify ethical issues and presents a four-step model which is use-

TABLE 17-1 Typical Stakeholders of a Corporation
Shareholders
Bondholders
Creditors
Employees
Management
Board of Directors
Customers
Suppliers
Government
Local Communities
Other Users of Shared Resources: people and animals that might be affected by corporate use of land, water, and air.

ful for guiding the analysis of the ethical issues that have been identified. The chapter concludes with a description of some of the major ethical issues related to MCSs and some suggestions for encouraging ethical behavior from organizational employees.

THE IMPORTANCE OF GOOD ETHICAL ANALYSES

High potentials for unethical behaviors are costly to individuals, organizations, markets, and societies. They create a need for extra laws and additional regulatory agencies from governments; and extra rules, reviews, or supervision within organizations. These extra enforcement mechanisms are incomplete, imperfect, expensive, and have the typical drawbacks of rigid action controls. Good ethics is the glue that holds organizations and societies together. It causes people not to be "unreservedly opportunistic [but to] constrain their own behavior out of an ethical sensibility or conscience."[4]

Lapses in ethics are often precursors of more serious problems, such as fraud. In a financial reporting context, one study found that companies which were guilty of violating generally accepted accounting principles (GAAP) were likely to be aggressive in their financial reporting in periods prior to the violation.[5] The aggressive financial reporting, which many interpret as less than ethical, but not quite illegal, seems to be one step on a "slippery slope" which can lead to costly, fraudulent activities.[6]

To control unethical behaviors within an organization, managers need well developed ethical reasoning skills. Just as they need good skills in their technical disciplines in order to make good business judgments, managers need moral expertise to make good ethical judgments. Senior managers should serve as *moral exemplars,* or role models, within their organizations. They should also design their MCS to promote moral points of view and ethical behaviors. A number of highly specific controls, including some policies and procedures and elements of measurement and reward systems, stem from ethical analyses. Some controls help ensure ethical behaviors in areas where totally precise organizational prescriptions are impossible; including training sessions, codes of conduct, and credos that help employees identify and think through ethical issues.

Managers without a solid foundation in ethics can make a number of mistakes that can lead to high probabilities of unethical behaviors within their organizations. First, they sometimes fail to recognize ethical issues when they arise. One common problem is that untrained people sometimes equate ethical and legal issues; they conclude that if an action is not illegal, it must be ethical. This is clearly not true. While many laws do prohibit immoral practices, it is impossible to write laws to prohibit all unethical actions. It is not even desirable to do so. Lying is usually considered to be immoral; however, laws prohibiting lying would not be enforceable, and even if they were, the enforcement would not be cost effective. As a consequence, lying is against the law only in the most important circumstances; that is, perjury. On the other hand, many would argue that some laws themselves are not morally defensible, such as those requiring racial segregation, those allowing abortion, or those causing huge payments to be made to victims of relatively minor accidents.

Second, some untrained people try to address ethical issues with simple rules, such as "Always tell the truth" or "Do no harm." Many times these rules work, but other times they do not. It is sometimes ethical to lie for worthwhile purposes, such as to thwart the efforts of someone who is threatening even greater harm.

A prominent example of a simple ethical rule is the *Golden Rule:* "Do unto others as you would have them do unto you." This rule works only in the rare situation where the values of the person invoking the rule are shared by all others. Untrained people are not able to understand when the rule works and when it does not, and they are incapable of defending their moral views.

Another simple rule is usually phrased as, "Act as if your family and friends had full knowledge of your actions and their implications," or "Don't take actions that you would not like to see described in the newspaper (or on television) tomorrow morning." Another variation of this rule is phrased in the form of a question, "Would the boy or girl in you be proud of the man or woman you have become?" This conscience-based rule works for honest managers in many situations, but it too fails when the manager is unaware either of the full implications of the actions or the full range of values and interests of all of the parties affected by the action.

IDENTIFYING ETHICAL ISSUES

The first challenge in adapting ethics thinking to managerial settings is in recognizing ethical issues. The ethics literature includes numerous normative models of behavior. Almost all of these models recognize that in a social context, ethics is about how actions affect the interests of other people. Every ethical issue involves multiple parties (stakeholders) one or more of whom benefits while others are harmed or put at risk by a particular action. The characterizations of harm or risk are made in terms of one or more major ethical principles, rules, or values which are embedded in one or more of the normative models of behavior. The following sections briefly describe four major traditions in moral philosophy: utilitarianism, rights and duties, justice, and virtue.[7]

Utilitarianism

Utilitarianism judges the rightness of actions solely on the basis of their consequences. (It is sometimes referred to as *consequentialism.*) In this model, an action is morally right if it maximizes the sum total of good in the world; that is, it produces at least as much net good (benefits less costs and harms) as any other action that could have been performed. Sometimes this objective is phrased as, "the greatest good for the greatest number of people." Utilitarianism does not mean that the right action is the one that produces the most good for the person performing the act, but rather the one that produces the most good for all parties affected by the action.

Utilitarianism is one of the most influential ethical models in business because of its tradition in economics. Utilitarian-type thinking has been accepted by many businesses, and it has been embedded in many public policy decision procedures, such as welfare economics and cost-benefit analyses.

Utilitarianism is not without its critics. These critics point to the problems of quantifying net goodness. The benefits of some goods; such as happiness, freedom from stress, and a risky possibility of additional profits sometime in the future, must be measured, aggregated, and compared across individuals. Critics also point out that utilitarianism is concerned only with aggregate social welfare, not with the distribution of that welfare. It ignores individuals, so small benefits provided to a large number of people can conceal major harm done to some small segments of society.

Rights and Duties

A second major ethical model focuses on *rights and duties.* It argues that all individuals have some basic rights to which they are entitled regardless of the consequences to others. The purpose of these rights is to enable individuals to pursue or, if they choose, not to pursue, certain interests or activities. Moral rights provide a moral justification for doing certain things. In certain circumstances, the rights may include a right to work, a right to freedom of speech, a right of association, and a right to receive fair and accurate disclosures about investments they have made or might make.

The rights model discounts considerations about both aggregate social welfare and the ways in which it is distributed. Where the moral rights exist, they are absolute. They must be provided regardless of the effects on social welfare or justice.

Duties are the converse of rights. Every right can be defined in terms of the moral duties others have not to interfere with that individual's right. Freedom of speech can be defined as an obligation for others not to interfere with that right.

The rights and duties model also has its critics. They point out, correctly, that rights can easily proliferate and that there is lack of agreement as to the limits of the rights and how each of the rights should be balanced against other conflicting rights.

Justice

A third major ethical model is built on notions of *justice* and fairness, two terms that are used interchangeably. Justice means that all individuals are given their due; equals are treated equally, and unequals are treated unequally.

Justice and fairness issues are often divided into four categories. *Distributive justice* is concerned with the fair distribution of benefits and burdens across members of a stakeholder group. *Retributive justice* refers to the fairness of the punishments meted out to wrong- or evil-doers. *Compensatory justice* is concerned with the fairness of the compensation people are given when others wrong them. *Pro-*

cedural justice is concerned with the fairness of decision processes; equal opportunity, but not necessarily equal outcomes.

The strength of the justice model lies in the fact that it raises ethical concerns that are different from those raised by the utilitarian and rights and duties models. The weakness of the justice standards is that they ignore effects on both aggregate social welfare and individuals.

Virtues

Virtues are positive aspects of character which are acquired by virtuous individuals.[8] Prominent examples are integrity, loyalty, and courage. Individuals with integrity have the intent to do what is ethically right without regard to self-interest. *Integrity* has many components; including honesty, fairness, and conscientiousness. *Loyalty* is faithfulness to one's allegiances. People have many loyalties; to other persons, organizations, religions, professions, and causes. When loyalties conflict, their relative strength dictates how the conflict is resolved. *Courage* is the strength to stand firm in the face of difficulty or pressure.

Action controls, such as policies and procedures, cannot be made both specific and complete. Virtues fill in the gaps and provide guidance as to what is the right thing to do and are an element of personnel/cultural control. Virtues provide their own *intrinsic* rewards. Virtuous individuals value, and hence pursue, these rewards.

Virtues are often reflected in codes of conduct. The Standards of Ethical Conduct for Management Accountants published by the Institute of Management Accountants is shown in Table 17-2. These standards, which describe role-related norms, are organized into four areas of virtue: competence, confidentiality, integrity, and objectivity. Similarly, the Financial Executives Institute's Code of Ethics uses virtue concepts. It requires members to "conduct [their] business and personal affairs at all times with honesty and integrity." Similarly, Table 17-3 shows the financial reporting and accounting records section of Caterpillar's Code of Worldwide Business Conduct and Operating Principles. The key word in this code is integrity. Integrity refers both to the information in the financial statements and the people involved in creating, processing, and recording the accounting information.

Parts of these codes of conduct define how individuals ought to behave; in other words, what an individual's duty is. Pure virtue theory does not deal directly with duties, but it is often easy to derive duties from individual virtues.

Virtue theory also has its critics. The list of potential virtues is long, and the critics argue that it is not obvious which set of virtues should be applied in any given setting. Some characteristics considered virtues can actually impede ethical behavior as, for example, courage is sometimes essential for managers to commit fraud. It is difficult to know whether particular virtues exist in any individuals, how to develop virtues in individuals and groups of individuals, and how to recognize when day-to-day pressures are eroding the virtues.

These models, utilitarianism, right and duties, justice, and virtues, identify four main types of moral considerations. Some people prefer to use (or emphasize) a utilitarian approach to ethical issues, and others prefer one of the other approaches. Decision makers must recognize that none of these models is complete. While some moral issues are usefully studied using just one of the models, none of the models captures all of the factors that must be taken into account in making

TABLE 17-2 Standards of Ethical Conduct for Management Accountants

Management accountants have an obligation to the organizations they serve, their profession, the public, and themselves to maintain the highest standards of ethical conduct. In recognition of this obligation, the Institute of Management Accountants, formerly the National Association of Accountants, has promulgated the following standards of ethical conduct for management accountants. Adherence to these standards is integral to achieving the Objectives of Management Accounting. Management accountants shall not commit acts contrary to these standards nor shall they condone the commission of such acts by others within their organizations.

Competence
Management accountants have a responsibility to:

- Maintain an appropriate level of professional competence by ongoing development of their knowledge and skills.
- Perform their professional duties in accordance with relevant laws, regulations, and technical standards.
- Prepare complete and clear reports and recommendations after appropriate analyses of relevant and reliable information.

Confidentiality
Management accountants have a responsibility to:

- Refrain from disclosing confidential information acquired in the course of their work except when authorized, unless legally obligated to do so.
- Inform subordinates as appropriate regarding the confidentiality of information acquired in the course of their work and monitor their activities to assure the maintenance of that confidentiality.
- Refrain from using or appearing to use confidential information acquired in the course of their work for unethical or illegal advantage either personally or through third parties.

Integrity
Management accountants have a responsibility to:

- Avoid actual or apparent conflicts of interest and advise all appropriate parties of any potential conflict.
- Refrain from engaging in any activity that would prejudice their ability to carry out their duties ethically.
- Refuse any gift, favor, or hospitality that would influence or would appear to influence their actions.
- Refrain from either actively or passively subverting the attainment of the organization's legitimate and ethical objectives.
- Recognize and communicate professional limitations or other constraints that would preclude responsible judgment or successful performance of an activity.
- Communicate unfavorable as well as favorable information and professional judgments or opinions.
- Refrain from engaging in or supporting any activity that would discredit the profession.

Objectivity
Management accountants have a responsibility to:

- Communicate information fairly and objectively.
- Disclose fully all relevant information that could reasonably be expected to influence an intended user's understanding of the reports, comments, and recommendations presented.

Resolution of Ethical Conflict
In applying the standards of ethical conduct, management accountants may encounter problems in identifying unethical behavior or in resolving an ethical conflict. When faced with significant ethical issues, management accountants should follow the established policies of the organization bearing on the resolution of such conflict. If these policies do not resolve the ethical conflict, management accountants should consider the following course of action:

TABLE 17-2 *(cont.)*

- Discuss such problems with the immediate superior except when it appears that the superior is involved, in which case the problem should be presented initially to the next higher managerial level. If satisfactory resolution cannot be achieved when the problem is initially presented, submit the issues to the next higher managerial level.

  If the immediate superior is the chief executive officer, or equivalent, the acceptable reviewing authority may be a group such as the audit committee, executive committee, board of directors, board of trustees, or owners. Contact with levels above the immediate superior should be initiated only with the superior's knowledge, assuming the superior is not involved.
- Clarify relevant concepts by confidential discussion with an objective advisor to obtain an understanding of possible courses of action.
- If the ethical conflict still exists after exhausting all levels of internal review, the management accountant may have no other recourse on significant matters than to resign from the organization and to submit an informative memorandum to an appropriate representative of the organization.

Except where legally prescribed, communication of such problems to authorities or individuals not employed or engaged by the organization is not considered appropriate.

Statements on Management Accounting: Objectives of Management Accounting, Statement No. 1B, June 17, 1982.

moral judgments across a broad range of issues. Moral philosophers have been unable to construct a comprehensive model to provide guidance as to when the considerations from one model should dominate the considerations from another. Informed moral reasoning must rely on elements of each of the traditions.

TABLE 17-3 Financial Reporting and Accounting Records Section of Caterpillar's Code of Worldwide Business Conduct and Operating Principles

Investors, creditors, and other persons having legitimate interest in the company have a right to material information that is timely and accurate.

To ensure reliability, Caterpillar's financial reporting is directed toward factual representations, objectivity, and consistency. This means the measurements, descriptions, and explanations employed reflect no bias toward a predetermined result.

The integrity of Caterpillar financial reporting and accounting records is based on validity, accuracy, and completeness of basic information supporting entries to the company's books of account. Every accounting or financial entry should reflect exactly that which is described by the supporting information. All employees involved in creating, processing, or recording such information are held responsible for its integrity.

There must be no concealment of information from (or by) management, or from the company's independent auditors.

Profit center and service center financial reports are based on the specific accountabilities assigned to each by the Executive Office and are reconciled to the company's external reports. These statements provide focused information to help run the business, assess managerial performance, and determine incentive compensation. The same standards of integrity that apply to the external financial reporting also apply to the financial statements that are used as internal management tools.

Employees who become aware of possible omission, falsification, or inaccuracy of accounting and financial entries, or basic data supporting such entries, are held responsible for reporting such information. These reports are to be made as specified by corporate procedure.

ANALYZING ETHICAL ISSUES

An ethical judgment cannot be considered to be proper unless the decision makers consider all the important elements of the issue and use logical reasoning to reach a conclusion. The following sections describe a structured, four-step framework that is useful in guiding a proper process of ethical and decision making.[9]

Step 1. Determine the facts. The first step is to uncover the facts that define the problem or potential issue. The relevant facts usually address questions about what, who, where, when, and how.

Step 2: Define the ethical issues. The second step is to identify the competing interests that create a possible ethical issue. Decision makers should list the significant stakeholders and phrase the issue in terms of one or more of the models described in the preceding section. Has someone benefited at someone's else's expense? Are somebody's rights being violated? Has someone been treated unfairly? Has someone acted without integrity?

Step 3: Specify the alternative actions and their probable consequences. List the major alternative courses of action. These typically include doing nothing and various forms of compromise. Identify the positive and negative and short- and long-term consequences for each of these alternatives. A good analysis will often reveal an unanticipated result of major importance as, for example, short-run gains or losses may be seen to be overridden by long-run considerations.

Step 4: Compare the alternatives with respect to ethical considerations, and choose the best alternative. Choose the alternative that best fits your (or your organization's) primary ethical principles or values.

Some ethical issues lead to conclusions with which most people will agree. It is easy to conclude that in most situations to lie, cheat, or steal. Many ethical issues do not have a single correct answer; experts who have gone through a careful ethical analysis can rightly disagree. They can reach different conclusions about the implications of particular facts. Even if the outcomes are unequivocal, they can reach different conclusions if they use (or emphasize) different ethical models or different values within a single model. To sort through the differences in perceptions and perspectives, ethical issues should be subjected to rigorous analysis using a decision-structuring framework, such as the four-step model described above. Anything less is merely casual opinion-giving which is subject to misinterpretation and error.

SOME COMMON MANAGEMENT CONTROL-RELATED ETHICAL ISSUES

Many ethical issues are imbedded within and around MCSs. Some people use ethics arguments to question the basic foundations MCSs and capitalistic economies which empower management to make economic decisions. Many critics argue that corporate restructurings and downsizings are unethical because they put profits (and management bonuses) before employee welfare. Others counter, however, that the restructurings are necessary responses to changes in the environment. While they may cause pain to displaced employees, they help ensure that the restructured businesses remain competitive and able to gainfully employ their remaining employees. Such large political economy-related ethics questions are, however, beyond the scope of this book. The following sections of this chapter identify and briefly discuss four more mundane, but common, management control-related ethical issues: (1) creating budget slack, (2) managing earnings, (3) responding to flawed control indicators, and (4) using results measures that are "too good." These issues are important, and the analyses required to deal with them are also representative of those that could be used to analyze other issues that might be faced.

The Ethics of Creating Budgetary Slack

Many performance targets, particularly those used at managerial organization levels, are negotiated between employees and their superiors. Negotiation processes provide opportunities for lower-level parties to "game" the process, to distort their positions in order to be given more easily achievable targets. This distortion is commonly known as *sandbagging* or *creating slack*. As was discussed in Chapter 6, putting slack in budgets is quite common.[10]

Is slack creation ethical? When employees create slack, they are exploiting their position of superior knowledge about business possibilities. They are failing to disclose to their superiors all of their information and informed insights and are actually presenting a distorted picture of the possibilities. Creating budget slack can be interpreted to be in violation of several of the obligations listed under integrity and objectivity in the IMA's Standards of Ethical Conduct (see Table 17-2). The integrity standard requires management accountants to "refrain from either actively or passively subverting the attainment of the organization's legitimate and ethical objectives." The objectivity standard requires management accountants to "communicate information fairly and objectively."

Analysis in a utilitarianism framework also suggests that slack creation creates an ethical issue. Typically, employees creating budget slack will benefit personally from their act. Slack protects employees against unforeseen bad luck, such as an economic downturn or an increase in costs, thus increasing the probability that the employees will meet their performance targets and earn performance-dependent rewards. If the reward/performance function is continuous, as is typical, slack increases the size of the rewards that will be earned.

An ethical issue is raised because slack creation is often costly to some stakeholders, especially the firm, its owners, and possibly creditors. Budgets containing slack are often less than optimally motivating. When achievement of an organization's goal is assured, the effort of the employees in the organization may decline. Achievement of a downward-biased annual profit target may be largely assured by August. What are the effects on the employees' behaviors after August? Managers know they do not want to exceed their target by too much because that would cause them to be given a higher, more difficult target for next year. They may not work as hard; they may make unnecessary expenditures to consume the excess; and they may be motivated to play games to save the profit not needed in the current year.

Slack creation also appears less than fair to the users of the budget submissions, (upper management). The users will rely on the information in the budget to make investment, resource allocation, and performance evaluation decisions that will become distorted.

On the other hand, some arguments can be raised to support the contention that creation of slack *is* ethical. Many managers, perhaps even a vast majority of them, argue that creating slack is a rational response within a results control system. They do not view slack as a distortion, but as a means of protecting themselves from the downside potential of an uncertain future. Viewed this way, slack serves a function identical to that of the accepted management accounting practices of variance analysis and flexible budgeting; both of which are used to eliminate the effects on the performance measures of some uncontrollable factors, and in so doing shielding managers from the risk these factors create. This protection from risk is particularly valuable in firms which treat the budget forecasts as promises from the manager to the corporation, with dismissal being the penalty for failure.

Some managers also argue that budget slack is sometimes necessary to address the imbalance of power that is inherent in a hierarchical organization. It helps protect lower-level managers from evaluation unfairness that can be caused by imperfect performance measures or evaluation abuses by superiors.

Finally, managers who defend the creation of slack also point out that it is an accepted part of their organization's budget negotiating process. Managers at all levels of the organization negotiate for slack in their budgets, and everyone is aware of the behavioral norm. Indeed, they point out, many top-level managers were promoted into their positions precisely because they were good at negotiating for slack and, hence, for achieving their budget targets consistently. In many organizations, superiors actually want their subordinates to create slack because they also benefit. The superiors' targets are usually consolidations of targets of their subordinates, so they enjoy the same reduction in risk and increase in the expected values of their rewards as the slack creators. When creation of slack is widespread and the practice is encouraged, can we say that the organization's culture is encouraging unethical behavior, or does it indicate that in this community, at least, creation of slack is an acceptable behavior norm?

In making judgments as to whether slack creation is ethical in any specific setting, many factors must be considered, including:

- how good the performance measures are (the extent to which they reflect the manager's (or entity's) true performance and are unaffected by factors the managers cannot control),
- whether budget targets are treated as a rigid promise from managers to the corporation,
- whether the manager's intent in creating the slack primarily reflects self-interest,
- whether (or how much) superiors are aware of the slack,
- whether the superiors encourage the creation of slack,
- whether the amount of slack is "material", or
- whether the individual(s) involved are bound by one or more of the sets of standards of professional conduct. (Most accountants are. Most managers are not.)

Overall judgments about the ethics of creating slack in each specific situation will depend on the ethical framework(s) used and the relative emphases placed on them.

The Ethics of Managing Earnings

A second important ethical issue involves the data manipulation problem discussed in Chapter 6. A common form of manipulation is *earnings management,* which can be defined to include any action which changes reported earnings while providing no real economic advantage to the organization and, sometimes, actually causing harm.[11] Generally earnings management actions are designed either to *boost* earnings to achieve a budget target or increase stock price, or to *smooth* earnings patterns to give the impression of higher earnings predictability and lower corporate risk. Some actions are designed to *reduce* earnings to save profits for a future period when they might be needed or to lower stock price to facilitate a management buyout.

As with slack creation, earnings management can be seen as unethical, at least sometimes, for any of several reasons. First, most of the actions are not apparent to either external or internal users of financial statements. Those engaging in earnings management may be deriving personal advantage through deception. Second, many people, and most professional associations, believe that professional managers and accountants have a duty to disclose fairly presented information. Third, the distortions can be interpreted as not being consistent with managers' and accountants' integrity obligations to be honest, fair, and truthful. Fourth, the rewards earned from managing earnings are not fair when the reported performance is only cosmetic, not real.

As in the area of slack, however, managers may have good justifications for managing earnings. They might be using their private information about company prospects to smooth out some meaningless, short-term perturbations in the earnings measures to provide more, rather than less, informative performance signals to financial statement users.[12] They might be taking actions necessary to protect themselves from rigid, unfair performance evaluations. They might also be taking actions that make it unnecessary for them to take other, more damaging actions; such as laying off employees or suspending research and development expenditures in the face of a budget shortfall.

Interestingly, most people judge accounting methods of managing earnings more harshly than they judge operating methods. This is true even though the purposes of the two earnings management methods are identical, and the economic effects of the operating methods are typically far more costly to the firm.[13] (As discussed in Chapter 6, accounting methods of managing earnings involve the selection of accounting methods and the flexibility in applying those methods to affect reported earnings. Operating methods involve the altering of actual operating decisions, such as the timing of sales or discretionary expenditures.) Most people seem to regard aggressive financial reporting as ethically questionable, and the standards for judging reporting aggressiveness (particularly consistency with generally accepted accounting principles) are clearer than those that are used for judging management decision making.

It is easy to see that many situational factors are likely to influence judgments as to when earnings management actions are ethical. Some of the most important considerations include: (1) the direction of the manipulation (boost, shrink, or merely smooth profits), (2) the size (materiality) of the effect, (3) the timing (quarter-versus year-end, random timing versus immediately preceding a bond offering), (4) the method used (play with reserves, defer discretionary expenditure, change accounting policy), (5) the managers' intent regarding the informativeness of the numbers (and disclosures), (6) the clarity of the rules prohibiting the action, and (7) the degree of repetition (one-time use versus on-going use of the action after a warning). Because it is difficult to distinguish right from wrong, it is difficult for managers to develop a set of rules to control earnings management actions. This lack of control undoubtedly contributes to the high incidence of earnings management.

The Ethics of Responding to Flawed Control Indicators

Results targets and action prescriptions provide signals to employees as to what the organization considers important. When the targets and prescriptions are not defined properly, they can actually motivate behaviors that employees know are not in the organization's best interest. The employees earn the rewards for doing what they are asked to do, but the organization suffers. These situations seem to be relatively common. Recent surveys have shown that nearly 10 percent of employees admitted that in the last year they had done things at work they would be ashamed or embarrassed to tell their children, and nearly one-third of the employees sometimes feel pressured to engage in misconduct to achieve business objectives.[14]

One commonly cited flawed-response example, myopia, was discussed in detail in Chapter 12. Myopia occurs when companies place a high emphasis on achievement of short-term profit targets, even though some profit-increasing activities (for example, reducing investments in research and development) diminish shareholder value. Other common examples occur where organizations allow their policies and procedures to become obsolete. Many fraud cases involve employees taking unethical and illegal actions which they perceive to be necessary for their company to thrive or survive.

What should employees do if they know the results measures or action prescriptions are flawed? Should they act to generate the results for which they will be rewarded, or should they sacrifice their own self-interest in favor of what they believe to be best for the organization? When they face this classic conflict of interest, most employees will choose to follow the rules of the reward system, perhaps while lobbying to get the measures changed. This behavioral norm may not be ethical. Management accountants have professional standards of ethical conduct (duties) that require them to further their organization's legitimate interests. Managers are not bound by those standards, but they should be bound by a sense of loyalty (a virtue) to their organization.

The Ethics of Using Control Indicators That Are Too Good

Another ethical issue relates to the use of control indicators that are *too good.* Highly, perhaps excessively, tight control indicators have been made possible by advances in technology. Networking Dynamics Corporation of Glendale, California, a software company, sells computer surveillance programs to allow supervisors to look at employees' personal computer screens.[15] One called Peek requires the employee's approval on each occasion. Another program called Spy allows access to the screen without the employee's knowledge or approval.

Many other examples of electronic eavesdropping also exist. Supervisors can listen in on employees' telephone conversations or sales calls; cameras can record all the actions some employees take; computers can count the number of keystrokes by data entry clerks and telephone operators to gauge productivity; and personal location devices can track a person's whereabouts throughout the work day. The U.S. Federal Office of Technology Assessment has estimated the number of employees whose employers are monitoring in detail the time they spend on computers or on the phone with customers is approximately 10 million.[16]

What is the ethical issue? Numbers of correct keystrokes and reports of individuals' locations-by-time may be good results measures in certain situations. They may describe what the organizations want from their employees, and they can be measured accurately and on a timely basis. There may be a conflict between the employer's right to know what is going on and the employees' rights to autonomy or freedom from controls which are considered oppressive.[17] Some employees' have labeled the use of such tight controls as an electronic sweatshop. A study of telephone operators found that knowing that somebody might be listening significantly increased stress-related health complaints.[18]

Questions relevant to determinations of whether use of such measures is ethical include:

- Is use of the measures secret or freely disclosed to the employees? For example, are supervisors listening after they have assured employees of privacy?
- Were the employees involved in establishing the system (making it fair)?
- When supervisors use such tight controls, do they emphasize quality, and not just quantity?
- Do they use the measures just for monitoring employees in training, or do they also monitor experienced employees?

SPREADING GOOD ETHICS WITHIN AN ORGANIZATION

Ethical progress within an organization typically proceeds in stages.[19] In an early stage, when the organization is small, the organization becomes an extension of the founder or top management group. The founder acts as a role model, setting the ethical tone, and is usually able to monitor employees' compliance with that tone.

In a later stage of development, organizations predominantly use action accountability-type controls. Corporate specialists develop lists of specific standards, rules, and regulations embodying good ethical principles. They communicate these lists either through corporate policies and procedures manuals, corporate codes of conduct, or less formal sets of memoranda. These rules clarify the meaning of good ethics, make it clear that ethical behavior is valued, and provide ethical guidance to employees who are incapable of thinking through ethical issues themselves.

After the rules are communicated, the managers take steps to ensure that the employees follow the rules. Sometimes companies ask key employees to sign a statement certifying that they have abided by the rules. Table 17-4 shows the annual certification statement that managers at The Seagram Company are asked to sign. Signed statements and trust are not sufficient. Managers must also endeavor to maintain a good internal control system so that potential violators know there is a high probability they will be caught. Monitoring should be done by both employees' superiors and internal auditors. Violators of the rules must be sanctioned. These sanctions help give people the courage to resist counterproductive pressures.

Organizations at more advanced stages of ethical development place a higher emphasis on personnel/cultural controls. They recognize that virtues are often learned by observations of exemplary behavior, so they identify and publicize moral exemplars. They ensure that the proper tone is set at the top. They often appoint an ombudsperson who is designated to help employees facing ethical issues. The more advanced stage of corporate ethical development tends to produce a commitment to ethical standards and a continuous improvement of the ethical structures and environment.

TABLE 17-4 Annual Certification Statement Managers at The Seagram Company are Asked to Sign

CERTIFICATION

I hereby certify that I have read the Annual Compliance Letter and the Manual of Seagram Policies and Procedures for Worldwide Business Conduct (revised January 1994) and the Conflicts of Interest Policy (revised January 1996); that I have abided by and will continue to abide by said Policies and Procedures; and that I have not engaged in and I am not aware of any activity or transaction which directly or indirectly violates the letter or spirit of the Seagram Policies and Procedures for Worldwide Business Conduct, the Conflicts of Interest Policy (revised January 1996) or any other Seagram Compliance Policy except as may be set forth below.

____________________ ____________________

Signature Company Country

____________________ ____________________

Print Name Title Date

EXCEPTIONS

Describe fully any matters which raise a question as to compliance with the Seagram Policies and Procedures for Worldwide Business Conduct, the Conflicts of Interest Policy (revised January 1996) or any other Seagram Compliance Policy.

____

____

____

____

____

____

____

PLEASE SIGN AND RETURN WITHIN THIRTY (30) DAYS TO:

Daniel R. Paladino
Vice President-Legal and Environmental Affairs
c/o Joseph E. Seagram & Sons, Inc.
P.O. Box 1623
F.D.R. Station
New York, New York 10150-1623
U.S.A.

CONCLUSION

This chapter has provided a brief introduction to the topic of ethics as it relates to the design and use of an MCS. To create the right ethical environment, the managers must have moral expertise and know where and how to provide it.

The sampling of issues discussed in this chapter should have made it obvious that many important ethical issues are not black or white. One cannot conclude unequivocally that, for example, creating budget slack or managing earnings is always unethical. Many situational factors must be considered in making ethical judgments. Rational, well-informed individuals can reach different conclusions because they use or emphasize different ethical models. The "greyness" of the answers, however, makes it even more important for managers to subject the various ethical issues to a formal analysis. They must understand how and why individuals will reach different ethical conclusions, and, importantly, they must take a stand as to how they want employees in their organization to behave.

Once managers have conducted their ethical analyses and reached their conclusions as to what is right, they must create a good ethical environment. Employees face many pressures and temptations which can cause them to act unethically. They can easily bow to performance deadlines and crises, reward temptations, pressures for conformity, and even counterproductive direct orders from their superiors. Unless managers act to minimize and deflect these pressures and temptations on a fairly consistent basis, their company's ethical climate will be weakened. Managers must help guide the behaviors of their employees who are incapable of thinking through ethical issues (distinguishing right from wrong) themselves.

Every organization has an ethical climate of some sort; either good, bad, or mixed. It is important for managers to build a good ethical climate, one which respects the rights, duties, and interests of stakeholders inside and outside the firm. A company that fosters unethical behaviors from its employees, even those which benefit the company in the short-run, will probably eventually find itself the victim of its own policies. This company is more likely to attract people who feel comfortable bending rules. This company will probably also tempt highly ethical, honest people to bend the rules. Weakened ethical climates can lead to unethical behaviors which can damage or destroy individual and organizational reputations. Once ethical climates are weakened and reputations are damaged, they can be quite difficult to rebuild.

Notes

1. J. C. Gaa and R. G. Ruland, "Ethics in Accounting: An Overview of Issues, Concepts and Principles," in J. Gaa and R. G. Ruland, eds. *Ethical Issues in Accounting* (Sarasota, Fla.: American Accounting Association, 1997).
2. R. E. Freeman, *Strategic Management: A Stakeholder Approach* (Boston: Pitman, 1984).
3. American Institute of Certified Public Accountants, *Code of Professional Conduct,* 1988.
4. E. Noreen, "The Economics of Ethics: A New Perspective on Agency Theory," *Accounting Organizations and Society* (1988), pp. 359.
5. M. D. Beneish, "Do Detected and Undetected Earnings Managers Differ?", unpublished working paper, Duke University, June 1995.
6. K. A. Merchant, *Fraudulent and Questionable Financial Reporting: A Corporate Perspective* (Morristown, N.J.: Financial Executives Research Foundation, 1987).
7. This chapter provides only a brief introduction to these ethical models. Those interested in further reading in this area should consult one of the many books on business ethics.
8. This section adapted from J. C. Gaa and R. G. Ruland, "Ethics in Accounting: An Overview of Issues, Concepts and Principles," in J. C. Gaa and R. G. Ruland (eds.) *Ethical Issues in Accounting* (Sarasota, Fla.: American Accounting Association, 1997).
9. This framework was adapted from the seven-step model described in W. W. May (ed.), *Ethics in the Accounting Curriculum: Cases & Readings* (Sarasota, Fla.: American Accounting Association), 1990.

10. S. Umapathy, *Current Budgeting Practices in U.S. Industry: The State of the Art* (New York: Quorum, 1987).
11. K. A. Merchant and J. Rockness, "The Ethics of Managing Earnings: An Empirical Investigation," *Journal of Accounting and Public Policy* (Spring 1994), pp. 79–94. Other performance measures can also be "managed" in the same way. For example, studies have shown evidence of balance sheet "windowdressing," particularly by banks. The ethical principles are the same, regardless of the measure being manipulated.
12. Evidence suggesting this result has been provided by D. W. Collins and L. DeAngelo, "Accounting Information and Corporate Governance: Market and Analyst Reactions to Earnings of Firms Engaged in Proxy Contests," *Journal of Accounting and Economics*, 13, no. 3 (1990), pp. 213–247; and A. Hunt, S. E. Moyer, and T. Shevlin, "Earnings Volatility, Earnings Management, and Equity Value," unpublished working paper, University of Washington, 1995.
13. K. A. Merchant and J. Rockness, "The Ethics of Managing Earnings: An Empirical Investigation," *Journal of Accounting and Public Policy* (Spring 1994), pp. 79–94. Other performance measures can also be "managed" in the same way. For example, studies have shown evidence of balance sheet "windowdressing," particularly by banks. The ethical principles are the same, regardless of the measure being manipulated.
14. "Employees Say It's Hard to Be Ethical In Some Organizations," *Internal Auditor* (February 1995), p. 9.
15. G. Bylinsky, "How Companies Spy on Employees," *Fortune* (November 4, 1991), pp. 131–140.
16. A. Bernstein, "How to Motivate Workers: Don't Watch 'Em," *Business Week* (April 29, 1991), p. 56.
17. G. Bylinsky, "How Companies Spy on Employees," *Fortune* (November 4, 1991), pp. 131–140.
18. G. Bylinsky, "How Companies Spy on Employees," *Fortune* (November 4, 1991), pp. 131–140.
19. J. A. Petrick and G. E. Manning, "Paradigm Shifts in Quality Management and Ethics Development," *Business Forum* 18, no. 4 (September 1993), p. 15.

Two Budget Targets

In the three years since he had been appointed manager of the Mobile Communications Division (MCD) of Advanced Technologies Corporation (ATC), Joe supervised the preparation of two sets of annual budget numbers. When ATC's bottom-up budgeting process began, Joe instructed his subordinates to set aggressive performance targets because he believed such targets would push everyone to perform at their best.

Then, before Joe presented his budget to his superiors, he added some *management judgment.* He made the forecasts of the future more pessimistic, and he added some allowances for *performance contingencies* to create what he called the *easy plan.* Sometimes the corporate managers questioned some of Joe's forecasts and asked him to raise his sales and profit targets somewhat. However, MCD operated in a rapidly-growing, uncertain market which Joe understood better than did his superiors, and Joe was a skillful and forceful negotiator. In each of the past three years, the end result was that the targets in the official budget for MCD were highly achievable. MCD's performance had exceeded the targets in the easy plan by an average of 40 percent, and Joe earned large bonuses. Joe did not show his superiors the targets his subordinates were working toward, but some of Joe's direct reports were aware of the existence of the easy plan.

In his subjective evaluations of his subordinates' performances for the purposes of assigning bonuses and merit raises, Joe compared actual performance with the aggressive targets. In the last three years, only approximately 25 percent of the aggressive targets had been achieved. Joe did not fire any of his managers for failing to achieve their targets, but he reserved the vast majority of the discretionary rewards for the managers who had achieved their targets.

Professor Kenneth A. Merchant wrote this case as a basis for class discussion rather than to illustrate either effective or ineffective handling of an administrative situation.

Conservative Accounting in the General Products Division

The year 1991 was a good one for the General Products Division (GPD) of Altman Industries, Inc., a large industrial products manufacturer. Sales and profits in the division were significantly above plan due largely to unexpectedly brisk sales of a new product introduced at the end of last year. The good fortune started Robert Standish, the GPD general manager, thinking about how he could save some of this year's profits for periods in which he might need them more. He believed that GPD's plan for next year would be tough to achieve because the corporation as a whole was not doing well, and corporate managers would expect GPD to show growth even above this year's abnormally high sales and profit levels. And already in September, he was sure that his division's profit would exceed the level above which no additional bonuses were awarded for higher performance—120 percent of plan—and he wanted to save some of this year's profits so that he could report them in a year in which they would augment his bonus and those of his direct reports.

Robert asked his staff to do what they could before the end of the year to *stash some acorns* that he could use in future years. He suggested to Joanne, his controller, that she start preparing the pessimistic scenarios that could be used to justify additional reserves and start thinking about how expenses could be accelerated and revenues deferred at year-end.

Joanne was uncomfortable. She reminded Robert that among the company accounting policies was a statement that assets and reserves should be fairly reported based on the existing facts and circumstances and not be used to manage income. Furthermore, because of continuing order declines, the company was looking for ways to report higher, not lower, profits in the current year and that if the situation did not turn around quickly, layoffs were threatened.

But Robert explained that GPD would still be reporting very high profits; he just wanted to save a portion of the excess above plan. And in any case, GPD couldn't help the corporation much because it was so small in comparison with the entire corporation.

QUESTIONS

1. Do you approve of Robert's actions? Are they smart or stupid from the perspective of the division? From the perspective of the corporation?
2. Should Joanne tell anyone of Robert's request?

Professor Kenneth A. Merchant wrote this case as a basis for class discussion rather than to illustrate either effective or ineffective handling of an administrative situation.

Education Food Services at Central Maine State University

Pam Worth, Manager of Education Food Services at Central Maine State University (CMSU), is meeting with a researcher to explain some apparent discrepancies in last year's budgeted figures and the actuals. The researcher, a faculty member at another university, is doing field studies in the food service business. Pam is explaining why she always tries to hide some slack in her numbers when she prepares her budget. She says that it is her understanding that she is just doing what others in her company and in her industry do. She agreed to speak to the researcher only with guarantees of strict confidentiality.

> I like to have a moderate cushion in my budget. The stakes are high. If I make my budget, my performance review will be good, almost regardless of whatever else I do during the period, and I will earn my 20 percent bonus. If I miss my budget without valid reasons, I may not be allowed to keep my job.
>
> More than that, however, the cushion in the budget allows me to do a better job. I don't have to worry that my staff is working at peak efficiency all the time, so I don't have to supervise every action. That is better for the staff, also; they hate it when I'm looking over their shoulders. The cushion also allows me to buy things that I can use to provide the university better service. For example, this year I was able to buy several portable bars that we have used already for some parties.

Pam, an accounting graduate of Northern University, is an employee of Contract Food Services Corporation (CFSC), a large corporation that provides food on a contract basis to universities, hospitals, and businesses. Pam runs a profit center that provides services only to one university—CMSU. Her operation provides food at two major, on-campus cafeterias serving 12,000 students and nearly 2,000 faculty and staff. Pam also has responsibility for the vending machine business on campus, and her employees sometimes provide catering services for on-campus business meetings. Pam's operation employs 59 regular employees and between 150 and 180 students on a part-time basis. Annual revenues are slightly in excess of $3 million.

Relations between CFSC and CMSU are governed by a contract that is renegotiated each January for the following academic year. The contract defines the responsibilities of each party. For example, CMSU administrators are given the power to review and approve CFSC's service plans and prices. The university provides all equipment costing over $100. CFSC sets the menus and hires the employees.

The contract also defines limits on the profits CFSC can earn from the CMSU operation. CFSC earns 100 percent of the profits from the food operation up to a limit of 10 percent profit on sales. Beyond that limit, profits are split equally with CMSU. The contract is set this way as an incentive to CFSC managers to provide extra quality and services after they have ensured themselves a reasonable profit.

Budgets are prepared on a bottom-up basis. In July, corporate headquarters personnel send planning guidelines and assumptions (e.g., employee benefits, inflation) to all operating units. The operating managers forecast their customer counts, which determines their food requirements, and then estimate their operating costs for the 18-month period starting in January. Since the university owns the buildings and equipment, the bulk of CFSC's costs are for food and labor.

After the units' budgets are prepared, a series of budget *challenge* rounds are held to review the numbers at successively higher CFSC's consolidation levels—district, region, division, group, and corporate. If the numbers meet the managers' profit expectations, the budgets are accepted. Typ-

Prepared by Kenneth A. Merchant, University of Southern California

ically, however, each of the managers in the hierarchy is asked to raise his or her profit targets. These requests lead to a series of meetings designed to explore whether revenue projections should be raised or cost projections cut. The size of these profit-increase requests are not predictable, but in recent years they have ranged from zero to 15 percent.

Pam explains that she routinely hides some cushion in both labor and food costs:

> I can build the budget cushion in a lot of places. This year for example:
>
> - I kept the proportion of meals served on board contracts (which are more lucrative for us) equivalent to last year's level even though I know that proportion will be growing because the trend is to have more students living on campus.
> - I planned for a number of labor hours at $7.15 when I knew that I would hire students for those hours, and students don't earn that much.
> - I planned no efficiency improvements when I know we almost always improve our efficiency. There is a learning curve in this business. My superiors know about this learning curve too—they ran operations just like this—but they don't object to my having a cushion. It is to their advantage to have me meet my budget too.
>
> These types of things add up. I put just enough in so that I am sure I will be able to meet my budget targets even after corporate management squeezes some of my cushion out in their reviews.
>
> I know more about what is happening at CMSU than anyone else. My bosses can't come here and check every assumption that I have in the plan. They don't have the time. My immediate boss, for example, is responsible for nine units spread over a fairly large geographic area.
>
> You can easily identify new managers—they submit budgets that are realistic. Experienced managers build in pads for themselves. It's a bit devious, sure, but it's not theft. It's just playing with projections. The money's there. Besides, if you don't build a cushion for yourself, you're not going to survive for long in this business.

The Incident at Waco Manufacturing

In 1986, Waco Manufacturing, a leading supplier of custom machined parts to the automotive industry, installed a security and information system in one of its manufacturing plants. Transceivers (devices that can both transmit and receive radio signals) were embedded in the plant corridors every 25 feet and in badges worn by all employees. This technology supported almost continuous tracking of the location of each employee, a capability that fostered many interesting applications. For example, a telephone call to an employee would ring at the phone nearest that person, which often was not the individual's office phone.

THE INCIDENT

During a third quarter performance review in September 1987, area manager Monique Saltz informed Monk Barber, a plant engineering manager, that she was unhappy that a new set of designs for composite-based products, required in the 1987 plan, was behind schedule. "I have repeatedly met with Sherman McCoy, Telly Frank, and Wanda Gogan, the three engineers assigned to this project," Barber explained, "and I have tried to impress upon them the importance of this set of designs. They simply have not responded. I am at wits' end."

When Saltz subsequently met with McCoy, Frank, and Gogan, Gogan expressed surprise. "I don't know quite how to say this," she told Saltz, "but I had no idea that this project was so important. In fact, I cannot remember meeting with Mr. Barber about the composite design project. We knew it was coming, but we had no idea of its importance." Frank and McCoy concurred. Later that day, Saltz described the situation to plant manager Shelly Tomaso who suggested that they review the plant record of employee locations as recorded by the transceiver system. Tomaso and Saltz looked first at the record and then at each other—since the beginning of 1987, Barber, McCoy, Frank, and Gogan had never all been in the same room at the same time.

Professor John J. Sviokla prepared this case as the basis for class discussion rather than to illustrate either effective or ineffective handling of an administrative situation.

Don Russell: Experiences of a Controller/CFO

In February 1991, Don Russell, chief financial officer (CFO) at Eastern Technologies, Inc. (ETI) was mulling over a critical decision. Don had joined ETI only 14 months earlier and had gradually become convinced that the company's financial accounting was excessively aggressive. He thought a sizable correcting entry should be made immediately. But if the correction was made, ETI would report a large loss that would trigger violations of debt financing covenants and place the company's survival in jeopardy.

ETI's chairman and president were strongly against making the correcting entry. They reminded Don that the company had a plan to shore up its operations and to get cheaper financing in place and that the plan needed time to work. But Don was not convinced that top management's plan was viable.

Don felt that ETI's accounting reports were misleading to decision makers both outside and inside the company. This caused him particular concern because he had seen the dangers of manipulating earnings reports at his previous employer. But he knew that if he forced the change now, he would lose his job. Even if ETI survived, he was sure he would be fired for "not being a team player." As he noted to an observer,

> It is frightening to know that you're going to be out the door almost immediately after you make the decision. It's even more frightening to me right now because I've just gone through a divorce and remarriage, and now I've got six kids and annual alimony payments of $60,000.

He also thought about the effect the decision would have on the value of the tens of thousands of ETI stock options he had been given. The options would be worth several hundred thousand dollars when exercised, and half of them could be exercised in two months.

EARLY CAREER

Don Russell joined the audit staff of the Chicago office of Touche & Young (T&Y) in July 1973 immediately upon graduation from the University of Illinois. His advancement was rapid. In 1983 he was promoted to senior manager and was given indications that he was on the track toward partnership. Over the 1975–80 period, Don attended DePaul University's evening MBA program and earned his degree in management information systems. T&Y gradually shifted his work responsibilities to take advantage of his systems expertise. By 1984, Don's time was split almost equally between auditing and systems consulting.

In 1985, Don left T&Y to become corporate controller for Cook & Spector, Inc. (C&S), a large ($4 billion sales) consumer products division of Queen's Industries, a major British corporation. C&S had been acquired by Queen's in 1984. Don was familiar with C&S because it was one of his major audit clients. He explained why he decided to take the job:

> When the headhunter first approached me about the job, I wasn't interested. C&S had an antiquated accounting system. It was a huge company, but they still had a manual accounts receivable system. They did no planning; no budgeting. It was ridiculous. But C&S's top managers told me, "You have carte blanche to make whatever changes you think are necessary. You have complete control." So I was intrigued by the challenge.
>
> It was also a great career opportunity. C&S was a large, reasonably profitable corporation with some outstanding brand names. And my job was significant. I had 250 people working for me. I reported to the CFO, and the only other person reporting to him was the Treasurer who had eight people

Professor Kenneth A. Merchant wrote this case as the basis for class discussion rather than to illustrate either effective or ineffective handling of an administrative situation. The case describes a real situation, but the facts have been disguised, and any resemblance to actual people or events is unintentional.

working for him. So I thought I would probably be next in line for the CFO job.

CONTROLLERSHIP EXPERIENCES AT COOK & SPECTOR

Systems Development Activities

Don started at C&S in August 1985. He spent his first six months planning the changes he wanted to make to the firm's accounting information systems. Then over the next three years he implemented major changes. He changed the chart of accounts so that the firm could produce profit-and-loss statements down to the product level; the new system had 500,000 account/cost center combinations. He installed new general ledger, accounts receivable, and accounts payable systems that would operate in a modern database environment. And he implemented a standard cost system in the firm's 42 factories. About the cost system change, he observed, "C&S had had only an actual cost system. The monthly costs fluctuated wildly and weren't useful. They didn't provide a reflection of what was going on."

After the accounting systems were computerized, Don found it easy to reduce costs in the controller's department. He reduced his accounting staff from 250 to 110 and saved the company over $4 million per year.

Earnings Management Activities

In 1985, for a variety of reasons, C&S's profit performance was running $45 million ahead of the $200 million plan. To *save* the profit for periods when it might be needed, Don established several types of large reserves. For example, C&S had been aggressive in expensing the acquisition costs incurred as part of the Queen's acquisition process, so Don set up a large reserve ($53 million) for taxes, in case the IRS disallowed the expense deductions. He also set up reserves for unknown liabilities because, "Everybody realized that the company had a poor accounting system." Don believed at the time that the reserves were justified and that, "It's better to be safe than sorry. If it turns out that we were overly conservative, it's no big deal."

These reserves had to be spread across the 34 line items in the income statements of each of the over 600 product lines in 60 divisions in a way that would not attract the attention of the analysts on Queen's corporate staff or the auditors. Don accomplished this task without significant questions being raised.

In 1986, company sales and profits were below forecast and top management told Don they wanted to use some of the reserves. They said they wanted to report an 8 percent increase in earnings and to increase significantly the amount of expenditures on new product development to help the company grow in the future. Don was able to free up the reserves to satisfy these requests.

Corporate Recognition

Don's superiors were ecstatic about his efforts. He had modernized the company's accounting systems; had saved the company $4 million in overhead annually; and had demonstrated great skill in managing the accounting profit numbers. After a year with the company, he was promoted to Vice President/Controller.

Don was flush with success:

> Every management meeting I was held up as the ideal. I remember one top-level meeting when they flashed my picture on the screen and said, 'Follow this guy's lead. This is the way you should manage your department.' One time the president called me *the Monet of the accounting profession.*
>
> My head was exploding. At T&Y, they keep telling you you are worthless to keep you there and to keep your salary down. All of a sudden I'm important, and I'm making a lot of money. After I had been at C&S six months, I gave them my six month plan, and I got a $30,000 bonus right there on the spot. I was in shock. I had never had that much free money in my life. Plus I was involved. I attended all the key management meetings.

Concerns about Earnings Management

During his third year at C&S, Don began to have concerns about his manipulations of reserves. He said:

> I hadn't really thought much about my manipulations of reserves. I thought I was being a team player. This is how the company had been run for years. It had a record of 33 consecutive years of increasing quarterly earn-

> ings. But real results, with recessions and everything else that happens, don't happen that way. So I hadn't invented earnings management at C&S, although we were probably now doing it on a grander scale than had been done before.
>
> But it suddenly dawned on me that something was horribly wrong. We were pristine in reporting for taxes because I sent my tax manager to the operating units to make sure real data were going to the IRS. But we didn't care if real data were going to Queen's. All of a sudden we had two years that weren't comparable and we really didn't know where we were. When people looked back at trends, they were looking at distorted numbers. And because we spread the reserves around, we had distorted all the product P&Ls.

Don attempted to drain the reserves out of the product-level profit and loss statements, but the complexity was overwhelming because each of the 60 divisions and over 600 product lines would now have two P&Ls each. Plus the draining provoked a number of arguments with the operating managers because the divisions had been manipulating the numbers on their own. They had not really spent the promotion expense by product as was reported, and they had their own buried reserves. In fact, the division reserves probably totalled more than those created at corporate-level. So even if Don could eliminate the distortions he had caused, the product statements that would result still would not yield accurate information.

Don's concern about the earning management activities rose in 1988:

> The year 1988 looked like another down year and everybody was saying, 'We need more product development because last year's development didn't work.' And the president, of course, was saying we need another 8 percent increase in income.
>
> I told the president that we can't allow the reserves within the division. Every year we'd have something like a $200 million target, but we'd have $40 million in reserves ready to help us. So everybody would get their bonuses; the executive parking lot was filled with BMW 750s and Mercedes. I was doing well also. My regular salary was around $130,000, but my total compensation was nearly $230,000.
>
> While the company was reporting profits, I thought we were headed in a downward spiral. The old products were still extremely profitable, but we were spending a huge amount of money on new products and were disguising the fact that the new products were a lot less profitable. There was no linkage between bonuses and a strategic plan, just a link to an accounting number that was not tied to a plan. It was just an accounting game. We were getting our bonuses for nothing—actually worse than nothing because we were making bad decisions.

Attempts to Change the Company's Financial Goals and Measurement System

To improve company decision making and reduce the temptations to manage earnings, Don decided to try to change C&S' financial goals and measurements system. He was particularly concerned that the potentially lucrative bonuses, ranging up to 70 to 100 percent of base salary, were based on operating profit numbers that were too easy to manipulate.

He began a fact-finding study. He began interviewing all the C&S division heads on his own and soon realized that the company was not doing any real strategic planning. He found that company planning involved just settling on a set of revenue and profit numbers that looked reasonable. C&S operating managers were unwilling to tell Queen's about their real plans, such as for new products, because they were worried that they would *have egg on their face* if they weren't able to accomplish their plans.

Among the questions Don asked in the interviews was "What are the most important decisions you make on a monthly and annual basis, and what information do you use in making those decisions?" The manager of the largest operating unit said, "On a monthly basis, one of the most important decisions I make is how much profit to recognize."

Don's reaction:

> I was floored. This is one of the most senior managers in a huge company, and he was

telling me that one of his most important decisions is how to manipulate the numbers. His operating decisions are secondary. His first role, he viewed, was to give the president the profit number he wanted that month.

And this guy wasn't unique. Everyone else I talked with reinforced this message. Managers who missed their monthly budget targets would take a lot of flak. The president would quickly call them and ask, 'What are you doing? How are you correcting the problem? Cut your advertising! Fire some people! . . .' This drilled into me what happens when you allow manipulations. People don't focus on real problems.

Don planned to take his interview observations to the president and tell him:

> We've got a big problem here because we're not managing the company the way we should be. We're spending four times the amount of product development and capital expenditures we need because it's easy to get Queen's to approve them. But Queen's assumes we are making good decisions, and we're not.

But Don wanted to be able to propose an alternative, and he set out looking for "the Holy Grail of more reasonable financial reporting."

Don learned that some companies were experimenting with an approach to planning that focused on changes in shareholder value. This focused measurement attention on hard numbers—cash flows—rather than the easily manipulatable operating profit. He studied these approaches and proposed their use to top management, but they were completely opposed to any changes. They did not understand why they would want to make such a drastic change when the company and its management team were doing so well.

The Decision to Leave

As the pace of accounting systems change slowed, Don's job became more routine, and he became bored. He began listening for other career opportunities. He thought he wanted to become a chief financial officer so that he could work more in finance areas where he had had no experience. And he thought he would like eventually to move into a line management position.

In early 1989, a headhunter approached Don with an opportunity to interview for the position of CFO of Eastern Technologies, Inc. (ETI), a public, communications-services company. ETI was growing rapidly and was raising large amounts of money both from banks and direct placements. He interviewed for the job and accepted it when it was offered. He joined ETI December 1, 1989.

CFO EXPERIENCES AT EASTERN TECHNOLOGIES

The Company

ETI, headquartered in Stamford, Connecticut, was founded in 1978 as a cable television firm. It had several cable franchises in New England and the New York metropolitan area. The company had been profitable since the early 1980s. It went public in 1984 with an initial offering price of $11.00 per share. For the 1988 fiscal year (ended June 30), revenues were $30 million and profits were just above $1 million. The 1988 year-end stock price was $8.75.

In 1987, ETI's founder, a skilled electronics engineer, decided to diversify the company's operations into the fast-growing area of satellite broadcasting. This business involves sending broadcast signals, such as from a concert or a sporting event, to a broadcast satellite that relays the signal to a network of large dish antennas on the ground. These antennas then distribute the signals to users, such as local television stations.

To finance the construction of antennas and distribution networks throughout the Northeast, ETI raised considerable bank financing. By the end of 1987, ETI's debt-equity ratio was 4 to 1, but management figured the company still needed $10 million of additional capital. They approached a prominent investment banking firm to make a bond offering. The investment bankers showed ETI management how easy it was to raise money with high yield bonds, and the company eventually made a much larger offering—of $25 million. When the bonds sold, the company had considerable cash but a debt-equity ratio of 6 to 1.

ETI management used the extra cash to accelerate the expansion of facilities and to acquire a Baltimore-based broadcasting firm of similar size to ETI. Growth exploded as the company signed more and more long-term contracts with customers. Revenues totalled $81 million in 1989, almost three times the 1988 level. But after-tax profits were just under $1 million, as the company had to book a large loss in the fourth quarter of the year to cover *one-time start-up problems* with the new technology.

ETI made another acquisition in February 1990. This acquisition was of a Southern California-based consulting firm that provided specialized communications services primarily to firms in the defense industry. The two acquired companies were run as largely autonomous divisions within the ETI corporate structure.

Transition of Power

When Don joined ETI, his major concern was whether ETI's president, Joe Blevins, would allow him autonomy in his CFO role. Joe was a former T&Y audit partner who had joined ETI in 1987. But Don found Joe's approach to the transition of power to be quite reasonable. Joe asked Don to focus his initial attention on improving the company's operating systems: ETI had no computerized systems, no planning, and no budgeting, and the controller was weak. But Joe let Don sit in on the discussions with bankers and investment bankers to help him learn the treasury functions which he would eventually assume.

Don quickly found that ETI's financial focus was on earnings per share, and he vowed to change the focus to cash flow. Joe said, however, "You don't really understand the market. I'll listen to your thoughts, but EPS is what the analysts care about. Cash flow may be the latest *voodoo* thought, but it's not very realistic." Still, Don thought Joe would be open-minded, and he believed he could convince Joe to change.

Don, however, had a lot of work to do before he could focus on changes in the company's planning and measurement processes. He focused his attention first on ETI's chart of accounts. Billing was done manually, and expenses were assigned only to highly aggregated accounts. For example, the company paid huge bills for satellite rental and telephone services with no attempt to trace the expenses to contracts or even product lines. Another complicating factor: Many of the charges were not billed regularly, so expenses had to be accrued. But the bases on which the accruals were done were not well thought out, and the company's monthly profit figures fluctuated wildly. Don knew he could not prepare a credible budget without a better understanding of where the expenses were coming from and what lines of business were more profitable than others. That understanding required a better accounting system. He wanted eventually to be able to produce reliable budgets and operating reports at department, and even project, levels of the organization.

Changing the chart of accounts proved to be a difficult process because few people in the company understood what Don was trying to do. The controller was not supportive. He was comfortable with the current chart of accounts and liked the fact that it was easy to work with. Don observed that, "It didn't matter to him that it did not provide meaningful information. He thought of accounts just as pots that you throw expenses into. If you make the system more complex, the assignment of expenses takes more thought."

Don also had to spend time integrating the systems of the newly acquired subsidiaries. He found ETI to be much more dynamic than C&S. At C&S he had time to plan what he wanted to do. At ETI he had to implement changes quickly and hope to fine-tune the systems later.

ETI's First Budgeting Process

Don led ETI through its first formal budgeting process in June–July 1990. Most of the numbers work was done by accounting personnel after they had consulted with the operating managers. Budgets were prepared for each division using the categories in Don's new chart of accounts.

When the budget for fiscal year 1991 was consolidated, it showed a $2 million loss. But nobody was sure if the budget was realistic. This was the first budget that had been prepared at the division level, and no division-level historical reports were available for comparison purposes. It also quickly became apparent that budgeting mistakes had been made. For example, management soon discovered that a major contract had been left out of the budget. Operating managers had failed to pass the information to accounting personnel, and two months into the year some significant unbudgeted expenses had to be paid.

ETI's Financial Reporting Strategy

After the budget was prepared, Don began an analysis of why the budget showed a loss for FY 1991 even though ETI had been reporting profits for years. It became obvious to him that the satellite communications business was in reality very unprofitable. ETI had been reporting profits because the company had implemented an extremely aggressive financial reporting strategy. Joe Blevins had a theory that all start-ups are unprofitable in the beginning and that aggressive accounting policies are necessary to make the company look profitable so that money can be raised. The profits catch up later.

Joe used a number of methods of boosting earnings, including the following:

1. Virtually all repairs and maintenance were capitalized. Because there was so much development going on, Joe's position was that all the engineers' and technicians' time was spent working on construction or making modifications that add capability to the equipment. Therefore all the costs were capitalizable.
2. Most interest was capitalized because it was deemed to be the cost of financing the construction in progress. For example, Don found that "We had deferred $3.5 million in interest for construction of a new video control center. We claimed it hadn't been put into service until May 1990 because we were still getting the bugs out of it, but it had actually been up and running since mid-1988 and certainly met the GAAP criterion of *substantially complete.* Don also found that "Nothing ever came out of construction in progress. They just kept capitalizing more and more interest."
3. Most equipment was being depreciated on a 12-year life. But electronic equipment, which comprised the bulk of the equipment, probably has a maximum five-year life, and some of the expensive tubes have a maximum 24-month life.
4. As many expenditures as possible (for example, travel) were classified as being related to one of the acquisitions so that they would add to goodwill and be amortized over 40 years instead of being expensed immediately. Also, if any parts of the acquired businesses were suffering operating losses, those losses were capitalized. On the other hand, a gain of over a half million dollars on sale of a portion of a communications relay station acquired in an acquisition was recorded directly as profit instead of as an adjustment to the price of the acquisition. Don noted, "We told the auditors we were just selling the rights to that asset since the buyers obviously couldn't take the asset with them. The auditors swallowed hard but accepted it."

The auditors had not objected strenuously to ETI's financial reports because they did not understand the technology. Satellite communications was a relatively new business that was just starting to grow. Few equipment retirements had taken place as yet, so it was difficult to tell what the true equipment lives were. Don found out that, "When the auditors asked questions about the 12-year depreciation lives, Joe would always point to the large antennas and say, 'They will be there for 100 years.' That's true, but not much of the company's equipment cost is in the antennas."

Don also noted:

> The auditors had a feeling that there was some repairs and maintenance being capitalized, but they never really found it. When they did their investigations, the engineers would tell them, 'We're just fine-tuning the equipment, getting it ready to use.' The auditors weren't thorough enough. If they had studied it carefully, they would have found, for example, that it takes $400,000 per year to maintain each of the fancy video tape decks. If the company doesn't do the maintenance, Sony won't guarantee the machines.

By the end of FY 1990, Don judged that of the $10 million in capital additions for the year, $3.5 million was in interest and another $2 million was for items that should have been classified as repairs and maintenance expense and engineering salaries. If those expenses were moved to the income statement, ETI would show a huge loss. But as long as ETI management could get funds for more capital additions, they would keep deferring those expenses.

Year End 1990

Don went to Joe and proposed a large accounting adjustment, of nearly $2 million, approximately twice the amount ETI would otherwise report as 1990 profit. But Joe was in the middle of an important series of negotiations that had begun in 1989 with National Telephone Corporation (NTC), a large telecommunications company. NTC had offered to buy a new offering of ETI stock at a substantial premium over market prices and to allow ETI to participate as a partner in the start of a whole new type of business—satellite telephone communications. This business, which was in an early development stage, involved having special telephones manufactured by NTC send a signal to a satellite positioned to handle such transmissions. The satellite would relay the call to a ground station which fed it into the regular phone network. This business was seen to have a large potential market in providing easy telephone communications to remote areas and to passengers in airplanes throughout the world. NTC was attempting to set up a worldwide satellite communications network and was promising to give ETI the East Coast franchise. ETI managers knew that the NTC deal was important both for the opportunity to enter a new business and for the infusion of cash which would allow the retirement of some expensive bonds.

So when Don proposed the accounting adjustment, Joe said,

> No! No! No! You don't understand. We've got NTC going to hand us an enormous amount of money, and that will solve the problem. We must report the profits they're expecting or they'll back away from us. Let's get through this year and digest these acquisitions. Our interest costs will be lower next year because we will be able to renegotiate our loans. Let's focus on the future. I'll talk to the auditors.

Don attended the meeting with the auditors, but said, "I had to leave the room because it was so outrageous."

The auditors gave the ETI 1990 financial statements an unqualified opinion, although they told the Board of Directors that the statements were *pushing the edge on aggressive reporting.* In response to a question about how the auditors approved the statements, Don replied:

> When I was at T&Y, I felt relatively certain that nobody could get anything by me. By the time I'd left C&S, I realized that auditors provide *no* safety net. There is no way you can have relatively untrained people (even those with up to five years experience), no matter how many you have, come up against financial people in a company with similar backgrounds but with a lot more experience and a full year to decide how they want to shape the financial picture they want to present to the world.
>
> I think Joe also had an effect on the auditors. He has an explosive personality. I have watched him call the auditors, even the partner, into his office and literally shriek at them. He grossly overreacts to things; he's not emotionally mature. I think they're afraid of him. Even when they realize their mistakes, they feel a natural pressure to go along to keep their client afloat. They hope it works out.

Even though Don felt ETI should not be reporting as it did, he knew he did not know what the proper accounting should be because he had spent his time focusing on improving the company's systems. Furthermore, he felt that the problem would be fixed in 1991 as a lot of goodwill amortization and depreciation of equipment put in service would have to be recognized as expense. Don was also appeased because management had agreed to limit expenditures, and Joe had finally agreed to let him change the company's measurement focus from EPS to cash flows.

Don wrote the management-discussion-and-analysis section of ETI's 1990 annual report. In it he indicated that fiscal year 1991 would be a year of restructuring, that the company would be amortizing its expenses over a much shorter period and, consequently, that profits would be much lower. His feeling at the time:

> I felt that I had done a reasonable job of telling people what was going on. I was signalling that the trend should not be plotted from these results. I thought if people looked at cash flows, they would understand what was going on. We had disclosed how much interest we had capitalized. I thought that someone who was smart and took the time would be able to draw the right conclusions from our disclosures.

Fiscal Year 1991

The budget proved to be reasonably accurate in the first quarter of fiscal year 1991, and Don was convinced that the company would actually report something close to the $2 million dollar loss that had been forecast unless changes were made. He showed his analysis to top management and made them promise to make significant cuts in expenditures. They committed to cut people and travel, to delay the capital additions, and even to sell some assets.

But at the end of the second quarter (January 1991), the manager of the satellite video division dropped his $3.5 million operating profit projection for the year to $1.5 million, so company profits were now forecast at an $4 million loss for the year. Don visited the presidents of all the divisions and asked them to raise their profit forecasts for the year, but they said that was impossible. For example, the president of the most profitable division said he had made a bad error and fired a couple of salespeople and his sales were below plan. Plus he said he had budgeted an aggressive level of sales that he had known from the beginning he could not deliver.

Don was now quite concerned. The rest of ETI's top management team still did not put great faith in the budget numbers, and they had not cut costs as sharply as Don would have liked. And they still believed that the negotiation with NTC pointed the way to the company's future. Don knew their stance perpetuated the pressures for aggressive financial reporting.

Don wondered what he should do. Should he continue to work on improving the company's accounting and budgeting systems and keep trying to convince top management that ETI had a serious financial problem on its hands? Or should he force the issue by making the accounting adjustment and hope that the company (and his job) survived the loss?

Section VI: Significant Situational Influences on Management Control Systems

CHAPTER 18

Influences of Uncertainty/Programmability, Diversification Strategy, and Business Strategy on MCSs

It should have been apparent in the discussions of controls in prior chapters that there is no universally best management control system (MCS) which applies to all situations in all organizations. Managers involved in designing, implementing, and using MCSs must consider a large number of *contingent factors;* that is, situational factors which, individually and collectively, affect either the effectiveness or the costs of the various controls and control features. Figure 18-1 depicts the general contingency framework within which control system design issues should be considered. This figure shows that the effects of the various elements and characteristics of MCSs on the various control outcomes depend on any of a number of contingent factors.

The second section of this book highlighted the importance of several of the contingent factors which affect the feasibility and effectiveness of action and results controls. These include (1) knowledge as to what actions or results are desirable, (2) employees' abilities to take the action or influence the results, and (3) managers' abilities to prevent the action from being taken (or track the actions taken, or measure the results generated). In later sections of the book, many more elements and characteristics of MCSs have been discussed, including planning and budgeting systems, responsibility structures, variance analyses, and transfer prices. The use and effects of each of these variables are also affected by many contingent factors.

Because the range of organizational settings is huge, literally thousands of sometimes-relevant contingent factors exist. Table 18-1 shows a rather lengthy, but necessarily incomplete, list of some of these factors, each of which does, or at least probably should, affect one or more MCS choices. To provide some structure to Table 18-1, the contingent factors are classified into three categories: organization and people factors, mission and strategy factors, and environmental and technology factors. Each of the factors in Table 18-1 affects one or more relationships between an MCS variable and an important outcome variable (degree of control, cost, or dysfunctional side-effects). Sometimes failure to consider even one of these situational factors can make the difference between an excellent and a disastrous MCS choice.

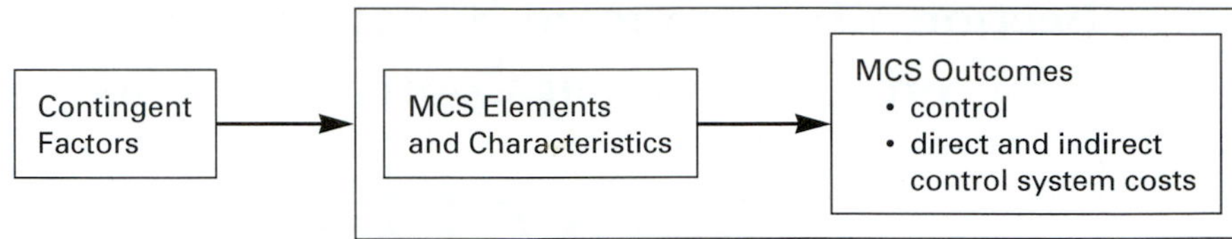

FIGURE 18-1 A General MCS Contingency Framework

The situational contingencies are complex because (1) many of the situational factors listed in Table 1 include multiple variables (for example, the organizational form factor includes, among others, for-profit and non-profit corporations; state-owned, closely-held, and widely-held corporations; partnerships, sole proprietorships, company-owned subsidiaries, and franchises); (2) many of the factors are related (for example, while environmental uncertainty, business risk, length of the business cycle, and decision reversibility are distinguishable from each other, they are all intercorrelated); and (3) many of the factors interact with each other to produce MCS-related effects (one factor may not produce an effect except in the presence of another factor).

Research has only begun to sort out the many complex MCS-related relationships. Even if all of the effects of each of these factors on MCS elements and MCS-related outcomes were well understood, space constraints would not permit their detailed discussion in a general purpose textbook. A few of these factors which have not been well discussed in prior chapters, but which are important in a broad range of settings, require extra highlighting. This chapter pulls together and augments discussions of the effects of three important situational factors: (1) uncertainty/programmability, (2) diversification (corporate) strategy, and (3) business strategy.

The discussion in this chapter is limited to MCSs and their effects in profit-making corporations in what can be called Anglo-American countries (United States, United Kingdom, Canada, Australia, and New Zealand). Chapter 19 describes some of the unique management control problems faced in corporations based in other countries. Chapter 20 does the same with organizations whose primary objective is other than creating value (making a profit) for an ownership group.

UNCERTAINTY/LACK OF PROGRAMMABILITY

Uncertainty and lack of programmability are discussed together because they tend to be highly correlated and their effects are quite similar. These two descriptors are usually used at different levels of analysis, however. Uncertainty is most often used to describe conditions at corporate or business-unit levels, although it is occasionally used at task levels. Programmability is used exclusively at task or activity levels.

Uncertainty refers to the broad set of factors that, individually and collectively, make it difficult or impossible to predict the future in a given area. Uncertainty can stem from changes (or potential changes) in natural conditions (weather or political disturbances) or in the actions of competitors, customers, suppliers (including labor), and regulators. Uncertainty is higher where the pace of technological change is higher. It is generally higher the farther one tries to look into the future. Uncertainty about payoffs is higher in industries where the natural business cycle, the lag between investment and the payoff from that investment, is longer. Uncertainty can also stem from a lack of critical information,

TABLE 18-1 Examples of Situational Factors Relevant in Some MCS Situations

Organization and People Factors
- Organizational form
- Ownership structure
- Organization size
- Organization structure
- Degree of diversification
- Organizational interdependence
- Industry
- Asset specificity/decision reversibility
- Organizational performance
- Debt covenants
- Information asymmetry between superiors and subordinates
- Corporate culture
- Organizational resources (stress)
- Management style
- Backgrounds/capabilities/personalities of people employed
- Distance from headquarters to operating unit(s)
- Individual's proximity to retirement age

Mission and Strategy Factors
- Diversification (corporate) strategy
- Strategic mission
- Business (competitive) strategy
- Critical success factors

Environmental and Technology Factors
- National culture and infrastructure
- Regional culture
- Environmental uncertainty
- Environmental stability
- Environmental complexity
- Intensity of competition
- Government regulatory environment
- Task programmability
- Length of production cycle
- Length of sales cycle
- Decision reversibility
- Stability of product line
- Production technologies (for example, batch, process, or mass production)
- Production routineness
- Production interdependence
- Pace of technological change
- Research and development intensity
- Business risk

perhaps because of the absence of an industry association or supporting government agency which could supply information about forthcoming demand, supply, and competitive conditions and improve companies' abilities to predict the future accurately.

Programmability refers to the degree to which means-end relationships regarding specific tasks are understood. Highly programmable tasks are repetitive and standardized, rather than being novel and customized, and the link between the highly programmable tasks and outcomes is stable and known. With highly programmable tasks, uncertainty about the future is low.

Uncertainty and lack of programmability have some powerful effects on

MCSs. Lack of programmability, particularly, makes action controls impossible, or at least difficult, to use. Action controls are effective only if there is knowledge as to which actions are desirable and if those actions are consistently desirable. If managers want to use action controls in uncertain situations, they have to develop knowledge about the desirable actions, which usually means they must become personally involved in the activities being controlled. They must use more intensive preaction reviews, get involved in more face-to-face meetings with the employees being controlled, and/or use more direct observation and supervision.[1]

When action controls are deemed to be infeasible or impractical, managers generally place a high reliance on results controls. Results controls can be used even in highly uncertain settings, as employees can be rewarded for generating more of what is known to be desirable; such as, more sales or profit. Unfortunately, uncertainty and lack of programmability limit the effectiveness of results controls. Results controls are not effective where employees do not know how to generate more output, and uncertainty and lack of programmability often hinder their abilities to know.

Further, even when employees know how to do better, results controls will not be optimally effective unless properly challenging performance targets are set. In uncertain, unprogrammable situations, it is almost inevitable that targets will be too easy or too difficult. Because information asymmetry between superiors and subordinates is likely to be relatively high, subordinates can add slack to their budgets relatively easily. In addition, the targets will include many uncontrollables caused by forecasting errors regarding, for example, the state of the economy, competitors' actions, and sources and prices of supplies. These uncontrollables will adversely affect the reliability of performance evaluations.

Third, uncertainty/lack of programmability combined with the inevitable use of results controls will cause employees to bear business risk. This risk brings into play all the conditions discussed in Chapter 14; the organization will either have to compensate employees for bearing the greater risk or take steps to limit that risk. To limit managers' risk, firms facing an uncertain environment might choose not to regard managers' budget targets as firm commitments to the organization and, consequently, to interpret unfavorable budget variances as clear indicators of poor performance.[2] If they do so, the firms will give up some generally-functional short-term performance pressure. Alternatively, if the firms decide to treat budget targets as performance commitments from their managers, it is more likely that they will find it desirable to implement systems using contingency planning, flexible performance targets, variance analyses, or subjective performance evaluations; to use shorter planning and measurement periods (increased reporting frequency); and/or to make greater investments in environmental scanning mechanisms and forecasting procedures to reduce their uncertainty.

Fourth, high uncertainty/lack of programmability tends to have some broad effects on organization structures and decision making and communication patterns. Firms facing relatively high uncertainty will tend to decentralize their operations, have more participative, relatively bottom-up planning and budgeting process, and make important decisions only after relatively intensive consultations among larger groups of managers.

The broad effects of uncertainty/programmability are well illustrated with a production example. In the old mass production system invented by Henry Ford, uncertainty was low/programmability was high. The production function of the organization was buffered from the environment so uncertainty was, in the short run, effectively zero. Production managers could then standardize behaviors and processes and produce in large runs or batches. Tasks were divided into many separate parts; laborers specialized, employees' actions were dictated by rules, decision making was centralized, and many vertical levels of management were used to provide coordination.

In recent years, however, many organizations are using one or more elements of the so-called "new manufacturing processes." These include flexible manufacturing systems (FMS), just-in-time production (JIT), total quality management (TQM), and elimination of nonvalue-added activities. These new processes have sharply increased uncertainty/lack of programmability in production areas of the organizations because they require rapid adjustments to the marketplace and because they increase the diversity of potential responses and the interdependence of the tasks performed by line personnel. More control must be exercised by line personnel on the shop floor. As a result, organizations that use the new manufacturing processes tend to have flat organization structures and use few formal work rules and less hierarchical control. Jobs loose much of their formal definition; duties are continuously redefined; the number of middle managers is reduced; and the workforce is asked to be adaptive.[3] There is more teamwork; greater use of control through socialization mechanisms; less monitoring information; coordination through personal, lateral channels rather than by standard operating procedures; and less rewards based on individual performance. The result is that the production environment is more adaptive as the workforce is encouraged to solve problems and implement solutions. The control system must be defined more loosely because more things can go wrong.

CORPORATE (DIVERSIFICATION) STRATEGY

An organization's *corporate strategy,* which is sometimes referred to as its *diversification strategy,* is another situational factor with significant effects on MCSs. The setting of corporate strategy determines what businesses a company wants to be in and how resources should be allocated among those businesses.[4] One important way of viewing corporate strategies is to array them along a continuum from related to unrelated diversification. Firms pursuing *related diversification* do not stray far from their core business activity. They diversify in order to realize economic benefits from the exploitation of economies of scope stemming from relationships among their divisions. Firms pursuing *unrelated diversification* are not concerned with restricting their focus to their core business. They pursue business opportunities wherever they exist, and they manage those businesses by exploiting the economic benefits of an internal capital market. The theory is that in certain situations internal methods of allocating resources are superior because the internal decision makers are more informed than those who drive external financial markets and the internal processes are more efficient.[5] To realize fully the benefits of either the related or unrelated forms of diversification, the firm must adopt appropriate and effective administrative systems, including an MCS.

An important distinguishing characteristic of firms which are diversified into related businesses is high interdependence among sub-units. These related-diversified organizations should design their MCS to take advantage of this interdependence by using several features. The first feature is relatively elaborate planning and budgeting systems requiring large amounts of interpersonal communication. These systems force the business unit managers to communicate with each other and make it more likely that the managers can keep their interrelated activities coordinated and that they can find and exploit synergies.

A second feature which related-diversified businesses are likely to use is performance-dependent incentive compensation systems that base rewards to some extent on group performance. A common example is to base some portion (for example, half) of managers' bonuses on the performance of the next higher-level entity in the organization, which may be called a department, a group, a sector, or the entire corporation. These group performance-based rewards provide a signal that cooperation is important.

Third, related-diversified businesses are likely to spend considerable resources solving transfer pricing problems, as discussed in Chapter 15. Transfer pricing problems become particularly acute if some business units supply others and no competitive price is observable from outside markets.

An important distinguishing characteristic of firms which are diversified into unrelated businesses is *information asymmetry* between top-level managers and sub-unit managers. As an organization with unrelated businesses becomes larger, it becomes more complex. Top-level corporate managers are unable to remain informed about all the developments in all of their diverse business units' operating areas.

Decentralization and heavy reliance on financial controls are common responses to information asymmetry. Corporate managers can reduce their information processing requirements by pushing the locus of decision making lower in the organization. They can effect good control by relying on financial results controls, particularly built around profit and investment center responsibility structures.[6] The financial measures help the corporate managers in comparing diverse businesses.

These choices will, however, cause many performance discussions among top- and lower-level managers to be largely in financial terms (regarding sales or profits and returns). The corporate managers are often not able to converse in an informed way using the language and performance standards unique to each business (for example, yield rates, occupancy rates, renewal rates). Because they do not have the detailed industry knowledge, the corporate managers will also tend to judge the performances of the diverse organizational units objectively; that is, they will tend to use relatively little subjectivity in their evaluations.

With such a system, the lower-level managers usually have considerable pressure for financial performance, yet they have relatively high autonomy. They tend to participate heavily in the setting of their performance targets, and they have considerable discretion as to how to achieve their financial targets. If the autonomy is combined with the use of less-than-perfect financial measures (as several earlier chapters have noted is common), the managers are likely to engage in some dysfunctional behaviors, such as myopia and game-playing.

BUSINESS STRATEGY

The term *business strategy* encompasses two related concepts: strategic mission (or goals) and competitive strategy. *Strategic mission* can be defined across a single continuum from the early to late stages of a business's life cycle: build, hold, harvest, and divest.[7] At one extreme, the build mission implies goals of increased sales and market share, even at the expense of short-term earnings and cash flows. Toward the other extreme, the harvest mission aims at maximizing short-term earnings and cash flows, even at the expense of market share. A divest involves a decision to exit from a business, either immediately through a sale or liquidation or through a slower process of disinvestment.

Competitive strategy defines how a business or strategic business unit (SBU) chooses to compete in its industry and tries to achieve a competitive advantage relative to its competitors. An SBU is an operating unit with a distinct set of products or services that faces a well-defined set of competitors. Different SBUs within the same firm can pursue different business strategies.

Two competitive strategy typologies are often cited. Porter defined two primary methods of deriving a competitive advantage: low cost or product (or service) differentiation.[8] A low cost strategy involves offerings of relatively standardized, undifferentiated products, vigorous pursuit of cost reductions, generation of volume to exploit economies of scale and to move down the experience curve, acquisition of process engineering skills and, as much as is possible, establishment of a routinized task environment. A differentiation strategy involves creation of something that is perceived by customers as unique and valuable. Firms pursuing this strategy pay more attention to product innovation, brand image, and customer service.

Another competitive strategy typology, developed by Miles and Snow, distinguishes between defenders and prospectors.[9] The defining variable is the rate at which the company (or SBU) alters its products and markets relative to its competitors. *Defenders* are organizations that have a narrow and stable product line. They tend to employ a mass production, routine technology. Managers in these businesses tend to have extensive knowledge of their areas of operations. They focus on making operations efficient and tend not to pay much attention to product and market developments. *Prospectors*, on the other hand, are continually examining the environment for product/market opportunities. They rely on product innovation and market development to bring change to their environment, and therefore face a more uncertain task environment.

An extensive strategy literature discusses the conditions that lead a business to adopt a particular strategic mission or competitive strategy, but these are outside the scope of this textbook. What is important here is the impact of whatever mission/strategy has been selected on one or more MCS characteristics. Most importantly, strategic missions and competitive strategies are important to MCS designers because they define to everyone in the organization what is critical to success. A business' critical success factors should, in turn, be directly related to the results measures included in a results control system. This relationship has been supported empirically. One study found that greater reliance on long-run criteria (sales growth, market share, or new product development) in the determination of the incentive bonus for SBU general managers had a stronger positive impact on effectiveness in build SBUs than in harvest SBUs.[10] Further, greater reliance on subjective performance evaluations had more significant positive impact on effectiveness in build units than in harvest units; it actually had a negative effect in harvest units. The emphasis placed on short-term performance criteria was equal for all SBUs.

Competitive strategies should translate into results measures equally strongly. Businesses endeavoring to be low cost producers, and those defending existing businesses, should control their lower-level employees' behaviors through standardized operating procedures designed to maximize efficiency. For motivating managers, their results measures should emphasize cost reductions (process innovation) and budget achievement. Conversely, businesses competing on the

basis of differentiation, and those prospecting for new markets, should have a more participative decision making environment and should reward employees and managers based on any of a number of nonfinancial performance indicators; such as product innovation, market development, customer service, and growth, as well as, secondarily, financial indicators such as budget achievement.[11]

CONCLUSION

This chapter has identified some of the many situational factors that can influence MCS choices and the effects of those choices. The appropriateness of each MCS choice does depend on the situation! The chapter also described some of the better known, relatively simple MCS-related effects of three important situational factors: uncertainty/programmability, diversification strategy, and business strategy. Similar discussions could be presented with regard to other factors, although our understanding of many of the effects is incomplete and unreliable.

Some of these factors can create MCS design conflicts. A business unit in an uncertain environment, but with a low cost strategy, faces conflicts between the desire to stay inward focused and efficient and the need to scan the environment to gather information that might indicate a structural change in the industry. MCS theory provides managers little guidance as to which demands are most important. In this example should managers focus on the demands of the uncertain environment or the low cost strategy, or try to deal with both? Alternatively, the proper question might be: In what situations should they try to deal with both sets of demands?

Despite the incomplete state of knowledge about the effects of various forms of MCSs in various situations, managers must cope. The main message in the chapter is that managers must be sensitive to these situational factors. They must be aware of the key dimensions of the situations in which they are managing and either adapt their MCS to the situational contingencies with which they are faced or find ways to alter their situation.

Notes

1. Simons calls this "interactive control." R. L. Simons, *Levers of Control* (Boston: Harvard Business School Press, 1995).
2. V. Govindarajan, "A Contingency Approach to Strategy Implementation at the Business Unit Level" Integrating Administrative Mechanisms with Strategy," *Academy of Management Journal*, 31, no. 4 (1988), pp. 828–853.
3. See P. L. Nemetz and L. W. Fry, "Flexible Manufacturing Organizations: Implications for Strategy Formulation and Organizational Design," *Academy of Management Review* 13:4 (1988).
4. See A. Hax and N. Maljuf, *The Strategy Concept and Process: A Pragmatic Approach* (Englewood Cliffs, N.J.: Prentice-Hall, 1991).
5. See C. W. L. Hill, "Internal Capital Market Controls and Financial Performance in Multidivisional Firms," *Journal of Industrial Economics*, 37, no. 1 (September 1988), pp. 67–83; C. W. L. Hill and R. E. Hoskisson, "Strategy and Structure in the Multi-Product Firm, *Academy of Management Review* 12 (April 1987), pp. 331–341; and O. E. Williamson, *Markets and Hierarchies: Analysis and Antitrust Implications* (New York: Free Press, 1975).
6. See N. A. Berg, "What's Different About Conglomerate Management?" *Harvard Business Review* 47, no. 6 (November–December 1969), pp. 112–120; J. W. Lorsch and S. A. Allen,

Managing Diversity and Interdependence: An Organizational Study of Multidivisional Firms (Boston: Harvard Business School Press, 1973); K. N. M. Dundas and P. R. Richardson, "Implementing the Unrelated Product Strategy," *Strategic Management Journal*, 3, no. 4 (1982), pp. 287–301; and J. L. Kerr, "Diversification Strategies and Managerial Rewards: An Empirical Study," *Academy of Management Journal*, 28, no. 1 (March 1985), pp. 155–179.

7. See J. Fisher and V. Govindarajan, "Incentive Compensation Design, Strategy Business Unit Mission, and Competitive Strategy," *Journal of Management Accounting Research* (Fall 1993), pp. 129–144.
8. M. E. Porter, *Competitive Strategy* (New York: Free Press, 1980).
9. R. E. Miles and C. C. Snow, *Organizational Strategy, Structure and Process* (New York: McGraw-Hill, 1978).
10. V. Govindarajan and A. K. Gupta, "Linking Control Systems to Business Unit Strategy: Impact on Performance," *Accounting, Organizations and Society*, 10 (1985), pp. 51–66.
11. See R. Simons, "The Role of Management Control Systems and Business Strategy: An Empirical Analysis," *Accounting, Organizations and Society*, 12, no. 4 (1987), pp. 357–374.

Monsanto Company

CONTROL OF R&D AT THE ANIMAL SCIENCES DIVISION

I. The Problem

In July 1987, managers at Monsanto Company were debating whether the company's management systems were facilitating or hindering corporate efforts to implement a strategic shift involving redeployment of assets away from commodity chemical businesses and toward the discovery of new biotechnology applications. Howard Schneiderman, corporate senior vice president of R&D and chief scientist, was an outspoken critic of the company's systems:

> Our system of evaluating performance based on short-term financial results has trained our operating managers not to take risks. They will not bet on a horse until the race is almost finished and the horse is leading. They tend to think about this year's profits, and that is natural because they are rewarded for only incremental improvements. They are penalized for missing budget targets, but do not get the big rewards for going way over plan.

Others, however, defended the company's systems. They noted that Monsanto was making large investments in biotechnology R&D despite its need to maintain a solid earnings record. Some even argued that because the biotechnology investments were the greatest risk that Monsanto had ever taken, the company perhaps should temper the scientists' natural bias toward optimism by requiring a more realistic focus on the projects' potential for commercial success. These managers suggested that people with greater knowledge of the specific markets to be served by the new products should be involved more intensively and much earlier in the review process of new R&D investments. This involvement would increase the likelihood that the company's R&D efforts would lead to commercial successes.

This case describes the Monsanto Company, its management systems, and, to illustrate the reasons for the R&D debate, it describes the history of the somatotropin program, a major biotechnology-based research effort designed to develop animal growth hormones.

II. Company Background

A. The Company

Monsanto Company, headquartered in St. Louis, Missouri, was a large, multinational company engaged in developing, manufacturing, and marketing a broad range of high-quality products, including chemicals, pharmaceuticals, low-calorie sweeteners (such as NutraSweet), industrial process controls, synthetic fibers, plastics, and electronic materials. Its sales reached $6.9 billion in 1986, and it employed 52,000 people in 100 countries.

In 1987, the company had six operating groups (see Exhibit 1 for a partial corporate organization chart). The largest group was the Monsanto Chemical Company, the original business, which still accounted for about 60 percent of total corporate sales.

The Monsanto Agricultural Company, the second-largest group, accounted for 17 percent of total sales. As shown in Exhibit 2, the Agricultural Company had two operating divisions, Crop Chemicals and Animal Sciences. Crop Chemicals was a leading worldwide producer of herbicides, with widely recognized patented products such as Lasso and Roundup. Animal Sciences focused on animal nutrition and growth products, only a few of which had already been introduced to the mar-

This case was prepared by Lourdes Ferreira, Research Assistant, under the supervision of Professor Kenneth A. Merchant, as a basis for class discussion rather than to illustrate either effective or ineffective handling of an administrative situation.

ket. Exhibit 3 summarizes financial data about these two divisions.

From 1982 to 1987, Monsanto had made a strategic shift toward faster-growing markets, away from the commodity chemicals that had provided most of its sales and profits. As stated in the 1986 Annual Report, "Monsanto is determined to be a leader in its chosen markets for the 1990s, but we must deliver results in the short term as well as generate the resources needed for the coming decades. We will achieve this goal by aggressively managing good business, by inventing and licensing new products that meet customers' needs, and by moving out of businesses that prove unable to meet targets." One of these targets was explicitly stated in the 1985 and 1986 letters from the CEO to the shareholders: "For the shareholders . . . this promise means aiming for a return on equity year after year in the 20 percent range."

B. Planning and Budgeting

Monsanto had two planning processes, long-range planning and annual budgeting. The long-range plan, which covered a horizon of ten years, projected growth rates for operating income, working capital, R&D, and fixed assets for each planning entity.

In June, after senior managers had reviewed and approved the long-range plan, they sent the guidelines contained in the long-range projections to the operating units, which would then start preparing the following year's budget (Monsanto's fiscal year coincided with the calendar year). During October and November, the budgets the operating units submitted were consolidated and presented to and negotiated with senior management. In December, senior management approved the final budget.

C. Performance Measurement

The operating units' primary financial measures of performance were net income, return on capital employed (ROCE), and net cashflow. The company defined net income as operating income less corporate charges, interest and taxes. ROCE was computed as the ratio between net income plus after-tax interest expenses and average capital employed, which corresponded to the operating unit's net worth. Net cash flow was calculated by a formula that adjusted the net income number to reflect actual cash uses and sources (e.g., depreciation, capital expenditures). These measures were intended to indicate performance of each business as a *stand-alone company.*

The weightings of importance among these measures could vary from year to year, depending on the areas that corporate management identified as critical for each operating unit to focus on. For example, the emphasis on cash flow had been increasing in the chemical businesses.

Each quarter, division managers had to prepare reports comparing budgeted and actual net income. The corporate philosophy was that managers should have aggressive goals that were as likely to be achieved as to be missed. The budget served as the basis for incentive compensation and promotions.

D. Incentive Compensation

Since 1984, Monsanto had used a Performance Incentive Plan, which tied annual bonus payments to each operating unit's achievement of an annual net income target. The first step to determine the bonuses was to assess corporate performance and measure it against the annual corporate target. Then the CEO would recommend to the Executive Compensation and Development Committee of the Board of Directors on allocation of the bonus pool to each profit center, based on how well the operating unit had performed against its financial targets. Finally, the distribution of bonuses to each participant depended on job level and individual attainment of the annual goals. The job level determined the maximum percentage of salary that could be paid out as bonus, but the Compensation and Development Committee and the CEO had considerable discretion to determine bonus payments above this limit. Typically, however, bonuses for operating managers did not exceed 50 percent of their base salary.

The Performance Incentive Plan established that the bonuses would be paid two-thirds in cash and one-third in restricted stock. The restrictions on the company stock lapsed after three years if Monsanto's stock price performed at least as well as the Standard & Poor's 400 during the same period.

Also in 1984, the Board approved a new Long-Term Incentive Plan in addition to the Performance Incentive Plan. Pursuant to the

Long-Term Plan, incentive payments depended on the corporation's achieving its goals for earnings per share and return on capital over three-year performance cycles. So far, however, corporate performance had not reached the goals stated in the long-term plan, and no payment of long-term awards had been made.

III. Research and Development Process

As an aid in managing its sizable R&D effort, Monsanto classified R&D activities into three categories. Class I was dedicated to maintaining existing businesses and the supply of technical services. Class II included efforts to expand business assets and markets, and to reduce costs of existing processes. Class III activities focused on developing new products. Exhibit 4 illustrates how the company increasingly moved its emphasis from Class I to Class III R&D activities, reflecting a growing concern with the introduction of new products.

R&D activities in Class III normally went through three phases of development before commercialization. The first phase began when scientists discovered a new product lead. In biotechnology, this phase involved the major technical efforts to isolate the specific gene responsible for the biological phenomenon under study (e.g., the gene responsible for growth in human cells, for disease resistance in plant cells, or for production of a certain hormone). Once the gene had been isolated, the process of duplicating it in a laboratory setting was greatly facilitated. Laboratory duplication still involved gene splicing techniques but Monsanto scientists had leading expertise in gene splicing. This first phase of research for new product development could take two or three years to be completed. If successful, it generated a new *probe.*

The second phase of discovery involved applying the new technical concept or probe to the development of a new product candidate. The discovery phase of R&D was the most technically challenging, and the research processes could take as long as four years. Only if this phase was satisfactorily completed would the R&D activity constitute an ongoing project.

In the third phase, R&D for a new product became a multiyear project focused on commercial and regulatory issues. On the commercial side, emphasis was on production costs, delivery systems (e.g., tablet or liquid form injection), and marketability. On the regulatory side, the tests involved meeting all safety and clinical standards set by regulatory agencies until the product was finally approved for consumer use. Compared with the two other stages, this was by far the most expensive and also the longest, often taking at least five years to complete.

R&D costs typically increased sharply as development moved closer to the testing stage for commercial applications. As Cliff Baile, R&D director of the Animal Sciences Division, noted "It is at least ten times cheaper to discover a new concept than to make it into a product."

IV. Decentralization of R&D Activities and Assignment of Costs

In 1985, Monsanto started a major decentralization effort that eventually could involve significant structural changes in its R&D activities, possibly including the transfer of all R&D then done at the corporate to the operating unit level. One of the primary objectives of such an organizational change was to decentralize the R&D effort as much as possible to place it directly under the control of the operating unit whose business would benefit from the R&D investment. The general managers in charge of the operating units would become responsible for their own R&D costs.

An R&D decentralization study concluded that the company should continue to conduct R&D activities in emerging fields such as biotechnology at a corporate level but that the operating units should undertake an increasing role in the effort. The study also developed better bases for further assigning corporate R&D costs to the operating units. Until 1985, for example, most of the R&D costs associated with biotechnology were fully retained at the corporate level, but after the changes, a larger part of these costs were assigned to the operating units.

By 1987, the R&D staffs at the operating unit level were capable of performing most types of R&D activities that were based primarily on existing technologies. When it came to developing new biotechnology-based technology, however, they were more dependent on corporate R&D. Corporate R&D also provided the operating units some support services, such as bioprocess research and use of analytical laboratories and an information center, on a fee-for-service basis.

Exhibit 5 shows where Monsanto's R&D costs were incurred. The operating units directly controlled about 80 percent of total R&D costs because of the various R&D activities conducted at the operating unit level. Corporate R&D controlled the remaining 20 percent of total R&D costs, 10 percent of which was retained at corporate level in 1986 and 10 percent which were charged back to the operating units, either on a fee-for-service basis (9 percent) or based upon net investment (1 percent). As is shown in Exhibit 5, there had been a marked increase in the extent of costs allocated to the operating units between 1985 and 1986.

The costs retained at corporate R&D related to biotechnology research, which served primarily the pharmaceutical, agricultural, and animal sciences divisions. These operating units were not charged for R&D in new areas such as biotechnology for two main reasons. One was that this kind of research was generic. It benefitted several operating units simultaneously, and it was virtually meaningless to try to allocate the costs to operating units. For instance, research on technology for gene splitting could benefit product lines in either agriculture or health care and possibly other businesses in ways that were difficult to anticipate.

The other reason for retaining control over biotechnology expenditures at corporate R&D was the concern that this investment was crucial for the company's long-term future, and it therefore should not be consigned to the operating units, which operated under short-term pressure. As Schneiderman explained:

> Corporate can't afford to fund all the R&D efforts alone. We need to push these costs down to the operating groups that generate enough cash flow to sustain these major investments. The ideal would be for corporate to engage only in the very basic research and to hand a project to the respective operating unit as soon as it reaches a stage when we can start talking about commercialization. The problem is that I have to be sure that there are enough people at the operating level who are really interested in the project. Otherwise, they will cut the R&D funding for the project as soon as the budget pressure starts to get to them. Operating managers often like to treat R&D expenditures as variable costs.

V. Effect of Profit Pressures on R&D

During the budget negotiation process, when the consolidated initial submissions from the operating units did not reach the corporate profit objectives, as was usual, senior management had to negotiate revisions with the operating unit managers. In December 1986, for example, the consolidated budget proposals from all operating units did not meet the corporate target for 1987. Thus, Richard Mahoney, the chairman and CEO, had to revise most entities' budgets to increase the estimated earnings per share. The operating managers, however, had the discretion to decide how the earnings increase would be achieved (e.g., through sales promotions, reductions in the cost of goods sold, or cuts in R&D expenditures).

The corporate R&D group, which was operated as a cost center, was affected. Schneiderman had to reduce the 1987 budget for corporate R&D from nearly $93 million to $90.5 million. Exhibit 6 shows the final breakdown of the 1987 R&D budget by cost category.

The operating units also had to reduce their R&D budgets to meet the tougher bottom-line targets. For example, Nick Reding, group president of Monsanto Agricultural Company, had to reduce his R&D budget by $15 million to a total of $135 million (about 12 percent of sales). The division managers for Crop Chemicals and Animal Sciences had, in turn, to revise their R&D budgets to adjust to the new targets. Adhering to corporate R&D's budget philosophy, the operating managers had to propose *stretch* budget targets having less than a 50 percent chance to be met. Reding, however, usually kept a provision in the budget for the Agricultural Company to cover possible budget overruns by his operating managers.

During the fiscal year, if division managers had to spend more on R&D than budgeted, they would first have to consult with the group president before making any commitments, unless the extra R&D expenditures would not cause a material decrease in operating income. On the other hand, if the operating manager had a windfall gain during the year, he or she could negotiate to invest the additional income in projects beyond the original R&D budget, as long as the operating income target was met and actions taken did not result in permanent additions to R&D expense (e.g., people).

When deciding which R&D projects to cut, Reding, in consultation with his operating managers, considered several aspects of the future potential of the projects in progress. A primary criterion was the level of capital requirements and how they affected the total portfolio of projects. He also assessed qualitative aspects, such as the probability of technological success, the total market potential for the new product, the market share that Monsanto could expect, and the regulatory requirements for final approval. He based his judgments on reports from the operating managers. Current projects, being closer to completion, usually had priority over new ones, which represented higher risks to the company.

In his original 1987 budget, Lee Miller, general manager of the Animal Sciences division, submitted a budget proposing additions of 25 percent in technology expenses. Nick Reding vetoed the additions because he felt that to meet his goal of controlling the growth in R&D expenditures he could not afford any more increases. The Agricultural Company had spent more than 12 percent of sales on R&D in 1985, and corporate had asked for tighter control over these costs. As a consequence, the Animal Sciences division was asked to limit its R&D expenditures to a maximum of 50 percent of its sales. Exhibit 7 shows that even after these budget cuts, the Animal Sciences division had $35 million in losses in 1986 and a budget of $43 million in losses for 1987.

VI. Funding New R&D Projects

Generally, the closer a project was to the commercialization stage, the more the operating unit bore its costs. However, in the case of pioneering R&D projects, which required developing new technologies, corporate R&D funded the projects directly, with no charges to the operating unit. In 1987, for instance (Exhibit 6), corporate R&D budgeted $42.9 million in R&D costs that it would retain—under the control of Howard Schneiderman—to fund primarily biotechnology research.

There was considerable discussion among the operating units about the use of corporate resources for a centralized R&D effort. The managers in the chemical businesses often felt that corporate management rejected their capital requests and favored the divisions engaged in biotechnology research, such as Animal Sciences, G. D. Searle, (the pharmaceutical company) or the corporate biotechnology product discovery efforts. Some Monsanto Chemical Company managers, who generated substantial cash flow from their mature businesses, had been known to wish secretively that biotechnology efforts would fail so that corporate R&D would release more resources for them to invest in their own businesses.

Some managers of the growing businesses also were critical of the commitment of funds to corporate R&D efforts. They would have preferred to fund and manage R&D, even the technically sophisticated biotechnology discovery efforts, with their own resources. They argued that only with direct responsibility for R&D could they ensure that the projects being worked on were commercially relevant.

Howard Schneiderman felt differently, however. He commented on the need for managing emerging technologies such as biotechnology at the corporate level:

> Operating managers have a strong incentive to think short term, to focus on this year's income, rather than the long-term potential of some R&D investments. If left on their own to fund innovative and risky R&D projects, they would simply choose not to. We could possibly change this short-term focus, or myopia, if we were willing to deemphasize budgets and use other control mechanisms or change the management compensation schemes substantially, for example, by giving royalties from successful projects to the respective managers.

VII. The Somatotropin Projects

To illustrate the effects of profit pressure on R&D for new product development, the example of the somatotropin projects is discussed in the following sections. Somatotropin, which is produced in the pituitary gland of animals, is a protein hormone responsible for growth.

A. Bovine Somatotropin

In 1980, Monsanto (and some other large chemical companies) started funding major research on bovine somatotropin (BST). Monsanto-sponsored preliminary experiments by universities showed that BST, which occurs naturally in cows, could increase milk production by as much as 10 to 25 percent when the cows were injected with supplemental BST with a corresponding increase of 5 to 10 percent in feed efficiency.

Based on those results, the company decided to invest in the development of a BST probe. The technical process to produce BST in commercial quantity was similar to the one already used for commercial production of insulin for human medical treatment. By 1984, the Monsanto scientists had successfully isolated the BST protein hormone and started working on the product development phase.

After extensive testings and product improvements, BST reached the project phase, and Monsanto filed for preliminary approval from the Food and Drug Administration (FDA), the U.S. regulatory agency responsible for approving any new drug that could affect animal or human health. In 1986, the FDA granted permission for long-term trials of BST to assess its efficacy and effect on animal safety. In the same year, the Animal Sciences division started funding BST on its own, without sharing the R&D costs with the corporate group. By then, BST had become a multiyear project aimed at offering the product for commercialization, scheduled to start before 1990.

The long-term trials confirmed that BST could increase annual milk production by as much as 25 percent and that it had no adverse effects on humans or animals. Monsanto expected the FDA to release the product for commercialization in 1990. Because of its technological advantage over its competitors, the company hoped to have a several-year-lead on its competition for registration and commercial production of BST.

One of the factors likely to delay FDA approval, however, was the reaction of some milk producers, who submitted a petition requesting that the FDA examine BST's impact on the milk-producing industry. They alleged that some industry projections forecasted milk surpluses for the 1990s, even without using BST. If the new product succeeded in increasing milk efficiency, milk prices would be lowered and many small farmers could be driven out of the industry. Other industry representatives argued that BST could actually improve flexibility in milk production, because it would allow production of the current level of output with fewer cows or increased production from the current number of cows. And, unlike other dairy industry technology advances, BST required little, if any, additional capital investment.

Because forecasting the exact percentage of farmers who would adopt BST was difficult, a careful evaluation of the commercial aspects of the R&D effort was important. As Lee Miller, general manager of the Animal Sciences division, noted: "In an industry subject to intense regulation, we can't fail to consider the real potential for commercialization that BST offers." BST would allow farmers the flexibility to increase production readily to achieve the full allowable revenue or to avert overproduction, which might result in penalties.

The company estimated that from the consumer's viewpoint, BST would be immediately self-financing. Assuming a typical scenario, a farmer could order a month's supply of BST and, by the third or fourth day into the month, could count on increased milk production at less feed per pound of milk produced. The increased output could probably be sold even before the BST and feed bills were due. The cost of BST to the dairy farmers, however, was difficult to estimate because manufacturing costs for BST producers were not yet final and no reliable estimate of what price it would sell for.

Reports from preliminary consumer surveys conducted in 1986 suggested that BST adoption would be gradual. Dairy farmers had said that they would use BST initially on a maximum of 50 to 60 percent of their cows and increase it later, if warranted, but revised estimates for 1990–1995 indicated that total milk production increases attributable to BST would be less than 2 percent per year. Companies investing in BST research projected the net benefit to the dairy farmers would be a return of $2 for every $1 invested, but about one-half of the dairy farmers surveyed stated that they would not buy the new product unless they expected a minimum return of $3 for $1 spent.

Several other issues concerning BST's market potential also remained unresolved. For example, farmers with larger herds (more than 500 cows) responded that they would not use BST if it were available only in dosages for daily injections. More than half of the farmers surveyed expressed concerns about possible adverse effects on the cow's health and reproductive efficiency. Others worried if consumers would respond negatively to milk from cows injected with BST. An overwhelming majority of farmers, however, still maintained they would like to see animal health companies continue to invest in BST research.

B. Porcine Somatotropin

In December 1984, while conducting research on BST, Cliff Baile, the Director of Animal Sciences R&D, and his research team at Monsanto identified a lead for another somatotropin product, PST (for porcine somatotropin). PST was a protein hormone naturally produced in swine pituitary glands to stimulate growth in pigs. As with BST, PST could be produced in commercial quantities following the biotechnology processes in which Monsanto scientists were experts.

The first R&D phase suggested that PST could improve feed efficiency, reduce feed intake, accelerate animal growth, and even reduce fat deposits, with a corresponding increase in pork protein content. The PST hormone helped regulate a pig's metabolism, and increased the development of muscle rather than fat. Since a pig's production of fat requires about four times the energy as production of muscle, the more muscle produced, the less feed needed to promote a pig's growth.

The increased feed efficiency would result in lower production costs and fewer days for the hogs to reach market weight. This was particularly important because feed costs represented 65 to 75 percent of total production costs. Furthermore, the leaner pork meat would meet consumer's current taste preferences and quality for a grade-price premium. Preliminary trials were a success, much to the satisfaction of Cliff Baile. Being a part-time hog farmer himself, he could evaluate the new product's tremendous potential for farmers.

In 1986, the company scientists isolated the PST hormone and developed the probe in the lab. They initially tried to use the same molecule from BST, but found that some modifications needed to be made. In June 1986, they successfully completed the PST production process. The challenge then was to ensure corporate approval of funding for more intensive investigations to develop commercial applications. PST would then become an ongoing project and be tested for commercial and regulatory purposes.

Cliff Baile remembered the various presentations he had made to senior management to request funding for the PST project. The financial arguments in PST's favor were that it could generate \$100–200 million per year in sales; and Monsanto had a perceived cost advantage over its competitors in PST production, so the sales would be profitable. The company had already anticipated the need to invest substantial amounts in the BST project, which used a closely related technology. The marginal costs of investing in PST would add just a fraction to what they had been investing in BST, about \$60 million, to be spent over a period of about 10 years. Company scientists estimated that PST would be available for commercialization in the mid-1990s, once the FDA had granted final approval for consumer use.

In mid-1986, it was difficult to estimate the economic impact of PST on the pork industry. Predictions of PST prices and potential gains to hog farmers were unreliable at that point because Monsanto had little idea of how much it would cost to produce PST in commercial quantities.

Studies conducted by independent university researchers forecasted that PST would increase pork production, which might cause pork prices to decline, with a corresponding increase in retail sales. However, if consumers were willing to pay premium prices for the leaner pork, prices would not have to fall due to increased production, and pork producers would reap net profits from PST adoption, no matter the size of their scale of operations. As with BST, there were still questions about how farmers would respond to the need for daily PST injections or for increased dietary nutrients to the hogs treated with PST.

Lee Miller, general manager of the Animal Sciences division, and his boss, Nick Reding, the group president of Monsanto Agricultural Company, were both sympathetic to the idea of pursuing the PST research. But the fiscal year was nearly half over when Cliff Baile requested funding for this new project. The Agricultural Company, with an already tough budget target to meet, could not afford to fund additional corporate bioprocess development work for PST at that point. Both Miller and Reding anticipated that PST development costs would escalate quickly. Of the total of $60 million necessary to bring PST to commercialization, about 10 percent, or $6 million, would be required for the first year, but after the fourth or fifth year, costs with the PST project could easily increase to $20 million per year, or almost one third of the total R&D costs that the Animal Sciences division had budgeted for fiscal year 1987.

On the other hand, it seemed that if Monsanto stopped working on PST at that point, it might lose any competitive advantages of patenting it before its competitors. Therefore, Reding told Baile to *find a way* to fund PST. Baile knowing that Howard Schneiderman, a leading scientist in biotechnology, would support PST, made his pitch for funding directly to him.

Schneiderman accepted Baile's argument that the Agricultural Company could not fund corporate bioprocess development costs for PST at that point, but he encouraged him to pursue the development. To cover the costs, Schneiderman retained $500,000 of this expense in corporate biotechnology product discovery.

At the end of 1986, Baile requested $6 million to $7 million to be dedicated to PST, which would then become a regular, multiyear project. His request was approved, after several negotiations with Miller, Schneiderman, and Reding. Corporate management decided to grant Animal Sciences the resources to fund PST on its own. The final R&D budget for Animal Sciences, including $6 million for PST, was approved by Richard Mahoney in early 1987.

VIII. General Controversies about R&D Funding

Monsanto's chairman and CEO, Richard Mahoney, was personally committed to making the company a leader in biotechnology, but he was also under pressure from the financial community to ensure that Monsanto would report earnings-per-share growth at least comparable to the market returns. In an interview, Mahoney commented on the balance that must be struck between profit goals and R&D requirements:

> We keep telling scientists that we're not in business for the pursuit of knowledge, but for the pursuit of products. Everything at the end of the line has to turn into a product. Unless we sell products, nothing happens. But I also know that good research doesn't happen overnight. I tell researchers I pray for patience every night—and I want it right now.

Corporate management was particularly concerned about the net unallocated R&D cost retained at the corporate level. This was the number that would become part of external reports and that would be closely monitored by the financial analyst community. Monsanto, with a reputation for making sound investments in R&D, wanted to ensure investors would not draw the erroneous impression that R&D expenditures were getting out of control just because more R&D was being funded at the corporate level.

As with most biotechnology projects, the returns from BST and PST were quite uncertain. For example, the company had started investing in BST back in 1980, and the project was still undergoing several tests in 1987 to obtain FDA final approval for commercialization. The regulatory authorities demanded extensive, multiyear trials to guarantee that the product would not adversely affect safety when consumed by humans.

Projects such as BST and PST presented risks on several dimensions, including technological uncertainties, potential competition from other chemical companies, and the inherent financial hazards associated with substantial investments. As Ron Stovall, controller for the Agricultural Company, explained,

> With BST, for example, Monsanto will probably have to invest several hundred million dollars before we can commercialize it. A product has to be a real commercial hit to pay off such major investments. Biotechnology may well be the highest risk this company has ever taken.

Richard Mahoney maintained that overfunding is one of the primary mistakes to avoid in industrial R&D.

> If I look back on the research mistakes we have made, it was usually due to overfunding. If we agree to pay $25 million over three years to see the first card, and after that time we don't get it, I don't want that project any more. But once the project has surfaced and has gotten up there, it is in the annual report, and it is hard to admit failure.

Monsanto had had a few projects that had to be discontinued after years of R&D investments because they failed at the commercialization stage. One example occurred in 1985, when it had to terminate a project on a plant growth regulator. In general, however, the whole area of genetically engineered plants had yielded very impressive scientific progress. In association with the Crop Chemicals division, the company was able to develop plants that were genetically resistant to common diseases and glyphosate (Roundup®) without the need for herbicides.

Lee Miller commented on how the uncertainty associated with R&D exacerbated the conflict among the various objectives he had to face.

> On one hand, I am supposed to invest in the long run and keep developing new products. I already spend 50 percent of my total revenues on R&D. But I also have a long-run target to reach a 20 percent return on equity in the 1990s, and I'm running sizable losses now. So I need to be very careful when allocating current resources. I wish we had a system to evaluate the commercial potential of new R&D investments more thoroughly. Some people believe that if you do good science, the market will follow, but it's not always true.

The corporate R&D group maintained close contact with the operating units to assess the new products' potentials for commercial success. For instance, before investing in developing probes for new pharmaceutical drugs, corporate R&D consulted the pharmaceutical division to determine if the potential product would be well received in the market. If the pharmaceutical division, which would ultimately have to sell the product, did not agree with the R&D project, corporate R&D would not pursue it.

One alternative for increasing discussions of commercial viability earlier in the R&D funding process was to form a commercial development group reporting directly to the CEO (at the same level of authority as Corporate R&D). This commercial group would get involved in all decisions about which research projects to fund. It would raise considerations about market needs, the company's marketing competitive advantages, and assessment of competitive products at the earliest possible stages of the R&D process.

Another alternative was to have a commercial staff at the operating unit level, reporting to the operating general manager. The managers who defended this suggestion asserted that the operating unit was the most knowledgeable about specific customer needs and maintained relationships with possible distribution channels thus being in the best position to assess market potential for new products.

R&D personnel were generally opposed to either of the aforementioned alternatives. They argue that if Monsanto allowed commercial emphasis to interfere with R&D projects at a too early stage it would thwart most of its opportunities for innovation. As Cliff Baile, director of R&D for Animal Sciences, commented:

> The people responsible for current products are the ones who bring in the cash so that they are also the ones with the most power. The people who do exploratory R&D have very little bargaining power. It is obvious that today's products will always get the division manager's attention. Potential products just don't provide enough motivation.

Other managers defended the current R&D system. As Will Carpenter, vice president for technology for Crop Chemicals, said:

> R&D can't be an end in itself. It is a means to get new products so that you can keep growing. But one will always need the financial discipline of controlling costs. And good financial controls are not incompatible with good R&D—they actually force us managers to establish priorities and focus our development efforts in products with the highest potential.

The multiyear nature of R&D projects posed some special financial problems. Some R&D people criticized the current process of annual R&D budgets. Cliff Baile explained:

> All my projects have at least a three-year horizon. Yet, it seems that every year I have to justify myself by asking for funding. What am I supposed to do if I don't get funding for my projects? Why don't they give me funding for three years?

The assignment of corporate R&D costs also was problematic. In 1987, for example, there was considerable debate about how Monsanto would fund the maintenance of the corporate bioprocess development facility, which conducted basic research for several operating units. As stated in the first quarter report of 1987, the Monsanto Life Sciences Research Center, which housed the bioprocess development facility, was "one of the largest and most sophisticated facilities in the world devoted to understanding the chemistry and biology of life." This $150 million facility had been dedicated in 1984 and employed approximately 1,200 scientists and support personnel. Until 1987, the bioprocess development facility had been conducting research related to several projects that were later handed over to the operating units. Yet, the problem remained about how corporate R&D would allocate the costs of that facility because it could not simply close it down on a temporary basis.

The Animal Sciences division, which typically had used more than half of the bioprocess development facility's capacity, now had fewer projects in progress, and its managers argued that they should pay only for the facility costs directly related to its own projects. From a corporate perspective, however, the facility had to be fully maintained in a state of readiness because Monsanto was deeply committed to biotechnology research and the company had to keep its scientists motivated and fully occupied. The company could not afford to have its scientists sit idle or leave when there was not enough volume to keep the facility fully operative. After several rounds of negotiations, corporate R&D, after curtailing other important research projects, decided to absorb the bioprocess development facility costs that could not be charged to the operating units on a fee-for-service basis.

Don Hughes, the controller for corporate R&D, wondered how the operating unit managers' increasing influence on R&D expenditures would affect the balance between the short-term pressure to meet the annual budget targets and the long-term need to invest in R&D:

> Does increasing operating unit influence on our key R&D growth programs enhance or mitigate our chances of meeting our goal of becoming an industry leader in innovative, high-quality products? I know there is pressure to level off our R&D spending across the company, including corporate R&D. We have got to make sure we get more *bang for our R&D buck* in terms of prioritizing those efforts to go after the most promising commercial opportunities if we are going to achieve our goals in biotechnology. How can we be sure we have the right incentive system in place so that the operating managers will prioritize these efforts toward increased commercial success?

These questions reflected senior management's concern about whether Monsanto had a problem in the way it funded R&D. If there was really a problem, what changes should be made to the company's management systems?

EXHIBIT 1 Partial Corporation Organization Chart, 1987

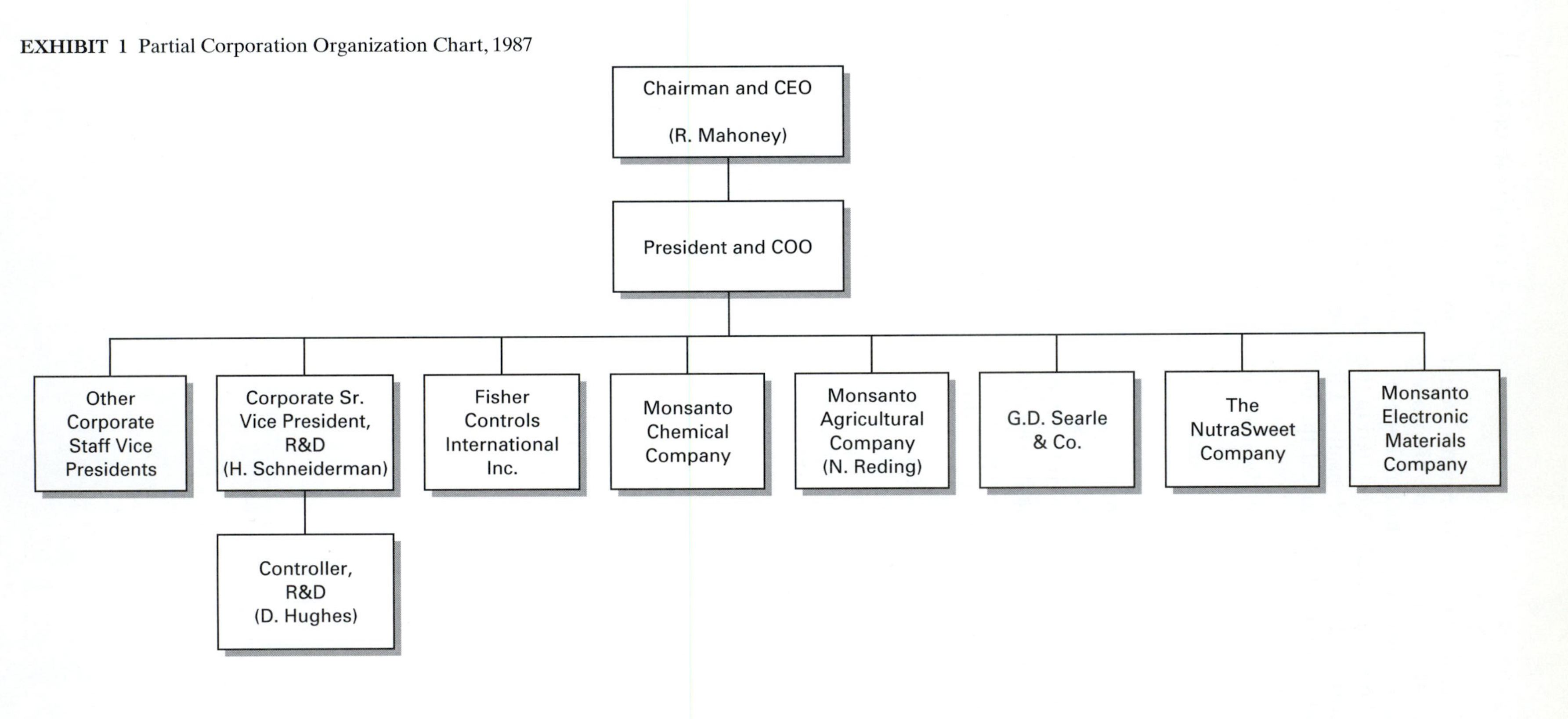

EXHIBIT 2 Organization Chart of Monsanto Agricultural Company, 1987

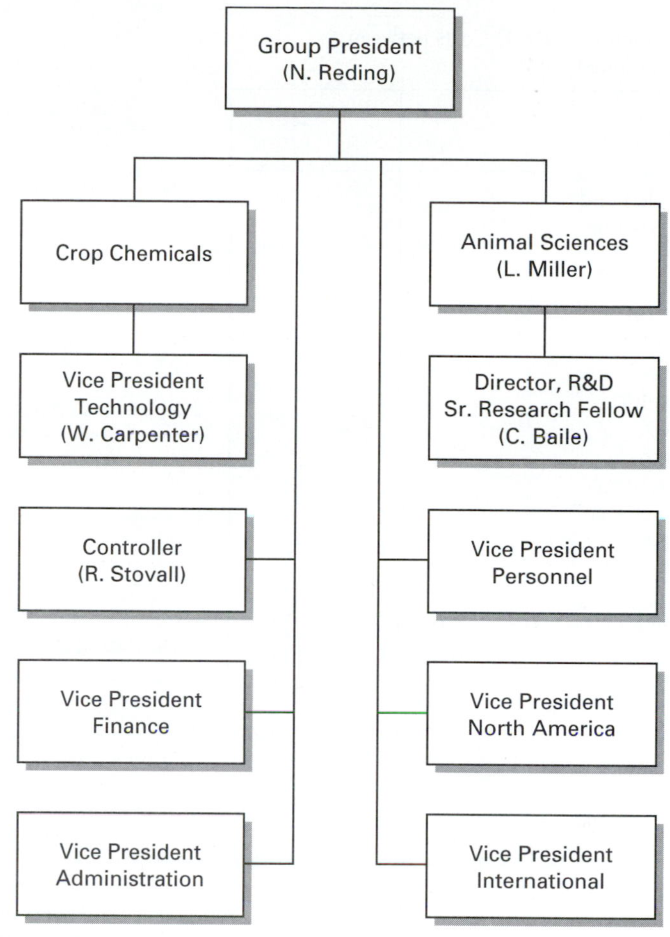

EXHIBIT 3 Financial Highlights of Monsanto Agricultural Company (U.S. $ millions)

	Crop Chemicals	*Animal Sciences*
Sales		
1986	1,067	86
1985	1,073	79
1984	1,256	82
Operating Income (Loss)		
1986	318	(35)
1985	177	(92)
1984	438	(49)
R&D Expenses		
1986	94	41
1985	110	32
1984	107	22

EXHIBIT 4 Corporate R&D Costs by Major Category (%)

	1986	*1985*	*1984*	*1983*	*1982*
Class I	26%	27%	29%	32%	32%
Class II	30	23	22	23	24
Class III	40	42	40	35	30
Other*	4	8	9	10	14
Total	100%	100%	100%	100%	100%

*Includes corporate unclassified administrative costs (e.g., maintenance of the central research laboratory).

EXHIBIT 5 Distribution of R&D Costs between Corporate and Operating Units

		1986 (%)		*1985 (%)*
Directly controlled and administered by the operating units		80%		80%
Controlled and administered by corporate R&D:				
Charged to operating units on a fee-for service basis-	9%		4%	
—Allocated to operating units as "corporate charge" based on net investment	1		3	
—Reported as part corporate R&D	10	20	10	20
Total R&D cost		100%		100%

EXHIBIT 7 Animal Sciences Division (U.S. $ millions)

	1987 Budget	*1986 Budget*
Sale	$ 127	$ 86
R&D	61	41
Other Operating Costs	109	80
Operating Income (Loss)	(43)	(35)

EXHIBIT 6 Budget vs. Actual Corporate R&D Costs (U.S. $ millions)

	1987 Budget	*1986 Actual*	*Excess of 1987 Budget Over 1986 Actual Costs*
Biotech Product Discovery*	42.9	40.6	2.3
Technology Management**	2.4	2.4	0
Distributed Research and Development***	45.2	49.9	(4.7)
Total Corporate R&D	90.5	92.9	(2.4)

*Retained at corporate R&D and reported as an operating segment.

**Allocated to the operating units as corporate overhead.

***Charged directly to operating companies based upon measured services rendered and/or negotiated amounts.

Graves Industries, Inc.

In April 1981, at the annual stockholders' meeting of Graves Industries, Inc., Henry Graves, the company's chairman, president, and CEO, announced a new strategic emphasis on flexible manufacturing systems equipment. The company planned to make major investments, over $100 million in research and development alone in the following four years, in a new Flexible Manufacturing Systems Division (FMSD).

The plan was to fund the new investments internally. Henry said he would be asking Graves Industries' existing divisions to cut costs and improve profitability while, of course, endeavoring to maintain the standards of excellence they had built. Managers throughout the company soon felt the added performance pressure. They responded in a variety of ways, not all of them positive.

GRAVES INDUSTRIES

Graves Industries was founded in the early 1920s as a manufacturer of industrial hardware and tooling. The company went public in 1926 and was listed on the New York Stock Exchange. Capitalizing on the rapid industrial growth during World War II, Graves Industries grew tremendously. Revenues climbed from $8.2 million in 1941 to $41.5 million in 1945. From 1946 to 1981, the company branched out into other areas of hardware and tooling—consumer hardware, automotive hardware, and marine hardware. (Exhibit 1 presents a financial summary of recent fiscal years.)

In the mid-1970s, Henry Graves, now the chairman and CEO, recognized that flexible manufacturing was becoming important in the hardware and other industries. He wanted Graves Industries to stay on the leading edge of technology. He knew the flexible manufacturing equipment business was complex and risky, but the potential market was large ($26 billion in 1982). Henry had the company start building numerically controlled (NC) tools in its Industrial division. In 1981, with the formation of the FMSD, Graves began allocating significantly more resources to this business.

ORGANIZATION

Graves Industries used a divisionalized organization structure (see Exhibit 2). The relatively autonomous operating divisions each included their own research and development, manufacturing, and marketing capabilities. Division staff managers reported directly to the division managers and had only relatively weak, *dotted line* relationships with corporate staff.

Headquarters staff monitored divisional performance by reviewing plans, budgets, capital requests, and financial reports. Formal reviews were held quarterly to discuss the actual results and the forecast for the year. If performance was in line with corporate financial goals, few inquiries were made. If negative variances resulted, however, headquarters gave divisions a great deal of attention and *help*.

Henry Graves believed it was very important for the company, and thus the divisions, to maintain a steady pattern of growth because "that is what the stock market values." Thus, consistency and predictability were the watchwords; surprises were to be avoided. One division president noted that, "There are only two things important in this company: profit, and turning it in a predictable fashion."

PROFIT PLANNING

Profit planning was performed in two distinct cycles: strategic planning and budgeting. Strategic planning involved creative thinking about corpo-

Professor Kenneth A. Merchant of the University of Southern California prepared this case as the basis for class discussion rather than to illustrate either effective or ineffective handling of an administrative situation. The case is based on knowledge of actual company situations, but the facts have been disguised.

rate strengths, weaknesses, opportunities, and threats in the next three-year period. The division managers had to submit a narrative analysis of their businesses and plans, supported by summary numerical schedules. Strategic plans were presented to top management in August and September.

After the strategic plans were approved, the divisions began working on their budgets. The budgets were expressed in terms of monthly income statements and balance sheets for the coming year. They were reviewed by top management and the board of directors in November and December. The budgets were considered a commitment of earnings and return on net assets (RONA) from division managers to the company and from the company to the board of directors.

While the intent of the profit planning process was *bottom-up,* it was typical for the division managers to have to adjust their targets after the review meetings. Henry Graves liked his managers to have aggressive budgets, and it was often said that "Henry always wants to take something from each division when he leaves the table."

MANAGEMENT INCENTIVE PLAN

Graves offered its management personnel a base salary slightly below that of its competitors and relied on a Management Incentive Plan (MIP) to help motivate and retain its key personnel. The MIP offered annual cash awards based on the actual vs. budgeted level of RONA achieved by the entity to which the individual was assigned (division or above). About 60 employees were enrolled in the MIP, including most managers down to one level below division manager.

The payouts in the plan were potentially lucrative. For example, the payouts for a division manager ranged up to 100 percent of salary. The incentive plan clearly attracted the attention of the managers. In a survey done several years after the plan was implemented, the managers included all reported that they understood the plan and that it affected their decision making.

BOARD OF DIRECTORS

The board of directors consisted of five members, two inside directors (Henry Graves and Steve Sinko, president of the Industrial Tools Division), and three outside directors. The outside directors were all either active or retired executives who were long-time acquaintances of Henry Graves. The board usually met four times a year to review the company's progress and plans.

The Audit Committee of the board was created in 1973 in response to the endorsement of the Security and Exchange Commission and the New York Stock Exchange for all publicly held companies to establish audit committees. At Graves, this committee was comprised of the three outside directors.

AUDITS

Since 1971, Graves had used a Big Eight accounting firm, Ernst, Mitchell and Sells (EMS) for its outside audits. Harvey Krantz had been the EMS partner on the Graves account for the last three years. Harvey and Henry Graves had developed an excellent working relationship during that period. They were members of the same country club; they were involved in many of the same activities; and they occasionally played golf together. In the last two years, however, the social relationship had been strained as Graves's pressure to fund the FMSD internally was passed on to the auditors; Harvey was asked to reduce the EMS audit fees significantly.

Graves's Internal Audit department consisted of a head auditor and three staff members. The internal audit staff ensured that corporate accounting policies were followed and verified that safeguards existed to protect the company's assets. The auditors' workload was heavy and even though they were scheduled to visit each division each year, sometimes they were able to perform audits only on alternate years.

In the following sections, activities in two divisions—the Marine Hardware Division and the Consumer Hardware Division—are described to illustrate how division managers reacted to the additional profit pressures being passed to them from the corporate level.

MARINE HARDWARE DIVISION

The Lohnes Marine Hardware Co. was founded in 1954 by Paul Lohnes. Paul, an avid sailboat builder, reasoned that a full-service marine hardware and tooling business that provided special services for sailboaters could be very successful.

By 1963 the company was well established in New England. Paul had the knowledge, but lacked the financial resources, for a large expansion.

In the fall of 1963, Graves Industries acquired 100 percent interest in Lohnes Marine Hardware. As part of the acquisition agreement, Paul remained as president of the new Marine Hardware division, and his organization, personnel policies, and accounting systems remained as they were before the acquisition. (See organization chart in Exhibit 3.) The only additional procedures required were a formal capital appropriation request and a monthly reporting of financial results to headquarters for consolidation. Corporate staff monitored division results (primarily sales, profits, and asset control), and occasionally asked Paul or his controller for explanations of variances from budget. Paul felt almost no corporate interference in his operations as long as his division's results were at or above the company's long-term growth targets of 8 percent in sales and profits and its budgets were being achieved.

However, during his tenure with Graves Industries, Paul discovered that good performance, although well-rewarded, was soon forgotten during the next fiscal year. An excellent year tended to make the following year's goals even higher. High performance targets had not been much of a problem for the Marine Hardware Division because a booming boat market caused it to be consistently among Graves' best-performing divisions. The Marine Hardware Division's sales grew from $4.1 million in 1963 to $88.4 million in 1982—a compound growth rate of 17.5 percent. The division almost always met its budget targets.

Performance started to become more challenging in the 1980s, however. The division had suffered because of the 1979 oil crisis; starting in 1982 it had much more aggressive profitability goals because of the company's reallocation of resources toward the FMSD; and it faced a general business downturn in 1984.

1983 Activities In late January 1983, Paul Lohnes met with key members of his staff—Patti Allen (sales and marketing), Jack Nelan (production and purchasing) and Don O'Grady (controllers) to discuss some performance-related ideas. Don pointed out that 1982 had been a relatively good year; sales had reached $88.4 million, slightly in excess of the division's goal of $85 million. In addition, the division had been able to maintain relatively large reserves. But Paul was worried about future prospects. He wanted to have more control over his reported sales and profits, and he wanted to have "a few nuts stored away for a possibly bad winter."

Paul told his staff that when the division was having a good period he wanted to meet the assigned goals and then be very conservative in operations and accounting so as to have a good start on making the goals for the next period. For example, if the division was near its quarterly target, Paul suggested it would be good to declare a shipping moratorium for the last week or two of the quarter to shift some sales to the next quarter. He also suggested increasing the reserves taken against inventory, accounts receivable, and potential liabilities. He reminded his staff that they should be discreet. Even though none of these actions was illegal, he did not want to cause waves at headquarters.

The year 1983 proved to be surprisingly good, and by mid-March the division had exceeded its quarterly sales goal. Patti imposed a shipping moratorium for the last ten days of March, and $3.8 million in finished goods were held until the first days of April. Even though she understood the need to smooth earnings, Patti did complain to Don and Paul that complete halts in shipping caused problems with workload scheduling, product damage, and delayed deliveries to customers. Paul agreed there were costs associated with this shipment policy, but he felt they could be minimized. Don built the division's obsolescence, liability, and bad debt reserves by a total of $900,000.

1984 Activities The long-anticipated downturn came in 1984; sales were very sluggish for the first two quarters. Paul and Don were worried but took no action other than maintaining their pressure on Sales and Marketing. When the third quarter continued the slow trend, Don started to liquidate some of the reserves, and by the end of 1984, reserves were reduced by $1.8 million. The auditors questioned these changes in reserves, but Don and Paul gave them an explanation based on an analysis of changes in inventory composition and estimates of forthcoming bad debt losses and expenses. The auditors were skeptical, but they eventually concurred with the changes.

Another big step taken by the division was the establishment of the Early Order Program for distributors and larger boat builders. Those who ordered early (e.g., the end of 1984 instead of early 1985) received large discounts. This program also provided liberal credit terms: No payments were due for 90 days, and no late-payment penalties were assessed until at least 120 days after receipt of the shipment. Some of the more aggressive salespeople told their clients to "order the stuff now and don't worry about any payment dates; just pay us when you sell it, and you get to pocket the extra margin." Although these terms were never formally sanctioned, a flurry of fourth-quarter sales brought the year-end results just above the budgeted goal of $108.0 million.

1985 Activities The first quarter of 1985 was slow due to all of the Early Orders that were placed in 1984. But by the middle of the second quarter, sales had picked up and were soon roaring along. In fact, third-quarter results were so good that $4.7 million had to be *transferred* to the fourth quarter, and the Early Order Program of 1984 was suspended.

By the end of 1985, the company had not only passed all required goals, it had a $10.4 million start on 1986 revenues and had restored $2.2 million in reserves. Once again the changing of the reserves was questioned, but the auditors accepted Don's explanation of *wanting to be conservative.*

Concern for the Future In January 1986, Don reviewed the financial results for 1985. It was another record year: Sales were up 12 percent and operating profits had increased 13 percent (see Exhibit 4). Don knew that Paul Lohnes would be very happy to see that the final profit figures were a couple of million dollars above budget. The company was also well positioned for a big jump on 1986's budgeted goals.

Don worried where all the smoothing of earnings would lead, however. The distress of 1994 reinforced in his mind the advice he had received early in his career, that "Only a fool does not have reserves salted away for rainy days." But now Don wondered if the division's reserves went beyond the bounds of reasonableness. He had hoped the earnings management would cease, but the financial demands from the FMSD were growing, and he expected corporate to start pressing all of the other divisions even more. Don also knew that Paul and Patti were already discussing new ways to smooth income. He wondered what he should do and whom he could speak to about this sensitive matter.

CONSUMER HARDWARE DIVISION

Graves Industries' Consumer Hardware division was founded in 1946. The division started out producing simple home tools, and eventually moved into producing a wide variety of high-quality tools and hardware. The Consumer Hardware division experienced slow, steady growth until the mid-1950s, when Henry Graves took over as divisional president. Henry expanded the product line and the distribution system. For the next 12 years the division enjoyed revenue growth at a compound annual rate of 11 percent.

In 1986 Henry was promoted to CEO. Leo Gladue, who had worked for the Graves for 22 years in the Industrial and Consumer Hardware divisions, was appointed as the Consumer Hardware division president. Leo was well regarded for his technical knowledge and his ability to get along with the distributors, but his knowledge of finance and accounting was considered relatively weak.

In the late 1970s and early 1980s, the division's growth began to slow. Sales targets were getting harder to reach, and the startup of the FMS division only compounded the problem as the Consumer Hardware division was expected to continue to achieve Graves' long-term growth target of 8 percent per year.

The Consumer Hardware division sold its goods to distributors who took title as soon as the orders were shipped. No goods were put on consignment, so sales revenue was recognized as soon as the goods were loaded on a truck. As was the industry standard, the Consumer Hardware division did offer large discounts for distributors who placed large orders early and used a wide variety of seasonal promotions as needed to stimulate sales.

Every now and then the Consumer Hardware division had been known to load some of the trucks in their fleet at the end of a fiscal period to generate *sales in place.* The loaded trucks would move a short distance away from the loading dock and park until it was time to make their deliveries.

1984 Activities The year 1984 was difficult for the Consumer Hardware division; the economy was slow and interest rates were high—the worst combination for a hardware and tool business. As midyear approached and predictions for the annual totals did not look good, Leo applied additional pressure to the Sales and Marketing department to *get more orders.* Sales and Marketing responded with a plan that they implemented but kept secret for a long time. Tim Bonsaint and John Ahern were the only senior managers to know about the plan in 1984. (See Exhibit 5 for an organizational chart.)

The Consumer Hardware division used approximately 30 distributors, but 8 of them generated 75 percent of Graves' business. Tim and John's plan was to ship additional, unordered products to the large distributors; these unordered shipments would be rotated among the large distributors and sent out along with their regular orders near the end of the month. These extra shipments would then be recorded as revenues. Four methods were used to cause the unordered product to be shipped including: (1) reentering a previously entered order; (2) doubling, tripling, or otherwise increasing the amount of product actually ordered; (3) creating fictitious orders on behalf of the distributors; and (4) shipping an unordered product when the product ordered was not in stock.

Once the unordered shipments were delivered, steps were taken to keep the goods from being returned or at least to delay their return. Overshipments were blamed on administrative and computer errors, and salespeople were directed to *make the sale stick* by (1) offering special prices or credit terms, (2) exchanging the goods for other Consumer Hardware division goods, (3) storing the goods (at Graves' expense) until needed, (4) arranging trades between distributors, and (5) ignoring the distributors' attempts to return the goods until the distributor had time to *digest* the shipment.

This plan worked rather well; even though the amount of *returned goods* increased, the net effect was to increase revenues by $2.8 million and operating profit by $600,000.

1985 Activities Leo knew that possibly a lot more than just his bonus was riding on making the division's assigned goals for 1985. Leo had argued that with a slow economy the division could only expect growth of 3 to 4 percent in 1985, but Henry Graves insisted that growth of at least 8 percent was possible. (See Exhibit 6 for financial results and budgets for 1982–85.)

Leo Gladue, unaware of Tim and John's scheme, scheduled a meeting for the second week in January 1985. He wanted his management team to review 1984 and started planning on where to come up with the additional sales required under the new budget. The financial officer, John Ahern, reported that the 1994 sales results had just come in over budget. Operating profits were close to budget, and after a few journal entries were made to reduce June reserves held against inventories and receivables, the operating profit and RONA targets would be met.

The next item on the agenda, the most important one, involved identifying new sources of revenues and cost savings that would make it possible to meet the new budget. The discussion went on for hours, but there were no clear solutions.

In the following week, the Sales and Marketing department decided to expand the overshipment program started at the end of 1984, and they decided not to tell Leo about the specifics of the program. Tim Bonsaint, the head of Sales and Marketing, just promised Leo that through "selective discounts and promotions we will increase the average order size of our largest distributors." The actual size of the overshipments was to be carefully controlled by Tim, using forecasts of actual quarterly and annual sales.

The Production and Purchasing department could do little to help with new revenues, but its manager, Kimberly Colson, knew she could have a large impact on controlling the expenses of the company's contracts with its suppliers. Some of Graves' suppliers sold both machines and parts to the division, and it was possible to alter contracts to adjust the amount of the expenditure to be capitalized. For example, Graves had a contract with the Riley Machine Company for $500,000; $200,000 of this amount was for two new ratchet machines, and the rest of the money was for 50,000 ratchet assemblies. By having Riley change the invoices to indicate that $300,000 was for the two machines, the price of the individual ratchet assemblies would drop by 33 percent. The extra $100,000 could be capitalized (and expensed over the life of the machines), and the immediate effect was an increase in profit.

Kim knew many variations on this scheme, such as adding a special *tooling charge* to the reduced base price of the ratchet. This tooling charge could be capitalized by the Consumer Hardware division, the price of the machines would not have to be changed, and Graves would still get the ratchets at the reduced price. And by mixing methods, no clear pattern would emerge. Such a system could easily be run by Kim and a few of her purchasing people, so she told Leo only that by putting pressure on suppliers, she had negotiated some price reductions on components.

The year 1985 was slow, and the Consumer Hardware division struggled; but with the assistance of the two special programs, it was able to meet its quarterly budget targets. Managers in the Sales and Marketing department projected that by the end of the year they would have *overshipped* (after returns) a total of $8.9 million in goods that increase operating profits by $1.8 million. And Production and Purchasing managers were able to negotiate contracts that reduced current expenses by $2.7 million ($2.2 million after depreciation). Not all of this went completely unnoticed, however. Toward the end of the year Leo started to ask questions about the higher-than-normal level of returns, complaints from distributors, and capital expenditures.

The auditors also noticed. In the first week of December, Roger Sexauer, the manager assigned to the Graves Industries audit, received a phone call from Don Hubbard, the senior assigned to the audit of the Consumer Hardware and Automotive divisions of Graves Industries. The conversation went approximately as follows:

ROGER: Hello, Don. What can I do for you?

DON: I am calling in regard to the Consumer Hardware Division audit. I have come across some unusual transactions, and I can't seem to get any reasonable answers from the company staff.

ROGER: What's the problem?

DON: One of my staff accountants was performing a review of capital expenditures for this past year and found some things that didn't seem right, such as large price hikes in what appears to be standard equipment for this division and an unusually large total of *tooling charges* and *tooling premiums.*

ROGER: Have you investigated the reason? Perhaps the equipment has been specially modified and, as a result, costs more. Also, this division has always had *tooling charges.* For any special product they want produced they help the supplier pay for the modifications to his equipment. Since this is a capital improvement they can capitalize the portion that they pay for.

DON: I know that, but I have checked a lot of this equipment myself and it all looks to be the same as the ones bought previously. When I ask people in Purchasing, they don't have a good answer. They say the differences are caused by inflation or some kind of internal modification. Now, as to the tooling charges, in 1984 they totaled $147,000. This year, through November, they total over $400,000.

ROGER: That is a sharp increase. Perhaps they have made modifications to the parts in question and the supplier has billed them to cover his fixed investment.

DON: I don't think so because the parts do not look like they have changed. However, this leads me to what I think is the heart of the matter. Do you remember when we asked Kim Colson about the decrease in price on some of the parts they were purchasing?

ROGER: Yes I do, and if I remember correctly, she said that since Graves had become such a large buyer for the output of some of their suppliers she was able to negotiate large discounts. Also, she said something to the effect that the suppliers had made so many of the items that their cost of production per item had gone down significantly.

DON: That's right. But when you stand back and look at the whole situation, the suppliers that gave them the large discounts on parts are the same ones that either raised their prices on capital equipment and/or are charging them for tooling charges.

ROGER: Now I see the picture. This is either an incredible coincidence or there is a systematic plan to capitalize current expenses and overstate profits.

Don estimated the total impact of the scheme to be about $1.7 million to $1.9 million, but it could be higher. So far, this equated to about 4 to 5 percent of the division's net income. Roger told Don to continue with the audit, but be extra careful. Roger said that he would talk to Harvey Krantz [the partner assigned to the Graves audit]. Roger told Don not to say anything to anyone at the company in the meantime. Roger thought about what Harvey would do if his suspicions were correct. The amount of money involved so far was large for the division, but perhaps immaterial from the standpoint of the entire company.

In the middle of December, Tim and John, after concluding that it was going to be virtually impossible to meet the 1985 targets and that it was increasingly difficult to keep their scheme going, decided they had better be honest with Leo. They were sure that with his support they could lay out a convincing story for the events of 1985 and get the auditors off their back. Kim also explained what she had been doing. As their stories came out, Leo sat dumbfounded. He began to wonder if something else could be done. Or should he just inform corporate headquarters? Or the internal or external auditors?

EXHIBIT 1 Consolidated Income Statements for Years Ending December 31 ($ millions)

	1981	*1982*	*1983*	*1984*	*1985*
Revenue	$476.3	$524.9	$580.0	$640.9	$708.2
Cost of sales	319.1	351.7	388.6	429.4	460.3
Gross margin	$157.2	$173.2	$191.4	$211.5	$247.9
R&D expense	20.2	31.0	36.0	44.0	58.3
SG&A expense	56.6	62.0	68.2	74.8	82.2
Operating profit	$80.4	$80.2	$87.2	$92.7	$107.4
Corporate expense	11.9	13.1	14.5	16.0	17.7
Interest expense	7.0	7.0	9.0	9.0	9.0
Profit before tax	$61.5	$60.1	$63.7	$67.7	$80.7
Income tax	28.3	27.6	29.3	31.1	37.1
Net income	$33.2	$32.5	$34.4	$36.6	$43.6

Source: Corporate records.

EXHIBIT 2 Corporate Organizational Chart

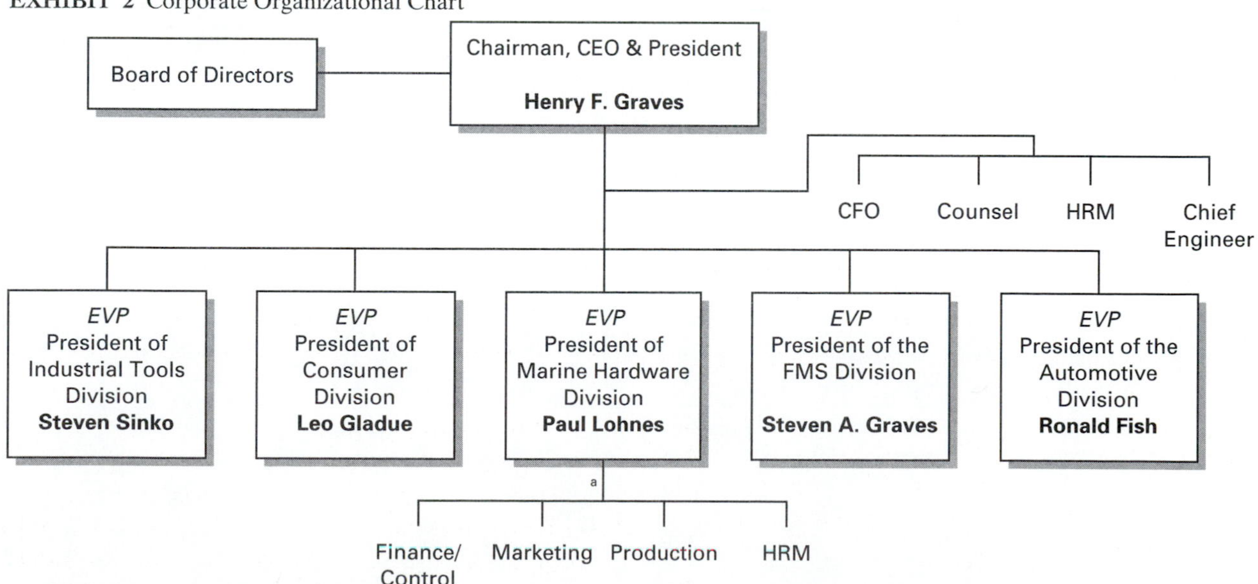

Source: Corporate records.
[a]Each division had a staff similar to the Marine Division.

EXHIBIT 3 Marine Hardware Division Organizational Chart

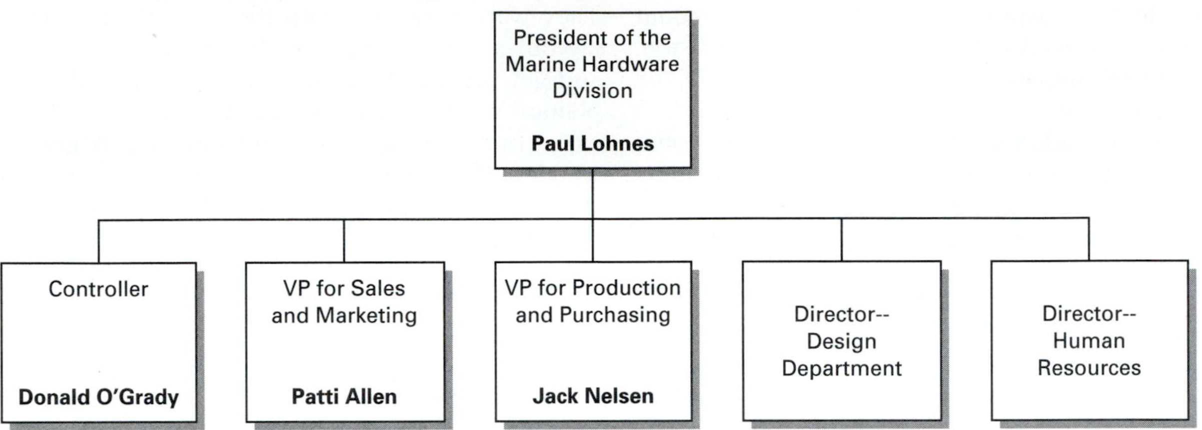

Source: Corporate records.

EXHIBIT 4 Marine Hardware Division, Divisional Income and Budget Statements for Fiscal Years Ending 30 December ($ millions)

	1982		*1983*		*1984*		*1985*	
	Budget	*Actual*	*Budget*	*Actual*	*Budget*	*Actual*	*Budget*	*Actual*
Revenue	$85.0	$99.4	$96.0	$99.1	$108.0	$109.2	$119.0	$122.2
Cost of sales	55.7	57.5	62.4	64.4	71.8	72.9	77.4	79.4
Gross margin	$29.3	$30.9	$33.6	$34.7	$ 36.2	$ 36.3	$ 41.6	$ 42.8
R&D expense	0.6	0.6	0.8	0.8	0.8	0.8	0.8	0.8
SG&A expense	10.8	10.9	11.2	12.1	11.8	11.3	14.0	14.8
Operating profit	$17.9	$19.4	$21.6	$21.8	$ 23.6	$ 24.2	$ 26.8	$ 27.2

Source: Corporate records.

EXHIBIT 5 Consumer Hardware Division Organizational Chart

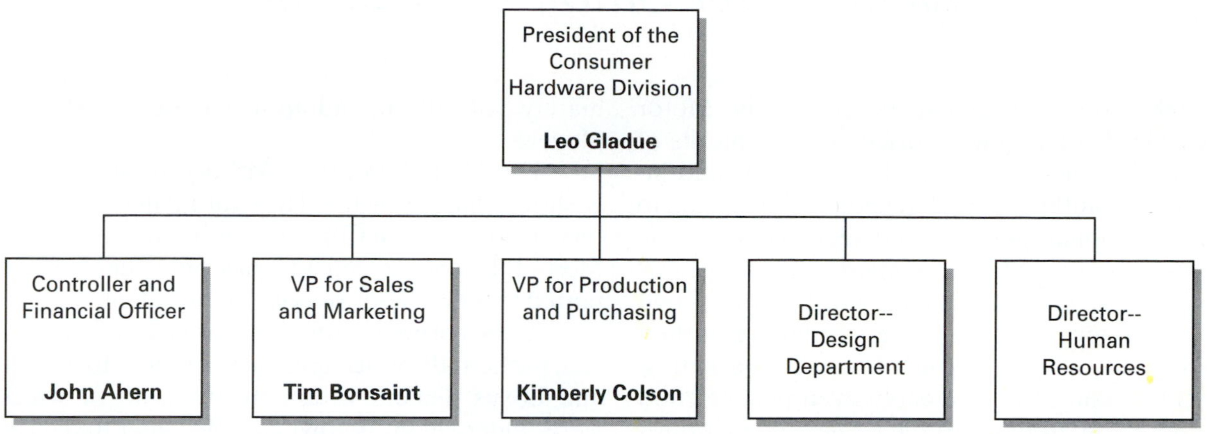

Source: Corporate records.

EXHIBIT 6 Consumer Hardware Division, Income and Budget Statements, 30 December 1985 ($ millions)

	1982		*1983*		*1984*		*1985*	
	Budget	*Actual*	*Budget*	*Actual*	*Budget*	*Actual*	*Budget*	*Actual*
Revenue	$125.0	$127.5	$139.0	$140.3	$153.5	$154.3	$168.0	
Cost of sales	80.0	81.6	89.0	89.2	98.2	98.3	107.5	
Gross margin	$ 45.0	$ 45.9	$ 50.0	$ 51.1	$ 55.3	$ 56.0	$ 60.5	
R&D expense	1.1	1.1	1.3	1.3	1.4	1.4	1.5	
SG&A expense	15.2	15.1	16.4	16.2	17.9	18.5	20.6	
Operating profit	$ 28.7	$ 29.6	$ 32.3	$ 33.6	$ 36.0	$ 36.1	$ 38.4	

Source: Corporate records.

Toyota Motor Sales, U.S.A., Inc.

In 1991, top-level managers at Toyota Motor Sales, U.S.A. (TMS) were discussing the merits of a significant organizational change that would increase the authority and responsibility given to TMS's regional general managers (GMs). The proponents for change argued that the GMs should be given authority for most of the activities that determined the success or failure of their region. The activities included finance, marketing, human resources, and possibly even port-of-entry operations, in addition to the dealer-support functions they already had. If these changes were made, then it would make sense to evaluate the GMs in terms of profit, rather than primarily sales.

Opponents of the change, however, feared that a profit target would force the regional GM's to focus excessively on short term profit and sacrifice TMS's goals of growth in the U.S. market and long term commitment to customers. They were also afraid that the regional managers were experienced with sales-related functions but lacked some of the experience necessary to fill a profit center manager's role effectively.

THE COMPANY

TMS was a wholly-owned subsidiary of Toyota Motor Corporation of Japan (TMC), the third largest automobile manufacturer in the world (after General Motors and Ford). TMS was founded in 1957 to operate as TMC's U.S. marketing and sales organization. TMS bought vehicles from TMC manufacturing plants in Japan (and, later, when plants were established, in the United States and Canada), sold them to Toyota dealers within the U.S., and helped the dealers sell them to customers. In 1990, TMS was the largest seller of import cars and trucks in the U.S., with sales of over one million units (market share of 7.6 percent), revenues of approximately $14 billion, and approximately 5,000 employees.[1]

Exhibit 1 shows the TMS organization chart. It shows that all of the TMS car-related functions reported to Bob McCurry, executive vice president. Most of the finance and administrative functions reported to Yale Gieszl, senior vice president.

TMS's primary function was to provide vehicles, parts, and service and sales support to Toyota and Lexus dealers within the U.S., all of which were independently owned and operated. The support for the 1,200 Toyota dealers was provided by nine regional offices and three distributorships with which TMS had contracts.[2] The nine regional offices, which were operated under a wholly owned TMS subsidiary, Toyota Motor Distributors (TMD), were located in the metropolitan areas of Portland (Oregon), San Francisco, Los Angeles, Denver, Kansas City, Chicago, Cincinnati, New York, and Boston. The three distributorships were Gulf States Toyota (Houston), Southeast Toyota (Deerfield Beach, Florida), and Central Atlantic Toyota (Baltimore) (see Exhibit 2). Gulf States Toyota and Southeast Toyota were privately owned distributors. Central Atlantic Toyota (CAT) was formerly a privately owned distributor that TMS acquired in 1990.

THE REGIONAL GENERAL MANAGER ROLE

The TMD regional GMs, who reported to Al Wagner (group vice president, Toyota Sales), had three primary responsibilities. First, they were re-

---

[1]In North America, TMC also operated manufacturing facilities, located in California, Kentucky, and Canada; technology centers, located in Michigan and California; and a design center located in California. These entities were not part of TMS's operations.

[2]Operations in Hawaii were contracted to an outside corporation which was not affiliated with TMS. Sales of Lexus vehicles were coordinated through four area offices reporting to the Group Vice President, Lexus Sales.

Research Assistant Patrick Henry and Professor Kenneth A. Merchant wrote this case as the basis for class discussion rather than to illustrate either effective or ineffective handling of an administrative situation.

sponsible for all dealer-related activities in their regions, which included retail vehicle sales, parts sales, and service. Second, they were responsible for supervising, training, and evaluating their employees. The regions employed between 40 and 70 employees, including field travelers (sales representatives), staff personnel, and regional management. (Exhibit 3 shows an organization chart for a representative region.) And third, they were responsible for achieving sales penetration, customer satisfaction, and operating budget objectives. A typical region had an annual operating budget of $12–16 million dollars. The regional operating budget was not a significant expense from the corporate standpoint because the amounts were small as compared with the national promotional budget, but expense control was still considered an integral part of the regional GMs' job.

The ways in which the regional GMs allocated their time varied significantly depending, for example, on their management style, the size of the region, the market conditions, and the quality of the regional dealer network. However, dealer-related activities, particularly involving new retail car and truck sales, usually took precedence over the GM's other roles. Most GM's spent more than 50 percent of their time on dealer-related matters, such as assisting in designing sales programs and improving dealer operations. According to Al Wagner, the group vice president for Toyota sales, regional GMs had to be *cheerleaders* in good economic times and *firefighters* in bad economic times. He explained that cheerleaders motivate and inspire their people and those of their dealers, while a firefighter attacks problems. The biggest potential problem in the firefighting role was dealer cash flow. Dealers financed their own inventories, and if sales were down, it was difficult to make interest payments. In bad economic times, this lack of cash could put dealers out of business and cause fewer Toyotas to be sold.

SALES FORECASTS AND PLANS

Accurate sales forecasts by car line/by region were important because Toyota vehicles were earmarked for a specific U.S. region on the production floor. Sales forecasts were prepared as part of Toyota's two formal planning processes: The first resulted in the preparation of a strategic plan with a horizon of five years or longer. The second produced an annual sales and profit plan.

The *strategic planning* process began with managers in TMS's Strategic and Product Planning Department making a prediction of the future automobile market segments. They based these predictions on demographic information, knowledge of forthcoming governmental regulations, and estimates of competitor plans, such as for model changes and new introductions. Second, they selected the segments in which TMS wanted to participate. And finally, they worked with TMC in Japan to formulate plans for the design of new models. (All production mix decisions were negotiated with Japan.) The strategic plan was reviewed in detail by TMS's board of directors.

The *annual planning* process involved several steps. First, TMS managers prepared a target for total unit sales and market share in the next year. This target, which was set by the end of July, was based on total market size estimates prepared by TMS corporate staff planners. Second, managers in the TMS Sales Administration and Marketing Departments developed a sales plan designed to achieve the unit sales target. They looked for growth areas among the models offered in their product lines and established pricing and incentive policies and advertising and promotion programs designed to effect the desired sales growth. They prepared sales projections by car line, region, and month.

The regional managers were not greatly involved in the sales planning process for two basic reasons. Some of the planning could be done more efficiently at the TMS level because vehicle sales were greatly affected by broad macroeconomic factors, seasonality, and corporate marketing plans that tended to influence all regions roughly equally. And the accuracy of the regional managers' plans had been found to be inconsistent in the past.

The third element in the annual planning process involved preparation of an expense budget. This budget, which was prepared by regional personnel based mostly from history, and the sales projections were reviewed by corporate and regional managers in a series of meetings held in August and September. The TMS plans were then sent to Japan at the end of September for comparison with sales plans that had been prepared by TMC corporate managers. Differences were ironed out, and TMC managers sent a revised, detailed sales plan to TMS managers in October. During the year, TMS managers updated their plans quarterly to reflect changes in market conditions and strategies.

CONSTANT PRODUCTION RATE POLICY

TMC had a policy of maintaining steady production rates in its manufacturing operations. This policy was established because it provided greater and more efficient utilization of fixed asset and labor resources and eased the suppliers' scheduling problems. TMC, like most large Japanese companies, offered its employees lifetime employment. This meant that labor costs were fixed, for all practical purposes: TMC did not lay off full-time employees even when sales were slow. In addition, TMC had to support its supplier network with a consistent demand schedule. TMC relied heavily on its supplier network because TMC's plants operated a just-in-time (JIT) or *kanban* inventory system, and these systems required reliable sources of supply. TMC had an extensive supplier network in Japan that required long lead times to supply some parts, and many of these companies depended on TMC for their survival. Constant production rates greatly facilitated their ability to meet TMC's needs.

ALLOCATION OF AUTOMOBILES TO REGIONS

TMC plants required a four-month vehicle order forecast lead time. The four months were necessary to allow the preparation of orders to its suppliers and the establishment and completion of the production schedules. Production of a particular grade could be shifted only very little in a three-month time frame. A major shift in production could take up to eight months.

One month before TMC plants shipped the completed vehicles, TMS would give the plant managers a firm order based on the current market conditions. If the four-month forecast was significantly incorrect, TMC might not be able to satisfy the revised order mix. The TMC system did not allow for redistribution of units among the regions after the order was placed. The regions could trade vehicles with each other after arrival at the ports, but this was rarely done because of the expense involved.

The assembled vehicles were shipped to one of the U.S. ports of entry. The port operations reported to H. Imai, group vice president, manufacturing liaison and distribution. When the cars reached the port, port personnel took them off the ship, added a window label and perhaps some accessories that had been ordered by the dealer but that the dealer did not want to install (e.g., roof rack), washed them, and loaded them on trucks or trains for shipment to the dealer. The ports were cost centers. Port personnel were responsible for maintaining good facilities, shipping vehicles on a timely basis, and minimizing labor costs (particularly overtime), port storage charges, and yard damage to the vehicles.

TMS managers were working with TMC plant managers to provide greater vehicle ordering flexibility. They wanted the plants to allow the shifting of the following month's production plus or minus 10 percent five days before the start of the month. This would allow the changing of August production on July 25. TMS managers were also lobbying to reduce the four-month required lead time to three months.

DEALER INCENTIVES

Like most automobile manufacturers, Toyota used dealer incentives to help sell the vehicles that had been allocated to the regions. TMS offered its dealers incentives for achieving predetermined sales volume targets by car line, and sometimes by grade (e.g., a 4-door model only). The incentives were primarily in the form of cash paid to the dealership, but sometimes cash or incentive trips were given to individual dealer salespeople or sales managers. In 1990, the total cost of the Toyota dealer incentive program in the U.S. was approximately $250 million, or about $250 per vehicle sold. The incentive programs were generally run on a 60-day cycle. Thus, there was a January/February program, a March/April program, and so on.

Most national dealer incentive programs were tiered. Here is a hypothetical example of such a program:

The Joe Jones Toyota dealership has a TMS-set target to sell 40 pickup trucks in July/August. The incentives promised the dealership are tiered, with greater unit incentives provided at higher sales levels.

PICKUPS SOLD	INCENTIVE/VEHICLE
1–24	$250
25–32	350
33–40	450
over 40	550

Toyota, and other car manufacturers, also frequently offered *fast start* incentives. Such incentives might be provided as follows:

> The Joe Jones Toyota dealership has a 60-day incentive to sell 40 pickups. If it sells 16 pickups in the first 30 days of the incentive program, then the dealer gets an additional $100 for each pickup sold in the second 30 days of the program.

Starting in 1991, TMS managers gave regional GMs the authority to allocate about $75 per vehicle in dealer incentives as they wished. These regionalized incentives were expected to total about $70 million, slightly over 30 percent of the total dealer incentive money budgeted for 1991. This change was made to allow the regional general managers to enhance the national incentive programs or to structure their own regional incentive programs to respond to local conditions (e.g., to move particular slow moving products).

The regional general managers liked having some authority over dealer incentives. For example, Bob Weldon, GM of the Cincinnati region, explained:

> In the June/July period, the national incentive program focused on trucks. But our dealers were overstocked on Camrys, so we put extra incentives on Camry sales. It worked. We had two very strong sales months, and we are now ready for the transition to the new model year. The dealers made money, and we are in a good position.

EVALUATION OF REGIONAL GENERAL MANAGERS

The nine regional GMs were evaluated by Al Wagner. Al's evaluations were often subjective, coming as a result of judgments made throughout the year based on Al's observations of the operation of the region.

Al did have access to considerable quantitative data that he could use to help him make his evaluations, however. For example, Exhibit 4 shows the Sales and Stock Summary report for June 1991 for each of the 12 sales areas and TMS in total (listed across the top). This report provided detail on car and truck sales, and it ranked the regions according to their percentage achievement of their retail sales objectives. Exhibit 5 shows a summary of various customer satisfaction indices for June 1991 and year-to-date. Exhibits 6 and 7 provide regional budget reports showing actual sales and expenses compared to plan and supporting details about the expenses. Monthly, Al also had full access to dealer records.

Only the expense line-items shown with an asterisk on Exhibit 7 were deemed controllable by the GMs. Some other expenses were not even allocated to the regional level. These included a LIFO inventory provision, the costs of employee benefits (e.g., group insurance, bonuses), some advertising and promotional costs (e.g., regional contributions to Toyota dealer associations, fleet incentives), and TMS administrative expenses.

Al said that he tended to evaluate the GMs in terms of four primary criteria: total unit sales, market penetration, customer satisfaction, and dealer profit. He did not like to rank the regions' performances against each other. He preferred to rate the managers as compared with their own region's history. He said,

> I don't like rankings. I dropped all rankings when I took this job. How can I compare a manager in Boston with one in Los Angeles? I cannot come up with meaningful, equal targets. And, furthermore, I don't want Boston to worry about what Los Angeles is doing.

GMs earned performance bonuses annually, but at mid-year they were paid an advance of approximately 45 percent of their projected bonus for the year. In a typical year, the highest performing regional manager would earn a bonus of approximately 25 percent of salary, while the lowest performing manager's bonus would be approximately ⅔ that amount. The bonus amounts varied somewhat depending on the manager's salary grade and TMS's sales and profit performance for the year but, according to Yale Gieszl, Toyota's bonus awards were "not as volatile as those in a typical U.S. car company which tend to be feast or famine." In recent years, the total bonus awards had varied only slightly from *normal,* because of TMS's overall performance.

Al Wagner did not think the link between performance and bonuses caused Toyota to attract people with any less talent. He said:

> People have gratifications other than money. After a few years, the other things become more important. For example, we give our people recognition and a sense of participation in what we're doing. Once a month we have a sales meeting with the GMs. They make a report and can talk all they want to the president and other executives in the company. That doesn't happen at General Motors, Ford, or Chrysler. It's a whole different climate here. That may sound corny, but it's very real. There are 50–60 people in the room. It means a lot.

THE CENTRAL ATLANTIC TOYOTA EXPERIMENT

As an experiment, TMS management was giving the management of Central Atlantic Toyota (CAT) more autonomy and operating flexibility than it allowed the nine TMD regional managers. CAT's operations were different from those of the TMD regions in three primary ways. First, CAT had its own finance, marketing, information systems, human resources, and port processing departments. Second, CAT managers had a profit plan and was thus more accountable for all of its costs than were the regional managers. And third, CAT's manager was given the title of subsidiary president. As a consequence the eight-member TMS executive committee, rather than the group vice president of sales, evaluated his performance. In effect, CAT was a hybrid between a TMD region and a private distributor.

This experiment seemed to have noticeable effects on the attitudes of CAT's management team. Dennis Clements, CAT's president/GM believed that he had more of a bottom-line mentality than when he was at GM. He said, "As president of CAT, I am always thinking of the financial implications of what goes on. For example, now when I leave a meeting, I turn out the lights because I know the costs have an effect on profitability."

A PROPOSAL FOR CHANGE

Some TMS managers believed that the regions should be made more like CAT. They wanted to give the regional GMs more authority and bottom-line (profit-and-loss) responsibility. They worried about the growing bureaucracy at TMS headquarters, and they believed that making the regions profit centers was a logical way to get the company to respond more quickly and more reliably to local market conditions. By making the regions into profit centers, these managers felt that the regional GM's could affect TMS profits and that the managers should be made aware of the costs and trade-offs associated with various administrative functions (e.g., finance, marketing, human resources) and port functions (e.g., work scheduling, accessorizing). They also believed that the current set of regional GM's was capable of balancing the necessary priorities and that making the regions into profit centers would further develop the GMs' managerial abilities. Yale Gieszl believed that, "They will step up to the challenge."

Other TMS corporate managers, however, argued that the regional managers should not have profit responsibility. Some believed that the profit measure would discount the importance of the other performance measures. Some feared that a profit target would force the regional GM's to focus excessively on short term profit and sacrifice TMS's goals of growth in the U.S. market and long term commitment to customers. Some believed that the change would cause significant operating and accounting issues. These managers pointed out that port operations would be a particular problem because the relationship between a port and a sales region was rarely one-to-one. For example, the Long Beach port facilities provided Toyotas to both the Los Angeles and Denver regions and Lexus automobiles to 70 percent of the U.S. Some opposing managers were also afraid that the regional managers were not capable of broader responsibilities. They noted that these managers were experienced with sales-related functions but might lack some of the experience necessary to assume a broader role. And finally some managers noted that the CAT experiment had not necessarily proven to be a success: Eight out of nine TMD regions had a higher share of the imported car market than did CAT during the 1991 recession.

Everybody agreed that a certain amount of decentralization to the regions was good and that the establishment of regionalized dealer incentives was a positive step. The remaining question was, as one manager put it, "When do you have too much of a good thing?" Some cynics also noted that even if more decentralization was desirable, they doubted that top management would be willing to let go since they had operated so long with centralized control.

EXHIBIT 1 Toyota Motor Sales—Organization Structure

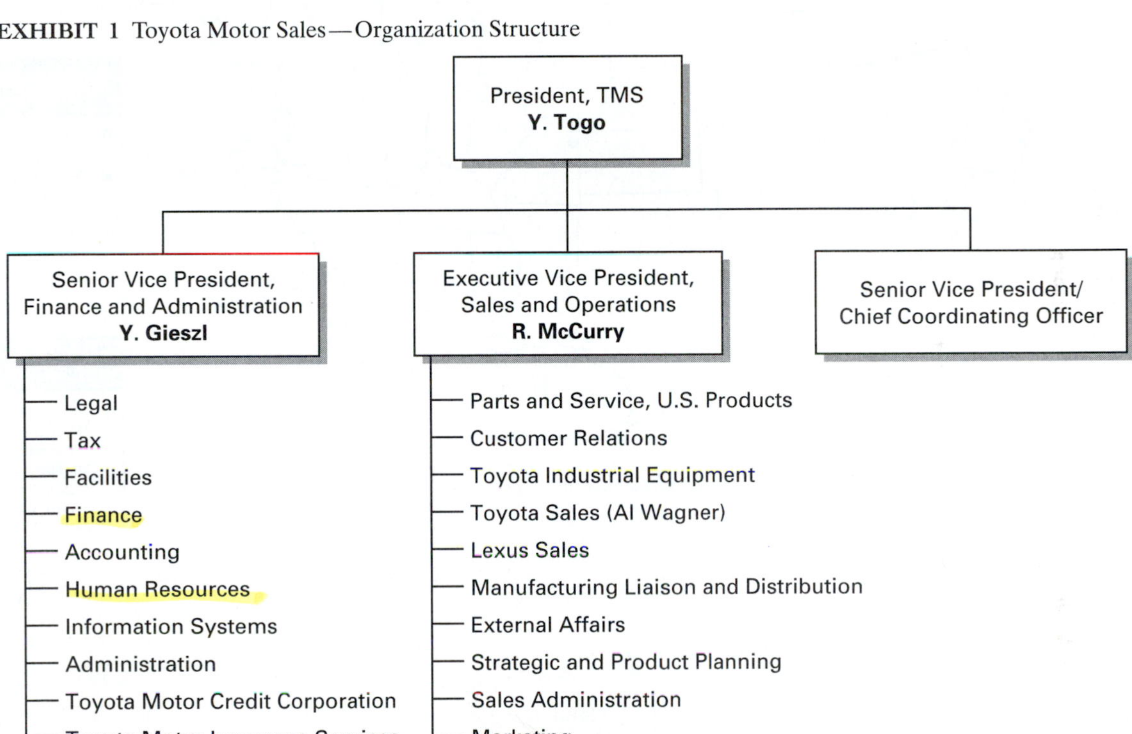

EXHIBIT 2 Location of TMS Facilities

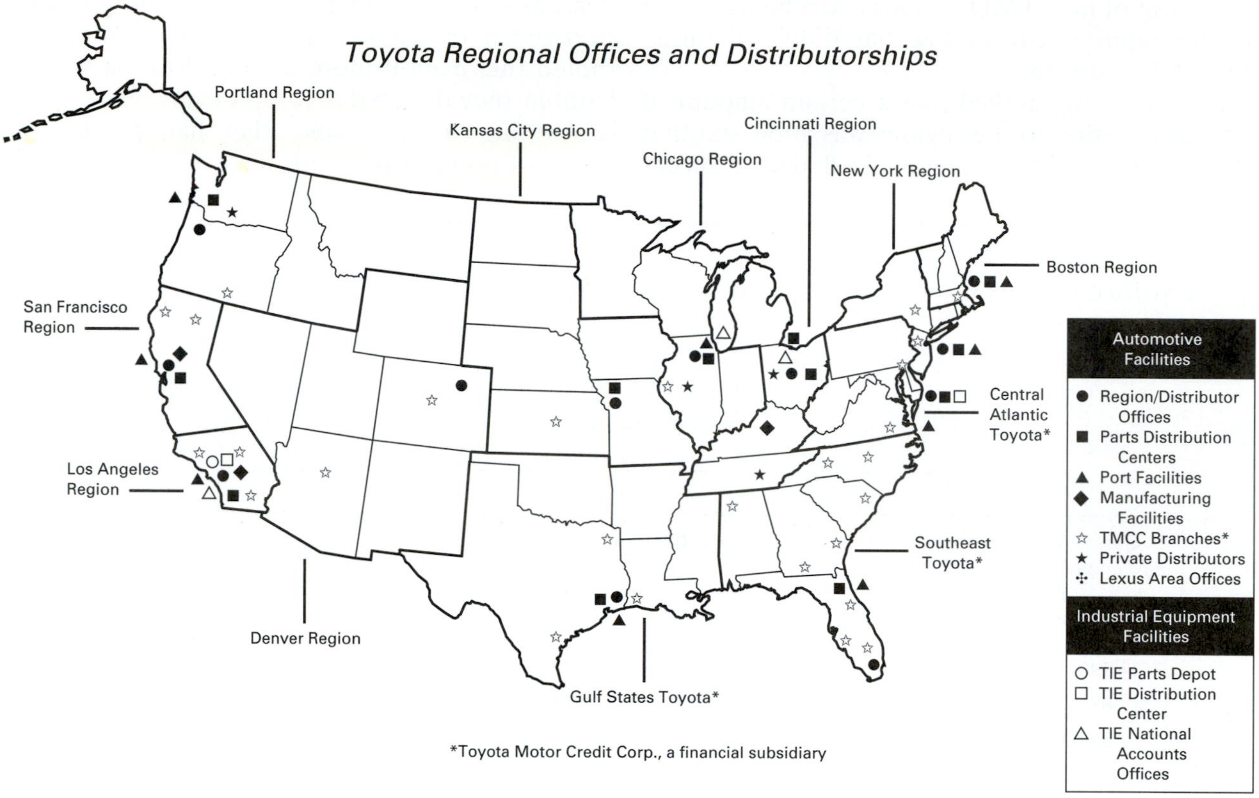

Toyota Regional Offices and Distributorships

Portland Region
Kansas City Region
Cincinnati Region
Chicago Region
New York Region
Boston Region
San Francisco Region
Central Atlantic Toyota*
Los Angeles Region
Southeast Toyota*
Denver Region
Gulf States Toyota*

*Toyota Motor Credit Corp., a financial subsidiary

Automotive Facilities

- ● Region/Distributor Offices
- ■ Parts Distribution Centers
- ▲ Port Facilities
- ◆ Manufacturing Facilities
- ☆ TMCC Branches*
- ★ Private Distributors
- ✣ Lexus Area Offices

Industrial Equipment Facilities

- ○ TIE Parts Depot
- □ TIE Distribution Center
- △ TIE National Accounts Offices

EXHIBIT 3 Representative Regional Organization Structure

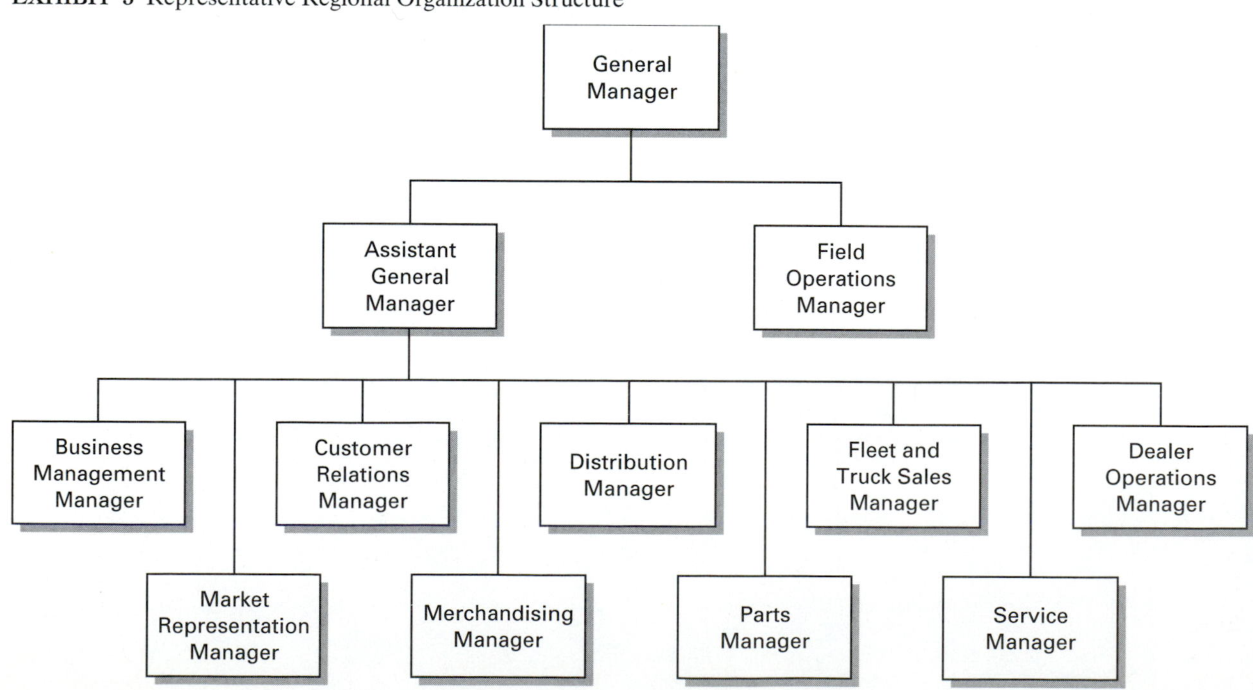

EXHIBIT 4 Sales and Stock Summary

V539DX-T10885										07/02/91 100.00 PERCENT OF MONTH REPORTED				
**** *Total Car* ****	*BOS*	*CHI*	*PTL*	*S.F.*	*N.Y.*	*CINN*	*K.C.*	*DEN*	*L.A.*	*SET*	*GST*	*CAT*	*190th*	*USA*
Daily Retail Sales	563	957	271	329	1,296	1,059	460	324	655	601	630	1,182	0	8,327
MTD Retail Sales	3,033	5,279	2,139	3,811	8,305	6,094	2,183	2,576	6,708	7,735	4,769	6,877	113	59,622
Retail Objective	2,950	4,510	2,110	3,920	8,080	5,260	1,870	2,290	7,200	7,020	4,470	5,520	0	55,200
% Retail Objective	102.8	117.1	101.4	97.2	102.8	115.9	116.7	112.5	93.2	110.2	106.7	124.6	.0	108.0
% OBJ. rank in USA	8	2	10	11	9	4	3	5	12	6	7	1		
Retail Dealer Stock	4,580	7,164	4,241	6,777	11,253	8,530	3,447	4,442	9,358	12,573	9,430	9,755	92	91,642
Retail Days Supply	38	34	50	44	34	35	39	43	35	41	49	35	20	30
% Retail Sales/Avail	39.8	42.4	33.5	35.9	42.4	41.6	38.7	36.7	41.7	38.0	33.5	41.3	.0	39.4
MTD Total Sales	3,314	5,587	2,241	4,094	8,764	6,699	2,272	2,977	7,035	8,164	5,022	8,425	113	64,707
Total Objective	3,090	4,690	2,190	4,020	8,165	5,560	1,930	2,540	7,300	7,345	4,625	7,045	0	58,500
% Total Objective	107.2	119.1	102.3	101.8	107.3	120.5	117.7	117.2	96.4	111.2	108.6	119.6	.0	110.6
Memo: MTD Fleet (J)	281	308	102	283	459	605	89	401	327	429	253	1,548	0	5,085
Memo: Fleet Obj	140	180	80	100	85	300	60	250	100	325	155	1,525	0	3,300
Memo: % Fleet Obj	200.7	171.1	127.5	283.0	540.0	201.6	148.3	160.4	327.0	132.0	163.2	101.5	.0	154.0
**** Total Truck ****														
Daily Retail Sales	52	79	126	95	93	172	121	145	182	108	134	197	0	1,504
MTD Retail Sales	294	498	1,187	1,587	619	918	464	959	2,172	1,229	1,191	1,150	0	12,268
Retail Objective	370	700	1,050	1,570	800	910	420	900	2,190	1,490	1,059	1,050	0	12,500
% Retail Objective	79.5	71.1	113.0	101.1	77.4	100.9	110.5	106.6	99.2	82.5	113.4	109.5	.0	98.1
% Obj. Rank in USA	10	12	2	6	11	7	3	5	8	9	1	4		
Retail Dealer Stock	631	1,132	1,880	2,507	1,693	1,271	657	1,557	3,393	2,563	1,571	2,027	41	20,923
Retail Days Supply	54	57	40	39	68	35	35	41	39	52	33	44	0	43
% Retail Sales/Avail	31.7	30.5	38.7	38.7	26.7	41.9	41.3	38.1	39.0	32.4	43.1	36.1	.0	36.9
MTD Total Sales	295	504	1,217	1,603	618	923	607	972	2,310	1,268	1,218	1,153	0	12,687
Total Objective	370	705	1,065	1,585	805	915	560	905	2,280	1,500	1,060	1,050	0	12,800
% Total Objective	79.7	71.5	114.3	101.1	76.8	100.9	108.4	107.4	101.3	84.5	114.9	109.7	.0	99.1
	1	6	30	16	1–	5	143	13	138	39	27	2	0	419
Memo: MTD Fleet (J)	0	5	15	15	5	5	140	5	90	10	10	0	0	300
Memo: Fleet Obj	.0	120.0	200.0	106.6	20.0–	100.0	102.1	260.0	153.3	390.0	270.0	.0	.0	139.6
Memo: % Fleet Obj														

EXHIBIT 5 National Customer Relations Owner Satisfaction Index June 1991

National — *Run Date: 06/21* ___ *CR82MX/CCR* ___

Region	*Current Month*					*Year to Date*				
	NVSDS INDEX/ RESPONSE	*NVSDS RECMD/ RESPONSE*	*TSS INDEX/ RESPONSE*	*TSS RECMD/ RESPONSE*	*OSI INDEX/ RESPONSE*	*NVSDS INDEX/ RESPONSE*	*NVSDS RECMD/ RESPONSE*	*TSS INDEX/ RESPONSE*	*TSS RECMD/ RESPONSE*	*OSI INDEX/ RESPONSE*
Los Angeles	94.5	91.9	92.9	89.9	90.9	94.4	91.9	92.3	89.5	90.7
	3,357	3,331	1,357	1,345	4,676	20,613	20,475	8,648	8,579	29,054
San Francisco	92.1	90.4	92.3	89.2	89.8	92.1	90.0	92.0	89.3	89.7
	1,947	1,935	803	796	2,731	12,326	12,255	5,526	5,468	17,723
Portland	93.4	90.9	91.2	87.2	89.1	93.4	90.7	91.1	88.2	89.5
	1,412	1,387	632	626	2,013	8,793	8,718	4,750	4,709	13,427
Denver	92.9	89.6	90.4	86.9	88.3	93.2	90.0	91.6	88.6	89.3
	1,315	1,304	633	627	1,931	8,498	8,446	4,665	4,610	13,056
New York	91.4	88.8	90.5	88.0	88.4	91.4	88.5	90.3	87.9	88.2
	3,515	3,493	1,874	1,846	5,339	21,578	21,454	12,509	12,380	33,834
Boston	94.2	91.0	91.8	90.3	90.7	93.8	91.2	91.7	89.9	90.6
	1,595	1,580	955	950	2,530	9,535	9,483	6,789	6,735	16,218
Chicago	93.9	92.0	91.6	89.7	90.9	93.9	91.6	91.4	89.1	90.4
	2,442	2,414	1,492	1,479	3,893	14,752	14,653	10,423	10,336	24,989
Cincinnati	93.9	92.6	92.2	89.9	91.3	94.1	92.4	91.8	89.8	91.1
	2,748	2,698	1,410	1,397	4,095	17,326	17,244	9,288	9,212	26,456
Kansas City	95.1	92.5	92.0	89.8	91.2	94.6	92.1	92.6	90.0	91.1
	1,112	1,067	576	571	1,638	7,057	7,011	4,287	4,246	11,257
Southeast	93.8	93.3	93.4	92.4	92.9	93.7	92.8	93.3	92.1	92.5
	4,370	4,308	1,769	1,753	6,061	25,234	25,090	11,630	11,547	36,637
Gulf States	92.9	91.7	92.2	90.8	91.3	93.1	91.5	91.1	89.1	90.3
	2,653	2,542	1,159	1,146	3,600	15,726	15,656	7,624	7,564	23,220
Cen. Atlantic	93.6	90.8	92.4	90.0	90.4	93.5	90.5	92.7	90.0	90.3
	3,446	3,376	1,397	1,383	4,759	20,188	20,060	9,393	9,393	29,364
National	93.4	91.4	92.0	89.8	90.6	93.4	91.2	91.8	89.5	90.4
	29,912	29,435	14,057	13,919	43,354	181,626	180,545	95,532	94,690	275,235

The OSI is a combination of NVSDS and service survey recommend questions

**OSI not calculated due to insufficient data

NVSDS	−0.1 BELOW MAY MTD	NVSDS	NO CHANGE FROM MAY YTD
TSS	−0.3 BELOW MAY MTD	TSS	NO CHANGE FROM MAY YTD
OSI	NO CHANGE FROM MAY MTD	OSI	+0.1 ABOVE MAY YTD
			NVSDS, TSS, OSI YTD BEST EVER

EXHIBIT 6 Budget Report for a Representative Region for Year Ended September 30, 1991 (000's)

	Actual	*Plan*	*Variance Fav (Unfav)*
Units	86,987	89,760	(2,773)
Sales	$1,045,000	$1,060,000	$(15,000)
Gross Profit	$ 21,312	$ 21,852	$ (540)
Expenses			
Personnel	2,815	2,920	105
Operating	2,785	2,714	(71)
Advertising & Promotion	7,175	7,337	162
Occupancy	1,837	1,845	8
General	2	1	(1)
Total Expenses	14,714	14,917	203
Operating Income	$ 6,598	$ 6,935	$ (337)

EXHIBIT 7 Expense Detail for a Representative Region for Year Ended September 30, 1991 (000's)

	Actual	*Plan*	*Variance Fav (Unfav)*
Personnel			
Salaries, Wages & Payroll Taxes	$2,749	$2,856	$107
*Overtime	11	15	4
*Temporary Help	21	17	(4)
Temporary Help–Disability related	10	—	(10)
*Other	24	32	8
	2,815	2,920	105
Operating			
*Travel and Transportation	1,029	963	(66)
*Telephone and Telegraph	365	350	(15)
*Meetings	324	362	38
*Supplies	78	75	(3)
*Postage	111	113	2
*RL Polk	120	120	—
*Dealer Training Expense	100	108	8
*Company Car	440	406	(34)
*Other	218	217	(1)
	2,785	2,714	(71)
Advertising & Promotion			
*Vehicle Incentives	6,959	7,181	222
*Local Promotion–Parts	129	37	(92)
*Local Promotion–Service	37	33	(4)
*Recognition and Awards	11	19	8
*Other	39	67	28
	7,175	7,337	162
Occupancy			
Rent Expenses—Intercompany	589	589	—
* —Equipment	26	29	3
Depreciation	19	26	7
Port Storage	970	970	—
*Utilities	83	73	(10)
*Security Service	13	15	2
Property Taxes–Real/Personal	114	114	—
*Janitor/Refuse Service	21	20	(1)
*Other	2	9	7
	1,837	1,845	8
*General	102	101	(1)
Total Expenses	$14,714	$14,917	$203

*These expenses are deemed "controllable." It is the responsibility of the Regional General Manager to maintain spending within the planned level.

CHAPTER 19

Control in International and Multinational Corporations

Previous chapters have discussed the elements of management control systems (MCSs) and many of the factors that cause them to vary among organizations and organizational units. These discussions explain a broad range of control practices in organizations around the world. It must be recognized, however, that most of the preceding discussion was based on evidence about the effects of controls in *for-profit* organizations operating *domestically* in what can be called *Anglo-American environments.* Some of the knowledge in the preceding discussions can be readily applied to other settings, but much of it cannot. Managers of organizations which operate in different environments often must make quite different control system choices, for any number of reasons. Even when they do make the same MCS choices, the effects are likely to be different.

As business markets and operations have become more global, cross-border investments have risen, forcing more managers to be aware of national differences. The managers of *multinational corporations* (those which operate in more than one country) must understand how they must adapt their management practices to make them work in their international locations. Many managers of organizations which operate in only a single country have also sought a greater understanding of international management practices, including control practices, because they are engaging in global benchmarking. *Global benchmarking* involves studying the extent to which elements of the management practices that successful foreign competitors are using can be profitably imported or emulated.

Adapting management and control practices across borders is complicated, and research on the topic is in its early stages. This chapter provides a discussion of, primarily, three sets of factors which have been shown to affect control system choices or outcomes across countries in a systematic manner: national culture, institutions, and local business environments.

This chapter also discusses the unique problems of controlling multinational corporations. Managers of multinational corporations must adapt the control practices they use in their home country to the set of unique factors faced in each of the countries in which they operate, or at least prepare for the potential differences in responses of local employees to their systems. If the control system adaptation is done improperly, the organization may suffer because it induces employee behaviors that are contrary to its interests or because it increases the costs of attracting and retaining good employees. These managers also have the additional problem of evaluating performances of managers whose results are measured in different currencies.

BEHAVIORAL SIMILARITIES ACROSS COUNTRIES

Clearly some of the effects, benefits, and costs of controls are universal because, at a certain basic level, people in all countries are alike. They have the same physiological needs (for example, water and food) and similar desires for safety, comfort, and accomplishment.

People around the world also tend to respond to the sets of incentives with which they are faced to further their own self-interests. It is well accepted that people in *capitalistic* economies react to monetary incentives, such as bonus plans; but so do people in *socialistic* economies. In Beijing China's socialistic economy, several different types of taxi fare structures exist. Drivers of one type of taxi earn only one yuan (about 12 U.S. cents) for the first kilometer of travel, but 1.5 yuan for every kilometer after the first. These drivers are highly motivated to find customers wanting long rides, and they are prone to refuse passengers who want only short trips. In addition, these taxi drivers' fares are not based on waiting time, so they are known to be aggressive (even reckless), to keep the wheels and meter running, and are prone to refuse to take passengers who want to travel on clogged streets. Conversely, another type of taxi fare structure provides its drivers with a relatively large fixed fare. These drivers are motivated to find short rides, and they are prone to refuse long rides.

China, in fact, passed a new labor law in early 1995 which provides for a transition away from secure, permanent employment towards performance-based employment. Nearly 90 percent of Chinese workers have signed new labor contracts with their employers.[1] Guangdong Kelon Electrical holdings, a southern China-based refrigerator manufacturer, is one company which now bases part of its managers' pay on both company profitability and the managers' individual performances. The company's chairman, Pan Ning, claims, "this gave directors a greater incentive to work harder to increase [the refrigerator maker's] profitability."[2]

These examples from China provide evidence that results controls should work anywhere in the world. Even in a country that has used a socialistic economy for many years, people respond to the environment in ways that further their own self-interests. Once again, money proves to be a powerful motivator.

CULTURAL DIFFERENCES ACROSS COUNTRIES

Despite the basic similarities in people around the world, there are also many differences. One important set of factors with potentially important influences on MCSs can be explained under the rubric *national culture.* National culture has been defined as ". . . the collective programming of the mind which distinguishes the members of one group or society from another. . ."[3] The national culture concept recognizes that people's tastes, norms, values, social attitudes, religions, personal priorities, and responses to interpersonal stimuli differ across nations. Of particular importance here is the fact that people of different national origins have different preferences for, and reactions to, management controls. National culture has a direct effect on MCSs because control problems are behavioral problems. When groups of employees perceive things differently or react to things differently, different control choices may have to be made.

Many definitions and taxonomies of national culture have been proposed. The most commonly cited are the four cultural dimensions identified in a major study by Geert Hofstede: individualism, power distance, uncertainty avoidance, and masculinity.[4] These four dimensions do not explain all the differences between people in different countries, but they explain a significant proportion. Each dimension has an implication for control systems (and for other aspects of management, including marketing and personnel policies).

The *individualism* (versus collectivism) dimension of national culture relates to individuals' self-concept; that is, whether individuals see themselves primarily as an individual (I) or as part of a group (we). Individuals from an individualistic culture tend to place their self-interests ahead of those of the group and prefer interpersonal conflict resolution over conflict suppression. Individuals in a collectivist culture are motivated by group interests and emphasize maintenance of interpersonal harmony.

The *power distance* dimension relates to the extent to which members of a society accept that institutional or organizational power is distributed unequally.

Uncertainty avoidance can be strong or weak. Individuals strong in uncertainty avoidance feel uncomfortable when the future is unknown and ambiguous.

The *masculinity* dimension relates to the preference for achievement, assertiveness, and material success (traits labeled masculine); as opposed to an emphasis on relationships, modesty, and the quality of life (traits labeled feminine).

A large body of data has shown that people from different countries vary significantly on these cultural dimensions, as shown in Table 19-1. These data show, for example, that as compared to the Taiwanese culture, the U.S. culture is much more individualistic and more masculine, while the Taiwanese culture is higher in both power distance and uncertainty avoidance.[5]

Each of the cultural dimensions has implications for control systems.[6] The individualism/collectivism dimension, in particular, appears to be so important that some researchers have suggested that high individualism is the key building block of American management theories.[7] Employees high in individualism tend to prefer individual-oriented, rather than group-oriented work arrangements, performance evaluations, and compensation. It is not surprising to see U.S. companies make relatively high use of individual incentives and efforts to remove the effects of uncontrollable factors from the performance evaluations. Most performance-related compensation in firms in countries relatively high in collectivism, on the other hand, is based on group performance; typically corporate profits. Higher collectivism may also provide some assurance that employees will not act myopically to emphasize their own short-term gains at the expense of what is best for their firm's long-term survival and success.

People who are high in power distance tend to prefer, or at least more willingly accept, greater centralization of decision-making authority and less participation in decision-making processes. Consequently, expect to see higher decentralization and greater employee participation in standard setting in firms in low power distance countries.

People high in uncertainty avoidance prefer to avoid, reduce, or deny risk and ambiguity. When designing control systems in high uncertainty avoidance countries, managers should, to the extent that is possible, agree on rules of behavior. Planning and budgeting systems should be more elaborate, with more ritual, to reduce employees' levels of anxiety. They should use more formal, rigid performance standards and less subjectivity in performance evaluations.

People high in masculinity tend to prefer basing rewards on performance. Those low in masculinity (high in femininity) prefer allocations based on need.

A dimension of national culture not picked up by the four Hofstede dimen-

TABLE 19-1 National Culture Scores for Thirty-nine Countries

Country	*Individualism (versus Collectivism)*	*Power Distance*	*Uncertainty Avoidance*	*Masculinity*
Argentina	46	49	86	56
Australia	90	36	51	61
Austria	55	11	70	79
Belgium	75	65	94	54
Brazil	38	69	76	49
Canada	80	39	48	52
Chile	23	63	86	28
Colombia	13	67	80	64
Denmark	74	18	23	16
Finland	63	33	59	26
France	71	68	86	43
Germany	67	35	65	66
Great Britain	89	35	35	66
Greece	35	60	112	57
Hong Kong	25	68	29	57
India	48	77	40	56
Iran	41	58	59	43
Ireland	70	28	35	68
Israel	54	13	81	47
Italy	76	50	75	70
Japan	46	54	92	95
Mexico	30	81	82	69
Netherlands	80	38	53	14
New Zealand	79	22	49	58
Norway	69	31	50	8
Pakistan	14	55	70	50
Peru	16	64	87	42
Phillipines	32	94	44	64
Portugal	27	63	104	31
Singapore	20	74	8	48
South Africa	65	49	49	63
Spain	51	57	86	42
Sweden	71	31	29	5
Switzerland	68	34	58	70
Taiwan	17	58	69	45
Thailand	20	64	64	34
Turkey	37	66	85	45
United States	91	40	46	62
Venezuela	12	81	76	73
39-Country Average	51	51	64	51

Source: G. H. Hofstede, *Culture's Consequences* (Beverly Hills, Calif.: Sage Publications, 1980).

sions relates to corporate goals. Managers in other countries, particularly those in Asia, are often more concerned with the interests of nonowner groups than are managers in the U.S. Surveys of the presidents and middle managers of large Japanese firms asked what the company's objectives were.[8] The presidents ranked pursuit of shareholders' profit only a distant fourth, with only 3.6 percent of the responses. Both groups ranked employees first among those entitled to the organization's profits.

Managers running a business for the benefit of many stakeholders; including employees, the communities in which the firm operates, customers, suppliers, and society as a whole, not primarily the owners or shareholders, will make different decisions. In MCS areas in particular, they will choose different performance measures and different ways of rewarding employees.

LOCAL INSTITUTIONS

Social, government, and legal institutions vary significantly across nations. These institutions include government agencies, corporate ownership structures, banking systems, labor unions, and bargaining and grievance resolution processes. Also important are the legal systems, including property rights, regulations, access to legal remedies, and the enforceability of contracts. Each of these factors can influence managers' abilities to influence employees' behaviors. Organizations in countries with strong labor unions often find it difficult to provide performance-based pay for incentive purposes. Most unions prefer basing pay on seniority.

One set of institutional factors deserving of special mention relates to the country's financial markets, their importance in raising money, and the extent of disclosures and types of information they demand. In many countries, equity capital markets are not particularly important for raising money. In their place, corporations raise money from banks and other financial institutions, or, as is particularly common in developing countries, from the state or from family sources.

Even in countries where financial markets are important, many managers do not believe that short-term accounting profits are reflected to a significant degree into stock prices. In developing countries, these beliefs may be correct because trading is often thin.

If senior managers do not believe that stock market valuations accurately reflect company values on a timely basis, they are much less likely to measure profits as frequently, less likely to give subordinates' short-term incentives, and less likely to engage in the short-sighted actions designed to manage earnings that were described in Chapter 12. The managers are also less likely to use stock-based reward instruments, such as restricted stock or stock options.

Another important stock market-related factor is the extent to which managers perceive a significant threat of hostile takeovers. The perceived threat of takeover is positively related to pressure to keep stock valuations high through, perhaps, maintenance of high short-term earnings; but it may be negatively related to motivation to perform.

The threat of hostile takeovers is quite low on the European continent. In Germany, hostile takeovers are virtually unheard of because the special position of banks, government antitrust policy, and the structure of the corporation all discourage them. A takeover would be virtually impossible without the support of the major banks because of their extensive stock holdings, their control over shares held on deposit, and the fact that they write the rules on takeovers.

Takeover guidelines, which are written and enforced by banks, not the legal system, require the bidder to inform appropriate stock exchanges of an offer, refrain from insider trading before publication of the offer, publish the terms of the offer, and give those who may have accepted a lower bid for their shares the higher prices in the event that a second offer is made. The government Cartel Office must clear any bid if the new organization would have more than DM2 billion in annual sales. The Cartel Office also has the authority to review the merger and require divestment *ex post.*

Several other structural aspects of German corporation and corporate law impede takeovers. Major changes to the corporation require 75 percent approval by shareholders. Golden parachutes are prohibited by law. Strict conflict-of-interest rules impede most management buyouts. Takeovers require employee support because companies with more than 2,000 workers have equal employee and shareholder representation on the supervisory board, called the *Aufsichtsrat,* the Germany counterpart to U.S. firms' board of directors.

Accounting regulations also differ dramatically across countries. German companies *cannot* report quarterly financial performance; thus, German managers are obviously not motivated to focus on short-term financial performance.

The basic purpose of accounting differs across countries. In the U.S., accounting rule-settings bodies, such as the Financial Accounting Standards Board, use decision usefulness (which is related to the extent and the transparency of disclosure) as its paramount guiding principle. In some other countries, accounting standard-setters, or law-makers, use prudence as their paramount principle. Prudent accounting rules are ultra-conservative. They emphasize creditor and employee protection, so they make it critically important that the wealth and earnings of a company never be overstated. Similarly, companies' accounting disclosures in countries emphasizing the prudence principle are not as extensive in many countries as they are in the decision-usefulness countries. It has been alleged that "more than 90 percent of German limited liability companies refuse to publish their accounts."[9]

DIFFERENCES IN LOCAL BUSINESS ENVIRONMENTS

Business environments differ significantly across countries. Elements of these environments can affect environmental uncertainty, inflation, labor availability, labor quality, and labor mobility. Each of these factors has MCS implications.

Risk- and Uncertainty-Related Factors

The MCS effects of high risk and high uncertainty were discussed in some detail in Chapter 18. Country-specific environmental uncertainty (or business risk) can be caused by many things. Some countries are inherently more risky places in which to do business. Military conflicts, kidnappings, bombings, and extortion threats can create major security problems. Some countries are also prone to corporate espionage and theft of corporate secrets by local competitors, perhaps even with the tacit approval of the host government.

Government activities are another important factor because they create *political risks.* Governments have, to a greater or lesser extent, powers that enable them to change organizational behaviors to serve certain objectives. These powers can have major effects on the value of companies' assets and the expected returns on those assets. Governments can distribute income through agricultural policies and tax laws. They can apply constraints through labor policies designed to reduce unemployment (forced production or prohibition of layoffs). They can design tax laws that dramatically affect the value of monetary compensation and other reward arrangements. They can exercise bureaucratic and quixotic control in issuing business permits, controlling prices, and restricting currency flows. They can enforce antitrust laws that make it difficult for corporations to share information that might be useful for benchmarking purposes. For this reason, corporate information sharing in the U.S. is formal. In most of Europe it is quite informal, as managers feel free to share information with old school classmates. In Japan, managers share information quite freely within their industrial groups (kieretsu).

In general, in nations where the government has greater powers and tends to use them more frequently, business risk is higher; however, governments can also act to lower business risk. Tariff barriers can protect corporations from competitive market forces. Governments can buy some of the companies' products (for example, agricultural products) to stabilize prices. They can provide direct subsidies in case of calamities. They can provide support for research and investment activities through grants or tax provisions. They can also help make available economic data that can be used for planning purposes (market sizes and shares or employee compensation levels) and competitive data that can be used for benchmarking (target-setting) and comparative performance evaluation purposes.

Risk also differs across countries because of the stage of economic development. Developing countries tend to contain mostly young, relatively small companies. These companies tend to have MCSs that are not as well-developed. They may have limited computerization, poor accounting and operating information, and relatively informal MCSs characterized by high use of subjective performance evaluations.

Company growth patterns also can affect risk through its influence on organizational learning. Firms that grow by acquisition learn from the management systems (including MCSs) being used in the organizations they acquire. This learning can lower risk.

As compared to the firms in many countries, U.S. firms are more likely to grow by acquisition, rather than internally. When firms grow by acquisition, they are likely to have to use, at least for a period of time, several variations of MCSs. The MCS variations may persist if they are superior for controlling the acquired businesses, even though it can be costly to maintain multiple sets of control mechanisms. What is important is that the acquisitions enhance organizational learning. The companies are exposed to multiple MCSs, and they can adapt the features that suit them best. This enhanced learning can improve control and lower uncertainty. In the absence of acquisitions, it is possible to derive much the same benefits by entering into joint ventures with companies in other countries.

Inflation

Inflation is another environmental factor that differs significantly across countries. Inflation and fluctuations in inflation, which affect the relative values of currencies, create *financial risk.* Valued in terms of a fixed currency, high inflation can cause a company's assets or an individual's compensation to deteriorate significantly in value in a short period of time.

High inflation, at the extreme hyperinflation, affects the congruence of financial measurement systems. It can lead to adoption of some form of inflation accounting which involves either the expressing of accounts and financial statements in terms of real (rather than nominal) amounts of expressing all assets and liabilities at current (or replacement) values. It can also lead to the use of some form of flexible budgeting, to shield managers from some uncontrollable inflation risks, or the partial abandonment of accounting measures of performance in favor of some nonfinancial measures; such as schedule achievement, production quality, commitment to research and development (R&D), and training of local staff.

Labor Availability

Companies operating in developing countries face limited availability of skilled and educated labor. When employees are not highly educated, decision making structures are usually more centralized, and MCSs tend to be more focused on action controls, rather than results controls. Small offices may contain only a few educated people. This makes it difficult to implement one of the basic internal control principles: separation of duties.

Labor Quality

Labor quality, even at managerial levels, can also differ significantly across companies. A study conducted during the mid-1960s showed dramatic differences in management characteristics and career patterns across countries.[10] In larger British industrial firms less than one-third of the top managers were university graduates, and more than a quarter had less than a secondary school education. Both proportions are low by international standards. In general, a managerial career was not considered to be a proper type of employment in the U.K. for upper- to middle-class individuals who had viable alternatives, and even individuals from the lower classes who succeeded in receiving prestigious types of higher education also tended to avoid industry. Promotions were based on job performance, and managers typically moved up in their organization through a single, narrow job function and did not receive broad experience.

The data from France, on the other hand, were quite different. Top management positions were considered to be prestigious. Career advancement of lower and middle managers was relatively independent of their performance after entering the firm, but education was a criterion for promotion. Over 80 percent of the chief executives in the 100 largest firms had higher education degrees, an 62 percent graduated from one of three elite universities.

These data have since aged and must now be viewed with caution. What was true twenty years ago might not be true today. The basic message is still valid: Employee characteristics and career patterns can be quite different across countries. The behavioral impacts of the controls can also vary from country to country.

Labor Mobility

The mobility of labor forces also varies significantly across countries. In the U.S., managers tend to change companies often over the course of their career. In many other countries, including Japan, most managers in the larger companies, at least, spend their entire careers with one company. When labor mobility is low, the need for implementing long-term incentive plans, which motivate managers both to think longer-term and to stay with the firm to earn their rewards, is reduced.

SPECIAL CONTROL ISSUES IN MULTINATIONAL ORGANIZATIONS

Multinational Organizations (MNOs), which own and manage business operations in multiple countries, are important institutions. Their revenues include more than half of the world's total trading value.[11] MNOs have many similarities with large domestic organizations in that they are usually characterized by a high degree of separation of ownership and control. Authority is decentralized to a relatively large number of decision makers, and control is exercised to a considerable extent through financial results controls.

Managers of MNOs have one important MCS-related advantage over their domestic organization counterparts: They are able to learn more quickly and more thoroughly about potentially desirable practices used in foreign countries. Those practices are known by employees in their foreign subsidiaries, and some of those practices can be readily adapted across countries. U.S. corporations have learned about just-in-time (JIT) production methods and target costing practices from Japanese corporations. On the other hand, some Japanese firms are looking more U.S.-like because they are abandoning the conventional Japanese practice of compensating and promoting employees based on seniority and instead making greater use of performance-dependent reward systems.

Generally, though, controlling MNOs is more difficult than controlling domestic organizations. First, MNO managers face a three-dimensional organizational problem. Their organizations are organized not only by function (marketing or production) and by product line, but also by geography. The geography dimension requires managers to adapt their control systems (and their strategies, organizations, and other management systems) to each of the national (and perhaps even regional) cultures in which they operate, as was discussed above. Second, MNO managers face the international transfer pricing problem that was discussed in Chapter 15. Third, MNO managers almost invariably have high information asymmetry between themselves and personnel in the foreign locations. The foreign personnel have specialized knowledge about their environments (local norms, tastes, regulations, and business risks). The high information asymmetry limits the corporate managers' abilities to use action controls, such as direct supervision and preaction reviews, because the corporate managers are not in a position to know when good judgments have been made. Action controls are also more expensive to use because of the geographical dispersion. Fourth, MNO managers almost invariably face the barriers of distance, time zones, and language. They cannot easily visit their foreign-based subordinates, although advancing information technologies have made communications much easier. Finally, they face the foreign currency translation problem, which is discussed in the following section.

At first glance, it is not obvious that results controls in MNOs should be complicated by the fact that the firms' profits are earned in multiple currencies. Results controls over foreign subsidiaries can be implemented using the same practices employed in most domestic corporations; by comparing performance measured in terms of the local currency with a preset plan also expressed in the local currency.

MNOs bear a real economic risk caused by fluctuating currency values. The values of foreign investments appreciate or depreciate based on the relative values of the home and foreign currencies. Through their performance evaluation practices, the MNO managers can make their subsidiary managers bear this risk or can shield them from it.

Most MNOs evaluate the managers of their foreign operations in terms of results measured in home-country currency. The home-country currency is the unit of measure in which the corporate financial objectives are stated; it is the currency most of the shareholders will be spending; and it is the unit of measure used to evaluate top management. It is natural for corporate managers to want to encourage subsidiary managers to take actions to increase home-currency-denominated profits.

Use of home-country currencies, however, causes problems when comparing performance versus an industry profit or rate-of-return norm. If the foreign currency is appreciating relative to the home currency, overseas units can earn comfortably above a satisfactory rate-of-return or show impressive sales gains while still not performing anywhere near the potential that is offered by foreign market opportunity. The converse is also true.

Evaluating managers of foreign subsidiaries in terms of the amount of home-country currency they earn subjects those managers to an extra risk: a foreign currency translation risk. The risk arises because the managers earn their cash returns (profits) in the foreign currency which fluctuates in value in comparison to home currency. When measured in home-country currency, the foreign subsidiaries' reported profits will be subjected to an extra, largely uncontrollable factor; the relative change in the size of the two monetary units over the measurement period. If the home currency appreciates in value relative to the local currency, then expressed in units of home currency, foreign subsidiary profits will be lower than they otherwise would have been. The subsidiary will be said to have a *foreign currency translation loss.* If the local currency appreciates in value relative to the home currency, then the converse is true; a *foreign currency translation gain* will be reported.

Tables 19-2 and 19-3 show a simple example illustrating the differences in exchange losses resulting from economic risk and translation risk. Table 19-2 shows the calculation of an exchange loss due to economic risk. The entity's assets and liabilities, both at the beginning and ending of the period, are expressed in current-value terms. Because this entity is assumed to do nothing during the period, the values expressed in local currency terms are identical. Because the local currency depreciated against the home currency, when the end-of-period local currency amounts are restated in home currency terms, an exchange loss of 260 is shown.

The only difference between Table 19-2 and Table 19-3 is that the latter's numbers reflect the standard accounting convention of expressing the entity's inventories and plant and equipment in historical cost, not current value, terms. Inventories and plant and equipment are shown at the amount it cost to build or buy them at the time they were acquired, regardless of their current value. Translation of the local currency amounts into home currency units results in a foreign exchange loss of 85. A loss is shown in both examples because the local currency depreciated in comparison to the home currency, but the numbers are significantly different. Because economic values are difficult to measure accurately, managers are normally held accountable for translation risk.

The amount of translation gain or loss can also vary significantly depending on the accounting convention used. The numbers shown in Table 19-3 use the current U.S. convention, described in Financial Accounting Statement (FAS) #52,

TABLE 19-2 Sample Calculation of Economic Loss

Notes: (1) All asets and liabilities expressed at *current market values* in home-currency units.
(2) Entity does nothing during the period.
(3) Local (foreign) currency (LC) depreciates against the home currency (HC). At the beginning of the period, 1 LC = 1 HC. At the end of the period, 2 LC = 1 HC.

	January 1, 19x1	*January 1, 19x2*	*January 1, 19x2*
Unit of Measure	Home Currency (= Local Currency)	Local Currency	Home Currency
Assets			
Cash	50	50	25
Accounts Receivable	100	100	50
Inventories	170	170	85
Plant and Equipment	500	500	250
Total Assets	820	820	410
Liabilities			
Accounts Payable	100	100	50
Long-term Debt	200	200	100
Total Liabilities	300	300	150
Net Worth	520	520	260
Foreign Exchange Loss		260	

TABLE 19-3 Sample Calculation of Translation Loss

Notes: (1) All assets and liabilities expressed following standard accounting conventions (inventories and plant and equipment at historical values) in home-currency units.
(2) Entity does nothing during the period. Assume units-of-production method of depreciation on plant and equipment.
(3) Local (foreign) currency (LC) depreciates against the home currency (HC). At the beginning of the period, 1 LC = 1 HC. At the end of the period, 2 LC = 1 HC.

	January 1, 19x1	*January 1, 19x2*	*January 1, 19x2*
Unit of Measure	Home Currency (= Local Currency)	Local Currency	Home Currency
Assets			
Cash	50	50	25
Accounts Receivable	100	100	50
Inventories	120	120	60
Plant and Equipment	200	200	100
Total Assets	470	470	235
Liabilities			
Accounts Payable	100	100	50
Long-term Debt	200	200	100
Total Liabilities	300	300	150
Net Worth	170	170	85
Foreign Exchange Loss		85	

which requires translation assets and liabilities at the exchange rate at the time of the statement.[12] FAS #52 was effective on January 1, 1983. From 1976 to 1982, the U.S. accounting rule for translation was expressed in FAS #8. FAS #8 required translation of real assets, such as inventories and plant and equipment, at the rates in effect when the assets were booked.

The most important control issue is whether to hold managers accountable for foreign exchange gains and losses, thus subjecting them to foreign currency translation risk. The issues involved here are identical to that discussed in the controllability chapter. The extra measurement noise caused by uncontrollable foreign exchange risk and various methods of measuring the gains and losses it can cause can affect judgments about the manager's performance.

It is easy to make the case that subsidiary managers who can influence the amount of the foreign exchange gain or loss should bear the foreign exchange risk. Most subsidiary managers can take actions that have foreign currency implications. Most have the authority to make significant cross-border investment product sourcing, or marketing decisions. Most have the authority to write purchase or sale contracts which are denominated in one currency or another. Some even have the authority to enter into foreign exchange transactions; such as hedging, currency swaps, or arbitrage. Most of these specialized hedging transactions require special skills most operating managers do not have. Authority in this area usually resides with an international finance department, usually at corporate level.[13]

If corporate managers decide that the managers of their foreign subsidiaries should not bear the foreign exchange risk, they can use any of four essentially identical methods:

1. Evaluate the manager in terms of local currency profits as compared to a local currency plan or budget,
2. Treat the foreign exchange gain or loss as "below" the income-statement line for which the manager is held accountable,
3. Evaluate the manager in terms of profits measured in home currency, but calculate a "foreign exchange variance" and treat it as uncontrollable,
4. Re-express the home currency budget for the subsidiary in local currency, using the end-of-year, not beginning-of-year exchange rate. This procedure creates a budget that "flexes" with exchange rates.

CONCLUSION

The MCS elements which are used, and which are most effective, vary systematically across organizations in different countries. This chapter has briefly discussed some of the most important country-level factors. Over time, good managers operating within a single national environment will learn what works and what does not.

Managers of multinational organizations face a more difficult challenge. They must simultaneously adapt their MCSs to multiple, diverse national environments, which themselves are probably changing, while attempting to minimize the cost of maintaining an effective system. They must also deal with the significant problem of measuring performance in terms of multiple currencies which are constantly changing in value with respect to each other.

Notes

1. M. Cao, "Law Protects Workers' Rights," *China Daily* (July 16, 1996), p. 4.
2. P. Chan, "No Profit Freeze for Refrigerator Maker," *Hong Kong Standard* (July 15, 1996), p. 3.
3. G. H. Hofstede, *Culture's Consequences* (Beverly Hills, Calif.: Sage Publications, 1980), p. 25.
4. Ibid. Hofstede's data are over 20-years old and were obtained from employees in only one firm (IBM), but numerous other studies have found support for Hofstede's taxonomy and findings. See the discussion in K. A. Merchant, C. Chow, and A. Wu, "Measurement Evaluation and Reward of Profit Center Managers: A Cross-Cultural Field Study," *Accounting, Organizations and Society,* 10 (October/November 1995), pp. 619–638.
5. It must be remembered that these data are representative only of averages within each country, not any specific individual or group of individuals. The individuals in some countries with strong cultural traditions, such as Japan, are relatively homogeneous, but they are quite diverse in other countries, such as the United States.
6. This discussion is adapted from S. Ueno and F. H. Wu, "The Comparative Influence of Culture on Budget Control Practices in the United States and Japan," *The International Journal of Accounting,* 28, no. 1 (1993), pp. 17–39 and from Merchant, Chow, and Wu, "Measurement," 1995.
7. See P. Harris and R. Moran, *Managing Cultural Difference* (Houston, Tex.: Gulf Publishing, 1987); J. Spence, "Achievement American Style: The Rewards and Costs of Individualism," *American Psychologist* (December 1985), pp. 1285–1295; E. Sampson, "Psychology and the American Ideal," *Journal of Personality and Social Psychology* (November 1977), pp. 767–782.
8. Survey results cited in *Nihon Sangyo Shimbun* (July 5, 1990). Cited by P. Milgrom and J. Roberts, *Economics Organization & Management* (Englewood Cliffs, N.J.: Prentice-Hall, 1992), p. 41.
9. K. Van Hulle, "Harmonization of Accounting Standards in the EC: Is It the Beginning or Is It the End?," *The European Accounting Review* (September 1993), p. 390. The German government has not taken any action against these delinquents, so the European Union has instituted an infringement procedure against Germany.
10. D. Granick, "National Differences in the Use of Internal Transfer Prices," *California Management Review* (Summer 1975), pp. 28–40.
11. A. Rugman and L. Eden, *Multinationals and Transfer Pricing* (London: Croom-Helm, 1985).
12. Under FAS #52, translation losses can be placed in a separate reserve account until the new asset (or liability) position is substantially or completely liquidated, or until it is determined that the new asset or liability position is permanently impaired.
13. See H. A. Davis and F. C. Militello, Jr., *Foreign Exchange Risk Management: A Survey of Corporate Practices* (Morristown, N.J.: Financial Executives Research Foundation, 1995).

Shell Brasil S.A.: Performance Evaluation in the Oil Products Division

In early March 1986, Roberto Boetger, vice president of the Oil Products Division of Shell Brasil S.A., was considering a major change in the control systems in his division. The previous week the Brazilian government had announced the Cruzado Plan, which introduced far-reaching economic and financial reforms, including a change in the national currency and a general one-year price freeze. The government plan, which took the country by surprise, intended to reduce annual inflation rates from 255 percent to less than 10 percent. Boetger felt that, with the Cruzado Plan in place, it might now be feasible to evaluate managers more objectively, based on financial measures of performance, instead of relying on subjective evaluations.

"Up to now, it has been relatively difficult to hold people responsible for not meeting the budget, because of the *masking effects* of many factors that are outside the manager's control, such as widely fluctuating inflation and exchange rates. If the Cruzado Plan is successful and inflation rates drop to 20 percent or less and stabilize, the budget targets will be much more meaningful. We could use actual vs. budget comparisons for evaluating managerial performance and, possibly, for providing managerial incentives. The problem is that we can still expect some residual effects of inflation and exchange rates to influence performance significantly in the future. Can we really tell, then, by comparing budget vs. actual, if a manager has done a good job?"

COMPANY BACKGROUND

Shell Brasil S.A. was the largest private company in Brazil and a wholly owned subsidiary of Royal Dutch/Shell Group, the largest corporation in the world outside the United States. The parent group had operating companies in over 100 countries in businesses such as oil and natural gas, chemicals, metals, and coal. In 1985 the group reported earnings of $3.9 billion in the oil business only, making it the largest oil company worldwide.

Shell Brasil was organized into three main divisions: oil products, chemicals, and metals (see Exhibit 1 for the organization chart). Besides these businesses, Shell had recently diversified into what it called *nontraditional businesses,* such as asphalt, motels (situated along highways, close to some of Shell's gas stations in the countryside), and a joint venture in forestry dedicated to growing eucalyptus and pine trees, which could be used for wood pellets, an alternative source of energy.

The oil business was subject to extensive government control. The government oil company, Petrobras, had a monopoly on oil exploration, and regulations also restricted oil distribution. For example, gas stations were not allowed to open during weekends since the oil price shocks; the location of gas stations was limited to certain areas; and distributors had to order oil supplies from Petrobras according to quotas, with lead times of up to three months. The government also set retail prices, which were updated periodically, according to cost information provided by all oil companies operating in Brazil.

Shell Brasil competed in the distribution of various oil products, acting both as a wholesaler to large clients (such as aviation companies) and as a retailer, through a network of 3,500 gas stations spread around Brazil, of which Shell owned about 30 percent, the rest belonging to franchisers. In the parts of the oil industry where the gov-

This case was prepared by Research Assistant Lourdes Ferreira, under the supervision of Professor Kenneth A. Merchant, as a basis for class discussion rather than to illustrate either effective or ineffective handling of an administrative situation.

ernment allowed private investments, Shell also operated as a manufacturer. In the production of lubricants, for example, the market leader was the government enterprise, Petrobras, with 23 percent market share, followed closely by Shell, with 21 percent market share. The Oil Products Division thus had a manager in charge of supplies and distribution of all of Shell's oil products, and an operations manager, responsible for manufacturing. The Oil Products Division had succeeded consistently, generating 60 percent of Shell Brasil's total sales volume and 70 percent of its profits. Despite price controls that limited operating margins in gasoline distribution to 2.5 percent, the oil business was a great cash generator with practically no credit sales.

At corporate, several services were provided to the operating divisions, as can be seen in Exhibit 1. In the Finance Division, the legal department was responsible for relations with shareholders, for taxes, and for legal support to the personnel functions at the operating levels. The treasury was a critical department for Shell Brasil, since it centralized the management of cash from all the different businesses. Daily this department dealt with about US$7 million, as a result of cash sales from the oil and chemical divisions. To keep idle cash to a minimum, the treasury department kept tight controls over the operations and maintained accounts with 18 different banks with branches all over Brazil.

PLANNING AND BUDGETING

The planning cycle at Shell Brasil consisted of three main stages: strategic planning, long-term financial planning, and operational budgeting. Strategic planning involved forming macroeconomic scenarios for the next 20 years and preparing the Country Plan Documentation (CPD). CPD focused on a time horizon of three years, and had the objective of quantifying the strategies necessary to meet the corporate goals. However, at this first stage management could not quantify some strategies in detail, so they presented targets such as *maintain market share* or *the Oil Products Division has to be a cash generator.*

Targets were often differentiated according to geographical characteristics. For instance, within the Oil Products Division targets varied depending on whether the unit was located in a metropolitan region or in the countryside. In the large cities, service levels and sales volume were key targets, while in the countryside the emphasis was on building new gas stations as fast as possible to guarantee future market share in a fast-growing segment. The Strategic Plan was approved by the parent group, generally around the end of August.

The Long-Term Financial Plan involved a review of the total resources the company would provide or need in the next five years. In recent years, Shell Brasil had consistently needed more resources than what it provided. The Long-Term Financial Plan was sent for approval to the parent group in November.

Operational budgeting, which started in December, began at the operating division level. Each manager presented revenue targets (based on forecasts for each customer account) and cost estimates for the upcoming year for each of the various businesses. By year end the three operating Vice Presidents (Oil Products, Chemicals and Metals divisions) and the finance and personnel vice presidents met with the President to discuss and approve the budget.

Once the budget was approved, any changes had to be approved at the vice president level. In situations where the forecasts proved to be very far from reality, the division could ask for a budget review, subject to direct approval by the President. Only a major disruption, however, such as a variation of 200 percent in the expected inflation rate, would cause a change in the plans. As John Beith, in charge of corporate planning, explained, "Variances are an essential part of any planning effort. In fact, one of the few things we can be sure about when putting a plan together is that we'll miss it! Brazilians sometimes tend to have a lot of expectations about the numbers in their plans, and later, when they find, year after year, that they missed the plan because of some unforeseen circumstances, they get so disappointed that some people simply lose their confidence in any plan."

PERFORMANCE MEASUREMENT

The operating divisions at Shell Brasil were evaluated on the basis of return on investment. Return was measured as profit after taxes and interest rates. The budget contained targets defined for three levels of profitability, called Margin I, Margin II, and Margin III, as shown in Exhibit 2. Margin I was a gross profit number. Margin II was division profit before allocations of indirect costs. Margin III was a fully allocated profit number, net of taxes. When computing the return on investment, Margin III was divided by total assets employed (defined as net working capital plus fixed assets). When Margin III was negative, management had to use Margin II to compute the return on investment. This happened in 1984 and 1985, but generally Margin III was the ultimate criterion for measuring profits. Despite continuous efforts by top management to find the best possible bases for allocating corporate costs at the division level, many managers still considered Margin III an unreliable indicator of the true contribution of the profit center to the performance of the whole company, because it depended on many factors outside the manager's control.

During the year each operating division prepared special reports for monthly, quarterly, and semiannual reviews. These reports compared actual results with the plans. Managers had to provide detailed explanations of the causes for variances only when failing by more than 5 percent to meet profitability targets. Managers often felt that it was much harder to explain unfavorable variances, so most of them preferred to set conservative targets.

Performance evaluation meetings were held every six months. Division managers had to rank all their subordinates according to how well they had met financial targets and other objectives, such as participating in leadership training programs, increasing sales volume, or opening new gas stations. In a first round, all employees in a division had to rank their peers (other employees at the same job level), and then each boss would review and consolidate the rankings of the subordinates. The personnel division collected these rankings with individual evaluation reports. The data were used for career planning, management succession, training, and internal transfer programs, as well as merit wage increases. Managers at all levels had to conduct interviews for preparing evaluation reports with each subordinate. Together they identified the factors that facilitated or prevented the achievement of each goal, including those that could not be quantified. The boss was also expected to serve as a counselor on career plans and to provide alternatives for improving performance.

Shell had attempted to reduce subjectivity in the evaluation process by setting performance targets at the beginning of each year and by quantifying the performance measures as much as possible. Some managers still felt uncomfortable, however, about giving a bad evaluation to their subordinates. In some instances managers ranked half of their subordinates as *perfectly acceptable* and the other half as *very good.* The problem was aggravated when the manager had to justify why his or her unit performed poorly if all subordinates had done such a good job.

ISOLATING UNCONTROLLABLES

In 1985 top management made some attempts to separate controllables from uncontrollables in the performance measures. Ian Wilson, corporate controller, commented: "Uncontrollables are outside factors that make you realize that you can't rely only on your own resources. Managers should be evaluated solely on their individual contribution." Unfortunately, however, management had difficulty in defining what was *controllable.*

For example, in the Oil Products Division, if a manager was responsible for opening new gas stations in the countryside, and despite all efforts in developing good plans for this operation, government officials decided not to grant the necessary authorization, then the manager would not be held responsible for failing to open the new stations. But if the manager disrupted some relationships with government officials because proper authorization was denied for the new gas stations, then the manager could be demoted, perhaps even fired.

Another example would be the frequent oil price increases. Approximately once a month the government determined price increases for different oil products, including gasoline. If a manager could forecast more or less accurately when the price increase would come, he or she could maximize inventory just before that day, and then sell everything later at the greater price. This gain could amount to a boost of about US$20 million in profits for a company as large as Shell.

To take advantage of these gains, some of Shell's competitors adopted various procedures not to sell just before the price increase was expected. For example, they would allege that delivery trucks had broken down or that the pumps were out of order in some gas stations, or they would intentionally reduce service levels to create large lines of customers. As a manager in the Oil Products Division commented, "We at Shell consider such procedures unethical. However, there are some ordinary business steps that a manager can take to maximize the gains with the oil price increases. For instance, a manager could anticipate purchases to maximize inventory around the time when he or she expects the price increase to occur. Should we reward such a manager even if the underlying cause for the large gains—the price increase announced by the government—was outside the manager's control?"

Two *uncontrollable* factors, inflation and the fluctuation in exchange rates, typically had a particularly significant impact on performance measurement, sometimes with opposite effects. This led management to consider explicitly these effects in computing Margins II and III.

A. Inflation:

Brazilian inflation rates, as high as 250 percent, caused major distortions in financial statements. Nevertheless, government regulations limited the adjustments that companies could make to account for inflation, allowing adjustments in just a few accounts, such as fixed assets. Due to other restrictions in the tax laws, companies in Brazil tended to use the same reporting system for tax and financial purposes. Thus, a large part of the reported results depended on the relative changes in prices over the period. In the Oil Products Division, for instance, management estimated that about 50 to 60 percent of reported profits were caused merely by inflation. For internal purposes, management prepared *what if* reports, that showed actual results adjusted for what they would have been, had inflation been just as expected. Even so, few people could understand the effects of inflation on various accounts. Some managers could enumerate between 20 and 30 effects of inflation with different magnitudes and which could have a positive or negative impact on the various line items in the budget. It was very hard to assess what their net result would be. The hardest effects to predict were changes in relative prices (e.g., how would the price of a finished product vary, compared with the variation in the price of one or more of its inputs).

As an approximation, management computed an *inflationary loss* estimate, according to the formula:

Inflationary Loss = Inflation Adjustment × Net Working Capital

where:

Inflation Adjustment	Percent adjustment that the government allowed for accounting for inflation during the period.
Net Working Capital	Balance, in U.S. dollars, outstanding at the beginning of the period.

Margin I, less the Inflationary Loss and Direct Costs, resulted in what was called Margin II. From Margin II the divisions deducted the Indirect Costs, and the result (Profit Before Taxes) was the basis for computing tax liability or savings. The total tax liability or savings for the company arose from consolidating the above computations supplied by each division.

B. Exchange Rate Changes:

Shell Brasil set budgets in dollars for all the different businesses, and used the targets contained in those budgets to control the performance of its general managers. Top management believed that results in dollars, rather than cruzeiros, better reflected real performance. One reason was that targets expressed in dollars would not be subject to the effects of the inflation of the cruzeiro, only to the inflation in dollars, which had been comparatively much smaller. Another reason was that the use of profitability measures denominated in dollars facilitated comparisons with the international competitive environment. Some managers, however, wondered why they should be held responsible for fluctuations in the exchange rates. They argued that they did their business in cruzeiros and had no control over exchange rates that were periodically established by the Brazilian government.

Besides the effects of changes in the value of the cruzeiro regarding the dollar, financial performance at Shell Brasil was also influenced by fluctuations in the exchange rate between cruzeiros and British pounds. The Dutch-British parent group required that Shell Brasil report its financial statements in British pounds to consolidate the corporate accounts worldwide. And when the president of Shell Brasil went to London to discuss budget reports, he would present the numbers, taking into consideration explicitly the effects of fluctuations in the exchange rates.

Devaluations of the cruzeiro concerning foreign currencies generally had a net negative effect on performance. Each time the Brazilian government established a new exchange rate, usually to devalue the cruzeiro, companies received more cruzeiros for their exports, but meanwhile they needed more cruzeiros to pay their foreign debt. Shell Brasil, like many other companies, had a substantial part of its current liabilities denominated in dollars and only a small percentage of revenues derived from exports. Because the government also controlled prices of many of Shell's products, the end result was that the frequent devaluations of the cruzeiro had a significant negative impact on performance of the different businesses at Shell.

For internal reporting purposes, the effects of variations in the exchange rates were computed by the Difference in Exchange (DIE) formula, as follows:

$$\frac{\text{Net Working Capital (NWC)}}{\text{Beginning Exchange Rate}} - \frac{\text{Net Working Capital}}{\text{Ending Exchange Rate}} = \begin{array}{c}\text{Beginning Loss}\\ \text{In Dollars (BLD)}\end{array}$$

$$\text{BLD} + \frac{\text{Variation in NWC}}{\text{Average Exch. Rate}} - \frac{\text{Variation in NWC}}{\text{Ending Exch. Rate}} = \text{DIE}$$

where:

Net Working Capital	Beginning Balance, in cruzeiros.
Variation in NWC	Difference between Net Working Capital of two consecutive periods.
Exchange Rate	Expressed as how many cruzeiros one needed to buy U.S. $1.

The DIE was deducted from Margin I, along with the direct costs, and the final result was Margin II. This Margin II could be very different from the Margin II calculated as Margin I minus direct costs and the Inflationary Loss, as explained earlier. If one considered the inflationary loss only, and not DIE, one would have a measure of what contribution the division made to the overall profit of the company, translated from cruzeiros to dollars at the current exchange rate at the end of the period. Yet, if one considered DIE only, and not the inflationary loss in cruzeiros, one would have a measure of the division's performance in dollars, allowing for the effect of the changes in the cruzeiro's value concerning the dollar during the period being evaluated. Management had to report the budget variances according to both criteria for computing Margin II (and, consequently, Margin III).

Exhibit 3 illustrates the evolution of the inflation rates of the cruzeiro and the dollar, and compares it with the changes in the exchange rate of the cruzeiro regarding the dollar, for the period 1981–1985. Respecting performance evaluation, these large variations in the inflation and exchange rates caused major uncontrollable variances from budget estimates. As a corporate manager explained, "When you receive a budget report that shows a big loss in dollars due to a major devaluation of the cruzeiro, or a loss in cruzeiros due to a jump in inflation, you often feel like you can't penalize the manager for missing the budget. However, you would expect that the manager would have reacted to these outside factors in some way, to offset some of these negative variances."

COMPENSATION POLICIES

Labor expenses at Shell Brasil accounted for over 50 percent of the company's total operating expenses, or about US$50 million per year. Shell compensated its managers on a salary basis, at levels designed to be competitive with total compensation (salary plus bonuses) packages offered by some large companies surveyed annually.

By 1986 an estimated 55 percent of the major companies in Brazil would be paying incentive bonuses. Part of Shell's reluctance to pay bonuses or other forms of compensation based on performance stemmed from the tradition among European companies against incentive plans. As a Shell executive explained, "We don't want our managers to be in a situation where one year they can earn a big bonus but they earn nothing the following year."

On some rare occasions, a small number of Shell managers (usually less than 5 percent of the total management team) would be eligible for either merit increases in salary (often associated with promotions) or cash bonuses, subject to approval by the Board of Directors. In its evaluation the Board emphasized two aspects—individual contribution and consistency. The individual contribution was defined as outstanding performance in relation to individual budget targets. Consistency, however, referred to long-term trends in performance. It was not enough to meet budget in any given year, because the Board was also looking for a consistent pattern of superior performance over a longer period, such as three to five years. The Board also used consistency to grant merit increases or bonuses to a manager who had *exceptional performance,* even if his or her division had not met budget in the current year. An obstacle to assessing *consistent performance* was that Shell frequently transferred people across functional departments and divisions to give high-potential employees varied experiences. Therefore, managers often had to change positions every two or three years.

Another problem with bonus payments was that managers received them only after the previous year's results had been thoroughly evaluated. This often delayed the delivery of bonus payments to midyear. By that time managers were already worried about meeting the current year's targets.

THE CRUZADO PLAN

The Cruzado Plan, which took effect on March 1, 1986, was a government attempt to eliminate one of the factors believed to be a root cause for inflation: the expectations of future inflation based on past price increases. So far the Brazilian economy had operated with an *indexation system* in which most prices were automatically raised according to variations in price indexes computed by the government. For some products, these price increases could occur weekly. The plan introduced two major reforms addressing this problem—all prices were frozen as of February 28, 1986, and a new monetary unit was created, the cruzado, equivalent to 1,000 old cruzeiros. The currency change was intended to erase inflationary memories.

The Cruzado Plan raised many questions about how to implement the generalized price freeze. A major concern was that, without the Plan, wages would have been readjusted on March 1 to account for inflation (wages in Brazil used to be adjusted twice a year, in March and November). Recognizing this, the Plan determined that wages should now be frozen at their average *real* value from the last six months. To this average, the government decided to add an 8 percent bonus. Furthermore, the Plan established a sliding scale mechanism that allowed automatic wage raises if the annual inflation rate reached 20 percent. The Plan also introduced unemployment benefits for the first time in Brazil. But no one knew how the labor unions would respond.

Another major problem with implementing of the price freeze was the required revisions in current long-term contracts. These contracts usually established adjustments in the periodic payments according to variations in the inflation or the exchange rates. Now the Plan prohibited any contracts (including investments) from having such provisions. Nevertheless, it was still reasonable to expect some residual inflation, even with the new price freeze. The Cruzado Plan considered this expected residual inflation by establishing a *conversion calendar,* that translated old cruzeiros into cruzados for every day of the year until March 1, 1987. Each day one needed more old cruzeiros to buy one cruzado. For example, on March 1, 1986, one cruzado was set as equivalent to 1,000 cruzeiros; six months later, one cruzado would be equivalent to 2,997.39 cruzeiros. This conversion calendar allowed for conversions into the new currency for payments established in cruzeiros in long-term contracts signed before the Plan. Another example was that if one had agreed before the Plan to pay 5 million cruzeiros on February 28, 1987, now one would have to pay about only 1,000 cruzados on that same date.

THE CRUZADO PLAN'S EFFECT ON SHELL'S MANAGEMENT

A wave of optimism about the promised stronger economy swept Shell the day the Plan was announced, but uncertainty lingered concerning the repercussions that the Plan would trigger. For example, how long could the government enforce the price freeze? After over twenty years of military government, the first elected president—a civilian—had certainly strong popular support, which would provide the much needed help to implement the Cruzado Plan. Coming elections for the Congress in November, however, could change the political scenario substantially, especially because the new Congress would vote on a new constitutional reform. It seemed that there was more uncertainty about the next year than about the nineties. Despite all uncertainties, Shell had to continue to set prices and renegotiate contracts with suppliers, banks, and insurance companies. Top management had to act quickly to send instructions to all managers, spread out over the whole country, for the adoption of coherent policies that might change practically every aspect of the way they operated in their different businesses.

The Cruzado Plan particularly affected the distribution business. Manufacturers used to sell to wholesalers offering deferred payment terms (generally between one to three months) that incorporated an inflation forecast. Now, according to the new conversion calendar, which converted cruzeiros into cruzados at different rates daily, wholesalers and retailers would face increasing costs. This situation, combined with the price freeze, caused many managers in the distribution business to doubt whether they would be able to keep earning their expected returns. Some people even speculated about a crisis in supplies and the creation of an underground economy.

Luiz Fortes, Treasurer, perceived an increasing pressure to meet performance targets: "The Cruzado Plan forces us to look at real returns. For example, we are all used to thinking about returns in nominal terms, with a large inflationary component built-in. Now only the really best performers will be able to generate significant real returns and beat competition." Ian Wilson, the corporate controller, predicted some positive effects of the Plan: "It'll be much easier now to compare budget with actual results. We can be more confident about our forecasts. It's a good opportunity to implement tighter cost controls and to hold people accountable for financial targets. We'll be able to ask good questions when somebody misses the budget. We won't have all those masking effects any more." Some people at corporate, however, remained uncertain about how the Plan would change the role of budgets in the performance evaluation process. Some managers argued that criteria such as meeting targets for Margin III, for instance, would be more reliable in the future, because then costs and other factors would be estimated much more precisely. However, others argued that with frozen prices managers would have less control over their results, so that even simpler criteria, such as Margin I, would not capture the "real effort" that each person made to accomplish his or her goals.

William Mills, the vice president of personnel, agreed that it was time to review some control policies: "We may now have a unique opportunity to introduce some performance-based compensation plans. There are several alternatives for careful examination. For instance, should we tie compensation to the performance of the profit center only? To what extent should we measure performance over a longer period of time—say, five years?"

The planning department at corporate would have to revise most of its macroeconomic premises, especially about inflation and exchange rates. If the inflation rate exceeded the devaluation rate of the cruzado concerning the dollar, Shell Brasil could possibly end up with losses in cruzados but profits in dollars.

AN EXAMPLE: EVALUATION OF PERFORMANCE IN THE LUBRICANTS BUSINESS

Roberto Boetger, vice president of the Oil Products Division, had just received the latest budget forecasts for the lubricants business (Exhibit 5) accompanied by a review of the performance of this business in the last two years (see Exhibits 4A and 4B). The lubricants business, which required large amounts of working capital, was representative of how the inflation and exchange rate effects could alter the financial results substantially. As shown in Exhibits 4A and 4B, the lubricants business missed its budget targets for Margin II and III in 1984, but did better than budget in 1985. In both years, management had underestimated sales volume. This was consistent with a conservative attitude that some managers at Shell adopted when preparing budget estimates. In both 1984 and 1985 management had also underestimated inflation, so the actual inflationary loss produced negative variances in both years.

Following the other criteria for measuring Margins II and III, that is, taking into consideration DIE, both in 1984 and 1985 the actual variation in exchange rates was much higher than expected. This led to a bottom line (Margin III) loss of $8 million dollars in 1984. However, in 1985 the actual variation in exchange rates was lower than inflation, causing substantial savings in direct costs. Thus, the bottom line (Margin III) for 1985 resulted in neither gains or losses for the lubricants business.

Now, when reviewing the budget for the following years, corporate planning expected both the DIE and the inflationary effects to be much smaller. Yet, they also expected that the spread between the variation in exchange rates and inflation would increase substantially. In particular, for 1987 top management estimated that the effect of inflation would be much smaller than the DIE, so that lubricants would report profits in cruzados (and a consequent payment of taxes), but losses in dollars. In 1988 management expected these results to reverse. These forecasts and their underlying assumptions appear in Exhibit 5.

Even assuming that the forecasts for the next couple of years were reasonably accurate, top management at Shell Brasil still had to decide what criteria should be used to assess management performance. Should they leave the system unchanged and continue to depend on more subjective judgements? Or should they rely primarily on budget standards? If so, should performance be measured in cruzados, in dollars, or in British pounds? Should managers be held responsible for the three levels of profitability—Margins I, II, and III? What criteria should be used to compute the profitability margins?

EXHIBIT 1 Organization Chart

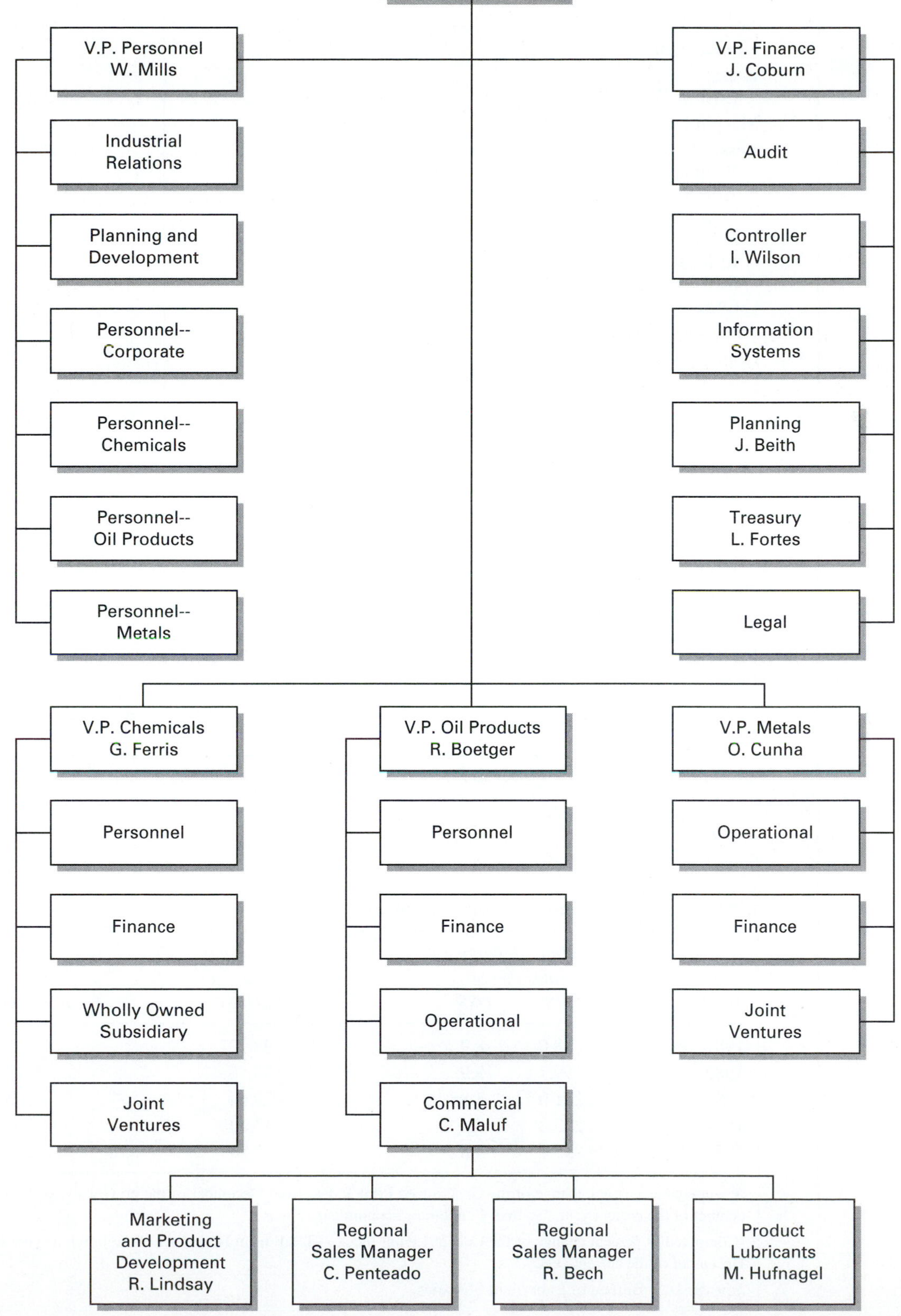

EXHIBIT 2 Format for Evaluation of Profitability Levels

		Budget		*Actual*
Net Revenues				
Less:				
Cost of Goods Sold		______		______
Margin I				
Less:				
Plant costs				
Administrative expenses				
Depreciation				
Freight costs				
Interests				
Sales and distribution				
Other direct costs				
Total direct costs		______		______
Contribution				
Less:				
	DIE	Inflationary Loss	DIE	Inflationary Loss
Margin II				
Less:				
Corporate overhead				
Publicity and other sales expenses				
Other allocated costs[a]				
Total indirect costs	___	______	___	______
Profit before taxes				
Less:				
Income taxes	___	______	___	______
Margin III				

[a]Examples include corporate services such as legal assistance, computer support, and auditing.

EXHIBIT 3 Performance of Brazilian Economy

Year	*Annual Inflation Rates (%) of: CR$*[a]	*US$*[b]	*Exchange Rates: Yearly Averages (CR$/US$)*	*% Change in Yearly Average Exchange Rate*
1981	88.0	8.9	98.12	—
1982	99.7	3.9	193.56	97.3
1983	211.0	3.8	629.64	225.3
1984	223.8	4.0	2,132.00	238.6
1985	235.1	3.8	7,037.50	230.0

[a]Computed as percent change of the Generalized Price Index, from December of the previous year through December of the current year. (Source: Conjuntura Economica).

[b]Computed as percent change of the Cost of Living Index—Total, from December of the previous year through December of the current year.

Source: U.S. Bureau of Labor and Statistics.

EXHIBIT 4A Variance Analysis of the Lubricants Business—1984 (U.S. $ millions)

	Budget		*Actual*	
	With DIE	*With Inflation*	*With DIE*	*With Inflation*
Net Revenues	128	128	160	160
Less:				
Cost of Goods Sold	84	84	111	111
Margin I	44	44	49	49
Less:				
Direct Costs	6	6	4	4
DIE Effect	34	—	43	—
Inflationary Loss	—	33.1	—	43.4
Margin II	4	4.9	2	1.6
Less:				
Indirect Costs	16	16	17	17
Profit (Loss) Before Taxes	(12)	(11.1)	(15)	(15.4)
Less:				
Income Tax Savings	5	5	7	7
Margin III	(7)	(6.1)	(8)	(8.4)

Other Data:	*Budget*	*Actual*
Sales Volume (1,000 m3)	140.5	168.0
Inflation (%)	200.0	223.8
% Variation in Exchange Rates (Cr$/US$)	210.0	238.6

EXHIBIT 4B Variance Analysis of the Lubricants Business—1985 (U.S.$ millions)

	Budget		*Actual*	
	With DIE	*With Inflation*	*With DIE*	*With Inflation*
Net Revenues	133	133	169	169
Less:				
Cost of Goods Sold	91	91	111	111
Margin I	42	42	58	58
Less:				
Direct Costs	12	12	7	7
DIE Effect	36	—	39	—
Inflationary Loss	—	38	—	39
Margin II	(6)	(8)	12	12
Less:				
Indirect Costs	12	12	12	12
Profit (Loss) Before Taxes	(18)	(20)	0	0
Less:				
Income Tax Savings	9	9	0	0
Margin III	(9)	(11)	0	0

Other Data:	*Budget*	*Actual*
Sales Volume (1,000 m3)	140.5	173.0
Inflation (%)	230.0	235.1
% Variation in Exchange Rates (Cr$/US$)	220.0	230.0

EXHIBIT 5 Forecasts for 1987/1988—Lubricants

Assumptions:

	1987			*1988*		
	Beginning		*Ending*	*Beginning*		*Ending*
Net Working Capital (Cz$ millions)	447.0		851.2	851.2		914.6
Exchange Rates (Cz$/US$)	15.0		23.0	23.0		37.0
DIE Effect (US$ millions)		14.1			14.4	
Inflationary Adjustment (%)		21.5			53.2	
Inflationary Loss (US$ millions)		6.4			19.7	

Forecasts (US$ millions):

	1987		*1988*	
	With DIE	*With Inflation*	*With DIE*	*With Inflation*
Margin I	47.9	47.9	49.8	49.8
Less:				
Direct Costs	16.1	16.1	16.3	16.3
Inflationary Loss	—	6.4	—	19.7
DIE	14.1	—	14.4	—
Margin II	17.7	25.4	19.1	13.8
Less:				
Indirect Costs	13.0	13.0	13.0	13.0
Profit Before Taxes	4.7	12.4	6.1	0.8
Less:				
Income Tax (45%)	5.6	5.6	0.4	0.4
Margin III	(0.9)	6.8	5.7	0.4

CIBA-GEIGY (A)
Information and Control System

In October 1983, Hans-Peter Schär, a member of the Executive Committee at Ciba-Geigy, reflected on his company's experience with its somewhat unique information and control system:

> We are very happy with our information and control system. The measures we use for evaluating managerial performance are a little different from those used in most companies—the primary goals set for our operating units are in terms of contribution, not net income, and we use direct costing and current cost accounting—but we have used this basic system for 10 years now, with good results, I think. We have the information we need to manage our businesses. That is not to say we can't improve, however, because, in fact, we are always considering refinements.

THE COMPANY

Ciba-Geigy was a large diversified corporation that was created in October 1970 as the result of a merger between two long-established Basel, Switzerland companies, CIBA Limited and J.R. Geigy S.A. Ciba-Geigy was truly a worldwide company, as in 1982, it employed nearly 80,000 people in 60 countries on five continents, and only 2 percent of its total sales of nearly SFr 14 billion (see Exhibit 1) were realized in its home country, Switzerland.

Ciba-Geigy used a matrix form of organization to ensure management attention both to products and geographical areas, and a large group of central staff functions supported both types of operating organizations (see Exhibit 2). These organizational elements are described as follows.

Product Division

One dimension of the matrix included seven product divisions, all involved in businesses related to one or more of what were considered to be the company's four franchise areas: chemistry, pharmaceuticals, agriculture, and physics. (The divisions are described in Exhibit 3.) The divisions were divided into a total of 41 strategic business units (SBUs).

The product divisions used a departmental form of organization, generally with managers responsible for research and development, production, marketing, and PIC (planning, information, and control) reporting to the division manager (see Exhibit 4). Most of the divisions also had one or more unique organizational functions; for example, the Pharmaceuticals Division (generally referred to as Pharma) had a Manager of Medicine who was responsible for clinical testing of products.

The factors that determined success were quite different between the divisions. One extreme was the Dyestuffs and Chemicals Division (D&C) which made products that were predominantly in very mature, even declining markets. In these markets, little innovation was occurring, and considerable production overcapacity existed, and that kept profits low. Thus, D&C's keys for success were marketing effectiveness, to maintain as much volume as possible, and cost control, particularly in production areas. Pharma, on the other hand, was profitable and growing rapidly. Continued growth, however, depended on continuous development of new products, and R&D was considered Pharma's most critical function. The R&D investments were significant, totalling about 14 percent of sales, and they involved considerable

This case was prepared by Professor Kenneth A. Merchant as a basis for class discussion rather than to illustrate either effective or ineffective handling of an administrative situation.

risk because the period of time before a new product could be brought to market was lengthy—up to 10 to 15 years due to legal requirements for medical testing—and because the competitive and political pressures could be intense. The other product divisions were between these two extremes, with some mature and some growth segments.

Group Companies

The other dimension of the matrix organization was geographically oriented. The managers of the 120 so-called Group Companies had responsibilities usually in a specific geographical area[1] which, in the case of most smaller countries, was an entire country. The Group Companies varied widely in size, with annual revenues ranging from only a few million to hundreds of millions of Swiss francs. Many Group Companies had responsibilities for sales and production, and some of the larger ones also controlled their own research and development facilities.

The Group Companies were organized into central functions and divisions which paralleled the product divisions of the parent company but did not necessarily include all the divisions (see Exhibit 5). The division managers were responsible for sales within the Group Company's geographical area, and they had strong dotted-line responsibility to managers in their respective product divisions.

Top Management and Central Functions

At the top of the Ciba-Geigy executive organization was a 9-member executive committee commonly referred to as the KL (abbreviation for Konzernleitung). The KL was responsible for the development and implementation of business policies, the setting of strategic targets for the product divisions and the company as a whole, the allocation of resources, and the basic organization structure and management principles guiding the company. Each member of the KL was a *KL patron* to particular product divisions, Group Companies, and/or the central functions that served both. Being a KL patron meant providing a liaison, with defined authorities and responsibilities, between the particular operating segment or staff function and the KL. (For specific examples of KL member responsibilities, see Exhibit 6.)

The central functions, located in Basel, included a full set of staff activities, including finance, control and management services, purchasing, research and development (for clearly specified tasks which were not in competition with divisional franchises), and personnel (for Swiss-based organizations only).

Distribution of Authority

In the late 1970s, the KL made a conscious effort to give the business unit managers greater control over the responsibility for operations, but it retained centralized control over important strategic decisions. Dr. Schär explained:

> We try to keep the important strategic decisions, which mainly involve questions of allocations of resources—money, people and facilities—centralized. We are guided in this allocation process because we have identified approximately 40 business segments (SBUs), and we allocate the bulk of the resources to the segments which we feel have the best prospects for the future. Other than that, we're decentralized. Every division is a business in itself. The managers have to develop plans, such as for research, marketing, and diversification, to serve their strategic mission within the constraints of the resources that have been allocated to them.

Jean Orsinger (Head of Pharma Division) agreed that he had significant operating autonomy:

> I definitely feel Ciba-Geigy is a decentralized company. They (the KL) tell me I have worldwide product responsibility, and I feel like I have it. We have a high rate of approvals for things we want to do. I cannot complain of a lot of interference.

THE ROI MEASURE AND COMPANY ACCOUNTING POLICIES

Ciba-Geigy's long-term financial objectives were set in terms of return on investment (ROI), and ROI was considered the single most important measure of financial success. ROI measures are, of

[1]Some of the Group Companies had responsibilities in a specific domain or area of franchise which was not a geographical area. For example, several Group Companies were established solely as distribution centers for other Group Companies.

course, dependent on the accounting rules used, and Ciba-Geigy was in a unique position of being able to choose its own set of accounting rules because Swiss multinationals did not have a legal obligation to publish any consolidated financial statements.[2]

Instead of using one of the sets of rules in most common use (e.g., those in use in the U.K. or U.S.),[3] Ciba-Geigy management chose to use a set of rules which they thought best presented the *true economic picture.*

The Ciba-Geigy accounting rules different from those in use in most companies in three important ways: use of current cost accounting, direct costing, and the operating income concept. These were described in company documents as follows:

- *Current Cost Accounting.* Fixed assets (building, equipment) are adjusted to inflated *current* values by specific indices. Inventories are valued at current cost of replacement. This is done to eliminate the *fictitious profit* that occurs when actual monetary value is confronted with historical costs. Current cost accounting (CCA) adjusts costs to the same inflation level as sales. Compared to historical cost accounting, which is based on the historical (paid) cost of assets, it leads to higher depreciation and material cost and consequently lower—but realistic—profits in the income statement. (A reconciliation between Ciba-Geigy income as reported and what it would have been using historical cost accounting rules is shown in Exhibit 7.)
- *Direct Costing.* All inventories are valued at variable cost, not at total product cost. The period costs incurred to produce intermediate or final products are not capitalized; they are charged directly to the income statement. Compared to an accounting system based on full cost, this has three effects. First, inventory values shown on the balance sheet are lower, compared on the same basis (i.e., historical cost accounting or CCA). Second, profits are more directly related to sales. Third, inventory build-up leads to lower profits, as compared to full costing, and inventory depletion leads to higher profits.
- *Operating Income Concept.* Only those transactions are charged to the income statement that are the result of operating activities. All extraordinary expenses, such as exchange gains and losses, writeoffs of goodwill from acquisitions, and revaluations of fixed assets to current costs, are charged or credited directly to equity on the balance sheet. (A summary of the extraordinary transactions occurring on a consolidated basis in 1982 were presented in the Ciba-Geigy annual report in a statement called *Movement of Equity Funds*. This is shown in Exhibit 8.)

Dr. Schär elaborated on the rationale behind the choice of this particular set of rules:

> We had been discussing the problems of performance measurements and the alternatives for years, back in the 1960s, and it was the general conviction that we needed to improve our measurement systems. At the time of the merger (1970), we were in a unique position to install something new, as everybody knew they would have to adapt to something different from what they were used to. There was minimal resistance to change.
>
> Geigy had just installed a responsibility accounting system based on direct costing (DC), and that made a lot of sense to us. With DC, the relationship between sales and profit is much more direct; what's happening to sales tends to show immediately on the profit level. We think that makes sense, because as sales increase you would expect profits to increase, and vice versa. With a full cost system, you can see sales decrease and profits stay level, or even go up. An accounting system with those characteristics has some weak points, I think. The main advantage of DC is that it shortens management reaction time, as managers tend to react quickly when they see profits fall. They might, for example, adjust prices or production levels.

---

[2]Most did so because of requests from Swiss stock exchanges. No particular set of accounting rules was required, or even suggested. Ciba-Geigy had published consolidated statements since 1971.

[3]Particular entities within Ciba-Geigy were required to submit sets of financial reports to various legal (and sometimes quasi-legal) authorities using a variety of accounting rules. Usually the financial reporting rules were dictated by the laws of the area in which the Ciba-Geigy legal entity was based. In some cases, a set of financial statements using still another set of accounting rules for tax purposes also had to be submitted. In Switzerland, for example, the accounting laws, which dated from the 1930s, were heavily biased in favor of conservatism to ensure the companies' continued prosperity (and thus to protect shareholders and creditors). In these legal accounts, Swiss companies were allowed to create hidden reserves by writing assets down to very small values. But these writedowns were generally not allowable for tax purposes.

Current cost accounting also made a lot of sense to us. Both CIBA and Geigy had had quite a bit of business experience in Latin America in the 1960s, and what we learned about inflation from that experience convinced us of the need for CCA. Look at the last 10 years and deduct the total Swiss inflation from our equity. You will see that we have kept the real value of our assets, and our substance intact. This is not the case for a lot of our competitors. With the high inflation of the past years, a lot of them were lost. They didn't realize that they paid our dividends they didn't earn—they paid out cash they had in fact borrowed from the banks!

Use of the operating income concept is based on our desire to have the income statement reflect operating performance only. Thus, we exclude everything that operating management cannot influence from the income statement.

EVALUATING PERFORMANCE OF OPERATING UNITS

Two types of evaluations of the financial performance of the Ciba-Geigy operating units were made: *managerial* performance was evaluated in terms of contribution and a contribution-based profitability measure called the *performance factor; economic* performance was evaluated in terms of return on investment (ROI). These approaches are described below.

Evaluating Managerial Performance

Contribution was used as the primary indicator of managerial performance because Ciba-Geigy management believed in the responsibility accounting principle which says that managers should be charged only with those costs and expenses which they could control.[4] The basic managerial control report was the Contribution Statement (shown in Exhibit 9), the key elements of which can be described as follows:

1. *Variable* costs and expenses varied directly with production or sales volume. *Variable Production Costs* included direct material, import duties, and purchasing costs only; direct labor was considered a fixed (period) cost, except in the U.S.
2. *Contribution Before Services* reflected all revenues and cost/expenses which originated in the specific organizational unit.
3. *Balance of Services* was a summary of the division's charges and credits for products and services provided within the company. Services were charged/credited as part of what was called the *Service Analysis* only if they were:
   - clearly originated by an organization unit;
   - objectively measurable; and
   - of economic significance.
4. *Contribution After Service* was a measure of performance in a wider sense than Contribution Before Services, as it reflected the revenues and costs/expenses of the services each unit provided and/or requested and consumed, in addition to local revenues and cost/expenses.

Contribution-based financial reports were produced at many levels of aggregation, from corporate summaries of the results of the product divisions and group companies down to the level of individual products. Examples are shown in Exhibits 10 and 11. Exhibit 10 shows a contribution report for a large group company and its five divisions; the group company headquarters and locally incurred financing expenses were not allocated to the divisions because they were not under the control of the division managers. Exhibit 11 shows a corporate summary with the totals for each of the product divisions.

The product divisions (but not the Group Companies) were also evaluated on a contribution-based profitability measure called the *Performance Factor* (PF). PF was computed as follows:

$$PF = \frac{\text{Contribution After Services}}{\text{Average Assets}^{5}\text{ Directly Employed by Division}} \times 10$$

The quotient was multiplied by 10 so that the PF number would be a different order of magnitude from and would not be confused with the

[4]In Ciba-Geigy terminology, the label *cost* was used only for revenue-diminishing items which rose in connection with production. All costs were, therefore, included in the standard cost calculations. All other revenue-diminishing items were given the label *expenses.*

[5]The assets were valued on a current cost basis, net of depreciation.

ROI numbers, the quotient of which was multiplied by 100. (Exhibit 12 shows a sample PF calculation.)

PF was not computed for Group Companies because it was not considered a reliable performance indicator. This was because most of the Group Companies were not complete businesses (i.e., they did not include all the major business functions), and it was felt that too many nearly arbitrary allocations of costs/expenses and, especially, assets were needed to calculate PF for them.

While Contribution After Services and PF were the primary financial goals for operating managers, performance-based incentives based on these measures were not an important part of the Ciba-Geigy's compensation package. Ciba-Geigy managers in the U.S. and Australia only were rewarded for performance which was measured partially in terms of contribution and PF, and even in these two locations the potential awards were small (10 to 15 percent of salary).

Evaluating Economic Performance

Ciba-Geigy management also found it useful to measure the economic performances of the product divisions in terms of ROI after allocations of indirect function expenses and assets and taxes. The ROI formula was as follows:

$$\text{ROI} = \frac{\text{Profit after taxes} + \text{interest expense}^{6}}{\text{Total divisional} + \text{functional assets}} \times 100$$

Each product division had a medium- to long-term financial target expressed in terms of ROI (as well as PF).

ROI, like PF, was much more difficult to calculate for the Group Companies than for the product divisions because most of the Group Companies were not close to being complete organizational entities.

TARGET SETTING PROCESSES

To establish performance targets for the operating units, Ciba-Geigy used three distinct planning processes: long-range planning, middle-range planning, and budgeting.

Long-Range Planning

Long-range (LR) planning was a largely qualitative, creative activity which involved looking at the general environment, long-term market prospects, competitive trends, and market positions (present and aspired to) in order to develop statements of the divisions' missions, policies, and basic strategies down to the SBU level. The KL and the product divisions took the lead in LR planning and sought input from Group Company and functional personnel only as required. The output from the LR planning process included a general mission statement for each division, a list of actions to be taken, and some quantitative targets in terms of a few key figures, including sales (built up from assumptions about prices and volumes, and expressed in constant 1981 Swiss francs), market share, PF, ROI, and cash flow, all for a point or period in time 7 to 10 years in the future. Long-range plans were not prepared for group companies or central functions.

LR planning was an ongoing process, as strategic discussions between divisional management and the KL took place whenever the need arose. The full LR planning process took place more or less every five years.

Middle-Range Planning

The other two planning processes—middle-range (MR) planning, and budgeting—took place annually. The timing of the communication processes between division headquarters and the divisions in the Group Companies necessary to complete these cycles is shown in Exhibit 13.

MR planning involved setting three-year strategies and targets for each division, SBU, and the largest Group Companies. In developing MR plans, the product divisions took the lead and conducted meetings with the key group company heads and division managers.

The MR plan itself consisted mainly of a qualitative analysis of the opportunities and risks that could be foreseen over the next three-year period, but a number of quantitative targets were also set for the major operating units and consolidated into a corporate MR plan. These included:

- Sales
- Contribution, Before and After Service Analysis
- Performance Factor
- ROI
- Personnel

[6]Interest expense was included in the numerator of the ROI calculation to reflect total return on the assets employed irrespective of whether they were financed by debt or equity.

- Receivables (Outstanding in Days)
- Inventory (Months Cover)
- Capital Expenditures

In addition to the above list, some division managers required some other quantitative MR targets from the division managers in the Group Companies. In particular divisions, these included targets for market shares, specific items of period expense, and product-specific performances (e.g., date of introduction of a new product). The central functions and the smaller Group Companies were not required to submit MR plans.

The MR planning process had been evolving over the years. Prior to 1978, MR target setting was largely a top-down process, as the KL gave targets to each product division and Group Company. Often these targets conflicted, and the bargaining processes needed to resolve the conflicts between the managers of the product divisions and the Group Companies were sometimes lengthy and heated.

In later years, the product divisions were given primary responsibility for developing MR targets. This was done both in order to increase the operating authority felt lower in the organization, and because the KL members realized that the targets depended critically on the product strategies; geographies were not the primary dimension in MR target setting. In the new MR planning process, the target *ideas* for the first planning year were prepared by divisional management after discussions and negotiations with managers in the Group Companies as necessary.

Any conflicts that might exist were expected to be resolved in the discussions that took place among the heads of the headquarters division, the local division, and the group company. In such discussions, the views of the heads of the headquarters division were given greater weight because the divisions were responsible for the implementation of the worldwide objectives. In the unlikely event that an issue could not be solved in these discussions, the problem was submitted to the KL patron(s) of the division and group company involved.

After they were finalized, the MR target ideas were approved by the responsible KL patrons. Then in May they were submitted to Central Control. Central Control consolidated and analyzed the targets and forwarded them with comments to the KL for review.

Another MR planning change (which started in 1980) was that more emphasis was placed on planning at the SBU level, instead of focusing just on the individual product and operating unit levels.

Budgeting

After the KL patron approved the MR plans for each division, the managers of the divisions and Group Companies prepared budgets for the next year. Budgeting involved identifying major action programs and setting detailed contribution targets for each responsibility center, down to, in some cases, the level of individual products. The budgets were the basis for the evaluations of performance during the next fiscal year.

By early October, the Group Companies were expected to have gotten far enough into the budgeting process so that the *October check* could be made; this involved telling if the first year of the MR plan could still be achieved. If it could not, perhaps because of changes in major environmental assumptions, a division/Group Company dialogue had to be reestablished to consider new action programs or to change the targets for the budget year. By the end of November, the budgets had to be submitted to headquarters. The total divisional budgets and the corporate consolidation were reviewed and approved by the LK as a body.

At the end of each quarter during the year, an abbreviated version of the budgeting process was used to prepare revised estimates for the year. The original budget was not changed, however; it served as the reference point in the local consolidated budget control processes for the whole year.

PERFORMANCE REPORTING AND REVIEW

Ciba-Geigy produced an extensive set of performance reports. The quarterly reports concentrated on contribution statements and included the following:

1. Contribution Before and After Service Analysis (Product Divisions and Group Companies), with the following variance analyses:
   - sales variances, broken into exchange rate parity, price and volume/mix variances;

- contribution variances from *budget*, both as converted in Swiss francs at actual exchange rates and assuming no change in exchange rates (shown in Exhibit 14 for a group company);
- contribution variance from *last year*, both actual and assuming no change in exchange rates.

2. Key figures, including personnel count and expenses, receivables, and inventories (Product Divisions and Group Companies).

Complete balance sheet data and allocations of indirect costs were prepared only annually; as a consequence, PF and ROI figures were available only on an annual basis.

In accordance with its desire to return more operating authority to the operating units, the KL had cut back its reviews of operating results sharply in 1981. Quarterly reviews of results and budget revisions were still scheduled, but starting in 1981, in quarters 1 through 3 the KL reviewed only a few key consolidated numbers and the comments submitted by the various organizational entities. In addition, the comments required from group companies were reduced in volume from 10–12 pages formerly, down to 1–2 pages, or nothing if results were *essentially on target.*

At year end, the KL reviewed the annual results, the variances and their consequences, and the planned actions, but this review was very brief if the business unit's objectives had been achieved. The time spent on the annual review had also been reduced, from 2–3 days prior to 1981, to 1 day.

As always, however, all managers were expected to report important and unforeseen developments or events, as well as major financial variances, immediately to their immediate superior. This was usually done informally either orally or by memorandum, but these *flash reports* were taken seriously.

SERVICE ANALYSIS

One of the dangers in reporting on a contribution basis was that the indirect costs not charged to the operating units in the contribution statement could get out of control. To minimize the risk of this happening, Ciba-Geigy management took several steps:

1. Central function managers were made clearly responsible for controlling costs, and the burden of showing need for increased resources was clearly placed on them.
2. A *service analysis* was institutionalized to give the divisions a direct influence on the quantity and quality of the services provided them. (See page 7 of this case.)
3. Every two or three years, the operating units were asked to evaluate and estimate the value of the services that were being provided to them from the central functions. This value estimate was compared to the cost being incurred.
4. Efforts were made to run every activity possible on a chargeout basis so that the operating managers would see the costs of the services they used. Sometimes this involved moving an activity out of a central function organization into an operating unit. For example, in 1979 Pharma took over responsibility for the Analytical Department (quality control) even though this activity, which had been an allocated part of the central research function, served several divisions. Costs of this department then were charged (and credited) as part of the service analysis in the division contribution statements.
5. A service was centralized (i.e., performed by a Central Function) only if it could be shown that it could be performed relatively efficiently and economically on that basis. Services that were performed centrally were to be adapted to the requirements of the recipient (e.g., competitive environment of a division) as necessary. Under certain circumstances, divisions were given the option of commissioning services from outside the company instead of using the services of a Central Function.

COMMENTS ABOUT THE CIBA-GEIGY INFORMATION AND CONTROL SYSTEM

Ciba-Geigy managers were generally satisfied with the company's information and control system. Here are some representative comments:

Paul Mark (Control, Group Companies):

> Although it looks complicated, our information system is about as simple as it could be. We cannot have a simple information system to cover our complicated organization. We produce and sell thousands of products, and in some unusual environments around the world. Plus there are numerous exceptions. For example, the management in Hong Kong is responsible for the pigment business in Indonesia. Singapore is responsible for

the dyes business in Jakarta, and so on. We could try to express all this in simpler terms, but the managers would say the numbers don't reflect their activities.

Mr. Orsinger (Head of Pharma Division):

I am quite happy with our information system. It is relatively simple, and it gives us the information we need to manage the division. I am also satisfied with being held accountable for the Performance Factor measure. If we don't reach it, we have only ourselves to blame.

Dr. Schär (KL member):

We need a lot of information to run this business. Although the key numbers in our system are based on contribution or ROI, depending on the specific purpose, we realize that it is dangerous to bring everything down to a single number and then rely on it—people can jiggle things around to meet the figures. For example, if sales are down, the division or company head could reduce R&D to meet the contribution objective, but in the long term, that could be disastrous. So we have a set of goals, and we make many measurements. We want to make sure that the major development efforts are carried through even if the profits are not what we expect in the first year.

Since Ciba-Geigy's information and control system had apparently served Ciba-Geigy well, the obvious question then was: Why had more companies not adopted the Ciba-Geigy-type of information system? In response to this question, Dr. Schär responded:

I think there are a couple of reasons why other companies don't use the type of system we have. One reason is that the introduction of these concepts are difficult in an ongoing business. People have a natural resistance to change, and in any case, a lot of training is required. It may take a crisis or a clean slate, such as we had at the time of the merger, to make the implementation doable.

Another, perhaps more important reason why our information system is relatively rare, is that many managers, particularly in the U.S., are paid on the basis of stock options or profits and they have an interest in showing annual and even quarterly increases. CCA brings income down, so that would directly affect their own compensation and DC makes income more volatile. Where is the incentive for these managers to install such a system? In Ciba-Geigy, we have very few management incentives based on income and we are not oriented to short-term stock performance. We have no option plans, and we are not interested in having shareholders who buy today and sell tomorrow, although we are, of course, very interested in having people invest in our stock for the long-term.

EXHIBIT 1 CIBA-GEIGY Group of Companies Summary of Financial Results at Current Value

	1982 SFr.m.	*1981 SFr.m.*	*Change, %*
Revenue			
Group sales to third parties	13,808	13,599	+1
Interest, royalties, and revenue from associated (non-consolidated) companies	253	237	+7
	14,061	**13,836**	**+2**
Expenditure			
Raw materials, intermediates and finished products (variable product costs, including inward freight and duties)	4,360	4,450	−2
Wages, salaries, bonuses and welfare benefits	4,206	4,095	+3
Interest payable	439	462	−5
Depreciation on fixed assets	836	818	+2
Other expenditure, including taxes	3,598	3,490	+3
	13,439	**13,315**	**+1**
Group operating profit	**622**	**521**	**+19**
As a percentage of sales	4.5	3.8	
Group operating cash flow	**1,458**	**1,339**	**+9**
As a percentage of sales	10.6	9.8	

EXHIBIT 2 Organization

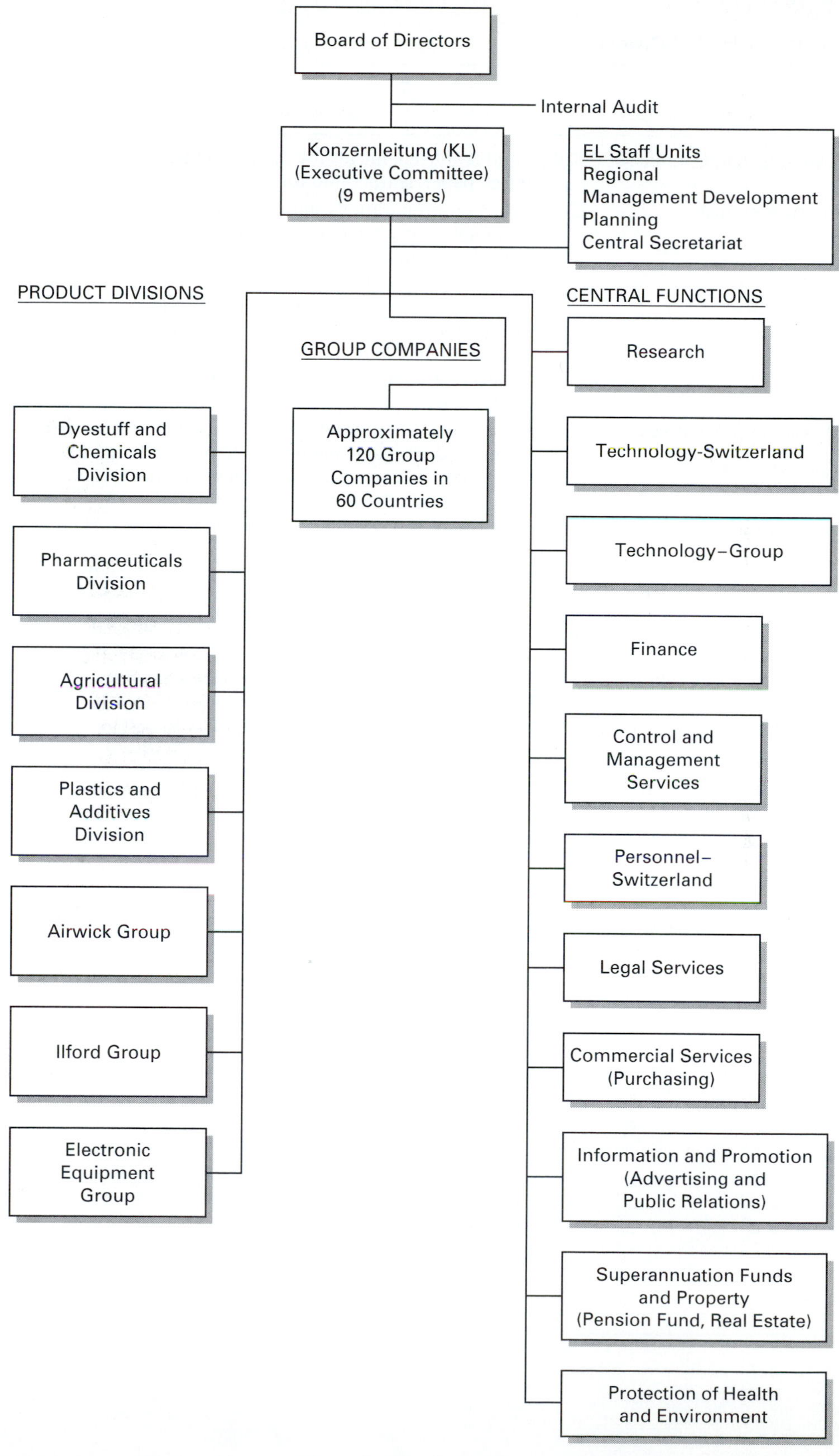

Board of Directors
Internal Audit
Konzernleitung (KL)
(Executive Committee)
(9 members)
EL Staff Units
Regional
Management Development
Planning
Central Secretariat
PRODUCT DIVISIONS
GROUP COMPANIES
CENTRAL FUNCTIONS
Dyestuff and Chemicals Division
Pharmaceuticals Division
Agricultural Division
Plastics and Additives Division
Airwick Group
Ilford Group
Electronic Equipment Group
Approximately 120 Group Companies in 60 Countries
Research
Technology-Switzerland
Technology–Group
Finance
Control and Management Services
Personnel–Switzerland
Legal Services
Commercial Services (Purchasing)
Information and Promotion (Advertising and Public Relations)
Superannuation Funds and Property (Pension Fund, Real Estate)
Protection of Health and Environment

EXHIBIT 3 Product Division

Division	*Main Products*	*1982 Revenues (million SFr)*	*Number of SBUS*
Dyestuffs and Chemicals	Colors and textile chemicals for dyeing and treating of fabrics, paper, leather and fur.	2,133	5
Pharmaceuticals	Cardiovascular preparations, antirheumatics and other anti-inflammatory preparations, psychotropic and neurotropic drugs, and medicines and drugs for treatment of various infectious diseases.	4,083	11
Agricultural	Products to improve the yield and quality of food crops, livestock and natural fibres (e.g., herbicides, insecticides, micronutrients), high performance hybrid seeds, products for animal health and for use in public health and hygiene.	3,451	5
Plastics and Additives	Epoxy resins and other thermosetting synthetic resin systems, organic and inorganic pigments and pigment preparations, additives like antioxidants, light and heat stabilizers and ultraviolet curing agents.	2,580	13
Airwick*	Consumer products, including household products (e.g., air fresheners, floor, rug and furniture care products), garden products (e.g., lawn care products), and personal hygiene products (e.g., mouthwashes, breath fresheners).	679	1
Ilford*	Black-and-white photographic materials (e.g., film, printing and enlarging papers), color materials and chemicals.	424	2
Electronic Equipment*	Broad range of electronic equipment, including color measuring instruments, telecommunications security systems, electronic analytical and precision balances, systems for the counting of small mass produced parts, and thermal analysis systems.	458	4

*These organizations were given the label "Group" instead of Division for historical reasons; they were significantly smaller than the other four organizations, and their products were not sold under Ciba-Geigy brand names.

EXHIBIT 4 Typical Product Division Organization

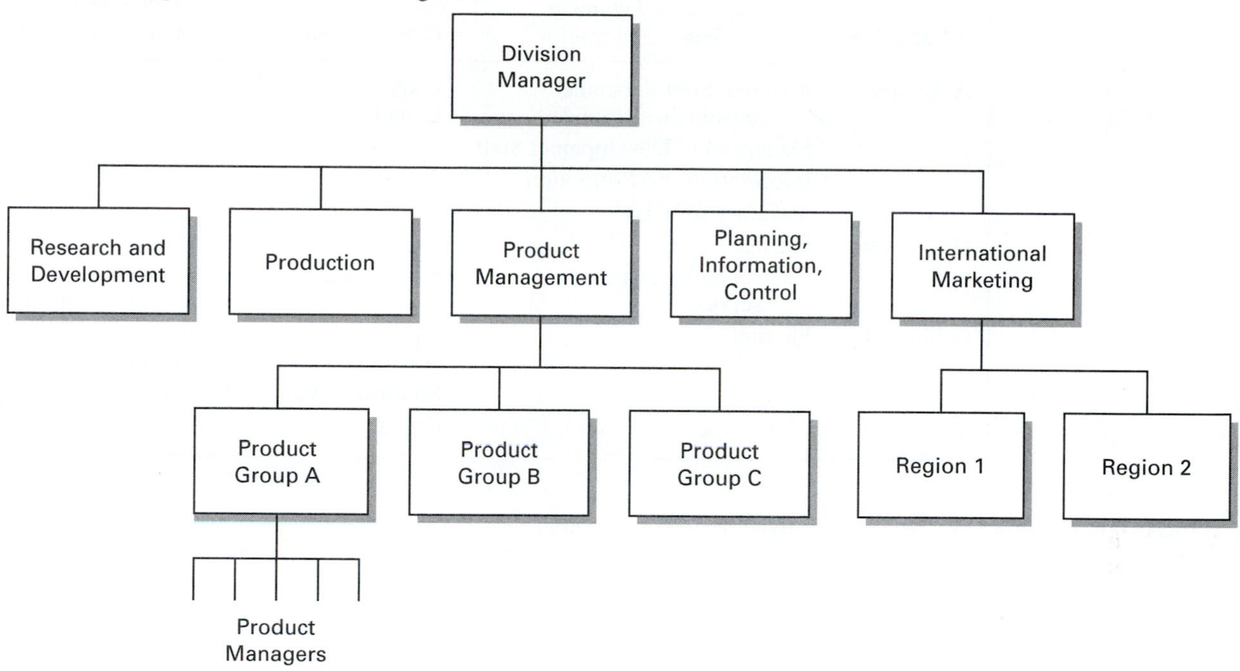

EXHIBIT 5 Typical Group Company Organization

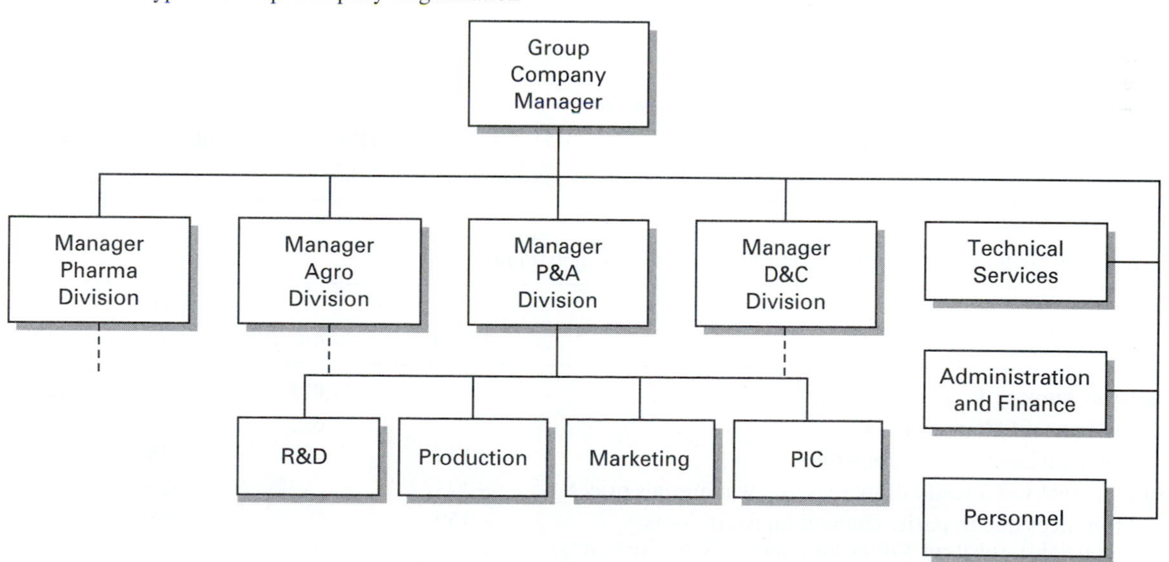

EXHIBIT 6 Examples of Responsibilities of KL Members

KL Member	*LIAISON TO:* *Operating Entities or Central Functions*	*Group Companies*	*Committee Assignments*
A. Bodmer	Regional Staff Personnel outside Switzerland Management Development Staff Information and Promotion Secretary (of KL)	USA Canada	
H. P. Schär	Finance Control and Management Services	Latin America Eastern Europe	Finance Insurance Information Systems
G. Staehelin	Pharma Airwick	Japan Australia Southwest Asia China	Insurance Third World Ecology

EXHIBIT 7 Group Profit by Conventional (Historical-Cost) Accounting

	1982 SFr.m.	*1981 SFr.m.*	*Change, %*
Current-value Group operating profit	**622**	**521**	**+19**
Add Revaluation of stocks as a result of increased raw materials prices	123	316	
Add Difference beween current-value and historical-cost depreciation on fixed assets	248	238	
Less Valuation differences due to parity changes on the financial status item 'Other long-term assets,' current assets and liabilities	291	425	
Approximate historical-cost Group profit	**702**	**650**	**+8**
as a percentage of sales	5.1	4.8	
Add Book depreciation (historical-cost basis) on fixed assets	588	580	
Approximate historical-cost cash flow	**1290**	**1230**	**+5**
as a percentage of sales	9.3	9.0	

EXHIBIT 8 CIBA-GEIGY Group of Companies Movement of Equity Funds

	1982 SFr.m.	*SFr.m.*	*1981 SFr.m.*	*SFr.m.*
Group equity at January 1		**11,018**		**10,848**
Group operating profit after taxation		+622		+521
Adjustment of fixed assets to current value	+709		+576	
Revaluation of stocks as a result of increased raw materials prices	+123		+316	
Valuation differences due to parity changes on fixed assets	−159		−525	
on the financial status item 'Other long-term assets,' current assets and liabilities	**−291**		**−425**	
Total valuation adjustments		+382		−58
Restructuring costs		−71		−96
Other equity changes		−152		−91
Distribution of profits (dividend and directors' percentages of CIBA-GEIGY Limited)		−120		−106
Group equity at December 31		**11,679**		**11,018**

EXHIBIT 9 Summary Division Contribution Statement—Division DC (For year ended December 31, 1982) (SFr millions)

Sales	2,133
Var. Product Costs	788
Var. Expenses	93
Marginal Contribution	1,252
Period Costs	(801)
Other Income/Expenses	12
Variances & Adjustments	(25)
Div. Contribution before Services	438
Balance of Services	(109)
Div. Contribution after Services	329

NOTE: Numbers are disguised.

EXHIBIT 10 Company Contribution—Group Company X (for year ended December 31, 1982) (SFr millions)

	DIVISIONS					
	DC	*PH*	*AC*	*PA*	*AW*	*Total*
Sales	83	218)	338	133)	98	870
Var. Product	(25)	(13)	(117)	(62)	(31)	(248)
Var. Expenses	(5)	(6)	(18)	(3)	(13)	(45)
Marginal Contribution	53	199	203	68	54	577
Period Costs	(10)	(82)	(50)	(12)	(31)	(185)
Other Income/Expenses	—	(1)	2	—	1	2
Variances & Adjustments	(1)	(5)	—	(2)	(1)	(9)
Contribution before Services and Expenses	42	111	155	54	23	385
Balance of Services	(2)	(9)	(4)	(4)	(8)	(27)
Contribution after Services	40	102	151	50	15	358
Group Company Expenses						(51)
Financing Expenses						(23)
Company Contribution after Services and Expenses						284

NOTE: Numbers are disguised.

EXHIBIT 11 Consolidated Contribution and Operating Profit (for year ended December 31, 1982) (Sfr millions)

	◁			*DIVISIONS*			▷	
	DC	*PH*	*AC*	*PA*	*AW*	*IL*	*EL*	*Total*
Sales	2,133	4,083	3,451	2,580	679	424	458	13,808
Variable Costs/Expenses	(881)	(1,288)	(1,959)	(1,250)	(301)	(200)	(195)	(6,074)
Marginal Contribution	1,252	2,795	1,492	1,330	378	224	263	7,734
Period Costs/Expenses	(814)	(1,807)	(852)	(768)	(197)	(144)	(135)	(4,717)
Contribution Before Services	438	988	640	562	181	80	128	3,017
Balance of Services	(109)	(58)	(98)	(69)	(24)	(8)	(17)	(383)
Contribution after Services	329	930	542	493	157	72	111	2,634
Other Expenses								
Central Function Expenses (unallocated)								(1,871)
Interest Expense (unallocated)								(346)
Income from Associated Companies								205
Consolidated Operating Profit								622

NOTE: Numbers are disguised.

EXHIBIT 12 Performance Factor Calculation—Division DC (for year ended December 31, 1982) (SFr millions)

Division Contribution after Services:		329 (from Exhibit 9)
Assets Employed (at end of year):		
Receivables from Third Parties	390	
Inventories	466	
Total working capital	856	
Buildings	4,277	
Machines	1,487	
Other	310	
Total Fixed Assets	6,074	
Total Assets	6,930	

Performance Factor:

$$\frac{\text{Division Contribution}}{\text{Ave. Assets Employed by Division}} \times 10 = \frac{329}{(6{,}530 + 6{,}930) \div 2} \times 10 = .49$$

(This calculation assumes that Total Assets at the end of 1981 was 6,530.)

NOTE: Numbers are disguised.

EXHIBIT 13 Coordination of Target-Setting Processes between Product Divisions and Group Company Divisions

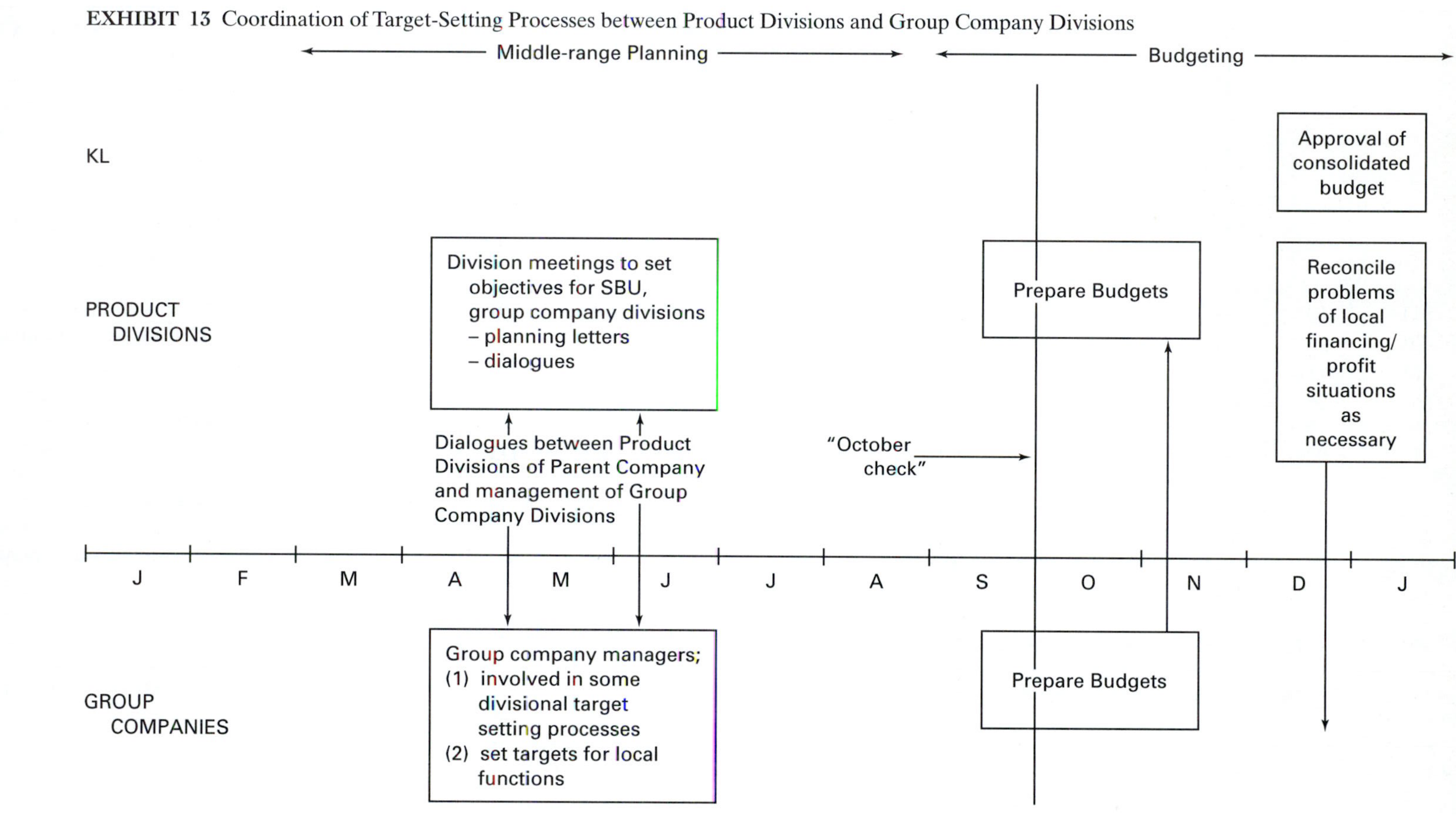

EXHIBIT 14 Variance Analysis—Group Company X (for year ended December 31, 1982) (SFr millions)

	DIVISIONS										TOTAL GROUP COMPANY		
	DC		PH		AC		PA		AW				
Company Contribution	*Actual*	*% Budget*	*Actual*	*% Budget*	*Actual*	*% Budget*	*Actual*	*% Budget*	*Actual*	*% Budget*	*Actual*	*Actual % Budget*	*Curr. Adj. % Budg.*
Sales to Third Parties	83	93	218	91	338	114	133	102	98	91	870	101	108
Var. Production Costs	(25)	97	(13)	76	(117)	101	(62)	104	(31)	91	(248)	99	102
Var. Expenses	(5)	103	(6)	115	(18)	136	(3)	80	(13)	101	(45)	113	121
Marginal Contribution	53	90	199	91	203	122	68	102	54	88	577	101	110
Period Costs	(10)	90	(82)	90	(50)	96	(12)	89	(31)	82	(185)	90	97
Variances and Adjustments	(1)	130	(6)	225	2	—	(2)	293	—	—	(7)	341	367
Contribution Before Expenses and Services	42	90	111	90	155	136	54	104	23	87	385	106	116
Group Company Expenses											(51)	91	97
Financing Expenses											(23)	92	98
Company Contribution											310	111	122
Balance of Services	(2)	90	(9)	91	(4)	113	(4)	107	(8)	86	(27)	95	102
Contribution After Services	40	90	102	89	151	137	50	103	15	88	358	107	118
Analysis of Variances													
Currency Effects—Div. Contr.	(4)		(8)		(16)		(7)		(2)		(36)		
Non Div. Exp.											5		
											(31)		
Marginal Contribution			(4)		55		9		(3)		57		
Period costs—Division					1		(1)		1		2		
Central Function											1		
Other (Financing)											1		
Total Variances	(4)		(12)		40		1		(4)		30		

NOTE: Numbers are disguised.

Teco Electric & Machinery Co. Ltd.

In July 1995, Mr. T. S. Hsieh, president of TECO Electric & Machinery Co., Ltd., explained that he thought much of the company's success over the years was due to the *spirit of TECO.* The TECO spirit existed because top-level managers hired good people, ran the corporation in a democratic way, encouraged employees to perform as a team, and made sure successes were enjoyed not only by shareholders but also employees, the society, and the corporation itself.

Mr. Hsieh thought one important factor helping to create the TECO spirit was a management decision to evaluate performance using *value-added,* rather than profit, as the primary corporate measure of success. Value-added was calculated by subtracting from sales revenues all payments to outsiders (for example, suppliers, subcontractors). TECO managers believed that the use of value-added focused attention on the right issues and created less conflict between shareholders and employees.

In the last few years, however, some issues regarding the use of value-added had arisen. Mr. Fred P. C. Wang, vice chairman of the TECO board was quick to explain that, "We are not considering abandoning value-added. The concept is perfect. But maybe we need to adjust it." The issues being discussed related to the calculation of value-added, the optimal way for sharing value added between employees and shareholders, and employee understanding and acceptance of the measure.

THE COMPANY

TECO was founded in 1956 as Tong-Yuen Electric Company[1] in San Chung City, a suburb of Taipei, Taiwan (Republic of China) with an initial capitalization of NT$3 million (US$200 thousand). Its initial product was induction motors.

Since its inception, TECO's stated mission was to generate customer satisfaction, create profit, and promote social prosperity. To fulfill the company's mission, TECO's management endeavored to build an excellent organization that emphasized technology and the creation of "a harmony between managers and employees." The basic strategy involved both continuous improvement of core businesses and expansion of long-term horizons through well-considered diversification into businesses that leveraged core strengths.

Guided by these principles and strategies, TECO management responded in the early 1970s to the development of a more affluent society in Taiwan and the international oil crisis in 1972 by shifting the company's focus more toward home appliances and high technology information systems products, both of which were designed to increase energy savings and efficiencies. This led to the introduction of a broad range of new products, including refrigerators, clothes washers and dryers, air conditioners, televisions, video cassette recorders, calculators, computer monitors and terminals, printers, robots, facsimile machines, and personal computers.

In addition to developing technology and marketing strengths internally, over the years TECO formed alliances with leading international companies to enhance its strategic position. Among its alliance partners were General Electric, Whirlpool, Westinghouse, Toshiba, Ericsson, Pitney Bowes, and Royal Co. Ltd. of Japan.

By 1994, TECO had grown to become one of the twenty largest private-sector companies in Taiwan with more than 3,500 employees and sales of NT$17.1 billion.[2] It had established a network

[1]The company adopted TECO as its official English name in 1978.

[2]At the time of the case, 1 NT$ = approximately US$.04.

Professor Kenneth A. Merchant wrote this case with the assistance of Professor Anne Wu (National Chengchi University, Taiwan, R.O.C.) as a basis for class discussion rather than to illustrate either effective or ineffective handling of an administrative situation.

of overseas subsidiaries and affiliates to serve markets in Southeast Asia, Australia, North America, and Europe. Exhibit 1 shows highlights of TECO's 13-year financial results.

The company made its initial public stock offering in 1973. The number of shareholders grew from 437 in 1973 to more than 50,000 in 1995. Unlike many Taiwanese firms, no single family controlled a significant proportion of TECO stock.

ORGANIZATION

Throughout its early history, TECO operated with a functional form of organization. In 1978, facing an increased number of product lines which made it difficult to coordinate manufacturing and sales for each product line centrally, management tried to implement a decentralized profit center form of organization. But this early attempt failed because the organization proved to be too complex. It had too many profit centers; every product line and the sales and marketing functions within each product line were set up as profit centers. A number of conflicts arose, such as about transfer prices. Top management was too busy at the time to resolve these problems, so the profit center organization was discontinued after a one-year test period.

In 1985, TECO management began the implementation of a more modest form of divisionalization. They divided the company into three division—home automation, factory automation, and information technology—each of which was to be run as a profit center. It took three years to design the performance measures and reports, to allocate the assets to divisions and, most importantly, to train the managers to use the new system. The system was formally introduced at the end of 1987. Exhibit 2 shows TECO's 1995 organization chart.[3]

[3]The Information Systems division was spun off in 1989 as TECO Information Systems Co. Ltd., with TECO still owning 70 percent of the stock. This separation was made to allow the division to respond better to the dynamic nature of the information product markets and technologies. TECO managers found that the information systems personnel, who were more creative, needed different systems and higher pay scales.

THE VALUE-ADDED MEASURE OF PERFORMANCE

Value added was the most important measure of performance within TECO. It was used for evaluating management performances and for distributing bonus monies. Value added was calculated by subtracting from revenues the amounts of value provided to outsiders, which included direct materials, utility expenses, depreciation, indirect expenses (excluding payroll), and subcontract fees and other purchases from outsiders. What remained were the amounts of value provided to:

1. employees (salaries, bonuses, benefits);
2. shareholders (dividends, directors' compensation, retained earnings);
3. society (taxes, donations, interest) (*Banks are social shareholders*).

Regarding the value contributed to society: TECO's management recognized that much of the company's success was due to the Taiwan's considerable success. In TECO's 1993 Annual Report, in a section titled "The Company's Ideals: Contributing to the Good of Society and Country," they acknowledged that, "Our debt to society must be repaid" and that "We measure our enterprise's success in terms of how this debt is repaid.

TECO implemented the value-added concept in 1966. Mr. Shieh, TECO's president, was quick to explain, however, that "We didn't invent value-added; we borrowed it from the Japanese." TECO's chairman had visited a Japanese university, read about the system, and adapted it for use in TECO.[4]

Value-added was used within TECO for deciding *how big the pie is for employee bonuses.* In the opinion of TECO management, value added was superior to profit as a measure of entity performance both because it was more consistent with the company's values and because it generated less conflict between shareholders and employees. The basic difference between profit and value-added is that with the profit concept, the residual goes to the shareholders; with the value added concept, the residual goes both to the shareholders and to the people whose efforts created the value added (the employees).

[4]The value-added measure was not in widespread use in either Japan or Taiwan, although a few companies did use it.

After the *size of the value-added pie* was calculated, management had to decide how it should be divided between employees and shareholders. Initially 25 percent was allocated to employees. Over the years, however, more competitive market conditions had caused TECO's value-added return to decrease, and prices and incomes in Taiwan had increased. In response to these changes, TECO managers gradually raised the employees' share of the value added. The last change, made in 1990, raised the employee's share from 40 to 43 percent. The sharing rule was changed only infrequently. The shares were generally fixed for at least five years and were changed only when they were challenged.

TECO used the value added system in all of its domestic and foreign locations. TECO managers believed it worked equally well in all locations except Southeast Asia. Mr. Shieh, said, "U.S. and Australian managers love it. But managers in Southeast Asia seem to have trouble understanding the company's philosophy of sharing the value created."

INCENTIVE COMPENSATION

The employee's share of the corporate value-added created a pool of funds to be allocated to individuals as bonuses. The pool was translated into an average number of days of salary to be given in bonuses and was allocated to individuals according to the following formula:

Individual bonus
= average bonus (number of days of salary) × individual's daily salary × number of days employed in the current year × entity performance percent × individual performance percent × (1 + extra-job pay percentage)

Explanation of the last three factors in the individual bonus formula:

1. The entity performance percent was based on 50 percent on corporate value-added and 50 percent on the performance of the subunit to which the employee was assigned, both as compared to plan. For division managers and division-staff managers, the subunit was the division. Subunit performance was measured using a variety of indicators. For example, in 1995 for the top-level managers in one division, the factors considered in calculating the entity performance percent and the factor weightings were:

PERFORMANCE AS COMPARED TO PLAN	**FACTOR WEIGHTING (%)**
Corporate value added	50
Sales	15
Sales growth rate	7.5
Return on assets	15
Value added per NT$ payroll	12.5
	100% (max.)

Entity performance was also measured in 18 subunits that were smaller than a division. Eight of these subunits were within the factory automation division; four were within the home automation division; and six were within corporate staff.

Plans for each of these elements of performance were set in a mostly top-down manner by corporate managers. But as part of the planning process, the corporate managers solicited input from division and corporate staff managers.

No automatic adjustments were made for the effects of uncontrollable factors (for example, typhoon damage to a plant), but the president was given the power to adjust the entity performance percent upward by up to five percent if uncontrollable circumstances so warranted or if he wanted to reward managers for aspects of their performance that had not yet been reflected in the financial measures (for example, effective implementation of a new system, development of a useful social relationship). To date, however, he had never exercised this adjustment right.

2. The individual performance percent was based on each individual's performance rating, on a scale from 1 (highest) to 5 (lowest), based on achievement of tailored MBO targets. The list of MBO performance areas for a representative division manager are shown in Exhibit 3, and those for a representative product manager are shown in Exhibit 4. These lists show that the individual performance evaluations were based on a combination of quantitative indicators and subjective assessments.

The evaluations were then forced into an approximately normal distribution, with 5 percent of the employees earning the highest rating of *one,* 20 percent earning a *two,* 50 percent earning a *three,* and so on. These ratings were then translated into a performance percent for use in the bonus formula as follows:

PERFORMANCE RATING	PERFORMANCE PERCENT
1	140%
2	130%
3	120%
4	110%
5	100%

It was a conscious management decision to give the lowest rated employees a performance percent of 100 percent, not a lower figure such as zero. Mr. Michael S. F. Liu, senior manager in the corporate planning department, explained, "This is part of Chinese philosophy, to make people feel good."

3. The extra-job pay percent was designed to ensure that higher level employees received larger bonuses. The extra-pay percentages were:

division manager	40%
manager	20%
product-line manager	10%
all lower-level employees	0%

These calculations resulted in average bonuses for all types of employees that were approximately 40 percent of salary in a good year for the corporation, 35 percent in a normal year, and 30 percent in a bad year. In 1994, TECO awarded its employees 176 days of base pay in bonus, the highest in the company's history.

CURRENT ISSUES

While they judged that the value-added system was generally working well, TECO managers were preparing to discuss three issues that had arisen. One related directly to the formula for calculating value-added. Some within the firm had raised questions as to whether depreciation and interest expense should be included or excluded from value-added and whether adjustments should be made for uncontrollable changes in the company's situation. Depreciation was becoming a more significant expense item as the company automated its production processes. Interest expense had become a concern because debt levels were no longer roughly constant, as they had been a decade ago. Furthermore, the company was taking on different kinds of debt, such as overseas convertible bonds rather than bank loans. Finally, some employees worried that uncontrollable changes in, for example, Taiwan's GDP or TECO's competition, could have significant, unfair effects on the value-added measure.

A second issue was created by uncertainty about the optimal sharing of the corporate value-added. Among the questions the managers were discussing were: Should the allocation percentage be changed more frequently to adapt to changing conditions? Should the company have a formula that automatically determined the allocation percentage? If so, what factors should be in the formula? For example, should the degree of automation be considered? Could the formula be used to provide incentives for employees to increase productivity, such as by dropping the employee's share if automation efforts were lagging? Should labor market conditions be considered? Labor was currently tight in Taiwan, and higher percentage might enhance the company's ability to attract the best employees.

The third issue related to how best to explain the value-added system to lower-level employees, particularly those with low levels of education. The system had not worked particularly well with manufacturing personnel in the factory automation division. These employees had low education levels: they had trouble understanding the system; and they did not think that the goals given them were reasonable. In recent years, these employee's bonuses had been based only on division subunit performance, and managers believed that the failure to link bonuses to individual performance had hindered efforts to improve productivity in the plant.

On the other hand, the system had worked well with the manufacturing people in the home automation division. As compared with those in factory automation, these employees were younger, were better educated (most had graduated at least from junior high school), and were engaged in more simpler, assembly-type work, the outputs of which were easier to distinguish for evaluation purposes.

EXHIBIT 1 13-Year Financial Highlights

	Sales	*Gross Margin*	*Net Income After Tax*	*Total Assets*	*Equity*
1982	NT$3.7	NT$0.8	NT$0.2	NT$4.1	NT$2.0
1983	5.0	1.2	0.4	4.7	2.2
1984	7.0	1.6	0.7	5.9	2.7
1985	6.7	1.5	0.5	5.6	3.0
1986	7.5	1.6	0.7	6.6	3.3
1987	9.3	2.0	1.0	8.7	4.1
1988	11.2	2.3	1.1	10.6	4.9
1989	12.2	2.3	0.9	12.9	7.0
1990	9.6	2.3	1.1	12.1	7.7
1991	10.3	2.7	1.3	13.4	8.7
1992	11.9	2.9	1.3	14.8	9.4
1993	14.2	3.4	1.6	16.4	10.4
1994	17.1	4.0	2.0	21.2	12.1

EXHIBIT 2 1991 Organization Chart

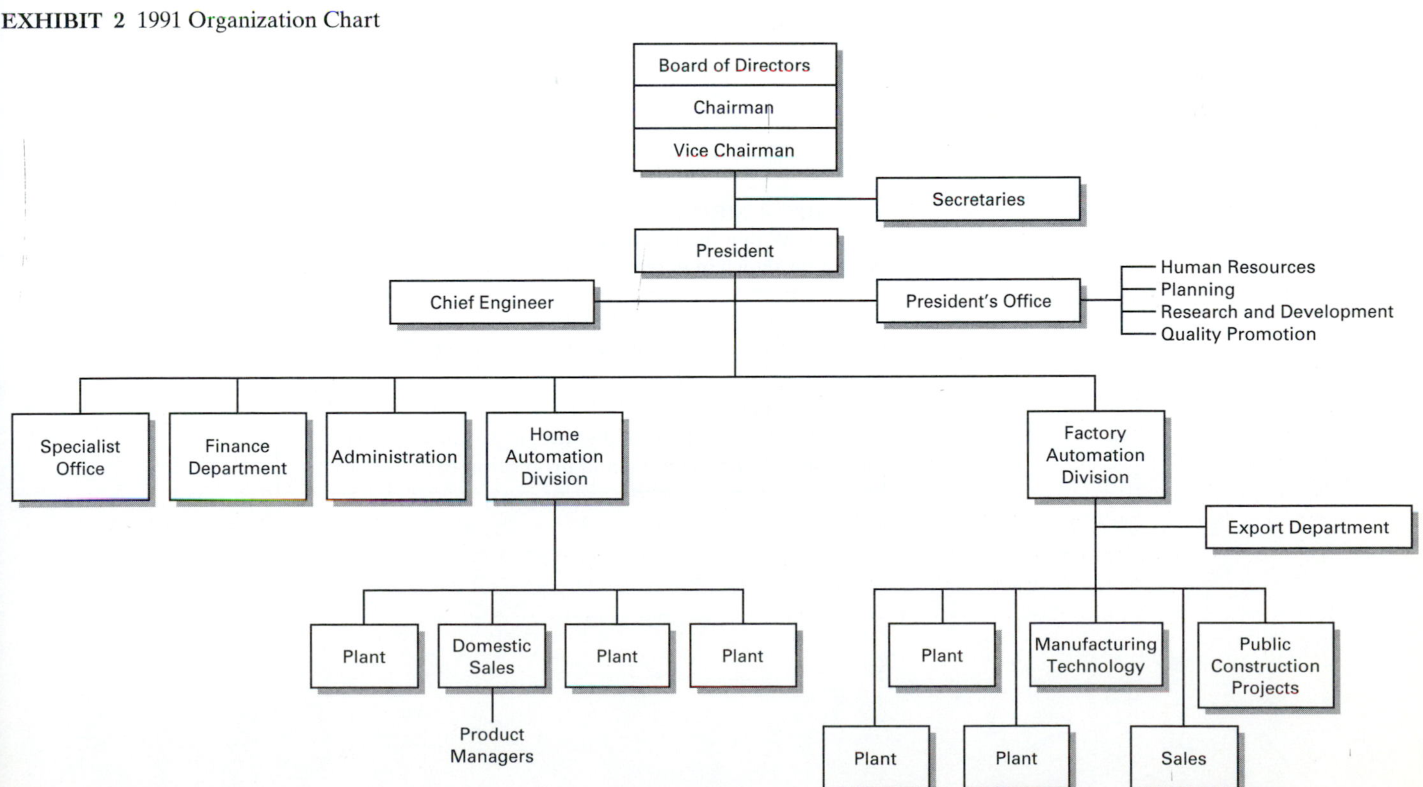

EXHIBIT 3 MBO Performance Areas for a Representative Division Manager (importance weighting shown in parentheses)

A. short-term (60%)
   1. return on assets
   2. competitive power
      a. market share
      b. sales growth
   3. productivity
      a. labor (value added/payroll expense)
      b. asset (value added/total assets)

B. long-term (40%)
   1. planning
      a. middle-long term planning (5–10 years). Subjective evaluation of the direction the business is taking.
      b. market planning. Subjective evaluation of the near-term strategic direction for the business unit, given the competition and industry situation.
   2. merchandise
      a. new products/models
      b. strategic product sales[1]/total sales
      c. technology (e.g., productivity, product standardization, waste reduction)
   3. human resource development (education, training, rotation)

[1]Strategic products tended to be high volume, profitable products or products that promised high profits in the near future

EXHIBIT 4 MBO Targets for a Representative Product Manager Within the Home Automation Division (importance weighting shown in parentheses)

1. product sales attained (35%)
2. growth in gross profit for product line (17%)
3. market share (17%)
4. inventory turnover (17%)
5. sales development of a strategic product (17%)
6. control of marketing and promotion expenses (3%)

CHAPTER 20

Control in Not-for-Profit Organizations

Prior chapters in this textbook have focused on MCSs in profit-seeking organizations. Not-for-profit organizations deserve some specific focus because they are important and in some ways are quite different from profit-seeking organizations.

Not-for-profit organizations fill a number of important societal roles. All (or virtually all) government organizations, churches, museums, labor unions, and political and fraternal organizations are not-for-profit organizations. Collectively, not-for-profit organizations comprise a large portion of the world's economy.

Not-for-profit organizations have many things in common with for-profit organizations. Most of them provide services (or, less commonly, products), and they have to compete with other organizations to be the chosen provider. They have professional managers who develop objectives, strategies, and budgets. Their managers delegate authority and hold their subordinates accountable in specific performance areas.

Not-for-profit organizations' MCS alternatives and challenges are often quite different than those faced by for-profit organizations. Understanding what is different about not-for-profit organizations and how those differences affect their MCSs is the focus of this chapter.

DIFFERENCES BETWEEN FOR-PROFIT AND NOT-FOR-PROFIT ORGANIZATIONS

The defining difference between for-profit and not-for-profit organizations is the organization's mission or goal. A *not-for-profit organization* is an organization whose primary purpose is anything other than to make a profit (or, more precisely, to create wealth for its owners). Its primary purpose is typically to provide some kind of public service. The not-for-profit category includes a large and diverse set of organizations, so the types of services provided varies widely. These services can be charitable, religious, scientific, literary, or educational. Included in the not-for-profit category are *governmental organizations* at federal, state, and local levels, and their various institutions, authorities, agencies, and programs. Also included are a large number of private organizations operated for *public benefit,* such as museums, hospitals, universities, and schools. Some not-for-profit organizations, such as religious organizations and charitable foundations, serve various *private benefit* purposes; and some, such as cooperatives, and labor, fraternal, trade, and homeowners' associations, are operated for the *mutual benefit* of the members.

Unlike for-profit organizations, not-for-profit organizations do not have any outside equity interest. That means that while somebody may control them, nobody owns them. Many not-for-profit organizations earn revenues by selling services or products, such as by charging admissions to see a museum exhibit or a theatrical presentation. Others are given money by a third party in exchange for providing their service; for example, a government entity might provide a school district $3,000 for every child taught. Money (cash flows and surpluses of revenues over expenses) is only a constraint; it is not an overriding goal. Some subentities within not-for-profit organizations do have goals to earn profits: governments run lotteries, hospitals run gift shops, the Girl Scouts sell cookies, and universities sell athletic tickets. In earning their profits they compete with for-profit organizations; however, profit is not their primary purpose. Whatever profits are earned in the subentities are used to further the organizations' overriding goals. Not-for-profit organizations are legally prohibited from distributing whatever income or profits they may have earned to anyone. They do not pay dividends. All the resources they acquire must be used to further the organizations' primary purposes.

All not-for-profit organizations have in common the above purpose- and ownership-related characteristics. They also tend to have some characteristics with MCS implications that apply to them far more than they apply to for-profit organizations. The following sections describe these characteristics and their MCS implications.

GOAL AMBIGUITY AND CONFLICT

As discussed earlier, MCSs should be designed to enhance the probability that the organization's goals will be achieved, and assessments about the MCS effectiveness should be predicated upon judgments of the likelihood (or degree of) goal achievement. Goal clarity exists in for-profit organizations; the primary goal is to maximize shareholder value. Managers of publicly-owned corporations can easily obtain timely feedback on their goal achievement by monitoring their company's stock performance and comparing it to those of their competitors and the overall market.

This goal clarity does not exist in many not-for-profit organizations. Usually many constituencies have an interest in the organization, its goals, and its performance. These constituencies often do not agree; their values and interests conflict.[1]

The managers of a museum may perceive that their primary goal is to run their central museum facility as effectively and efficiently as possible. Others with some say, however, (members of their board of directors, their management team, local government officials, or members of the community) might perceive that the museum's goals are to make museum materials and exhibits accessible to the community-at-large, even to those who are unable to travel to the central location. Neighbors might be most concerned about traffic congestion and lack of parking. Still others, such as those in the local government, might be more concerned with cost reduction goals than service goals. Resolving these conflicts and differences in perceptions requires special decision making mechanisms.

Conflict is inevitable in government organizations. These organizations are often directed from a number of sources, including the executive, legislative, and judicial branches of government and, possibly, from federal, state, and local levels.

Law enforcement organizations have to respond to laws passed and rulings made by all levels of legislatures, regulatory agencies, and courts. Their funding, and their consequent accountability, may also be to multiple authorities. Managers of these organizations face external pressure because the press and public in democratic societies have access to considerable information. Some key officials (a sheriff or district attorney) may face reelection pressures and have a need to please the public-at-large and (hopefully not) potentially large campaign donors. This diffusion of direction greatly complicates management. At a minimum, it provides for more goal complexity. In many cases, the goals given to the organization from its various constituencies can conflict.

Without clarity as to what goals should be achieved and how trade-offs among them should be made, it is difficult, if not impossible, to judge how well the organization's control system or, indeed, how well the management team, is performing. Some not-for-profit organizations struggle with this fundamental problem. It must be resolved before the overall control system can be designed effectively.

DIFFICULTY IN MEASURING PERFORMANCE

Even if a not-for-profit organization's goals are quite clear to all, managers of these organizations do not have at their disposal any single, quantitative bottom-line performance indicator, like the profit indicator in for-profit organizations.[2] The degree of achievement of the organization's overall goals, the provision of quality service to constituencies, usually cannot be measured accurately in financial terms. If a school's goal is to educate children, how is success to be judged? How are improvements in writing skills, mathematics knowledge, science knowledge, and physical education skills to be measured? Because one set of skills can be compromised in favor of others, what importance is to be placed on each set of skills?

Without a single, quantifiable performance indicator, the tasks of management and management control are greatly complicated. It becomes difficult to

- measure organizational performance in light of the overall goals and, thus, to use results control even at the broad organization level,
- analyze the benefits of alternative investments or courses of action,
- decentralize the organization and hold subunit managers accountable for specific areas of performance that relate exactly to the organization's overriding goal, and
- compare the performances of subunits performing dissimilar activities.

ACCOUNTING DIFFERENCES

The financial statements prepared by not-for-profit organizations have varied widely from those used in for-profit organizations in both form and content. A comprehensive standard for general-purpose external financial statements provided by not-for-profit organizations did not exist in the U.S. until the Financial Accounting Standards Board issued Financial Accounting Statement #117 in June 1993 (effective for fiscal years beginning after December 15, 1994). As a consequence, some not-for-profit organizations have provided consolidated financial statements; others have not. Some organizations have provided cash flow information; most did not. FAS Statement #117 is expected to improve the relevance, understandability, and comparability of not-for-profit organizations' financial statements.

The individual accounting standards used by not-for-profit organizations for operating transactions have also historically been different from those used in for-profit organizations. Depreciation is probably the single most important area of difference. In the U.S., depreciation of long-lived tangible assets was required for not-for-profit organizations starting only in 1990 by Financial Accounting Statements #93 and #99. Government organizations are still exempted; they recognize depreciation expense only in their funds that account for business-like activities. Most experts, however, now conclude that the accounting used in not-for-profit organizations' accounting should be identical to that used in for-profit organizations, with one exception: Not-for-profit organizations need separate accounts, called funds, to segregate operating transactions from contributed capital transactions.

For-profit organizations acquire their resources by selling stock, borrowing money, and earning profits through the selling of the goods and services they provide. Their managers can use those resources any legal way they wish.[3] Most of the resources obtained by not-for-profit organizations, on the other hand, are donated or granted to the organization. The terms of the donation or grant can *restrict* the purposes for which those resources can be used. The restriction may involve use of the resources for a specific purpose (for example, to conduct research about cancer), a particular type of expenditure (for example, a new building), or a particular time period (for example, not until after the year 2000).

Ensuring that each of these donations or grants is used for only its intended purpose places extra demands on the managers of not-for-profit organizations. Some of these restrictions are legal obligations; others are moral obligations from the organization to the donor. To satisfy this extra dimension of accountability these restrictions involve, most not-for-profit organizations use *fund accounting.* Fund accounting separates resources restricted for different purposes from each other. Each fund has its own set of financial statements, balance sheet, and statement of changes in fund balance. Each not-for-profit organization also has a *general fund* which is used to account for all operating transactions and resources not included in any of the restricted funds.

Most not-for-profit organizations prepare consolidated financial reports. The fund accounting counterpart for the for-profit organizations' income statement, which can be called a *statement of activities,* an *operating statement,* or a *statement of income and expenses,* provides important information about the financial performance of the organization. Table 20-1 shows a representative operating statement, in this case for the University of Southern California. This statement shows that the University raised $1.152 billion in revenue in FY 1995, but $55 million of those revenues were restricted, either temporarily or permanently (the two middle columns). There were a few adjustments, particularly loan cancellations, which reduced total revenues to $1.152 billion. Expenses totalled $1.005 billion. The University was able to invest the surplus of $147 million in its assets, most particularly buildings and various forms of restricted funds.

The statement of activities is quite informative because if resource inflows are persistently less than resource outflows, the organization will not survive. On the other hand, having inflows exceed outflows by too great a margin is not good either. It indicates that the organization is not fulfilling its primary mission, providing service, as well as it could with the resources it has available.

It must be recognized, however, that consolidated financial statements for not-for-profit organizations can be misleading. Consolidation obscures the resource restrictions. A consolidated cash balance may not be usable for paying the organization's operating expenses if the use of some of that cash is restricted.

EXTERNAL SCRUTINY

Most not-for-profit organizations do not directly serve, and have to answer to, a group with ultimate authority, like a shareholder group. They do not have to answer to a number of external constituencies, however, often including donors, government entities, alumni, and society-at-large. These external constituencies often ask a lot. This is natural because most not-for-profit organizations were established to provide valuable social services, and these organizations are not bound by the necessity to report ever-increasing profits. High societal expectations lead to high demands for accountability. Sometimes benefactors, or the general public, bring direct political pressure on the organization. If an organization is perceived not to be performing appropriately, donations can be withheld, and managers and boards of directors can be forced out of office. Government regulators can shut the organizations down or place additional restrictions on them.

TABLE 20-1 Consolidated Statement of Activities University of Southern California for the Year Ended June 30, 1995

	Total Unrestricted Net Assets	*Temporarily Restricted Net Assets*	*Permanently Restricted Net Assets*	*Total Net Assets*
Revenues				
Student tuition and fees	$ 415,007,000			$ 415,007,000
Endowment income	24,794,000		$ 54,000	24,848,000
Investment and other income	14,215,000	$ 135,000	352,000	14,702,000
Net appreciation (depreciation) in fair value of investments	87,242,000	2,868,000	5,738,000	95,848,000
Government contracts and grants	142,703,000			142,703,000
Recovery of indirect costs	53,170,000			53,170,000
Gifts and pledges	94,728,000	8,879,000	36,768,000	140,375,000
Sales and service	14,179,000			14,719,000
Auxiliary enterprises	97,772,000			97,772,000
LAC/USC Medical Center services	79,579,000			79,579,000
Clinical practices	7,607,000			7,607,000
Kenneth Norris Jr. Cancer Hospital	50,183,000			50,183,000
Other	15,979,000			15,979,000
Total Revenues	**1,097,158,000**	**11,882,000**	**42,912,000**	**1,151,952,000**
Loan cancellations and loss provisions	469,000	704,000	(180,000)	993,000
Present value adjustment to annuities payable		92,000	(794,000)	(702,000)
Net assets released from restrictions	11,059,000	(13,306,000)	2,247,000	
	1,108,686,000	**(628,000)**	**44,185,000**	**1,152,243,000**

(continued)

TABLE 20-1 (Continued)

	Total Unrestricted Net Assets	*Temporarily Restricted Net Assets*	*Permanently Restricted Net Assets*	*Total Net Assets*
Expenses				
Educational and general activities	799,559,000			799,559,000
Health care services	134,594,000			134,594,000
Depreciation	51,600,000			51,600,000
Interest on indebtedness	19,637,000			19,637,000
Total Expenses	**1,005,390,000**			**1,005,390,000**
Transfers within Unrestricted Net Assets:				
Mandatory transfers for external debt service				
Student loan matching requirement				
Unrestricted gifts designated for long-term investment				
Internal loan repayments				
Accumulated gains used for spending rule				
Other miscellaneous nonmandatory transfers				
Property, plant, and equipment acquisitions				
Increase (Decrease) in Net Assets	**103,296,000**	**(628,000)**	**44,185,000**	**146,853,000**
Transfer operating surplus to departmental net assets				
Beginning Net Assets	**978,426,000**	**46,653,000**	**491,352,000**	**1,516,431,000**
Ending Net Assets	**$1,081,722,000**	**$46,025,000**	**$535,537,000**	**$1,663,284,000**

Source: University of Southern California, *Financial Report, 1995.*

This high scrutiny from parties external to the organization places extra control system-related demands on not-for-profit organizations; particularly the organizations' governing body, such as its board of directors, which represents the external constituencies, must be informed, active, and proactive. Unfortunately, however, members of many not-for-profit organizations' board of directors are selected for reasons that do not qualify them to exercise organizational oversight optimally. They may have been selected because they are potentially large donors to the organization or because they are good friends of a high-ranking government official. In addition, most not-for-profit board members are paid little or nothing for their services, so they can be easily distracted from their tasks. The consequence is that, as one set of authors concluded, "Effective governance by the board of a not-for-profit organization is a rare and unnatural act.[4] When the organization's internal oversight fails, direct pressure is more likely to be brought from external constituencies.

The sometimes-intense external scrutiny can also shape some decision making processes, including some MCS-related processes. Planning and budgeting processes are likely to be more important and more time-consuming because the external parties must be heard and their concerns must be accommodated. The setting of management compensation levels and formulas can also be subject to considerable political pressure.

LEGAL CONSTRAINTS

Many not-for-profit organizations face legal constraints that are more extensive than those faced by for-profit organizations. They must comply with many specific laws and conditions attached to the revenues (donations and grants) they raise. Compliance with these constraints almost automatically calls for the use of action controls, and it increases control costs.

EMPLOYEE CHARACTERISTICS

Employees of not-for-profit organizations often have some characteristics that distinguish them from those in for-profit organizations, and those characteristics can have both positive and negative control implications. The compensation paid employees of many not-for-profit organizations is not competitive with those paid employees at for-profit organizations. This can cause control problems if employee quality is diminished, as one of the main control problems, personal limitations, may be salient. On the other hand, many not-for-profit organizations tend to attract employees who are highly committed to their organization's goals. They find it easier to relate to the organization's goal, whether that is providing shelter for the homeless, food for the hungry, or a cure for AIDS, than to a goal merely to provide more value for shareholders. Some not-for-profit employees even work with an idealistic fervor. This high commitment minimizes the other control problems: lack of direction and lack of motivation. Control, then, can be more easily achieved through personnel/cultural means.

SERVICES PROVIDED

Most not-for-profit organizations provide services, rather than tangible products. Service businesses have a different set of critical success factors that must be controlled well. In particular, service businesses tend to be labor intensive. It is often difficult to avoid control problems by replacing labor with machines. Utilization of capacity is critical because services cannot be inventoried in order to dampen demand fluctuations. Quality is a more difficult concern because the organization's output is not tangible, so it cannot be visually inspected.

CONCLUSION

Control in not-for-profit organizations has both similarities with and differences from control in for-profit organizations. The basic needs for good control are the same. Managers of not-for-profit organizations have to address the same set of control problems; lack of direction, lack of motivation, and lack of ability, as do their for-profit counterparts. They also have basically the same set of control tools; action, results, and personnel/cultural controls, at their disposal.

MCSs in not-for-profit organizations are often not as well developed as are those in for-profit organizations. Not-for-profit managers have historically not been as well trained in modern management methods, and have struggled with their more difficult management and control problems and tight resource constraints. As their organizations mature, these managers implement many of the control features used in for-profit organizations. When the United Way charity ran into financial problems in 1992, among the changes made was the implementation of a new financial control system. For the first time in the organization's history, middle-level managers were held accountable for achieving budget targets, and managers' expense reports were reviewed by volunteer auditors.

It is true, however, that MCSs often must differ significantly in not-for-profit organizations. A command-and-control style of management is not effective in these organizations. Managers cannot just make decisions, issue commands, and find that the commands are obeyed quickly. They must spend considerable time managing elaborate, open decision processes designed to build consensus. Even then these decisions often get tied up in a lengthy approval process involving multiple regulators and overseers. Managers cannot easily define results measures and motivate behavior through financial incentives. The goals are not always clear; the important results are often difficult to measure; internal auditors cannot just be ordered into a department to do a performance audit; and the provision of incentives may be impossible. There are no stock options to offer. Bonuses are often specifically prohibited by law or the employees' labor contracts. Even where feasible, sizable bonuses may be politically unwise. Some successful managers of for-profit organizations who have moved into not-for-profit organizations have attempted to implement for-profit organization-type controls. More often than not they have failed, particularly in the public sector organizations.[5]

There are, however, a few success stories that suggest lessons not-for-profit managers can learn from for-profit managers. Richard Riordan, a successful businessman who was elected mayor of Los Angeles in 1993, implemented mission statements and formal results-oriented performance evaluations backed up by, in some cases, merit pay. His changes have produced some successes, but he still laments, "In government there is too much talk about process and not enough talk about results."[6] William Popejoy, who served a short stint as the chief executive officer of Orange County, California, but resigned in 1995 in frustration, agrees. He said, "Even after everything, I still think government can be run more like a business. It must be run more like a business or it will overwhelm us."[7]

Notes

1. G. Hofstede, "Management Control of Public and Not-for-Profit Activities," *Accounting, Organizations and Society,* 6, no. 3 (1981), pp. 193–211.
2. See P. Smith, "Outcome-Related Performance Indicators and Organizational Control in the Public Sector," *British Journal of Management,* 4, no. 3 (1993), pp. 135–151.
3. Most for-profit organizations also have funds (pension funds, trust funds, and charitable foundation funds) that must be kept separate from the entity's main operating accounts. These restricted funds, however, typically make up a tiny fraction of the entity's total assets.
4. See B. E. Taylor, R. P. Chait, and T. P. Holland, "The New Work of the Nonprofit Board," *Harvard Business Review* (September/October 1996), p. 36.
5. D. Vrana, "CEOs Learn the Bottom Line of Public Life," *Los Angeles Times* (August 10, 1995), p. 1.
6. Ibid., p. 22.
7. Ibid., p. 23.

City of Yorba Linda, California

Arthur Simonian, the city manager of Yorba Linda, California, introduced some refinements in the city's budget process and content for the budget cycle for the fiscal years 1991–92 and 1992–93 (ended June 30). The city's department directors were given more responsibility for making their expenditure projections; a budget manual was created by the Finance Department to assist department personnel with budgeting duties; and more detail was required regarding the purposes of the programs proposed and measurements used to evaluate the programs.

The budgeting cycle encompassed the period January–June 1991. On June 18, 1991, the City Council of the City of Yorba Linda approved the budget. For the second time in city history, however, the budget was not unanimously approved. The final vote was four in favor and one abstention. The abstaining council member raised several issues, the most important of which was a 24.9 percent increase in police service costs.

BACKGROUND

The city of Yorba Linda, located in northern Orange County, California, was incorporated in 1967 as a general law city.[1] Yorba Linda is known as the birthplace of Richard Nixon, the 37th president of the United States, and is the home of the Nixon Presidential Library. Since 1980 Yorba Linda had been growing at a rate of about 3,000 people per year. In 1991, the city had 53,000 residents living in approximately 18.5 square miles.

Yorba Linda used a city manager form of government. Mr. Simonian, the city manager, was a full-time employee appointed by the City Council to manage all city departments except Legal Services (see organization chart in Exhibit 1). The city's budget included 68 full-time employee positions for general city operations and 17 for library operations.

A City Council set city policy. The council was comprised of five city residents elected on an at-large basis for a four-year, part-time term. The council met twice each month, and sessions, except those dealing with personnel or litigation matters, were open to the public. Council members were paid $500 per month for their services. One council member was elected by the council to serve a one-year, largely ceremonial term as mayor. A mayor pro tem performed the mayoral duties when the mayor was unavailable.

Yorba Linda was a contract city, meaning that the city contracted with public and private agencies to provide many of its services. The neighboring City of Brea provided police protection. The County of Orange provided fire, paramedic, public bus transportation, and sewage treatment services. And private agencies provided a variety of other services, including water, trash collection, cable television, engineering, legal, maintenance, public construction, and recreation program instruction. The contract approach enabled the city to cut back or delay noncritical services or projects when revenues were not available.

City revenues, which totalled slightly less than $30 million per year, were derived primarily from state and local sources. State funds included state subventions and grants. In the subvention process, the state collected fees and taxes (e.g., motor vehicle license fees, gas taxes, cigarette taxes) and redistributed the funds back to the cities, usually on the basis of population. The state also awarded grants intended for specific purposes, such as the improvement of park facilities. Some grants were awarded on a per-capita basis, while others were awarded based on a competition. Yorba Linda's primary local sources of revenues were property taxes, sales taxes, franchise

[1]A general law city is governed by the laws of the state of California. The alternative, a charter city, is governed by its own laws.

Research Assistant Patrick Henry and Professor Kenneth A. Merchant wrote this case as the basis for class discussion rather than to illustrate either effective or ineffective handling of an administrative situation.

fees and building permit fees. United States federal government monies were also available to cities, but the City of Yorba Linda rarely applied for them.

California state law required cities to use fund accounting. Fund accounting creates a clear separation between operating and capital transactions and helps ensure that the restrictions placed on revenues (e.g., use only for parks, traffic safety, or library improvement) were adhered to. Yorba Linda summarized its operations in six major fund categories: general fund, special revenue funds, capital revenue funds, special assessment funds, reserve funds, and restricted funds. Exhibit 2 shows estimates of fund balances at the end of fiscal year 1990–91 and estimates of revenues and expenditures for fiscal year 1991–92. Each fund had its own self-balancing set of accounts. Revenues not restricted to a specific purpose were put into the city's general fund.

THE BUDGETING SYSTEM

Purposes of Budgeting

All cities in California were required by state law to have an annual budget. These budgets had two primary purposes. They provided city managers the authority to make expenditures. Without this budget authority, the city council would have to approve expenditures individually. The budgets also provided control over expenditures by providing benchmarks against which to compare reports of actual expenditures.

By law, city budgets had to be balanced, but Yorba Linda maintained reserves to ensure a balanced budget even when faced with nonrecurring expenses, such as capital additions and unexpected emergencies. The Yorba Linda City Council established a goal of maintaining a general fund reserve level equal to 50 percent of the operating budget. This assured the city's capability of continuing operations for six months in the event of a major catastrophe. In view of Yorba Linda's many contractual arrangements (e.g., fire, police), the Council also thought it wise for the city to be prepared to deliver services if a contractor defaulted or otherwise became unable to perform vital services. Because Yorba Linda had enjoyed a sustained period of prosperity, city managers had come close to achieving the City Council's goal for general fund reserves: the 1991 ending balance was exactly 50 percent of the operating budget; the lowest balance was 41 percent in 1988; and the projection for fiscal 1993 was 53 percent.

Mr. Simonian had three basic goals for the city's budgeting process, all intended to ensure that the process provided a forum for discussion leading to the establishment of good city policies and priorities. First, he wanted the budget to be easy for members of the City Council to understand. The Yorba Linda council members had little or no formal training in public administration or policy. (Figure 1 shows the full-time occupations of the 1991–92 Yorba Linda city councillors.) Second, he wanted the budget to be understandable by members of the community. The citizens were the ultimate customers of the city services, and Mr. Simonian wanted them to understand city priorities and to get involved in the budget-setting process. Typically only two or three citizens attended a budget hearing. Third, he wanted to encourage the city department directors to analyze current and projected activities and their available resources so that priorities could be evaluated.

Comparisons of actual program performance as compared to budget were not considered in department performance evaluations. These evaluations tended to be totally subjective. The evaluations were not linked with monetary awards. The city had no bonus system, and the salaries of most managers and their subordinates were at maximum for their job classification. These personnel received cost-of-living salary increases only.

FIGURE 1 Yorba Linda City Council Members and their Occupations

Mark Schwing (Mayor)	aerospace company manager
Irwin M. Fried (Mayor Pro Tem)	lawyer
John M. Gullixson	lawyer
Henry W. Wedaa	book company owner
William E. Wisner	shoe store owner

Evolution of the Budgeting System

The Yorba Linda city budgeting system had been evolving over the last decade. In 1986, Mr. Simonian implemented a program budget to replace the line-item budget that had been used for many years. With the line-item budget, amounts of most line-items were quite small, and the city manager found that the council members had a tendency to get lost in the detail. The Council would ask questions such as, "Why are telephone charges going up 13 percent next year?" and lose focus on the programs being planned and their objectives. The program budget identified the objectives of every major project/program and resources required.

In 1986, the city also began using a multi-year budgeting approach. Mr. Simonian thought that planning for two years was better than annual planning since many programs and most capital projects lasted longer than one year. Thus in odd years, city administrators issued a new two-year budget to the city council for approval. In even years, qualified revisions were made and submitted for approval.

In odd years, the budgeting process took place over the period November–June in two distinct phases. The first phase involved preparation of the capital improvement projects (CIP) budget, a five-year capital plan designed to make council members aware of upcoming capital expenses. City managers submitted the CIP budget to Council in December for approval by March. The second phase involved the preparation of the two-year operating budget. Mr. Simonian presented the operating budget to Council in mid-April. The council had to approve a budget by mid-June since Yorba Linda's fiscal year ended on June 30th.

Mr. Simonian designed the budget to facilitate the setting of policies and priorities. It presented the council members with options. If, for instance, the council members wanted to accelerate construction of a community center in the 1991–92 fiscal year, the budget showed them where the money could come from. The city council established final priorities.

During the year, Mr. Simonian tried to keep budget revisions to a minimum. But as part of a mid-year financial performance review, the city council sometimes authorized additional expenditures for projects that occurred after the budget was prepared. Typically departmental budgets were not changed unless, for example, a major piece of equipment broke and needed replacing. At the mid-year review, council also looked at the second year of the budget, sometimes making changes, such as to accelerate the commencement of a particular project.

Several changes were made to the budgeting process and budget content for the 1991–93 cycle. First, the department managers were given responsibility for making all their expenditure projections, including personnel costs. Second, a budget manual, with guidelines, samples, forms, standard costs, and the chart of accounts, was distributed to assist department personnel in the preparation of their budgets. Third, the budget instructions called for more detail than had been asked for in the past about the purpose of each departmental program, program accomplishments over the past budget cycle, objectives for the next two years, and the criteria that department managers believed should be used for measuring achievement of the objectives. (Exhibits 3 and 4 show two program budget examples. Exhibit 3 shows the budget submission for the Contract Classes program of the Parks & Recreation Department. Exhibit 4 shows the submission for the Records/Office Automation Management Program of the City Clerk's Office.) And fourth, the budget calendar was expanded for three weeks to allow managers more time to define the program portion of the budget.

THE PROCESS OF SETTING THE 1991–92 AND 1992–93 BUDGETS

Revenue Projections

Revenue projections were made by Gordon Vessey, finance director. Mr. Vessey typically projected revenues conservatively to ensure that the city exceeded its revenue goals. For 1991–93, however, he and the city manager endeavored to make the revenue projections *more realistic.* They knew finances would be tight during this period and did not want to cut programs unnecessarily.

As is shown in Exhibit 5, Yorba Linda's revenues were expected to decline from fiscal year 1991. General fund revenues, the most significant component of revenues, had been declining since fiscal 1988–89, but personnel in the city manager's office were pursuing four major initiatives to increase general fund revenues. First, programs and incentives to encourage commercial development were continued. The city manager expected the

Yorba Linda Auto Plaza, Price Club, and other new commercial developments to generate additional sales tax revenues in future years. Second, franchise fees were expected to increase, due in large part to a restructuring of the cable television franchise fee. Third, building permit fees were expected to return in 1989–90 levels within the next two years. And fourth, property taxes, the largest single revenue source, were expected to continue to increase. Property taxes generated $3.6 million in revenues in 1991–92 and $4.0 million in 1992–93. Overall, Mr. Vessey projected general fund revenues for 1991–92 and 1992–93 to increase by 16.6 percent and 7.9 percent, respectively.

Mr. Vessey expected special revenues to remain constant over the next two years. He knew gas tax revenues would increase because of a recent five cent per gallon state gas tax increase, but he expected gains from the gas tax to be offset by a decline in special revenue grant monies. He expected capital revenues to decline considerably in 1991–92 because of a sharp reduction in developer fees. Special assessments, fees charged to residents for landscaping and street lights in their district, had provided a reliable source of revenue in past years with consistent increases each year, and Gordon expected these revenues to continue to grow. Mr. Vessey projected increases in public library revenues in 1991–92 and 1992–93 of 13.9 percent and 11.3 percent, respectively. The city established a dedicated fund for library revenues as a result of the Library District's merger with the city in 1985. As part of the transition process, the City Council committed to guarantee the monies for library operations. Virtually all the library revenues were collected from property taxes. So overall, Mr. Vessey projected moderate increases in total city revenues to $23.2 million in 1991–92 and $25.5 in 1992–93.

Expenditure Projections

As was discussed above, the Yorba Linda department directors prepared all aspects of their expenditure budgets in the 1991–93 budget cycle. In a letter included within the budget manual, Mr. Simonian cautioned the directors to be conservative in their plans. He reminded them that the city had expended 20 percent of General Fund Reserve balances in the 1990–91 fiscal year and that this trend could not continue if the city was to maintain its healthy fiscal base. Thus, he asked them to take a "*hard* and *realistic* look at their current level of operations," to make a "critical evaluation of existing services and programs," and to make a review and prioritization of general operations. Mr. Simonian realized that department directors tended to budget on a line-item basis: If they spent $1,000 last year, they tended to budget $1,000, plus inflation, for the next year. Because finances were tight, he asked the directors to look carefully at each item and eliminate or reduce items when possible.

The initial expenditure budget submission was too high, so Mr. Simonian asked the directors to identify potential reductions of 5 percent and 10 percent from original requests. He thought it was *prudent* to involve the department managers in the cutting process. The potential reductions were discussed in a series of management meetings. Final cuts did not fall equally on all departments. City management attempted to preserve services and programs traditionally preferred by the residents of Yorba Linda. Plus, reductions were easier to make in larger departments and in departments where directors were inclined to build in slack. Many of the targeted reductions in the budget focused on capital outlay items that city and department managers believed could be deferred to future years without significant impact on operations or services. Exhibit 6 shows a comparison of expenditures by department for fiscal year 1990–91 compared with budgeted figures for fiscal years 1991–92 and 1992–93.

The proposed budget contained several significant changes in the operating expenses of the city council, city manager, city clerk, police, and parks and recreation department. The city council's budget was higher than normal in 1990–91 due to public relations efforts associated with the dedication of the Nixon Library. The city manager's office incurred an expense of $100,000 in 1990–91 for consulting fees associated with waste management plans, but Mr. Simonian knew the city would require fewer services of this type over the next two years. The city clerk's budget was increased 9 percent in 1992–93 to allow for administration of the November 1992 election. The budget for police services was increased by 24.9 percent in 1991–92 and 10 percent in 1991–93 because of proposed salary increases and additional patrol hours to improve response times and enhance enforcement of the most serious accident-causing traffic violations. The parks and recreation budget for 1992–93 was increased in anticipation of the opening of a new community center projected to be constructed.

Budget changes were also made for capital improvements, capital projects, and the library. Yorba Linda undertook many capital improvements in 1991. Significant expenses were for remodeling the library, land acquisition for and design of the community center, street maintenance, and street improvements. The library was scheduled for completion in early 1992 and the community center for early 1993, which accounted for the 42.5 percent decrease in the budget for 1992–93. The capital project account differed from the capital improvement account in that capital projects were funded with bonded debt. One of the most prominent capital projects in the city's history, the Gypsum Canyon Bridge, was completed in the 1990–91 budget cycle. As a result, the absence of expenditures related to this project accounted for a large portion of the 63.2 percent decrease in capital projects for 1991–92. The Yorba Linda Public Library had been operating in a temporary facility since April 1990. Upon completion of the library remodel, library services were to be increased in operating, maintenance, and capital expense, which accounted for the projected 16.0 percent increase.

As in past years, Mr. Simonian proposed a balanced operating budget (as required by law). But this budget cycle differed from past budgets in the property tax monies in the amount of $1.4 million in 1991–92 and $1.1 million in 1992–93 were allocated to the general fund in order to balance the operating budget. The city had begun receiving property tax money in 1984, and the city manager's goal had been not to rely on property tax money to operate the general fund. But this goal was temporarily abandoned in this budget cycle because of the recession.

In total, city expenditures proposed for 1991–92 and 1992–93 were $30.3 million and $26.5 million, respectively, as shown in Exhibit 7. The general fund balance was projected to be $5.4 million at fiscal year end 1991–92 and $6.3 million at fiscal year end 1992–93.

BUDGET APPROVAL

After the proposed budget was prepared, Mr. Simonian met with City Council members individually to answer questions and resolve objections. In addition, he held a departmental budget staff work session with the Council in early May. This session was open to the public.

Council member John Gullixson voiced disagreement with portions of the budget, particularly proposed increases in the cost of police services. According to terms of the five-year contract approved in 1991 with the neighboring city of Brea, Yorba Linda was charged for police patrol hours, traffic control hours, detective hours, and an allocated portion of overhead for the Brea police force. Brea police overhead was charged to Yorba Linda based on the proportion of police force person-hours used. In 1991, this charge was 48 percent of Brea police department overhead costs. A 24.9 percent increase in police service costs was projected for fiscal year 1991–92 because of projections of expanded services provided to Yorba Linda and an average 7.5 percent salary increase for police force personnel. This increase in police service costs was of concern to Mr. Gullixson. He believed police personnel were overpaid and was disturbed that Brea was making money on the contract since Brea did not have to cover the full overhead costs for a police force.

Mr. Simonian, however, believed that the police contract was an equitable arrangement and that using Brea services was a good way to provide services to Yorba Linda. He explained, for example, that if Yorba Linda had its own police force, it would have to employ full time detectives for vice and narcotics. By contracting, the city only had to pay for the hours of detective service actually used. He noted that if Yorba Linda had its own police force, it would have to cover all the overhead costs associated with the force. And he pointed out that Yorba Linda's police costs were low in comparison with most other cities in Orange County. So he pressed for approval of the budget over Mr. Gullixson's objections.

The City Council met formally on June 18, 1992 to consider the budget. Because of the earlier budget sessions, there was little discussion at this meeting. Mr. Gullixson had not changed his mind about his objection to increased costs of police service. But the budget was approved and adopted with four favorable votes and with Mr. Gullixson abstaining.

EXHIBIT 1 Organization Chart

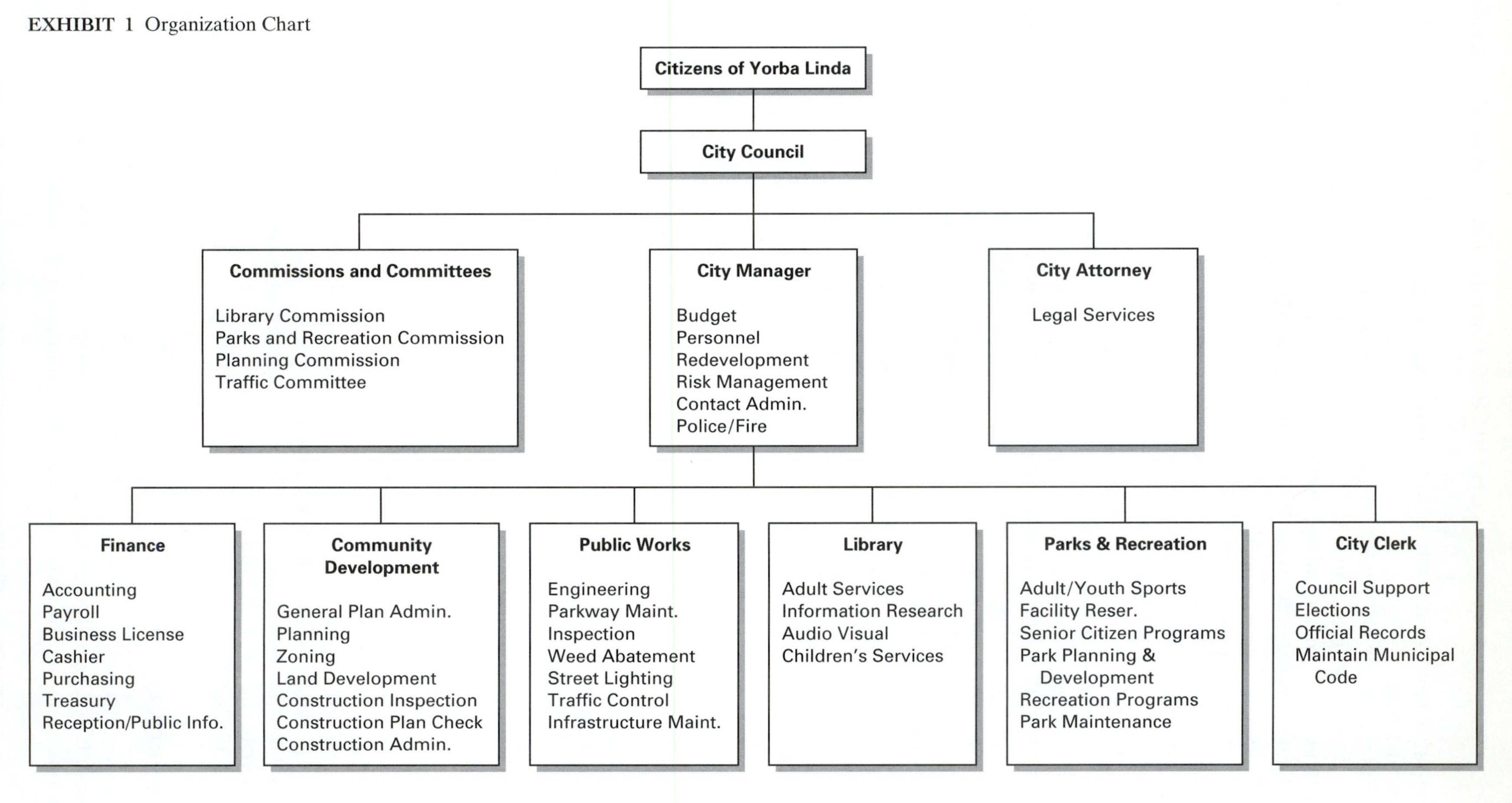

Citizens of Yorba Linda
City Council
Commissions and Committees
Library Commission
Parks and Recreation Commission
Planning Commission
Traffic Committee
City Manager
Budget
Personnel
Redevelopment
Risk Management
Contact Admin.
Police/Fire
City Attorney
Legal Services
Finance
Accounting
Payroll
Business License
Cashier
Purchasing
Treasury
Reception/Public Info.
Community Development
General Plan Admin.
Planning
Zoning
Land Development
Construction Inspection
Construction Plan Check
Construction Admin.
Public Works
Engineering
Parkway Maint.
Inspection
Weed Abatement
Street Lighting
Traffic Control
Infrastructure Maint.
Library
Adult Services
Information Research
Audio Visual
Children's Services
Parks & Recreation
Adult/Youth Sports
Facility Reser.
Senior Citizen Programs
Park Planning & Development
Recreation Programs
Park Maintenance
City Clerk
Council Support
Elections
Official Records
Maintain Municipal Code

EXHIBIT 2 Annual Budget Fund Analysis

Fund	Description	Fiscal Year 91/92					
		Estimated Fund Balance 6/30/91	*Projected Revenues 91/92*	*Total Available 91/92*	*Projected Expenditures 91/92*	*Fund Transfer In (Out)*	*Estimated Fund Balance 6/30/92*
General Fund							
001	General fund	9,097,067	13,541,300	22,638,367	12,007,000	(2,020,756)	8,610,611
						*Library loan balance $800,000	
Special Revenue Funds							
002	Gas Tax	874,388	887,500	1,761,888	0	(1,420,171)	341,717
003	Aid to Cities	57,872	760,500	818,372	0	(351,771)	466,601
004	Traffic Safety	36,101	225,000	261,101	0	(225,000)	36,101
006	Housing & Community Development	0	15,000	15,000	0	(15,000)	0
026	Street Light Energy	470,765	20,000	490,765	0	0	490,765
	*Total Special Revenue Funds	1,439,126	1,908,000	3,347,126	0	(2,011,942)	1,335,184
Capital Improvement Fund							
008	Capital Improvements	(272,707)	0	(272,707)	14,391,900	10,719,498	(3,945,109)
Capital Projects Funds							
005	Street Improvements	221,861	0	221,861	0	(50,000)	171,861
010	Traffic Signal Development	344,172	0	344,172	0	(234,600)	109,572
014	Park In-Lieu West	366,545	20,000	386,545	0	(225,827)	160,718
014	Park In-Lieu East	359,702	1,500,000	1,859,702	0	(1,562,169)	297,533
014	Park In-Lieu (Designated)	450,000	0	450,000	0	0	450,000
011 & 015	Master Plan of Drainage & Sewers	621,203	820,000	1,441,203	115,000	(1,013,440)	312,763
027	Public Improvement East	417,528	35,000	452,528	0	(348,000)	104,528
	Debt Service Funds						
007	Weir Canyon 79-1 Redemption	114,250	0	114,250	0	0	114,250
028	Atwood 85-1 Redemption	0	6,200	6,200	6,200	0	0
030	Savi 83-1 Refund Issue Redemption	1,186,842	458,000	1,644,842	1,431,000	0	213,842
031	Savi 83-1 Redemption	306,017	175,000	481,017	350,000	0	151,017
033	Pub Fin Auth/Cop Redemption Fund	1,433,288	0	1,433,288	0	0	1,433,288
	*Total Capital Projects Funds	5,821,408	3,014,200	8,835,608	1,882,200	(3,434,036)	3,519,372

EXHIBIT 2 Annual Budget Fund Analysis *Continued*

		Fiscal Year 91/92					
Fund	*Description*	*Estimated Fund Balance 6/30/91*	*Projected Revenues 91/92*	*Total Available 91/92*	*Projected Expenditures 91/92*	*Fund Transfer In (Out)*	*Estimated Fund Balance 6/30/92*
Special Assessment Funds							
012	Street Lighting District #2	284,089	576,500	860,589	615,000	(61,500)	184,089
016	Greenbelt Maintenance District #1	31,364	22,900	54,264	47,800	(4,780)	1,684
017	Landscape Maint Assmt District #5	218,326	34,400	252,726	29,900	(2,990)	219,836
019	Landscape Maint Assmt District #3	58,485	993,200	1,051,685	906,300	(90,630)	54,755
020	Landscape Maintenance District #7	25,289	24,800	50,089	46,200	(4,620)	(731)
021	Landscape Maintenance District #8	18,420	7,400	25,820	11,400	(1,140)	13,280
022	Landscape Maintenance District #9	35,362	17,800	53,162	20,100	(2,010)	31,052
023	Landscape Assessment District #1	(73,957)	846,700	772,743	611,600	(61,160)	99,983
024	Landscape Assessment District #2	11,572	388,600	400,172	328,700	(32,870)	38,602
025	Sewer Maintenance District #1	77,122	77,500	154,622	56,600	(5,660)	92,362
	*Total Special Assessment Funds	686,072	2,989,800	3,675,872	2,673,600	(267,360)	734,912
Reserve Funds							
034	Continuation Wages Reserve	33,787	100,000	133,787	15,000	15,000	133,787
035	Liability Insurance Reserve	1,024,631	100,000	1,124,631	470,000	372,000	1,026,631
037	Savi 83-1 Bond Reserve	79,228	5,000	84,228	0	0	84,228
038	Unemployment Insurance Reserve	20,000	2,000	22,000	2,000	2,000	22,000
039	Liability Benefit Reserve	263,238	19,000	282,238	0	0	282,238
041	Pub Fin Auth/Cop Reserve Fund	403,986	0	403,986	0	0	403,986
042	Savi 83-1 Refund Issue Bond Reserve	188,590	0	188,590	0	0	188,590
045 & 047	Sinking Funds Reserve	695,834	75,000	770,834	0	125,000	895,834
046	Community Center Reserve	232,230	205,000	437,230	0	0	437,230
048	Bridge Restoration Reserve	876,247	70,000	946,247	0	0	946,247
051	Library Remodel Reserve	382,432	0	382,432	0	(845,706)	(463,274)
	*Total Reserve Funds	4,200,203	576,000	4,776,203	487,000	(331,706)	3,957,497
Restricted Funds							
050	Yorba Linda Public Library	301,546	1,705,000	2,006,546	1,514,000	(466,747)	25,799
Redevelopment Agency (Memo Entry)							
069	Redevelopment Agency					(2,186,951)	
	*** Total All Funds	21,655,147	23,734,300	45,389,447	32,955,700	2,186,951	13,774,992
						ref: RDA Fund Bal	

EXHIBIT 3 Budget Submission for Contract Classes Program, Parks & Recreation Department

STATEMENT OF PURPOSE:

The purpose of the Contract Classes Division is to provide varied and comprehensive recreational opportunities for City residents of all ages based upon a self-supporting fee basis.

ACTIVITY SUMMARY:

89/90 & 90/91 Accomplishments:

1. Increased Tennis program's enrollment by over 20%.
2. Established Aquatics program with 520 participants.
3. Initiated "Santa Visits" program
4. Coordinated July 4th Fireworks Spectacular celebration with attendance of 5,000 in 1989 increasing to 10,000 in 1990
5. Provided over 100 different classes to the public during each quarterly session
6. Generated over $225,000 in revenue from contract classes participation

91/92 & 92/93 Goals:

1. Continue to offer a variety of contractual programs to meet the diversified interests of the community
2. Expand the aquatics program to include water safety awareness

OBJECTIVES:

1. Increase department's knowledge of community's interest areas
2. Provide qualified contract instructors for new classes/activities
3. Provide water safety awareness instructional lessons for children and adults and other information to general public regarding safe pool practices at the home

MEASUREMENTS:

1. Conduct community survey regarding their interest by June 1992
2. Provide a minimum of two new contract instructors per quarterly session
3. Publish and provide a pool safety flyer to the general public and all participants in the aquatics program

	Actual Expenditures 06/30/1990	*Actual Expenditures 03/31/1991*	*Department Requests 1991/92*	*City Mgr Proposed 1991/92*	*Department Requests 1992/93*	*City Mgr Proposed 1992/93*
Personnel Services	17,602	34,825	46,900	49,200	49,800	52,300
Maintenance & Operations	18,259	10,450	21,800	21,600	22,800	22,800
Contractual Services	114,264	125,474	140,000	140,000	146,000	146,000
Capital Outlay						
TOTAL DEPARTMENT	150,125	170,750	208,700	210,800	218,600	221,100
CONTRACTUAL SERVICES (Line Item Detail)						
Recreation/Instructors			7,000	7,000	8,000	8,000
Recreation/Classes	103,429	95,406	115,000	115,000	119,000	119,000
Special Events	10,835	30,069	18,000	18,000	19,000	19,000
TOTAL CONTRACTUAL SERVICES	114,264	125,474	140,000	140,000	146,000	146,000

EXHIBIT 4 Budget Submission for Records/Office Automation Management Program, City Clerk's Department

DEPARTMENT: City Clerk — Department No 001.4.132
DIVISION/PROGRAM: Records/Office Automation Management

STATEMENT OF PURPOSE:

The purpose of the Records/Office Automation Management Division is to improve productivity and provide a cost-effective use of resources in the City Clerk's Department by maintaining an effective Records Management System for the storage, preservation and retrieval of official City/RDA records.

ACTIVITY SUMMARY:

89/90 & 90/91 Accomplishments:

1. Completed physical inventory of records
2. Separated RDA from City records
3. Established file patterns and master File indexes with cross reference system for City and RDA records
4. Attended graduate level "Managing Successful Records Management Programs" seminar
5. Implemented new computer system
6. Attended computer hardware/software application workshops

91/92 & 92/93 Goals:

1. Complete Comprehensive Records Management System
2. Implement database software on computer system
3. Develop Legislative History Program

OBJECTIVES:

1. Continue implementation of systematic records plan for retention, storage, destruction and microfilming of records
2. Selection and acquisition of database for implementation of records program

MEASUREMENTS:

1. Development of Records Retention and Destruction Schedules, and written policy regarding disposition of records
2. Installation of database and development of Legislative History Program

	Actual Expenditures 06/30/1990	*Actual Expenditures 03/31/1991*	*Department Requests 1991/92*	*City Mgr Proposed 1991/92*	*Department Requests 1992/93*	*City Mgr Proposed 1992/93*
Personnel Services	17,650	14,063	27,700	26,600	29,500	28,100
Maintenance & Operations	7,236	4,277	9,600	9,600	9,900	9,900
Contractual Services	113		3,100	3,800	3,300	4,000
Capital Outlay			1,300	1,300		
TOTAL DEPARTMENT	24,998	18,341	41,700	41,300	42,700	42,000
CONTRACTUAL SERVICES (Line Item Detail)						
Misc Other Contract Services	113		3,100	3,800	3,300	4,000
TOTAL CONTRACTUAL SERVICES	113		3,100	3,800	3,300	4,000

EXHIBIT 5 Annual Budget Revenues

Account Number	Account Title	*Actual Revenues 87/88*	*Actual Revenues 88/89*	*Actual Revenues 89/90*	*Actual Revenues 90/91*	*Projected Revenues 91/92*	*Projected Revenues 92/93*
Revenue Summary							
	General fund	9,919,107	13,234,564	12,326,222	12,966,927	13,541,300	14,604,300
	Special Revenue Funds	1,174,402	1,046,333	1,201,358	1,947,536	1,908,000	2,084,500
	Capital Revenue Funds	23,313,834*	4,038,583	5,445,348	6,777,323**	3,014,200	2,431,800
	Special Assessment Funds	1,851,858	2,113,953	2,380,172	2,798,568	2,989,800	4,131,500
	Reserve Funds	2,236,324	170,074	235,021	279,549	576,000	318,000
	Public Library Fund	1,313,905	1,494,073	1,733,987	1,855,724	1,705,000	1,897,000
	***Total City Revenues	39,809,430	22,097,580	23,322,108	26,625,627	23,734,300	25,467,100

*Includes a bond sale of $16,027,794.

**Includes bond proceeds of $3,949,850.

EXHIBIT 6 Expenditures by Department

Department	*1990/91 Projected Expenditures*	*1991/92 Proposed Expenditures*	*% Change*	*1992/93 Proposed Expenditures*	*% Change*	*Average % Change (2 Years)*
City Council	$ 153,000	$ 94,200	−38.4%	$ 95,900	1.8%	−18.3%
City Manager	$ 580,400	$ 473,600	−18.4%	$ 483,100	2.0%	−8.2%
City Clerk	$ 206,600	$ 212,900	3.0%	$ 232,100	9.0%	6.0%
Finance	$ 344,300	$ 352,800	2.5%	$ 360,400	2.2%	2.3%
Legal Services	$ 132,000	$ 133,000	0.8%	$ 140,600	5.7%	3.2%
Government Buildings	$ 174,700	$ 142,600	−18.4%	$ 156,200	9.5%	−4.4%
Continuation Wages	$ 10,000	$ 15,000	50.0%	$ 15,000	0.0%	25.0%
Liability Insurance	$ 470,000	$ 470,000	0.0%	$ 490,000	4.3%	2.1%
Unemployment Insurance	$ 2,000	$ 2,000	0.0%	$ 2,000	0.0%	0.0%
Police	$ 3,773,600	$ 4,713,200	24.9%	$ 5,184,500	10.0%	17.4%
Community Development	$ 1,652,400	$ 1,651,400	−0.1%	$ 1,442,200	−12.7%	−6.4%
Public Works	$ 2,684,500	$ 2,669,900	−0.5%	$ 2,734,200	2.4%	0.9%
Parks & Recreation	$ 1,447,100	$ 1,574,900	8.8%	$ 1,871,100	18.8%	13.8%
Total Operating Budget	$11,630,600	$12,505,500	7.5%	$13,207,300	5.6%	6.6%
Capital Improvements	$11,013,600	$12,663,000	15.0%	$ 7,275,000	−42.5%	−13.8%
Capital Projects	$ 2,669,900	$ 982,200	−63.2%	$ 898,800	−8.5%	−35.9%
Special Assessments	$ 2,201,700	$ 2,670,400	21.3%	$ 3,531,900	32.3%	26.8%
Library	$ 1,302,100	$ 1,510,100	16.0%	$ 1,550,200	2.7%	9.3%
Total Expenditures	$28,817,900	$30,331,200	5.3%	$26,463,200	−12.8%	−3.8%

EXHIBIT 7 Annual Budget Expenditures

Account Number	Account Title	*Actual Revenues 87/88*	*Actual Revenues 88/89*	*Actual Expenditures 89/90*	*Actual Expenditures 90/91*	*Adopted Expenditures 91/92*	*Adopted Expenditures 92/93*
	Expenditure Summary						
	Operating Budget	7,995,958	9,374,920	10,176,504	11,327,782	12,494,000	13,172,500
	Capital Improvements	5,774,384	3,515,392	5,135,104	10,018,072	14,391,900	5,005,000
	Capital Projects	10,495,508	13,100,277	6,081,755	4,051,292	1,882,200	898,800
	Special Assessments	1,622,488	1,870,539	2,188,885	2,373,050	2,673,600	3,531,900
	Public Library	1,054,484	1,133,702	1,365,748	1,264,025	1,514,000	1,540,000
	***Total City Expenditures	26,942,822	28,994,830	24,947,996	29,034,221	32,955,700	24,148,200

Waikerie Co-Operative Producers Ltd.

The 1993 Budget Report for Waikerie Co-Operative Producers Ltd., an Australian citrus co-operative, listed "the four singularly most important factors in the operation of the co-operative":

1. Are we making a profit and close to budget on our cash flow?
2. Are we paying a competitive price for all produce supplied?
3. Is our volume of handling near or better than our estimate?
4. Are our sales targets being achieved?

The budget for fiscal year 1993 was calculated "with these factors uppermost in all considerations," but Duncan Beaton, general manager of the co-operative had concerns in each of these areas. The co-operative had had a negative operating surplus in each of the last two fiscal years and its managers were forecasting another, in large part because it was operating at less than 50 percent of its capacity. Some grower-members were complaining that the co-operative was not paying a competitive price for produce (although Duncan was not convinced that their criticisms were valid). And Waikerie managers found it difficult to prepare even reasonably accurate sales and budget targets both because of volatility in the produce markets and less than complete cooperation from the grower-members.

THE CO-OPERATIVE

Waikerie Producers was the largest citrus packer in Australia. Because Australia produced only 1 percent of the world's citrus, however, it was still a small organization; 1992 revenues totalled A$8.4 million (excluding fruit revenue of approximately A$20 million paid directly to growers).[1] (Exhibit 1 shows an organization chart.) The co-operative was located at Waikerie, a town of 5,000 people approximately 150 kilometers northeast of Adelaide, South Australia. Waikerie, and the small towns around it, were in a region called *The Riverland,* the largest of five citrus growing regions in Australia.

The co-operative existed to serve its grower-members. It was founded in 1914 to pack dried fruit (e.g., apricots, raisins). It began packing oranges in 1920, and the operating emphasis shifted gradually to citrus, rather than dried fruit, reflecting the agricultural production in the region. The peak year for packing dried fruit was 1944. The co-operative had been exporting citrus fruit under the *Riverland* brand since 1936.

The co-operative's most important functions were the packing and marketing of fruit, primarily oranges, but also grapefruit, lemons, mandarins, and dried fruit. It also provided its members with a broad range of other services, including fruit price forecasts, growing advice (e.g., how to minimize mold infestations, how to reduce irrigation to reduce fruit blemishes), bulk (e.g., fertilizer) and hardware supplies, transport, and equipment sales and servicing. All of the grower-members were relatively small: The average grower's holdings in the Riverland area were 20–25 acres; the largest was 500 acres.

The grower members delivered citrus fruit to the co-operative in 60-bushel bins. The major packing seasons were as follows: Navel oranges—primarily April to September; Valencia oranges—August to May; grapefruit—June to November; lemons—May to October; mandarins—May to October; dried fruit—December to February. Waikerie Producers chose a fiscal year ending 31 March, in the slow season, toward the end of the Valencia season but before the beginning of the Navel season.

The larger, higher quality citrus fruit was washed, dipped in fungicide, waxed, sorted by grade (export or standard) and size, stamped with the *Riverland* logo, and packed in 30-liter (4/5

[1]At the time of the case, A$1 was worth approximately U.S.$.70.

Professor Kenneth A. Merchant wrote this case as a basis for class discussion rather than to illustrate either effective or ineffective handling of an administrative situation.

bushel) boxes or 3-kilo mesh bags. This fruit was sold either directly to larger retailers or to sales agents. Smaller, lower quality (e.g., blemished) fruit was sold by the truckload to be made into juice. Waikerie Producers maintained a strict quality standard to protect its brandname: About 70 percent of the product sent was sold to be made into juice; this compared to approximately 60 percent at other packers.

To join the co-operative, members were required to purchase at least A$300 worth of co-operative shares, the current market value of which was approximately A$67 per share. If the co-operative earned a surplus, 50 percent of the surplus was rebated to the members, and 50 percent was held back as a rotating reserve.

The members elected a board of directors, comprised of seven grower-members, to a two-year term. The board met not less than once a month; in 1991 it met 20 times. The board members usually had altruistic and prestige motives for serving. They were paid little for their services: the members earned $1,000 a year; the chairman earned $5,000.

Waikerie Producers had the capacity to sort and pack 6,500 cases per day, but it was operating at an average of only 2,000–2,500 cases per day. In 1989, Waikerie managers made what was, in retrospect, a strategic error. They added more automated sorting and packing equipment to reduce unit costs through economies of scale, but the additions coincided with a downturn in the market for Australian fruit and a dramatic rise in interest charges. Because of the industry overcapacity, they were unable to sell the excess equipment.

The whole Riverland area had significant citrus packing overcapacity. Virtually every small town in the Riverland area had its own citrus packing co-operative. The area also contained a few private packers, each of which was a small, privately owned, family business. The packing co-operatives generally abided by the six internationally accepted principles of co-operation shown in Exhibit 2. The last of these principles prohibited competition among co-operatives, so the packing co-operatives tended to specialize geographically and were looking for ways to share resources (e.g., marketing, administration) to reduce unit costs. The private packers had some operating advantages over the co-operatives because, for example, they could discriminate among growers (e.g., offer special terms to large growers), they could choose not to accept all the fruit the growers wanted to send them, and they could keep their strategic information confidential. Despite these advantages, however, the private packers were also suffering from the decline in the industry. For example, the town of Waikerie alone used to have 20 private packers, but competition had driven all but one out of business.

CITRUS MARKETING

Waikerie Producers sold its packed fruit at market prices which were set (by variety and size) weekly. Figure 1 shows the market prices being offered in July 1992. Juice prices were lower than, but were closely linked to, the local market price. The co-operative paid the growers the market price less packing and freight costs which, in 1992, averaged approximately $5.50 and $1.00 per 4/5 bushel, respectively. The prices paid to growers were identical for all fruit (in any one grade and size) processed in a pool (of a week or fortnight in duration). Assignment to a pool depended on the delivery date to the co-operative. All growers with fruit in a given pool were paid the same prices for each specific grade. The growers were paid 30 days after the month of delivery.

In 1992, Waikerie producers began offering its grower-members supply contracts. Growers who committed to deliver a certain quantity of fruit to the co-operative were guaranteed a minimum price. If the market price turned out to be greater than the guaranteed minimum, the growers would be paid the market price. The contract system was designed both to provide the grower-members with some pricing stability and to encourage them to ship more fruit in a more consistent stream to the co-operative.

The co-operative supplied the growers' juice-quality citrus to their associate co-operative, Berrivale Orchards, the largest orange juicer in Australia and located in a town adjacent to Waik-

FIGURE 1 Orange Prices per 30-litre box—July 1992

Export, large fruit	$11.00
Export, small fruit	$ 9.50
Local	$7.00–10.00

erie. Approximately 50 percent of the juicer's daily capacity was used for fresh-squeezed juice; the balance was for concentrate. The price for the deliveries for fresh-squeezed juice was set at $170/T.[2] The balance of the juice oranges were sold at the prevailing market price, which in July 1992 was $60/T.

FINANCIAL PLANNING

Waikerie Producers' managers prepared an annual plan in considerable detail. (They planned beyond one year only sketchily.) The annual plan was seen as important because, as was stated in the 1992 Budget Report, "At this crucial period in the life of our co-operative, we must elucidate where we go and how we plan to get there, and then have a consensus which we can pursue for the ultimate benefit of our co-operative and members."

The annual planning process began in November with a grower survey. The grower-members were asked for an estimate of how much tonnage, by variety, they would be sending the co-operative in the forthcoming fiscal year (starting 1 April). A field officer visited each grower to inspect the orchards and to impress upon them the importance of completing the questionnaire. Even so, estimates were received from only about 60 percent of the members. After they received the questionnaires, Waikerie managers consolidated the estimates, extrapolated them to an estimate of total fruit receipts, and added their judgment. Duncan Beaton described the planning philosophy:

> We try to be realistic to the best of our ability. There are so many external factors, such as frost, drought, sooty mould infestations, and changes in the levels of duties. We look at a moving average for the last five years and add our knowledge of the current market and a factor for optimism/pessimism.

Despite the attention paid to the crop estimates, however, Waikerie managers were not satisfied with the accuracy of these estimates. Most years the actual volume of fruit sent to the co-operative was less than estimated, as can be seen in Figure 2.

FIGURE 2 Total Tonnage: Estimate versus Actual Received

Fiscal Year	*Estimate*	*Actual*
91/2	44,520	41,810
90/1	56,524	54,317
89/90	44,316	40,273
88/9	49,407	46,512
87/8	53,520	57,890

Concurrently, Cliff Carthew, Waikerie's chief financial officer, worked with the department managers to estimate costs and cash flows for the coming fiscal year. Considerable time was spent thinking about how to reduce costs to ensure that the co-operative could make payments to members that are *competitive and worthy of support.* As a result, staffing levels were reduced, and no capital expenditures were planned for 1993.

Cliff then set the unit packing costs to be charged to grower-members, which were based on estimates of the full cost of the service plus a modest profit margin. Cliff estimated the costs for many different packing types, 14 for oranges alone. He began by estimating the standard labor cost per minute. This calculation is shown in Exhibit 3. Then he multiplied the standard labor costs per minute by the standard labor minutes per operation, as calculated in a time-and-motion study conducted in 1990. Third, he estimated material costs, which varied with the size of the package and the types of materials used, by requesting quotations from suppliers of major items (e.g., cartons) and estimating the costs of other materials for each pack type (see Exhibit 4). Fourth, he added an allocation of overhead (see Exhibit 5) and transportation. These allocations were crude. For example, the transportation charge of six cents per carton had not been reestimated in several years. The packing costs also included an allocation of interest, and because of Waikerie's high borrowing to buy automated equipment, this was a relatively large number that caused Waikerie's packing costs to be higher than many of the other packers. Finally, Cliff added a small profit margin as a cushion. A summary of the costs of three representative pack types is shown in Exhibit 6.

Duncan admitted that Waikerie's system of

[2]One ton of fruit was equivalent to 48 30-litre (4/5 bushel) boxes.

estimating costs was crude, but he thought it was ahead of most packers. "A lot of packers don't do any costing at all. They don't know their costs." Despite the potential for inaccuracies, Waikerie managers tried to keep the packing charges constant for the whole fiscal year. A few times, however, the costs had varied because of significant changes in volumes or large cost factors.

The ideal was to plan for, and then deliver, a small surplus of, perhaps, less than A$500,000. That small surplus would ensure a satisfactory cash flow while providing the opportunity to reduce interest costs and exposure to adverse market conditions plus provide a small rebate. Duncan Beaton said, "It would be nice to have a big surplus year to recoup the losses we have had recently, but it is not our goal to increase our surplus each year." However, because times were tough, losses were forecast in both 1992 and 1993.

The Waikerie board of directors approved the budget in the middle of March. As they had been apprised of financial issues during the preparation of the budget, there were usually no last minute issues to be settled. The original budget remained fixed for the year, but managers prepared frequent updates of volume forecasts. The co-operative produced an extensive set of formal reports comparing actual with budgeted numbers on a monthly basis.

PERFORMANCE EVALUATIONS AND INCENTIVES

Performance evaluations at Waikerie Producers were done informally. Even for manager-level personnel, there was no formal annual review. Waikerie's practices stemmed from Duncan Beaton's philosophy. He described formal performance evaluations as *a bit traumatic.* He preferred to talk to his subordinates about performance-related issues *somewhat steadily.*

The co-operative offered no bonuses of any kind. Duncan Beaton explained:

> I have thought about it a lot, but I would want to base bonuses on performance, and I can't do it based on profit. In production areas, we have done a lot of one-of projects which are hard to evaluate. In the hardware store, I have evaluated the manager based on sales, but even there evaluations are difficult. Profit is not a good performance measure because he can't really raise profit margins when he is supplying shareholders in a small town, but I don't want him to cut prices excessively to increase sales either."

CONCERNS FOR THE FUTURE

As fiscal year 1993 began, Waikerie managers knew that difficult operating conditions were continuing. The market for Australian citrus was shrinking, and prices were very competitive. The bad market conditions forced Waikerie managers to put some growers on quota. They were allowed to ship only the quantity remaining in their original volume estimate.

Some citrus growers in the Riverland were being encouraged to move to alternate crops, such as grapes, potatoes, carrots, leaf vegetables, melons, or tomatoes, which were even more risky than oranges. But these crops provided greater flexibility because the grower could make annual decisions on what to grow. Citrus growers, typically, can replant only approximately 10 percent of their crop each year. If this crop shift took place, Waikerie Producers could face a gradually shrinking market for some time.

During the difficult times, grower loyalty to the co-operative was declining, and there was a lot of *co-op bashing.* Duncan Beaton explained that, "The growers complain about everything—the board, management, prices." In particular, he noted that the growers had become increasingly insistent on high returns, and they did not think the co-operative was offering competitive prices. Duncan believed Waikerie Producers was within 10 percent of the best price available to the growers, but he found it difficult to verify the growers' claims because packers in the Riverland area, both co-operative and private, did not willingly disclose their prices and packing charges. He was aware of some attempts that some growers were trying to *beat the co-op,* for example, by getting an estimate from the co-operative and then taking it to private packers to see if they would better it.

It was clear to Duncan that Waikerie Producers would have to become more efficient to get an increasing share of a smaller market. He thought that Waikerie Producers was large enough to build more special relationships with supermarkets in order to sell directly, rather than on the open market. He also wanted the co-operative to provide consistently superior service and to offer special promotions so that the Riverland product could compete without always being sold at lowest price.

It was also clear that Waikerie management was handicapped by their inability to prepare reasonably accurate annual financial plans. The summary income statement comparisons of budget vs. actual shown in Exhibit 7 reveals some significant variances. Crop forecasts were one part of the problem. Consequently, in a note to members accompanying the 1993 budget, Waikerie managers wrote:

Crop forecasting, particularly of citrus, has become more difficult and more time-consuming, and ultimately has proved less accurate each year. . . . Our projection of volumes in all activities is critical to the budgetary process, and it is only as a result of this exercise that we can propose a budget. . . . Each year we spend more time and effort to create our estimates, which appear to be less accurate through varying levels of support from our grower suppliers. As the estimate is the singularly most critical factor in the calculations, this causes us much concern.

EXHIBIT 1 Organization Structure

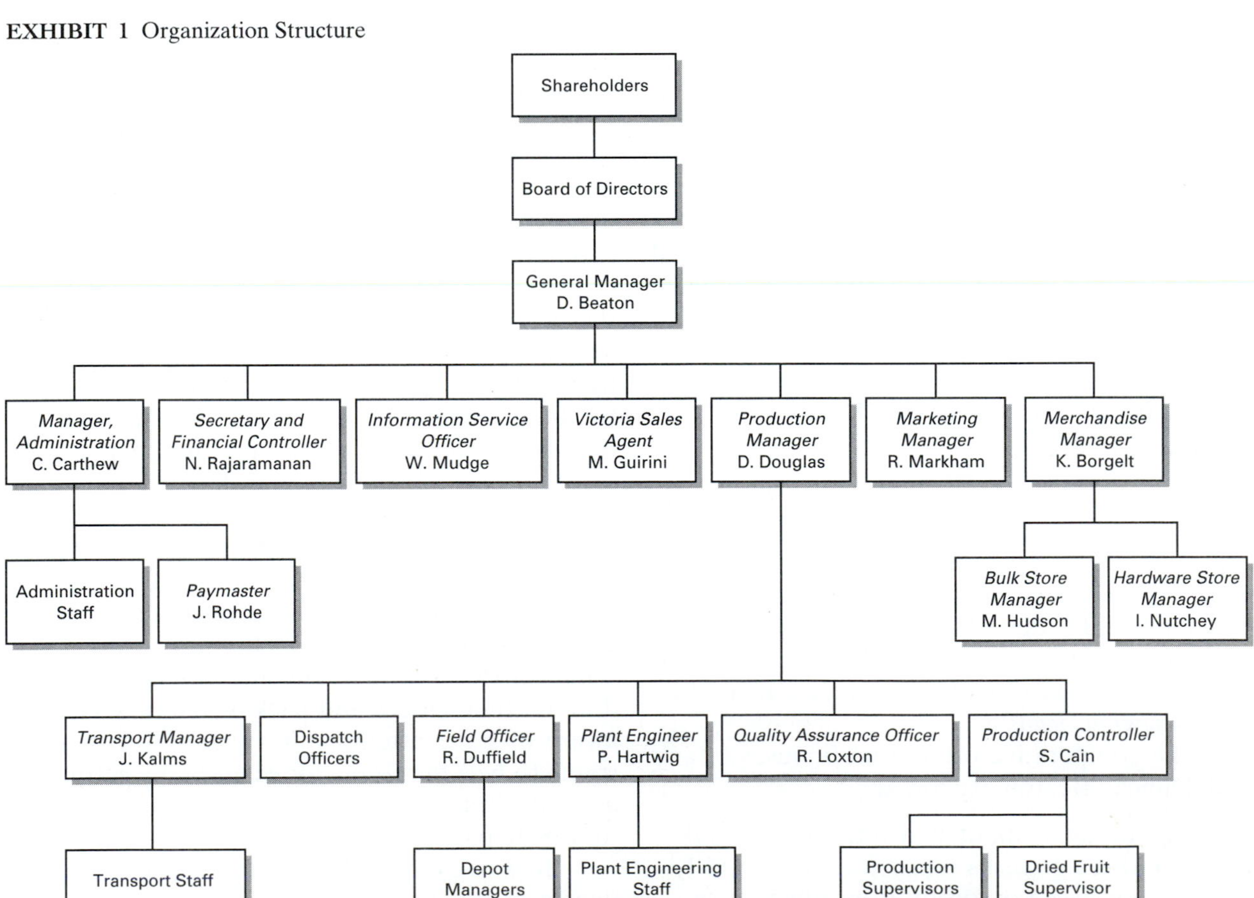

EXHIBIT 2 International Principles of Co-operation

1. OPEN AND VOLUNTARY MEMBERSHIP
   Membership of a co-operative society should be voluntary and available without artificial restriction or any social, political, racial, or religious discrimination, to all persons who can make use of the co-operative's services and are willing to accept the responsibilities of membership.
2. DEMOCRATIC CONTROL
   Co-operative societies are democratic organizations. Their affairs should be administered by persons elected or appointed in a manner agreed by the members and accountable to them. Members of primary societies should enjoy equal rights of voting (one member, one vote) and participation in decisions affecting their societies. In other than primary societies, the administration should be conducted on a democratic basis in a suitable form.
3. LIMITED INTEREST ON SHARES
   Share capital should only receive a strictly limited rate of interest, if any.
4. EQUITABLE DISTRIBUTION OF SURPLUS
   Surplus or savings arising out of the operations of a society belong to the members of that society and should be distributed in such a manner as would avoid one member gaining at the expense of others. This may be done by decision of the members at the Annual General Meeting as follows:
   a. By provision for development of the business of the co-operative (rotation reserves, 5 years);
   b. By provision of common service;
   c. By distribution among members in proportion to their transactions with the Society.
5. CO-OPERATIVE EDUCATION
   All co-operative societies should make provision for the education of their members, officers, and employees and of the general public, in the principles and techniques of co-operation, both economic and democratic.
6. CO-OPERATION AMONGST CO-OPERATIVES
   All co-operative organisations, in order to best serve the interest of their members and their communities should actively co-operate in every practical way with other co-operatives at local, national, and international levels.

EXHIBIT 3 Estimate of Standard Cost of Labour for Fiscal Year 1993

Labour rate at 31/1/90	$ 9.00/hr
+increase in January	.36
	9.36
+increases during year (8.16%)	10.12/hr
+cost of operating at only 50% efficiency	10.12
	20.24
+oncost* of 35%	7.09
Standard hourly rate	$27.33
Standard minute rate	$ 0.4556
In fiscal year 1992:	
Standard minute rate = $.383	
Increase = .0726 or 19%	

*employee benefits

EXHIBIT 4 Cost of Packing Materials for Three Representative Types of Packages

	*C6 CTN**	*3KG P/P***	*Bulk Wood†*
Carton-top	$.5153	$.9565	
Carton-tray	.6381		
Glue	.0150		
Wraps			
Labels			
Taping			
Fungicides	.1700		
Wax	.0600	.2300	.2300
Tags		.3360	
Headers		.1200	
Enclosures		.0850	
Make-up		.3000	
Total materials	$1.3984	$2.0275	$.2300
Assume 20% inflation on all	$1.6781	$2.4330	$.2760

*A C6 CTN is a 30 litre (or 0.8 bushel) export carton.

**A 3KG/P/P is 3 kilogram net bags in prepack cartons, 6 to a carton, and equivalent to 0.8 bushels/carton.

†Bulk wood is loose oranges in a wooden bin. Each bin holds 20 0.8-bushel-equivalent units.

EXHIBIT 5 Overhead Cost Budget

	1993	*1992*
Direct labour-related	$ 606,300	$ 454,020
Direct labour oncost	212,205	158,907
Indirect labour	231,673	210,794
Repair labour	98,518	70,514
Indirect and repair labour oncost	115,567	98,460
Variable costs	398,215	335,256
Other income	(42,180)	(33,074)
Fixed costs	1,119,890	1,108,130
Total overhead costs	$2,740,188	$2,403,007
Packed cases	885,800	1,007,300
Needed overhead cost recovery/case	$ 3.09	$ 2.36

EXHIBIT 6 Packing Costing Summary for Three Representative Pack Types

	C6 Carton	*3KG P/P*	*Bulk Wood*
Std. Mins.	1.85	1.71	0.50
Labour per pack	0.8429	0.7791	0.2278
Matl. per pak	1.6781	2.4330	0.2760
Pack overhead	3.09	3.09	3.09
Transportation to shed @ 4¢	0.060	0.060	0.060
Profit @ 20¢	0.20	0.20	0.20
Total packing cost	5.8710	6.5621	3.8538

Note: A C6 CTN is a 30 litre (or 0.8 bushel) export carton.

A 3KG P/P is 3 kilogram net bags in prepack cartons, 6 to a carton, and equivalent to 0.8 bushels/carton.

Bulk wood is loose oranges in a wooden bin. Each bin holds 20 0.8-bushel-equivalent units.

EXHIBIT 7 Income Statement Budget versus Actual—Citrus Packing Only

	Total 1992		*March*		*February*		*January*		*December*		*November*	
	Act.	*Budg.*	*Act.*	*Budg.*	*Act.*	*Budg.*	*Act.*	*Budg.*	*Act.*	*Budg.*	*Act.*	*Budg.*
Sales/Packing Charges Income	$3,681.6	$4,075.8	$125.6	$ 97.2	$226.7	$251.8	$201.5	$254.1	$245.5	$247.0	$172.3	$301.4
Cost of Goods/Services Sold	1,035.7	1,332.3	(122.3)	41.9	76.6	81.4	70.1	78.7	77.0	79.6	98.3	97.3
Added Value/Gross Margin	2,645.9	2,743.5	247.9	55.3	150.1	170.4	131.5	175.5	168.5	167.3	74.0	204.1
Direct Labour and Oncost*	1,282.5	1,501.7	49.0	45.0	90.3	81.9	91.5	81.7	93.3	91.6	136.6	110.6
Gross Contribution Margin	1,363.5	1,241.8	198.9	10.2	59.9	88.6	40.0	93.7	75.2	75.7	(62.6)	93.5
Indirect & Repair Labour and Oncost*	351.6	354.3	24.2	29.4	27.0	29.5	26.6	29.4	24.9	29.4	32.7	29.5
Net Contribution Margin	1,011.9	887.5	174.7	(19.2)	32.9	59.2	13.3	64.2	50.4	46.3	(95.3)	64.0
Variable Costs*	352.3	346.3	18.4	18.7	22.7	23.0	30.1	23.8	22.5	24.6	26.7	35.2
Other Income†	(143.9)	(21.3)	(105.5)	(1.7)	(12.1)	(1.8)	(2.6)	(1.8)	(.9)	(1.8)	1.0	(1.7)
Divisional Contribution	803.4	562.6	261.6	(36.1)	22.4	38.0	(14.2)	42.2	28.7	23.4	(122.8)	30.6
Fixed Costs††	$ 928.5	$ 971.6	$ 11.9	$ 79.7	$ 77.2	$ 79.8	$ 77.3	$ 77.6	$ 79.7	$ 80.8	$ 83.3	$ 81.0
Net Operating Surplus	($ 125.1)	($ 409.0)	($249.7)	($115.8)	($ 54.8)	($ 41.8)	($ 91.6)	($ 35.4)	($ 50.9)	($ 57.4)	($206.2)	($ 50.3)

October		*September*		*August*		*July*		*June*		*May*		*April*	
Act.	*Budg.*	*Act.*	*Budg.*	*Act.*	*Budg.*	*Act.*	*Budg.*	*Act.*	*Budg.*	*Act.*	*Budg.*	*Act.*	*Budg.*
$308.7	$373.0	$491.8	$415.0	$491.7	$768.1	$506.6	$672.2	$381.3	$482.1	$332.0	$115.6	$197.8	$98.3
85.9	133.6	152.5	135.3	176.3	243.4	145.8	205.2	111.7	163.8	102.0	36.5	61.8	35.6
222.7	239.4	339.4	279.7	315.4	524.7	360.7	467.0	269.7	318.4	230.0	78.9	136.0	62.8
60.0	159.4	147.7	137.7	146.8	236.3	148.3	218.2	156.4	166.5	78.9	144.8	83.7	27.9
162.7	80.0	191.7	142.0	168.6	288.4	212.4	248.8	113.3	151.9	151.1	(65.9)	52.3	34.9
24.3	29.5	36.2	29.5	29.9	29.4	31.0	29.5	39.7	29.9	24.5	29.7	30.6	29.6
138.4	50.5	155.5	112.5	138.7	259.0	181.4	219.3	73.6	122.0	126.6	(95.6)	21.7	5.3
22.3	31.3	37.7	30.3	36.7	45.0	47.1	42.0	32.8	30.2	29.6	23.6	25.7	18.6
(.8)	(1.8)	(5.6)	(1.8)	(.7)	(1.8)	(.6)	(1.8)	3.5	(1.7)	(43.3)	(1.8)	(23.7)	(1.8)
116.8	21.0	123.4	84.1	102.7	215.7	134.9	108.3	37.3	93.5	140.3	(117.4)	(27.7)	(11.5)
$ 78.9	$ 82.0	$ 84.5	$ 82.0	$ 82.9	$ 81.9	$ 84.1	$ 82.5	$ 81.3	$ 81.9	$ 80.8	$ 81.8	$106.6	$80.6
$ 38.0	$ 61.1	$ 38.9	$ 2.0	$ 19.8	$133.9	$ 50.8	$ 96.5	$ 44.0	$ 11.7	$ 59.5	($199.1)	$134.3	($92.2)

*Oncost includes the costs of employing labour (e.g. annual leave, sick leave, holidays, superannuation, payroll taxes)

**General costs over which the supervisor has control (e.g., advertising, repair and maintenance, power, stationery)

†Income gained not as a direct result of selling (e.g., rebates, rental, commissions, recharges)

††Costs incurred irrespective of the level of activity (e.g. depreciation, interest, rent)

University of Southern California: Revenue Center Management System

In 1991, several faculty groups at the University of Southern California (USC) voiced public criticism of the university's Revenue Center Management System (RCMS). The RCMS, which had been used since 1981, was the key element of USC's decentralized financial control system. It provided top university managers the ability to hold the heads of each operating unit (e.g., school deans) accountable for the financial consequences of their decisions.

In February 1991, 56 faculty members from 13 university units sent an open letter to Steven Sample, the newly appointed university president, criticizing the RCMS. This letter, which was not based on any careful study and which proposed no alternatives to the current system, claimed that the RCMS had turned the university into "a collection of independent and competing units, whose only legitimacy is built on their ability to produce revenues." It went on to state that "among units whose fields do not create wealthy entrepreneurs or professionals the concept has produced polarization between units and a chronic concern for survival." The concern for survival, in turn, leads faculty to try to serve larger numbers of students to raise enrollment revenues, but at the expense of education quality.

In May, the University Research Committee approved a subcommittee report based on a study of the RCMS that had been underway for over a year. This study was the first serious faculty review of the USC RCMS. Contrary to the open letter, this committee report concluded that RCMS was *generally working well.* But the report did say that some modifications to the RCMS were needed to eliminate, or at least reduce, some *perverse incentives* for deans and faculty members. These perverse incentives included discouragement of innovation, multidisciplinary research, and the seeking of outside research grants, and encouragement of course proliferation. The report made specific suggestions to relieve some of the problems.

Both faculty groups called on the university administration to examine the RCMS and to consider an appropriate and timely response to their criticisms. Preparation of the response became the responsibility of USC's central financial staff, in particular Dennis Dougherty, senior vice president-finance and John Curry, vice president-budget and planning. Dennis, John, and their staffs had to decide whether the criticisms were valid, and if so, how the system could be altered to alleviate the problems.

THE UNIVERSITY OF SOUTHERN CALIFORNIA

The University of Southern California was established in 1880 as a private, research institution of higher education. Located on the perimeter of downtown Los Angeles, USC was a diverse and complex organization. It ran 22 colleges and schools, more than any other private university in the United States, and offered over 200 degree programs. It enrolled over 28,000 students from all 50 states and 113 countries, employed over 2,000 full time faculty members, and had annual operating revenues of over $800 million. Exhibit 1 shows a university organization chart. Exhibit 2 shows an *income statement.* (The *restricted* and *unrestricted* nature of some of the revenue and expense items is explained later in the case.)

As a research university, USC's goals included the creation, as well as the transmission, of knowledge. Thus USC's faculty were expected to engage in basic or applied research as well as perform their teaching. USC supported its activities primarily by generating tuition revenues, securing research sponsorship, and attracting philanthropic

Research Assistant Marily Fassett and Professor Kenneth A. Merchant wrote this case as the basis for class discussion rather than to illustrate either effective or ineffective handling of an administrative situation.

contributions. Because its endowment was relatively small, the university was heavily dependent on tuition revenue. But it was successful in generating sponsored research funds, ranking 14th among the nation's universities.

THE FINANCIAL MANAGEMENT SYSTEM PRIOR TO RCMS

Prior to the implementation of RCMS, decision making power was centralized, with one senior administrative officer playing a key role in all major resource allocation decisions. Dennis Dougherty remembered that, "The old system was heavily based on personal negotiation. The resource allocation decisions were made behind the scenes in a 'smoke-filled room.'"

Also in the old system, financial accountability for the unit heads was weak. Each university unit had its own financial statement, but the statements were not complete, as some revenues were neither traced nor allocated to the units that generated them, and unit heads were not sanctioned for producing unfavorable variances as compared to their budget. David Shawaker, finance director for the School of Engineering, recalled:

> Certain players would consistently overrun their budgets, and some had substantial overruns. Most of the overruns were due to undergenerated revenues rather than cost overruns. No one had any explicit financial incentive to manage differently. (But there were some real, significant informal incentives.)

RCMS DESIGN PRINCIPLES

The RCMS was designed in 1981 by a Task Force on Budget Incentives appointed by James Zumberge, the university president. The Task Force based much of the RCMS design on the system used at the University of Pennsylvania which, in turn, was adapted from the system in use at General Electric Company. Reginald Jones, the then-chairman of GE was on the Board of Trustees at Penn, and he insisted that this kind of system would provide a better alignment of authority and responsibility, and better university management.

The Task Force developed the following nine management principles to guide their development of the RCMS:[1]

1. Responsibility should be commensurate with authority, and vice versa.
2. Decentralization should be proportional to organizational size and complexity.
3. Locally optimal decisions are not always globally optimal: central leverage is required to implement corporate (global) priorities.
4. Outcome measures are preferable to process controls.
5. Accountability is only as good as the tools which measure it.
6. Quantitative measures of performance tend to drive out qualitative measures (a variant of Gresham's Law).
7. Outcomes should matter: Plans that work should lead to rewards, plans which fail should lead to sanctions.
8. Resource-expanding incentives are preferable to resource-dividing ones.
9. People play better games when they own the rules.

The new RCMS system had to include three basic elements that would permit a decentralized management system within the university. First, the university had to be divided into responsibility centers. Second, the performance reports, including methods for tracing or allocating shared revenues and costs to the primary operating units, had to be designed. And third, the extent of decision authority to be delegated to the operating units needed to be clarified.

RESPONSIBILITY CENTERS

The university was divided into two types of responsibility centers: revenue centers and administrative centers. Revenue centers were organizational units to which revenues could be uniquely attributed. Some of these, the colleges, schools, and research institutes, were called *academic* revenue centers. The other revenue centers, including athletics, residence halls, bookstores, parking op-

[1] J. R. Curry, "Afterword: The USC Experience with Revenue Center Management," in E. L. Whalen, *Responsibility Center Budgeting: An Approach to Decentralized Management for Institutions of Higher Education.* Bloomington, IN: Indiana University Press, 1991, p. 178.

erations, and food services, were called *auxiliary* revenue centers. The administrative centers were entities that did not generate revenues directly but performed activities which supported the revenue centers. Examples included Admissions and Financial Aid, Business Affairs, Financial Services, Legal Services, Library, Office of the President, and Registrar.

Most of the responsibilities for raising revenues and expending resources were delegated to the revenue center managers. The central administration maintained some power to implement university-wide goals. As noted in the 1985 USC Financial Report:

> At USC, we believe that the primary planning takes place at the operating unit level: the school or auxiliary enterprise, or the administrative unit. We believe that people closest to the action know their programs, their customers, and their markets best; they are the best informed and, therefore, the most capable of strategic thinking. The role of central planners is primarily one of coordinating and monitoring.

The central administration maintained the power to hold the responsibility center managers accountable for attaining their targets. The academic revenue center managers (i.e., school deans) were evaluated in terms of their units' academic excellence (research and teaching), generation of sponsored research grants, faculty development, fundraising, and bottom-line financial performance. Their performances were reviewed formally every five years.

PERFORMANCE REPORTS

USC produced an elaborate set of reports to facilitate control of each responsibility center's operations. A monthly financial report presented the current month's and year-to-date performance as compared to budget. Other reports provided information on gifts, grants, enrollments, students, personnel, space usage, and the detailed items affecting the revenues and expenses of each responsibility center. The financial reports included four primary categories of accounts: revenues, direct expenses, indirect expenses, and participation/subvention. These are explained as follows.

Revenues

The university generated two types of revenues: restricted and unrestricted. More than 25 percent of the total funds available to support operations were restricted, meaning that they were given to the university for a specific purpose or project. These funds came from grants and contracts from the federal government and other sponsors of specific research projects, from gifts from private donors and foundations, and from income from endowments to support specific individuals and/or activities. The restricted revenue funds had to be used only for the specific purpose for which they were given and were not allowed to be transferred to an unrestricted account without prior permission from the central administration.

The other revenues were unrestricted in purpose. They came from tuition and fees, unrestricted gifts, and indirect cost recoveries from government contracts. Tuition revenue was credited 100 percent to the revenue center offering the course taken. The indirect cost recoveries were determined by formula negotiated with each funding source. For example, in fiscal year 1991, UCS's indirect cost recovery rate on U.S. government projects was 60.5 percent of direct costs; that is, for every $1.00 reported as the approved direct costs of a research project, the university received an additional 60.5 cents to help cover indirect costs. But on projects funded by the Kellogg Foundation, the recovery rate was only 8 percent.

Expenses

The direct expenses of a revenue center included the costs of the people and equipment directly assigned to that center. Indirect expenses included the costs of shared resources, such as buildings, utilities, and various kinds of support provided by the administrative centers. The indirect expenses were allocated to the revenue centers on the basis of cause and effect, benefit derived, or common practice. Exhibit 3 shows the indirect cost pools generated by the various administrative centers and the rules that governed their allocation. John Curry, vice president of budget and planning, acknowledged that the allocations were based on:

> . . . imperfect rules, some of which were totally arbitrary. We used Federal government

allocation guidelines as a guide, but we also put together a group of deans and administrators and hammered the rules out.

Dennis Dougherty concurred:

> Allocation of indirect costs is done with thumbnail methods that are much less precise than precise. No study was done, but the allocations are somewhat thoughtful. We developed rules of thumb and tried to remove blatant inaccuracies.

FIGURE 1 1991 Summary Income Statements ($ millions)

	School of Business	*School of Music*
Unrestricted income	$64.1	$10.8
Indirect income	(4.1)	2.5
TOTAL INCOME	60.0	13.3
Direct Expense	38.0	8.2
Indirect Expense	22.0	5.0
TOTAL EXPENSE	$60.0	$13.3

Participations and Subventions

University administrators used a system of *participations* and *subventions* to maintain a degree of control over university-wide resource allocation decisions and to even out the distribution of monies between revenue centers. The participations were contributions required from all revenue centers in equal proportion to further the objectives and well-being of the total university. Each revenue center contributed 20 percent of the sum of its tuition and fees, sales and service income, and indirect cost recoveries. These contributions were redistributed to revenue centers as block grants called subventions. In the revenue center financial reports, the participations were shown as negative indirect income, while the subventions were shown as positive indirect income.

The participation/subvention feature of RCMS provided university administrators a means to implement university priorities and goals. When they made their allocations of subventions, the administrators, particularly the provost and president, tended to focus on two key factors: (1) differentials in the costs of educating students in different fields; and (2) the revenue centers' cost/quality ratios.

The cost of educating students varied widely between schools. Some schools could educate their students effectively by teaching them in large sections, while other had to provide instruction in small classes or in expensive laboratories. John Curry explained:

> The cost of educating a music major is large, especially in a conservatory-like program like ours. The dominant mode of instruction is one-on-one: a master pianist and pupil on the same bench. Business education is much less expensive; as accounting and finance can be taught well to classes of 25 or 50, or even more. But we as a university have decided to charge both music and business students the same tuition. Common price, but most uncommon *unit* costs!

Part of the subvention allocations was aimed at evening out this cost disparity. This pattern can be seen in Figure 1 which shows the 1991 summary income statement numbers for the schools of Business and Performing Arts.

The other major factor underlying the subvention allocation was a subjectively determined cost/academic excellence ratio that represented what the university administrators perceived they were receiving for their investment. This is illustrated in Figure 2. A school located near point number 3, such as USC's School of Music, with both high cost of instruction and high academic excel-

FIGURE 2 Cost/Academic Excellence Ratios

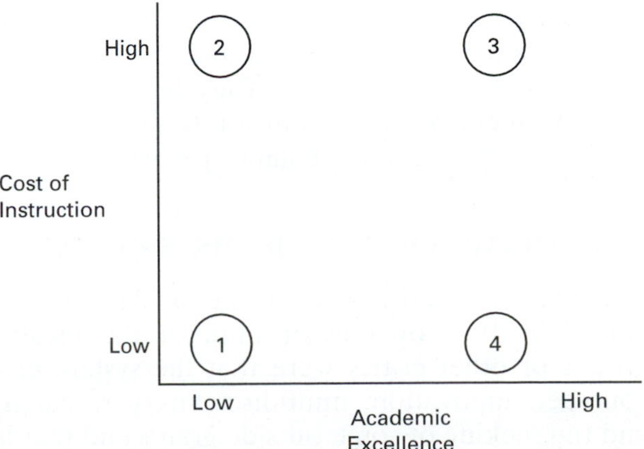

lence, is most likely to get a disproportionately high subvention. It offers high quality programs and research productivity but is unable to cover its costs through tuitions. A school located near point number 4 is valuable to the university because it offers high quality and financial independence. It can probably provide funds that can be used in other parts of the university, but administrators will be careful to allow it to keep enough funds to maintain its excellence. A school located near point number 2 is in trouble. It is a candidate for new leadership or program discontinuance.

INTERCENTER BANK

The RCMS included one other significant element, an Intercenter Bank. This bank provided the revenue centers the opportunity to carry unrestricted funds across fiscal year boundaries. It thus provided revenue center managers incentives to produce year-end surpluses rather than just to meet a break-even bottom-line. And it reduced the *use-it-or-lose it* mentality, present in some not-for-profit organizations, which causes managers to spend all the money that had been approved in their budget before year end.

The Intercenter Bank was used both by revenue centers reporting surpluses and by those reporting losses. If a revenue center had a surplus (i.e., a positive unrestricted fund balance at the end of the year), it was given an account in the bank and provided interest on the account balance at the annual treasury-bill rate as of July 1st of the year just started. These revenue center managers were allowed to spend their account's principal balance in future years, but only up to a maximum of 20 percent of the balance each year. Conversely, revenue centers with a deficit were assigned a loan from the bank and charged interest at the treasury-bill rate. They had to budget for repayment of the loan at a rate of at least 20 percent of the beginning balance per year.

CRITICISMS OF THE RCMS SYSTEM

The five basic criticisms of the RCMS system voiced in 1991 by one or both of the faculty groups or other critics were that the system discouraged innovation, multidisciplinary research, and the seeking of some outside grants and that it encouraged both proliferation of redundant and inappropriate courses and end-of-period financial gameplaying.

1. Discouragement of Innovation

The discouragement-of-innovation criticism, which the Research Committee considered the most important problem, stemmed from three concerns. First, some critics believed that the RCMS system forced deans to think of their mission more in financial terms and not in terms of their academic mission. The open letter to president Sample stated:

> The system in place makes few allowances for the various missions and contributions of the academic units of the university. Those units unable to show a *profit* under current budgetary formulas are condemned to live in a deficit situation, to depend upon subventions given after demeaning negotiations, and to face inferior status among other units in the university.

Many believed that the financial pressure discouraged innovation and even teaching quality. The committee report noted that, "Innovators whose ideas do not imply immediate income feel that no one in the system will give those ideas a sympathetic hearing, and so are discouraged from innovating. And one critic added that, "Faculty under pressure to produce income are not focused on students." Some critics even believed that the emphasis on financial performance would lead university administrators to hire deans with, perhaps, more financial management abilities than leadership vision for their school.

Second, another group of critics believed that innovation and initiative were stifled because RCMS institutionalized decentralization only to the level of the deans and, thus, did not go far enough. Deans were unlikely to carry the delegation any further and, as a consequence, the university was stripped of the entrepreneurial energies of many faculty leaders. And third, some critics observed that much of the power and discretionary funds had been taken from the top-level administrators and their roles essentially became those of administrators, not leaders. One critic noted that, "Neither president Zumberge nor provost Pings has become identified with any public position. All the leadership that is being exerted is coming from the [good] deans."

As a partial solution, the Research Committee report suggested that USC should create a Research Leadership Fund of at least $1 million per year to be used for time-limited support of innovative projects. These projects should involve large expenditures, of at least $50,000/year, because another program was already in place to provide smaller grants to support individual faculty research projects. In the new program, administrators or researchers would apply for funds, and the approval process would be administered by the Vice Provost for Research.

2. Discouragement of Multidisciplinary Research

The Research Committee report expressed concern about the discouragement of multidisciplinary research because the committee members thought that the best research, particularly that of an applied nature, should involve researchers with different skills and perspectives. Some faculty members believed that since RCMS emphasized financial priorities, most deans could not see the financial benefits of multidisciplinary research. They also noted that such research could even be a financial drain on a revenue center, depending on how the costs and revenues of the cross-revenue-center work were shared. Ward Edwards, the chairman of the subcommittee of the University Research Committee that prepared the report critical of RCMS said:

> The biggest obstacle to multidisciplinary research is territoriality. Any efforts to institutionalize a turf, which is what RCMS does, will lead to action to protect that turf. I can give you perhaps 20 examples where this system has stifled interdisciplinary work. For example, I know of instances in which deans have upbraided faculty members for getting involved with someone from outside their revenue center.

The subcommittee members could not find much evidence that USC professors were engaging in significant amounts of multidisciplinary research, and they blamed the RCMS, at least in part. They proposed that overhead revenue for multi-revenue centers projects be assigned in a manner proportional to the costs the units will occur. They also suggested that the Research Leadership Fund could be used explicitly to encourage multidisciplinary research proposals.

3. Discouragement of the Seeking of Outside Grants

The Research Committee report noted that some personnel are discouraged from seeking some outside funding grants. These grants appear *unprofitable* to the unit because they do not provide for full recovery of the expenses charged to the revenue center. For example, the U.S. government recovery rate of 60.5 percent, which was higher than the recovery rates allowed by many foundations, did not cover the overall USC average overhead rate which was approximately 68 percent of direct costs. And the actual overhead rates in some departments, such as science departments which had to maintain expensive laboratories, were much higher than the university average.

The research committee urged university administrators to study their allocation methods and to consider discontinuing the allocation of some categories of expenses, such as the relatively fixed indirect expenses (e.g., space, general administration). This change would allow units to price at least some research grants on a marginal cost basis.

4. Encouragement of Course Proliferation

The critics who believed that the RCMS encouraged course proliferation based their belief on the knowledge that a school earned tuition revenue only if students signed up for courses they offered. Thus many schools, and even departments, offered similar or even identical courses (e.g., statistics, communications) in order to retain all of its students' tuition dollars at their school. The faculty voicing this criticism believed that it would be more likely for courses to be taught in the department best suited to offer it if the pressure for revenue generation was lessened. Some RCMS critics also noted that some schools offered *gut* (excessively easy) courses that might be deemed inappropriate for an institute of higher education (e.g., a course that just shows movies) or tolerated professors who grade *liberally* to keep their courses popular because popularity brings with it additional revenues.

5. Encouragement of End-of-Period Financial Gameplaying

Neither the committee report nor the open letter mentioned the problem of end-of-period financial gameplaying, but some other critics within the university believed that RCMS encouraged such actions. They noted many examples of revenue center managers moving revenues and expenses between fiscal years depending on whether they were in a budget surplus or deficit position. These managers were motivated to do so because meeting their budget target was an important part of their job. Most of them believed that if they failed to achieve their budget two years in a row, they would probably be replaced.

The managers had used many methods of moving monies between reporting periods. For example, they could ask donors to accelerate or delay their contributions, or they could deposit June donations immediately or wait until after July 1, the start of the new fiscal year. And they could move expenses between years by, for example, accelerating or delaying discretionary expenditures or by asking faculty and staff members to submit requests for reimbursement of expenditures already made in the current or following fiscal year.

The deans and many others within the university did not consider such manipulations unethical because they had observed top-level university administrators taking the same types of actions. The university had never posted a deficit for a fiscal year, but sometimes administrators had to take end-of-year actions to maintain that record. They believed the continuing record of budget achievement and surpluses was desirable because it provided evidence that the school was well run and contributed to the high-quality (AA) bond rating USC was given by Moody's and Standard and Poor's. Both of these indicators facilitated the raising of capital and donations from alumni, foundations, and the investment community. As Dennis Dougherty noted, "Big donors will not give to a school running a deficit. They assume the people there can't handle the money."

A REQUIRED RESPONSE

Dennis Dougherty and John Curry knew they would have to respond to the criticisms of the RCMS system. But Dennis noticed that, "Some of the people who have the greatest problems with the RCMS system are those who were the best at negotiating behind closed doors when we had the old system." He also believed that some of these criticisms were merely inevitable side-effects of the use of a system—a decentralized organization structure combined with financial accountability—that had great benefits. But both he and John were convinced that the system could probably be improved.

EXHIBIT 1 Organization Chart

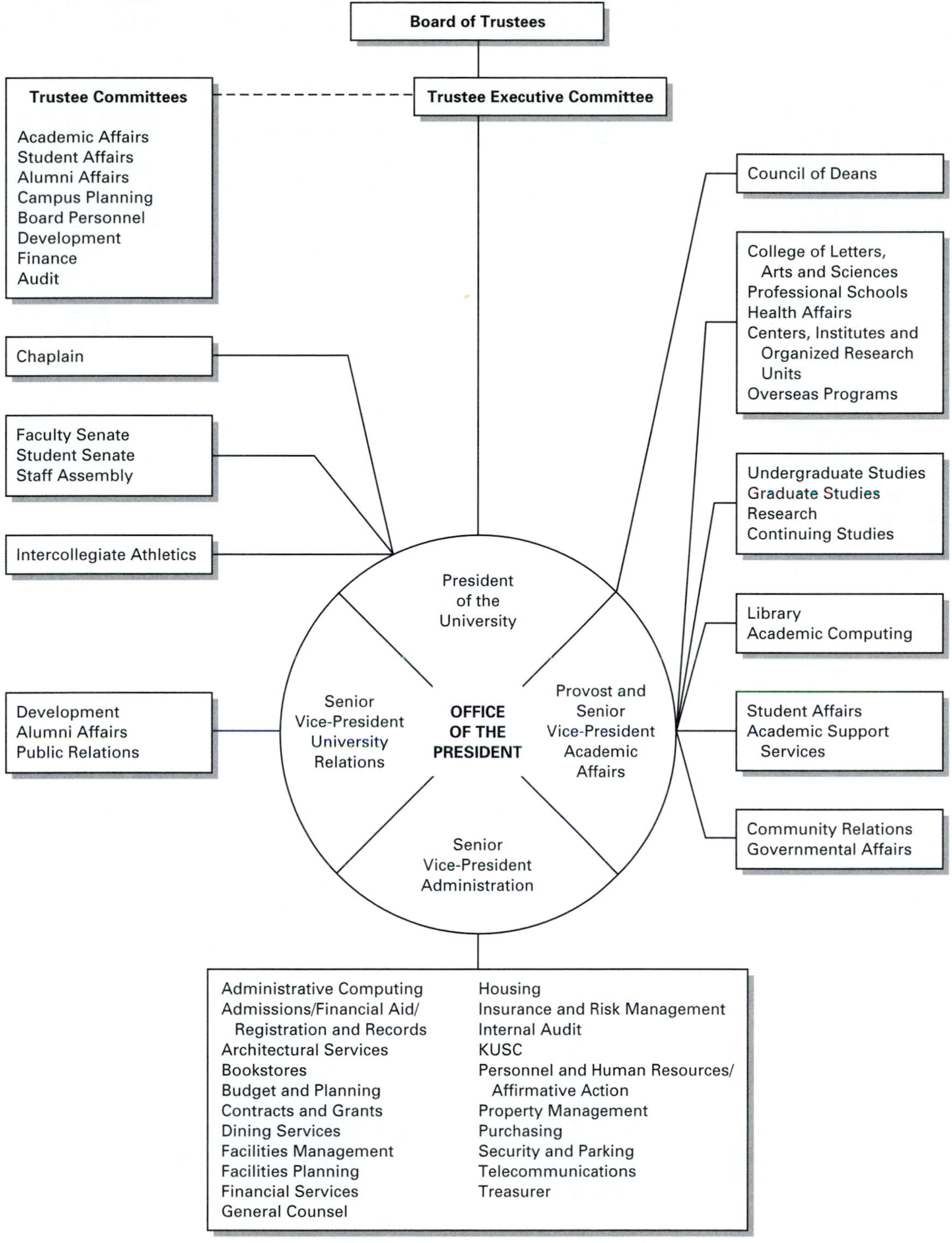

Organizational Chart

University of Southern California

January 15, 1988

The Office of the President is an extension of the President and is comprised of the President and the Senior Vice President to whom the President has delegated authority and responsibility for the wide areas of the University's operations assigned to them.

EXHIBIT 2 Summary of Current Funds Revenue & Expense

(in $1,000)		*Unrestricted Budget*						*Restricted Budget*	
		1989–90 Unrestricted Budget	*1990–91 Unrestricted Budget*	*1990–91 % from 1989–90*	*1989–90 Patient Care Budget*	*1990–91 Patient Care Budget*	*1990–91 % from Budget*	*1989–90 Budget*	*1990–91 Budget*
Revenues	Tuition & Fees	328,480	335,527	2.15%					
	Endowment Income							9,473	9,947
	Unrestricted to University	3,869	4,582	18.43%					
	Unrestricted to Centers	3,707	4,375	18.02%					
	Investment Income	10,592	11,713	10.58%	1,500	1,918	27.87%		
	Gifts							23,000	24,150
	Unrestricted to University	2,950	3,850	30.51%					
	Unrestricted to Centers	11,047	13,522	22.40%					
	Contracts & Grants							128,388	135,679
	Recovery of Indirect Costs								
	Endowments	1,434	1,790	24.83%					
	Gifts	1,542	1,734	12.45%					
	Contracts & Grants	41,738	44,796	7.33%	2,100	2,595	23.57%		
	Sales & Service, Auxiliary Enterprises & Other Sources	117,111	126,642	8.14%	66,856	115,684	73.03%		
	Total Revenues	522,470	548,531	4.99%	70,456	120,197	70.60%	160,861	169,775
Expenses	Compensation								
	Faculty Salaries	92,840	100,599	8.36%	22,890	40,475	76.82%	49,052	52,486
	Other Salaries & Wages	155,535	160,832	3.41%	23,593	37,890	60.60%	31,087	32,952
	Fringe Benefits	71,337	75,285	5.53%	9,535	15,884	66.59%	22,917	24,063
	Total Compensation	319,712	336,716	5.32%	56,018	94,249	68.25%	103,056	109,501
	Equipment								
	Library	3,989	4,383	9.88%					
	Other than Library	6,849	7,393	7.94%	44	81	84.09%	18,000	18,900
	Student Aid	52,773	54,439	3.16%				21,492	22,996
	Telephone	7,180	8,042	12.01%	66	120	81.82%		
	M & S, Travel & Others	98,548	90,858	−7.80%	14,175	25,701	81.31%	18,313	18,378
	Utilities	14,503	16,447	13.40%					
	Debt Service	18,916	30,253	59.93%	153	46	−69.93%		
	Total Expense	522,470	548,531	4.99%	70,456	120,197	70.60%	160,861	169,775

EXHIBIT 3 Indirect Cost Pools

Direct	*Administrative Center (Source)*	*Allocation in Proportion to Revenue Center Destination*
Student Aid	Admissions & Fin. Aid	Number of students enrolled
Operations & Maintenance	Business Affairs	Costs incurred in specific buildings and the net square footage occupied
Telephone Office	Business Affairs	Number of lines and instruments
Computer Usage	University Computing Center	Use
Library	Library	Acquisitions and use
Student Services	Admissions & Fin. Aid, Fin. Services, Student Affairs, Registrar	Total undergraduate and/or graduate tuition units
Cultural Services	Academic Administration	Use
Development	University Relations	5-year average gift receipts
General Administration	Fin. Services, Business Affairs, Office of the President Office of the University Budget, Treasurer . . .	Total direct expense
General Expense	Legal Services, Business Affairs, Office of the President (i.e., corporate obligations)	Total direct expense

Index

A

B

C

D

E

F

G

H

I

J

K

L

M

N

O

P